Recommended by **Teachers**
Trusted by **Toppers**

All in One®

ACCOUNTANCY
Class 12

EVERYTHING YOU NEED TO SCORE

- Simplified Theory
- Illustrations & Practice Questions
- CBQs; MCQs, A-R, Case Based
- Board Questions Upto 2025
- Sample Question Papers

CBSE Exams 2026

Authors
Anshul Sharma
Sarvesh Kumar Mittal

arihant
SUCCESS AND NOTHING LESS

arihant
SUCCESS AND NOTHING LESS

ARIHANT PRAKASHAN

(School Division Series)

卐 *ADMINISTRATIVE & PRODUCTION OFFICES*

Regd. Office

'Ramchhaya' 4577/15, Agarwal Road, Darya Ganj, New Delhi -110002
Tele: 011- 47630600, 43518550; Fax: 011- 23280316

卐 *Head Office*

Kalindi, TP Nagar, Meerut (UP) - 250002, Tel: 0121-7156203, 7156204

卐 *SALES & SUPPORT OFFICES*

Agra, Ahmedabad, Bengaluru, Bareilly, Chennai, Delhi, Guwahati, Hyderabad, Jaipur, Jhansi, Kolkata, Lucknow, Nagpur & Pune.

PO No : TXT-XX-XXXXXXX-X-XX

Published By Arihant Publications (India) Ltd.

For further information about the books published by Arihant, log on to www.arihantbooks.com or e-mail at info@arihantbooks.com

Follow us on

卐 *PRICE* ₹600.00

PRODUCTION TEAM

Publishing Managers	*Cover Designer*	*Inner Designer*
Mahendra Singh Rawat & Keshav Mohan	Salman Shaikh	Ankit Tyagi
Project Head	*Page Layouting*	*Proof Reader*
Saurabh Gupta	Amit Bansal	Apoorvi

Index *cum* Study Planner

One Book- Endless Features

to Help you Succeed

In this Chapter

At the start of each chapter, all the topics of the chapter have been listed, so that students may know what they are going to study.

01

CHAPTER

When two or more persons join hands to set up a business and share its profits and losses, they are said to be in partnership.

Accounting for Partnership Firm: Fundamentals

YOUR STUDY GOALS

1.1 Introduction to Partnership
1.2 Profit and Loss Appropriation Account
1.3 Partners' Capital Accounts
1.4 Appropriation and Charge Items
1.5 Past Adjustments
1.6 Guarantee of Profits

YOUR PRACTICE GOAL

- Topicwise Solved Questions (35 Solved Questions)
- Numerical Questions [46 Questions (Unsolved)]
- Theoretical Questions [4 Questions (with answers)]

1.1 Introduction to Partnership

According to Section 4 of the **Indian Partnership Act, 1932,** "Partnership is the relation between persons who have agreed to share the profits of a business carried on by all or any of them acting for all."

Essential Features of Partnership

1. **Number of Persons** Two or more persons and all such persons must be competent to contract.
2. **Agreement** Either written or oral.
3. **Motive** Carrying on a business (which must be legal) and earning profit.
4. **Mutual Agency** Business can be carried on by all or by any one of them, acting for all. Partners are agents as well as the principals of the firm.

Smart Study Chart

To quickly recall the Concepts, Smart Study Charts are given at many places.

Smart Study **Chart No. 1**

Partnership Deed

Meaning

Partnership comes into existence as a result of agreement among the partners. The document containing the terms and conditions of the agreement in writing among partners is called the 'partnership deed'.

Importance

Partnership deed and its registration is not compulsory but written agreement is considered beneficial due to following reasons

- Helps in settlement of dispute with respect to terms of partnership.
- Serves as an evidence in the court of law.
- Regulates the rights, duties and liabilities of each partner.

Contents of Partnership Deed

The partnership deed usually contains the following details

- Name and address of all the partners
- Name and address of the firm
- Principal place of business
- Nature of business
- Date of commencement of the partnership
- Rules regarding operation of bank accounts
- Capital to be contributed by each partner
- Interest on capitals, drawings and loan
- Salary/Commission to partners
- Profit and loss sharing ratio
- Accounting period of the firm
- Mode of auditor's appointment, if any
- The rights, duties and liabilities of each partner
- Treatment of loss arising out of insolvency of one or more partners
- Method of settlement of disputes among the partners
- Valuation of goodwill
- Any other matter relating to the conduct of business

Complete Theory in Each Chapter

Each chapter has Complete, Easy to Understand and Simplified theory covering latest syllabus. Theory is developed in such a way that it is suitable for all types of learners.

1.1 Introduction to Partnership

According to Section 4 of the **Indian Partnership Act, 1932,** "Partnership is the relation between persons who have agreed to share the profits of a business carried on by all or any of them acting for all."

Essential Features of Partnership

1. **Number of Persons** Two or more persons and all such persons must be competent to contract.
2. **Agreement** Either written or oral.
3. **Motive** Carrying on a business (which must be legal) and earning profit.
4. **Mutual Agency** Business can be carried on by all or by any one of them, acting for all. Partners are agents as well as the principals of the firm.
5. **Sharing of Profits** As per agreement or as per provision of Partnership Act. However, it is not essential that the losses are also shared by all partners.
6. **Liability** Each partner is liable individually and collectively with all other partners to third party for all the acts of the firm, while he is a partner. Also, liability of a partner is unlimited.

One Book- Endless Features

to Help you Succeed

Mind Map

A quick revision visual tool for the complete chapter.

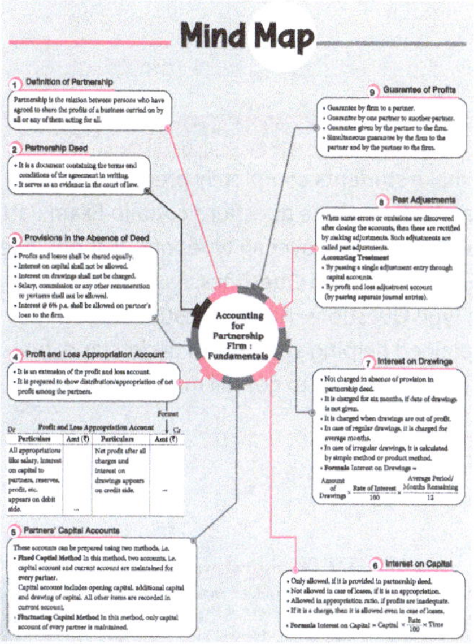

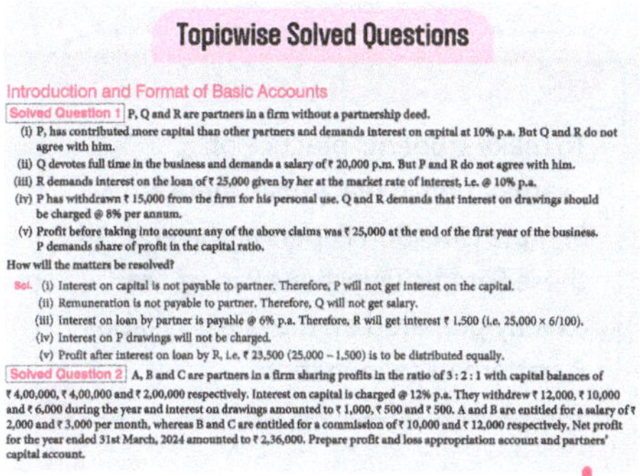

Topicwise Solved Questions

Introduction and Format of Basic Accounts

Solved Question 1 P, Q and R are partners in a firm without a partnership deed.

(i) P, has contributed more capital than other partners and demands interest on capital at 10% p.a. But Q and R do not agree with him.
(ii) Q devotes full time in the business and demands a salary of ₹ 20,000 p.m. But P and R do not agree with him.
(iii) R demands interest on the loan of ₹ 25,000 given by her at the market rate of interest, i.e. @ 10% p.a.
(iv) P has withdrawn ₹ 15,000 from the firm for his personal use. Q and R demands that interest on drawings should be charged @ 8% per annum.
(v) Profit before taking into account any of the above claims was ₹ 25,000 at the end of the first year of the business. P demands share of profit in the capital ratio.

How will the matters be resolved?

Sol. (i) Interest on capital is not payable to partner. Therefore, P will not get interest on the capital.
(ii) Remuneration is not payable to partner. Therefore, Q will not get salary.
(iii) Interest on loan by partner is payable @ 6% p.a. Therefore, R will get interest ₹ 1,500 (i.e. 25,000 × 6/100).
(iv) Interest on P drawings will not be charged.
(v) Profit after interest on loan by R, i.e. ₹ 23,500 (25,000 − 1,500) is to be distributed equally.

Solved Question 2 A, B and C are partners in a firm sharing profits in the ratio of 3 : 2 : 1 with capital balances of ₹ 4,00,000, ₹ 4,00,000 and ₹ 2,00,000 respectively. Interest on capital is charged @ 12% p.a. They withdrew ₹ 12,000, ₹ 10,000 and ₹ 6,000 during the year and interest on drawings amounted to ₹ 1,000, ₹ 500 and ₹ 500. A and B are entitled for a salary of ₹ 2,000 and ₹ 3,000 per month, whereas B and C are entitled for a commission of ₹ 10,000 and ₹ 12,000 respectively. Net profit for the year ended 31st March, 2024 amounted to ₹ 2,36,000. Prepare profit and loss appropriation account and partners' capital account.

Topicwise Solved Questions

Topicwise Solved Questions have been given after the theory. These Questions have been solved in detail, so that students can learn the problem solving process completely.

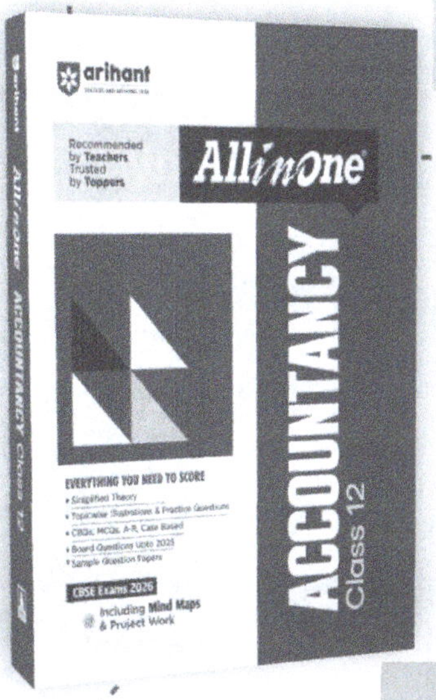

Topicwise Practice Questions

To make students understand the chapter in a smooth part-by-part manner, practice questions have been given in each chapter. These questions help students to assess the understanding of related concepts completely.

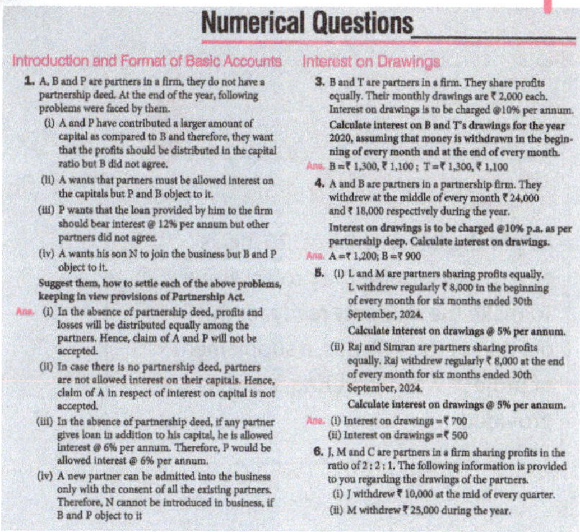

Numerical Questions

Introduction and Format of Basic Accounts

1. A, B and P are partners in a firm, they do not have a partnership deed. At the end of the year, following problems were faced by them.
   (i) A and P have contributed a larger amount of capital as compared to B and therefore, they want that the profits should be distributed in the capital ratio but B did not agree.
   (ii) A wants that partners must be allowed interest on the capitals but P and B object to it.
   (iii) P wants that the loan provided by him to the firm should bear interest @ 12% per annum but other partners did not agree.
   (iv) A wants his son N to join the business but B and P object to it.

   Suggest them, how to settle each of the above problems, keeping in view provisions of Partnership Act.

Ans. (i) In the absence of partnership deed, profits and losses will be distributed equally among the partners. Hence, claim of A and P will not be accepted.
(ii) In case there is no partnership deed, partners are not allowed interest on their capitals. Hence, claim of A in respect of interest on capital is not accepted.
(iii) In the absence of partnership deed, if any partner gives loan in addition to his capital, he is allowed interest @ 6% per annum. Therefore, P would be allowed interest @ 6% per annum.
(iv) A new partner can be admitted into the business only with the consent of all the existing partners. Therefore, N cannot be introduced in business, if B and P object to it

Interest on Drawings

3. B and T are partners in a firm. They share profits equally. Their monthly drawings are ₹ 2,000 each. Interest on drawings is to be charged @10% per annum.
   Calculate interest on B and T's drawings for the year 2020, assuming that money is withdrawn in the beginning of every month and at the end of every month.

Ans. B = ₹ 1,300, ₹ 1,100 ; T = ₹ 1,300, ₹ 1,100

4. A and B are partners in a partnership firm. They withdrew at the middle of every month ₹ 24,000 and ₹ 18,000 respectively during the year.
   Interest on drawings is to be charged @10% p.a. as per partnership deep. Calculate interest on drawings.

Ans. A = ₹ 1,200; B = ₹ 900

5. (i) L and M are partners sharing profits equally. L withdrew regularly ₹ 8,000 in the beginning of every month for six months ended 30th September, 2024.
   Calculate interest on drawings @ 5% per annum.
   (ii) Raj and Simran are partners sharing profits equally. Raj withdrew regularly ₹ 8,000 at the end of every month for six months ended 30th September, 2024.
   Calculate interest on drawings @ 5% per annum.

Ans. (i) Interest on drawings = ₹ 700
(ii) Interest on drawings = ₹ 500

6. J, M and C are partners in a firm sharing profits in the ratio of 2 : 2 : 1. The following information is provided to you regarding the drawings of the partners.
   (i) J withdrew ₹ 10,000 at the mid of every quarter.
   (ii) M withdrew ₹ 25,000 during the year.

One Book- Endless Features
to Help you Succeed

Theoretical and Objective Questions

To make students completely prepared for examination, these questions contain Exam Pattern Questions. They cover all types of questions, like; MCQs, Case Based Questions, Assertion-Reason & SA Type Questions. All the questions are fully explained helping students to understand, how to write the answers to get full marks in the exam.

Theoretical Questions

Short Answer Type Questions

1. State any four features of a partnership.

Ans. Following are the features of partnership

(i) There must be atleast two persons to form a partnership and all such persons must be competent to contract.

(ii) Partnership comes into existence by an agreement, either oral or written.

(iii) The partnership agreement between/among the partners must be to share profits or losses of the business.

(iv) A partnership must be formed to do a lawful business.

3. List any four contents of partnership deed.

Ans. The contents of partnership deed are

(i) Name and address of all the partners.

(ii) Name and address of the firm.

(iii) Capital to be contributed by each partner.

(iv) Date and commencement of the partnership.

4. In the absence of partnership deed, specify the rules relating to the following **NCERT**

(i) Sharing of profits and losses

(ii) Interest on partner's capital

(iii) Interest on partner's drawings

(iv) Interest on partner's loan

Objective Questions

Multiple Choice Questions (MCQs)

1. Persons who have entered into partnership are individually called .... and collectively called .... .

(a) owners, organisation (b) agents, firm

(c) partners, business (d) partners, firm

2. Under what circumstances, a partner can get exemption from sharing losses in a firm?

(a) If he is a senior citizen (b) If he is a minor

(c) If he is retiring partner (d) All of these

5. Which of the following statement is incorrect?

(a) Each partner is an owner as well as agent in the firm

(b) Partnership firm has a separate legal entity

(c) Share of profits and losses in agreed ratio

(d) Capital of partners may be fixed or fluctuating

6. A charitable dispensary is run by 15 members. A new member wants to join them. The new member is of the opinion that partnership deed must be written while other members refused to do that.

They said this is not a partnership Give reason(s) in

Project 1 Comprehensive

Case Study of an Individual, Willing to Set-up a Small-scale Business in Retail Sector

Mr Sultan Raza, a business school graduate from US came back to India with a thought to open a retail outlet on a small-scale with an initial capital investment of ₹ 5,00,000 for selling packaged and frozen foods in Mumbai, as people in Mumbai are quite busy and don't have time for cooking. He then finalised the business plan, capital requirement, etc. He opened a bank account with Punjab National Bank, in which he deposited ₹ 3,50,000.

He selected a suitable place for the store, renovated it, purchased furniture of ₹ 1,00,000 and paid the amount by cheque. He employed a helper for his shop.

The other transactions during the year were

Particulars	Amt (₹)
Purchases	
On Credit (from Ajay)	2,00,000
On Cash (from Ashok)	80,000
Sales	
On Credit (from Vijay)	1,40,000
On Cash (from Vinod)	1,00,000
Paid Travelling Expenses in Cash	30,000
Paid Salary to Helper in Cash	20,000
Received from Debtor Vijay in Full Settlement by Cheque	1,30,000
Deposited Cash into Bank	50,000
Paid to Creditor Ajay by Cheque in Full Settlement	1,95,000

He withdrew for his personal use an amount of ₹ 30,000 by cheque. *You are required to*

1. Journalise these transactions after considering the following information
   (a) Value of goods unsold on 31st March, 2025, valued at cost ₹ 1,70,000
   (b) Depreciate furniture @ 2%
   (c) Telephone bill for the month of March 2025 not yet paid ₹ 15,000
2. Open ledger and prepare trial balance.
3. Prepare financial statements for the year ended 31st March, 2025 and also calculate the profitability ratios i.e. gross profit ratio, net profit ratio and also comment on the profitability of the company, comparing its performance with the industry standards. Industry standard being 50% and 20% respectively for gross profit and net profit.

Detailed Study of the Project

Introduction

The project is to prepare accounting record of Mr Sultan Raza for the accounting year 2024-25 and also to prepare trial balance, trading and profit and loss account and balance sheet. Necessary data has been provided for the project work.

Project Work

Sample Question Papers

To make students practice of examination in real sense, there are 3 Sample Question Papers at the end. All these Sample Questions Papers are exactly prepared on the latest syllabus & pattern of examination.

SAMPLE QUESTION PAPER 1

A Highly Simulated Sample Question Paper for CBSE Class XII Examination

ACCOUNTANCY

Time : 3 Hours **Max. Marks : 80**

General Instructions

1. This question paper contains **34** questions. **All** questions are compulsory.
2. This question paper is divided into **two** Parts: **Part A** and **B**.
3. **Part-A** and **B** are compulsory for all the candidates.
4. Question Nos. **1 to 16** (Part-A) and **27 to 30** (Part-B) are multiple choice questions carrying **1** mark each.
5. Question Nos. **17 to 20** (Part-A) and **31 & 32** (Part-B) are short answer type questions, carrying **3** marks each.
6. Question Nos. from **21, 22** (Part-A) and **33** (Part-B) are long answer type-I questions, carrying **4** marks each.
7. Question Nos. from **23 to 26** (Part-A) and **34** (Part-B) are long answer type-II questions, carrying **6** marks each.
8. There is no overall choice. However, an internal choice has been provided in few questions in each of the parts.

PART-A

(Accounting for Partnership Firms and Companies)

1. If a partner withdraws equal amount at end of each quarter, then .... are to be considered for interest on total drawings. (1)

(a) 5.5 months (b) 6 months

(c) 4.5 months (d) 7.5 months

2. A company issued 25,000 shares and received applications for 35,000 shares. Company wants to allot shares to everyone who has applied. What will be the ratio for allotment? (1)

(a) 6:7 (b) 7:5 (c) 5:7 (d) 7:6

3. V, S and T are partners in a firm with profit sharing ratio 3 : 2 : 1 respectively. The extract of their balance sheet is as follows

Liabilities	Amt (₹)	Assets	Amt (₹)
Workmen Compensation Reserve	48,000		

At the time of retirement of T, if liability for workmen compensation to the extent of ₹ 24,000 is to be created, then at what amount will workmen compensation reserve be shown in new balance sheet? (1)

(a) ₹ 48,000 (b) ₹ 72,000

(c) ₹ 24,000 (d) Not to be shown in new balance sheet

Or Sonu and Monu are partners sharing profits and losses in the ratio of 3 : 2. Tonu is admitted for 1/5th share in profits of the firm which he gets entirely from Sonu. Find out the new profit sharing ratio.

(a) 12 : 8 : 5 (b) 8 : 12 : 5

(c) 2 : 2 : 1 (d) 2 : 2 : 2

Project Work

As per the latest syllabus, 20 marks have been kept for the project work. To make the students ready for this portion of the syllabus, a supplement of project work (covering 3 projects) is provided.

Latest Course Structure

PART A : Accounting for Partnership Firms and Companies — 60 Marks

UNIT 1 Accounting for Partnership Firms — 36 Marks

Units/Topics	Learning Outcomes
• Partnership: features, Partnership Deed. • Provisions of the Indian Partnership Act 1932 in the absence of partnership deed. • Fixed v/s fluctuating capital accounts. Preparation of Profit & Loss Appropriation account- division of profit among partners, guarantee of profits. • Past adjustments (relating to interest on capital, interest on drawing, salary and profit sharing ratio). • Goodwill: Meaning, nature, factors affecting, need for valuation and methods of valuation - average profit, super profit and capitalization. **Note:** Interest on partner's loan is to be treated as a charge against profits. Goodwill to be adjusted through partners capital/current account. **Accounting for Partnership Firms : Reconstitution and Dissolution** • **Change in the Profit Sharing Ratio** among the existing partners - sacrificing ratio, gaining ratio, accounting for revaluation of assets and reassessment of liabilities and treatment of reserves, accumulated profits and losses. Preparation of revaluation account and balance sheet. • **Admission of a Partner** effect of admission of a partner on change in the profit sharing ratio, treatment of goodwill (as per AS 26), treatment for revaluation of assets and reassessment of liabilities, treatment of reserves, accumulated profits and losses, adjustment of capital accounts and preparation of capital, current account and balance sheet.	**After going through this unit, the students will be able to:** • State the meaning of partnership, partnership firm and partnership deed. • Describe the characteristic features of partnership and the contents of partnership deed. • Discuss the significance of provision of Partnership Act in the absence of partnership deed. • Differentiate between fixed and fluctuating capital, outline the process and develop the understanding and skill of preparation of Profit and Loss Appropriation Account. • Develop the understanding and skill of preparation of profit and loss appropriation account involving guarantee of profits. • Develop the understanding and skill of making past adjustments. • State the meaning, nature and factors affecting goodwill. • Develop the understanding and skill of valuation of goodwill using different methods. • State the meaning of sacrificing ratio, gaining ratio and the change in profit sharing ratio among existing partners. • Develop the understanding of accounting treatment of revaluation assets and re-assessment of liabilities and treatment of reserves and accumulated profits by preparing revaluation account and balance sheet.

- **Retirement and Death of a Partner** effect of retirement / death of a partner on change in profit sharing ratio, treatment of goodwill (as per AS 26), treatment for revaluation of assets and reassessment of liabilities, adjustment of accumulated profits, losses and reserves, adjustment of capital accounts and preparation of capital, current account and balance sheet. Preparation of loan account of the retiring partner.
- Calculation of deceased partner's share of profit till the date of death. Preparation of deceased partner's capital account and his executor's account.
- **Dissolution of a partnership firm:** Meaning of dissolution of partnership and partnership firm, types of dissolution of a firm. Settlement of accounts - preparation of realization account, and other related accounts: capital accounts of partners and cash/bank a/c (excluding piecemeal distribution, sale to a company and insolvency of partner(s)).

Note

(i) If the realised value of tangible assets is not given, it should be considered as realised at book value itself.

(ii) If the realised value of intangible assets is not given, it should be considered as nil (zero value).

(iii) In case, the realization expenses are borne by a partner, clear indication should be given regarding the payment there of.

- Explain the effect of change in profit sharing ratio on admission of a new partner.
- Develop the understanding and skill of treatment of goodwill as per As-26, treatment of revaluation of assets and re-assessment of liabilities, treatment of reserves and accumulated profits, adjustment of capital accounts and preparation of capital, current account and balance sheet of the new firm.
- Explain the effect of retirement/death of a partner on change in profit sharing ratio.
- Develop the understanding of accounting treatment of goodwill, revaluation of assets and re-assessment of liabilities and adjustment of accumulated profits, losses and reserves on retirement/death of a partner and capital adjustment.
- Develop the skill of calculation of deceased partner's share till the time of his death and prepare deceased partner's and executor's account.
- Discuss the preparation of the capital accounts of the remaining partners and the balance sheet of the firm after retirement / death of a partner.
- Understand the situations under which a partnership firm can be dissolved.
- Develop the understanding of preparation of realisation account and other related accounts.

UNIT 2 Accounting for Companies

24 Marks

Units/Topics

Accounting for Share Capital

- Features and types of companies
- Share and share capital: nature and types.
- Accounting for share capital: issue and allotment of equity and preference shares, Public subscription of shares - over subscription and under subscription of shares; issue at par and at premium, calls in advance and arrears (excluding interest), issue of shares for consideration other than cash.
- Concept of Private Placement and Employee Stock Option Plan (ESOP), sweat equity.
- Accounting treatment of forfeiture and re-issue of shares.
- Disclosure of share capital in company's Balance Sheet.

Learning Outcomes

After going through this unit, the students will be able to:

- State the meaning of share and share capital and differentiate between equity shares and preference shares and different types of share capital.
- Understand the meaning of private placement of shares and Employee Stock Option Plan.
- Explain the accounting treatment of share capital transactions regarding issue of shares.
- Develop the understanding of accounting treatment of forfeiture and re-issue of forfeited shares.
- Describe the presentation of share capital in the balance sheet of the company as per schedule III part I of the Companies Act 2013.

Accounting for Debentures

- Debentures: Meaning, types, Issue of debentures at par, at a premium and at a discount. Issue of debentures for consideration other than cash; Issue of debentures with terms of redemption; debentures as collateral security-concept, interest on debentures (Concept of TDS is excluded). Writing off discount/loss on issue of debentures.

Note : Discount or loss on issue of debentures to be written off in the year debentures are allotted from Security Premium Reserve (if it exists) and then from Statement of Profit and Loss as Financial Cost (AS 16).

- Explain the accounting treatment of different categories of transactions related to issue of debentures.
- Develop the understanding and skill of writing of discount/loss on issue of debentures.
- Understanding the concept of collateral security and its presentation in balance sheet.
- Develop the skill of calculating interest on debentures and its accounting treatment.
- State the meaning of redemption of debentures.

PART B : Financial Statement Analysis

20 Marks

UNIT 3 Analysis of Financial Statements

12 Marks

Units/Topics	Learning Outcomes
• **Financial Statements of a Company:** Meaning, nature, uses and importance of financial statement. Statement of Profit and Loss and Balance Sheet in the prescribed form with major headings and sub headings (as per Schedule III to the Companies Act, 2013). **Note:** Exceptional items, extraordinary items and profit (loss) from discontinued operations are excluded. • **Financial Statement Analysis:** Meaning, objectives, importance and limitations. • **Tools for Financial Statement Analysis:** Comparative statements, common size statements, ratio analysis and cash flow analysis. • **Accounting Ratios:** Meaning, objectives, advantages, classification and computation. • **Liquidity Ratios:** Current ratio and Quick ratio. • **Solvency Ratios**: Debt to Equity Ratio, Total Asset to Debt Ratio, Proprietary Ratio and Interest Coverage Ratio. Debt to Capital Employed Ratio. • **Activity Ratios:** Inventory Turnover Ratio, Trade Receivables Turnover Ratio, Trade Payables Turnover Ratio, Fixed Asset Turnover Ratio, Net Asset Turnover Ratio and Working Capital Turnover Ratio. • **Profitability Ratios:** Gross Profit Ratio, Operating Ratio, Operating Profit Ratio, Net Profit Ratio and Return on Investment.	**After going through this unit, the students will be able to:** • Develop the understanding of major headings and sub-headings (as per Schedule III to the Companies Act, 2013) of balance sheet as per the prescribed norms / formats. • State the meaning, objectives and limitations of financial statement analysis. • Discuss the meaning of different tools of 'financial statements analysis'. • Develop the skill of preparation of comparative and common size statement. • State the meaning, objectives and significance of different types of ratios. • Develop the understanding of computation of current ratio and quick ratio. • Develop the skill of computation of debt equity ratio, total asset to debt ratio, proprietary ratio and interest coverage ratio. • Develop the skill of computation of inventory turnover ratio, trade receivables and trade payables ratio and working capital turnover ratio and others. • Develop the skill of computation of gross profit ratio, operating ratio, operating profit ratio, net profit ratio and return on investment.

Note: *Net Profit ratio is to be calculated on the basis of profit before and after tax.*

UNIT 4 Cash Flow Statement

8 Marks

Units/Topics	Learning Outcomes
• Meaning, objectives, benefits, cash and cash equivalents, classification of activities and preparation [as per AS 3 (Revised) (Indirect Method only] **Note:** (i) Adjustments relating to depreciation and amortization, profit or loss on sale of assets including investments, dividend (both final and interim) and tax. (ii) Bank overdraft and cash credit to be treated as short term borrowings. (iii) Current Investments to be taken as Marketable securities unless otherwise specified.	**After going through this unit, the students will be able to:** • State the meaning and objectives of cash flow statement. • Develop the understanding of preparation of Cash Flow Statement using indirect method as per AS 3 with given adjustments.

Note: *Previous years' proposed dividend to be given effect, as prescribed in AS-4, events occurring after the balance sheet date. Current years' proposed dividend will be accounted for in the next year after it is declared by the shareholders.*

PART C : Project Work

20 Marks

Please refer to the guidelines published by CBSE.

Accountancy -1 Class XII NCERT Publication

Accountancy -II Class XII NCERT Publication

PART A
Accounting for Partnership Firms and Companies

01
CHAPTER

When two or more persons join hands to set up a business and share its profits and losses, they are said to be in partnership.

Accounting for Partnership Firm: Fundamentals

▼ **YOUR STUDY GOALS**

▼ **YOUR PRACTICE GOAL**

- Topicwise Solved Questions (35 Solved Questions)
- Numerical Questions [46 Questions (Unsolved)]
- Theoretical Questions [4 Questions (with answers)]
- Objective Questions (64 Qs ; MCQs, A-R, Statements, Matching, Case)

1.1 Introduction to Partnership

According to Section 4 of the **Indian Partnership Act, 1932,** "Partnership is the relation between persons who have agreed to share the profits of a business carried on by all or any of them acting for all."

Essential Features of Partnership

1. **Number of Persons** Two or more persons and all such persons must be competent to contract.
2. **Agreement** Either written or oral.
3. **Motive** Carrying on a business (which must be legal) and earning profit.
4. **Mutual Agency** Business can be carried on by all or by any one of them, acting for all. Partners are agents as well as the principals of the firm.
5. **Sharing of Profits** As per agreement or as per provision of Partnership Act. However, it is not essential that the losses are also shared by all partners.
6. **Liability** Each partner is liable individually and collectively with all other partners to third party for all the acts of the firm, while he is a partner. Also, liability of a partner is unlimited.

Smart Study Chart No. 1

Partnership Deed

Meaning

Partnership comes into existence as a result of agreement among the partners. The document containing the terms and conditions of the agreement in writing among partners is called the 'partnership deed'.

Importance

Partnership deed and its registration is not compulsory but written agreement is considered beneficial due to following reasons

- Helps in settlement of dispute with respect to terms of partnership.
- Serves as an evidence in the court of law.
- Regulates the rights, duties and liabilities of each partner.

Contents of Partnership Deed

The partnership deed usually contains the following details

- Name and address of all the partners
- Name and address of the firm
- Principal place of business
- Nature of business
- Date of commencement of the partnership
- Rules regarding operation of bank accounts
- Capital to be contributed by each partner
- Interest on capitals, drawings and loan
- Salary/Commission to partners
- Profit and loss sharing ratio
- Accounting period of the firm
- Mode of auditor's appointment, if any
- The rights, duties and liabilities of each partner
- Treatment of loss arising out of insolvency of one or more partners
- Method of settlement of disputes among the partners
- Valuation of goodwill
- Any other matter relating to the conduct of business

Provisions in the Absence of Partnership Deed

Matters	Provisions of the Indian Partnership Act, 1932
Sharing of profits/losses	Shared equally by the partners
Interest on capital	Not paid to partners
Interest on drawings	Not charged from partners
Interest on loan by partner	Interest on loan is paid @ 6% p.a.
Remuneration to partner	No remuneration is to be paid to any partner

1.2 Profit and Loss Appropriation Account

The profit and loss appropriation account is an extension of the profit and loss account. It is prepared to show **distribution/appropriation of net profit among the partners** (whereas profit and loss account is prepared to ascertain net profit).

Format of Profit and Loss Appropriation Account

Profit and Loss Appropriation Account

Dr for the year ended... Cr

Particulars		Amt (₹)	Particulars		Amt (₹)
To Interest on Capital A/c			By Profit and Loss A/c (Net Profit subject to Appropriations)		...
A	...		By Interest on Drawings A/c		
B	...	...	A	...	
To Partners' Salaries A/c		...	B	...	...
To Reserve A/c		...			
To Partners' Commission A/c		...			
To Profit transferred to					
*A's Capital A/c	...				
**(or A's Current A/c)					
*B's Capital A/c	...				
**(or B's Current A/c)		...			
		...			...

Commission on profit to manager or partner on this amount

After all charges only

No charges on credit side

Divisible profit/ Distributable profit

**Under fluctuating capital method* ***Under fixed capital method*

Journal Entries Relating to Items of Profit and Loss Appropriation Account

1. **Transfer of profit from profit and loss account to profit and loss appropriation account**

Profit and Loss A/c	Dr
To Profit and Loss Appropriation A/c	

2. **Transfer of loss from profit and loss account to profit and loss appropriation account**

Profit and Loss Appropriation A/c	Dr
To Profit and Loss A/c	

3. **For allowing interest on capital**
   - **Adjusting Entry**

Interest on Capital A/c	Dr
To Partners' Capital*/Current**/A/cs (Individually)	

- **Closing Entry**

Profit and Loss Appropriation A/c	Dr
To Interest on Capital A/c	

4. **For partner's salaries/commission**

- **Adjusting Entry**

Partners' Salaries/Commission A/c	Dr
To Partner's Capital*/Current** A/cs (Individually)	

- **Closing Entry**

Profit and Loss Appropriation A/c	Dr
To Partner's Salaries/Commission A/c	

5. **For charging interest on drawings**

- **Adjusting Entry**

Partners' Capital*/Current** A/cs (Individually)	Dr
To Interest on Drawings A/c	

- **Closing Entry**

Interest on Drawings A/c	Dr
To Profit and Loss Appropriation A/c	

6. **For transfer to reserve out of profits**

Profit and Loss Appropriation A/c	Dr
To Reserve A/c	

7. **For transfer of credit balance of profit and loss appropriation account (Being profit)**

Profit and Loss Appropriation A/c	Dr
To Partner's Capital*/Current** A/cs	

8. **For transfer of debit balance of profit and loss appropriation account (Being loss)**

Partner's Capital*/Current**A/cs (Individually)	Dr
To Profit and Loss Appropriation A/c	

** When capitals are fluctuating ** When capitals are fixed*

1.3 Partners' Capital Accounts

All transactions relating to partners of the firm are recorded in the books of the firm through their capital accounts. In a partnership firm, there are two methods by which partners' capital accounts may be maintained. These are

- Fixed capital method
- Fluctuating capital method

Note Unless otherwise stated, the partners' capitals should be assumed to be fluctuating.

Smart Study Chart No. 2

Partners' Capital Account

Fixed Capitals

- Under this method, the capitals of the partners remain fixed unless additional capital is introduced or a part of the capital is withdrawn by the partners.
- Two accounts are maintained under fixed capital method i.e. capital account and current account.

Fluctuating Capitals

Under this method, only one account is maintained i.e. capital account.

Format of Accounts Maintained under Fixed Capital Method

Dr **Partners' Capital Account** Cr

Particulars	X (₹)	Y (₹)	Z (₹)	Particulars	X (₹)	Y (₹)	Z (₹)
To Cash/Bank A/c (Withdrawal of capital)	...	...	...	By Balance b/d	...	...	...
To Balance c/d	...	...	...	By Cash/Bank A/c (Additional Capital)	...	...	...
	...	...	...		...	...	...

Dr **Partners' Current Account** Cr

Particulars	X (₹)	Y (₹)	Z (₹)	Particulars	X (₹)	Y (₹)	Z (₹)
*To Balance b/d (In case of Debit Opening Balance)	...	...	...	*By Balance b/d (In case of Credit Opening Balance)	...	...	...
To Drawings A/c	...	...	...	By Interest on Capital A/c	...	...	...
To Interest on Drawings A/c	...	...	...	By Commission A/c	...	...	...
To Profit and Loss Appropriation A/c (Loss)	...	...	...	By Salary A/c	...	...	...
*To Balance c/d	...	...	...	By Profit and Loss Appropriation A/c (Profit)	...	...	...
				*By Balance c/d	...	...	...
	...	...	...		...	...	...

**Any one will appear*

Format of Account Maintained under Fluctuating Capital Method

Dr **Partners' Capital Account** Cr

Particulars	X (₹)	Y (₹)	Z (₹)	Particulars	X (₹)	Y (₹)	Z (₹)
*To Balance b/d (In case of Debit Opening Balance)	...	...	...	*By Balance b/d (In case of Credit Opening Balance)	...	...	...
To Cash/Bank A/c (Withdrawal of Capital)	...	...	...	By Cash/Bank A/c (Additional Capital)	...	...	...
To Drawings A/c	...	...	...	By Interest on Capital A/c	...	...	...
To Interest on Drawings A/c	...	...	...	By Salary A/c	...	...	...
To Profit and Loss Appropriation A/c (Loss)	...	...	...	By Commission A/c	...	...	...
*To Balance c/d	...	...	...	By Profit and Loss Appropriation A/c (Profit)	...	...	...
				*By Balance c/d	...	...	...
	...	...	...		...	...	...

**Any one will appear*

1.4 Appropriation and Charge Items

Appropriation implies distribution of available net profits left out after providing all expenses. Appropriations are provided only in case a firm has profits (and not in case of losses).

Smart Study Chart No. 3

Appropriation of Profit and Charge Against Profit

Appropriation

- Appropriation implies distribution of available net profits left out after providing all expenses. Appropriations are provided only in case a firm has profits (and not in case of losses).
- Appropriations are recorded (debited) to the profit and loss appropriation account.
- e.g. Interest on capital of partners, interest on drawings, salary or commission to a partner.

Charge

- Charges implies deduction of expenses from the profits in order to compute net profit/net loss during the accounting year.
- Charges are provided under all circumstances irrespective of profits or losses. Charges are recorded (debited) to the profit and loss account.
- e.g. Interest on loan from partner/outsider, salary/commission to employees/manager, rent to a partner/outsider.

These appropriation and charge items mentioned above are discussed in detail ahead.

1. Interest on Drawings

The amount withdrawn by partners in cash or in kind for their personal use is termed as **drawings**. Drawings may be against profits or against capital. No interest is charged on drawings, if partnership agreement is silent about interest on drawings. Interest on drawings is an income/gain for the firm and hence is credited to profit and loss appropriation account.

Calculation of Interest on Drawings

Drawings at Regular Interval

$$\text{Interest on Drawings} = \text{Annual Drawings} \times \frac{\text{Rate of Interest}}{100} \times \frac{\text{Average Period}}{12}$$

Time of Drawings	Average Period	Time of Drawings	Average Period
Monthly Drawings for 12 Months		**Half Yearly Drawings for 12 months**	
In the beginning of every month	6.5	In the beginning of the period	9
In the middle of every month	6	In the middle of the period	6
At the end of every month	5.5	At the end of the period	3
Quarterly Drawings for 12 Months		**Monthly Drawings for 6 Months**	
In the beginning of every quarter	7.5	In the beginning of the period	3.5
In the middle of every quarter	6	In the middle of the period	3
At the end of every quarter	4.5	At the end of the period	2.5

Drawings at Irregular Intervals

Important Points to Consider

- Drawings can be either out of profits or out of capital.
- Interest will not be charged in case of drawings out of capital.
- In the absence of any information, drawings will be considered as out of profits.

1. **When Date is given**

In this case, interest on drawings is calculated with the help of following methods

(i) **Simple Method** In this method, interest on drawings is calculated for every individual drawings considering the time for which it is used. Following table will be used

Date of Drawings	Amount of Drawings (₹)	Number of Months Remaining in the Year	Interest @ ...... % (₹)
...	...	...	...
...	...	...	...

$$\text{Interest on Drawings} = \text{Amount of Drawings} \times \frac{\text{Rate of Interest}}{100} \times \frac{\text{Months Remaining}}{12}$$

(ii) **Product Method** In this method, individual drawings are multiplied by the months remaining in the year and interest for one month (if period taken is in months) or for one day (if period taken is in days) is calculated on the total of such products. Following table will be used

Date of Drawings (A)	Amount of Drawings (B) (₹)	Number of Months Remaining in the Year (C)	Product (D) D = B × C (₹)
...	...	...	...
...	...	...	...

$$\text{Interest on Drawings} = \text{Total of Product} \times \frac{\text{Rate of Interest}}{100} \times \frac{1}{12} \text{ or } \frac{1}{365}$$

2. **When Date is not given**

In this case, total amount withdrawn is given but the date of withdrawals are not specified. In such case, it is assumed that the amount was withdrawn evenly throughout the year. Interest on total drawings is calculated for 6 months.

2. Interest on Capital

Interst on capital is generally allowed to compensate partners for contributing capital to the firm in excess of profit sharing ratio.

$$\text{Interest on Capital} = \text{Amount of Capital} \times \frac{\text{Rate}}{100} \times \text{Time}$$

- Interest on capital is always calculated on opening capital along with the additional capital introduced by partners (for the accounting period is remained in business).
- If question provides closing capital, then opening capital will be calculated first by using following formula

Opening Capital = Closing Capital + Drawing – Profits – Additional Capital

Smart Study Chart No. 4

Different Cases Related to Interest on Capital

Case 1 When partnership agreement says interest on capital is to be provided as a charge.
Treatment Interest on capital is fully allowed whether there is a profit or loss because charges are fully provided irrespective of the amount of profit or loss.

Case 2 When partnership agreement is silent as to interest on capital.
Treatment Interest on capital is not allowed in this case.

Case 3 When partnership agreement provides that interest on capital is to be allowed, but is silent as to the treatment of interest as a charge or appropriation.
Treatment Interest on capital will be allowed only if there are profits

- **Situation 1** In case of loss, no interest will be allowed.
- **Situation 2** In case there are sufficient profits, i.e. when profit before interest is equal to or more than the interest, full interest on capital will be allowed.
- **Situation 3** In case of insufficient profits, i.e. when profit before interest is less than the interest, profits will be distributed proportionately in the ratio of capital of each partner.

3. Salary or Commission to a Partner

Salary or commission to a partner is to be allowed only if the partnership agreement provides for the same

Commission as percentage of net profit **before** charging such commission	Commission as percentage of net profit **after** charging such commission
$= \text{Net Profit before Commission} \times \dfrac{\text{Rate of Commission}}{100}$	$= \text{Net Profit after Commission} \times \dfrac{\text{Rate of Commission}}{100 + \text{Rate of Commission}}$

4. Rent Paid to a Partner

It is a charge against the profits as it is payable to a partner for using his/her personal property in business. Alternatively, it can also be paid in cash.

Journal Entries relating to Rent Paid to a Partner

If rent have become due but is not yet paid	Rent A/c To Rent Payable A/c (Being the amount of rent have become due)	Dr
If rent is paid in cash	Rent A/c To Cash/Bank A/c (Being rent paid in cash)	Dr
For transferring rent to profit and loss account	Profit and Loss A/c To Rent A/c (Being rent charged to profit and loss account)	Dr

5. Interest on Loan

It includes two types which are discussed below

Smart Study Chart No. 5

Interest on Loan

By the Partner to the Firm

- If a partner advances a loan to the firm, he is entitled to receive interest at an agreed rate of interest. If there is no agreement as to the rate of interest, partner is entitled to interest on loan @ 6% per annum.
- Interest on partner's loan is a charge against the profits and it is to be allowed whether there are profits or not.

Journal Entries to Record Interest on Partner's Loan of Firm

For interest due on partner's loan	Interest on Partner's Loan A/c Dr To Partner's Loan A/c
For transferring the interest on partner's loan	Profit and Loss A/c Dr To Interest on Partner's Loan A/c

To the Partner by the Firm

When a partner takes a loan from the firm, interest is charged on such loan if partnership deed provide for the same or when the partners have agreed to the rate of interest to be charged on such loan.

Journal Entries to Record Partner's Loan from Firm

For charging interest on loan to a partner	Partner's Capital/Current A/c Dr To Interest on Partner's Loan A/c
For closing the interest on partner's loan account	Interest on Partner's Loan A/c Dr To Profit and Loss A/c

Appropriations are more than Available Profit

Sometimes, it is possible that amount of appropriations are more than the available profit.

In such a situation, firstly, the amount that should have been appropriated is determined for each partner. Then, the amount of appropriations so determined for each partner becomes the ratio for distribution of available profits among the partners.

1.5 Past Adjustments

If after closing the accounts of a partnership firm, some errors or omissions are discovered in the accounts, then such errors and omissions are rectified by making adjustments, instead of altering the closed accounts in the next accounting period. Such adjustments are called past adjustments, as they relate to past period. Accounting for past adjustments is made directly through the capital accounts of the concerned partners.

Usually, the following types of adjustments are effected

- When interest on capitals may have been omitted by mistake or have been wrongly treated.
- When interest on drawings may have been omitted.
- When salary or commission payable to a partner has been omitted.
- When profit sharing ratio has been changed with effect from some past date (i.e. retrospectively).
- When profits and losses have been distributed among the partners in wrong ratio.

Smart Study Chart No. 6

Rectification of Errors

Case I When a Single Adjustment Entry is Passed

In this case, a single adjusting entry is passed by debiting and crediting the partners' capital/current account with net effect (amount) of all the errors (past adjustments).

Steps to Pass Adjusting Journal Entry

***Step* 1** Calculate the amount already recorded by the way of share of profit, interest on capital, salary, commission, etc.

***Step* 2** Calculate the amount which should have been recorded by the way of interest on capital, salary or commission or share of profit, etc.

***Step* 3** Calculate the difference between the amounts calculated as per Step 1 and the amount calculated as per Step 2.

***Step* 4** Find out the partner who received excess and the partner who received less.

***Step* 5** Pass the adjusting journal entry by debiting the capital account of partner who received excess and by crediting the capital account of partner who received less.

Case II When Separate Adjustment Entries are Passed

In this case, separate journal entries are passed in place of one single adjustment entry and analytical table is also not prepared to determine the net effect of all adjustments.

Instead, separate journal entries are passed for each error or omission by debiting or crediting the profit and loss adjustment account.

After all the adjustment entries are passed, profit and loss adjustment account is closed by debiting or crediting the partner's capital/current accounts.

Format of Adjustment Table (To Be Used in Case I)

Statement Showing Adjustment to be Made

Particulars	X (₹)	Y (₹)	Total (₹)
A. **Amounts Already Recorded**			
Interest on Capital	...	...	...
Interest on Drawings	(...)	(...)	(...)
Salary/Commission to Partner	...	...	...
Share of Profit	...	...	...
	...	...	...
B. **Amounts which should have been Recorded**			
Interest on Capital	...	...	...
Interest on Drawings	(...)	(...)	(...)
Salary/Commission to Partner	...	...	...
Share of Profit	...	...	...
	...	...	...
Net Effect (A – B)	...	...	...

JOURNAL

Date	Particulars		LF	Amt (Dr)	Amt (Cr)
	Gaining Partners' Capital A/c	(Who received excess) Dr		...	
	To Sacrificing Partners' Capital A/c	(Who received less)			...

1.6 Guarantee of Profits

A partner may be admitted into the firm with a guarantee of minimum profit, which means that if his share of profit is less than that of guaranteed profit, then he would be paid the guaranteed share of profit. The guarantee may be provided by one or some or all of the partners in an existing ratio or in some other agreed ratio.

Different conditions regarding guarantee of profits

1. **Guarantee by the Firm to a Partner**
   - If a specific partner is guaranteed a certain amount, he must be paid atleast that much amount.
   - He may get more, if his share of profit according to the profit sharing ratio is more.
2. **Guarantee by One Partner to Another Partner**

   In this case, the deficiency is borne by the partner giving guarantee.
3. **Guarantee Given by the Partner to the Firm**

   Partners may guarantee the certain minimum amount of profit or income earned by him for the firm.
4. **Simultaneous Guarantee by the Firm to the Partner and by the Partner to the Firm**
   - In this situation, guarantee given to the firm by the partner will be applied first.
   - If the profit earned by the partner falls short of the guaranteed minimum amount, the deficiency will be debited to the partner's capital/current account and credited to profit and loss appropriation account of the firm.
   - It will increase the amount of total profit.
   - The minimum guaranteed amount will be paid to the partner out of total profit and remaining amount of profit will be distributed among other partners.

Mind Map

Accounting for Partnership Firm : Fundamentals

1 Definition of Partnership

Partnership is the relation between persons who have agreed to share the profits of a business carried on by all or any of them acting for all.

2 Partnership Deed

- It is a document containing the terms and conditions of the agreement in writing.
- It serves as an evidence in the court of law.

3 Provisions in the Absence of Deed

- Profits and losses shall be shared equally.
- Interest on capital shall not be allowed.
- Interest on drawings shall not be charged.
- Salary, commission or any other remuneration to partners shall not be allowed.
- Interest @ 6% p.a. shall be allowed on partner's loan to the firm.

4 Profit and Loss Appropriation Account

- It is an extension of the profit and loss account.
- It is prepared to show distribution/appropriation of net profit among the partners.

Format

Dr **Profit and Loss Appropriation Account** Cr

Particulars	Amt (₹)	Particulars	Amt (₹)
All appropriations like salary, interest on capital to partners, reserves, profit, etc. appears on debit side.	...	Net profit after all charges and interest on drawings appears on credit side.	...

5 Partners' Capital Accounts

These accounts can be prepared using two methods, i.e.

- **Fixed Captial Method** In this method, two accounts, i.e. capital account and current account are maintained for every partner.
  Capital account includes opening capital, additional capital and drawing of capital. All other items are recorded in current account.
- **Fluctuating Capital Method** In this method, only capital account of every partner is maintained.

6 Interest on Capital

- Only allowed, if it is provided in partnership deed.
- Not allowed in case of losses, if it is an appropriation.
- Allowed in appropriation ratio, if profits are inadequate.
- If it is a charge, then it is allowed even in case of losses.
- **Formula** Interest on Capital $= \text{Capital} \times \frac{\text{Rate}}{100} \times \text{Time}$

7 Interest on Drawings

- Not charged in absence of provision in partnership deed.
- It is charged for six months, if date of drawings is not given.
- It is charged when drawings are out of profit.
- In case of regular drawings, it is charged for average months.
- In case of irregular drawings, it is calculated by simple method or product method.
- **Formula** Interest on Drawings =

$$\text{Amount of Drawings} \times \frac{\text{Rate of Interest}}{100} \times \frac{\text{Average Period/ Months Remaining}}{12}$$

8 Past Adjustments

When some errors or omissions are discovered after closing the accounts, then these are rectified by making adjustments. Such adjustments are called past adjustments.

Accounting Treatment

- By passing a single adjustment entry through capital accounts.
- By profit and loss adjustment account (by passing separate journal entries).

9 Guarantee of Profits

- Guarantee by firm to a partner.
- Guarantee by one partner to another partner.
- Guarantee given by the partner to the firm.
- Simultaneous guarantee by the firm to the partner and by the partner to the firm.

Topicwise Solved Questions

Introduction and Format of Basic Accounts

Solved Question 1 **P, Q and R are partners in a firm without a partnership deed.**

(i) P, has contributed more capital than other partners and demands interest on capital at 10% p.a. But Q and R do not agree with him.

(ii) Q devotes full time in the business and demands a salary of ₹ 20,000 p.m. But P and R do not agree with him.

(iii) R demands interest on the loan of ₹ 25,000 given by her at the market rate of interest, i.e. @ 10% p.a.

(iv) P has withdrawn ₹ 15,000 from the firm for his personal use. Q and R demands that interest on drawings should be charged @ 8% per annum.

(v) Profit before taking into account any of the above claims was ₹ 25,000 at the end of the first year of the business. P demands share of profit in the capital ratio.

How will the matters be resolved?

Sol. (i) Interest on capital is not payable to partner. Therefore, P will not get interest on the capital.

(ii) Remuneration is not payable to partner. Therefore, Q will not get salary.

(iii) Interest on loan by partner is payable @ 6% p.a. Therefore, R will get interest ₹ 1,500 (i.e. 25,000 × 6/100).

(iv) Interest on P drawings will not be charged.

(v) Profit after interest on loan by R, i.e. ₹ 23,500 (25,000 – 1,500) is to be distributed equally.

Solved Question 2 **A, B and C are partners in a firm sharing profits in the ratio of 3 : 2 : 1 with capital balances of ₹ 4,00,000, ₹ 4,00,000 and ₹ 2,00,000 respectively. Interest on capital is charged @ 12% p.a. They withdrew ₹ 12,000, ₹ 10,000 and ₹ 6,000 during the year and interest on drawings amounted to ₹ 1,000, ₹ 500 and ₹ 500. A and B are entitled for a salary of ₹ 2,000 and ₹ 3,000 per month, whereas B and C are entitled for a commission of ₹ 10,000 and ₹ 12,000 respectively. Net profit for the year ended 31st March, 2024 amounted to ₹ 2,36,000. Prepare profit and loss appropriation account and partners' capital account.**

Sol. Dr **Profit and Loss Appropriation Account** Cr

Particulars		Amt (₹)	Particulars		Amt (₹)
To Interest on Capital A/c			By Net Profit		2,36,000
A's Capital A/c	48,000		By Interest on Drawings		
B's Capital A/c	48,000		A's Capital A/c	1,000	
C's Capital A/c	24,000	1,20,000	B's Capital A/c	500	
To Partners' Salary A/c			C's Capital A/c	500	2,000
A's Capital A/c	24,000				
B's Capital A/c	36,000	60,000			
To Partners' Commission A/c					
B' Capital A/c	10,000				
C's Capital A/c	12,000	22,000			
To Divisible Profits					
A's Capital A/c	18,000				
B's Capital A/c	12,000				
C's Capital A/c	6,000	36,000			
		2,38,000			2,38,000

Dr **Partners' Capital Account** Cr

Particulars	A (₹)	B (₹)	C (₹)	Particulars	A (₹)	B (₹)	C (₹)
To Drawings	12,000	10,000	6,000	By Balance b/d	4,00,000	4,00,000	2,00,000
To Interest on Drawings	1,000	500	500	By Interest on Capital A/c	48,000	48,000	24,000
To Balance c/d	4,77,000	4,95,500	2,35,500	By Partners' Salary	24,000	36,000	—
				By Partners' Commission	—	10,000	12,000
				By Divisible Profit	18,000	12,000	6,000
	4,90,000	5,06,000	2,42,000		4,90,000	5,06,000	2,42,000

Interest on Drawings

Solved Question 3 **Calculate the interest on drawings of Mr. Karan Sharma @ 10% per annum in each of the following alternative cases.**

(i) If he withdrew ₹ 5,000 per month in the beginning of every month.
(ii) If he withdrew ₹ 5,000 per month at the end of every month.
(iii) If he withdrew ₹ 5,000 per month in the middle of every month.
(iv) If he withdrew ₹ 5,000 in the beginning of every month for 6 months.
(v) If he withdrew ₹ 5,000 at the middle of every month for 6 months.
(vi) If he withdrew ₹ 5,000 at the end of every month for first 6 months.
(vii) If he withdrew ₹ 5,000 in the beginning of every month for 9 months.
(viii) If he withdrew ₹ 5,000 at the end of every month for 9 months.
(ix) If he withdrew ₹ 5,000 in the middle of every month for 9 months.
(x) If he withdrew ₹ 5,000 in the beginning of each quarter.
(xi) If he withdrew ₹ 5,000 at the end of each quarter.
(xii) If he withdrew ₹ 5,000 at the middle of each quarter.

Sol. Interest on Drawings $= \text{Annual Drawings} \times \frac{\text{Rate}}{100} \times \frac{\text{Average Period}}{12}$

(i) Interest on Drawings $= (5{,}000 \times 12) \times \frac{10}{100} \times \frac{6.5}{12} =$ ₹ 3,250

(ii) Interest on Drawings $= (5{,}000 \times 12) \times \frac{10}{100} \times \frac{5.5}{12} =$ ₹ 2,750

(iii) Interest on Drawings $= (5{,}000 \times 12) \times \frac{10}{100} \times \frac{6}{12} =$ ₹ 3,000

(iv) Interest on Drawings $= (5{,}000 \times 6) \times \frac{10}{100} \times \frac{3.5}{12} =$ ₹ 875

(v) Interest on Drawings $= (5{,}000 \times 6) \times \frac{10}{100} \times \frac{3}{12} =$ ₹ 750

(vi) Interest on Drawings $= (5{,}000 \times 6) \times \frac{10}{100} \times \frac{8.5}{12} =$ ₹ 2,125

(vii) Interest on Drawings $= (5{,}000 \times 9) \times \frac{10}{100} \times \frac{5}{12} =$ ₹ 1,875

(viii) Interest on Drawings $= (5{,}000 \times 9) \times \frac{10}{100} \times \frac{4}{12} =$ ₹ 1,500

(ix) Interest on Drawings $= (5{,}000 \times 9) \times \frac{10}{100} \times \frac{4.5}{12} =$ ₹ 1,687.5

(x) Interest on Drawings $= (5{,}000 \times 4) \times \frac{10}{100} \times \frac{7.5}{12} =$ ₹ 1,250

(xi) Interest on Drawings $= (5{,}000 \times 4) \times \frac{10}{100} \times \frac{4.5}{12} =$ ₹ 750

(xii) Interest on Drawings $= (5{,}000 \times 4) \times \frac{10}{100} \times \frac{6}{12} =$ ₹ 1,000

Solved Question 4 **Calculate the interest on drawings of Rakesh in the following cases**

(i) If he withdrew ₹ 90,000 during the year and interest is charged @10% p.a.
(ii) If he withdrew ₹ 7,500 per month during the year and interest is charged @10% p.a.
(iii) If he withdrew ₹ 2,00,000 during the year and interest in charged @10%.

Sol. (i) Assuming that drawings were made evenly throughout the year, interest on drawings has been calculated for an average period of 6 months.

Interest on Drawings $= 90{,}000 \times 10/100 \times 6/12 =$ ₹ 4,500

(ii) Total Drawings = 7,500 × 12 = ₹ 90,000

Interest on Drawings = 90,000 × 10/100 × 6/12 = ₹ 4,500

(iii) Interest on Drawings = $2,00,000 \times \frac{10}{100}$ = ₹ 20,000 (Time will not be considered as 'p.a.' word is not suffixed with rate)

Solved Question 5 **Dinesh is a partner in a firm. He withdrew the following amounts during the year 2023.**

Date	1st May	1st August	30th September	31st January	31st March
Amt (₹)	4,000	10,000	4,000	12,000	4,000

Interest on drawings to be charged @ $7\frac{1}{2}$% per annum. Calculate the amount of interest to be charged on Dinesh's drawings for the year ending 31st March, 2023 by (i) Simple method and (ii) Product method.

Sol. (i) **Simple Method**

Calculation of Interest on Dinesh's Drawings

Date	Amt (₹)	Number of months upto 31st March	Interest @ 7.5% (₹)
1st May, 2023	4,000	11 months	275 $\left(4,000 \times 7.5 / 100 \times \frac{11}{12}\right)$
1st August, 2023	10,000	8 months	500 $\left(10,000 \times 7.5 / 100 \times \frac{8}{12}\right)$
30th September, 2023	4,000	6 months	150 $\left(4,000 \times 7.5 / 100 \times \frac{6}{12}\right)$
31st January, 2024	12,000	2 months	150 $\left(12,000 \times 7.5 / 100 \times \frac{2}{12}\right)$
31st March, 2024	4,000	0 month	0
Total	34,000		1,075

(ii) **Product Method**

Calculation of Interest on Dinesh's Drawings

Date	Amt (₹)	Period	Product (₹)
1st May, 2023	4,000	11 months	44,000
1st August, 2023	10,000	8 months	80,000
30th September, 2023	4,000	6 months	24,000
31st January, 2024	12,000	2 months	24,000
31st March, 2024	4,000	0 month	—
Total			1,72,000

Interest = $1,72,000 \times \frac{7.5}{100} \times \frac{1}{12}$ = ₹ 1,075

Interest on Capital

Solved Question 6 **A and B are partners sharing profits and losses in the ratio of 3 : 2. Their capital accounts showed balances of ₹ 1,50,000 and ₹ 2,00,000 respectively on 1st January, 2020. Show the treatment of interest on capital and distribution of profits for the year ending 31st March, 2024 in each of the following alternatives.**

(i) If the partnership deed is silent as to the payment of interest on capital and the profit for the year is ₹ 50,000.

(ii) If partnership deed provides for interest on capital @ 8% per annum and the firm incurred a loss of ₹ 50,000 during the year.

(iii) If partnership deed provides for interest on capital @ 8% per annum and the firm earned a profit of ₹ 50,000 during the year.

(iv) If the partnership deed provides for interest on capital @ 8% per annum and the firm earned a profit of ₹ 14,000 during the year.

(v) If the partnership deed provides interest on capital @ 8% is to be treated as a charge and the profit for the year is ₹ 50,000.

(vi) If the partnership deed provides interest @ 8% on capital is to be treated as a charge and the profit for the year is ₹ 14,000.

(vii) If the partnership deed provides interest on capital @ 8% is to be treated as a charge and firm incurred the loss for the year amounted to ₹ 10,000.

Sol. (i) Dr **Profit and Loss Account** Cr

Particulars		Amt (₹)	Particulars	Amt (₹)
To Profit transferred to			By Profit and Loss A/c (Profit for the Year)	50,000
A's Capital A/c	30,000			
B's Capital A/c	20,000	50,000		
		50,000		50,000

Working Note

If the partnership deed is silent, no interest will be allowed on capitals. However, the whole amount of profit will be distributed among the partners in their profit sharing ratio.

(ii) Dr **Profit and Loss Account** Cr

Particulars	Amt (₹)	Particulars		Amt (₹)
To Profit and Loss A/c (Loss for the Year)	50,000	By Loss transferred to		
		A's Capital A/c	30,000	
		B's Capital A/c	20,000	50,000
	50,000			50,000

Important Problem Solving Points

- Interest on capital will not be provided in case of loss.
- Profit and loss appropriation account will not be prepared in case of loss.
- Alternatively, loss can be distributed through profit and loss adjustment account.

(iii) Dr **Profit and Loss Appropriation Account** Cr

Particulars		Amt (₹)	Particulars	Amt (₹)
To Interest on Capital A/cs			By Profit and Loss A/c	50,000
A (1,50,000 × 8%)	12,000		(Profit for the Year)	
B (2,00,000 × 8%)	16,000	28,000		
To Profit transferred to				
A's Capital A/c	13,200			
B's Capital A/c	8,800	22,000		
		50,000		50,000

(iv) Dr **Profit and Loss Appropriation Account** Cr

Particulars		Amt (₹)	Particulars	Amt (₹)
To Interest on Capital A/c			By Profit and Loss A/c	14,000
A	6,000			
B	8,000	14,000		
		14,000		14,000

Working Note

Interest on Capital

$$A = 1,50,000 \times \frac{8}{100} = ₹\ 12,000 \qquad \text{A will get} = \frac{12,000}{28,000} \times 14,000 = ₹\ 6,000$$

$$B = 2,00,000 \times \frac{8}{100} = ₹\ 16,000 \qquad \text{B will get} = \frac{16,000}{28,000} \times 14,000 = ₹\ 8,000$$

₹ 28,000

(v) Dr **Profit and Loss Account** Cr

Particulars		Amt (₹)	Particulars	Amt (₹)
To Interest on Capital A/cs			By Profit for the Year	50,000
A (1,50,000 × 8%)	12,000			
B (2,00,000 × 8%)	16,000	28,000		
To Profit transferred to Profit and Loss Appropriation A/c		22,000		
		50,000		50,000

Dr **Profit and Loss Appropriation Account** Cr

Particulars		Amt (₹)	Particulars	Amt (₹)
To Profit transferred to Capital A/cs			By Profit and Loss A/c (Net Profit)	22,000
A (22,000 × 3/5)	13,200			
B (22,000 × 2/5)	8,800	22,000		
		22,000		22,000

(vi) Dr **Profit and Loss Account** Cr

Particulars		Amt (₹)	Particulars		Amt (₹)
To Interest on Capital A/cs			By Profit for the Year		14,000
A	12,000		By Loss transferred to Capital A/cs		
B	16,000	28,000	A (14,000 × 3/5)	8,400	
			B (14,000 × 2/5)	5,600	14,000
		28,000			28,000

(vii) Dr **Profit and Loss Account** Cr

Particulars		Amt (₹)	Particulars		Amt (₹)
To Loss for the Year		10,000	By Loss transferred to Capital A/cs		
To Interest on Capital A/cs			A (38,000 × 3/5)	22,800	
A	12,000		B (38,000 × 2/5)	15,200	38,000
B	16,000	28,000			
		38,000			38,000

Solved Question 7 *(When additional capital and withdrawal of capital are given)* **G and K are partners in a firm with capital balances of ₹ 5,00,000 and ₹ 7,00,000 at the beginning of the year. G brings additional capital of ₹ 1,00,000 on 30th June, 2023 and K withdrew ₹ 1,00,000 from his capital on 1st January, 2024. Interest on capital is to be provided @15% p.a. and interest on drawings @ 10%. G withdrew ₹ 3,000 per month at the begining of each month and K withdrew ₹ 4,000 per month during the year. Calculate interest on capital and drawings.**

Sol. G's Interest on Capital = (5,00,000 × 15/100 × 3/2) + (6,00,000 × 15/100 × 9/12) = 18,750 + 67,500 = ₹ 86,250

K's Interest on Capital = (7,00,000 × 15/100 × 9/12) + (6,00,000 × 15/100 × 3/12) = 78,750 + 22,500 = ₹ 1,01,250

$$\text{G's Interest on Drawings} = 36{,}000 \times \frac{10}{100} = ₹\ 3{,}600$$

$$\text{K's Interest on Drawings} = 48{,}000 \times \frac{10}{100} = ₹\ 4{,}800$$

Solved Question 8 *(When closing capital is given)* **Om and Sai are partners sharing profits and losses in the ratio of 3 : 1. Their capitals at the end of the financial year 2023-24 were ₹ 1,50,000 and ₹ 75,000. During the year 2023-24, Om's drawings were ₹ 20,000 and the drawings of Jai were ₹ 5,000. Profit before charging interest on capital for the year was ₹ 16,000 which was duly credited to their accounts. Jai had brought additional capital of ₹ 16,000 on 30th September, 2023. Calculate interest on capital @ 12% per annum for the year 2023-24.**

Sol.

Statement Showing Calculation of Capital at the Beginning

Particulars	Om (₹)	Jai (₹)
Capital at the End	1,50,000	75,000
(+) Drawings During the Year	20,000	5,000
	1,70,000	80,000
(–) Share of Profit (Credited)	(12,000)	(4,000)
	1,58,000	76,000
(–) Additional Capital	—	(16,000)
Capital in the Beginning	1,58,000	60,000

$$\text{Interest on Om's Capital} = 1{,}58{,}000 \times \frac{12}{100} = ₹\ 18{,}960$$

$$\text{Interest on Jai's Capital} = \left(60{,}000 \times \frac{12}{100}\right) + \left(16{,}000 \times \frac{12}{100} \times \frac{6}{12}\right) = 7{,}200 + 960 = ₹\ 8{,}160$$

Other Appropriation and Charge Items

Solved Question 9 (*Partner's commission and interest on loan*) **Rajesh and Vikram are partners sharing profits in a 3 : 2 ratio, with capitals of ₹ 75,000 and ₹ 45,000, respectively. They have agreed on an interest rate of 9% per annum on capital. Additionally, Vikram is entitled to an annual salary of ₹ 6,750. Rajesh also lent the firm ₹ 75,000 on 1st April, 2023, without any agreement. Rajesh is entitled for a commission of 5% of net profit after charging such commission. For the financial year 2023-24, the firm earned a profit of ₹ 18,750 after Vikram's salary.**

Prepare the profit and loss appropriation account to illustrate the distribution of profit for the year ending 31st March, 2024.

Sol.

Profit and Loss Appropriation Account
Dr for the year ended 31st March, 2024 Cr

Particulars		Amt (₹)	Particualrs	Amt (₹)
To Interest on Capital			By Net Profit	21,000
Rajesh's Capital	6,750		(18,750 + 6,750 – 4,500**)	
Vikram's Capital	4,050	10,800		
To Salary A/c				
Vikram's Capital		6,750		
To Commission				
Rajesh's Capital**		1,000		
To Profit transferred to				
Rajesh's Capital	1,470			
Vikram's Capital	980	2,450		
		21,000		21,000

$$^{*}\text{Interest on Rajesh's Loan} = 75{,}000 \times \frac{6}{100} = ₹\ 4{,}500$$

$$^{**}\text{Rajesh's Commission} = 21{,}000 \times \frac{5}{105} = ₹\ 1{,}000$$

Solved Question 10 (*Partner's commission and rent to partner*) **Ravi, Sam and Priya established a partnership firm on 1st April, 2023. They contributed ₹ 1,25,000, ₹ 1,00,000 and ₹ 75,000, respectively, as their capitals and agreed to share profits and losses in the ratio of 3 : 1 : 1. Business is being carried from the property owned by Priya on a monthly rent of ₹ 4,000. Ravi is to be paid a salary of ₹ 2,500 per month and Sam will receive a commission 6% of net profit after charging all the expenses including such commission. It is also stipulated that interest on capital will be allowed at 6% per annum. The net profit as per the profit and loss account for the year ending 31st March, 2024 was ₹ 1,49,000.**

Prepare the proft and loss appropriation account to illustrate the distribution of profit among the partners.

Sol.

Profit and Loss Appropriation Account
for the year ended 31st March, 2024

Dr | | | | Cr

Particulars		Amt (₹)	Particualrs	Amt (₹)
To Interest on Capital			By Net Profit (1,49,000 – 48,000**)	1,01,000
Ravi's Capital	7,500			
Sam's Capital	6,000			
Priya's Capital	4,500	18,000		
To Salary A/c				
Ravi's Capital		30,000		
To Commission				
Sam's Capital**		3,000		
To Profit transferred to				
Ravi's Capital	30,000			
Sam's Capital	10,000			
Priya's Capital	10,000	50,000		
		1,01,000		1,01,000

*Rent to Priya $= 4{,}000 \times 12 =$ ₹ 48,000

** Sam's Commission $= (1{,}01{,}000 - 18{,}000 - 30{,}000) \times \frac{6}{106} =$ ₹ 3,000

Profit and Loss Appropriation Account and Partners' Capital Account

Solved Question 11 **S and G are partners in a firm sharing profit and loss equally. On 1st April, 2023, the capital of the partners were ₹ 4,00,000 and ₹ 3,00,000 respectively. The profit and loss appropriation account of the firm showed a net profit of ₹ 7,50,000 for the year ended 31st March, 2024. The terms of partnership deed provided the following**

(i) Transfer 10% of distributable profits to reserve fund.

(ii) Interest on capitals @ 6% per annum.

(iii) Interest on drawings @ 6% per annum. Drawings being S ₹ 80,000 and G ₹ 60,000 during the year.

Pass necessary journal entries and prepare profit and loss appropriation, account for the year ended 31st March, 2024.

Sol.

JOURNAL

Date	Particulars		LF	Amt (Dr)	Amt (Cr)
	Profit and Loss Appropriation A/c	Dr		42,000	
	To S's Capital A/c				24,000
	To G's Capital A/c				18,000
	(Being interest on capital paid)				
	Profit and Loss Appropriation A/c	Dr		71,220	
	To Reserve Fund A/c				71,220
	(Being amount transferred to reserve fund)				
	S's Capital A/c	Dr		2,400	
	G's Capital A/c	Dr		1,800	
	To Profit and Loss Appropriation A/c				4,200
	(Being interest on drawings charged)				
	Profit and Loss Appropriation A/c	Dr		6,40,980	
	To S's Capital A/c				3,20,490
	To G's Capital A/c				3,20,490
	(Being profit distributed among partners)				

Profit and Loss Appropriation Account
Dr **for the year ended 31st March, 2024** Cr

Particulars		Amt (₹)	Particulars		Amt (₹)
To Interest on Capital A/cs			By Net Profit as per Profit and Loss A/c		7,50,000
S (4,00,000 × 6/100)	24,000		By Interest on Drawings A/cs		
G (3,00,000 × 6/100)	18,000	42,000	S (80,000 × 6/100 × 6/12)	2,400	
To Reserve Fund A/c		71,220	G (60,000 × 6/100 × 6/12)	1,800	4,200
To Profit Transferred to Partners' Capital A/cs					
S	3,20,490				
G	3,20,490	6,40,980			
		7,54,200			7,54,200

Working Notes

1. In the absence of date of drawings, interest on drawings has been calculated on an average basis for 6 months.
2. **Calculation of Amount Transferred to Reserve Fund**

Distributable Profits = Profit + Interest on Drawings – Interest on Capital

$= 7,50,000 + 2,400 + 1,800 - 24,000 - 18,000 = ₹\ 7,12,200$

Amount transferred to reserve fund $= 7,12,200 \times \frac{10}{100} = ₹\ 71,220$

Solved Question 12 *(Calculation of partners' commission)* **Sonu and Rachit are partners in a firm. Sonu is to get a commission of 10% of net profit before charging any commission. Rachit is to get a commission of 10% of net profit after charging all commissions. Net profit before charging any commission was ₹ 55,000 for the year ended 31st march, 2020. Find out the commissions of Sonu and Rachit. Also, show the distribution of profit.**

Sol. Sonu's commission as percentage of net profit before charging such commission

$$= \text{Net Profit before Commission} \times \frac{\text{Rate of Commission}}{100} = 55,000 \times \frac{10}{100} = ₹\ 5,500$$

Rachit's commission as percentage of net profit after charging such commission

$$= \text{Net Profit before Commission} \times \frac{\text{Rate of Commission}}{100 + \text{Rate of Commission}}$$

$$= (55,000 - 5,500) \times \frac{10}{110} = 49,500 \times \frac{10}{110} = ₹\ 4,500$$

Profit and Loss Appropriation Account
Dr **for the year ended 31st March, 2020** Cr

Particulars		Amt (₹)	Particulars	Amt (₹)
To Sonu's Commission A/c		5,500	By Profit and Loss Account (Net Profit)	55,000
To Rachit's Commission A/c		4,500		
To Profit transferred to Capital A/cs				
Sonu	22,500			
Rachit	22,500	45,000		
		55,000		55,000

Solved Question 13 **Arun and Barun were partners sharing profits in the ratio of 3 : 2 Their capitals were ₹ 50,000 and ₹ 30,000 respectively. Partnership deed provided for interest on capital @6% p.a. to Arun and Barun and quarterly salary of ₹ 1,000 to Barun. Arun had given a loan of ₹ 1,00,000 on 1st October, 2021 to the firm without any agreement about interest. For the year 2021-22, the profits earned were ₹ 26,800.**

Prepare profit and loss appropriation account of the firm for the year ended 31st March, 2022. **CBSE 2023**

Sol.

Profit and Loss Appropriation Account
for the year ended on 31st March, 2022

Dr | | | | | Cr

Particulars		Amt (₹)	Particulars	Amt (₹)
To Interest on Capital A/c			By Profit and Loss A/c (26,800 –3,000)	23,800
Arun	3,000			
Barun	1,800	4,800		
To Salary A/c – Barun		4,000		
To Profit Transferred to Partners' Capital A/c				
Arun	9,000			
Barun	6,000	15,000		
		23,800		23,800

Solved Question 14 **Misha and Prisha were partners in a firm sharing profits and losses in the ratio of 3 : 2. On 1st April, 2022, their capital accounts showed balances of ₹ 50,000 and ₹ 30,000 respectively. During the year, Misha withdrew ₹ 12,900 while Prisha withdrew ₹ 9,600. They were allowed interest on capital @ 10% p.a. Interest on drawings of ₹ 660 was charged on Misha's drawings and ₹ 540 on Prisha's drawings. Prisha had advanced a loan of ₹ 20,000 to the firm on 1st August, 2022. The net profit for the year ended 31st March, 2023 amounted to ₹ 22,600.**

Prepare profit and loss appropriation account for the year ended 31st March, 2023. **CBSE 2024**

Sol.

Profit and Loss Appropriation Account
for the year ended 31st March, 2023

Dr | | | | | | Cr

Particulars		Amt (₹)	Particulars		Amt (₹)
To Interest on Capital			By Profit and Loss (Net Profit)		22,600
Misha's Capital	5,000		By Interest on Drawings		
Prisha's Capital	3,000	8,000	Misha's Capital	660	
To Profit transferred to			Prisha's Capital	540	1,200
Misha's Capital	9,480				
Prisha's Capital	6,320	15,800			
		23,800			23,800

Note Interest on loan is not considered as net profit is given.

Solved Question 15 ***(When the firm incurs loss)*** **A and B are partners in a firm sharing profits and losses in the ratio of 2 : 3. Their fixed capitals as on 1st April, 2023 were ₹ 3,00,000 and ₹ 4,00,000 respectively. As per partnership deed, both partners are to get salary of ₹ 12,500 each and interest on capital @ 8% p.a. They are to be charged interest on drawings @ 10% p.a. Drawings during the year ended 31st March, 2024 were A ₹ 5,000 per month and B ₹ 60,000 during the year. Firm incurred a loss of ₹ 50,000 during the year before above adjustments.**

Pass journal entries and prepare an account showing the distribution of profit/loss.

Sol.

JOURNAL

Date	Particulars		LF	Amt (Dr)	Amt (Cr)
2024					
Mar 31	Profit and Loss Appropriation A/c	Dr		50,000	
	To Profit and Loss A/c				50,000
	(Being transfer of net loss)				
Mar 31	A's Current A/c	Dr		3,000	
	B's Current A/c	Dr		3,000	
	To Interest on Drawings A/c				6,000
	(Being interest charged on drawings)				
Mar 31	Interest on Drawings A/c	Dr		6,000	
	To Profit and Loss Appropriation A/c				6,000
	(Being transfer of interest on drawings to profit and loss appropriation account)				

Date	Particulars		LF	Amt (Dr)	Amt (Cr)
Mar 31	A's Current A/c	Dr		17,600	
	B's Current A/c	Dr		26,400	
	To Profit and Loss Appropriation A/c				44,000
	(Being loss transferred to partner's current accounts)				

Profit and Loss Appropriation Account
Dr for the year ended 31st March, 2024 Cr

Particulars	Amt (₹)	Particulars		Amt (₹)
To Profit and Loss A/c (Net Loss)	50,000	By Interest on Drawings A/cs		
		A	3,000	
		B	3,000	6,000
		By Loss transferred to		
		A's Current A/c (2/5)	17,600	
		B's Current A/c (3/5)	26,400	44,000
	50,000			50,000

Working Notes

1. **Interest on Drawings**

   A's Drawings $= 5{,}000 \times 12 = 60{,}000 \times \frac{10}{100} \times \frac{6}{12} =$ ₹ 3,000; B's Drawings $= 60{,}000 \times \frac{10}{100} \times \frac{6}{12} =$ ₹ 3,000

   In the absence of actual date of drawings, interest thereon has been calculated for an average period of 6 months.
2. Salary and interest on capital will not be provided in case of loss.
3. Although, profit and loss appropriation account is not prepared in case of loss, it has been prepared in this question because 'interest on drawings' is to be credited to this account.

Solved Question 16 ***(When appropriations are more than available profits)*** **Varun and Vivek were partners in a firm sharing profits in the ratio of 3 : 2. The balance in their capital and current accounts as on 1st April, 2022 were as under**

Particulars	Varun (₹)	Vivek (₹)
Capital Accounts	3,00,000 (Cr)	2,00,000 (Cr)
Current Accounts	1,00,000 (Cr)	28,000 (Dr)

The partnership deed provided that Varun was to be paid a salary of ₹ 5,000 p.m. whereas Vivek was to get a commission of ₹ 30,000 for the year. Interest on capital was to be allowed @ 8% p.a. whereas interest on drawings was to be charged @ 6% p.a. The drawings of Varun were ₹ 3,000 at the beginning of each quarter while Vivek withdrew ₹ 30,000 on 1st September, 2022. The net profit of the firm for the year, 2022-23, before making the above adjustments was ₹ 1,20,000.

Prepare profit and loss appropriation account and partners' capital and current accounts. **CBSE SQP 2025**

Sol.

Profit and Loss Appropriation Account
Dr for the year ended on 31st March, 2023 Cr

Particulars		Amt (₹)	Particulars		Amt (₹)
To Partners' Current A/c			By Profit and Loss A/c (Net Profit)		1,20,000
Varun	78,508		By Interest on Drawings		
Vivek	42,992	1,21,500	Varun	450	
			Vivek	1,050	1,500
		1,21,500			1,21,500

Note As divisible profits are insufficient, so available profits are distributed in ratio of appropriations i.e. 42 : 23.
Varun = 60,000 + 24,000 = ₹ 84,000; Vivek = 30,000 + 16,000 = ₹ 46,000 = 84: 46 *or* 42 : 23

Partners' Capital Account
Dr Cr

Particulars	Varun (₹)	Vivek (₹)	Particulars	Varun (₹)	Vivek (₹)
To Balance c/d	3,00,000	2,00,000	By Balance b/d	3,00,000	2,00,000
	3,00,000	2,00,000		3,00,000	2,00,000

Dr **Partners' Current Account** Cr

Particulars	**Varun(₹)**	**Vivek (₹)**	**Particulars**	**Varun (₹)**	**Vivek (₹)**
To Balance c/d	—	28,000	By Balance b/d	1,00,000	—
To Drawings	12,000	30,000	By Profit and Loss Appropriation A/c	78,508	42,992
To Interest on Drawings	450	1,050	By Balance c/d	—	16,058
To Balance c/d	1,66,058	—			
	1,78,508	59,050		1,78,508	59,050

Solved Question 17 **Parul and Rajul were partners in a firm, sharing profits and losses in the ratio of 5 : 3. The balance in their fixed capital accounts on 1st April, 2023 were: Parul ₹ 6,00,000 and Rajul ₹ 8,00,000. The partnership deed provided for allowing interest on capital at 12% per annum. The net profit of the firm for the year ended 31th March, 2024 was ₹ 1,26,000.**

Prepare profit and loss appropriation account for the year ended 31st March, 2024. Show your working clearly. **CBSE 2025**

Sol.

Profit and Loss Appropriation Account

Dr as at 31st March, 2024 Cr

Particulars	**Amt (₹)**	**Particulars**	**Amt (₹)**
Interest on Capital		By Net Profit	1,26,000
Parul's Capital	54,000		
Rajul's Capital	72,000		
	1,26,000		1,26,000

Working Notes

1. Total Appropriation = Parul's Interest on Capital + Rajul's Interest on Capital
   $= (6,00,000 \times 12\%) + (8,00,000 \times 12\%) = 72,000 + 96,000 = ₹\ 1,68,000$
2. Total appropriation is greater than profit available hence profit of ₹ 1,26,000 will be distributed in appropriation ratio, i.e. 72,000 : 96,000

   Parul's share $= 1,26,000 \times \frac{72,000}{1,68,000} = ₹\ 54,000$; Rajul's share $= 1,26,000 \times \frac{96,000}{1,68,000} = ₹\ 72,000$

Solved Question 18 **Anu and Manu are partners sharing profit in proportion of 3 : 2 with capitals of ₹ 4,00,000 and ₹ 3,00,000 respectively. Interest on capital is agreed @ 5% per annum. Manu is to be allowed an annual salary of ₹ 30,000 which has not been withdrawn. During 2023-24, the net profit amounted to ₹ 1,42,500. A provision of 5% of the profits is to be made in respect of commission to the manager.**

Anu will get commission @ 2% of turnover. Manu will get commission of 5% on profits after deduction of interest, salary and commission (including his own commission) turnover for the year was ₹ 6,00,000.

Prepare profit and loss appropriation account and partners' capital account.

Sol.

Profit and Loss Appropriation Account

Dr for the year ended 31st March, 2024 Cr

Particulars		**Amt (₹)**	**Particulars**	**Amt (₹)**
To Partner's Salary A/c (Manu's Capital A/c)		30,000	By Net Profit as per Profit and Loss A/c	1,42,500
To Interest on Capital A/cs				
Anu	20,000			
Manu	15,000	35,000		
To Commission A/c				
Anu	12,000			
Manu	3,119	15,119		
To Profit transferred to				
Anu's Capital A/c	37,429			
Manu's Capital A/c	24,952	62,381		
		1,42,500		1,42,500

Dr **Partners' Capital Account** **Cr**

Date	Particulars	Anu (₹)	Manu (₹)	Date	Particulars	Anu (₹)	Manu (₹)
2022				2021			
Mar 31	To Balance c/d	4,69,429	3,73,071	Apr 1	By Balance b/d	4,00,000	3,00,000
				2022			
				Mar 31	By Partner's Salary A/c	—	30,000
				Mar 31	By Interest on Capital A/c	20,000	15,000
				Mar 31	By Commission A/c	12,000	3,119
				Mar 31	By Profit and Loss Appropriation A/c	37,429	24,952
		4,69,429	3,73,071			4,69,429	3,73,071

Working Notes

1. **Calculation of Interest on Capital**

   Anu $= 4{,}00{,}000 \times \frac{5}{100} =$ ₹ 20,000; Manu $= 3{,}00{,}000 \times \frac{5}{100} =$ ₹ 15,000

2. **Calculation of Commission**

   Anu $= 6{,}00{,}000 \times \frac{2}{100} =$ ₹ 12,000; Manu $= (1{,}42{,}500 - 30{,}000 - 35{,}000 - 12{,}000) \times 5/105 =$ ₹ 3,119

3. Since net profit is given, it is assumed that managers' commission is already charged.

Solved Question 19 **X and Y started business on 1st April, 2023 with capitals of ₹ 1,50,000 and ₹ 1,00,000 respectively. According to the partnership deed, Y is to get salary of ₹ 2,500 per month, X is to get 10% commission on profit after allowing salary to Y and interest is to be allowed on capital @ 6% p.a. Profit sharing ratio between the two partners is 3 : 2. During the year, the firm earned profit of ₹ 1,25,000. X had given loan of ₹ 50,000 to the firm on 1st April, 2023. Interest on loan was allowed @ 8% p.a. Y was given loan of ₹ 1,00,000 on which interest was charged ₹ 5,500. Manager was to be allowed commission of ₹ 1,500.**

Pass journal entries for distribution of profit and prepare profit and loss appropriation account and capital account. The firm closes its books of account on 31st March every year.

Sol.

JOURNAL

Date	Particulars	LF	Amt (Dr)	Amt (Cr)
2024				
Mar 31	Profit and Loss A/c Dr		1,25,000	
	To Profit and Loss Appropriation A/c			1,25,000
	(Being transfer of net profit to profit and loss appropriation account)			
Mar 31	Y's Salary A/c Dr		30,000	
	To Y's Capital A/c			30,000
	(Being salary due to Y @ ₹ 2,500 per month)			
Mar 31	X's Commission A/c Dr		9,500	
	To X's Capital A/c			9,500
	(Being commission due to X)			
Mar 31	Profit and Loss Appropriation A/c Dr		39,500	
	To Y's Salary A/c			30,000
	To X's Commission A/c			9,500
	(Being salary and commission to partners transferred to profit and loss appropriation account)			
Mar 31	Interest on Capital A/c Dr		15,000	
	To X's Capital A/c			9,000
	To Y's Capital A/c			6,000
	(Being interest on capitals allowed to partners @ 6% p.a.)			
Mar 31	Profit and Loss Appropriation A/c Dr		15,000	
	To Interest on Capital A/c			15,000
	(Being interest on capital transferred to profit and loss appropriation account)			

Date	Particulars		LF	Amt (Dr)	Amt (Cr)
Mar 31	Profit and Loss Appropriation A/c	Dr		70,500	
	To X's Capital A/c (70,500 × 3/5)				42,300
	To Y's Capital A/c (70,500 × 2/5)				28,200
	(Being distribution of profit among the partners)				

Profit and Loss Appropriation Account
Dr **for the year ended 31st March, 2024** Cr

Particulars		Amt (₹)	Particulars	Amt (₹)
To Salary—Y's Capital A/c		30,000	By Profit and Loss A/c (Net Profit)	1,25,000
To Commission—X's Capital A/c		9,500		
To Interest on Capital—X's Capital A/c		9,000		
To Interest on Capital—Y's Capital A/c		6,000		
To Profit transferred to				
X's Capital A/c (3/5)	42,300			
Y's Capital A/c (2/5)	28,200	70,500		
		1,25,000		1,25,000

Profit and Loss Account
Dr **for the year ended 31st March, 2024** Cr

Particulars	Amt (₹)	Particulars	Amt (₹)
To Interest on X's Loan (50,000 × 8%)	4,000	By Profit before Interest	1,25,000
To Manager's Commission	1,500	By Interest on Y's Loan	5,500
To Net Profit transferred to Profit and Loss Appropriation A/c	1,25,000		
	1,30,500		1,30,500

Dr **Partners' Capital Account** Cr

Date	Particulars	X (₹)	Y (₹)	Date	Particulars	X (₹)	Y (₹)
	To Balance c/d	2,10,800	1,64,200		By Balance b/d	1,50,000	1,00,000
					By Profit	42,300	28,200
					By Salary A/c	—	30,000
					By Commission A/c	9,500	—
					By Interest on Capital A/c	9,000	6,000
		2,10,800	1,64,200			2,10,800	1,64,200

Past Adjustments

Solved Question 20 **Mohan, Suhaan and Adit were partners in a firm sharing profits and losses in the ratio of 3 : 2 : 1. Their fixed capitals was ₹ 2,00,000, ₹ 1,00,000 and ₹ 1,00,000 respectively. For the year ended 31st March, 2023, interest on capital was credited to their accounts @ 8% p.a instead of 5% p.a.**
Pass necessary adjusting journal entry. Show your workings clearly. CBSE 2024

Sol. **In the Books of Mohan, Suhaan and Adit**
JOURNAL

Date	Particulars		LF	Amt (Dr)	Amt (Cr)
	Adit's Current A/c	Dr		1,000	
	To Suhaan's Current A/c				1,000
	(Being adjustment entry for interest on capital credited at a higher rate)				

Working Note

Statement of Adjustment

Particulars	Mohan (₹)	Suhaan (₹)	Adit (₹)
Interest on Capital to be Debited	(6,000)	(3,000)	(3,000)
Profit to be Credited now (₹ 12,000 in 3 : 2 : 1)	6,000	4,000	2,000
(Adjustment)	—	1,000 (Cr)	(1,0000) (Dr)

Note Full credit be given if working notes are prepared in any other form.

Solved Question 21 **Puneet, Shan and Raj are partners having fixed capitals of ₹ 2,00,000, ₹ 1,60,000 and ₹ 1,20,000 respectively. They share profits in the ratio of 3 : 1 : 1. The partnership deed provided for the following which were not recorded in the books.**

(i) Interest on capital @ 5% per annum.

(ii) Salary to Puneet ₹ 1,500 per month and to Raj ₹ 1,000 per month.

(iii) Transfer of profit to general reserve ₹ 10,000. Net profit for the year ended 31st March, 2024 was ₹ 1,00,000.

Pass necessary rectifying entry for the above adjustments in the books of the firm. Also, show your workings clearly.

Sol. **JOURNAL**

Date	Particulars		LF	Amt (Dr)	Amt (Cr)
	Puneet's Current A/c	Dr		10,400	
	Shan's Current A/c	Dr		4,800	
	To Raj's Current A/c				5,200
	To General Reserve A/c				10,000
	(Being the adjustment entry passed)				

Adjustment Table

Particulars	Puneet (₹)	Shan (₹)	Raj (₹)	Total (₹)
I. **Amount Already Recorded** (Dr)				
Share of Profit, i.e. ₹ 1,00,000 in 3 : 1 : 1	60,000	20,000	20,000	1,00,000
II. **Amount which should have been Recorded** (Cr)				
Interest on Capital	10,000	8,000	6,000	24,000
Salary	18,000	—	12,000	30,000
Share of Profit, i.e. ₹ 36,000 in 3 : 1 : 1	21,600	7,200	7,200	36,000
	49,600	15,200	25,200	90,000
Net Effect (I – II)	10,400 (Dr)	4,800 (Dr)	5,200 (Cr)	10,000 (Cr)

Working Notes

1. **Calculation of Interest on Capital**

Puneet $= 2{,}00{,}000 \times \frac{5}{100} =$ ₹ 10,000 ; Shan $= 1{,}60{,}000 \times \frac{5}{100} =$ ₹ 8,000 ; Raj $= 1{,}20{,}000 \times \frac{5}{100} =$ ₹ 6,000

Salary = Puneet $(1{,}500 \times 12) =$ ₹ 18,000 ; Raj $(1{,}000 \times 12) =$ ₹ 12,000

2. **Calculation of Adjusted Profits**

Adjusted Profits = Given Profit – Transfer to Reserve – Interest on Capital – Salary]

$= 1{,}00{,}000 - 10{,}000 - 24{,}000\,(10{,}000 + 8{,}000 + 6{,}000) - 30{,}000\,(18{,}000 + 12{,}000) =$ ₹ 36,000

Solved Question 22 ***(Omission of interest on capital, salary, etc. for more than one year)*** **A, B and C were partners in a firm. On 1st April, 2023, their fixed capitals stood at ₹ 50,000, ₹ 25,000 and ₹ 25,000 respectively. As per the provisions of the partnership deed**

(i) A was entitled to a salary of ₹ 5,000 per annum.

(ii) All the partners were entitled to interest on capital @ 5% per annum.

(iii) Profits were to be shared in the ratio of capitals.

The net profits for the year ending 31st March, 2023 of ₹ 33,000 and 31st March, 2024 of ₹ 45,000 were divided equally without providing for the above terms.

Pass an adjustment journal entry to rectify the above error.

Sol. **Adjustment Table**

Particulars	A (₹)	B (₹)	C (₹)	Total (₹)
I. **Amount Already Recorded** (Dr)				
Profit (1 : 1 : 1) 31st March, 2023	11,000	11,000	11,000	33,000
31st March, 2024	15,000	15,000	15,000	45,000
	26,000	26,000	26,000	78,000

Particulars	A (₹)	B (₹)	C (₹)	Total (₹)
II. **Amount which should have been Recorded** (Cr)				
Salary 31st March, 2023	5,000	—	—	5,000
31st March, 2024	5,000	—	—	5,000
Interest on Capital 31st March, 2023	2,500	1,250	1,250	5,000
31st March, 2024	2,500	1,250	1,250	5,000
Profits (Capital ratio i.e. 2 : 1 : 1) 31st March, 2023	11,500	5,750	5,750	23,000
31st March, 2024	17,500	8,750	8,750	35,000
	44,000	17,000	17,000	78,000
Net Effect (I – II)	18,000 (Cr)	9,000 (Dr)	9,000 (Dr)	Nil

JOURNAL

Date	Particulars		LF	Amt (Dr)	Amt (Cr)
	B's Current A/c	Dr		9,000	
	C's Current A/c	Dr		9,000	
	To A's Current A/c				18,000
	(Being interest on capital and salary not provided previously and profit distributed wrongly, now adjusted)				

Working Note

Calculation of Adjusted Profit

31st March, 2023 = 33,000 – 5,000 (Salary) – 5,000 (Interest on capital) = ₹ 23,000

31st March, 2024 = 45,000 – 5,000 (Salary) – 5,000 (Interest on capital) = ₹ 35,000

Solved Question 23 **Jatin, Keshav and Lalit were partners in a firm with fixed capitals of ₹ 1,20,000, ₹ 1,00,000 and ₹ 80,000 respectively. As per the partnership deed, there was a provision for allowing interest on capitals @ 10% p.a., but entries for the same had not been made for the last two years.**

The profit sharing ratio during the last two years was as follows

Year	Jatin	Keshav	Lalit
2021-22	5	3	2
2022-23	1	1	1

Pass an adjustment entry of the beginning of the third year, i.e., on 1st April, 2023. **CBSE 2024 C**

Sol.

In the Books of Jatin, Keshav and Lalit
JOURNAL

Date	Particulars		LF	Amt (Dr)	Amt (Cr)
2023					
Apr 1	Jatin's Current A/c	Dr		1,000	
	To Keshav's Current A/c				1,000
	(Being omission of interest on capital, now rectified)				

Working Notes

Adjustment Table

Particulars	Jatin		Keshav		Lalit	
	Dr (₹)	Cr (₹)	Dr (₹)	Cr (₹)	Dr (₹)	Cr (₹)
Interest on Capital to be Credited						
2021-22	—	12,000	—	10,000	—	8,000
2022-23	—	12,000	—	10,000	—	8,000
Profit of ₹ 30,000 reversed in ratio of 5 : 3 : 2 for 2021-22	15,000	—	9,000	—	6,000	—
Profits of ₹ 30,000 reversed in ratio of 1 : 1 : 1 for 2022-23	10,000	—	10,000	—	10,000	—
Net Effect	1,000	—	—	1,000	—	—

Solved Question 24 *(Distribution of profits in wrong ratio)* **Prem, Maya and Nita shared profits in the ratio of 3 : 2 : 1. The profits of the last three years were ₹ 1,40,000, ₹ 84,000 and ₹ 1,06,000 respectively. These profits were by mistake, shared equally for all the three years. It is now decided to correct the error. Pass necessary journal entry for the same.**

Sol.

Adjustment Table

Particulars	Prem (₹)	Maya (₹)	Nita (₹)
I. **Amounts Already Recorded** (3,30,000 in 1 : 1 : 1)	1,10,000	1,10,000	1,10,000
II. **Amounts which should have been Recorded** (3,30,000 in 3 : 2 : 1)	1,65,000	1,10,000	55,000
Net Effect (I – II)	55,000 (Cr)	Nil	55,000 (Dr)

JOURNAL

Date	Particulars		LF	Amt (Dr)	Amt (Cr)
	Nita's Capital A/c	Dr		55,000	
	To Prem's Capital A/c				55,000
	(Being the adjustment made for profit divided in wrong ratio)				

Solved Question 25 **A, B and C are partners in a firm. Their capital accounts stood at ₹ 1,50,000, ₹ 75,000 and ₹ 75,000 respectively on 1st April, 2020. As per the provisions of the deed**

(i) C was to be allowed a remuneration of ₹ 18,000 per annum,

(ii) Interest @ 5% p.a. was to be provided on capitals and

(iii) Profits were to be distributed in the ratio of 2 : 2 : 1.

Ignoring the above terms, net profit of ₹ 90,000 for the year ended 31st March, 2020 was distributed among the three partners equally. Pass the journal entries to rectify the above errors.

Sol.

JOURNAL

Date	Particulars		LF	Amt (Dr)	Amt (Cr)
2020					
Apr 1	A's Capital A/c	Dr		30,000	
	B's Capital A/c	Dr		30,000	
	C' s Capital A/c	Dr		30,000	
	To Profit and Loss Adjustment A/c				90,000
	(Being share of profit wrongly credited to partners', now reversed)				
	Profit and Loss Adjustment A/c	Dr		18,000	
	To C's Capital A/c				18,000
	(Being remuneration credited to C's capital account)				
	Profit and Loss Adjustment A/c	Dr		15,000	
	To A's Capital A/c				7,500
	To B's Capital A/c				3,750
	To C's Capital A/c				3,750
	(Being interest on capitals @ 5% p.a. credited to capital account of respective partners)				
	Profit and Loss Adjustment A/c	Dr		57,000	
	To A's Capital A/c				22,800
	To B's Capital A/c				22,800
	To C's Capital A/c				11,400
	(Being divisible profit credited to partners' capital accounts in the ratio of 2 : 2 : 1)				

Guarantee of Profits

Solved Question 26 **D, B and T are partners in a firm sharing profits in the ratio of 2 : 1 : 1. Their capital balances as on 1st April, 2023 were ₹ 6,00,000, ₹ 4,00,000 and ₹ 4,00,000 respectively. Interest on capital will be provided at 10% p.a. net profit at the end of the year amounted to ₹ 2,15,000. Prepare profit and loss appropriation account if**

(i) B's share of profit is guaranteed by D to be not less than ₹ 20,400 in any financial year.

(ii) B's share of profit is guaranteed to be not less than ₹ 20,400 in any financial year.

(iii) B's share of profit is guaranteed by D and T to be not less than ₹ 20,400. Deficiency to be borne in the ratio of 3 : 2.

Sol. (i) Dr **Profit and Loss Appropriation Account** Cr

Particulars		Amt (₹)	Particulars	Amt (₹)
To Interest on Capital			By Net Profit	2,15,000
D's Capital A/c	60,000			
B's Capital A/c	40,000			
T's Capital A/c	40,000	1,40,000		
To Divisible Profits				
D's Capital A/c	37,500			
(–) Transferred to B	(1,650)	35,850		
B's Capital A/c	18,750			
(+) Transferred from D	1,650	20,400		
T's Capital A/c		18,750		
		2,15,000		2,15,000

(ii) Dr **Profit and Loss Appropriation Account** Cr

Particulars		Amt (₹)	Particulars	Amt (₹)
To Interest on Capital			By Net Profit	2,15,000
D's Capital A/c	60,000			
B's Capital A/c	40,000			
T's Capital A/c	40,000	1,40,000		
To Divisible Profits				
D's Capital A/c	37,500			
(–) Transferred to B	(1,100)	36,400		
B's Capital A/c	18,750			
(+) Transferred from D	1,100			
(+) Transferred from T	(550)	20,400		
T's Capital A/c	18,750			
(–) Transferred to B	(550)	18,200		
		2,15,000		2,15,000

(iii) Dr **Profit and Loss Appropriation Account** Cr

Particulars		Amt (₹)	Particulars	Amt (₹)
To Interest on Capital			By Net Profit	2,15,000
D's Capital A/c	60,000			
B's Capital A/c	40,000			
T's Capital A/c	40,000	1,40,000		
To Divisible Profits				
D's Capital A/c	37,500			
(–) Transferred to B	(990)	36,510		
B's Capital A/c	18,750			
(+) Transferred from D	990			
(+) Transferred from T	660	20,400		

Particulars		Amt (₹)	Particulars	Amt (₹)
T's Capital A/c	18,750			
(–) Transferred to B	(660)	18,090		
		2,15,000		2,15,000

Solved Question 27 *(When guarantee of minimum profits is given to an incoming partner by existing partners in a certain ratio)* **Vikas and Vivek were partners in a firm sharing profits in the ratio of 3 : 2. On 1st April, 2023, they admitted Vandana as a new partner for $\frac{1}{8}$th share in the profits with a guaranteed profit of ₹ 1,50,000. The new profit sharing ratio between Vivek and Vikas will remain the same but they decided to bear any deficiency on account of guarantee to Vandana in the ratio 2 : 3. ₹ 90,000 of the trading profits will be transferred to reserve account. The profit of the firm for the year ended 31st March, 2024 was ₹ 9,90,000.**

Prepare profit and loss appropriation account of Vikas, Vivek and Vandana for the year ended 31st March, 2024.

Sol.

Profit and Loss Appropriation Account
for the year ended 31st March, 2024

Dr — Cr

Particulars		Amt (₹)	Particulars	Amt (₹)
To Reserve A/c		90,000	By Net Profit as per Profit and Loss A/c	9,90,000
To Profit Transferred to Capital A/c				
Vikas [(9,00,000 – 1,12,500) × 3/5]	4,72,500			
(–) To Vandana	(22,500)	4,50,000		
Vivek (7,87,500 × 2/5)	3,15,000			
(–) To Vandana	(15,000)	3,00,000		
Vandana (9,00,000 × 1/8)	1,12,500			
(+) From Vikas	22,500			
(+) From Vivek	15,000	1,50,000		
		9,90,000		9,90,000

Working Note

Vandana's share in profit $= 9{,}00{,}000 \times \frac{1}{8} =$ ₹ 1,12,500; Minimum profit guaranteed to Vandana = ₹ 1,50,000

Deficiency = ₹ 37,500 (1,50,000 – 1,12,500) is to be borne by Vivek and Vikas in 2 : 3 ratio.

Deficiency to be borne by Vivek $= 37{,}500 \times \frac{2}{5} =$ ₹ 15,000; Deficiency to be borne by Vikas $= 37{,}500 \times \frac{3}{5} =$ ₹ 22,500

Solved Question 28 **Aakash and Baadal entered into partnership on 1st October, 2023 with the capitals of ₹ 80,00,000 and ₹ 60,00,000 respectively. They decided to share profits and losses equally. Partners were entitled to interest on capital @ 10% per annum as per the provisions of the partnership deed.**

Baadal is given a guarantee that his share of profit, after charging interest on capital will not be less than ₹ 7,00,000 per annum. Any deficiency arising on that account shall be met by Aakash. The profit of the firm for the year ended 31st March, 2024 amounted to ₹ 13,00,000,

Prepare profit and loss appropriation account for the year ended 31st March, 2024. **CBSE 2025**

Sol.

Profit and Loss Appropriation Account
as at 31st March, 2024

Dr — Cr

Particulars		Amt (₹)	Particulars	Amt (₹)
To Interest on Capital			By Net Profit	13,00,000
Aakash's Capital (80,00,000 × 10/100 × 6/12)	4,00,000			
Baadal's Capital (60,00,000 × 10/100 × 6/12)	3,00,000	7,00,000		
To Profit transferred to Capital Account				
Aakash	3,00,000			
(–) Deficiency Met	(50,000)	2,50,000		
Baddal	3,00,000			
(+) Deficiency Received from Aakash	50,000	3,50,000		
		13,00,000		13,00,000

Working Notes

1. Baadal is given a guarantee of minimum profit of ₹ 7,00,000 per annum

   Guarantee from 1st October, 2023 to 31st March, 2024 $= \frac{7,00,000}{2} =$ ₹ 3,50,000

2. Deficiency met by Aakash = Guaranteed Amount – Actual Share of Profit of Baadal

   $= 3,50,000 - \left(6,00,000 \times \frac{1}{2}\right) =$ ₹ 50,000

Comprehensive Questions

Solved Question 29 **Y, V and R were partners in a firm sharing profits in the ratio of 4 : 3 : 3. Their fixed capitals on 1st April, 2023 were ₹ 9,00,000, ₹ 5,00,000 and ₹ 4,00,000 respectively. On 1st November, 2023, Y gave a loan of ₹ 80,000 to the firm. As per the partnership agreement**

(i) The partners were entitled to an interest on capital @ 6% p.a.

(ii) Interest on partners' drawings was to be changed @ 8% p.a.

The firm earned profits of ₹ 2,53,000 (after interest on Y's loan) during the year 2023-24. Partners' drawings for the year amounted to Y ₹ 80,000 V ₹ 70,000 R ₹ 50,000.

Prepare profit and loss appropriation account for the year ending 31st March, 2024.

Sol.

Profit and Loss Appropriation Account
for the year ended 31st March, 2024

Dr | Cr

Particulars		Amt (₹)	Particulars		Amt (₹)
To Interest on Capital			By Profit and Loss A/c (Net Profit)		2,53,000
Y's Current A/c	54,000		By Interest on Drawings		
V's Current A/c	30,000		Y's Current A/c	3,200	
R's Current A/c	24,000	1,08,000	V's Current A/c	2,800	
To Profit transferred to			R's Current A/c	2,000	8,000
Y's Current A/c	61,200				
V's Current A/c	45,900				
R's Current A/c	45,900	1,53,000			
		2,61,000			2,61,000

Working Notes

1. **Calculation of Interest on Partner's Drawings**

   Interest on Y's Drawings $= 80,000 \times 8/100 \times 6/12 =$ ₹ 3,200 ; Interest on V's Drawings $= 70,000 \times 8/100 \times 6/12 =$ ₹ 2,800

   Interest on R's Drawings $= 50,000 \times 8/100 \times 6/12 =$ ₹ 2,000

   Since, date of drawings is not given in the question so interest has been calculated for an average period of 6 months.

2. **Calculation of Interest on Partner's Capital**

   Interest on Y's Capital $= 9,00,000 \times 6/100 =$ ₹ 54,000; Interest on V's Capital $= 5,00,000 \times 6/100 =$ ₹ 30,000

   Interest on R's Capital $= 4,00,000 \times 6/100 =$ ₹ 24,000

Solved Question 30 **P, Q and R were partners in a firm trading in garments. They were sharing profits in the ratio of 5 : 3 : 2. Their capitals on 1st April, 2017 were ₹ 6,00,000, ₹ 8,00,000 and ₹ 16,00,000 respectively. P withdrew ₹ 20,000 from the firm on 15th September, 2017 and Q instead of withdrawing cash from the firm, took garments amounting to ₹ 48,000 from the firm. On the other hand, R withdrew ₹ 4,00,000 from her capital on 1st January, 2018.**

The partnership deed provides for charging interest on drawings @ 6% per annum. After the final accounts were prepared, it was discovered that interest on drawings had not been charged. Give the necessary adjusting journal entry and show the working notes clearly.

Sol.

Adjustment Table

Particulars	P (₹)	Q (₹)	R (₹)	Total (₹)
I. **Amount to be Debited**				
Interest on Drawings	650	1,560	—	2,210
II. **Amount to be Credited**				
Profit of ₹ 2,860 Shared in Ratio of 5 : 3 : 2	1,105	663	442	2,210
Net Effect (I – II)	455 (Cr)	897 (Dr)	442 (Cr)	Nil

JOURNAL

Date	Particulars	LF	Amt (Dr)	Amt (Cr)
	Q's Capital A/c Dr		897	
	To P's Capital A/c			455
	To R's Capital A/c			442
	(Being the adjustment entry passed)			

Working Note

Calculation of Interest on Drawings

$P = 20{,}000 \times \frac{6}{100} \times \frac{6.5}{12} = ₹ 650$; $Q = 48{,}000 \times \frac{6}{100} \times \frac{6.5}{12} = ₹ 1{,}560$

Solved Question 31 **On 31st March, 2018, the balance in the capital accounts of Abhir, Bobby and Vineet, after making adjustments for profits and drawings were ₹ 8,00,000, ₹ 6,00,000 and ₹ 4,00,000 respectively.**

Subsequently, it was discovered that interest on capital and interest on drawings had been omitted. The partners were entitled to interest on capital @ 10% p.a. and were to be charged interest on drawings @ 6% p.a. The drawings during the year were Abhir ₹ 20,000 drawn at the end of each month, Bobby ₹ 50,000 drawn at the beginning of every half year and Vineet ₹ 1,00,000 withdrawn on 31st October, 2017. The net profit for the year ended 31st March, 2018 was ₹ 1,50,000. The profit sharing ratio was 2 : 2 : 1. Pass necessary adjusting entry for the above adjustments in the books of the firm. Also, show your workings clearly. CBSE 2019

Sol.

JOURNAL

Date	Particulars	LF	Amt (Dr)	Amt (Cr)
2018				
Apr 1	Bobby's Capital A/c Dr		14,402	
	To Abhir's Capital A/c			10,112
	To Vineet's Capital A/c			4,290
	(Being an adjustment entry passed for past adjustment)			

Calculation of Opening Capital

Particulars	Abhir (₹)	Bobby (₹)	Vineet (₹)
Capital at the End	8,00,000	6,00,000	4,00,000
(+) Drawings	2,40,000	1,00,000	1,00,000
	10,40,000	7,00,000	5,00,000
(–) Profit	(60,000)	(60,000)	(30,000)
Capital at the Beginning	9,80,000	6,40,000	4,70,000

Calculation of Amount to be Adjusted

Particulars	Abhir (₹)	Bobby (₹)	Vineet (₹)	Total (₹)
Amount to be Debited				
Profit	60,000	60,000	30,000	1,50,000
Interest on Drawings	6,600	4,500	2,500	13,600
	66,600	64,500	32,500	1,63,600

Particulars	Abhir (₹)	Bobby (₹)	Vineet (₹)	Total (₹)
Amount to be Credited				
Interest on Capital @ 10% p.a.	76,712	50,098	36,790	1,63,600
Interest on Capital will be allowed to the Extent of Maximum Profit Available	10,112 (Cr)	14,402 (Cr)	4,290 (Dr)	Nil

Working Notes

1. **Calculation of Interest on Drawings**

$\text{Abhir} = 20{,}000 \times 12 \times \frac{6}{100} \times \frac{5.5}{12} = ₹\,6{,}600$; $\text{Bobby} = 50{,}000 \times 2 \times \frac{6}{100} \times \frac{9}{12} = ₹\,4{,}500$; $\text{Vineet} = 1{,}00{,}000 \times \frac{6}{100} \times \frac{5}{12} = ₹\,2{,}500$

2. **Calculation of Interest on Capital**

Abhir = 9,80,000 × 10% = ₹ 98,000
Bobby = 6,40,000 × 10% = ₹ 64,000
Vineet = 4,70,000 × 10% = ₹ 47,000
= ₹ 2,09,000

$\text{Abhir} = \frac{98{,}000}{2{,}09{,}000} \times 1{,}63{,}600 = ₹\,76{,}712$; $\text{Bobby} = \frac{64{,}000}{2{,}09{,}000} \times 1{,}63{,}600 = ₹\,50{,}098$; $\text{Vineet} = \frac{47{,}000}{2{,}09{,}000} \times 1{,}63{,}600 = ₹\,36{,}790$

Solved Question 32 **Abhay, Siddharth and Kusum are partners in a firm sharing profits in the ratio of 5 : 3 : 2. Kusum is guaranteed a minimum amount of ₹ 10,000 as per share in the profits. Any deficiency arising on that account shall be met by Siddharth. Profits for the years ending 31st March, 2017 and 2018 are ₹ 40,000 and ₹ 60,000 respectively. Prepare profit and loss appropriation account.** **NCERT**

Sol.

Profit and Loss Appropriation Account
for the year ended 31st March, 2017

Dr | Cr

Particulars		Amt (₹)	Particulars	Amt (₹)
To Profit Transferred to Capital A/c			By Net Profit as per Profit and Loss A/c	40,000
Abhay's		20,000		
Siddharth's	12,000			
(−) Deficiency of Kusum	(2,000)	10,000		
Kusum's Capital A/c	8,000			
(+) Siddharth's Guarantee	2,000	10,000		
		40,000		40,000

Profit and Loss Appropriation Account
for the year ended 31st March, 2018

Dr | Cr

Particulars		Amt (₹)	Particulars	Amt (₹)
To Profit Transferred to Capital A/c			By Net Profit as per Profit and Loss A/c	60,000
Abhay's	30,000			
Siddharth's	18,000			
Kusum's	12,000	60,000		
		60,000		60,000

Working Note

In the year ending on 31st March, 2018, the profit share of partner Kusum is already above guaranteed amount, thus there is no need of adjustment.

Solved Question 33 **Jay, Vijay and Karan were partners of an architect firm sharing profits in the ratio of 2 : 2 : 1. Their partnership deed provided the following**

(i) A monthly salary of ₹ 15,000 each to Jay and Vijay.

(ii) Karan was guaranteed a profit of ₹ 5,00,000 and Jay guaranteed that he will earn an annual fee of ₹ 2,00,000. Any deficiency arising because of guarantee to Karan will be borne by Jay and Vijay in the ratio of 3 : 2.

During the year ended 31st March, 2018, Jay earned fee of ₹ 1,75,000 and the profits of the firm amounted to ₹ 15,00,000. Showing your workings clearly prepare profit and loss appropriation account and the capital account of Jay, Vijay and Karan for the year ended 31st March, 2018. **CBSE 2019**

Sol. **Profit and Loss Appropriation Account**

Dr for the year ended 31st March, 2018 Cr

Particulars		Amt (₹)	Particulars	Amt (₹)
To Salary Jay's Capital A/c (15,000 × 12)		1,80,000	By Profit	15,00,000
Vijay's Capital A/c (15,000 × 12)		1,80,000	By Jay's Capital A/c (Shortfall of Guaranteed Fee)	25,000
To Profit transferred to Partner's Capital A/c				
Jay	4,66,000			
(–) Transfer to Karan (2,67,000 × 3/5)	(1,60,200)	3,05,800		
Vijay	4,66,000			
(–) Transfer to Karan (2,67,000 × 2/5)	(1,06,800)	3,59,200		
Karan	2,33,000			
(+) Shortage	2,67,000	5,00,000		
		15,25,000		15,25,000

Dr **Partners' Capital Account** Cr

Particulars	Jay (₹)	Vijay (₹)	Karan (₹)	Particulars	Jay (₹)	Vijay (₹)	Karan (₹)
To Profit and Loss Appropriation A/c (Shortage of Guaranteed Fee)	25,000	—	—	By Balance b/d	—	—	—
To Balance c/d	—	—	—	By Profit and Loss Appropriation A/c (Salary)	1,80,000	1,80,000	—
				By Profit and Loss Appropriation A/c (Profit)	3,05,800	3,59,200	5,00,000

Note In the absence of any information of capital at the beginning, it is not possible to close capital account and calculate capital at the end. Alternatively, we can calculate the balance also.

Missing Information

Solved Question 34 **X and Y are partners with capitals of ₹ 2,50,000 and ₹ 1,50,000 respectively, sharing profits in the ratio of 2 : 1. The terms of partnership for the year ended 31st March, 2018 are as follows**

(i) Interest on capital is to be allowed @ 9% p.a.

(ii) X is to get a salary of ₹ 2,000 per month.

(iii) Interest on Y's loan account of ₹ 1,00,000 for the whole year.

(iv) Interest on drawings of partners at 12% per annum. Drawings being X ₹ 30,000 and Y ₹ 36,000.

(v) 5% of the distributable profit should be transferred to general reserve.

Fill in the missing figures in the following accounts

Profit and Loss Account

Dr for the year ended 31st March, 2018 Cr

Particulars	Amt (₹)	Particulars	Amt (₹)
To Interest on Y's Loan	....	By Profit before Interest	....
To Profit transferred to Profit and Loss Appropriation A/c	....		
	....		....

Profit and Loss Appropriation Account
for the year ended 31st March, 2018

Dr | | | | | Cr

Particulars		Amt (₹)	Particulars		Amt (₹)
To Interest on Capital A/c			By Profit and Loss A/c (Net Profit)		....
X	....		By Interest on Drawings A/cs		
Y	....	....	X	...	
To Salary (X)		....	Y	...	...
To General Reserve A/c		....			
To Profit transferred to					
X's Capital A/c	57,000				
Y's Capital A/c	....	....			
		....			....

Sol.

Profit and Loss Account
for the year ended 31st March, 2018

Dr | | | Cr

Particulars	Amt (₹)	Particulars	Amt (₹)
To Interest on Y's Loan	**6,000**	By Profit before Interest	**1,52,040**
To Profit transferred to Profit and Loss Appropriation A/c	**1,46,040**		
	1,52,040		**1,52,040**

Profit and Loss Appropriation Account
for the year ended 31st March, 2018

Dr | | | | | Cr

Particulars		Amt (₹)	Particulars		Amt (₹)
To Interest on Capital A/c			By Profit		**1,46,040**
X	**22,500**		By Interest on Drawings A/cs		
Y	**13,500**	**36,000**	X	**1,800**	
To Salary (X)		**24,000**	Y	**2,160**	**3,960**
To General Reserve A/c		**4,500**			
To Profit transferred to					
X's Capital A/c	57,000				
Y's Capital A/c	**28,500**	**85,500**			
		1,50,000			**1,50,000**

Solved Question 35 **P and Q are partners sharing profits in the ratio of 3 : 2. Interest on capital is allowed at 10% p.a. and charged on drawings at the same rate. Fill up the missing figures in the following accounts**

Profit and Loss Appropriation Account
for the year ended 31st March, 2019

Dr | | | | | Cr

Particulars		Amt (₹)	Particulars		Amt (₹)
To Salary to Q		....	By Profit and Loss A/c (Net Profit)		....
To		....	By Interest on Drawings A/cs		
To Profit transferred to			P	5,000	
....	....		Q	3,000	8,000
....	....	2,40,000			
		....			5,68,000

Partners' Capital Account

Dr | | | | | | Cr

Particulars	P (₹)	Q (₹)	Particulars	P (₹)	Q (₹)
To	....	....	By	....	....
	....	....		....	....

Dr **Partners' Current Account** Cr

Particulars	P (₹)	Q (₹)	Particulars	P (₹)	Q (₹)
To	....	....	By Balance c/d	32,000	44,000
To	....	....	By	....	....
To	....	....	By Interest on Capital A/c	1,60,000	1,20,000
			By	....	....
	....	....		....	....

Sol.

Profit and Loss Appropriation Account
for the year ended 31st March, 2019

Dr Cr

Particulars		Amt (₹)	Particulars		Amt (₹)
To Salary to Q (Balancing Figure)		**48,000**	By Profit and Loss A/c (Net Profit)		**5,60,000**
To **Interest on Capital A/cs**			By Interest on Drawings A/cs		
P	**1,60,000**		P	5,000	
Q	**1,20,000**	**2,80,000**	Q	3,000	8,000
To Profit transferred to					
P's Current A/c (3/5)	**1,44,000**				
Q's Current A/c (2/5)	**96,000**	2,40,000			
		5,68,000			5,68,000

Dr **Partners' Capital Account** Cr

Particulars	P (₹)	Q (₹)	Particulars	P (₹)	Q (₹)
To **Balance c/d**	**16,00,000**	**12,00,000**	By **Balance b/d**	**16,00,000**	**12,00,000**
	16,00,000	**12,00,000**		**16,00,000**	**12,00,000**

Dr **Partners' Current Account** Cr

Particulars	P (₹)	Q (₹)	Particulars	P (₹)	Q (₹)
To **Drawings A/c**	**1,00,000**	**60,000**	By Balance c/d	32,000	44,000
To **Interest on Drawings A/c**	**5,000**	**3,000**	By **Salary A/c**	—	**48,000**
To **Balance c/d**	**2,31,000**	**2,45,000**	By Interest on Capital A/c	1,60,000	1,20,000
			By **Profit and Loss Appropriation A/c**	**1,44,000**	**96,000**
	3,36,000	**3,08,000**		**3,36,000**	**3,08,000**

Working Notes

1. P's Capital $= 1{,}60{,}000 \times \frac{100}{10} =$ ₹ 16,00,000 ; Q's Capital $= 1{,}20{,}000 \times \frac{100}{10} =$ ₹ 12,00,000
2. Interest on drawings must have been charged for an average period of six months.

   Hence, P's Drawings $= 5{,}000 \times \frac{100}{10} \times \frac{12}{6} =$ ₹ 1,00,000 ; Q's Drawings $= 3{,}000 \times \frac{100}{10} \times \frac{12}{6} =$ ₹ 60,000

Numerical Questions

Introduction and Format of Basic Accounts

1. A, B and P are partners in a firm, they do not have a partnership deed. At the end of the year, following problems were faced by them.

(i) A and P have contributed a larger amount of capital as compared to B and therefore, they want that the profits should be distributed in the capital ratio but B did not agree.

(ii) A wants that partners must be allowed interest on the capitals but P and B object to it.

(iii) P wants that the loan provided by him to the firm should bear interest @ 12% per annum but other partners did not agree.

(iv) A wants his son N to join the business but B and P object to it.

Suggest them, how to settle each of the above problems, keeping in view provisions of Partnership Act.

Ans. (i) In the absence of partnership deed, profits and losses will be distributed equally among the partners. Hence, claim of A and P will not be accepted.

(ii) In case there is no partnership deed, partners are not allowed interest on their capitals. Hence, claim of A in respect of interest on capital is not accepted.

(iii) In the absence of partnership deed, if any partner gives loan in addition to his capital, he is allowed interest @ 6% per annum. Therefore, P would be allowed interest @ 6% per annum.

(iv) A new partner can be admitted into the business only with the consent of all the existing partners. Therefore, N cannot be introduced in business, if B and P object to it.

2. T, M and S are partners in a firm sharing profits in the ratio of 4 : 3 : 3 respectively with capital balances of ₹ 3,00,000, ₹ 1,20,000 and ₹ 1,20,000 respectively. As per partnership deed they're entitled for interest on their capitals @ 12%, p.a. M is entitled for a monthly salary of ₹ 3,000 and T is entitled for a commission of ₹ 30,000 respectively. Drawings of the partners amounted to ₹ 10,000, ₹ 8,000 and ₹ 7,000 and interest thereon amounted to ₹ 1,000, ₹ 800 and ₹ 700 respectively. Net profit for the year ended 31st March, 2024 amounted to ₹ 1,43,300.

Prepare profit and loss appropriation account and partner's capital account.

Ans. Divisible Profit = ₹ 15,000 ; Partners' Capital Account T = ₹ 3,61,000, M = ₹ 1,66,100, S = ₹ 1,31,200

Interest on Drawings

3. B and T are partners in a firm. They share profits equally. Their monthly drawings are ₹ 2,000 each. Interest on drawings is to be charged @10% per annum. **Calculate interest on B and T's drawings for the year 2020, assuming that money is withdrawn in the beginning of every month and at the end of every month.**

Ans. B = ₹ 1,300, ₹ 1,100 ; T = ₹ 1,300, ₹ 1,100

4. A and B are partners in a partnership firm. They withdrew at the middle of every month ₹ 24,000 and ₹ 18,000 respectively during the year.

Interest on drawings is to be charged @10% p.a. as per partnership deep. Calculate interest on drawings.

Ans. A = ₹ 1,200; B = ₹ 900

5. (i) L and M are partners sharing profits equally. L withdrew regularly ₹ 8,000 in the beginning of every month for six months ended 30th September, 2024.

Calculate interest on drawings @ 5% per annum.

(ii) Raj and Simran are partners sharing profits equally. Raj withdrew regularly ₹ 8,000 at the end of every month for six months ended 30th September, 2024.

Calculate interest on drawings @ 5% per annum.

Ans. (i) Interest on drawings = ₹ 700

(ii) Interest on drawings = ₹ 500

6. J, M and C are partners in a firm sharing profits in the ratio of 2 : 2 : 1. The following information is provided to you regarding the drawings of the partners.

(i) J withdrew ₹ 10,000 at the mid of every quarter.

(ii) M withdrew ₹ 25,000 during the year.

(iii) C withdrew ₹ 40,000 on 30st September.

Calculate interest on drawings it is charged @ 6% p.a.

Competency Based Que

Ans. J = ₹ 1,200, M = 750, C = ₹ 1,200

7. **X and Y two partners, drew for private use ₹ 2,40,000 and ₹ 1,60,000. What will be their interest on drawings if?**

(i) Interest in chargeable @ 6% p.a.

(ii) Interest is chargeable @ 6%

Ans. (i) X = ₹ 7,200, Y= ₹ 4,800

(ii) X = ₹ 14,400, Y= ₹ 9,600

Hint When the date of drawings is not given, interest on drawings is calculated on the total amount of drawings for a period of 6 months.

8. Rakesh and Roshan are partners sharing profits in the ratio of 3 : 2 with capitals of ₹ 40,000 and ₹ 30,000 respectively.

They withdrew from the firm the following amounts for their personal use

	Date	Amt (₹)
Rakesh	31st May, 2017	600
	30th June, 2017	500
	31st August, 2017	1,000
	1st November, 2017	400
	31st December, 2017	1,500
	31st January, 2018	300
	1st March, 2018	700
Roshan	At the beginning of each month	400

Interest is to be charged @ 6% per annum on drawings. Calculate Rakesh's interest on drawings by simple and product method assuming that books of accounts are closed on 31st March, 2018, every year.

Ans. Rakesh = ₹ 126.50

Interest on Capital

9. P, Q and R are partners in a firm sharing profits equally with capital balances of ₹ 5,00,000, ₹ 6,60,000 and ₹ 7,20,000 respectively on 1st April, 2023. Interest on capital is provided @ 7% p.a. On 1st August 2023 R withdrew ₹ 30,000 from his capital. On 1st October, 2023 P brings additional capital of ₹ 1,00,000.

Calculate interest on capital for the year ended 31st March, 2024.

Ans. P = ₹ 38,500, Q = ₹ 46,200, R = ₹ 49,000

10. Ram and Vij started business on 1st January, 2023 with capitals of ₹ 1,20,000 and ₹ 80,000 respectively. During the year, Ram introduced ₹ 20,000 as additional capital on 1st July, 2023. They both withdrew ₹ 1,000 per month for household expenses in lieu of profits. Interest on capital is to be allowed @ 10% per annum.

Calculate the interest on capital payable to Ram and Vij for the year ending 31st December, 2023.

Competency Based Que

Ans. Ram = ₹ 13,000, Vij = ₹ 8,000

11. Rakshit and Malik are partners in a firm sharing profits and losses in the ratio of 4 : 1. On 1st April, 2021, their capitals were ₹ 1,20,000 and ₹ 80,000 respectively. On 1st December, 2021, they decided that the total capital of the firm should be ₹ 3,00,000 to be contributed by them in the ratio of 2 : 1. According to the partnership deed, interest on capital is allowed to the partners @ 6% p.a.

Calculate interest on capital to be allowed for the the year ending 31st March, 2022. **CBSE 2023**

12. From the following balance sheet of P and Q, calculate interest on capital @ 8% per annum for the year ended 31st March, 2024. **Competency Based Que**

Balance Sheet
as at 31st March, 2024

Liabilities	Amt (₹)	Assets	Amt (₹)
P's Capital A/c	3,20,000	Fixed Assets	6,00,000
Q's Capital A/c	2,80,000	Drawings (P)	80,000
Profit and Loss Appropriation A/c (2023-24)	2,00,000	Other Assets	1,20,000
	8,00,000		8,00,000

During the year, P's drawings were ₹ 80,000 and Q's drawings were ₹ 1,00,000. Profit for the year was ₹ 3,00,000.

Ans. Interest on Capital P = ₹ 21,600, Q = ₹ 26,400

Other Appropriation and Charge Items

13. B, S and F were partners in a firm, sharing profits in the ratio of 4 : 3 : 3. Their fixed capitals as on 1st April, 2023, were ₹ 27,00,000, ₹ 15,00,000 and ₹ 12,00,000 respectively. On 1st November, 2023, B provided a loan of ₹ 2,40,000 ot the firm. According to their partnership agreement.

(i) The partners were entitled to interest on their capital at a rate of 6% per annum.

(ii) Interest on the partners' drawings was to be charged at 8% per annum.

The firm generated profits of ₹ 7,65,000 (before accounting for interest on B's loan) during the financial yeat 2023-24. the partners' drawings for the year were as follows

B ₹ 2,40,000, S ₹ 2,10,000 and F ₹ 1,50,000

Prepare the profit and loss appropriation account for the year ending 31st March, 2024.

Ans. Divisible Profit = ₹ 4,59,000; B's Loan = ₹ 6,000

14. Rahul and Karan are partners sharing profits in the ratio of 3 : 2, with capitals of ₹ 1,25,000 and ₹ 75,000, respectively. Interest on capital is agreed at 6% per annum. Karan is to be allowed an annual salary of ₹ 6,250. The manager is to receive a commission of ₹ 12,500. Rahul has also provided a loan of ₹ 1,25,000 to the firm on 1st April, 2023, without any agreement. During the year 2023-2024, the profits earned amounted to ₹ 56,125.

Prepare the profit and loss appropriation account to show the distribution of profit for the year ending 1st March, 2024.

Ans. Divisible Profit = ₹ 17,875

Note Manager's commission will be deducted from profit.

15. On 1st April, 2023, X and Y started a partnership firm. They contributed capitals of ₹ 9,00,000 and ₹ 6,75,000, respectively. Additionally, X provided a loan of ₹ 1,50,000 to the firm on the same data. The following agreement were made

(i) Interest on the partner's loan will be charged at 10% p.a. and interest on capital allowed @ 8% p.a.

(ii) Y will receive ₹ 3,000 per month as rent for providing office space to the firm.

(iii) X is entitled to a commission of 10% on the net profit after charging all the expenses including such commission.

The total profit generated during the year amounted to ₹ 3,97,000.

Prepare the profit and loss appropriation account to show the distribution of profit for the year ending 31st March, 2024. **Competency Based Que**

Ans. Divisible Profit = ₹ 2,00,000; X's Commission = ₹ 20,000

Profit and Loss Appropriation Account and Partners' Capital Account

16. A, B and C are partners in a firm sharing profits in the ratio of 2 : 2 : 1. On 1st April, 2023 their capital balances were ₹ 3,00,000, ₹ 3,00,000 and ₹ 1,50,000 respectively. Interest on capital is to be charged @ 10% p.a. A and B are entitled for a salary of ₹ 2,000 and ₹ 3,000 per month. C is to get a commission of ₹ 18,000. Net profit at the end of the year amounted to ₹ 1,60,500.

Prepare profit and loss appropriation account and partners' capital account for the year ended 31st March, 2024.

Ans. Divisible Profit = ₹ 7,500; Partners' Capital Account A = ₹ 3,57,000, B = ₹ 3,69,000, C = ₹ 1,84,500

17. Akhil and Nikhil were partners sharing profits and losses in the ratio of 3 : 2. Their fixed capitals were ₹ 1,00,000 and ₹ 80,000 respectively. Interest on capital was agreed @ 6% p.a. Nikhil was to be allowed an annual salary of ₹ 9,200. During the year 2021-22, the net profit prior to the calculation of interest on capital but after charging Nikhil's salary amounted to ₹ 1,20,000.

Prepare profit and loss appropriation account of the firm for the year ending 31st March, 2022. **CBSE 2023**

Ans. Divisible Profit = ₹ 1,09,200

18. Aman and Vikram were parnters in a firm sharing profits in the ratio of their capital contributed at the start of the business, which were ₹ 1,60,000 and ₹ 1,20,000, respectively. According to the partnership agreement, interest on capital and drawings are set at 12% and 10% per annum, respectively. Aman and Vikram receive a monthly salary of ₹ 4,000 and ₹ 6,000, respectively. The profits for the year ending 31st March, 2024 before making the above appropriations, were ₹ 2,00,600. The drawings of Aman and Vikram were ₹ 80,000 and ₹ 1,00,000, respectively.

Prepare the profit and loss appropriation account for the year ended 31st March, 2024.

Ans. Divisible Profit = ₹ 56,000

19. Pavan and Karan were partners in a firm sharing profits in the ratio of 3 : 2. Their fixed capitals as of 1st April, 2023, were Pavan ₹ 20,000 and Karan ₹ 40,000. They agreed to allow interest on capital at 12% per annum and charge interest on drawings at 15% per annum. The firm earned a profit of ₹ 6,000 before making any adjustments for the year ending 31st March, 2024. The drawings made by Pavan and Karan during the year were ₹ 600 and ₹ 1,000, respectively.

Showing your calculations clearly, prepare the profit and loss appropriation account for Pavan and Karan. The interest on capital will be allowed even if the firm incurs a loss.

Ans. Net Loss transferred to Partners' Capital Account = ₹ 1,080

20. Sonu and Rajat started a partnership firm on 1st April, 2023. They contributed ₹ 8,00,000 and ₹ 6,00,000 respectively as their capitals and decided to share profits and losses in the ratio of 3 : 2.

The partnership deed provided that Sonu was to be paid a salary of ₹ 20,000 per month and Rajat a commission of 5% on turnover. It also provided that interest on capital be allowed @ 8% p.a. Sonu withdrew ₹ 20,000 on 1st December, 2023 and Rajat withdrew ₹ 5,000 at the end of each month. Interest on drawings was charged @ 6% p.a.

The net profit as per profit and loss account for the year ended 31st March, 2024 was ₹ 4,89,950. The turnover of the firm for the year ended 31st March, 2024 amounted to ₹ 20,00,000.

Pass necessary journal entries for the above transactions in the books of Sonu and Rajat. **CBSE 2019**

Ans. Divisible Profit = ₹ 40,000

21. The partnership agreement between Mann and Shaan provides that

(i) Profits with be shared equally.

(ii) Mann will be allowed a salary of ₹ 400 per month.

(iii) Shaan who manages the sales department will be allowed a commission equal to 10% of the net profits, after allowing Mann's salary.

(iv) 7% interest will be allowed on partners' fixed capital.

(v) 5% interest will be charged on partners' annual drawings.

(vi) The fixed capitals of Mann and Shaan are ₹ 1,00,000 and ₹ 80,000 respectively. Their annual drawings were ₹ 16,000 and ₹ 14,000 respectively. The next profit for the year ending 31st March, 2024 amounted to ₹ 40,000.

Prepare firm's profit and loss appropriation account.

NCERT; Competency Based Que

Ans. Divisible Profit = ₹ 20,580

22. X and Y are partners in a firm sharing profits and losses in the ratio of 3 : 2. Their fixed capitals as on 1st April, 2023, were ₹ 6,00,000 and ₹ 4,00,000 respectively.

Their partnership deed provided for the following

(i) Partners are to be allowed interest on their capitals @ 10% per annum.

(ii) They are to be charged interest on drawings @ 4 % per annum.

(iii) X is entitled to a salary of ₹ 2,000 per month.

(iv) Y is entitled to a commission of 5% of the correct net profit of the firm before charging such commission.

(v) X is entitled to a rent of ₹ 3,000 per month for the use of his premises by the firm.

The net profit of the firm of the year ended 31st March, 2024, before providing for any of the above clauses was ₹ 4,00,000. Both partners withdrew ₹ 5,000 at the beginning of every month for the entire year.

You are required to prepare a profit and loss appropriation account for the year ended 31st March, 2024.

Competency Based Que

Ans. Divisible Profit = ₹ 2,24,400

Hint Commission 5% on 3,64,000 = ₹ 18,200

23. P and Q established a partnership firm on 1st April, 2023. They each contributed capital of ₹ 12,00,000 and ₹ 9,00,000, respectively and agreed to share profits and losses in the ratio of 3 : 2. According to the partnership agreement, P would receive a monthly salary of ₹ 30,000, while Q would earn a commission of 5% on the firm's turnover. The agreement also stated that interest on capital would be provided at a rate of 8% per annum. P withdrew ₹ 30,000 on 1st December, 2023 and Q withdrew ₹ 7,500 at the end of each month. Interest on drawings was charged at 6% per annum. The net profit as per the profit and loss account for the year ending 31st March, 2024, was ₹ 7,34,925 and the firm's turnover for the same period amounted to ₹ 30,00,000.

Prepare the profit and loss appropriation account for the year ended 31st March, 2024.

Ans. Divisible Profit = ₹ 60,000

24. Ayaan and Rohan are partners in a business, sharing profits and losses in the ratio of 3 : 2. As of 1st April, 2023, their fixed capital contributions were ₹ 18,00,000 and ₹ 12,00,000, respectively. According to their partnership agreement, the following terms apply

(i) Both partners are entitled to interest on their capital at a rate of 10% per annum.

(ii) Interest on drawings is charged at a rate of 4% per annum.

(iii) Ayaan receives a salary of ₹ 6,000 per month.

(iv) Rohan earns a commission equal to 5% of the firm's net profit before his commission is deducted.

(v) Ayaan is entitled to a monthly rent of ₹ 9,000 for the use of his premises by the firm.

The net profit of the firm for the year ending 31st March, 2024, before any adjustments for the above items, was ₹ 12,00,000. Both partners withdrew ₹ 15,000 at the beginning of each month throughout the year.

You are required to prepare the profit and loss appropriation account for the year ending 31st March, 2024.

Ans. Divisible Profit = ₹ 6,73,200

Past Adjustments

25. Ajay, Manish and Sachin were partners sharing profits in the ratio 5 : 3 : 2. Their capitals were ₹ 6,00,000, ₹ 8,00,000 and ₹ 11,00,000 as on 1st April, 2021. As per partnership deed, interest on capitals were to be provided @ 10% p.a. For the year ended 31st March, 2022, profits of ₹ 2,00,000 were distributed without providing for interest on capitals.

Pass an adjustment entry and show the workings clearly. **CBSE SQP 2023**

26. Ananya, Bhavi and Chandni were partners in a firm with capitals of ₹ 3,00,000, ₹ 2,00,000 and ₹ 1,00,000 respectively.

According to the provisions of the partnership deed

(i) Ananya and Chandni were each entitled to a monthly salary of ₹ 1,500.

(ii) Bhavi was entitled to a salary of ₹ 4,000 per annum.

The profit for the year ended 31st March, 2022, ₹ 80,000 was divided between the partners in their profit sharing ratio of 3 : 3 : 2 without providing for the above adjustments.

Pass the necessary adjustment entry to rectify the above omissions in the books of the firm. Show your working notes clearly.

27. On 31st March, 2023, the capitals of Raghav and Diya stood at ₹ 4,00,000 and ₹ 3,00,000 respectively, after the necessary adjustment in respect of drawings and net profit. Subsequently, it was discovered that interest on capital @ 10% p.a. had been omitted. The net profit for the year ended 31st March, 2023 amounted to ₹ 1,00,000.

During the year ended 31st March, 2023, Raghav's drawings were ₹ 2,000 drawn at the beginning of each month, while Diya's drawings were ₹ 3,000 drawn at the beginning of each quarter.

Pass the necessary adjustment entry.

28. A, B and C are partners. Their fixed capitals as on 31st March, 2024 were : A ₹ 50,000, B ₹ 40,000 and C ₹ 30,000.

Give the necessary adjusting entry if interest on capital was credited @10% per annum instead of 8% per annum.

Ans. Debit A's current account and Credit R's current account with ₹ 200 respectively.

29. P, Q and R are partners. Their fixed capitals as on 31st March, 2024 were P ₹ 1,00,000, Q ₹ 2,00,000, R ₹ 3,00,000. Profits for the year 2023-24 amounting to ₹ 1,20,000 were distributed.

Give the necessary adjusting entry, if interest on capital was credited @10% per annum instead of 12% per annum.

Ans. Debit P's current account and Credit R's current account with ₹ 2,000 respectively.

30. The partners of a firm distributed the profits for the year ended 31st March, 2024, ₹ 75,000 in the ratio of 2 : 2 : 1 without providing for the following adjustments

(i) X and Y were entitled to a salary of ₹ 750 per quarter.

(ii) Z was entitled to a commission of ₹ 9,000.

(iii) X and Z had guaranteed a minimum profit of ₹ 25,000 p.a. to Y.

(iv) Profits were to be shared in the ratio of 3 : 3 : 2.

Pass necessary journal entry for the above adjustments in the books of the firm. **Competency Based Que**

31. M, N and O are partners and their capitals on 1st April, 2024 were P ₹ 2,00,000, Q ₹ 4,00,000 and R ₹ 6,00,000.

The following appropriations are provided for

(i) Interest on capital @ 10% per annum.

(ii) Interest on drawings @ 6% irrespective of time period.

(iii) M as a working partner received a salary of ₹ 3,000 per month.

(iv) N is paid a commission of ₹ 8,000.

After providing the above items, remaining profit was ₹ 90,000 which was distributed by the partners in the ratio of their capitals.

The drawings of the partners were P ₹ 10,000, Q ₹ 12,000 and O ₹ 16,000. There was no partnership deed in the business.

Give necessary adjustment entry. **Competency Based Que**

Ans. Debit O with ₹ 20,134 and Credit M and N with ₹ 13,507 and ₹ 6,627 respectively.

32. A, B and C are partners in a firm. They contributed ₹ 75,000 each, as capital three years ago. At that time, C agreed to look after the business as A and B were busy. The profits for the past three years were ₹ 45,000, ₹ 30,000 and ₹ 60,000 respectively. While going through the books of accounts, A noticed that profit had been distributed in 1 : 1 : 2 ratio.

When he enquired from C about this, C answered that, since he looked after the business he should get more profit.

A disagreed and it was decided to distribute profits equally with retrospective effect for the last three years.

You are required to make necessary corrections in the books of accounts of A, B and C by passing an adjustment entry. **Competency Based Que**

Ans. Debit C with ₹ 22,500 and Credit A and B with ₹ 11,250 each.

33. The capital accounts of A, B and C stood at ₹ 20,000, ₹ 15,000 and ₹ 10,000 respectively after the necessary adjustments in respect of drawings and net profit for the year ended 31st March, 2024.

It was subsequently ascertained that interest on capital @ 10% p.a. was not taken into account while arriving at the divisible profits for the year.

Drawing during the year 2023-24 had been A ₹ 500 per month, B ₹ 1,500 quarterly and C ₹ 3,000.

The net profit for the year amounted to ₹ 18,000 and partners shared profits and losses in the ratio of 2 : 2 : 1.

You are required to pass the necessary journal entries to rectify the lapse in accounting. **Competency Based Que**

Ans. Opening Capitals A = ₹ 18,800, B = ₹ 13,800, C = ₹ 9,400; Corrected Net Profit = ₹ 13,800

Hint (i) Entry will be passed for withdrawing the profit of ₹ 18,000 already distributed among the partners.

(ii) Entries will be passed for interest on capital ₹ 4,200.

(iii) Entry will be passed for distributing the corrected net profit of ₹ 13,800 among the partners.

Guarantee of Profits

34. Chaman, Burman and Aman were partners in a firm sharing profits and losses in the ratio of 3 : 2 : 1. Aman was guaranteed a minimum amount of ₹ 60,000 as firm his share of profit every year. The net profit for the year ended 31st March, 2023 amounted to ₹ 1,20,000.

Pass necessary journal entries in the books of the firm showing the distribution of profit amongst the partners. CBSE 2024

35. Mohan, Sohan and Suresh were partners in a firm sharing profits in the ratio of 2 : 2 : 1. Suresh was guaranteed a profit of ₹ 70,000. Any deficiency on account of guarantee to Suresh was to be borne by Mohan and Sohan in 3 : 2 ratio. The profit of the firm for the year ended 31st March, 2022 amounted to ₹ 2,00,000.

Prepare profit and loss appropriation account of the firm for the year ended 31st March, 2022.

Ans. Mohan = ₹ 62,000, Sohan = 68,000, Suresh = ₹ 70,000

36. X, Y and Z were in partnership sharing profits in the ratio of 1 : 2 : 3. Their fixed capitals on 1st April, 2023 were X ₹ 30,000; Y ₹ 45,000 and Z ₹ 1,00,000.

Their partnership deed provided for the following

(i) X provides his personal office to the firm for business use charging yearly rent of ₹ 15,000.

(ii) Interest on capital @ 8% p.a. and interest on drawings @ 10% p.a.

(iii) X was allowed salary @ ₹ 1,000 per month.

(iv) Y was allowed a commission of 10% of net profit as shown by profit and loss account, after charging such commission.

(v) Z was guaranteed a profit of ₹ 30,000 after making all the adjustments.

The net profit of the firm for the year ended 31st March, 2024 was ₹ 1,03,000 before making above adjustments.

You are informed that X has withdrawn ₹ 500 at the beginning of each month, Y has withdrawn ₹ 500 at the end of each month and Z has withdrawn ₹ 2,400 at the beginning of each quarter.

Prepare profit and loss appropriation account and partners' current account. Competency Based Que

Ans. Divisible Profit = ₹ 55,200; Share of Profit X = ₹ 8,400, Y = ₹ 16,800, Z = ₹ 30,000
Balances of Current Accounts X = ₹ 16,475, Y = ₹ 23,125, Z = ₹ 27,800

Hint (i) Commission to Y = ₹ 8,000
(ii) Total Interest on Drawings = ₹ 1,200

37. Three chartered accountants P, Q and R form a partnership, profits being divisible in the ratio of 3 : 2 : 1 subject to the following

(i) R's share of profits guaranteed to be not less than ₹ 30,000 per annum.

(ii) Q gives a guarantee to the effect that gross fee earned by him for the firm shall be equal to his average gross fee of the preceding five years when he was carrying on profession alone which on an average works out at ₹ 50,000.

The profits for the first year of the partnership are ₹ 1,50,000. The gross fee earned by Q for the firm is ₹ 32,000.

You are required to show profit and loss appropriation account after giving effect to the above. Competency Based Que

Ans. P's Share = ₹ 82,800, Q's Share = ₹ 37,200, R's share = ₹ 30,000

Comprehensive Questions

38. B, R and P were partners in a firm having capitals of ₹ 6,000, ₹ 6,000 and ₹ 8,000 respectively. Their current account balance were B ₹ 1,000, R ₹ 500 and P ₹ 200 (Dr).

According to the partnership deed, the partners were entitled to interest on capital @ 5% p.a. P being the working partner was also entitled to a salary of ₹ 600 p.a. The profits were to be divided as

(i) The first ₹ 2,000 in proportion to their capitals.

(ii) Next ₹ 3,000 in the ratio of 5 : 3 : 2.

(iii) Remaining profits to be shared equally.

The firm made a profit of ₹ 15,600 before charging any of the above items.

Prepare profit and loss appropriation account. Competency Based Que

Ans. Profit transferred to Partners' Current Account
B = ₹ 5,100, R = ₹ 4,500, P = ₹ 4,400

39. P, Q and R were partners with fixed capital of ₹ 40,000, ₹ 32,000 and ₹ 24,000. After distributing the profit of ₹ 48,000 for the year ended 31st March, 2022 in their agreed ratio of 3 : 1 : 1 it was observed that.

(i) Interest on capital was provided at 10% p.a. instead of 8% p.a.

(ii) Salary of ₹ 12,000 was credited to P instead of Q.

You are required to pass a single journal entry in the beginning of the next year to rectify the above omission. CBSE SQP 2024; Competency Based Que

40. Cheese and Slice are equal partners. Their capitals as on 1st April, 2022 were ₹ 50,000 and ₹ 1,00,000 respectively. After the account for the financial year ending 31st March, 2023 have been prepared, it is observed that interest on capital @ 6% per annum and salary to Cheese @ ₹ 5,000 per annum, as provided in the partnership deed has not been credited to the partners' capital account before distribution of profits.

You are required to given necessary rectifying entries using profit and loss adjustment account. CBSE SQP 2024; Competency Based Que

41. Manoj and Nitin were partners in a firm sharing profits and losses in the ratio of 2 : 1. On 31st March, 2023, the balances in their capital accounts after making adjustments for profits and drawings were ₹ 90,000 and ₹ 80,000 respectively.

The net profit for the year ended 31st March, 2023, amounted to ₹ 30,000.

During the year Manoj withdrew ₹ 40,000 and Nitin withdrew ₹ 20,000. Subsequently, it was noticed that interest on capital @10% p.a. was not provided to the partners. Also interest on drawings to Manoj ₹ 3,000 and to Nitin ₹ 2,000 was not charged.

Pass necessary adjusting journal entry. Show your workings clearly. **Competency Based Que**

42. A, B, C and D are partners sharing profits and losses in the ratio of 3 : 3 : 2 : 2. Their capitals as on 1st April, 2023 were ₹ 5,00,000, ₹ 5,00,000, ₹ 4,00,000 and ₹ 3,00,000 respectively.

D's share of profit (excluding interest on capital) has been guaranteed by the firm should not be less than ₹ 1,50,000. C's share of profits (including interest on capital and salary) guaranteed by A is not less than ₹ 1,55,000. The profits for the year ended 31st March, 2024 were ₹ 6,50,000 before interest on capital @ 10% per annum and salary to C ₹ 2,500 per month.

Show the distribution of profit by preparing profit and loss appropriation account. **Competency Based Que**

Ans. Profit transferred to Capital Accounts A = ₹ 1,02,500, B = ₹ 1,12,500, C = ₹ 85,000, D = ₹ 1,50,000

43. Mona, Sona and Kona entered into partnership on 1st October, 2023 to share profits and losses in the ratio of 4 : 3 : 3. Mona, however, personally guaranteed that Kona's share of profit after charging interest on capital @ 10% per annum would not be less than ₹ 80,000 in any year.

The capital contributions were : Mona ₹ 3,00,000, Sona ₹ 2,00,000 and Kona ₹ 1,50,000. The profit for the year ended 31st March, 2024 amounted to ₹ 1,60,000.

Prepare profit and loss appropriation account. **Competency Based Que**

Ans. Net Profit = ₹ 1,27,500; Share of Profit
Mona = ₹ 49,250, Sona = ₹38,250, Golu = ₹ 40,000

Hint Guaranteed amount for half-year $= 80{,}000 \times \frac{1}{2}$
$= ₹\ 40{,}000$

Missing Information

44. M and N are partners in a firm. M gets a commission of 10% on net profit before charging any commission and N gets a commission of 10% after charging M's commission and his own commission. Their profit sharing ratio is 3 : 2.

Calculate the missing figures from the following profit and loss appropriation account for the year ended 31st March, 2024. **Competency Based Que**

Profit and Loss Appropriation Account
for the year ended 31st March, 2024

Dr | | Cr

Particulars		Amt (₹)	Particulars	Amt (₹)
To Partners' Commission A/c			By Profit and Loss A/c (Net Profit)	...
M	26,400			
N	...	...		
To Partner's Salary – M		...		
To Share of Profit transferred to Partners' Capital Accounts				
M	...			
N	80,000	...		...
		...		...

45. **Fill in the missing figures in the following accounts.** **Competency Based Que**

Profit and Loss Account
for the year ended 31st March, 2024

Dr | | Cr

Particulars	Amt (₹)	Particulars	Amt (₹)
To Manager's Commission (6% of profit before charging commission)	36,000	By Profit before Manager's Commission	...
To Net Profit transferred to Profit and Loss Appropriation A/c	...		
	...		...

Profit and Loss Appropriation Account
for the year ended 31st March, 2024

Dr | | | | Cr

Particulars		Amt (₹)	Particulars	Amt (₹)
To Interest on Capital A/c (@ 10% p.a.)			By Net Profit transferred from Profit and Loss Account	5,64,000
P	1,50,000			
Q	1,20,000	2,70,000		
To Partner's Salary – P		54,000		
To Profit transferred to Partners' Capital Accounts				
P (3/5)	...			
Q (2/5)	...	...		

46. **M and J are partners sharing profits in the ratio of 3 : 2. Their partnership deed provided for allowing interest on capital @ 10% p.a. and charging interest on drawings @ 12% p.a. The incomplete profit and loss appropriation account for the year ended 31st March, 2024, partners' capital and current accounts are given below** **Competency Based Que**

Profit and Loss Appropriation Account
for the year ended 31st March, 2024

Dr | | | | Cr

Particulars		Amt (₹)	Particulars		Amt (₹)
To Interest on Capital A/c			By Profit and Loss A/c		
M's Current A/c	...		Net Profit b/d		...
J's Current A/c	...	...	By Interest on Drawings		
To Salary			M's Current A/c	...	
J's Current A/c		...	J's Current A/c	...	
To Profit transferred to					
M's Current A/c	72,000				
J's Current A/c	...	...			
		1,70,400			1,70,400

Partners' Capital Acccount

Dr | | | | Cr

Particulars	M (₹)	J (₹)	Particulars	M (₹)	J (₹)
To Balance c/d	...	...	By Balance b/d	...	...
	...	...		...	...

Partners' Current Account

Dr | | | | Cr

Particulars	M (₹)	J (₹)	Particulars	M (₹)	J (₹)
To Bank (Drawings)	6,000	5,400	By Balance b/d	46,800	41,400
To ...	...	...	By Interest on Capital	10,800	14,400
To ...	...	...	By ...	...	...
			By ...	...	...
	...	...		...	...

Complete the profit and loss appropriation account for the year ended 31st March, 2024, partners' capital account and current account.

Theoretical Questions

Short Answer Type Questions

1. State any four features of a partnership.

Ans. Following are the features of partnership

(i) There must be atleast two persons to form a partnership and all such persons must be competent to contract.

(ii) Partnership comes into existence by an agreement, either oral or written.

(iii) The partnership agreement between/among the partners must be to share profits or losses of the business.

(iv) A partnership must be formed to do a lawful business.

2. Give any three points highlighting the importance of partnership deed.

Ans. Partnership deed and its registration is not compulsory but it is always better to have the agreement in writing for the following reasons

(i) It helps in settling any dispute or doubt with regard to the terms of partnership.

(ii) It serves as an evidence in the court of law.

(iii) It regulates the rights, duties and liabilities of each partner.

3. List any four contents of partnership deed.

Ans. The contents of partnership deed are

(i) Name and address of all the partners.

(ii) Name and address of the firm.

(iii) Capital to be contributed by each partner.

(iv) Date and commencement of the partnership.

4. In the absence of partnership deed, specify the rules relating to the following NCERT

(i) Sharing of profits and losses

(ii) Interest on partner's capital

(iii) Interest on partner's drawings

(iv) Interest on partner's loan

(v) Salary to a partner

Ans. (i) Profits and losses are to be shared equally irrespective of the type of partner (active or sleeping) or the amount of capital contributed by them.

(ii) No interest is to be allowed on capital.

(iii) No interest is to be charged on drawings made by the partners.

(iv) Interest @ 6% per annum is to be allowed on loans and advances.

(v) Partners are not entitled to any salary, commission or any other remuneration.

Objective Questions

Multiple Choice Questions (MCQs)

1. Persons who have entered into partnership are individually called .... and collectively called .... .

(a) owners, organisation (b) agents, firm
(c) partners, business (d) partners, firm

2. Under what circumstances, a partner can get exemption from sharing losses in a firm?

(a) If he is a senior citizen (b) If he is a minor
(c) If he is retiring partner (d) All of these

3. Maximum number of partners which should not exceed for partnership business is ....

(a) 50 (b) 40
(c) 60 (d) 30

4. The central government can prescribe maximum number of members in a partnership firm which cannot exceed

(a) 50 members (b) 100 members
(c) 200 members (d) 150 members

5. Which of the following statement is incorrect?

(a) Each partner is an owner as well as agent in the firm
(b) Partnership firm has a separate legal entity
(c) Share of profits and losses in agreed ratio
(d) Capital of partners may be fixed or fluctuating

6. A charitable dispensary is run by 15 members. A new member wants to join them. The new member is of the opinion that partnership deed must be written while other members refused to do that.

They said this is not a partnership. Give reason(s) in favour of other members. Competency Based Que

(a) There is no business
(b) There is no sharing of profits
(c) There is no motive of profit-making
(d) All of the above

7. Vibha and Asha are partners in a firm. Asha withdrew ₹ 1,000 at the end of each quarter during the year ended 31st March, 2022. Interest on drawings will be calculated for an average period of CBSE 2023

(a) 6 months (b) $4\frac{1}{2}$ months
(c) $7\frac{1}{2}$ months (d) $6\frac{1}{2}$ months

8. **X and Y are partners in a firm sharing profits in 3 : 2. X withdrew ₹ 15,000 during the year. Interest is charged @10% p.a. on drawings. The entry for interest on drawings charged, assuming capitals of partners were fixed, will be** Competency Based Que

(a) X's Capital A/c Dr 750
To Interest on Drawings A/c 750
(b) X's Current A/c Dr 750
To Interest on Drawings A/c 750
(c) X's Current A/c Dr 1,500
To Interest on Drawings A/c 1,500
(d) X's Capital A/c Dr 1,500
To Interest on Drawings A/c 1,500

9. **Radhika, Mehar and Shubha were partners in a firm sharing profits and losses in the ratio of 9 : 8 : 7. If Radhika's share of profit at the end of the year amounted to ₹ 5,40,000, Shubha's share of profit will be** CBSE 2025

(a) ₹ 5,40,000 (b) ₹ 4,80,000
(c) ₹ 60,000 (d) ₹ 4,20,000

10. **Kanha, Resham and Nisha were partners in a firm. Nisha had given a loan of ₹ 1,00,000 to the firm @ 10% p.a. The accountant of the firm is emphasising that interest on loan will be paid @ 6% p.a. At what rate the interest on loan will be paid to Nisha?** CBSE 2024; Competency Based Que

(a) 6% p.a. (b) 10% p.a.
(c) 8% p.a.
(d) No interest on loan will be paid

11. **Hina and Neena are partners in a firm. Neena withdrew ₹ 10,000 per month at the beginning of each month during the year ended 31st March, 2022. Interest on drawings was to be charged @ 6% per annum.**

Interest on Neena's drawings for the year ended 31st March, 2022 will be CBSE 2023

(a) ₹ 3,900 (b) ₹ 325
(c) ₹ 3,600 (d) ₹ 3,300

12. **The difference between the fixed capital method and fluctuating capital method of maintaining partner's capitals is whether or not the transactions other than .... are recorded in the capital accounts of the partners.** CBSE Term I 2021; Competency Based Que

(a) additional capital introduced
(b) withdrawal of capital
(c) partner's loan (d) Both (a) and (b)

13. **The partnership deed should be property drafted and prepared as per the provisions of the ..... and preferably registered with the .... .** CBSE Term I 2021

(a) Indian Partnership Act, 1932, Registrar of Companies
(b) Indian Partnership Act, 1932, Registrar of Firms
(c) Stamp Act, Registrar of Companies
(d) Stamp Act, Registrar of Firms

14. **A manager gets 5% commission on net profit before charging such commission. Profit is ₹ 1,00,000. Commission will be ₹ ....**

(a) 5,00,000 (b) 5,000
(c) 50,000 (d) 1,05,000

15. **Nikhil and Sharat were partners in a firm sharing profits and losses in the ratio of 4 : 3. Nikhil withdrew ₹ 6,000 on the first day of every quarter for the year ended 31st March, 2023. Interest on drawings is to be charged @ 5% p.a. Interest on Nikhil's drawings will be calculated for** Competency Based Que

(a) 6 months (b) 4.5 months
(c) 7.5 months (d) 3 months

16. **Which of the following statements are incorrect?** Competency Based Que

(a) Co-ownership will amount to partnership if some income is being generated from it
(b) The written agreement among the partners is called partnership deed
(c) Additional capital introduced will be credited to partners' capital account in both methods, i.e. fixed and fluctuating methods
(d) Drawings out of capital will be debited to partners' account in case of fixed capitals

17. **Daksh and Mayank are parthers sharing profits equally. Interest on capital is provided @ 7.5% p.a. on their capitals. Interest on capital credited to their capital accounts ₹ 11,250 and ₹ 13,125 respectively.**
Their opening capital balances will be Competency Based Que

(a) ₹ 1,50,000, ₹ 1,60,000
(b) ₹ 1,60,000, ₹ 1,75,000
(c) ₹ 1,75,000, ₹ 1,90,000
(d) ₹ 1,50,000, ₹ 1,75,000

18. **On 1st January, 2023, Abhished, a partner, advanced a loan of ₹ 3,00,000 to the firm. In the absence of a partnership agreement, the amount of interest on the loan for the year ending 31st March, 2023 will be** CBSE 2024

(a) ₹ 18,000
(b) ₹ 4,500
(c) ₹ 9,000
(d) No interest will be provided

19. The clauses of the partnership deed can be altered.
(a) With the consent of active partners only
(b) With the consent of all the partners except sleeping partner
(c) With the consent of all the partners irrespective of type of partner
(d) With the consent of managing partner only

20. Omkar and Shiva were partners in a firm. Omkar was entitled to a salary of ₹ 20,000 p.a. while Shiva was entitled to a salary of ₹ 50,000 p.a. Net profit for the year ended 31st March, 2023 after charging salary of Omkar and Shiva was ₹ 5,60,000. The total amount credited to Omkar's capital account will be
CBSE 2024; Competency Based Que
(a) ₹ 2,45,000 (b) ₹ 2,65,000
(c) ₹ 3,15,000 (d) ₹ 3,00,000

21. Rights of a partner consists which of the following?
(a) Right to inspect books of accounts
(b) Right to not allow the admission of new partner
(c) Right to conduct affairs of business
(d) All of the above

22. Current accounts of the partners are not opened, when capitals are ....
(a) fixed (b) fluctuating
(c) Both (a) and (b) (d) None of these

23. Nandita and Prabha were partners in a firm. Nandita withdrew ₹ 3,00,000 during the year for personal use. The partnership deed provides for charging interest on drawings @ 10% p.a. Interest on Nandita's drawings for the year ended 31st March, 2024 will be
CBSE 2025
(a) ₹ 9,000 (b) ₹ 30,000
(c) ₹ 18,000 (d) ₹ 15,000

24. Which of the following items cannot be recorded in the capital account of partners if the capital account of partners are fixed? CBSE 2024
(a) Drawings (b) Withdrawal of capital
(c) Introduction of additional capital
(d) Opening balance of capital

25. Which one of the following items is not dealt through profit and loss appropriation account? CBSE 2024
(a) Interest on capital (b) Interest on drawings
(c) Rent paid to partners (d) Partner's salary

26. Rahul, Samarth and Ayaan were partners sharing profits and losses in the ratio of 5 : 4 : 3. Ayaan's fixed capital balance as on 31st March, 2024 was ₹ 2,70,000. Which of the following items would have affected this capital balance? CBSE SQP 2025
(a) Profit/Loss for the year
(b) Additional capital introduced
(c) Reduction in capital due to capital adjustment
(d) Both (b) and (c)

27. Ram and Shyam inherited a 2 BHK flat from their father and the both agreed and rented the flat immediately for an annual rent of ₹ 2,40,000. This is an example of Competency Based Que
(a) partnership (b) limited partnership
(c) co-ownership (d) Both (a) and (c)

28. Which of the following is an essential element of a partnership firm, except
(a) two or more persons (b) agreement
(c) mutual agency (d) limited liability

29. A and B are partners in a firm sharing profit in the ratio of 3 : 2. Their Balance Sheet as on 31st March, 2021 was as follows

Liabilities	Amt (₹)	Assets		Amt (₹)
A's Capital	30,000	Drawings		
B's Capital	10,000	A	4,000	
		B	2,000	6,000
		Other Assets		34,000
	40,000			40,000

Net profit of the year ended 31st March, 2021, ₹ 5,000 was divided without providing for interest on capital @ 10% p.a. What will be the amount of interest on A's capital? CBSE Term I 2021; Competency Based Que
(a) ₹ 3,000 (b) Nil
(c) ₹ 3,100 (d) ₹ 2,700

30. Vanya and Aanaya were partners in a firm sharing profit and losses in the ratio of 3 : 2. Their capital were ₹ 5,00,000 and ₹ 1,00,000 respectively. Vanya was entitled to interest on capital @ 8% p.a. and Aanya was entitled to salary @ ₹ 5,000 per month. The net profit before any appropriation was ₹ 1,75,000. Vanya's share in divisible profit will be
CBSE 2024; Competency Based Que
(a) ₹ 45,000 (b) ₹ 30,000
(c) ₹ 37,500 (d) ₹ 40,000

31. Salary/Commission to a partner is a/an .... profit.
(a) charge against (b) appropriation of
(c) Either (a) or (b) (d) None of these

32. Which of the following is the adjusting entry for recording commission allowed to a partner?
Competency Based Que
(a) Partner's Capital A/c Dr
To Partner's Commission A/c
(b) Partner's Commission A/c Dr
To Partner's Current A/c
(c) Profit and Loss Appropriation A/c Dr
To Partner's Commission A/c
(d) Partner's Commission A/c Dr
To Profit and Loss Appropriation A/c

33. **Anthony a partner was being guaranteed that his share of profits will not be less than ₹ 60,000 p.a. Deficiency, if any was to be borne by other partners Amar and Akbar equally. For the year ended 31st March, 2024 the firm incurred loss of ₹ 1,80,000.**

What amount will be debited to Amar's capital account in total at the end of the year? CBSE SQP 2025; Competency Based Que

(a) ₹ 60,000 (b) ₹ 1,20,000 (c) ₹ 90,000 (d) ₹ 80,000

34. **Ikka, Dukka and Teeka were partners sharing profits and losses in the ratio of 2 : 2 : 1. Their fixed capital balances were ₹ 5,00,000, ₹ 4,00,000 and ₹ 3,00,000 respectively. For the year ended 31st March, 2024 profits of ₹ 84,000 were distributed without providing for interest on capital @ 10% p.a. as per the partnership deed. While passing an adjustment entry, which of the following is correct?** CBSE SQP 2025; Competency Based Que

(a) Teeka will be debited by ₹ 4,200
(b) Teeka will be credited by ₹ 4,200
(c) Teeka will be credited by ₹ 6,000
(d) Teeka will be debited by ₹ 6,000

35. **A and B are partners with capital balances of ₹ 3,00,000 and ₹ 4,00,000. Interest on capital @ 8% p.a. was omitted to be provided by the accountant of the firm, in the adjustment entry.** Competency Based Que

(a) Debit A by and Credit B by ₹ 3,000
(b) Debit A by and Credit B by ₹ 4,000
(c) Debit B by and Credit A by ₹ 4,000
(d) Debit A by and Credit B by ₹ 28,000

36. **Sonia and Roma are equal partners with fixed capitals of ₹ 8,00,000 and ₹ 6,00,000 respectively. After closing the accounts for the year ending 31st March, 2022 it was discovered that interest on capitals was provided @ 8% instead of 10% p.a. In the adjusting entry** Competency Based Que

(a) Sonia will be debited by ₹ 56,000 and Roma will be credited by ₹ 56,000
(b) Sonia will be debited by ₹ 96,000 and Roma will be credited by ₹ 96,000
(c) Sonia will be debited by ₹ 2,000 and Roma will be credited by ₹ 2,000
(d) Sonia will be credited by ₹ 2,000 and Roma will be debited by ₹ 2,000

37. **Ashu and Nishu are equal partners with fixed capitals of ₹ 25,00,000 and ₹ 10,00,000 respectively. After closing the accounts for the year ending 31st March, 2022 it was discovered that interest on capitals was provided @ 6% instead of 5% p.a. In the adjusting entry.** Competency Based Que

(a) Ashu will be debited by ₹ 7,500 and Nishu will be credited by ₹ 7,500
(b) Ashu will be credited by ₹ 7,500 and Nishu will be debited by ₹ 7,500
(c) Ashu will be debited by ₹ 25,000 and Nishu will be debited by ₹ 25,000
(d) Ashu will be credited by ₹ 10,000 and Nishu will be credited by ₹ 10,000

38. **Eliza, Fenn and Garry were partners in a firm sharing profits and losses in the ratio of 4 : 3 : 1. Fenn was guaranteed ₹ 25,000 as his share in the profits. Any deficiency arising on that account was to be met by Eliza. The firm earned a profit of ₹ 80,000 for the year ended 31st March, 2024. The amount of profit credited to Fenn's capital account will be** CBSE 2025; Competency Based Que

(a) ₹ 30,000 (b) ₹ 40,000 (c) ₹ 25,000 (d) ₹ 10,000

Assertion-Reason

Direction (Q.No. 39 to 45) *Read the following Assertion (A) and Reason (R) and choose the correct alternative from the following*

Alternatives

(a) Both Assertion (A) and Reason (R) are true and Reason (R) is the correct explanation of Assertion (A)
(b) Both Assertion (A) and Reason (R) are true, but Reason (R) is not the correct explanation of Assertion (A)
(c) Assertion (A) is true, but Reason (R) is false
(d) Assertion (A) is false, but Reason (R) is true

39. **Assertion** (A) Each partner is a principal as well as an agent for all the other partners.

Reason (R) As per the definition of Partnership Act, partnership business may be carried on by all the partners or any of them acting for all. CBSE 2024

40. **Assertion** (A) Partners' current accounts maintained under 'fixed capital method' may show a debit or a credit balance.

Reason (R) In the 'fixed capital method', all items like share of profit or loss interest on capital, drawings, interest on drawings, etc. are recorded in the partners' capital account. CBSE 2024

41. **Assertion** (A) The maximum number of partners in a partnership firm are 50.

Resason (R) The maximum number of partners are prescribed by the Partnership Act, 1932. CBSE 2024 C

42. **Assertion** (A) It is considered desirable to have a partnership agreement in writing.

Reason (R) It helps in settling any disputes with regard to the terms of partnership and acts as an evidence in the court of law.

43. **Assertion** (A) Partners distribute profits and losses in their profit sharing ratio and not in the ratio of their capitals.

Reason (R) As per partnership deed if appropriations are more than the amount of profit available for distribution, profit is distributed in the ratio of capital.

44. **Assertion** (A) The maximum number of partners in a partnership firm is 50.

Reason (R) By virtue of the Companies Act, 2013, the Central Government is empowered to prescribe maximum number of partners in a firm. The Central Government has prescribed the maximum number of partners in a firm to be 50. **CBSE 2025**

45. **Assertion** (A) The fixed capital account balance of a partner may change due to additional capital introduced or capital withdrawn or both, during the year.

Reason (R) Under fixed capital method, the partner's capital accounts balance always remains same. **CBSE Term I 2021**

Two Statements Based MCQs

Direction (Q.No. 46 to 52) *Read the following statements carefully and choose the correct alternative*

Alternatives

(a) Both the statements are correct
(b) Both the statements are incorrect
(c) Statement I is correct and Statement II is incorrect
(d) Statement I is incorrect and Statement II is correct

46. **Statement I** A partnership cannot be formed for charitable purpose.

Statement II Rent paid to a partner for use of his personal property for business is debited to profit and loss account.

47. **Statement I** Not all the partners are entitled to participate in the conduct of the affairs of its business.

Statement II The element of mutual agency is the most important element in a partnership.

48. **Statement I** Partners share profits of the business and losses as well.

Statement II Business is carried by all or any of them acting for all.

49. **Statement I** In the absence of a partnership deed, partners share profits and losses in the ratio of their capital contribution.

Statement II Interest on capital is provided to partners only if it is mentioned in the partnership deed.

50. **Statement I** Two or more person carry common business as per agreement.

Statement II There must be a written agreement among all partners.

51. **Statement I** Private properties of the partners cannot be used to pay the firm's debts.

Statement II The oral agreement is equally valid just like a written agreement.

52. **Statement I** In fixed capital method, two account are prepared.

Statement II In fluctuating capital method, only one account is prepared.

Matching

53. **Match the following**

Column I	Column II
A. Drawings at the beginning of every month	(i) 7.5
B. Drawings at the beginning of every quarter	(ii) 6.5
C. Drawings at the end of every month	(iii) 5.5

Codes

	A	B	C		A	B	C
(a)	(i)	(ii)	(iii)	(b)	(ii)	(i)	(iii)
(c)	(ii)	(i)	(iii)	(d)	(iii)	(ii)	(i)

54. **Match the following in the absence of partnership deed**

Column I	Column II
A. Interest on capital	(i) Is not allowed
B. Interest on loan	(ii) Is not charged
C. Interest on drawings	(iii) Allowed @ 6% p.a.

Codes

	A	B	C		A	B	C
(a)	(i)	(iii)	(ii)	(b)	(ii)	(iii)	(i)
(c)	(ii)	(i)	(iii)	(d)	(iii)	(ii)	(i)

55. **Match the following in case of fixed capitals**

Column I	Column II
A. Drawings out of profits	(i) Dr side of partner' current account
B. Drawings out of capital	(ii) Dr side of partners' capital account
C. Additional capital introduced	(iii) Cr side of partners' capital account

Codes

	A	B	C		A	B	C
(a)	(i)	(iii)	(ii)	(b)	(i)	(ii)	(iii)
(c)	(ii)	(i)	(iii)	(d)	(iii)	(ii)	(i)

56. **Match the following if interest on drawings is charged @ 12% p.a.**

Column I	Column II
A. Drawn ₹ 1,000 in the beginning of every month	(i) Interest on drawings = ₹ 720
B. Drawn ₹ 1,000 in the end of every month	(ii) Interest on drawings = ₹ 660
C. Drawn ₹ 1,000 every month	(iii) Interest on drawings = ₹ 780

Codes

	A	B	C		A	B	C
(a)	(i)	(ii)	(iii)	(b)	(ii)	(iii)	(i)
(c)	(ii)	(i)	(iii)	(d)	(iii)	(ii)	(i)

57. Match the following

Column I	Column II
A. Interest on drawings	(i) Credit side, profit and loss account
B. Commission to a partner	(ii) Credit side, profit and loss appropriation account
C. Interest on partner's loan	(iii) Debit side, profit and loss appropriation account
D. Interest received on loan	(iv) Debit side, profit and loss account

Codes

	A	B	C	D		A	B	C	D
(a)	(i)	(ii)	(iii)	(iv)	(b)	(i)	(iv)	(ii)	(iii)
(c)	(ii)	(iii)	(iv)	(i)	(d)	(iv)	(iii)	(ii)	(i)

Case Based MCQs

Direction *Read the following case study and answer the questions 58 to 60 on the basis of the same*

X and Y are partners in a firm sharing profits and losses equally. On 1st April, 2018, the capitals of the partners were ₹ 2,00,000 and ₹ 1,50,000 respectively. The profit and loss appropriation account of the firm showed a net profit of ₹ 3,75,000 for the year ended 31st March, 2019. The terms of partnership deed provided the following

(i) Transfer 10% of distributable profits to reserve fund.

(ii) Interest on capitals @ 6% p.a.

(iii) Interest on drawings @ 6% p.a. Drawings being X ₹ 40,000 and Y ₹ 30,000. The partners decided to provide clean drinking water and build toilets in a nearby school.

58. What is the average period for which interest on drawings will be calculated?

(a) 3 (b) 6
(c) 9 (d) 12

59. The total interest on capital provided is ₹ ....

(a) 9,000 (b) 12,000 (c) 21,000 (d) None of these

60. The amount transferred to reserve fund is ₹ ....

(a) 37,500 (b) 35,610 (c) 37,710 (d) None of these

Direction *Read the following case study and answer the questions 61 and 62 on the basis of the same*

Kavita, Savita and Madhu were partners in firm with capitals of ₹ 6,00,000, ₹ 4,00,000 and ₹ 2,00,000 respectively. After providing interest on capital @ 10% p.a. the profits are divisible as follows Kavita 1/3, Savita 1/2 and Madhu 1/6. Kavita personally guaranteed that Savita's share of profit after charging interest on capital would not be less than ₹ 1,00,000 in any year. The profit for the year ending 31st March, 2022 amounted to ₹ 3,00,000 before providing interest on capital. **CBSE 2023**

61. Savita's share of profit is short of the guaranteed amount by

(a) ₹ 40,000 (b) ₹ 70,000 (c) ₹ 20,000 (d) ₹ 10,000

62. The total profits of the firm after adjustment of guaranteed amount will be distributed between he partners as

(a) Kavita ₹ 60,000, Savita ₹ 40,000 and Madhu ₹ 20,000
(b) Kavita ₹ 50,000, Savita ₹ 1,00,000 and Madhu ₹ 30,000
(c) Kavita ₹ 60,000, Savita ₹ 90,000 and Madhu ₹ 30,000
(d) Kavita ₹ 60,000, Savita ₹ 1,00,000 and Madhu ₹ 20,000

Direction *Read the following case study and answer the questions 63 and 64 on the basis of the same*

Aditi and Saurabh were partners in a firm sharing profits and losses in the ratio of 2 : 1. On 1st April, 2022, their capitals were ₹ 5,00,000 and ₹ 4,00,000 respectively. Before any appropriation, the firm earned a net profit of ₹ 81,000 for the year ended 31st March, 2023. According to the partnership deed, interest on capital was to be provided @ 10% p.a. **CBSE 2024**

63. Interest on capital will be provided to Aditi and Saurabh in which of the following ratio?

(a) 5 : 4 (b) 2 : 1 (c) 1 : 1 (d) 8 : 1

64. Interest on Aditi's capital will be

(a) ₹ 50,000 (b) ₹ 45,000
(c) ₹ 40,500 (d) ₹ 54,000

Answers

1. (d) partners, firm
2. (b) If he is a minor
3. (a) 50
4. (b) 100 members
5. (b) Partnership have unlimited liabilities because they don't have separate legal entity.
6. (d) For partnership, there must be a business but in the question a member wants to join a charitable dispensary. Also, they work to provide social service and not to earn profits.
7. (b) $4\frac{1}{2}$ months
8. (b) Interest on Drawings $= 15,000 \times \frac{10}{100} \times \frac{6}{12} =$ ₹ 750
9. (d) Total Profit = Share of Profit of Radhika × Reciprocal of her share $= 5,40,000 \times \frac{24}{9} =$ ₹ 14,40,000

Shubha's Share in Profit = 14,40,000 × 7/24 = ₹ 4,20,000

10. (b) 10% p.a.

11. (a) Interest on Neena's Drawings

$$= (10{,}000 \times 12) \times \frac{6}{100} \times \frac{6.5}{12} = ₹\,3{,}900$$

12. (d) Both (a) and (b)

13. (d) Stamp Act, Registrar of Firms

14. (b) $1{,}00{,}000 \times \frac{5}{100} = ₹\,5{,}000$

15. (c) 7.5 months

16. (a) Co-ownership is not a partnership even if it is generating some income.

17. (d) **Opening Capitals**

Daksh $= 11{,}250 \times \frac{100}{7.5} = ₹\,1{,}50{,}000$

Mayank $= 13{,}125 \times \frac{100}{7.5} = ₹\,1{,}75{,}000$

18. (b) Interest on loan $= 3{,}00{,}000 \times \frac{6}{100} \times \frac{3}{12} = ₹\,4{,}500$

19. (c) With the consent of all the partners irrespective of type of partner

20. (d) Omkar's Profit Share $= 5{,}60{,}000 \times \frac{1}{2} = 2{,}80{,}000$

(+) Salary to Omkar = 20,000

= 3,00,000

21. (d) All of the above 22. (b) fluctuating

23. (d) Interest on Drawings $= 3{,}00{,}000 \times \frac{10}{100} \times \frac{6}{12} = ₹\,15{,}000$

24. (a) Drawings

25. (c) Rent paid to partners is a charge against profit and thus will be dealt through profit and loss account.

26. (d) Both (b) and (c) 27. (c) co-ownership

28. (d) limited liability

29. (d) Interest on A's Capital $= (30{,}000 - 3{,}000) \times 10\%$

$= ₹\,2{,}700$

30. (a) Vanya's Profit Share $= (1{,}75{,}000 - 40{,}000 - 60{,}000) \times \frac{3}{5}$

$= ₹\,45{,}000$

31. (b) appropriation of

32. (b) Partner's Commission A/c Dr
  To Partner's Current A/c

33. (b) Anthony's share in losses $= 1{,}80{,}000 \times \frac{1}{3} = ₹\,60{,}000$

Guarantee provided to Anthony = ₹ 60,000

Total amount payable to Anthony = ₹ 1,20,000

Deficiency to be borne by Amar

$$= 1{,}20{,}000 \times \frac{1}{2} = ₹\,60{,}000$$

Loss debited to Amar's capital account

$$= 1{,}80{,}000 \times \frac{1}{3} = ₹\,60{,}000$$

∴ Total amount debited to Amar's capital account

= Deficiency + Loss = 60,000 + 60,000 = ₹ 1,20,000

34. (b) **Statement Showing Adjustments**

Particulars	Ikka (₹)	Dukka (₹)	Teeka (₹)	Firm (₹)
Profit Debited	33,600	33,600	16,800	84,000
Profit Credited (5 : 4 : 3)	35,000	28,000	21,000	84,000
	1,400 Cr	5,600 Dr	4,200 Cr	—

Interest on Capital

Ikka $= 5{,}00{,}000 \times \frac{10}{100} = ₹\,50{,}000$

Dukka $= 4{,}00{,}000 \times \frac{10}{100} = ₹\,40{,}000$

Teeka $= 3{,}00{,}000 \times \frac{10}{100} = ₹\,30{,}000$

Ratio of interest on capital = 5 : 4 : 3

Since the appropriations are more than the available profit, the profit will be distributed in the ratio of appropriation i.e. 5 : 4 : 3.

35. (b) Debit A by and Credit B by ₹ 4,000

36. (d) Sonia will be credited by ₹ 2,000 and Roma will be debited by ₹ 2,000

37. (a) Ashu will be debited by ₹ 7,500 and Nishu will be credited by ₹ 7,500

38. (a) Fenn's share in profits $= 80{,}000 \times \frac{3}{8} = ₹\,30{,}000$ which is more than the guaranteed amount. Hence Fenn's capital account will be credited with ₹ 30,000.

39. (a) Both Assertion (A) and Reason (R) are true and Reason (R) is the correct explanation of Assertion (A)

40. (c) In the 'fixed capital method', all items like share of profit or loss, interest on capital, drawings, interest on drawings, etc. are recorded in the partners' correct account.

41. (c) The maximum number of partners are prescribed by the Indian Companies Act, 2013.

42. (a) Both Assertion (A) and Reason (R) are true and Reason (R) is the correct explanation of Assertion (A)

43. (c) As per partnership deed if appropriations are more than the amount of profit available for distribution, profit is distributed in the ratio of appropriations.

44. (a) Both Assertion (A) and Reason (R) are true and Reason (R) is the correct explanation of Assertion (A)

45. (c) Under fixed capital method, the partner's capital accounts balance always remains same.

46. (a) Both the statements are correct

47. (d) Every partner has a right to participate in the conduct of the affairs of its business.

48. (a) Both the statements are correct

49. (d) As per the Indian Partnership Act, 1932, if there is no partnership deed, profits and losses are shared equally, not in the ratio of capital contribution.

50. (c) Agreement whether written or verbal is optional in case of a partnership firm.

51. (d) Partnership have unlimited liabilities, therefore the private properties of the partners can also be used to pay the firm's debts

52. (a) Both the statements are correct

53. (b) (ii) (i) (iii)

54. (a) (i) (iii) (ii)

55. (b) (i) (ii) (iii)

56. (d) A. Interest on Drawings $= 12{,}000 \times \frac{12}{100} \times \frac{6.5}{12}$

B. Interest on Drawings $= 12{,}000 \times \frac{12}{100} \times \frac{5.5}{12}$

C. Interest on Drawings $= 12{,}000 \times \frac{12}{100} \times \frac{6}{12}$

57. (c) (ii) (iii) (iv) (i)

58. (b) 6

59. (c) 21,000

60. (b) 35,610

Hint **to the case study solutions 58-60**

Profit and Loss Appropriation Account

Dr for the year ending 31st March, 2019 Cr

Particulars		Amt (₹)	Particulars	Amt (₹)
To Interest on Capital A/cs **[59]**			By Net Profit as per Profit and Loss A/c	3,75,000
X (2,00,000 × 6/100)	12,000		By Interest on Drawings A/cs	
Y (1,50,000 × 6/100)	9,000	21,000	X (40,000 × 6/100 × 6/12)	1,200
To Reserve Fund A/c **[60]**		35,610	Y (30,000 × 6/100 × 6/12)	900
To Profit Transferred to Partners' Capital A/cs				
X	1,60,245			
Y	1,60,245	3,20,490		
		3,77,100		3,77,100

Note In the absence of date of drawings, interest on drawings has been calculated on an average basis for 6 months. **[58]**

61. (d) Savita's share = ₹ 90,000 ; Guarantee = ₹ 1,00,000 ; Deficiency = 1,00,000 − 90,000 = ₹ 10,000

62. (b)

Profit and Loss Appropriation Account

Dr for the year ended...... Cr

Particulars		Amt (₹)	Particulars	Amt (₹)
To Interest on Capital			By Net Profit	3,00,000
Kavita	60,000			
Savita	40,000			
Madhu	20,000	1,20,000		
To Profit transferred to				
Kavita (1,80,000 × 1/3)	60,000			
(−) Guarantee to Savita	(10,000)	50,000		
Savita (1,80,000 × 1/2)	90,000			
(+) Deficiency from Kavita	10,000	1,00,000		
Madhu (1,80,000 × 1/6)		30,000		
		3,00,000		3,00,000

63. (a)

Interest on Capital	Amt (₹)
Aditi (5,00,000 × 10%)	50,000
Saurabh (4,00,000 × 10%)	40,000
	90,000

which is more than available profit i.e. ₹ 81,000. Thus, available profit will be divided in partners' capital ratio.

64. (b) Interest on Aditi's Capital $= 81{,}000 \times \frac{5}{9} =$ ₹ 45,000

02

CHAPTER

In partnership, goodwill represents the firm's reputation and earning potential, increasing its value.

Accounting for Partnership Firm: Goodwill

▼ **YOUR STUDY GOALS**

▼ **YOUR PRACTICE GOAL**

- Topicwise Solved Questions (19 Solved Questions)
- Numerical Questions [22 Questions (Unsolved)]
- Theoretical Questions [5 Questions (with answers)]
- Objective Questions (62 Qs; MCQs, A-R, Statements, Matching, Case)

2.1 Meaning of Goodwill

Goodwill refers to the reputation or good name of a business that helps it to earn more profits than others. Goodwill is earned by a firm through the hard work and honesty of its owners.

As per **Lord Lindley**, "The term goodwill is generally used to denote the benefit arising from connections and reputations."

Nature of Goodwill

Goodwill is an intangible asset (an asset which cannot be seen and touched) and not a fictitious asset, because it has a realisable value and fictitious assets don't have a realisable value. Goodwill can be sold, but sale of goodwill is possible only along with the sale of entire business.

Characteristics or Features of Goodwill

- It is an intangible and valuable asset.
- It helps in earning excess profits.
- Its value is liable to constant fluctuation.
- It is valuable only when entire business is sold.
- It is difficult to place an exact value of goodwill.
- It is an attractive force that brings customers regularly to the place of business.

Need for Valuation of Goodwill Valuation

- At the time of change in profit sharing ratio amongst the existing partners.
- At the time of admission of a new partner.
- At the time of retirement or death of a partner.
- When the partnership firm is sold.
- At the time of amalgamation of partnership firm.

Factors Affecting the Value of Goodwill

Factor	Description
Nature of Business	If the nature of the products, in which the firm deals, are in high demand, the profit of the firm will be higher and therefore the value of goodwill will increase.
Efficiency of Management	If the management is capable and competent, the firm will earn high profits. It will thus, increase the value of goodwill.
Location	If the business is located at a favourable place, it will result in good sales and also increase in the value of goodwill.
Market Situation	If a firm deals in a business where the demand for the products is higher than the supply, it will lead to lower capital requirement and higher profit. It will thus, increase the value of goodwill.
Quality of Product	If the firm enjoys good reputation for its product's quality, there will be higher sales and the value of its goodwill will increase.
Risk Involved	If the risk involved in the business is more, the value of goodwill will be less. On the contrary, if the risk involved in the business is less, the value of goodwill will be higher.
Longer Establishment of Business	Older businesses that have build up good reputation over a period of time, have broader customer base and thus are likely to have more goodwill.
Special Advantages	Firms enjoying special advantages like import licenses, favourable and long-term contracts for supply of materials, low rate and assured supply of electricity, patents, etc. enjoy higher value of goodwill.

Smart Study Chart No. 1

Classification of Goodwill

Purchased Goodwill
This goodwill is acquired by paying consideration in cash or kind for a business. According to Accounting Standard 26, it is recorded in the books of accounts since a monetary consideration is paid for it.

↓

Features
- It arises on purchase of business.
- It is recorded in books of accounts.
- It is shown as an asset in the balance sheet.
- It is amortized over its estimated useful life.

Self-generated Goodwill
This goodwill is internally generated or earned through an organisation's efforts, such as better quality or customer service. As per AS-26, it is not recorded as no monetary consideration is paid for it.

↓

Features
- It is internally generated.
- It is not recorded in accounts per AS-26.
- It's valuation is subjective.

2.2 Methods of Valuation of Goodwill

Goodwill, being an intangible asset, is difficult to value precisely. Various methods are available for valuing the goodwill of a partnership firm and the value may differ depending on the method used.

The important methods of valuation of goodwill are as follows

- Average profit method
- Super profit method
- Capitalisation method

I. Average Profit Method

Goodwill under average profit method can be calculated using simple average profit method or weighted average profit method.

Average profit method involves two approaches

1. Simple Average Profit Method

Goodwill is calculated by multiplying average profits by a certain number of years' purchase.

Average profit is the total profit divided by the number of years purchased.

Number of year's purchase refers to the period during which the business is expected to earn the same profits due to past efforts. The method assume that a new business will not be able to earn profit in its early years, so goodwill compensates for the established business's prior performance.

2. Weighted Average Profit Method

In this method, goodwill is calculated by multiplying the weighted average profit by the number of years' purchase.

Each year's profit is assigned a weight, with the highest weight given to the profit of most recent year.

Then, profits are multiplied by their respective weights and the sum of these products is divided by the total of weights to get the weighted average profit.

This is then multiplied by the year's purchase to determine goodwill.

The weighted average method is preferred over the simple average method as it gives more importance to recent profits, reflecting future earning potential. It is particularly useful when profits show a rising or falling trend.

Steps to Calculate Goodwill using Simple Average Profit Method

***Step* 1** Find actual (normal) profits of each given year by deducting abnormal gains and non-business incomes and adding abnormal losses and non-business expenses.

***Step* 2** Calculate the total normal profits by adding each year's profit.

***Step* 3** Find Average Profit

$$= \frac{\text{Total Actual (Normal) Profits of given Number of Years}}{\text{Given Number of Years}}$$

***Step* 4** Find value of Goodwill = Average Profit × Number of Years' Purchase

Steps to Calculate Goodwill using Weighted Average Profit Method

***Step* 1** Calculate weighted average profit as follows using weighted average profit method

Year (A)	**Profit** (B)	**Weight** (C)	**Product** (₹) (B × C = D)
...	...	...	...
...	...	...	...
...	...	...	...

$$\text{Weighted Average Profit} = \frac{\text{Total of Products}}{\text{Total of Weights}}$$

***Step* 2** Value of Goodwill = Weighted Average Profit × Number of Years' Purchase

II. Super Profit Method

In business, a certain level of profit is generally expected. However, actual profits may exceed or fall short of this normal profit. When actual profits exceed the normal profit, the excess is called **super profit**. In this method, goodwill is calculated by multiplying the super profit by a specified number of years.

Steps to Calculate Goodwill using Super Profit Method

***Step* 1** Find average profits.

***Step* 2** Find normal profits

Normal Profits = Average Capital Employed × Normal Rate of Return/100

Capital Employed (By assets approach)
= Total Assets (Excluding goodwill, non-trade investments and fictitious assets) − External Liabilities

or Capital Employed (By liabilities approach)
= Capital + Reserves − Fictitious Assets − Non-trade Investments

or Average Capital Employed

$$= \frac{\text{Opening Capital Employed} + \text{Closing Capital Employed}}{2}$$

***Step* 3** Find Super Profits = Average (Actual) Profits − Normal Profits

***Step* 4** Value of Goodwill = Super Profits × Number of Years' Purchase

III. Capitalisation Method

Under this method, goodwill can be calculated in two ways

- Capitalisation of average profit
- Capitalisation of super profit

1. Capitalisation of Average Profit

This method calculates goodwill by subtracting the capital employed from the capitalised value of average profits, based on the normal rate of return. The capitalised value is ascertained by capitalising profits earned at the normal rate of profit.

Steps to calculate goodwill using average profits

Step 1 Calculate Average (actual) Profits $= \dfrac{\text{Total Actual Profits of given Years Before Abnormal and Non-business Items}}{\text{Numbers of Years}}$

Step 2 Calculate Capitalised Value of Average Profits = Average Profits $\times \dfrac{100}{\text{Normal Rate of Return}}$

Step 3 Determine the value of net assets, on the date of valuation of goodwill.

Net Assets = All Assets (other than goodwill, fictitious assets and non-trade investments) at their Current Values – Outside Liabilities

Step 4 Find value of Goodwill = Capitalised Value of Profits – Actual Capital Employed

2. Capitalisation of Super Profit

In this method, goodwill is calculated by the capitalisation of super profits on the basis of normal rate of return.

Steps to calculate goodwill using super profits

Step 1 Calculate capital employed (net assets) of the firm

Net Assets = All Assets (except goodwill, fictitious assets and non-trade investments) – Outside Liabilities

Step 2 Calculate Normal Profits on Capital Employed = Capital Employed $\times \dfrac{\text{Normal Rate of Return}}{100}$

Step 3 Calculate Average Profits of past years.

Step 4 Calculate Super Profits = Average Profits – Normal Profits

Step 5 Calculate Goodwill = Super Profits $\times \dfrac{100}{\text{Normal Rate of Return}}$

Mind Map

Accounting for Partnership Firm : Goodwill

1 Meaning of Goodwill

- It refers to the reputation or good name of business that helps it to earn more profits than others.
- It is an intangible asset and not a fictitious asset, as it has a realisable value.

2 Features of Goodwill

- It is an intangible and valuable asset.
- It helps in earning excess profits.
- It's value fluctuates.
- It is valuable when entire business is sold.
- It is difficult to calculate it's exact value.

3 Need for Valuation of Goodwill

- At the time of change in profit sharing ratio.
- At the time of admission of a new partner.
- At the time of retirement or death of a partner.
- When the partnership firm is sold.
- When the partnership firm is amalgamated.

4 Factors Affecting Goodwill

- Nature of business
- Efficiency of management
- Location
- Market situation
- Quality of product
- Risk involved
- Longer establishment of business

5 Classification of Goodwill

- **Purchase Goodwill** It is acquired by paying consideration in cash or kind and recorded in the books of accounts as per AS-26.
- **Self-generated Goodwill** It is internally generated through an organisation's efforts and not recorded in the books of accounts as per AS-26.

6 Methods of Valuation of Goodwill

Various methods are available for valuing the goodwill of a partnership firm and value may differ depending on the method used.

These methods are

- Average profit method
- Super profit method
- Capitalisation method

7 Average Profit Method

- **Simple Average Profit Mehod**

  Goodwill = Average Profit × Number of Year's Purchase
- **Weighted Average Profit Method**

  Goodwill = Weighted Average Profit × Number of Year's Purchase

Note *Average profit is calculated after adjustments of abnormal profit and losses, etc.*

8 Super Profit Method

- Super profit is the excess of average profit over normal profit.
- Goodwill = Super Profit × Number of Year's Purchase

  Where, Super Profit = Average Profits – Normal Profits

  $$\text{Normal Profits} = \text{Capital Employed} \times \frac{\text{Normal Rate of Return}}{100}$$

  Here, Capital Employed = Total Assets (Excluding goodwill, non-trade investments and fictitious assets) – External Liabilities or Capital + Reserves – Fictitious Assets – Non-trade Investments

9 Capitalisation Method

- **Capitalisation of Average Profit**

  Goodwill = Capitalised Value of Profits – Actual Capital Employed

  $$\text{Here, Capitalised Value of Profits} = \text{Average Profits} \times \frac{100}{\text{Normal Rate of Return}}$$
- **Capitalisation of Super Profit**

  $$\text{Goodwill} = \text{Super Profit} \times \frac{100}{\text{Normal Rate of Return}}$$

Topicwise Solved Questions

Average Profit Method

Solved Question 1 **Calculate the goodwill of the firm on the basis of 4 year's purchase of average profit of last 5 years. Profits of last 5 years were : 2020 ₹ 50,000, 2021 ₹ 80,000, 2022 ₹ 30,000 (loss), 2023 ₹ 1,60,000, 2024 ₹ 2,00,000.**

Sol. Average Profit = (50,000 + 80,000 + (30,000) + 1,60,000 + 2,00,000)/5

= ₹ 92,000

Goodwill = 92,000 × 4 = ₹ 3,68,000

Solved Question 2 **Following information is provided to you. Profit for the year ended**

2020	**–**	**₹ 10,000**	**2021**	**–**	**₹ 12,500**
2022	**–**	**₹ 20,000**	**2023**	**–**	**₹ 40,000**
2024	**–**	**₹ 60,000**			

(i) There as a gain on sale of furniture of ₹ 2,500. The furniture was sold on 1st October, 2020.

(ii) A compensation was paid to the workers of ₹ 10,000 on 1st January, 2022.

Goodwill is valued at 4 years' purchase of average profit of last 5 years'.

Sol. Adjusted Profit of 2021 = 12,500 – 2,500 = ₹ 10,000

Adjusted Profit of 2022 = 20,000 + 10,000 = ₹ 30,000

Average Profit = Total Profit/Number of Years

= (10,000 + 10,000 + 30,000 + 40,000 + 60,000)/5

= ₹ 30,000

Goodwill = Average Profit × Number of Years' Purchase

= 30,000 × 4 = ₹ 1,20,000

Solved Question 3 **The profits and losses for the last five years were**

2020 — ₹ 6,000 (including an abnormal gain of ₹ 2,000)
2021 — ₹ 14,000 (excluding ₹ 4,000 as insurance premium)
2023 — ₹ 4,000 (after charging an abnormal loss of ₹ 2,000)
2023 — ₹ 6,000
2024 — ₹ 2,000 (loss)

Calculate the amount of goodwill on the basis of 3 years' purchase of last 5 years profits and losses.

Sol. **Calculation of Goodwill**

Average Maintainable Profits	**Amt (₹)**
Profit for 2020 (6,000 – 2,000)	4,000
Profit for 2021 (14,000 – 4,000)	10,000
Profit for 2022 (4,000 + 2,000)	6,000
Profit for 2023	6,000
	26,000
(–) Loss for 2024	(2,000)
Total Profit for last Five Years	24,000

Average Profits = Total Profits / Number of Years

$= \frac{24,000}{5} =$ ₹ 4,800

Goodwill = Average Profits × Number of Years' Purchase

= 4,800 × 3 = ₹ 14,400

Solved Question 4 **B, M and C are partners sharing profits and losses equally. They agree to admit G for equal share. For this purpose, value of goodwill is to be calculated on the basis of four years' purchase of average profit of last five years. These profits were**

Years	Amt (₹)
2020	60,000 (Profit)
2021	1,40,000 (Profit)
2022	2,00,000 (Profit)
2023	2,80,000 (Profit)
2024	2,40,000 (Loss)

On 1st January, 2024, a moped costing ₹ 40,000 was purchased and debited to travelling expenses account, on which depreciation is to be charged @ 25%. Calculate the value of goodwill after adjusting the above.

Sol. **Calculation of Average Profit**

Years	**Amt (₹)**	
2020	60,000	(Profit)
2021	1,40,000	(Profit)
2022	2,00,000	(Profit)
2023	2,80,000	(Profit)
2024	(2,10,000)	(Loss) (WN)
Total Profit	4,70,000	

Average Profit $= \frac{4,70,000}{5} =$ ₹ 94,000

Goodwill = Average Profit × Number of Years' Purchase

= 94,000 × 4

= ₹ 3,76,000

Working Note

In 2024, a moped costing ₹ 40,000 was purchased but it was wrongly debited to travelling expenses account. After rectification, the loss of 2024 will be reduced by ₹ 40,000.

The depreciation on moped ₹ 10,000 (25% of 40,000) was not charged to profit and loss account of 2024.

Therefore, the final loss of 2024 will be

= 2,40,000 – 40,000 + 10,000

= ₹ 2,10,000

Solved Question 5 The profit of firm for past years are as follows

Years	Profit (₹)	Years	Profit (₹)
2020	2,40,000	2021	2,55,000
2022	2,70,000	2023	3,00,000
2024	3,30,000		

The weight to be used are 1, 2, 3, 4 and 5 for the years from 2020-2024. Calculate the value of goodwill on the basis of two year's purchase of weighted average profit.

Sol.

Years	Profit (₹)	Weight	Product (₹)
2020	2,40,000	1	2,40,000
2021	2,55,000	2	5,10,000
2022	2,70,000	3	8,10,000
2023	3,00,000	4	12,00,000
2024	3,30,000	5	16,50,000
Total		15	44,10,000

Weighted Average Profit = 44,10,000/15 = ₹ 2,94,000

Goodwill = 2,94,000 × 2 = ₹ 5,88,000

Solved Question 6 Calculate goodwill of a firm on the basis of three years purchase of the weighted average profits of the last four years. The profits of the last four years were **CBSE SQP 2023**

Year (ending 31st March)	2020	2021	2022	2023
Amt (₹)	28,000	27,000	46,900	53,810

(i) On 1st April, 2020 a major plant repair was undertaken for ₹ 10,000 which was charged to revenue. The said sum is to be capitalised for goodwill calculation subject to adjustment of depreciation of 10% on reducing balance method.

(ii) For the purpose of calculating goodwill, the company decided that the years ending 31st March, 2020 and 31st March, 2021 be weighted as 1 each (being Covid affected) and for year ending 31st March, 2022 and 31st March, 2023 weights be taken as 2 and 3 respectively.

Sol.

Year (Ending 31st March)	Adjusted Profit (₹)	Weights	Product (₹)
2020	28,000	1	28,000
2021	36,000	1	36,000
2022	46,000	2	92,000
2023	53,000	3	1,59,000
Total		7	3,15,000

Adjusted Profits	2020 (₹)	2021 (₹)	2022 (₹)	2023 (₹)
Given Profits	28,000	27,000	46,900	53,810
(+) Capital Expenditure Charged to Revenue	—	10,000	—	—
(–) Unprovided Depreciation (WN)	—	(1,000)	(900)	(810)
Adjusted Profits	28,000	36,000	46,000	53,000

Weighted Average Profit = 3,15,000/7 = ₹ 45,000

Goodwill = 45,000 × 3 = ₹ 1,35,000

Working Notes

Calculation of Depreciation

1. In 2021 = 10% of ₹ 10,000 = 10,000 × 10/100 = ₹ 1,000
2. In 2022 = 10% of ₹ 9,000 = 9,000 × 10/100 = ₹ 900
3. In 2023 = 10% of ₹ 8,100 = 8,100 × 10/100 = ₹ 810

Super Profit Method

Solved Question 7 On 1st April, 2022, the capital of the firm of Ashu and Madhav is ₹ 1,50,000. The normal rate of return on capital employed is 10%. Average profits of the firm are ₹ 23,000. Calculate goodwill of the firm based on three years' purchase of super profits.

Sol. Normal Profit = 10/100 × 1,50,000 = ₹ 15,000

Average Profit = ₹ 23,500

Super Profit = Average Profits – Normal Profit

= 23,500 – 15,000 = ₹ 8,500

Goodwill = Super Profits × Number of Year's Purchase

= 8,500 × 3 = ₹ 25,500

Solved Question 8 The capital of the firm of Ansh and Bani is ₹ 10,00,000 and the market rate of interest is 15%. Annual salary to the partner is ₹ 60,000 each. The profit for the last three years ₹ 3,00,000, ₹ 3,60,000 and ₹ 4,20,000.

Goodwill of the firm is to be valued on the basis of two years' purchase of last three years' average super profits. Calculate the goodwill of the firm. **CBSE 2019**

Sol. Capital Employed = ₹ 10,00,000

Normal Rate of Return = 15%

Normal Profit = 10,00,000 × 15% = ₹ 1,50,000

3 Years' Average Profit

$$= \frac{3,00,000 + 3,60,000 + 4,20,000}{3}$$

= ₹ 3,60,000

Average Profit after Partners Salary

= 3,60,000 – (60,000 × 2)

= ₹ 2,40,000

Super Profit = Average Profit – Normal Profit

= 2,40,000 – 1,50,000

= ₹ 90,000

Goodwill = Super Profit × Number of Years' Purchase

= 90,000 × 2

= ₹ 1,80,000

Solved Question 9 Aayush and Krish are partners sharing profits and losses equally. They decided to admit Vansh for an equal share in the profits. For this purpose, the goodwill of the firm was to be valued at four years purchase of super profits.

The balance sheet of the firm on 31st March, 2023 before admission of Vansh was as follows

Balance Sheet of Aayush and Krish
as at 31st March, 2023

Liabilities		Amt (₹)	Assets	Amt (₹)
Capital A/cs			Machinery	75,000
Aayush	90,000		Furniture	15,000
Krish	50,000	1,40,000	Stock	30,000
General Reserve		20,000	Debtors	20,000
Loan		25,000	Cash	50,000
Creditors		5,000		
		1,90,000		1,90,000

The normal rate of return is 12% per annum. Average profit of the firm for the last four years was ₹ 30,000. Calculate Vansh's share of goodwill. **CBSE 2024**

Sol. Capital Employed | **Amt (₹)**

Aayush's Capital	90,000
Krish's Capital	50,000
(+) General Reserve	20,000
	1,60,000

$$\text{Normal Profit} = \text{Capital Employed} \times \frac{\text{Nomal Rate of Return}}{100}$$

$$= 1,60,000 \times \frac{12}{100} = ₹\ 19,200$$

Average profit = ₹ 30,000

Super Profit = Average Profit − Normal Profit
= 30,000 − 19,200 = ₹ 10,800

Goodwill = Super Profit × Number of Years' Purchase
= 10,800 × 4 = ₹ 43,200

$$\text{Vansh's Share of Goodwill} = 43,200 \times \frac{1}{3} = ₹\ 14,400$$

Solved Question 10 **P and Q are partners in M/s PQR Ltd. They admit S as partner *w.e.f.* 1st April, 2020. They agreed to value goodwill at 3 years' purchase by super profit method for which they decided to take average of last 5 years profits.**

The profits for the last five years were

Year Ended	Amt (₹)
31st March, 2020	1,00,000 (Including gain of ₹ 12,500 from sale of fixed asset)
31st March, 2021	85,000 (Including abnormal loss of ₹ 25,000)
31st March, 2022	1,05,000
31st March, 2023	1,15,000
31st March, 2024	1,25,000

Capital employed in the firm is ₹ 7,50,000 and normal rate of return in similar business is 10%.

Calculate value of goodwill.

Sol. Calculation of Actual Normal Profit

Year	Profit (₹)	Adjustment (₹)	Normal Profit (₹)
31st March, 2020	1,00,000	(12,500)	87,500
31st March, 2021	85,000	25,000	1,10,000
31st March, 2022	1,05,000	—	1,05,000
31st March, 2023	1,15,000	—	1,15,000
31st March, 2024	1,25,000	—	1,25,000
			5,42,500

$$\text{Actual Average Profit} = \frac{\text{Total Normal Profit}}{\text{Number of Years}}$$

$$= \frac{5,42,500}{5} = ₹\ 1,08,500$$

Calculation of Normal Profit

Capital Employed = ₹ 7,50,000

Normal Rate of Return = 10%

$$\therefore \quad \text{Normal Profit} = 7,50,000 \times \frac{10}{100} = ₹\ 75,000$$

Calculation of Super Profit

Super Profit = Actual Average Profit − Normal Profit
= 1,08,500 − 75,000 = ₹ 33,500

Value of Goodwill

Goodwill = Super Profit × Number of Years' Purchase
= 33,500 × 3 = ₹ 1,00,500

Solved Question 11 **Asha and Babita were partners in a firm. Their capitals were ₹ 15,00,000 and ₹ 10,00,000 respectively. The normal rate of return was 15%. The profits of the last four years were**

	Amt (₹)
2019-20	2,50,000
2020-21	(50,000)
2021-22	8,00,000
2022-23	5,00,000

The closing stock for the year 2022-23 was undervalued by ₹ 1,00,000. Goodwill is to be valued at two years purchase of the last four years' average super profits. Calculate the value of goodwill. **CBSE 2024 C**

Sol. Capital Employed = Asha's Capital + Babita's Capital
= 15,00,000 + 10,00,000 = ₹ 25,00,000

$$\text{Normal Profits} = \text{Capital Employed} \times \frac{\text{Normal Rate of Return}}{100}$$

$$= 25,00,000 \times \frac{15}{100} = ₹\ 3,75,000$$

Calculation of Adjusted Profit

Year	Adjusted Profit (₹)
2019-20	2,50,000
2020-21	(50,000)
2021-22	8,00,000
2022-23	6,00,000 (5,00,000 + 1,00,000)
Total	16,00,000

So, Average Profit $= \frac{16,00,000}{4} =$ ₹ 4,00,000

Now, Super Profit = Average Profit − Normal Profit

Super Profit = 4,00,000 − 3,75,000 = ₹ 25,000

Now, Goodwill = Super Profit × Number of Years' Purchase

= 2 × 25,000 = ₹ 50,000

Capitalisation Method

Solved Question 12 **A firm earned average profit of ₹ 3,00,000 during the last few years. The normal rate of return of the industry is 15%. The assets of the business were ₹ 17,00,000 and its liabilities were ₹ 2,00,000. Calculate the goodwill of the firm by capitalisation of average profits.** CBSE 2019

Sol. Average Profit = ₹ 3,00,000

Normal Rate of Return = 15%

Capitalised Value of Average Profits

$= \frac{\text{Average Profit}}{\text{Normal Rate of Return}} \times 100$

$= \frac{3,00,000}{15} \times 100 =$ ₹ 20,00,000

Capital Employed = Total Assets − Liabilities

= 17,00,000 − 2,00,000 = ₹ 15,00,000

Goodwill = Capitalised Value of Average Profit − Capital Employed

= 20,00,000 − 15,00,000 = ₹ 5,00,000

Solved Question 13 **A and B are partners in a business. Balance in capital and current accounts on 31st March, 2020 were**

	Capital Account (₹)	Current Account (₹)
A	2,50,000	40,000
B	1,75,000	10,000 (Dr)

Profits of the last five consecutive years ending 31st March, 2020 were : ₹ 30,000, 2021 Loss ₹ 20,000, 2022 ₹ 65,000, 2023 ₹ 1,00,000 and 2020 ₹ 1,25,000.

General reserve appeared in the books at ₹ 25,000. If the normal rate of return is 10%, find the value of goodwill by capitalisation of average profit method.

Sol. Average Profits

$= \frac{30,000 - 20,000 + 65,000 + 1,00,000 + 1,25,000}{5}$

= ₹ 60,000

Capitalised Value of Average Profits

$= \text{Average Profit} \times \frac{100}{\text{Normal Rate of Return}}$

$= 60,000 \times \frac{100}{10} =$ ₹ 6,00,000

Capital Employed = Capital Accounts + Current Accounts + General Reserve

= 2,50,000 + 1,75,000 + 40,000 − 10,000 + 25,000

= ₹ 4,80,000

Goodwill = Capitalised Value of Average Profits − Capital Employed

= 6,00,000 − 4,80,000 = ₹ 1,20,000

Solved Question 14 **A business has earned average profits of ₹ 1,00,000 during the last few years and the normal rate of return in similar business is 10%. Find out the value of goodwill by**

(i) Capitalisation of super profit method.

(ii) Super profit method if the goodwill is valued at 3 years' purchase of super profit.

The assets of the business were ₹ 10,00,000 and its external liabilities ₹ 1,80,000.

Sol. Actual Average Profit = ₹ 1,00,000

Normal Rate of Return = 10%

Total Assets = ₹ 10,00,000

External Liabilities = ₹ 1,80,000

Capital Employed = Total Assets − External Liabilities

= 10,00,000 − 1,80,000

= ₹ 8,20,000

$\text{Normal Profit} = \text{Capital Employed} \times \frac{\text{Normal Rate of Return}}{100}$

$= 8,20,000 \times \frac{10}{100} =$ ₹ 82,000

Super Profit = Average Profit − Normal Profit

= 1,00,000 − 82,000 = ₹ 18,000

(i) Calculation of goodwill by capitalisation of super profit method

$\text{Goodwill} = \frac{\text{Super Profit}}{\text{Normal Rate of Return}} \times 100$

$= \frac{18,000 \times 100}{10} =$ ₹ 1,80,000

(ii) Calculation of goodwill by super profit method

Goodwill = Super Profit × Number of Years' Purchase

= 18,000 × 3

= ₹ 54,000

Comprehensive Illustrations

Solved Question 15 **Pearl and Ruby were partners in a firm with a combined capital of ₹ 2,50,000. The normal rate of return was 10%.**

The profits of the last four years were as follows

Year	Amt (₹)
2019-20	35,000
2020-21	25,000
2022-22	32,000
2022-23	33,000

The closing stock for the year 2022-23 was overvalued by ₹ 5,000.

Calculate goodwill of the firm based on three years' purchase of the last four years' average super profit. CBSE 2024

Sol. **Calculation of Normal Adjusted Profit**

Year	Profit (₹)	Adjustment (₹)	Adjusted Profit (₹)
2019-20	35,000	—	35,000
2020-21	25,000	—	25,000
2021-22	32,000	—	32,000
2022-23	33,000	(5,000)	28,000
Total			1,20,000

Average Profit = (Total Adjusted Profit) / No. of Years

$= \frac{1,20,000}{4} = ₹ 30,000$

Normal Profit = Capital Employed $\times \frac{\text{Normal Rate of Return}}{100}$

$= 2,50,000 \times \frac{10}{100} = ₹ 25,000$

Super Profit = Average Profit − Normal Profit

$= 30,000 - 25,000 = ₹ 5,000$

Goodwill = Super Profit × Number of Years' Purchase

$= 5,000 \times 3 = ₹ 15,000$

Solved Question 16 **Amit and Kartik are partners sharing profits and losses equally. They decided to admit Saurabh for an equal share in the profits. For the purpose, the goodwill of the firm was to be valued at four years' purchase of super profit. The balance sheet of the firm on Saurabh's admission was as follows** **CBSE SQP 2025**

Liabilities		Amt (₹)	Assets	Amt (₹)
Capital A/cs			Fixed Assets (Tangible)	75,000
Amit	90,000		Furniture	15,000
Kartik	50,000	1,40,000	Stock	30,000
Creditors		5,000	Debtors	20,000
General Reserve		20,000	Cash	50,000
Bills Payable		25,000		
		1,90,000		1,90,000

The normal rate of return is 12% p.a. Average profit of the firm for the last four years was ₹ 30,000. Calculate Saurabh's share of goodwill.

Sol. Capital of Firm = 1,40,000 + 20,000 (Reserve) = ₹ 1,60,000

Normal Profit = 1,60,000 × 12/100 = ₹ 19,200

Average Profit = ₹ 30,000

Super Profit = Average Profit − Normal Profit

= 30,000 − 19,200 = ₹ 10,8000

Goodwill = 4 (Super Profit) = 4 (10,800) = ₹ 43,200

Saurabh's Share of Goodwill = 1/3 of ₹ 43,200 = ₹ 14,400

Solved Question 17 **From the following information, calculate value of goodwill of M/s Hari & Sons**

(i) At three years' purchase of average profit.
(ii) At three years' purchase of super profit.
(iii) On the basis of capitalisation of super profit.
(iv) On the basis of capitalisation of average profit.

Additional Information

(a) Average capital employed in the business ₹ 7,00,000.
(b) Net trading results of the firm for the past years
2022 – ₹ 1,47,600 (profit)
2023 – ₹ 1,48,100 (loss)
2024 – ₹ 4,48,700 (profit)
(c) Rate of interest expected from capital having regard to the risk involved 18%.
(d) Remuneration to each partner for his service ₹ 500 per month.
(e) Assets (excluding goodwill) ₹ 7,54,762, liabilities ₹ 31,329.

Sol. (i) Calculation of goodwill at three years' purchase of average profit

Average Profit $= \frac{1,47,600 - 1,48,100 + 4,48,700}{3}$

$= \frac{4,48,200}{3} = ₹ 1,49,400$

*Average Profit for Goodwill

= 1,49,400 − Remuneration of Partners

= 1,49,400 − (500 × 12 × 2)

= 1,49,400 − 12,000 = ₹ 1,37,400

Goodwill = Average Profit* × Number of Years' Purchase

= 1,37,400 × 3 = ₹ 4,12,200

(ii) Calculation of goodwill at three years' purchase of super profit

Normal Profit = Average Capital Employed × Normal Rate of Return

$= 7,00,000 \times \frac{18}{100} = ₹ 1,26,000$

**Super Profit = Average Profit* − Normal Profit

= 1,37,400 − 1,26,000

= ₹ 11,400

Goodwill = Super Profit** × Number of Years' Purchase

= 11,400 × 3 = ₹ 34,200

(iii) Calculation of goodwill under capitalisation of super profit

Goodwill = Super Profit** $\times \frac{100}{\text{Normal Rate of Return}}$

$= 11,400 \times \frac{100}{18}$

= ₹ 63,333.33

(iv) Calculation of goodwill under capitalisation of average profit

Goodwill = Total Capitalised Value of Business − Net Assets

Total Capitalised Value of the Firm

$= \frac{\text{Average Profit}^{*} \times 100}{\text{Normal Rate of Return}}$

$= \frac{1,37,400 \times 100}{18} = ₹ 7,63,333$

Net Assets = Total Assets (excluding goodwill) – Outsiders' Liabilities
= 7,54,762 – 31,329 = ₹ 7,23,433
Goodwill = 7,63,333 – 7,23,433 = ₹ 39,900

Missing Information

Solved Question 18 **The goodwill of DGH and Co. is valued at ₹ 10,00,000 at 2 years' purchase of average profit of last 5 years. Find out the missing values.**

Average Profit = (5,00,000 + 6,00,000 – 2,00,000 + ... + 7,00,000)/5 = ...

Goodwill = ... × ... = ₹ 10,00,000

Sol. Average Profit = (5,00,000 + 6,00,000 – 2,00,000 + **9,00,000** + 7,00,000)/5 = **5,00,000**

Goodwill = **5,00,000** × **2** = ₹ 10,00,000

Solved Question 19 **Goodwill of the firm is valued at ₹ 2,50,000 at 2 years' purchase of average profit. Determine the missing value.**

Total Profits = 1,25,000 + ... + 1,50,000 – 50,000 + 1,75,000 = ₹...

Average Profit = $\frac{\text{Total Profits}}{\text{Number of Years}} = \frac{...}{5} = ...$

Goodwill = ... × 2 = ₹ 2,50,000

Sol. Total Profits
= 1,25,000 + **2,25,000** + 1,50,000 – 50,000 + 1,75,000
= ₹ **6,25,000** *(Step 3)*

Average Profit = $\frac{\textbf{6,25,000}}{5}$ = ₹ **1,25,000** *(Step 2)*

Goodwill = **1,25,000** × 2 = ₹ 2,50,000 *(Step 1)*

Working Note

Total Profit = Average Profit × 5 = ₹ 6,25,000

Numerical Questions

Average Profit Method

1. Calculate value of goodwill on the basis of three years' purchase of average profit of the preceding five years which were as follows

Year	Amt (₹)
2023-24	4,00,000
2022-23	7,50,000
2021-22	9,00,000
2020-21	2,00,000 (Loss)
2019-20	6,50,000

Ans. Goodwill = ₹ 15,00,000

2. Babu purchased Chavi's business with effect from 1st January, 2024. It was agreed that the firm's goodwill is to be valued at two years' purchase of normal average profit of the last three years.

The profits of Chavi's business for the last three years were

2021 – ₹ 80,000 (including an abnormal gain of ₹ 10,000)

2022 – ₹ 1,00,000 (after charging an abnormal loss of ₹ 20,000)

2023 – ₹ 90,000 (excluding ₹ 10,000 as insurance premium on firm's property now to be insured)

Calculate value of the firm's goodwill.

Ans. Value of Goodwill = ₹ 1,80,000

3. The profits and losses for the last five years of a business are as follows **Competency Based Que**

1st Year – ₹ 15,000 (includes an abnormal gain of ₹ 5,000)
2nd Year – ₹ 35,000 (excludes an insurance premium of ₹ 10,000)
3rd Year – ₹ 10,000 (after deducting an abnormal loss of ₹ 5,000)
4th Year – ₹ 15,000
5th Year – ₹ 5,000 (Loss)

Calculate the value of goodwill based on 3 years' purchase of the average profits of the last 5 years.

Ans. Goodwill = ₹ 36,000

4. M, N and S are partners sharing profits and losses equally. They agree to admit T for equal share. For this purpose goodwill is to be valued at 3 year's purchase of average profits of last 5 years' which were as follows

	Amt (₹)
31st March, 2020	30,000 (Profit)
31st March, 2021	75,000 (Profit)
31st March, 2022	10,000 (Loss)
31st March, 2023	1,00,000 (Profit)
31st March, 2024	92,500 (Profit)

On 1st October, 2023, a computer costing ₹ 20,000 was purchased and debited to office expenses account on which depreciation is to be charged @ 25% p.a.

Calculate the value of goodwill.

Ans. Goodwill = ₹ 1,83,000

Hint Adjusted profit of 2024 will be 92,500 + 20,000 – 2,500 (Depreciation) = ₹ 1,10,000.

5. X and Y are partners sharing profits in the ratio of 3 : 2. They have decided to admit Z as a partner from 1st April, 2024, under the following terms

(i) Z will receive a 2/5th share of the profits.

(ii) The goodwill of the firm is to be valued at two years' purchase of the average profit for the last three years. The profits for the previous three years ending on 31st March are as follows

2024 – Profit of ₹ 45,000 (after deducting a loss of ₹ 60,000 due to fire damage to stock)

2023 – Loss of ₹ 1,20,000 (includes ₹ 1,65,000 paid as voluntary retirement compensation)

2022 – Profit of ₹ 1,65,000 (includes a gain of ₹ 45,000 from the sale of fixed assets)

You are required to calculate the value of the firm's goodwill. Competency Based Que

Ans. Goodwill = ₹ 1,80,000

6. Calculate the value of goodwill on the basis of three years' purchase of weighted average profit of last 5 years while assigning weights 1, 2, 3, 4 and 5 to the years 2020, 2021, 2022, 2023 and 2024. Profits of the said years' were : ₹ 20,000, ₹ 24,000, ₹ 30,000, ₹ 25,000 and ₹ 18,000 respectively.

Ans. Goodwill = ₹ 69,600

7. Calculate the goodwill of a firm based on three years' purchase of the weighted average profits of the last four years. Competency Based Que

The profits for the past four years are

2021 – ₹ 10,100 2022 – ₹ 12,400

2023 – ₹ 10,000 2024 – ₹ 15,000

The weights assigned to each year are

2021 – 1; 2022 – 2 ; 2023 – 3 and 2024 – 4

Additional information provided

(i) On 1st September, 2023, a major plant repair costing ₹ 3,000 was charged to revenue. This amount should be capitalised for goodwill calculation, with depreciation at 10% per annum on the reducing balance method.

(ii) The closing stock for the year 2022 was overvalued by ₹ 1,200.

(iii) An annual charge of ₹ 2,400 should be deducted to cover management costs for goodwill valuation.

Ans. Goodwill = ₹ 32,892

Super Profit Method

8. The average net profits expected of the firm in future are ₹ 2,38,000 per year and capital invested in the business by the firm is ₹ 12,25,000. The rate of interest expected from capital invested in this class of business is 12%.

The remuneration of the partners is estimated to be ₹ 28,000 for the year.

You are required to find out the value of goodwill on the basis of 2 years purchase of super profits.

Ans. Goodwill = ₹ 1,26,000

9. A firm earned the following net profits during the last 4 years

Years	Profit (₹)	Years	Profit (₹)
2003	4,05,000	2004	5,40,000
2005	7,20,000	2006	8,10,000

Capital employed in the firm is ₹ 45,00,000. The normal rate of profit is 10%.

Calculate the value of the goodwill on the basis of 4 year purchase of super profit.

Ans. Goodwill = ₹ 6,75,000

10. MJP & Co. earned net profits during the past three years as follows

Years	Amt (₹)
31st March, 2024	4,60,000
31st March, 2023	4,00,000
31st March, 2022	3,40,000

Capital investment in the firm throughout the above mentioned period has been ₹ 8,00,000. Having regard to the risk involved, 15% is considered to be a fair return on the capital. The remuneration of the partners during this period is estimated to be ₹ 2,00,000 per annum.

Calculate value of goodwill on the basis of two years' purchase of average super profit earned during the above mentioned three years. Competency Based Que

Ans. Goodwill = ₹ 1,60,000

11. The firm expects to earn an average net profit of ₹ 1,36,000 per year in the future and the total capital invested in the business is ₹ 7,00,000. It is expected that the business should earn a 12% return on this capital. The partners are estimated to take ₹ 16,000 per year as their remuneration.

You need to calculate the value of goodwill based on 2 years' purchase of super profits.

Ans. Goodwill = ₹ 72,000

12. P and Q are partners. They admit R into partnership *w.e.f.* 1st April, 2024. They agreed to value goodwill at 3 years' purchase of super profit method for which they decided to average profits for last 5 years. The profits for the last 5 years were

	Amt (₹)
2020	75,000
2021	90,000
2022	50,000
2023	1,30,000 (including abnormal loss ₹ 50,000)
2024	1,20,000 (including abnormal gain ₹ 20,000)

The firm has total assets of ₹ 10,00,000 and outside liabilities of ₹ 2,50,000 as on that date. Normal rate of return in similar business is 10%.

Calculate value of goodwill. Competency Based Que

Ans. Goodwill = ₹ 72,000

Hint Capital Employed = Total Assets – Outside Liabilities

= 10,00,000 – 2,50,000

13. On 1st April 2023, ABC Enterprises had total assets of ₹ 1,87,500, which included cash of ₹ 12,500. The firm's creditors on that date amounted to ₹ 12,500. It also had a reserve of ₹ 25,000, while the partners' capital account showed a balance of ₹ 1,50,000.

Given that the normal rate of return is 20% and the goodwill of the firm is valued at ₹ 60,000 based on four years' purchase of super profit, calculate the average profit per year of ABC Enterprises.

Ans. Average Profit = ₹ 50,000

Capitalisation Method

14. The capital invested in a firm is ₹ 1,84,000 and the rate of return in the similar business is 12%. The firm earns the following profit in the last 4 years

2021 – ₹ 24,000 2023 – ₹ 32,000

2022 – ₹ 28,000 2024 – ₹ 36,000

Calculate the value of goodwill by capitalisation method.

Ans. Goodwill = ₹ 66,000

15. From the following particulars, calculate value of goodwill of a firm by applying capitalisation of average profit method.

(i) Profits of last five consecutive years are 2024 ₹ 1,08,000 ; 2023 ₹ 84,000 ; 2022 ₹ 78,000 ; 2021 ₹ 1,34,000 and 2020 ₹ 1,18,000.

(ii) Capitalisation rate 20%.

(iii) Net assets of the firm ₹ 4,00,000.

Ans. Goodwill = ₹ 1,22,000

Hint (i) Average profit = ₹ 1,04,400

(ii) Capital employed = Net assets of the firm

16. A business has earned average profit of ₹ 5,00,000 during the last few years and the normal rate of return in similar business is 10%.

Find value of goodwill by Competency Based Que

(i) Capitalisation of super profit method and

(ii) Super profit method if the goodwill is valued at 2 years' purchase of super profits.

Ans. (i) Goodwill = ₹ 12,50,000

(ii) Goodwill = ₹ 1,25,000

Comprehensive Questions

17. **(i) Calculate capital employed by liabilities side approach and assets side approach from the following balance sheet**

Liabilities		Amt (₹)	Assets	Amt (₹)
Capital A/cs			Land and Building	1,50,000
A	1,00,000		Goodwill	30,000
B	1,00,000	2,00,000	Investments (Trade)	50,000
General Reserve		90,000	Stock	50,000
Sundry Creditors		90,000	Sundry Debtors	70,000
Outstanding Expenses		10,000	Cash at Bank	30,000
			Deferred Revenue Expenditure (Advertisement Suspense)	10,000
		3,90,000		3,90,000

(ii) Calculate capital employed if in the above problem, non-trade investments were given instead of trade investments. Competency Based Que

Ans. (i) Capital Employed = ₹ 2,50,000

(ii) Capital Employed = ₹ 2,00,000

18. The following information relates to a partnership firm

(i) Profit/Losses for the last six years

1st Year — ₹ 10,000 (Profit)

4th Year — ₹ 30,000 (Profit)

2nd Year — ₹ 30,000 (Profit)

5th Year — ₹ 25,000 (Profit)

3rd Year — ₹ 5,000 (Loss)

6th Year — ₹ 36,000 (Profit)

(ii) Average capital employed is ₹ 1,00,000.

(iii) Rate of normal profit is 15%.

Find out the value of goodwill on the basis of Competency Based Que

(a) Four year's purchase of average profits.

(b) Four year's purchase of super profits.

(c) Capitalisation of super profits.

Ans. (a) On the basis of average profits = ₹ 84,000

(b) On the basis of super profits = ₹ 24,000

(c) On the basis of capitalisation of super profits = ₹ 40,000

19. A business has earned average profit of ₹ 5,00,000 during the last few years and the normal rate of return in similar business is 10%.

Find value of goodwill by Competency Based Que

(i) Capitalisation of super profit method and

(ii) Super profit method if the goodwill is valued at 2 years' purchase of super profits.

Ans. (i) Goodwill = ₹ 12,50,000 (ii) Goodwill = ₹ 1,25,000

20. **Determine the value of goodwill for partners X and Y based on the following information** Competency Based Que

(i) Calculate goodwill at two years' purchase of average profit.
(ii) Calculate goodwill at two years' purchase of super profit.
(iii) Calculate goodwill based on the capitalisation of super profit.
(iv) Calculate goodwill based on the capitalisation of average profit.

The following details are provided

(a) Average capital employed is ₹ 24,00,000.
(b) Profits for the firm over the past three years are
2021 – ₹ 3,60,000 2022 – ₹ 3,20,000
2023 – ₹ 5,20,000
(c) The normal rate of return is 10%.
(d) Each partner receives a monthly remuneration of ₹ 6,000.
(e) Total assets amount to ₹ 27,00,000 and total liabilities are ₹ 3,00,000.

Ans. (i) ₹ 5,12,000 (ii) ₹ 32,000
(iii) ₹ 1,60,000 (iv) ₹ 1,60,000

Missing Information

21. The goodwill of DGH and Co. is valued at ₹ 3,00,000 at 2 years' purchase of average profit of last 5 years.
Find out the missing values. Competency Based Que

Average Profit = (1,50,000 + 1,80,000 – 60,000 + ... + 2,10,000)/5 = ...

Goodwill = ... × ... = 3,00,000

22. **Find out the value of missing figures if goodwill of the firm is valued at ₹ 6,07,500 at 3 years' purchase of super profit.** Competency Based Que

Average Profit = ₹ 5,40,000
Normal Profit = ... × 15/100 = ...
Super Profit = 6,07,500 – ... = ...

Theoretical Questions

Short Answer Type Questions

1. **State any three circumstances other than (i) death of a partner (ii) admission of a partner and (iii) retirement of a partner, when need for valuation of goodwill of a firm may arise.** Competency Based Que

Or **On what occassions does the need for valuation of goodwill arise?**

Ans. The need for valuation of goodwill may arise

(i) **When there is a Change in Profit Sharing Ratio** In case the existing partners in the firm decide to mutually change the profit sharing ratio between them, there is a need to value the goodwill.
(ii) **When the Partnership Firm is sold as Going Concern** The need for valuation of goodwill arises, in case the partnership firm is sold to some other concern on going basis.
(iii) **When two Firms Amalgamate** The need for valuing also arises in case of amalgamation of two firms, i.e. merger or acquisition of two business.

2. **Enumerate the methods of valuation of goodwill.**

Ans. Following are the methods of valuation of goodwill

(i) Average profit method
(a) Simple average method
(b) Weighted average method
(ii) Super profit method
(iii) Capitalisation method
(a) Capitalisation of average profits
(b) Capitalisation of super profits

3. **Enumerate two main steps involved in valuing the goodwill according to super profits method.** Competency Based Que

Ans. The two main steps involved in valuing the goodwill according to super profits method are

(i) Ascertain super profits
Super Profits = Average (Actual) Profits – Normal Profits
(ii) Calculate goodwill
Value of Goodwill = Super Profits × Number of Years' Purchase

4. **Enumerate two main steps involved in valuing goodwill according to average profit method.**

Ans. (i) Ascertain average profit

$$\text{Average Profit} = \frac{\text{Total Profits of Given Number of Years}}{\text{Number of Years}}$$

(ii) Calculate goodwill
Goodwill = Average Profit × Number of Years' Purchase

5. What is the difference between average profit and super profit?

Ans. Difference between average profit and super profit

Basis	Average Profit	Super Profit
Meaning	It is average of the profits of past few years.	It is the excess of average profits over normal profit.
Normal Rate of Return	Normal rate of return is not relevant in the calculation of average profit.	Normal rate of return is considered while calculating the super profit.
Average Capital Employed	Average capital employed is not considered while calculating average profit.	Average capital employed is taken into account while calculating the super profit.
Relevance of Valuing Goodwill	Average profit is relevant for average profit method, super profit method and capitalisation method of valuation of goodwill.	Super profit is relevant for super profit method and capitalisation of super profit method of valuation of goodwill.

Objective Questions

Multiple Choice Questions (MCQs)

1. When does the valuation or adjustment of goodwill become necessary in a partnership firm?
(a) Only when the firm makes a profit
(b) During reconstitution of the firm
(c) When the firm's assets are sold
(d) Only when a partner leaves the firm

2. Which of the following events in a partnership firm typically requires the adjustment of goodwill?
(a) Increase in capital
(b) Change in the profit sharing ratio
(c) Purchase of new assets
(d) Payment of dividends

3. Goodwill adjustment is necessary at the time of which of the following?
(a) Admission of a partner
(b) Retirement of a partner
(c) Death of a partner
(d) All of the above

4. What is goodwill in the context of partnership accounts?
(a) A tangible asset (b) An intangible asset
(c) A liability (d) A current asset

5. Self-generated goodwill is an .... generated goodwill which arises from number of factors.
(a) externally (b) internally
(c) Both (a) and (b) (d) None of these

6. Goodwill is considered an intangible asset because it represents which of the following?
(a) The firm's physical infrastructure
(b) The firm's reputation and ability to earn excess profits
(c) The firm's future investments
(d) The firm's current liabilities

7. Goodwill helps firms bring ...... profits.
(a) excess (b) less
(c) similar (d) All of these

8. If a firm deals in a business where demand is ...... supply, then profits will increase and therefore goodwill will increase.
(a) higher than (b) lower than
(c) similar to (d) Both (a) and (b)

9. When a firm consistently earns profits that are equal to or below the industry average, what happens to its goodwill?
(a) The goodwill increases (b) The goodwill decreases
(c) The firm has no goodwill
(d) The goodwill remains constant

10. Find out that goodwill which is accounted for, as per Accounting Standard 26.
(a) Purchased goodwill only
(b) Self-generated goodwill only
(c) Both (a) and (b)
(d) Goodwill brought in by a partner

11. Which of the following factors can significantly increase the value of goodwill for a business?
Competency Based Que
(a) Poor management practices
(b) High demand for the products or services offered
(c) Location in a remote area
(d) High employee turnover

12. How does the location of a business impact its goodwill?
(a) It has no effect on goodwill
(b) A central location with high customer traffic generally increases goodwill
(c) Only rural locations have higher goodwill
(d) Location is less important than management efficiency

13. A business operating in a monopoly market condition is likely to experience

(a) decreased profits and lower goodwill
(b) normal profits and stable goodwill
(c) higher profits and an increased value of goodwill
(d) no impact on its goodwill

14. Which of the following events does not necessitate the valuation of goodwill in a partnership firm?

(a) Admission of a new partner
(b) Retirement of a partner
(c) Change in business location
(d) Death of a partner

15. What assumption underlies the average profits method of goodwill valuation? Competency Based Que

(a) A new business will earn high profits immediately
(b) A running business will experience a loss in the first few years
(c) A new business will not earn any profits during its initial years of operation
(d) Goodwill is only calculated when a partnership is dissolved

16. The capital of the firm of Ravi and Sita is ₹ 1,50,000, and the market rate of interest is 15%. Each partner receives an annual salary of ₹ 9,000. The profits for the last 3 years were ₹ 45,000, ₹ 54,000 and ₹ 63,000. If goodwill is to be valued at 2 years' purchase of the last 3 years' average super profits, what is the goodwill of the firm? Competency Based Que

(a) ₹ 24,000 (b) ₹ 27,000
(c) ₹ 36,000 (d) ₹ 18,000

17. The profits for last 3 years were
1st year = ₹ 6,000 (including abnormal gain ₹ 2,000)
2nd year = ₹ 4,000 (after charging abnormal loss ₹ 3,000)
3rd year = ₹ 2,500 (including abnormal income ₹ 1,500)
Calculate goodwill on the basis of 3 years' purchase of last 3 years profits and losses. Competency Based Que

(a) ₹ 12,500 (b) ₹ 12,000
(c) ₹ 13,000 (d) ₹ 16,000

18. Why is the average profits method important for someone purchasing a running business? Competency Based Que

(a) It provides a fixed price for the business without considering profits
(b) It helps estimate the profits that the purchaser is likely to receive in the first few years
(c) It solely focuses on the asset valuation of the business
(d) It calculates goodwill based on the current market trends

19. .... is the total profit divided by the total number of years for which profit or loss is given.

(a) super profit (b) weighted profit
(c) normal profit (d) average profit

20. For the valuation of goodwill, any abnormal gains will be .... from the profits.

(a) included
(b) excluded
(c) Either (a) or (b) depending upon the nature of the business
(d) Either (a) or (b) depending upon the method of calculating goodwill

21. Capital employed in a business is ₹ 2,00,000. Normal rate of return on capital employed is 15%. During the year, the firm earned a profit of ₹ 48,000. Calculate goodwill on the basis of 3 years' purchase of super profit. Competency Based Que

(a) ₹ 54,000 (b) ₹ 60,000
(c) ₹ 50,000 (d) ₹ 48,000

22. Super profit is

(a) excess of past profits over current profits
(b) excess of normal profit over average profit
(c) excess of average profit over normal profit
(d) excess of market value over book value

23. How are super profits calculated in the context of goodwill valuation?

(a) By adding normal profits to actual profits
(b) By deducting normal profits from average profits
(c) By multiplying actual profits by the number of years' purchase
(d) By averaging the profits over the last five years

24. Goodwill will be .... if super profit is negative.

(a) negative
(b) positive
(c) Either (a) or (b) (d) Neither (a) nor (b)

25. A partnership firm has capital employed of ₹ 6,00,000. Its average profits are ₹ 80,000. The normal rate of return in similar type of business is 10%. The amount of super profits are CBSE 2023; Competency Based Que

(a) ₹ 60,000 (b) ₹ 8,000
(c) ₹ 20,000 (d) ₹ 52,000

26. A firm earns ₹ 1,20,000 as its annual profits. The normal rate of profit being 10%. Assets of firm are ₹ 14,40,000 and liabilities are ₹ 4,40,000. Find value of goodwill by capitalisation method. Competency Based Que

(a) ₹ 4,00,000 (b) ₹ 2,80,000
(c) ₹ 2,00,000 (d) ₹ 3,60,000

27. **Keshav and Karan were partners in a firm sharing profits equally. The capitalised value of average profits of the firm was ₹ 18,00,000. Assets of the firm were ₹ 20,00,000 (excluding goodwill) and liabilities were ₹ 5,00,000. The value of goodwill of the firm by capitalisation of average profits method will be**

CBSE 2023; Competency Based Que

(a) ₹ 2,00,000 (b) ₹ 3,00,000
(c) ₹ 4,00,000 (d) ₹ 3,50,000

28. **Amit and Sumit were partners in a firm with capitals of ₹ 3,00,000 and ₹ 2,00,000 respectively. The normal rate of return was 20% and the capitalised value of average profits was ₹ 8,50,000. The goodwill of the firm by capitalisation of average profit method will be ....**

CBSE Term I 2021; Competency Based Que

(a) ₹ 10,00,000 (b) ₹ 1,50,000
(c) ₹ 3,50,000 (d) ₹ 5,00,000

29. **The profit earned by a firm after retaining ₹ 15,000 to its reserve was ₹ 75,000. The firm had total tangible assets worth ₹ 10,00,000 and outside liabilities ₹ 3,00,000. The value of the goodwill as per capitalisation of average profit method was valued as ₹ 50,000. Determine the rate of normal rate of return.**

CBSE SQP 2025; Competency Based Que

(a) 10% (b) 5%
(c) 12% (d) 8%

30. **Average profit of firm is ₹ 3,00,000. Total tangible assets in the firm are ₹ 28,00,000 and outside liabilities are ₹ 8,00,000. In same type of business, normal rate of return is 10% of capital employed. Calculate goodwill by capitalisation of super profit method.**

Competency Based Que

(a) ₹ 14,00,000
(b) ₹ 16,00,000
(c) ₹ 18,00,000 (d) ₹ 10,00,000

Assertion-Reason

Direction (Q. No. 31 to 40) *Read the following Assertion (A) and Reason (R) and choose the correct alternative from the following*

Alternatives

(a) Both Assertion (A) and Reason (R) are true and Reason (R) is the correct explanation of Assertion (A)
(b) Both Assertion (A) and Reason (R) are true, but Reason (R) is not the correct explanation of Assertion (A)
(c) Assertion (A) is true, but Reason (R) is false
(d) Assertion (A) is false, but Reason (R) is true

31. **Assertion** (A) Goodwill needs to be valued and adjusted during the reconstitution of a partnership firm.

Reason (R) Goodwill represents the future economic benefits from past efforts and the firm's reputation.

32. **Assertion** (A) Goodwill is an intangible asset.

Reason (R) Goodwill is the value of the reputation of a firm in respect of profits expected in future, over and above the normal profits. **CBSE 2023**

33. **Assertion** (A) Goodwill is the present value of a firm's anticipated expected earnings.

Reason (R) The capitalised value attached to the differential profit capacity of a business is called goodwill.

34. **Assertion** (A) The factors which affect profits, also affect goodwill.

Reason (R) Profits are directly related to goodwill.

35. **Assertion** (A) Goodwill is recorded as an asset in the books of accounts only when it has been purchased.

Reason (R) Internally generated goodwill cannot be reliably measured and accounting standards do not permit it to be recorded.

36. **Assertion** (A) Goodwill is classified as an intangible asset, making it challenging to determine its precise value.

Reason (R) The valuation of goodwill can vary significantly depending on the method used for calculation.

37. **Assertion** (A) Self-generated goodwill is the internally generated or hard earned goodwill.

Reason (R) It arises due to continued hardwork of the organisation, its better quality products, etc.

38. **Assertion** (A) A centrally located business generally has higher goodwill than one in a remote location.

Reason (R) A firm that produces high value added products tends to earn higher profits, leading to increased goodwill.

39. **Assertion** (A) Typically, the valuation of goodwill is necessary during the sale of a business.

Reason (R) In a partnership firm, the valuation of goodwill can be required when there is a change in the profit sharing ratio among the existing partners.

40. **Assertion** (A) In average profit method, it is assumed that the newly setup business will not be able to earn any profits during the first few years.

Reason (R) The person purchasing the existing business will have to pay a sum which is the anticipated profits of first 'few years', i.e. goodwill.

Two Statements Based MCQs

Direction (Q. No. 41 to 48) *Read the following statements carefully and choose the correct alternative*

Alternatives

(a) Both the statements are correct
(b) Both the statements are incorrect
(c) Statement I is correct and Statement II is incorrect
(d) Statement I is incorrect and Statement II is correct

41. **Statement I** Goodwill is only adjusted at the time of a partner's death.

Statement II Goodwill is considered an intangible asset in the balance sheet of a firm.

42. **Statement I** Goodwill in the balance sheet represents self-generated goodwill.

Statement II Continuous losses will put no impact on the goodwill of the firm.

43. **Statement I** Purchased goodwill is acquired by paying cash only.

Statement II Favourable location affects the value of goodwill of the firm.

44. **Statement I** Goodwill is an intangible asset that represents the reputation of a business.

Statement II Goodwill is only recorded in the books when it is purchased.

45. **Statement I** A firm that earns super profits will have a higher goodwill value.

Statement II Goodwill is always automatically created for all firms regardless of profit levels.

46. **Statement I** Normal profit is calculated to value goodwill by adding abnormal gains and deducting abnormal losses.

Statement II Goodwill is a fictitious asset and is not saleable.

47. **Statement I** The average profits method is useful for calculating the anticipated profits a purchaser can expect from a business.

Statement II This method calculates goodwill based solely on the most recent year's profits.

48. **Statement I** While calculating capital employed, trade investments are taken as part of capital employed whereas non-trade investments are excluded.

Statement II Average profit method involves two approaches.

Matching

49. **Match the following terms with their correct descriptions**

Column I	Column II
A. Goodwill	(i) Profits above the normal expected return
B. Super profits	(ii) Intangible asset representing business reputation
C. Normal profits	(iii) Profits that an average firm in the industry earns
D. Capitalisation of goodwill	(iv) Determining the value of goodwill based on profits

Codes

	A	B	C	D
(a)	(ii)	(i)	(iii)	(iv)
(b)	(iv)	(ii)	(i)	(iii)
(c)	(ii)	(iii)	(i)	(iv)
(d)	(iii)	(iv)	(ii)	(i)

50. **Match the following**

Column I	Column II
A. Intangible asset	(i) Method of goodwill valuation
B. Nature of business	(ii) Feature of goodwill
C. Super profit	(iii) Factor affecting goodwill
D. Self-generated	(iv) Type of goodwill

Codes

	A	B	C	D
(a)	(iii)	(ii)	(iv)	(i)
(b)	(ii)	(iii)	(iv)	(i)
(c)	(iii)	(ii)	(i)	(iv)
(d)	(ii)	(iii)	(i)	(iv)

51. **Match the following factors affecting the value of goodwill with their description**

Column I	Column II
A. Nature of business	(i) The business's operational location influencing customer access
B. Location	(ii) High value added products leading to increased profits
C. Efficiency of management	(iii) Strong management leading to productivity and cost savings
D. Market situation	(iv) Limited competition enabling higher profit margins

Codes

	A	B	C	D
(a)	(ii)	(i)	(iii)	(iv)
(b)	(i)	(ii)	(iii)	(iv)
(c)	(ii)	(iii)	(i)	(iv)
(d)	(iii)	(ii)	(i)	(iv)

52. **Match the following components of goodwill valuation with their calculations**

Column I	Column II
A. Average profit	(i) Actual Profits – Normal Profits
B. Normal profit	(ii) Total Capital × Normal Rate of Return
C. Super profit	(iii) Total Average Profits/Number of Years
D. Goodwill	(iv) Super Profit × Number of Years' Purchase

Codes

	A	B	C	D		A	B	C	D
(a)	(iii)	(ii)	(i)	(iv)	(b)	(iv)	(iii)	(ii)	(i)
(c)	(i)	(ii)	(iv)	(iii)	(d)	(ii)	(iv)	(i)	(iii)

53. **Match the following components of goodwill valuation with their calculations**

Column I (Components)	Column II (Calculations)
A. Average profit	(i) Average Profits × Number of Years' Purchase
B. Capitalisation of average profits	(ii) Net Assets – Capitalised Value of Average Profits
C. Super profit	(iii) Super Profits × 100/Normal Rate of Return
D. Capitalisation of super profits	(iv) Super Profit × Number of Years' Purchase

Codes

	A	B	C	D		A	B	C	D
(a)	(ii)	(i)	(iii)	(iv)	(b)	(i)	(ii)	(iv)	(iii)
(c)	(i)	(iii)	(ii)	(iv)	(d)	(i)	(ii)	(iii)	(iv)

Case Based MCQs

Direction *Read the following case study and answer the questions 54 to 56 on the basis of the same*

Rashid and Komal are partners in a firm. Over the years, they have built a legacy and reputation because of the kind of products that they sell. They believe that they should calculate the goodwill of firm for better future purposes. The accountants introduced them to the concept of goodwill by stating certain features of goodwill. On the basis of certain factors, the accountant laid certain guidelines for calculation of goodwill. The accountant then calculated the goodwill by taking into consideration the following facts about business

- The capital of partners are Rashid ₹ 30,000 and Komal ₹ 20,000
- During the last financial year, firm earned a profit of ₹ 15,000.
- The normal rate of return on the business is 20%.

54. **Which of these features stated by accountant about goodwill is incorrect?**

(a) It is not a fictitious asset
(b) It is not valuable when business is sold
(c) It does not keep its value constant
(d) All of the above

55. **What is the capitalised value of business?**

(a) ₹ 1,50,000 (b) ₹ 75,000
(c) ₹ 5,00,000 (d) ₹ 25,000

56. **What is the goodwill value by super profit method if goodwill is valued at 4 years' purchase of super profits?**

(a) ₹ 5,000 (b) ₹ 75,000 (c) ₹ 20,000 (d) ₹ 25,000

Direction *Read the following case study and answer the questions 57 to 59 on the basis of the same*

In a small town known for its vibrant community, a bakery named 'Sweet Delights,' owned by the hardworking couple Maya and Raj, had become a local favourite. Their delectable pastries and warm atmosphere attracted many customers and the business thrived.

To evaluate their financial performance and explore potential expansion, Maya and Raj discovered that their average profit was ₹ 80,000. However, this amount included an undervaluation of stock averaging ₹ 8,000. With an investment of ₹ 8,00,000 in the bakery and a normal rate of return of 8%, they set out to calculate their average profits after adjusting for stock, the normal profits, the super profits and ultimately the goodwill of their bakery.

57. **Normal profits of the firm are**

(a) ₹ 80,000 (b) ₹ 88,000
(c) ₹ 72,000 (d) ₹ 64,000

58. **Super profits of the firm is**

(a) ₹ 80,000 (b) ₹ 88,000
(c) ₹ 68,000 (d) ₹ 24,000

59. **Goodwill of the firm as per super profit method on the basis of 7 years' purchase is**

(a) ₹ 1,80,000 (b) ₹ 1,88,000
(c) ₹ 1,68,000 (d) ₹ 1,24,000

Direction *Read the following case study and answer the questions 60 to 62 on the basis of the same*

Tony and Rony started a partnership firm, TR CDs to manufacture music CDs way back in 1990. Now since the music CDs are out of business, they plan to sell the business to one of the major content production houses in Mumbai. For the purpose of selling business, they reached to their accountant to calculate the goodwill and other financial advice.

He suggested that since the CDs are very less in demand, their goodwill value will be hampered. Nonetheless, the framework for goodwill calculation was decided as 'The goodwill be valued at 4 years' purchase of super profits.'

The following financial information was obtained at the end of this transaction

- Assets ₹ 8,000
- Creditors ₹ 1,000
- Normal rate of return 10%
- Goodwill of the firm ₹ 1,000

60. Which factor affecting the goodwill was highlighted by accountant?

(a) Efficiency of management (b) Market situation
(c) Nature of business (d) Special advantages

61. What is the super profit of business?

(a) ₹ 250 (b) ₹ 1,000
(c) ₹ 500 (d) ₹ 1,250

62. What is the normal profit of business?

(a) ₹ 850 (b) ₹ 800 (c) ₹ 750 (d) ₹ 700

Answers

1. (b) During reconstitution of the firm
2. (b) Change in the profit sharing ratio
3. (d) All of the above
4. (b) An intangible asset
5. (b) internally
6. (b) The firm's reputation and ability to earn excess profits
7. (a) excess
8. (a) higher than
9. (c) The firm has no goodwill
10. (a) Purchased goodwill only
11. (b) High demand for the products or services offered
12. (b) A central location with high customer traffic generally increases goodwill
13. (c) higher profits and an increased value of goodwill
14. (c) Change in business location
15. (c) A new business will not earn any profits during its initial years of operation
16. (b) Average Profit = (45,000 + 54,000 + 63,000)/3

$= 54{,}000 - 18{,}000 = ₹\ 36{,}000$

Normal Profit = $1{,}50{,}000 \times 15/100 = ₹\ 22{,}500$

Super Profit = $36{,}000 - 22{,}500 = ₹\ 13{,}500$

Goodwill = $13{,}500 \times 2 = ₹\ 27{,}000$

17. (b) Average Profits $= \dfrac{\text{Total Operating Profits}}{\text{Number of Years}}$

Average Profits

$$= \frac{(6{,}000-2{,}000)+(4{,}000+3{,}000)+(2{,}500-1{,}500)}{3}$$

$= ₹\,4{,}000$

Goodwill = Average Profits × Number of Years' Purchase

$= 4{,}000 \times 3 = ₹\ 12{,}000$

18. (b) It helps estimate the profits that the purchaser is likely to receive in the first few years
19. (d) average profit
20. (b) excluded
21. (a) Normal Profit = Capital Employed $\times \dfrac{\text{Normal Rate of Return}}{100}$

$= 2{,}00{,}000 \times \dfrac{15}{100} = ₹\ 30{,}000$

Super Profit = Actual Average Profit − Normal Profit

$= 48{,}000 - 30{,}000 = ₹\ 18{,}000$

Goodwill = Super Profit × Number of Years' Purchase

$= 18{,}000 \times 3 = ₹\ 54{,}000$

22. (c) excess of average profit over normal profit
23. (b) By deducting normal profits from average profits
24. (d) There will be no goodwill if super profit is negative
25. (c) Normal Profit = Capital Employed $\times \dfrac{\text{Normal Rate of Return}}{100}$

$= 6{,}00{,}000 \times \dfrac{10}{100} = ₹\ 60{,}000$

Super Profit = Average Profit − Normal Profit

$= 80{,}000 - 60{,}000 = ₹\ 20{,}000$

26. (c) Capitalised Value of Firm $= \dfrac{\text{Actual Profits} \times 100}{\text{Normal Rate of Return}}$

$= \dfrac{1{,}20{,}000}{10} \times 100 = ₹\ 12{,}00{,}000$

∴ Net Assets of Firm = Total Assets − Total Liabilities

$= 14{,}40{,}000 - 4{,}40{,}000 = ₹\ 10{,}00{,}000$

Goodwill = Capitalised Value of Firm − Net Assets of Firm

∴ Goodwill $= 12{,}00{,}000 - 10{,}00{,}000 = ₹\ 2{,}00{,}000$

27. (b) Net Assets $= 20{,}00{,}000 - 5{,}00{,}000 = ₹\ 15{,}00{,}000$

Capitalised Value = ₹ 18,00,000

Goodwill $= 18{,}00{,}000 - 15{,}00{,}000 = ₹\ 3{,}00{,}000$

28. (c) Goodwill = Capitalised Value of Profits − Actual Capital Employed

$= 8{,}50{,}000 - (3{,}00{,}000 + 2{,}00{,}000) = ₹\ 3{,}50{,}000$

29. (c) Net Assets $= 10,00,000 - 3,00,000 =$ ₹ 7,00,000

Captialised Value of the Firm = Goodwill + Net Assets

$= 50,000 + 7,00,000 =$ ₹ 7,50,000

Capitalised Value of the Firm $= \frac{\text{Average Profit} \times 100}{\text{Normal Rate of Return}}$

Normal Rate of Return $= \frac{90,000 \times 100}{7,50,000} = 12\%$

30. (d) Capital Employed (Net Assets)

= Total Assets − Total Liabilities

$= 28,00,000 - 8,00,000$

= ₹ 20,00,000

Normal Profit $= 20,00,000 \times \frac{10}{100} =$ ₹ 2,00,000

Super Profit $= 3,00,000 - 2,00,000 =$ ₹ 1,00,000

So, Goodwill $= \frac{\text{Super Profit}}{\text{Normal Rate of Return}} \times 100$

$= \frac{1,00,000}{10} \times 100 =$ ₹ 10,00,000

31. (a) Both Assertion (A) and Reason (R) are true and Reason (R) is the correct explanation of Assertion (A)
32. (b) Both Assertion (A) and Reason (R) are true, but Reason (R) is not the correct explanation of Assertion (A)
33. (b) Both Assertion (A) and Reason (R) are true, but Reason (R) is not the correct explanation of Assertion (A)
34. (a) Both Assertion (A) and Reason (R) are true and Reason (R) is the correct explanation of Assertion (A)
35. (a) Both Assertion (A) and Reason (R) are true and Reason (R) is the correct explanation of Assertion (A)
36. (b) Both Assertion (A) and Reason (R) are true, but Reason (R) is not the correct explanation of Assertion (A)
37. (a) Both Assertion (A) and Reason (R) are true and Reason (R) is the correct explanation of Assertion (A)
38. (b) Both Assertion (A) and Reason (R) are true, but Reason (R) is not the correct explanation of Assertion (A)
39. (b) Both Assertion (A) and Reason (R) are true, but Reason (R) is not the correct explanation of Assertion (A)
40. (b) Both Assertion (A) and Reason (R) are true, but Reason (R) is not the correct explanation of Assertion (A)
41. (d) Statement I is incorrect and Statement II is correct
42. (b) Both the statements are incorrect
43. (d) Statement I is incorrect and Statement II is correct
44. (a) Both the statements are correct
45. (c) Statement I is correct and Statement II is incorrect
46. (b) While calculating normal business profit, any abnormal gain is excluded by deducting from and any abnormal loss is included by adding to past profits. Goodwill is an intangible asset.
47. (c) Statement I is correct and Statement II is incorrect
48. (a) Both the statements are correct
49. (a) (ii) (i) (iii) (iv)
50. (d) (ii) (iii) (i) (iv)
51. (a) (ii) (i) (iii) (iv)
52. (a) (iii) (ii) (i) (iv)
53. (b) (i) (ii) (iv) (iii)
54. (b) Goodwill is valuable when the business is sold as it is calculated to adjust for the reputation that the business has earned over the years.
55. (b) Total Capitalised Value of the Firm $= \frac{15,000 \times 100}{20}$

= ₹ 75,000

56. (c) Normal Profit $= 50,000 \times \frac{20}{100} =$ ₹ 10,000

Average Profit = ₹ 15,000

Super Profit $= 15,000 - 10,000 =$ ₹ 5,000

Goodwill of the Firm = Super Profit × Number of Years' Purchase

$= 5,000 \times 4 =$ ₹ 20,000

57. (d) Normal profit is calculated using the formula

Normal Profit = Capital Invested $\times \frac{\text{Normal Rate of Return}}{100}$

Normal Profit $= 8,00,000 \times \frac{8}{100} =$ ₹ 64,000

58. (d) Super profit is calculated as follows

Super Profit = Adjusted Average Profit − Normal Profit

Super Profit $= 88,000 - 64,000 =$ ₹ 24,000

59. (c) Goodwill is calculated using the formula

Goodwill = Super Profit × Years' Purchase

In this case, the number of years' purchase is 7

Goodwill $= 24,000 \times 7 =$ ₹ 1,68,000

60. (c) Nature of business
61. (a) Goodwill = Super Profit × Number of Years' Purchase

1,000 = Super Profit × 4

Super Profit = ₹ 250

62. (d) Normal Profit $= (8,000 - 1,000) \times \frac{10}{100} =$ ₹ 700

03
CHAPTER

When existing partners decide to change their profit sharing ratio, it results in a reallocation of future profits and losses. It requires adjustments for goodwill, revaluation of assets and liabilities and settlement of any compensation among partners.

YOUR STUDY GOALS

YOUR PRACTICE GOAL

- Topicwise Solved Questions (19 Solved Questions)
- Numerical Questions [23 Questions (Unsolved)]
- Theoretical Questions [3 Questions (with answers)]
- Objective Questions (61 Qs ; MCQs, A-R, Statements, Matching, Case)

Reconstitution of a Partnership Firm :

Change in Profit Sharing Ratio Among the Existing Partners

3.1 Reconstitution of a Partnership Firm

Any change in the existing partnership agreement results in the reconstitution of a firm. This means that the existing agreement between partners comes to an end, a new one is formed and the firm continues.

Reconstitution can take place due to

- Change in the profit sharing ratio of existing partners
- Admission of a new partner
- Retirement of a partner
- Death of a partner
- Amalgamation of two partnership firms

Change in Profit Sharing Ratio

When existing partners agree to change their profit sharing ratio, it constitutes to reconstitution of the firm without admission, retirement, death or amalgamation. This results in a gain of additional share in future profits of firm for some partners while a loss of a part thereof for other partners.

e.g. If A and B previously shared profits 3 : 2 but now decide to share them equally, then A will sacrifice 1/10 of his share and B will gain the same amount.

Adjustments for Change in Profit Sharing Ratio

- Determination of sacrificing and gaining ratio.
- Accounting treatment of reserves, accumulated profits or losses.
- Revaluation of assets and reassessment of liabilities.
- Accounting treatment of goodwill.
- Adjustment of capital (if agreed).

Smart Study Chart No. 1

Determination of Sacrificing and Gaining Ratios
(These ratios show how much a partner gives up or gains in profits)

→ **Sacrificing Ratio**
It is the proportion of profit that a partner gives up.
Formula = Old Share – New Share

→ **Gaining Ratio**
It is the proportion of profit that a partner gains.
Formula = New Share – Old Share

The **gaining partner** compensates the **sacrificing partner** for his/her reduced share by paying a proportionate amount of goodwill.

3.2 Accounting Treatment of Goodwill

When partners change their profit sharing ratio, the gaining partner must compensate the sacrificing partner by paying goodwill in the gaining ratio. The accounting treatment for this adjustment is as follows

- Calculate the share gained and share sacrificed

Sacrificing/Gaining Share = Old Share – New Share

- Calculate the compensation payable by gaining partner(s) to sacrificing partner(s)

Compensation = Firm's Goodwill × Share of Profit Gained

- Write-off the existing goodwill (if any) by passing the following journal entry

All Partners' Capital*/Current** A/c [In old ratio]	Dr
To Goodwill A/c	
[With existing book value of goodwill]	

- Pass the adjustment entry for premium for goodwill paid by gaining partner

Gaining Partner's Capital*/Current** A/c [In gaining ratio]	Dr
To Sacrificing Partner's Capital*/Current** A/c [In sacrificing ratio]	

**Under fluctuating capital method. **Under fixed capital method.*

Accounting Standard (AS) 26 Intangible Assets

Accounting Standard-26 states that internally generated goodwill shall not be recognised as an asset because it is not an identifiable resource, controlled by the entity that can be measured reliably at cost.

Para 16 of Accounting Standard-10 (Accounting for Fixed Assets) states that goodwill can be recorded in the books only if money or money's worth has been paid for it. This implies that goodwill will be recorded in the books only when it is purchased.

As per AS-26, if goodwill is raised, it should be written-off immediately and it should be adjusted through partners' capital accounts.

3.3 Accounting Treatment of Reserves, Accumulated Profits or Losses

The accounting treatment of reserves, accumulated profits or losses can be studied under two situations

Smart Study Chart No. 2

Accounting Treatment

Situation I

Transfer of Reserves and Accumulated Profits/Losses to Capital Accounts

When the profit sharing ratio changes, any existing reserves or accumulated profits/losses are transferred to the partners' capital/current accounts in the old profit sharing ratio. This is because these amounts pertain to the period before the change and must be shared in old profit sharing ratio.

Situation II

When Reserves and Accumulated Profits/Losses are not Transferred to Capital Accounts

If partners choose not to transfer reserve and accumulated profits/losses to capital accounts, they can make one adjusting entry involving the capital accounts of sacrificing and gaining partners. This is because at present, they share these reserves and profits in the old profit sharing ratio, but in the future, they will share them in the new profit sharing ratio.

Journal Entries to be Passed in Situation I

1. **For Transfer of Reserves and Accumulated Profits**

Reserve/Profit and Loss A/c	Dr
Profit and Loss A/c (Cr Balance)	Dr
Workmen's Compensation Reserve A/c	Dr
(Excess of reserve over actual liability)	
Investments Fluctuation Reserve A/c	Dr
(Excess of reserve over the difference between book value and market value)	
To All Partners' Capital/Current A/cs	
(Individually in old ratio)	

2. **For Transfer of Accumulated Losses**

All Partners' Capital/Current A/cs	Dr
(Individually in old ratio)	
To Profit and Loss A/c (Dr Balance)	
To Deferred Revenue Expenditure A/c	

Steps to Pass Journal Entry in Situation II

Step 1 Calculate the net effect of reserves and accumulated profits/losses

Accumulated Profits	...
(+) Reserves	...
(−) Accumulated Losses	(...)
Net Effect	...

Step 2 Calculate sacrificing/gaining share

Sacrificing/Gaining Share = Old Share − New Share

Step 3 Calculate share of gaining and sacrificing partners in the net reserves and accumulated profits/losses

For Gaining Partner = Net Effect × Share Gained

For Sacrificing Partner = Net Effect × Share Sacrificed

Step 4 Pass the single adjusting entry

In Case of Profit	In Case of Loss
Gaining Partner's Capital/Current A/c Dr To Sacrificing Partner's Capital/Current A/c	Sacrificing Partner's Capital/Current A/c Dr To Gaining Partner's Capital/Current A/c

Workmen Compensation Reserve

This is a reserve created out of profits to meet the possible liability towards workmen, i.e. pay compensation to employees if any, that may arise in future. Accounting treatment in each of the instance is specified below

Case	Treatment
When there is no claim against workmen compensation reserve	The journal entry to this effect is Workmen Compensation Reserve A/c Dr To Partners' Capital/Current A/cs [In old ratio]
When claim for workmen compensation is lower than the amount of workmen compensation reserve	The journal entry passed is Workmen Compensation Reserve A/c Dr To Provision for Workmen Compensation Claim A/c To Partners' Capital/Current A/cs [In old ratio]

Case	Treatment		
When the claim for workmen compensation is equal to workmen compensation reserve	The journal entry passed is		
	Workmen Compensation Reserve A/c	Dr	
	To Provision for Workmen Compensation Claim A/c		
When claim for workmen compensation is more than the amount of workmen compensation reserve	The journal entries passed are		
	• Workmen Compensation Reserve A/c	Dr	
	Revaluation A/c	Dr	
	To Provision for Workmen Compensation Claim A/c		
	• Partners' Capital/Current A/cs	Dr	[In old ratio]
	To Revaluation A/c		

Investment Fluctuation Reserve

Investment fluctuation reserve is a reserve created out of profits to meet the fall in the market value of investments. The different situations which can arise are

Case	Treatment	
When book value and market value of investments is same	The journal entry to this effect is	
	Investment Fluctuation Reserve A/c	Dr
	To Partners' Capital/Current A/cs	[In old profit sharing ratio]
When the market value of investments is less than the book value	In this case, there are three possibilities	
	(i) **When Fall in Value is Less than Investment Fluctuation Reserve**	
	Investment Fluctuation Reserve A/c	Dr
	To Investment A/c	[Book Value – Market Value]
	To Partners' Capital/Current A/cs	[In old ratio]
	(ii) **When Fall in Value is Equal to Investment Fluctuation Reserve**	
	Investment Fluctuation Reserve A/c	Dr
	To Investment A/c	
	(iii) **When Fall in Value is More than Investment Fluctuation Reserve**	
	• Investment Fluctuation Reserve A/c	Dr
	Revaluation A/c	Dr
	To Investment A/c	
	• Partners' Capital/Current A/cs	Dr
	To Revaluation A/c	[In old ratio]
When the market value of investments is more than the book value of investments	The required journal entries will be	
	• Investment Fluctuation Reserve A/c	Dr
	To Partners' Capital A/c	[In old ratio]
	• Investments A/c	Dr
	To Revaluation A/c	
	• Revaluation A/c	Dr
	To Partners' Capital/Current A/c	[In old ratio]

3.4 Revaluation of Assets and Reassessment of Liabilities

When there is a change in the profit sharing ratio among partners, assets are revalued and liabilities reassessed because their actual value might differ from those shown in the balance sheet. Any gain or loss arising from this revaluation belongs to the period prior the change in the profit sharing ratio and must be shared in the old profit sharing ratio by the partners.

Two alternatives are available for this purpose, which are as follows

Smart Study Chart No. 3

Revaluation/Reassessment

Alternative I

Revised Values to be Recorded in Books

In this method, a 'revaluation account' (also called 'profit and loss adjustment account') is opened. This account records gains by crediting increase in asset values and decrease in liabilities while losses are debited when assets value decreases or liabilities increase. Also, unrecorded assets are credited and unrecorded liabilities are debited.

The resulting profit or loss from revaluation is shared among partners in their old profit sharing ratio. If the account's credit side is higher than the debit side, there's a profit and if the debit side is higher, there's a loss. The new balance sheet will show the revised values of assets and liabilities.

Alternative II

Revised Values are Not Recorded in Books

If partners agree to record the net effect of revaluation without changing the old values of assets and liabilities, then a single entry is made that involves the capital accounts of gaining and sacrificing partners.

The profit or loss from revaluation is adjusted through the capital accounts and the assets and liabilities continue to appear at their original values in the balance sheet of the new firm.

Accounting Entries to Record Revaluation of Assets and Reassessment of Liabilities (For Alternative I)

Case	Entry	
For increase in the value of asset	Assets A/c (Individually) To Revaluation A/c	Dr
For decrease in the value of asset	Revaluation A/c To Assets A/c (Individually)	Dr
For increase in the amount of liability	Revaluation A/c To Liabilities A/c (Individually)	Dr
For decrease in the amount of liability	Liabilities A/c (Individually) To Revaluation A/c	Dr
For an unrecorded asset	Unrecorded Assets A/c To Revaluation A/c	Dr
For an unrecorded liability	Revaluation A/c To Unrecorded Liability A/c	Dr
For profit on revaluation (i.e. if total of credit side exceeds the total of debit side)	Revaluation A/c To Partners' Capital/Current A/cs (Old ratio) (Individually)	Dr
For loss on revaluation (i.e. if total of debit side exceeds the total of credit side)	Partners' Capital/Current A/cs (Old ratio) (Individually) To Revaluation A/c	Dr

Format of Revaluation Account (Alternative I)

Dr **Revaluation Account** Cr

Particulars	Amt (₹)	Particulars	Amt (₹)
To Decrease in Value of Assets (Loss)	...	By Increase in Value of Assets (Profit)	...
To Increase in Value of Liabilities (Loss)	...	By Decrease in Value of Liabilities (Profit)	...
To Unrecorded Liabilities (At an agreed value)	...	By Unrecorded Assets (At an agreed value)	...
To Profit Transferred to Old Partners' Capital/ Current A/cs (In Old Ratio)*	...	By Loss Transferred to Old Partners' Capital/ Current A/cs (In Old Ratio)*	...
	...		...

**Any one will appear.*

Steps to be Taken for Adjustment Entry (Alternative II)

***Step* 1** Calculation of the net effect of revaluation

Increase in the value of assets	...
(+) Decrease in amount of liabilities	...
(–) Decrease in value of assets	(...)
(–) Increase in amount of liabilities	(...)
Net effect on revaluation	...

***Step* 2** To find share of sacrifice/gain by partners

(i) Their old share	...
(ii) Their new share	...
Difference (i – ii)	...

***Step* 3** Calculation of proportional amount of net effect of revaluation

For Gaining Partner

Proportional amount of net effect of revaluation (for gaining partner) = Share Gained × Net Effect of Revaluation

For Sacrificing Partner

Proportional amount of net effect of revaluation (for sacrificing partner) = Share Sacrificed × Net Effect of Revaluation

***Step* 4** Pass the following journal entries

For Profit on Revaluation

Gaining Partners' Capital/Current A/c	Dr
To Sacrificing Partners' Capital/Current A/c	

For Net Loss on Revaluation

Sacrificing Partners' Capital/Current A/c	Dr
To Gaining Partners' Capital/Current A/c	

3.5 Adjustment of Capital

At the time of change in profit sharing ratio, the partners may agree that their capitals should also be adjusted according to their new profit sharing ratio. Thus, an adjustment will be done to give effect to it.

Steps involved in adjusting the capital of partner are as follows

***Step* 1** Calculate the sacrifice/gain made by all the partners.

***Step* 2** Calculate the adjusted old capitals of all the partners (after all adjustments have been made, i.e. goodwill, reserves, profit/loss on revaluation, etc). It is the total capital of the firm. (Alternatively, the total capital of the firm may be given in the question).

***Step* 3** Calculate the new capitals of all the partners = Total Capital × New Share of Partners

***Step* 4** Calculate the actual cash to be paid-off or brought in by old partners by comparing their new capitals with adjusted old capitals (i.e. *step* 3 and *step* 4)

***Step* 5** Adjust the surplus by paying-off or by transfer to the credit of his current account and adjust the deficiency by asking the concerned partner to bring in the required amount or by transfer to the debit of his current account. In the absence of any information, adjustment in capitals is done through cash account.

Mind Map

Reconstitution of a Partnership Firm : Change in Profit Sharing Ratio among the Existing Partners

1 Reconstitution of a Partnership Firm

Any change in existing partnership agreement leads to reconstitution of a firm. It takes place due to

- Change in profit sharing ratio among existing partners.
- Admission of a new partner.
- Retirement of a partner.
- Death of a partner.
- Amalgamation of two partnership firms.

2 Sacrificing Ratio and Gaining Ratio

- Sacrificing Ratio = Old Share – New Share
- Gaining Ratio = New Share – Old Share
- The partner whose share is increased, is called gaining partner.
- The partner whose share is decreased, is called sacrificing partner.

3 Accounting Treatment of Goodwill

- **Existing Goodwill** It is written-off among all partners by debiting them in old ratio.
- **Valued Goodwill** It is adjusted through capital accounts of partners by debiting gaining partners in their gaining ratio and by crediting sacrificing partners in their sacrificing ratio.

4 Accounting Treatment of Reserves, Accumulated Profits or Losses

- **When Reserves and Accumulated Profits/Losses are to be transferred to Capital Accounts**
  - It means partners want to distribute the same or do not want to carry the balances in new balance sheet.
  - In such a case, reserves and profits are credited to all partners' capital/current account in their old ratio and losses are debited to all partners' capital/current account in their old ratio.
- **When Reserves and Accumulated Profits/Losses are not to be transferred to Capital Accounts**
  - It means partners do not want to distribute the same or want to carry the balances in new balance sheet. A single adjustment entry is passed for this adjustment.
  - In such a case, net effect, i.e profits/reserves – losses, is calculated.
  - If net effect is 'profit', then gaining partner is debited and sacrificing partner is credited with their respective share.
  - If net effect is 'loss', then sacrificing partner is debited and gaining partner is credited with their respective share.

6 Adjustment of Capital

Step 1 Calculate sacrifice/gain made by all partners.

Step 2 Calculate adjusted capital after all adjustments. It is the total capital of the firm.

Step 3 Calculate new capitals, i.e. Total Capital × New Share of Partners.

Step 4 Compare adjusted capital with new capital to calculate actual cash to be paid-off or brought in by partners.

Step 5 Adjust the surplus or deficiency in cash or by transfer to credit or debit of partner's current account, as the case may be.

5 Revaluation of Assets and Reassessment of Liabilities

- **When Revised Values are to be Recorded in Books**
  In this situation, **revaluation account** is prepared. Gain is recorded on credit side and loss is recorded on debit side. Final profit/loss is shared among partners in their old profit sharing ratio.
- **When Revised Values are not to be Recorded in Books**
  In this situation, net effect is calculated and a single adjustment entry is passed.
  - If net effect is 'profit', gaining partner is debited and sacrificing partner is credited with their respective share.
  - If net effect is 'loss', sacrificing partner is debited and gaining partner is credited with their respective share.

Format

Revaluation Account

Dr | | | Cr

Particulars	Amt (₹)	Particulars	Amt (₹)
To Decrease in Value of Assets (Loss)	...	By Increase in Value of Assets (Profit)	...
To Increase in Value of Liabilities (Loss)	...	By Decrease in Value of Liabilities (Profit)	...
To Unrecorded Liabilities (At an agreed value)	...	By Unrecored Assets (At an agreed value)	...
To Profit Transferred to Old Partners' Capital/Current A/c (In old ratio)	...	By Loss Transferred to Old Partners' Capital/Current A/c (In old ratio)	...
	...		...

Topicwise Solved Questions

Sacrificing/Gaining Ratio

Solved Question 1 **A, B and C are partners in a firm sharing profits in the ratio of 3 : 2 : 1. From 1st April, 2023, they decided to share future profits in the ratio of 4 : 2 : 1. Calculate their sacrificing/gaining ratio.**

Sol. Sacrificing/Gaining Ratio = Old Share – New Share

So, $A = \frac{3}{6} - \frac{4}{7} = (-)\frac{3}{42}$ (Gain)

B's share $= \frac{2}{6} - \frac{2}{7} = \frac{2}{42}$ (Sacrifice)

C's share $= \frac{1}{6} - \frac{1}{7} = \frac{1}{42}$ (Sacrifice)

Solved Question 2 **P, Q and R are partners sharing profits and losses in the ratio of 5 : 3 : 2. Calculate the new profit sharing ratio and sacrificing/gaining ratio in each of the following cases**

(i) If R acquires 1/10th share from Q.

(ii) If R acquires 1/10th share equally from P and Q.

(iii) If R acquires 1/3rd share of P and 1/4th share of Q.

(iv) If P, Q and R decide to share the future profits and losses equally.

(v) If R gets $\frac{1}{10}$th share in the future.

Sol. (i) P's new share $= \frac{5}{10}$

Q's new share $= \frac{3}{10} - \frac{1}{10} = \frac{3-1}{10} = \frac{2}{10}$

R's new share $= \frac{2}{10} + \frac{1}{10} = \frac{2+1}{10} = \frac{3}{10}$

∴ New profit sharing ratio = P : Q : R = 5 : 2 : 3

Sacrificing/Gaining Share = Old Share – New Share

$P = \frac{5}{10} - \frac{5}{10}$ = Nil

$Q = \frac{3}{10} - \frac{2}{10} = \frac{3-2}{10} = \frac{1}{10}$ Sacrifice

$R = \frac{2}{10} - \frac{3}{10} = \frac{2-3}{10} = \left(\frac{1}{10}\right)$ Gain

(ii) P's new share $= \frac{5}{10} - \left(\frac{1}{10} \times \frac{1}{2}\right)$

$= \frac{5}{10} - \frac{1}{20} = \frac{10-1}{20} = \frac{9}{20}$

Q's new share $= \frac{3}{10} - \left(\frac{1}{10} \times \frac{1}{2}\right) = \frac{3}{10} - \frac{1}{20} = \frac{6-1}{20} = \frac{5}{20}$

R's new share $= \frac{2}{10} + \frac{1}{10} = \frac{2+1}{10} = \frac{3}{10}$

New profit sharing ratio = P : Q : R

$= \frac{9}{20} : \frac{5}{20} : \frac{3}{10} = 9:5:6$

Sacrificing/Gaining Share = Old Share – New Share

$P = \frac{5}{10} - \frac{9}{20} = \frac{10-9}{20} = \frac{1}{20}$ Sacrifice

$Q = \frac{3}{10} - \frac{5}{20} = \frac{6-5}{20} = \frac{1}{20}$ Sacrifice

$R = \frac{2}{10} - \frac{6}{20} = \frac{4-6}{20} = \left(\frac{2}{20}\right)$ Gain

(iii) P's new share $= \frac{5}{10} - \left(\frac{5}{10} \times \frac{1}{3}\right) = \frac{5}{10} - \frac{5}{30}$

$= \frac{15-5}{30} = \frac{10}{30}$

Q's new share $= \frac{3}{10} - \left(\frac{3}{10} \times \frac{1}{4}\right) = \frac{3}{10} - \frac{3}{40}$

$= \frac{12-3}{40} = \frac{9}{40}$

R's new share $= \frac{2}{10} + \left(\frac{5}{10} \times \frac{1}{3}\right) + \left(\frac{3}{10} \times \frac{1}{4}\right)$

$= \frac{2}{10} + \frac{5}{30} + \frac{3}{40} = \frac{24+20+9}{120} = \frac{53}{120}$

∴ New profit sharing ratio $= \frac{10}{30} : \frac{9}{40} : \frac{53}{120}$

or 40 : 27 : 53

Sacrificing/Gaining Share = Old Share – New Share

$P = \frac{5}{10} - \frac{40}{120} = \frac{60-40}{120} = \frac{20}{120}$ Sacrifice

$Q = \frac{3}{10} - \frac{27}{120} = \frac{36-27}{120} = \frac{9}{120}$ Sacrifice

$R = \frac{2}{10} - \frac{53}{120} = \frac{24-53}{120} = \left(\frac{29}{120}\right)$ Gain

(iv) Sacrificing/Gaining Share = Old Share – New Share

$P = \frac{5}{10} - \frac{1}{3} = \frac{15-10}{30} = \frac{5}{30}$ Sacrifice

$Q = \frac{3}{10} - \frac{1}{3} = \frac{9-10}{30} = \left(\frac{1}{30}\right)$ Gain

$R = \frac{2}{10} - \frac{1}{3} = \frac{6-10}{30} = \left(\frac{4}{30}\right)$ Gain

(v) Let profit = 1

R's share $= \frac{1}{10}$; Remaining profit $= 1 - \frac{1}{10} = \frac{9}{10}$

P and Q will share remaining profit in their old profit sharing ratio, i.e. 5 : 3

Thus P's new share $= \frac{9}{10} \times \frac{5}{8} = \frac{45}{80}$

Q's new share $= \frac{9}{10} \times \frac{3}{8} = \frac{27}{80}$

R's share $= \frac{1}{10} \times \frac{8}{8} = \frac{8}{80}$

New profit sharing ratio of P, Q, R will be 45 : 27 : 8

Sacrificing/Gaining Share = Old Share – New Share

$P = \frac{5}{10} - \frac{45}{80} = \frac{40-45}{80} = \left(\frac{5}{80}\right)$ Gain

$Q = \frac{3}{10} - \frac{27}{80} = \frac{24-27}{80} = \left(\frac{3}{80}\right)$ Gain

$R = \frac{2}{10} - \frac{8}{80} = \frac{16-8}{80} = \frac{8}{80}$ Scarifice

Accounting for Goodwill

Solved Question 3 **Anant, Gulab and Khushbu were partners in a firm sharing profits in the ratio of 5 : 3 : 2. From 1st April, 2019, they decided to share the profits equally. For this purpose, the goodwill of the firm was valued at ₹ 2,40,000. Pass necessary journal entry for the treatment of goodwill on change in the profit sharing ratio. If goodwill is adjusted through partners' capital account.**

Sol. JOURNAL

Date	Particulars	LF	Amt (Dr)	Amt (Cr)
2019 Apr 1	Gulab's Capital A/c Dr		8,000	
	Khushbu's Capital A/c Dr		32,000	
	To Anant's Capital A/c			40,000
	(Being share of goodwill adjusted on change in profit sharing ratio)			

Working Notes

1. **Calculation of Sacrificing/Gaining Share**

Sacrificing/Gaining Share = Old Share – New Share

Anant $= \frac{5}{10} - \frac{1}{3} = \frac{15-10}{30} = \frac{5}{30}$ Sacrifice

Gulab $= \frac{3}{10} - \frac{1}{3} = \frac{9-10}{30} = \left(\frac{1}{30}\right)$ Gain

Khushbu $= \frac{2}{10} - \frac{1}{3} = \frac{6-10}{30} = \left(\frac{4}{30}\right)$ Gain

2. **Share of Goodwill**

Anant = 2,40,000 × 5/30 = ₹ 40,000

Gulab = 2,40,000 × 1/30 = ₹ 8,000

Khushbu = 2,40,000 × 4/30 = ₹ 32,000

Solved Question 4 **D, J and S were partners in a firm sharing profits in the ratio of 3 : 2 : 1. They decided to change their future profit share to 1 : 1 : 1. For that, goodwill of the firm was valued at 2 years' purchase of average profit of last 3 years. Profits for the last years were: 2020-21 ₹ 1,00,000, 2021-22 ₹ 70,000, 2022-23 ₹ 50,000, 2023-24 ₹ 60,000.**

Pass necessary journal entry for goodwill.

Sol. Average Profit = (70,000 + 50,000 + 60,000)/3 = ₹ 60,000

Goodwill = 60,000 × 2 = ₹ 1,20,000

Sacrificing/Gaining Share

$D = \frac{3}{6} - \frac{1}{3} = \frac{1}{6}$ (Sacrifice) ; $J = \frac{2}{6} - \frac{1}{3} = 0$

$S = \frac{1}{6} - \frac{1}{3} = (-)\frac{1}{6}$ (Gain)

JOURNAL

Date	Particulars	LF	Amt (Dr)	Amt (Cr)
	S's Capital A/c (WN) Dr		10,000	
	To D's Capital A/c			10,000
	(Being share of goodwill adjusted to change in profit sharing ratio)			

Working Note

Share of Goodwill $= 60,000 \times \frac{1}{6} =$ ₹ 10,000

Solved Question 5 **Kumar, Gupta and Kavita were partners in a firm sharing profits and losses equally. The firm was engaged in the storage and distribution of canned juice and its godowns were located at three different places in the city. Each godown was being managed individually by Kumar, Gupta and Kavita. Because of increase in business activities at the godown managed by Gupta, he had to devote more time.**

Gupta demanded that his share in the profits of the firm be increased, to which Kumar and Kavita agreed. The new profit sharing ratio was agreed to be 1 : 2 : 1. For this purpose, the goodwill of the firm was valued at two years' purchase of the average profits of last five years. The profits of the last five years were as follows

Year	Profit (₹)
I	4,00,000
II	4,80,000
III	7,33,000
IV (Loss)	(33,000)
V	2,20,000

You are required to

(i) Calculate the goodwill of the firm.

(ii) Pass necessary journal entry for the treatment of goodwill on change in profit sharing ratio of Kumar, Gupta and Kavita.

Sol. (i) **Calculation of Goodwill of the Firm**

Average Profits

$= \frac{4,00,000 + 4,80,000 + 7,33,000 - 33,000 + 2,20,000}{5}$

$$= \frac{18,00,000}{5} = ₹\ 3,60,000$$

Goodwill = Average Profits × Number of Years' Purchase

$$= 3,60,000 \times 2 = ₹\ 7,20,000$$

(ii) **JOURNAL**

Date	Particulars	LF	Amt (Dr)	Amt (Cr)
	Gupta's Capital A/c Dr		1,20,000	
	To Kumar's Capital A/c			60,000
	To Kavita's Capital A/c			60,000
	(Being Gupta's share of goodwill recorded on change in profit sharing ratio)			

Working Note

Calculation of Sacrifice or Gain of each Partner

Sacrificing/Gaining Share = Old Share – New Share

$$\text{Kumar} = \frac{1}{3} - \frac{1}{4} = \frac{4-3}{12} = \frac{1}{12} \text{ Sacrifice}$$

$$\text{Gupta} = \frac{1}{3} - \frac{2}{4} = \frac{4-6}{12} = \left(\frac{2}{12}\right) \text{ Gain}$$

$$\text{Kavita} = \frac{1}{3} - \frac{1}{4} = \frac{4-3}{12} = \frac{1}{12} \text{ Sacrifice}$$

$$\text{Gupta will pay for goodwill} = 7,20,000 \times \frac{2}{12} = ₹\ 1,20,000$$

Accounting Treatment of Reserves, Profits or Losses

Solved Question 6 **Anu, Manu, Sonu and Rohan were partners in a firm sharing profits and losses in the ratio of 1 : 2 : 1 : 2. With effect from 1st April, 2023, they decided to share profits and losses in the ratio of 2 : 4 : 1 : 3. Their balance sheet showed general reserve of ₹ 90,000. The goodwill of the firm was valued at ₹ 4,50,000.**

Pass necessary journal entries for the above on account of changing in the profit sharing ratio. Show your working clearly. **CBSE 2024**

Sol. **In the Books of Anu, Manu, Sonu and Rohan**

JOURNAL

Date	Particulars	LF	Amt (Dr)	Amt (Cr)
2023				
Apr 1	General Reserve A/c Dr		90,000	
	To Anu's Capital A/c			15,000
	To Manu's Capital A/c			30,000
	To Sonu's Capital A/c			15,000
	To Rohan's Capital A/c			30,000
	(Being distribution of general reserve in old profit sharing ratio)			
Apr 1	Anu's Capital A/c Dr		15,000	
	Manu's Capital A/c Dr		30,000	
	To Sonu's Capital A/c			30,000
	To Rohan's Capital A/c			15,000
	(Being adjustment for goodwill on account of change in profit sharing ratio)			

Working Note

Calculation of Gain/Sacrifice

Gaining Share = New Share – Old Share

$$\text{Anu} = \frac{2}{10} - \frac{1}{6} = \frac{1}{30} \text{ (Gain)}; \qquad \text{Manu} = \frac{4}{10} - \frac{2}{6} = \frac{2}{30} \text{ (Gain)}$$

$$\text{Sonu} = \frac{1}{10} - \frac{1}{6} = (-)\frac{2}{30} \text{ (Sacrifice)}$$

$$\text{Rohan} = \frac{3}{10} - \frac{2}{6} = (-)\frac{1}{30} \text{ (Sacrifice)}$$

Solved Question 7 **Mahesh, Ramesh and Naresh were partners in a firm sharing profits in the ratio of 5 : 3 : 2. From 1st April, 2023, they decided to share profits equally. On that date, there was a balance of ₹ 3,60,000 in general reserve and a debit balance of ₹ 1,80,000 in the profit and loss account.**

Pass single adjustment journal entry for the above on account of change in the profit sharing ratio. **CBSE 2024**

Sol. **In the Books of Mahesh, Ramesh and Naresh**

JOURNAL

Date	Particulars	LF	Amt (Dr)	Amt (Cr)
2023				
Apr 1	Ramesh's Capital A/c Dr		6,000	
	Naresh's Capital A/c Dr		24,000	
	To Mahesh's Capital A/c			30,000
	(Being adjustment made for general reserve and debit balance of profit and loss account on account of change in profit sharing ratio among partners)			

Working Notes

1. **Items to be Adjusted**

	Amt (₹)
General Reserve	3,60,000
Profit and Loss Account (Dr)	(1,80,000)
	1,80,000

2. **Calculation of Sacrifice/Gain**

Sacrificing Share = Old Share – New Share

$$\text{Mahesh} = \frac{5}{10} - \frac{1}{3} = \frac{5}{30} \text{ (Sacrifice)}$$

$$\text{Ramesh} = \frac{3}{10} - \frac{1}{3} = (-)\frac{1}{30} \text{ (Gain)}$$

$$\text{Naresh} = \frac{2}{10} - \frac{1}{3} = (-)\frac{4}{30} \text{ (Gain)}$$

Solved Question 8 (*Treatment of workmen compensation reserve*) **Ram, Raj and Rohan are partners sharing profits and losses in the ratio of 4 : 3 : 2. They decide to share the future profits and losses in the ratio of 2 : 3 : 4 with effect from 1st April, 2024. An extract of their balance sheet as at 31st March, 2024 is as under**

Balance Sheet (An extract)
as at 31st March, 2024

Liabilities	Amt (₹)	Assets	Amt (₹)
Workmen Compensation Reserve	45,000		

Show the accounting treatment under the following alternative cases

(i) If there is no other information.
(ii) If a claim on account of workmen's compensation is estimated at ₹ 22,500.
(iii) If a claim on account of workmen's compensation is estimated at ₹ 49,500.
(iv) If a claim on account of workmen's compensation is estimated at ₹ 45,000.

Sol. **JOURNAL**

Date	Particulars	LF	Amt (Dr)	Amt (Cr)
2024 Apr 1				
(i)	Workmen Compensation Reserve A/c Dr		45,000	
	To Ram's Capital A/c			20,000
	To Raj's Capital A/c			15,000
	To Rohan's Capital A/c			10,000
	(Being the transfer of workmen compensation reserve to partners' capital accounts in their old profit sharing ratio)			
(ii)	Workmen Compensation Reserve A/c Dr		45,000	
	To Provision for Workmen Compensation Claim A/c			22,500
	To Ram's Capital A/c			10,000
	To Raj's Capital A/c			7,500
	To Rohan's Capital A/c			5,000
	(Being the transfer of surplus workmen compensation reserve to partners' capital accounts in their old profit sharing ratio)			
(iii) (a)	Workmen Compensation Reserve A/c Dr		45,000	
	Revaluation A/c Dr		4,500	
	To Provision for Workmen Compensation Claim A/c			49,500
	(Being the provision created and shortfall charged to revaluation account)			
(b)	Ram's Capital A/c Dr		2,000	
	Raj's Capital A/c Dr		1,500	
	Rohan's Capital A/c Dr		1,000	
	To Revaluation A/c			4,500
	(Being the transfer of loss on revaluation to partners' capital accounts in their old profit sharing ratio)			
(iv)	Workmen Compensation Reserve A/c Dr		45,000	
	To Provision for Workmen Compensation Claim A/c			45,000
	(Being the provision made for workmen compensation claim)			

Solved Question 9 (*Treatment of investment fluctuation reserve*) **Suraj, Mahesh and Tarun are partners sharing profits and losses in the ratio of 4 : 3 : 2. They decide to share future profits and losses in the ratio of 2 : 3 : 4 with effect from 1st April, 2024.**

An extract of their balance sheet as at 31st March, 2024 is as under

Balance Sheet (An extract)
as at 31st March, 2024

Liabilities	Amt (₹)	Assets	Amt (₹)
Investment Fluctuation Reserve	36,000	Investments (At Cost)	4,00,000

Show the accounting treatment under the following alternative cases

(i) If there is no other information.
(ii) If the market value of investments is ₹ 4,00,000.
(iii) If the market value of investments is ₹ 3,82,000.
(iv) If the market value of investments is ₹ 4,36,000.
(v) If the market value of investments is ₹ 3,46,000.
(vi) If the market value of investments is ₹ 3,64,000.

Sol.

JOURNAL

Date	Particulars		LF	Amt (Dr)	Amt (Cr)
2024 Apr 1					
(i)	Investment Fluctuation Reserve A/c	Dr		36,000	
	To Suraj's Capital A/c				16,000
	To Mahesh's Capital A/c				12,000
	To Tarun's Capital A/c				8,000
	(Being the transfer of investment fluctuation reserve to partners' capital account in their old profit sharing ratio)				
(ii)	Same solution as given in (i)				
(iii)	Investment Fluctuation Reserve A/c	Dr		36,000	
	To Investments A/c (4,00,000 – 3,82,000)				18,000
	To Suraj's Capital A/c				8,000
	To Mahesh's Capital A/c				6,000
	To Tarun's Capital A/c				4,000
	(Being the transfer of excess investment fluctuation reserve to partners' capital account in their old profit sharing ratio)				
(iv) (a)	Investment Fluctuation Reserve A/c	Dr		36,000	
	To Suraj's Capital A/c				16,000
	To Mahesh's Capital A/c				12,000
	To Tarun's Capital A/c				8,000
	(Being the transfer of investment fluctuation reserve to partners' capital account in their old profit sharing ratio)				
(b)	Investments A/c (4,36,000 – 4,00,000)	Dr		36,000	
	To Revaluation A/c				36,000
	(Being the value of investments brought up to market value)				
(c)	Revaluation A/c	Dr		36,000	
	To Suraj's Capital A/c				16,000
	To Mahesh's Capital A/c				12,000
	To Tarun's Capital A/c				8,000
	(Being the transfer of excess investment fluctuation reserve and balance of revaluation to partners' capital account in their old profit sharing ratio)				
(v) (a)	Investment Fluctuation Reserve A/c	Dr		36,000	
	Revaluation A/c	Dr		18,000	
	To Investment A/c (4,00,000 – 3,46,000)				54,000
	(Being fall in the value of investments adjusted through investment fluctuation reserve and shortfall charged to revaluation account)				
(b)	Suraj's Capital A/c	Dr		8,000	
	Mahesh's Capital A/c	Dr		6,000	
	Tarun's Capital A/c	Dr		4,000	
	To Revaluation A/c				18,000
	(Being transfer of loss on revaluation to partner's capital account in their old profit sharing ratio)				
(vi)	Investment Fluctuation Reserve A/c	Dr		36,000	
	To Investment A/c (4,00,000 – 3,64,000)				36,000
	(Being fall in the value of investment is equal to investment fluctuation reserve account)				

Working Note

In the absence of any information, it is assumed that the market value of investments equals its cost. Thus, it is assumed that market value of investments is ₹ 4,00,000.

Solved Question 10 Anubha and Yuvika were partners in a firm sharing profits and losses in the ratio of 3 : 2. From 1st April, 2024, they decided to share future profits and losses in the ratio of 2 : 3. On this date, their balance sheet showed a balance of ₹ 50,000 in general reserve and a debit balance of ₹ 2,50,000 in profit and loss account. Partners decided to write-off profit and loss account but decided not to distribute the general reserve. Pass the necessary journal entries for the above transactions on the reconstitution of the firm. Show your workings clearly. **CBSE 2025**

Sol. **JOURNAL**

Date	Particulars	LF	Amt (Dr)	Amt (Cr)
2024 Apr 1	Anubha's Capital A/c Dr		1,50,000	
	Yuvika's Capital A/c Dr		1,00,000	
	To Profit and Loss A/c			2,50,000
	(Being loss written-off in old ratio)			
	Yuvika's Capital A/c $\left(50,000 \times \frac{1}{5}\right)$ Dr		10,000	
	To Anubha's Capital A/c			10,000
	(Being adjustment entry passed from general reserve)			

Working Note

Calculation of Gaining and Sacrificing Ratio

Anubha $= \frac{3}{5} - \frac{2}{5} = \frac{1}{5}$ Sacrifice; Yuvika $= \frac{2}{5} - \frac{3}{5} = (-)\frac{1}{5}$ Gain

Solved Question 11 Sanjeev, Mohan and Ashish are partners sharing profits and losses in the ratio of 2 : 3 : 4. They decide to share future profits and losses in the ratio of 4 : 3 : 2. They also decided to record the effect of the following without affecting their book values.

Particulars	Amt (₹)
General Reserve	80,000
Profit and Loss A/c (Cr)	40,000
Advertisement Suspense A/c (Dr)	30,000

You are required to give the necessary single journal entry.

Sol. **Calculation of Net Effect of Reserves and Accumulated Profits/Losses**

	Amt (₹)
General Reserve	80,000
(+) Profit and Loss A/c	40,000
	1,20,000
(−) Advertisement Suspense A/c	(30,000)
Net Effect	90,000

Calculation of Sacrificing/Gaining Share of Partners

Old ratio = 2 : 3 : 4; New ratio = 4 : 3 : 2

Sacrificing/Gaining Share = Old Share − New Share

Sanjeev $= \frac{2}{9} - \frac{4}{9} = \left(\frac{2}{9}\right)$ Gain ; Mohan $= \frac{3}{9} - \frac{3}{9} =$ Nil

Ashish $= \frac{4}{9} - \frac{2}{9} = \frac{2}{9}$ Sacrifice

Calculation of Share of Gaining and Sacrificing Partners in the Net Reserves and Accumulated Profits/Losses

For Sanjeev (Gaining partner) $= 90,000 \times \frac{2}{9} =$ ₹ 20,000

For Ashish (Sacrificing partner) $= 90,000 \times \frac{2}{9} =$ ₹ 20,000

JOURNAL

Date	Particulars	LF	Amt (Dr)	Amt (Cr)
	Sanjeev's Capital A/c Dr		20,000	
	To Ashish's Capital A/c			20,000
	(Being the adjustment for general reserve, profit and loss account balance and advertisement suspense account on change in profit sharing ratio)			

Revaluation/Reassessment

Solved Question 12 Parth, Raman and Zaisha are partners in a firm manufacturing furniture. They have been sharing profits and losses in the ratio of 5 : 3 : 2. From 1st April, 2017, they decided to share future profits and losses in the ratio of 2 : 5 : 3.

Their balance sheet showed a debit balance of ₹ 4,000 in profit and loss account, balance of ₹ 36,000 in general reserve and a balance of ₹ 12,000 in workmen's compensation reserve. It was agreed that

(i) The goodwill of the firm be valued at ₹ 76,000.

(ii) The stock (book value of ₹ 40,000) was to be depreciated by 8%.

(iii) Creditors amounting to ₹ 900 were not likely to be claimed.

(iv) Claim on account of workmen's compensation amounted to ₹ 20,000.

(v) Investments (book value ₹ 38,000) were revalued at ₹ 40,000.

Pass necessary journal entries for the above. **CBSE 2018 C**

Sol. **In the Books of the Parth, Raman and Zaisha**

JOURNAL

Date	Particulars	LF	Amt (Dr)	Amt (Cr)
2017 Apr 1	Parth's Capital A/c Dr		2,000	
	Raman's Capital A/c Dr		1,200	
	Zaisha's Capital A/c Dr		800	
	To Profit and Loss A/c			4,000
	(Being debit balance of profit and loss account distributed in old ratio)			

Date	Particulars	LF	Amt (Dr)	Amt (Cr)
Apr 1	General Reserve A/c Dr		36,000	
	To Parth's Capital A/c			18,000
	To Raman's Capital A/c			10,800
	To Zaisha's Capital A/c			7,200
	(Being general reserve distributed in old ratio)			
Apr 1	Revaluation A/c Dr		8,000	
	Workmen Compensation Reserve A/c Dr		12,000	
	To Provision for Workmen Compensation Claim A/c			20,000
	(Being liability created for workmen compensation claim)			
Apr 1	Revaluation A/c Dr		3,200	
	To Stock A/c			3,200
	(Being decrease in value of stock)			
Apr 1	Investments A/c Dr		2,000	
	Creditors A/c Dr		900	
	To Revaluation A/c			2,900
	(Being increase in value of investments and amount not likely to be claimed by creditors)			
Apr 1	Parth's Capital A/c Dr		4,150	
	Raman's Capital A/c Dr		2,490	
	Zaisha's Capital A/c Dr		1,660	
	To Revaluation A/c			8,300
	(Being loss on revaluation transferred in old ratio)			
Apr 1	Raman's Capital A/c Dr (2/10 of 76,000)		15,200	
	Zaisha's Capital A/c Dr (1/10 of 76,000)		7,600	
	To Parth's Capital A/c (3/10 of 76,000)			22,800
	(Being adjustment for goodwill on account of change in profit sharing ratio)			

Working Notes Amt (₹)

1. Revaluation account debited with (8,000 + 3,200) 11,200
   Revaluation account credited with (2,900)
   Therefore, loss on revaluation 8,300
2. **Calculation of Sacrifice or Gain**
   Old ratio = 5 : 3 : 2 ; New ratio = 2 : 5 : 3
   Parth $= \frac{5}{10} - \frac{2}{10} = \frac{3}{10}$ Sacrifice
   Raman $= \frac{3}{10} - \frac{5}{10} = \left(\frac{2}{10}\right)$ Gain; Zaisha $= \frac{2}{10} - \frac{3}{10} = \left(\frac{1}{10}\right)$ Gain

Solved Question 13 **Nisha, Meenu and Sara were partners in a partnership firm sharing profits and losses in the ratio of 2 : 2 : 1.**

With effect from 1st April, 2023, they agreed to share profits and losses equally. On that date, there was a general reserve of ₹ 50,000 in the books of the firm.

It was agreed that

(i) Goodwill of the firm be valued at ₹ 3,00,000.

(ii) Profit on revaluation of assets and reassessment of liabilities amounted to ₹ 30,000.

Pass necessary journal entries for the above transactions in the books of the firm. **CBSE 2024**

Sol. Sacrificing/(Gaining) Share = Old Share – New Share

Nisha $= \frac{2}{5} - \frac{1}{3} = \frac{6-5}{15} = \frac{1}{15}$; Meenu $= \frac{2}{5} - \frac{1}{3} = \frac{6-5}{15} = \frac{1}{15}$

Sara $= \frac{1}{5} - \frac{1}{3} = \frac{3-5}{15} = \left(\frac{2}{15}\right)$ Gain

JOURNAL

Date	Particulars	LF	Amt (Dr)	Amt (Cr)
	General Reserve A/c Dr		50,000	
	To Nisha's Capital A/c			20,000
	To Meenu's Capital A/c			20,000
	To Sara's Capital A/c			10,000
	(Being general reserve transferred to partners' capital account in their old profit sharing ratio)			
	Revaluation A/c Dr		30,000	
	To Nisha's Capital A/c			12,000
	To Meenu's Capital A/c			12,000
	To Sara's Capital A/c			6,000
	(Being profit on revaluation transferred to partners' capital account)			
	Sara's Capital Dr (3,00,000 × 2/15)		40,000	
	To Nisha's Capital A/c (3,00,000 × 1/15)			20,000
	To Meenu's Capital A/c (3,00,000 × 1/15)			20,000
	(Being treatment of goodwill due to change in profit sharing ratio)			

Solved Question 14 **Ashok, Bhim and Chetan were partners in a firm sharing profits in the ratio of 3 : 2 : 1. Their balance sheet as on 31st March 2024 was as follows**

Balance Sheet

Liabilities		Amt (₹)	Assets	Amt (₹)
Sundry Creditors		1,00,000	Cash at Bank	10,000
General Reserve		60,000	Sundry Debtors	60,000
Bills Payables		40,000	Stock	80,000
Capital A/cs			Plant and Mach.	2,00,000
Ashok	2,00,000		Building	1,00,000
Bhim	1,00,000		Land	1,00,000
Chetan	50,000	3,50,000		
		5,50,000		5,50,000

Ashok, Bhim and Chetan decided to share the future profits equally. For this, it was agreed that

(i) Goodwill of the firm be valued at ₹ 3,00,000.

(ii) Land to be revalued at ₹ 1,60,000 and building to be depreciated by 6%.

(iii) Creditors of ₹ 12,000 were not likely to be claimed and hence be written-off.

Prepare revaluation account and partners' capital account.

Sol. Dr **Revaluation Account** Cr

Particulars		Amt (₹)	Particulars	Amt (₹)
To Building A/c		6,000	By Land A/c	60,000
To Revaluation Profit			By Creditors A/c	12,000
Ashok	33,000			
Bhim	22,000			
Chetan	11,000	66,000		
		72,000		72,000

Dr **Partners' Capital Account** Cr

Particulars	Ashok (₹)	Bhim (₹)	Chetan (₹)	Particulars	Ashok (₹)	Bhem (₹)	Chetan (₹)
To Ashok's Capital A/c	—	—	50,000	By Balance b/d	2,00,000	1,00,000	50,000
To Balance c/d	3,13,000	1,42,000	21,000	By Revaluation Profit	33,000	22,000	11,000
				By General Reserve	30,000	20,000	10,000
				By Chetan's Capital A/c	50,000	—	—
	3,13,000	1,42,000	71,000		3,13,000	1,42,000	71,000

Working Notes

1. **Sacrificing Gaining Ratio** Ashok $= \frac{3}{6} - \frac{1}{3} = \frac{1}{6}$; Bhim $= \frac{2}{6} - \frac{1}{3} = \text{Nil}$; Chetan $= \frac{1}{6} - \frac{1}{3} = \left(\frac{1}{6}\right)$ Gain

2. **Goodwill** Chetan's Capital A/c $\left(3{,}00{,}000 \times \frac{1}{6}\right)$ Dr 50,000

To Ashok's Capital A/c 50,000

Solved Question 15 **X, Y and Z are partners sharing profits and losses in the ratio of 3 : 3 : 2. Their balance sheet as at 31st March, 2024 was as follows**

Balance Sheet
as at 31st March, 2024

Liabilities		Amt (₹)	Assets	Amt (₹)
Sundry Creditors		12,000	Cash at Bank	18,500
General Reserve		18,000	Sundry Debtors	22,000
Capital A/cs			Stock	60,000
X	1,00,000		Machinery	79,500
Y	75,000		Building	1,00,000
Z	75,000	2,50,000		
		2,80,000		2,80,000

Partners decided that with effect from 1st April, 2024, they would share profits and losses in the ratio of 4 : 3 : 2. It was agreed that

(i) Stock be valued at ₹ 55,000.

(ii) Machinery is to be depreciated by 10%.

(iii) A provision for doubtful debts is to be made on debtors @ 5%.

(iv) Building to be appreciated by 20%.

(v) A liability for ₹ 1,250 included in sundry creditors is not likely to arise.

Partners agreed that the revised values are to be recorded in the books. They do not, however want to distribute the general reserve. You are required to prepare journal entries, capital accounts of the partners and the revised balance sheet.

Sol.

JOURNAL

Date	Particulars		LF	Amt (Dr)	Amt (Cr)
2024					
Apr 1	Revaluation A/c	Dr		14,050	
	To Stock A/c				5,000
	To Machinery A/c				7,950
	To Provision for Doubtful Debts A/c				1,100
	(Being decrease in the value of assets and provision made for doubtful debts)				
	Building A/c	Dr		20,000	
	Sundry Creditors A/c	Dr		1,250	
	To Revaluation A/c				21,250
	(Being increase in the value of building and decrease in creditors)				
	Revaluation A/c	Dr		7,200	
	To X's Capital A/c				2,700
	To Y's Capital A/c				2,700
	To Z's Capital A/c				1,800
	(Being the transfer of profit on revaluation to the capital accounts of partners in old ratio)				
	X's Capital A/c	Dr		1,250	
	To Y's Capital A/c				750
	To Z's Capital A/c				500
	(Being the adjustment for general reserve on change in profit sharing ratio)				

Dr **Revaluation Account** Cr

Particulars		Amt (₹)	Particulars	Amt (₹)
To Stock A/c		5,000	By Building A/c	20,000
To Machinery A/c		7,950	By Sundry Creditors A/c	1,250
To Provision for Doubtful Debts A/c		1,100		
To Profit on Revaluation Transferred to				
X's Capital A/c	2,700			
Y's Capital A/c	2,700			
Z's Capital A/c	1,800	7,200		
		21,250		21,250

Dr **Partners' Capital Account** Cr

Particulars	X (₹)	Y (₹)	Z (₹)	Particulars	X (₹)	Y (₹)	Z (₹)
To Y's Capital A/c	750	—	—	By Balance b/d	1,00,000	75,000	75,000
To Z's Capital A/c	500	—	—	By Revaluation A/c	2,700	2,700	1,800
To Balance c/d	1,01,450	78,450	77,300	By X's Capital A/c	—	750	500
	1,02,700	78,450	77,300		1,02,700	78,450	77,300

Balance Sheet
as at 1st April, 2024

Liabilities		Amt (₹)	Assets		Amt (₹)
Sundry Creditors		10,750	Cash at Bank		18,500
General Reserve		18,000	Sundry Debtors	22,000	
Capital A/cs			(–) Provision for Doubtful Debts	(1,100)	20,900
X	1,01,450		Stock		55,000
Y	78,450		Machinery		71,550
Z	77,300	2,57,200	Building		1,20,000
		2,85,950			2,85,950

Working Note

Adjustment for General Reserve

Old Ratio of A, B and C = 3 : 3 : 2 ; New Ratio of A, B and C = 4 : 3 : 2

Sacrifice or Gain X = $\frac{3}{8}-\frac{4}{9}=\left(\frac{5}{72}\right)$ Gain ; Y = $\frac{3}{8}-\frac{3}{9}=\frac{3}{72}$ Sacrifice ; Z = $\frac{2}{8}-\frac{2}{9}=\frac{2}{72}$ Sacrifice

Since X has gained, he will be debited from $\frac{5}{72}$ of general reserves of 18,000 = ₹ 1,250

Since Y has sacrificed, he will be credited from $\frac{3}{72}$ of general reserves of 18,000 = ₹ 750

Since Z has sacrificed, he will be credited from $\frac{2}{72}$ of general reserves of 18,000 = ₹ 500

Solved Question 16 ***(When assets and liabilities have to be shown in their original values and goodwill is also required to be adjusted)*** **Z, E and N are partners sharing profits and losses in the ratio of 3 : 2 : 1. Their balance sheet as on 31st December, 2017 was as follows**

Balance Sheet

as at 31st December, 2017

Liabilities		Amt (₹)	Assets		Amt (₹)
Sundry Creditors		1,74,000	Cash at Bank		60,000
Reserves		84,000	Sundry Debtors	1,24,000	
Profit and Loss A/c (Profit)		42,000	(–) Provision for Doubtful Debts	(4,000)	1,20,000
Capital A/cs			Stock		3,60,000
Z	6,00,000		Furniture		60,000
E	6,00,000		Plant and Machinery		4,00,000
N	1,00,000	13,00,000	Land and Buildings		6,00,000
		16,00,000			16,00,000

The partners agreed that from 1st January, 2018, they will share profits and losses in the ratio of 4 : 4 : 1. They agreed that

(i) Stock is to be valued at 20% less.

(ii) Provision for doubtful debts to be increased by ₹ 3,000.

(iii) Furniture is to be depreciated by 20% and plant and machinery by 15%.

(iv) ₹ 7,000 are outstanding for salaries.

(v) Land and buildings are to be valued at ₹ 7,00,000.

(vi) Goodwill is valued at ₹ 90,000.

Neither want to record the altered values of assets and liabilities in the books nor want to distribute the reserves and accumulated profit. They also decided not to show goodwill in the books. You are required to pass a single journal entry to give effect to the above. Also, prepare capital accounts of partners and balance sheet.

Sol. Calculation of Net Effect of Revaluation

	Amt (₹)
Loss due to decrease in the value of stock	(72,000)
Loss due to increase in the value of provision for doubtful debts	(3,000)
Loss due to decrease in the value of furniture	(12,000)
Loss due to decrease in the value of plant and machinery	(60,000)
Loss due to unrecorded liability (i.e. outstanding salary)	(7,000)
	(1,54,000)
Profit due to increase in the value of land and buildings	1,00,000
Loss on revaluation	(54,000)
Adjustment for goodwill	90,000
Adjustment for reserves	84,000
Adjustment for profit and loss account (Profit)	42,000
	1,62,000

Calculation of Sacrificing/Gaining Share

Old ratio of Z, E and N = 3 : 2 : 1; New ratio of Z, E and N = 4 : 4 : 1

Sacrificing/Gaining Share = Old Share – New Share

$Z = \frac{3}{6} - \frac{4}{9} = \frac{9-8}{18} = \frac{1}{18}$ Sacrifice ; $E = \frac{2}{6} - \frac{4}{9} = \frac{6-8}{18} = \left(\frac{2}{18}\right)$ Gain ; $N = \frac{1}{6} - \frac{1}{9} = \frac{3-2}{18} = \frac{1}{18}$ Sacrifice

Calculation of the Proportionate Amount

For Z (Sacrificing partner) $= 36,000 \times \frac{1}{18} =$ ₹ 2,000 (Cr); For E (Gaining partner) $= 36,000 \times \frac{2}{18} =$ ₹ 4,000 (Dr)

For N (Sacrificing partner) $= 36,000 \times \frac{1}{18} =$ ₹ 2,000 (Cr)

JOURNAL

Date	Particulars		LF	Amt (Dr)	Amt (Cr)
2018					
Jan 1	E's Capital A/c	Dr		18,000	
	To Z's Capital A/c				9,000
	To N's Capital A/c				9,000
	(Being the adjustment for revaluation of assets and liabilities and for reserves, profits and goodwill on change in profit sharing ratio)				

Note Increase in the value of assets and decrease in the value of liabilities are profit for the firm.

Dr **Partners' Capital Account** Cr

Particulars	Z (₹)	E (₹)	N (₹)	Particulars	Z (₹)	E (₹)	N (₹)
To Z's Capital A/c	—	9,000	—	By Balance b/d	6,00,000	6,00,000	1,00,000
To N's Capital A/c	—	9,000	—	By E's Capital A/c	9,000	—	9,000
To Balance c/d	6,09,000	5,82,000	1,09,000				
	6,09,000	6,00,000	1,09,000		6,09,000	6,00,000	1,09,000

Balance Sheet
as at 1st January, 2018

Liabilities		Amt (₹)	Assets		Amt (₹)
Creditors		1,74,000	Cash		60,000
Reserves		84,000	Debtors	1,24,000	
Profit and Loss A/c (Profit)		42,000	(–) Provision for Doubtful Debts	(4,000)	1,20,000
Capital A/cs			Stock		3,60,000
Z	6,09,000		Furniture		60,000
E	5,82,000		Plant		4,00,000
N	1,09,000	13,00,000	Building		6,00,000
		16,00,000			16,00,000

Adjustment of Capital

Solved Question 17 **A, B, C and D were partners in a firm sharing profits in the ratio of 3 : 2 : 3 : 2. On 1st April, 2024 their balance sheet was as follows**

Balance Sheet
as at 1st April, 2024

Liabilities		Amt (₹)	Assets	Amt (₹)
Sundry Creditors		90,000	Fixed Assets	8,25,000
Workmen Compensation Reserve		25,000	Current Assets	3,00,000
Capital A/cs				
A	2,00,000			
B	2,50,000			
C	2,50,000			
D	3,10,000	10,10,000		
		11,25,000		11,25,000

From the above date the partners decided to share the future profits in the ratio of 4 : 3 : 2 : 1. For this purpose the goodwill of the firm was valued at ₹ 2,70,000.
It was also considered that
(i) Claim against workmen compensation reserve will be estimated at ₹ 30,000 and fixed assets will be depreciated by ₹ 25,000.
(ii) The capitals of the partners will be adjusted according to the new profit sharing ratio by opening current accounts of the partners.

Prepare revaluation account, partners' capital account and the balance sheet of the reconstituted firm. **CBSE 2017**

Sol. Dr **Revaluation Account** Cr

Particulars	Amt (₹)	Particulars		Amt (₹)
To Depreciation on Fixed Assets A/c	25,000	By Loss on Revaluation Transferred Partner's to Capital A/cs		
To Provision for Workmen Compensation Fund	5,000	A	9,000	
		B	6,000	
		C	9,000	
		D	6,000	30,000
	30,000			30,000

Dr **Partners' Capital Account** Cr

Particulars	A (₹)	B (₹)	C (₹)	D (₹)	Particulars	A (₹)	B (₹)	C (₹)	D (₹)
To Revaluation A/c	9,000	6,000	9,000	6,000	By Balance b/d	2,00,000	2,50,000	2,50,000	3,10,000
To C's Capital A/c	27,000	—	—	—	By A's Capital A/c	—	—	27,000	—
To D's Capital A/c	—	27,000	—	—	By B's Capital A/c	—	—	—	27,000
To Current A/c (Balancing Figure)	—	—	72,000	2,33,000	By Current A/c (Balancing Figure)	2,28,000	77,000	—	—
To Balance c/d	3,92,000	2,94,000	1,96,000	98,000					
	4,28,000	3,27,000	2,77,000	3,37,000		4,28,000	3,27,000	2,77,000	3,37,000

Balance Sheet
as at...

Liabilities		Amt (₹)	Assets		Amt (₹)
Capital A/cs			Fixed Assets	8,25,000	
A	3,92,000		(−) Depreciation	(25,000)	8,00,000
B	2,94,000		Current Assets		3,00,000
C	1,96,000		Current A/cs		
D	98,000	9,80,000	C	72,000	
Current A/cs			D	2,33,000	3,05,000
A	2,28,000				
B	77,000	3,05,000			
Workmen Compensation Reserve		30,000			
Sundry Creditors		90,000			
		14,05,000			14,05,000

Working Notes

1. **Calculation of Sacrificing/Gaining Share**

Sacrificing/Gaining Share = Old Share − New Share

$A = \frac{3}{10} - \frac{4}{10} = \frac{3-4}{10} = \left(\frac{1}{10}\right)$ Gain ; $B = \frac{2}{10} - \frac{3}{10} = \frac{2-3}{10} = \left(\frac{1}{10}\right)$ Gain; $C = \frac{3}{10} - \frac{2}{10} = \frac{3-2}{10} = \frac{1}{10}$ Sacrifice ; $D = \frac{2}{10} - \frac{1}{10} = \frac{2-1}{10} = \frac{1}{10}$ Sacrifice

2. **Calculation of Goodwill**

A's share of goodwill = $2,70,000 \times \frac{1}{10}$ = ₹ 27,000; B's share of goodwill = $2,70,000 \times \frac{1}{10}$ = ₹ 27,000

C's share of goodwill = $2,70,000 \times \frac{1}{10}$ = ₹ 27,000; D's share of goodwill = $2,70,000 \times \frac{1}{10}$ = ₹ 27,000

3. **Journal Entry Showing Adjustment for Goodwill**

A's Capital A/c	Dr	27,000	
B's Capital A/c	Dr	27,000	
To C's Capital A/c			27,000
To D's Capital A/c			27,000

While posting in ledger, it has been assumed that A pays to C and B pays to D.

4. **Calculation of Adjusted Capitals**

Adjusted capital of A = ₹ 1,64,000; Adjusted capital of B = ₹ 2,17,000

Adjusted capital of C = ₹ 2,68,000 ; Adjusted capital of D = ₹ 3,31,000

Total combined capital = ₹ 9,80,000

New capital of A = $9,80,000 \times \frac{4}{10}$ = ₹ 3,92,000; New capital of B = $9,80,000 \times \frac{3}{10}$ = ₹ 2,94,000

New capital of C = $9,80,000 \times \frac{2}{10}$ = ₹ 1,96,000; New capital of D = $9,80,000 \times \frac{1}{10}$ = ₹ 98,000

Missing Information

Solved Question 18 *(Evaluation Question)* **A, B, C are partners sharing profits and losses in the ratio of 5 : 3 : 2. They decide to share future profits and losses equally with effect from 1st April, 2020. Complete the missing information in the following table**

JOURNAL

Date	Particulars		LF	Amt (Dr)	Amt (Cr)
2020					
Apr 1	....	Dr		...	
	....	Dr		...	
	....	Dr		...	
	To Goodwill A/c				...
	(Being the existing goodwill ₹ 15,000 written-off in old ratio on change in profit sharing ratio)				
	....	Dr		3,000	
	C's Capital A/c	Dr		...	
	To				...
	(Being the adjustment made for goodwill valued at ₹ 90,000 on change in profit sharing ratio)				

Sol.

JOURNAL

Date	Particulars		LF	Amt (Dr)	Amt (Cr)
2017					
Apr 1	**A's Capital A/c (15,000 × 5/10)**	Dr		**7,500**	
	B's Capital A/c (15,000 × 3/10)	Dr		**4,500**	
	C's Capital A/c (15,000 × 2/10)	Dr		**3,000**	
	To Goodwill A/c				**15,000**
	(Being the existing goodwill written-off in old ratio on change in profit sharing ratio)				
	B's Capital A/c (90,000 × 1/30)	Dr		3,000	
	C's Capital A/c (90,000 × 4/30)	Dr		**12,000**	
	To A's Capital A/c (90,000 × 5/30)				**15,000**
	(Being the adjustment made for goodwill valued at ₹ 90,000 on change in the profit sharing ratio)				

Working Note

Calculation of Sacrificing/Gaining Share

Sacrificing/Gaining Share = Old Share − New Share

$A = \frac{5}{10} - \frac{1}{3} = \frac{15-10}{30} = \frac{5}{30}$ Sacrifice; $B = \frac{3}{10} - \frac{1}{3} = \frac{9-10}{30} = \left(\frac{1}{30}\right)$ Gain; $C = \frac{2}{10} - \frac{1}{3} = \frac{6-10}{30} = \left(\frac{4}{30}\right)$ Gain

Compensation payable by B (Gaining partner) to A (Sacrificing partner) = $90{,}000 \times \frac{1}{30}$ = ₹ 3,000

Compensation payable by C (Gaining partner) to A (Sacrificing partner) = $90{,}000 \times \frac{4}{30}$ = ₹ 12,000

Solved Question 19 **M, J and P are partners sharing profits and losses in the ratio of 2 : 2 : 1. From 1st April 2024, they decided to share future profits in 1 : 1 : 1, following revaluation account and capital account were drawn, in which some values are missing.**

Revaluation Account

Dr | | | | | Cr

Particulars		Amt (₹)	Particulars	Amt (₹)
To Furniture A/c		40,000	By Machinery A/c	...
To Provision for Doubtful Debts A/c		5,000	By Bank Overdraft A/c	20,000
To Prepaid Expenses A/c		...		
To Gain (Profit) Transferred to				
M's Capital A/c	...			
J's Capital A/c	...			
P's Capital A/c	...	...		
		80,000		80,000

Partners' Capital Account

Dr | | | | | | | Cr

Particulars	M (₹)	J (₹)	P (₹)	Particulars	M (₹)	J (₹)	P (₹)
To Advertisement Suspense A/c	...	...	...	By Balance b/d	...	...	...
To Balance c/d	1,50,000	1,40,000	1,30,000	By Revaluation A/c	8,000	8,000	4,000
	1,54,000	1,44,000	1,32,000		1,54,000	1,44,000	1,32,000

You are required to complete the accounts.

Sol.

Revaluation Account

Dr | | | | | Cr

Particulars		Amt (₹)	Particulars	Amt (₹)
To Furniture A/c		40,000	By Machinery A/c	**60,000**
To Provision for Doubtful Debts A/c		5,000	By Bank Overdraft A/c	20,000
To Prepaid Expenses A/c		**15,000**		
To Gain (Profit) Transferred to				
M's Capital A/c	**8,000**			
J's Capital A/c	**8,000**			
P's Capital A/c	**4,000**	**20,000**		
		80,000		80,000

Partners' Capital Account

Dr | | | | | | | Cr

Particulars	M (₹)	J (₹)	P (₹)	Particulars	M (₹)	J (₹)	P (₹)
To Advertisement Suspense A/c	**14,000**	**8,000**	**3,000**	By Balance b/d	**1,46,000**	**1,36,000**	**1,28,000**
To Balance c/d	1,40,000	1,36,000	1,29,000	By Revaluation A/c	8,000	8,000	4,000
	1,54,000	1,44,000	1,32,000		1,54,000	1,44,000	1,32,000

Numerical Questions

Sacrificing/Gaining Ratio

1. P, Q and R are partners in a firm sharing profits equally. They decided to share future profits in the ratio of 5 : 3 : 2.

Calculate their gaining/sacrificing ratio.

Ans. P Gain = 5/30 ; Q Sacrifice = 1/30; R Sacrifice = 4/30

2. M, N and S are partners sharing profits in the ratio of 5 : 3 : 2. With effect from 1st April, 2024, they decide to share profits and losses in the ratio of 5 : 2 : 3.

Calculate each partners' gain or sacrifice due to the change in ratio.

Ans. S gains = $\frac{1}{10}$ th share ; N sacrifices = $\frac{1}{10}$ th share

3. Ram, Krishna and Shiva are partners sharing profits in the ratio of 2 : 2 : 1.

Calculate the new profit sharing ratio and sacrificing ratio, if Krishna acquires $\frac{1}{15}$th share from Ram.

Ans. New Profit Sharing Ratio = 5 : 7 : 3

Sacrifice made by Ram = $\frac{1}{15}$

Accounting for Goodwill

4. D, E and F are partners sharing profits and losses in the ratio of 5 : 4 : 1. On 1st April, 2024, they decided to share future profits in 9 : 6 : 5. For that, the goodwill of the firm is valued at ₹ 1,00,000.

Pass necessary journal entry.

Ans. Debit F's capital account by ₹ 15,000 and Credit D's capital account by ₹ 5,000 and E's capital account by ₹ 10,000

5. Chintu, Montoo and Shitu are partners in a business sharing profits in the ratio of 3 : 4 : 2. From 1st April, 2024, they decide to share profits equally. Goodwill was valued at ₹ 90,000, as on that date.

Pass journal entry to give effect to the above adjustment. If goodwill is adjusted through partners capital accounts.

Ans. Debit Shitu's capital account and Credit Montoo's capital account with ₹ 10,000

6. P, R and M were partners in a firm sharing profits in the ratio of 3 : 2 : 1. From 1st April, 2024, they decided to share future profits in 2 : 2 : 1.

To account for this change, the goodwill of the firm was valued at 2 years' purchase of the average profit of the last 4 years.

The profits for the previous years were as follows

2020-21 = ₹3,20,000; 2021-22 = ₹ 1,50,000

2022-23 = ₹50,000 ; 2023-24 = ₹ 80,000

Pass the necessary journal entry for goodwill.

Ans. Debit R's capital account by ₹ 10,000, M's capital account ₹ 5,000 and Credit P's capital account by ₹ 15,000

7. Anita, Asha and Amrit are partners sharing profits in the ratio of 3 : 2 : 1 respectively. From 1st April, 2024, they decided to share profits in the ratio of 1 : 1 : 1. The partnership deed provided that in the event of any change in profit sharing ratio, the goodwill should be valued at three years' purchase of the average of five years' profits.

The profits and losses of the preceding five years are

Year	Profit (₹)
2020	1,20,000
2021	3,00,000
2022	3,40,000
2023	3,80,000 (Loss)
2024	1,40,000

Showing the working clearly, give the necessary journal entry to record the above change. **Competency Based Que**

Ans. Amrit gains and Anita sacrifices 1/6th share. Debit Amrit's capital account and Credit Anita's capital account with ₹ 1,00,000

Accounting Treatment of Reserves, Profits or Losses

8. Riya, Tara, Simran and Arjun were partners in a firm sharing profits and losses in the ratio of 1 : 2 : 1 : 2. From 1st April, 2023, they agreed to change the profit sharing ratio to 3 : 2 : 3 : 2.

Their balance sheet reflected a general reserve of ₹ 2,25,000 and debit balance of profit and loss account of ₹ 15,000.

Pass the necessary journal entries to account for the change in the profit sharing ratio, clearly showing your calculations.

9. Nisha, Priya, Kabir and Aditya were partners in a firm sharing profits and losses in the ratio of 1 : 1 : 1 : 1. From 1st April, 2024, they agreed to change the profit sharing ratio to 2 : 3 : 2 : 1. Their balance sheet reflected a general reserve of ₹ 1,50,000 and the firm's goodwill was valued at ₹ 7,50,000.

Pass the necessary journal entries to account for the change in the profit sharing ratio, clearly showing your calculations.

10. S and D are partners in a firm sharing profits in the ratio of 3 : 2. From 1st April, 2024 they decided to share future profits in the ratio of 2 : 1. Workmen compensation reserve is appearing in their balance sheet as ₹ 40,000.

Pass necessary journal entries if Competency Based Que

(i) **There is no claim in respect of workmen compensation.**
(ii) **A claim on account of workmen compensation is estimated at ₹ 25,000.**
(iii) **A claim on account of workmen compensation is estimated at ₹ 40,000.**
(iv) **A claim on account of workmen compensation is estimated at ₹ 52,000.**

11. The balance sheet of U and V shows investment at ₹ 1,50,000 and investment fluctuation reserve of ₹ 70,000. They were sharing profits equally but from 1st April, 2024, they decided to share future profits in the ratio of 3 : 2.

Pass necessary journal entries if Competency Based Que

(i) **There is no other information.**
(ii) **The market value of the investment is ₹ 1,00,000.**
(iii) **The market value of the investment is ₹ 80,000.**
(iv) **The market value of the investment is ₹ 50,000.**
(v) **The market value of the investment is ₹ 1,80,000.**

12. Mita, Gopal and Farhan were partners sharing profits and losses in the ratio of 3 : 2 : 1. On 31st March, 2024, they decided to change profit sharing ratio to 5 : 3 : 2. On this date, balance sheet showed deferred advertisement expenditure ₹ 30,000 and contingency reserve ₹ 9,000. Goodwill was valued at ₹ 4,80,000.

Pass the necessary journal entries for the above transactions in the books of the firm on its reconstitution.

13. B, M and C are sharing profits and losses in the ratio of 5 : 3 : 2. They decide to share future profits and losses in the ratio of 2 : 3 : 5 with effect from 1st April, 2024.

They also decide to record the effect of the following without affecting their book figures, by passing a single adjusting entry.

Particulars	Book Figure (₹)
General Reserve	60,000
Contingencies Reserve	10,000
Profit and Loss A/c (Cr)	30,000
Advertisement Suspense A/c (Dr)	40,000

Ans. C gains and B sacrifices 3/10th share. Debit C and Credit B with ₹ 18,000

14. P and J were in partnership sharing profits in the ratio of 2 : 3. With effect from 1st May, 2024 they agreed to share profits in the ratio of 1 : 2. For this purpose the goodwill of the firm is to be valued at two year's purchase of the average profits of last three years, which were ₹ 75,000, ₹ 70,000 and ₹ 1,10,000 respectively. Reserves appear in the books at ₹ 55,000. Partners do not want to distribute the reserves.

You are required to give effect to the change by passing a single journal entry.

Ans. Debit J and Credit P by ₹ 15,000

Revaluation/Reassessment

15. Reeha, Meenu and Sara were partners in a partnership firm sharing profits and losses in the ratio of 2 : 2 : 1. With effect from 1st April, 2023, they agreed to share profits and losses equally. On that date, there was a general reserve of ₹ 50,000 in the books of the firm. It was agreed that

(i) Goodwill of the firm be valued at ₹ 3,00,000.
(ii) Profit on revaluation of assets and reassessment of liabilities amounted to ₹ 30,000.

Pass necessary journal entries for the above transactions in the books of the firm. CBSE 2024

16. M, N and O are partners in a firm sharing profits and losses in the ratio of 3 : 3 : 2. Their balance sheet as on 31st March, 2023 is as follows

Balance Sheet

Liabilities		Amt (₹)	Assets	Amt (₹)
Sundry Creditors		48,000	Cash at Bank	54,000
General Reserve		72,000	Sundry Debtors	1,00,000
Capital A/cs			Stock	2,40,000
M	4,00,000		Machinery	3,18,000
N	4,00,000		Building	4,00,000
O	2,00,000	10,00,000	Advert. Expen.	8,000
		11,20,000		11,20,000

Partners decided that from now onwards they will share profits and losses in the ratio of 4 : 3 : 2. Further adjustments include

(i) Machinery is to be depreciated by 10%.
(ii) A provision for doubtful debt is to be made @ 5% of debtors.

(iii) Stock is to be valued at 2,20,000.
(iv) Building is to be appreciated by 20%.
(v) A liability of ₹ 6,000 included in sundry creditors is not likely to arise.

The partners decided to retain the general reserve in the books.

Pass necessary journal entries. **Competency Based Que**

17. Frank, George and Hemant were partners in a firm sharing profits in the ratio of 5 : 3 : 2. They decided to change their profit sharing ratio to 2 : 5 : 3 with effect from 1st April, 2023. Their balance sheet as at 31st March, 2023 was as follows

Balance Sheet of Frank, George and Hemant
as at 31st March, 2023

Liabilities		Amt (₹)	Assets	Amt (₹)
Capital A/cs			Land	5,00,000
Frank	4,00,000		Building	3,00,000
George	3,00,000		Machinery	2,00,000
Hemant	2,00,000	9,00,000	Stock	1,50,000
Creditors		5,00,000	Debtors	2,50,000
Employees' Provident Fund		1,00,000	Cash	3,00,000
General Reserve		2,00,000		
		17,00,000		17,00,000

It was decided that
(i) The value of land having appreciated be brought up to ₹ 6,50,000.
(ii) Goodwill of the firm was valued at ₹ 2,00,000. Goodwill was not to appear in the books of the firm.

Pass the necessary journal entries in the books of the firm. **CBSE 2024**

18. M and N are partners sharing profits and losses in the ratio of 4 : 3. Their balance sheet as at 31st March, 2024 stood as follows

Balance Sheet
as at 31st March, 2019

Liabilities		Amt (₹)	Assets	Amt (₹)
Sundry Creditors		14,000	Cash	10,000
Reserve		21,000	Sundry Debtors	60,000
Capital A/cs			Stock	70,000
M	1,20,000		Fixed Assets	75,000
N	60,000	1,80,000		
		2,15,000		2,15,000

They decided that with effect from 1st April, 2024, they will share profits and losses in the ratio of 2 : 1. For this purpose they decided that
(i) Fixed assets are to be depreciated by 10%.
(ii) A provision of 6% be made on debtors for doubtful debts.
(iii) Stock be valued at ₹ 95,000.
(iv) An amount of ₹ 1,850 included in creditors is not likely to be claimed.

Partners decided to record the revised values in the books. However, they do not want to disturb the reserves.

You are required to prepare journal entries, capital accounts of the partners and the revised balance sheet. **Competency Based Que**

Ans. Profit on Revaluation = ₹ 15,750; Adjustment for Reserve Dr M by ₹ 2,000 and Cr N by ₹ 2,000; Capitals of M = ₹ 1,27,000 and N = ₹ 68,750; Balance Sheet Total = ₹ 2,28,900

19. The balance sheet of Raj, Rahul and Rohan who are sharing profits in the ratio of 2 : 3 : 1, as at 31st March, 2024 is given below

Balance Sheet
as at 31st March, 2024

Liabilities		Amt (₹)	Assets	Amt (₹)
Capital A/cs			Goodwill	24,000
Raj	2,00,000		Land and Building	5,00,000
Rahul	4,00,000		Investments (Market Value ₹ 92,000)	1,00,000
Rohan	6,00,000	12,00,000	Stock	1,60,000
Workmen Compensation Reserve		40,000	Debtors	6,00,000
Investment Fluctuation Reserve		20,000	Bank	5,92,000
Provision for Doubtful Debts		20,000	Advertisement Suspense A/c	24,000
Sundry Creditors		6,00,000		
Employees Provident Fund		1,20,000		
		20,00,000		20,00,000

Raj, Rahul and Rohan decide to alter their profit sharing ratio as 3 : 2 : 1 from 1st April, 2024.

(i) Goodwill is to be valued at 2 years' purchase of average profits of last three completed years. The profits were Year I = ₹ 96,000, Year II = ₹ 1,86,000, Year III = ₹ 2,76,000.
(ii) Land and building was found undervalued by ₹ 40,000 and stock was found overvalued by ₹ 76,000.
(iii) Provision for doubtful debts is to be made equal to 5% of the debtors.
(iv) Claim on account of workmen compensation is ₹ 16,000.
(v) 10% of the sundry creditors be written back as no longer payable.
(vi) Out of the amount of insurance which was debited entirely to profit and loss account ₹ 10,000 be carried forward as an unexpired insurance.

Prepare the necessary ledger accounts and the balance sheet. **Competency Based Que**

Ans. Profit on Revaluation = ₹ 24,000; Partners' Capital Account Raj = ₹ 1,42,000, Rahul = ₹ 4,68,000, Rohan = ₹ 6,02,000; Balance Sheet Total = ₹ 18,88,000; Goodwill = ₹ 3,72,000; Raj gains and Rahul sacrifices 1/16th share

20. Z, J and M are partners sharing profits and losses in the ratio of 5 : 3 : 2. Their balance sheet as at 31st March, 2024 was as follows

Balance Sheet
as at 31st March, 2024

Liabilities		Amt (₹)	Assets		Amt (₹)
Sundry Creditors		80,000	Cash in Hand		12,500
Salaries Payable		15,000	Bank Balance		62,500
General Reserve		40,000	Bills Receivable		5,000
Profit and Loss A/c		15,000	Sundry Debtors	50,000	
Capital A/cs			(–) Provision for Doubtful Debts	(5,000)	45,000
Z	1,50,000		Stock		1,00,000
J	90,000		Funiture		25,000
M	60,000	3,00,000	Computers		1,50,000
			Air Conditioners		50,000
		4,50,000			4,50,000

Profit sharing ratio among the partners was agreed to be 2 : 2 : 1 *w.e.f.* 1st April, 2024. They agreed to the following

(i) Stock to be increased to ₹ 1,10,000.
(ii) Provision for doubtful debts to be reduced by ₹ 1,000.
(iii) Furniture to be reduced by 20%.
(iv) Computers to be reduced to ₹ 1,35,000.
(v) Goodwill of the firm is valued at ₹ 50,000.

The partners decided to carry the assets and liabilities at their existing values. They also decided that general reserve and profit and loss account balances be carried at the same values.

Pass an adjustment entry giving effect to the above arrangement and prepare balance sheet after adjustments.

Competency Based Que

Ans. Debit J and Credit Z with ₹ 9,600; Z sacrifice and J gains 1/10 the share ; Balance Sheet Total = ₹ 4,50,000 ; Net Amount to be Adjusted = ₹ 96,000

Adjustment of Capital

21. A, B and C were partners in a firm sharing profits and losses in the ratio of 2 : 2 : 1. On 31st March, 2024, their balance sheet was as follows

Balance Sheet
as at 31st March, 2024

Liabilities		Amt (₹)	Assets	Amt (₹)
Capitals A/cs			Land and Building	1,50,000
A	1,00,000		Stock	80,000
B	75,000		Debtors	40,000
C	45,000	2,20,000	Cash at Bank	5,000
General Reserve		20,000		
Creditors		35,000		
		2,75,000		2,75,000

From 1st April, 2024, they decided to share future profits in the ratio of 1 : 2 : 3. For this purpose the following were agreed upon

(i) Goodwill of the firm was valued at ₹ 2,25,000.

(ii) Land and building will be appreciated by 20%.

(iii) Capital of the partners will be in proportion to their new profit sharing ratio. For this purpose, current accounts will be opened.

Pass necessary journal entries for the above transactions in the books of the firm and prepare partners' capital account and balance sheet. **Competency Based Que**

Ans.

Particulars	A (₹)	B (₹)	C (₹)
Existing Capital	1,72,500	1,10,000	(–) 12,500
Required Capital	45,000	90,000	1,35,000
Transferred to Current Accounts	1,27,500 (Cr)	20,000 (Cr)	1,47,500 (Dr)

Balance Sheet Total = ₹ 3,05,000

Missing Information

22. S, M and J are partners in a firm sharing profits in 3 : 3 : 2 ratio. They decide to share profits equally *w.e.f.* 1st April, 2024. On that date, the profit and loss account shows the credit balance of ₹ 30,000. They decide that profit and loss account will remain as it is.

You are required to fill up the following journal entry **Competency Based Que**

JOURNAL

Date	Particulars	LF	Amt (Dr)	Amt (Cr)
2024				
Apr 1	.... Dr		...	
	To			...
	To			...
	(Being the adjustment made for credit balance of profit and loss account due to change in profit sharing ratio)			

23. P, Q and R are partners sharing profit and loss in the ratio of 2 : 5 : 5. From 1st April 2024 they decided to share profit and loss in the ratio of 3 : 5 : 7.

You are required to fill up the following journal entry. **Competency Based Que**

JOURNAL

Date	Particulars	LF	Amt (Dr)	Amt (Cr)
2024				
Apr 1	P's Capital A/c Dr		...	
	R's Capital A/c Dr		4,05,000	
	To Q's Capital A/c			...
	(Being adjustment for goodwill due to change in profit sharing ratio)			

Theoretical Questions

Short Answer Type Questions

1. How will you treat goodwill in case of change in the profit sharing ratio of the existing partners?

Ans. At the time of change in profit sharing ratio, the gaining partner (i.e. the partner whose share has increased) must compensate the sacrificing partner (i.e. the partner whose share has been reduced) by way of payment to him as goodwill in the gaining ratio.

Gaining Partner's Capital/Current A/c Dr
[In gaining ratio]
To Sacrificing Partner's Capital/Current A/c
[In sacrificing ratio]

2. How will you deal with reserves and accumulated profits at the time of change in the profit sharing ratio among the existing partners? **Competency Based Que**

Or **State the ratio in which partners share the accumulated profits when there is a change in profit sharing ratio amongst the existing partners.**

Ans. If at the time of change in profit sharing ratio, any reserves and accumulated profits (general reserve, reserve fund or credit balance of profit and loss account) or losses (debit balance of profit and loss account) exist in the books of the firm, then these should be transferred to existing partner's capital accounts (if capitals are fluctuating) or current accounts (if capitals are fixed) in their old profit sharing ratio.

3. Briefly explain the need for revaluation of assets and liabilities on the reconstitution of a partnership firm.

Ans. Revaluation of assets and reassessment of liabilities is necessary because the change in the value of assets and liabilities belong to the period prior to reconstitution.

Hence, any gain or loss on revaluation must be shared in the old profit sharing ratio by the partners. Moreover, such revaluation is necessary so that revised value of assets and liabilities may appear in the balance sheet of the new firm.

Objective Questions

Multiple Choice Questions (MCQs)

1. **In case of change in profit sharing ratio, if the question is silent, then accumulated profit or losses are**

(a) distributed (b) not distributed
(c) adjusted (d) None of these

2. **Revaluation account is prepared ...... the value of assets.**

(a) to revise (b) not to revise
(c) to distribute (d) None of these

3. **In case of change in profit sharing ratio, when revised values are not to be recorded in the books, then steps to be followed are** Competency Based Que

(i) Pass a single adjustment entry.
(ii) To find share of sacrifice/gain by partners.
(iii) Calculation of the net effect of revaluation.
(iv) Calculation of proportional amount of net effect of revaluation.

Codes

(a) (ii), (iii), (iv), (i) (b) (iii), (ii), (iv), (i)
(c) (iv), (iii), (ii), (i) (d) None of these

4. **At the time of change in profit sharing ratio, general reserve existing in the balance sheet is transferred to capital accounts of partner in their**

(a) sacrificing ratio (b) gaining ratio
(c) old profit sharing ratio (d) new profit sharing ratio

5. **Ratio is which one or more partners of the firm forego, i.e. sacrifice their share of profits in favour of one or more partners of the firm is**

(a) sacrificing ratio (b) gaining ratio
(c) Either (a) or (b) (d) No change in ratio

6. **At the time of change in profit sharing ratio, gaining partner is .... and sacrificing partner is .... for the adjustment of goodwill.**

(a) debited, credited (b) credited, debited
(c) debited, debited (d) credited, credited

7. **Which of the following is not a part of change in profit sharing ratio?**

(a) Dissolution of partnership firm
(b) Accounting for goodwill
(c) Determination of sacrificing and gaining ratio
(d) Accounting of reserves, accumulated profits and losses

8. **If the existing profit sharing ratio among X, Y and Z of 3 : 2 : 1 is changed to 1 : 2 : 3, then the partner(s) whose share will be unaffected is/are** Competency Based Que

(a) X (b) Y
(c) Z (d) None of these

9. **If the existing profit sharing ratio among X, Y and Z of 5 : 4 : 1 is changed to 1 : 4 : 5, then the partner(s) whose share will be affected is/are ....**

(a) X, Y (b) Y, Z
(c) X, Z (d) None of these

10. **Ratio in which partners acquire additional share of profit from other partner or partners is**

(a) sacrificing ratio (b) gaining ratio
(c) new ratio (d) old ratio

11. **In which of the following circumstances, there is a need to change the profit sharing ratio?**

(a) When a new partner is admitted
(b) When a partner retires (c) When a partner dies
(d) All of the above

12. **If profit sharing ratio changes, sacrificing ratio is determined so that .... partner can compensate share of goodwill to the .... partner.**

(a) gaining, sacrificing (b) sacrificing, gaining
(c) old, new (d) None of these

13. **If the partners of a firm decide to change their profit sharing ratio, the gaining partner compensates the sacrificing partner by paying the proportionate amount of ....**

(a) capital (b) goodwill
(c) Both (a) and (b) (d) None of these

14. **Anisha, Deepa and Charu were partners sharing profits and losses in the ratio of 5 : 3 : 2. On 31st March, 2024, they decided to change their profit sharing ratio to 2 : 3 : 5. Each partner's gain or sacrifice due to change in profit sharing ratio will be** CBSE 2025; Competency Based Que

(a) Anisha's sacrifice $\frac{3}{10}$; Charu's gain $\frac{3}{10}$
(b) Anisha's gain $\frac{3}{10}$; Charu's sacrifice $\frac{3}{10}$
(c) Anisha's sacrifice $\frac{3}{10}$; Deepa's gain $\frac{3}{10}$
(d) Deepa's gain $\frac{3}{10}$; Charu's sacrifice $\frac{3}{10}$

15 **'A', 'B' and 'C' are partners sharing profits in the ratio of 2 : 2 : 1. At the time of reconstitution of firm, they agreed to write-off goodwill which is shown in balance sheet as an intangible assets amounting to ₹ 50,000. Journalise it.** Competency Based Que

(a) Goodwill A/c	Dr	50,000	
To A's Capital A/c			20,000
To B's Capital A/c			20,000
To C's Capital A/c			10,000

(b) A's Capital A/c Dr 20,000
B's Capital A/c Dr 20,000
To Goodwill A/c 40,000

(c) A's Capital A/c Dr 20,000
B's Capital A/c Dr 20,000
C's Capital A/c Dr 10,000
To Goodwill A/c 50,000

(d) A's Capital A/c Dr 10,000
B's Capital A/c Dr 20,000
To C's Capital A/c 30,000

16. **'A' and 'B' are partners in a firm. They share their profits and losses in the ratio of 3 : 2. They have decided that their new profits (losses) sharing ratio will be 1 : 1. At that time their goodwill is valued at ₹ 30,000.**

Calculate amount of goodwill which will be given by B to A.

(a) ₹ 2,500 (b) ₹ 2,400
(c) ₹ 2,800 (d) ₹ 3,000

17. **Workmen compensation reserve is a reserve created out of profits to meet the ....**

(a) capital reserve shortage
(b) general reserve shortage
(c) workmen compensation liability
(d) None of the above

18. **A, B and C were partners in a firm sharing profits in the ratio of 2 : 5 : 3. They decided to change the profit-sharing ratio to 2 : 1 : 1 w.e.f. 1st January, 2025. After the revaluation of assets and liabilities, revaluation account showed a loss of ₹ 1,80,000. The amount to be debited to C's capital account on account of loss on revaluation will be**

(a) ₹ 45,000 (b) ₹ 54,000
(c) ₹ 36,000 (d) ₹ 90,000

19. **Preet and Saral were partners sharing profits and losses in the ratio of 3 : 2. On 31st March, 2024 they decided to change their profit sharing ratio to 1 : 1. On the date of reconstitution goodwill of the firm was valued at ₹ 1,00,000.**

The journal entry for treatment of goodwill on account of change in profit sharing ratio will be

CBSE 2025; Competency Based Que

(a) Preet's Capital A/c Dr 1,00,000
To Saral's Capital A/c 1,00,000

(b) Saral's Capital A/c Dr 1,00,000
To Preet's Capital A/c 1,00,000

(c) Preet's Capital A/c Dr 10,000
To Saral's Capital A/c 10,000

(d) Saral's Capital A/c Dr 10,000
To Preet's Capital A/c 10,000

20. **The credit balance of profit and loss account appearing in the balance sheet of the firm is transferred to**

(a) partners' capital account
(b) partners' capital account in old ratio
(c) partners' capital ratio in new ratio
(d) None of the the above

21. **'A', 'B' and 'D' are partners in a firm sharing profits (losses) in the ratio of 3 : 2 : 1. They change their ratio into 2 : 1 : 2 for future profits. At that time their balance sheet shows the following balances.**

Investment fluctuation reserve = ₹ 6,000
Investment = ₹ 25,000
Now, the market value of investments is ₹ 22,000. Distribute investment fluctuation reserve among partners. **Competency Based Que**

(a) Investment Fluctuation Reserve A/c Dr 6,000
To A's Capital A/c 3,000
To B's Capital A/c 2,000
To D's Capital A/c 1,000

(b) Investment Fluctuation Reserve A/c Dr 6,000
To A's Capital A/c 6,000

(c) A's Capital A/c Dr 6,000
To B's Capital A/c 3,000
To D's Capital A/c 3,000

(d) Investment Fluctuation Reserve A/c Dr 6,000
To Investment A/c 3,000
To A's Capital A/c 1,500
To B's Capital A/c 1,000
To D's Capital A/c 500

22. **Arun, Babita and Charu are partners in a firm sharing profits in the ratio of 3 : 3 : 2. They decided to share future profits and losses in the ratio of 1 : 1 : 1 with effect from 1st April, 2021. They decided to record the effect of the following without affecting their book values.**

(i) Profit and loss account (Cr) ₹ 8,000.
(ii) General reserve ₹ 4,000.

The necessary adjusting entry for the same will be

CBSE Term I 2021; Competency Based Que

(a) Charu's Capital A/c Dr 1,000
To Arun's Capital A/c 500
To Babita's Capital A/c 500

(b) Arun's Capital A/c Dr 500
Babita's Capital A/c Dr 500
To Charu's Capital A/c 1,000

(c) Charu's Capital A/c Dr 1,000
To Babita's Capital A/c 1,000

(d) Charu's Capital A/c Dr 3,000
To Arun's Capital A/c 1,500
To Babita's Capital A/c 1,500

23. **Malika, Meera and Madhu were partners sharing profits in the ratio of 2 : 2 : 1. They decided to share future profits in the ratio of 7 : 5 : 3 with effect from 1st April, 2021. Their balance sheet as on that date showed a balance of ₹ 30,000 in advertisement suspense account.**

Amount, that will be debited/credited to the capital accounts of Malika, Meera and Madhu if they decide to carry forward the amount of advertisement suspense account. **CBSE Term I 2021; Competency Based Que**

(a) ₹ 12,000 (Dr); ₹ 12,000 (Dr) and ₹ 6,000 (Dr) respectively to the capital accounts of Malika, Meera and Madhu
(b) Debit ₹ 10,000 each to all partner's capital accounts
(c) Debit Meera's capital account and credit Malika's capital account by ₹ 2,000
(d) Debit Malika's capital account and credit Meera's capital account by ₹ 2,000 each

24. **If there is an unrecorded asset, it will be**

(a) debited to revaluation account
(b) credited to revaluation account
(c) credited to capital account
(d) debited to capital account

25. **Deepa, Elton and Frank were partners in a firm sharing profits in the ratio of 2 : 2 : 1. With effect from 1st April, 2023 they decided to change their profit sharing ratio as 1 : 2 : 2. There existed a debit balance of profit and loss account of ₹ 50,000 in the books of the firm on the date of change in profit sharing ratio. The partners decided to retain the debit balance of profit and loss account in the books. The adjustment entry will be** **CBSE 2024 C; Competency Based Que**

(a) Deepa's Capital A/c	Dr	10,000	
To Frank's Capital A/c			10,000
(b) Deepa's Capital A/c	Dr	5,000	
To Frank's Capital A/c			5,000
(c) Frank's Capital A/c	Dr	10,000	
To Deepa's Capital A/c			10,000
(d) Frank's Capital A/c	Dr	5,000	
To Deepa's Capital A/c			5,000

26. **Calculate net effect of revaluation when revised values are to be recorded in books.**

(i) Stock is to be valued at 10% less (Book value ₹ 3,00,000).
(ii) Provision for bad debts is no more required, (Shown in balance sheet for ₹ 4,000).
(iii) An outstanding salary which is unrecorded of ₹ 16,000.

(a) ₹ 40,000 profit
(b) ₹ 42,000 profit
(c) ₹ (42,000) loss
(d) None of the above

27. **Joey, Sam and Tex were partners sharing profits and losses in the ratio 5 : 3 : 2. With effect from 1st April, 2024, they decided to share future profits and losses in the ratio 2 : 1 : 1.**

For which of the following balances tax will be credited at the time of reconstitution of firm, if the firm decided to continue with available accumulated profits and losses balances. **CBSE SQP 2025; Competency Based Que**

(a) General Reserve ₹ 2,00,000 and Profit and Loss (Dr) ₹ 1,20,000
(b) General Reserve ₹ 2,00,000 and Profit and Loss (Cr) ₹ 2,50,000
(c) Deferred Revenue Expenditure ₹ 50,000 and Profit and Loss (Cr) ₹ 80,000
(d) Deferred Revenue Expenditure ₹ 50,000 and Profit and Loss (Dr) ₹ 80,000

28. **Som, Pam and Ron were partners in a firm sharing profits in the ratio of 7 : 2 : 1. With effect from 1st April, 2023 they decided to change their profit sharing ratio to 1 : 2 : 7. There existed a credit balance in the profit and loss account of ₹ 1,00,000 on the date of change in profit sharing ratio in the books of the firm.**

The partners decided to retain the credit balance in profit and loss account in the books. The adjustment entry will be **CBSE 2024 C; Competency Based Que**

(a) Ron's Capital A/c	Dr	20,000	
To Som's Capital A/c			20,000
(b) Ron's Capital A/c	Dr	60,000	
To Som's Capital A/c			60,000
(c) Som's Capital A/c	Dr	20,000	
To Ron's Capital A/c			20,000
(d) Som's Capital A/c	Dr	60,000	
To Ron's Capital A/c			60,000

29. **A, B and C are partners in a firm sharing profits in the ratio of 3 : 2 : 1. They decided to change their ratio to 2 : 1 : 1 with effect from 1st April, 2022. They also decide to take over the furniture of ₹ 30,000 at book value.**

This transaction will be recorded on the

(a) debit side of revaluation account
(b) credit side of partners' account
(c) credit side of revaluation account
(d) None of the above

Assertion-Reason

Direction (Q.No. 30 to 39) *Read the following Assertion (A) and Reason (R) and choose the correct alternative from the following*

Alternatives

(a) Both Assertion (A) and Reason (R) are true and Reason (R) is the correct explanation of Assertion (A)
(b) Both Assertion (A) and Reason (R) are true, but Reason (R) is not the correct explanation of Assertion (A)
(c) Assertion (A) is true, but Reason (R) is false
(d) Assertion (A) is false, but Reason (R) is true

30. **Assertion** (A) A change in the profit sharing ratio among existing partners is a form of reconstitution of a firm.

Reason (R) In this form of reconstitution, the same partners continue to conduct the business of the firm without any change in membership.

31. **Assertion** (A) A change in profit sharing ratio amounts to dissolution of partnership firm.

Reason (R) Existing agreement comes to an end and a new agreement comes into existence.

32. **Assertion** (A) Reconstitution of a partnership refers to a change in the existing agreement, involving mutual terms and conditions among partners.

Reason (R) Consequently, the previous agreement between the partners is terminated and a new agreement is formed.

33. **Assertion** (A) A change in the profit sharing ratio among existing partners can lead to gain for some partners and loss for others.

Reason (R) Partners may sometimes decide to alter their existing profit sharing ratio without any admission or retirement of a partner.

34. **Assertion** (A) It is important to compute sacrificing and gaining ratio at the time of change in profit sharing ratio.

Reason (R) Sacrificing partner compensates the gaining partner by paying him proportionate amount of goodwill.

35. **Assertion** (A) When there is a change in the profit sharing ratio, the gaining partner should compensate the sacrificing partner for goodwill based on the gaining ratio.

Reason (R) During the reconstitution of a partnership, reserves and accumulated profits are distributed among partners according to the old ratio.

36. **Assertion** (A) When reserves and accumulated profits/losses are adjusted through capital accounts, they appear in the balance sheet of new firm at the old figures.

Reason (R) If partner decide to record net effect of reserves, etc. a single adjusting entry involving the capital accounts of sacrificing and gaining partners is passed.

37. **Assertion** (A) At the time of a change in the profit sharing ratio among partners, adjustments for accumulated profits and reserves should be made to reflect the new sharing agreement.

Reason (R) Adjusting for accumulated profits and reserves ensures that each partner's capital account reflects their entitlement based on the updated profit sharing ratio.

38. **Assertion** (A) It is essential to determine the sacrificing and gaining ratios of partners when there is a change in the profit sharing ratio.

Reason (R) This determination ensures that the gaining partner compensates the sacrificing partner for the loss in their share of future profits.

39. **Assertion** (A) At the time of reconstitution of firm, assets are revalued and liabilities are reassessed.

Reason (R) The change in the value of assets and liabilities belongs to the period prior to reconstitution and any gain or loss on revaluation is shared in the old ratio by the partners.

Two Statement Based MCQs

Direction (Q.No. 40 to 47) *Read the following statements carefully and choose the correct alternative*

Alternatives

(a) Statement I is correct and Statement II is incorrect
(b) Statement II is correct and Statement I is incorrect
(c) Both the statements are correct
(d) Both the statements are incorrect

40. **Statement I** A change in the profit sharing ratio among partners implies a reconstitution of the firm.

Statement II Changing the profit sharing ratio requires the admission of a new partner.

41. **Statement I** A reconstitution of a partnership can occur without admitting, retiring or losing any partner.

Statement II In a change in profit sharing ratio, the total gain by one or more partners must equal the total sacrifice made by the other partner(s).

42. **Statement I** When the profit sharing ratio changes, it is necessary to revalue assets and reassess liabilities.

Statement II Adjusting accumulated profits or losses is not needed during a change in the profit sharing ratio.

43. **Statement I** Change in profit sharing among partners increases the combined shares of the partners.

Statement II Old profit share of a partner if deducted from his new profit share, is gained profit share.

44. **Statement I** When partners agree to adjust the profit sharing ratio, they need to determine the sacrificing and gaining ratio.

Statement II The adjustment of goodwill is not relevant when there is a change in the profit sharing ratio.

45. **Statement I** The gaining partner compensates the sacrificing partner by paying him a proportionate amount of goodwill at the time of a change in profit sharing ratio.

Statement II The sacrificing partner's share in profits is increased as a result of the change in the profit sharing ratio.

46. **Statement I** The sacrificing ratio is calculated by subtracting the new share from the old share of a partner.

Statement II The gaining ratio is calculated by adding the new share and the old share of a partner.

47. **Statement I** At the time of changing the profit sharing ratio, assets are revalued and liabilities are reassessed to reflect their actual values in the balance sheet.

Statement II Any gain or loss from the revaluation of assets and liabilities is shared among the partners in the new profit sharing ratio.

Matching

48. Match the following terms related to profit sharing adjustments with their descriptions

Column I (Terms)	Column II (Descriptions)
A. Reconstitution of partnership	(i) A partner's decrease in share due to a new ratio
B. Gain in profit sharing ratio	(ii) The redistribution of shares of profit
C. Scrifice in profit sharing ratio	(iii) A partner's increase in future share of profits
D. New profit sharing ratio	(iv) The agreed division of profits among partners now

Codes

	A	B	C	D		A	B	C	D
(a)	(ii)	(iii)	(i)	(iv)	(b)	(i)	(iv)	(iii)	(ii)
(c)	(ii)	(iv)	(iii)	(i)	(d)	(iii)	(ii)	(i)	(iv)

49. Match the following adjustments required at the time of change in profit sharing ratio with their descriptions

Column I (Adjustments)	Column II (Descriptions)
A. Sacrificing ratio	(i) Calculating decrease in partners' share of profits
B. Goodwill adjustment	(ii) Compensating partners for loss of profit share
C. Revaluation of assets	(iii) Adjusting the book values to current values
D. Reserves and accumulated profits	(iv) Distributing profits accumulated before change

Codes

	A	B	C	D		A	B	C	D
(a)	(i)	(ii)	(iii)	(iv)	(b)	(ii)	(i)	(iv)	(iii)
(c)	(i)	(iv)	(ii)	(iii)	(d)	(iii)	(i)	(iv)	(ii)

50. Match the following terms related to profit sharing ratio with their definitions

Column I (Terms)	Column II (Descriptions)
A. Sacrificing ratio	(i) Ratio of profit increase for gaining partners
B. Gaining ratio	(ii) The ratio in which partners give up their share
C. Gaining partner	(iii) Partner who has lost share in profit
D. Sacrificing partner	(iv) Partner whose share in profit has increased

Codes

	A	B	C	D		A	B	C	D
(a)	(ii)	(i)	(iv)	(iii)	(b)	(i)	(ii)	(iii)	(iv)
(c)	(ii)	(iii)	(i)	(iv)	(d)	(iv)	(i)	(ii)	(iii)

51 Match the following

Column I	Column II
A. Employees provident fund	(i) Accumulated loss
B. Advertisement expenditure	(ii) Statutory liability
C. Machinery replacement fund	(iii) Accumulated profit
D. General reserve	(iv) Accumulated depreciation

Codes

	A	B	C	D		A	B	C	D
(a)	(iii)	(ii)	(i)	(iv)	(b)	(iii)	(ii)	(iv)	(i)
(c)	(ii)	(i)	(iv)	(iii)	(d)	(i)	(ii)	(iv)	(iii)

52. Match the following

Column I	Column II
A. Unrecorded liability recorded	(i) Credit revaluation account
B. Increase in value of land	(ii) Debit revaluation account
C. Profit on revaluation	(iii) Credit partners' capital account
D. Loss on revaluation	(iv) Debit partners' capital account

Codes

	A	B	C	D		A	B	C	D
(a)	(i)	(ii)	(iii)	(iv)	(b)	(i)	(ii)	(iv)	(iii)
(c)	(ii)	(i)	(iii)	(iv)	(d)	(ii)	(i)	(iv)	(iii)

Case Based MCQs

Direction *Read the following case study and answer the questions 53 to 55 on the basis of the same*

Karan and Pragya are partners in a firm sharing profits in the ratio of 2 : 3. The balance sheet of the firm as on 31st March, 2020 is given below

Balance Sheet
as at 31st March, 2020

Liabilities		Amt (₹)	Assets	Amt (₹)
Creditors		6,20,000	Bills Receivable	3,60,000
Bills Payable		1,80,000	Stock	16,00,000
Capital A/cs			Machinery	18,40,000
Karan	16,00,000		Land and Building	10,00,000
Pragya	24,00,000	40,00,000		
		48,00,000		48,00,000

The partners decided to share profits in equal ratio with effect from 1st April, 2020. The following adjustments were agreed upon

(i) Land and building was valued at ₹ 16,00,000 and machinery at ₹ 16,40,000 and were to appear at revalued amounts in the balance sheet.

(ii) The goodwill of the firm was valued at ₹ 80,000, but it was not to appear in books.

53. What was the entry passed in revaluation account with respect to machinery?

(a) Debit machinery account ₹ 2,00,000; Credit revaluation account ₹ 2,00,000

(b) Debit revaluation account ₹ 2,00,000; Credit machinery account ₹ 2,00,000

(c) Debit machinery account ₹ 16,40,000; Credit revaluation account ₹ 16,40,000

(d) Debit revaluation account ₹ 16,40,000; Credit machinery account ₹ 16,40,000

54. What was the final profit/loss of revaluation account?

(a) Loss ₹ 8,00,000
(b) Profit ₹ 8,00,000
(c) Profit ₹ 4,00,000 (d) Loss ₹ 4,00,000

55. What was the gain/sacrifice of share for Karan?

(a) Gain = 1/10 (b) Sacrifice = 1/10
(c) Sacrifice = 1/5 (d) Gain = 1/5

Direction *Read the following case study and answer the questions 56 to 58 on the basis of the same*

Anil and Sunil are partners in a firm sharing profits in the ratio of 3 : 2. They decided that *w.e.f.* 1st April, 2019, they will share the profits equally. The balance sheet of Anil and Sunil as at 31st March, 2019 is given below

Balance Sheet
as at 31st March, 2019

Liabilities		Amt (₹)	Assets	Amt (₹)
Creditors		48,000	Cash in Hand	32,000
Outstanding Expenses		12,000	Debtors	28,800
Capital A/cs			Stock	67,200
Anil	2,40,000		Furniture	49,600
Sunil	2,40,000	4,80,000	Machinery	3,62,400
		5,40,000		5,40,000

Goodwill of the firm is to be valued on the basis of two years' purchase of average net profit. The average net profit expected in future by the firm is ₹ 16,000 p.a.

56. What is the goodwill of the firm?

(a) ₹ 8,000 (b) ₹ 16,000 (c) ₹ 32,000 (d) ₹ 64,000

57. What was Anil's gain or sacrifice?

(a) Gain = 1/10 (b) Sacrifice = 1/10
(c) Sacrifice = 1/5 (d) Gain = 1/5

58. What was the treatment in Sunil's account for goodwill adjustment?

(a) Debit ₹ 6,400 (b) Credit ₹ 6,400
(c) Debit ₹ 3,200 (d) Credit ₹ 3,200

Direction *Read the following case study and answer the questions 59 to 61 on the basis of the same*

X, Y and Z are partners in a firm called Stellar Textiles, sharing profits in the ratio of 3 : 2 : 1. As their business continues to expand, they decide to purchase a new shop and increase their investment in the business. Partner Z contributes ₹ 2,00,000 but requests to have at least 25% of the total share of profits. After discussions, X and Z come to an agreement and all partners decide to share future profits in the new ratio of 8 : 7 : 5. At the time of this agreement, the firm's financial records show a general reserve of ₹ 60,000.

Additionally, the goodwill of the firm is valued at ₹ 30,000. The value of the land has appreciated by ₹ 20,000, while the value of the buildings is set to depreciate by ₹ 50,000.

59. The sacrificing (gaining) shares of the partners will be

(a) X = 2/30 (Sacrifice), Y = 1/30 (Sacrifice), Z = 3/30 (Gain)
(b) X = 6/60 (Gain), Y = 1/60 (Sacrifice), Z = 5/60 (Sacrifice)
(c) X = 6/60 (Sacrifice), Y = 1/60 (Gain), Z = 5/60 (Gain)
(d) X = 2/30 (Gain), Y = 1/30 (Gain), Z = 3/30 (Sacrifice)

60. They have decided not to distribute the general reserve. The share of the general reserve compensated to X will be

(a) ₹ 30,000 (b) ₹ 24,000 (c) ₹ 3,000 (d) ₹ 6,000

61. For the adjustment of goodwill, Y's share will be

(a) debited by ₹ 10,000 (b) debited by ₹ 500
(c) credited by ₹ 10,000 (d) credited by ₹ 500

Answers

1. (a) distributed
2. (a) to revise
3. (b) (iii), (ii), (iv), (i)
4. (c) old profit sharing ratio
5. (a) sacrificing ratio
6. (a) debited, credited
7. (a) Dissolution of partnership firm
8. (b) Y
9. (c) X, Z
10. (b) gaining ratio
11. (d) All of the above
12. (a) gaining, sacrificing
13. (b) goodwill
14. (a) Anisha $= \frac{5}{10} - \frac{2}{10} = \frac{3}{10}$ Sacrifice

    Deepu $= \frac{3}{10} - \frac{3}{10} =$ Nil; Charu $\frac{2}{10} - \frac{5}{10} = -\frac{3}{10}$ Gain
15. (c) When goodwill appears in the books of firm, it is written-off by debiting all partners capital accounts in their old profit ratio and crediting goodwill account. Share of partners will be computed as follows

    A's Share $= 50{,}000 \times \frac{2}{5} =$ ₹ 20,000

    B's Share $= 50{,}000 \times \frac{2}{5} =$ ₹ 20,000

    C's Share $= 50{,}000 \times \frac{1}{5} =$ ₹ 10,000
16. (d) Sacrifice/Gaining Ratio = Old Ratio – New Ratio

    A's Sacrificing Ratio $= \frac{3}{5} - \frac{1}{2} = \frac{6-5}{10} = \frac{1}{10}$ Sacrifice

    B's Sacrificing Ratio $= \frac{2}{5} - \frac{1}{2} = \frac{4-5}{10} = \left(\frac{1}{10}\right)$ Gain

    So, 'B' will give to 'A' $= 30{,}000 \times \frac{1}{10} =$ ₹ 3,000
17. (c) workmen compensation liability
18. (b) C's share in losses = 1,80,000 × 3/10 = ₹ 54,000
19. (d) Preet's Sacrifice $= \frac{3}{5} - \frac{1}{2} = \frac{6-5}{10} = \frac{1}{10}$ Sacrifice

    Saral's Gain $= \frac{2}{5} - \frac{1}{2} = \frac{4-5}{10} = (-)\frac{1}{10}$ Gain

    Saral will compensate ₹ 10,000 $\left(1{,}00{,}000 \times \frac{1}{10}\right)$ to Preet
20. (b) partners' capital account in old ratio
21. (d) Investment fluctuation reserve is created as a safeguard against loss due to fluctuation in market price of investments.

    In the given example, ₹ 3,000 (25,000 – 22,000) will be used to cover loss due to fall in the price of investments and the balance ₹ 3,000 will be distributed among partners in their old ratio.
22. (a) Sacrificing/Gaining Ratio

    Arun $= \frac{3}{8} - \frac{1}{3} = \frac{1}{24}$; Babita $= \frac{3}{8} - \frac{1}{3} = \frac{1}{24}$

    Charu $= \frac{2}{8} - \frac{1}{3} = \left(\frac{2}{24}\right)$

    Amount to be compensated by Charu

    $= (8{,}000 + 4{,}000) \times \frac{2}{24} =$ ₹ 1,000
23. (d) Gaining Ratio

    Malika $= \frac{7}{15} - \frac{2}{5} = \frac{1}{15}$; Meera $= \frac{5}{15} - \frac{2}{5} = \left(\frac{1}{15}\right)$

    Madhu $= \frac{3}{15} - \frac{1}{5} =$ Nil

    Amount to be compensated by Malika

    $= 30{,}000 \times \frac{1}{15} =$ ₹ 2,000
24. (b) credited to revaluation account
25. (a) Deepak's Capital A/c Dr 10,000

    To Frank's Capital A/c 10,000
26. (c) To ascertain the effect of revaluation, we will prepare revaluation account in the following manner

Dr **Revaluation Account** Cr

Particulars	Amt (₹)	Particulars	Amt (₹)
To Stock	30,000	By Prov. for Bad Debts	4,000
To Outstanding Salary	16,000	By Loss on Revaluation to be Transferred to Partners' Capital A/c	42,000
	46,000		46,000

27. (d) Deferred Revenue Expenditure ₹ 50,000 and Profit and Loss (Dr) ₹ 80,000
28. (b) Ron's Capital A/c Dr 60,000

    To Som's Capital A/c 60,000
29. (d) Asset taken over by partners will be recorded on the debit side of partners' capital account.
30. (b) Both Assertion (A) and Reason (R) are true, but Reason (R) is not the correct explanation of Assertion (A)

31. (c) A change in profit sharing ratio amounts to dissolution of partnership only, not partnership firm.
32. (b) Both Assertion (A) and Reason (R) are true, but Reason (R) is not the correct explanation of Assertion (A)
33. (b) Both Assertion (A) and Reason (R) are true, but Reason (R) is not the correct explanation of Assertion (A)
34. (d) Gaining partner compensates the sacrificing partner by paying him proportionate amount of goodwill.
35. (b) Both Assertion (A) and Reason (R) are true, but Reason (R) is not the correct explanation of Assertion (A)
36. (a) Both Assertion (A) and Reason (R) are true and Reason (R) is the correct explanation of Assertion (A)
37. (a) Both Assertion (A) and Reason (R) are true and Reason (R) is the correct explanation of Assertion (A)
38. (a) Both Assertion (A) and Reason (R) are true and Reason (R) is the correct explanation of Assertion (A)
39. (a) Both Assertion (A) and Reason (R) are true and Reason (R) is the correct explanation of Assertion (A)
40. (a) Statement I is correct and Statement II is incorrect
41. (c) Both the statements are correct
42. (a) Statement I is correct and Statement II is incorrect
43. (b) Statement II is correct and Statement I is incorrect
44. (a) Statement I is correct and Statement II is incorrect
45. (a) Statement I is correct and Statement II is incorrect
46. (a) Statement I is correct and Statement II is incorrect
47. (a) Statement I is correct and Statement II is incorrect
48. (a) (ii) (iii) (i) (iv)
49. (a) (i) (ii) (iii) (iv)
50. (a) (ii) (i) (iv) (iii)
51. (c) (ii) (i) (iv) (iii)
52. (c) (ii) (i) (iii) (iv)
53. (b)

Revaluation A/c	Dr	2,00,000	
To Machinery A/c			2,00,000
(Being value of machinery depreciated)			

54. (c) Profit on Land and Building = 16,00,000 – 10,00,000 = ₹ 6,00,000

(–) Loss on Machinery = 18,40,000 – 16,40,000 = ₹ 2,00,000

Profit (Balance) = 6,00,000 – 2,00,000 = ₹ 4,00,000

55. (a) Sacrificing Ratio = Old Share – New Share

$$\text{Karan} = \frac{2}{5} - \frac{1}{2} = \frac{4-5}{10} = \left(\frac{1}{10}\right)\text{Gain}$$

$$\text{Pragya} = \frac{3}{5} - \frac{1}{2} = \frac{6-5}{10} = \frac{1}{10}\text{ Sacrifice}$$

56. (c) Average Profit = ₹ 16,000

Goodwill = 16,000 × 2 = ₹ 32,000

57. (b) **Calculation of Sacrificing and Gaining Ratio**

$$\text{Anil} = \frac{3}{5} - \frac{1}{2} = \frac{6-5}{10} = \frac{1}{10}\text{ Sacrifice}$$

$$\text{Sunil} = \frac{2}{5} - \frac{1}{2} = \frac{4-5}{10} = \left(\frac{1}{10}\right)\text{Gain}$$

58. (c) Sunil's Sacrifice/Gain = Old Share – New Share

$$= \frac{2}{5} - \frac{1}{2} = \left(\frac{1}{10}\right)$$

i.e. gain so his account will be debited for goodwill adjustment

Amount of Goodwill Adjustment = Gaining Share × Value of Firm's Goodwill

$$= \frac{1}{10} \times 32,000 = ₹\ 3,200$$

59. (c) **Calculating the Sacrificing and Gaining Shares**

X's Sacrifice = Old Share – New Share

= 3/6 – 8/20 = (30 – 24)/60 = 6/60 Sacrifice

Y's Sacrifice = 2/6 – 7/20 = (20 – 21)/60 = (1/60) Gain

Z's Gain = 1/6 – 5/20 = (10 – 15)/60 = (5/60) Gain

60. (d) The share of the general reserve compensated to X = 60,000 × 6/60 = ₹ 6,000
61. (b) Y's Share = 30,000 × 1/60 = ₹ 500

04

CHAPTER

Admission of a partner takes place when a new partner joins an existing firm, contributing capital and/or goodwill. This requires the consent of all existing partners as per the partnership agreement.

YOUR STUDY GOALS

YOUR PRACTICE GOAL

- Topicwise Solved Questions (39 Solved Questions)
- Numerical Questions [47 Questions (Unsolved)]
- Theoretical Questions (7 Questions (with answers)]
- Objective Questions (71 Qs ; MCQs, A-R, Statements, Matching, Case)

Reconstitution of a Partnership Firm : Admission of a Partner

4.1 Meaning of Admission of a Partner

Admission of a partner is one of the modes of reconstituting the firm under which old partnership comes to an end and a new one between all partners (including incoming partner) comes into existence.

According to **Section 31(1)** of **Indian Partnership Act, 1932**, "A person can be admitted as a new partner only with the consent of all the existing partners, unless otherwise agreed upon."

So, even a minor can be admitted as a partner to share profits with the consent of all the partners (Section 30).

Purpose of Admitting a New Partner

- For procuring additional capital for expansion of business.
- For acquiring additional managerial skills.
- To increase goodwill of the business by admitting a reputed person.
- To get benefit from the efficiency of an experienced person.

Rights Acquired by a New Partner

A new partner acquires two main rights in the firm

1. **Right to Share Future Profits** For this, the new partner contributes a premium for goodwill.
2. **Right to Share in the Assets** The new partner provides capital, either in cash or kind, for this right.

The new partner is also liable for the firm's liabilities and losses. However, he is personally liable only for those liabilities which are incurred after his admission.

Effects of Admission of a New Partner

When a new partner joins

- The old partnership ends, a new one is formed and the firm continues.
- Existing partners' shares reduce as the new partner gains a share in future profits.
- The new partner contributes capital and becomes liable for the firm's debts while gaining rights to its assets.
- Adjustments are made for accumulated profits and losses.
- Assets are revalued and liabilities reassessed and the net change is adjusted in old partners' capital accounts.
- The firm's goodwill is valued and paid to sacrificing partners by the gaining partners through capital accounts.

Adjustments Required

At the Time of Admission of a New Partner

- Computation of new profit sharing and sacrificing ratio.
- Adjustment for goodwill.
- Adjustment for accumulated profits, reserves and losses.
- Adjustment for profit/loss from revaluation of assets and liabilities.
- Adjustment of capital (if agreed).

4.2 New Profit Sharing Ratio and Sacrificing Ratio

- The ratio in which all the partners (including incoming partner) share the future profits and losses of the firm is known as the new profit sharing ratio.

$$\text{New Profit Sharing Ratio} = \text{Old Share} - \text{Sacrificing Share}$$

- The ratio in which old partners have agreed to sacrifice their share of profit in favour of the new partner is called sacrificing ratio.

$$\text{Sacrificing Ratio} = \text{Old Share} - \text{New Share}$$

Different Cases for Calculation of New Profit Sharing Ratio and Sacrificing Ratio

Case	Steps
New (incoming) **partner acquires his share from old** (existing) **partners in their old profit sharing ratio**	1. Calculate combined share of old partners by deducting new partner's share from 1. 2. Calculate old partners' new share as part of the combined share. 3. Convert the new shares of all the partners and find out the new profit sharing ratio. **In this case, the sacrificing ratio will be the same as the old ratio.*
New (incoming) **partner acquires his share from old partners in a particular ratio**	1. Deduct old partners' sacrifice from their share and calculate new share. 2. Add sacrifices made by old partners to find out new partner's share. 3. Convert the new shares of all partners into ratio and find out new profit sharing ratio. 4. Sacrifice made by old partners should be converted into sacrificing ratio.
New (incoming) **partner acquires his share by surrender of a particular fraction of shares by the old** (existing) **partners**	1. Calculate old partners' sacrifice as part of their shares. 2. Deduct sacrifices from old share and find out new share of old partners. 3. Add sacrifices of old partners to ascertain new partner's share. 4. Convert the new shares of all the partners into ratio and find out new profit sharing ratio. 5. Convert the sacrifice of old partners to determine their sacrificing ratio.
New partner gets his share in a specified ratio, which is different from the old ratio of the old partners	1. Calculate the sacrifice made by old partners by multiplying the given share with the ratio given. 2. *Steps* 2, 3 and 4 are the same as given in *case* 3.

Case	Steps
Entire sacrifice has been made by one of the partners	1. Find the new share of the sacrificing partner by deducting the share of the new partner from his share. 2. Convert the new shares of all the partners into ratio and find out the new profit sharing ratio. **There is no need to calculate the sacrificing ratio in this case, as the entire sacrifice is made by one partner only.*
Relative ratio between old partners changes in the new firm	1. Find out the remaining share left after giving new partner his share of profits. 2. Divide the remaining share in the ratio in which old partners decide to share future profits. 3. Find out the new profit sharing ratio. 4. Find out the sacrificing ratio by deducting new share from old share.
One of the existing partners retains his original share	1. Calculate combined share of old partners by deducting new partner's share and share of existing partner (who retains his old share) from 1. 2. Calculate old partner's (excluding the partner who retained his share) new share as part of the combined share. 3. Convert the new shares of all the partners and find out the new profit sharing ratio.
Calculation of sacrificing ratio, if new ratio is given	1. Calculate the sacrifice made by old partners by deducting new share from old share. 2. Convert the sacrifice made by old partners in a ratio to find the sacrificing ratio.
One partner is admitted, followed by the admission of another partner.	1. Calculate the new profit sharing ratio as per the given condition, after the admission of first partner. 2. Calculate the new profit sharing ratio, taking the ratio calculated in step 1 as old ratio, as per the given condition. 3. Sacrificing ratio will be computed as the difference between the share of partners as computed in *step 2* and *step 1*.

4.3 Treatment of Goodwill

When a new partner is admitted, he acquires his share of future profits from the existing partner's, who must be compensated.

This compensation, called goodwill, is based on the sacrifice made by each existing partner.

Compensation Amount = Value of Goodwill × Share Sacrificed

Various Cases Related to Accounting Treatment of Goodwill

***Case* 1 When premium for goodwill is paid privately by a new partner**

In case a new partner pays premium privately, it will not be recorded because it is an out of business (not related to business) transaction.

***Case* 2 When premium for goodwill is brought in by new partner in cash and retained in the business**

- **Write-off the existing goodwill (if any) appearing in the books**

Old Partners' Capital/Current A/cs (In old ratio)	Dr
To Goodwill A/c	

- **For bringing premium for goodwill and capital in cash by a new partner**

Cash/Bank A/c	Dr
To New Partner's Capital A/cs (With share of capital)	
To Premium for Goodwill A/c (With share of goodwill)	

- **For sharing of premium for goodwill by sacrificing partners**

Premium for Goodwill A/c (With share of goodwill) Dr
  To Sacrificing Partners' Capital/Current A/cs
  (In sacrificing ratio)

Case 3 **When premium for goodwill is brought in kind**

- **For assets brought in by the new partner**

Assets A/c (Individually) Dr
  To New Partner's Capital A/c (With amount of capital)
  To Premium for Goodwill A/c
  (With share of goodwill brought in)

- **For sharing of premium for goodwill by sacrificing partners**

Premium for Goodwill A/c Dr
  To Sacrificing Partners' Capital A/c (In sacrificing ratio)

Case 4 **When premium for goodwill is brought in by new partner and is withdrawn by old** (sacrificing) **partners fully or partly**

First three entries will be the same as discussed in *case 2.*

- **For withdrawal of premium money by sacrificing partners fully or partly**

Sacrificing Partners' Capital/Current A/cs Dr
  To Cash/Bank A/c (Amount withdrawn)

Case 5 **When a new partner brings only a part of premium for goodwill in cash**

First two entries will be the same as discussed in *case 2.*

- **For credit given to sacrificing partners by incoming partner's full share of goodwill**

Premium for Goodwill A/c Dr
  (With share of goodwill brought in)
Incoming Partner's Current A/c
  (With unpaid share of goodwill)
  To Sacrificing Partners' Capital/Current A/cs
  (In sacrificing ratio)

Case 6 **When new or incoming partner is not able to bring his share of premium for goodwill in cash**

New Partner's Current A/c (For his share of goodwill) Dr
  To Sacrificing Partners' Capital/Current A/cs
  (In sacrificing ratio)

Case 7 **When amount of goodwill is to be inferred on the basis of the partners' capitals** (hidden goodwill)

Hidden or inferred goodwill is the excess of desired total capital of the firm over the actual combined capital of all partners.

In case, the value of goodwill is not given at the time of admission of a new partner, it is to be inferred on the basis of net worth (capital) of firm.

Calculation of Hidden Goodwill

	Particulars	Amt (₹)
A.	Net worth (including goodwill) on the basis of capital brought in by incoming partner (Incoming Partner's Capital × Reciprocal of Share of Incoming Partner)	...
B.	(–) Net worth (excluding goodwill of the new firm including incoming partner's capital)	(...)
C.	Value of goodwill (A – B)	...

Net Worth = Total Assets – Total Outside Liabilities

or Net Worth = Total of adjusted capitals of all the partners

4.4 Adjustment for Reserves and Accumulated Profits/Losses

At a time of partner's admission, any reserves and accumulated profits or losses in the firm's books should be transferred to the old partners' capital or current accounts in their old profit sharing ratio.

New partners are not entitled to any share in these profits and have no obligation for past or accumulated losses.

Accounting Treatment of Reserves/Profits

Free Reserves to be Credited to Old Partners' Capital Accounts

- Reserve fund
- General reserve
- Capital reserve
- Retained earnings
- Undistributed profits
- Profit and loss account (Credit) balance
- Contingency reserve

Journal entry for transfer of reserves and accumulated profits

General Reserve A/c	Dr
Profit and Loss A/c	Dr
Capital Reserve A/c	Dr
Contingency Reserve A/c	Dr
To Old Partners' Capital/Current A/cs (Individually in old ratio)	

Reserves Transferred with Restrictions

- **Workmen Compensation Reserve**
  This reserve compensates workers for injuries sustained at work, as per the provisions of Workmen Compensation Act. At the time of partner's admission, it is reassessed. The new value may differ from the existing fund maintained by firm. Journal entries will be same as in case of change in profit sharing ratio.
- **Investment Fluctuation Reserve**
  This reserve, created out of profits, addresses fall in investments' market value. At the time of partner's admission, its treatment depends on the current market value of investments. Accounting treatment will be same as in case of change in profit sharing ratio among existing partners.

Items to be Debited to Old Partners' Capital Accounts

- Profit and loss account (Debit) balance
- Advertisement suspense account
- Preliminary expenses account
- Miscellaneous expenditure account
- Deferred revenue expenditure account

Journal entry to transfer

Old Partners' Capital/Current A/cs (In old ratio)	Dr
To Profit and Loss A/c	
To Deferred Revenue Expenditure A/c	

Reserves Not to be Distributed

Following reserves should never be distributed as they are neither profits nor free reserves

- Employees provident fund
- Taxation fund
- Employees savings fund
- Machinery replacement fund

4.5 Revaluation of Assets and Reassessment of Liabilities

- At the time of admission of a new partner, assets are revalued and liabilities are reassessed to ascertain the profit/loss and adjust it in the old partners' capital accounts in their old profit sharing ratio, as it belongs to the old partners.
- For this purpose, **revaluation account** of the firm is prepared. This is also known as **profit and loss adjustment account.**
- It is a nominal account in nature.
- When revaluation account is prepared, the assets and liabilities appear in the balance sheet of new firm at their revised figures.

Accounting Treatment

Journal entries to be passed on revaluation of assets and liabilities are summarised as follows

Transaction	Entry	
(i) For increase in the value of asset	Assets A/c (Individually) To Revaluation A/c	Dr
(ii) For reduction in the value of asset	Revaluation A/c To Assets A/c (Individually)	Dr
(iii) For appreciation in the amount of liability	Revaluation A/c To Liabilities A/c (Individually)	Dr
(iv) For reduction in the amount of liability	Liabilities A/c (Individually) To Revaluation A/c	Dr
(v) For an unrecorded asset	Unrecorded Assets A/c (Individually) To Revaluation A/c	Dr
(vi) For an unrecorded liability	Revaluation A/c To Unrecorded Liability A/c (Individually)	Dr
(vii) For profit on revaluation (i.e. if total of credit side exceeds the total of debit side)	Revaluation A/c To Old Partners' Capital/Current A/cs (Old profit sharing ratio)	Dr
(viii) For loss on revaluation (i.e. if total of debit side exceeds the total of credit side)	Old Partners' Capital/Current A/cs (Old profit sharing ratio) (Individually) To Revaluation A/c	Dr

Format of Revaluation Account

Dr **Revaluation Account** Cr

Particulars	Amt (₹)	Particulars	Amt (₹)
To Decrease in Value of Assets	...	By Increase in Value of Assets	...
To Increase in Value of Liabilities	...	By Decrease in Value of Liabilities	...
To Unrecorded Liabilities	...	By Unrecorded Assets	...
*To Profit Transferred to Old Partners' Capital/Current A/cs (In old ratio)	...	*By Loss Transferred to Old Partners' Capital/Current A/cs (In old ratio)	...
	...		...

* *Either profit or loss will appear.*

4.6 Adjustment of Capital

When a new partner joins, the partners may agree to adjust their capitals to align with their profit sharing ratio. This can be done in several ways

- Adjusting the capitals of existing partners based on the incoming partner's capital.
- Determining the new partner's capital on the basis of firm's total capital.
- Adjusting the old partners' capitals in accordance with the new profit sharing ratio.
- When the total capital of the new firm is specified.
- When all partners' capitals (including the new partner) are to be adjusted.
- When only the old partners' capitals are to be adjusted.

Smart Study Chart No. 1

Adjustment of Capital

Adjusting the Capitals of Old Partners on the Basis of Incoming Partner's Capital

Step 1 Calculate the new profit sharing ratio.

Step 2 Calculate total capital of new firm as under

Total Capital = New Partner's Capital × Reciprocal of Proportion of Share of New Partner

Step 3 Calculate new capitals of old partners by dividing total capital in their new ratio.

Step 4 Calculate adjusted old capitals of old partners by preparing their capital accounts.

Step 5 Calculate the surplus/deficiency in each of the old partner's capital account by comparing the new capital with adjusted old capital (i.e. New Capital – Adjusted Old Capital).

Step 6 Adjust the surplus by paying-off or by transfer to the credit of partner's current account and adjust the deficiency by bringing in the required amount by partner or by transfer to debit of his current account.

JOURNAL

In case the adjusted old capital is less than the new capital	Cash A/c or Concerned Partner's Current A/c Dr To Concerned Partner's Capital A/c
In case the adjusted old capital is more than the new capital	Concerned Partner's Capital A/c Dr To Cash A/c or Concerned Partner's Current A/c

**In the absence of any information, surplus or deficiency should be adjusted in cash and not by transfer to current account.*

Determining the New Partner's Capital on the Basis of Total Capital of the Firm

Step 1 Calculate the new profit sharing ratio.

Step 2 Calculate the adjusted old capitals of old partners (after all adjustments have been made, i.e. goodwill, reserves, profit/loss on revaluation, etc).

Step 3 Calculate the total capital of new firm as follows

Total Capital = Combined Adjusted Old Capitals of Old Partners × Reciprocal of Proportion of Share of Old Partners

Step 4 Calculate the proportionate capital of new partner as follows

New Partner's Capital = Total Capital × Proportion of Share of New Partner

**Students should read the question carefully whether new partner's capital is to be computed on the basis of total capital (as discussed above) or on the basis of adjusted combined capitals of old partners.*

In case of latter, new partner's share will be computed with the help of the following formula

New Partner's Capital = Combined Adjusted Capitals of Old Partners × Share of New Partner

Mind Map

Reconstitution of a Partnership Firm : Admission of a Partner

1 Admission of a Partner

A person can be admitted as a new partner only with the consent of all the existing partners, unless otherwise agreed upon.

Purpose of Admitting a New Partner

- For procuring additional capital for expansion of business.
- For acquring additional managerial skills.
- To increase goodwill of the business by admitting a reputed person.
- To get benefit from the efficiency of an experienced person.

Adjustments Required

- Calculation of new profit sharing ratio and sacrificing ratio.
- Adjustment of goodwill.
- Adjustment for reserves, accumulated profits and losses.
- Revaluation of assets and reassessment of liabilities.
- Adjustment of capital.

2 New Profit Sharing Ratio and Sacrificing Ratio

- New Profit Sharing Ratio = Old Share – Sacrificing Share
- Sacrificing Ratio = Old Share – New Share

3 Accounting Treatment of Goodwill

- When premium for goodwill is paid by new partner privately, it will not be recorded.
- When premium for goodwill is brought in by new partner and retained in business
  - Write-off existing goodwill (if any) among old partners in old ratio.
  - Premium for goodwill is credited to sacrificing partners in sacrificing ratio.
- When premium for goodwill is brought in by new partner and is withdrawn by sacrificing (old) partners fully or partly, then entry for amount withdrawal will be made.
- When new partner is not able to bring premium for goodwill, then it is adjusted through his current account.

4 Adjustment for Reserves, Accumulated Profits and Losses

- **When Reserves and Accumulated Profits/Losses are to be transferred to Capital Accounts**
  - It means partners want to distribute the same or do not want to carry the balances in new balance sheet.
  - In such a case, reserves and profits are credited to existing partners' capital/current account in their old ratio and losses are debited to their capital/current account in old ratio.
- **When Reserves and Accumulated Profits/Losses are not to be transferred to Capital Accounts**
  - It means partners do not want to distribute the same or want to carry the balances in new balance sheet. A single adjustment entry is passed for this adjustment.
  - In such a case, net effect, i.e. profits/reserves – losses, is calculated.
  - If net effect is 'profit', then gaining partner is debited and sacrificing partner is credited with their respective share.
  - If net effect is 'loss', then sacrificing partner is debited and gaining partner is credited with their respective share.

5 Revaluation of Assets and Reassessment of Liabilities

Following journal entries are passed

• Increase in Assets Value (Individually)	Dr
Decrease in Liabilities Value (Individually)	Dr
Unrecorded Assets A/c (Individually)	Dr
To Revaluation A/c	
• Revaluation A/c	Dr
To Decrease in Assets Value (Individually)	
To Increase in Liabilities Value (Individually)	
To Unrecorded Liabilities A/c (Individually)	
• Revaluation A/c (For profit)	Dr
To Old Partners' Capital/Current A/c	
• Old Partners' Capital/Current A/c	Dr
To Revaluation A/c (For loss)	

6 Adjustment of Capital

- **On the Basis of Capital of Incoming Partner**
  - Calculate Capital of New Firm = New Partner's Capital × Reciprocal of his Share
  - Calculate new capital of old partners by dividing total Capital in their new ratio.
  - Calculate adjusted old capitals of old partners.
  - Calculate surplus/deficiency by comparing adjusted capital of old partners with their new capital.
  - Adjust the surplus by paying-off and deficiency by bringing in the required amount by partner.
- **Determining New Partner's Capital on the Basis of Total Capital of the Firm**
  - Calculate adjusted old capitals of old partners.
  - Calculate New Capital of the Firm = Total Adjusted Capital of Old Partners × Reciprocal of Proportion of Share of Old Partners
- Calculate new partner's capital according to new capital of the firm.

  New Partner's Capital = Total Capital × Proportion of His Share

Topicwise Solved Questions

New Profit Sharing Ratio and Sacrificing Ratio

Solved Question 1 **A and B are partners in a firm sharing profit in the ratio of 4 : 1. On 1st April, 2024 they decided to admit C as a partner into the firm for 1/5th share in profit. Calculate their new profit sharing ratio.**

Sol. Let the profit be 1.

Remaining share $= 1 - \frac{1}{5} = \frac{4}{5}$

A's new share $= \frac{4}{5} \times \frac{4}{5} = \frac{16}{25}$

B's new share $= \frac{1}{5} \times \frac{4}{5} = \frac{4}{25}$

C's share $= \frac{1}{5} \times \frac{5}{5} = \frac{5}{25}$

New profit sharing ratio = 16 : 4 : 5

Solved Question 2 **A and B are equal partners. They admit X and Y with 1/5 and 1/6 share respectively. Determine the profit sharing ratio of all partners.**

Sol. Let total profit of the firm be 1

X's share $= \frac{1}{5}$; Y's share $= \frac{1}{6}$

Remaining share of A and B

$= 1 - \left(\frac{1}{5} + \frac{1}{6}\right) = \frac{30 - (6+5)}{30} = \frac{19}{30}$ to be shared equally by A and B

Hence, A's share $= \frac{19}{30} \times \frac{1}{2} = \frac{19}{60}$; B's share $= \frac{19}{30} \times \frac{1}{2} = \frac{19}{60}$

∴ New profit sharing ratio of A, B, X and Y

$= \frac{19}{60} : \frac{19}{60} : \frac{1}{5} : \frac{1}{6} = \frac{19:19:12:10}{60}$ *or* 19 : 19 : 12 : 10

Solved Question 3 **M and L are partners in a firm sharing profits in the ratio of 3 : 1. They admitted A into the business on 1st April, 2024 for 2/3rd share into the business, which he acquired 1/2nd from M and 1/6th from L. Calculate their new profit sharing ratio.**

Sol. M's new share $= \frac{3}{4} - \frac{1}{2} = \frac{1}{4} \times \frac{3}{3} = \frac{3}{12}$

L's new share $= \frac{1}{4} - \frac{1}{6} = \frac{1}{12}$;

A's share $= \frac{2}{3} \times \frac{4}{4} = \frac{8}{12}$

New profit sharing ratio = 3 : 1 : 8

Solved Question 4 **P and M are partners in a firm sharing profits in the ratio of 2 : 1. They decided to admit C into the partnership. For C's admission, P surrendered 1/3rd of his share and M surrendered 1/5th of his share. Calculate their new profit sharing ratio.**

Sol. P's sacrifice $= \frac{2}{3} \times \frac{1}{3} = \frac{2}{9}$

P's new share $= \frac{2}{3} - \frac{2}{9} = \frac{4}{9} \times \frac{5}{5} = \frac{20}{45}$

M's sacrifice $= \frac{1}{3} \times \frac{1}{5} = \frac{1}{15}$

M's new share $= \frac{1}{3} - \frac{1}{15} = \frac{4}{15} \times \frac{3}{3} = \frac{12}{45}$

C's new share $= \frac{2}{9} + \frac{1}{15} = \frac{7}{45}$

New profit sharing ratio = 20 : 12 : 7

Solved Question 5 **Sumit and Binit were partners in a firm sharing profits and losses in the ratio of 3 : 1. Ramit was admitted as a new partner for $\frac{1}{6}$th share in the profit. Ramit acquired $\frac{2}{5}$th of his share from Sumit. How much share did Ramit acquire from Binit?** **CBSE 2018**

Sol. Rani share $= \frac{1}{6}$

Share acquired from Sumit $= \frac{2}{5} \times \frac{1}{6} = \frac{2}{30}$

Share acquired from Binit = Ramit's Share − Share acquired from Sumit

$= \frac{1}{6} - \frac{2}{30} = \frac{5-2}{30} = \frac{3}{30}$

Solved Question 6 **C and B are partners sharing profits in the ratio of 2 : 1. They admitted I into partnership for 1/3rd share. I acquired his share from C and B in the ratio of 3 : 2. Calculate their new profit sharing ratio.**

Sol. C's sacrifice $= \frac{2}{3} \times \frac{3}{5} = \frac{6}{15}$

C's new share $= \frac{2}{3} - \frac{6}{15} = \frac{4}{15}$

B's sacrifice $= \frac{1}{3} \times \frac{2}{5} = \frac{2}{15}$; B's new share $= \frac{1}{3} - \frac{2}{15} = \frac{3}{15}$

I's share $= \frac{6}{15} + \frac{2}{15} = \frac{8}{15}$

New profit sharing ratio = 4 : 3 : 8

Solved Question 7 **P, Q and R are partners sharing profits in 2 : 2 : 1 ratio. They admitted S for $\frac{1}{8}$th share which he acquired entirely from P. Calculate new profit sharing ratio.** **NCERT**

Sol. P's new share $= \frac{2}{5} - \frac{1}{8} = \frac{16-5}{40} = \frac{11}{40}$

Q's share $= \frac{2}{5}$; R's share $= \frac{1}{5}$; S's share $= \frac{1}{8}$

New profit sharing ratio $= \frac{11}{40} : \frac{2}{5} : \frac{1}{5} : \frac{1}{8}$ *or* 11 : 16 : 8 : 5

Solved Question 8 **Rao and Swami are partners in a firm sharing profits and losses in 3 : 2 ratio. They admit Ravi as a new partner for 1/8th share in the profits. The new profit sharing ratio between Rao and Swami is 4 : 3. Calculate new profit sharing ratio and sacrificing ratio.** **NCERT**

Sol. Remaining share left after Ravi's admission $= 1 - \frac{1}{8} = \frac{7}{8}$

Rao's share in remaining profits $= \frac{7}{8} \times \frac{4}{7} = \frac{4}{8}$

Swami's share in remaining profits $= \frac{7}{8} \times \frac{3}{7} = \frac{3}{8}$

Ravi's share $= \frac{1}{8}$

$\therefore$ New profit sharing ratio = 4 : 3 : 1

Sacrifice made by Rao = Old Share – New Share

$= \frac{3}{5} - \frac{4}{8} = \frac{24-20}{40} = \frac{4}{40}$

Sacrifice made by Swami $= \frac{2}{5} - \frac{3}{8} = \frac{16-15}{40} = \frac{1}{40}$

$\therefore$ Sacrificing ratio = 4 : 1

Solved Question 9 **N, G and O are partners in a firm sharing profits in the ratio of 3 : 2 : 1. They decided to admit S into the firm for 1/5th share in profits. G will retain his original share. Find out their new profit-sharing ratio.**

Sol. Let the profit be 1.

Remaining share $= 1 - \frac{1}{5} - \frac{2}{6} = \frac{19}{30}$

N's new share $= \frac{3}{4} \times \frac{19}{30} = \frac{57}{120}$

G's share $= \frac{2}{6} \times \frac{20}{20} = \frac{40}{120}$

O's new share $= \frac{1}{4} \times \frac{19}{30} = \frac{19}{120}$

S's share $= \frac{1}{5} \times \frac{24}{24} = \frac{24}{20}$

New profit sharing ratio = 57 : 40 : 19 : 24

Solved Question 10 **Ramesh and Suresh are partners in a firm sharing profits in the ratio of 4 : 3. They admitted Mohan as a new partner. The profit sharing ratio of Ramesh, Suresh and Mohan will be 2 : 2 : 3. Calculate the gain or sacrifice of old partner.**

Sol. Sacrifice made by Ramesh $= \frac{4}{7} - \frac{2}{7} = \frac{2}{7}$

Sacrifice made by Suresh $= \frac{3}{7} - \frac{2}{7} = \frac{1}{7}$

Sacrificing ratio = 2 : 1

Solved Question 11 **On 1st April, 2020, S and C entered into partnership for sharing profits in the ratio of 4 : 3. They admitted T as a new partner on 1st April, 2023 for 1/5th share which she acquired equally from S and C. On 1st April, 2024, they admitted P as a new partner for 1/7th share in profits which he acquired from S and C in 7 : 3 ratio. Calculate**

(i) New profit sharing ratio of S, C and T for the year 2023-24.

(ii) New profit sharing ratio of S, C, T and P on P's admission.

Sol. (i) **Calculation of New Profit Sharing Ratio of S, C and T for the Year 2023-24**

T is admitted for $\frac{1}{5}$th share.

T acquired profit share from S $= \frac{1}{5} \times \frac{1}{2} = \frac{1}{10}$

T acquired profit share from C $= \frac{1}{5} \times \frac{1}{2} = \frac{1}{10}$

S's New Share = Old Share – Sacrificed Share

$= \frac{4}{7} - \frac{1}{10} = \frac{40-7}{70} = \frac{33}{70}$

C's New Share = Old Share – Sacrificed Share

$= \frac{3}{7} - \frac{1}{10} = \frac{30-7}{70} = \frac{23}{70}$

New profit sharing ratio will be

$= \frac{33}{70} : \frac{23}{70} : \frac{1}{5} = \frac{33:23:14}{70}$ *or* 33 : 23 : 14

(ii) **Calculation of New Profit Sharing Ratio of S, C, T and P**

Old ratio = 33 : 23 : 14

P is admitted for 1/7th share, which he acquired from S and C in 7 : 3 ratio.

P acquired share from S $= \frac{1}{7} \times \frac{7}{10} = \frac{7}{70}$

P acquired share from C $= \frac{1}{7} \times \frac{3}{10} = \frac{3}{70}$

S's new share $= \frac{33}{70} - \frac{7}{70} = \frac{26}{70}$

$$\text{C's new share} = \frac{23}{70} - \frac{3}{70} = \frac{20}{70}$$

$$\text{New ratio} = \frac{26}{70} : \frac{20}{70} : \frac{14}{70} : \frac{1}{7} = \frac{26}{70} : \frac{20}{70} : \frac{14}{70} : \frac{10}{70}$$

or 13 : 10 : 7 : 5

Treatment of Goodwill

Solved Question 12 **S and M are partners in a firm sharing profits equally. On 1st April, 2023 they decided to admit C into the firm for 1/5th share in profits. C brings ₹ 25,000 as his capital and ₹ 4,500 as his share of goodwill. Pass necessary journal entries.**

Sol. **JOURNAL**

Date	Particulars	LF	Amt (Dr)	Amt (Cr)
	Cash A/c Dr		29,500	
	To C's Capital A/c			25,000
	To Premium for Goodwill A/c			4,500
	(Being C brings his share of capital and goodwill in cash)			
	Premium for Goodwill A/c Dr		4,500	
	To S's Capital A/c			2,250
	To M's Capital A/c			2,250
	(Being premium for goodwill distributed between sacrificing partners)			

Working Note

Sacrificing ratio = 1 : 1

Solved Question 13 **Arti and Bharti are partners in a firm sharing profits in 3 : 2 ratio. They admitted Sarthi as a new partner and the new profit sharing ratio will be 2 : 1 : 1. Sarthi brought in ₹ 10,000 for her share of goodwill and ₹ 1,00,000 as capital. Goodwill already appeared in the books of Arti and Bharti at ₹ 5,000.**

Pass necessary journal entries in the books of the new firm for the above transactions.

Sol. **JOURNAL**

Date	Particulars	LF	Amt (Dr)	Amt (Cr)
	Arti's Capital A/c Dr (5,000 × 3/5)		3,000	
	Bharti's Capital A/c Dr (5,000 × 2/5)		2,000	
	To Goodwill A/c			5,000
	(Being the existing goodwill written-off in old ratio)			
	Bank A/c Dr		1,10,000	
	To Prem. for Goodwill A/c			10,000
	To Sarthi's Capital A/c			1,00,000
	(Being Sarthi's share of capital and goodwill brought in cash)			

Date	Particulars	LF	Amt (Dr)	Amt (Cr)
	Premium for Goodwill A/c Dr		10,000	
	To Arti's Capital A/c (10,000 × 2/5)			4,000
	To Bharti's Capital A/c (10,000 × 3/5)			6,000
	(Being the premium for goodwill shared by the old partners on the basis of their sacrifice, i.e. 2 : 3)			

Working Note

Old ratio = 3 : 2; New ratio = 2 : 1 : 1

Sacrificing Ratio = Old Share − New Share

$$\text{Arti} = \frac{3}{5} - \frac{2}{4} = \frac{12-10}{20} = \frac{2}{20}$$

$$\text{Bharti} = \frac{2}{5} - \frac{1}{4} = \frac{8-5}{20} = \frac{3}{20}$$

Sacrificing ratio = 2 : 3

Solved Question 14 **M, N and O were partners in a firm sharing profits and losses in the ratio of 5 : 3 : 2. On 1st April, 2024, they admitted S as a new partner in the firm for 1/5th share in the profits. On S's admission the goodwill of the firm was valued at 3 years purchase of last five average profits. The profits during the last five years were**

Year Ended 31st March	2020	2021	2022	2023	2024
Profit (₹)	4,00,000	3,00,000	2,00,000	50,000	(50,000)

Calculate the value of the goodwill of the firm. Pass necessary journal entry for the treatment of goodwill on S's admission.

CBSE 2019 (M)

Sol. Average Profit

$$= \frac{4,00,000 + 3,00,000 + 2,00,000 + 50,000 + (50,000)}{5}$$

= ₹ 1,80,000

Firm's Goodwill = Average Profit × Number of Years' Purchase

= 1,80,000 × 3 = ₹ 5,40,000

S's Share of Goodwill = 5,40,000 × 1/5 = ₹ 1,08,000

JOURNAL

Date	Particulars	LF	Amt (Dr)	Amt (Cr)
2024				
Apr 1	Cash A/c Dr		1,08,000	
	To Premium for Goodwill A/c			1,08,000
	(Being goodwill brought in by new partner)			
	Premium for Goodwill A/c Dr		1,08,000	
	To M's Capital A/c			54,000
	To N's Capital A/c			32,400
	To O's Capital A/c			21,600
	(Being premium for goodwill distributed among old partners in sacrificing ratio)			

Working Note

It is not clearly mentioned in the question that new partner S bring his share of goodwill in cash or not. So, it is assumed that goodwill premium is brought in cash.

Solved Question 15 **R and S are partners in a firm sharing profits in the ratio of 3 : 2. They admit T as a new partner. The new profit sharing ratio of R, S and T will be 5 : 5 : 3. T contributed the following assets towards his capital and for his share of goodwill.**

Stock ₹ 1,67,000, debtors ₹ 1,40,000 (less provision for doubtful debts of 5%), land ₹ 1,00,000, plant and machinery ₹ 1,80,000. On the date of admission of T, the goodwill of the firm was valued at ₹ 13,00,000.

Record the necessary journal entries in the books of the firm on T's admission.

Sol. JOURNAL

Date	Particulars	LF	Amt (Dr)	Amt (Cr)
	Stock A/c Dr		1,67,000	
	Debtors A/c Dr		1,40,000	
	Land A/c Dr		1,00,000	
	Plant and Machinery A/c Dr		1,80,000	
	To Prov. for Doubtful Debts A/c			7,000
	To Premium for Goodwill A/c (13,00,000 × 3/13)			3,00,000
	To T's Capital A/c (Balancing figure)			2,80,000
	(Being stock, debtors, land, plant and machinery contributed by T on his admission as his capital and his share of goodwill)			
	Premium for Goodwill A/c Dr		3,00,000	
	To R's Capital A/c (3,00,000 × 14/15)			2,80,000
	To S's Capital A/c (3,00,000 × 1/15)			20,000
	(Being the share of T in goodwill credited to sacrificing partners in their sacrificing ratio)			

Working Note

Calculation of Sacrificing Ratio

Sacrificing Ratio = Old Share − New Share

$$R = \frac{3}{5} - \frac{5}{13} = \frac{39-25}{65} = \frac{14}{65}$$

$$S = \frac{2}{5} - \frac{5}{13} = \frac{26-25}{65} = \frac{1}{65}$$

$$\text{Sacrificing ratio} = \frac{14}{65} : \frac{1}{65} = 14 : 1$$

Solved Question 16 **G and A are partners sharing profits and losses in the ratio of 4 : 3. They admit S as a partner. He will bring ₹ 28,000 as his share of goodwill. S's share in the future profits or losses will be 1/4th. G and A decided to withdraw half the goodwill credited to their capital accounts. Pass necessary journal entries.**

Sol. JOURNAL

Date	Particulars	LF	Amt (Dr)	Amt (Cr)
	Cash A/c Dr		28,000	
	To Premium for Goodwill A/c			28,000
	(Being S brings his share of goodwill in cash)			
	Premium for Goodwill A/c Dr		28,000	
	To G's Capital A/c			16,000
	To A's Capital A/c			12,000
	(Being premium for goodwill distributed between sacrificing partners)			
	G's Capital A/c Dr		8,000	
	A's Capital A/c Dr		6,000	
	To Cash A/c			14,000
	(Being half share of goodwill withdrawn in cash)			

Working Note

Sacrificing ratio = 4 : 3

Solved Question 17 **Aditya and Balan are partners sharing profits and losses in 3 : 2 ratio. They admitted Christopher for 1/4th share in the profits. The new profit sharing ratio agreed was 2 : 1 : 1. Christopher brought ₹ 50,000 for his capital. His share of goodwill was agreed to at ₹ 15,000. Christopher could bring only ₹ 10,000 out of his share of goodwill. Record necessary journal entries in the books of the firm.** **NCERT**

Sol. JOURNAL

Date	Particulars	LF	Amt (Dr)	Amt (Cr)
	Cash A/c Dr		60,000	
	To Christopher's Capital A/c			50,000
	To Premium for Goodwill A/c			10,000
	(Being cash ₹ 50,000 as capital and ₹ 10,000 as premium paid by Christopher)			
	Premium for Goodwill A/c Dr		10,000	
	Christopher's Current A/c Dr (15,000 – 10,000)		5,000	
	To Aditya's Capital A/c			6,000
	To Balan's Capital A/c			9,000
	(Being premium ₹ 10,000 and remaining ₹ 5,000 unpaid adjusted from new partner's capital and distributed in sacrificing ratio)			

Note In case new partner does not give his full share of goodwill in cash, the balance will be adjusted from his current account.

Working Note

Old ratio = 3 : 2; New ratio = 2 : 1 : 1

Sacrificing Ratio = Old Share − New Share

$$\text{Aditya} = \frac{3}{5} - \frac{2}{4} = \frac{12-10}{20} = \frac{2}{20};\quad \text{Balan} = \frac{2}{5} - \frac{1}{4} = \frac{8-5}{20} = \frac{3}{20}$$

∴ Sacrificing ratio = 2 : 3

Solved Question 18 X and Y are partners in a firm sharing profits in the ratio of 5 : 3. On 1st March, 2024, they admitted Z as a new partner. The new profit sharing ratio will be 4 : 3 : 2. Z brought in ₹ 50,000 in cash as his share of capital but could not bring any amount for goodwill in cash. The firm's goodwill on Z's admission was valued at ₹ 90,000. X and Y decided that Z can bring his share of premium for goodwill later or it can be adjusted against his share of profits. At the time of Z's admission, goodwill existed in the books of the firm at ₹ 1,20,000.

You are required to pass necessary journal entries in the books of the firm on Z's admission.

Sol. JOURNAL

Date	Particulars	LF	Amt (Dr)	Amt (Cr)
2024				
Mar 1	X's Capital A/c Dr		75,000	
	Y's Capital A/c Dr		45,000	
	To Goodwill A/c			1,20,000
	(Being goodwill already existing in the books, now written-off in old ratio i.e. 5 : 3)			
Mar 1	Bank A/c Dr		50,000	
	To Z's Capital A/c			50,000
	(Being amount brought in by Z as his capital)			
Mar 1	C's Current A/c Dr $\left(\frac{2}{9} \text{ of } 90{,}000\right)$		20,000	
	To X's Capital A/c			16,250
	To Y's Capital A/c			3,750
	(Being Z's share of goodwill credited to X and Y in their sacrificing ratio i.e. 13 : 3)			

Working Note

Calculation of Sacrificing Ratio

Sacrificing Ratio = Old Ratio − New Ratio

$$\text{X's sacrifice} = \frac{5}{8} - \frac{4}{9} = \frac{45-32}{72} = \frac{13}{72}$$

$$\text{Y's sacrifice} = \frac{3}{8} - \frac{3}{9} = \frac{27-24}{72} = \frac{3}{72}$$

Thus, sacrificing ratio between X and Y = 13 : 3

Solved Question 19 X and Y are partners sharing profits and losses in the ratio of 5 : 4. On 1st April, 2024, they admit Z as a new partner for 1/6th share in the profits of the firm and the new ratio agreed upon is 3 : 2 : 1.

Goodwill, at the time of Z's admission is to be valued on the basis of capitalisation of the average profits of the last three years. Profits for the last three years were

Year ended 31st March, 2022	₹ 39,000 (including an abnormal loss of ₹ 9,000).
Year ended 31st March, 2023	₹ 83,000 (including an abnormal gain of ₹ 8,000).
Year ended 31st March, 2024	₹ 72,000.

On 1st April, 2024, the firm had assets of ₹ 8,00,000. Its creditors amounted to ₹ 3,60,000. The firm had a reserve fund of ₹ 40,000 while partners' capital accounts showed a balance of ₹ 4,00,000. The normal rate of return expected from this class of business is 13%. Z brings in ₹ 2,00,000 for her capital but is unable to bring in cash for her share of goodwill.

You are required to

(i) Calculate Z's share of goodwill in the firm (Show your workings clearly).

(ii) Pass journal entries at the time of Z's admission.

Sol. (i) **Calculation of Z's Share of Goodwill in the Firm**

Calculation of Average Normal Profit

Year Ended	Profit	Amt (₹)
31st March, 2022	(39,000 + 9,000)	48,000
31st March, 2023	(83,000 − 8,000)	75,000
31st March, 2024		72,000
		1,95,000

$$\text{Average Profit} = \frac{1{,}95{,}000}{3} = ₹\ 65{,}000$$

Capitalised Value of Average Profits

$$= \frac{\text{Average Normal Profit}}{\text{Normal Rate of Return}} \times 100$$

$$= \frac{65{,}000}{13} \times 100 = ₹\ 5{,}00{,}000$$

Capital Employed (Net Assets) = Total Assets − Outside Liabilities

= 8,00,000 − 3,60,000

= ₹ 4,40,000

Goodwill = Capitalised Value of Average Profits − Net Assets

= 5,00,000 − 4,40,000

= ₹ 60,000

$$\text{Z's Share of Goodwill} = 60{,}000 \times \frac{1}{6} = ₹\ 10{,}000$$

(ii) JOURNAL

Date	Particulars	LF	Amt (Dr)	Amt (Cr)
2024				
Apr 1	Bank A/c Dr		2,00,000	
	To Z's Capital A/c			2,00,000
	(Being amount of capital brought in cash)			
Apr 1	Z's Current A/c Dr		10,000	
	To X's Capital A/c			3,333
	To Y's Capital A/c			6,667
	(Being Z's share of goodwill credited to sacrificing partners in their sacrificing ratio of 1 : 2)			

Working Note

Calculation of Sacrificing Ratio

X's sacrifice $= \frac{5}{9} - \frac{3}{6} = \frac{10-9}{18} = \frac{1}{18}$; Y's sacrifice $= \frac{4}{9} - \frac{2}{6} = \frac{8-6}{18} = \frac{2}{18}$

Sacrificing ratio $= \frac{1}{18} : \frac{2}{18}$ *or* 1 : 2

Solved Question 20 **D and E are partners in a firm sharing profits in the ratio of 3 : 2 respectively. The fixed capital of D is ₹ 2,40,000 and of E is ₹ 1,50,000. On 1st April, 2024 they admitted H as a new partner for 1/5th share in future profits. H brought ₹ 1,50,000 as his capital. Calculate value of goodwill of the firm and record necessary journal entries on H's admission.**

Sol. New Firm's Capital $= 1{,}50{,}000 \times \frac{5}{1} =$ ₹ 7,50,000

Total Capital of All the Partners = 2,40,000 + 1,50,000 + 1,50,000

= ₹ 5,40,000

Firm's goodwill = 7,50,000 − 5,40,000 = ₹ 2,10,000

H's Share of Goodwill $= 2{,}10{,}000 \times \frac{1}{5} =$ ₹ 42,000

JOURNAL

Date	Particulars	LF	Amt (Dr)	Amt (Cr)
	Cash A/c Dr		1,50,000	
	To H's Capital A/c			1,50,000
	(Being H brings his share of capital in cash)			
	H's current A/c Dr		42,000	
	To D's Current A/c			25,200
	To E's Current A/c			16,800
	(Being adjustment of goodwill)			

Solved Question 21 **X and Y are partners with fixed capitals of ₹ 40,000 and ₹ 30,000 respectively. They admit Z as a new partner with 1/5th share in the profits of the firm. Z brings ₹ 40,000 as his capital and sufficient cash for his share of goodwill. Profit and loss (Debit balance) on that date amounted to ₹ 60,000 and general reserve given in the balance sheet ₹ 20,000. Their current accounts (Credit balance) are ₹ 30,000 and ₹ 20,000. Calculate hidden goodwill.**

Sol. **Calculation of Z's Share of Goodwill** **Amt (₹)**

Net worth of new firm on the basis of capital brought in by Z $\left(40{,}000 \times \frac{5}{1}\right)$	2,00,000
(−) Net worth of new firm (40,000 + 30,000 − 60,000 + 20,000 + 30,000 + 20,000 + 40,000)	(1,20,000)
	80,000

Z's share in goodwill $= 80{,}000 \times \frac{1}{5} =$ ₹ 16,000

Note While calculating hidden goodwill, when capitals are fixed, capitals will remain same (if no capital is withdrawn or introduced).

Solved Question 22 **A and S are partners in a firm. They admit P as a new partner with 1/5th share in the profits of the firm.**

P brings ₹ 5,00,000 as his share of capital. The value of the total assets of the firm was ₹ 15,00,000 and outside liabilities were valued at ₹ 5,00,000 on that date. Give the necessary journal entry to record goodwill at the time of P's admission. Also show your workings.

Sol. **JOURNAL**

Date	Particulars	LF	Amt (Dr)	Amt (Cr)
	P's Capital A/c Dr		2,00,000	
	To A's Capital A/c			1,00,000
	To S's Capital A/c			1,00,000
	(Being adjustment entry passed for goodwill)			

Working Notes

1. **Calculation of P's Share of Goodwill** **Amt (₹)**

Net worth of new firm on the basis of capital brought in by P (5,00,000 ×5)	= 25,00,000
(−) Net worth (excluding goodwill) of new firm	= (15,00,000)
(Adjusted capitals of Old Partners + Incoming Partner's Capital) [(15,00,000 − 5,00,000) + 5,00,000]	
Value of goodwill	= 10,00,000

P's share of goodwill $= 10{,}00{,}000 \times \frac{1}{5}$

= ₹ 2,00,000

2. Sacrificing ratio will be equal to old profit sharing ratio.

Adjustment for Reserves and Accumulated Profits/Losses

Solved Question 23 **Leela and Meeta were partners in a firm sharing profits and losses in the ratio of 5 : 3. On 1st April, 2024, they admitted Om as a new partner. On the date of Om's admission, the balance sheet of Leela and Meeta showed a balance of ₹ 16,000 in general reserve and ₹ 24,000 (Cr) in profit and loss account.**

Record necessary journal entries for the treatment of these items on Om's admission. The new profit sharing ratio between Leela, Meeta and Om was 5 : 3 : 2. **NCERT**

Sol. **JOURNAL**

Date	Particulars	LF	Amt (Dr)	Amt (Cr)
	General Reserve A/c Dr		16,000	
	To Leela's Capital A/c (16,000 ×5/8)			10,000
	To Meeta's Capital A/c (16,000 ×3/8)			6,000
	(Being general reserve distributed among old partners in old profit sharing ratio)			

Date	Particulars	LF	Amt (Dr)	Amt (Cr)
	Profit and Loss A/c Dr		24,000	
	To Leela's Capital A/c (24,000 × 5/8)			15,000
	To Meeta's Capital A/c (24,000 × 3/8)			9,000
	(Being profit and loss account credit balance distributed among old partners in old profit sharing ratio)			

Solved Question 24 Amit and Viney are partners in a firm sharing profits and losses in 3 : 1 ratio. On 1st April, 2024, they admitted Ranjan as a partner. On Ranjan's admission, the profit and loss account of Amit and Viney showed a debit balance of ₹ 40,000, advertisement suspense account showed a balance of ₹ 4,000.

Record necessary journal entry for the treatment of the same.

Sol. **JOURNAL**

Date	Particulars	LF	Amt (Dr)	Amt (Cr)
	Amit's Capital A/c Dr		33,000	
	Viney's Capital A/c Dr		11,000	
	To Profit and Loss A/c			40,000
	To Advertisement Suspense A/c			4,000
	(Being debit balance of profit and loss account and advertisment suspense account transferred to capital accounts of old partners)			

Solved Question 25 D and I are partners sharing profits in the ratio of 3 : 2. They admitted P as a partner for 1/4th share. P paid ₹ 40,000 as his capital and ₹ 20,000 for premium in cash.

At the time of admission of P, workmen reserve amounting to ₹ 15,000 and debit balance of profit and loss account amounting to ₹ 12,000 appeared in the balance sheet.

Pass necessary journal entries to record the above transactions.

Sol. **JOURNAL**

Date	Particulars	LF	Amt (Dr)	Amt (Cr)
	Cash A/c Dr		60,000	
	To P's Capital A/c			40,000
	To Premium for Goodwill A/c			20,000
	(Being P brings his share of capital and goodwill in cash)			
	Premium for Goodwill A/c Dr		20,000	
	To D's Capital A/c			12,000
	To I's Capital A/c			8,000
	(Being premium for goodwill distributed between sacrificing partners)			
	Workmen Reserve A/c Dr		15,000	
	To D's Capital A/c			9,000
	To I's Capital A/c			6,000
	(Being workmen reserve distributed among old partners in their old profit sharing ratio)			
	D's Capital A/c Dr		7,200	
	I's Capital A/c Dr		4,800	
	To Profit and Loss A/c			12,000
	(Being debit balance of profit and loss account is transferred to capital accounts of old partners in their old profit sharing ratio)			

Solved Question 26 Sunny and Ujjwal were partners in a firm sharing profits and losses in the ratio of 3 : 2. On 1st April, 2024 Timmy was admitted as a new partner for 1/5th share in profits which he acquired equally from Sunny and Ujjwal. On the date of Timmy's admission the balance sheet of Sunny and Ujjwal showed investments at ₹ 5,00,000 and a balance of ₹ 2,00,000 in investment fluctuation reserve.

Pass necessary journal entries for treatment of investment fluctuation reserve on the date of Timmy's admission in each of the following cases

(i) Market value of investments was ₹ 5,00,000.

(ii) Market value of investments was ₹ 3,00,000.

(iii) Market value of investments was ₹ 2,00,000. **CBSE 2025**

Sol. **JOURNAL**

Date	Particulars	LF	Amt (Dr)	Amt (Cr)
2024 Apr 1				
(i)	Investment Fluctuation Reserve A/c Dr		2,00,000	
	To Sunny's Capital A/c			1,20,000
	To Ujjwal's Capital A/c			80,000
	(Being whole reserve distributed in old ratio as market value is equal to book value)			
(ii)	Investment Fluctuation Reserve A/c Dr		2,00,000	
	To Investment A/c			2,00,000
	(Being whole reserves credited to investment account on account of decrease in value of ₹ 2,00,000)			
(iii)	Investment Fluctuation Reserve A/c Dr		2,00,000	
	Revaluation A/c Dr		1,00,000	
	To Investment A/c			3,00,000
	(Being investment reduced by ₹ 3,00,000 and shortfall debited to revalution account)			
	Sunny's Capital A/c Dr		60,000	
	Ujjwal's Capital A/c Dr		40,000	
	To Revaluation A/c			1,00,000
	(Being loss transferred to partner's capital account in old ratio)			

Revaluation/Reassessment

Solved Question 27 **Krishna and Suresh were partners in a firm sharing profits in the ratio of 3 : 1. On 1st April, 2024 they admitted Rahul as a new partner for 1/5th share in profits of the firm. On the date of Rahul's admission the balance sheet of Krishna and Suresh showed a general reserve of ₹ 1,20,000 a debit balance of ₹ 60,000 in profit and loss account and workmen compensation fund of ₹ 1,50,000.**

The following was agreed upon on Rahul's admission

(i) Rahul will bring ₹ 1,50,000 as his capital and his share of goodwill premium in cash.

(ii) Goodwill of the firm be valued at ₹ 2,40,000.

(iii) There was a claim of workmen compensation for ₹ 1,70,000.

(iv) The partners decided to share future profits in the ratio of 3 : 1 : 1.

Pass the necessary journal entries for the above on Rahul's admission.

Sol.

JOURNAL

Date	Particulars		LF	Amt (Dr)	Amt (Cr)
	General Reserve A/c	Dr		1,20,000	
	To Krishna's Capital A/c (1,20,000 × 3/4)				90,000
	To Suresh's Capital A/c (1,20,000 × 1/4)				30,000
	(Being general reserve distributed between old partners in old ratio)				
	Krishna's Capital A/c (60,000 × 3/4)	Dr		45,000	
	Suresh's Capital A/c (60,000 × 1/4)	Dr		15,000	
	To Profit and Loss A/c				60,000
	(Being debit balance of profit and loss distributed between old partners in old ratio)				
	Workmen Compensation Fund A/c	Dr		1,50,000	
	Revaluation A/c	Dr		20,000	
	To Claim for Workmen Compensation Fund A/c				1,70,000
	(Being claim against workmen compensation fund adjusted)				
	Krishna's Capital A/c (20,000 × 3/4)	Dr		15,000	
	Suresh's Capital A/c (20,000 × 1/4)	Dr		5,000	
	To Revaluation A/c				20,000
	(Being loss on revaluation distributed among old partners in old ratio)				
	Cash A/c	Dr		1,98,000	
	To Rahul's Capital A/c				1,50,000
	To Premium for Goodwill A/c (2,40,000 × 1/5)				48,000
	(Being cash brought in by Rahul for capital and premium for goodwill)				
	Premium for Goodwill A/c	Dr		48,000	
	To Krishna's Capital A/c (48,000 × 3/4)				36,000
	To Suresh's Capital A/c (48,000 × 1/4)				12,000
	(Being the premium for goodwill adjusted through sacrificing partners capital account)				

Working Note

Calculation of Sacrificing Ratio

Sacrificing Ratio = Old Share – New Share

$$\text{Krishna} = \frac{3}{4} - \frac{3}{5} = \frac{15-12}{20} = \frac{3}{20}; \qquad \text{Suresh} = \frac{1}{4} - \frac{1}{5} = \frac{5-4}{20} = \frac{1}{20}$$

Sacrificing ratio = 3 : 1

Solved Question 28 **Anikesh and Bhavesh are partners in a firm sharing profits in the ratio of 7 : 3. Their balance sheet as on 31st March, 2023 was as follows**

Balance Sheet of Anikesh and Bhavesh
as at 31st March, 2023

Liabilities	Amt (₹)	Assets		Amt (₹)
Creditors	60,000	Cash		36,000
Outstanding Wages	9,000	Debtors	54,000	
General Reserve	15,000	(–) Provision for Doubtful Debts	(6,000)	48,000

Liabilities		Amt (₹)	Assets	Amt (₹)
Capital A/cs			Stock	60,000
Anikesh	1,20,000		Furniture	1,20,000
Bhavesh	1,80,000	3,00,000	Machinery	1,20,000
		3,84,000		3,84,000

On 1st April, 2023 Chahat was admitted for 1/4th share in the profits on the following terms

(i) Chahat will bring ₹ 90,000 as her capital and ₹ 30,000 as her share of goodwill premium.

(ii) Outstanding wages will be paid. **(iii) Stock will be reduced by 10%.**

(iv) A creditor of ₹ 6,300, not recorded in the books, was to be taken into account.

Pass necessary journal entries for the above transactions in the books of the firm. **CBSE 2024**

Sol. **In the Books of Anikesh and Bhavesh**

JOURNAL

Date	Particulars		LF	Amt (Dr)	Amt (Cr)
	General Reserve A/c	Dr		15,000	
	To Anikesh's Capital A/c				10,500
	To Bhavesh's Capital A/c				4,500
	(Being general reserve balance transferred to partners' capital account in old ratio)				
	Cash/Bank A/cs	Dr		1,20,000	
	To Chahat's Capital A/c				90,000
	To Premium for Goodwill A/c				30,000
	(Being amount brought in by Chahat as her capital and her share of goodwill)				
	Premium for Goodwill A/c	Dr		30,000	
	To Anikesh's Capital A/c				21,000
	To Bhavesh's Capital A/c				9,000
	(Being goodwill premium brought in by new partner shared by old partners in their sacrificing ratio)				
	Outstanding Wages A/c	Dr		9,000	
	To Cash/Bank A/cs				9,000
	(Being outstanding wages paid)				
	Revaluation A/c	Dr		12,300	
	To Stock A/c				6,000
	To Creditors A/c				6,300
	(Being decrease in the value of stock and increase in the value of creditors on revaluation recorded)				
	Anikesh's Capital A/c	Dr		8,610	
	Bhavesh's Capital A/c	Dr		3,690	
	To Revaluation A/c				12,300
	(Being loss on revaluation of assets and reassessment of liabilities transferred to partners' capital account in old ratio)				

Solved Question 29 **Chander and Damini were partners in a firm sharing profits and losses equally. On 31st March, 2024 their balance sheet was as follows**

Balance Sheet

as on 31st March, 2024

Liabilities		Amt (₹)	Assets	Amt (₹)
Sundry Creditors		1,04,000	Cash at Bank	30,000
Capitals A/cs			Bills Receivable	45,000
Chander	2,50,000		Debtors	75,000
Damini	2,16,000	4,66,000	Furniture	1,10,000
			Land and Building	3,10,000
		5,70,000		5,70,000

On 1st April, 2024, they admitted Elina as a new partner for 1/3rd share in the profits on the following conditions

(i) Elina will bring ₹ 3,00,000 as her capital and ₹ 50,000 as her share of goodwill premium, half of which will be withdrawn by Chander and Damini.

(ii) Debtors to the extent of ₹ 5,000 were unrecorded.

(iii) Furniture will be reduced by 10% and 5% provision for bad and doubtful debts will be created on bills receivables and debtors.

(iv) Value of land and building will be appreciated by 20%.

(v) There being a claim against the firm for damages, a liability to the extent of ₹ 8,000 will be created for the same.

Prepare revaluation account and partners' capital account. **CBSE 2018**

Sol. Dr **Revaluation Account** Cr

Particulars		Amt (₹)	Particulars	Amt (₹)
To Furniture A/c		11,000	By Debtors A/c	5,000
To Provision for Doubtful Debts A/c		6,250	By Land and Building A/c	62,000
To Claim for Damages A/c		8,000		
To Profit Transferred to Partner's Capital A/cs				
Chander	20,875			
Damini	20,875	41,750		
		67,000		67,000

Dr **Partners' Capital Account** Cr

Particulars	Chander (₹)	Damini (₹)	Elina (₹)	Particulars	Chander (₹)	Damini (₹)	Elina (₹)
To Bank A/c	12,500	12,500	—	By Balance b/d	2,50,000	2,16,000	—
To Balance c/d	2,83,375	2,49,375	3,00,000	By Bank A/c	—	—	3,00,000
				By Premium for Goodwill A/c	25,000	25,000	—
				By Revaluation A/c	20,875	20,875	—
	2,95,875	2,61,875	3,00,000		2,95,875	2,61,875	3,00,000

Working Notes

1. Provision for Doubtful Debts $= (45{,}000 + 75{,}000 + 5{,}000) \times \frac{5}{100} =$ ₹ 6,250

2. **JOURNAL**

Date	Particulars		LF	Amt (Dr)	Amt (Cr)
	Bank A/c	Dr		3,50,000	
	To Elina's Capital A/c				3,00,000
	To Premium for Goodwill A/c				50,000
	Premium for Goodwill A/c	Dr		50,000	
	To Chander's Capital A/c				25,000
	To Damini's Capital A/c				25,000
	Chander's Capital A/c	Dr		12,500	
	Damini's Capital A/c	Dr		12,500	
	To Bank A/c				25,000

Solved Question 30 **P and Q sharing profits in the ratio of 3 : 2 had the following balance sheet as at 31st March, 2018.**

Balance Sheet
as at 31st March, 2018

Liabilities		Amt (₹)	Assets		Amt (₹)
Creditors		1,50,000	Cash		50,000
General Reserve		1,20,000	Debtors	2,00,000	
Capital A/cs			(–) Provision for Doubtful Debts	(8,000)	1,92,000
P	5,40,000		Patents		1,48,000
Q	3,60,000	9,00,000	Investments		80,000
Current A/cs			Machinery		7,20,000
P	1,00,000		Goodwill		1,00,000
Q	20,000	1,20,000			
		12,90,000			12,90,000

On 1st April, 2018, they decided to admit R on the following terms

(i) A provision of 5% is to be created on debtors.
(ii) Accrued income of ₹ 15,000 does not appear in the books and ₹ 50,000 are outstanding for salaries.
(iii) The present market value of investments is ₹ 60,000. P takes over the investments at this value.
(iv) The new profit sharing ratio of partners will be 4 : 3 : 2.
(v) R will bring in ₹ 2,00,000 as his capital.
(vi) R is to pay in cash an amount equal to his share in the firm's goodwill valued at twice the average profit of the last three years which were ₹ 2,50,000, ₹ 2,60,000 and ₹ 3,00,000 respectively.
(vii) Half the amount of goodwill is withdrawn by the old partners.

Prepare revaluation account, partners' capital account, partners' current account and the opening balance sheet of the new firm.

Sol. Dr **Revaluation Account** Cr

Particulars	Amt (₹)	Particulars		Amt (₹)
To Provision for Doubtful Debts A/c	2,000	By Accrued Income A/c		15,000
To Outstanding Salaries A/c	50,000	By Loss Transferred to		
To Investments A/c	20,000	P's Current A/c	34,200	
		Q's Current A/c	22,800	57,000
	72,000			72,000

Dr **Partners' Capital Account** Cr

Particulars	P (₹)	Q (₹)	R (₹)	Particulars	P (₹)	Q (₹)	R (₹)
To Balance c/d	5,40,000	3,60,000	2,00,000	By Balance b/d	5,40,000	3,60,000	—
				By Cash A/c	—	—	2,00,000
	5,40,000	3,60,000	2,00,000		5,40,000	3,60,000	2,00,000

Dr **Partners' Current Account** Cr

Particulars	P (₹)	Q (₹)	Particulars	P (₹)	Q (₹)
To Investments A/c	60,000	—	By Balance b/d	1,00,000	20,000
To Revaluation A/c	34,200	22,800	By General Reserve A/c	72,000	48,000
To Goodwill A/c	60,000	40,000	By Premium for Goodwill A/c	84,000	36,000
To Cash A/c	42,000	18,000			
To Balance c/d	59,800	23,200			
	2,56,000	1,04,000		2,56,000	1,04,000

Opening Balance Sheet (Balance sheet of the reconstituted firm)
as at 1st April, 2018

Liabilities		Amt (₹)	Assets		Amt (₹)
Creditors		1,50,000	Cash		3,10,000
Outstanding Salaries		50,000	Debtors	2,00,000	
Capital A/cs			(–) Provision for Doubtful Debts	(10,000)	1,90,000
P	5,40,000		Accrued Income		15,000
Q	3,60,000		Patents		1,48,000
R	2,00,000	11,00,000	Machinery		7,20,000
Current A/cs					
P	59,800				
Q	23,200	83,000			
		13,83,000			13,83,000

Working Notes

1. As there are current account balances appearing in the balance sheet, it means that the capital accounts are fixed. Hence, all transactions relating to the capital accounts will be passed through the current accounts.
2. Goodwill appearing in the balance sheet is written-off by the old partners in their old profit sharing ratio.

3. Calculation of Goodwill

   $\text{Average Profit} = \frac{2,50,000 + 2,60,000 + 3,00,000}{3} = ₹\ 2,70,000$

   Goodwill = 2,70,000 × 2 = ₹ 5,40,000

   R brings in his share of goodwill in cash.

   Therefore, the amount of goodwill brought in by $R = 5,40,000 \times \frac{2}{9} = ₹\ 1,20,000$

4. Sacrificing ratio $P = \frac{3}{5} - \frac{4}{9} = \frac{27-20}{45} = \frac{7}{45}$; $Q = \frac{2}{5} - \frac{3}{9} = \frac{18-15}{45} = \frac{3}{45}$ *or* 7 : 3

Solved Question 31 **Rajinder and Vijay were partners in a firm sharing profits in the ratio 3 : 2. On 31st March, 2023 their balance sheet was as follows**

Liabilities		Amt (₹)	Assets		Amt (₹)
Capital A/cs			Fixed Assets (Tangible)		3,60,000
Rajinder	3,00,000		Goodwill		50,000
Vijay	1,50,000	4,50,000	Investments		40,000
Current A/cs			Stock		74,000
Rajinder	50,000		Debtors	1,00,000	
Vijay	10,000	60,000	(−) Provision for Doubtful Debts	(4,000)	96,000
Creditors		75,000	Bank		25,000
General Reserve		60,000			
		6,45,000			6,45,000

With an aim to expand business it is decided to admit Ranvijay as a partner on 1st April, 2023 on the following terms

(i) Provision for doubtful debts is to be increased to 6% of debtors.

(ii) An outstanding bill for repairs ₹ 50,000 to be accounted in the books.

(iii) An unaccounted interest accrued of ₹ 7,500 be provided for.

(iv) Investment were sold at book value.

(v) Half of stock was taken by Rajinder at ₹ 42,000 and remaining stock was also to be revalued at the same rate.

(vi) New profit sharing ratio of partners will be 5 : 3 : 2.

(vii) Ranvijay will bring ₹ 1,00,000 as capital and his share of goodwill which was valued at twice the average profit of the last three years ended 31st March, 2023, 2022 and 2021 were ₹ 1,50,000, ₹ 1,30,000 and ₹ 1,70,000 respectively.

Pass necessary journal entries. **CBSE 2024**

Sol. **In the Books of Rajinder, Vijay and Ranvijay**

JOURNAL

Date	Particulars		LF	Amt (Dr)	Amt (Cr)
(i)	Revaluation A/c	Dr		52,000	
	To Provision for Doubtful Debts A/c				2,000
	To Outstanding Bill for Repairs A/c				50,000
	(Being increase in provision for doubtful debts and outstanding bill accounted)				
(ii)	Accrued Interest A/c	Dr		7,500	
	Stock A/c	Dr		5,000	
	To Revaluation A/c				12,500
	(Being increase in stock and accrued interest accounted)				
(iii)	Rajinder's Current A/c	Dr		23,700	
	Vijay's Current A/c	Dr		15,800	
	To Revaluation A/c				39,500
	(Being loss on revaluation transferred to partner's current account)				
(iv)	Bank A/c	Dr		40,000	
	To Investment A/c				40,000
	(Being investment sold at book value)				
(v)	Rajinder's Current A/c	Dr		42,000	
	To Stock A/c				42,000
	(Being stock taken over by Rajinder)				

Date	Particulars		LF	Amt (Dr)	Amt (Cr)
(vi)	General Reserve A/c	Dr		60,000	
	To Rajinder's Current A/c				36,000
	To Vijay's Current A/c				24,000
	(Being general reserve distributed)				
(vii)	Rajinder's Current A/c	Dr		30,000	
	Vijay's Current A/c	Dr		20,000	
	To Goodwill A/c				50,000
	(Being goodwill written-off)				
(viii)	Bank A/c	Dr		1,60,000	
	To Ranvijay's Capital A/c				1,00,000
	To Premium for Goodwill A/c (WN)				60,000
	(Being new partner brings capital and share of goodwill)				
(ix)	Premium for Goodwill A/c	Dr		60,000	
	To Rajinder's Current A/c				30,000
	To Vijay's Current A/c				30,000
	(Being premium distributed in sacrificing ratio)				

Working Note

Valuation of Goodwill

Average Profit $= \frac{1{,}50{,}000 + 1{,}30{,}000 + 1{,}70{,}000}{3} =$ ₹ 1,50,000; Goodwill $= 1{,}50{,}000 \times 2 =$ ₹ 3,00,000

Ranvijay's Goodwill $= 3{,}00{,}000 \times \frac{2}{10} =$ ₹ 60,000

Solved Question 32 *(New partner does not bring his share of goodwill in cash)* **X and Y are partners in a firm. Their balance sheet as at 31st March, 2024 was**

Balance Sheet

as at 31st March, 2024

Liabilities		Amt (₹)	Assets		Amt (₹)
Workmen Compensation Reserve		2,800	Cash		5,000
Outstanding Expenses		1,500	Sundry Debtors	40,000	
Creditors		15,000	(–) Provision for Doubtful Debts	(2,000)	38,000
Capital A/cs			Stock		10,000
X	25,000		Machinery		19,300
Y	30,000	55,000	Profit and Loss A/c		2,000
		74,300			74,300

On 1st April, 2024, they admitted Z as a new partner on the following conditions

(i) Z brings in ₹ 20,000 as his share of capital but he is unable to bring any amount for goodwill.

(ii) The new profit sharing ratio will be 3 : 2 : 1.

(iii) Claim towards workmen compensation is ₹ 1,500.

(iv) Bad debts amounting to ₹ 3,000 are to be written-off.

(v) Creditors are to be paid ₹ 1,000 more.

(vi) ₹ 1,000 be provided for an unrecorded liability for damages.

(vii) Outstanding expenses be brought down to ₹ 600.

(viii) R, an old customer whose account was written-off as bad debts, has promised to pay ₹ 1,250 in settlement of her dues.

(ix) Goodwill is valued at $1\frac{1}{2}$ years' purchase of the average profit of last three years, less ₹ 6,000. The profits of last three years amounted to ₹ 5,000, ₹ 10,000 and ₹ 15,000 respectively.

Prepare revaluation account, capital accounts of partners' and the opening balance sheet.

Sol. Dr **Revaluation Account** Cr

Particulars	Amt (₹)	Particulars		Amt (₹)
To Bad Debts A/c (WN 2)	1,000	By Outstanding Expenses A/c		900
To Creditors A/c	1,000	By Loss Transferred to Partner's Capital A/cs		
To Damages Payable A/c	1,000	X's	1,050	
		Y's	1,050	2,100
	3,000			3,000

Dr **Partners' Capital Account** Cr

Particulars	X (₹)	Y (₹)	Z (₹)	Particulars	X (₹)	Y (₹)	Z (₹)
To Profit and Loss A/c	1,000	1,000	—	By Balance b/d	25,000	30,000	—
To Revaluation A/c (Loss)	1,050	1,050	—	By Workmen Compensation			
To Balance c/d	23,600	30,100	20,000	Reserve A/c (WN 1)	650	650	—
				By Z's Current A/c (WN 3 and 4)	—	1,500	—
				By Cash A/c	—	—	20,000
	25,650	32,150	20,000		25,650	32,150	20,000

Opening Balance Sheet of the Reconstituted Firm
as at 1st April, 2024

Liabilities		Amt (₹)	Assets	Amt (₹)
Workmen Compensation Reserve		1,500	Cash	25,000
Outstanding Expenses		600	Stock	10,000
Damages Payable		1,000	Sundry Debtors	37,000
Creditors		16,000	Machinery	19,300
Capital A/cs			Z's Current A/c	1,500
X	30,100			
Y	30,100			
Z	20,000	73,700		
		92,800		92,800

Working Notes

1. Workmen compensation reserve appears in the balance sheet as ₹ 2,800, whereas the workmen compensation claim is ₹ 1,500. Therefore, surplus of ₹ 1,300 is transferred to the capital accounts of the old partners in their old profit sharing ratio.
2. Provision for doubtful debts appearing in the balance sheet is ₹ 2,000, whereas actual bad debts amounted to ₹ 3,000. Therefore, ₹ 1,000 will be debited to the revaluation account as loss.
3. Goodwill = $(10{,}000^{*} \times 3/2) - 6{,}000 = 15{,}000 - 6{,}000 =$ ₹ 9,000

   Z's share of Goodwill = $9{,}000 \times 1/6 =$ ₹ 1,500. He has not brought his share of goodwill in cash.

   *Average Profit = $\dfrac{5{,}000 + 10{,}000 + 15{,}000}{3} =$ ₹ 10,000
4. Sacrifice of Share = Old Share – New Share

   X's Sacrifice $= 1/2 - 3/6 = 0$; Y's Sacrifice $= 1/2 - 2/6 = 1/6$

   Hence, Y alone has sacrificed
5. There will be no entry for the promise made by R it is an event and not a transaction. However, there is another view that promise to pay should be recognised as gain (i.e. bad debts recovered), in this situation following entry will be passed

   Sundry Debtors A/c Dr 1,250

   To Revaluation A/c 1,250

Alternate solution, when promise to pay is taken as income i.e. bad debts recovered

Dr **Revaluation Account** Cr

Particulars	Amt (₹)	Particulars		Amt (₹)
To Bad Debts A/c (WN 2)	1,000	By Outstanding Expenses A/c		900
To Creditors A/c	1,000	By Sundry Debtors A/c		1,250
To Damages Payable A/c	1,000	By Loss Transferred to Partner's Capital A/cs		
		X	425	
		Y	425	850
	3,000			3,000

Dr **Partners' Capital Account** Cr

Particulars	X (₹)	Y (₹)	Z (₹)	Particulars	X (₹)	Y (₹)	Z (₹)
To Profit and Loss A/c	1,000	1,000	—	By Balance b/d	25,000	30,000	—
To Revaluation A/c (Loss)	425	425	—	By Workmen Compensation Reserve A/c (WN 1)	650	650	—
To Balance c/d	24,225	30,725	20,000	By Z's Current A/c	—	1,500	—
				By Cash A/c	—	—	20,000
	25,650	32,150	20,000		25,650	32,150	20,000

Adjustment of Capital

Solved Question 33 **Charu and Harsha were partners in a firm sharing profits in the ratio of 3 : 2. On 1st April, 2024, their balance sheet was as follows**

Balance Sheet
as at 1st April, 2024

Liabilities		Amt (₹)	Assets	Amt (₹)
Creditors		17,000	Cash	6,000
General Reserve		4,000	Debtors	15,000
Workmen Compensation Fund		9,000	Investments	20,000
Investment Fluctuation Fund		11,000	Plant	14,000
Provision for Bad Debts		2,000	Land and Building	38,000
Capital A/cs				
Charu	30,000			
Harsha	20,000	50,000		
		93,000		93,000

On the above date Vaishali was admitted for 1/4th share in the profits of the firm on the following terms

(i) Vaishali will bring ₹ 20,000 for her capital and ₹ 4,000 for her share of goodwill premium.

(ii) All debtors were considered good.

(iii) The market value of investments was ₹ 15,000.

(iv) There was a liability of ₹ 6,000 for workmen compensation.

(v) Capital accounts of Charu and Harsha are to be adjusted on the basis of Vaishali's capital by opening current accounts.

Prepare revaluation account and partners' capital account.

Sol. Dr **Revaluation Account** Cr

Particulars		Amt (₹)	Particulars	Amt (₹)
To Gain (Profit) Transferred to Partners' Capital A/cs			By Provision for Bad Debts A/c (WN 1)	2,000
Charu	1,200			
Harsha	800	2,000		
		2,000		2,000

Dr **Partners' Capital Account** Cr

Particulars	Charu (₹)	Harsha (₹)	Vaishali (₹)	Particulars	Charu (₹)	Harsha (₹)	Vaishali (₹)
To Partners' Current A/cs (Balancing Figure)	5,400	3,600	—	By Balance b/d	30,000	20,000	—
				By General Reserve A/c	2,400	1,600	—
To Balance c/d (WN 2)	36,000	24,000	20,000	By Cash A/c	—	—	20,000
				By Premium for Goodwill A/c	2,400	1,600	—
				By Revaluation A/c	1,200	800	—
				By Workmen Compensation Fund A/c (WN 4)	1,800	1,200	—
				By Investment Fluctuation Fund A/c (WN 3)	3,600	2,400	—
	41,400	27,600	20,000		41,400	27,600	20,000

Working Notes

1. 'All debtors were considered good' means provision for bad debts is no longer required and hence should be credited to revaluation account.
2. **Calculation of Partners' Capitals on the basis of Vaishali's Capital**

   Since, Vaishali brings in ₹ 20,000 as her capital for 1/4th share in profits.

   Total capital of the new firm would be = 20,000 × 4 = ₹ 80,000

   Charu's capital in new firm would be $= 80{,}000 \times \frac{3}{4} \times \frac{3}{5} =$ ₹ 36,000; Harsha's capital in new firm would be $= 80{,}000 \times \frac{3}{4} \times \frac{2}{5} =$ ₹ 24,000
3. Investment fluctuation fund is maintained to meet the fall in market value of investments.

	Amt (₹)
Book Value of Investments (Given in the balance sheet)	20,000
(−) Market Value of Investments	(15,000)
Investment Fluctuation Fund required to set-off Loss	5,000
Balance of Investment Fluctuation Fund (Given in the balance sheet)	11,000
(−) Investment Fluctuation Fund Required to set-off Loss	(5,000)
Surplus of Investment Fluctuation Fund	6,000

Surplus of investment fluctuation fund is transferred to old partners' capital accounts in their old profit sharing ratio.

4.

Balance of Workmen Compensation Fund (Given in the balance sheet)	9,000
(−) Workmen Compensation Fund Required to cover Liability	(6,000)
Surplus of Workmen Compensation Fund	3,000

Surplus of workmen compensation fund is transferred to old partners' capital accounts in their old profit sharing ratio.

Solved Question 34 **Shubhi and Revanshi were partners in a firm sharing profits and losses in the ratio of 3 : 2. Their balance sheet as at 31st March, 2023 was as follows**

Balance Sheet of Shubhi and Revanshi
as at 31st March, 2023

Liabilities		Amt (₹)	Assets	Amt (₹)
Capital A/cs			Fixed Assets	90,000
Shubhi	60,000		Stock	38,000
Revanshi	32,000	92,000	Debtors	30,000
General Reserve		30,000	Cash	52,000
Bank Loan		18,000		
Creditors		70,000		
		2,10,000		2,10,000

On 1st April, 2023 they admitted Pari into the partnership on the following terms

(i) Pari will bring ₹ 50,000 as her capital and ₹ 50,000 for her share of premium for goodwill for 1/4th share in the profits of the firm.
(ii) Fixed assets were depreciated @ 30%.
(iii) Stock was valued at ₹ 45,000.
(iv) Bank loan was paid-off.
(v) After all adjustments capitals of Shubhi and Revanshi were to be adjusted taking Pari's capital as the base. Actual cash was to be paid-off or brought in by the old partners as the case may be.

Prepare revaluation account and partners' capital account. CBSE 2024

Sol. Dr **Revaluation Account** Cr

Particulars	Amt (₹)	Particulars		Amt (₹)
To Fixed Assets A/c	27,000	By Stock A/c		7,000
		By Loss Transferred to Partner's Capital A/cs		
		Shubhi	12,000	
		Revanshi	8,000	20,000
	27,000			27,000

Dr **Partners' Capital Acccount** Cr

Particulars	Shubhi (₹)	Revanshi (₹)	Pari (₹)	Particulars	Shubhi (₹)	Revanshi (₹)	Pari (₹)
To Revaluation Ac	12,000	8,000	—	By Balance b/d	60,000	32,000	—
To Cash A/c	6,000	—	—	By General Reserve A/c	18,000	12,000	—
To Balance c/d	90,000	60,000	50,000	By Cash A/c	—	—	50,000
				By Premium for Goodwill A/c	30,000	20,000	—
				By Cash A/c	—	4,000	—
	1,08,000	68,000	50,000		1,08,000	68,000	50,000

Working Notes

1. **Adjustment of Capital**

   Now firm's capital $= 50{,}000 \times \frac{4}{1} = ₹\ 2{,}00{,}000$

2. **New Profit Sharing Ratio**

   Let profits be 1

   Remaining Share $= 1 - \frac{1}{4} = \frac{3}{4}$; Shubhi's new share $= \frac{3}{5} \times \frac{3}{4} = \frac{9}{20}$; Revanshi's new share $= \frac{2}{5} \times \frac{3}{4} = \frac{6}{20}$

   New profit sharing ratio = 9 : 6 : 5

   Shubi's new capital $= 2{,}00{,}000 + \frac{9}{20} = ₹\ 90{,}000$; Revanshi's new capital $= 2{,}00{,}000 \times \frac{6}{20} = ₹\ 60{,}000$

Solved Question 35 **Ashish and Nimish were partners in a firm sharing profits and losses in the ratio of 3 : 2. On 31st March, 2024 their balance sheet was as follows**

Balance Sheet of Ashish and Nimish
as at 31st March, 2024

Liabilities		Amt (₹)	Assets		Amt (₹)
Capital A/cs			Plant and Machinery		2,90,000
Ashish	3,10,000		Furniture		2,20,000
Nimish	2,90,000	6,00,000	Debtors	90,000	
General Reserve		50,000	(–) Provision for Doubtful Debts	(1,000)	89,000
Workmen's Compensation Fund		20,000	Stock		1,40,000
Creditors		1,10,000	Cash		41,000
		7,80,000			7,80,000

On 1st April, 2024, Geeta was admitted into the partnership for 1/4th share in the profits on the following terms

(i) Goodwill of the firm was valued at ₹ 2,00,000.
(ii) Geeta brought ₹ 3,00,000 as her capital and her share of goodwill premium in cash.
(iii) Bad debts amounted to ₹ 2,000. Create a provision for doubtful debts @ 5% on debtors.
(iv) Furniture was found undervalued by ₹ 65,400.
(v) Stock was taken over by Nimish for ₹ 1,30,000.
(vi) The liability against workmen's compensation fund was determined at ₹ 30,000.
(vii) After the above adjustments, the capitals of Ashish and Nimish were to be adjusted taking Geeta's capital as the base. Excess or shortage was to be adjusted by opening current accounts.

Prepare revalution account, partners' capital accounts and the balance sheet of the firm after Geeta's admission.

CBSE 2020 Modified

Sol. Dr **Revaluation Account** Cr

Particulars		Amt (₹)	Particulars	Amt (₹)
To Bad Debts		1,000	By Furniture	65,400
To Provision for Doubtful Debts		4,400		
To Stock		10,000		
To Workmen Compensation Fund		10,000		
To Profit Transferred to Partner's Capital A/cs				
Ashish	24,000			
Nimish	16,000	40,000		
		65,400		65,400

Dr **Partners' Capital Account** Cr

Particulars	Ashish (₹)	Nimish (₹)	Geeta (₹)	Particulars	Ashish (₹)	Nimish (₹)	Geeta (₹)
To Stock	—	1,30,000	—	By Balance b/d	3,10,000	2,90,000	—
To Balance c/d	5,40,000	3,60,000	3,00,000	By Cash	—	—	3,00,000
				By Premium for Goodwill	30,000	20,000	—
				By General Reserve	30,000	20,000	—
				By Revaluation	24,000	16,000	—
				By Current A/c	1,46,000	1,44,000	—
	5,40,000	4,90,000	3,00,000		5,40,000	4,90,000	3,00,000

Balance Sheet
as at 1st April, 2024

Liabilities		Amt (₹)	Assets		Amt (₹)
Workmen's Compensation Fund		30,000	Debtors	90,000	
Creditors		1,10,000	(–) Bad Debts	(2,000)	
Capital A/cs				88,000	
Ashish	5,40,000		(–) Provision for Doubtful Debts	(4,400)	83,600
Nimish	3,60,000		Furniture		2,85,400
Geeta	3,00,000	12,00,000	Plant and Machinery		2,90,000
			Cash		3,91,000
			Ashish's Current A/c		1,46,000
			Nimish's Current A/c		1,44,000
		13,40,000			13,40,000

Working Notes

1. $\frac{1}{4}$th share capital = ₹ 3,00,000 ; Total capital = 3,00,000 × 4 = ₹ 12,00,000

   Ashish capital $= 12{,}00{,}000 \times \frac{9}{20} =$ ₹ 5,40,000 ; Nimish capital $= 12{,}00{,}000 \times \frac{6}{20} =$ ₹ 3,60,000

2. Geeta's share $= \frac{1}{4}$th ; Remaining share $= 1 - \frac{1}{4} = \frac{3}{4}$; Ashish's share $= \frac{3}{4} \times \frac{3}{5} = \frac{9}{20}$; Nimish's share $= \frac{3}{4} \times \frac{2}{5} = \frac{6}{20}$

   Geeta's share $= \frac{1}{4} \times \frac{5}{5} = \frac{5}{20}$; New ratio = 9 : 6 : 5

Solved Question 36 **Leena and Rohit are partners in a firm sharing profits in the ratio of 3 : 2. On 31st March, 2024, their balance sheet was as follows**

Balance Sheet of Leena and Rohit
as at 31st March, 2024

Liabilities	Amt (₹)	Assets		Amt (₹)
Sundry Creditors	80,000	Cash		42,000
Bills Payable	38,000	Debtors	1,32,000	
General Reserve	50,000	(–) Provision for Doubtful Debts	(2,000)	1,30,000

Liabilities		Amt (₹)	Assets	Amt (₹)
Capital A/cs			Stock	1,46,000
Leena	1,60,000		Plant and Machinery	1,50,000
Rohit	1,40,000	3,00,000		
		4,68,000		4,68,000

On the above date Manoj was admitted as a new partner for 1/5 th share in the profits of the firm on the following terms

(i) Manoj brought proportionate capital. He also brought his share of goodwill premium of ₹ 80,000 in cash.

(ii) 10% of the general reserve was to be transferred to provision for doubtful debts.

(iii) Claim on account of workmen's compensation amounted to ₹ 40,000.

(iv) Stock was overvalued by ₹ 16,000.

(v) Leena, Rohit and Manoj will share future profits in the ratio of 5 : 3 : 2.

Prepare revaluation account, partners' capital account and the balance sheet of the reconstituted firm. **CBSE 2019 (M)**

Sol. Dr **Revaluation Account** Cr

Particulars	Amt (₹)	Particulars		Amt (₹)
To Claim for Workmen's Compensation	40,000	By Loss Transferred to Partner's Capital A/cs		
To Stock	16,000	Leena	33,600	
		Rohit	22,400	56,000
	56,000			56,000

Dr **Partners' Capital Account** Cr

Particulars	Leena (₹)	Rohit (₹)	Manoj (₹)	Particulars	Leena (₹)	Rohit (₹)	Manoj (₹)
To Revaluation Loss	33,600	22,400	—	By Balance b/d	1,60,000	1,40,000	—
To Balance c/d	1,93,400	1,75,600	92,250	By General Reserve	27,000	18,000	—
				By Premium for Goodwill	40,000	40,000	—
				By Cash	—	—	92,250
	2,27,000	1,98,000	92,250		2,27,000	1,98,000	92,250

Dr **Cash Account** Cr

Particulars	Amt (₹)	Particulars	Amt (₹)
To Balance b/d	42,000	By Balance c/d	2,14,250
To Premium for Goodwill	80,000		
To Manoj's Capital	92,250		
	2,14,250		2,14,250

Balance Sheet
as at 1st April, 2024

Liabilities		Amt (₹)	Assets		Amt (₹)
Claim for Workmen's Compensation		40,000	Debtors	1,32,000	
Sundry Creditors		80,000	(−) Provision for Doubtful Debts	(7,000)	1,25,000
Bills Payable		38,000	Stock		1,30,000
Capital A/cs			Plant and Machinery		1,50,000
Leena	1,93,400		Cash		2,14,250
Rohit	1,75,600				
Manoj	92,250	4,61,250			
		6,19,250			6,19,250

Working Notes

1. **Calculation of Sacrifice Ratio**

   Leena Sacrifice $= \frac{3}{5} - \frac{5}{10} = \frac{6-5}{10} = \frac{1}{10}$; Rohit Sacrifice $= \frac{2}{5} - \frac{3}{10} = \frac{4-3}{10} = \frac{1}{10}$

   Sacrificing ratio = 1 : 1

		Amt (₹)
2. General Reserve	=	50,000
Transferred to Provision for Doubtful Debts	=	(5,000)
To be Distributed among Old Partners in Old Ratio	=	45,000
3. Leena's Capital	=	1,93,400
Rohit's Capital	=	1,75,600
	=	3,69,000

Manoj's Share $= \frac{1}{5}$; Remaining Share $= 1 - \frac{1}{5} = \frac{4}{5}$; $\frac{4}{5}$th Share Capital = ₹ 3,69,000

$\frac{1}{5}$th Share Capital $= 3,69,000 \times \frac{5}{4} \times \frac{1}{5} =$ ₹ 92,250

Solved Question 37 **Bittu and Chintu were partners in a firm sharing profit and losses in the ratio of 4 : 3. Their balance sheet as at 31st March, 2024 was as follows**

Balance Sheet of Bittu and Chintu
as at 31st March, 2024

Liabilities		Amt (₹)	Assets	Amt (₹)
Capital A/cs			Fixed Assets	15,40,000
Bittu	8,00,000		Stock	3,50,000
Chintu	6,00,000	14,00,000	Debtors	1,40,000
General Reserve		2,10,000	Bank	70,000
Creditors		4,90,000		
		21,00,000		21,00,000

On 1st April, 2024. Diya was admitted in the firm for $\frac{1}{7}$th share in the profits on the following terms

(i) New profit sharing ratio between Bittu, Chintu and Diya will be 3 : 3 : 1.
(ii) Fixed assets were found to be overvalued by ₹ 1,40,000.
(iii) Creditors were paid ₹ 4,20,000 in full settlement.
(iv) Diya brought proportionate capital and ₹ 5,60,000 as her share of goodwill premium by cheque.

Prepare revaluation account and partners' capital account. **CBSE 2025**

Sol. Dr **Revaluation Account** Cr

Particulars	Amt (₹)	Particulars		Amt (₹)
To Fixed Assets	1,40,000	By Creditors		7,40,000
		By Loss on Revaluation		
		Bittu's Capital	40,000	
		Chintu's Capital	30,000	70,000
	1,40,000			1,40,000

Dr **Partners' Capital Account** Cr

Date	Particulars	Bittu (₹)	Chintu (₹)	Diya (₹)	Date	Particulars	Bittu (₹)	Chintu (₹)	Diya (₹)
2024					2024				
Apr 1	To Loss on Revaluation	40,000	30,000	—	Apr 1	By Balance b/d	8,00,000	6,00,000	—
	To Balance c/d	14,40,000	6,60,000	3,50,000		By Premium for Goodwill	5,60,000	—	—
						By General Reserve A/c	1,20,000	90,000	—
						By Bank A/c	—	—	3,50,000
		14,80,000	6,90,000	3,50,000			14,80,000	6,90,000	3,50,000

Working Notes

1. Calculation of Gaining and Sacrificing Ratio

Bittu $= \frac{4}{7} - \frac{3}{7} = \frac{1}{7}$ Sacrificie

Chintu $= \frac{3}{7} - \frac{3}{7} =$ Nil

2. Calculation of Diya's Capital brought in

New Capital of Firm = Adjusted Capital of Old Partners × Reciprocal of the Share

$= 21,00,000 \times \frac{7}{6} =$ ₹ 24,50,000

Diya's Capital $= 24,50,000 \times \frac{1}{7} =$ ₹ 3,50,000

Missing Information

Solved Question 38 **M and J are partners sharing profits in the ratio of 7 : 3. Their capitals were ₹ 3,00,000 and ₹ 2,25,000 respectively. They admitted P as a new partner for 1/6th share in fulture profit. P brought his share of capital but he was unable to bring his share of premium for goodwill. Fill in the missing figures, to record capital and goodwill.**

JOURNAL

Date	Particulars		LF	Amt (Dr)	Amt (Cr)
	Bank A/c	Dr		1,50,000	
	To P's Capital A/c				...
	(Being the amount of capital contributed by P)				
	P's Current A/c	Dr		...	
	To				...
	To				...
	(Being P's share of goodwill credit to old partners in their sacrificing ratio)				

Sol.

JOURNAL

Date	Particulars		LF	Amt (Dr)	Amt (Cr)
	Bank A/c	Dr		1,50,000	
	To P's Capital A/c				**1,50,000**
	(Being the amount of capital contributed by P)				
	P's Current A/c	Dr		**37,500**	
	To **M's Capital A/c**				**26,250**
	To **J's Capital A/c**				**11,250**
	(Being P's share of goodwill credit to old partners in their sacrificing ratio)				

Working Note

Calculation of Hidden Goodwill and New Partner's Share in Goodwill

P's share in profits = 1/6

Total capital of the firm based on Z's capital = 1,50,000 × 6/1 =		₹ 9,00,000
(–) Capital M, J and P (3,00,000 + 2,25,000 + 1,50,000)	=	₹ (6,75,000)
Value of goodwill of the firm	=	₹ 2,25,000

P's share of goodwill $= 2,25,000 \times \frac{1}{6} =$ ₹ 37,500

Solved Question 39 **Mohit and Naman were partners in a firm sharing profits in the ratio of 3 : 1. Omkar was admitted as a partner for 1/5th share in profits on 1st January, 2024. From the information given below, complete revaluation account, partners' capital accounts and the balance sheet of the new firm.**

Dr **Revaluation Account** Cr

Particulars		Amt (₹)	Particulars	Amt (₹)
To Stock A/c		16,000	By Plant A/c	...
To Provision for Doubtful Debts A/c		13,000	By Land and Building A/c	17,500
To Creditors A/c		...		
To Profit Transferred to Partner's Capital A/cs				
Mohit	...			
Naman	8,000	...		
		1,00,000		...

Dr **Partners' Capital Account** Cr

Particulars	Mohit (₹)	Naman (₹)	Omkar (₹)	Particulars	Mohit (₹)	Naman (₹)	Omkar (₹)
To Balance c/d	...	...	...	By	3,00,000	2,30,000	—
				By	...	...	—
				By Cash A/c	—	—	2,50,000
				By Premium for Goodwill A/c	30,000	10,000	—
	...	...	...		...	...	...

Balance Sheet (After admission)
as at 1st January, 2024

Liabilities		Amt (₹)	Assets		Amt (₹)
Creditors		62,500	Cash		...
Bills Payable		80,000	Debtors	60,000	
Outstanding Salary		...	(–) Provision for Doubtful Debts	(...)	47,000
Capital A/cs			Stock		84,000
Mohit	...		Plant		3,30,000
Naman	...		Land and Building		2,57,000
Omkar	...	...			
		10,08,500			...

Sol.

Dr **Revaluation Account** Cr

Particulars		Amt (₹)	Particulars	Amt (₹)
To Stock A/c		16,000	By Plant A/c	**82,500**
To Provision for Doubtful Debts A/c		13,000	By Land and Building A/c	17,500
To Creditors A/c		**39,000**		
To Profit Transferred to Partner's Capital A/cs				
Mohit	**24,000**			
Naman	8,000	**32,000**		
		1,00,000		**1,00,000**

Dr **Partners' Capital Account** Cr

Particulars	Mohit (₹)	Naman (₹)	Omkar (₹)	Particulars	Mohit (₹)	Naman (₹)	Omkar (₹)
To Balance c/d	**3,54,000**	**2,48,000**	**2,50,000**	By **Balance b/d**	3,00,000	2,30,000	—
				By **Revaluation A/c**	**24,000**	**8,000**	—
				By Cash A/c	—	—	2,50,000
				By Premium for Goodwill A/c	30,000	10,000	—
	3,54,000	**2,48,000**	**2,50,000**		**3,54,000**	**2,48,000**	**2,50,000**

Balance Sheet (After admission)
as at 1st January, 2024

Liabilities		Amt (₹)	Assets		Amt (₹)
Creditors		62,500	Cash (2,50,000 + 40,000)		**2,90,000**
Bills Payable		80,000	Debtors	60,000	
Outstanding Salary		**14,000**	(–) Provision for Doubtful Debts	**(13,000)**	47,000
Capital A/cs			Stock		84,000
Mohit	**3,54,000**		Plant		3,30,000
Naman	**2,48,000**		Land and Building		2,57,500
Omkar	**2,50,000**	**8,52,000**			
		10,08,500			**10,08,500**

Numerical Questions

New Profit Sharing Ratio and Sacrificing Ratio

1. H and D are partners in a firm sharing profits in the ratio of 2 : 1. On 1st April, 2024, they decided to admit U as a partner for 3/4th share in profits.

Calculate their new profit sharing ratio.

Ans. New Profit Sharing Ratio = 2 : 1 : 9

2. **Ganga and Yamuna are partners in a firm sharing profits in the ratio of 2 : 1. Saraswati and Narmada are admitted for 1/6th and 1/8th shares respectively.**

Ans. New Profit Sharing Ratio = 34 : 17 : 12 : 9
Sacrificing Ratio = 2 : 1

3. D and K are partners sharing profits and losses in the ratio of 3 : 2. They decided to admit M into the partnership for 20% share in profits.

Calculate their new profit sharing ratio.

Ans. New Profit Sharing Ratio = 12 : 8 : 5

4. A and S are partners in a firm sharing profits in the ratio of 2 : 1. They admitted G into the partnership on 1st April, 2024 for 1/3rd share into the business, which he acquired 3/15th from A and 2/15th from S.

Calculate their new profit sharing ratio.

Ans. New Profit Sharing Ratio = 7 : 3 : 5

5. Radha and Lokesh are partners sharing profits and losses in the ratio of 3 : 2. Deepa, a new partner is admitted who acquired 1/9th share from Radha and 1/18th from Lokesh.

Calculate the new profit sharing ratio and sacrificing ratio.

Ans. New Profit Sharing Ratio = Radha : Lokesh : Deepa
= 44 : 31 : 15

Sacrificing Ratio of Radha and Lokesh = 10 : 5 = 2 : 1

6. Ram and Shyam are partners in a firm sharing profits in the ratio of 3 : 2. They admit Ghanshyam as a new partner. Ram surrenders 1/4th of his share and Shyam 1/3rd of his share in favour of Ghanshyam.

Calculate new profit sharing ratio of Ram, Shyam and Ghanshyam.

Ans. New Profit Sharing Ratio = 27 : 16 : 17

7. A and B are partners in a firm sharing profits in the ratio of 3 : 1. They admit C as a new partner for 1/5th share. C acquired 1/4th of his share from A.

How much share did C acquire from A?

Ans. 3/20

8. A, B and C are partners sharing profits in 3 : 2 : 2 ratio. They admitted D as a new partner for 1/5th share which he acquired from A, B and C in 2 : 2 : 1 ratio respectively.

Calculate new profit sharing ratio. Competency Based Que

Ans. New Profit Sharing Ratio = 61 : 36 : 43 : 35

9. A and B are partners sharing profits in the ratio of 5 : 4. They admit C for 1/10th share, which he acquires in equal proportion from both A and B.

Find new profit sharing ratio.

Ans. New Profit Sharing Ratio = 91 : 71 : 18

10. I, N and C are partners in a firm sharing profits in the ratio of 2 : 2 : 1. They decided to admit D into the firm for 1/4th share in profits. N will retain his original share.

Find out their new profit sharing ratio.

Ans. New Profit Sharing Ratio = 14 : 24 : 7 : 15

11. A and B are partners sharing profits in the ratio of 5 : 3. They admit C for 1/4th share and agree to share future profits between them in the ratio of 2 : 1.

Calculate new profit sharing ratio and sacrificing ratio.

Ans. New Profit Sharing Ratio = 2 : 1 : 1
Sacrificing Ratio = 1 : 1

12. Sandeep and Navdeep are partners in a firm sharing profits in 5 : 3 ratio. They admit C into the firm and the new profit sharing ratio was agreed at 4 : 2 : 1.

Calculate the sacrificing ratio.

Ans. Sacrificing Ratio = Sandeep : Navdeep = 3 : 5

13. Sakshi and Saksham are partners sharing profits in the ratio of 2 : 1. On 1st April, 2017, they admitted Saurabh as a partner for 1/6th share which he acquired in the ratio of 2 : 3 from them. On 1st April, 2018, they admitted Vishal as a partner for 1/4th share which he acquired equally from all the partners.

Calculate Competency Based Que

(i) New profit sharing ratio after Saurabh's admission.

(ii) New profit sharing ratio after Vishal's admission.

Ans. (i) Profit Sharing Ratio after Saurabh's Admission = 18 : 7 : 5

(ii) Profit Sharing Ratio after Vishal's Admission = 93 : 27 : 15 : 45

14. Manish and Nirjhar are partners sharing profits in the ratio of 4 : 1. Manish surrenders 1/4th from his share and Nirjhar surrenders 1/5th of his share in favour of Vardaan.

Calculate the new ratio and sacrificing ratio.

Competency Based Que

Ans. New Ratio = 55 : 16 : 29 ; Sacrificing Ratio = 25 : 4

Treatment of Goodwill

15. X and Y are partners sharing profits in 3 : 2 ratio. Z is admitted for 1/5th share. He contributed ₹ 50,000 as capital and pays the proportionate amount of goodwill to X and Y privately. At the time of Z's admission, goodwill is valued at ₹ 30,000.

Journalise.

Ans. Only entry for capital brought in by partners would be passed, no entry will be passed for goodwill as it is paid privately.

16. Bablu and Guddu are partners in a firm sharing profits in the ratio of 2 : 1. From 1st April, 2024 they decided to admit Munna into the firm for 1/3rd share. Munna gets his share from Bablu and Guddu equally. Munna brings ₹ 1,20,000 as capital and his share of goodwill in cash. Goodwill of the firm was ₹ 75,000.

Pass necessary journal entries.

17. Kia and Mia are partners sharing profits and losses in the ratio of 4 : 1. They agreed to admit Tia into the partnership on 1st April, 2018 for 1/3rd share in profits. It was agreed that Kia, Mia and Tia would share profits equally in future. Tia brought in ₹ 5,000 as goodwill (premium) for her 1/3rd share in profits.

Record the necessary journal entries in the books of the firm.

Ans. Kia's Sacrifice $= \frac{7}{15}$; Mia's Gain $= \frac{2}{15}$

Tia will be credited with ₹ 7,000

18. X and Y are partners sharing profits and losses in the ratio of 2 : 1. They admit Z as a partner for 1/5th share. Z brings in ₹ 2,50,000 as his capital and his share of goodwill in cash. For this purpose, the goodwill of the firm is to be calculated at three year's purchase of the average profits of the total last four years.

The profits of the last four years ending 31st March were

Year	Profit (₹)	
2020-21	80,000	(after charging loss of ₹ 12,720 on sale of plant)
2021-22	70,000	(after charging voluntary retirement compensation of ₹ 25,000)
2022-23	1,25,000	
2023-24	1,20,000	

The following information is provided

(i) On 1st October, 2021, the firm had purchased a computer for ₹ 30,000 and it was debited to stationery expenses. Depreciation is to be charged on computer @ 20% p.a. on the diminishing balance method.

(ii) The closing stock ending 31st March, 2022 and 2023 were overvalued by ₹ 10,000 and ₹ 15,000 respectively.

(iii) To cover the operating cost, an annual charge of ₹ 5,000 should be made for the purpose of valuation of goodwill.

Pass necessary journal entries on admission of Z.

Competency Based Que

Ans. Adjusted Profit = 2020-21 = ₹ 87,720, 2021-22 = ₹ 1,07,000, 2022-23 = ₹ 1,09,600, 2023-24 = ₹ 1,25,680

19. S and W are partners sharing profits and losses in the ratio of 2 : 3. On 1st April, 2024, they admitted A into partnership for 1/4th share in profits. A brought in ₹ 10,000 for his capital and ₹ 3,600 as premium for his 1/4th share in the profits. The new profit sharing ratio of S, W and A is agreed to be 3 : 3 : 2. S and W withdraw the premium money from business.

Pass the necessary journal entries.

20. A and B are partners sharing profits in 4 : 3 ratio. C joins partnership for 2/7th share in the profits which he acquires 3/4 from A and 1/4 from B. Z brings in ₹ 1,50,000 for his capital and ₹ 60,000 for goodwill. Half of the amount of goodwill is withdrawn by the old partners.

Pass necessary entries and new profit sharing ratio.

Competency Based Que

Ans. New Profit Sharing Ratio = 5 : 5 : 4

21. Bhumi and Parul were partners in a firm sharing profits in the ratio of 3 : 2. Their capitals were ₹ 3,20,000 and ₹ 2,00,000.

They admitted Rakshit on 1st April, 2018 as a new partner for 1/5th share in the future profits. Rakshit brought ₹ 2,40,000 as his capital.

Calculate the value of goodwill of the firm and necessary journal entries for the above transactions.

22. Vishu and Nishu were sharing profits and losses in the ratio of 2 : 1 respectively. They admitted Ishu for 2/7th share. The actual value of goodwill, however, on that date was ₹ 84,000. Ishu contributed the following assets towards the payment of his capital and goodwill. Cash ₹ 4,000, sundry debtors ₹ 20,000, stock ₹ 24,000, machinery ₹ 20,000.

Pass the journal entries to give effect to the above. Also give the new profit sharing ratio. **Competency Based Que**

Ans. New Profit Sharing Ratio = 10 : 5 : 6

23. P and Q who share profits in the ratio of 3 : 2 had capitals of ₹ 4,00,000 and ₹ 3,00,000 respectively. They agree to admit R into partnership from 1st April, 2024 on the following terms in return for 1/3rd share in future profits.

(i) That R should bring in ₹ 4,00,000 as capital.

(ii) That as R is unable to bring in his share of goodwill in cash, goodwill of the firm is valued at ₹ 3,00,000.

Record necessary journal entries in the books of the firm. Competency Based Que

Ans. Debit R's capital with ₹ 1,00,000 and credit P and Q's capitals with ₹ 60,000 and ₹ 40,000 respectively

24. X and Y are partners sharing profits and losses as 2 : 1. They admit Z as a new partner and new profit sharing ratio becomes 2 : 1 : 1. Goodwill of firm is valued at ₹ 60,000. Z does not bring any amount for goodwill.

Show the necessary journal entries when goodwill account is opened.

25. Hardik and Shlok are partners in a firm sharing profits equally. They decided to admit Varshika into the partnership for 1/3rd share in profits. Varshika brings ₹ 45,000 as capital but she was unable to bring goodwill in cash. Goodwill of the firm is valued at ₹ 30,000. Goodwill appearing in the books of accounts was ₹ 11,000.

Pass necessary journal entries. Competency Based Que

26. A and B are partners in a firm. They admit C as a partner for 1/4th share in profits. C brings ₹ 1,00,000 as his share of capital. Value of total assets of the firm is ₹ 2,70,000 and outside liabilities are valued at ₹ 50,000 on that date.

Give necessary entry to record goodwill at the time of C's admission.

Ans. Value of Goodwill = ₹ 80,000

C's Share of Goodwill = ₹ 20,000

27. A and B are partners sharing profits in 2 : 3. C and D are admitted and profit sharing ratio becomes 3 : 4 : 3 : 2. Goodwill is valued at ₹ 1,50,000. C brings required goodwill and ₹ 1,00,000 cash for capital. D brings in ₹ 50,000 cash and motor vehicle for ₹ 40,000 as his capital in addition to the required amount of goodwill in cash.

Show the necessary journal entries. Competency Based Que

Ans. Sacrificing Ratio = 9 : 16 ; C's Share of Goodwill = ₹ 37,500; D's Share of Goodwill = ₹ 25,000

Amount of capital and goodwill brought in by D

Bank A/c	Dr 75,000	
Motor Vehicle A/c	Dr 40,000	
To D's Capital A/c		90,000
To Premium for Goodwill A/c		25,000

Adjustment for Reserves and Accumulated Profits/Losses

28. Sunny and Bobby are partners in a firm sharing profits and losses in the ratio of 5 : 3. On 1st April, 2024, they admitted Abhay as a partner for 1/5th share. On that date, their balance sheet showed a balance of ₹ 64,000 in general reserve and a credit balance of ₹ 24,000 in profit and loss account.

Pass the necessary journal entries for the treatment of these items on Abhay's admission.

29. A and B are partners in a firm sharing profits and losses in the ratio of 3 : 2. On 1st April, 2024, they adimit C as a partner for 1/5th share in profits. On that date, there was a balance of ₹ 15,000 in advertisement suspense account and a debit balance of ₹ 2,000 in the profit and loss account of the firm.

Pass necessary journal entries regarding adjustment of reserve and accumulated profit/loss.

30. B and S are partners sharing profits in the ratio of 3 : 2. They admitted T as a partner for 1/4th share. T paid ₹ 40,000 as his capital and ₹ 20,000 for premium in cash. At the time of admission of T, general reserve amounting to ₹ 24,000 and profit and loss account amounting to ₹ 12,000 appeared in the balance sheet.

Pass necessary journal entries to record the above transactions.

31. P, Q, R were partners sharing profits and losses in the ratio of 6 : 3 : 1. They take D into partnership with effect from 1st April, 2020. The new profit sharing ratio between P, Q, R and S will be 3 : 3 : 3 : 1. The following balances appear in their balance sheet

	Book Values (₹)
General Reserve	15,000
Contingency Reserve	6,000
Profit and Loss Account (Cr)	9,000
Advertisement Suspense Account (Dr)	12,000
Goodwill	10,000

Pass the necessary journal entries through the partners' current account. Competency Based Que

32. K and S were partners in a firm sharing profits in the ratio of 3 : 1. On 1st April, 2023, they admitted R as a partner for 1/5th share in profits of the firm. On the date of R's admission, the balance sheet of K and S showed a general reserve of ₹ 48,000, a debit balance of ₹ 24,000 in profit and loss account and workmen compensation fund of ₹ 60,000.

The following was agreed upon on R's admission.

(i) R will bring ₹ 60,000 as his capital and his share of goodwill premium in cash.

(ii) Goodwill of the firm be valued at ₹ 68,000.

(iii) The partners decided to share future profits in the ratio of 3 : 1 : 1.

(iv) Goodwill appears in the balance sheet of the firm at ₹ 96,000.

Pass necessary journal entries for the above on R's admission. **Competency Based Que**

Revaluation/Reassessment

33. Rochelle and Mandana are partners sharing profits and losses in the ratio of 3 : 2. Keith is admitted as a partner for 1/5th share.

Make entries in the firm's journal, for the following adjustments.

(i) The value of buildings increased by ₹ 2,00,000.

(ii) The landlord has decided to waive the outstanding rent of ₹ 5,000 appearing in the books.

(iii) Prepaid insurance of ₹ 2,500 is to be brought into account.

(iv) Investments and investment fluctuation fund appear in the balance sheet at ₹ 50,000 and ₹ 5,000 respectively. Presently, the value of investments is ₹ 42,000.

(v) On 31st December, 2015, goods of ₹ 20,000 were received by the firm on account of credit purchases. This transaction has not yet been recorded in the books of the firm. (Unrecorded creditors of ₹ 20,000 and unrecorded stock of ₹ 20,000).

Ans. Profit on Revaluation = ₹ 2,04,500

34. Pass journal entries to record the following transactions on the admission of a new partner **Competency Based Que**

(i) Stock is undervalued by 10% (Book value of stock ₹ 27,000).

(ii) Stock is overvalued by 10% (Book value of stock ₹ 33,000).

(iii) Value of land and building is to be increased to ₹ 4,00,000 (Book value ₹ 3,00,000).

(iv) A debtor whose due of ₹ 20,000 was written-off as bad debts last year, paid ₹ 15,000 in full settlement.

(v) An old customer, whose account was written-off as bad debts has promised to pay ₹ 30,000 in full settlement of his account of ₹ 50,000.

(vi) A liability for claim, included in creditors for ₹ 40,000 is settled at ₹ 32,000.

(vii) A computer purchased on 1st October, 2016 for ₹ 80,000 debited to office expense account is to be brought into account on 31st March, 2018 charging depreciation @ 10% p.a. on written down value basis.

(viii) Unrecorded investments worth ₹ 10,000.

(ix) Unrecorded liabilities towards suppliers for ₹ 3,000.

(x) An item of ₹ 1,200 included in sundry creditors is not likely to be claimed, hence should be written back.

35. Given below is the balance sheet of A and B, who are carrying on partnership business on 31st March, 2024. A and B share profits and losses in the ratio of 2 : 1.

Balance Sheet of A and B
as on 31st March, 2024

Liabilities		Amt (₹)	Assets	Amt (₹)
Bills Payable		10,000	Cash in Hand	10,000
Creditors		58,000	Cash at Bank	40,000
Outstanding Expenses		2,000	Sundry Debtors	60,000
Capitals A/cs			Stock	40,000
A	1,80,000		Plant	1,00,000
B	1,50,000	3,30,000	Buildings	1,50,000
		4,00,000		4,00,000

C is admitted as a partner on the date of the balance sheet on the following terms

(i) C will bring in ₹ 1,00,000 as his capital and ₹ 60,000 as his share of goodwill for 1/4th share in the profits.

(ii) Plant is to be appreciated to ₹ 1,20,000 and the value of buildings is to be appreciated by 10%.

(iii) Stock is found overvalued by ₹ 4,000.

(iv) A provision for bad and doubtful debts is to be created at 5% of debtors.

(v) Creditors were unrecorded to the extent of ₹ 1,000.

Pass the necessary journal entries and prepare the revaluation account.

Ans. Revaluation Profit = ₹ 27,000

36. The balance sheet of Subhash and Ramesh, who share profits equally is given below

Balance Sheet
as at 31st March, 2024

Liabilities		Amt (₹)	Assets	Amt (₹)
Capital A/cs			Cash in Hand	25,000
Subhash	5,00,000		Debtors	50,000
Ramesh	3,75,000	8,75,000	Stock	2,50,000
Creditors		1,00,000	Furniture and Fittings	50,000
Outstanding Salaries		10,000	Plant and Machinery	2,00,000
Provision for Tax		15,000	Land and Building	4,30,000
Bank Overdraft		5,000		
		10,05,000		10,05,000

On the given date, Arpit is admitted for $\frac{3}{7}$th share and the following adjustments are agreed upon

(i) Outstanding salaries are of a clerk, Jagdish, who has left the job and is untraceable. Therefore, it is decided to write-off the salaries.
(ii) Provision for tax is to be increased upto ₹ 17,500.
(iii) Bank reconciliation statement revealed overdraft as per passbook at ₹ 4,500.
(iv) Included in debtors, is an amount of ₹ 3,500 owed by Dinesh, who has left the city. So, it is decided to write-off the above amount.
(v) At the end of the year, stock worth ₹ 20,000 lying with the customers, is not brought to account.
(vi) Furniture and fittings are found overvalued by ₹ 1,00,000 and plant and machinery by ₹ 20,000.
(vii) Land and buildings are undervalued by ₹ 1,00,000.
(viii) Ramesh uses a laptop which has been purchased from firm's funds. This laptop has not been shown in the above balance sheet. Its value has been agreed upon at ₹ 12,500.
(ix) Both the partners purchased smartphones from the firm's money. These smartphones are valued at ₹ 5,000 each.

Prepare revaluation account to give effect to the above transactions. **Competency Based Que**

Ans. Profit on Revaluation = ₹ 1,16,500

Hint Overdraft as per passbook has no relevance, Hence, it will not be considered.

37. A and B are partners in a firm sharing profits and losses in the ratio of 3 : 2. On 31st March, 2024, their balance sheet was as under

Balance Sheet
as at 31st March, 2024

Liabilities		Amt (₹)	Assets		Amt (₹)
Sundry Creditors		8,000	Cash in Hand		600
Public Deposits		30,500	Cash at Bank		1,400
Bank Overdraft		3,000	Stock		16,000
Outstanding Liabilities		1,000	Prepaid Insurance		500
Capital A/cs			Sundry Debtors	14,400	
A	24,000		(−) Provision for Doubtful Debts	(400)	14,000
B	20,000	44,000	Plant and Machinery		24,000
			Land and Building		25,000
			Furniture		5,000
		86,500			86,500

On the above date, the partners decide to admit C as a partner on the following terms

(i) The new profit sharing ratio will be 5 : 3 : 2, respectively.

(ii) C shall bring ₹ 16,000 as his capital.

(iii) C is unable to bring in any cash for his share of goodwill. Partners therefore, decide to calculate goodwill on the basis of C's share in the profit and the capital contribution made by him to the firm.

(iv) Plant and machinery would be increased by ₹ 6,000.

(v) Stock would be increased to ₹ 20,000.

(vi) Provision for doubtful debts is to be maintained at ₹ 2,000. Value of land and building has appreciated by 20%. Furniture has depreciated by 10%.

(vii) There is an additional liability of ₹ 4,000 being outstanding salary payable to employees of the firm. This liability is not included in the outstanding liabilities, stated in the above balance sheet. Partners decide to show this liability in the books of accounts of the reconstituted new firm.

Prepare revaluation account and partners' capital account of A, B and C. **Competency Based Que**

Ans. Profit on Revaluation = ₹ 8,900 ; Value of Goodwill = ₹ 11,100 ; C's Share of Goodwill = ₹ 2,220 to be credited to A and B in sacrificing ratio i.e. equally Partners' Capital Account A = ₹ 30,450, B = ₹ 24,670, C = ₹ 16,000

38. X, Y and Z are partners in a firm sharing profits in the ratio of 3 : 2 : 1. On 1st April, 2024, their balance sheet is as follows

Balance Sheet
as at 1st April, 2024

Liabilities		Amt (₹)	Assets	Amt (₹)
Capital A/cs			Y's Current Account	7,000
X	1,75,000		Land and Building	1,75,000
Y	1,50,000		Plant and Machinery	67,500
Z	1,25,000	4,50,000	Furniture	80,000
Current A/cs			Investments	36,500
X	4,000		Bills Receivable	17,000
Z	6,000	10,000	Sundry Debtors	43,500
General Reserve		15,000	Stock	1,37,000
Profit and Loss Account		7,000	Bank	43,500
Creditors		80,000		
Bills Payable		45,000		
		6,07,000		6,07,000

On the above date, A is admitted on the following terms

(i) A will bring ₹ 50,000 as his capital and will get 1/6th share in profits.

(ii) He will bring necessary amount for his share of goodwill premium. Goodwill of the firm was valued at ₹ 90,000.

(iii) The new profit sharing ratio will be 2 : 2 : 1 : 1.

(iv) A bill receivable of ₹ 7,004 discounted with bank was dishonoured, which is to be recorded in the books of account.

(v) Value of stock, furniture and investments is reduced by 20% whereas the value of land and building and plant and machinery will be appreciated by 20% and 10% respectively.

Prepare revaluation account, partners' current account, capital account and balance sheet. **Competency Based Que**

Ans. Loss on Revaluation = ₹ 8,950 ; Partners' Current Account Balance X = ₹ 1,00,525, Y = ₹ 47,350, Z = ₹ 83,175;
Partners' Capital Account Balance X = ₹ 1,00,000, Y = ₹ 1,00,000, Z = ₹ 50,000, A = ₹ 50,000 ; Balance Sheet Total = ₹ 6,56,050

39. A and B are partners in a firm, sharing profits and losses equally. Their balance sheet as at 31st March, 2024 was as follows

Balance Sheet
as at 31st March, 2024

Liabilities		Amt (₹)	Assets		Amt (₹)
Sundy Creditors		21,000	Cash at Bank		20,000
General Reserve		15,000	Sundry Debtors	22,000	
Capital A/cs			(–) Provision for Doubtful Debts	(1,000)	21,000
A	45,000		Stock		10,000
B	40,000	85,000	Plant and Machinery		60,000
			Goodwill		10,000
		1,21,000			1,21,000

C was to be taken as a partner for 1/4th share in the profits of the firm, with effect from 1st April, 2024 on the following terms

(i) Bad debts amounting to ₹ 1,500 to be written-off.
(ii) Stock to be taken over by A at ₹ 12,000.
(iii) Plant and machinery to be valued at ₹ 50,000.
(iv) Goodwill of the firm to be valued at ₹ 20,000.
(v) C to bring in ₹ 50,000 as his capital. He was unable to bring in cash his share of goodwill.
(vi) General reserve not to be distributed. For this, it was decided that C would compensate the old partners through his current account.

You are required to

(a) Pass journal entries on the date of C's admission.

(b) Prepare the capital accounts and the balance sheet of the reconsituted firm. **Competency Based Que**

Ans. Loss on Revaluation = ₹ 8,500 ; Capital Accounts A = ₹ 28,125, B = ₹ 35,125, C = ₹ 50,000 ; Balance Sheet Total = ₹ 1,49,250

Adjustment of Capital

40. Divya and Ekta were partners in a firm sharing profits in the ratio of 3 : 1. On 31st March, 2023 they admitted Sona as a new partner for 1/4th share in the profits of the firm. Their balance sheet on that date was as follows

Balance Sheet of Divya and Ekta
as at 31st March, 2023

Liabilities		Amt (₹)	Assets		Amt (₹)
Capital A/cs			Land and Building		5,00,000
Divya	10,00,000		Machinery		6,00,000
Ekta	7,00,000	17,00,000	Stock		1,50,000
General Reserve		3,20,000	Debtors	4,00,000	
Creditors		5,40,000	(–) Provision for Doubtful Debts	(30,000)	3,70,000
			Investments		5,00,000
			Cash		4,40,000
		25,60,000			25,60,000

Sona will bring ₹ 4,00,000 as her capital and her share of goodwill in cash. It was agreed that

(i) Goodwill of the firm was valued at ₹ 2,40,000.
(ii) Land and building were valued at ₹ 7,12,000.
(iii) Provision for doubtful debts was found to be in excess by ₹ 8,000.
(iv) A liability for ₹ 20,000 included in creditors was not likely to arise.
(v) The capitals of Divya and Ekta will be adjusted on the basis of Sona's capital by opening current accounts.

Prepare revaluation account and partners' capital account. **Competency Based Que**

Ans. Revaluation Profit = 2,40,000; Partners' Capital Account Divya = ₹ 9,00,000, Ekta = ₹ 3,00,000, Sona = ₹ 4,00,000

41. On 31st March, 2024, the balance sheet of A and B, who shared profits in 3 : 2 ratio, was as follows

Balance Sheet
as at 31st March, 2024

Liabilities		Amt (₹)	Assets		Amt (₹)
Creditors		20,000	Cash		5,000
Profit and Loss A/c		15,000	Sundry Debtors	20,000	
Capital A/cs			(–) Provision for Doubtful Debts	(700)	19,300
A	40,000		Stock		25,000
B	30,000	70,000	Plant and Machinery		35,000
			Patents		20,700
		1,05,000			1,05,000

On this date, C was admitted as a partner on the following conditions

(i) C will get 4/15th share of profits.
(ii) C had to bring ₹ 30,000 as his capital to which amount other partners' capitals shall have to be adjusted.
(iii) He would pay cash for his share of goodwill which would be based on 2.5 years' purchase of average profits of past 4 years.
(iv) The assets would be revalued as sundry debtors at book value less 5% provision for bad debts, stock at ₹ 20,000, plant and machinery at ₹ 40,000.
(v) The profits of the firm for the year's ending on 31st March, 2021, 2022 and 2023 were ₹ 20,000, ₹ 14,000 and ₹ 17,000, respectively.

Prepare revaluation account, partners' capital account and balance sheet of a new firm. **Competency Based Que**

Ans. Loss on Revaluation = ₹ 300 ; New Profit Sharing Ratio = 33 : 22 : 20 ; Sacrificing Ratio = 3 : 2 ; Capital Account A = ₹ 49,500, B = ₹ 33,000, C = ₹ 30,000 ; Balance Sheet Total = ₹ 1,32,500

42. Sarah and Varsha were partners in a firm sharing profits and losses in the ratio of 3 : 2. Their balance sheet as at 31st March, 2023 was as follows

Balance Sheet of Sarah and Varsha
as at 31st March, 2023

Liabilities		Amt (₹)	Assets		Amt (₹)
Capital A/cs			Plant and Machinery		2,00,000
Sarah	60,000		Stock		30,000
Varsha	50,000	1,10,000	Debtors	50,000	
Workmen's Compensation Fund		20,000	(–) Provision for Doubtful Debts	(5,000)	45,000
Provident Fund		1,20,000	Cash		25,000
Creditors		50,000			
		3,00,000			3,00,000

On 1st April, 2023, they decided to admit Tasha as a new partner for 1/4th share in the profits of the firm on the following terms

(i) Tasha brought ₹ 40,000 as her capital and ₹ 20,000 as her share of premium for goodwill.
(ii) Plant and machinery was valued at ₹ 1,90,000.
(iii) An item of ₹ 20,000, included in creditors, is not likely to be claimed and should be written-off.
(iv) Capitals of the partners in the new firm are to be in the new profit sharing ratio on the basis of Tasha's capital, by bringing or paying off cash, as the case may be.

Prepare revaluation account and partners' capital account. **CBSE 2024; Competency Based Que**

Ans. Profit on Revaluation = ₹ 10,000 ; Partners' Capital Account Sarah = ₹ 72,000, Varsha = ₹ 48,000, Tasha = ₹ 40,000

43. X and Y are partners and the profit is divided as follows $\frac{1}{2}$ to X; $\frac{1}{3}$ to Y and $\frac{1}{6}$ carried to a reserve account. They admit Z as a partner on 1st April, 2024 at which date the balance sheet of the firm was as under

Balance Sheet
as at 1st April, 2024

Liabilities		Amt (₹)	Assets	Amt (₹)
Creditors		80,000	Cash at Bank	10,000
Outstanding Expenses		6,000	Debtors	1,10,000
Reserve		45,000	Stock	90,000
Capital A/cs			Plant and Machinery	75,000
X	1,59,000		Buildings	1,00,000
Y	1,00,000	2,59,000	Advertisement Expenditure	5,000
		3,90,000		3,90,000

Following terms were agreed upon
(i) Stock is undervalued by 10%.
(ii) Depreciation of ₹ 15,000 had been omitted on plant and machinery for the year ended 31st March, 2024.
(iii) Creditors include a contingent liability of ₹ 25,000 which has been decided by the court at ₹ 21,500.
(iv) In respect of debtors, the following debts proved bad or doubtful ₹ 7,500 due from P – bad to the full extent ; ₹ 10,000 due from Q – insolvent, estate expected to pay only 40%.
(v) Goodwill of the firm is value at ₹ 30,000. However, Z is unable to bring his share of goodwill in cash.
(vi) Z is given 1/5th share of profits which he acquires equally from X and Y. Z is to bring in capital proportionate to his share of profits in the firm.

You are required to prepare revaluation account, capital account and the new balance sheet of the firm.

Competency Based Que

Ans. Loss on Revaluation = ₹ 15,000 ; Capital Accounts X = ₹ 1,77,000, Y = ₹ 1,13,000, Z = ₹ 72,500 ;
Balance Sheet Total = ₹ 4,45,000

44. Anshu and Vihu were partners in a firm sharing profits and losses in the ratio of 3 : 2. Their Balance Sheet as at 31st March, 2023 was as follows

Balance Sheet of Anshu and Vihu
as at 31st March, 2023

Liabilities		Amt (₹)	Assets		Amt (₹)
Creditors		80,000	Cash		40,000
General Reserve		50,000	Debtors	36,000	
Investment Fluctuation Fund		10,000	(–) Provision for Doubtful Debts	(2,000)	34,000
Capitals A/cs			Stock		30,000
Anshu	1,44,000		Investments		40,000
Vihu	80,000	2,24,000	Plant and Machinery		2,20,000
		3,64,000			3,64,000

On 1st April, 2023, Mani was admitted into partnership for 1/5th share in the profits of the firm on the following terms
(i) Mani brought ₹ 20,000 as her share of goodwill and proportionated capital.
(ii) Provision for doubtful debts was to be maintained at 10% on debtors.
(iii) Market value of investments was ₹ 35,000.
(iv) The value of plant and machinery be increased by ₹ 6,600.

Prepare revaluation account and partners' capital account. **CBSE 2024 C**

Ans. Revaluation Profit = ₹ 5,000; Partners' Capital Account Anshu = ₹ 1,92,000, Vishu = ₹ 1,12,000, Moni = ₹ 76,000

45. A and B are partners sharing profits in the ratio of 3 : 2. Their balance sheet on 31st March, 2024 stood as under

Balance Sheet
as at 31st March, 2024

Liabilities		Amt (₹)	Assets		Amt (₹)
Capital A/cs			Machinery		66,000
A	70,000		Furniture		30,000
B	60,000	1,30,000	Investments		40,000
General Reserve		20,000	Stock		46,000
Bank Loan		18,000	Debtors	38,000	
Creditors		72,000	(–) Provision for Doubtful Debts	(4,000)	34,000
			Cash		24,000
		2,40,000			2,40,000

On this date, they admitted C for 25% share in profits on following terms

(i) C brings capital proportionate to his share after all adjustments and ₹ 8,000 for goodwill out of his share of ₹ 14,000.
(ii) Depreciate furniture by 10%.
(iii) Half of investments were to be taken over by A and B in their profit sharing ratio and remaining valued at ₹ 26,000.
(iv) New ratio will be 3 : 3 : 2.
(v) C brings 25% of the combined capital of A and B as capital.

Prepare revaluation account, partners' capitals account and balance sheet.

Ans. Profit on Revaluation = ₹ 3,000; Balance in Capital Accounts A = ₹ 84,400, B = ₹ 62,600, C = ₹ 36,750; Balance Sheet Total = ₹ 2,73,750

Missing Information

46. B and D are partners sharing profits in the ratio of 7 : 3. Their capitals were ₹ 40,000 and ₹ 30,000 respectively. They admitted M as a new partner for 1/6th share in future profits M brought his share of capital but he was unable to bring his share of premium for goodwill.

Fill in the missing figures, to record capital and goodwill. **Competency Based Que**

JOURNAL

Date	Particulars	LF	Amt (Dr)	Amt (Cr)
	Bank A/c Dr		20,000	
	To Z's Capital A/c			...
	(Being the amount of capital contributed by Z)			
	Z's Current A/c Dr		...	
	To			...
	To			...
	(Being M's share of goodwill credit to old partners in their sacrificing ratio)			

47. Complete the following accounts and balance sheet by filling the missing amount. **Competency Based Que**

Dr **Revaluation Account** Cr

Particulars		Amt (₹)	Particulars	Amt (₹)
To Bad Debts A/c		400	By Land and Building A/c	22,000
To Provision for Doubtful Debts A/c		1,500	By Sundry Creditors	...
To Stock A/c		2,000		
To Plant and Machinery A/c		2,000		
To Gain (Profit) Transferred to				
X's Capital A/c	...			
Y's Capital A/c	...	...		
		...		...

Dr **Partners' Capital Account** Cr

Particulars	X (₹)	Y (₹)	Z (₹)	Particulars	X (₹)	Y (₹)	Z (₹)
To Balance c/d	2,16,000	1,44,000	90,000	By Balance b/d	...	...	...
				By Revaluation A/c (Gain)	10,500	7,000	
				By Bank A/c	—	—	90,000
				By Z's Current A/c	12,000	8,000	—
				By Bank A/c (Deficit)	1,01,500	61,000	—
	2,16,000	1,44,000	90,000		2,16,000	1,44,000	90,000

Balance Sheet
as at 31st March, 2024

Liabilities		Amt (₹)	Assets		Amt (₹)
Capital A/c			Land and Building		82,000
X	2,16,000		Plant and Machinery		68,000
Y	1,44,000		Stock		3,600
Z	90,000	4,50,000	Debtors	32,000	
Sundry Creditors		23,600	(–) Bad Debts	(2,000)	
Bills Payable		...		30,000	
			(–) Provision for Doubtful Debts	(...)	...
			Z's Current Account		...
			Cash at Bank		27,65,00
		...			...

Theoretical Questions

Short Answer Type Questions

1. What is sacrificing ratio? Why is it calculated? **NCERT; All India 2014 C; 2011**

Ans. The ratio in which old partners have agreed to sacrifice their share of profit in favour of the new partner is called sacrificing ratio. It is necessary to determine the sacrificing ratio, to determine the amount of compensation in the form of goodwill that the new partner should pay to the old partners for the share of profits sacrificed by them.

Sacrificing Ratio = Old Share – New Share

2. Differentiate between new profit sharing ratio and sacrificing ratio.

Ans. Difference between new profit sharing ratio and sacrificing ratio

Basis	New Profit Sharing Ratio	Sacrificing Ratio
Meaning	It is the ratio in which all partners will share the future profits of the firm.	It is the ratio in which old partners sacrifice their share in profits, in favour of new partner.
Purpose for Computation	It is computed, so that future profits could be shared.	It is computed to ascertain the sacrifice made by the partners.
Concerned with	It is concerned with all the partners.	It is concerned with only sacrificing partners.
Formula for Computation	New Profit Sharing Ratio = Old Share – Share Sacrificed	Sacrificing Ratio = Old Share – New Share

3. Explain how will you deal with goodwill when new partner is not in a position to bring his share of goodwill in cash? **NCERT; Competency Based Que**

Ans. If a new partner does not bring his share of goodwill in cash, then his capital account is debited for his share of goodwill and sacrificing partners' capital accounts are credited in their sacrificing ratio.

Following entry is passed in this case

New Partners' Capital/Current A/c Dr
  To Sacrificing Partners' Capital/Current A/c

4. Explain various methods for the treatment of goodwill on the admission of a new partner.

Ans. Various methods for the treatment of goodwill are

(i) When premium for goodwill is paid privately by a new partner.

(ii) When premium for goodwill is brought in by new partner in cash and retained in the business.

(iii) When premium for goodwill is brought in kind.

(iv) When premium for goodwill is brought in by new partner and is withdrawn by old (sacrificing) partners fully or partly.

(v) When a new partner brings only a part of premium for goodwill in cash.

(vi) When new or incoming partner is not able to bring his share of premium for goodwill in cash.

5. On admission of a new partner in a firm, an accountant is of the opinion that reserves and accumulated profits should not be distributed as there is not legal requirement and also he is of the opinion that even if they are not distributed, they will remain in business and they can be distributed when a partner retires or when the firm is dissolved. Is the accountant correct? **Competency Based Que**

Ans. No, the accountant is not correct because if the reserves and accumulated profits are distributed at the time of retirement or dissolution, they will have to be distributed among all the partners including the new partner in the profit sharing ratio at the time of distribution. It will mean that the new partner will also be given a share out of reserves and accumulated profits. It will not be correct because it puts the new partner to advantage and old partners to disadvantage.

6. How will you deal with accumulated profits and losses reserves on the admission of a new partner?

Ans. If at the time of admission of a partner, any reserves and accumulated profits (general reserve, reserve fund or credit balance of profit and loss account) or losses (debit balance of profit and loss account) exist in the books of the firm, then these should be transferred to old partner's capital accounts (if capital are fluctuating) or current accounts (if capital are fixed) in their old profit sharing ratio. The new partners are not entitled to have any share in such accumulated profit and also are not required to contribute towards accumulated losses.

7. Why there is a need for revaluation of assets and liabilities on the admission of a partner?

2014 (C); NCERT; Competency Based Que

Ans. There is a need revaluation of assets and liabilities on the admission of a partner, so that profit/loss on such revaluation upto the date of admission may be ascertained and adjusted in the old partners' capital accounts in their old profit sharing ratio, as it belongs to the old partners. For this purpose, revaluation account of the firm is prepared. This is also known as 'profit and loss adjustment account'. Revaluation account is a nominal account in nature.

Objective Questions

Multiple Choice Questions (MCQs)

1. According to Section 31 (1) of the Indian Partnership Act, 1932, a new partner can be admitted to a firm

(a) only with the consent of all existing partners
(b) with the consent of the majority of partners
(c) without consent if the new partner brings additional capital
(d) only if the existing partnership agreement allows it

2. Which amongst the following adjustment(s) is/are required at the time of admission of a new partner?

(a) Computation of new profit sharing ratio and sacrificing ratio
(b) Adjustment for goodwill
(c) Revaluation of assets (d) All of the above

3. A minor can be admitted as a partner in a partnership firm

(a) without any restrictions
(b) to share profits with the consent of all partners
(c) only if the minor has experience
(d) by law, a minor cannot be admitted as a partner

4. A, B and C are partners in a firm. If D is admitted as a new partner **NCERT**

(a) old firm is dissolved
(b) old firm and old partnership is dissolved
(c) old partnership is reconstituted
(d) None of the above

5. Piyush, Rajesh and Avinash were partners in a firm sharing profits and losses equally. Shiva admitted as a new partner for an equal share. Shiva brought his share of capital and premium for goodwill in cash.

The premium for goodwill amount will be divided among **CBSE 2024**

(a) old partner in old ratio
(b) new partners in new ratio
(c) new partners in sacrificing ratio
(d) old partners in sacrificing ratio

6. Upon admission, a new partner gains the right to

(a) share in future profits and assets of the firm
(b) sole ownership of the business
(c) have no liabilities
(d) remove existing partners

7. When a new partner is admitted to a firm, what happens to the old partnership?
(a) It continues with no changes
(b) It comes to an end and a new partnership comes into existence
(c) It is put on hold temporarily
(d) It remains the same but with reduced profits

8. Which of the following adjustments are made at the time of admission of a new partner?
(a) Goodwill and new liabilities only
(b) Only the assets are adjusted
(c) Capital contribution is removed
(d) Accumulated profits, losses, assets and liabilities

9. A and B share profits and losses in the ratio of 3 : 1, C is admitted into partnership for 1/4th share. The sacrificing ratio of A and B is **NCERT**
(a) equal (b) 3 : 1
(c) 2 : 1 (d) 3 : 2

10. 'A', 'B' and 'C' share profits and losses in the ratio of 3 : 2 : 1. 'D' is admitted with 1/6th share which he gets entirely from 'A'. New ratio will be
(a) 2 : 2 : 1 : 1 (b) 3 : 1 : 1 : 1
(c) 2 : 2 : 2 : 1 (d) None of these

11. Akshita and Anurag are partners in a firm sharing profits in the ratio of 2 : 1. Akshat is admitted in the firm with $\frac{1}{3}$ share in profits. Akshat acquires $\frac{2}{3}$ of his share from Akshita and 1/3 of his share from Anurag. The new profit sharing ratio of Akshita, Anurag and Akshat will be **CBSE 2023; Competency Based Que**
(a) 3 : 2 : 4 (b) 4 : 3 : 2
(c) 2 : 1 : 1 (d) 4 : 2 : 3

12. A and B are partners sharing profits in the ratio of 3 : 1. They admit C for 1/4 th share in the future profits. The new profit sharing ratio will be **NCERT**
(a) $A=\frac{9}{16}, B=\frac{3}{16}, C=\frac{4}{16}$
(b) $A=\frac{8}{16}, B=\frac{4}{16}, C=\frac{4}{16}$
(c) $A=\frac{10}{16}, B=\frac{2}{16}\ C=\frac{4}{16}$ (d) $A=\frac{8}{16}, B=\frac{9}{16}, C=\frac{10}{16}$

13. String and Kite were partners sharing profits and losses in the ratio 5 : 3. They admitted spinner as a new partner. String sacrificed 1/4 from his share and Kite sacrificed 1/6 of his share. What will be the new ratio? **CBSE SQP 2025; Competency Based Que**
(a) 6 : 5 : 5 (b) 9 : 5 : 10
(c) 15 : 10 : 7 (d) 35 : 21 : 40

14. Gupta and Sharma are partners in a firm sharing profits in the ratio of 4 : 1. They admitted Preeti as a new partner for 1/4th share in the profits, which she acquired wholly from Gupta.

New profit sharing ratio of Gupta, Sharma and Preeti will be **CBSE 2024; Competency Based Que**
(a) 2 : 1 : 1 (b) 11 : 4 : 5
(c) 3 : 3 : 2 (d) 7 : 5 : 4

15. Renu, Trilok and Mansi were partners in a firm sharing profits and losses in the ratio of 9 : 6 : 5. Hina was admitted as a partner for 1/10th share in the profits which she acquired equally from Renu and Trilok. The new profit sharing ratio after Hina's admission will be **CBSE 2024 C; Competency Based Que**
(a) 5 : 5 : 2 : 8 (b) 5 : 5 : 8 : 2
(c) 8 : 2 : 5 : 5 (d) 8 : 5 : 5 : 2

16. Ashu and Ria were partners in a firm sharing profits and losses in the ratio of 4 : 3. They admitted Nitu for a 3/7th share in the profits of the firm, which she took 2/7th from Ashu and 1/7th from Ria. The new profit sharing ratio between Ashu, Ria and Nitu will be **CBSE 2024 C**
(a) 4 : 3 : 3 (b) 2 : 1 : 3
(c) 2 : 2 : 3 (d) 4 : 3 : 2

17. X and Y were partners sharing profits in the ratio of 3 : 2. Z was admitted as a new partner for 1/5th share. X sacrificed 3/20 from his share and Y sacrificed 1/20 from his share in favour of Z, the new profit sharing ratio would be **CBSE Term I 2021; NCERT; Competency Based Que**
(a) 9 : 7 : 4 (b) 8 : 8 : 4
(c) 6 : 10 : 4 (d) 10 : 6 : 4

18. Krish and Laksh were partners in a firm sharing profits and losses in the ratio of 4 : 1. They admitted Rani as a new partner. Krish sacrificed 1/4th of his share and Laksh sacrificed 1/5th of his share in favour of Rani. Rani's share in the profits of the reconstituted firm will be. **CBSE 2020; Competency Based Que**
(a) $\frac{2}{5}$ (b) $\frac{6}{25}$ (c) $\frac{9}{30}$ (d) $\frac{1}{9}$

19. Arun, Bashir and Joseph were partners in a firm sharing profits and losses in the ratio of 5 : 3 : 2. They admitted Daksh as a new partner who acquired his share entirely from Arun. If Arun sacrificed 1/5th from his share to Daksh, Daksh's share in the profits of the firm will be **CBSE 2025**
(a) $\frac{1}{10}$ (b) $\frac{1}{5}$ (c) $\frac{3}{10}$ (d) $\frac{2}{5}$

20. **When goodwill existing in the books is written-off at the time of admission of a partner, it is transferred to partners' capital account in their ....**

(a) new profit sharing ratio (b) old profit sharing ratio
(c) sacrificing ratio (d) None of these

21. **The amount of compensation a new partner pays as goodwill is calculated by** **Competency Based Que**

(a) dividing the firm's total capital by the number of partners
(b) dividing the value of goodwill by the new partner's profit share
(c) multiplying the value of goodwill by the share sacrificed by existing partners
(d) adding the profit shares of all partners

22. **When a new partner brings his share of goodwill in cash, the amount is debited to ....**

(a) capital account (b) cash account
(c) revaluation account (d) None of these

23. **Kamini, Lata and Meera were partners in a firm sharing profits and losses equally. Neel was admitted as a new partner for an equal share in the profits of the firm. Neel brought his share of capital and premium for goodwill in cash. On the date of admission of Neel, goodwill appeared in the books at ₹ 1,20,000. The existing goodwill is to be written-off among** **CBSE 2024 C**

(a) old partners in old ratio
(b) new partners in new ratio
(c) sacrificing partners in sacrificing ratio
(d) old partners in sacrificing ratio

24. **Suhas and Vilas were partners in a firm with capitals of ₹ 4,00,000 and ₹ 3,00,000 respectively. They admitted Prabhas as a new partner for 1/5th share in future profits. Prabhas brought ₹ 2,00,000 as his capital. Prabhas' share of goodwill will be** **CBSE 2025; Competency Based Que**

(a) ₹ 1,00,000 (c) ₹ 10,00,000
(b) ₹ 9,00,000 (d) ₹ 20,000

25. **Mani and Neeru are partners in a firm sharing profits in the ratio of 5 : 3. On 1st April, 2024 they admitted Lily as a new partner on the following terms**

(i) The new profit sharing ratio will be 2 : 3 : 3.
(ii) Lily will bring ₹ 1,00,000 for her capital and the necessary amount of goodwill premium in cash.
(iii) Goodwill of the firm was valued at ₹ 1,40,000.

The journal entry for treatment or goodwill premium brought by Lily will be **CBSE Term I 2021; Competency Based Que**

(a)	Premium for Goodwill A/c	Dr	52,500	
	To Mani's Capital A/c			37,500
	To Neeru's Capital A/c			15,000
(b)	Premium for Goodwill A/c	Dr	52,500	
	To Mani's Capital A/c			52,500
(c)	Premium for Goodwill A/c	Dr	52,500	
	Neeru's Capital A/c	Dr	12,500	
	To Mani's Capital A/c			65,000
(d)	Lily's Current A/c	Dr	1,40,000	
	To Mani's Capital A/c			1,00,000
	To Neeru's Capital A/c			40,000

26. **Pulkit and Ravinder were partners in a firm sharing profits and losses in the ratio of 3 : 2. Sikander was admitted as a new partner for 1/5th share in the profits of the firm. Pulkit, Ravinder and Sikander decided to share future profits in the ratio of 2 : 2 : 1. Sikander brought ₹ 5,00,000 as his capital and ₹ 10,00,000 as his share of premium for goodwill. The amount of premium for goodwill that will be credited to the old partners' capital accounts will be** **CBSE 2025**

(a) Pulkit's Capital Account ₹ 10,00,000
(b) Pulkit's Capital Account ₹ 6,00,000 and Ravinder's Capital Account ₹ 4,00,000
(c) Pulkit's Capital Account ₹ 5,00,000 and Ravinder's Capital Account ₹ 5,00,000
(d) Pulkit's Capital Account ₹ 2,00,000

27. **Rohit, Virat and Shikhar were partners sharing profits and losses in the ratio 3 : 1 : 1. Their capital balance as on 31st March, 2024 was ₹ 3,00,000, ₹ 2,70,000 and ₹ 2,50,000 respectively.**

On the same date, they admitted Hardik as a new partner for 20% share. Hardik was to bring ₹ 80,000 for his share of goodwill and 1/5 of the combined capital of all the partners of new firm. What will be the total amount brought in by Hardik on his admission as a new partner? **CBSE SQP 2025; Competency Based Que**

(a) ₹ 2,25,000 (b) ₹ 1,80,000
(c) ₹ 2,60,000 (d) ₹ 3,05,000

28. **Asha and Nisha are partners' sharing profit in the ratio of 2 : 1. Asha's son Ashish was admitted for 1/4 th share of which 1/8 th was gifted by Asha to her son. The remaining was contributed by Nisha. Goodwill of the firm is valued at ₹ 40,000.**

How much of the goodwill be credited to the old partners' capital account? **NCERT; Competency Based Que**

(a) ₹ 2,500 each
(b) ₹ 5,000 each
(c) ₹ 20,000 each
(d) None of the above

29. **At the time of admission of a partner, undistributed profits appearing in the balance sheet of old firm is transferred to capital account of** NCERT

(a) old partners in old profit sharing ratio
(b) old partners in new profit sharing ratio
(c) all the partner in the new profit sharing ratio
(d) None of the above

30. **Reserve or general reserve appearing in the balance sheet will be divided among old partners during admission in .... ratio.**

(a) gaining (b) new
(c) sacrificing (d) old

31. **Kajal and Laura were partners in a firm sharing profits and losses in the ratio of 5 : 3. They admitted Maddy for for 1/4th share in future profits. Maddy brought ₹ 8,00,000 as his capital and ₹ 4,00,000 as his share of premium for goodwill. Kajal, Laura and Maddy decided to share profits in future in the ratio of 2 : 1 : 1. After all adjustments in respect of goodwill, revaluation of assets and liabilities, etc. Kajal's capital was ₹ 15,00,000 and Laura's capital was ₹ 8,00,000. It was agreed that partners' capitals should be in proportion to their new profit sharing ratio taking Maddy's capital as base. The adjustment was made by bringing in or withdrawing the necessary cash as the case may be. The cash brought in by Kajal was** CBSE 2025

(a) ₹ 1,00,000 (b) ₹ 8,00,000
(c) ₹ 16,00,000 (d) ₹ 12,00,000

32. **At the time of admission of a partner, the balance sheet of the firm showed a workmen compensation reserve of ₹ 80,000. The claim for workmen compensation was estimated at ₹ 1,00,000. The shortfall of ₹ 20,000 will be** CBSE 2024

(a) debited to revaluation account
(b) credited to revaluation account
(c) debited to partners' capital account
(d) credited to partners' capital account

33. **Seema and Teena are partners in a firm sharing profits and losses in the ratio of 3 : 2. They agreed to admit Reena into partnership for l/5th share of profits on 1st April, 2024. On that date, workmen's compensation fund stood in the balance sheet at ₹ 50,000. The liability against workmen's compensation fund is determined at ₹ 20,000 which is to be paid later in the year.**
What will be the journal entry for the treatment of workmen compensation fund on the admission of new partner Reena? CBSE Term I 2021; Competency Based Que

(a) Workmen Compensation Fund A/c Dr 30,000
  To Seema's Capital A/c 18,000
  To Teena's Capital A/c 12,000

(b) Workmen Compensation Fund A/c Dr 50,000
  To Revaluation A/c 20,000
  To Seema's Capital A/c 18,000
  To Teena's Capital A/c 12,000

(c) Workmen Compensation Fund A/c Dr 50,000
  To Workmen Compensation Claim A/c 20,000
  To Seema's Capital A/c 18,000
  To Teena's Capital A/c 12,000

(d) Workmen Compensation Fund A/c Dr 50,000
  To Seema's Capital A/c 30,000
  To Teena's Capital A/c 20,000

34. **Decrease in the value of assets at the time of admission of a partner is debited to ....**

(a) capital account (b) cash account
(c) revaluation account (d) None of these

35. **Gopal and Govind are partners in a firm sharing profits equally. They admitted Chetan for 1/3rd share in profits. On admission debtor whose dues of ₹ 5,000 were earlier written-off as bad debts, paid ₹ 4,000 in full, settlement. Bad debts recovered ₹ 4,000 will be debited to .... and credited to ....** CBSE Term I 2021; Competency Based Que

(a) cash/bank account, revaluation account
(b) bad debts recovered account, bad debts account
(c) cash/bank account, bad debts account
(d) revaluation account, bad debts recovered account

36. **Increase in the value of liabilities at the time of admission of a partner is .... to revaluation account.**

(a) credited (b) debited
(c) No treatment required (d) None of these

37. **The amount earlier written-off as bad debt now received is .... in revaluation account.**

(a) credited (b) debited
(c) Not recorded (d) None of these

38. **At the time of admission of new partner Vasu, old partners Paresh and Prabhav had debtors of ₹ 6,20,000 and a Provision for Doubtful Debts (PDD) of ₹ 20,000 in their books. As per terms of admission, assets were revalued and it was found that debtors worth ₹ 15,000 had turned bad and hence should be written-off. Which journal entry reflects the correct accounting treatment of the above situation?** CBSE SQP 2025; Competency Based Que

(a) Bad Debts A/c Dr 15,000
  To Debtors A/c 15,000
 Prov. for Doubtful Debts A/c Dr 15,000
  To Bad Debts A/c 15,000

(b) Bad Debts A/c Dr 15,000
 To Debtors A/c 15,000
 Revaluation A/c Dr 15,000
 To Prov. for Doubtful Debts A/c 15,000
(c) Revaluation A/c Dr 15,000
 To Debtors A/c 15,000
(d) Bad Debts A/c Dr 15,000
 To Revaluation A/c 15,000

39. Ram and Shyam were partners sharing profits and losses in the ratio of 3 : 2. Their balance sheet shows building at ₹ 1,60,000. They admitted Mohan as a new partner for 1/4th share. In additional information it is given that building is undervalued by 20%.

The share of loss/gain of revaluation of Shyam is ……… and current value of building shown in new balance sheet is ………… .

CBSE SQP 2025; Competency Based Que

(a) gain ₹ 12,800, value ₹ 1,92,000
(b) loss ₹ 12,800, value ₹ 1,28,000
(c) gain ₹ 16,000, value ₹ 2,00,000
(d) gain ₹ 40,000, value ₹ 2,00,000

40. 'X' and 'Y' share profits in the ratio of 3 : 2. 'X's' capital is ₹ 90,000, 'Y's' capital is ₹ 50,000. 'M' is admitted for 1/5th share in profits.

What is the amount of capital which 'M' should bring?

Competency Based Que

(a) ₹ 35,000 (b) ₹ 32,000 (c) ₹ 2,00,000 (d) ₹ 1,24,000

41. Santa and Banta are partners in a firm sharing profits in the ratio of 3 : 2. Kanta was admitted as a new partner for 1/5th share of profits. On Kanta's admission it was decided that machinery would be appreciated by 10% (Book value ₹ 80,000) and building would be depreciated 20% (Book value ₹ 2,00,000).

Unrecorded debtors of ₹ 1,250 would be brought to books. There was a liability of ₹ 2,750 included in sundry creditors that is not to be paid. What will be the gain/loss on revaluation? **CBSE Term I 2021; Competency Based Que**

(a) Loss ₹ 28,000 (b) Loss ₹ 40,000
(c) Profit ₹ 28,000 (d) Profit ₹ 40,000

42. Alex, Benn and Cole wee partners in a firm sharing profits and losses in the ratio of 5 : 3 : 2. They admitted Dona as a new partner for 1/5th share in the future profits. Dona agreed to contributed proportionate capital. On the date of admission, capitals of Alex, Benn and Cole after all adjustments were : ₹ 1,20,000, ₹ 80,000 and ₹ 1,00,000 respectively.

The amount of capital brought in by Dona will be

CBSE 2024; Competency Based Que

(a) ₹ 75,000 (b) ₹ 60,000 (c) ₹ 65,000 (d) ₹ 70,000

43. 'A' and 'B' carry on business and share profits and losses in the ratio of 3 : 2. Their respective capitals are ₹ 1,20,000 and ₹ 54,000. 'C' is admitted for 1/5th share in profit and brings ₹ 1,20,000 as his share of capital. Capitals of 'A' and 'B' to be adjusted according to 'C's' share.

Calculate the amount required to bring by 'A'.

Competency Based Que

(a) ₹ 30,000 (b) ₹ 1,68,000
(c) ₹ 60,000 (d) ₹ 28,000

44. Arjun, Babita and Charlie were partners in a firm sharing profits in the ratio of 2 : 2 : 1. They admitted Dheeraj for 1/5th share in the profits of the firm. He has to contribute proportionate capital to acquire 1/5th share in future profits.

On the date of admission, the capitals after all adjustments relating to goodwill and revaluation of assets and liabilities were : Arjun ₹ 62,000, Babita ₹ 52,000 and Charlie ₹ 36,000. The capital brought by Dheeraj will be **CBSE 2024 C**

(a) ₹ 37,500 (b) ₹ 30,000
(c) ₹ 32,500 (d) ₹ 35,000

Assertion-Reason

Direction (Q.No. 45 to 54) *Read the following Assertion (A) and Reason (R) and choose the correct alternative from the following*

Alternatives

(a) Both Assertion (A) and Reason (R) are true and Reason (R) is the correct explanation of Assertion (A)
(b) Both Assertion (A) and Reason (R) are true, but Reason (R) is not the correct explanation of Assertion (A)
(c) Assertion (A) is true, but Reason (R) is false
(d) Assertion (A) is false, but Reason (R) is true

45. Assertion (A) When a new partner is admitted to a firm, the existing partnership comes to an end and a new partnership agreement comes into existence.

Reason (R) Admission of a new partner results in reconstitution of the firm and requires consent from all existing partners.

46. Assertion (A) The new partner's capital contribution is essential to the firm at the time of admission.

Reason (R) A new partner's capital contribution provides resources for potential business expansion or acquisition.

47. Assertion (A) It is necessary to ascertain new profit sharing ratio for old partners when a new partner is admitted.

Reason (R) New partner acquires his share from old partners which reduces old partners' share in profits.

48. **Assertion** (A) Upon the admission of a new partner, the goodwill of the firm is often adjusted through the capital accounts of the partners.

Reason (R) The goodwill adjustment ensures that the sacrificing partners compensate the gaining partners for any reduction in their profit sharing ratio.

49. **Assertion** (A) Revaluation of assets and reassessment of liabilities are essential adjustments when a new partner is admitted to a firm.

Reason (R) Revaluation helps allocate gains or losses from asset and liability adjustments among partners in the new profit sharing ratio.

50. **Assertion** (A) When a new partner is admitted, he compensates the existing partners for their sacrifice in future profits by paying an amount called goodwill.

Reason (R) The amount of goodwill is calculated based on the share sacrificed by the existing partners.

51. **Assertion** (A) In certain cases, the premium for goodwill paid by the incoming partner is not recorded in the books of accounts.

Reason (R) Sometimes, the incoming partner pays his share of goodwill privately to the sacrificing partners, outside the business.

52. **Assertion** (A) If the amount of any liability is understated, then revaluation account will be debited to restore the liability's amount to its actual value.

Reason (R) Increase in the amount of liability is a profit for the firm.

53. **Assertion** (A) The balance of memorandum revaluation account (second part) is transferred to partners' capital account in old profit sharing ratio.

Reason (R) Sometimes, partners decide to show the assets and liabilities in the books of the new firm at their existing values.

54. **Assertion** (A) It is necessary to revalue assets and liabilities of a firm in case of admission of a partner.

Reason (R) It is because the incoming partner is neither put to an advantage nor to a disadvantage due to change in the value of assets and liabilities. **CBSE Term I 2021**

Two Statements Based MCQs

Direction (Q.No. 55 to 62) *Read the following statements carefully and choose the correct alternative*

Alternatives

(a) Statement I is correct and Statement II is incorrect
(b) Statement II is correct and Statement I is incorrect
(c) Both the statements are correct
(d) Both the statements are incorrect

55. **Statement I** A new partner can be admitted with the consent of all existing partners.

Statement II A minor can be admitted as a partner without the consent of all partners.

56. **Statement I** A new partner can only acquire a share in the firm's assets.

Statement II A new partner has the right to share future profits of the firm.

57. **Statement I** The existing partnership agreement does not need any change when a new partner is admitted.

Statement II A new partner must bring capital to gain rights in the firm's assets.

58. **Statement I** A new partner's personal liability starts only after his admission.

Statement II A newly admitted partner is liable for liabilities incurred before his admission.

59. **Statement I** On admission, the new partner's share of profit increases the combined share of the old partners.

Statement II The goodwill of the firm is adjusted through the capital accounts of the sacrificing and gaining partners.

60. **Statement I** The new partner compensates the existing partners based on their past profits only.

Statement II The compensation paid by the new partner for goodwill is calculated based on the share sacrificed by the existing partners.

61. **Statement I** At the time of admission of a partner, unrecorded assets or liabilities are transferred to profit and loss account.

Statement II The ratio in which all partners including the incoming partner share future profits and losses is known as old profit sharing ratio.

62. **Statement I** Undistributed profits and general reserves are transferred to partners current accounts, if capital accounts are fixed.

Statement II Newly admitted partner does not have the right on the assets of firm.

Matching

63. **Match the following terms with their definitions:**

Column I (Terms)	Column II (Definitions)
A. Gaining partner	(i) Share of profit reduced due to admission of new partner
B. Sacrificing partner	(ii) Share of profit increased due to admission of new partner
C. Goodwill	(iii) Amount paid to compensate sacrificing partner
D. Capital contribution	(iv) Amount brought by the new partner

Codes

	A	B	C	D		A	B	C	D
(a)	(ii)	(i)	(iii)	(iv)	(b)	(iv)	(ii)	(i)	(iii)
(c)	(ii)	(iii)	(iv)	(i)	(d)	(i)	(iii)	(ii)	(iv)

64. **Match the following purposes of admitting a new partner with their descriptions**

Column I (Purposes)		Column II (Descriptions)	
A.	Additional capital	(i)	To expand the business financially
B.	Managerial skills	(ii)	To improve business operations
C.	Increase goodwill	(iii)	By associating with a reputed individual
D.	Efficiency benefit	(iv)	By gaining experienced partners

Codes

	A	B	C	D		A	B	C	D
(a)	(i)	(ii)	(iii)	(iv)	(b)	(ii)	(i)	(iv)	(iii)
(c)	(i)	(iii)	(ii)	(iv)	(d)	(iii)	(iv)	(i)	(ii)

65. **Match the adjustments with their descriptions**

Column I (Adjustments)	Column II (Descriptions)
A. New profit sharing and sacrificing ratio	(i) Ensures correct allocation of profits between old and new partners
B. Goodwill adjustment	(ii) Compensates existing partners for profit sacrifices made
C. Revaluation of assets and liabilities	(iii) Accounts for current value of firm's assets and obligations
D. Capital adjustment	(iv) Balances partner's capital accounts as per new agreement

Codes

	A	B	C	D		A	B	C	D
(a)	(i)	(ii)	(iii)	(iv)	(b)	(ii)	(i)	(iv)	(iii)
(c)	(i)	(iv)	(ii)	(iii)	(d)	(iii)	(ii)	(i)	(iv)

Case Based MCQs

Direction *Read the following case study and answer the questions 66 to 68 on the basis of the same*

Given below is the balance sheet of A and B who are partners in a firm sharing profits in the ratio of 3 : 2.

Balance Sheet
as at 1st April, 2024

Liabilities		Amt (₹)	Assets	Amt (₹)
Sundry Creditors		3,00,000	Land and Buildings	4,00,000
Profit and Loss A/c		1,00,000	Plant and Machinery	3,00,000
Capital A/cs			Stock	70,000
A	4,00,000		Debtors	1,80,000
B	2,00,000	6,00,000	Bank	50,000
		10,00,000		10,00,000

On the same date, C is admitted as a partner on the following terms

(i) A gives 1/3rd of his share, while B gives 1/10th from his share to C.

(ii) Goodwill is valued at 2 years' purchase of the average profits of the last 5 years, which were ₹ 50,000 (loss); ₹ 1,20,000; ₹ 10,000 (loss); ₹ 3,00,000 and ₹ 3,40,000 respectively. C does not bring his share of goodwill in cash.

66. **What was the sacrificing ratio of A and B?**

(a) 1 : 1 (b) 3 : 10
(c) 3 : 2 (d) 2 : 1

67. **What was the amount of firm's goodwill?**

(a) ₹ 84,000
(b) ₹ 1,40,000
(c) ₹ 1,64,000
(d) ₹ 2,80,000

68. **What was the C's share of goodwill?**

(a) ₹ 84,000 (b) ₹ 1,40,000
(c) ₹ 1,64,000 (d) ₹ 2,80,000

Direction *Read the following case study and answer the questions 69 to 71 on the basis of the same*

A and B are partners in a firm sharing profits in the ratio of 5 : 2. On 1st April, 2024 their balance sheet was as follows

Balance Sheet
as at 1st April, 2024

Liabilities	Amt (₹)	Assets	Amt (₹)
A's Capital A/c	80,000	Bank	10,000
B's Capital A/c	70,000	Stock	20,000
Creditors	30,000	Debtors	30,000
		Plant and Machinery	40,000
		Building	80,000
	1,80,000		1,80,000

On the above date, they admitted C as a new partner on the following terms

(i) That the new profit sharing ratio will be 2 : 3 : 3.
(ii) That C will bring ₹ 1,00,000 for her capital and the necessary amount of goodwill premium in cash.
(iii) Goodwill of the firm is valued at ₹ 1,40,000.

69. **What was the share of A's sacrifice?**

(a) 5/56 (b) 13/28
(c) 3/7 (d) 3/8

70. **Who is/are the gaining partner(s) in this case?**

(a) A (b) B
(c) C (d) Both (b) and (c)

71. **What was C's share of goodwill?**

(a) ₹ 12,500 (b) ₹ 52,500
(c) ₹ 1,40,000 (d) ₹ 2,80,000

Answers

1. (a) only with the consent of all existing partners
2. (d) All of the above
3. (b) to share profits with the consent of all partners
4. (c) old partnership is reconstituted
5. (d) old partners in sacrificing ratio
6. (a) share in future profits and assets of the firm
7. (b) It comes to an end and a new partnership comes into existence
8. (d) Accumulated profits, losses, assets and liabilities
9. (b) 3 : 1
10. (a) 'A's' Share $= \frac{3}{6} - \frac{1}{6} = \frac{2}{6}$; 'B's' Share $= \frac{2}{6}$

 'C's' Share $= \frac{1}{6}$ and 'D's' Share $= \frac{1}{6}$

 New Profit Sharing Ratio $= 2:2:1:1$
11. (d) Akshat acquires from Akshita $= \frac{2}{3} \times \frac{1}{3} = \frac{2}{9}$

 Akshat acquires from Anurag $= \frac{1}{3} \times \frac{1}{3} = \frac{1}{9}$

 Akshita's share $= \frac{2}{3} - \frac{2}{9} = \frac{6-2}{9} = \frac{4}{9}$

 Anurag's share $= \frac{1}{3} - \frac{1}{9} = \frac{3-1}{9} = \frac{2}{9}$

 New Profit Sharing Ratio $= \frac{4}{9} : \frac{2}{9} : \frac{1}{3}$ *or* $4:2:3$
12. (a) C's share $= \frac{1}{4}$; Total share $= 1$

 Remaining share of A and B $= 1 - \frac{1}{4} = \frac{3}{4}$

 A's New Share $= \frac{3}{4} \times \frac{3}{4} = \frac{9}{16}$

 B's New Share $= \frac{3}{4} \times \frac{1}{4} = \frac{3}{16}$

 C's New Share $= \frac{1}{4} \times \frac{4}{4} = \frac{4}{16}$

 $\therefore$ New Profit Sharing Ratio $= 9:3:4$
13. (a) String's New Share $= \frac{5}{8} - \frac{1}{4} = \frac{5-2}{8} = \frac{3}{8} \times \frac{6}{6} = \frac{18}{48}$

 Kite's Sacrifice $= \frac{3}{8} \times \frac{1}{6} = \frac{3}{48}$

 Kite's New Share $= \frac{3}{8} - \frac{3}{48} = \frac{18-3}{48} = \frac{15}{48}$

 Spinner's New Share $= \frac{1}{4} + \frac{3}{48} = \frac{12+3}{48} = \frac{15}{48}$

 $\Rightarrow 18:15:15$ *or* $6:5:5$
14. (b) Preeti's share $= \frac{1}{4}$th share, which she acquired from Gupta

 Gupta's New Share $= \frac{4}{5} - \frac{1}{4} = \frac{16-5}{20} = \frac{11}{20}$

 Sharma's share $= \frac{1}{5}$

 $\therefore$ New profit sharing ratio of Gupta, Sharma and Preeti $= \frac{11}{20} : \frac{1}{5} : \frac{1}{4} = 11:4:5$
15. (d) Share sacrificed by Renu in favour of Hina

 $= \frac{1}{10} \times \frac{1}{2} = \frac{1}{20}$

 Share sacrificed by Trilok in favour of Hina

 $= \frac{1}{10} \times \frac{1}{2} = \frac{1}{20}$

 New share of Renu $= \frac{9}{20} - \frac{1}{20} = \frac{8}{20}$

 New share of Trilok $= \frac{6}{20} - \frac{1}{20} = \frac{5}{20}$

 Share of Mansi $= \frac{5}{20}$; Share of Hina $= \frac{1}{10} \times \frac{2}{2} = \frac{2}{20}$

 New Profit Sharing Ratio $= 8:5:5:2$
16. (c) Share sacrificed by Ashu $= \frac{4}{7} - \frac{2}{7} = \frac{2}{7}$

 Share sacrificed by Ria $= \frac{3}{7} - \frac{1}{7} = \frac{2}{7}$

 Nitu's share = 3/7; New Profit Sharing Ratio $= 2:2:3$
17. (a) Z's share $= \frac{1}{5}$; X sacrifice $= \frac{3}{20}$; Y sacrifice $= \frac{1}{20}$

 X's New Share $= \frac{3}{5} - \frac{3}{20} = \frac{12-3}{20} = \frac{9}{20}$

 Y's New Share $= \frac{2}{5} - \frac{1}{20} = \frac{8-1}{20} = \frac{7}{20}$

 Z's New Share $= \frac{3}{20} + \frac{1}{20} = \frac{4}{20}$

 $\therefore$ New Profit Sharing Ratio $= 9:7:4$
18. (b) $\frac{6}{25}$
19. (b) $\frac{1}{5}$
20. (b) old profit sharing ratio
21. (c) multiplying the value of goodwill by the share sacrificed by existing partners
22. (b) cash account
23. (a) old partners in old ratio
24. (d) Hidden Goodwill = Capital of Firm taking Prabhas Base − Net Worth

$= (2,00,000 \times 5) - (2,00,000 + 4,00,000 + 3,00,000)$

$= 10,00,000 - 9,00,000 = ₹\ 1,00,000$

Prabhas' share in goodwill $= 1,00,000 \times \frac{1}{5} = ₹\ 20,000$

25. (b) Premium for Goodwill A/c Dr 52,500
To Mani's Capital A/c 52,500

26. (d) Only Pulkit is sacrificing as $= \frac{3}{5} - \frac{2}{5} = \frac{1}{5}$ Sacrifice

Pulkit's capital will be credited with ₹ 2,00,000 as premium for goodwill.

Pulkit's share in premium for goodwill = ₹ 10,00,000 $\times \frac{1}{5} = ₹\ 2,00,000$

27. (d) Let Hardik's capital be x

Combined capital of all the partners

$= 3,00,000 + 2,70,000 + 2,50,000 + 80,000 + x$

$= 9,00,000 + x$

Hardik's capital $= \frac{9,00,000 + x}{5} \Rightarrow x = \frac{9,00,000 + x}{5}$

$x = ₹\ 2,25,000$

Total amount brought in $= 2,25,000 + 80,000$

$= ₹\ 3,05,000$

28. (c) Asha sacrifice $= \frac{1}{8}$

Nisha sacrifice $= \frac{1}{4} - \frac{1}{8} = \frac{2-1}{8} = \frac{1}{8}$

Sacrificing ratio = 1 : 1

∴ Amount of goodwill credited to old partners' capital account $= 40,000 \times \frac{1}{2} = ₹\ 20,000$

29. (a) old partners in old profit sharing ratio

30. (d) old

31. (a) Capital of new firm taking Maddy's capital as base $= 8,00,000 \times 4 = ₹\ 32,00,000$

New capital of Kajal $= 32,00,000 \times \frac{1}{4} = ₹\ 16,00,000$

Cash brought in by Kajal = New Capital – Adjusted Capital

$= 16,00,000 - 15,00,000$

$= ₹\ 1,00,000$

32. (a) debited to revaluation account

33. (c) Workmen Compensation Fund A/c Dr 50,000
To Workmen Compensation Claim A/c 20,000
To Seema's Capital A/c 18,000
To Teena's Capital A/c 12,000

34. (c) revaluation account

35. (a) cash/bank account, revaluation account

36. (b) debited **37.** (a) credited

38. (a) Bad Debts A/c Dr 15,000
To Debtors A/c 15,000
Prov. for Doub. Debts A/c Dr 15,000
To Bad Debts A/c 15,000

39. (c) If the building is undervalued by 20%, the recorded value will be equal to 80%, i.e. 100% – 20%.

Current value of building $= \frac{1,60,000}{80} \times 100 = ₹\ 2,00,000$

∴ Profit on revaluation $= 2,00,000 - 1,60,000 = ₹\ 40,000$

Shyam's share in revaluation profit $= 40,000 \times \frac{2}{5}$

$= ₹\ 16,000$

40. (a)

Particulars	Amt (₹)
'X's' Capital	90,000
'Y's' Capital	50,000
Capital of 'X' and 'Y' for $\frac{4}{5}$th share $\left(\text{i.e. } 1 - \frac{1}{5}\right)$	1,40,000
Total Capital of Firm $\left(1,40,000 \times \frac{5}{4}\right)$	1,75,000
'M's' Share in Capital $\left(1,75,000 \times \frac{1}{5}\right)$	35,000

41. (a) Gain/Loss on Revaluation

$= 8,000 - 4,000 + 1,250 + 2,750 = ₹\ (28,000)$

42. (a) Dona's Capital $= (1,20,000 + 80,000 + 1,00,000) \times \frac{5}{4} \times \frac{1}{5}$

$= ₹\ 75,000$

43. (b) Old ratio = 3 : 2; 'C's' share $= \frac{1}{5}$; Capital = ₹ 1,20,000

Total capital of firm based on 'C's' share

$= 1,20,000 \times \frac{5}{1} = ₹\ 6,00,000$

Remaining share $= 1 - \frac{1}{5} = \frac{4}{5}$

New profit sharing ratio

'A's' New Share $= \frac{4}{5} \times \frac{3}{5} = \frac{12}{25}$

'B's' New Share $= \frac{4}{5} \times \frac{2}{5} = \frac{8}{25}$; 'C's' Share $= \frac{1}{5} \times \frac{5}{5} = \frac{5}{25}$

New profit sharing ratio = 12 : 8 : 5

'A's' capital based on new share

$= 6,00,000 \times \frac{12}{25} = ₹\ 2,88,000$

∴ Capital to bring in by 'A' $= 2,88,000 - 1,20,000$

$= ₹\ 1,68,000$

44. (a) ₹ 37,500

45. (a) Both Assertion (A) and Reason (R) are true and Reason (R) is the correct explanation of Assertion (A)
46. (a) Both Assertion (A) and Reason (R) are true and Reason (R) is the correct explanation of Assertion (A)
47. (a) Both Assertion (A) and Reason (R) are true and Reason (R) is the correct explanation of Assertion (A)
48. (c) Assertion (A) is true, but Reason (R) is false
49. (b) Both Assertion (A) and Reason (R) are true, but Reason (R) is not the correct explanation of Assertion (A)
50. (b) Both Assertion (A) and Reason (R) are true, but Reason (R) is not the correct explanation of Assertion (A)
51. (a) Both Assertion (A) and Reason (R) are true and Reason (R) is the correct explanation of Assertion (A)
52. (c) Increase in the amount of liability is a loss for the firm.
53. (d) The balance of memorandum revalution account (second part) is transferrred to all partners' capital account (including new partner) in new ratio as the value of assets and liabilities are not to be changed.
54. (a) Both Assertion (A) and Reason (R) are true and Reason (R) is the correct explanation of Assertion (A)
55. (a) Statement I is correct and Statement II is incorrect
56. (b) Statement II is correct and Statement I is incorrect
57. (b) Statement II is correct and Statement I is incorrect
58. (a) Statement I is correct and Statement II is incorrect
59. (b) Statement II is correct and Statement I is incorrect
60. (b) Statement II is correct and Statement I is incorrect
61. (b) At the time of admission of a partner, unrecorded assets or liabilities are transferred to revalution account. The ratio in which all the partners including the incoming partner share future profits is known as new profit sharing ratio.
62. (a) Statement I is correct and Statement II is incorrect
63. (a) (ii) (i) (iii) (iv)
64. (a) (i) (ii) (iii) (iv)
65. (a) (i) (ii) (iii) (iv)
66. (d) **Calculation of Sacrificing Ratio**

    Share surrendered by A $= \frac{3}{5} \times \frac{1}{3} = \frac{1}{5}$

    Share surrendered by B $= \frac{1}{10}$

    Sacrificing ratio $= \frac{1}{5} : \frac{1}{10} \Rightarrow \frac{2}{10} : \frac{1}{10} \Rightarrow 2:1$
67. (d) **Valuation of Goodwill**

    Average Profit

    $= \frac{(50{,}000) + 1{,}20{,}000 + (10{,}000) + 3{,}00{,}000 + 3{,}40{,}000}{5}$

    $=$ ₹ 1,40,000

    Goodwill at 2 years' purchase $= 1{,}40{,}000 \times 2 =$ ₹ 2,80,000
68. (a) C's Share of Goodwill $= 2{,}80{,}000 \times \frac{3}{10} =$ ₹ 84,000
69. (b) 13/28
70. (d) B is an old partner, however, he will gain due to change in profit sharing ratio. C is incoming partner and therefore gains a share in the profits/losses of the firm.
71. (b) C's Share of Goodwill = 3/8 × 1,40,000 = ₹ 52,500

05
CHAPTER

A partner may retire from the firm after giving due notice in advance. It results to an end of old partnership but the firm continues with new partnership between remaining partners.

YOUR STUDY GOALS

YOUR PRACTICE GOAL

- Topicwise Solved Questions (44 Solved Questions)
- Numerical Questions [54 Questions (Unsolved)]
- Theoretical Questions [9 Questions (with answers)]
- Objective Questions (70 Qs ; MCQs, A-R, Statements, Matching, Case)

Reconstitution of a Partnership Firm : Retirement/Death of a Partner

5.1 Retirement of a Partner

Retirement of a partner means retiring from the firm, i.e. ceasing to be a partner of the firm. As a result, an old partnership comes to an end and a new one between the remaining (continuing) partners comes into existence. However, the firm continues its business.

According to **Section 32(1)** of the **Indian Partnership Act, 1932**, a partner may retire

- With the consent of all the other partners (Whether expressed or implied).
- In accordance with an express agreement by partners.
- By giving notice in writing, to all other partners. (In case of **partnership at will**).

Liability of a Retiring Partner

Liability for the Acts before Retirement [Section 32(2)] A retiring partner remains liable for all the acts of firm upto the date of his retirement unless discharged from his liability by an agreement between himself, third party and the continuing partners.

Liability for the Acts after Retirement [Section 32(3)] A retiring partner also continues to be liable to third parties for firm's acts even after his retirement, until a public notice of his retirement is given.

Adjustments Required at the Time of Retirement of a Partner

- New profit sharing ratio and gaining ratio.
- Adjustment for goodwill
- Adjustment of profit/loss on revaluation of assets and reassessment of liabilities.
- Adjustment of accumulated profits, reserves and losses.
- Computation of retiring partner's dues and payment.
- Adjustment of capitals (if agreed).

New Profit Sharing Ratio

This is the ratio in which remaining partners decide to share the future profits and losses, after an outgoing partner leaves.

New Ratio = Old Share + Acquired Gaining Share

Unless agreed otherwise, continuing partners acquire the outgoing partner's share in their old profit sharing ratio.

Gaining Ratio

This is the ratio in which remaining partners acquire the outgoing (retired or deceased) partner's share.

Gaining Ratio = New Share − Old Share

Calculation of New Profit Sharing Ratio and Gaining Ratio

Case	Explanation
One partner retires and the new profit sharing ratio among the remaining partners is not given	When a partner retires and the new profit sharing ratio is not given, then new profit sharing ratio and gaining ratio can be calculated by omitting retiring partner's share. So, it will be assumed that the remaining partners continue to share profits and losses in the remaining ratio.
Gains of continuing partners are separately given	In case, gains of continuing partners are separately given, then new share of continuing partners may be calculated by adding their gain to their old share. New Share = Old Share + Gain The shares gained will be converted to a ratio to find the gaining ratio.
The remaining partners acquire share of the retiring partner in specified ratio	In this case, the share taken by each partner is computed separately and then added to their old share.
To find gaining ratio when old ratio and new ratio are given	In this case, gaining ratio is computed by taking out the difference between old share and new share i.e. Gaining Ratio = New Share − Old Share
Entire share of retiring partner is taken by only one partner	In case the entire share of retiring partner is taken by one partner, the acquired share will be added to that particular partner's share.
To find new profit sharing ratio when gaining ratio is given	In this case, gaining share is added to old share to find out the new profit sharing ratio.

Accounting Treatment of Goodwill

The retiring or deceased partner is entitled to his share of goodwill, as it has been earned through the efforts of all existing partners. Since, his share of profits will be taken by the remaining partners, so the continuing partners should compensate the retiring or deceased partner. This compensation is called **goodwill**. The goodwill value is calculated as per the partners' agreement at the time of retirement or death.

Point to Remember

AS-26 states that goodwill is to be recorded in the books only when some consideration in money or money's worth has been paid for it i.e. only purchased goodwill is recorded in the books.

Adjustment for goodwill is made by following given steps

Step 1 **Write-off goodwill** (if any) **already appearing in the books.**

All Partners' Capital/Current A/c	Dr	[In old ratio including reitiring partner]
To Goodwill A/c		[With existing book value of goodwill]

Step 2 **Give credit to retiring/deceased** (i.e. outgoing) **partner for his share of goodwill.**

Continuing/Gaining Partners' Capital*/Current** A/c	Dr	[In gaining ratio]
To Outgoing/Sacrificing Partner's Capital*/Current** A/c		[With his share of goodwill]

**Under fluctuating capital method.* ***Under fixed capital method.*

Sometimes on retirement of a partner, a continuing partner may also sacrifice a part of his profit share. In this case, such partner is also compensated alongwith the outgoing partner.

JOURNAL

Continuing Partners' Capital/Current A/c	Dr	[Who have gained]
To Retiring Partners' Capital/Current A/c		[Who have sacrificed]
To Continuing Partners' Capital/Current A/c		[Who have sacrificed]

Hidden Goodwill

Sometimes, the firm agrees to settle the retiring or deceased partner's account by payment of a lumpsum amount. If such amount is in excess of his capital and share in reserves/revaluation of assets and liabilities, etc., the excess will be treated as his share of goodwill.

Adjustment for Reserves, Accumulated Profits and Losses

At the time of retirement of a partner any reserve, accumulated profits or losses, etc. appearing in the balance sheet of the firm is distributed among all the partners (including retiring partner) in their old profit sharing ratio.

Smart Study Chart No. 1

Journal Entries

For Distribution of Reserves and Accumulated Profits

General Reserve A/c	Dr
Reserve Fund A/c	Dr
Profit and Loss A/c (Cr Balance)	Dr
To All Partner's Capital/Current A/cs (In old ratio)	

For Distribution of Accumulated Losses

All Partner's Capital/Current A/cs (In old ratio)	Dr
To Profit and Loss A/c	
To Advertisement Expenditure A/c	

Revaluation of Assets and Reassessment of Liabilities

At the time of retirement of a partner, the assets are revalued and liabilities are reassessed to determine retiring partner's share in profit/loss arising from such revaluation and adjust it in capital account.

For this purpose, **revaluation account** is prepared. Any profit or loss arising from revaluation of assets and liabilities is divided among all the partners including the retiring one.

Revaluation account is prepared in the same manner as discussed in the chapter 'admission of a partner'. But with the exception that any profit or loss arising from revaluation of assets and liabilities is divided among all the partners including the retiring partner.

5.2 Computation of Amount Due to a Retiring Partner

The amount due to a retiring partner is ascertained by preparing retiring partner's capital account, after taking into account the following

Smart Study Chart No. 2

Items to be Considered

Items to be Credited

- Opening balance of capital and current account of a retiring partner.
- His share in the profit of revaluation account.
- His share of reserves/accumulated profits.
- His share of goodwill of the firm.
- His share of profit till the date of his retirement.
- His salary/commission due till the date of his retirement.
- Interest on capital (if allowed) till the date of his retirement.

Items to be Debited

- Drawings and interest thereon, of the retiring partner.
- Share in the accumulated losses of past year(s).
- Share in the loss of revaluation account.

Format of Retiring Partner's Capital Account

Dr **Retiring Partner's Capital Account** Cr

Particulars	Amt (₹)	Particulars	Amt (₹)
To Revaluation A/c (Share in Loss)	...	By Balance b/d	...
To Share in Accumulated Losses	...	By Profit and Loss Suspense A/c (Share in Profit for Current year till the Date of Retirement)	...
To Cash A/c (Drawings till Retirement)	...	By Revaluation A/c (Share in Gain)	...
To Interest on Drawings A/c	...	By Share of Goodwill	...
To Goodwill A/c (Share in Existing Goodwill Written-off)	...	By Share in Accumulated Profits	
To Retiring Partner's Loan A/c (Transfer) (Balancing Figure)	...	General Reserve A/c	...
		Profit and Loss A/c	...
		By Interest on Capital A/c (Due till the Date of his Retirement)	...
		By Salary/Commission A/c (Due till the Date of his Retirement)	...
	...		...

If the question doesn't specify how to settle a retiring partner's account, the amount owed is transferred to his loan account and recorded as

Retiring Partner's Capital A/c	Dr
To Retiring Partner's Loan A/c	

This loan account appears as a liability in the balance sheet.

Section 37 of the Indian Partnership Act, 1932

Under Section 37 of the Indian Partnership Act, 1932, if an outgoing partner's due amount is unpaid in full or part, then

- he is entitled to either interest, a share in profits or nothing, as mutually agreed by the partners.
- If no agreement is in place, then outgoing partner or his representatives may choose between
  - Interest at 6% per annum on the outstanding balance or
  - A share in the profits proportional to the outstanding amount in relation to the total capital, which can be calculated using the formula provided below

$$\text{Share in Profit} = \frac{\text{Outstanding Amount of Outgoing Partner}}{\text{Capital of All Partner} + \text{Balance of Outgoing Partner}} \times \text{Profit from the Date of the Last Balance Sheet till Date of Death or Retirement of a Partner}$$

Smart Study Chart No. 3

Method of Payment of Amount due to Retiring Partner

Payment in Lumpsum

Retiring Partner's Capital A/c To Cash/Bank A/c	Dr

Payment in Installments

For amount due transferred to retiring partner's loan account	Retiring Partner's Capital A/c To Retiring Partner's Loan A/c	Dr
On interest being provided	Interest on Loan A/c To Retiring Partner's Loan A/c	Dr
On payment of instalment with interest	Retiring Partner's Loan A/c To Cash/Bank A/c	Dr

Payment in part Cash and in part Installments (As a Loan)

Retiring Partner's Capital A/c To Cash/Bank A/c To Retiring Partner's Loan A/c	Dr

5.3 Adjustment of Capital

After the retirement of a partner, the remaining partners may decide that their capitals should be adjusted in proportion to their profit sharing ratio. The capitals of the continuing partners may be required to be adjusted in any one of the following cases

Case	Steps
Total capital of the new firm is given	1. Calculate new profit sharing ratio and gaining ratio of continuing partners (if not given). 2. Calculate the adjusted old capitals of continuing partners (i.e. after all other adjustments). 3. Calculate the new capitals of continuing partners by dividing the total capital in their new profit sharing ratio. 4. Calculate the surplus/deficiency in each of the continuing partners' capital accounts by comparing the new capitals with the adjusted old capitals. 5. Adjust the surplus by paying-off or by transfer to current account and adjust the deficiency by asking the concerned partner to bring in necessary amount or by debiting his current account.
The total capital of the new firm is not given (When total capital of the new firm is to be in new profit sharing ratio)	1. Calculate the adjusted old capitals of continuing partners after all other adjustments. 2. Calculate total capital of the new firm as follows Total Capital of the New Firm = Aggregate of Adjusted Old Capitals of Continuing Partners. 3. Calculate the new capitals of continuing partners by dividing the total capital in their new profit sharing ratio. 4. Calculate the surplus/deficiency in each of the continuing partners' capital account by comparing the new capitals with the adjusted old capitals. 5. Adjust the surplus by paying-off or by transfer to the credit of current account and adjust the deficiency by asking the concerned partner to bring in the necessary amount or by transfer to the debit of his current account.
The total capital of the new firm is to be same as before retirement of a partner	1. Calculate the adjusted old capitals of continuing partners after all other adjustments. 2. Calculate the new capitals of continuing partners by dividing the total capital (same as before the retirement of a partner) in their new profit sharing ratio. 3. Calculate the surplus/deficiency in each of the continuing partners' capital account by comparing the new capitals with the adjusted old capitals. 4. Adjust the surplus by paying-off or by transfer to the credit of current account and adjust the deficiency by asking the concerned partner to bring in the necessary amount or by transfer to the debit of his current account.

Case	Steps
The outgoing partner is to be paid through cash brought in by the continuing partners in such a way as to make their capitals proportionate to their new profit sharing ratio	1. Calculate the adjusted old capitals of continuing partners after all other adjustments. 2. Calculate total capital of the new firm as follows Total capital of the new firm = Aggregate of adjusted old capitals of continuing partners + Shortage of cash to be brought in by continuing partners in order to make payment to outgoing partner. 3. Calculate the new capitals of continuing partners by dividing the total capital in their new profit sharing ratio. 4. Calculate the surplus/deficiency in each of the continuing partners' capital accounts by comparing the new capitals with the adjusted old capitals. 5. Adjust the surplus by paying-off or by transfer to the credit of current account and adjust the deficiency by asking the concerned partner to bring in the necessary amount or by transfer to the debit of his current account.
The partners are required to maintain a minimum cash/bank balance	1. Calculate the adjusted old capitals of continuing partners after all other adjustments. 2. Calculate total capital of the new firm as follows Total capital of the new firm = Aggregate of adjusted old capitals of continuing partners + Shortage of cash to be brought in by continuing partners in order to make payment to outgoing partner + Bank balance required to be maintained – Existing bank balance 3. Calculate the new capitals of continuing partners by dividing the total capital (as calculated in *step 2*) in their new profit sharing ratio. 4. Calculate the surplus/deficiency by comparing the new capitals with the adjusted old capitals. 5. Adjust the surplus by paying-off or by transfer to the credit of current account and adjust the deficiency by asking the concerned partner to bring in the necessary amount or by transfer to the debit of his current account.

5.4 Death of a Partner

A partnership comes to an ends immediately upon a partner's death, though the firm may continue with the remaining partners. The deceased partner's executors are entitled to his share according to the partnership agreement, which is calculated similarly as in case of a retiring partner.

The basis key differences between retirement and death of a partner are

- Retirement can be planned from a specific date, while death can occur anytime during the year.
- In retirement, payment is made to the partner while in death, it is made to the deceased partner's legal representatives.

Smart Study Chart No. 4

Computation of Amount Due to the Deceased Partner

Items to be Credited
- Balance in the deceased partner's capital account
- Share in firm's goodwill
- Share of profits from the start of the year to the date of death
- Profit share from assets revaluation and liability reassessment
- Accumulated profits or reserves
- Interest on capital (up to the date of death, if specified in the partnership deed)
- Salary and commission (up to the date of death, if specified in the partnership deed)

Items to be Debited
- Loss on assets revaluation and liabilities reassessment, if any
- Accumulated losses
- His drawings
- Interest on drawings and his share of loss up to the date of death

Format of Deceased Partner's Capital Account

Deceased Partner's Capital Account

Dr | | | Cr

Particulars	Amt (₹)	Particulars	Amt (₹)
To Revaluation A/c (Share in Loss)	...	By Balance b/d	...
To Share in Accumulated Losses	...	By Profit and Loss Suspense A/c (Share in Profit for Current Year till Death)	...
To Cash A/c (Drawings till Death)	...		
To Profit and Loss Suspense A/c (Share in Loss for Current Year till Death)	...	By Revaluation A/c (Share in Gain)	...
		By Share of Goodwill	...
To Interest on Drawings A/c	...	By Share in Accumulated Profits	...
To Goodwill A/c (Share in Existing Goodwill Written-off)	...	General Reserve A/c	...
		Profit and Loss A/c	...
To Deceased Partner's Executor's A/c (Transfer) (Balancing Figure)	...	By Interest on Capital A/c	...
		By Salary, Commission A/c	...
	...		...

The adjustment are made in the deceased partner's capital account and the balance is then transferred to a new account opened in the name of the deceased partner's executors, The journal entry is

Deceased Partner's Capital A/c	Dr
To Deceased Partner's Executor's A/c	

Computation of Specific Items of Deceased Partner's Capital Account

Following issues need to be discussed before ascertaining the amount payable to the executors of a deceased partner

I. Share in Profits

The calculation of deceased partner's share in profits earned from the date of last balance sheet to date of death/retirement, involves the following two steps

***Step* 1** Determination of firm's profits from the date of last balance sheet to the date of death/retirement. Subject to agreement, such profits may be determined either on time basis or on sales basis using previous year's profits or average profits of the past years

Basis	Explanation
On Time Basis	In this method, profit of previous year or average profit of past years and the time for which deceased partner remained in business during the current year, are taken into consideration. Then, proportionate profit upto the date of death is calculated assuming that the profits are earned evenly throughout the year as under Profit from the date of last balance sheet to the date of death $= \frac{\text{(Number of days or months from the date of last balance sheet to the date of death)}}{\text{365 Days or 12 Months}}$ $\times$(Previous year's profits or average profits of a given number of past years)
On Turnover or Sales Basis	In this method, profit and total sales of the previous year are taken into consideratioin and then profit of the current year is estimated on the basis of the previous year's sales and the sales upto the date of death as under Profit from the date of last balance sheet to the date of death $= \frac{\text{(Sales from the date of the last balance sheet to the date of death)}}{\text{(Previous year's sales or average sales of a given number of past years)}}$ $\times$(Previous year's profits or average profits of a given number of past years)

***Step* 2** **Calculation of outgoing partner's share in profits.**

Outgoing partner's share in profits = Profits of the firm for the period beginning with the date of accounting year and ending with the date of death as computed in *step 1* × Proportion of share of outgoing partner

Accounting Treatment of Deceased Partner's Share in Profits

Through Profit and Loss Suspense Account

This method is used when the new profit sharing ratio of continuing partners does not differ from their old profit sharing ratio.

(i) **In case of profit**	Profit and Loss Suspense A/c To Deceased Partner's Capital A/c	Dr

Note In this case, profit and loss suspense account will appear on the assets side of the balance sheet.

(ii) **In case of loss**	Deceased Partner's Capital A/c To Profit and Loss Suspense A/c	Dr

Note In this case, profit and loss suspense account will appear on the liabilities side of the balance sheet.

Through Capital Transfer

In case, new ratio of continuing partners differs from their old profit sharing ratio, then outgoing partner's share of profit must be adjusted through capital accounts of gaining partners only.

(i) **In case of profit**	Gaining Partners' Capital A/c To Deceased Partner's Capital A/c	Dr	[Gaining ratio] [Share of profit]
(ii) **In case of loss**	Deceased Partner's Capital A/c To Gaining Partners' Capital A/c	Dr	[Share of loss] [Gaining ratio]

II. Treatment of Goodwill

It is same as in the case of retirement of a partner.

Following entry is passed for the treatment of goodwill

Gaining Partners' Capital A/c	Dr	[In gaining ratio]
To Deceased Partner's Capital A/c		[With his share of goodwill]

Settlement of Deceased Partner's Executor's Account

The payment to the executors of the deceased partner is made as is stated in the partnership deed or as agreed to by the remaining partners and the executors.

The payment may be made either in full in one instalment or more than one instalment.

1. **When Payment is Made in Full in One Instalment**
   The accounting entry is

Deceased Partner's Executor's A/c	Dr
To Bank A/c	

2. **When Payment is Made in more than One Instalment** Unless agreed otherwise, the executors are entitled to interest @ 6% per annum. The executors can opt to take share of profits instead of interest. The share of profits is ascertained by dividing the profits in the ratio of deceased partner's capital to total capital employed.
   The accounting entry is

(i) **When interest is due**	Interest A/c To Deceased Partner's Executor's A/c	Dr
(ii) **When instalment is paid**	Deceased Partner's Executor's A/c To Bank A/c	Dr

Mind Map

Reconstitution of a Partnership Firm : Retirement/Death of a Partner

1 Retirement/Death of a Partner

Retirement/Death of a partner means ceasing to be a partner of the firm.
As per Section 32(1) of Indian Partnership Act, 1932, a partner may retire

- With the consent of all the other partners.
- If there is an express agreement by the partners.
- By giving notice in writing to all other partners of his intention to retire.

2 Liability of a Retiring Partner

- A retiring partner remains liable for all acts of firm upto the date of his retirement.
- A retiring partner may also continue to be liable after retirement until a public notice is given about his retirement.

3 New Ratio/Gaining Ratio

- New Ratio = Old Share + Acquired Gaining Share
- Gaining Ratio = New Share – Old Share

4 Accounting Treatment of Goodwill

- Write-off existing goodwill (if any) among old partners in old ratio.
- Give credit to retiring/deceased partner for his share of goodwill.
- Sometimes, excess amount is paid to retiring/deceased partner, such excess is treated as his share of goodwill.

5 Accounting Treatment of Reserves, Accumulated Profits and Losses

- For distribution of reserves and accumulated profits

General Reserve A/c	Dr
Reserve Fund A/c	Dr
Profit and Loss A/c (Cr. Balance)	Dr
To All Partners' Capital/Current A/c	

- For distribution of accumulated losses

All Partners' Capital/Current A/c	Dr
To Profit and Loss A/c	
To Advertisement Expenditure A/c	

6 Revaluation of Assets and Reassessment of Liabilities

- At the time of retirement or death of a partner, assets are revalued and liabilities are reassessed to determine outgoing partner's share in profit/loss arising from such revaluation.
- For this purpose, revaluation account is prepared in same manner as discussed in Chapter-3.

7 Amount due to a Retiring Partner

- The amount due to a retiring/deceased partner is computed by preparing his capital account.
- Retiring partner can be using any of the following methods
  - Payment of full amount in lumpsum.
  - Payment in installments.
  - Partly payment and remaining treated as loan.
- In case question is silent, his balance is transferred to his loan account.

8 Adjustment of Capital

1. ***When Total Capital of New Firm is Given***
   Calculate new capital as per new capital of firm and compare with adjusted capital.
   Afterwards, adjust with cash or current account, as the case may be.
2. ***When total capital of firm is not given*** New capital of new firm will be equal to adjusted capitals of remaining partners. Afterwards, follow the step as given in point 1 above.
3. ***When total capital is same as before retirement***
   Follow steps as given in point 1.
4. ***When outgoing partner is paid by cash brought in by the remaining partners in such a way as to make their capitals proportionate to new ratio***
   Capital of New Firm
   = Total Adjusted Capital of Old Partners + Shortage of Cash to be Brought in.
   Afterwards, follow steps as given in point 1.
5. ***When a minimum bank balance is maintained***
   Capital of New Firm = Total Adjusted Capital of Remaining Partners + Shortage of Cash + Required Bank Balance – Existing Bank Balance.
   Afterwards, follow steps as given in point 1.

9 Calculation of Deceased Partner's Share of Profits

- Calculation of deceased partner's share in profit upto the date of death/retirement

– On Time Basis $= \dfrac{\text{Days/Months} \times \text{Average Profit}}{\text{365 days/12 months}}$

– On Turnover Basis $= \dfrac{\text{(Sales till Date of Death} \times \text{Average Profit)}}{\text{Previous Year Sales or Average Sales}}$

- Outgoing Partner's Share = Profit as calculated above × Share of Outgoing Partner

Topicwise Solved Questions

New Profit Sharing Ratio

Solved Question 1 **P, Q and R are partners in a firm sharing profits in the ratio of 3 : 2 : 1. On 1st April, 2024, Q decided to retire from the firm. Calculate the new ratio of remaining partners.**

Sol. Q's share = 2/6

P and R will gain Q's share in the ratio of 3 : 1

P's gain $= \frac{3}{4} \times \frac{2}{6} = \frac{6}{24}$; P's new share $= \frac{3}{4} + \frac{6}{24} = \frac{24}{24}$

R's gain $= \frac{1}{4} \times \frac{2}{6} = \frac{2}{24}$; R' new share $= \frac{1}{4} + \frac{2}{24} = \frac{8}{24}$

New profit sharing ratio = 24 : 8 = 3 : 1

Solved Question 2 **K, L and Z are partners sharing profit in the ratio of 4 : 3 : 2 respectively. L retired and surrendered 1/9 th of his share of profit to K and remaining in favour of Z. Calculate the new profit sharing ratio and gaining ratio of K and Z.**

Sol. Old ratio between K, L and Z = 4 : 3 : 2

Share surrendered in favour of K by L $= \frac{3}{9} \times \frac{1}{9} = \frac{3}{81}$

Share surrendered in favour of Z by L

$= \frac{3}{9} - \frac{3}{81} = \frac{27-3}{81} = \frac{24}{81}$

New share of K $= \frac{4}{9} + \frac{3}{81} = \frac{36+3}{81} = \frac{39}{81}$

New share of Z $= \frac{2}{9} + \frac{24}{81} = \frac{18+24}{81} = \frac{42}{81}$

∴ New ratio = 39 : 42 *or* 13 : 14

Gaining ratio $= \frac{3}{81} : \frac{24}{81} = 1 : 8$

Solved Question 3 **D, J and I are partners in a firm sharing profits equally. I decided to retire on 1st April, 2024. I's share is acquired by D and J in the ratio of 3 : 2. Calculate the new ratio of D and J.**

Sol. I's share acquired by D $= \frac{1}{3} \times \frac{3}{5} = \frac{3}{15}$

D's new share $= \frac{3}{5} + \frac{3}{15} = \frac{12}{15}$

I's share acquired by J $= \frac{1}{3} \times \frac{2}{5} = \frac{2}{15}$

J's new share $= \frac{2}{5} + \frac{2}{15} = \frac{8}{15}$

New profit sharing ratio = 12 : 8 = 3 : 2

Solved Question 4 **Ashok, Anil and Ajay are partners sharing profit and loss in the ratio of $\frac{1}{2}, \frac{3}{10}$ and $\frac{1}{5}$. Anil retires from the firm. Ashok and Ajay decide to share future profit and loss in the ratio of 3 : 2. Calculate the gaining ratio.**

Sol. Old ratio of Ashok, Anil and Ajay $= \frac{1}{2} : \frac{3}{10} : \frac{1}{5} = 5 : 3 : 2$

New share of Ashok and Ajay = 3 : 2

Gaining Ratio = New Ratio – Old Ratio

Ashok's gain $= \frac{3}{5} - \frac{5}{10} = \frac{6-5}{10} = \frac{1}{10}$

Ajay's gain $= \frac{2}{5} - \frac{2}{10} = \frac{4-2}{10} = \frac{2}{10}$

Gaining ratio of Ashok and Ajay = 1 : 2

Solved Question 5 **P, Q and R are partners sharing profits in the ratio of 2 : 2 : 1. Q retires and his share is taken by R. Calculate new profit sharing ratio of P and R.**

Sol. Share taken by R from Q $= \frac{2}{5}$

R's New Share = Old Share + Share taken from Q

R's New Share $= \frac{1}{5} + \frac{2}{5} = \frac{3}{5}$; P's New Share $= \frac{2}{5}$ (unchanged)

New ratio of P and R $= \frac{2}{5} : \frac{3}{5} = 2 : 3$

Solved Question 6 **Jayant, Kartik and Leena were partners in a firm sharing profits and losses in the ratio 5 : 2 : 3. Kartik died and Jayant and Leena decided to continue the business. Their gaining ratio was 2 : 3. Calculate the new profit sharing ratio of Jayant and Leena.** **CBSE 2018**

Sol. Jayant's old share $= \frac{5}{10}$

Jayant's gaining share $= \frac{2}{5} \times \frac{2}{10} = \frac{4}{50}$

Jayant's New Share = Old Share + Gaining Share

$= \frac{5}{10} + \frac{4}{50} = \frac{25+4}{50} = \frac{29}{50}$

Leena's old share $= \frac{3}{10}$

Leena's gaining share $= \frac{3}{5} \times \frac{2}{10} = \frac{6}{50}$

Leena's new share $= \frac{3}{10} + \frac{6}{50} = \frac{15+6}{50} = \frac{21}{50}$

New profit sharing ratio = Jayant : Leena = 29 : 21

Solved Question 7 M, N and O are partners sharing profits in the ratio 4 : 3 : 2. M retires from the firm and it is decided that profit sharing ratio between N and O will be same as existing between M and N. Calculate new ratio and gaining ratio.

Sol. Ratio between M and N = 4 : 3

Hence, New Ratio between N and O will be 4 : 3

Calculation of Gaining Ratio

Gaining Ratio = New Ratio − Old Share

$$\text{N's Gains} = \frac{4}{7} - \frac{3}{9} = \frac{36-21}{63} = \frac{15}{63}$$

$$\text{O's Gains} = \frac{3}{7} - \frac{2}{9} = \frac{27-14}{63} = \frac{13}{63}$$

Hence, Gaining ratio of N and O = $\frac{15}{63} : \frac{13}{63} = 15 : 13$

Accounting Treatment of Goodwill

Solved Question 8 Varun, Tarun, Arun and Barun were partners in a firm sharing profits in the ratio of 5 : 3 : 2 : 2. Arun retired on 31st March, 2023. Varun, Tarun and Barun decided to share future profits equally. On Arun's retirement, goodwill of the firm was valued at ₹ 9,00,000. Showing your workings clearly, pass the necessary journal entry for treatment of goodwill on Arun's retirement without opening goodwill account. **CBSE 2024**

Sol. **In the Books of Varun, Tarun, Arun and Barun**

JOURNAL

Date	Particulars	LF	Amt (Dr)	Amt (Cr)
2023				
Mar 31	Tarun's Capital A/c Dr		75,000	
	Barun's Capital A/c Dr		1,50,000	
	To Varun's Capital A/c			75,000
	To Arun's Capital A/c			1,50,000
	(Being share of goodwill adjusted to capital accounts of partners in their gaining ratio 1 : 2)			

Working Note

Calculation of Gaining Share

Gaining Share = New Share − Old Share

$$\text{Varun's Gain} = \frac{1}{3} - \frac{5}{12} = (-)\frac{1}{12} \text{ (Sacrifice)}$$

$$\text{Tarun's Gain} = \frac{1}{3} - \frac{3}{12} = \frac{1}{12}; \quad \text{Barun's Gain} = \frac{1}{3} - \frac{2}{12} = \frac{2}{12}$$

Solved Question 9 P, Q and R are partners in a firm sharing profits in the ratio of 3 : 2 : 1. Q retired on 31st March, 2024 from the firm. The goodwill of the firm was valued at ₹ 24,000. On the same date, goodwill appearing in the books of accounts amounted to ₹ 75,000. Pass necessary journal entries.

Sol. **JOURNAL**

Date	Particulars	LF	Amt (Dr)	Amt (Cr)
2024				
Mar 31	P's Capital A/c Dr		6,000	
	R's Capital A/c Dr		2,000	
	To Q's Capital A/c			8,000
	(Being amount of goodwill adjusted in gaining ratio 3 : 1)			
	P's Capital A/c Dr		37,500	
	Q's Capital A/c Dr		25,000	
	R's Capital A/c Dr		12,500	
	To Goodwill A/c			75,000
	(Being amount of goodwill written-off in old profit sharing ratio)			

Solved Question 10 Arjun, Bhim and Nakul are partners sharing profit and loss in the ratio of 14 : 5 : 6 respectively. Bhim retires and surrenders his 5/25th share in favour of Arjun. The goodwill of the firm is valued at 2 years' purchase of super profit based on average profit of last 3 years.

The profit of the last three years are ₹ 50,000, ₹ 55,000 and ₹ 60,000 respectively. The normal profit of the similar firms are ₹ 30,000. Goodwill already appears in the books of the firm at ₹ 75,000. The profit for the first year after the Bhim's retirement was ₹ 1,00,000. Give necessary journal entries to adjust goodwill and distribute profit and showing your workings clearly.

Sol. **JOURNAL**

Date	Particulars	LF	Amt (Dr)	Amt (Cr)
	Arjun's Capital A/c Dr (75,000 × 14/25)		42,000	
	Bhim's Capital A/c Dr (75,000 × 5/25)		15,000	
	Nakul's Capital A/c Dr (75,000 × 6/25)		18,000	
	To Goodwill A/c			75,000
	(Being amount of goodwill written-off in old ratio)			
	Arjun's Capital A/c Dr		10,000	
	To Bhim's Capital A/c			10,000
	(Being amount of goodwill adjusted in gaining ratio)			
	Profit and Loss Appropriation A/c Dr		1,00,000	
	To Arjun's Capital A/c (1,00,000 × 19/25)			76,000
	To Nakul's Capital A/c (1,00,000 × 6/25)			24,000
	(Being profit distributed among partners)			

Working Notes

1. **Calculation of New Ratio and Gaining Ratio between Arjun and Nakul**

   Old ratio of Arjun, Bhim and Nakul = 14 : 5 : 6

   Bhim surrenders in favour of Arjun = $\frac{5}{25}$ share

   Arjun's new share = $\frac{14}{25}+\frac{5}{25}=\frac{14+5}{25}=\frac{19}{25}$; Nakul's share = $\frac{6}{25}$

   New ratio of Arjun and Nakul = 19 : 6

   Gaining Ratio = New Share − Old Share

   Arjun = $\frac{19}{25}-\frac{14}{25}=\frac{19-14}{25}=\frac{5}{25}$

   Nakul = $\frac{6}{25}-\frac{6}{25}=\frac{6-6}{25}=0$

2. **Calculation of Bhim's Share of Goodwill**

   Actual Average Profit = $\frac{50{,}000+55{,}000+60{,}000}{3}$

   = ₹ 55,000

   Normal Profit = ₹ 30,000

   Super Profit = Average Profit − Normal Profit

   = 55,000 − 30,000 = ₹ 25,000

   Firm's Goodwill = 25,000 × 2 = ₹ 50,000

   Bhim's share of goodwill = 50,000 × $\frac{5}{25}$ = ₹ 10,000

   (to be contributed by Arjun alone)

Solved Question 11 **W, X, Y and Z are partners in a firm sharing profits and losses in the ratio of 2 : 2 : 1 : 1. X and Y decided to retire from the firm. The goodwill of the firm was valued at ₹ 4,50,000. W and Z decided to share future profits and losses in the ratio of 3 : 2.**

Pass necessary journal entry for the treatment of goodwill.

Sol. **Calculation of Gaining Ratio**

W gains = $\frac{3}{5}-\frac{2}{6}=\frac{18-10}{30}=\frac{8}{30}$

Z gains = $\frac{2}{5}-\frac{1}{6}=\frac{12-5}{30}=\frac{7}{30}$

As such gaining ratio between W and Z = 8 : 7

JOURNAL

Date	Particulars		LF	Amt (Dr)	Amt (Cr)
	W's Capital A/c (8/15 × 2,25,000)	Dr		1,20,000	
	Z's Capital A/c (7/15 × 2,25,000)	Dr		1,05,000	
	To X's Capital A/c				1,50,000
	To Y's Capital A/c				75,000
	(Being X's and Y's share of goodwill debited to the gaining partners in their gaining ratio of 8 : 7)				

Working Note

X's Share of Goodwill = 4,50,000 × $\frac{2}{6}$ = ₹ 1,50,000

Y's Share of Goodwill = 4,50,000 × $\frac{1}{6}$ = ₹ 75,000

₹ 2,25,000

Solved Question 12 **X, Y and Z are partners sharing profits in the ratio of 4 : 3 : 1. Y retires, giving his share of profits to X and Z for ₹ 4,050; ₹ 1,800 being paid by X and ₹ 2,250 by Z. Profit for the year after Y's retirement was ₹ 5,250.**

You are required (i) to give necessary journal entries to record the transfer of Y's share to X and Z (ii) to calculate new profit sharing ratio and distribute the profits between X and Z.

X and Z bring the necessary amount.

Sol. (i) **JOURNAL**

Date	Particulars		LF	Amt (Dr)	Amt (Cr)
	X's Capital A/c	Dr		1,800	
	Z's Capital A/c	Dr		2,250	
	To Y's Capital A/c				4,050
	(Being share of goodwill credited to him by debiting gaining partners in their gaining ratio of 4 : 5)				
	Cash/Bank A/c	Dr		4,050	
	To X's Capital A/c				1,800
	To Z's Capital A/c				2,280
	(Being amount brought by X and Z to pay Y on his retirement)				
	Y's Capital A/c	Dr		4,050	
	To Cash/Bank A/c				4,050
	(Being amount paid to Y on his retirement for selling his share)				
	Profit and Loss Appropriation A/c	Dr		5,250	
	To X's Capital A/c				3,500
	To Z's Capital A/c				1,750
	(Being amount of profit distributed after Y's retirement in their new profit sharing ratio) (WN 2)				

(ii) **Calculation of New Profit Sharing Ratio**

X and Z paid ₹ 4,050 to Y in the ratio of ₹ 1,800 : ₹ 2,250 or 4 : 5. Hence, they will divide Y's profit share between themselves in the same ratio, i.e. 4 : 5. Their new profit shares will be

New Profit Share = Old Profit Share + Gain	A	C
(a) Existing profit share	4/8	1/8
(b) Profit share of Y acquired	$3/8 \times 4/9 = 1/6$	$3/8 \times 5/9 = 5/24$
(c) New profit share (a + b)	$4/8 + 1/6 = 2/3$	$1/8 + 5/24 = 1/3$

Thus, new profit sharing ratio of X and Z will be 2/3 : 1/3 *or* 2 : 1.

Working Notes

1. X and Z bring in cash for acquiring Y 's profit share and after that cash is given to Y in consideration.
2. X's share of profit = 5,250 × 2/3 = ₹ 3,500 ; Z's share of profit = 5,250 × 1/3 = ₹ 1,750

Solved Question 13 **Riya, Shreya and Niya are partners sharing profit in the ratio of 1 : 2 : 3. Niya retires and her capital, after making adjustments for reserves and profits on revaluation stands at ₹ 4,40,000. Riya and Shreya agreed to pay her ₹ 5,00,000 in full settlement of her claim. Record necessary journal entry for the treatment of goodwill, if the new profit sharing ratio is decided at 1 : 3.**

Sol. **JOURNAL**

Date	Particulars		LF	Amt (Dr)	Amt (Cr)
	Riya's Capital A/c (60,000 × 1/6)	Dr		10,000	
	Shreya's Capital A/c (60,000 × 5/6)	Dr		50,000	
	To Niya's Capital A/c				60,000
	(Being Niya's share of goodwill adjusted to the capital accounts of Riya and Shreya in their gaining ratio of 1 : 5)				

Working Notes

1. **Calculation of Gaining Ratio**

Gaining Ratio = New Share − Old Share

Riya $= \frac{1}{4} - \frac{1}{6} = \frac{3-2}{12} = \frac{1}{12}$; Shreya $= \frac{3}{4} - \frac{2}{6} = \frac{9-4}{12} = \frac{5}{12}$; Gaining ratio $= \frac{1}{12} : \frac{5}{12}$ *or* 1 : 5

2. **Calculation of Hidden Goodwill**

	Amt (₹)
Amount agreed to be paid in full settlement	5,00,000
(−) Niya's capital after all adjustments	(4,40,000)
Hidden goodwill	60,000

Adjustment for Reserves, Accumulated Profits and Losses

Solved Question 14 **Bat, Cat and Rat were partners sharing profits and losses in the ratio 5 : 3 : 2. Cat retired and on that date there was a balance of investment of ₹ 4,00,000 and investment fluctuation reserve of ₹ 1,00,000 was appearing in the balance sheet.**

Pass necessary journal entries for investment fluctuation reserve in the following cases

(i) Market value of investments was ₹ 4,80,000. **(ii) Market value of investments was ₹ 3,80,000.**
(iii) Market value of investments was ₹ 2,90,000.

CBSE SQP 2025

Sol. **JOURNAL**

Date	Particulars		Amt (Dr)	Amt (Cr)
(i)	Investment Fluctuation Reserve A/c	Dr	1,00,000	
	To Bat's Capital A/c			50,000
	To Cat's Capital A/c			30,000
	To Rat's Capital A/c			20,000
	(Being investment fluctuation reserve distributed)			
	Investment A/c	Dr	80,000	
	To Revaluation A/c			80,000
	(Being increase in investment recorded)			
	Revaluation A/c	Dr	80,000	
	To Bat's Capital A/c			40,000
	To Cat's Capital A/c			24,000
	To Rat's Capital A/c			16,000
	(Being gain on revaluation transferred to partners)			

Date	Particulars		Amt (Dr)	Amt (Cr)
(ii)	Investment Fluctuation Reserve A/c	Dr	1,00,000	
	To Bat's Capital A/c			40,000
	To Cat's Capital A/c			24,000
	To Rat's Capital A/c			16,000
	To Investment A/c			20,000
	(Being decrease in investment recorded and balance investment fluctuation reserve distributed)			
(iii)	Investment Fluctuation Reserve A/c	Dr	1,00,000	
	Revaluation A/c	Dr	10,000	
	To Investment A/c			1,10,000
	(Being decrease in investment recorded)			
	Bat's Capital A/c	Dr	5,000	
	Cat's Capital A/c	Dr	3,000	
	Rat's Capital A/c	Dr	2,000	
	To Revaluation A/c			10,000
	(Being loss on revaluation distributed among the partners)			

Revaluation/Reassessment

Solved Question 15 **Balance sheet of P, Q and R sharing profit and loss in the ratio of 5 : 3 : 2 as at 31st March, 2024 is as under**

Balance Sheet
as at 31st March, 2024

Liabilities		Amt (₹)	Assets		Amt (₹)
Sundry Creditors		15,000	Cash at Bank		27,000
Capital A/cs			Debtors	16,000	
P	46,000		(–) Provision for Doubtful Debts	(800)	15,200
Q	34,000		Stock		12,800
R	25,000	1,05,000	Plant and Machinery		35,000
			Land and Building		30,000
		1,20,000			1,20,000

Q retires from the firm on 1st April, 2024. P and R decided to share future profit and loss in the ratio of 3 : 1 respectively. Following adjustments are agreed.

(i) An amount of ₹ 1,100 included in sundry debtors be written-off as it is no longer receivable.
(ii) A provision for doubtful debts be maintained at 5%.
(iii) Stock be written down by ₹ 1,055.
(iv) Land and building be written up by ₹ 11,000.
(v) Plant and machinery be reduced to ₹ 34,000.
(vi) An amount of ₹ 700 included in sundry creditors be written back as no longer payable.
(vii) A provision of ₹ 600 be made for an outstanding repair bill.
(viii) An old computer previously written-off was sold for ₹ 2,000 as scrap.

To give effect to the above adjustments, you are required to record necessary journal entries and prepare the revaluation account.

Sol.

JOURNAL

Date	Particulars		LF	Amt (Dr)	Amt (Cr)
2024					
Apr 1	Bad Debts A/c	Dr		1,100	
	To Debtors A/c				1,100
	(Being bad debts written-off)				
Apr 1	Provision for Doubtful Debts A/c	Dr		800	
	Revaluation A/c (1,100 – 800)	Dr		300	
	To Bad Debts A/c				1,100
	(Being balance in bad debts account transferred)				

Date	Particulars		LF	Amt (Dr)	Amt (Cr)
Apr 1	Revaluation A/c	Dr		745	
	To Provision for Doubtful Debts A/c				745
	(Being provision for doubtful debts created @ 5% on 14,900, i.e. 16,000 – 1,100)				
Apr 1	Revaluation A/c	Dr		1,055	
	To Stock A/c				1,055
	(Being fall in value of stock recorded)				
Apr 1	Land and Building A/c	Dr		11,000	
	To Revaluation A/c				11,000
	(Being increase in value of building recorded)				
Apr 1	Revaluation A/c	Dr		1,000	
	To Plant and Machinery A/c				1,000
	(Being fall in value of plant and machinery recorded)				
Apr 1	Sundry Creditors A/c	Dr		700	
	To Revalution A/c				700
	(Being amount of creditors no longer payable written back)				
Apr 1	Revalution A/c	Dr		600	
	To Provision for Repairs A/c				600
	(Being provision for repairs created)				
Apr 1	Bank A/c	Dr		2,000	
	To Revaluation A/c				2,000
	(Being old computer sold completely written-off)				
Apr 1	Revaluation A/c	Dr		10,000	
	To A's Capital A/c				5,000
	To B's Capital A/c				3,000
	To C's Capital A/c				2,000
	(Being transfer of gain on revaluation)				

Dr **Revaluation Account** Cr

Particulars		Amt (₹)	Particulars	Amt (₹)
To Bad Debts A/c (1,100 – 800)		300	By Land and Building A/c	11,000
To Stock A/c		1,055	By Sundry Creditors A/c	700
To Plant and Machinery A/c		1,000	By Bank A/c (Sale of Old Computer)	2,000
To Outstanding Repairs A/c		600		
To Provision for Doubtful Debts A/c		745		
To Gain (Profit) Transferred to				
P's Capital A/c	5,000			
Q's Capital A/c	3,000			
R's Capital A/c	2,000	10,000		
		13,700		13,700

Solved Question 16 **D, E and F were partners in a firm sharing profits in the ratio of 5 : 2 : 3. On 31st March, 2024 their balance sheet was as follows**

Liabilities		Amt (₹)	Assets	Amt (₹)
Creditors		53,000	Cash	16,000
Bills Payable		62,000	Bank	17,000
General Reserve		2,00,000	Stock	18,000
Capital A/cs			Debtors	1,99,000
D	7,00,000		Investments	1,15,000
E	5,00,000		Machinery	7,50,000
F	6,00,000	18,00,000	Land and Building	10,00,000
		21,15,000		21,15,000

On the above date D retired from the firm and the following was agreed upon
(i) Goodwill of the firm was valued at ₹ 1,00,000. D's share of goodwill was adjusted through the capital accounts of remaining partners.
(ii) Investments were to be brought to their market value which was ₹ 85,000.
(iii) Machinery was to be depreciated to ₹ 7,00,000.
(iv) Land and building was to be appreciated to ₹ 12,00,000.
(v) The balance in D's capital account was transferred to his loan account.

Prepare revaluation account and D's capital account on his retirement. **CBSE Term II 2022**

Sol. Dr **Revaluation Account** Cr

Particulars		Amt (₹)	Particulars	Amt (₹)
To Investments A/c		30,000	By Land and Building A/c	2,00,000
To Machinery A/c		50,000		
To Profit on Revaluation Transferred to Partner's Capital A/cs				
D	60,000			
E	24,000			
F	36,000	1,20,000		
		2,00,000		2,00,000

Dr **D's Capital Account** Cr

Date	Particulars	Amt (₹)	Date	Particulars	Amt (₹)
2022			2022		
Mar 31	To D's Loan A/c	9,10,000	Mar 31	By Balance b/d	7,00,000
			Mar 31	By General Reserve A/c	1,00,000
			Mar 31	By Revaluation A/c	60,000
			Mar 31	By E's Capital A/c	20,000
			Mar 31	By F's Capital A/c	30,000
		9,10,000			9,10,000

Solved Question 17 Sameer, Yasmin and Saloni were partners in a firm sharing profit and loss in the ratio of 4 : 3 : 3. On 31st March, 2024, their balance sheet was as follows

Balance Sheet
as at 31st March, 2024

Liabilities		Amt (₹)	Assets		Amt (₹)
Creditors		1,10,000	Cash		80,000
General Reserve		60,000	Debtors	90,000	
Capital A/cs			(−) Provision for Doubtful Debts	(10,000)	80,000
Sameer	3,00,000		Stock		1,00,000
Yasmin	2,50,000		Machinery		3,00,000
Saloni	1,50,000	7,00,000	Building		2,00,000
			Patents		60,000
			Profit and Loss A/c		50,000
		8,70,000			8,70,000

On the above date, Sameer retired and it was agreed that
(i) Debtors of ₹ 4,000 will be written-off as bad debts and a provision of 5% on debtors for bad and doubtful debts will be maintained.
(ii) An unrecorded creditor of ₹ 20,000 will be recorded.
(iii) Patents will be completely written-off and 5% depreciation will be charged on stock, machinery and building.
(iv) Yasmin and Saloni will share the future profit in the ratio of 3 : 2.
(v) Goodwill of the firm on Sameer's retirement was valued at ₹ 5,40,000.

Pass necessary journal entries for the above transactions in the books of the firm on Sameer's retirement.

Sol.

JOURNAL

Date	Particulars		LF	Amt (Dr)	Amt (Cr)
2024					
Mar 31	General Reserve A/c	Dr		60,000	
	To Sameer's Capital A/c				24,000
	To Yasmin's Capital A/c				18,000
	To Saloni's Capital A/c				18,000
	(Being general reserve distributed among old partners in old ratio)				
Mar 31	Sameer's Capital A/c	Dr		20,000	
	Yasmin's Capital A/c	Dr		15,000	
	Saloni's Capital A/c	Dr		15,000	
	To Profit and Loss A/c				50,000
	(Being balance of profit and loss account distributed among old partners in old ratio)				
Mar 31	Yasmin's Capital A/c	Dr		1,62,000	
	Saloni's Capital A/c	Dr		54,000	
	To Sameer's Capital A/c				2,16,000
	(Being Sameer's share of goodwill adjusted)				
Mar 31	Revaluation A/c	Dr		1,10,000	
	To Patents A/c				60,000
	To Stock A/c (1,00,000 × 5%)				5,000
	To Machinery A/c (3,00,000 × 5%)				15,000
	To Building A/c (2,00,000 × 5%)				10,000
	To Creditors A/c				20,000
	(Being decrease in the value of assets and increase in the value of liabilities recorded)				
Mar 31	Provision for Doubtful Debts A/c	Dr		1,700	
	To Revaluation A/c				1,700
	(Being decrease in the value of provision recorded)				
Mar 31	Sameer's Capital A/c	Dr		43,320	
	Yasmin's Capital A/c	Dr		32,490	
	Saloni's Capital A/c	Dr		32,490	
	To Revaluation A/c				1,08,300
	(Being loss on revaluation distributed among old partners)				
Mar 31	Sameer's Capital A/c	Dr		4,76,680	
	To Sameer's Loan A/c				4,76,680
	(Being amount due to Sameer transferred to his loan account)				

Working Notes

1. **Calculation of Gaining Ratio**

Gaining Ratio = New Share – Old Share

Yasmin $= \frac{3}{5} - \frac{3}{10} = \frac{6-3}{10} = \frac{3}{10}$; Saloni $= \frac{2}{5} - \frac{3}{10} = \frac{4-3}{10} = \frac{1}{10}$

Gaining ratio = 3 : 1

2. **Provision for Bad Debts**

	Amt (₹)	
Debtors	90,000	
(–) Bad Debts	(4,000)	which will be adjusted against provision for bad debts.
	86,000	

Provision for doubtful debts @ 5% $= \left(86{,}000 \times \frac{5}{100}\right) =$ ₹ 4,300

		Amt (₹)
Existing provision after adjusting bad debts (10,000 – 4,000)	=	6,000
(–) New provision	=	(4,300)
Excess provision	=	1,700

3. **Calculation of Sameer's Share of Goodwill**

Firm's goodwill = ₹ 5,40,000; Sameer's share $= 5,40,000 \times \frac{4}{10}$ = ₹ 2,16,000

To be contributed by Yasmin and Saloni in their gaining ratio i.e. 3 : 1.

4. **Loss on Revaluation**

It can be ascertained by preparing revaluation account in the following manner

Dr **Revaluation Account** Cr

Particulars	Amt (₹)	Particulars		Amt (₹)
To Patents A/c	60,000	By Provision for Doubtful Debts A/c		1,700
To Stock A/c	5,000	By Loss on Revaluation Transferred to Partner's Capital A/cs		
To Machinery A/c	15,000	Sameer	43,320	
To Building A/c	10,000	Yasmin	32,490	
To Creditors A/c	20,000	Saloni	32,490	1,08,300
	1,10,000			1,10,000

Solved Question 18 **Rishi, Shashi and Trishi were partners in a firm sharing profits and losses in proportion of $\frac{1}{2}, \frac{1}{6}$ and $\frac{1}{3}$ respectively. Their balance sheet as at 31st March, 2023 was as follows**

Balance Sheet of Rishi, Shashi and Trishi
as at 31st March, 2023

Liabilities		Amt (₹)	Assets	Amt (₹)
Capital A/cs			Fixed Assets	80,000
Rishi	36,000		Stock	20,000
Shashi	30,000		Debtors	30,000
Trishi	20,000	86,000	Cash	40,000
General Reserve		30,000		
Creditors		54,000		
		1,70,000		1,70,000

Shashi retired from the firm on 1st April, 2023 on the following terms

(i) Fixed assets were valued at ₹ 56,000.

(ii) Stock was taken over by Shashi at ₹ 26,000.

(iii) Goodwill of the firm was valued at ₹ 18,000 on Shashi's retirement.

(iv) Balance in Shashi's capital account was transferred to her loan account.

Prepare revaluation account and partners' capital account. **CBSE 2024**

Sol. Dr **Revaluation Account** Cr

Particulars	Amt (₹)	Particulars		Amt (₹)
To Fixed Assets A/c	24,000	By Stock A/c		6,000
		By Loss Transferred to Partner's Capital A/cs		
		Rishi	9,000	
		Shashi	3,000	
		Trishi	6,000	18,000
	24,000			24,000

Dr **Partners' Capital Account** Cr

Particulars	Rishi (₹)	Shashi (₹)	Trishi (₹)	Particulars	Rishi (₹)	Shashi (₹)	Trishi (₹)
To Revaluation A/c	9,000	3,000	6,000	By Balance b/d	36,000	30,000	20,000
To Stock A/c	—	26,000	—	By General Reserve A/c	15,000	5,000	10,000
To Shashi's Capital A/c	1,800	—	1,200	By Rishi's Capital A/c	—	1,800	—
To Shashi's Loan A/c	—	9,000	—	By Trishi's Capital A/c	—	1,200	—
To Balance c/d	40,200	—	22,000				
	51,000	38,000	30,000		51,000	38,000	30,000

Solved Question 19 **A, B and C were partners in a firm sharing profit and losses in proportion to their fixed capitals. Their balance sheet as at 31st March, 2017 was as follows**

Balance Sheet
as at 31st March, 2017

Liabilities		Amt (₹)	Assets		Amt (₹)
Capital A/cs			Bank		21,000
A	5,00,000		Stock		9,000
B	3,00,000		Debtors	15,000	
C	2,00,000	10,00,000	(–) Provision for Doubtful Debts	(1,500)	13,500
General Reserve		75,000	A's Loan		35,500
Creditors		23,000	Plant and Machinery		2,00,000
Outstanding Salary		7,000	Land and Building		6,00,000
B's Loan		15,000	Profit and Loss Account (For the year ending 31st March, 2017)		2,41,000
		11,20,000			11,20,000

On the date of above balance sheet, C retired from the firm on the following terms

(i) **Goodwill of the firm will be valued at two year's purchase of the average profits of last three years. The profit for the year ended 31st March, 2015 and 31st March, 2016 were ₹ 4,00,000 and ₹ 3,00,000 respectively.**
(ii) **Provision for bad debts will be maintained at 5% of the debtors.**
(iii) **Land and building will be appreciated by ₹ 90,000 and plant and machinery will be reduced to ₹ 1,80,000.**
(iv) **A agreed to repay his loan.**
(v) **The loan repaid by A was to be utilised to pay C. The balance of the amount payable to C was transferred to his loan account bearing interest @ 12% per annum.**

Prepare revaluation account, partners' current account, partners' capital account and the balance sheet of the reconstituted firm. **CBSE SQP 2018**

Sol. Dr **Revalution Account** Cr

Particulars		Amt (₹)	Particulars	Amt (₹)
To Plant and Machinery A/c		20,000	By Provision for Doubtful Debts A/c	750
To Profit Transferred to			By Land and Building A/c	90,000
A's Current A/c	35,375			
B's Current A/c	21,225			
C's Current A/c	14,150	70,750		
		90,750		90,750

Dr **Partners' Current Account** Cr

Date	Particulars	A (₹)	B (₹)	C (₹)	Date	Particulars	A (₹)	B (₹)	C (₹)
2017					2017				
Mar 31	To C's Current A/c	38,250	22,950	—	Mar 31	By Revaluation A/c	35,375	21,225	14,150
Mar 31	To Profit and Loss A/c	1,20,500	72,300	48,200	Mar 31	By A's Current A/c	—	—	38,250
Mar 31	To C's Capital A/c	—	—	42,150	Mar 31	By B's Current A/c	—	—	22,950
					Mar 31	By General Reserve A/c	37,500	22,500	15,000
					Mar 31	By Balance c/d	85,875	51,525	—
		1,58,750	95,250	90,350			1,58,750	95,250	90,350

Dr **Partners' Capital Account** Cr

Date	Particulars	A (₹)	B (₹)	C (₹)	Date	Particulars	A (₹)	B (₹)	C (₹)
2017					2017				
Mar 31	To Bank A/c	—	—	35,500	Mar 31	By Balance b/d	5,00,000	3,00,000	2,00,000
Mar 31	To C's Loan A/c	—	—	2,06,650	Mar 31	By C's Current A/c	—	—	42,150
Mar 31	To Balance c/d	5,00,000	3,00,000	—					
		5,00,000	3,00,000	2,42,150			5,00,000	3,00,000	2,42,150

Balance Sheet
as at 31st March, 2017

Liabilities		Amt (₹)	Assets		Amt (₹)
Capital A/cs			Bank		21,000
A	5,00,000		Stock		9,000
B	3,00,000	8,00,000	Debtors	15,000	
C's Loan		2,06,650	(–) Provision for Doubtful Debts	(750)	14,250
Creditors		23,000	Plant and Machinery		1,80,000
Outstanding Salary		7,000	Land and Building		6,90,000
B's Loan		15,000	A's Current A/c		85,875
			B's Current A/c		51,525
		10,51,650			10,51,650

Working Note

Valuation of Goodwill

$$\text{Average Profit} = \frac{4{,}00{,}000 + 3{,}00{,}000 - 2{,}41{,}000 \text{ (Given in B / S)}}{3} = ₹\ 1{,}53{,}000$$

Goodwill at 2 year's purchase $= 1{,}53{,}000 \times 2 = ₹\ 3{,}06{,}000$; C's share $= 3{,}06{,}000 \times \frac{2}{10} = ₹\ 61{,}200$

Entry for Goodwill

A's Current A/c $\left(61{,}200 \times \frac{5}{8}\right)$	Dr	38,250	
B's Current A/c $\left(61{,}200 \times \frac{3}{8}\right)$	Dr	22,950	
To C's Current A/c			61,200

Methods of Payment of Amount due to Retiring Partner

Solved Question 20 **The balance sheet of A, B and C who shared profits and losses in the ratio 3 : 3 : 2 respectively was as follows on 31st March, 2021**

Liabilities		Amt (₹)	Assets	Amt (₹)
Capitals A/cs			Machinery	31,600
A	24,000		Furniture	6,400
B	10,000		Stock	8,500
C	8,000	42,000	Debtors	4,300
Reserve		4,800	Cash at Bank	4,700
Creditors		8,700		
		55,500		55,500

A retired from the business on 1st April, 2021. Revaluation of assets were made as
Machinery ₹ 34,000, furniture ₹ 5,000, stock ₹ 9,600, debtors ₹ 4,000 and goodwill of the firm is valued at ₹ 10,000.
A was paid ₹ 6,225 immediately and the balance was transferred to a loan account for payment in 3 equal yearly instalments together with interest @ 6% p.a.
Show revaluation account and partners' capital account of the firm immediately after A's retirement and his loan account till finally paid-off.

Sol. Dr **Revaluation Account** Cr

Particulars		Amt (₹)	Particulars	Amt (₹)
To Furniture A/c		1,400	By Machinery A/c	2,400
To Debtors		300	By Stock A/c	1,100
To Profit Transferred to Partner's Capital A/cs				
A	675			
B	675			
C	450	1,800		
		3,500		3,500

Dr **Partners' Capital Account** Cr

Particulars	A (₹)	B (₹)	C (₹)	Particulars	A (₹)	B (₹)	C (₹)
To A's Capital A/c	—	2,250	1,500	By Balance b/d	24,000	10,000	8,000
To Bank A/c	6,225	—	—	By Revaluation Profit	675	675	450
To A's Bank A/c	24,000	—	—	By B's Capital A/c	2,250	—	—
To Balance c/d	—	10,225	8,150	By C's Capital A/c	1,500	—	—
				By Reserve A/c	1,800	1,800	1,200
	30,225	12,475	9,650		30,225	12,475	9,650

Dr **A's Loan Account** Cr

Date	Particulars	Amt (₹)	Date	Particulars	Amt (₹)
2022			2021		
Mar 31	To Bank A/c (8,000 + 1,440)	8,440	Apr 1	By A's Capital A/c	24,000
Mar 31	To Balance c/d	16,000	2022 Mar 31	By Interest A/c $\left(24,000 \times \frac{6}{100}\right)$	1,440
		25,440			25,440
2023			2022		
Mar 31	To Bank A/c (8,000 + 960)	8,960	Apr 1	By Balance b/d	16,000
Mar 31	To Balance c/d	8,000	2023 Mar 31	By Interest A/c $\left(16,000 \times \frac{6}{100}\right)$	960
		16,960			16,960
2024			2023		
Mar 31	To Bank A/c (8,000 + 480)	8,480	Apr 1	By Balance b/d	8,000
			2024 Mar 31	By Interest A/c $\left(8,000 \times \frac{6}{100}\right)$	480
		8,480			8,480

Solved Question 21 (*When amount of instalment includes interest*) **Banwari, Girdhari and Murari are partners in a firm sharing profits and losses in the ratio of 4 : 5 : 6. On 31st March, 2024, Girdhari retired. On that date the capitals of Banwari, Girdhari and Murari before the necessary adjustments stood at ₹ 2,00,000, ₹ 1,00,000 and ₹ 50,000, respectively. On Girdhari's retirement, goodwill of the firm was valued at ₹ 1,14,000. Revaluation of assets and reassessment of liabilities resulted in a profit of ₹ 6,000. General reserve stood in the books of the firm at ₹ 30,000. The amount payable to Girdhari was transferred to his loan account. Banwari and Murari agreed to pay Girdhari two yearly instalments of ₹ 75,000 each including interest @ 10% per annum on the outstanding balance during the first two years and the balance including interest in the third year. The firm closes its books on 31st March every year.**

Prepare Girdhari's loan account till it is finally paid showing the working notes clearly. **CBSE 2018 (M)**

Sol. Dr **Girdhari's Loan Account** Cr

Date	Particulars	Amt (₹)	Date	Particulars	Amt (₹)
2022			2021		
Mar 31	To Bank A/c	75,000	Apr 1	By Girdhari's Capital A/c	1,50,000
Mar 31	To Balance c/d	90,000	2022 Mar 31	By Interest A/c	15,000
		1,65,000			1,65,000
2023			2022		
Mar 31	To Bank A/c	75,000	Apr 1	By Balance c/d	90,000
Mar 31	To Balance c/d	24,000	2023 Mar 31	By Interest A/c	9,000
		99,000			99,000
2024			2023		
Mar 31	To Bank A/c	26,400	Apr 1	By Balance b/d	24,000
			2024 Mar 31	By Interest A/c	2,400
		26,400			26,400

Working Note

Girdhari's Capital Account

Dr Particulars	Amt (₹)	Particulars	Cr Amt (₹)
To Girdhari's Loan A/c	1,50,000	By Balance b/d	1,00,000
		By Share in Goodwill $\left(1,14,000 \times \frac{5}{15}\right)$	38,000
		By Revaluation Profit $\left(6,000 \times \frac{5}{15}\right)$	2,000
		By General Reserve $\left(30,000 \times \frac{5}{15}\right)$	10,000
	1,50,000		1,50,000

Solved Question 22 *(When amount is to be paid in semi-annual instalments)* **A, B and C were in partnership sharing profits and losses in the ratio of 2 : 3 : 1. B retired from the firm. After all the adjustments, his capital account shows a credit balance of ₹ 1,10,000 as on 1st April, 2022. 'B' is to be paid ₹ 30,000 by cheque immediately and balance in four equal semi-annual instalments along with interest @ 10% p.a. from on the unpaid amount. Prepare B's loan account till he is paid the amount due to him. The firm closes its books on 31st March every year.**

Sol.

B's Loan Account

Dr Date	Particulars	Amt (₹)	Date	Particulars	Cr Amt (₹)
2022			2022		
Sept 30	To Bank A/c (20,000 + 4,000)	24,000	Apr 1	By B's Capital A/c	80,000
2023			Sept 30	By Interest A/c (80,000 × 10/100 × 6/12)	4,000
Mar 31	To Bank A/c (20,000 + 3,000)	23,000	2023		
Mar 31	To Balance c/d	40,000	Mar 31	By Interest A/c (60,000 × 10/100 × 6/12)	3,000
		87,000			87,000
2023			2023		
Sept 30	To Bank A/c (20,000 + 2,000)	22,000	Apr 1	By Balance b/d	40,000
2024			Sept 30	By Interest A/c (40,000 × 10/100 × 6/12)	2,000
Mar 31	To Bank A/c (20,000 + 1,000)	21,000	2024		
			Mar 31	By Interest A/c (20,000 × 10/100 × 6/12)	1,000
		43,000			43,000

Adjustment of Capital

Solved Question 23 **Prina, Qadir and Kian were partners in a firm sharing profits in the ratio of 7 : 2 : 1. On 31st March, 2023 their balance sheet was as follows**

Balance Sheet of Prina, Qadir and Kian
as at 31st March, 2023

Liabilities		Amt (₹)	Assets		Amt (₹)
Capital A/cs			Land		12,00,000
Prina	9,60,000		Building		9,00,000
Qadir	8,40,000		Furniture		3,60,000
Kian	9,00,000	27,00,000	Stock		6,60,000
General Reserve		3,00,000	Debtors	6,00,000	
Workmen's Compensation Reserve		5,40,000	(–) Provision for Doubtful Debts	(30,000)	5,70,000
Creditors		3,60,000	Cash at Bank		2,10,000
		39,00,000			39,00,000

On the above date Qadir retired on the following terms

(i) Goodwill of the firm was valued at ₹ 12,00,000.
(ii) Land was to be appreciated by 30% and building was to be depreciated by ₹ 3,54,000.
(iii) A provision of 6% is to be maintained on debtors.
(iv) Liability for workmen's compensation was determined at ₹ 1,40,000.
(v) Amount payable to Qadir was transferred to his loan account.

(vi) Total capital of the new firm was fixed at ₹ 16,00,000 which will be adjusted according to their new profit ratio by opening current accounts.

Prepare revaluation account and partners' capital account. **CBSE 2024**

Sol. Dr **Revaluation Account** Cr

Particulars	Amt (₹)	Particulars	Amt (₹)
To Building A/c	3,54,000	By Land A/c	3,60,000
To Provision for Doubtful Debts	6,000		
	3,60,000		3,60,000

Dr **Partners' Capital Account** Cr

Particulars	Prina (₹)	Qadir (₹)	Kian (₹)	Particulars	Prina (₹)	Qadir (₹)	Kian (₹)
To Qadir's Capital A/c	2,10,000	—	30,000	By Balance b/d	9,60,000	8,40,000	9,00,000
To Qadir's Loan A/c	—	12,20,000	—	By Workmen Compensation Reserve A/c	2,80,000	80,000	40,000
To Kian's Current	—	—	7,40,000	By Prina's Capital A/c (Goodwill)	—	2,10,000	—
To Balance c/d	14,00,000	—	2,00,000	By Kian's Capital A/c (Goodwill)	—	30,000	—
				By General Reserve A/c	2,10,000	60,000	30,000
				By Pian's Current A/c	1,60,000	—	—
	16,10,000	12,20,000	9,70,000		16,10,000	12,20,000	9,70,000

Working Note

Adjustment of Capital

Prina $= 16,00,000 \times \frac{7}{8} =$ ₹ 14,00,000 ; Kian $= 16,00,000 \times \frac{1}{8} =$ ₹ 2,00,000

Solved Question 24 Arnav, Bhavi and Chavi were in partnership sharing profits and losses in the ratio of 3 : 2 : 1. On 31st March, 2023 their balance sheet was as follows

Balance Sheet of Arnav, Bhavi and Chavi
as at 31st March, 2023

Liabilities		Amt (₹)	Assets		Amt (₹)
Capital A/cs			Plant and Machinery		3,00,000
Arnav	1,80,000		Furniture		20,000
Bhavi	1,60,000		Debtors	3,50,000	
Chavi	1,00,000	4,40,000	(–) Provision for Doubtful Debts	(20,000)	3,30,000
		2,50,000	Cash in Hand		10,000
			Profit and Loss Account		30,000
		6,90,000			6,90,000

Chavi retired on the above date. It was agreed that

(i) Plant and machinery be valued at ₹ 4,30,000 (ii) The existing provision for bad debts was to be increased by 50%.

(iii) Chavi's share of goodwill was valued at ₹ 80,000 and the same was to be treated without opening goodwill account.

(iv) The total amount to be paid to Chavi was brought in by Arnav and Bhavi in such a way as to make their capitals in proportion to their new profit sharing ratio.

Prepare revaluation account and partners' capital account. **CBSE 2024**

Sol. Dr **Revaluation Account** Cr

Particulars		Amt (₹)	Particulars	Amt (₹)
To Provision for Doubtful Debts A/c		10,000	By Plant and Machinery A/c	1,30,000
To Profit Transferred to Partners' Capital A/cs				
Arnav	60,000			
Bhavi	40,000			
Chavi	20,000	1,20,000		
		1,30,000		1,30,000

Dr **Partners' Capital Account** Cr

Particulars	Arnav (₹)	Bhavi (₹)	Chavi (₹)	Particulars	Arnav (₹)	Bhavi (₹)	Chavi (₹)
To Chavi's Capital A/c	48,000	32,000	—	By Balance b/d	1,80,000	1,60,000	1,00,000
To Profit and Loss A/c	15,000	10,000	5,000	By Revaluation A/c	60,000	40,000	20,000
To Cash A/c	—	—	1,95,000	By Arnav's Capital A/c	—	—	48,000
To Balance c/d	3,18,000	2,12,000	—	By Bhavi's Capital A/c	—	—	32,000
				By Cash A/c	1,41,000	54,000	—
	3,81,000	2,54,000	2,00,000		3,81,000	2,54,000	2,00,000

Working Note

Adjustment of Capital

Total Capital of the Firm = 1,77,000 + 1,58,000 + 1,95,000 = ₹ 5,30,000

New Profit Sharing Ratio = 3 : 2

Arnav's New Capital = $5{,}30{,}000 \times \frac{3}{5}$ = ₹ 3,18,000 ; Bhavi's New Capital = $5{,}30{,}000 \times \frac{2}{5}$ = ₹ 2,12,000

Solved Question 25 **Following is the balance sheet of P, Q and R as at 31st March, 2024, who have agreed to share profits and losses in proportion of their capitals.**

Balance Sheet
as at 31st March, 2024

Liabilities		Amt (₹)	Assets		Amt (₹)
Capital A/cs			Land and Building		2,00,000
P	2,00,000		Machinery		3,00,000
Q	3,00,000		Closing Stock		1,00,000
R	2,00,000	7,00,000	Sundry Debtors	1,10,000	
General Reserve		35,000	(−) Provision for Doubtful Debts	(10,000)	1,00,000
Workmen's Compensation Fund		15,000	Cash at Bank		1,00,000
Sundry Creditors		50,000			
		8,00,000			8,00,000

On 31st March, 2024, P desired to retire from the firm and the remaining partners decided to carry on the business. It was agreed to revalue the assets and reassess the liabilities on the following basis

(i) Land and building to be appreciated by 30%. **(ii) Machinery be depreciated by 20%.**

(iii) There were bad debts of ₹ 17,000.

(iv) The claim on account of workmen's compensation was estimated at ₹ 8,000.

(v) Goodwill of the firm was valued at ₹ 1,40,000 and P's share of goodwill be adjusted against the capital accounts of the continuing partners Q and R who have decided to share future profits in the ratio of 4 : 3 respectively.

(vi) Capital of the new firm in total will be the same as before the retirement of P and will be in the new profit sharing ratio of the continuing partners.

(vii) Amount due to P be settled by paying ₹ 50,000 in cash and the balance by transferring to her loan account which will be paid later on.

Prepare revaluation account, capital accounts of partners' and balance sheet of the firm after P's retirement.

Sol. Dr **Revaluation Account** Cr

Particulars	Amt (₹)	Particulars		Amt (₹)
To Machinery A/c	60,000	By Land and Building A/c		60,000
To Bad Debts A/c (WN 1)	7,000	By Loss Transferred to		
		P's Capital A/c	2,000	
		Q's Capital A/c	3,000	
		R's Capital A/c	2,000	7,000
	67,000			67,000

Dr **Partners' Capital Account** Cr

Particulars	P (₹)	Q (₹)	R (₹)	Particulars	P (₹)	Q (₹)	R (₹)
To Revaluation A/c (Loss)	2,000	3,000	2,000	By Balance b/d	2,00,000	3,00,000	2,00,000
To P's Capital A/c (Goodwill) (WN 3)	—	20,000	20,000	By General Reserve A/c	10,000	15,000	10,000
To Bank A/c	50,000	—	—	By Workmen's Compensation Fund A/c (WN 2)	2,000	3,000	2,000
To P's Loan A/c	2,00,000	—	—	By Q's Capital A/c	20,000	—	—
To Balance c/d (WN 5)	—	4,00,000	3,00,000	By R's Capital A/c	20,000	—	—
				By Bank A/c (Balancing Figure)	—	1,05,000	1,10,000
	2,52,000	4,23,000	3,22,000		2,52,000	4,23,000	3,22,000

Balance Sheet
as at 31st March, 2024

Liabilities		Amt (₹)	Assets	Amt (₹)
Capital A/cs			Land and Building	2,60,000
Q	4,00,000		Machinery	2,40,000
R	3,00,000	7,00,000	Closing Stock	1,00,000
P's Loan		2,00,000	Sundry Debtors	93,000
Workmen's Compensation Claim		8,000	Cash at Bank (WN 4)	2,65,000
Sundry Creditors		50,000		
		9,58,000		9,58,000

Working Notes

1. **Accounting Entries for Bad Debts**

JOURNAL

Date	Particulars		LF	Amt (Dr)	Amt (Cr)
2024					
Mar 31	Bad Debts A/c	Dr		17,000	
	To Sundry Debtors A/c				17,000
	Provision for Doubtful Debts A/c	Dr		10,000	
	Revaluation A/c	Dr		7,000	
	To Bad Debts A/c				17,000

2. Balance of workmen's compensation fund ₹ 7,000 (i.e. 15,000 – 8,000 claim) is credited to partners' capital accounts in their old profit sharing ratio, i.e. 2 : 3 : 2.
3. P's share of goodwill $= 1{,}40{,}000 \times \frac{2}{7} =$ ₹ 40,000, which is contributed by Q and R in gaining ratio.

   It is calculated as follows

   Gaining Ratio = New Share – Old Share

   $Q = \frac{4}{7} - \frac{3}{7} = \frac{1}{7}$; $R = \frac{3}{7} - \frac{2}{7} = \frac{1}{7}$

   Gaining ratio of Q and R $= \frac{1}{7} : \frac{1}{7}$ or $1:1$

   Q's contribution $= 40{,}000 \times \frac{1}{2} =$ ₹ 20,000 ; R's contribution $= 40{,}000 \times \frac{1}{2} =$ ₹ 20,000

4. Dr **Bank Account** Cr

Particulars	Amt (₹)	Particulars	Amt (₹)
To Balance b/d	1,00,000	By P's Capital A/c	50,000
To Q's Capital A/c	1,05,000	By Balance c/d	2,65,000
To R's Capital A/c	1,10,000		
	3,15,000		3,15,000

5. Total capital of the firm before P's retirement = ₹ 7,00,000

   Q's capital in the new firm $= 7{,}00{,}000 \times \frac{4}{7} =$ ₹ 4,00,000; R's capital in the new firm $= 7{,}00{,}000 \times \frac{3}{7} =$ ₹ 3,00,000

Solved Question 26 Rupal, Shanu and Trisha were partners in a firm sharing profits and losses in the ratio of 4 : 3 : 1. Their balance sheet as at 31st March, 2024 was as follows

Balance Sheet of Rupal, Shanu and Trisha
as at 31st March, 2024

Liabilities		Amt (₹)	Assets	Amt (₹)
Capital A/cs			Fixed Assets	8,20,000
Rupal	8,00,000		Stock	2,80,000
Shanu	6,00,000		Debtors	5,00,000
Trisha	2,00,000	16,00,000	Cash	7,20,000
General Reserve		3,20,000		
Creditors		4,00,000		
		23,20,000		23,20,000

Trisha retired from the firm on 1st April, 2024 on the following terms

(i) Trisha's share of profit was entirely taken by Shanu.
(ii) Fixed assets were found to be undervalued by ₹ 2,40,000.
(iii) Stock was revalued at ₹ 2,00,000.
(iv) Goodwill of the firm was valued at ₹ 8,00,000 on Trisha's retirement.
(v) The total capital of the new firm was fixed at ₹ 16,00,000 which was adjusted according to the new profit sharing ratio of the partners. For this necessary cash was paid-off or brought in by the partners as the case may be.

Prepare revaluation account and partners' capital account. **CBSE 2025**

Sol. Dr **Revaluation Account** Cr

Particulars		Amt (₹)	Particulars	Amt (₹)
To Stock		80,000	By Fixed Assets	2,40,000
To Gain on Revaluation				
Rupal's Capital	80,000			
Shanu's Capital	60,000			
Trisha's Capital	20,000	1,60,000		
		2,40,000		2,40,000

Dr **Partners' Capital Account** Cr

Date	Particulars	Rupal (₹)	Shanu (₹)	Trisha (₹)	Date	Particulars	Rupal (₹)	Shanu (₹)	Trisha (₹)
2024					2024				
Apr 1	To Trisha's Capital A/c	—	1,00,000	—	Apr 1	By Balance c/d	8,00,000	6,00,000	2,00,000
Apr 1	To Trisha's Loan A/c	—	—	3,60,000	Apr 1	By Revaluation A/c	80,000	60,000	20,000
Apr 1	To Cash A/c	2,40,000	—	—	Apr 1	By General Reserve	1,60,000	1,20,000	40,000
Apr 1	To Balance c/d	8,00,000	8,00,000	—	Apr 1	By Shanu's Capital A/c	—	—	1,00,000
					Apr 1	By Cash A/c	—	1,20,000	—
		10,40,000	9,00,000	3,60,000			10,40,000	9,00,000	3,60,000

Working Notes

1. **New Capital**

Rupal $= 16{,}00{,}000 \times \frac{1}{2} =$ ₹ 8,00,000; Shanu $= 16{,}00{,}000 \times \frac{1}{2} =$ ₹ 8,00,000

2. **New Ratio**

Rupal $= \frac{4}{8}$; Shanu $= \frac{3}{8} + \frac{1}{8} = \frac{4}{8}$; New Ratio = 1 : 1

3. **Calculation of Cash brought in or Paid-off**

		Amt (₹)	
Rupal	New capital	8,00,000	
	Adjusted capital	10,40,00	
		2,40,000	(withdrawn)
Shanu	New capital	8,00,000	
	Adjusted capital	6,80,000	
		1,20,000	(brought in)

Solved Question 27 **P, Q and R were equal partners. Their balance sheet as at 31st March, 2024 is**

Balance Sheet
as at 31st March, 2024

Liabilities		Amt (₹)	Assets		Amt (₹)
Bills Payable		20,000	Bank		20,000
Creditors		40,000	Stock		20,000
General Reserve		30,000	Furniture		28,000
Profit and Loss A/c		6,000	Debtors	45,000	
Capital A/cs			(−) Provision for Doubtful Debts	(5,000)	40,000
P	60,000		Land and Building		1,20,000
Q	40,000				
R	32,000	1,32,000			
		2,28,000			2,28,000

Q retired on 1st April, 2024. P and R decided to continue the business as equal partners on the following terms

(i) **Goodwill of the firm was valued at ₹ 57,600.**

(ii) **The provision for doubtful debts to be maintained @ 10% on debtors.**

(iii) **Land and building to be increased to ₹ 1,32,000.** (iv) **Furniture to be reduced by ₹ 8,000.**

(v) **Rent outstanding (not provided for as yet) was ₹ 1,500.**

The remaining partners decided to bring in sufficient cash in the business to pay-off Q and to maintain a bank balance of ₹ 24,800. They also decided to readjust their capitals as per their new profit sharing ratio.

Prepare the necessary ledger accounts and the balance sheet.

Sol. Dr **Revaluation Account** Cr

Particulars		Amt (₹)	Particulars	Amt (₹)
To Furniture A/c		8,000	By Provision for Doubtful Debts A/c	500
To Outstanding Rent A/c		1,500	By Land and Building A/c	12,000
To Profit Transferred to Partner's Capital A/cs				
P	1,000			
Q	1,000			
R	1,000	3,000		
		12,500		12,500

Dr **Partners' Capital Account** Cr

Particulars	P (₹)	Q (₹)	R (₹)	Particulars	P (₹)	Q (₹)	R (₹)
To Q's Capital A/c (Goodwill)	9,600	—	9,600	By Balance b/d	60,000	40,000	32,000
To Bank A/c	—	72,200	—	By General Reserve A/c	10,000	10,000	10,000
To Balance c/d (WN)	87,900	—	87,900	By Profit and Loss A/c	2,000	2,000	2,000
				By P's Capital A/c	—	9,600	—
				By R's Capital A/c	—	9,600	—
				By Revaluation A/c (Profit)	1,000	1,000	1,000
				By Bank A/c (Balancing Figure)	24,500	—	52,500
	97,500	72,200	97,500		97,500	72,200	97,500

Dr **Bank Account** Cr

Date	Particulars	Amt (₹)	Date	Particulars	Amt (₹)
2024			2024		
Apr 1	To Balance b/d	20,000	Apr 1	By Q's Capital A/c	72,200
Apr 1	To P's Capital A/c	24,500	Apr 1	By Balance c/d	24,800
Apr 1	To R's Capital A/c	52,500			
		97,000			97,000

Balance Sheet
as at 1st April, 2024

Liabilities		Amt (₹)	Assets		Amt (₹)
Capital A/cs			Land and Building		1,32,000
P	87,900		Furniture		20,000
R	87,900	1,75,800	Stock		20,000
Creditors		40,000	Debtors	45,000	
Bills Payable		20,000	(–) Provision for Doubtful Debts	(4,500)	40,500
Outstanding Rent		1,500	Bank		24,800
		2,37,300			2,37,300

Working Note

Capital of the New Firm = Balance of P's Capital Account and R's Capital Account (63,400 + 35,400) + Amount Payable to Q (72,200) + Bank Balance Required (24,800) – Existing Bank Balance (20,000) = ₹ 1,75,800

Allternatively

Capital of P and R in the New Firm		Amt (₹)
Assets will remain as		
Land and Building	1,32,000	
Furniture	20,000	
Stock	20,000	
Debtors	45,000	
Bank (Required)	24,800	2,41,800
(–) Creditors	(40,000)	
Bills Payable	(20,000)	
Outstanding Rent	(1,500)	
Provision for Doubtful Debts	(4,500)	(66,000)
Capital of the New Firm		1,75,800

Capital of P and R in the new firm = 1,75,800 × 1/2 = ₹ 87,900

Death of a Partner

Solved Question 28

(i) X, Y and Z were partners in a firm. The firm closes its books on 31st March every year. On 31st December, 2021, X died. The partnership deed provided that the share of deceased partner in the profits of the firm till the date of his death will be calculated on the basis of last year's profit. The profit for the year ended 31st March, 2021 was ₹ 6,00,000.

Calculate X's share in the profits of the firm till the date of his death and pass the necessary journal entry for the same in the books of the firm. **CBSE Term II 2022**

(ii) P, Q and R are partners in a firm whose books are closed on 31st March, each year. P died on 30th June, 2024 and according to the agreement the share of profits of a deceased partner up to the date of the death is to be calculated on the basis of the average profits for the last five years. The net profits for the last 5 years have been : 2020 ₹ 7,000, 2021 ₹ 9,000, 2022 ₹ 8,000, 2023 ₹ 5,000 (loss) and 2024 ₹ 8,000. Calculate P's share of the profits upto the date of death and pass necessary journal entry assuming

(a) There is no change in the profit sharing ratio of remaining partners.

(b) There is change in the profit sharing ratio of remaining partners, new ratio being 3 : 2.

Sol. (i) Calculation of X's share in the profits till 31st December, 2021 $= 6{,}00{,}000 \times \frac{9}{12} \times \frac{1}{3} =$ ₹ 1,50,000

JOURNAL

Date	Particulars		LF	Amt (Dr)	Amt (Cr)
2021					
Dec 31	Profit and Loss Suspense A/c	Dr		1,50,000	
	To X's Capital A/c				1,50,000
	(Being X's share of profits till the date of death adjusted)				

(ii) Total Profit $= 7{,}000 + 9{,}000 + 8{,}000 - 5{,}000 + 8{,}000 =$ ₹ 27,000

Average Profit $= 27{,}000 \div 5 =$ ₹ 5,400

3 month's profit i.e. from 1st April, 2020 to 30th June, 2020 $= 5{,}400 \times \frac{3}{12} =$ ₹ 1,350

$\frac{1}{3}$rd share of X upto the date of death $= 1{,}350 \times \frac{1}{3} =$ ₹ 450

(a) When there is no change in the profit sharing ratio of Y and Z.

JOURNAL

Date	Particulars		LF	Amt (Dr)	Amt (Cr)
2024					
June 30	Profit and Loss Suspense A/c	Dr		450	
	To P's Capital A/c				450
	(Being P's share of profit till the date of his death)				

(b) When there is change in the profit sharing ratio of Q and R and their new ratio is 3 : 2.

Gaining Ratio = New Ratio – Old Ratio

Q Gains $= \frac{3}{5} - \frac{1}{3} = \frac{9-5}{15} = \frac{4}{15}$; R Gains $= \frac{2}{5} - \frac{1}{3} = \frac{6-5}{15} = \frac{1}{15}$

Hence, Gaining Ratio of Q and R = 4 : 1

JOURNAL

Date	Particulars		LF	Amt (Dr)	Amt (Cr)
2024					
Jun 30	Q's Capital A/c $\left(450 \times \frac{4}{5}\right)$	Dr		360	
	R's Capital A/c $\left(450 \times \frac{1}{5}\right)$	Dr		90	
	To P's Capital A/c				450
	(Being Q's share of profit debited to remaining partners in their gaining ratio 4 : 1)				

Solved Question 29 **Simar, Tanvi and Umara were partners in a firm sharing profits and losses in the ratio of 5 : 6 : 9. On 31st March, 2024 their balance sheet was as follows**

Balance Sheet of Simar, Tanvi and Umara
as at 31st March, 2024

Liabilities		Amt (₹)	Assets	Amt (₹)
Capitals			Fixed Assets	25,00,000
Simar	13,00,000		Stock	10,00,000
Tanvi	12,00,000		Debtors	8,00,000
Umara	14,00,000	39,00,000	Cash	7,00,000
General Reserve		7,00,000	Profit and Loss Account (2023-24)	2,00,000
Trade Payables		6,00,000		
		52,00,000		52,00,000

Umara died on 30th June, 2024. The partnership deed provided for the following on the death of a partner

(i) Goodwill of the firm be valued at 3 years purchase of average profits for the last 5 years. The profit/loss for the previous four years were 2022-23 ₹ 3,10,000 (loss); 2021-22 ₹ 3,00,000 (profit); 2020-21 ₹ 4,00,000 (profit); 2019-20 ₹ 2,50,000 (profit)

(ii) Umara's share of profit or loss till the date of her death was to be calculated on the basis of profit or loss for the year ended 31st March, 2024.

(a) Calculate goodwill of the firm.

(b) Pass the necessary journal entry for the treatment of goodwill on Umara's death.

(c) Calculate Umara's share in the profit or loss of the firm till the date of her death.

(d) Pass the necessary journal entry to record Umara's share of profit or loss till the date of her death. **CBSE 2025**

Sol. (a) Goodwill = Average Profits × Number of Year's Purchase = 88,000 × 3 = ₹ 2,64,000

$$\text{Average Profits} = \frac{(3,10,000) + 3,00,000 + 4,00,000 + 2,50,000 + (2,00,000)}{5} = \frac{4,40,000}{5} = ₹\ 88,000$$

JOURNAL

(b)

Date	Particulars		LF	Amt (Dr)	Amt (Cr)
	Simar's Capital A/c	Dr		54,000	
	Tanvi's Capital A/c	Dr		64,800	
	To Umara's Capital A/c				1,18,800
	(Being goodwill credited to Umara by Simar and Tanvi in gaining ratio)				

Working Note

Umara's share in goodwill = $2,64,000 \times \frac{9}{20}$ = ₹ 1,18,800; Gaining ratio of Simar and Tanvi = 5 : 6

(c) Loss for the year ended 31st March, 2024 = ₹ 2,00,000

Hence, Umara's share in loss till 30th June, 2024 = $2,00,000 \times \frac{9}{20} \times \frac{3}{12}$ = ₹ 22,500

JOURNAL

(d)

Date	Particulars		LF	Amt (Dr)	Amt (Cr)
	Umara's Capital A/c	Dr		22,500	
	To Profit and Loss Suspense A/c				22,500
	(Being entry recorded for Umara's share in loss)				

Solved Question 30 **Aamir, Bashir and Chirag were partners in a firm sharing profit and losses in the ratio of 3 : 3 : 2. Chiraj died on 30th September, 2023. Aamir and Bashir decided to share profits and losses in future in the ratio of 1 : 2. On the day of Chirag's death, goodwill of the firm was valued at ₹ 5,40,000.**

Calculate gaining ratio and pass necessary journal entry to record the treatment of goodwill (without opening goodwill account).

Sol. Gain = New Share − Old Share

Aamir's Gain = 1/3 − 3/8 = (−) 1/24 (Sacrifice) ; Bashir's Gain = 2/3 − 3/8 = 7/24 (Gain)

In the Books of Aamir, Bashir and Chirag

JOURNAL

Date	Particulars		LF	Amt (Dr)	Amt (Cr)
2023					
Sep 30	Bashir's Capital A/c	Dr		1,57,500	
	To Aamir's Capital A/c				22,500
	To Chirag's Capital A/c				1,35,000
	(Being goodwill treated on Chirag's death without opening goodwill account)				

Settlement of Accounts

Solved Question 31 **Jay, Kamal and Lata are partners in a business. As of 1st April, 2024, their capital account balances are as follow Jay with ₹ 5,00,000, Kamal with ₹ 5,25,000 and Lata with ₹ 4,62,500. Kamal passed away on 30th September, 2024. According to the partnership agreement, the following provisions apply in the event of a partner's death**

(i) Interest on capital is provided at a rate of 10% per annum.

(ii) The legal representatives of the deceased partner will receive ₹ 43,750 for Kamal's share of goodwill.

(iii) Kamal's share of profit until the date of his death is to be calculated based on sales. Sales for the entire year 2023-24 amounted to ₹ 18,75,000, while sales from 1st April, 2024, to 30th September, 2024, were ₹ 3,75,000. The firm's profit for the financial year 2023-24 was ₹ 3,75,000.

Prepare Kamal's capital account to determine the amount payable to his legal representatives, given that the firm closes its books on 31st March each year.

Sol. Dr **Kamal's Capital Account** Cr

Particulars	Amt (₹)	Particulars	Amt (₹)
To Kamal's Executor's A/c (Transferred)	6,20,000	By Balance b/d	5,25,000
		By Interest on Capital A/c $\left(5,25,000 \times \frac{10}{100} \times \frac{6}{12}\right)$	26,250
		By Jay's Capital A/c (Goodwill)	21,875
		By Lata's Capital A/c (Goodwill)	21,875
		By Profit and Loss Suspense A/c (WN)	25,000
	6,20,000		6,20,000

Working Note

Calculation of profit upto date of death

% of Profit on Sales $= \frac{3,75,000}{18,75,000} \times 100 = 20\%$; Profit on Sales (20% of 3,75,000) = ₹ 75,000

Kamal's Share of Profit $= 75,000 \times \frac{1}{3} =$ ₹ 25,000

Solved Question 32 **Arun, Varun and Karan were partners in a firm sharing profits in the ratio of 4 : 3 : 3. On 31st March, 2024, their balance sheet was as follows**

Balance Sheet
as at 31st March, 2024

Liabilities		Amt (₹)	Assets	Amt (₹)
Creditors		17,000	Cash	8,000
Bills Payable		12,000	Debtors	13,000
Karan's Loan		28,000	Bills Receivables	9,000
Capital A/cs			Furniture	27,000
Arun	70,000		Machinery	1,25,000
Varun	68,000	1,38,000	Karan's Capital	13,000
		1,95,000		1,95,000

On 30th September, 2024, Karan died. The partnership deed provided for the following to the executors of the deceased partner.

(i) His share in the goodwill of the firm calculated on the basis of three years' purchase of the average profits of the last four years. The profits of the last four years were ₹ 1,90,000, ₹ 1,70,000, ₹ 1,80,000 and ₹ 1,60,000 respectively.

(ii) His share in the profits of the firm till the date of his death calculated on the basis of the average profits of the last four years.

(iii) Interest @ 8% per annum on the credit balance, if any, in his capital account.

(iv) Interest on his loan @ 12% per annum.

Prepare Karan's capital account to be presented to his executors, assuming that his loan and interest on loan were transferred to his capital account.

Sol. Dr **Karan's Capital Account** Cr

Particulars	Amt (₹)	Particulars	Amt (₹)
To Balance b/d	13,000	By Karan's Loan A/c	28,000
To Karan's Executor's A/c	2,00,430	By Arun's Capital A/c	90,000
		By Varun's Capital A/c	67,500
		By Profit and Loss Suspense A/c (Profit upto Death)	26,250
		By Interest on Loan A/c $\left(28,000 \times \frac{12}{100} \times \frac{6}{12}\right)$	1,680
	2,13,430		2,13,430

Working Notes

1. **Calculation of Share of Goodwill**

   $\text{Average Profit} = \frac{1,90000 + 1,70,000 + 1,80,000 + 1,60,000}{4} = ₹\ 1,75,000$

   $\text{Goodwill} = \text{Average Profit} \times \text{Number of Years' Purchase} = 1,75,000 \times 3 = ₹\ 5,25,000$

   $\text{Karan's Share} = 5,25,000 \times \frac{3}{10} = ₹\ 1,57,500$

2. **Calculation of Profit upto Death**

   Average profit = ₹ 1,75,000 ; Karan's share of profit $= 1,75,000 \times \frac{3}{10} \times \frac{6}{12} = ₹\ 26,250$

3. As there is no credit balance in capital account of Karan, he will not get interest on capital.

Solved Question 33 Azhar, Sumit and Robit were partners in a firm sharing profits and losses in the ratio of 3 : 1 : 1. Their balance sheet as at 31st March, 2023, was as follows

Balance Sheet of Azhar, Sumit and Robit
as at 31st March, 2023

Liabilities		Amt (₹)	Assets	Amt (₹)
Creditors		90,000	Bank	20,000
General Reserve		60,000	Stock	40,000
Capital A/cs			Debtors	1,50,000
Azhar	60,000		Fixed Assets	60,000
Sumit	40,000			
Robit	20,000	1,20,000		
		2,70,000		2,70,000

Robit died on 30th June, 2023. According to the partnership deed, Robit's legal representatives were entitled to

(i) Balance in his capital account.
(ii) His share of general reserve.
(iii) Interest on capital @10% p.a.
(iv) His share of goodwill. Goodwill of the firm was valued on the basis of thrice the average of the past four years' profits.
(v) His share in profits up to the date of death on the basis of the profit for the last year.

Profit for the previous year were

Year	Amt (₹)	Year	Amt (₹)
2019-20	**3,000**	**2020-21**	**28,000**
2021-22	**16,000**	**2022-23**	**15,000**

Prepare Robit's capital account to be rendered to his legal representatives. CBSE 2024

Sol.

Dr **Robit's Capital Account** Cr

Particulars	Amt (₹)	Particulars	Amt (₹)
To Robit's Executor's Legal Representatives A/c	41,650	By Balance b/d	20,000
		By General Reserve A/c	12,000
		By Interest on Capital A/c	500
		By Azhar's Capital A/c	6,300
		By Sumit's Capital A/c	2,100
		By Profit and Loss Suspense A/c	750
	41,650		41,650

Working Notes

1. $\text{Goodwill} = 3 \times \frac{56,000}{4} = ₹\ 42,000$

   Robit's share in firm's goodwill $= 42,000 \times 1/5 = ₹\ 8,400$

   Gaining ratio between Azhar and Sumit = 3 : 1

2. Robit's share in the profit upto the date of death $= 15,000 \times 1/5 \times 3/12 = ₹\ 750$

Solved Question 34 Aditi, Renu and Varsha were partners in a firm sharing profits and losses in the ratio of 3 : 2 : 5. On 31st March, 2023 their balance sheet was as under. **CBSE 2024**

Balance Sheet of Aditi, Renu and Varsha
as at 31st March, 2023

Liabilities		Amt (₹)	Assets	Amt (₹)
Capitals A/cs			Buildings	6,00,000
Aditi	5,00,000		Machinery	3,00,000
Renu	4,00,000		Stock	1,00,000
Varsha	3,00,000	12,00,000	Patents	1,50,000
General Reserve		1,00,000	Debtors	2,50,000
Creditors		2,00,000	Cash	1,00,000
		15,00,000		15,00,000

Varsha died on 31st July, 2023. The partnership deed provided for the following, on the death of a partner

(i) **Interest on capital was to be provided @ 6% p.a.**

(ii) **Goodwill of the firm was to be valued at 3 years purchase of average profits of the previous five years which were ₹ 90,000.**

(iii) **Varsha's share of profit or loss till the date of death was to be calculated on the basis of sales. Sales for the year ended 31st March, 2023 amounted to ₹ 60,00,000 and that from 1st April, 2023 to 31st July, 2023 amounted to ₹ 15,00,000. The profit for the year ended 31st March, 2023 was ₹ 12,00,000.**

Prepare Varsha's capital account to be rendered to her executors.

Sol. **In the Books of Aditi, Renu and Varsha**
Varsha's Capital Account

Dr Cr

Particulars	Amt (₹)	Particulars	Amt (₹)
To Varsha's Executor's A/c	6,41,000	By Balance b/d	3,00,000
		By General Reserve A/c	50,000
		By Aditi's Capital A/c	81,000
		By Renu's Capital A/c	54,000
		By Interest on Capital A/c	6,000
		By Profit and Loss Suspense A/c	1,50,000
	6,41,000		6,41,000

Working Notes

1. **Calculation of Goodwill**

   Firm's Goodwill $= 3 \times 90{,}000 =$ ₹ 2,70,000 ; Varsha's Share of Goodwill $= 2{,}70{,}000 \times 5/10 =$ ₹ 1,35,000

2. **Calculation of Profit**

   Profit $= 12{,}00{,}000 / 60{,}00{,}000 \times 15{,}00{,}000 =$ ₹ 3,00,000 ; Varsha's Share of Profit $= 3{,}00{,}000 \times 5/10 =$ ₹ 1,50,000

Solved Question 35 X, Y and Z were partners sharing profits and losses in the ratio of 5 : 3 : 2. On 31st March, 2024, their balance sheet was as follows

Balance Sheet
as at 31st March, 2024

Liabilities		Amt (₹)	Assets	Amt (₹)
Capital A/cs			Goodwill	2,500
X	33,750		Patents	13,000
Y	23,750		Machinery	15,600
Z	18,500	76,000	Investments	1,500
Investment Fluctuation Reserve		1,750	Stock	5,000
Workmen Compensation Reserve		1,750	Sundry Debtors	6,000
Sundry Creditors		25,500	Loan to Z	20,500
			Cash at Bank	2,900
			Advertisement Expenditure	500
			Profit and Loss A/c (Year ended 31st March, 2024)	37,500
		1,05,000		1,05,000

Z died on 1st August, 2024. Z had withdrawn ₹ 2,500 during the period from 1st April, 2024 to the date of death. It was agreed between his executors and the remaining partners that

(i) Goodwill will be valued at $2\frac{1}{2}$ years' purchase of average of four completed years' profits. Profits for the years ended 31st March, were

Year (₹)	2021	2022	2023
Profits (₹)	50,500	7,000	8,000

(ii) Z's share of profit from the beginning of the accounting year till the date of death be calculated on the basis of the average of three completed years' profit before death.

(iii) Patents were undervalued by ₹ 8,500, machinery was overvalued by ₹ 1,600.

(iv) Market value of investment on 1st August, 2024 was ₹ 2,100.

Prepare Z's capital account and Z's executors' account.

Sol. Dr **Z's Capital Account** Cr

Particulars	Amt (₹)	Particulars	Amt (₹)
To Drawings A/c	2,500	By Balance b/d	18,500
To Goodwill A/c (2,500 × 2/10)	500	By Revaluation A/c (WN 1)	1,500
To Profit and Loss A/c (37,500 × 2/10)	7,500	By X's Capital A/c (WN 2)	2,187
To Profit and Loss Suspense A/c (WN 3)	500	By Y's Capital A/c (WN 2)	1,313
To Advertisement Expenditure A/c $\left(500 \times \frac{2}{10}\right)$	100	By Investment Fluctuation Reserve A/c (1,750 × 2/10)	350
		By Workmen Compensation Reserve A/c (1,750 × 2/10)	350
To Loan to Z A/c	20,500	By Z's Executors' A/c (Balancing Figure)	7,400
	31,600		31,600

Dr **Z's Executors' Account** Cr

Particulars	Amt (₹)	Particulars	Amt (₹)
To Z's Capital A/c	7,400	By Bank A/c*	7,400

*Deficiency of Z's capital account (i.e. Debit balance) met by Z's executors.

Working Notes

1. Dr **Revaluation Account** Cr

Particulars		Amt (₹)	Particulars	Amt (₹)
To Machinery A/c		1,600	By Patents A/c	8,500
To Gain Transferred to Partner's Capital A/cs			By Investments A/c	600
X (7,500 × 5/10)	3,750			
Y (7,500 × 3/10)	2,250			
Z (7,500 × 2/10)	1,500	7,500		
		9,100		9,100

2. **Z's Share of Goodwill**

Firm's Goodwill $= \frac{50{,}500 + 7{,}000 + 8{,}000 - 37{,}500}{4} \times 2.5 =$ ₹ 17,500

Z's Share of Goodwill = 17,500 × 2/10 = ₹ 3,500, which is contributed by X and Y in their gaining ratio, i.e. 5 : 3.

X's Contribution = 3,500 × 5/8 = ₹ 2,187 ; Y's Contribution = 3,500 × 3/8 = ₹ 1,313

3. **Z's Share of Profit/Loss till Date of Death**

Average Profit/Loss till Date of Death

Average Profit/Loss of Last 3 years $= \frac{7{,}000 + 8{,}000 - 37{,}500}{3} =$ ₹ (7,500)

Z's Share of Profit/Loss = (7,500) × 4/12 × 2/10 = ₹ 500

Comprehensive Questions (Retirement and Death)

Solved Question 36 **Inder, Jonny and Kapil were partners in a firm sharing profits and loss in the ratio of 9 : 3 : 4. Their balance sheet as at 31st March, 2023 was as follows**

Balance Sheet of Inder, Jonny and Kapil
as at 31st March, 2023

Liabilities		Amt (₹)	Assets	Amt (₹)
Capital A/cs			Fixed Assets	1,20,000
Inder	90,000		Stock	60,000
Jonny	75,000		Debtors	1,00,000
Kapil	60,000	2,25,000	Cash	35,000
General Reserve		80,000		
Creditors		10,000		
		3,15,000		3,15,000

Kapil retired from the firm on 31st March, 2023 on the following terms

(i) Bad debts amounting to ₹ 5,000 were to be written-off.
(ii) Fixed assets were revalued at ₹ 96,000.
(iii) Stock was undervalued by ₹ 29,000.
(iv) Creditors were paid-off.
(v) Goodwill of the firm was valued at ₹ 80,000 and Kapil's share of goodwill was to be adjusted in the accounts of Inder and Jonny.
(vi) New profit sharing ratio between Inder and Jonny was 3 : 2.

Pass the necessary journal entries in the books of the firm on Kapil's retirement. **CBSE 2024**

Sol.

In the Books of Inder, Jonny and Kapil
JOURNAL

Date	Particulars		LF	Amt (Dr)	Amt (Cr)
2023					
Mar 31	General Reserve A/c	Dr		80,000	
	To Inder's Capital A/c				45,000
	To Jonny's Capital A/c				15,000
	To Kapil's Capital A/c				20,000
	(Being general reserve distributed among old partners in old ratio)				
Mar 31	Bad Debts A/c	Dr		5,000	
	To Debtors A/c				5,000
	(Being bad debts written-off)				
Mar 31	Revaluation A/c	Dr		5,000	
	To Bad Debts A/c				5,000
	(Being bad debts transferred to revaluation account)				
Mar 31	Stock A/c	Dr		29,000	
	To Revaluation A/c				29,000
	(Being value of stock increased by ₹ 12,000)				
Mar 31	Revaluation A/c	Dr		24,000	
	To Fixed Asset A/c				24,000
	(Being fixed assets reduced by ₹ 24,000)				
Mar 31	Creditors A/c	Dr		10,000	
	To Cash A/c				10,000
	(Being creditors paid-off)				
Mar 31	Inder's Capital A/c	Dr		3,000	
	Jonny's Capital A/c	Dr		17,000	
	To Kapil's Capital A/c				20,000
	(Being goodwill adjusted on retirement)				
Mar 31	Kapil's Capital A/c	Dr		1,00,000	
	To Kapil's Loan A/c				1,00,000
	(Kapil's final balance in capital transferred to his loan account)				

Solved Question 37 **Prateek, Charu and Sirima were partners in a firm sharing profits in the ratio of 3 : 2 : 1. Prateek retired from the firm on 31st March, 2023. Charu and Sirima decided that the capital of the new firm will be ₹ 6,30,000. The capital accounts of Charu and Sirima after all adjustments on the date of retirement showed as credit balance of ₹ 4,35,000 and ₹ 1,89,000 respectively. Calculate the amount of actual cash to be brought into the firm or to be paid to the partners. Also pass necessary journal entries.** **CBSE 2024**

Sol. **Calculation of Amount of Cash to be brought into the Firm or to be paid to the Partners**

Particulars	Charu (₹)	Sirima (₹)
New Capital (₹ 6,30,000 in new ratio 2 : 1)	2/3 ×6,30,00 = 4,20,000	1/3 ×6,30,000 = 2,10,000
Adjusted Capital	4,35,000	1,89,000
	Paid 15,000	Brought 21,000

In the Book of Prateek, Charu and Sirima
JOURNAL

Date	Particulars		LF	Amt (Dr)	Amt (Cr)
2023					
Mar 31	Cash A/c	Dr		21,000	
	To Sirima's Capital A/c				21,000
	(Being cash brought in by Sirima on retirement of Prateek)				
Mar 31	Charu's Capital A/c	Dr		15,000	
	To Cash A/c				15,000
	(Being cash paid to Charu on retirement of Prateek)				

Solved Question 38 **J, H and K were partners in a firm sharing profits in the ratio of 5 : 3 : 2. On 31st March, 2024 their balance sheet was as follows**

Balance Sheet
as at 31st March, 2024

Liabilities		Amt (₹)	Assets		Amt (₹)
Creditors		42,000	Land and Building		1,24,000
Investment Fluctuation Fund		20,000	Motor Vans		40,000
Profit and Loss A/c		80,000	Investments		38,000
Capital A/cs			Machinery		24,000
J	1,00,000		Stock		30,000
H	80,000		Debtors	80,000	
K	40,000	2,20,000	(–) Provision for Doubtful Debts	(6,000)	74,000
			Cash		32,000
		3,62,000			3,62,000

On the above date H retired and J and K agreed to continue the business on the following terms

(i) Goodwill of the firm was valued at ₹ 1,02,000. **(ii) There was a claim of ₹ 8,000 for workmen's compensation.**
(iii) Provision for bad debts was to be reduced by ₹ 2,000.
(iv) H will be paid ₹ 14,000 in cash and the balance will be transferred in his loan account which will be paid in four equal yearly instalments together with interest @ 10% per annum.
(v) The new profit sharing ratio between J and K will be 3 : 2 and their capitals will be in their new profit sharing ratio. The capital adjustments will be done by opening current accounts.

Prepare revaluation account, partners' capital account and balance sheet of the new firm.

Sol. Dr **Revaluation Account** Cr

Particulars	Amt (₹)	Particulars		Amt (₹)
To Claim for Workmen Compensation Fund A/c	8,000	By Provision for Doubtful Debts A/c		2,000
		By Loss Transferred to Partner's Capital A/cs		
		J	3,000	
		H	1,800	
		K	1,200	6,000
	8,000			8,000

Dr **Partners' Capital Account** Cr

Particulars	J (₹)	H (₹)	K (₹)	Particulars	J (₹)	H (₹)	K (₹)
To Loss on Revaluation A/c	3,000	1,800	1,200	By Balance b/d	1,00,000	80,000	40,000
To H's Capital A/c	10,200	—	20,400	By Investment Fluctuation Fund A/c	10,000	6,000	4,000
To Cash A/c	—	14,000	—	By Profit and Loss A/c	40,000	24,000	16,000
To H's Loan A/c	—	1,24,800	—	By J's Capital A/c	—	10,200	—
To Current A/c (Balancing Figure)	31,680	—	—	By K's Capital A/c	—	20,400	—
To Balance c/d	1,05,120	—	70,080	By Current A/c (Balancing Figure)	—	—	31,680
	1,50,000	1,40,600	91,680		1,50,000	1,40,600	91,680

Balance Sheet
as at 31st March, 2024

Liabilities		Amt (₹)	Assets		Amt (₹)
Creditors		42,000	Land and Building		1,24,000
J's Current A/c		31,680	Motor Van		40,000
Claim for Workmen Compensation		8,000	Investments		38,000
H's Loan A/c		1,24,800	Machinery		24,000
Capital A/cs			Stock		30,000
J	1,05,120		Debtors	80,000	
K	70,080	1,75,200	(−) Provision for Doubtful Debts	(4,000)	76,000
			Cash (32,000 − 14,000)		18,000
			K's Current A/c		31,680
		3,81,680			3,81,680

Working Notes

1. **Calculation of Gaining Ratio**

   Gaining Ratio = New Share − Old Share

   $J = \frac{3}{5} - \frac{5}{10} = \frac{6-5}{10} = \frac{1}{10}$; $K = \frac{2}{5} - \frac{2}{10} = \frac{4-2}{10} = \frac{2}{10}$

   Gaining ratio = 1 : 2

2. **Adjustment for Goodwill**

   Firm's goodwill = ₹ 1,02,000

   H's share of goodwill $= 1,02,000 \times \frac{3}{10} =$ ₹ 30,600 will be debited to gaining partners i.e. J and K in gaining ratio i.e. 1 : 2

   J's share $= 30,600 \times \frac{1}{3} =$ ₹ 10,200; K's share $= 30,600 \times \frac{2}{3} =$ ₹ 20,400

3. **Adjustment of Capital**

	Amt (₹)
J's capital after adjustment =	1,36,800
K's capital after adjustment =	38,400
Total capital of new firm =	1,75,200

   J's adjusted capital $= 1,75,200 \times \frac{3}{5} =$ ₹ 1,05,120 ; K's adjusted capital $= 1,75,200 \times \frac{2}{5} =$ ₹ 70,080

Solved Question 39 **Meghna, Mehak and Mandeep were partners in a firm whose balance sheet as on 31st March, 2023 was as under**

Balance Sheet

Liabilities		Amt (₹)	Assets	Amt (₹)
Creditors		28,000	Cash	27,000
General Reserve		7,500	Debtors	20,000
Capital A/cs			Stock	28,000
Meghna	20,000		Furniture	5,000
Mehak	14,500			
Mandeep	10,000	44,500		
		80,000		80,000

Mehak retired on this date under following terms

(i) To reduce stock and furniture by 5% and 10% respectively.

(ii) To provide for doubtful debts at 10% on debtors.

(iii) Goodwill was valued at ₹ 12,000.

(iv) Creditros of ₹ 8,000 were settled at ₹ 7,100.

(v) Mehak should be paid-off and the entire sum payable to Mehak shall be brought in by Meghna and Mandeep in such a way that their capitals should be in their new profit sharing ratio and a balance of ₹ 25,000 is maintained in the cash account.

Prepare revaluation account and partners' capital account of the new firm. **CBSE SQP 2025**

Sol. Dr **Revaluation Account** Cr

Particulars	Amt (₹)	Particulars		Amt (₹)
To Stock A/c	1,400	By Creditors A/c		900
To Furniture A/c	500	By Loss Transferred to Partner's Capital A/cs		
To Provision for Doubtful Debts	2,000	Meghna	1,000	
		Mehak	1,000	
		Mandeep	1,000	3,000
	3,900			3,900

Dr **Partners' Capital Account** Cr

Particulars	Meghna (₹)	Mehak (₹)	Mandeep (₹)	Particulars	Meghna (₹)	Mehak (₹)	Mandeep (₹)
To Revaluation	1,000	1,000	1,000	By Balance b/d	20,000	14,500	10,000
To Mehak	2,000	—	2,000	By General Reserve	2,500	2,500	2,500
To Cash	—	20,000	—	By Meghna	—	2,000	
To Balance c/d	27,050	—	27,050	By Mandeep		2,000	
				By Cash	7,550	—	17,550
	30,050	21,000	30,050		30,050	21,000	30,050

Working Note

Adjustment of Capital

Capital Balances of Partners after all the Adjustments = 19,500 + 20,000 + 9,500 + 5,100 (Cash) = ₹ 54,100

Meghna's New Capital $= 54{,}100 \times \frac{1}{2} =$ ₹ 27,050 ; Mandeep's New Capital $= 54{,}100 \times \frac{1}{2} =$ ₹ 27,050

Solved Question 40 A, B and C were partners sharing profits and losses in the ratio of 2 : 2 : 1. C died on 1st July, 2023 on which date the capitals of A, B and C after all necessary adjustments stood at ₹ 74,000, ₹ 6,750 and ₹ 42,250 respectively. A and B continued to carry on the business for six months without setting the accounts of C. During the period of six months from 1st July, 2023, a profit of ₹ 20,500 is earned using the firm's property. State which of the two options available u/s 37 of the Indian Partnership Act, 1932 should be exercised by executors of C and why? **CBSE SQP 2025**

Sol. (i) Share in the subsequent profits attributable to the use of his balance $= \frac{42{,}250 \times 20{,}500}{1{,}80{,}000} =$ ₹ 4,812

(ii) Interest @ 6% p.a. on the use of his balance = 42,250 × 6/12 × 6/100 ₹ 1,267.50

C should exercise option (i) since the amount payable to him under this option is more as compared to the amount payable to him under option (ii).

Solved Question 41 X, Y and Z were partners sharing profits and losses equally. Y died on 1st October, 2023 and total amount transferred to Y's executor's was ₹ 15,60,000. Y's executors were being paid ₹ 3,60,000 immediately and balance was to be paid in four equal quarterly instalments, together with interest @ 6% p.a. Pass entries till payment of first two instalments.

Sol. **JOURNAL** **CBSE SQP 2025**

Date	Particulars		Amt (Dr)	Amt (Cr)
2023 Oct 1	Y's Capital A/c	Dr	15,60,000	
	To Y's Executor's A/c			15,60,000
	(Being balance in capital transferred to executor's account)			

Date	Particulars		Amt (Dr)	Amt (Cr)
Oct 1	Y's Executor's A/c To Bank A/c (Being payment made to the executor)	Dr	3,60,000	3,60,000
Dec 31	Interest A/c To Y's Executor's A/c (Being interest due)	Dr	18,000	18,000
Dec 31	Y's Executor's A/c To Bank A/c (Being payment made to the executor)	Dr	3,18,000	3,18,000
2024 Mar 31	Interest A/c To Y's Executor's A/c (Being Interest due)	Dr	13,500	13,500
Mar 31	Y's Executor's A/c To Bank A/c (Being payment made to the executor)	Dr	3,13,500	3,13,500

Solved Question 42 **Sandeep, Maheep and Amandeep were partners in a firm sharing profits in the ratio of 2 : 2 : 1. The firm closes its books on 31st March every year. On 30th June, 2020 Maheep died. The partnership deed provided that on the death of a partner his executors will be entitled to the following**

(i) Balance in his capital account which amounted to ₹ 15,000 and interest on capital till date of death which amounted to ₹ 5,000.
(ii) His share in the profits of the firm till the date of his death amounted to ₹ 20,000.
(iii) His share in the goodwill of the firm. The goodwill of the firm on Maheep's death was valued at ₹ 1,50,000.
(iv) Loan to Maheep amounted ₹ 20,000.

It was agreed that the amount will be paid to his executor in three equal yearly instalments with interest @10% p.a. The first instalment was to be paid on 30th June, 2021.

Calculate the amount to be transferred to Maheep's executors account and prepare the executor's account till it is finally settled.

Sol. Maheep dues to be transferred to executors = 1,15,000 + 5,000 + 20,000 + 60,000 – 20,000 = ₹ 1,80,000

Dr **Maheep's Executors Account** Cr

Date	Particulars	Amt (₹)	Date	Particulars	Amt (₹)
2021			2020		
Mar 31	To Balance c/d	1,93,500	Jun 30	By Maheep's Capital A/c	1,80,000
			2021		
			Mar 31	Interest (9 months)	13,500
		1,93,500			1,93,000
2021			2021		
Jun 30	To Bank (II Instalment)	78,000	Apr 1	By Balance b/d	1,93,500
2022			June 30	By Interest (3 months)	4,500
Mar 31	To Balance c/d	1,29,000	2022		
			Mar 31	By Interest (9 months)	9,000
		2,07,000			2,07,000
2022			2022		
Jun 30	To Bank (II Instalment)	72,000	Apr 1	By Balance b/d	1,29,000
2023			Jun 30	By Interest (3 months)	3,000
Mar 31	To Balance c/d	64,000	2023		
			Mar 31	By Interest (9 months)	4,500
		1,36,500			1,36,500
2023			2023		
June 30	To Bank (III Instalment)	66,000	Apr 1	By Balance b/d	64,500
			Jun 30	By Interest (3 months)	1,500
		66,000			66,000

Missing Information

Solved Question 43 **Anshul, Babita and Chander were partners in a firm running a successful business of car accessories. They had agreed to share profits and losses in the ratio of 1/2 : 1/3 : 1/6 respectively. After running business successfully and without any disputes for 10 years, Babita decided to retire due to old age and the Anshul and Chander decided to share future profits and losses in the ratio of 3 : 2. The accountant passed the following journal entry for Babita share of goodwill and missed some information. Fill in the missing figures in the following journal entry and calculate the gaining ratio.**

JOURNAL

Date	Particulars		LF	Amt (Dr)	Amt (Cr)
	Anshul's Capital A/c	Dr		...	
	Chander's Capital A/c	Dr		21,000	
	To Babita's Capital A/c				...
	(Being Chander's share of goodwill debited to the amounts of continuing partners in their gaining ratio)				

Sol.

JOURNAL

Date	Particulars		LF	Amt (Dr)	Amt (Cr)
	Anshul's Capital A/c	Dr		**9,000**	
	Chander's Capital A/c	Dr		21,000	
	To Babita's Capital A/c				**30,000**
	(Being Chander's share of goodwill debited to the amounts of continuing partners in their gaining ratio)				

Working Note

Gaining Ratio = 3 : 7

Anshul $= \frac{3}{5} - \frac{3}{6} = \frac{18-15}{30} = \frac{3}{30}$; Chander $= \frac{2}{5} - \frac{1}{6} = \frac{12-5}{30} = \frac{7}{30}$

Solved Question 44 **S, B and M were partners in a firm sharing profits and losses in the ratio of 5 : 3 : 2. The profits of the firm for the year ending on 31st March, 2024 was ₹ 5,85,000. M dies on 1st August, 2024. Determine the missing values in the following journal entry.**

JOURNAL

Date	Particulars		LF	Amt (Dr)	Amt (Cr)
2021					
Aug 1	Profit and Loss Suspense A/c	Dr		...	
	To M's Capital A/c				...
	(Being M's share of profit (based on last year's profit) till the date of his death credited)				

Sol.

JOURNAL

Date	Particulars		LF	Amt (Dr)	Amt (Cr)
2021					
Aug 1	Profit and Loss Suspense A/c	Dr		**39,000**	
	To M's Capital A/c				**39,000**
	(Being M's share of profit (based on last year's profit) till the date of his death credited)				

Working Note

Calculation of M's Share in Profit

Total Profit for the Last Year = ₹ 5,85,000

Period (1st April, 2021 to 1st August, 2021) = 4 Months

Profit for 4 months = 5,85,000 × 4/12 = ₹ 1,95,000

M's share of estimated profit = 1,95,000 × 2 / 10 = ₹ 39,000

Numerical Questions

New Profit Sharing Ratio

1. P, Q and R were partners in a firm sharing profits in the ratio of 3 : 2 : 1. On 31st March, 2024, R decided to retire.

Calculate the new ratio and the gaining ratio of P and Q.

Ans. New Ratio = 3 : 2; Gaining Ratio = 3 : 2

2. P, Q and R were partners sharing profit in the ratio of 5 : 4 : 1. P retires from the firm.

Calculate new profit sharing ratio.

Ans. New Ratio = 4 : 1

3. X, Y and Z are partners sharing profit and loss in the ratio of 4 : 3 : 2. Z retires from the business. X is acquiring 4/9th of Z's share and balance is acquired by Y.

Calculate the new profit sharing ratio and gaining ratio.

Ans. Gaining Ratio of X and Y = 4 : 5; New Ratio will be = 44 : 37

4. D, L and F were partners in a firm sharing profits in the ratio of 2 : 1 : 1. D retired on 31st March, 2024 and his share was acquired by L and F in the ratio of 3 : 2.

Calculate the new and gaining ratio of L and F.

Ans. New Ratio = 11 : 9; Gaining Ratio = 3 : 2

5. P, Q and R share profit as 1/2 to P, 1/3 to Q and 1/6 to R. Q retires and his share is taken up by P and R in the ratio of 1 : 3.

Calculate the new profit sharing ratio.

Ans. New Profit Sharing Ratio = 7 : 5

6. Shiv, Mohan and Hari were partners in a firm sharing profit in the ratio of 5 : 5 : 4. Mohan retired and his share was divided equally between Shiv and Hari.

Calculate new profit sharing ratio.

Ans. New Ratio = 15 : 13

7. P, Q and R are partners sharing profit and loss in the ratio of 2 : 2 : 1. Q retires and his share is entirely taken by R.

Calculate the new ratio.

Ans. New Ratio of P and R = 2 : 3

8. X, Y and Z are partners sharing profits in 4 : 3 : 1 ratio. Y retires and gaining ratio between X and Z is 4 : 5.

Calculate new profit sharing ratio.

Ans. New Profit Sharing Ratio = 2 : 1

9. C, D and E are partners sharing the profits and losses in the ratio of 16 : 4 : 1. D retires. It is decided that the profit sharing ratio between C and E will be the same as existing between D and E.

Calculate the new profit sharing ratio and gaining ratio.

Ans. New Ratio = 4 : 1; Gaining Ratio = 1 : 4

Accounting Treatment of Goodwill

10. Ravi, Guru, Mani and Sonu were partners in a firm sharing profits in the ratio of the 2 : 2 : 2 : 1. On 31st January, 2023, Sonu retired. On Sonu's retirement the goodwill of the firm was valued at ₹ 1,40,000. The new profit sharing ratio among Ravi, Guru and Mani was agreed as 5 : 1 : 1.

Showing your workings clearly, pass necessary journal entry for the treatment of goodwill in the books of the firm on Sonu's retirement without opening goodwill account. Competency Based Que

Ans. Debit Ravi's capital account by ₹ 60,000 and Credit Sonu's capital account by ₹ 20,000, Guru's capital account by ₹ 20,000 and Mani's capital account by ₹ 20,000

11. L, M, N and O are partners sharing profit and loss in the ratio of 3 : 3 : 2 : 2 . O retires and L, M and N decide to share the future profit in the ratio of 3 : 2 : 1. Goodwill of the firm is valued at ₹ 1,80,000. Goodwill already appears in the books of the firm at ₹ 50,000. The profit for the first year after O's retirement was ₹ 3,00,000.

Give the necessary journal entries.

Ans. Debit L and M with ₹ 36,000 and ₹ 6,000 respectively and Credit N and O with ₹ 6,000 and ₹ 36,000 respectively.

12. X, Y and Z were partners in a firm sharing profits in the ratio of 6 : 4 : 5. Their capitals were ₹ 1,00,000, ₹ 80,000 and ₹ 60,000. On 1st April, 2024, Y retired from the firm. New profit sharing ratio between X and Z decided as 11 : 4. On Y's retirement, the goodwill of the firm was valued at ₹ 1,80,000. Goodwill already appears in the books of accounts at ₹ 1,50,000.

Pass necessary journal entries in the books of accounts.

Ans. Debit X by ₹ 60,000 and Credit Y by ₹ 48,000 and Z by ₹ 12,000

13. P, Q, R and S are partners in a firm sharing profits in the ratio of 2 : 2 : 1 : 1. P and R decided to retire from the firm. The goodwill of the firm was valued at ₹ 45,000. Q and S decided to share future profits in the ratio of 5 : 3.

Pass necessary journal entry for the treatment of goodwill.

Ans. Debit Q by ₹ 13,125 and S by ₹ 9,375 and credit P by ₹ 15,000 and R by ₹ 7,500

14. D, E and F are partners sharing profits and losses in the ratio of 4 : 3 : 1 respectively. E retires, selling his share of profit to D and F for ₹ 5,40,000, ₹ 2,40,000 being paid by D and ₹ 3,00,000 by F.

You are required

(i) To give necessary journal entry to record the above said sale of E's share to D and F.

(ii) To calculate the new profit sharing ratio.

Ans. (ii) New Profit Sharing Ratio = 2 : 1

15. A, B and C are partners sharing profits and losses in the ratio of 3 : 2 : 1. B retires selling his share to A and C for ₹ 80,000, ₹ 50,000 being paid by A and ₹ 30,000 by C. The profit for the year after B's retirement is ₹ 1,20,000.

Pass entries to (i) record the sale of B's share to A and C and (ii) distribute the profit between A and C.

Ans. New Profit Sharing Ratio = 17 : 7

16. P, Q and R are partners sharing profit in the ratio of $\frac{4}{9}:\frac{3}{4}:\frac{2}{9}$. Q retires and his capital after making adjustments for reserves and gain (profit) on revaluation stands at ₹ 1,39,200. P and R agreed to pay him ₹ 1,50,000 in full settlement of his claim.

Record necessary journal entry for adjustment of goodwill if the new profit sharing ratio is decided at 5 : 3.

Ans. Hidden Goodwill = ₹ 10,800; Gaining Ratio = 13 : 11; Debit P's capital account and R's capital account with ₹ 5,850 and ₹ 4,950 respectively and Credit Q's capital account with ₹ 10,800

Adjustment for Reserves, Accumulated Profits and Losses

17. D, J and I were in partnership sharing profits and losses in the proportions of 3 : 2 : 1. On 1st April, 2024, J retires from the firm. The following information is provided to you

(i) Investment fluctuation reserve stood at ₹ 15,000 in balance sheet. The value of investment is increased by ₹ 6,000.

(ii) General reserve stood in the balance sheet at ₹ 35,000.

Give journal entries for above adjustments.

18. A, B and C are partners in a firm sharing profit and loss in the ratio of 3 : 2 : 1. C retires from the firm on 31st March, 2024. On the date of C's retirement, the following balances appeared in the books of the firm.
General reserve ₹ 1,80,000
Profit and loss account (Dr) ₹ 30,000
Workmen compensation reserve ₹ 24,000 which was no more required
Employees' provident fund ₹ 20,000

Pass necessary journal entries for the adjustment of these items on C's retirement. Competency Based Que

Revaluation/Reassessment

19. X, Y and Z were in partnership sharing profits in proportion to their capitals. Their balance sheet on 31st March, 2024 was as follows

Balance Sheet
as at 31st March, 2024

Liabilities		Amt (₹)	Assets		Amt (₹)
Creditors		1,56,000	Cash		1,60,000
Reserve		60,000	Debtors	2,00,000	
Capital A/cs			(−) Provision for Doubtful Debts	(4,000)	1,96,000
X	9,00,000		Stock		1,80,000
Y	6,00,000		Machinery		4,80,000
Z	3,00,000	18,00,000	Buildings		10,00,000
		20,16,000			20,16,000

On the above date, Y retired owing to ill health and the following adjustments were agreed upon.

(i) Buildings to be appreciated by 10%.
(ii) Provision for doubtful debts to be increased to 5% of debtors.
(iii) Machinery to be depreciated by 15%.
(iv) A provision to be made for outstanding repairs bill of ₹ 30,000.
(v) Included in the value of creditors is ₹ 18,000 for an outstanding legal claim, which is not likely to arise.
(vi) Out of the insurance premium paid ₹ 20,000 is for the next year. The amount was debited to profit and loss account.

Record necessary journal entries and prepare the revaluation account. Competency Based Que

Ans. Profit on Revaluation = ₹ 30,000

20. Rohit, Raj and Rajan were partners in a firm sharing profits in the ratio of 4 : 2 : 1. On 31st March, 2020, Rohit retired. The following is their balance sheet

Balance Sheet
as at 31st March, 2020

Liabilities		Amt (₹)	Assets	Amt (₹)
Creditors		30,000	Cash	14,000
Bills Payable		4,000	Stock	30,000
General Reserve		21,000	Debtors	22,000
Capital A/cs			Building	40,000
Rohit	60,000		Plant	53,000
Raj	40,000		Motor Van	26,000
Rajan	30,000	1,30,000		
		1,85,000		1,85,000

(i) The assets and liabilities were revalued at Stock ₹ 24,000, debtors ₹ 21,000, building ₹ 45,200, plant ₹ 50,000 and creditors ₹ 28,000.
(ii) Goodwill of the firm was valued at ₹ 52,500.
(iii) Amount due to Rohit will be transferred to his loan account.

Prepare revaluation account and partners' capital account.

Ans. Revaluation Loss = ₹ 2,800; Partners' Capital Account Raj = ₹ 25,200, Rajan = ₹ 22,600; Rohit's Loan = ₹ 1,00,400

21. On 31st December, 2024, the balance sheet of M/s Sachin, Saurav and Rahul sharing profits and losses in proportion to their capitals stood as follows

Balance Sheet
as at 31st December, 2024

Liabilities		Amt (₹)	Assets		Amt (₹)
Sundry Creditors		10,800	Cash		8,000
Capital A/cs			Sundry Debtors	10,000	
Sachin	45,000		(−) Provision for Doubtful Debts	(200)	9,800
Saurav	30,000		Inventory		9,000
Rahul	15,000	90,000	Plant and Machinery		24,000
			Buildings		50,000
		1,00,800			1,00,800

On that date, Saurav retires from the firm and the remaining partners decide to carry on.

The following readjustments of assets and liabilities have been agreed upon before the ascertainment of the amount payable to Saurav

(i) Out of the fire insurance premium paid during 2024, ₹ 1,000 be carried forward as unexpired.
(ii) Buildings be appreciated by 10%.
(iii) Provision for doubtful debts be brought up to 5% on debtors.
(iv) Plant and machinery be depreciated by 5%.
(v) A provision for ₹ 1,500 be made in respect of an outstanding bill for repairs.
(vi) Goodwill of the entire firm be at ₹ 18,000 and Saurav's share of the same adjusted in the account of Sachin and Rahul, who share future profits in the proportion of 3/4th and 1/4th respectively.
(vii) Saurav be paid ₹ 5,000 in cash and the balance be transferred to his loan account.

Prepare revaluation account, partners' capital account and the balance sheet of the firm of Sachin and Rahul.

Competency Based Que

Ans. Profit on Revaluation = ₹ 3,000; Balance in Partners' Capital Account Sachin = ₹ 42,000; Rahul = ₹ 14,000; Total of Balance Sheet = ₹ 1,00,300

22. Trisha, Urvi and Varsha were partners in a firm sharing profits and losses in the ratio of 5 : 4 : 1.

Their balance sheet as at 31st March, 2023 was as follows

Balance Sheet of Trisha, Urvi and Varsha
as at 31st March, 2023

Liabilities		Amt (₹)	Assets	Amt (₹)
Capital A/cs			Fixed Assets	4,00,000
Trisha	2,00,000		Stock	1,00,000
Urvi	1,30,000		Debtors	1,50,000
Varsha	1,00,000	4,30,000	Cash	2,00,000
General Reserve		1,50,000		
Creditors		2,70,000		
		8,50,000		8,50,000

Trisha retired on 1st April, 2023 and the partners agreed to the following terms

(i) Fixed assets were found overvalued by ₹ 80,000.
(ii) Stock was taken over by Trisha at ₹ 80,000.
(iii) Goodwill of the firm was valued at ₹ 1,00,000 on Trisha's retirement and Trisha's share by goodwill was adjusted through the capital accounts of remaining partners.
(iv) New profit sharing ratio between the remaining partners was agreed at 2 : 3.
(v) Trisha was paid ₹ 50,000 on retirement and the balance was transferred to her loan account.

Pass necessary journal entries in the books of the firm on Trisha's retirement. **CBSE 2024 C**

23. The balance sheet of Arpan, Raman and Shubham who were sharing profits in the ratio of 5 : 3 : 2, is given below as at 31st March, 2015.

Liabilities		Amt (₹)	Assets	Amt (₹)
Capital A/cs			Land	4,00,000
Arpan	7,20,000		Building	3,80,000
Raman	4,15,000		Plant and Machinery	4,65,000
Shubham	3,45,000	14,80,000	Furniture and Fittings	77,000
Reserve Fund		1,80,000	Stock	1,85,000
Sundry Creditors		1,24,000	Sundry Debtors	1,72,000
Outstanding Expenses		16,000	Cash in Hand	1,21,000
		18,00,000		18,00,000

Raman retires on the above date and the following adjustments are agreed upon his retirement.

(i) Stock was valued at ₹ 1,72,000.
(ii) Furniture and fittings were valued at ₹ 80,000.
(iii) An amount of ₹ 10,000 due from Mr. Deepak, a debtor, was doubtful and a provision for the same was required.
(iv) Goodwill of the firm was valued at ₹ 2,00,000 but it was decided not to show goodwill in the books of accounts.
(v) Raman was paid ₹ 40,000 immediately on retirement and the balance was transferred to his loan account.
(vi) Arpan and Shubham were to share future profits in the ratio of 3 : 2.

Prepare revaluation account and partners' capital account.

Ans. Revaluation Loss = ₹ 20,000; Partners' Capital Account Arpan = ₹ 7,80,000, Shubham = ₹ 3,37,000; Raman's Loan Account = ₹ 4,83,000

Methods of Payment of Amount Due to Retiring Partner

24. A, B and C were in partnership sharing profits and losses in 3 : 2 : 1. C retired from the firm on 1st April, 2020. After adjustments, his capital account shows a credit balance of ₹ 50,000 on the date of retirement. C is to be paid in four equal annual instalments from 31st March, 2021 with interest @ 10%. p.a.

Prepare C's loan account until he is paid the amount due to him. The firm closes its books on 31st March every year. **Competency Based Que**

25. A, B and C were in partnership sharing profits and losses equally. C retired from the firm. After adjustment, his capital account shows a credit balance of ₹ 50,000 as on 1st April, 2023. C is to be paid in two equal instalments of ₹ 18,750 each including interest @ 10% p.a. on the outstanding balance of each year and the balance including interest in the third year.

Prepare C's loan account till he is paid the amount due to him.

26. Raj, Samir and Kabir are partners in a firm. Samir decides to retire from the firm. On the date of his retirement, an amount of ₹ 2,70,000 is due to him. Raj and Kabir agree to pay him this amount in instalments at the end of each year and Samir consents to the arrangement. **NCERT; Competency Based Que**

Prepare Samir's loan account in the following scenarios

(i) When the payment is made in four yearly instalments, with interest at 12% per annum on the unpaid balance.

(ii) When the payment is made in three yearly instalments of ₹ 20,000 each, including interest at 12% per annum on the outstanding balance for the first three years and the remaining balance, including interest, is paid in the fourth year.

27. A, B and C were in partnership sharing profits and losses equally. B retired from the firm. After all adjustments, his capital account shows a credit balance of ₹ 55,000 as on 1st April, 2024.

B is to be paid ₹ 15,000 by cheque immediately and balance in four equal semi-annual instalments along with interest @ 10% on the unpaid amount.

Prepare B's loan account till he is paid the amount due to him. The firm closes its books on 31st March, every year. **Competency Based Que**

Adjustment of Capital

28. Chirag, Nidhi and Meera were partners in a firm sharing profits in the ratio of 3 : 2 : 1. Chirag retired from the firm on 31st March, 2023. Nidhi and Meera decided that the capital of the new firm would be ₹ 15,75,000. The capital accounts of Nidhi and Meera, after all adjustments on the date of retirement, showed a credit balance of ₹ 10,87,500 and ₹ 4,72,500, respectively.

Calculate the amount of actual cash to be brought into the firm or to be paid to the partners. Also, pass the necessary journal entries.

Ans. Cash brought in by Meera = ₹ 52,500; Cash paid to Nidhi = ₹ 37,500

29. L, M and N were partners in a firm sharing profit and losses in the ratio of 2 : 2 : 3. On 31st March, 2023, their balance sheet was as follows

Liabilities		Amt (₹)	Assets	Amt (₹)
Creditors		80,000	Land and Building	5,00,000
Bank Overdraft		22,000	Machinery	2,50,000
Long-term Debts		2,00,000	Furniture	3,50,000
Capital A/cs			Investments	1,00,000
L	6,25,000		Stock	4,00,000
M	4,00,000		Debtors	2,00,000
N	5,25,000	15,50,000	Bank	20,000
Employees Provident Fund		38,000	Deferred Advertisement Expenditure	70,000
		18,90,000		18,90,000

On 31st March, 2023, M retired from the firm and remaining partners decided to carry on business. It was decided to revalue assets and liabilities as under

(i) Land and building be appreciated by ₹ 2,40,000 and machinery be depreciated 10%.

(ii) 50% of investments were taken by the retiring partner at book value.

(iii) Provision for doubtful debts was to be made at 5% on debtors.

(iv) Stock will be valued at market price which is ₹ 1,00,000 less than the book value.

(v) Goodwill of the firm be valued at ₹ 5,60,000 which will be in proportion of profit sharing ratio of L and N.

(vi) The total capital of the new firm will be ₹ 32,00,000 which will be in proportion of profit sharing ratio of L and N.

(vii) Gain on revaluation account amounted to ₹ 1,05,000.

Prepare partners' capital account and balance sheet of firm after M's retirement. **Competency Based Que**

Ans. Partners' Capital Account L = ₹ 12,80,000, N = ₹ 19,20,000; M's Loan = ₹ 5,20,000; Balance Sheet = ₹ 40,60,000

30. Arjun, Ravi and Kiran are partners in a firm sharing profits in the ratio of 3 : 2 : 1. Ravi retires. After making all adjustments related to revaluation, goodwill and accumulated profit, the capital accounts of Arjun and Kiran showed a credit balance of ₹ 24,000 and ₹ 12,000, respectively.

It was decided to adjust the capitals of Arjun and Kiran in their new profit sharing ratio.

You are required to calculate the new capitals of the partners and record necessary journal entries for bringing in or withdrawing the required amounts.

Competency Based Que

Ans. Cash to be brought in Arjun = ₹ 3,000, Kiran = ₹ 3,000

31. V, W and X were carrying out a business as partners and sharing profits in the ratio of 2 : 1 : 1. Their balance sheet at 31st December, 2024 was as under

Balance Sheet
as at 31st December, 2024

Liabilities		Amt (₹)	Assets		Amt (₹)
Bills Payable		10,600	Buildings		70,000
Sundry Creditors		11,000	Plant and Machinery		78,000
Capital A/cs			Stock		16,000
V	7,500		Debtors	22,000	
W	5,000		(–) Provision for		
X	5,500	1,80,000	Doubtful Debts	(400)	21,600
Profit and Loss A/c		1,400	Bank		7,500
			Cash		9,900
		2,03,000			2,03,000

V decided to retire on that date because of health problems.

In this regard, following adjustments were agreed upon

(i) The value of buildings to be increased to ₹ 96,000.

(ii) The provision for bad and doubtful debts on debtors to be maintained at 3%.

(iii) Plant and machinery should be valued at 20% less.

(iv) Goodwill of the firm is valued at ₹ 36,000 and V's share is to be adjusted in the remaining partners' accounts.

(v) W and X agree that the capital of the new firm would be in their new profit sharing ratio and adjustments to be made through cash.

You are required to prepare revaluation account, partners' capital account and balance sheet.

Ans. Profit V = ₹ 5,070, W = ₹ 2,535, X = ₹ 2,535; V's Loan Account = ₹ 98,770; Partners' Capital Accounts W = ₹ 46,385, X = ₹ 46,385; Total of Balance Sheet = ₹ 2,13,140

32. The balance sheet of Sun, Moon and Star sharing profits and losses in the ratio of 2 : 3 : 2 is given below

Balance Sheet

as at ...

Liabilities		Amt (₹)	Assets		Amt (₹)
Capital A/cs			Land and Buildings		2,40,000
Sun	2,40,000		Machinery		3,60,000
Moon	3,60,000		Closing Stock		1,20,000
Star	2,40,000	8,40,000	Sundry Debtors	1,32,000	
Workmen Compensation Reserve		18,000	(−) Provision for Doubtful Debts	(12,000)	1,20,000
Sundry Creditors		60,000	Cash at Bank		1,20,000
Employees Provident Fund		42,000			
		9,60,000			9,60,000

On same date, Sun desired to retire on the following terms

(i) Land and buildings be appreciated by 30%. (ii) Machinery be depreciated by 30%.

(iii) Bad debts ₹ 22,200.

(iv) The claim on account of workmen compensation fund was estimated at ₹ 9,600.

(v) Goodwill of the entire firm be valued at ₹ 1,68,000. Moon and Star decided to share the future profits and losses in the ratio of 3 : 4.

(vi) The total capital of the firm is to be the same as before retirement. Individual capitals be in their profit sharing ratio.

(vii) Amount due to Sun is to be settled by paying ₹ 60,000 in cash and balance by transferring to loan account.

Prepare revaluation account, capital accounts of partners, balance sheet of new firm.

Ans. Loss on Revaluation = ₹ 46,200; Capital Account Balances Moon = ₹ 3,60,000, Star = ₹ 4,80,000; Sun's Loan = ₹ 2,17,200; Balance Sheet Total = ₹ 11,68,800

33. Ajay, Brajesh and Chandan are partners in a firm, sharing profits in the ratio of 4 : 3 : 3. Upon Ajay's retirement and after completing all adjustments related to general reserves, goodwill, revaluation and other items, their capital account balances stood at ₹ 1,05,000, ₹ 90,000, and ₹ 75,000, respectively.

It was agreed that the amount due to Ajay would be contributed by Brajesh and Chandan in such a way that their capitals would be proportionate to their profit sharing ratio.

Calculate the amounts that Brajesh and Chandan need to bring in and prepare the necessary journal entries for these contributions. Also, record the journal entry for the payment made to Ajay. Following Ajay's retirement, the new profit sharing ratio between Brajesh and Chandan will be 1 : 1. **Competency Based Que**

Ans. Brajesh contributing = ₹45,000 and Chandan contributing = ₹ 60,000

34. Ajay, Bhavesh and Charan are partners in a firm, sharing profits in the ratio of 5 : 3 : 2. On 1st April, 2024, Bhavesh decides to retire. On that date, after making all necessary adjustments, the capital balances of Ajay, Bhavesh and Charan stand at ₹ 15,552, ₹ 13,176 and ₹ 4,032 respectively, with a cash and bank balance of ₹ 1,440. Bhavesh is to be paid his share using funds brought in by Ajay and Charan so that their capitals become proportionate to the new profit sharing ratio of 3/5 for Ajay and 2/5 for Charan.

Calculate the amounts that the continuing partners, Ajay and Charan, need to bring in or adjust, ensuring that a minimum cash and bank balance of ₹ 1,080 is maintained. Also, prepare the necessary journal entries.

Competency Based Que

35. Sonu, Nonu and Tonu are partners in a firm sharing profits and losses in the ratio of 3 : 2 : 1. Their balance sheet is as under

Balance Sheet
as at 31st March, 2024

Liabilities		Amt (₹)	Assets		Amt (₹)
Creditors		30,000	Cash in Hand		18,000
Bills Payable		16,000	Debtors	25,000	
General Reserve		12,000	(−) Provision for Doubtful Debts	(3,000)	22,000
Capital A/cs			Stock		18,000
Sonu	40,000		Furniture		30,000
Nonu	40,000		Machinery		70,000
Tonu	30,000	1,10,000	Goodwill		10,000
		1,68,000			1,68,000

Nonu retired on the following terms

(i) Provision for doubtful debts will be raised by ₹ 1,000.
(ii) Stock will be depreciated by 10% and furniture by 5%.
(iii) There is an outstanding claim for damages of ₹ 1,100 and it is to be provided for in the books.
(iv) Creditors will be written back by ₹ 6,000.
(v) Goodwill of the firm is valued at ₹ 22,000, which is not to be shown in the books of the new firm.
(vi) Nonu is paid in full with the cash brought in by Sonu and Tonu in such a manner that their capitals are in proportion to their profit sharing ratio of 3 : 2.

Prepare the revaluation account, partners' capital account and the balance sheet of new firm.

Ans. Profit on Revaluation = ₹ 600; Gaining Ratio = 3 : 7; Amount due to Outgoing Partner = ₹ 48,200; Total New Capital = ₹ 1,12,600; New Capital Sonu = ₹ 67,560, Tonu = ₹ 45,040; Cash brought in by Sonu = ₹ 28,460, Tonu = ₹ 19,740; Balance Sheet Total = ₹ 1,53,700

Death of a Partner

36. M, N and J are partners in a firm. On 1st August, 2024, due to illness, J died. J's share in the profits of current year will be calculated on the basis of last year's profits. Profits for the year ended 31st March, 2024 amounted to ₹ 4,65,000. Bad debts amounted to ₹ 15,000 are to be adjusted.

Pass necessary journal entries.

Ans. J's Profit = ₹ 50,000

37. M, N and O were partners in a firm, N died on 31st August, 2024. N's share of profit from the closure of the last accounting year till the date of death was to be calculated on the basis of the average of three completed years of profits before death. Profits for the years ending 31st March, 2022-23 and 2024 were ₹ 4,000; ₹ 5,000 and ₹ 7,200 respectively. The firm closes its books on 31st March every year.

Calculate N's share of profit till the date of her death and pass the necessary journal entry for the same assuming

(i) There is no change in the profit sharing ratio of M and N
(ii) There is change in the profit sharing ratio of M and N and the new ratio is 7 : 5.

38. A, B and C were partners sharing profits and losses in the ratio of 2 : 2 : 1. C died on 31st March, 2024. Profits and sales for the calendar year 2023 were ₹ 2,00,000 and ₹ 20,00,000 respectively. Sales during January to March, 2024 were ₹ 1,50,000.

You are required to calculate share of profit of C upto the date of death.

Ans. Percentage of Profit to Sales = 10%; Profit for the period January to March 2018 = ₹ 30,000; C's share of Profit = ₹ 6,000

39. Gita, Hina and Isha were partners in a firm sharing profits and losses in the ratio of 3 : 3 : 2. Gita died. Hina and Isha decided to share profits and losses in the future, equally.

On the day of Gita's death, goodwill of the firm was valued at ₹ 8,00,000.

Calculate gaining ratio and pass necessary journal entry to record treatment of goodwill on Gita's death.

Ans. Gaining Ratio = 1 : 2

40. P, Q and R are partners in a firm sharing profits in the ratio of 1 : 1 : 3 respectively. Their capital accounts showed the following balances on 31st March, 2024. P ₹ 70,000; Q ₹ 65,000 and R ₹ 2,10,000. Firm closes its accounts every year on 31st March. P died on 30th September, 2024.

In the event of death of any partner, the partnership deed provides for the following

(i) Interest on capital will be calculated at the rate of 6% per annum.

(ii) The deceased partner's share in the goodwill of the firm will be calculated on the basis of 2 years' purchase of the average profit of last three years. The profits of the firm for the last three years were ₹ 90,000, ₹ 1,00,000 and ₹ 1,10,000 respectively.

(iii) Her share in the reserve fund of the firm will be paid. The reserve fund of the firm was ₹ 60,000 at the time of P's death.

(iv) Her share of profit till the date of death will be calculated on the basis of sales. It is also specified that the sales during the year 2023-24 were ₹ 20,00,000. The sales from 1st April, 2024 to 30th September, 2024 were ₹ 4,00,000. The profit of the firm for the year ending 31st March, 2024 was ₹ 2,00,000.

Prepare P's capital account to be presented to his legal representative. Competency Based Que

Ans. Transferred to P's Executor's Account = ₹ 1,32,100; P's Share in Goodwill = ₹ 40,000; Gaining Ratio = 1 : 3; P's Share of Current Year's Profit = ₹ 8,000

41. Ram, Ravi and Rohan were partners profits in the ratio of 2 : 3 : 1. On 31st March, 2023, their balance sheet was as follows

Balance Sheet of Ram, Ravi and Rohan
as on 31st March, 2023

Liabilities		Amt (₹)	Assets		Amt (₹)
Creditors		3,62,000	Cash		14,000
General Reserve		18,000	Bank		2,96,000
Capital A/cs			Stock		80,000
Ram	1,00,000		Debtors	3,00,000	
Ravi	2,00,000		(–) Provision for		
Rohan	3,00,000	6,00,000	Doubtful Debts	(10,000)	2,90,000
			Investments		50,000
			Land		2,50,000
		9,80,000			9,80,000

Rohan died on 30th September, 2023. On the death of a partner the partnership deed provided for the following

(i) Goodwill was to be valued at two years purchase of average profit of last three years. The profits for the last three years were : 2020-21 ₹ 45,000, 2021-22 ₹ 90,000 and 2022-23 ₹ 1,35,000.

(ii) Deceased partner's share of profit till the date of his death will be calculated on the basis of average profit of last three years.

Prepare Rohan's capital account to be rendered to his executors. CBSE 2024

Ans. Amount Transferred to Rohan's Executor's Account = ₹ 3,40,500

42. P, Q and R were partners in a firm sharing profits in the ratio of 5 : 3 : 2. On 31st March, 2024, their balance sheet was as under

Balance Sheet
as at 31st March, 2024

Liabilities		Amt (₹)	Assets	Amt (₹)
Creditors		11,000	Buildings	20,000
Reserves		6,000	Machinery	30,000
Capital A/cs			Stock	10,000
P	30,000		Patents	11,000
Q	25,000		Debtors	8,000
R	15,000	70,000	Cash	8,000
		87,000		87,000

P died on 1st October, 2024. It was agreed between his executors and the remaining partners that

(i) Goodwill to be valued at 2½ years' purchase of the average profits of the previous four years, which were I = ₹ 13,000, II = ₹ 12,000, III = ₹ 20,000 and IV = ₹ 15,000.

(ii) Patents be valued at ₹ 8,000, machinery at ₹ 28,000 and buildings at ₹ 25,000.
(iii) Profit for the year 2024-25 be taken as having accrued at the same rate as that of the previous year.
(iv) Interest on capital be provided at 10% per annum.
(v) Half of the amount due to P to be paid immediately to the executor and the balance transferred to his (executor) loan account.

Prepare P's capital account and P's executor's account as on 1st October, 2024.

Ans. Deceased Partner's Share : Goodwill = ₹ 18,750, Profits = ₹ 3,750, Reserve = ₹ 3,000; Interest on Capital = ₹ 1,500; Total Amount due = ₹ 57,000; Bank Overdraft = ₹ 20,500

43. A, B and C were partners sharing profits and losses in the ratio of 5 : 3 : 2 respectively. On 31st December, 2023, their balance sheet stood as under

Balance Sheet
as at 31st December, 2023

Liabilities		Amt (₹)	Assets	Amt (₹)
Sundry Creditors		50,000	Goodwill	25,000
Employees Provident Fund		5,000	Leasehold	1,00,000
Contingency Reserve		20,000	Patents	30,000
Employees Compensation Reserve		10,000	Machinery	1,50,000
			Stock	50,000
Capital A/cs			Debtors	40,000
A	1,50,000		Cash at Bank	40,000
B	1,25,000			
C	75,000	3,50,000		
		4,35,000		4,35,000

C died on 1st May, 2024 and it was agreed that

(i) Goodwill to be valued at $2\frac{1}{2}$ years' purchase of last four years' average profits which were I = ₹ 65,000, II = ₹ 60,000, III = ₹ 80,000 and IV = ₹ 75,000.
(ii) Machinery be valued at ₹ 1,40,000, patents be valued at ₹ 40,000, leasehold be valued at ₹ 1,25,000 on 1st May, 2024.
(iii) For the purpose of calculating C's share in the profits to 2024, the profits in 2024 should be taken to have accrued on the same scale as in 2023.
(iv) A sum of ₹ 21,000 to be paid immediately to the executors of C and the balance to be paid in four equal half-yearly instalments together with interest @ 10% per annum.

Pass the necessary journal entries to record the above transactions and C's executor's account for 2024.

Competency Based Que

Ans. Deceased Partner's Share : Goodwill = ₹ 35,000, Profit = ₹ 5,000, Reserves = ₹ 6,000; Profit on Revaluation = ₹ 5,000; Total Amount due = ₹ 1,21,000; Goodwill Written-off = ₹ 5,000; Half Yearly Interest I = ₹ 5,000, II = ₹ 1,250

44. Pankaj, Rajat and Samay were partnes in a firm sharing profits and losses in the ratio of 7 : 2 : 1. Their balance sheet as at 31st March, 2023 was as follows

Balance Sheet of Pankaj, Rajat and Samay
as at 31st March, 2023

Liabilities		Amt (₹)	Assets	Amt (₹)
Capital A/cs			Machinery	2,10,000
Pankaj	3,00,000		Furniture	1,00,000
Rajat	2,00,000		Stock	1,50,000
Samay	1,00,000	6,00,000	Debtors	1,60,000
General Reserve		1,00,000	Bank	2,50,000
Creditors		1,70,000		
		8,70,000		8,70,000

Rajat died on 30th June, 2023. It was agreed between his executors and remaining partners that

(i) Goodwill be valued at two years purchase of average profits of the previous four year which were ₹ 5,00,000.
(ii) Share of profit up to the date of death will be on the calculated on the basis of average profits of the past four years. Rajat's share of profit amounted to ₹ 25,000.
(iii) Interest on capital is to be provided @ 10% p.a.
(iv) Half the amount due to Rajat is to be paid immediately.

Prepare Rajat's capital account and Rajat's executor's account as on 30th June, 2023. **CBSE 2024 C**

Ans. Amount transferred to Rajat's Executor's Account = ₹ 4,50,000

45. L, M and N were partners in a firm sharing losses in the ratio of 3 : 2 : 1. N died on 31st March, 2024. The balance sheet of the firm as at that date was as under

Balance Sheet
as at 31st March, 2024

Liabilities		Amt (₹)	Assets	Amt (₹)
Capital A/cs			Plant and Machinery	1,20,000
L	1,20,000		Furniture and Fittings	75,000
M	80,000		Investments	20,000
N	40,000	2,40,000	Stock-in-trade	32,000
L's Current A/c		8,000	Sundry Debtors	25,000
M's Current A/c		2,500	Bills Receivable	11,000
Reserve		30,000	Cash at Bank	11,000
Bills Payable		17,000	Cash in Hand	18,500
Sundry Creditors		20,000	Z's Current A/c	5,000
		3,17,500		3,17,500

The following decisions were taken by the remaining partners

(i) A provision for doubtful debts is to be raised at 5% on debtors.
(ii) While plant and machinery is to be depreciated by 10%, furniture and stock-in-trade are to be appreciated by 5% and 10% respectively.
(iii) Advertising expenses ₹ 2,100 are to be carried forward to the next accounting year and therefore, it is to be adjusted through the revaluation account.
(iv) Goodwill of the firm is valued at ₹ 30,000.
(v) The fixed capital method is to be converted into the fluctuating capital method by transferring the current account balances to the respective partners' capital account.

Prepare the revaluation and partners' capital account.

Ans. Loss on Revaluation = ₹ 4,200; Capital Account Balances L = ₹ 1,37,900, M = ₹ 89,100; N's Executors = ₹ 44,300

Comprehensive Questions (Retirement and Death)

46. P, Q, R were partners in a firm sharing profits in 5 : 3 : 2 ratio. On 31st March, 2024 Z retired from the firm. On the date of R's retirement the balance sheet of the firm was as follows

Balance Sheet of P, Q and R
as at 31st March, 2024

Liabilities		Amt (₹)	Assets		Amt (₹)
Creditors		2,700	Bank		8,000
Bills Payable		1,300	Debtors	2,000	
Outstanding Rent		2,250	(–) Provision for Doubtful Debts	(50)	1,950
Provision for Legal Claims		5,750	Stock		2,100
Capital A/cs			Furniture		8,750
P	12,700		Land and Building		20,000
Q	9,000				
R	7,100	28,800			
		40,800			40,800

On R's retirement it was agreed that

(i) Land and building will be appreciated by 5% and furniture will be depreciated by 20%.
(ii) Provision for doubtful debts will be made at 5% on debtors and provision for legal claims will be made ₹ 6,000.
(iii) Goodwill of the firm was valued at ₹ 6,000.
(iv) ₹ 7,000 from R's capital account will be transferred to his loan account and the balance will be paid to him by cheque.

Prepare revaluation account, partners' capital account and balance sheet of P and Q after R's retirement.

Competency Based Que

Ans. Loss on Revaluation X = ₹ 1,050; Balance Amount paid to R by Cheque = ₹ 1,090; Capital Accounts X = ₹ 11,425, Q = ₹ 8,235; Balance Sheet Total = ₹ 38,910

47. P, Q and R are partners sharing profits in the ratio of their capitals. Their balance sheet as at 31st March, 2024 is as under

Liabilities		Amt (₹)	Assets	Amt (₹)
Capital A/cs			Bank	4,480
P	20,000		Sundry Debtors	17,200
Q	20,000		Stock	30,000
R	10,000	50,000	Furniture and Fittings	4,600
Reserve Fund		4,000		
Sundry Creditors		2,000		
Outstanding Expenses		280		
		56,280		56,280

P retired on this date.

Additional Information

(i) Furniture and fittings were undervalued by ₹ 400.

(ii) An amount of ₹ 1,200 due from X, a debtor, was doubtful and a provision for the same is required.

(iii) Stock be valued at 90%.

(iv) Goodwill of the firm be valued at ₹ 6,000.

(v) ₹ 10,000 be transferred to P's loan account bearing interest @ 10% p.a. and balance be paid through bank. Bank overdraft be arranged, if required.

(vi) Q and R will share future profits in 5 : 3

Prepare necessary ledger accounts and balance sheet of the firm after P's retirement. **Competency Based Que**

Ans. Loss on Revaluation = ₹ 3,800; Amount Paid to P = ₹ 12,480; Bank Overdraft = ₹ 8,000; Capital Accounts Q = ₹ 18,730, R = ₹ 8,990; Balance Sheet Total = ₹ 48,000; Gaining Ratio = 9 : 7

48. X, Y and Z were partners in a firm sharing profits in 2 : 2 : 1 ratio. On 1st April, 2024 their balance sheet was as follows

Liabilities		Amt (₹)	Assets	Amt (₹)
Bank Loan		12,800	Cash	51,300
Sundry Creditors		25,000	Bills Receivable	10,800
Capital A/cs			Debtors	35,600
X	80,000		Stock	44,600
Y	50,000		Furniture	7,000
Z	40,000	1,70,000	Plant and Machinery	19,500
Profit and Loss A/c		9,000	Building	48,000
		2,16,800		2,16,800

Y retired from the firm on 1st April, 2024 and his share was ascertained on the revaluation of assets as follows Stock ₹ 40,000, Furniture ₹ 6,000, Plant and machinery ₹ 18,000; Building ₹ 40,000, ₹ 1,700 were to be provided for doubtful debts. The goodwill of the firm was valued at ₹ 12,000. Y was to be paid ₹ 21,680 in cash on retirement and the balance in three equal quarterly instalments (starting from 30th June, 2021) alongwith interest @ 12% p.a.

Prepare revaluation account, partners' capital account, Y's loan account and balance sheet on 1st April, 2024. **Competency Based Que**

Ans. Loss on Revaluation = ₹ 16,800; Y's Loan Account = ₹ 30,000; Capital Account X = ₹ 73,680, Z = ₹ 36,840; Balance Sheet Total = ₹ 1,78,320

49. X, Y and Z were partners sharing profits in 3 : 2 : 1. Y retires and his claim including capital and entitlements from the firm including his share of goodwill of the firm is ₹ 50,000. After this amount was determined, it was found that there was an unrecorded piece of furniture, valued at ₹ 12,000 which had to be recorded upon recording this piece of furniture, the revised amount due to Y was determined and settled by giving him this piece of furniture and balance in cash.

Pass necessary journal entries. **Competency Based Que**

50. On 31st March, 2024 the balance sheet of M, N and O who were sharing profits and losses in proportion to their capitals stood as

Liabilities		Amt (₹)	Assets		Amt (₹)
Creditors		10,800	Cash at Bank		13,000
Bills Payable		5,000	Debtors	10,000	
Capital A/cs			(–) Provision for Doubtful Debts	(200)	9,800
M	45,000		Stock		9,000
N	30,000		Machinery		24,000
O	15,000	90,000	Freehold Premises		50,000
		1,05,000			1,05,800

N retired and following adjustments were agreed to determine the amount payable to N

(i) Out of the amount of insurance premium debited to profit and loss account, ₹ 1,000 be carried forward as prepaid insurance.

(ii) Freehold premises be appreciated by 10%.

(iii) Provision for doubtful debts is brought upto 5% on debtors.

(iv) Machinery be reduced by 5%.

(v) Liability for workmen compensation to the extent of ₹ 1,500 would be created.

(vi) Goodwill of the firm be fixed at ₹ 18,000 and Q's share of the same be adjusted into the capital accounts of M and N who will share future profits in the ratio of 3/4th and 1/4th.

(vii) Total capital of the firm as newly constituted be fixed at ₹ 60,000 between M and O in the proportion of 3/4th and 1/4th after passing entries in their accounts for adjustments i.e. actual cash to be paid or to be brought in by continuing partners as the case may be.

(viii) N be paid ₹ 5,000 in cash and the balance be transferred to his loan account.

Prepare capital accounts of partners' and the balance sheet of the firm of M and O. **Competency Based Que**

51. X, Y and Z carried on business in partnership, sharing profits and losses in the proportion of 3 : 2 : 1. Their capitals as per the balance sheet as at 31st March, 2024 were X = ₹ 60,000, Y = ₹ 40,000, Z = ₹ 30,000. On 31st December, 2024, Z died. You are instructed to prepare an account for presentation to his executors, having regard to the following facts.

(i) Capital carried interest at 12% per annum.

(ii) Z's drawings from 1st April, 2024 to the date of his death amounting to ₹ 9,000.

(iii) Z's share of profits for the portion of the current financial year for which he lived was to be taken at the sum calculated on the average of the last three completed years.

(iv) Goodwill of the firm be valued on the basis of two years' purchase of the average profit of last three completed years. The annual profits of last three completed years were ₹ 35,000 ; ₹ 32,000 and ₹ 38,000 respectively.

Pass necessary journal entries and show the account of the executors of Z. **Competency Based Que**

Ans. Amount due to Z's Executors = ₹ 39,740 including ₹ 11,666 for goodwill and ₹ 4,374 for profit.

52. Madhav, Raghav and Purav were partners in a firm sharing profits and losses in the ratio of 3 : 1 : 1. Their balance sheet as at 31st March, 2023 was as follows

Balance Sheet of Madhav, Raghav and Purav
as at 31st March, 2023

Liabilities		Amt (₹)	Assets	Amt (₹)
Creditors		1,00,000	Bank	20,000
General Reserve		50,000	Stock	1,10,000
Capital A/cs			Investment	70,000
Madhav	60,000		Furniture	35,000
Raghav	1,00,000		Building	1,15,000
Purav	40,000	2,00,000		
		3,50,000		3,50,000

Purav died on 30th September, 2023. According to partnership deed, his legal representatives are entitled to the following

(i) Balance in his capital account.

(ii) Share of profit upto the date of death to be calculated on the basis of last year's profit.

(iii) Share of goodwill calculated on the basis of three years purchase of average profits of last four years.

(iv) Interest on capital @ 12% p.a.

Purav's share of profit was ₹ 3,000 and the average profit of last four years were ₹ 50,000. Purav's drawings upto the date of death were ₹ 10,000.

Prepare Purav's capital account to be rendered to his legal representatives. **Competency Based Que**

Ans. Amount transferred to Purva's Executor's Account = ₹ 75,400

Missing Information

53. On 31st December, 2024 the balance sheet of M/s X, Y and Z sharing profits and losses in proportion to $\frac{1}{2}:\frac{1}{3}:\frac{1}{6}$ stood as follows

Liabilities		Amt (₹)	Assets		Amt (₹)
Creditors		10,800	Cash at Bank		8,000
Capital A/cs			Debtors	10,000	
X	45,000		(−) Provision	(200)	9,800
Y	30,000		Stock		9,000
Z	15,000	90,000	Machinery		24,000
			Land and Building		50,000
		1,00,800			1,00,800

On that date, Y wants to retire from the firm and the remaining partners decide to carry on. X and Z decided to share future profits in the proportion of 4/7 and 3/7 respectively.

Fill in the missing figures in revaluation account and capital account of the partners' and the balance sheet of the firm.

Competency Based Que

Dr **Revaluation Account** Cr

Particulars		Amt (₹)	Particulars	Amt (₹)
To Provision for Doubtful Debts A/c		300	By ...	...
To ...		...	By ...	...
To Outstanding Repairs A/c		1,500		
To Profit transferred to				
X's Capital A/c	...			
Y's Capital A/c	...			
Z's Capital A/c	...	...		
		...		...

Dr **Partners' Capital Account** Cr

Particulars	X (₹)	Y (₹)	Z (₹)	Particulars	X (₹)	Y (₹)	Z (₹)
To Y's Capital A/c (Goodwill)	18,000	—	...	By Balance b/d	...	...	...
To Bank A/c	—	...	—	By Revaluation	...	...	...
To Y's Loan A/c	—	...	—	By X's Capital A/c (Goodwill)	—	...	—
To Balance c/d	...	—	...	By Z's Captial A/c (Goodwill)	—	...	—
	...	...	...		...	...	...

Balance Sheet of the Firm (After Y's Retirement)
as at 31st December, 2024

Liabilities		Amt (₹)	Assets		Amt (₹)
Creditors		...	Cash at Bank		...
Outstanding Repairs		...	Debtors	10,000	
Y's Loan		34,400	(−) Provision	(...)	...
Capital A/cs			Stock		...
X	...		Unexpired Insurance		1,000
Z	...	...	Machinery		22,800
			Land and Building		55,000
		...			...

54. Ashok, Babu and Chetan were partners in a firm sharing profits in the ratio of 4 : 3 : 3. The firm closes its books on 31st March every year. On 31st December, 2024 Ashok died. The partnership deed provided that on the death of a partner his executors will be entitled to the following

(i) Balance in his capital account. On 1st April, 2024, there was a balance of ₹ 90,000 in Ashok's capital account.

(ii) Interest on capital @ 12% per annum.

(iii) His share in the profits of the firm in the year of his death will be calculated on the basis of rate of net profit on sales of the previous year, which was 25%. The sales of the firm till 30th December, 2024 were ₹ 4,00,000.

(iv) His share in the goodwill of the firm. The goodwill of the firm on Ashok's death was valued at ₹ 4,50,000.

The partnership deed also provided for the following deductions from the amount payable to the executor of the deceased partner.

(a) His drawings in the year of his death. Ashok's drawings till 31st December, 2024 were ₹ 15,000.

(b) Interest on drawing @ 12% per annum which was calculated as ₹ 1,500.

The accountant of the firm prepared Ashok's capital account to be presented to the executor of Ashok but in a hurry he left it incomplete.

Ashok's capital account as prepared by the firm's accountant is given below

Dr **Ashok's Capital Account** Cr

Date	Particulars	Amt (₹)	Date	Particulars	Amt (₹)
2024			2024		
Dec 31	....	15,000	Apr 1	....	90,000
Dec 31	....	....	Dec 31	....	8,100
Dec 31	....	....	Dec 31	....	40,000
			Dec 31	....	90,000
			Dec 31	....	90,000
		3,18,100			3,18,100

You are required to complete Ashok's capital account. Competency Based Que

Theoretical Questions

1. Why is it necessary to calculate new profit sharing ratio at the time of retirement of a partner?

Ans. When a partner retires, remaining partners gain the share of profits of the retiring partner. This increases the remaining partners' share of profits. Hence, it becomes necessary to calculate new profit sharing ratio of remaining partners so that the basis of sharing future profits is known.

2. Distinguish between sacrificing ratio and gaining ratio. **NCERT**

Or **Give any one distinction between sacrificing ratio and gaining ratio.**

Ans. Difference between sacrificing ratio and gaining ratio

Basis	Sacrificing Ratio	Gaining Ratio
Meaning	It is the ratio in which old partners agree to sacrifice their share of profit in favour of new partner/partners.	It is the ratio in which continuing partners acquire the share of profit from outgoing partner/partners.
Objective	It is calculated to ascertain the share of profit and loss given up by the existing partners in favour of new partner/partners.	It is calculated to ascertain the share of profit and loss acquired by the remaining partners (of the new firm in case of retirement) from the retiring or deceased partner.
Time	It is calculated at the time of admission of new partner/partners.	It is calculated at the time of retirement/death of old partner/partners.
Calculation	Sacrificing Ratio = Old Share – New Share	Gaining Share = New Share – Old Share
Effect	It reduces the profit sharing ratio of the existing partners.	It increases the profit sharing ratio of the remaining partners.

3. Why a retiring/deceased partner is entitled to a share of goodwill of the firm? **NCERT; Competency Based Que**

Ans. When an existing partner of a firm decides to retire from the firm, the remaining partner(s) will gain in future profits. The remaining partner who gains by acquiring an additional right to share future profits must compensate the outgoing partner who sacrifices by foregoing his right to share future profits. The amount of compensation must be equal to the proportionate value of firm's goodwill.

4. Explain the treatment of goodwill at the time of retirement or on the event of death of a partner. **NCERT**

Ans. In case of retirement or death of a partner, the adjustment for goodwill will be made through partner's capital accounts.

The retiring or deceased partner's capital account will be credited with his share of good will and continuing partner's capital accounts will be debited in their gaining ratio.

The following journal entry will be recorded

Continuing Partner's Capital A/cs Dr
[In the gaining ratio]
To Retiring/Deceased Partner's Capital A/c
[With his share of goodwill]
(Being retiring/deceased partner's share of goodwill adjusted to continuing partners in the gaining ratio)

5. Why is it necessary to distribute accumulated reserves, profits and losses at the time of retirement of a partner? **Competency Based Que**

Ans. At the time of retirement of a partner, all reserves, accumulated profits or losses upto the date of retirement/death of a partner are transferred to the capital accounts of all the partners (including outgoing partner) in their old profit sharing ratio so that the due share of an outgoing partner in the reserves, accumulated profits/losses gets adjusted in his capital account (or current account) because such reserves profits/losses relate to pre-retirement period.

6. Why do firms revalue assets and reassess their liabilities on retirement or on the event of death of a partner? **NCERT; Competency Based Que**

Ans. At the time of retirement of a partner, the assets and liabilities are revalued, so that the profit/loss on revaluation upto the date of retirement/death of a partner may be ascertained and adjusted in all partners' capital accounts in their old profit sharing ratio because such profit or loss on revaluation relates to pre-retirement period.

7. Can a retiring partner or legal representative of a deceased partner share in the subsequent profits? **Competency Based Que**

Or

What will happen if retired or deceased partner's dues are not settled immediately?

Ans. If the amount due to the retiring partner or legal representative of a deceased partner is not settled and the business is carried on, the retiring partner or legal representative of a deceased partner at his option is entitled to receive either interest @ 6% per annum till the amount is paid-off or a share of the profit which has been earned by using the amount due to him.

8. What are the modes of payment of amount due to the retiring partner?

Ans. Following are the modes of payment of amount due to retiring partner
(i) Payment of full amount in lumpsum.
(ii) Payment in instalments.
(iii) Payment partly in cash and remaining amount to be treated as loan.

9. How will you compute the amount payable to a deceased partner? NCERT

Ans. The amount payable to a deceased partner can be computed as follows

Particulars	Amt (₹)
Opening Balance of Capital	...
(+) Share of Goodwill	...
Share of Profits up to Date of Death	...
Share of Reserves	...
Share of Profit on Revaluation of Assets and Liabilities	...
Interest on Capital and Salary up to Date of Death	...
Salary/Commission up to the Date of Death	...
(−) Share of Exsting Goodwill Written-off	(...)
Share of Loss up to Date of Death	(...)
Share of Accumulated Losses	(...)
Share of Loss on Revaluation of Assets and Liabilities	(...)
Drawings up to Date of Death	(...)
Interest on Drawings up to Date of Death	(...)
Amount Payable to Deceased Partner	...

Objective Questions

Multiple Choice Questions (MCQs)

1. What document must be revised when a partner retires?
(a) Partnership deed
(b) Memorandum of association
(c) Articles of association
(d) Firm's license

2. A retiring partner remains liable for acts of the firm until
(a) all partners sign a discharge agreement
(b) a public notice of retirement is given
(c) the partnership deed is renewed
(d) the firm changes its name

3. Which of the following adjustments is made when a partner retires?
(a) Only goodwill is adjusted
(b) Only liabilities are reassessed
(c) Profit sharing ratio and goodwill are adjusted
(d) Only accumulated losses are adjusted

4. Under the Indian Partnership Act, 1932, a partner can retire by giving written notice if
(a) the partnership is at will
(b) the partnership deed explicitly forbids it
(c) all partners disagree
(d) there are two or more partners remaining

5. If there is no agreement to discharge the retiring partner from liabilities, they remain liable for
(a) acts until a new partnership deed is created
(b) only personal debts
(c) firm's acts until a public notice of retirement
(d) future firm losses

6. Which section of the Indian Partnership Act, 1932, addresses a partner's retirement?
(a) Section 32
(b) Section 21
(c) Section 40
(d) Section 28

7. On retirement/death of a partner, the remaining partner(s) who have gained due to change in profit sharing ratio should compensate the
(a) retiring partners only
(b) remaining partners (who have sacrificed) as well as retiring partners
(c) remaining partners only (who have sacrificed)
(d) None of the above

8. What is the new profit sharing ratio formula?
(a) Old Share − Gaining Share
(b) Old Share + Gaining Share
(c) New Share − Old Share
(d) New Share + Old Share

9. In the absence of any information regarding the acquisition of share in profit of the retiring/deceased partner by the remaining partners, it is assumed that they will acquire his/her share Competency Based Que
(a) old profit sharing ratio
(b) new profit sharing ratio
(c) equal ratio
(d) None of these

10. .... ratio is calculated at the time of retirement of a partner and change in profit sharing ratio.
(a) Sacrificing
(b) Gaining
(c) New
(d) Old

11. Ishan, Jatin and Kapil were partners in a firm sharing profits and losses in the ratio of 5 : 4 : 1. Jatin retired and his share was taken up by Ishan and Kapil in the ratio 1 : 1. The new profit sharing ratio between Ishan and Kapil after Jatin's retirement will be **CBSE 2025; Competency Based Que**

(a) 5 : 1 (b) 1 : 1
(c) 5 : 4 (d) 7 : 3

12. Anju, Divya and Bobby were partners in a firm sharing profits and losses in the ratio of 3 : 2 : 1. Bobby retired. The new profit sharing ratio between Anju and Divya after Bobby's retirement was 5 : 3. The gaining ratio of remaining partners will be

(a) 3 : 2 (b) 8 : 7
(c) 3 : 1 (d) 2 : 3

13. Mita, Veena and Atul were partners in a firm sharing profits and losses in the ratio of 3 : 2 : 1. Atul retired and his share was taken over by Mita and Veena in the ratio of 1: 4. The new profit sharing ratio between Mita and Veena after Atul's retirement will be **CBSE 2024; Competency Based Que**

(a) 3 : 2 (b) 8 : 7
(c) 3 : 1 (d) 2 : 3

14. Pooja, Nita and Anita were partners in a firm sharing profits and losses in the ratio of 3 : 2 : 1. Pooja retired and her share is taken up by Nita and Anita equally. The new profit sharing ratio of Nita and Anita will be **CBSE 2023; Competency Based Que**

(a) 2 : 1 (b) 7 : 5
(c) 1 : 1 (d) 3 : 2

15. Anu, Bina and Roy were partners in a firm sharing profits and losses in the ratio of 3 : 2 : 1. Roy retired and his share was acquired by Anu. The new profit sharing ratio between Anu and Bina after Roy's retirement will be **CBSE 2024 C; Competency Based Que**

(a) 3 : 2 (b) 3 : 1
(c) 1 : 1 (d) 2 : 1

16. Asha, Yug and Zubin were partners in a firm sharing profits and losses in the ratio of 4 : 3 : 2. Zubin retired. Zubin's share was acquired equally by Asha and Yug. The new profit sharing ratio between Asha and Yug after Zubin's retirement was **CBSE 2024 C; Competency Based Que**

(a) 3 : 2 (b) 5 : 4 (c) 4 : 3 (d) 2 : 1

17. On retirement/death of a partner, the retiring/deceased partner's capital account will be credited with **NCERT**

(a) his/her share of goodwill
(b) goodwill of the firm
(c) shares of goodwill of remaining partners
(d) None of the above

18. The journal entry for written-off goodwill already appearing in the books of account at the time of retirement of partner is

(a) All Partner's Capital A/c Dr
  To Goodwill A/c
(b) Goodwill A/c Dr
  To All Partner's Capital A/c
(c) Goodwill A/c Dr
  To Retiring Partner's Capital A/c
(d) None of the above

19. When is the gaining ratio equal to the old profit sharing ratio?

(a) When continuing partners gain in their old ratio
(b) When a new partner is admitted
(c) When partners change the profit sharing ratio
(d) When the old profit sharing ratio is dissolved

20. Gobind, Hari and Partap are partners. On retirement of Gobind, the goodwill already appears in the balance sheet at ₹ 24,000.

The goodwill will be written-off **Competency Based Que**

(a) by debiting all partners' capital accounts in their old profit sharing ratio
(b) by debiting remaining partners' capital accounts in their new profit sharing ratio
(c) by debiting retiring partners' capital accounts from his share of goodwill
(d) None of the above

21. Chaman, Raman and Suman are partners sharing profits in the ratio of 5 : 3 : 2. Raman retires, the new profit sharing ratio between Chaman and Suman will be 1 : 1. The goodwill of the firm is valued at ₹ 1,00,000. Raman's share of goodwill will be adjusted **Competency Based Que**

(a) by debiting Chaman's capital account and Suman's capital account with ₹ 15,000 each
(b) by debiting Chaman's capital account and Suman's capital account with ₹ 21,429 and ₹ 8,571 respectively
(c) by debiting only Suman's capital account with ₹ 30,000
(d) by debiting Raman's capital account with ₹ 30,000

22. 'P', 'Q' and 'R' are partners sharing profits in the ratio of 2 : 1 : 1. 'R' retires and assets and liabilities are revalued, resulting in a profit of ₹ 12,000. 'R's' share will be **Competency Based Que**

(a) ₹ 6,000 (b) ₹ 3,000
(c) ₹ 2,000 (d) None of these

23. Aman, Aadhar and Avinash were partners and sharing profits in the ratio of 3 : 2 : 1. Avinash retired from the firm on 1st July, 2022. On the date of Avinash's retirement, the balance sheet showed a debit balance of ₹ 1,20,000 in this profit and loss account. For calculating the amount payable to Avinash, this balance will be transferred **CBSE 2023; Competency Based Que**

(a) to the debit side of the capital accounts of Aman and Aadhar in old profit sharing ratio
(b) to the debit side of the capital accounts of Aman, Aadhar and Avinash in old profit sharing ratio
(c) to the credit side of the capital accounts of Aman and Aadhar in new profit sharing ratio
(d) to the credit side of the capital accounts of Aman and Aadhar in their gaining ratio

24. **Riya, Rita and Renu were partners in a firm. On 31st March, 2023 Renu retired. The amount payable to Renu ₹ 2,17,000 was transferred to her loan account. Renu agreed to receive interest on this amount as per the provisions of Partnership Act, 1932. The rate at which interest would be paid to Renu is** CBSE 2024; Competency Based Que

(a) 9% p.a. (b) 6% p.a. (c) 12% p.a. (d) 10% p.a.

25. **Partner's capital account is debited**
(a) to record the general reserve
(b) to record the gain on revaluation
(c) to record the profit and loss account (debit)
(d) to record the shortage of capital brought in

26. **Revaluation account is prepared to give effect to**
(a) change in value of assets only
(b) change in value of liabilities only
(c) change in value of assets and liabilities
(d) undistributed profits or losses

27. **Increase in liabilities at the time of retirement of a partner is**
(a) credited to revalution account
(b) debited to revalution account
(c) debited to profit and loss account
(d) debited to profit and loss appropriation account

28. **Balance of revalution account, in case of fixed capitals is transferred to partner's .... account.**
(a) capital
(b) current
(c) Either (a) or (b)
(d) None of the above

29. **Nidhi, Kunal and Kabir are partners in a firm sharing profits in the ratio of 2 : 1 : 2. Kunal retired and the balance in his capital account after making necessary adjustments on account of reserves, revaluation of assets and reassessment of liabilities was ₹ 80,000. Nidhi and Kabir agreed to pay him ₹ 1,00,000 in full settlement of his claim. Kunal's share of goodwill of the firm, on his retirement was** CBSE 2023; Competency Based Que

(a) ₹ 4,000 (b) ₹ 20,000
(c) ₹ 16,000 (d) ₹ 1,80,000

30. **Kriti, Hina and Nidhi were partners sharing profits in the ratio of 3 : 2 : 1. Nidhi retired. On the date of her retirement, workmen compensation fund stood in the balance sheet at ₹ 1,50,000. Workmen compensation claim was ₹ 1,20,000. How much amount of workmen compensation fund will be credited to Nidhi's capital account?** CBSE 2024; Competency Based Que

(a) ₹ 30,000 (b) ₹ 10,000
(c) ₹ 5,000 (d) ₹ 15,000

31. **Rohit, Udit and Mohit were partners in a firm sharing profits in the ratio of 3 : 2 : 1. Mohit retired. The balance in his capital account after making the necessary adjustments on account of reserves and revaluation of assets and liabilities was ₹ 1,80,000. Rohit and Udit agreed to pay him ₹ 2,00,000 in full settlement of his claim. Mohit's share of goodwill in the firm was** CBSE 2024; Competency Based Que

(a) ₹ 1,80,000 (b) ₹ 2,00,000 (c) ₹ 40,000 (d) ₹ 20,000

32. **Sakshi, Kiara and Gunjan were partners in a firm sharing profits and losses in the ratio of 3 : 2 : 1. Kiara retired on 1st April, 2023. After all adjustments the amount due to Kiara was ₹ 5,00,000. The payment was to be made in two yearly instalments of ₹ 2,50,000 each plus interest @ 10% per annum on the unpaid balance. The amount of first instalment paid on 31st March, 2024 will be** CBSE 2025; Competency Based Que

(a) ₹ 3,00,000 (b) ₹ 2,75,000
(c) ₹ 5,50,000 (d) ₹ 2,50,000

33. **The amount due to the deceased partner is paid to his ....**
(a) wife (b) relatives
(c) legal heir (d) None of these

34. **Aditi, Sukriti and Niti were partners sharing profits in the ratio of 2 : 2 : 1. Sukriti died on 30th June, 2023. Net profit for the year ended 31st March, 2023 was ₹ 4,50,000. If the deceased partner's share of profit is to be calculated on the basis of previous year's profit, the amount of profit credited to Sukriti's capital account will be** Competency Based Que

(a) ₹ 90,000 (b) ₹ 45,000
(c) ₹ 1,80,000 (d) ₹ 1,12,500

35. **Nicku, Mala and Ritu were partners in a firm sharing profits in the ratio of 5 : 3 : 2. Nicku died on 30th September, 2023. The deceased partner was entitled to his share of profit up to the date of death which was to be calculated on the basis of previous year's profit. The previous year's profit was ₹ 80,000. Nicku's share of profit will be** CBSE 2024; Competency Based Que

(a) ₹ 10,000 (b) ₹ 20,000
(c) ₹ 30,000 (d) ₹ 40,000

36. **Aarohi, Bhuvan and Charu were partners in a firm sharing profits and losses in the ratio of 1 : 2 : 6. Charu died. Aarohi and Bhuvan acquired Charu's share in the ratio of 2 : 1. The new profit sharing ratio between Aarohi and Bhuvan after Charu's death will be**

Competency Based Que

(a) 2 : 1 (b) 1 : 2 (c) 5 : 4 (d) 4 : 5

37. **Aditya, Vishesh and Nimesh were partners in a firm sharing profits and losses equally. Aditya died on 1st July, 2023. Remaining partners decided to continue the business of the firm and decided to share future profits in the ratio of 4 : 3. The gaining ratio of Vishesh and Nimesh will be** **CBSE 2024; Competency Based Que**

(a) 4 : 3 (b) 3 : 2 (c) 5 : 2 (d) 1 : 1

38. **A, Band C were partners sharing profits and losses equally. B died on 31st August, 2023 and total amount transferred to B's executors was ₹ 13,20,000. B's executors were being paid ₹ 1,20,000 immediately and balance was to be paid in four equal semi-annual instalments together with interest @ 10% p.a.**

Total amount of interest to be credited to B's executor's account for the year ended 31st March, 2024 will be?

CBSE SQP 2025; Competency Based Que

(a) ₹ 70,000 (b) ₹ 67,500 (c) ₹ 60,000 (d) ₹ 77,000

Assertion-Reason

Direction (Q.No. 39 to 48) *Read the following Assertion (A) and Reason (R) and choose the correct alternative from the following*

Alternatives

(a) Both Assertion (A) and Reason (R) are true and Reason (R) is the correct explanation of Assertion (A)
(b) Both Assertion (A) and Reason (R) are true, but Reason (R) is not the correct explanation of Assertion (A)
(c) Assertion (A) is true, but Reason (R) is false
(d) Assertion (A) is false, but Reason (R) is true

39. **Assertion** (A) A retiring partner is not liable for any acts of the firm after their retirement.

Reason (R) Public notice of the retirement is required to relieve the partner of liability to third parties.

40. **Assertion** (A) Retirement of a partner requires a new partnership deed.

Reason (R) The retiring partner's dues are settled based on the terms of the new deed.

41. **Assertion** (A) Goodwill is adjusted only when a partner retires.

Reason (R) Goodwill represents the firm's reputation and must be reassessed whenever there is a change in the partnership.

42. **Assertion** (A) Retirement of a partner results into a reconstitution of the firm.

Reason (R) In retirement, old partnership agreement discontinues and new partnership agreement come into existence.

43. **Assertion** (A) The new profit sharing ratio is determined after an outgoing partner leaves the partnership.

Reason (R) Remaining partners automatically acquire the outgoing partner's share in their new profit sharing ratio.

44. **Assertion** (A) The gaining ratio represents the ratio in which continuing partners take over the outgoing partner's share.

Reason (R) The gaining ratio is calculated by adding the new share to the old share.

45. **Assertion** (A) The executor of a deceased partner has the right to claim their share of any accumulated profits, but they are not responsible for covering accumulated losses.

Reason (R) Accumulated profits or losses are considered to belong to all partners collectively and should be distributed to each partner's capital account based on the previous profit sharing agreement.

46. **Assertion** (A) If the amount of any asset is understated, then revaluation account will be debited to restore asset amount to its actual value.

Reason (R) Increase in the value of an asset is profit for the firm.

47. **Assertion** (A) Accumulated profits and losses will be debited and credited to all the partners' capital account.

Reason (R) Accomulated profits and losses are distributed among partners in old profit sharing ratio.

48. **Assertion** (A) Profit or loss on the revaluation of assets and liabilities is a capital profit.

Reason (R) Capital profits are recurring in nature.

Two Statement Based MCQs

Direction (Q.No. 49 to 56) *Read the following statements carefully and choose the correct alternative*

Alternatives

(a) Statement I is correct and Statement II is incorrect
(b) Statement II is correct and Statement I is incorrect
(c) Both the statements are correct
(d) Both the statements are incorrect

49. **Statement I** A retiring partner is discharged from all liabilities for the firm's actions before retirement.

Statement II A retiring partner is liable for firm acts until a public notice of retirement is given.

50. **Statement I** Upon the retirement of a partner, the business of the firm is discontinued.

Statement II A new partnership deed is created upon the retirement of a partner.

51. **Statement I** A partner can retire only with the consent of all other partners.

Statement II A partner may retire by giving a written notice in a partnership at will.

52. **Statement I** Adjustment of goodwill is necessary at the time of partner's retirement.

Statement II Accumulated profits and reserves are adjusted only upon the firm's dissolution.

53. **Statement I** New profit sharing ratio is the ratio in which remaining partners decide to share future profits and losses.

Statement II Gaining ratio is calculated by subtracting the new share from the old share.

54. **Statement I** The new profit sharing ratio is calculated as the old share plus the acquired gaining share.

Statement II Unless otherwise agreed, continuing partners acquire the outgoing partner's share in their gaining ratio.

55. **Statement I** Revaluation account is prepared at the time of retirement of a partner.

Statement II The amount due to the retiring partner, if not paid in cash is transferred to his loan account.

56. **Statement I** In the event of death, the combined share of the continuing partners will decrease.

Statement II A partner can retire from the firm with the consent of all the partners.

Matching

57. **Match the concepts with their descriptions**

Column I (Terms)		Column II (Definitions)
A. Liability for Acts pre-retirement	(i)	Based on new partnership terms
B. Liability for Acts post-retrement	(ii)	Requires public notice for discharge
C. Adjustment of goodwill	(iii)	Applies to acts up to the retirement date
D. New partnership deed	(iv)	Compensates for the firm's reputation

Codes

	A	B	C	D		A	B	C	D
(a)	(iii)	(ii)	(iv)	(i)	(b)	(ii)	(iii)	(i)	(iv)
(c)	(iv)	(iii)	(ii)	(i)	(d)	(i)	(ii)	(iii)	(iv)

58. **Match the following adjustments with their descriptions**

Column I (Terms)		Column II (Definitions)
A. Profit sharing ratio	(i)	Reallocation based on partner contribution changes
B. Accumulated profits	(ii)	Settlement of retiring partner's share
C. Capital adjustment	(iii)	Reflects new ratios after retirement
D. Payment to retiring partner	(iv)	Distributed or adjusted for remaining partners

Codes

	A	B	C	D
(a)	(iii)	(iv)	(i)	(ii)
(b)	(iv)	(iii)	(i)	(ii)
(c)	(ii)	(i)	(iv)	(iii)
(d)	(i)	(ii)	(iii)	(iv)

59. **Match the following liabilities with their conditions**

Column I (Terms)		Column II (Definitions)
A. Liability until notice	(i)	Discharged by mutual agreement
B. Pre-retirement liability	(ii)	Applies if no public notice given
C. Partnership at will	(iii)	Allows withdrawal by written notice
D. Discharge by agreement	(iv)	Limited to acts until retirement

Codes

	A	B	C	D		A	B	C	D
(a)	(ii)	(iv)	(iii)	(i)	(b)	(i)	(ii)	(iii)	(iv)
(c)	(iii)	(i)	(ii)	(iv)	(d)	(iv)	(iii)	(ii)	(i)

60. **Match the terms with their correct definitions**

Column I (Terms)		Column II (Definitions)
A. New profit sharing ratio	(i)	Old share plus acquired gaining share
B. Gaining ratio	(ii)	Difference between new share and old share
C. Continuing partners	(iii)	Partners who remain after one exits
D. Outgoing partner	(iv)	Partner who leaves the partnership

Codes

	A	B	C	D		A	B	C	D
(a)	(i)	(ii)	(iii)	(iv)	(b)	(ii)	(i)	(iv)	(iii)
(c)	(iii)	(iv)	(i)	(ii)	(d)	(iv)	(iii)	(ii)	(i)

61. **Match the columns (at the time of retirement of partners situations)**

Column I (Items/Transactions)	Column II (Entry)
A. Increase in liabilities	(i) Credit–Revaluation account
B. Bad debts recovered	(ii) Credit–Partners' capital account
C. Accumulated losses	(iii) Debit – Revaluation account
D. Profit and loss (Cr)	(iv) Debit–Partners' capital account

Codes

	A	B	C	D		A	B	C	D
(a)	(iii)	(i)	(ii)	(iv)	(b)	(i)	(iii)	(iv)	(ii)
(c)	(i)	(iii)	(ii)	(iv)	(d)	(iii)	(i)	(iv)	(ii)

Case Based MCQs

Direction *Read the case study and answer the questions 62 to 64 on the basis of the same*

Ravi is a partner in a firm and he decides to retire due to health reasons. He informs all partners in writing of his intention, as the firm operates as a partnership at will. Before his retirement, Ravi had signed a contract on behalf of the firm with a client. After his retirement, Ravi noticed that the firm continued to fulfill the contract and he wanted to know his liabilities. The remaining partners agreed to settle Ravi's share based on the revaluation of assets and goodwill adjustments.

62. **What is the legal condition for Ravi's retirement as per the Indian Partnership Act, 1932?**

(a) Consent of all partners is mandatory
(b) He must wait until a new partnership deed is created
(c) Written notice to all partners is sufficient
(d) He must wait for public notice before retirement

63. **Is Ravi liable for the contract he signed before retirement?**

(a) Yes, unless discharged by an agreement
(b) No, as he retired with notice
(c) Yes, for all contracts made by the firm
(d) No, if the remaining partners do not involve him

64. **What adjustments are required in the firm's accounts upon Ravi's retirement?**

(a) Only accumulated profits
(b) Revaluation of assets and goodwill adjustments
(c) No adjustments if the firm is at will
(d) Both (a) and (b)

Direction *Read the following case study and answer the questions 65 to 67 on the basis of the same*

Alpha, Beta and Gamma are partners sharing profits in the ratio of 3 : 2 : 1. Beta retired from the firm. On that date, the balance sheet of the firm was as follows

Balance Sheet
as at 31st March, 2020

Liabilities		Amt (₹)	Assets		Amt (₹)
Creditors		15,000	Bank		7,600
General Reserve		12,000	Furniture		41,000
Bills Payable		12,000	Stock		9,000
Outstanding Salary		2,200	Premises		80,000
Provision for Legal Damages		6,000	Debtors	6,000	
			(–) Provision for Doubtful Debts	(400)	5,600
Capital A/cs					
Alpha	46,000				
Beta	30,000				
Gamma	20,000	96,000			
		1,43,200			1,43,200

Additional Information

(i) Premises to be appreciated by 20%, stock to be depreciated by 10% and provision for doubtful debts was to be maintained @ 5% on debtors. Further, provision for legal damages is to be increased by ₹ 1,200 and furniture to be brought upto ₹ 45,000.
(ii) Goodwill of the firm is valued at ₹ 42,000.
(iii) ₹ 26,000 from Beta's capital account be transferred to his loan account and balance to be paid through bank, if required, necessary loan may be obtained from bank.
(iv) New profit sharing ratio of Alpha and Gamma is decided to be 5 : 1.

65. **What will be the gaining ratio of Alpha and Gamma?**

(a) 1 : 1
(b) Entire Beta's share taken by Gamma only
(c) Entire Beta's share taken by Alpha only
(d) None of the above

66. **What is the value of Beta's share of goodwill?**

(a) ₹ 7,000
(b) ₹ 14,000
(c) ₹ 21,000
(d) Cannot be determined from the given data

67. **20% appreciation in the value of premises would be recorded as**

(i) Revaluation account debited by ₹ 16,000.
(ii) Revaluation account credited by ₹ 16,000.
(iii) Premises increased by ₹ 16,000 in the assets side of the balance sheet.
(iv) Premises decreased by ₹ 16,000 in the assets side of the balance sheet.

Codes

(a) (i) and (iv)
(b) (ii) and (iv)
(c) (i) and (iii)
(d) (ii) and (iii)

Direction *Read the following case study and answer the questions 68 to 70 on the basis of the same*

Arjun, Bhim and Nakul are partners sharing profits and losses in the ratio of 14 : 5 : 6. Bhim retires and gives $\frac{5}{25}$th of his share to Arjun and remaining share to Nakul. Goodwill of the firm is valued at 2 years' purchases of super profits based on average profits of last 3 years. Profit for the last 3 years are ₹ 50,000, ₹ 55,000 and ₹ 60,000 respectively. Normal profits for the similar firm are ₹ 30,000.

Goodwill already exist in the books of the firm at ₹ 75,000. Profit for the first year after Bhim's retirement was ₹ 1,00,000.

68. **What will be gaining ratio of remaining partners?**
(a) 26 : 19
(b) 1 : 4
(c) 4 : 1
(d) 19 : 26

69. **What will be the amount of super profit?**
(a) ₹ 55,000
(b) ₹ 25,000
(c) ₹ 50,000
(d) None of the above

70. **The new profit sharing ratio of remaining partners would be**
(a) 19 : 26 (b) 3 : 2
(c) 15 : 10 (d) 26 : 19

Answers

1. (a) Partnership deed
2. (b) a public notice of retirement is given
3. (c) Profit sharing ratio and goodwill are adjusted
4. (a) the partnership is at will
5. (c) firm's acts until a public notice of retirement
6. (a) Section 32
7. (b) remaining partners (who have sacrificed) as well as retiring partners
8. (b) Old Share + Gaining Share
9. (a) old profit sharing ratio
10. (b) Gaining
11. (d) Ishan's New Ratio = Old Share + Share Taken

$$=\frac{5}{10}+\left(\frac{4}{10}\times\frac{1}{2}\right)=\frac{5}{10}+\frac{4}{20}=\frac{7}{10}$$

Kapil's New Ratio = Old Share + Share Taken

$$=\frac{1}{10}+\left(\frac{4}{10}\times\frac{1}{2}\right)=\frac{1}{10}+\frac{2}{10}=\frac{3}{10}$$

12. (c) Gaining Ratio

$$\text{Anju}=\frac{5}{8}-\frac{3}{6}=\frac{30-24}{48}=\frac{6}{48}; \text{Diya}=\frac{3}{8}-\frac{2}{6}=\frac{18-16}{48}=\frac{2}{48}$$

Gaining Ratio = 3 : 1

13. (b) Mita's Gain $=\frac{1}{6}\times\frac{1}{5}=\frac{1}{30}$

Veena's Gain $=\frac{1}{6}\times\frac{4}{5}=\frac{4}{30}$

Mita's New Share $=\frac{3}{6}+\frac{1}{30}=\frac{16}{30}$

Veena's New Share $=\frac{2}{6}+\frac{4}{30}=\frac{14}{30}$

New Profit Sharing Ratio = 8 : 7

14. (b) Share acquired by Nita from Pooja $=\frac{3}{6}\times\frac{1}{2}=\frac{3}{12}$

Share acquired by Anita from Pooja $=\frac{3}{6}\times\frac{1}{2}=\frac{3}{12}$

Nita's New Share $=\frac{3}{12}+\frac{2}{6}=\frac{3+4}{12}=\frac{7}{12}$

Anita's New Share $=\frac{3}{12}+\frac{1}{6}=\frac{3+2}{12}=\frac{5}{12}$

New ratio = 7 : 5

15. (d) Anu's New Share $=\frac{3}{6}+\frac{1}{6}=\frac{4}{6}$

Bina's Share $=\frac{2}{6}$; New Profit Sharing Ratio = 4 : 2 *or* 2 : 1

16. (b) Gain of remaining partners

Asha $=\frac{2}{9}\times\frac{1}{2}=\frac{2}{18}$; Yug $=\frac{2}{9}\times\frac{1}{2}\times\frac{2}{18}$

New profit share

Asha $=\frac{4}{9}+\frac{2}{18}=\frac{10}{18}$; Yug $=\frac{3}{9}+\frac{2}{18}=\frac{8}{18}$ = 10 : 8 *or* 5 : 4

17. (a) his/her share of goodwill
18. (a) Any goodwill appearing in the books of accounts is written-off by debiting old partners capital account and crediting goodwill account in old ratio.
19. (a) When continuing partners gain in their old ratio
20. (a) by debiting all partners' capital accounts in their old profit sharing ratio
21. (c) Gaining Ratio = New Ratio − Old Ratio

Chaman gains $=\frac{1}{2}-\frac{5}{10}=\frac{5-5}{10}$ = Nil

Suman gains $=\frac{1}{2}-\frac{2}{10}=\frac{5-2}{10}=\frac{3}{10}$

Firm's goodwill = ₹ 1,00,000

Raman's share of goodwill $= 1{,}00{,}000 \times \frac{3}{10} =$ ₹ 30,000 will be paid by Suman (gaining partner).

22. (b) 'R's' share in revaluation profits $= 12{,}000 \times \frac{1}{4} =$ ₹ 3,000
23. (b) to the debit side of the capital accounts of Aman, Aadhar and Avinash in old profit sharing ratio
24. (b) 6% p.a.
25. (c) to record the profit and loss account (debit)
26. (c) change in value of assets and liabilities
27. (b) debited to revalution account
28. (b) current
29. (b) Kunal's Share of Goodwill = 1,00,000 – 80,000 = ₹ 20,000
30. (c) Nidhi's Share $= 30{,}000 \times \frac{1}{6} =$ ₹ 5,000
31. (d) Goodwill = 2,00,000 – 1,80,000 = ₹ 20,000
32. (a) Interest due on 31st March, 2024 $= 5{,}00{,}000 \times \frac{10}{100}$

= ₹ 50,000

Amount of First Instalment = 2,50,000 + 50,000 = ₹ 3,00,000
33. (c) legal heir
34. (b) Sukriti's profit share $= 4{,}50{,}000 \times \frac{2}{5} \times \frac{3}{12} =$ ₹ 45,000
35. (b) Nicku's share of profit $= 80{,}000 \times \frac{5}{10} \times \frac{6}{12} =$ ₹ 20,000
36. (c) Gain of remaining partners

Aarohi $= \frac{6}{9} \times \frac{2}{3} = \frac{12}{27} = \frac{4}{9}$; Bhuvan $= \frac{6}{9} \times \frac{1}{3} = \frac{6}{27} = \frac{2}{9}$

New profit share

Aarohi $= \frac{1}{9} + \frac{4}{9} = \frac{5}{9}$; Bhuvan $= \frac{2}{9} + \frac{2}{9} = \frac{4}{9}$

New ratio = 5 : 4
37. (c) Gaining ratio

Vishesh $= \frac{4}{7} - \frac{1}{3} = \frac{12-7}{21} = \frac{5}{21}$; Nimesh $= \frac{3}{7} - \frac{1}{3} = \frac{9-7}{21} = \frac{2}{21}$

Gaining ratio = 5 : 2
38. (b) Interest paid on 31st March, 2024

$$= \left(12{,}00{,}000 \times \frac{10}{100} \times \frac{6}{12}\right) + \left(9{,}00{,}000 \times \frac{10}{12} \times \frac{1}{12}\right)$$

= 60,000 + 7,500 = ₹ 67,500
39. (b) Both Assertion (A) and Reason (R) are true, but Reason (R) is not the correct explanation of Assertion (A)
40. (c) Assertion (A) is true, but Reason (R) is false
41. (d) Assertion (A) is false, but Reason (R) is true
42. (a) Both Assertion (A) and Reason (R) are true and Reason (R) is the correct explanation of Assertion (A)
43. (c) Assertion (A) is true, but Reason (R) is false
44. (c) Assertion (A) is true, but Reason (R) is false
45. (d) Assertion (A) is false, but Reason (R) is true
46. (d) If the amount of any asset is understated, then revaluation account will be credited to restore asset amount to its actual value because increase in the value of an asset is profit for the firm.
47. (d) Accumulated profits are credited and losses are debited to partners' capital account in old profit sharing ratio.
48. (c) The profit that is earned through capital items is called the capital profit. It is not recurring in nature.
49. (b) Statement II is correct and Statement I is incorrect
50. (b) Statement II is correct and Statement I is incorrect
51. (b) Statement II is correct and Statement I is incorrect
52. (a) Statement I is correct and Statement II is incorrect
53. (a) Statement I is correct and Statement II is incorrect
54. (a) Statement I is correct and Statement II is incorrect
55. (a) Statement I is correct and Statement II is incorrect
56. (b) Statement II is correct and Statement I is incorrect
57. (a) (iii) (ii) (iv) (i)
58. (a) (iii) (iv) (i) (ii)
59. (a) (ii) (iv) (iii) (i)
60. (a) (i) (ii) (iii) (iv)
61. (d) (iii) (i) (iv) (ii)
62. (c) Written notice to all partners is sufficient
63. (a) Yes, unless discharged by an agreement
64. (d) Both (a) and (b)
65. (c) Old profit sharing ratio = 3 : 2 : 1; New profit sharing ratio = 5 : 1

Gaining Ratio = New Profit Sharing Ratio – Old Profit Sharing Ratio

Alpha $= \frac{5}{6} - \frac{3}{6} = \frac{1}{6}$; Gamma $= \frac{1}{6} - \frac{1}{6} = 0$
66. (b) Beta's share of goodwill $= 42{,}000 \times \frac{1}{3} =$ ₹ 14,000
67. (d) Book value of premises = ₹ 80,000

20% appreciation $= 80{,}000 \times \frac{20}{100} =$ ₹ 16,000

As there is increase in the value of asset, it will be credited to revaluation account by ₹ 16,000 and premises' increased value will be shown in the balance sheet.
68. (b) Profit surrendered by Bhim to Arjun $= \frac{5}{25} \times \frac{5}{25} = \frac{1}{25}$

Profit surrendered by Bhim to Nakul $= \frac{5}{25} \times \frac{20}{25} = \frac{4}{25}$

∴ Gaining ratio of Arjun and Nakul would be 1 : 4
69. (b) Average Profit = (50,000 + 55,000 + 60,000)/3 = ₹ 55,000

Super Profit = Average Profit – Normal Profit

= 55,000 – 30,000 = ₹ 25,000
70. (b) New share of Arjun $= \frac{14}{25} + \frac{1}{25} = \frac{15}{25}$

New share of Nakul $= \frac{6}{25} + \frac{4}{25} = \frac{10}{25}$

Thus, the new profit sharing ratio of Arjun and Nakul

$= \frac{15}{25} : \frac{10}{25} = 15 : 10$ *or* $3 : 2$

06

CHAPTER

Dissolution of a Partnership Firm

Dissolution of partnership firm refers to the closure of its business, where the partnership agreement comes to an end and assets are liquidated to settle liabilities.

YOUR STUDY GOALS

6.1 Meaning of Dissolution

6.2 Accounting Treatment at the Time of Dissolution

YOUR PRACTICE GOAL

- Topicwise Solved Questions (22 Solved Questions)
- Numerical Questions [25 Questions (Unsolved)]
- Theoretical Questions [6 Questions (with answers)]
- Objective Questions (61 Qs ; MCQs, A-R, Statements, Matching, Case)

6.1 Meaning of Dissolution

Dissolution means breaking up or extinction, i.e. discontinuance of existing relationship among the partners. Under the Indian Partnership Act, 1932, the dissolution may be either of partnership or of a firm.

Dissolution of Partnership

It refers to the change in the existing relationship between partners but the firm may continue its business as before.

The partnership is deemed to have been dissolved in any of the following cases

- In case of change in existing profit sharing ratio among partners.
- In case of admission of a new partner.
- In case of retirement of a partner.
- In case of death of a partner.
- In case of insolvency of a partner.
- In case of completion of the venture, if partnership is formed for that.
- In case of expiry of the period of partnership, if partnership is for a specific period of time.

Dissolution of a Firm

Dissolution of a firm means business of the firm is closed (i.e. discontinued) and the firm is wound up. According to **Section 39** of the **Indian Partnership Act, 1932**, "Dissolution of the firm means dissolution of partnership among all the partners in the firm."

At the time of dissolution of firm, all assets are sold and liabilities are paid. Balance, if any, is paid to partners at the time of settlement of their accounts and shortfall in meeting outside liabilities, is met from the private assets of partners.

It may be noted that dissolution of partnership may not necessarily involve dissolution of firm, but dissolution of firm necessarily brings in dissolution of the partnership.

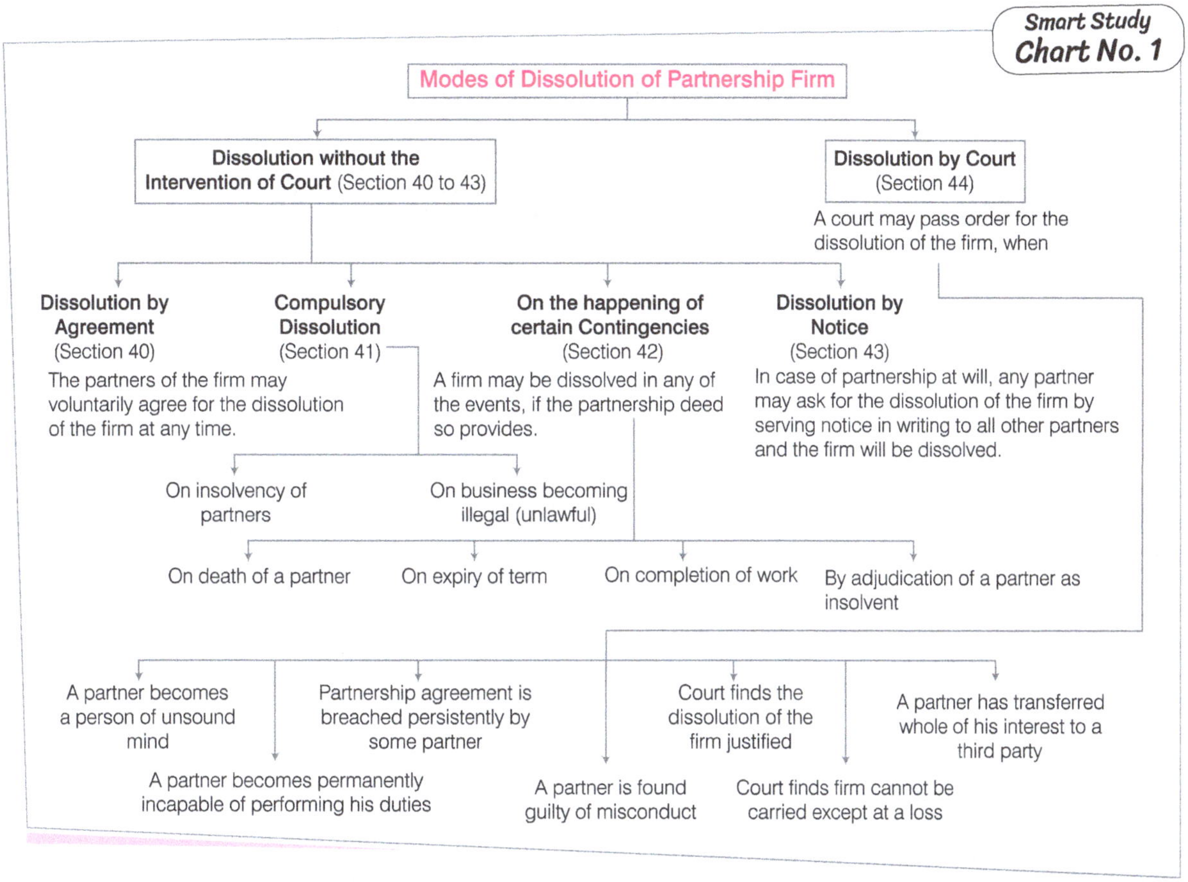

Settlement of Accounts in Case of Dissolution of Firm (Section 48)

Sub-section	Explanation
Treatment of Losses [Section 48(a)]	Losses including deficiencies of capital shall be paid in the following manner • First out of profits. • Next out of capital. • Lastly, if necessary, by the partners individually in their profit sharing ratio.
Application of Assets [Section 48(b)]	The assets of the firm, including any sum contributed by the partners to make up deficiencies, shall be applied in the following manner • First to pay firm's debts to the third parties i.e. outside parties. • Then to pay loans from partners. • Then to pay capitals of partners. • Lastly, the surplus (if any) shall be distributed among the partners in their profit sharing ratio.

Treatment of Firm's Debts and Private Debts (Section 49)

Firm's Debts Debts which the firm owes to its outsiders are known as firm's debts.

Private Debts Debts which a partner owes in his personal capacity are known as private debts.

Where both the debts of the firm and private debts of a partner co-exist, the following rules, as stated in Section 49 of the Act, shall apply

- Firm's property is applied first in payment of firm's debts and if there is any surplus, then the share of each partner is applied in the payment of his private debts or paid to him.
- Partner's private property is applied first in payment of his private debts and the surplus (if any), will be used in payment of firm's debts (if the firm's liabilities exceed the firm's assets).

6.2 Accounting Treatment at the Time of Dissolution

When a firm is dissolved, all assets are realised, liabilities are paid-off and the balance, if any is distributed among the partners. The books of the firm are closed by preparing the following accounts

- Realisation Account
- Partners' Capital Account
- Partners' Loan Account
- Cash/Bank Account

Realisation Account

Realisation account is opened at the time of dissolution of a firm. It is a nominal account and prepared to determine the profit or loss on the realisation of assets and payment of liabilities. It is prepared by transferring to it the firm's assets and liabilities, amount realised from the sale of assets, payment of liabilities and expenses incurred on realisation. The balance in the account is either profit or loss, which is transferred to the capital accounts of the partners in their profit sharing ratio.

Journal Entries for Dissolution of a Firm

1. Closing Asset Accounts

All assets accounts (excluding cash/bank balance, fictitious assets, accumulated losses, if any) are closed by transferring them to the debit of realisation account at their book value.

Key Points to Consider

- **Cash/Bank Balance** Not transferred as it is already in liquid form.
- **Fictitious Assets/Accumulated Losses** Transferred to partners' capital/current accounts (debit side) in the old profit sharing ratio.

Entry

Realisation A/c To Various Assets A/c (Individually)	Dr	[With the book values]

Balance Sheet

Liabilities	Assets
	Fixed Assets Debtors Cash Preliminary Expenses

Realisation Account

To Fixed Assets To Debtors	

2. For Transfer of Goodwill

Goodwill appearing in the balance sheet is treated like any other asset and is transferred to the realisation account at its book value.

Entries

Particulars	If goodwill appears in the balance sheet		If goodwill does not appear in the balance sheet	
(i) **On transfer to realisation account**	Realisation A/c To Goodwill A/c	Dr	No entry	
(ii) **If it is realised in cash**	Bank/Cash A/c To Realisation A/c	Dr	Bank/Cash A/c To Realisation A/c	Dr
(iii) **If one of the partners agrees to pay for goodwill**	Concerned Partner's Capital A/c To Realisation A/c	Dr	Concerned Partner's Capital A/c To Realisation A/c	Dr

**If the question is silent about realisation of goodwill, it is assumed that goodwill has no value and no amount is realised for it.*

3. Closing Liabilities Accounts

External liabilities (e.g. Creditors, bills payable, bank overdraft, partner's spouse's loan, etc.) and provisions are closed by transferring them to the credit of the realisation account.

Key Points to Consider

- **Exclusions** Liabilities exclude accumulated profits and partner related liabilities.
- **Reserves and Accumulated Profits** Transferred to partners' capital/current accounts in old profit sharing.
- **Partner's Loan** Not an external liability. It is settled after external liabilities but before partner capital accounts.

Entry

Liabilities A/c (Individually) To Realisation A/c	Dr	[With the book values]

Balance Sheet

Liabilities	Assets
Capital Creditors Bills Payable General Reserve Profit and Loss A/c	

Realisation Account

	By Creditors By Bills Payable

4. For Transfer of Reserves and Provisions

Provisions which have a credit balance will be transferred to the credit of realisation account.

Provision for Depreciation A/c	Dr	[With the book values]
Provision for Bad Debts A/c	Dr	[With the book values]
Provision for Discount on Debtors A/c	Dr	[With the book values]
Investment Fluctuation Fund A/c	Dr	[With the book values]
To Realisation A/c		

Provisions which have a debit balance will be transferred to the debit of realisation account.

Realisation A/c To Provision for Discount on Creditors A/c	Dr	[With the book values]

5. For Cash Realised on Sale of All Assets (Whether Recorded or Unrecorded)

Cash/Bank A/c To Realisation A/c	Dr	[With the realised values]

In the absence of any information regarding realisation of assets (tangible or intangible), tangible assets should be considered as realised at book value itself and intangible assets should be considered as nil (zero value).

Realisation Account

To Fixed Assets To Debtors	By Cash/Bank A/c (Realised Value of Assets)

6. For Cash Paid for External Liabilities (Whether Recorded or Unrecorded)

Realisation A/c To Cash/Bank A/c	Dr	[With the actual amount paid]

In the absence of any information regarding settlement of any outside liabilities, it is assumed an amount equal to the book value of such liability is paid.

Realisation Account

To Cash/Bank A/c (Liabilities Paid)	By Creditors By Bills Payable

7. For an Asset Taken Over by Any Partner

Partner's Capital A/c To Realisation A/c	Dr	[With the agreed value]

Realisation Account

	By Partner's Capital A/c (Assets taken Over)

Concerned Partner's Capital Account

To Realisation A/c (Assets taken Over)	

8. For a Liability Discharged by Any Partner

Realisation A/c Dr To Partner's Capital A/c	[With the agreed value]

Realisation Account

To Partner's Capital A/c (Liability taken Over)	

Concerned Partner's Capital Account

	By Realisation A/c (Liability taken Over)

9. For Assets Given Away to Creditors

- When a creditor accepts an asset as full and final settlement.
  No journal entry is required.
- When a creditor accepts his payment partly by taking over an asset and partly his payment in cash, the following entry will be made for cash payment only

Realisation A/c	Dr
To Cash/Bank A/c	

- When a creditor accepts an asset where value of asset is more than the amount due to him, he will pay cash to the firm for the difference

Cash/Bank A/c	Dr
To Realisation A/c	

10. For Realisation Expenses

When realisation expenses are paid by the firm on its own behalf	Realisation A/c Dr To Cash/Bank A/c	[Actual amount of expenses]
When expenses are paid by a partner on firm's behalf	Realisation A/c Dr To Concerned Partner's Capital A/c	[Actual amount of expenses]
When expenses are paid by firm on behalf of a partner who has to bear such expenses	Partner's Capital A/c Dr To Cash/Bank A/c	[Actual amount of expenses]
When expenses are paid by the partner and borne by the partner	No journal entry is required in this case.	
When a partner is paid a fixed amount for the purpose of bearing realisation expenses and actual expenses are borne by a partner	Realisation A/c Dr To Partner's Capital A/c	[With the guaranteed fixed amount]
When a partner is paid a fixed amount for the purpose of bearing realisation expenses and the actual expenses are borne by the firm	Realisation A/c Dr To Partner's Capital A/c Realisation A/c Dr To Cash/Bank A/c	[Actual amount of expenses]
When expenses are paid by one partner on behalf of another partner	Partner's Capital A/c Dr To Partner's Capital A/c	[Partner who borne the expenses] [Partner who pays the expenses]
When expenses are borne by the firm but partly paid by the firm and balance by a partner	Realisation A/c Dr To Cash/Bank A/c To Concerned Partner's Capital A/c	 [Amount paid by firm] [Amount paid by partner]

**If question is silent about the treatment of realisation expenses, it is assumed that the expenses are paid and borne by the firm.*

11. Accounting Treatment of Unrecorded Assets and Unrecorded Liabilities

- **For Unrecorded Assets**

Cash/Bank A/c Dr Partner's Capital A/c Dr To Realisation A/c	[If sold for cash] [If taken by a partner]

**If the unrecorded assets are taken by a creditor, no entry is passed.*

Realisation Account

	By Cash/Bank A/c (Unrecorded Assets Realised)

- **For Unrecorded Liabilities**

Realisation A/c Dr To Cash/Bank A/c To Partner's Capital A/c	 [If paid in cash] [If partner has agreed to pay]

Realisation Account

To Cash/Bank A/c (Unrecorded Liabilities Paid-off)	

Key Point
It is to be noted that unrecorded assets and unrecorded liabilities are not transferred to realisation account (since there is no account for such assets and liabilities, there is no case for their transfer).

12. For Transferring Profit/Loss on Realisation

- In case of profit on realisation

Realisation A/c Dr To Partners' Capital A/c	[In profit sharing ratio]

- In case of loss on realisation

Partners' Capital A/c Dr To Realisation A/c	

Step to Prepare a Realisation Account

Step 1 Transfer all assets (except cash in hand, cash at bank and fictitious assets) to the debit side of realisation account.

Step 2 Transfer outside liabilities to the credit side of realisation account.

Step 3 Show the disposal of assets on the credit side of realisation account with the actual amount received.

Step 4 Show the payment of outside liabilities at agreed value or book value on the debit side of realisation account.

Step 5 Make the payment of realisation expenses on the debit side of realisation account.

Step 6 Show the disposal of unrecorded assets on the credit side of realisation account.

Step 7 Show the payment of unrecorded liabilities on the debit side of realisation account.

Step 8 Transfer investment fluctuation fund, depreciation/replacement reserve on credit side of realisation account.

Step 9 Close the realisation account. Excess of credit side represents profit and will be transferred to credit side of partners' capital accounts. Excess of debit side shows loss which will be transferred to the debit side of partners' capital accounts.

Format of Realisation Account

Dr **Realisation Account** Cr

Particulars	Amt (₹)	Particulars	Amt (₹)
To Sundry Assets A/c (Excluding cash, bank, fictitious assets, accumulated losses, debit balance of partners' capital/current accounts, loans to partner(s))	At their respective book values	By Sundry Liabilities A/c (Excluding partners' capitals, loan from partner(s), reserve, accumulated profits, etc)	At their respective book values
		By Provision on any Asset A/c	...
To Provision on any Liability A/c	...	By Bank/Cash A/c (Amount received on realisation of assets)	Amount realised
To Bank/Cash A/c (Amount paid for discharging liabilities)	Amount paid	By Bank/Cash A/c (Amount received from unrecorded assets)	...
To Bank/Cash A/c (Amount paid for unrecorded liabilities)	...	By Partner's Capital/Current A/c (Assets taken over by a partner recorded or unrecorded)	Agreed value of the cost
To Bank/Cash A/c (Expenses on realisation)	Expenses paid		
To Partner's Capital/Current A/c (Liability taken over by a partner or remuneration/ commission paid to him or any expenses beared by him)	Amount paid	By Partners' Capital/Current A/c (Loss on realisation)* (Transferred to partners' capital accounts in their profit sharing ratio)	...
To Partners' Capital/Current A/c (Profit on realisation)* (Transferred to partners' capital accounts in their profit sharing ratio)	...		
	...		...

**Any one of two accounts will appear.*

Partners' Capital Account

This account records the balances of partners' capital and current accounts. Any assets taken over by a partner is debited and any liability taken over is credited in the capital account. Under the fixed capital method, partners maintain separate current accounts, which may show a credit or debit balance. These balances are transferred to the respective capital accounts to close current accounts.

The entries are as follows

(i) In case of debit balance in a current account of a partner	(ii) In case of credit balance in a current account of a partner
Concerned Partner's Capital A/c Dr To Concerned Partner's Current A/c	Concerned Partner's Current A/c Dr To Concerned Partner's Capital A/c

In addition to the transfer of current account balances, realisation profit/loss, reserves and undistributed profit/loss are also transferred to partners' capital accounts.

On Transfer of Realisation Profit/Loss

Realisation profit/loss is credited/debited to partners' capital accounts in their profit sharing ratio by passing the following journal entry

(i) In case of realisation profit	(ii) In case of realisation loss
Realisation A/c Dr To Partners' Capital A/c	Partners' Capital A/c Dr To Realisation A/c

On Transfer of Undistributed Profits/Losses and Reserves

Undistributed profits (such as general reserve, reserve fund, credit balance of profit and loss account, etc.) are transferred to partners' capital accounts in their profit sharing ratio.

General Reserve A/c	Dr
Reserve Fund A/c	Dr
Profit and Loss A/c	Dr
Workmen's Compensation Fund A/c	Dr
To Partners' Capital A/c	

Undistributed losses or fictitious assets (i.e. debit balance of profit and loss account, advertisement expenses, etc.) appearing on the assets side of the balance sheet are transferred to partners' capital accounts in their profit sharing ratio.

Partners' Capital A/c	Dr
To Profit and Loss A/c	
To Advertisement Expenses A/c	

Quick Review : Treatment of Reserves in Different Situations

Reserve	Distribute to the Partners	Transfer to Realisation Account
General reserve	Always	Never
Investment fluctuation reserve	If investment does not exist in the balance sheet.	If investment exists in the balance sheet.
Workmen compensation reserve	When there is no liability for workmen compensation.	When there is any liability on account of this fund.
Contingency reserve	Always	Never
Machinery replacement fund	If machinery does not exist in the balance sheet.	If machinery exists in the balance sheet.
Reserve for discount on creditors	If creditors does not exist in the balance sheet.	If creditors exist in the balance sheet.

For Final Settlement with Partners

After the transfer of profit/loss on realisation, undistributed profits, reserves, etc. to the capital accounts of the partners, the balances of capital accounts are closed in the following manner

(i) When partner is required to bring in cash to clear-off his debit balance	(ii) When a partner is paid to settle his claims
Cash/Bank A/c Dr To Partners' Capital A/c	Partners' Capital A/c Dr To Cash/Bank A/c

Format of Partners' Capital Account

Dr **Partners' Capital Account** Cr

Particulars	X (₹)	Y (₹)	Particulars	X (₹)	Y (₹)
To Balance b/d (Debit balance)	...	...	By Balance b/d (Credit balance)	...	...
To Profit and Loss A/c (Debit balance)	...	...	By General Reserve A/c	...	...
To Advertisement Suspense A/c	...	...	By Profit and Loss A/c (Credit balance)	...	...
To Realisation A/c (Assets taken over)	...	...	By Workmen's Compensation Fund A/c	...	...
			By Realisation A/c (Liabilities taken over)	...	...
To Realisation A/c (Loss on realisation)	...	...	By Realisation A/c (Profit on realisation)	...	...
			By Cash/Bank A/c (Cash brought in)	...	...
To Cash/Bank A/c (Excess cash paid)	...	...			
	...	...		...	...

Partners' Loan Account

If any loan is advanced by a partner to the firm, it will be paid-off only after all the outside liabilities are paid in full. Thus, partner's loan account is not transferred to realisation account and a separate account is prepared namely partner's loan account and is paid-off by passing the following entry

Partner's Loan A/c	Dr
To Bank A/c	

The loan account, showing a credit balance, appears on the liabilities side of the balance sheet. It should be paid separately before paying the partner's capital.

Key Point

When a partner's capital account shows a debit balance after all adjustments, his loan account (to firm) should be transferred to his capital account to the extent of debit balance.

Loan by Firm to Partner

When a firm advances loan to a partner, it is an asset for the firm. Following journal entry is passed in this case

Partner's Capital A/c	Dr
To Loan to Partner A/c	

Partner's loan account will show a debit balance and will appear on assets side in the balance sheet of the firm. It should be settled through partner's capital account.

Bank or Cash Account

In the case of dissolution of a partnership firm, cash account (or bank account) is prepared and closed at the end. Bank or cash account is a real account. On debit side of this account, opening balance, amount realised through sale of assets and any amount bought in by the partners have to be shown. On the credit side, all the payments for liabilities, realisation expenses and final settlement made to partners are shown.

In case both cash and bank balances appear in balance sheet, it is always better to open a single account, i.e. either cash account or bank account. If cash account is prepared, the bank balance should be withdrawn from the bank and posted to the debit of cash account and if bank account is prepared, then cash in hand should be deposited in the bank account.

Format of Cash/Bank Account

Dr **Cash/Bank Account** Cr

Particulars	Amt (₹)	Particulars	Amt (₹)
To Balance b/d (Cash in hand or Cash at bank)	...	By Balance b/d (Bank overdraft)	...
To Realisation A/c (Assets realised)	...	By Realisation A/c (Liabilities paid)	...
To Partner's Capital A/c (Cash brought in by partner)	...	By Realisation A/c (Realisation expenses paid)	...
		By Partner's Loan A/c (Partner's loan paid)	...
		By Partner's Capital A/c (Excess cash paid to partner)	...
	...		...

Mind Map

Dissolution of a Partnership Firm

1 Meaning of Dissolution of a Firm

According to Section 39 of the Indian Partnership Act, 1932, "Dissolution of the firm means dissolution of partnership among all the partners in the firm."

2 Modes of Dissolution of Partnership Firm

1. **Dissolution without the Intervention of Court**
   - Dissolution by agreement (Sec 40)
   - Compulsory dissolution (Sec 41)
   - On the happening of certain contingencies (Sec 42)
   - Dissolution by notice (Sec 43)
2. **Dissolution by Court**
   - When partner becomes a person of unsound mind
   - When partner becomes permanently incapable
   - When agreement is breached by some partner consistently
   - When partner is found guilty of misconduct
   - When court finds dissolution of firm justified
   - When court finds firm cannot be carried except at a loss
   - When a partner has transferred whole of his interest to a third party

3 Settlement of Accounts

1. **Treatment of Losses** [Section 48 (a)]
   - First, out of profits
   - Next, out of capital
   - Lastly, if necessary, by the partners individually in their profit sharing ratio
2. **Application of Assets** [Section 48 (b)]
   - First, to pay firm's debts to third parties, i.e. outside parties
   - Then, to pay loan from partners
   - Then, to pay capital of partners
   - Lastly, the surplus (if any) shall be distributed among the partners in their profit sharing ratio

4 Treatment of Firm's Debts and Private Debts (Section 49)

- Firm's property is applied first in payment of firm's debts and surplus (if any), then the share of each partner is applied in the payment of his private debt or paid to him.
- Partner's private property is applied first in payment of his private debts and the surplus (if any), will be used in payment of firms debts.

8 Bank or Cash Account

- On the debit side of this account, opening balance, amount realised through sale of assets and any amount brought in by the partners have to be shown.
- On the credit side, all the payments for liabilities, realisation expenses and final settlement made to partners are shown.

7 Partners' Loan Account

- If any loan is advanced by a partner to firm, it will be paid-off only after all outside liabilities are paid in full.
- It is not transferred to realisation account and a separate account is prepared namely partner's loan account.

6 Partner's Capital Account

- Balances of partners capital accounts and current accounts are recorded in this account.
- Any asset of the firm taken over by the partner is debited and any liability taken over is credited in the capital account.
- Realisation profits or losses, reserves and undistributed profits or losses are also transferred to partner's capital account.
- Lastly, if there is a balance in capital account, they are paid and if there is any deficiency in capital, partners bring cash.

Dr **Realisation Account** Cr

Particulars	Amt (₹)	Particulars	Amt (₹)
To Sundry Assets A/c (Excluding cash, bank, fictitious assets, accumulated losses, debit balance of partner's capital/current accounts, loans to partner(s))	At their respective book values	By Sundry Liabilities A/c (Excluding partners' capitals, loan from partner(s), reserve, accumulated profits, etc)	At their respective book values
To Provision on any Liability A/c	...	By Provision on any Asset A/c	...
To Bank/Cash A/c (Amount paid for discharging liabilities)	Amount paid	By Bank/Cash A/c (Amount received on realisation of assets)	Amount realised
To Bank/Cash A/c (Expenses on realisation)	Expenses paid	By Bank/Cash A/c (Amount received from unrecorded assets)	...
To Partner's Capital/Current A/c (Liability taken over by a partner or remuneration/ commission paid to him or any expenses beared by him)	Amount paid	By Partner's Capital/Current A/c (Assets taken over by a partner recorded or unrecorded)	Agreed value of the cost
To Partner's Capital/Current A/c (Profit on realisation)* (Transferred to partners' capital accounts in their profit sharing ratio)	...	By Partner's Capital/Current A/c (Loss on realisation)* (Transferred to partners' capital accounts in their profit sharing ratio)	...
	...		...

* Any one of two account will appear

Format

5 Realisation Account

It is opened at the time of dissolution of a firm. It is a nominal account and prepared to determine the profit and loss on the realisation of assets and payment of liabilities.

Topicwise Solved Questions

Journal Related to Dissolution

Solved Question 1 Lal and Pal were partners in a firm sharing profits in the ratio of 3 : 7. On 1st April, 2024 their firm was dissolved. After transferring assets (other than cash) and outsider's liabilities to realisation account, you are given the following information.

(i) A creditor of ₹ 3,60,000 accepted machinery valued at ₹ 5,00,000 and paid to the firm ₹ 1,40,000.

(ii) A second creditor for ₹ 50,000 accepted stock at ₹ 45,000 in full settlement of his claim.

(iii) A third creditor amounting to ₹ 90,000 accepted ₹ 45,000 in cash and investments worth ₹ 43,000 in full settlement of his claim.

(iv) Loss on dissolution was ₹ 15,000.

Pass necessary journal entries for the above transactions in the books of firm assuming that all payments were made by cheque.

Sol. **JOURNAL**

Date	Particulars		LF	Amt (Dr)	Amt (Cr)
(i)	Bank A/c	Dr		1,40,000	
	To Realisation A/c				1,40,000
	(Being payment received from creditors)				
(ii)	No entry will be passed as liability is settled against asset.				
(iii)	Realisation A/c	Dr		45,000	
	To Bank A/c				45,000
	(Being partial payment made to creditors through cheque)				
(iv)	Lal's Capital A/c (15,000 × 3/10)	Dr		4,500	
	Pal's Capital A/c (15,000 × 7/10)	Dr		10,500	
	To Realisation A/c				15,000
	(Being loss on realisation transferred to partners' capital account in the ratio 3 : 7)				

Solved Question 2 Pass the necessary journal entries for the following transactions on the dissolution of firm of A, B and C (who were sharing profits in the ratio of 2 : 2 : 1) after the transfer of all assets (other than cash) and external liabilities to realisation account.

(i) Debtors were of ₹ 1,24,200. A, takes over debtors amounted to ₹ 1,20,000 at ₹ 1,17,200 and the remaining debtors were sold to a debt collecting agency at 50% of the value.

(ii) Sundry assets were of ₹ 1,17,000. B, is to take over some sundry assets at ₹ 72,000 (being 10% less than the book value). C is to take over remaining sundry assets at 80% of the book value.

(iii) C, assumes the responsibility of discharge of Mrs. C's loan of ₹ 11,500 together with accrued interest of ₹ 2,300.

(iv) The amount of sundry assets transferred to realisation account was ₹ 80,000. 60% of them have been sold at a profit of ₹ 2,000. 20% of the remaining were sold at a discount of 30% and remaining were taken over by A (a partner) at book value.

Sol. **JOURNAL**

Date	Particulars		LF	Amt (Dr)	Amt (Cr)
(i) (a)	A's Capital A/c	Dr		1,17,200	
	To Realisation A/c				1,17,200
	(Being some debtors taken over by A)				
(b)	Cash/Bank A/c [(1,24,200 – 1,20,000) × 50/100]	Dr		2,100	
	To Realisation A/c				2,100
	(Being the remaining debtors sold to a debt collecting agency)				

Date	Particulars		LF	Amt (Dr)	Amt (Cr)
(ii) (a)	B's Capital A/c To Realisation A/c (Being sundry assets of value ₹ 80,000 $\left(72,000 \times \frac{100}{90}\right)$ taken over by B at ₹ 72,000)	Dr		72,000	72,000
(b)	C's Capital A/c [(1,17,000 – 80,000) × 80/100] To Realisation A/c (Being the remaining sundry assets taken over by C)	Dr		29,600	29,600
(iii)	Realisation A/c To C's Capital A/c (11,500 + 2,300) (Being Mrs. C's loan paid by C)	Dr		13,800	13,800
(iv) (a)	Bank A/c To Realisation A/c (Being assets having book value of ₹ 48,000 were sold for ₹ 50,000 and assets having book value of ₹ 6,400 were sold for ₹ 4,480) (WN 1)	Dr		54,480	54,480
(b)	A's Capital A/c To Realisation A/c (WN 2) (Being assets having book value of ₹ 25,600 were taken over by A at this value)	Dr		25,600	25,600

Working Notes

1. **Calculation of Amount Realised from Assets**

	Amt (₹)
60% of ₹ 80,000	48,000
(+) Profit on sale	2,000
A	50,000
20% of the remaining assets [i.e. (20/100) × (80,000 – 48,000)]	6,400
(–) 30% discount	(1,920)
B	4,480

Total amount realised from assets (A + B) = 50,000 + 4,480 = ₹ 54,480

2. **Calculation of Value of Assets taken over by C**

	Amt (₹)
Total book value of assets	80,000
(–) Book value of assets sold (i.e. 48,000 + 6,400)	(54,400)
	25,600

Solved Question 3 **Pass journal entries for the following transactions.**

(i) Realisation expenses amounted to ₹ 40,000.

(ii) Realisation expenses amounted to ₹ 20,000 were paid by a partner.

(iii) Realisation expenses amounted to ₹ 20,000 were paid by the firm on behalf of a partner.

(iv) A partner was paid remuneration (including expenses) of ₹ 30,000 to carry out dissolution of the firm. Actual expenses were ₹ 40,000.

(v) Dissolution expenses were ₹ 32,000. Out of the paid expenses, ₹ 12,000 were to be borne by the firm and the balance by a partner, ₹ 32,000 are paid by the firm.

(vi) Dissolution expenses were ₹ 32,000, ₹ 12,000 were to be borne by the firm and the balance by a partner. The expenses were paid by a partner.

(vii) Realisation expenses of ₹ 20,000 were to be borne and paid by a partner.

(viii) Rohit, a partner is paid remuneration of ₹ 20,000 for dissolution of the firm. Realisation expenses of ₹ 32,000 are met by the firm.

(ix) Rohit, a partner agreed to take over the responsibility of completing dissolution at an agreed remuneration of ₹ 4,000 and to bear all realisation expenses. Actual realisation expenses amounted to ₹ 3,200 were paid by Rohit out of his private funds.

(x) Rohit, one of the partners was to receive 2% of the value of assets realised as remuneration for completing the dissolution work and was to bear realisation expenses. Realisation expenses were ₹ 4,000 paid by Rohit. The assets (including cash at bank ₹ 12,000) realised ₹ 6,12,000.

(xi) Rohit, one of the partners was to receive 2% of the net cash realised from dissolution and was to bear realisation expenses. Realisation expenses were ₹ 4,000. The assets (including cash at bank ₹ 12,000) realised ₹ 6,12,000 and cash paid for outsiders' liabilities amounted to ₹ 1,60,000.

(xii) Realisation expenses of ₹ 2,000 were to be borne by Raju, a partner. However, it was paid by Sanju.

Sol.

JOURNAL

Date	Particulars		LF	Amt (Dr)	Amt (Cr)
(i)	Realisation A/c	Dr		40,000	
	To Cash/Bank A/c				40,000
	(Being the dissolution expenses paid)				
(ii)	Realisation A/c	Dr		20,000	
	To Partner's Capital A/c				20,000
	(Being the dissolution expenses paid by the partner credited to his capital account)				
(iii)	Partner's Capital A/c	Dr		20,000	
	To Cash/Bank A/c				20,000
	(Being the dissolution expenses paid by the firm on behalf of the partner debited to his capital account)				
(iv)	Realisation A/c	Dr		30,000	
	To Partner's Capital A/c				30,000
	(Being the remuneration to partner credited to his capital account)				
(v)	Realisation A/c	Dr		12,000	
	Partner's Capital A/c	Dr		20,000	
	To Cash/Bank A/c				32,000
	(Being the dissolution expenses paid by the firm, firm's share of expenses debited to realisation account and balance to partner's capital account)				
(vi)	Realisation A/c	Dr		12,000	
	To Partner's Capital A/c				12,000
	(Being the realisation expenses paid by the partner credited to his capital account)				
(vii)	No entry is to be passed				
(viii) (a)	Realisation A/c	Dr		20,000	
	To Rohit's Capital A/c				20,000
	(Being the remuneration payable to Rohit for dissolution of the firm)				
(b)	Realisation A/c	Dr		32,000	
	To Cash/Bank A/c				32,000
	(Being the realisation expenses paid)				
(ix)	Realisation A/c	Dr		4,000	
	To Rohit's Capital A/c				4,000
	(Being the remuneration due to Rohit)				
(x)	Realisation A/c	Dr		12,000	
	To Rohit's Capital A/c				12,000
	(Being the remuneration for dissolution work due to Rohit, i.e. 2% of ₹ 6,00,000 i.e. 6,12,000 – 12,000)				
(xi) (a)	Realisation A/c	Dr		8,800	
	To Rohit's Capital A/c				8,800
	(Being the remuneration for dissolution due to Rohit, i.e. 2% of ₹ 4,40,000 i.e. 6,00,000 – 1,60,000)				
(b)	No entry for realisation expenses is passed assuming that Rohit has paid the same out of his private funds.				
(xii)	Raju's Capital A/c	Dr		2,000	
	To Sanju's Capital A/c				2,000
	(Being realisation expenses to be borne by Raju, paid by Sanju)				

Solved Question 4 Pass necessary journal entries for the following transactions on dissolution of the firm of Rajesh, Somesh and Yogesh after various assets (other than cash) and third party liabilities have been transferred to realisation account.

(i) Rajesh took over stock of ₹ 4,00,000 at a discount of 20%.

(ii) Somesh agreed to take over the firm's furniture, not recorded in the books of the firm at ₹ 80,000.

(iii) Land and building of the book value of ₹ 60,00,000 was sold for ₹ 90,00,000 through a broker who charged 10% commission.

(iv) Ashish, an old customer, whose account for ₹ 70,000 was written-off as bad in the previous year, paid 60% of the amount.

(v) Sundry creditors of ₹ 3,00,000 were settled at a discount of 10%.

(vi) Realisation expenses amounting to ₹ 21,000 were paid by Yogesh. **CBSE 2025**

Sol.

JOURNAL

Date	Particulars		LF	Amt (Dr)	Amt (Cr)
(i)	Rajesh's Capital A/c (4,00,000 – 80,000)	Dr		3,20,000	
	To Realisation A/c				3,20,000
	(Being stock taken over by Rajesh)				
(ii)	Somesh's Capital A/c	Dr		80,000	
	To Realisation A/c				80,000
	(Being unrecorded furniture taken over by Somesh)				
(iii)	Bank A/c (90,00,000 – 9,00,000)	Dr		81,00,000	
	To Realisation A/c				81,00,000
	(Being land and building realised recorded at net amount i.e. after broker's commission)				
(iv)	Bank A/c (70,000 × 60%)	Dr		42,000	
	To Realisation A/c				42,000
	(Being bad debt recovered recorded)				
(v)	Realisation A/c (3,00,000 – 30,000)	Dr		2,70,000	
	To Bank A/c				2,70,000
	(Being sundry creditors settled at 10% discount)				
(vi)	Realisation A/c	Dr		21,000	
	To Yogesh's Capital A/c				21,000
	(Being realisation expenses paid by Yogesh credited to his capital account)				

Solved Question 5 Ajay and Brajesh share profits and losses in a ratio of 4 : 3. They have decided to dissolve their partnership and all assets and liabilities have been transferred to the realisation account. Prepare journal entries to account for the following transactions during the dissolution.

(i) A loan of ₹ 2,52,000 was repaid.

(ii) Ajay was responsible for all dissolution expenses and received a commission of ₹ 8,400 for handling them.

(iii) Debit balance of profit and loss account appeared on the books with a balance of ₹ 1,96,000.

(iv) Brajesh took over stock valued at ₹ 11,200 for an agreed amount of ₹ 9,800.

(v) An unrecorded typewriter was sold for ₹ 24,500.

(vi) An outstanding bill for damages of ₹ 10,500 was paid-off.

Sol.

JOURNAL

Date	Particulars		LF	Amt (Dr)	Amt (Cr)
(i)	Realisation A/c	Dr		2,52,000	
	To Bank A/c				2,52,000
	(Being loan discharged)				
(ii)	Realisation A/c	Dr		8,400	
	To Ajay's Capital A/c				8,400
	(Being the commission allowed to Ajay)				
(iii)	Ajay's Capital A/c	Dr		1,12,000	
	Brajesh's Capital A/c	Dr		84,000	
	To Profit and Loss A/c				1,96,000
	(Being debit balance of profit and loss account written-off)				

Date	Particulars		LF	Amt (Dr)	Amt (Cr)
(iv)	Brajesh's Capital A/c	Dr		9,800	
	To Realisation A/c				9,800
	(Being stock taken over by Brajesh)				
(v)	Bank A/c	Dr		24,500	
	To Realisation A/c				24,500
	(Being unrecorded typewriter realised)				
(vi)	Realisation A/c	Dr		10,500	
	To Bank A/c				10,500
	(Being outstanding bill for damages paid-off)				

Solved Question 6 **Pass the necessary journal entries for the following transactions on the dissolution of the partnership firm of Tina and Rina after the various assets (other than cash and bank) and external liabilities have been transferred to realisation account.**

(i) There was an outstanding bill for repairs for which ₹ 20,000 were paid.

(ii) The firm had stock of ₹ 80,000. Tina took over 50% of the stock at a discount of 20% while the remaining stock was sold-off for ₹ 52,000.

(iii) The firm had 100 shares of ₹ 10 each which were taken over by the partners at market value of ₹ 20 per share in their profit sharing ratio of 3 : 2.

(iv) Realisation expenses of ₹ 4,000 were paid by Rina.

(v) Tina had given a loan of ₹ 40,000 to the firm which was duly paid.

(vi) Rina agreed to pay off her husband's loan of ₹ 10,000 at a discount of 10%. **CBSE 2024**

Sol.

In the Books of Tina and Rina
JOURNAL

Date	Particulars		LF	Amt (Dr)	Amt (Cr)
(i)	Realisation A/c	Dr		20,000	
	To Bank/Cash A/c				20,000
	(Being an outstanding bill for repairs paid)				
(ii)	Tina's Capital A/c	Dr		32,000	
	Cash/Bank A/c	Dr		52,000	
	To Realisation A/c				84,000
	(Being stock partially taken over by Tina, a partner and partially realised)				
(iii)	Tina's Capital A/c	Dr		1,200	
	Rina's Capital A/c	Dr		800	
	To Realisation A/c				2,000
	(Being shares acquired by partners in their profit sharing ratio)				
(iv)	Realisation A/c	Dr		4,000	
	To Rina's Capital A/c				4,000
	(Being realisation expenses paid by Rina credited to her capital account)				
(v)	Tina's Loan A/c	Dr		40,000	
	To Bank/Cash A/c				40,000
	(Being partner's loan paid)				
(vi)	Realisation A/c	Dr		9,000	
	To Rina's Capital A/c				9,000
	(Being loan taken over by Rina, a partner)				

Solved Question 7 **Pass necessary journal entries on the dissolution of a partnership firm in the following cases**

(i) L a partner, was appointed to look after the dissolution process for which he was given a remuneration of ₹ 10,000.

(ii) Dissolution expenses ₹ 8,000 were paid by the partner, M.

(iii) Dissolution expenses were ₹ 5,000.

(iv) P a partner, was appointed to look after the process of dissolution for which he was allowed a remuneration of ₹ 7,000. P agreed to bear the dissolution expenses. Actual dissolution expenses ₹ 4,000 were paid by P.

(v) N a partner, was appointed to look after the process of dissolution for which he was allowed a remuneration of ₹ 9,000. N agreed to bear the dissolution expenses. Actual dissolution expenses ₹ 4,000 were paid by the firm.

(vi) Q a partner was appointed to look after the process of dissolution for which he was allowed a remuneration of ₹ 18,000. Q agreed to take over stock worth ₹ 18,000 as his remuneration. The stock had already been transferred to realisation account.

Sol.

JOURNAL

Date	Particulars		LF	Amt (Dr)	Amt (Cr)
(i)	Realisation A/c To L's Capital A/c (Being remuneration payable to L)	Dr		10,000	10,000
(ii)	Realisation A/c To M's Capital A/c (Being dissolution expenses payable to M)	Dr		8,000	8,000
(iii)	Realisation A/c To Bank A/c (Being realisation expenses paid)	Dr		5,000	5,000
(iv)	Realisation A/c To P's Capital A/c (Being remuneration allowed to P and dissolution expenses paid by him)	Dr		7,000	7,000
(v) (a)	Realisation A/c To N's Capital A/c (Being remuneration payable to N)	Dr		9,000	9,000
(b)	N's Capital A/c To Cash A/c (Being realisation expenses paid by firm on behalf of N)	Dr		4,000	4,000
(vi)	No Entry **Alternatively**				
(a)	Realisation A/c To Q's Capital A/c (Being remuneration allowed to Q)	Dr		18,000	18,000
(b)	Q's Capital A/c To Realisation A/c (Being stock taken by Q as remuneration)	Dr		18,000	18,000

Solved Question 8 Nandu, Bandu and Chandu were partners in a firm. On 31st March, 2023 they decided to dissolve the firm. Pass necessary journal entries for the following transactions after the various assets (other than cash and bank) and outside liabilities have been transferred to realisation account.

(i) Stock of ₹ 1,40,000 was taken by Nandu at a discount of 30%.

(ii) Creditors to whom the firm owed ₹ 40,000 accepted stock at ₹ 4,000 and the balance amount was paid to them by a cheque.

(iii) An old computer which had been written-off completely from the books was sold for ₹ 4,000, whereas its estimated market value was ₹ 10,000.

(iv) Chandu had given a loan of ₹ 1,00,000 to the firm, which was paid to him through a cheque.

(v) ₹ 24,000 were recovered from a debtor which was written-off as bad debt in the previous year.

(vi) Bandu was appointed to look after the dissolution work for which he was allowed a remuneration of ₹ 26,000. Bandu agreed to bear the dissolution expenses. Actual dissolution expenses of ₹ 36,000 were paid by Bandu. **CBSE 2024**

Sol.

In the Books of Nandu, Bandu and Chandu

JOURNAL

Date	Particulars		LF	Amt (Dr)	Amt (Cr)
(i)	Nandu's Capital A/c To Realisation A/c (Being stock taken over by Nandu at 30% discount)	Dr		98,000	98,000
(ii)	Realisation A/c To Bank A/c (Being creditors paid by cheque)	Dr		36,000	36,000

Date	Particulars		LF	Amt (Dr)	Amt (Cr)
(iii)	Cash/Bank A/c	Dr		4,000	
	To Realisation A/c				4,000
	(Being old computer sold)				
(iv)	Chandu's Loan A/c	Dr		1,00,000	
	To Bank A/c				1,00,000
	(Being Chandu's loan paid through cheque)				
(v)	Cash/Bank A/c	Dr		24,000	
	To Realisation A/c				24,000
	(Being bad debts previously written-off recovered)				
(vi)	Realisation A/c	Dr		26,000	
	To Bandu's Capital A/c				26,000
	(Being remuneration allowed to Bandu for carrying out dissolution work)				

Solved Question 9 **Alok and Dhruv were partners sharing profits in the ratio of 3 : 2. Given journal entries under following situation at the time of dissolution of firm.**

(i) Workmen compensation reserve in the balance sheet was ₹ 37,500.

(ii) Workmen compensation reserve was ₹ 30,000 and liability for it was ₹ 17,500.

(iii) Workmen compensation reserve was ₹ 30,000 and liability was ₹ 37,500.

(iv) Workmen compensation reserve was ₹ 30,000 and liability was ₹ 30,000.

(v) Workmen compensation reserve was nil and liability was ₹ 7,500.

Sol.

JOURNAL

Date	Particulars		LF	Amt (Dr)	Amt (Cr)
(i)	Workmen Compensation Reserve A/c	Dr		37,500	
	To Alok's Capital A/c				22,500
	To Dhruv's Capital A/c				15,000
	(Being balance of workmen compensation reserve transferred to partners' capital accounts in the profit sharing ratio)				
	Note Since, amount of liability is not given, it is assumed to be nil.				
(ii) (a)	Workmen Compensation Reserve A/c	Dr		17,500	
	To Realisation A/c				17,500
	(Being workmen compensation reserve to the extent of liability transferred to realisation account)				
(b)	Workmen Compensation Reserve A/c	Dr		12,500	
	To Alok's Capital A/c				7,500
	To Dhruv's Capital A/c				5,000
	(Being surplus of workmen compensation reserve transferred to partner's capital accounts in their profit sharing ratio)				
(c)	Realisation A/c	Dr		17,500	
	To Bank A/c				17,500
	(Being liability on account of workmen compensation paid)				
(iii) (a)	Workmen Compensation Reserve A/c	Dr		30,000	
	To Realisation A/c				30,000
	(Being balance of workmen compensation reserve transferred to realisation account)				
(b)	Realisation A/c	Dr		37,500	
	To Bank A/c				37,500
	(Being liability on account of workmen compensation paid)				
(iv) (a)	Workmen Compensation Reserve A/c	Dr		30,000	
	To Realisation A/c				30,000
	(Being balance of workmen compensation reserve transferred to realisation account)				

Date	Particulars		LF	Amt (Dr)	Amt (Cr)
(b)	Realisation A/c	Dr		30,000	
	To Bank A/c				30,000
	(Being liability on account of workmen compensation paid)				
(v)	Realisation A/c	Dr		7,500	
	To Bank A/c				7,500
	(Being liability on account of workmen compensation paid)				

Realisation Account

Solved Question 10 **Aadish and Shreyansh were partners in a firm sharing profits and losses in the ratio of 3 : 2. On 31st March, 2024 their balance sheet was as follows**

Balance Sheet of Aadish and Shreyansh
as at 31st March, 2024

Liabilities		Amt (₹)	Assets		Amt (₹)
Creditors		90,000	Cash at Bank		20,000
Mrs. Aadish's Loan		30,000	Stock		24,000
Shreyansh's Loan		30,000	Investments		30,000
General Reserve		45,000	Debtors	20,000	
Capital A/cs			(−) Provision for Doubtful Debts	(2,000)	18,000
Aadish	1,00,000		Plant		1,00,000
Shreyansh	97,000	1,97,000	Advertisement Suspense A/c		2,00,000
		3,92,000			3,92,000

The firm was dissolved on 31st March, 2024 on the following terms

(i) Debtors realised ₹ 17,000 and plant realised 10% more than the book value.
(ii) Aadish promised to pay Mrs. Aadish's loan and took away stock at ₹ 20,000.
(iii) Shreyansh took away half of the investments at a discount of 10%. Remaining investments realised ₹ 4,500.
(iv) Creditors were paid-off at a discount of 10%. **(v) Expenses of realisation amounted to ₹ 7,000.**

Prepare realisation account. **CBSE 2023**

Sol. Dr **Realisation Account** Cr

Particulars		Amt (₹)	Particulars		Amt (₹)
To Sundry Assets A/c			By Creditors A/c		90,000
Stock	24,000		By Provision for Doubtful Debts		2,000
Investment	30,000		By Mrs. Aadish's Loan A/c		30,000
Debtors	20,000		By Bank A/c (Assets)		
Plant	1,00,000	1,74,000	Debtors	17,000	
To Bank A/c (Creditors) (90,000 – 9,000)		81,000	Plant	1,10,000	
To Aadish's Capital A/c (Mrs. Aadish's Loan)		30,000	Investment	4,500	1,31,500
To Bank A/c (Realisation Expenses)		7,000	By Aadish's Capital A/c (Stock)		20,000
			By Shreyansh's Capital A/c (Investment) (15,000 – 1,500)		13,500
			By Loss Transferred to Capital A/c		
			Aadish	3,000	
			Shreyansh	2,000	5,000
		2,92,000			2,92,000

Solved Question 11 Archana, Vandana and Arti were partners in a firm sharing profits and losses in the ratio of 5 : 3 : 2. Their balance sheet on 31st March, 2023 was as follows

Balance Sheet of Archana, Vandana and Arti
as at 31st March, 2023

Liabilities		Amt (₹)	Assets	Amt (₹)
Capital A/cs			Investments	80,000
Archana	80,000		Plant	1,00,000
Vandana	70,000		Stock	40,000
Arti	60,000	2,10,000	Debtors	50,000
General Reserve		30,000	Cash at Bank	30,000
Creditors		60,000		
		3,00,000		3,00,000

The firm was dissolved on the above date

(i) Assets were realised as follows
Debtors ₹ 40,000, Stock ₹ 50,000, Plant ₹ 60,000

(ii) 25% of the investments were taken over by Vandana at ₹ 18,000. Remaining investments were taken over by Archana at 10% less than its book value.

(iii) Expenses of realisation ₹ 20,000 were paid by Arti.

Prepare realisation account. **CBSE 2024**

Sol. Dr **Realisation Account** Cr

Particulars	Amt (₹)	Particulars		Amt (₹)
To Investments A/c	80,000	By Creditors A/c		60,000
To Plant A/c	1,00,000	By Bank A/c		
To Stock	40,000	Debtors	40,000	
To Debtors A/c	50,000	Stock	50,000	
To Bank	60,000	Plant	60,000	1,50,000
To Arti's Capital A/c	20,000	By Vandana's Capital A/c		18,000
		By Archana's Capital A/c		54,000
		By Loss Transferred to Partners' Capital A/cs		
		Archana	34,000	
		Vandana	20,400	
		Arti	13,600	68,000
	3,50,000			3,50,000

Solved Question 12 Ashish and Kanav were partners in a firm sharing profits and losses in the ratio of 3 : 2. On 31st March, 2024 their balance sheet was as follows

Balance Sheet of Ashish and Kanav
as at 31st March, 2024

Liabilities		Amt (₹)	Assets	Amt (₹)
Trade Creditors		42,000	Bank	35,000
Empolyees' Provident Fund		60,000	Stock	24,000
Mrs. Ashish's Loan		9,000	Debtors	19,000
Kanav's Loan		35,000	Furniture	40,000
Workmen's Compensation Fund		20,000	Plant	2,10,000
Investment Fluctuation Reserve		4,000	Investments	32,000
Capital A/cs			Profit and Loss A/c	10,000
Ashish	1,20,000			
Kanav	80,000	2,00,000		
		3,70,000		3,70,000

On the above date they decided to dissolve the firm.

(i) Ashish agreed to take over furniture at ₹ 38,000 and pay-off Mrs. Ashish's loan.

(ii) Debtors realised ₹ 18,500 and plant realised 10% more.

(iii) Kanav took over 40% of the stock at 20% less than the book value. Remaining stock was sold at a gain of 10%.

(iv) Trade creditors took over investments in full settlement.

(v) Kanav agreed to take over the responsibility of completing dissolution at an agreed remuneration of ₹ 12,000 and to bear realisation expenses. Actual expenses of realisation amounted to ₹ 8,000.

Prepare realisation account. **CBSE 2019**

Sol. Dr **Realisation Account** Cr

Particulars		Amt (₹)	Particulars		Amt (₹)
To Sundry Assets			By Sundry Liabilities		
Stock	24,000		Creditors	42,000	
Debtors	19,000		Employees Provident Fund	60,000	
Furniture	40,000		Mrs. Ashish's Loan	9,000	
Plant	2,10,000		Investment Fluctuation Reserve	4,000	1,15,000
Investments	32,000	3,25,000	By Ashish's Capital (Furniture)		38,000
To Ashish's Capital (Mrs. Ashish Loan)		9,000	By Kanav's Capital (40% Stock) (WN 1)		7,680
To Bank (Employees Provident Fund)		60,000	By Bank		
To Kanav's Capital (Realisation Expenses)		12,000	Debtors	18,500	
To Profit Transferred to			Plant	2,31,000	
Ashish's Capital A/c	12,012		60% Stock (WN 2)	15,840	2,65,340
Kanav's Capital A/c	8,008	20,020			
		4,26,020			4,26,020

Working Notes

		Amt (₹)
1. 40% Stock = 24,000 × 40%	=	9,600
(−) 20%	=	(1,920)
	=	7,680
2. 60% Stock = 24,000 × 60%	=	14,400
(+) 10%	=	1,440
	=	15,840

Solved Question 13 **The balance sheet of Abhishek, Aditya and Arjun sharing profits in the ratio of 3 : 2 : 1, respectively stood as follows on 31st March, 2022.**

Balance Sheet
as at 31st March, 2022

Liabilities		Amt (₹)	Assets	Amt (₹)
Creditors		2,01,600	Cash	14,800
Investment Fluctuation Fund		40,000	Stock	80,400
Reserve Fund		48,000	Debtors	2,50,400
Capital A/cs			Investments	64,000
Abhishek	1,20,000		Furniture	26,000
Aditya	80,000		Buildings	94,000
Arjun	40,000	2,40,000		
		5,29,600		5,29,600

The firm was dissolved as on that date. For the purpose of dissolution, the investments were valued at ₹ 72,000 and stock at ₹ 70,000. Abhishek agreed to take over investments and Aditya to take over stock. Arjun took over the furniture at book value. Debtors and buildings realised ₹ 2,28,000 and ₹ 1,00,000 respectively. Expenses of realisation amounted to ₹ 1,800. In addition, one bill for ₹ 2,000 under discount was dishonoured and had to be taken up by the firm. Prepare the necessary ledger accounts to close the books of the firm.

Sol. Dr **Realisation Account** Cr

Particulars		Amt (₹)	Particulars		Amt (₹)
To Stock A/c		80,400	By Creditors		2,01,600
To Debtors A/c		2,50,400	By Investment Fluctuation Fund		40,000
To Investment A/c		64,000	By Abhishek's Capital A/c		72,000
To Furniture A/c		26,000	By Aditya's Capital A/c		70,000
To Building A/c		94,000	By Arjun's Capital A/c		26,000
To Cash A/c			By Cash A/c		
Creditors	2,01,600		Debtors	2,28,000	
Realisation Expenses	1,800		Building	1,00,000	32,800
Bill Under Discount	2,000	2,05,400			
To Realisation Profit					
Abhishek	8,700				
Aditya	5,800				
Arjun	2,900	17,400			
		7,37,600			7,37,000

Dr **Partners' Capital Account** Cr

Particulars	Abhishek (₹)	Aditya (₹)	Arjun (₹)	Particulars	Abhishek (₹)	Aditya (₹)	Arjun (₹)
To Realisation A/c	72,000	70,000	26,000	By Balance b/d	1,20,000	80,000	40,000
To Cash A/c	80,700	31,800	24,900	By Realisation Profit	8,700	5,800	2,900
				By Reserve Fund	24,000	16,000	8,000
	1,52,700	1,01,800	50,900		1,52,700	1,01,800	50,900

Dr **Cash Account** Cr

Particulars	Amt (₹)	Assets	Amt (₹)
To Balance b/d	14,800	By Realisation A/c	2,05,400
To Realisation A/c	3,28,000	By Abhishek's Capital A/c	80,700
		By Aditya's Capital A/c	31,800
		By Arjun Capital A/c	24,900
	3,42,800		3,42,800

Solved Question 14 **A, B and C shared profits in the ratio of 3 : 2 : 1. They dissolved the firm and appointed A to realise the assets. A is to receive 5% commission on the sale of assets (except cash) and is to bear all expenses of realisation. The position of the firm was as follows**

Balance Sheet
as at 31st March, 2024

Liabilities		Amt (₹)	Assets	Amt (₹)
Bank Overdraft		12,500	Cash in Hand	11,250
Creditors		30,000	Debtors	26,150
Provident Fund		6,000	Stock	18,000
Investment Fluctuation Fund		3,000	Investments	7,500
Commission Received in Advance		4,000	Plant	45,600
Capital A/cs			Profit and Loss A/c	27,000
A	45,000			
B	30,000			
C	5,000	80,000		
		1,35,500		1,35,500

Additional Information

(i) **A realised the assets are follows debtors ₹ 15,000; Stock ₹ 13,000; Investment at 75% value; Plant at ₹ 21,375. Expenses of realisation met by A amounted to ₹ 2,050.**

(ii) **Commission received in advance in returned to the customers after deducting ₹ 1,500 for work done.**

(iii) Firm had to pay ₹ 3,600 for outstanding salaries, not provided for earlier.
(iv) Compensation to employees paid by firm amounted to ₹ 4,900. This liability was not provided for in the above balance sheet.
(v) ₹ 12,500 had to be paid for provident fund.

Prepare necessary accounts.

Sol. Dr **Realisation Account** Cr

Particulars	Amt (₹)	Particulars		Amt (₹)
To Debtors	26,150	By Bank Overdraft (WN 3)		12,500
To Stock	18,000	By Creditors		30,000
To Investments	7,500	By Provident Fund		6,000
To Plant	45,600	By Investment Fluctuation Fund		3,000
To A's Capital A/c (5% on 55,000)	2,750	By Commission Received in Advance		4,000
To Bank A/c (Advance Commission Returned)	2,500	By Bank A/c		
To Bank A/c (Outstanding Salaries Paid)	3,600	Debtors	15,000	
To Bank A/c (Compensation Paid)	4,900	Stock	13,000	
To Bank A/c (Bank Overdraft Paid)	12,500	Investments	5,625	
To Bank A/c (Creditors and Provident Fund)	42,500	Plant	21,375	55,000
		By Loss Transferred to		
		A's Capital A/c	27,750	
		B's Capital A/c	18,500	
		C's Capital A/c	9,250	55,500
	1,66,000			1,66,000

Dr **Partners' Capital Account** Cr

Particulars	A (₹)	B (₹)	C (₹)	Particulars	A (₹)	B (₹)	C (₹)
To Profit and Loss A/c	13,500	9,000	4,500	By Balance b/d	45,000	30,000	5,000
To Realisation A/c (Loss)	27,750	18,500	9,250	By Realisation A/c (Commission)	2,750	—	—
To Bank A/c	6,500	2,500	—	By Bank A/c	—	—	8,750
	47,750	30,000	13,750		47,750	30,000	13,750

Dr **Bank Account** Cr

Particulars	Amt (₹)	Particulars	Amt (₹)
To Cash A/c (Deposited)	11,250	By Realisation A/c (Commission Returned)	2,500
To Realisation A/c (Assets Realised)	55,000	By Realisation A/c (Outstanding Salary)	3,600
To C's Capital A/c	8,750	By Realisation A/c (Compensation)	4,900
		By Realisation A/c (Bank Overdraft)	12,500
		By Realisation A/c (Creditors and Provident Fund)	42,500
		By A's Capital A/c	6,500
		By B's Capital A/c	2,500
	75,000		75,000

Working Notes

1. There will be no entry for the expenses of realisation, as these are met by A personally.
2. Following entry be passed for commission payable to A on the sale of assets

Realisation A/c	Dr	2,750	
To A's Capital A/c			2,750

3. Bank overdraft will be first transferred to credit of realisation account and then paid-off.

Comprehensive Illustrations

Solved Question 15 **Following is the balance sheet of X and Y as at 31st March, 2024**

Balance Sheet
as at 31st March, 2024

Liabilities	Amt (₹)	Assets	Amt (₹)
Sundry Creditors	30,000	Cash in Hand	500
Bills Payable	8,000	Cash at Bank	8,000

Liabilities		Amt (₹)	Assets		Amt (₹)
Mrs. X's Loan		5,000	Stock-in-trade		5,000
Mrs. Y's Loan		10,000	Investments		10,000
General Reserve		10,000	Debtors	20,000	
Investments Fluctuation Fund		1,000	(–) Provision for Doubtful Debts	(2,000)	18,000
Capital A/cs			Plant and Machinery		20,000
X	10,000		Building		15,000
Y	10,000	20,000	Goodwill		4,000
			Profit and Loss A/c		3,500
		84,000			84,000

The firm was dissolved on 31st March, 2024 and following was agreed

(i) X promised to pay Mrs. X's loan and took stock-in-trade at ₹ 4,000.

(ii) Y took half the investments @ 10% discount.

(iii) Debtors realised ₹ 19,000.

(iv) Creditors and bills payable were due on an average basis of one month after 31st March, but they were paid immediately on 31st March @ 6% discount per annum.

(v) Plant realised ₹ 25,000, building ₹ 40,000, goodwill ₹ 6,000 and remaining investments at ₹ 4,500.

(vi) There was an old typewriter in the firm which had been written-off completely from the books. It is now estimated to realise ₹ 300. It was taken away by Y at this estimated price.

(vii) Realisation expenses were ₹ 1,000.

Show the realisation account, partners' capital account and bank account in the books of the firm.

Sol. Dr **Realisation Account** Cr

Particulars		Amt (₹)	Particulars		Amt (₹)
To Sundry Assets A/c			By Sundry Liabilities A/c		
Stock-in-trade	5,000		Sundry Creditors	30,000	
Investments	10,000		Bills Payable	8,000	
Debtors	20,000		Mrs. X's Loan	5,000	
Plant and Machinery	20,000		Mrs. Y's Loan	10,000	
Building	15,000		Investments Fluctuation Fund	1,000	
Goodwill	4,000	74,000	Provision for Doubtful Debts	2,000	56,000
To X's Capital A/c (Mrs. X's Loan)		5,000	By X's Capital A/c (Stock)		4,000
To Bank A/c (Liabilities Paid)			By Y's Capital A/c (Investments)		4,500
Creditors (30,000 – 150) (WN)	29,850		By Bank A/c (Assets Realised)		
Bills Payable (8,000 – 40) (WN)	7,960		Debtors	19,000	
Realisation Expenses	1,000		Plant and Machinery	25,000	
Mrs. Y's Loan	10,000	48,810	Building	40,000	
To Profit Transferred to			Goodwill	6,000	
X's Capital A/c	15,745		Investments	4,500	94,500
Y's Capital A/c	15,745	31,490	By Y's Capital A/c (Typewriter)		300
		1,59,300			1,59,300

Dr **Partners' Capital Account** Cr

Particulars	X (₹)	Y (₹)	Particulars	X (₹)	Y (₹)
To Realisation A/c	4,000	4,500	By Balance b/d	10,000	10,000
To Realisation A/c	—	300	By Realisation A/c	5,000	—
To Profit and Loss A/c	1,750	1,750	By Realisation A/c (Profit)	15,745	15,745
To Bank A/c (Final Settlement)	29,995	24,195	By General Reserve A/c	5,000	5,000
	35,745	30,745		35,745	30,745

Dr **Bank Account** Cr

Particulars	Amt (₹)	Particulars	Amt (₹)
To Balance b/d	8,000	By Realisation A/c (Liabilities Paid)	48,810
To Cash A/c	500	By X's Capital A/c (Final Payment)	29,995
To Realisation A/c (Assets Realised)	94,500	By Y's Capital A/c (Final Payment)	24,195
	1,03,000		1,03,000

Working Note

Discount on creditors $= 30,000 \times \frac{6}{100} \times \frac{1}{12} =$ ₹ 150; Discount on bills payable $= 8,000 \times \frac{6}{100} \times \frac{1}{12} =$ ₹ 40

Solved Question 16 Abhay, Bikram and Chris were partners in a firm sharing profits and losses equally. They decided to dissolve their partnership firm on 31st March, 2023. The firm's balance sheet on the data of dissolution was as follows

Balance Sheet of Abhay, Bikram and Chris
as at 31st March, 2023

Liabilities		Amt (₹)	Assets	Amt (₹)
Capital A/cs			Plant and Machinery	80,000
Abhay	68,000		Furniture	45,000
Bikram	1,00,000		Motor Car	1,25,000
Chris	77,000	2,45,000	Stock	30,000
Creditors		1,20,000	Debtors	70,000
			Cash at Bank	15,000
		3,65,000		3,65,000

The following information is available

(i) **Plant and machinery was taken over by Abhay at an agreed valuation of ₹ 75,000.**
(ii) **Furniture realised ₹ 40,000.**
(iii) **Motor car was taken over by Bikram for ₹ 1,30,000.**
(iv) **Debtors realised 10% less.**
(v) **10% of the stock was taken over by Chris for ₹ 4,500. The remaining stock was sold for ₹ 30,000.**
(vi) **Realisation expenses amounted to ₹ 5,000.**

Prepare realisation account. **CBSE 2024**

Sol. Dr **Realisation Account** Cr

Particulars		Amt (₹)	Particulars		Amt (₹)
To Sundary Assets			By Sundry Liabilities		
Plant and Machinery	80,000		Creditors		1,20,000
Furniture	45,000		By Abhay's Capital A/c (P & M)		75,000
Motor Car	1,25,000		By Bikram's Capital A/c (Car)		1,30,000
Stock	30,000		By Chris's Capital A/c (Stock)		4,500
Debtors	70,000	3,50,000	By Bank A/c		
To Bank A/c			Debtors	63,000	
Expenses	5,000		Stock	30,000	
Creditors	1,20,000	1,25,000	Furniture	40,000	1,33,000
			By Loss Transferred to Partners' Capital A/cs		
			Abhay	4,166	
			Bikram	4,167	
			Chris	4,167	12,500
		4,75,000			4,75,000

Solved Question 17 X, Y and Z sharing profits equally, dissolved their firm on 30th March, 2024, on which date their balance sheet was as follows

Balance Sheet
as at 31st March, 2024

Liabilities		Amt (₹)	Assets		Amt (₹)
Sundry Creditors		3,100	Bank		630
Reserve for Contingency		1,800	Debtors		5,500
Profit and Loss A/c		1,200	Stock		8,100
X's Wife Loan		1,200	Furniture		2,000
Bank Loan at 12%		2,000	Plant		5,370
Capital A/cs			Current A/c		
X	6,000		Z		2,200
Y	5,000				
Z	2,000	13,000			
Current A/cs					
X	1,000				
Y	500	1,500			
		23,800			23,800

Additional Information

(i) There is a bill for ₹ 500 under discount. This bill was received from 'Z'. Z proved insolvent and 60% were received from his estate.

(ii) It was found that an investment not recorded in the books is worth ₹ 800. This is taken over by one of the creditors at this value.

(iii) X agreed to accept furniture in full settlement of his wife's loan.

(iv) Bank loan was repaid alongwith interest for nine months.

(v) Assets realised as follows debtors ₹ 2,450, stock ₹ 6,000, plant ₹ 2,800.

Prepare necessary accounts.

Sol. Dr **Realisation Account** Cr

Particulars	Amt (₹)	Particulars		Amt (₹)
To Debtors	5,500	By Sundry Creditors		3,100
To Stock	8,100	By X's Wife Loan		1,200
To Furniture	2,000	By Bank Loan at 12%		2,000
To Plant	5,370	By Bank (Assets Realised)		11,250
To Bank (Payment for Bill Discounted)	500	By Bank (Recovery from B/R Dishonoured)		300
To Bank (Payment to Creditors 3,100 – 800)	2,300	By Loss Transferred to		
To Bank (Payment of Bank Loan)	2,180	X's Current A/c	2,700	
		Y's Current A/c	2,700	
		Z's Current A/c	2,700	8,100
	25,950			25,950

Dr **Partners' Current Account** Cr

Particulars	X (₹)	Y (₹)	Z (₹)	Particulars	X (₹)	Y (₹)	Z (₹)
To Balance b/d	—	—	2,200	By Balance b/d	1,000	500	—
To Realisation A/c (Loss)	2,700	2,700	2,700	By Reserve for Contingency	600	600	600
				By Profit and Loss A/c	400	400	400
				By Capital A/c (Transfer)	700	1,200	3,900
	2,700	2,700	4,900		2,700	2,700	4,900

Dr **Partners' Capital Account** Cr

Particulars	X (₹)	Y (₹)	Z (₹)	Particulars	X (₹)	Y (₹)	Z (₹)
To Current A/c (Transfer)	700	1,200	3,900	By Balance b/d	6,000	5,000	2,000
To Bank A/c (Final Payment)	5,300	3,800	—	By Bank A/c (Deficit brought in)	—	—	1,900
	6,000	5,000	3,900		6,000	5,000	3,900

Dr **Bank Account** Cr

Particulars	Amt (₹)	Particulars	Amt (₹)
To Balance b/d	630	By Realisation A/c (Bill Discounted)	500
To Realisation A/c (Assets Realised)	11,250	By Realisation A/c (Creditors)	2,300
To Realisation A/c (Recovery from B/R Dishonoured)	300	By Realisation A/c (Bank Loan)	2,180
To Z's Capital A/c	1,900	By X's Capital A/c	5,300
		By Y's Capital A/c	3,800
	14,080		14,080

Working Notes

1. The firm has to pay ₹ 500 to the bank for the dishonour of the discounted bill, of which 60% i.e. ₹ 300 has been received from Z. Following entries will be passed for it

(i) Bank A/c	Dr	300	
To Realisation A/c			300
(ii) Realisation A/c	Dr	500	
To Bank A/c			500

2. No separate entry will be passed for the investments of ₹ 800, as these are taken over by the creditors. Creditors will be paid at the net figure of 3,100 − 800 = ₹ 2,300.
3. Wife's loan has not been paid in cash. It has been settled by giving away furniture. Therefore, no entry will be passed for the discharge of wife's loan.
4. When partner's current accounts are given in the question, it means that the capitals are fixed. In such a case profit or loss on realisation, accumulated profits and reserves should be transferred to current accounts.

Solved Question 18 **Pratham and Mohit were partners in a firm sharing profits in the ratio of 3 : 2. The court ordered for the dissolution of their partnership firm on 31st March, 2024. Pratham was deputed to realise the assets and to pay the liabilities. He was paid ₹ 1,000 as commission for his services. The financial position of the firm on 31st March, 2024 was as follows**

Balance Sheet
as at 31st March, 2024

Liabilities		Amt (₹)	Assets		Amt (₹)
Creditors		80,000	Building		1,20,000
Mrs. Pratham's Loan		40,000	Investments		30,600
Mohit's Loan		24,000	Debtors	34,000	
Investment Fluctuation Fund		8,000	(−) Provision for Doubtful Debts	(4,000)	30,000
Capital A/cs			Bills Receivable		37,400
Pratham	42,000		Cash		6,000
Mohit	42,000	84,000	Profit and Loss A/c		8,000
			Goodwill		4,000
		2,36,000			2,36,000

Following was agreed upon

(i) Pratham agreed to pay-off his wife's loan.
(ii) Debtors realised ₹ 24,000.
(iii) Mohit took away all investments at ₹ 27,000.
(iv) Building realised ₹ 1,52,000.
(v) Creditors were payable after 2 months. They were paid immediately at 10% discount.
(vi) Bills receivable were settled at a loss of ₹ 1,400.
(vii) Realisation expenses amounted to ₹ 2,500.

Prepare realisation account, partner's capital account and cash account to close the books of the firm.

Sol. Dr **Realisation Account** Cr

Particulars		Amt (₹)	Particulars		Amt (₹)
To Building		1,20,000	By Creditors		80,000
To Investments		30,600	By Mrs. Pratham's Loan		40,000
To Debtors		34,000	By Investment Fluctuation Fund		8,000
To Bills Receivable		37,400	By Provision for Doubtful Debts		4,000
To Goodwill		4,000	By Cash A/c		
To Pratham's Capital A/c		40,000	Debtors	24,000	
To Cash A/c – Creditors		72,000	Building	1,52,000	
To Pratham's capital A/c (Realisation Expenses)		1,000	Bills Receivable	36,000	2,12,000
To Profit Transferred to Partner's Capital A/cs			By Mohit's Capital A/c		27,000
Pratham	19,200				
Mohit	12,800	32,000			
		3,71,000			3,71,000

Dr **Partners' Capital Account** Cr

Particulars	Pratham (₹)	Mohit (₹)	Particulars	Pratham (₹)	Mohit (₹)
To Realisation A/c		27,000	By Balance b/d	42,000	42,000
To Profit and Loss A/c	4,800	3,200	By Realisation A/c	41,000	—
To Cash A/c	97,400	24,600	By Realisation Profit	19,200	12,800
	1,02,200	54,800		1,02,200	54,800

Dr **Cash Account** Cr

Particulars	Amt (₹)	Particulars	Amt (₹)
To Balance b/d	6,000	By Realisation A/c	72,000
To Realisation A/c	2,12,000	By Mohits' Loan	24,000
		By Pratham's Capital A/c	97,400
		By Mohit's Capital A/c	24,600
	2,18,000		2,18,000

Solved Question 19 **Anju, Manju and Sanju who were sharing profits in the ratio of 2 : 2 : 1 decided to dissolve the firm when their balance sheet was as follows**

Balance Sheet
as at 31st March, 2024

Liabilities		Amt (₹)	Assets	Amt (₹)
Creditors		50,000	Cash	60,000
Bank Loan		35,000	Debtors	75,000
Employees' Provident Fund		15,000	Stock	40,000
Investment Fluctuation Fund		10,000	Investments	20,000
Commission Received in Advance		8,000	Plant	50,000
Capital A/cs			Profit and Loss A/c	3,000
Anju	50,000			
Manju	50,000			
Sanju	30,000	1,30,000		
		2,48,000		2,48,000

Anju was appointed to realise the assets. Anju was to receive 5% commission on the sale of assets (except cash) and was to bear all expenses of realisation. Anju realised the assets as follows

Debtors 20% less, stock ₹ 35,500, investments 80%, plant 90% of the book value.

Expenses of realisation amounted to ₹ 7,500 paid by the firm on Anju's behalf. Commission received in advance was returned to the customers after deducting ₹ 3,000. Firm had to pay ₹ 8,500 of outstanding salary not provided for earlier. Compensation paid to employees amounted to ₹ 17,000. This liability was not provided for in the above balance sheet ₹ 20,000 has to be paid for provident fund. Prepare realisation account, capital accounts of partners and cash account.

Sol. Dr **Realisation Account** Cr

Particulars		Amt (₹)	Particulars		Amt (₹)
To Sundry Assets A/c			By Sundry Liabilities A/c		
Debtors	75,000		Creditors	50,000	
Stock	40,000		Bank Loan	35,000	
Investments	20,000		Employees' Provident Fund	15,000	
Plant	50,000	1,85,000	Investment Fluctuation Fund	10,000	1,10,000
To Cash A/c			By Commission Received in Advance		8,000
Creditors	50,000		By Cash A/c		
Bank Loan	35,000		Debtors	60,000	
Provident Fund	20,000		Stock	35,500	
Commission Received in Advance	5,000		Investments	16,000	
Outstanding Salaries	8,500		Plant	45,000	1,56,500
Compensation	17,000	1,35,500	By Realisation Loss Transferred to		
To Anju's Capital A/c (Commission)		7,825	Anju's Capital A/c	21,530	
			Manju's Capital A/c	21,530	
			Sanju's Capital A/c	10,765	53,825
		3,28,325			3,28,325

Dr **Partners' Capital Account** Cr

Particulars	Anju (₹)	Manju (₹)	Sanju (₹)	Particulars	Anju (₹)	Manju (₹)	Sanju (₹)
To Profit and Loss A/c	1,200	1,200	600	By Balance b/d	50,000	50,000	30,000
To Realisation A/c	21,530	21,530	10,765	By Realisation A/c	7,825	—	—
To Cash A/c	7,500	—	—				
To Cash A/c (Final Payment)	27,595	27,270	18,635				
	57,825	50,000	30,000		57,825	50,000	30,000

Dr **Cash Account** Cr

Particulars	Amt (₹)	Particulars	Amt (₹)
To Balance b/d	60,000	By Realisation A/c	1,35,500
To Realisation A/c	1,56,500	By Anju's Capital A/c (Realisation Expenses)	7,500
		By Anju's Capital A/c	27,595
		By Manju's Capital A/c	27,270
		By Sanju's Capital A/c	18,635
	2,16,500		2,16,500

Solved Question 20 **P and Q sharing profits and losses in the ratio of 3 : 2 agreed upon the dissolution of the firm on 31st March, 2024 at which date their balance sheet was as follows**

Balance Sheet
as at 31st March, 2024

Liabilities		Amt (₹)	Assets		Amt (₹)
Trade Creditors		40,000	Cash		3,000
Bills Payable		12,500	Bank		15,000
Loan by Q		7,500	Stock		40,000
Reserve		17,000	Sundry Debtors	33,000	
Profit and Loss A/c		5,500	(−) Provision for Doubtful Debts	(3,000)	30,000
Capital A/cs			Loan to P		5,000
P	45,000		Plant and Machinery		15,000
Q	15,000	60,000	Land and Building		16,500
			Furniture		5,000
			Goodwill		7,500
			Prepaid Insurance		500
			Advertisement Expenditure		5,000
		1,42,500			1,42,500

The firm was dissolved on the given data and following transactions took place

(i) P took 50% of the stock at a discount of 20%.
(ii) Remaining stock was sold at a profit of 30%.
(iii) ₹ 6,000 out of sundry debtors were not recovered.
(iv) Land and building realised ₹ 70,000.
(v) Half of the trade creditors accepted plant and machinery at 10% less than the book value and cash of ₹ 2,500 in full settlement of their claims.
(vi) Remaining trade creditors were paid at a discount of 10%.
(vii) Realisation expenses were ₹ 2,500.
(viii) X an old customer, whose account was written-off as bad debt in the previous year, paid ₹ 250.
(ix) A contingent liability of ₹ 500 was discharged.
(x) Furniture was sold for ₹ 5,000.

Prepare realisation account, partner's loan account, partners' capital account and bank account.

Sol. Dr **Realisation Account** Cr

Particulars		Amt (₹)	Particulars		Amt (₹)
To Sundry Assets (Transfer)			By Provision for Doubtful Debts		3,000
Stock	40,000		By Trade Creditors		40,000
Sundry Debtors	33,000		By Bills Payable		12,500
Plant and Machinery	15,000		By P's Capital A/c (Stock)		16,000
Land and Building	16,500		By Bank A/c (Assets Realised)		
Furniture	5,000		Stock (Remaining)	26,000	
Goodwill	7,500		Sundry Debtors	27,000	
Prepaid Insurance	500	1,17,500	Land and Building	70,000	
To Bank A/c (Liabilities Paid)			Furniture	5,000	1,28,000
Trade Creditors	20,500		By Bank A/c (Bad Debts Recovered)		250
Bills Payable	12,500	33,000			
To Bank A/c (Realisation Expenses)		2,500			
To Bank A/c (Unrecorded Liability)		500			

Particulars		Amt (₹)	Particulars	Amt (₹)
To Gain (Profit) on Realisation Transfered to				
P's Capital A/c	27,750			
Q's Capital A/c	18,500	46,250		
		1,99,750		1,99,750

Dr **Loan by Q's Account** Cr

Particulars	Amt (₹)	Particulars	Amt (₹)
To Bank A/c	7,500	By Balance c/d	7,500

Dr **Partners' Capital Account** Cr

Particulars	P (₹)	Q (₹)	Particulars	P (₹)	Q (₹)
To Realisation A/c (Stock)	16,000	—	By Balance b/d	45,000	15,000
To Advertisement Expenditure A/c	3,000	2,000	By Realisation A/c (Gain/Profit)	27,750	18,500
To Loan to P's A/c	5,000	—	By Reserve A/c	10,200	6,800
To Bank A/c (Final Payment)	62,250	40,500	By Profit and Loss A/c	3,300	2,200
	86,250	42,500		86,250	42,500

Dr **Loan to P's Account** Cr

Particulars	Amt (₹)	Particulars	Amt (₹)
To Balance b/d	5,000	By P's Capital A/c	5,000

Dr **Bank Account** Cr

Particulars	Amt (₹)	Particulars	Amt (₹)
To Balance c/d	15,000	By Realisation A/c (Liabilities Paid)	33,000
To Cash A/c	3,000	By Realisation A/c (Expenses)	2,500
To Realisation A/c (Assets Realised)	1,28,000	By Realisation A/c (Unrecorded Liability)	500
To Realisation A/c (Bad Debts Recovered)	250	By Q's Loan A/c	7,500
		By P's Capital A/c (Final Payment)	62,250
		By Q's Capital A/c (Final Payment)	40,500
	1,46,250		1,46,250

Missing Information

Solved Question 21 **M, N and K were partners sharing profits in the ratio of 3 : 2 : 1. On 1st March, 2024, their firm was dissolved. The assets were realised and liabilities were paid-off. The accountant prepared realisation account, partners' capital account and cash account, but forgot to post few amounts in these accounts. You are required to complete these below given accounts by posting correct amounts.**

Dr **Realisation Account** Cr

Particulars		Amt (₹)	Particulars		Amt (₹)
To Sundry Assets A/c			By Provision for Doubtful Debts A/c		1,000
Machinery	10,000		By Sundry Creditors A/c		15,000
Stock	21,000		By S's Loan A/c		13,000
Debtors	20,000		By Repairs and Renewals Reserve A/c		1,200
Prepaid Insurance	400		By Cash A/c (Assets Sold)		
Investments	3,000	54,400	Machinery	8,000	
To M's Capital A/c (S's Loan)		13,000	Stock	14,000	
To Cash A/c (Creditors Paid)		15,000	Debtors	16,000	38,000

Particulars	Amt (₹)	Particulars	Amt (₹)
To Cash A/c (Dishonoured Bill Paid)	5,000	By M's Capital A/c (Investments)	2,000
To Cash A/c (Expenses)	800	By	...
	88,200		88,200

Dr **Partners' Capital Account** Cr

Particulars	M (₹)	N (₹)	K (₹)	Particulars	M (₹)	N (₹)	K (₹)
To ...	...	...	...	By	...	...	...
To ...	...	...	...	By	...	...	...
To Cash A/c	12,000	9,000	...	By Cash A/c	...	...	1,000
	23,000	15,000	3,000		23,000	15,000	3,000

Dr **Cash Account** Cr

Particulars	Amt (₹)	Particulars	Amt (₹)
To Balance b/d	2,800	By Realisation A/c (Creditors Paid)	15,000
To Realisation A/c (Sale of Assets)	38,000	By Dishonoured Bill A/c	5,000
To K's Capital A/c	1,000	By	...
		By M's Capital A/c	12,000
		By N's Capital A/c	9,000
	41,800		41,800

Sol. Dr **Realisation Account** Cr

Particulars		Amt (₹)	Particulars		Amt (₹)
To Sundry Assets A/c			By Provision for Doubtful Debts A/c		1,000
Machinery	10,000		By Sundry Creditors A/c		15,000
Stock	21,000		By S's Loan A/c		13,000
Debtors	20,000		By Repairs and Renewals Reserve A/c		1,200
Prepaid Insurance	400		By Cash A/c (Assets Sold)		
Investments	3,000	54,400	Machinery	8,000	
To M's Capital A/c (S's Loan)		13,000	Stock	14,000	
To Cash A/c (Creditors Paid)		15,000	Debtors	16,000	38,000
To Cash A/c (Dishonoured Bill Paid)		5,000	By M's Capital A/c (Investments)		2,000
To Cash A/c (Expenses)		800	By **Loss Transferred to**		
			M's Capital A/c	**9,000**	
			N's Capital A/c	**6,000**	
			K's Capital A/c	**3,000**	**18,000**
		88,200			88,200

Dr **Partners' Capital Account** Cr

Particulars	M (₹)	N (₹)	K (₹)	Particulars	M (₹)	N (₹)	K (₹)
To **Realisation A/c** (Investments)	**2,000**	—	—	By **Balance b/d**	**10,000**	**15,000**	**2,000**
To **Realisation A/c** (Loss)	**9,000**	**6,000**	**3,000**	By **Realisation A/c** (S's Loan)	**13,000**	—	—
To Cash A/c	12,000	9,000	—	By Cash A/c	—	—	1,000
	23,000	15,000	3,000		23,000	15,000	3,000

Dr **Cash Account** Cr

Particulars	Amt (₹)	Particulars	Amt (₹)
To Balance b/d	2,800	By Realisation A/c (Creditors Paid)	15,000
To Realisation A/c (Sale of Assets)	38,000	By Dishonoured Bill A/c	5,000
To K's Capital A/c	1,000	By **Expenses Paid A/c**	**800**
		By M's Capital A/c	12,000
		By N's Capital A/c	9,000
	41,800		41,800

Solved Question 22 B, S and I were partners in a firm sharing profits in the ratio of 5 : 3 : 1. On 31st March, 2024 their firm was dissolved. Given below are the realisation account, partners' capital account and bank account of the firm. You are required to complete these accounts by posting the correct amounts.

Dr **Realisation Account** Cr

Particulars		Amt (₹)	Particulars		Amt (₹)
To Stock		25,000	By Provision for Doubtful Debts		12,500
To Debtors		62,500	By Sundry Creditors		41,500
To Plant and Machinery		1,00,000	By Bills Payable		8,500
To Bank A/c			By Mortgage Loan		37,500
Sundry Creditors	40,000		By Bank – Assets Realised		
Bills Payable	8,500		Stock	16,750	
Mortgage Loan	37,500	86,000	Debtors	31,250	
To Bank (Outstanding Repairs)		1,000	Plant and Machinery	90,000	1,38,000
To Bank (Expenses)		1,550	By Bank – Unrecorded Assets Realised		15,550
			By		...
		2,76,050			2,76,050

Dr **Partners' Capital Account** Cr

Particulars	B (₹)	S (₹)	I (₹)	Particulars	B (₹)	S (₹)	I (₹)
....	...	...	...	By Balance b/d	55,000	45,000	25,000
....	...	...	...	By General Reserve	6,250	3,750	1,250
	61,250	48,750	26,250		61,250	48,750	26,250

Dr **Bank Account** Cr

Particulars	Amt (₹)	Particulars	Amt (₹)
To Balance b/d	48,750	By Realisation (Liabilities)	86,000
To Realisation (Assets Realised)	1,38,000	By Realisation (Unrecorded Liabilities)	1,000
....	...	By	...
		By	...
	2,02,300		2,02,300

Sol. Dr **Realisation Account** Cr

Particulars	Amt (₹)	Particulars	Amt (₹)
To Stock	25,000	By Provision for Doubtful Debts	12,500
To Debtors	62,500	By Sundry Creditors	41,500
To Plant and Machinery	1,00,000	By Bills Payable	8,500

Particulars		Amt (₹)	Particulars		Amt (₹)
To Bank			By Mortgage Loan		37,500
Sundry Creditors	40,000		By Bank – Assets Realised		
Bills Payable	8,500		Stock	16,750	
Mortgage Loan	37,500	86,000	Debtors	31,250	
To Bank (Outstanding Repairs)		1,000	Plant and Machinery	90,000	1,38,000
To Bank (Expenses)		1,550	By Bank – Unrecorded Assets Realised		15,550
			By Loss Transferred to Partner's Capital A/cs		
			B	**12,500**	
			S	**7,500**	
			I	**2,500**	**22,500**
		2,76,050			2,76,050

Dr **Partners' Capital Account** Cr

Particulars	B (₹)	S (₹)	I (₹)	Particulars	B (₹)	S (₹)	I (₹)
To Realisation A/c	**12,500**	**7,500**	**2,500**	By Balance b/d	55,000	45,000	25,000
To Bank A/c (Balancing Figure)	**48,750**	**41,250**	**23,750**	By General Reserve	6,250	3,750	1,250
	61,250	48,750	26,250		61,250	48,750	26,250

Dr **Bank Account** Cr

Particulars	Amt (₹)	Particulars		Amt (₹)
To Balance b/d	48,750	By Realisation (Liabilities)		86,000
To Realisation (Assets Realised)	1,38,000	By Realisation (Unrecorded Liabilities)		1,000
To Realisation A/c (Unrecorded Assets)	15,550	**By Realisation A/c (Expenses)**		**1,550**
		By Bora's Capital A/c	**48,750**	
		By Singh's Capital A/c	**41,250**	
		By Ibrahim's Capital A/c	**23,750**	**1,13,750**
	2,02,300			2,02,300

Numerical Questions

Journal Related to Dissolution

1. Pass necessary journal entries for the following transactions at the time of dissolution of the firm

(i) Loan of ₹ 10,000 advanced by a partner to the firm was refunded.

(ii) X, a partner takes over an unrecorded asset (typewriter) at ₹ 300.

(iii) Undistributed balance (debit) of profit and loss account ₹ 30,000. The firm has three partners X, Y and Z.

(iv) The assets of the firm realised ₹ 1,25,000.

(v) Y who undertakes to carry out the dissolution proceedings is paid ₹ 2,000 for the same.

(vi) Creditors paid ₹ 28,000 in full settlement of their account of ₹ 30,000.

2. What journal entries will be passed in the books of Aman and Bhola sharing profits and losses in the ratio of 3 : 1, for the following transactions on dissolution of the firm?

(i) An unrecorded asset realised ₹ 50,000.

(ii) Stock worth ₹ 40,000 was taken by partner Aman.

(iii) Creditors were paid ₹ 60,000.

(iv) Bhola has to bear realisation expenses for which he will get ₹ 3,800. The actual expenses paid by Bholu were ₹ 3,000.

(v) There was a balance of ₹ 20,000 in the general reserve account on the date of dissolution.

(vi) Gain (profit) on realisation of ₹ 80,000 is to be distributed between partners Aman and Bhola in the ratio of 3 : 1.

3. What journal entries will be passed for the following transactions on the dissolution of a firm of partners P and Q?

(i) Old furniture which had been written-off in the books was sold for ₹ 10,000.

(ii) 'X' an old customer whose account for ₹ 5,000 was written-off as bad debt in the previous year, paid 70%.

(iii) 'P' agreed to take over firm's goodwill (Not recorded in the books of a firm) at ₹ 25,000.

(iv) There was an old computer which had been written-off from the books. It was estimated to realise ₹ 2,500. It is taken by 'Q' a partner at the estimated price less 30%.

(v) Investments costing ₹ 20,000 (Being 1,000 shares), had been written-off from the books. These investment (Shares) are valued @ ₹ 15 each and distributed between the partners in their profit sharing ratio.

4. What journal entries would be passed in the books of Jeet and Shivam sharing profits and losses in the ratio of 5 : 2, for the following transactions on the dissolution of a firm, after various assets (other than cash) and third party liabilities have been transferred to realisation account? Competency Based Que

(i) Realisation expenses amounted to ₹ 8,000. Shivam, one of the partners has to bear these expenses.

(ii) Shivam, one of the partners agreed to take over the creditor of ₹ 1,20,000 for ₹ 80,000.

(iii) Jeet, one of the partners has given a loan to the firm of ₹ 40,000. It was paid back to him at the time of dissolution.

(iv) Profit and loss account balance of ₹ 2,24,000 appeared on the assets side of the balance sheet.

(v) Deferred revenue advertising expenditure appeared at ₹ 1,12,000.

(vi) There was an unrecorded investment of ₹ 28,000.

(vii) Jeet, one of the partners has to bear all the realisation expenses for which he was given a commission of 2% of net cash realised from dissolution. Cash realised from assets was ₹ 1,00,000 and cash paid for liabilities amounted to ₹ 20,000.

5. Mohan, a partner in a firm undergoing dissolution, was entitled to a remuneration of 2% of the total assets realised, excluding cash and 10% of the amount distributed to the partners. The firm's sundry assets (including ₹ 36,000 in cash) were realised at ₹ 5,22,000, and sundry liabilities amounted to ₹ 1,41,030.

Calculate Mohan's remuneration, showing all calculations clearly and record the necessary journal entry for this remuneration.

Ans. Remuneration Payable to Mohan = ₹ 47,817

6. Journalise the following

(i) Expenses of realisation ₹ 4,000.

(ii) Expenses of realisation ₹ 5,000 were paid by a partner.

(iii) Realisation expenses of ₹ 6,000 were to be met by P, a partner but were paid by the firm.

(iv) X, a partner, was paid remuneration of ₹ 5,000 and he was to meet all expenses.

(v) Y, a partner, was paid remuneration of ₹ 7,500 and he was to meet all expenses.
Actual expenses amounted to ₹ 10,000 which were paid by the firm.

(vi) Realisation expenses amounting to ₹ 7,500 were paid by the firm. ₹ 5,000 were to be borne by a partner and the balance by the firm.

(vii) Z, a partner was allowed a remuneration of ₹ 12,500 and he was to meet all expenses. Firm paid an expense of ₹ 2,500.

7. **Pass the necessary journal entries for the following transactions on dissolution of the firm of Avyan and Shruti after various assets (other than cash) and third party liabilities have been transferred to realisation account.** **CBSE 2024**

(i) Sundry creditors amounting to ₹ 40,000 were settled at a discount of 10%.

(ii) An unrecorded computer of ₹ 50,000 was taken over by Shruit.

(iii) Creditors of ₹ 5,000 agreed to take over debtors of ₹ 8,000 in full settlement of their claim.

(iv) The firm had a debit balance of ₹ 42,000 in the profit and loss account on the date of dissolution.

(v) There was an old furniture with the firm which had been written-off completely from the books. This was sold for ₹ 9,000.

(vi) Realisation expenses amounting to ₹ 11,000 were paid by Shruti.

8. **Asha and Jaya are partners. They decided to dissolve their firm. Pass necessary entries assuming that various assets and external liabilities have been transferred to realisation account.** **Competency Based Que**

(i) Asha's loan was appearing on the liabilities side of balance sheet at ₹ 4,000. She accepted an unrecorded asset of ₹ 6,000 in full settlement of her account.

(ii) P, a creditor to whom ₹ 2,500 were due to be paid, accepted an unrecorded computer of ₹ 1,800 at a discount of 10% and the balance was paid to him in cash.

(iii) Q, an unrecorded creditor of ₹ 4,000 accepted an unrecorded vehicle of ₹ 2,000 at ₹ 2,500 and the balance was paid to him in cash.

(iv) There was a contingent liability in respect of bill discounted but not matured ₹ 2,000.

(v) Furniture of ₹ 2,000 and goodwill of ₹ 3,000 were appearing in the balance sheet but no other information was provided regarding these two items.

9. Sun and Kiran are partners sharing profits and losses equally. They decided to dissolve their firm assets and liabilities have been transferred to realisation account.

Pass necessary journal entries for the following **CBSE SQP 2024**

(i) All partners are agreed that the process of realisation at the time dissolution will be accomplished by Sun for which he will be paid ₹ 10,000 along with the amount of expense which amounted to 2% of total value realised from the assets on dissolution. Some assets were sold for cash at a cumulative value of ₹ 12,00,000 and the remaining were taken over by creditors at a valuation of ₹ 3,00,000.

(ii) Deferred advertisement expenditure account appeared in the books at ₹ 28,000.

(iii) Out of the stock of ₹ 1,20,000; Kiran (a partner) took over 1/3 of the stock at a discount of 25% and 50% of remaining stock was took over by a creditor of ₹ 30,000 in full settlement of his claim. Balance amount of stock was realised at ₹ 25,000.

(iv) An outstanding bill for repairs and renewal of ₹ 3,000 was settled through an unrecorded asset which was valued at ₹ 10,000. Balance being settled in cash.

10. **Pass necessary journal entries on the dissolution of a firm in the following cases** **Competency Based Que**

(i) X, a partner was appointed to look after the process of dissolution at a remuneration of ₹ 1,200 and he had to bear the dissolution expenses. Dissolution expenses ₹ 1,100 were paid by X.

(ii) Y, a partner was appointed to look after the process of dissolution and was allowed a remuneration of ₹ 1,500. Y agreed to bear dissolution expenses. Actual dissolution expenses ₹ 1,600 were paid by Z another partner on behalf of Y.

(iii) P, a partner was to look after the process of dissolution and for this work she was allowed a remuneration of ₹ 700. P agreed to bear dissolution expenses. Actual dissolution expenses ₹ 600 were paid from the firm's bank account.

(iv) Q, a partner, agreed to do the work of dissolution for ₹ 750. He took away stock of the same amount as his commission. The stock had already been transferred to realisation account.

(v) R, a partner agreed to do the work of dissolution for which he was allowed a commission of ₹ 1,000. He agreed to bear the dissolution expenses. Actual dissolution expenses paid by R were ₹ 1,200. These expenses were paid by R by drawing cash from the firm.

(vi) A debtor of ₹ 800 already transferred to realisation account agreed to pay the realisation expenses of ₹ 780 in full settlement of his account.

11. Vijay and Raj were partners sharing profits in the ratio of 3 : 2.

Record the necessary journal entries for each of the following situations during the dissolution of their firm.

(i) The workmen compensation reserve was ₹ 45,000 and the corresponding liability was ₹ 56,250.
(ii) No workmen compensation reserve was available, but there was a liability of ₹ 11,250.
(iii) Both the workmen compensation reserve and the liability were ₹ 45,000.
(iv) Workmen compensation reserve amounted to ₹ 45,000, while the liability was ₹ 26,250.
(v) The workmen compensation reserve listed in the balance sheet was ₹ 56,250.

12. A and B were partners in a firm sharing profits in the ratio of 3 : 2. On 31st March, 2024 the balance sheet of the firm was as follows

Balance Sheet
as at 31st March, 2024

Liabilities		Amt (₹)	Assets	Amt (₹)
Capital A/cs			Building	2,40,000
A	3,50,000		Furniture	1,75,000
B	1,50,000	5,00,000	Debtors	80,000
Sundry Creditors		97,000	Stock	75,000
A's Loan		20,000	Cash	47,000
		6,17,000		6,17,000

The firm was dissolved on 31st March, 2024 and the assets and liabilities were settled as following

(i) Building was taken over by the creditors as their full and final payment.
(ii) A accepted an unrecorded asset of ₹ 25,000 in full settlement of his loan.
(iii) Furniture was taken over by B for cash payment at 5% less than the book value.
(iv) Debtors were collected by a debt collection agency at a cost of ₹ 5,000.
(v) Stock realised ₹ 70,500.
(vi) B agreed to bear all realisation expenses. For this service B is to be allowed ₹ 500. Actual expenses on realisation amounted to ₹ 1,000.

Pass necessary journal entries for dissolution of the firm.
Competency Based Que

Realisation Account

13. A, B and C are in partnership sharing profits and losses equally. On 31st March, 2024, their balance sheet was as follows

Balance Sheet
as at 31st March, 2024

Liabilities		Amt (₹)	Assets	Amt (₹)
Creditors		13,000	Cash	1,500
B's Loan		2,500	Debtors	12,500
Bills Payable		500	Stock	29,000
Reserve Fund		3,000	Furniture	1,000
A's Current A/c		1,500	Machinery	5,000
B's Current A/c		1,500	C's Current A/c	3,000
Capital A/cs			Goodwill	10,000
A	20,000			
B	10,000			
C	10,000	40,000		
		62,000		62,000

On the date they dissolved their partnership the following arrangements were made among the partners

(i) A agrees to pay creditors.
(ii) B takes over the stock at an agreed valuation of ₹ 25,000.
(iii) C takes over goodwill at ₹ 15,000.
(iv) Bills payable were cleared-off, ₹ 10 being allowed for discount.
(v) The remaining assets were auctioned and realised ₹ 15,000. Expenses of realisation amounted to ₹ 120.
(vi) B's loan was also paid-off.

Prepare realisation account.

Ans. Loss on Realisation A = ₹ 810, B = ₹ 870, C = ₹ 870

14. Sonia and Rohit were partners in a firm sharing profits and losses in the ratio of 3 : 2. On 31st March, 2023 their balance sheet was as follows

Balance Sheet of Sonia and Rohit
as at 31st March, 2023

Liabilities		Amt (₹)	Assets	Amt (₹)
Capital A/cs			Building	2,00,000
Sonia	70,000		Machinery	1,40,000
Rohit	90,000	1,60,000	Furniture	80,000
General Reserve		80,000	Debtors	1,20,000
Sonia's Loan		1,30,000	Stock	60,000
Bank Loan		2,20,000	Cash at Bank	60,000
Creditors		70,000		
		6,60,000		6,60,000

The firm was dissolved on the above date on the following terms

(i) Building machinery and furniture realised ₹ 3,44,000.
(ii) Debtors realised 90% only.
(iii) Creditors took away half of the stock in full settlement of their account.

(iv) Remaining stock realised ₹ 72,000.

(v) Realisation expenses amounting to ₹ 14,000 were paid by Rohit.

Prepare realisation account.

CBSE 2024 C; Competency Based Que

Ans. Realisation Loss = ₹ 20,000

15. Sandhya Rathi and Meenakshi Gupta are partners in a firm, sharing profits and losses equally. On 1st April, 2024, the balance sheet of the firm is given as under

Balance Sheet
as at 1st April, 2024

Liabilities		Amt (₹)	Assets		Amt (₹)
Sundry Creditors		75,000	Cash		6,000
Bills Payable		30,000	Bank		30,000
Mr. Rathi's Loan		15,000	Stock		75,000
Reserve Fund		24,000	Book Debts	66,000	
Capital A/cs			(−) Provision for		
Sandhya Rathi	90,000		Doubtful Debts	(6,000)	60,000
Meenakshi Gupta	30,000	1,20,000	Plant and Machinery		45,000
			Land and Building		48,000
		2,64,000			2,64,000

The firm was dissolved on the date given above. The following transactions took place

(i) Sandhya Rathi undertook to pay Mr. Rathi's loan and took over 50% of the stock at a discount of 20%.

(ii) Book debts realised ₹ 54,000, balance of the stock was sold-off at a profit of 30% on cost.

(iii) Sundry creditors were paid out at a discount of 10%. Bills payable were paid in full.

(iv) Plant and machinery realised ₹ 75,000, land and building ₹ 1,20,000.

(v) Sandhya Rathi took over the goodwill of the firm at a valuation of ₹ 30,000.

(vi) Realisation expenses were ₹ 5,250.

Show realisation account, partners' capital account and bank account in the books of the firm.

Competency Based Que

Ans. Profit on Realisation = ₹ 1,32,000; Amount paid to Sandhya Rathi = ₹ 1,23,000, Meenakshi Gupta = ₹ 1,08,000

16. Following was the balance sheet of Siraj and Zahir as at 31st March, 2024.

Balance Sheet
as at 31st March, 2024

Liabilities		Amt (₹)	Assets	Amt (₹)
Creditors		76,000	Cash at Bank	23,000
Mrs. Suraj's Loan		20,000	Stock	12,000
Zaheer's Loan		30,000	Debtors	38,000
Reserve		10,000	Furniture	8,000
Capital A/cs			Plant	56,000
Siraj	20,000		Investments	20,000
Zahir	16,000	36,000	Profit and Loss A/c	15,000
		1,72,000		1,72,000

The firm was dissolved on 31st March, 2024 and both the partners agreed to the following

(i) Siraj agreeing to take over investments at an agreed value of ₹ 16,000. He also agreed to settle Mrs. Siraj's loan.

(ii) Other assets realised as stock ₹ 10,000, debtors ₹ 37,000, furniture ₹ 9,000, plant ₹ 50,000.

(iii) Expenses of realisation came to ₹ 3,200.

(iv) Creditors agreed to accept ₹ 74,000 in full settlement of their claims.

Prepare realisation account, partners' capital account and bank account.

Ans. Loss on Realisation = ₹ 13,200; Siraj to be Paid = ₹ 13,080, Zahir to be Paid = ₹ 8,720

Comprehensive Questions

17. X, Y and Z were partners in a firm sharing profits and losses in the ratio of 3 : 2 : 1.

Following was the balance sheet at the date of dissolution

Balance Sheet
as at 31st March, 2024

Liabilities		Amt (₹)	Assets		Amt (₹)
Creditors		18,500	Bank Balance		1,000
Mrs. X's Loan		5,000	Debtors	15,000	
X's Loan		8,000	(−) Provision	(1,000)	14,000
Investment Fluctuation Fund		7,500	Stock		80,000
			Investments		20,000
Capital A/cs			Plant		75,000
X	75,000		Goodwill		35,000
Y	66,000				
Z	45,000	1,86,000			
		2,25,000			2,25,000

Following transactions took place

(i) X took over the investments at 25% more than the book value.

(ii) Y took over debtors amounting to ₹ 5,000 at ₹ 4,000. Remaining debtors realised 75% of their book value.

(iii) Stock is sold for ₹ 59,000 and plant is sold for ₹ 40,000.

Expenses of realisation amounted to ₹ 1,000. It was also found that there is a liability for ₹ 8,000 for damages, which also had to be paid.

Prepare necessary accounts. **Competency Based Que**

Ans. Realisation Loss = ₹ 90,000; Partners' Capital Account X = ₹ 5,000, Y = ₹ 32,000, Z = ₹ 30,000; Bank Account = ₹ 1,07,500

18. X, Y and Z are partners sharing profits in the ratio of 5 : 3 : 2. They decided to dissolve the firm whose balance sheet is given below

Balance Sheet
at 31st March, 2024

Liabilities		Amt (₹)	Assets	Amt (₹)
Capital A/cs			Bank	84,000
X	2,40,000		Debtors	60,000
Y	1,80,000		Stock	72,000
Z	1,80,000	6,00,000	Furniture	1,50,000
Current A/cs			Patents	42,000
X	30,000		Building	3,84,000
Y	20,400	50,400	Z's Current A/c	14,400
Profit and Loss A/c		60,000		
Trade Creditors		72,000		
Workmen Compensation Fund		12,000		
Employees Provident Fund		6,000		
Loan from Mrs. X		6,000		
		8,06,400		8,06,400

Following transactions took place at the time of dissolution.

(i) Realisation expenses were to be fully borne by X for which he is to get a credit of ₹ 12,000. Actual realisation expenses paid out of firm's bank account amounted to ₹ 14,400.

(ii) Y took over stock for ₹ 66,000 and Z took over buildings for ₹ 4,80,000.

(iii) Other assets realised as follows debtors ₹ 57,600, furniture ₹ 1,16,400.

(iv) Patents did not realise anything and trade creditors were settled in full by paying them ₹ 66,000.

(v) Accounts of partners were settled after realising assets and paying outside liabilities.

Prepare realisation account, partners' current account, capital account and bank account. **Competency Based Que**

Ans. Profit on Realisation = ₹ 6,000; Final Payment X = ₹ 3,06,600, Y = ₹ 1,57,800, Z = ₹ 2,98,800

19. Following is the balance sheet of X and Y who share profits and losses in the ratio of 3 : 2 as at 31st March, 2024.

Balance Sheet
as at 31st March, 2024

Liabilities		Amt (₹)	Assets		Amt (₹)
Sundry Creditors		75,000	Cash at Bank		4,500
Bills Payable		30,000	Stock		25,000
Mrs. X's Loan		25,000	Debtors	40,500	
Workmen Compensation Reserve		8,000	(–) Provision for Doubtful Debts	(1,000)	39,500
Bank Loan		50,000	Bills Receivable		15,000
General Reserve		27,000	Investments		60,000
Capital A/cs			Plant and Machinery		80,000
X	30,000		Building		61,000
Y	40,000	70,000			
		2,85,000			2,85,000

On the above date, the firm was dissolved and the following arrangements were made

(i) X promised to pay Mrs. X's loan and took half of the investments @ 10% discount.

(ii) Stock and remaining investments were sold @ 10% discount.

(iii) Goodwill was taken by Y for ₹ 40,000. He also agreed to pay bills payable at a discount of 10%.

(iv) Debtors realised ₹ 35,000, bills receivable ₹ 13,500, plant and machinery ₹ 38,900 and building ₹ 1,20,000.

(v) There was a car in the firm, which was completely written-off from the books. It was taken over by X for ₹ 23,400.

(vi) Creditors were paid 90% in full and final settlement of their dues.

(vii) Expenses of dissolution amounted to ₹ 1,700.

Prepare realisation account, capital account of partners' and bank account in the books of the firm.

Ans. Profit on Realisation = ₹ 75,600; Payment to X = ₹ 70,960, Y = ₹ 71,240; Total of Bank Account = ₹ 2,61,400

20. Sunny and Bobby were partners in a firm sharing profits and losses in the ratio of 3 : 2, their balance sheet as at 31st March, 2024

Liabilities		Amt (₹)	Assets		Amt (₹)
Creditors		1,90,000	Bank		5,000
Bills Payable		1,10,000	Fixed Deposits		70,000
Employees Provident Fund		50,000	Stock		86,000
Mrs. Sunny's Loan		55,000	Investments		1,04,000
Bobby's Loan		85,000	Debtors	1,77,000	
Investment Fluctuation Fund		30,000	(–) Provision for Doubtful Debts	(12,000)	1,65,000
Capital A/cs			Other Fixed Assets		3,80,000
Sunny	2,20,0000		Deferred Revenue Expenditure		35,000
Bobby	1,20,000	3,40,000	Sunny's Loan		15,000
		8,60,000			8,60,000

The firm was dissolved on 31st March, 2024. The assets were realised and the liabilities were paid as under

(i) Sunny promised to pay-off Mrs. Sunny's loan.

(ii) Bobby took away stock at 20% discount and 80% of the investments at 10% discount.

(iii) Dharam, a debtor of ₹ 60,000 had to pay the amount due 2 months after the date of dissolution. He was allowed a discount of 9% p.a. for making immediate payment.

(iv) Creditors were paid ₹ 1,75,000 in full settlement of their claim.

(v) 90% of other fixed assets realised ₹ 1,98,000 and remaining were realised at discount of 15%.

(vi) Balance of investments were sold at 75% value and fixed deposits were realised at 110%.

(vii) There was an old furniture which has been written-off completely from the books, Bobby took away the same for ₹ 41,000 against his loan and balance to him was given in cash.

(viii) Realisation expenses ₹ 20,000 were paid by Sunny and Bobby equally on behalf of the firm.

You are required to prepare realisation account. **CBSE SQP 2025; Competency Based Que**

Ans. Realisation Loss = ₹ 96,320

21. Srijan, Raman and Manan were partners in a firm sharing profits and losses in the ratio of 2 : 2 : 1. On 31st March, 2024 their balance sheet was as follows

Balance Sheet
as at 31st March, 2024

Liabilities		Amt (₹)	Assets	Amt (₹)
Capital A/cs			Capital : Manan	10,000
Srijan	2,00,000		Plant	2,20,000
Raman	1,50,000	3,50,000	Investments	70,000
Creditors		75,000	Stock	50,000
Bills Payable		40,000	Debtors	60,000
Outstanding Salary		35,000	Bank	10,000
			Profit and Loss A/c	80,000
		5,00,000		5,00,000

On the above date they decided to dissolve the firm.

(i) Srijan was appointed to realise the assets and discharge the liabilities. Srijan was to receive 5% commission on sale of assets (except cash) and was to bear all expenses of realisation.

(ii) Assets were realised as follows

	Amt (₹)
Plant	85,000
Stock	33,000
Debtors	47,000

(iii) Investments were realised at 95% of the book value.
(iv) The firm had to pay ₹ 7,500 for an outstanding repair bill not provided for earlier.
(v) A contingent liability in respect of bills receivable, discounted with the bank had also materialised and had to be discharged for ₹ 15,000.
(vi) Expenses of realisation amounting to ₹ 3,000 were paid by Srijan.

Prepare realisation account, partners' capital account and bank account. **CBSE 2018; Competency Based Que**

Ans. Loss on Realisation = ₹ 2,02,575; Total of Bank Account = ₹ 3,08,015; Commission Payable to Srijan = ₹ 11,575; Partners' Capital Account = Srijan ₹ 98,545, Raman = ₹ 36,970, Manan = ₹ 66,515

22. A, S and Z were carrying on business and sharing profits and losses in the ratio of 2 : 2 : 1. They dissolved their firm as on 31st March, 2024. On that date, their balance sheet was as follows

Balance Sheet
as at 31st March, 2024

Liabilities		Amt (₹)	Assets	Amt (₹)
Trade Creditors		4,06,000	Cash	90,000
Reserve Fund		2,00,000	Spare Parts	3,20,000
Investment Fluctuation Reserve		1,60,000	Investments	2,20,000
Capital A/cs			Debtors	2,00,000
A	3,00,000		Leasehold	6,06,000
S	3,00,000			
Z	60,000	6,60,000		
Provision for Doubtful Debts		10,000		
		14,36,000		14,36,000

All assets (except cash and investments) were taken over by a company for ₹ 13,00,000. The investments were sold at ₹ 2,26,000, trade creditors were paid ₹ 3,90,000 and realisation expenses amounted to ₹ 60,000. A bill was received from Mr. X worth ₹ 20,000, which was under discount, now as Mr. X has become insolvent, a dividend of 50% was received from his estate.

Prepare realisation account, partners' capital account and cash account.

Ans. Profit on Realisation = ₹ 2,96,000; Partners' Capital Account A = ₹ 4,98,400, S = ₹ 4,98,400, Z = ₹ 1,59,200; Cash Account = ₹ 16,26,000

23. The following is the balance sheet of A and B as at 31st March, 2024

Balance Sheet
as at 31st March, 2024

Liabilities	Amt (₹)	Assets		Amt (₹)
Sundry Creditors	30,000	Cash in Hand		500
Bills Payable	8,000	Cash at Bank		8,000
Mrs. A's Loan	5,000	Stock-in-trade		5,000
Mrs. B's Loan	10,000	Investments		10,000
General Reserve	10,000	Debtors	20,000	
Investment Fluctuation Reserve	1,000	(–) Provision	(2,000)	18,000
A's Capital	10,000	Plant		20,000
B's Capital	10,000	Building		15,000
		Goodwill		4,000
		Advertisement Suspense A/c		3,500
	84,000			84,000

The firm was dissolved on 31st March, 2024 on the following terms

(i) A promised to pay Mrs. A's loan and took away stock-in-trade at ₹ 4,000.

(ii) B took away half of the investments at 10% discount.

(iii) Debtors realised ₹ 19,000.

(iv) Creditors and bills payable were due on an average basis of one month after 31st March, but they were paid immediately on 31st March at 6% discount p.a.

(v) Plant realised ₹ 25,000, building ₹ 40,000, goodwill ₹ 6,000 and remaining investments at ₹ 74,500.

(vi) There was an old typewriter in the firm which had been written-off completely from the books, it was estimated to realise ₹ 300, it was taken away by B at this estimated price.

You are required to prepare the realisation account, partners' capital account and bank account to close books of the firm.

Competency Based Que

Ans. Realisation Profit = ₹ 32,490; Partners' Capital Account A = ₹ 30,495, B = ₹ 24,695; Cash Account = ₹ 1,03,000

Missing Information

24. A and B were partners in a firm sharing profits and losses in the ratio 4 : 3. They decided to dissolve the firm on 1st May, 2024.

From the information given below, complete realisation account, partner's capital account and bank account

Competency Based Que

Dr **Realisation Account** Cr

Particulars		Amt (₹)	Particulars		Amt (₹)
To Sundry Assets			By Sundry Liabilities		
Machinery		56,000	Creditors		4,000
Stock		9,000	A's Wife's Loan		2,500
Debtors		5,500	By Bank		
To Bank			Machinery		48,000
Creditors		...	Debtors		1,000
To A's Capital A/c			By A's Capital A/c		
A's Wife's Loan		3,400	Stock	12,800	
To B's Capital A/c			Typewriter	7,000	19,800
Realisation Expenses		700	By B's Capital A/c		
To Profit Transferred to			Debtors		4,000
A's Capital A/c	400				
B's Capital A/c	300	700			
		79,300			79,300

Dr **Partners' Capital Account** Cr

Particulars	A (₹)	B (₹)	Particulars	A (₹)	B (₹)
To Realisation A/c	...	...	By ...	...	...
To Bank A/c	40,000	45,000	By ...	...	...
			By ...	...	...
	...	...		...	...

Dr **Bank Account** Cr

Particulars	Amt (₹)	Particulars	Amt (₹)
To Balance b/d	...	By Realisation A/c	...
To Realisation A/c	49,000	By A's Loan A/c	400
		By A's Capital A/c	40,000
		By B's Capital A/c	...
	...		...

25. Prakash, Kiran and Rishabh are partners in a firm sharing profit and losses in the ratio of 3 : 2 : 1. They decided to dissolve the firm on 1st November, 2014.

From the information given below, complete realisation account partner's capital accounts and bank account.

Competency Based Que

Dr **Realisation Account** Cr

Particulars		Amt (₹)	Particulars		Amt (₹)
To Sundry Assets			By Creditors	27,000	
Debtors	20,000		By Bills Payable	10,000	
Stock	25,200		By Mrs. Prakash Loan	5,000	42,000
Investments	20,000		By Bank (Assets Realised)		...
Bills Receivable	8,000		By Kiran's Capital A/c (Bills Receivable)		7,000
Machinery	60,000		By Bank (Unrecorded Asset)		1,200
Goodwill	6,000	1,39,200	By Bank (Goodwill)		5,000
To Kiran's Capital A/c			By Loss Transferred to		
Bills Payable	10,000		Prakash's Capital A/c	...	
Realisation Expenses	2,100	12,100	Kiran's Capital A/c	...	
To Prakash Capital A/c			Rishabh's Capital A/c	...	...
Wife's Loan	5,000				
Contingent Liability for Bill Discounted	8,000	13,000			
To Bank (Creditors)		...			
		1,86,800			1,86,800

Dr **Partners' Capital Account** Cr

Particulars	Prakash (₹)	Kiran (₹)	Rishabh (₹)	Particulars	Prakash (₹)	Kiran (₹)	Rishabh (₹)
To Balance b/d	...	...	6,000	By	75,000	50,000	...
To Profit and Loss A/c	9,900	...	3,300	By Realisation A/c (Bills Payable and Realisation Expenses)	...	...	...
To Realisation A/c (Bills Receivable)	...	...	...				
To Realisation A/c (Loss)	19,200	12,800	6,400	By Realisation A/c (Wife's Loan and Contingent Liability)	...	...	...
To Bank A/c (Final Payment)	...	...	...	By Bank A/c (Amount brought in)	...	...	...
	88,000	62,100	15,700		88,000	62,100	15,700

Dr **Bank Account** Cr

Particulars	Amt (₹)	Particulars	Amt (₹)
To	...	By Realisation A/c (Creditors)	...
To	...	By Prakash's Capital A/c	...
To	...	By Kiran's Capital A/c	35,700
To	...		
To Rishabh's Capital A/c	...		
	1,17,100		1,17,100

Theoretical Questions

Short Answer Type Questions

1. What is a realisation account? NCERT

Ans. Realisation account is opened on the dissolution of a firm. It is a nominal account. It is prepared to determine the profit or loss on the realisation of assets and payment of liabilities. It is prepared by transferring to it the firm's assets and liabilities, amount realised from the sale of assets, payment of liabilities and expenses incurred on realisation. The balance in the account is either profit or loss, which is transferred to the capital account of the partners in their profit sharing ratio.

2. On what account realisation account differs from revaluation account? NCERT

Ans. Differences between revaluation account and realisation account

Basis	Revaluation Account	Realisation Account
Purpose	The purpose of preparing revaluation account is to ascertain profit or loss on the revaluation of assets and reassessment of liabilities.	Realisation account is meant to ascertain profit or loss on the disposal of assets and payment of liabilities.
Situations	It is prepared in case of reorganisation or reconstitution of firm, i.e. admission, retirement and death of a partner.	It is prepared in case of dissolution of firm.
Transfer of Profit/Loss	Profit or loss on revaluation is transferred to old partners' capital accounts in case of admission and all partners' capital accounts in case of retirement.	In case of dissolution, profit or loss on realisation is transferred to all partners' capital accounts.
Repetition of Accounts	This account is repeated many times during the life time of business.	This account is prepared only once during the life time of business.
Closing of Accounts	Accounts of assets and liabilities shown in this account are not closed.	Accounts of assets and liabilities transferred here are closed.
Settlement of Accounts	Assets of the firm are revalued and liabilities are reassessed. The profit or loss is distributed among all the partners.	Assets of the firm are realised and liabilities are settled. The balance amount is distributed among all the partners.

3. State the difference between dissolution of partnership and dissolution of a firm.

Ans. Differences between dissolution of partnership and dissolution of a firm

Basis	Dissolution of Partnership	Dissolution of a Firm
Meaning	Dissolution of partnership is only a change in the partnership agreement. The firm may continue.	Dissolution of the firm is the discontinuance of all the business activities of the firm.
Books of Accounts	In this situation, books of accounts may not be closed.	Books of accounts are necessarily closed.
Dissolution	Dissolution of partnership does not mean dissolution of firm. The firm may not be discontinued.	Dissolution of the firm necessarily leads to dissolution of partnership.
Nature	Dissolution of the partnership is voluntary. It emerges out of the agreement.	Dissolution of the firm may be both voluntary and compulsory.
Court's Intervention	There is no intervention of court.	The court intervenes, if deemed necessary.

4. If partner's loan appears on the liabilities side of the balance sheet of the firm and the capital account of such partner shows a debit balance, how will you deal with such a loan? Competency Based Que

Ans. When a partner's capital account shows a debit balance, his loan (to firm) account should be transferred to his capital account to the extent of debit balance and the balance, if any, in his loan account (to firm) should always be paid-off separately.

5. State the accounting treatment for NCERT

(i) Unrecorded assets

(ii) Unrecorded liabilities

Ans. Unrecorded assets and liabilities are not transferred to realisation account because they do not appear in the books.

Following accounting procedure is followed

(i) **Unrecorded Assets** If amount is realised from sale of unrecorded assets, it is debited to cash/bank account and credited to realisation account, it being in the nature of gain.

If unrecorded asset is taken by one of the partners, it is debited to concerned partner's capital account and credited to realisation account.

(ii) **Unrecorded Liabilities** If unrecorded liability is paid, realisation account is debited and cash/bank account is credited with the amount paid, it being a loss.

If a partner agrees to pay unrecorded liability, realisation account is debited and concerned partner's capital account is credited.

No entry is passed if unrecorded assets is given to discharge a recorded or unrecorded liability.

6. On dissolution, mention how will you deal with the partners's loan if it appears on the

(i) Liabilities side of balance sheet

(ii) Assets side of balance sheet

NCERT; Competency Based Que

Ans. (i) If partners's loan appears on the liabilities side of balance sheet, it should be paid separately before making payment to a partner what is due to him on account of capital.

(ii) If partner's loan appears on the assets side of balance sheet, it should be settled through partner's capital account.

Objective Questions

Multiple Choice Questions (MCQs)

1. On dissolution, realisation account is debited with

(a) all assets
(b) all assets to be realised
(c) all liabilities
(d) all liabilities to be paid

2. Realisation account is a ...... account.

(a) real (b) personal
(c) nominal (d) None of these

3. The firm of A and B was dissolved on 31st March, 2024. According to the agreement, B had agreed to undertake the dissolution work for an agreed remuneration of ₹ 8,000 and bear all the realisation expenses.

Dissolution expenses were ₹ 5,000. The journal entry passed will be Competency Based Que

(a)	Realisation A/c	Dr	5,000	
	To Bank A/c			5,000
(b)	Realisation A/c	Dr	8,000	
	To Bank A/c			8,000
(c)	Realisation A/c	Dr	5,000	
	To B's Capital A/c			5,000
(d)	Realisation A/c	Dr	8,000	
	To B's Capital A/c			8,000

4. Dada, Yuvi and Viru were partners sharing profits and losses in the ratio 3 : 2 : 1. Their books showed work-men compensation reserve of ₹ 1,00,000 workmen claim amounted to ₹ 60,000.

How it will affect the books of accounts at the time of dissolution of firm? CBSE SQP 2025; Competency Based Que

(a) Only ₹ 40,000 will be distributed amongst partner's capital account
(b) ₹ 1,00,000 will be credited to realisation account and ₹ 60,000 will be paid-off
(c) ₹ 60,000 will be credited to realisation account and will be even paid-off. Balance ₹ 40,000 will be distributed amongst partners
(d) Only ₹ 60,000 will be credited to realisation account and will be even paid-off

5. Which of the following will be transferred to realisation account at the time of dissolution of firm?

CBSE 2023; Competency Based Que

(i) Provision for doubtful debts
(ii) Partners' loan
(iii) General reserve
(iv) Goodwill

Codes

(a) (i) and (iv) (b) (i), (ii) and (iv)
(c) (i), (iii) and (iv) (d) (i), (ii) and (iii)

6. P and Q are partners in a firm. They decided to dissolve the firm. Assets other than cash ₹ 1,60,000, cash ₹ 25,000, total liabilities ₹ 1,75,000. On dissolution, assets realised ₹ 1,25,000 and liabilities paid ₹ 1,40,000. Net profit or loss on realisation is Competency Based Que

(a) profit ₹ 25,000 (b) loss ₹ 25,000
(c) loss ₹ 15,000 (d) no profit, no loss

7. A, B, C are partners sharing profits in the ratio of 4 : 3 : 2. On firm's dissolution, firms total assets are ₹ 35,000, creditors are ₹ 7,500. Realisation expenses are ₹ 1,050. Assets realised 15% more than the book value creditors were paid 2% more.

For profit/loss on realisation B's capital account will debited/credited with Competency Based Que

(a) credit ₹ 4,050
(b) debit ₹ 1,350
(c) credit ₹ 1,350
(d) debit ₹ 1,200

8. On dissolution of a partnership firm, if realisation expenses are paid by the firm on behalf of a partner, then such expenses are debited to which of the following account?

(a) Realisation account (b) Partner's capital account
(c) Partner's loan account (d) Bank account

9. Wayne, Shann and Bryan were partners in a firm. Shann had advanced a loan of ₹ 1,00,000 to the firm. On 31st March, 2024 the firm was dissolved. After transferring various assets (other than cash and bank) and outside liabilities to realisation account, Shaan took over furniture of book value of ₹ 90,000 in part settlement of his loan amount. For the payment of balance amount of Shaan's loan, bank account will be credited with **CBSE 2025**

(a) ₹ 1,00,000 (b) ₹ 90,000 (c) ₹ 1,90,000 (d) ₹ 10,000

10. In the balance sheet, total debtors appear at ₹ 25,000 and provision for doubtful debts appear at ₹ 750. How much amount will be realised from debtors, if bad debts amount to ₹ 5,000 and remaining debtors are realised at a discount of 5%? **Competency Based Que**

(a) ₹ 19,000 (b) ₹ 18,250
(c) ₹ 18,287.5 (d) ₹ 19,750

11. On dissolution of a firm, partners' capital accounts balance was ₹ 31,500; creditors balance was ₹ 6,000 and profit and loss account debit balance was ₹ 3,000. Profit on realisation of assets was ₹ 3,900. Total amount realised from assets will be **Competency Based Que**

(a) ₹ 40,500 (b) ₹ 35,400
(c) ₹ 38,400 (d) None of these

12. On dissolution of a firm, out of the proceeds received from sale of assets .... will be paid first.

(a) outside creditors (b) outside debtors
(c) Either (a) or (b) (d) None of these

13. On dissolution of a firm, bank overdraft is transferred to **NCERT**

(a) cash account (b) bank account
(c) realisation account (d) partners' capital account

14. At the time of dissolution of a firm, the total assets were ₹ 6,00,000 and outside liabilities were ₹ 2,40,000. If assets realised ₹ 7,20,000 and realisation expenses of ₹ 8,000 were paid, the profit or loss on realisation will be **CBSE 2024**

(a) loss ₹ 1,20,000 (b) profit ₹ 1,20,000
(c) loss ₹ 1,12,000 (d) profit ₹ 1,12,000

15. Investment of ₹ 1,00,000 were not shown in the books. One of the creditor's took these investments in settlement of his debt of ₹ 1,10,000. How much amount will be payable to that creditor?

(a) Nil (b) ₹ 1,10,000 (c) ₹ 10,000 (d) ₹ 2,10,000

16. On dissolution of a firm, partner's loan account is transferred to **NCERT**

(a) realisation account
(b) partners' capital account
(c) partners' current account
(d) None of the above

17. After transferring liabilities like creditors and bills payables in the realisation account, in the absence of any information regarding their payment, such liabilities are treated as **NCERT**

(a) never paid (b) fully paid
(c) partly paid (d) None of these

18. Aavya, Mitansh and Praveen were partners in a firm. On 31st March, 2023, the firm was dissolved. Creditors took over furniture of book value of ₹ 50,000 at ₹ 45,000 in part settlement of their amount of ₹ 60,000. The balance amount was paid to them through cheque. The amount paid through cheque will be **CBSE 2024; Competency Based Que**

(a) ₹ 10,000 (b) ₹ 50,000 (c) ₹ 45,000 (d) ₹ 15,000

19. Lata, Mehu and Namita were partners in a firm sharing profits and losses in the ratio of 3 : 2 : 1. They decided to dissolve the firm on 31st March, 2023. Creditors took over stock of book value of ₹ 80,000 at 80%, in part settlement of their amount of ₹ 90,000. The balance amount was paid to the creditors by cheque. The amount paid by cheque to the creditors will be **CBSE 2024; Competency Based Que**

(a) ₹ 26,000 (b) ₹ 64,000 (c) ₹ 80,000 (d) ₹ 1,44,000

20. Sanya, Sarthak and Nitya were partners in a firm sharing profits and losses in the ratio of 4 : 3 : 1. They decided to dissolve the firm on 31st March, 2023. On this date, the firm had debtors amounting to ₹ 3,00,000 and provision for doubtful debts of ₹ 30,000. On dissolution, debtors for ₹ 20,000 proved bad and the remaining debtors realised 90%. Amount realised from the debtors will be **Competency Based Que**

(a) ₹ 3,00,000 (b) ₹ 2,25,000
(c) ₹ 2,80,000 (d) ₹ 2,52,000

21. X carried out dissolution of the firm for a remuneration of ₹ 10,000. He later agreed to take stock valued at ₹ 9,000 in settlement of his remuneration. What will be the journal entry? **Competency Based Que**

(a) X's Capital A/c	Dr	10,000	
To Stock A/c			9,000
To Realisation A/c			1,000
(b) X's Capital A/c	Dr	9,000	
To Realisation A/c			9,000
(c) Realisation A/c	Dr	9,000	
To X's Capital A/c			9,000

(d) No entry

22. On the dissolution of a partnership firm there were debtors of ₹ 34,000. Debtors of ₹ 1,000 became bad and 60% was realised from the remaining debtors. Which account will be debited and by how much amount on the realisation from debtors? **CBSE 2024; Competency Based Que**

(a) Realisation account by ₹ 33,000
(b) Profit and loss account by ₹ 1,000
(c) Cash account by ₹ 19,800
(d) Debtors account by ₹ 14,200

23. Pawan, a partner was appointed to look after the process of dissolution of firm for which he was allowed a remuneration of ₹ 75,000. Pawan agreed to bear the dissolution expenses. Actual dissolution expenses ₹ 60,000 were paid by Pawan. Pawan's capital account will be credited by

(a) ₹ 75,000 (b) ₹ 60,000 (c) ₹ 15,000 (d) ₹ 10,000

24. A firm is dissolved X, a partner carry out dissolution for which he will get ₹ 25,000 including expenses. Realisation expenses were ₹ 12,500 which were paid by the firm. Realisation account will be debited by

(a) ₹ 12,500 (b) ₹ 25,000
(c) ₹ 37,500 (d) None of these

25. Pawan, Kavita and Gaurav were partners in a firm. The firm was dissolved. Creditors took over furniture of book value of ₹ 60,000 at 10% less than the book value in part settlement of their amount of ₹ 60,000. The balance amount was paid to them through cheque. The amount paid through cheque will be **CBSE 2024 C**

(a) ₹ 5,000 (b) ₹ 6,000
(c) ₹ 54,000 (d) Nil

26. On the day of dissolution of the firm 'Roop Brothers' had partner's capital amounting to ₹ 21,50,000 external liabilities ₹ 35,000, cash balance ₹ 28,000 and profit and loss account (debit) ₹ 7,000. If realisation expense and loss on realisation amounted to ₹ 5,000 and ₹ 25,000 respectively, the amount realised by sale of assets **Competency Based Que**

(a) ₹ 1,64,000 (b) ₹ 1,45,000
(c) ₹ 1,57,000 (d) ₹ 1,50,000

27. Rama, a partner took over machinery of ₹ 50,000 in full settlement of her loan of ₹ 60,000. Machinery was already transferred to realisation account. How it will effect the realisation account? **CBSE SQP 2025**

(a) Realisation account will be credited by ₹ 60,000
(b) Realisation account will be credited by ₹ 10,000
(c) Realisation account will be credited by ₹ 50,000
(d) No effect on realisation account

28. At the time of dissolution machinery appears at ₹ 10,00,000 and accumulated depreciation for the machinery appears at ₹ 6,00,000 in the balance sheet of a firm. This machine is taken over by a creditor of ₹ 5,40,000 at 5% below the net value. The balance amount of the creditor was paid through bank. By what amount should the bank account be credited for this transaction? **CBSE SQP 2025; Competency Based Que**

(a) ₹ 60,000 (b) ₹ 1,60,000
(c) ₹ 5,40,000 (d) ₹ 4,00,000

29. On dissolution of a firm, unrecorded furniture of ₹ 2,500 was taken by a partner for ₹ 2,150.
Which account will be credited and by how much amount?

(a) Cash account by ₹ 2,150
(b) Realisation account by ₹ 700
(c) Partner's capital account by ₹ 2,500
(d) Realisation account by ₹ 2,150

Assertion-Reason

Direction (Q.No. 30 to 39) *Read the following Assertion (A) and Reason (R) and choose the correct alternative from the following*

Alternatives

(a) Both Assertion (A) and Reason (R) are true and Reason (R) is the correct explanation of Assertion (A)
(b) Both Assertion (A) and Reason (R) are true, but Reason (R) is not the correct explanation of Assertion (A)
(c) Assertion (A) is true, but Reason (R) is false
(d) Assertion (A) is false, but Reason (R) is true

30. **Assertion** (A) A partnership firm dissolves when the business becomes illegal.

Reason (R) An illegal business cannot be carried out under any circumstances.

31. **Assertion** (A) A firm is dissolved if a partner gives notice in writing in a partnership at will.

Reason (R) A partnership at will has no fixed term.

32. **Assertion** (A) Firm's debts are the debts which firm owes to its outsiders.

Reason (R) Private debts are the debts which partners' owes personally.

33. **Assertion** (A) Dissolution of firm means discontinuation of the firm.

Reason (R) Economic relationship between the partners comes to an end.

34. **Assertion** (A) Court does not intervene when dissolution of partnership takes place.

Reason (R) Dissolution of partnership takes place by mutual agreement between the partners. **CBSE 2024 C**

35. **Assertion** (A) Court does not intervene in case of dissolution of partnership.

Reason (R) Dissolution of partnership takes place by mutual agreement among partners.

36. **Assertion** (A) In partnership firm, the private assets of the partners can also be used to pay-off the firm's debts.

Reason (R) The liability of the partners for acts of the firm is limited.

37. **Assertion** (A) Loan from spouse of a partner is considered as external liability.

Reason (R) It is shown on the debit side of realisation.

38. **Assertion** (A) While transferring liabilities to realisation account, it does not include accumulated profits.

Reason (R) Reserves and accumulated profits are transferred on the credit side of partners' capital account in new profit sharing ratio.

39. **Assertion** (A) After dissolution, cash/bank account will have nil balance.

Reason (R) Assets whether recorded or unrecorded, are credited to realisation account when realised.

Two Statements Based MCQs

Direction (Q.No. 40 to 47) *Read the following statements carefully and choose the correct alternative*

Alternatives

(a) Statement I is correct and Statement II is incorrect
(b) Statement II is correct and Statement I is incorrect
(c) Both the statements are correct
(d) Both the statements are incorrect

40. **Statement I** Dissolution of a partnership always leads to dissolution of the firm.

Statement II A firm is compulsorily dissolved when all partners become insolvent.

41. **Statement I** A firm constituted for a fixed term dissolves automatically when the term expires.

Statement II A partnership firm can never be dissolved by a court.

42. **Statement I** Death of a partner always results in dissolution of a firm.

Statement II A firm can be dissolved if its business becomes illegal.

43. **Statement I** A partnership at will can be dissolved by notice in writing by any partner.

Statement II A firm can continue its business after the retirement of a partner.

44. **Statement I** A firm is compulsorily dissolved if all partners become incompetent to contract.

Statement II The dissolution of a firm is always initiated by a court order.

45. **Statement I** Losses in a partnership are first settled from the profits of the firm before being paid from the partners' capitals.

Statement II Private property of a partner can be used to pay firm's debts only after settling private liabilities.

46. **Statement I** Dissolution of firm means dissolution of partnership.

Statement II All assets inclusive of cash are transferred to realisation account.

47. **Statement I** Loan from the wife of the partner is just treated like a loan from partner himself.

Statement II At the time of dissolution of firm, the balance of partners' capital account is paid after making the payment to third party for their loans as well as partners loans.

Matching

48. Match the following

Column I	Column II
A. Loss on realisation	(i) Debit partners' capital account
B. Profit on realisation	(ii) Credit realisation account
C. Asset sold	(iii) Credit partners' capital account
D. Creditors paid	(iv) Debit realisation account

Codes

	A	B	C	D		A	B	C	D
(a)	(iii)	(i)	(iv)	(ii)	(b)	(i)	(iii)	(iv)	(ii)
(c)	(iii)	(i)	(ii)	(iv)	(d)	(i)	(iii)	(ii)	(iv)

49. Match the following types of dissolution with their causes

Column I (Type of Dissolution)	Column II (Cause)
A. Dissolution by agreement	(i) Death of a partner
B. Compulsory dissolution	(ii) Partners agree to dissolve
C. Dissolution by notice	(iii) Partnership at will
D. Dissolution by court	(iv) Partner becomes insane

Codes

	A	B	C	D		A	B	C	D
(a)	(iii)	(ii)	(iv)	(i)	(b)	(ii)	(iii)	(i)	(iv)
(c)	(iv)	(iii)	(ii)	(i)	(d)	(ii)	(i)	(iii)	(iv)

50. Match the following grounds of court ordered dissolution with their description

Column I (Ground)	Column II (Description)
A. Misconduct	(i) Partner incapable of duties
B. Incapacity	(ii) Persistent breach of agreement

Column I (Ground)		Column II (Description)
C. Breach of Agreement	(iii)	Adversely affects the business
D. Losses	(iv)	Business cannot continue

Codes

	A	B	C	D		A	B	C	D
(a)	(iii)	(ii)	(iv)	(i)	(b)	(ii)	(iii)	(i)	(iv)
(c)	(iv)	(iii)	(ii)	(i)	(d)	(iii)	(i)	(ii)	(iv)

51. Match the following

Column I		Column II
A. Partnership firm is deemed to be dissolved	(i)	when a partner has become of unsound mind
B. Court can make an order to dissolve the firm	(ii)	on expiry of the period of partnership
C. Partner owners in his personal capacity	(iii)	firm's debts
D. All partners are liable to	(iv)	private debts

Codes

	A	B	C	D		A	B	C	D
(a)	(ii)	(i)	(iv)	(iii)	(b)	(iii)	(i)	(iv)	(ii)
(c)	(i)	(iii)	(ii)	(iv)	(d)	(iv)	(iii)	(ii)	(i)

52. Match the following

Column I		Column II
A. Losses in partnership	(i)	Paid from capital of partners if profits are insufficient
B. Private property of partner	(ii)	Cannot include properties of wife and children
C. Partner's loans	(iii)	Paid before settling capital balances
D. Private liabilities	(iv)	Paid before firm's liabilities

Codes

	A	B	C	D		A	B	C	D
(a)	(i)	(ii)	(iii)	(iv)	(b)	(iii)	(i)	(iv)	(ii)
(c)	(ii)	(iv)	(i)	(iii)	(d)	(i)	(iii)	(ii)	(iv)

Case Based MCQs

Direction *Read the following case study and answer the question 53 to 55 on the basis of the same*

Ravi, Aman and Neha were partners in a trading firm sharing profits and losses equally. Over time, Aman became permanently incapacitated, making him unable to perform his duties as a partner. Ravi and Neha filed a suit to dissolve the partnership in March 2024. On the date of dissolution

- The firm's balance sheet showed the following
  - Capital Accounts = Ravi ₹ 3,00,000, Aman ₹ 2,40,000, Neha ₹ 3,60,000.
  - Total assets = ₹ 15,00,000
  - Liabilities = ₹ 6,00,000.
- The assets realised ₹ 12,00,000 and dissolution expenses were ₹ 1,50,000.
- An unrecorded asset (old machinery) was sold for ₹ 30,000.

53. What type of dissolution does this case represent?
(a) Dissolution by agreement (b) Dissolution by court
(c) Compulsory dissolution (d) Dissolution by notice

54. What was the net profit or loss on the realisation of assets?
(a) ₹ 4,50,000 profit (b) ₹ 4,20,000 loss
(c) ₹ 4,10,000 loss (d) No profit, no loss

55. Calculate the amount of Ravi's capital to be transferred to cash account.
(a) ₹ 1,50,000 (b) ₹ 1,20,000
(c) ₹ 1,10,000 (d) ₹ 1,60,000

Direction *Read the following case study and answer the questions 56 to 58 on the basis of the same*

Anju, Manju and Sanju who were sharing profits in the ratio of 2 : 2 : 1 decided to dissolve the firm when their balance sheet was as follows

Balance Sheet
as at ...

Liabilities		Amt (₹)	Assets	Amt (₹)
Creditors		50,000	Cash	60,000
Bank Loan		35,000	Debtors	75,000
Employees' Provident Fund		15,000	Stock	40,000
Investment Fluctuation Fund		10,000	Investments	20,000
Commission Received in Advance		8,000	Plant	50,000
Capital A/cs			Profit and Loss A/c	3,000
Anju	50,000			
Manju	50,000			
Sanju	30,000	1,30,000		
		2,48,000		2,48,000

Anju was appointed to realise the assets. Anju was to receive 5% commission on the sale of assets (except cash) and was to bear all expenses of realisation. Anju realised the assets as follows

Debtors 20% less, stock ₹ 35,500, investments 80%, plant 90% of the book value. Expenses of realisation amounted to ₹ 7,500 paid by the firm on Anju's behalf. Commission received in advance was returned to the customers after deducting ₹ 3,000. Firm had to pay ₹ 8,500 of outstanding salary not provided for earlier. Compensation paid to employees amounted to ₹ 17,000. This liability was not provided for in the above balance sheet. ₹ 20,000 has to be paid for provident fund.

56. **The amount received by firm after realisation of assets is ....**

(a) ₹ 1,56,500 (b) ₹ 1,85,000
(c) ₹ 1,88,000 (d) ₹ 2,45,000

57. **Commission charged by Anju amounted to ....**

(a) ₹ 9,275 (b) ₹ 8,000
(c) ₹ 7,825 (d) ₹ 6,000

58. **The amount of profit and loss received by Anju, Manju and Sanju is**

(a) ₹ 1,000, ₹ 1,000, ₹ 1,000
(b) ₹ 750, ₹ 750, ₹ 1,500
(c) ₹ 1,200, ₹ 1,200, ₹ 600
(d) ₹ 500, ₹ 500, ₹ 2,000

Direction *Read the following case study and answer the questions 59 to 61 on the basis of the same*

P, Q and R who were sharing the profits and losses in the ratio of 3 : 1 : 1 respectively decided to dissolve the firm when their balance sheet was as follows

Balance Sheet
as at ...

Liabilities		Amt (₹)	Assets		Amt (₹)
Sundry Creditors		1,20,000	Cash at Bank		64,000
Loan from Mrs. Q		30,000	Debtors	4,84,000	
General Reserve		2,00,000	(–) Provision for Doubtful Debts	(24,000)	4,60,000
Capital A/cs					
P	4,90,000		Stock		1,56,000
Q	1,80,000		Investments		3,40,000
R	1,20,000	7,90,000	Fixed Assets		20,000
			Advertisement Suspense A/c		1,00,000
		11,40,000			11,40,000

It was agreed that

(i) Goodwill is to be ignored.
(ii) P is to take over all the fixed assets at ₹ 4,000 less, debtors amounting to ₹ 4,00,000 at ₹ 3,44,000. The creditors of ₹ 1,20,000 to be assumed by P at that figure.
(iii) Q is to take over all stock at ₹ 1,40,000 and certain of the investment at ₹ 1,44,000 (being book value less 10%).
(iv) R is to take over the remaining investments at 90% of book value less ₹ 2,000 allowances and to assume responsibility for the discharge of the Mrs. Q's loan, together with accruing interest of ₹ 600 which has not been recorded in the books of the firm.
(v) The remaining debtors were sold to a debt collecting agency for 50% of book values.
(vi) P was entitled to receive ₹ 5,400 as remuneration for completing the dissolution work and was to bear the realisation expenses. The expenses of realisation ₹ 3,400 were paid by P out of his private funds.

59. **What is the book value of investment taken over by Q?**

(a) ₹ 1,60,000
(b) ₹ 1,29,600
(c) ₹ 1,44,000
(d) None of the above

60. **What is the agreed value of investment taken over by R?**

(a) ₹ 1,80,000
(b) ₹ 1,62,600
(c) ₹ 1,62,000
(d) ₹ 1,60,000

61. **Amount collected by selling debtors to collecting agency is ....**

(a) ₹ 20,000
(b) ₹ 42,000
(c) ₹ 21,000
(d) ₹ 12,000

Answers

1. (b) All the recorded assets except fictitious assets, cash in hand, cash at bank, debit balance of current/capital account of partners, are transferred to the realisation account at their book values.
2. (c) nominal
3. (d) In this case, the firm pays remuneration to a partner for carrying out dissolution work, so no further entry is passed in the books of the firm regarding actual payment of expenses.
4. (c) ₹ 60,000 will be credited to realisation account and will be even paid-off. Balance ₹ 40,000 will be distributed amongst partners.
5. (a) (i) and (iv)
6. (d)

Dr **Realisation Account** Cr

Particulars	Amt (₹)	Particulars	Amt (₹)
To Sundry Assets	1,60,000	By Sundry Liabilities	1,75,000
To Bank	1,40,000	By Bank	1,25,000
	3,00,000		3,00,000

7. (c)

Dr **Realisation Account** Cr

Particulars		Amt (₹)	Particulars	Amt (₹)
To Assets		35,000	By Creditors	7,500
To Bank A/c		1,050	By Bank A/c (Assets)	40,250
To Bank A/c (Liabilities)		7,650		
To Profit Transfered to Partner's Capital A/cs				
A	1,800			
B	1,350			
C	900	4,050		
		47,750		47,750

8. (b) Partner's capital account
9. (d) Balance amount to be paid for Shaan's loan

$$= 1,00,000 - 90,000 = ₹\ 10,000$$

10. (a)

	Amt (₹)
Debtors	25,000
(–) Bad Debts	(5,000)
	20,000
5% Discount	(1,000)
	19,000

11. (c)

Balance Sheet

Liabilities	Amt (₹)	Assets	Amt (₹)
Capital A/c	31,500	Profit and Loss A/c	3,000
Creditors	6,000	Assets (Balancing Fig.)	34,500
	37,500		37,500

Dr **Realisation Account** Cr

Particulars	Amt (₹)	Particulars	Amt (₹)
To Assets	34,500	By Creditors	6,000
To Bank A/c (Creditors)	6,000	By Bank A/c (Assets) (Balancing Figure)	38,400
To Profit	3,900		
	44,400		44,400

12. (a) outside creditors
13. (c) realisation account
14. (d) Profit on realisation $= (7,20,00 - 6,00,00) - 8,000$

$$= ₹\ 1,12,000 \text{ (Profit)}$$

15. (a) No entry is passed if unrecorded asset is taken over by the partner against a recorded or unrecorded liability
16. (d) None of the above
17. (b) fully paid
18. (d) Balance amount paid to creditors

$$= (60,000 - 45,000) = ₹\ 15,000$$

19. (a) Stock taken over $= 80,000 \times \frac{80}{100} = ₹\ 64,000$

Balance to be paid $= 90,000 - 64,000 = ₹\ 26,000$

20. (d) Amount realised from debtor

$$= (30,000 - 20,000) \times \frac{90}{100} = ₹\ 2,52,000$$

21. (d) No entry
22. (c) Amount of debtor $= (34,000 - 1,000) \times \frac{60}{100} = ₹\ 19,800$
23. (a) Whatever amount is paid to partner, will be recorded by the firm as dissolution expenses. It doesn't matter how much amount is paid by the partner.
24. (b) ₹ 25,000
25. (b) Amount paid through cheque

$$= 60,000 - \left(60,000 \times \frac{90}{100}\right) = 60,000 - 54,000$$

$$= ₹\ 6,000$$

26. (d) Book value of assets realised

$$= 15,000 + 35,000 - 8,000 - 7,000 = ₹\ 1,70,000$$

Realised value of assets $= 1,70,000 + 5,000 - 25,000$

$$= ₹\ 1,50,000$$

27. (a) Realisation account will be credited by ₹ 60,000
28. (b) Net value of machinery $= 10,00,000 - 6,00,000$

$$= ₹\ 4,00,000$$

Realised value of machinery $= 4,00,000 - 20,000$

$$= ₹\ 3,80,000$$

Balance amount of creditor $= 5,40,000 - 3,80,000$

$$= ₹\ 1,60,000$$

29. (d) Concerned Partner's Capital A/c Dr 2,150
To Realisation A/c 2,150

30. (a) Both Assertion (A) and Reason (R) are true and Reason (R) is the correct explanation of Assertion (A)

31. (a) Both Assertion (A) and Reason (R) are true and Reason (R) is the correct explanation of Assertion (A)

32. (b) Both Assertion (A) and Reason (R) are true, but Reason (R) is not the correct explanation of Assertion (A)

33. (a) Both Assertion (A) and Reason (R) are true and Reason (R) is the correct explanation of Assertion (A)

34. (a) Both Assertion (A) and Reason (R) are true and Reason (R) is the correct explanation of Assertion (A)

35. (b) Both Assertion (A) and Reason (R) are true, but Reason (R) is not the correct explanation of Assertion (A)

36. (d) Assertion (A) is false, but Reason (R) is true

37. (c) Loan taken from spouse or relative of a partner is shown on the credit side of realisation account.

38. (c) Reserves and accumulated profits are transferred on the credit side of partners' capital account in old profit sharing ratio.

39. (b) Cash/Bank account remains nil after making payment of all external and internal liabilities at the time of dissolution.

40. (b) Statement II is correct and Statement I is incorrect

41. (a) Statement I is correct and Statement II is incorrect

42. (b) Statement II is correct and Statement I is incorrect

43. (c) Both the statements are correct

44. (a) Statement I is correct and Statement II is incorrect

45. (c) Both the statements are correct

46. (c) Cash or bank balance is not transferred to realisation account because it does not required realisation as it is already in liquid form.

47. (a) Statement I is correct and Statement II is incorrect

48. (d) (i) (iii) (ii) (iv)

49. (d) (ii) (i) (iii) (iv)

50. (d) (iii) (i) (ii) (iv)

51. (a) (ii) (i) (iv) (iii)

52. (a) (i) (ii) (iii) (iv)

53. (b) Dissolution by court

54. (b) Realisation Loss = (12,00,000 + 30,000) – (15,00,000 + 1,50,000) = ₹ 4,20,000

55. (d) Ravi's closing balance = 3,00,000 – 1,40,000
= ₹ 1,60,000

56. (a) Amount received on Realisation
= Debtors + Stock + Investment + Plant
= 60,000 + 35,500 + 16,000 + 45,000 = ₹ 1,56,500

57. (c) Assets Realised = $1,56,500 \times \frac{5}{100}$ = ₹ 7,825

58. (c) It would be distributed among partners in their old profit sharing ratio.
Anju = 3,000 × 2/5 = ₹ 1,200
Manju = 3,000 × 2/5 = ₹ 1,200
Sanju = 3,000 × 1/5 = ₹ 600

59. (a) $1,44,000 \times \frac{100}{90}$ = ₹ 1,60,000

60. (d) Remaining investment = 3,40,000 – 1,60,000
= ₹ 1,80,000
Book value taken over by R = 1,80,000 × 90/100
= ₹ 1,62,000
Agreed value of investment = 1,62,000 – 2,000
= ₹ 1,60,000

61. (b) Remaining debtors = 4,84,000 – 4,00,000 = ₹ 84,000
Debtors honoured = $84,000 \times \frac{50}{100}$ = ₹ 42,000

07

CHAPTER

Share is the interest of a shareholder in a company measured by a sum of money, for the purpose of liability in the first place and of interest in the second.

▼ YOUR STUDY GOALS

▼ YOUR PRACTICE GOAL

- Topicwise Solved Questions (41 Solved Questions)
- Numerical Questions [47 Questions (Unsolved)]
- Theoretical Questions [8 Questions (with answers)]
- Objective Questions (81 Qs ; MCQs, A-R, Statements, Matching, Case)

Accounting for Share Capital

7.1 Meaning of a Company

A company is an incorporated association, which is an artificial person created by law, having a separate legal identify, with a perpetual succession and a common seal.

According to **Section 2(20)** of the **Companies Act, 2013**, "Company means a company incorporated under this Act or any previous company law."

Features of a Company

1. **Incorporated Association** A company is an artificial person created by law upon registration under the Companies Act, 2013.
2. **Voluntary Association** It is formed by individuals who willingly unite to conduct business.
3. **Separate Legal Entity** A company is distinct from its members, allowing it to own property, enter contracts, conduct business and sue or be sued.
4. **Limited Liability** Members' liability is limited to the unpaid amount on their shares. e.g. If a ₹ 100 share is partly paid at ₹ 60, then the member's liability is ₹ 40 only.
5. **Perpetual Succession** As a separate legal entity, a company remains unaffected by the death, insolvency or luancy of its members.

6. **Common Seal** Being an artificial entity, a company uses a common seal as its official signature on legal documents.
7. **Transferability of Shares** Shares can be freely transferred in case of public companies and with restriction in case of private companies.
8. **May Sue or Be Sued** A company, as a legal entity, can initiate or face legal proceedings for contract breaches.
9. **Separate Management and Ownership** The company is managed by directors elected by its members, separating ownership from management.

Smart Study **Chart No. 1**

Classification/Types of Companies

On the basis of Incorporation

- **Chartered Companies** Formed by a special charter, by king or sovereign. e.g. East India Company.
- **Statutory Companies** Established under special legislative acts. e.g. RBI.
- **Registered Companies** Incorporated under the Companies Act, 2013 or any previous applicable acts. e.g. Reliance, Tata Motors.

On the basis of Liability

- **Company Limited by Shares** As per Section 2(22) of the Companies Act, 2013, it is a company where members' liability is limited by the memorandum to the unpaid amount on their shares.
- **Unlimited Liability Company** According to Section 2(92) of the Companies Act, 2013, it is a company where members' liability is unlimited. So, in case of winding-up, the members' private property may be used to settle the company's debts.
- **Company Limited by Guarantee** As per Section 2(21) of the Companies Act, 2013, it is a company where members' liability is limited by the memorandum to the amount they agree to contribute to the company's assets during winding-up.

On the basis of Transferability of Shares

- **Private Company** As per Section 2(68) of the Companies Act, 2013, a private company is one which has minimum paid-up capital as prescribed and which by its articles restricts the right to transfer its shares, limits its members to 200 (excluding current and former employees), prohibits any invitation to the public to subscribe for its securities and ends its name with 'Private Limited.'
- **Public Company** As per Section 2(71) of the Companies Act, 2013, a public company is not a private company, meets the prescribed minimum capital requirements and includes private companies that are subsidiaries of non-private companies and ends its name with 'Limited.'
- **One Person Company** As per Section 2(62) of the Companies Act, 2013, a one person company is a private company that has only one member.

7.2 Share

As per **Section 2(84)** of the **Companies Act, 2013**, "share means a share in the capital of a company and includes stock." The capital of a company is divided into small units, each called a share.

Shares grant holders ownership rights, voting rights and a claim to the company's profits. They represent the shareholder's interest in the company through a contractual agreement.

Each share has a nominal or face value (e.g. ₹ 1, ₹ 2, ₹ 5, ₹ 10, etc.) and is numbered for identification.

Nature of Shares

As per Section 44 of the Companies Act, 2013, shares or debentures or other interest of any member in a company shall be movable property, transferable in the manner provided by the articles of the company.

According to Sale of Goods Act, 1930, "Goods mean any kind of movable property other than actionable claims and money and includes stock and shares."

So, on the basis of above two definitions, it can be concluded that shares are basically goods which can be bought, sold or gifted.

Smart Study Chart No. 2

Classes or Kind of Shares

Equity Shares

Equity shares do not carry preferential rights and are entitled to dividends and capital repayment after the claim of preference shares.
These can be further classified as

- **Shares With Voting Rights** Allow shareholders to vote on corporate policies and board matters.
- **Shares With Differential Rights** Provide varied rights to shareholders on dividends, voting, etc. as per Rule 4 of the Companies (Share Capital and Debentures) Rules, 2014.

Preference Shares

Preference shares grant two key rights to shareholders

- Priority in receiving a fixed or stipulated dividend before equity shareholders.
- Priority in the return of capital during the company's winding-up over equity shares.

On the basis of Payment of Dividend

- **Cumulative Preference Shares** These shares grant the right to receive arrears of dividends before equity shareholders.
- **Non-cumulative Preference Shares** These shares do not provide the right to receive arrears of dividends.

On the basis of Convertibility

- **Convertible Preference Shares** These shares can be converted into equity shares as per the terms of issue.
- **Non-convertible Preference Shares** These shares cannot be converted into equity shares unless stated otherwise.

On the basis of Redemption

- **Redeemable Preference Shares** These shares are repaid after a specified period. They have with a maximum maturity of 20 years in India.
- **Irredeemable Preference Shares** These shares are repayable only during the company's winding-up. This is prohibited under the Companies Act, 2013.

On the basis of Participation in Profits

- **Participating Preference Shares** These shares allow holders to share in surplus profits, In addition to the fixed dividend, after equity dividend distribution.
- **Non-participating Preference Shares** These shares provide only a fixed dividend without right to share in surplus profits.

Difference between Preference Shares and Equity Shares

Basis	Preference Shares	Equity Shares
Dividend Rate	Preference shares are paid dividend at a fixed rate.	The rate of dividend on equity shares vary from year to year and depending upon the availability of profits.
Arrears of Dividend	If dividend is not paid on these shares in any year, the arrears of dividend may accumulate (in case of cumulative preference shares).	In case of equity shares, no such recoupment is possible.
Redemption	Preference shares can be redeemed as provided by the articles and terms of issue.	Equity shares cannot be redeemed except under a scheme involving reduction of capital.
Payment of Dividend	These shares have a preferential right to receive dividend before any dividend is paid on equity shares.	Payment of dividend on equity shares is made only after dividend has been paid to preference shareholders.
Payment of Capital	In the event of winding-up, preference shareholders have a preferential right to receive capital, before capital or any amount thereof is returned to equity shareholders.	Equity share capital is paid only after full payment is made to preference shareholders.
Voting Rights	Preference shareholders do not have any voting right except when their interest is directly affected.	Equity shareholders enjoy voting rights.
Participation in Management	Preference shareholders do not have the right to participate in the management of the company.	Equity shareholders have full right to participate in the management of the company.
Trading on Equity	Preference shares help the owners to derive the benefit of trading on equity.	Availability of only equity share capital in the total capital of a concern involves high degree of risk and an element of uncertainty.
Company's Formation	A company with only preference shares cannot be formed.	A company may be formed only with equity shares.

7.3 Share Capital

A company, being an artificial person, cannot generate its own capital rather it is necessarily to be collected from several persons. These persons are known as shareholders and the amount contributed by them is called share capital.

Share capital is the amount that a company can raise or has raised by issue of shares. It is that part of the capital of a company, which is represented by the total nominal value of shares it has issued.

From an accounting perspective, share capital is **classified** as follows

1. Authorised Share Capital

As per Section 2(8) of the Companies Act, 2013, authorised capital (also known as nominal or registered capital) is the maximum share capital a company can issue, as specified in its Memorandum of Association.

A company cannot raise more capital than this specified limit. Authorised share capital can be equal or exceed issued share capital, but cannot be less than the issued capital.

2. Issued Capital

According to Section 2(50) of the Companies Act, 2013, issued capital is the portion of authorised capital offered to the public for subscription.

It includes shares issued for cash, shares taken by directors as qualifying shares and shares subscribed by signatories to the memorandum. Issued capital cannot exceed authorised capital.

3. Subscribed Capital

As per Section 2(86) of the Companies Act, 2013, subscribed capital is that part of issued capital which is subscribed by its members.

It includes shares issued for consideration other than cash, shares taken by directors and those subscribed by signatories to the memorandum as qualifying shares.

Subscribed capital can be further divided into

(i) **Subscribed and Fully Paid-up** When shareholders have fully paid the nominal value of the shares.

(ii) **Subscribed but not Fully Paid-up** When either the full nominal value is not called-up by the company or it is called but not fully paid by the shareholders.

4. Called-up Capital

As per Section 2(15) of the Companies Act, 2013, 'called-up capital' refers to the portion of share capital that the company has called (or demanded) from shareholders for payment.

5. Paid-up Capital

Section 2(64) of the Companies Act, 2013 defines 'paid-up share capital' as the total amount received or credited as paid-up by the company against shares issued. It excludes any other amount received by the company in relation to the shares.

6. Reserve Capital

It is the part of subscribed share capital that remains uncalled and can only be called in the event of the company's winding-up. Companies passing a resolution for reserve capital must show these shares as 'subscribed but not fully paid-up.'

Difference between Reserve Capital and Capital Reserve

Basis	Reserve Capital	Capital Reserve
Meaning	It refers to that portion of uncalled share capital which shall not be called-up except in the event of winding-up.	It is that reserve which is created out of capital profits such as profit on sale of fixed assets, profit on revaluation of fixed assets, premium on issue of shares and debentures, profit on redemption of debentures, etc. These profits are not earned in the normal course of business.
Creation	It is not necessary to create reserve capital.	It is necessary to create capital reserve in case of capital profits.
Special Resolution	A special resolution is required for its creation.	No special resolution is required for the creation of capital reserves.
With Respect to Amount	It refers to the amount which has not been received.	It refers to the amount which has already been received.
Disclosure	It is not shown in the company's balance sheet.	It is shown as the first item under the head, 'reserves and surplus' on the liabilities side of the balance sheet.
When it Can be Used?	It can be used only at the time of winding-up of the company.	It can be used to write-off capital losses or to declare a bonus share any time during the life of the company.

Disclosure of Share Capital in Company's Balance Sheet

As per Schedule III of Companies Act, 2013, share capital is to be disclosed in a company's balance sheet in the following manner

Balance Sheet
as at ...

Particulars	Note No.	Current Year (₹)	Previous Year (₹)
I. EQUITY AND LIABILITIES			
1. **Shareholders' Funds**			
*(i) Share Capital	1	...	...

**As per Schedule III, disclosure requirements relating to share capital are to be provided in notes to accounts. Also note number should be put against the item in the balance sheet.*

Notes to Accounts

Particulars		Amt (₹)
1. **Share Capital**		
Authorised Capital		
... Shares of ₹ ... each		...
Issued Capital		
... Shares of ₹ ... each		...
Subscribed Capital		
Subscribed and Fully Paid-up		
... Shares of ₹ ... each		...
Subscribed but not Fully Paid-up		
... Shares of ₹ ... each ... Called-up	...	
(–) *Calls-in-arrears (If any)	(...)	...
Shares Forfeited Account		...
Total		...

***Calls-in-arrears** *It is that part of the call money that has been called-up by the company but has not been received by the company.*

7.4 Issue of Shares

A company raises its capital by issuing shares, which may be issued

1. **For Cash** Shares issued by company in exchange for cash.
2. **For Consideration other than Cash** Shares are issued by company against purchase of fixed assets or other non-cash considerations.

Terms of Issue of Shares

Shares may be issued

Term of Issue	Description
At Par	When the issue price equals the face value (e.g. A ₹ 10 share issued at ₹ 10).
At Premium	When the issue price exceeds the face value (e.g. A ₹ 10 share issued at ₹ 15; premium = ₹ 5).
At Discount	When the issue price is below the face value. However, as per **Section 35** of the Companies Act, 2013, issuing shares at a discount is **prohibited**, except for sweat equity shares issued to employees or directors under Section 54.

Important Terms

Related to Issue of Shares

- **Securities Premium** The excess of issue price over face value is credited to the securities premium account as required by the Companies Act, 2013. It is treated as a capital receipt.

  The securities premium account appears under main head 'shareholders' funds' and sub-head 'reserves and surplus' in the balance sheet.

  According to Section 52(2) of the Companies Act, 2013, the premium received on securities can only be used for
  - Buying-back own shares.
  - Issuing fully paid bonus shares.
  - Writing-off expenses, commissions or discounts on the issue of securities or debentures.
  - Paying the premium on redeemable preference shares or debentures.
  - Writing-off preliminary expenses.
- **Buy-back of Shares** Buy-back implies the act of purchasing its own shares by company. Funds for buy-back can come from
  - Free reserves.
  - The securities premium reserve account.
  - Proceeds from shares or other specified securities.
- **Preliminary Expenses** These include costs incurred during the promotion and formation of a company, such as registration fees, stamp duty, legal fees and expenses for preparing and issuing a prospectus. These are written-off in the year they are incurred and are also called incorporation, promotion or formation expenses.

Smart Study Chart No. 3

Modes of Issuing Shares

Private Placement of Shares

This involves issuing shares to a select group of individuals, not to the general public. It is generally done by private or unlisted companies. A special resolution is required to be passed and all SEBI guidelines for preferential issues are applicable in private placement also. Shares issued *via* private placement are subject to a three-year lock-in period during which they cannot be sold.

Note Accounting entries for private placement are the same as for public issues.

Public Issue of Shares

This refers to offering shares to the general public for subscription, often through an Initial Public Offer (IPO).

Steps involved in Public Issue

Issuing Prospectus
A formal invitation to the public,detailing company information like name, address, directors, objectives, financial position, capital structure and terms of issue to attract investors.

Receiving Applications
The public applies for shares by submitting application money (minimum 25% of the issue price, per SEBI guidelines) through a scheduled bank. Based on the applications received, the issue may be fully subscribed, oversubscribed or undersubscribed.

Allotting Shares
After the application period ends, the bank forwards application money and letters to the company. The directors ensure that the minimum subscription requirement is met before allotting shares.

To Make Calls
If the full issue price is not collected during application and allotment, subsequent instalments are called calls (e.g. First call, second call, final call). Calls must follow the terms in the Articles of Association or in their absence, the provisions of Table F of the Companies Act.

Minimum Subscription

As per Section 39(1) of the Companies Act, 2013, minimum subscription is the amount specified in the prospectus that must be subscribed. Securities cannot be allotted unless this amount is fully paid and received by the company through cheque or other instruments.

SEBI mandates that at least 90% of the total issue must be subscribed before shares are allotted to the public. If this minimum amount is not subscribed and the application amount is not received within 30 days (or the period specified by SEBI) from the prospectus issue date, the received amount must be refunded within 15 days of issue closure.

Accounting Treatment of Issue of Shares for Cash

Accounting treatment for shares issued can be discussed under two heads i.e. when amount is payable in lumpsum and when amount is payable in instalments.

1. Shares Payable in Lumpsum

Shares are said to have been issued against lumpsum payment when amount is payable in one instalment.

Journal entries will be as follows

- **For receiving share application money**

Bank A/c	Dr
To Share Application and Allotment A/c	
(Being application money received)	

- **For allotment of shares**
  - **At Par**

Share Application and Allotment A/c	Dr
To Share Capital A/c	
(Being the shares allotted and application money transferred to share capital account)	

  - **At Premium**

Share Application and Allotment A/c	Dr
To Share Capital A/c (With the face value of shares)	
To Securities Premium A/c (With the amount of premium)	
(Being shares allotted and application money transferred to share capital account and securities premium account)	

2. Shares Payable in Instalments

The amount against the shares may be received in instalments. First instalment is called **application money** (it is paid alongwith the application). Second instalment is called **allotment money** (it is collected by the company at the time of allotment). After allotment of shares, the remaining part of share money, when called-up, is known as **call money**. It may be collected in one or more instalments. If only one call is made, then it is called first and final call in place of first call, otherwise the word 'final' will be added to the last instalment.

The issue price of shares can be received by the company in instalments and these instalments are referred to as

First instalment	⟶	Application money payable alongwith application
Second instalment	⟶	Allotment money payable at the time of allotment
Third, fourth instalment	⟶	First call, second call and so on
Last instalment	⟶	Final call

The journal entries required to be passed are

- **On receipt of application money**

Bank A/c	Dr
To Share Application A/c	

- **On allotment of shares**

Share Application A/c	Dr
To Share Capital A/c	

- **On making allotment due**
  - **At Par**

Share Allotment A/c	Dr
To Share Capital A/c	

  - **At Premium**

Share Allotment A/c	Dr
To Share Capital A/c	
To Securities Premium A/c	

- **On receipt of allotment money**

Bank A/c	Dr
To Share Allotment A/c	

- **On making the first call due**

Share First Call A/c	Dr
To Share Capital A/c	

- **On receipt of the first call**

Bank A/c	Dr
To Share First Call A/c	

7.5 Full Subscription, Undersubscription and Oversubscription of Shares

On the basis of applications received by the public, an issue may be fully subscribed, undersubscribed or oversubscribed.

Full Subscription of Shares

When the number of shares applied for is equal to the number of shares offered for subscription, the issue is said to be fully subscribed. e.g. GH Ltd. issued 25,000 equity shares of ₹ 10 each and received applications for 25,000 equity shares.

However, this is a very rare situation. In reality, shares are generally undersubscribed or oversubscribed.

Undersubscription of Shares

When the number of shares applied for is less than the number of shares offered for subscription, the issue is said to be undersubscribed. e.g. GH Ltd. issued 25,000 equity shares of ₹ 10 each and received applications for 22,000 shares.

Oversubscription of Shares

When the number of shares applied for is more than the number of shares offered for subscription, the issue is said to be oversubscribed. e.g. GH Limited issued 25,000 equity shares of ₹ 10 each and received applications for 30,000 shares.

In case of oversubscription, following **three alternatives** are available

1. **Rejection of Applications** In this case, some applications are accepted in full and excess applications are rejected outrightly and their application money is refunded. e.g. Applications are invited for 25,000 shares and applications are received for 35,000 shares. Applications for shares are in excess of 25,000 shares i.e. 10,000 shares are not accepted and their application money is refunded.
2. **Partial or Pro-rata Allotment** In this case, no application for shares is refused and no applicant is allotted the shares in full. Smaller number of shares are allotted to each applicant according to the number of shares applied by him. So, the excess application money received is normally adjusted towards the amount due on allotment.

   In case, the excess money is more than the amount due on allotment of shares, then it may either be refunded or credited to calls-in-advance account.

   e.g. Applications are invited for 25,000 shares and applications are received for 35,000 shares. Shares are allotted to all the applicants in the ratio of 25 : 35, i.e. 5 : 7.
3. **Combination of Pro-rata Allotment and Rejection** In this case, some applications are accepted in full, some applications are outrightly rejected and proportional allotment is made to the remaining. e.g. Applicants are allotted shares as, applications for 10,000 shares are accepted in full, applications for 5,000 shares are rejected and the balance applications are allotted on pro-rata basis, i.e. in the ratio of 3 shares for every 4 shares applied.

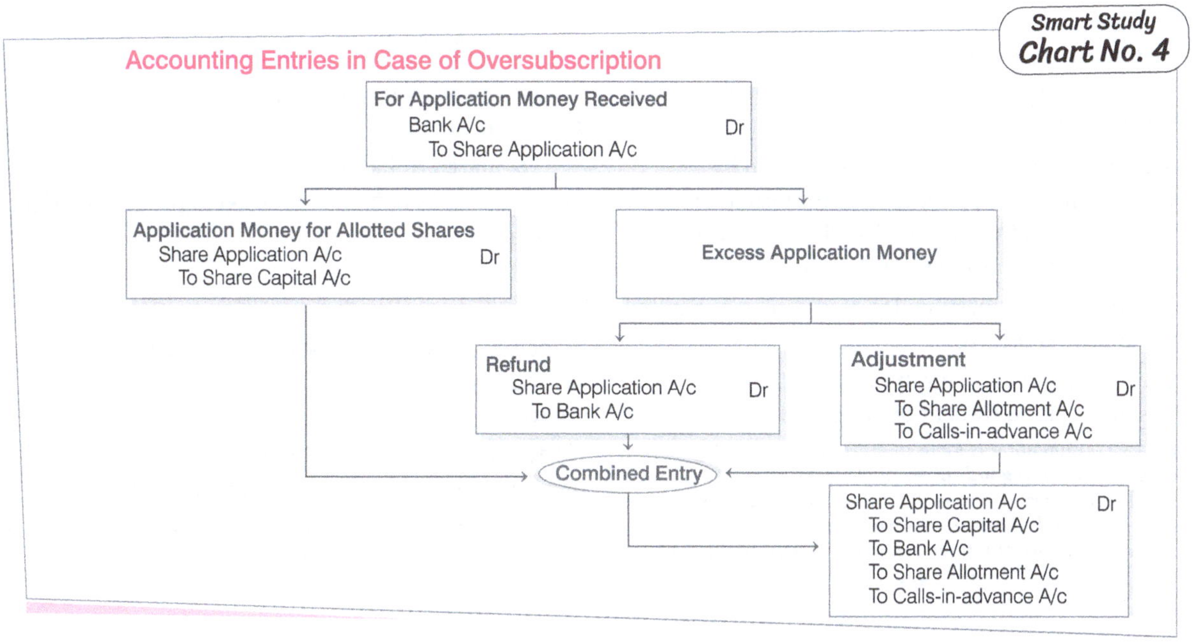

7.6 Issue of Shares for Consideration Other than Cash

Sometimes, a company issues shares in payment (consideration) against purchase of assets or business or to promoters/underwriters in appreciation for their services. This is referred to as 'issue of shares for consideration other than cash'. These shares can be issued either at par or at premium and the number of shares to be issued depends on the price at which the shares are issued and the amount payable.

These shares can be issued to vendors, promoters or underwriters as discussed ahead

I. Issue of Shares to Vendors

1. On Purchase of Assets or Business

In this regard, the purchase of assets and issue of shares are to be treated as two separate transactions.

Accounting Treatment

- **On purchase of assets**

Sundry Assets A/c (Individually) Dr
  To Vendor's A/c
(Being assets purchased from ...... vendor)

- **On purchase of business**

Sundry Assets A/c Dr
*Goodwill A/c Dr
  To Sundry Liabilities A/c
  To Vendor's A/c
  **To Capital Reserve A/c
(Being business purchased from vendor for purchase consideration of ...)

Purchase Consideration It is the amount paid by purchasing company in consideration for purchase of assets/business from the vendor. 'Vendor' is credited with purchase consideration payable to him.

It may be given in the question. If not, it can be computed using the following formula

Purchase Consideration = Sundry Assets – Sundry Liabilities, which is equivalent of 'net assets'

*If purchase consideration is more than net assets, then the difference is debited to **goodwill** account.*
***If purchase consideration is less than net assets, then the difference is credited to **capital reserve** account.*
Either goodwill or capital reserve account will appear at a time.

2. On Issue of Shares

- **Issue of shares at par**

Vendor's A/c Dr
  To Share Capital A/c
(Being ... shares of ₹ ... each issued to vendor)

$$\text{Number of Shares to be Issued} = \frac{\text{Amount Payable}}{\text{Issue Price (Face value)}}$$

- **Issue of shares at premium**

Vendor's A/c Dr
  To Share Capital A/c
  To Securities Premium A/c
(Being ... shares of ₹ ... each at a premium of ₹ ... issued to vendor)

$$\text{Number of Shares to be Issued} = \frac{\text{Amount Payable}}{\text{Issue Price (Face Value + Premium)}}$$

II. Issue of Shares to Promoters

The persons like individuals, firms or companies which promote the company are called promoters. Sometimes, companies issue shares to promoters for their services to the company.

Such issue of shares is put under the category of issue of shares for consideration other than cash. From accounting viewpoint, it is incorporation cost or formation expenses.

Accounting Treatment

Formation Expenses/Incorporation Cost/ Goodwill A/c Dr
  To Share Capital A/c
(Being ... shares of ₹ ... each issued to promoters of the company)

III. Issue of Shares to Underwriters

Underwriter is a person who works closely with the issuing body to determine the offering price of the securities.

Underwriters buys securities from the issuer and sells them to investor via the underwriter's distribution network. Sometimes, underwriters are issued shares as their fees by the issuing company.

Accounting Treatment

- **Making underwriting expenses due**

Underwriting (Commission) Expenses A/c	Dr
To Underwriters A/c	
(Being underwriting commission due)	

- **Issuing shares to underwriters**

Underwriters A/c	Dr
To Share Capital A/c	
(Being ... shares issued @ ₹ ... per share to underwriters)	

- **Transferring underwriting commission to statement of profit and loss**

Statement of Profit and Loss	Dr
To Underwriting Commission A/c	
(Being underwriting commission transferred to statement of profit and loss)	

Disclosure of Shares Issued for Consideration other than Cash in Balance Sheet

Shares issued for consideration other than cash are disclosed under subscribed share capital in the notes to accounts on share capital (either as subscribed and fully paid-up or subscribed but not fully paid-up, as the case may be).

7.7 Calls-in-arrears

When a shareholder fails to pay the amount due on allotment or calls, the unpaid amount is termed as calls-in-arrears. This amount may or may not be recorded in a Calls-in-arrears account. If permitted by the Article of Association, the company can charge interest on calls-in-arrears from the due date to the payment date. If the articles are silent, Table F of the Companies Act, 2013 applies, limiting the interest rate to 10% per annum.

Note Interest on calls-in-arrears is not included in the syllabus.

Disclosure in the Balance Sheet

While preparing balance sheet, calls-in-arrears are shown in notes to accounts as a deduction from subscribed but not fully paid-up capital.

Accounting Treatment

Calls-in-arrears can be dealt in the following ways

- Without opening calls-in-arrears account.
- By opening calls-in-arrears account.

Case 1 **Without Opening Calls-in-arrears Account**

In this method, the amount paid by the shareholders is credited to his call account. The call account will show debit balance equal to the total unpaid amount of each call. On receiving of calls-in-arrears amount, bank account is debited and relevant call account is credited.

Steps to Compute Calls-in-arrears in Case of Oversubscription

Step 1 Calculate the number of shares allotted (if shares applied are given) with the help of the following formula

$$\text{Allotted} = \frac{\text{Shares Applied} \times \text{Total Shares Issued}}{\text{Total Shares Applied}}$$

(If different categories are given, then total share issued and applied should be category specific).

or Calculate the number of shares applied (If shares allotted are given) with the help of the following formula

$$\text{Shares Applied} = \frac{\text{Shares Allotted} \times \text{Total Shares Applied}}{\text{Total Shares Issued}}$$

Step 2 Calculate the excess amount paid by the shareholder at the time of application by using the following formula

Excess Amount Paid = (Shares Applied – Shares Issued) × Application Money Per Share

Step 3 Calculate the amount due on allotment to be paid by the shareholder, with the help of the following formula

Amount Due on Allotment = Shares Issued to the Shareholder × Allotment Money Per Share

Step 4 Calls-in-arrears is the difference in the amounts computed is *step 3* and *step 2*.

Point to Remember

When shares are issued at premium, the steps to be followed will be the same as discussed above. However, it should be kept in mind that when shares are issued at premium, excess application money should be first adjusted towards the share capital and any amount over and above should be adjusted against securities premium.

Case 2 **By Opening Calls-in-arrears Account**

In this method, the amount of calls-in-arrears is transferred to an account namely calls-in-arrears account. If the amount of calls not paid by some shareholders is transferred to calls-in-arrears account, allotment and other call accounts will not show any balance.

The balance in calls-in-arrears account will show a debit balance equal to the total unpaid allotment and call money. Later, on receipt of amount, it is credited to calls-in-arrears account.

Accounting Entries of Calls-in-arrears

- **On non-receipt of call till the day fixed**

Calls-in-arrears A/c	Dr
To Relevant Call A/c	

- **On receipt of calls-in-arrears at a subsequent date**

Bank A/c	Dr
To Calls-in-arrears A/c	

7.8 Calls-in-advance

When a company receives money from allottees for calls not yet made, it is called calls-in-advance. It is credited to the calls-in-advance account. As per Section 50 of the Companies Act, 2013, a company can accept calls-in-advance only if authorised by its Articles of Association. The company pays interest on calls-in-advance as specified in its articles. If the articles are silent, Table F of the Companies Act, 2013 applies, which provides for interest at 12% per annum.

Note Interest on calls-in-advance is not included in the syllabus.

The journal entry passed to record this is

Bank A/c	Dr	[With the amount of call money received in advance]
To Calls-in-advance A/c		

It is adjusted when the respective call is made. The entry is

Calls-in-advance A/c	Dr
To (say) First Call A/c	

Disclosure in the Balance Sheet

Calls-in-advance is shown in the equity and liabilities part of the balance sheet under the head 'current liabilities' and sub-head 'other current liabilities.'

Difference between Calls-in-arrears and Calls-in-advance

Basis	Calls-in-arrears	Calls-in-advance
Meaning	It is the amount called-up by the company but not paid by shareholders.	It is the amount not called-up by the company but paid by shareholders.
Interest	Interest @ 10% is charged from members.	Interest @ 12% is given to members.
Disclosure	Amount is shown by way of deduction from called-up capital.	Amount is shown as a separate item under other current liability.

7.9 Forfeiture of Shares

Forfeiture refers to the cancellation of shares for non-payment of calls or allotment money, with the company seizing any amounts already paid. The shareholder's name is removed from the register of members.

e.g. If Raman buys 100 shares of RTATA Motors but fails to pay the final call of ₹ 4 per share, his shares are cancelled and the ₹ 600 paid will be forfeited.

If any shareholder fails to make the payment of allotment or call money, the company may forfeit such shares, subject to the following provisions of the Companies Act

- Articles of Association must empower the company to forfeit the shares.
- The company must give clear 14 days notice to the defaulting shareholder that unless he pays the amount together with interest, if any, by the specified date, the shares shall be forfeited. If the shareholder still does not pay, the company may forfeit the shares by passing an appropriate resolution.
- On forfeiture, the shares are cancelled and to that extent, share capital is reduced. The amount paid upto that date is not refunded to him, it is forfeited. The unpaid calls shown as calls-in-arrears, is also cancelled by passing a reverse entry.

Disclosure in the Balance Sheet

Unless the forfeited shares are reissued, the balance of the forfeited shares account is added to the paid-up capital. It is shown under subscribed share capital in the 'notes to accounts' on share capital under the head 'shareholders' funds' in the 'equity and liabilities' part of balance sheet.

Accounting Entries

At the time of passing the entry for forfeiture of shares, students must be careful about the following matters

- Amount called-up in respect of forfeited shares (₹ 10 per share in the illustration given above).
- Amount already received in respect of these shares (₹ 6 per share).
- Amount due, but has not been received in respect of these shares (₹ 4 per share).

Shares can be issued at par or at a premium.

Accounting entry for forfeiture will vary according to the following cases

***Case* 1 Forfeiture of Shares which were Issued at Par**

Share Capital A/c	Dr	[With called-up amount]
To Share Allotment A/c		[With amount due but not paid on allotment]
To Share Call A/c		[With amount due but not paid on call]
To Share Forfeiture A/c		[With amount already received]

When 'calls-in-arrears account' is maintained by the company, 'calls-in-arrears account' would be credited in the above entry instead of share allotment account and share call(s) account.

The entry will be

Share Capital A/c	Dr	[Called-up value]
To Calls-in-arrears A/c		[Total amount not received]
To Share Forfeiture A/c		[Amount received]

***Case* 2 Forfeiture of Shares which were Originally Issued at a Premium**

When shares issued at premium are forfeited, two possibilities exist which are

- Securities premium amount has been received.
- Securities premium amount has not been received.

Smart Study Chart No. 5

Accounting Treatment

When Securities Premium Amount has been Received

The amount received as securities premium is not cancelled, i.e. is not debited when the shares are forfeited. This amount is also not transferred to forfeited shares account.

It is due to the restrictions imposed by Section 52(2) of the Companies Act, 2013 which prescribes the purpose for securities premium utilisation.

The journal entry to be passed for forfeiture is given below

Share Capital A/c [Amount called-up, less premium]	Dr
To Share Allotment A/c [Amount not received]	
To Share Call A/c [Amount not received]	
To Share Forfeiture A/c [Amount received excluding securities premium]	

When Securities Premium Amount has not been Received

The amount of the premium credited to the securities premium account but not received is debited with the premium in respect of the forfeited shares.

The provisions of Section 52(2) of the Companies Act, 2013 are not violated since the amount is not received.

If premium has not been received, the following entry will be passed

Share Capital A/c [Amount called-up, less premium]	Dr
Securities Premium A/c [Premium amount called-up]	Dr
To Share Allotment A/c [Amount not received]	
To Share Call A/c [Amount not received]	
To Share Forfeiture A/c [Amount received]	

- In case, 'calls-in-arrears account' is maintained by the company, 'calls-in-arrears account' would be credited in the above entries instead of 'share allotment' and 'share call account'.

Forfeiture of Shares under Pro-rata Category

When shares belonging to pro-rata category are forfeited, the following accounting procedure is recommended

- Find the total number of shares applied (if not given) for by the shareholders whose shares are being forfeited.

  Apply the following formula

Number of Shares Applied for

$$= \frac{\text{Total Shares Applied under Pro-rata Category}}{\text{Total Shares Allotted under Pro-rata Category}} \times \text{Number of Shares Allotted by the Company to Shareholders}$$

or Calculate total number of shares allotted (If not given)

$$= \frac{\text{Total Shares Allotted under Pro-rata Category}}{\text{Total Shares Applied under Pro-rata Category}} \times \text{Number of Shares Applied by Shareholders}$$

- Multiply the number of shares as calculated above with the amount of application money. This gives total money sent by the shareholders with the application. This amount is forfeited on default and credited to share forfeited account.
- Deduct from the application money received, the amount due on application with the help of shares allotted. The result is the excess application money sent by the applicant in advance with the application. This money is available for adjustment towards allotment.
- Calculate the amount due on allotment and deduct it from the amount sent in advance with the application. The result is the amount in arrears on allotment. This amount is credited to share allotment account at the time of making entry for forfeiture.

7.10 Reissue of Forfeited Shares

The directors can either cancel or reissue the forfeited shares. Shares forfeited can be reissued at par, at premium or at a discount. In case, they are reissued at par, accounting entry will be

Bank A/c	Dr
To Share Capital A/c	

In case, shares are reissued at a discount, the amount of discount allowed on the reissue of forfeited shares must not exceed the amount forfeited on reissued shares. The discount allowed on reissue of forfeited shares should be debited to the 'share forfeiture account'.

The journal entry will be

Bank A/c	Dr	[With the amount received on reissue]
*Share Forfeiture A/c	Dr	[With the discount allowed on reissue]
To Share Capital A/c		[With the amount credited as paid-up]

*It is calculated as

= Number of Shares Reissued × (Paid-up Value − Reissue Price Per Share)

If the forfeited shares are reissued at premium (i.e. at a price higher than that of paid-up) the excess is credited to securities premium reserve account.

The journal entry will be

Bank A/c	Dr
To Share Capital A/c	
To Securities Premium A/c	

After the shares have been reissued, the balance (if any) in the share forfeited account is dealt in the way discussed below

Transfer of Balance in the Forfeited Shares Account after Reissue

1. When All Forfeited Shares are Reissued

If after the reissue of the forfeited shares, balance is left in the share forfeiture account, such balance is a capital profit and is transferred to the capital reserve account. The journal entry will be

Share Forfeiture A/c	Dr
To Capital Reserve A/c	
(Being the profit on reissue transferred to capital reserve)	

Point to Remember

If forfeited shares are reissued at par or premium, the whole of the amount forfeited on such shares is a gain of capital nature and is transferred to capital reserve account.

2. When Forfeited Shares are not Reissued

If only a part of forfeited shares is reissued, the discount cannot exceed the amount received on the reissued shares. Any excess is treated as a profit and transferred to the capital reserve.

The amount of forfeited shares not reissued, remains in the forfeited shares account, shown under subscribed share capital in the equity and liabilities section of the balance sheet.

Profit on Reissue =

$$\left(\frac{\text{Total Amount Forfeited}}{\text{Number of Shares Forfeited}} \times \text{Number of Shares Reissued}\right) - \left(\begin{array}{l}\text{Amount with which Forfeited Shares Account as Debited at the}\\ \text{Time of Reissue of such Shares}\\ \textit{or}\ \text{Reissue Discount}\end{array}\right)$$

7.11 Employee Stock Option Plan (ESOP)

ESOP allows a company to offer its directors, officers and employees the option to purchase a specified number of shares at a future date for a predetermined price, typically lower than the market price. These shares must be locked in for at least one year from the date of allotment.

A company may issue stock options if

- The shares are of the same class as those already issued.
- It is approved by a special resolution specifying the number of shares, market price and eligible employees or directors.
- At least one year has passed since the company began its operations.
- SEBI regulations are followed, if the shares are listed.

Some Important Terms

Term	Description
Preferential Allotment	Preferential allotment is the issuance of shares at a predetermined price to selected individuals, such as promoters, venture capitalists, financial institutions or suppliers, who aim to take a strategic stake in the company.
Sweat Equity Shares	Under Section 2(88) of the Companies Act, 2013, sweat equity shares are issued by a company to its employees or directors at a discount. These shares must be of the same class as already issued, approved by a special resolution and meet SEBI regulations. At least one year must have passed since the company began its operations. The accounting entries for sweat equity shares are the same as those for other equity shares.
Right Issue	Under Section 62 of the Companies Act, 2013, existing shareholders have the right to subscribe to a company's fresh share issue in proportion to their holdings. They can subscribe fully, partially, reject or renounce their right. Alternatively, the company can seek approval via a special resolution to offer the shares to the public.

Mind Map

Accounting for Share Capital

1 Meaning of Company

According to **Section 2(20)** of the Companies Act, 2013, company means a company incorporated under this Act or any previous company law.

2 Features of a Company

- Incorporated association under Companies Act, 2013
- Separate legal entity, i.e. distinct from its members.
- Limited liability of members
- Perpetual succession
- Common seal, i.e. signature of company
- Transferability of shares except in case of private company

3 Share

- According to **Section 2(84)** of the Companies Act, 2013, share means a share in the capital of a company and includes stock.
- Shares are classified into two categories, i.e. preference shares and equity shares.
- Preference shares carries the two rights, i.e. a right to receive dividend at a fixed rate before any dividend is paid on equity shares and right to return of capital on the winding-up of the company before that of equity shares.
- Equity shares are shares which are not preference shares. These can be classified as equity shares with voting rights and equity shares with differential rights.

4 Share Capital

Share capital can be classified as
- Authorised share capital
- Issued capital
- Subscribed capital, which can be categorised as
  - Subscribed and fully paid-up
  - Subscribed but not fully paid-up
- Called-up capital
- Paid-up capital
- Reserve capital

5 Issue of Shares

- Company may issue shares for cash or for consideration other than cash.
- A company can issue shares at par when shares are issued at their face value; at premium when shares are issued at a value that is higher than the face value and at discount (only sweat equity shares).
- Modes of issuing shares include private placement of shares (generally to group of persons privately) generally made by private company and public issue of shares (made to public in general).

6 Accounting Treatment of Shares

- Shares may be issued for an amount payable in lumpsum.
- Shares may be issued for an amount payable in installments.
- An issue may be fully subscribed, under subscribed or oversubscribed.
- When issue is oversubscribed, three alternatives is are available, i.e.
  - Excess application may be rejected
  - Company may allot partially, i.e. pro-rata basis
  - Company may allot partially and reject remaining applications
- Shares my be issued for consideration other than cash in case of purchase of assets or business, to promoters and to underwriters.

7 Calls-in-arrears and Calls-in-advance

- Amount not received against the amount called from the shareholder(s) is known as calls-in-arrears.
- When a company accepts money from the shareholder against the call not yet made, the amount received in advance is known as calls-in-advance.

8 Forfeiture of Shares

- It means cancellation of shares for non-payment of allotment or calls due and seizure of the amount already received from the defaulting shareholders.
- On forfeiture, the shares are cancelled and to that extent, share capital is reduced. The amount paid up to the date is not refunded, it is forfeited.

9 Reissue of Forfeited Shares

- The directors of a company can either cancel or reissue the forfeited shares. Shares forfeited can be reissued at par, at premium or at a discount.
- The profit on reissue of forfeited shares is transferred to capital reserve account.

Topicwise Solved Questions

Disclosure of Share Capital in Company's Balance Sheet

Solved Question 1 Sandesh Ltd. has an authorised capital of ₹ 30,00,000 divided into equity shares of ₹ 10 each. The company invited applications for issuing 70,000 shares. Applications for 69,000 shares were received. All calls were made and duly received except the first and final call of ₹ 2 per share on 3,000 shares. These shares were forfeited.

(i) Present the 'share capital' in the balance sheet of the company as per Schedule III, Part I of the Companies Act, 2013.

(ii) Also prepare 'notes to accounts' for the same. **CBSE 2023**

Sol. (i) **Balance Sheet** (An Extract)
as at ...

Particulars	Note No.	Amt (₹)
I. **EQUITY AND LIABILITIES**		
1. **Shareholders' Funds**		
Share Capital	1	6,84,000

(ii) **Notes to Accounts**

Particulars		Amt (₹)
1. **Share Capital**		
Authorised Share Capital		
3,00,000 Shares of ₹ 10 each		30,00,000
Issued Share Capital		
70,000 Shares of ₹ 10 each		7,00,000
Subscribed Share Capital		
Subscribed and Fully Paid-up		
66,000 Shares of ₹ 10 each		6,60,000
Subscribed but not Fully Paid-up		
3,000 Shares of ₹ 10 each	30,000	
(–) Calls-in-arrears (3,000 × 2)	(6,000)	24,000
		6,84,000

Solved Question 2 Shringar Ltd. was registered with an authorised capital of ₹ 5,00,000 divided into equity shares of ₹ 10 each. The company issued a prospectus inviting applications for 20,000 equity shares. The amount was payable as follows

On application — ₹ 3 per share On allotment — ₹ 5 per share

On first and final call — Balance

Applications were received for 19,000 equity shares and allotment was made to all the applicants. All the amounts were duly received except the first and final call on 5,000 shares.

Present the share capital in the company's balance sheet as per Schedule III, Part I of Companies Act, 2013. Also prepare 'notes to accounts' for the same. **CBSE 2024 C**

Sol. **Balance Sheet of Shringar Ltd.** (An Extract)
as at ...

Particulars	Note No.	Amt (₹)
I. **EQUITY AND LIABILITIES**		
1. **Shareholders' Funds**		
Share Capital	1	1,80,000

Notes to Accounts

Particulars		Amt (₹)
1. **Share Capital**		
Authorised Share Capital		
50,000 Equity Shares of ₹ 10 each		5,00,000
Issued Share Capital		
20,000 Equity Shares of ₹ 10 each		2,00,000
Subscribed Share Capital		
Subscribed and Fully Paid-up		
14,000 Equity Shares of ₹ 10 each		1,40,000
Subscribed but not Fully Paid-up		
5,000 Equity Shares of ₹ 10 each	50,000	
(–) Calls-in-arrears (5,000 × 2)	(10,000)	40,000
		1,80,000

Issue of Shares for Cash

Solved Question 3 ***(Issued at par, fully subscribed, payable in lumpsum)*** **Mayank Ltd. invited applications for 4,000 equity shares of ₹ 10 each at the issue price of ₹ 10. The amount payable alongwith application is ₹ 10. This issue was fully subscribed. Give the journal entries for the above transactions. Also prepare the balance sheet.**

Sol. JOURNAL

Date	Particulars	LF	Amt (Dr)	Amt (Cr)
	Bank A/c Dr To Equity Share Application and Allotment A/c (4,000 × 10) (Being the application money received on 4,000 equity shares of ₹ 10 each)		40,000	40,000
	Equity Share Application and Allotment A/c Dr To Equity Share Capital A/c (Being the share money transferred to share capital on allotment)		40,000	40,000

Important Problem Solving Point

In case, the issue price is payable in one instalment or lumpsum, then entry should be passed through share application and allotment account.

Balance Sheet
as at ...

Particulars	Note No.	Amt (₹)
I. **EQUITY AND LIABILITIES**		
1. **Shareholders' Funds**		
Share Capital	1	40,000
Total		40,000
II. **ASSETS**		
1. **Current Assets**		
Cash and Cash Equivalents	2	40,000
Total		40,000

Notes to Accounts

Particulars	Amt (₹)
1. **Share Capital**	
Authorised Share Capital	
... Equity Shares of ₹ 10 each	—
Issued Share Capital	
... Equity Shares of ₹ 10 each	—
Subscribed Share Capital	
Subscribed and Fully Paid-up	
4,000 Equity Shares of ₹ 10 each	40,000
2. **Cash and Cash Equivalents**	
Cash at Bank	40,000

Solved Question 4 *(Issued at par, fully subscribed, payable in instalments)* **Parth Ltd. was registered with a capital of ₹ 10,00,000 in shares of ₹ 20 each. It invited applications for 50,000 shares. The amount is payable as ₹ 5 on application, ₹ 10 on allotment and ₹ 5 on first and final call. The whole of above issue was applied for and amount was duly received. Give the journal entries for the above transactions.**

Sol.

JOURNAL

Date	Particulars		LF	Amt (Dr)	Amt (Cr)
	Bank A/c	Dr		2,50,000	
	To Share Application A/c (50,000 × 5)				2,50,000
	(Being application money received on 50,000 shares at ₹ 5 per share)				
	Share Application A/c	Dr		2,50,000	
	To Share Capital A/c				2,50,000
	(Being application money transferred to share capital account at the time of allotment)				
	Share Allotment A/c	Dr		5,00,000	
	To Share Capital A/c (50,000 × 10)				5,00,000
	(Being allotment money due on 50,000 shares at ₹ 7 per share)				
	Bank A/c	Dr		5,00,000	
	To Share Allotment A/c				5,00,000
	(Being receipt of ₹ 10 per share on 50,000 shares)				
	Share First and Final Call A/c	Dr		2,50,000	
	To Share Capital A/c (50,000 × 5)				2,50,000
	(Being first and final call money due on 50,000 shares @ ₹ 5 per share)				
	Bank A/c	Dr		2,50,000	
	To Share First and Final Call A/c				2,50,000
	(Being first and final call money received)				

Solved Question 5 **Urvashi Ltd. invited application for 60,000 shares of ₹ 15 per share at a premium of 5 per share, payable as ₹ 5 on application, ₹ 7 on allotment (including premium of ₹ 5) and balance on 2 equal instalments. All shares were applied and allotted. All the money was duly received. You are required to journalise these transactions.**

Sol.

JOURNAL

Date	Particulars		LF	Amt (Dr)	Amt (Cr)
(i)	Bank A/c	Dr		3,00,000	
	To Share Application A/c				3,00,000
	(Being application money received)				
(ii)	Share Application A/c	Dr		3,00,000	
	To Share Capital A/c				3,00,000
	(Being application money due)				
(iii)	Share Allotment A/c	Dr		4,20,000	
	To Share Capital A/c				1,20,000
	To Securities Premium A/c				3,00,000
	(Being allotment money due)				
(iv)	Bank A/c	Dr		4,20,000	
	To Share Allotment A/c				4,20,000
	(Being allotment money received)				
(v)	Share First Call A/c	Dr		2,40,000	
	To Share Capital A/c				2,40,000
	(Being first call money due)				
(vi)	Bank A/c	Dr		2,40,000	
	To Share First Call A/c				2,40,000
	(Being first call money received)				

Date	Particulars		LF	Amt (Dr)	Amt (Cr)
(vii)	Share Final Call A/c	Dr		2,40,000	
	To Share Capital A/c				2,40,000
	(Being final call money due)				
(viii)	Bank A/c	Dr		2,40,000	
	To Share Final Call A/c				2,40,000
	(Being final call money received)				

Undersubscription

Solved Question 6 *(Issue of shares at par, undersubscribed, payment in instalment)* **Parth Ltd. was registered with a capital of ₹ 10,00,000 in shares of ₹ 20 each. It invited applications for 50,000 shares. The amount is payable as ₹ 5 on application, ₹ 10 on allotment and ₹ 5 on first and final call. Give journal entries for the above transactions and also show the cash book of the firm, when the public has subscribed for 46,500 shares.**

Sol. JOURNAL

Date	Particulars		LF	Amt (Dr)	Amt (Cr)
	Share Application A/c	Dr		2,32,500	
	To Share Capital A/c (46,500 × 5)				2,32,500
	(Being application money received, transferred to capital account at the time of allotment)				
	Share Allotment A/c	Dr		4,65,000	
	To Share Capital A/c (46,500 × 10)				4,65,000
	(Being allotment money due)				
	Share First and Final Call A/c	Dr		2,32,500	
	To Share Capital A/c (46,500 × 5)				2,32,500
	(Being first and final call money due)				

Dr **Cash Book** Cr

Date	Particulars	Amt (₹)	Date	Particulars	Amt (₹)
	To Share Application A/c	2,32,500		By Balance c/d	9,30,000
	To Share Allotment A/c	4,65,000			
	To Share First and Final Call A/c	2,32,500			
		9,30,000			9,30,000

Important Problem Solving Point

When cash book is maintained, journal entries related to receipt of application, allotment or calls are not passed. Rather, they are recorded in cash book.

Solved Question 7 **Chirag Ltd. issued 10,000 equity shares of ₹ 10 each at premium of ₹ 2, payable as follows ₹ 3 on application, 6 on allotment (including premium) and ₹ 3 on first and final call. Company received applications for 7,000 shares. Pass necessary journal entries.**

Sol. JOURNAL

Date	Particulars		LF	Amt (Dr)	Amt (Cr)
(i)	Bank A/c	Dr		21,000	
	To Share Application A/c				21,000
	(Being application money received)				
(ii)	Share Application A/c	Dr		21,000	
	To Share Capital A/c				21,000
	(Being application money due)				

Date	Particulars		LF	Amt (Dr)	Amt (Cr)
(iii)	Share Allotment A/c	Dr		42,000	
	To Share Capital A/c				28,000
	To Securities Premium A/c				14,000
	(Being allotment money due)				
(iv)	Bank A/c	Dr		42,000	
	To Share Allotment A/c				42,000
	(Being allotment money received)				
(v)	Share First and Final Call A/c	Dr		21,000	
	To Share Capital A/c				21,000
	(Being first and final call money due)				
(vi)	Bank A/c	Dr		21,000	
	To Share First and Final Call A/c				21,000
	(Being first and final call money received)				

Oversubscription

Solved Question 8 **Daksh Ltd. invited applications for 10,000 shares of ₹ 10 each payable as follows ₹ 2 on application, ₹ 3 on allotment, ₹ 2 on first call and balance on final call. Applications were received for 15,000 shares. Applications were accepted for 10,000 shares and remaining applications were rejected. You are required to journalise these transactions.**

Sol.

JOURNAL

Date	Particulars		LF	Amt (Dr)	Amt (Cr)
(i)	Bank A/c	Dr		30,000	
	To Share Application A/c				30,000
	(Being application money received)				
(ii)	Share Application A/c	Dr		30,000	
	To Share Capital A/c				20,000
	To Bank A/c				10,000
	(Being application money due and rejected excess application received)				
(iii)	Share Allotment A/c	Dr		30,000	
	To Share Capital A/c				30,000
	(Being allotment money due)				
(iv)	Bank A/c	Dr		30,000	
	To Share Allotment A/c				30,000
	(Being allotment money received)				
(v)	Share First Call A/c	Dr		20,000	
	To Share Capital A/c				20,000
	(Being first call money due)				
(vi)	Bank A/c	Dr		20,000	
	To Share First Call A/c				20,000
	(Being first call money received)				
(vii)	Share Final Call A/c	Dr		30,000	
	To Share Capital A/c				30,000
	(Being final call money due)				
(viii)	Bank A/c	Dr		30,000	
	To Share Final Call A/c				30,000
	(Being final call money received)				

Solved Question 9 *(Issue of shares at premium, oversubscribed, payment in lumpsum)* **Annex Ltd. issued 1,00,000 shares of ₹ 10 each at a premium of 10% to the public for subscription. The whole amount was payable on application. Applications were received for 3,00,000 shares and the board decided to allot shares to all shareholders on pro-rata basis.**

Pass necessary journal entries for the above transactions in the books of Annex Ltd. **CBSE 2023**

Sol. JOURNAL

Date	Particulars	LF	Amt (Dr)	Amt (Cr)
	Bank A/c (3,00,000 × 11) Dr		33,00,000	
	To Share Application and Allotment A/c			33,00,000
	(Being application money received on 3,00,000 shares @ ₹ 11 per share inclusive of securities premium)			
	Share Application and Allotment A/c Dr		33,00,000	
	To Share Capital A/c (1,00,000 × 10)			10,00,000
	To Securities Premium A/c (1,00,000 × 1)			1,00,000
	To Bank A/c (2,00,000 × 11)			22,00,000
	(Being money received on application transferred to share capital account and securities premium on allotment and excess refunded)			

Solved Question 10 **Printkit Limited invited applications for issue of 80,000 equity shares of 10 each. The amount was payable as follows**

On application ₹ 3 per share, on allotment ₹ 2 per share, on first and final call balance

Applications for 1,50,000 shares were received. Applications for 10,000 shares were rejected and pro-rata allotment was made to the remaining applicants on the following basis

Category A — Applicants for 80,000 shares were allotted 40,000 shares.

Category B — Applicants for 60,000 shares were allotted 40,000 shares.

Excess money received on application was adjusted towards amount due on allotment and first and final call. All the amounts due on allotment and first and final call were duly received.

Pass necessary journal entries in the books of Printkit Limited. **CBSE 2024**

Sol. In the Books of Printkit Limited

JOURNAL

Date	Particulars	LF	Amt (Dr)	Amt (Cr)
(i)	Bank A/c Dr		4,50,000	
	To Equity Share Application A/c			4,50,000
	(Being application money received on 1,50,000 shares)			
(ii)	Equity Share Application A/c Dr		4,50,000	
	To Equity Share Capital A/c			2,40,000
	To Equity Share Allotment A/c			1,40,000
	To Calls-in-advance A/c			40,000
	To Bank A/c			30,000
	(Being application money transferred to share capital and excess amount adjusted to share allotment account and calls-in-advance; application money on 10,000 shares refunded)			
(iii)	Equity Share Allotment A/c Dr		1,60,000	
	To Equity Share Capital A/c			1,60,000
	(Being allotment money due on 80,000 shares)			
(iv)	Bank A/c Dr		20,000	
	To Equity Share Allotment A/c			20,000
	(Being allotment money received after adjusting excess application money)			
(v)	Equity Share First and Final Call A/c Dr		4,00,000	
	To Equity Share Capital A/c			4,00,000
	(Being share first and final call money due)			

Date	Particulars		LF	Amt (Dr)	Amt (Cr)
(vi)	Bank A/c	Dr		3,60,000	
	Calls-in-advance A/c	Dr		40,000	
	To Equity Share First and Final Call A/c				4,00,000
	(Being share first and final call money received after adjusting calls-in-advance)				

Solved Question 11 ***(Issue of shares at par, oversubscribed, payment in instalment)*** **Janta Papers Ltd. invited applications for 1,00,000 equity shares of ₹ 25 each payable as under**

On application	**₹ 5.00 per share**
On allotment	**₹ 7.50 per share**
On first call (due two months after allotment)	**₹ 6 per share**
On second and final call (due two months after first call)	**₹ 6.5 per share**

Applications were received for 4,00,000 shares on 1st January, 2018 and allotment was made on 1st February, 2018. Record journal entries in the books of the company to record these share capital transactions under each of the following circumstances

(i) The directors decide to allot 1,00,000 shares in full to selected applicants and the applications for the remaining 3,00,000 shares were rejected outright.

(ii) The directors decide to make a pro-rata allotment of 25% of the shares applied for to every applicant; to apply the balance of application money towards amount due on allotment and to refund the amount remaining thereafter.

(iii) The directors totally rejected applications for 2,00,000 shares, accepted full applications for 80,000 shares and made a pro-rata allotment of 20,000 shares to the remaining applicants. The excess of application money is to be adjusted towards allotment and calls to be made. **NCERT (Modified)**

Sol. (i) **First Alternative** Rejection of Applications

JOURNAL

Date	Particulars		LF	Amt (Dr)	Amt (Cr)
2018					
Jan 1	Bank A/c (4,00,000 ×5)	Dr		20,00,000	
	To Equity Share Application A/c				20,00,000
	(Being money received on applications for 4,00,000 shares @ ₹ 5 per share)				
Feb 1	Equity Share Application A/c	Dr		20,00,000	
	To Equity Share Capital A/c (1,00,000 ×5)				5,00,000
	To Bank A/c (3,00,000 ×5)				15,00,000
	(Being transfer of application money on 1,00,000 shares to share capital and money refunded on rejected applications)				
	Equity Share Allotment A/c	Dr		7,50,000	
	To Equity Share Capital A/c (1,00,000 ×7.5)				7,50,000
	(Being amount due on the allotment of 1,00,000 shares @ ₹ 7.5 per share)				
	Bank A/c	Dr		7,50,000	
	To Equity Share Allotment A/c				7,50,000
	(Being allotment money received)				
Apr 1	Equity Share First Call A/c (1,00,000 × 6)	Dr		6,00,000	
	To Equity Share Capital A/c				6,00,000
	(Being first call money due on 1,00,000 shares @ ₹ 6 per share)				
	Bank A/c	Dr		6,00,000	
	To Equity Share First Call A/c				6,00,000
	(Being first call money received)				

Date	Particulars		LF	Amt (Dr)	Amt (Cr)
Jun 1	Equity Share Second and Final Call A/c (1,00,000 × 6.5)	Dr		6,50,000	
	To Equity Share Capital A/c				6,50,000
	(Being second and final call money due on 1,00,000 shares @ ₹ 5 per share)				
	Bank A/c	Dr		6,50,000	
	To Equity Share Second and Final Call A/c				6,50,000
	(Being second and final call money received)				

(ii) **Second Alternative** Partial or Pro-rata Allotment

JOURNAL

Date	Particulars		LF	Amt (Dr)	Amt (Cr)
2018					
Jan 1	Bank A/c (4,00,000 ×5)	Dr		20,00,000	
	To Equity Share Application A/c				20,00,000
	(Being money received on applications for 4,00,000 shares @ ₹ 5 per share)				
Feb 1	Equity Share Application A/c	Dr		20,00,000	
	To Equity Share Capital A/c (1,00,000 ×5)				5,00,000
	To Equity Share Allotment A/c (1,00,000 ×7.5)				7,50,000
	To Bank A/c				7,50,000
	(Being transfer of application money on shares allotted to share capital, excess application amount credited to allotment account and money refunded on applications)				
	Equity Share Allotment A/c	Dr		7,50,000	
	To Equity Share Capital A/c (1,00,000 ×7.5)				7,50,000
	(Being amount due on the allotment of ₹ 1,00,000 shares @ 7.5 per share)				

Important Problem Solving Points

- Entry for receiving allotment money will not be passed as the full amount payable at the time of allotment has been received with application.
- The entries regarding the two calls would be the same as under the preceeding alternative.

(iii) **Third Alternative** Combination of Pro-rata Allotment and Rejection

JOURNAL

Date	Particulars		LF	Amt (Dr)	Amt (Cr)
2018					
Jan 1	Bank A/c (4,00,000 ×5)	Dr		20,00,000	
	To Equity Share Application A/c				20,00,000
	(Being money received on applications for 4,00,000 shares @ ₹ 5 per share)				
Feb 1	Equity Share Application A/c	Dr		20,00,000	
	To Equity Share Capital A/c				5,00,000
	To Equity Share Allotment A/c				1,50,000
	To Calls-in-advance A/c				2,50,000
	To Bank A/c (WN)				11,00,000
	(Being amount on share application adjusted to share capital, share allotment and calls-in-advance and the balance refunded including the money on rejected applications)				
	Equity Share Allotment A/c	Dr		7,50,000	
	To Equity Share Capital A/c (1,00,000 ×7.5)				7,50,000
	(Being amount due on the allotment of 1,00,000 shares @ ₹ 7.5 per share)				

Date	Particulars		LF	Amt (Dr)	Amt (Cr)
	Bank A/c	Dr		6,00,000	
	To Equity Share Allotment A/c				6,00,000
	(Being allotment money received)				
Apr 1	Equity Share First Call A/c	Dr		6,00,000	
	To Equity Share Capital A/c (1,00,000 × 6)				6,00,000
	(Being first call money due on 1,00,000 shares @ ₹ 6 per share)				
	Bank A/c	Dr		6,00,000	
	Calls-in-advance A/c	Dr		1,20,000	
	To Equity Share First Call A/c				7,20,000
	(Being calls-in-advance adjusted against first call and the balance money on call received)				
Jun 1	Equity Share Second and Final Call A/c	Dr		6,50,000	
	To Equity Share Capital A/c (1,00,000 × 6.5)				6,50,000
	(Being second and final call money due on 1,00,000 shares @ ₹ 5 per share)				
	Bank A/c	Dr		5,20,000	
	Calls-in-advance A/c	Dr		1,30,000	
	To Equity Share Second and Final Call A/c				6,50,000
	(Being calls-in-advance adjusted against second and final call and the balance money on call received)				

Note The balance of excess application money as a result of pro-rata distribution in journal entry 2 above is large enough to meet the demands on allotted shares in respect of the allotment and the two calls money, as well as to leave an amount to be refunded alongwith that on the rejected applications.

Working Note

Particulars		Amt (₹)
Excess Application Money		15,00,000
(–) Transfer		
Share Allotment		
20,000 shares @ ₹ 7.50	(1,50,000)	
Share Calls		
20,000 shares @ ₹ 12.50	(2,50,000)	(4,00,000)
Amount to be refunded (including that on the rejected applications)		11,00,000

Issue of Shares for Consideration Other than Cash

Solved Question 12 **Kumar Ltd. purchased assets of ₹ 6,30,000 from Bhanu Oil Ltd. Kumar Ltd. issued equity shares of ₹ 100 each fully paid in consideration. What journal entries will be made, if the shares are issued (i) at par and (ii) at premium of 20%.**

Sol.

JOURNAL

Date	Particulars		LF	Amt (Dr)	Amt (Cr)
	Sundry Assets A/c	Dr		6,30,000	
	To Bhanu Oil Ltd.				6,30,000
	(Being assets purchased from Bhanu Oil Ltd.)				
(i)	**When shares are issued at par**				
	Bhanu Oil Ltd.	Dr		6,30,000	
	To Equity Share Capital A/c (6,300 × 100)				6,30,000
	(Being 6,300 shares issued at par to Bhanu Ltd.)				
(ii)	**When shares are issued at premium**				
	Bhanu Oil Ltd.	Dr		6,30,000	
	To Equity Share Capital A/c (5,250 × 100)				5,25,000
	To Securities Premium A/c (5,250 × 20)				1,05,000
	(Being 5,250 shares are issued at 20% premium to Bhanu Ltd. in consideration of assets purchased)				

Working Note

$$\text{Number of Shares to be Issued} = \frac{\text{Amount Payable}}{\text{Face Value Per Share}}$$

Case (i) $\frac{6,30,000}{100} = 6,300$ shares *Case* (ii) $\frac{6,30,000}{(100+20)\ 120} = 5,250$ shares

Solved Question 13 **Chavi Ltd. purchased machinery from Neo Ltd. It was agreed that the purchase consideration will be paid by issuing 10,000 equity shares of ₹ 10 each at a premium of 10% and a bank draft of ₹ 50,000. Pass the necessary journal entries in the books of Chavi Ltd. for the above transactions.** **CBSE 2024**

Sol. **In the Books of Chavi Ltd.**

JOURNAL

Date	Particulars		LF	Amt (Dr)	Amt (Cr)
(i)	Machinery A/c	Dr		1,60,000	
	To Neo Ltd. A/c				1,60,000
	(Being machinery purchased from Neo Ltd.)				
(ii)	Neo Ltd. A/c	Dr		1,60,000	
	To Equity Share Capital A/c				1,00,000
	To Securities Premium A/c				10,000
	To Bank A/c				50,000
	(Being issued 10,000 equity shares of ₹ 10 each at a premium of 10% and bank draft in favour of Neo Ltd.)				
	Alternatively				
(ii) (a)	Neo Ltd. A/c	Dr		1,10,000	
	To Equity Share Capital A/c				1,00,000
	To Securities Premium A/c				10,000
	(Being issued 10,000 equity shares of ₹ 10 each at a premium of 10% to Neo Ltd.)				
(b)	Neo Ltd. A/c	Dr		50,000	
	To Bank A/c				50,000
	(Being payment made to Neo Ltd. by a bank draft)				

Solved Question 14 **Nikhil Ltd. purchased a running business from Sonia Ltd. The assets and liabilities consisted of the following**

Machinery ₹ 7,00,000, debtors ₹ 2,50,000, stock ₹ 5,00,000, building ₹ 11,50,000 and bills payable ₹ 2,50,000.

Pass necessary journal entries in the books of Nikhil Ltd. if

(i) The purchase consideration of ₹ 22,00,000 was discharged by issuing 20,000 fully paid equity shares of ₹ 100 each at a premium of 10%.

(ii) The purchase consideration of ₹ 24,00,000 was discharged by issuing 19,200 fully paid equity shares of ₹ 100 each at a premium of 25%.

Sol. **JOURNAL**

Date	Particulars		LF	Amt (Dr)	Amt (Cr)
(i)	Machinery A/c	Dr		7,00,000	
	Debtors A/c	Dr		2,50,000	
	Stock A/c	Dr		5,00,000	
	Building A/c	Dr		11,50,000	
	To Bills Payable A/c				2,50,000
	To Sonia Ltd.				22,00,000
	To Capital Reserve A/c				1,50,000
	(Being assets and liabilities taken over and balance credited to capital reserve)				

Date	Particulars		LF	Amt (Dr)	Amt (Cr)
	Sonia Ltd.	Dr		22,00,000	
	To Equity Share Capital A/c (20,000 × 100)				20,00,000
	To Securities Premium A/c (20,000 × 10)				2,00,000
	(Being 20,000 equity shares issued at a premium of 10%)				
(ii)	Machinery A/c	Dr		7,00,000	
	Debtors A/c	Dr		2,50,000	
	Stock A/c	Dr		5,00,000	
	Building A/c	Dr		11,50,000	
	Goodwill A/c	Dr		50,000	
	To Bills Payable A/c				2,50,000
	To Sonia Ltd.				24,00,000
	(Being assets and liabilities taken over and balance debited to goodwill account)				
	Sonia Ltd.	Dr		24,00,000	
	To Equity Share Capital A/c (19,200 × 100)				19,20,000
	To Securities Premium A/c (19,200 × 25)				4,80,000
	(Being 19,200 equity shares issued at a premium of 25%)				

Working Notes

1. Number of Shares $= \frac{22,00,000}{110} = 20,000$
2. Number of Shares $= \frac{24,00,000}{125} = 19,200$

Solved Question 15 **Rakesh Ltd. issued 3,500 shares of 10 each credited as fully paid to the promoters for helping on the incorporate of the company and also issued 3,000 shares of 10 each fully paid up to the underwriters for their underwriting services. Journalise these transactions.**

Sol.

JOURNAL

Date	Particulars		LF	Amt (Dr)	Amt (Cr)
(i)	Incorporation Expenses A/c	Dr		35,000	
	To Promotors				35,000
	(Being amount due to promotors for their services)				
(ii)	Promotors	Dr		35,000	
	To Share Capital A/c				35,000
	(Being shares issued to the promotors)				
(iii)	Underwriting Commission A/c	Dr		30,000	
	To Underwriter				30,000
	(Being commission of underwriters due)				
(iv)	Underwriter	Dr		30,000	
	To Share Capital				30,000
	(Being shares issued to underwriters)				

Calls-in-arrears

Solved Question 16 **Gold Rush Ltd. called the first call money of ₹ 3 per share on its 50,000 shares. Dibakar who holds 2,750 shares of the company failed to pay the above amount by the due date of 15th August. However, he later on paid the amount on 30th August. Journalise in the books when calls-in-arrears account is not to be opened.**

Sol.

JOURNAL

Date	Particulars		LF	Amt (Dr)	Amt (Cr)
Aug 15	Share First Call A/c	Dr		1,50,000	
	To Share Capital A/c				1,50,000
	(Being first call made due on 50,000 shares)				
Aug 15	Bank A/c	Dr		1,41,750	
	To Share First Call A/c				1,41,750
	(Being first call received on 47,250 shares)				

Date	Particulars		LF	Amt (Dr)	Amt (Cr)
Aug 30	Bank A/c	Dr		8,250	
	To Share First Call A/c				8,250
	(Being amount outstanding on account of first call on 2,750 shares received)				

Note If the question is silent, then entry for receiving calls-in-arrears will not be passed.

Solved Question 17 **Dureja Ltd. was registered with an authorised capital of 4,00,000 shares of 10 each. It invited applications for 2,40,000 shares payable as under**

2.50 on application, 2.50 on allotment, 2 on first call and 3 on final call. Vansh, who had been allotted 8,000 shares failed to pay the final call. Pass entries in the journal of Dureja Ltd.

Sol.

JOURNAL

Date	Particulars		LF	Amt (Dr)	Amt (Cr)
(i)	Bank A/c	Dr		6,00,000	
	To Share Application A/c				6,00,000
	(Being application money received)				
(ii)	Share Application A/c	Dr		6,00,000	
	To Share Capital A/c				6,00,000
	(Being application money due)				
(iii)	Share Allotment A/c	Dr		6,00,000	
	To Share Capital A/c				6,00,000
	(Being allotment money due)				
(iv)	Bank A/c	Dr		6,00,000	
	To Share Allotment A/c				6,00,000
	(Being allotment money received)				
(v)	Share First Call A/c	Dr		4,80,000	
	To Share Capital A/c				4,80,000
	(Being first call money due)				
(vi)	Bank A/c	Dr		4,80,000	
	To Share First Call A/c				4,80,000
	(Being first call money received)				
(vii)	Share Final Call A/c	Dr		7,20,000	
	To Share Capital A/c				7,20,000
	(Being final call money due)				
(viii)	Bank A/c	Dr		6,96,000	
	Calls-in-arrears A/c	Dr		24,000	
	To Share Final Call A/c				7,20,000
	(Being final call money received)				

Solved Question 18 **Gorank Ltd. issued 10,000 equity shares of ₹ 10 each payable at ₹ 2.50 on application, ₹ 3 on allotment, ₹ 2 on first call and the balance of ₹ 2.50 on the final call. All the shares were fully subscribed and paid except of a shareholder having 100 shares who could not pay for the final call. Give journal entries to record these transactions.**

Sol.

JOURNAL

Date	Particulars		LF	Amt (Dr)	Amt (Cr)
	Bank A/c (10,000 × 2.5)	Dr		25,000	
	To Equity Share Application A/c				25,000
	(Being money received on applications for 10,000 shares @ ₹ 2.50 per share)				
	Equity Share Application A/c	Dr		25,000	
	To Equity Share Capital A/c				25,000
	(Being transfer of application money on 10,000 shares to share capital)				

Date	Particulars		LF	Amt (Dr)	Amt (Cr)
	Equity Share Allotment A/c	Dr		30,000	
	To Equity Share Capital A/c (10,000 × 3)				30,000
	(Being amount due on the allotment of 10,000 shares @ ₹ 3 per share)				
	Bank A/c	Dr		30,000	
	To Equity Share Allotment A/c				30,000
	(Being allotment money received)				
	Equity Share First Call A/c	Dr		20,000	
	To Equity Share Capital A/c (10,000 × 2)				20,000
	(Being first call money due on 10,000 shares @ ₹ 2 per share)				
	Bank A/c	Dr		20,000	
	To Equity Share First Call A/c				20,000
	(Being first call money received)				
	Equity Share Second and Final Call A/c	Dr		25,000	
	To Equity Share Capital A/c (10,000 × 2.5)				25,000
	(Being final call money due)				
	Bank A/c	Dr		24,750	
	Calls-in-arrears A/c (100 × 2.5)	Dr		250	
	To Equity Share Second and Final Call A/c				25,000
	(Being final call money received except that of 100 shares)				

Calls-in-advance

Solved Question 19 **Vrijesh Ltd. with a registered capital of ₹ 50,00,000 in shares of ₹ 10 each issued 2,00,000 of such shares, payable ₹ 3 per share on application, ₹ 2 per share on allotment and ₹ 3 per share on first call. All the amounts payable on allotment were duly received. On the first call being made, one shareholder paid the entire balance on his holding of 6,000 shares. Give journal entries to record the transactions and draw up the company's balance sheet.**

Sol.

JOURNAL

Date	Particulars		LF	Amt (Dr)	Amt (Cr)
	Bank A/c	Dr		6,00,000	
	To Share Application A/c (2,00,000 × 3)				6,00,000
	(Being the application money on 2,00,000 shares @ ₹ 3 per share received)				
	Share Application A/c	Dr		6,00,000	
	To Share Capital A/c				6,00,000
	(Being the application money transferred to share capital account)				
	Share Allotment A/c	Dr		4,00,000	
	To Share Capital A/c (2,00,000 × 2)				4,00,000
	(Being the amount due on allotment on 2,00,000 shares @ ₹ 2 per share)				
	Bank A/c	Dr		4,00,000	
	To Share Allotment A/c				4,00,000
	(Being the allotment money received)				
	Share First Call A/c	Dr		6,00,000	
	To Share Capital A/c (2,00,000 × 3)				6,00,000
	(Being first call money due on 2,00,000 shares @ ₹ 3 per share)				
	Bank A/c (2,00,000 × 3 + 6,000 × 2)	Dr		6,12,000	
	To Share First Call A/c (2,00,000 × 3)				6,00,000
	To Calls-in-advance A/c (6,000 × 2)				12,000
	(Being first call money received on 2,00,000 shares @ ₹ 3 per share and ₹ 2 per share on 6,000 shares received in advance)				

Balance Sheet
as at...

Particulars	Note No.	Amt (₹)
I. **EQUITY AND LIABILITIES**		
1. **Shareholders' Funds**		
Share Capital	1	16,00,000
2. **Current Liabilities**		
Calls-in-advance		12,000
Total		16,12,000
II. **ASSETS**		
1. **Current Assets**		
Cash and Cash Equivalents (Cash at Bank)		16,12,000
Total		16,12,000

Notes to Accounts

Particulars	Amt (₹)
1. **Share Capital**	
Authorised Capital	
5,00,000 Shares of ₹ 10 each	50,00,000
Issued Capital	
2,00,000 Shares of ₹ 10 each	20,00,000
Subscribed Capital	
Subscribed but not Fully Paid-up	
2,00,000 Shares of ₹ 10 each ₹ 8 per Share Called-up	16,00,000

Solved Question 20 (*Calls-in-arrears and calls-in-advance in case of oversubscription*) **Poonam Ltd. issued 50,000 shares of ₹ 10 each at a premium of ₹ 2 per share payable as ₹ 3 on application, ₹ 5 including premium on allotment and balance in equal instalments over two calls. Applications were received for 92,000 shares and the allotment was done as under**

(i) Applications of 40,000 shares — Allotted 30,000 shares
(ii) Applications of 40,000 shares — Allotted 20,000 shares
(iii) Applications of 12,000 shares — Nil

Suresh who had applied for 2,000 shares of category (i) did not pay any money other than application money. Chandar who was allotted 800 shares of category (ii) paid the call money due alongwith allotment. All other allottees paid their dues as per schedule.

Pass necessary journal entries in the books of Poonam Ltd. for the above transactions.

Sol. **JOURNAL**

Date	Particulars		LF	Amt (Dr)	Amt (Cr)
	Bank A/c	Dr		2,76,000	
	To Share Application A/c (92,000 × 3)				2,76,000
	(Being share application money received on 92,000 shares @ ₹ 3 per share)				
	Share Application A/c	Dr		2,76,000	
	To Share Capital A/c (50,000 × 3)				1,50,000
	To Share Allotment A/c (30,000 × 3)				90,000
	To Bank A/c (12,000 × 3)				36,000
	(Being share application money transferred)				
	Share Allotment A/c (50,000 × 5)	Dr		2,50,000	
	To Share Capital A/c (50,000 × 3)				1,50,000
	To Securities Premium A/c (50,000 × 2)				1,00,000
	(Being allotment money due on 50,000 shares @ ₹ 5 per share including premium of ₹ 2 each)				

Date	Particulars		LF	Amt (Dr)	Amt (Cr)
	Bank A/c (WN)	Dr		1,57,200	
	To Equity Share Allotment A/c				1,54,000
	To Calls-in-advance A/c				3,200
	(Being allotment money received and calls-in-advance on 800 shares @ ₹ 4 per share)				
	Share First Call A/c	Dr		1,00,000	
	To Share Capital A/c (50,000 × 2)				1,00,000
	(Being first call money due on 50,000 shares @ ₹ 2 per share)				
	Bank A/c	Dr		95,400	
	Calls-in-advance A/c (800 × 2)	Dr		1,600	
	To Share First Call A/c (48,500 × 2)				97,000
	(Being first call money received on 48,500 shares @ ₹ 2 per share)				
	Share Final Call A/c	Dr		1,00,000	
	To Share Capital A/c (50,000 × 2)				1,00,000
	(Being final call money due on 50,000 shares @ ₹ 2 per share)				
	Bank A/c	Dr		95,400	
	Calls-in-advance A/c	Dr		1,600	
	To Share Final Call A/c				97,000
	(Being final call money received on 48,500 shares @ ₹ 2 per share)				

Working Note

	Applied Shares	Allotted Shares	
(i)	40,000	30,000	(Pro-rata allotment)
(ii)	40,000	20,000	(Pro-rata allotment)
(iii)	12,000	Nil	
	92,000	50,000	

Number of shares allotted to Suresh $= 2{,}000 \times \frac{30{,}000}{40{,}000} = 1{,}500$ shares

Surplus towards Allotment on Suresh's Shares		**Amt (₹)**
Application money received (2,000 × 3)		6,000
(–) Application money required (1,500 × 3)		(4,500)
Surplus towards allotment		1,500
Calculation of Amount Received on Allotment		
Allotment money due (50,000 × 5)		2,50,000
(–) Excess received with application (30,000 × 3)		(90,000)
		1,60,000
(–) Calls-in-arrears (Suresh)		
Due (1,500 × 5)	7,500	
(–) Surplus	(1,500)	(6,000)
		1,54,000
(+) Calls-in-advance (Chandar)		
First call (800 × 2)	1,600	
Final call (800 × 2)	1,600	3,200
Amount received with allotment		1,57,200

Solved Question 21 **Alexia Limited invited applications for issuing 1,00,000 equity shares of ₹ 10 each at premium of ₹ 10 per share.**

The amount was payable as follows

On application ₹ 9 per share (including premium ₹ 6 per share)

On allotment ₹ 8 per share (including premium ₹ 4 per share)

On first and final call ₹ 3 per share.

Applications were received for 1,50,000 equity shares and allotment was made as follows

Category A : Applicants for 90,000 shares were allotted 70,000 shares.

Category B : Applicants for 60,000 shares were allotted 30,000 shares.
Excess money received on application was adjusted towards allotment and first and final call.
Shekhar, who had applied for 1200 shares failed to pay the first and for final call. Shekhar belonged to category B.
Pass necessary journal entries for the above transactions in the books of Alexia Limited. Open calls-in-arrears and calls-in-advance account, wherever necessary. **CBSE 2025**

Sol. **JOURNAL**

Date	Particulars		LF	Amt (Dr)	Amt (Cr)
	Bank A/c (1,50,000 × 9)	Dr		13,50,000	
	To Equity Share Application A/c				13,50,000
	(Being application money received)				
	Equity Share Application A/c	Dr		13,50,000	
	To Security Premium A/c				6,00,000
	To Equity Share Capital A/c				3,00,000
	To Equity Share Allotment A/c				4,20,000
	To Calls-in-Advance A/c				30,000
	(Being application money adjusted and transferred to capital and security premium)				
	Equity Share Allotment A/c	Dr		8,00,000	
	To Security Premium A/c				4,00,000
	To Equity Share Capital A/c				4,00,000
	(Being allotment due)				
	Bank A/c (8,00,000 – 3,20,000)	Dr		3,80,000	
	To Equity Share Allotment A/c				3,80,000
	(Being remaining allotment money received)				
	Equity Share First and Final Call A/c	Dr		3,00,000	
	To Equity Share Capital A/c				3,00,000
	(Being call money due)				
	Calls-in-advance A/c	Dr		30,000	
	Bank A/c (3,00,000 – 30,000 – 1,200)	Dr		2,68,800	
	Calls-in-arrears A/c	Dr		1,200	
	To Equity Share First and Final Call A/c				3,00,000
	(Being amount after calls-in-arrears received)				

Working Notes

1. Number of allotted shares to Shekhar $= \frac{1,200 \times 30,000}{60,000} = 600$

Excess application money deposited by Shekhar [(1,200 – 600) × 9]	= ₹	5,400
Allotment money due to Shekhar (600 × 8)	= ₹	4,800
(–) Adjusted excess application money (including ₹ 2,400 of premium) allotment due after adjustment	= ₹	(4,800)
		Nil
First and final call money due to Shekhar (600 × 3)	= ₹	1,800
(–) Remaining excess application money (5,400 – 4,800)	= ₹	(600)
First and final call not received	= ₹	1,200

2. Total excess application money received (Category A) (90,000 – 70,000) × 9 = ₹ 1,80,000 adjusted on allotment

3. Total excess application money received (Category B) [(60,000 – 30,000) × 9] = ₹ 2,70,000

Allotment due (30,000 × 8)	= ₹	2,40,000
(–) Adjusted from excess	= ₹	(2,40,000)
		—
First and final call due (30,000 × 3)	= ₹	90,000
(–) Remaining excess adjusted (2,70,000 – 2,40,000)	= ₹	(30,000)
	= ₹	60,000

Forfeiture of Shares

Solved Question 22 **Zara Ltd. issued 10,000 equity shares of ₹ 10 each at par payable on application ₹ 2 per share, on allotment ₹ 3 per share, on first call ₹ 3 per share and on second call ₹ 2 per share. Z was allotted 80 shares. Pass necessary journal entry relating to the forfeiture of shares in each of the following alternative cases**

(i) If Z failed to pay allotment money and his shares were forfeited after allotment.

(ii) If Z failed to pay allotment money and on his subsequent failure to pay the first call, his shares were forfeited after the first call.

(iii) If Z failed to pay the first call and on his subsequent failure to pay the final call, his shares were forfeited.

Sol.

JOURNAL

Date	Particulars		LF	Amt (Dr)	Amt (Cr)
(i)	Equity Share Capital A/c (80 × 5)	Dr		400	
	To Equity Share Allotment A/c (80 × 3)				240
	To Share Forfeiture A/c (80 × 2)				160
	(Being 80 shares forfeited for non-payment of allotment money)				
(ii)	Equity Share Capital A/c (80 × 8)	Dr		640	
	To Equity Share Allotment A/c (80 × 3)				240
	To Equity Share First Call A/c (80 × 3)				240
	To Share Forfeiture A/c (80 × 2)				160
	(Being 80 shares forfeited for non-payment of allotment and first call money)				
(iii)	Equity Share Capital A/c (80 × 10)	Dr		800	
	To Equity Share First Call A/c (80 × 3)				240
	To Equity Share Final Call A/c (80 × 2)				160
	To Share Forfeiture A/c (80 × 5)				400
	(Being 80 shares forfeited for non-payment of first call and final call money)				

Solved Question 23 **JMC Ltd. dealing in aerospace fuel, issued 2,00,000 equity shares of ₹ 20 each, at a premium of ₹ 5 per share, payable as ₹ 8 per share on application, ₹ 10 per share on allotment (including premium), ₹ 7 per share on first and final call. The issue was fully subscribed.**

Pass journal entry for forfeiture of shares.

(i) All the amount was duly received except first and final call on 10,000 shares. Then shares were forfeited after first and final call.

(ii) All the amount was duly received except allotment money on 10,000 shares. These shares were forfeited immediately after allotment.

Sol. (i)

JOURNAL

Date	Particulars		LF	Amt (Dr)	Amt (Cr)
	Equity Share Capital A/c	Dr		2,00,000	
	To Equity Share First and Final Call A/c				70,000
	To Share Forfeiture A/c				1,30,000
	(Being 10,000 shares forfeited as per resolution dated ...)				

(ii)

JOURNAL

Date	Particulars		LF	Amt (Dr)	Amt (Cr)
	Equity Share Capital A/c	Dr		1,30,000	
	Securities Premium A/c	Dr		50,000	
	To Equity Share Allotment A/c				1,00,000
	To Share Forfeiture A/c				80,000
	(Being 10,000 shares forfeited as per resolution dated ...)				

Solved Question 24 Shivaji Limited was registered with an authorised capital of ₹ 8,00,000 divided into equity shares of ₹ 10 each.

It offered 50,000 equity shares to the public. The amount was payable as follows

On application	— ₹ 3 per share
On allotment	— ₹ 5 per share
On first and final call	— Balance

The issue was fully subscribed. All the amounts were duly received except the allotment and first and final call money on 4,000 equity shares. These equity shares were forfeited. Give journal entries to record these transactions.

Sol. JOURNAL

Date	Particulars		LF	Amt (Dr)	Amt (Cr)
	Bank A/c (50,000 × 3)	Dr		1,50,000	
	To Equity Share Application				1,50,000
	(Being application money received)				
	Equity Share Application A/c	Dr		1,50,000	
	To Equity Share Capital A/c				1,50,000
	(Being application money transferred to share capital)				
	Equity Share Allotment A/c	Dr		2,50,000	
	To Equity Share Capital A/c				2,50,000
	(Being amount on allotment due)				
	Bank A/c [2,50,000 – (4,000 ×5)]	Dr		2,30,000	
	Calls-in-arrears A/c	Dr		20,000	
	To Equity Share Allotment A/c				2,50,000
	(Being allotment money received except on 4,000 shares)				
	Equity Share First and Final Call A/c	Dr		1,00,000	
	To Equity Share Capital A/c				1,00,000
	(Being amount due on first and final call, recorded)				
	Bank A/c [1,00,000 – (4,000 × 2)]	Dr		92,000	
	Calls-in-arrears A/c	Dr		8,000	
	To Equity Share First and Final Call A/c				1,00,000
	(Being amount received except on 4,000 shares)				
	Equity Share Capital A/c (4,000 ×10)	Dr		40,000	
	To Calls-in-arrears A/c				28,000
	To Share Forfeiture A/c				12,000
	(Being 4,000 shares forfeited)				

Reissue of Forfeited Shares

Solved Question 25 Karishma who was allotted 200 equity shares of ₹ 10 each by a company, failed to pay the final call of ₹ 4 each. These shares were forfeited and reissued to Mona (i) at ₹ 10 each, (ii) at ₹ 9 each and (iii) at ₹ 12 each. Journalise the transactions in respect of forfeiture and reissue of shares.

Sol. JOURNAL

Date	Particulars		LF	Amt (Dr)	Amt (Cr)
	Equity Share Capital A/c (200 ×10)	Dr		2,000	
	To Equity Share Final Call A/c (200 × 4)				800
	To Forfeited Shares A/c (200 × 6)				1,200
	(Being the forfeiture of 200 equity shares for non-payment of final call money)				
(i)	**In case shares were issued at ₹ 10**				
	Bank A/c (200 × 10)	Dr		2,000	
	To Equity Share Capital A/c				2,000
	(Being the reissue of 200 equity shares as fully paid-up at ₹ 10 per share)				

Date	Particulars		LF	Amt (Dr)	Amt (Cr)
	Forfeited Shares A/c	Dr		1,200	
	To Capital Reserve A/c				1,200
	(Being the profit on reissue transferred to capital reserve)				
(ii)	**In case shares were reissued at ₹ 9** (i.e. discount)				
	Bank A/c (200 × 9)	Dr		1,800	
	Forfeited Shares A/c (200 × 1)	Dr		200	
	To Share Capital A/c (200 × 10)				2,000
	(Being the reissue of 200 equity shares as fully paid-up at ₹ 10 per share)				
	Forfeited Shares A/c	Dr		1,000	
	To Capital Reserve A/c				1,000
	(Being the profit on reissue transferred to capital reserve)				
(iii)	**In case shares were reissued at ₹ 12** (i.e. premium)				
	Bank A/c	Dr		2,400	
	To Share Capital A/c (200 × 10)				2,000
	To Securities Premium A/c (200 × 2)				400
	(Being the reissue of 200 equity shares at ₹ 12 per share)				
	Share Forefeiture A/c	Dr		1,200	
	To Capital Reserve A/c				1,200
	(Being the profit on reissue transferred to capital reserve)				

Solved Question 26 **A company forfeited certain number of shares of face value ₹ 10 each, for non-payment of final call money of ₹ 4. These shares were reissued at a discount of ₹ 5 and amount of ₹ 4,500 was transferred to capital reserve account. Pass the necessary journal entries to show the above transactions and prepare share forfeited account.** CBSE SQP 2025

Sol.

JOURNAL

Date	Particulars		LF	Amt (Dr)	Amt (Cr)
	Share Capital A/c	Dr		45,000	
	To Forfeited Shares A/c				27,000
	To Share Final Call A/c				18,000
	(Being 4,500 shares forfeited)				
	Bank A/c	Dr		22,500	
	Forfeited Shares A/c	Dr		22,500	
	To Share Capital A/c				45,000
	(Being 4,500 shares reissued)				
	Share Forfeiture A/c	Dr		4,500	
	To Capital Reserve A/c				4,500
	(Being balance of share forfeiture transferred to capital reserve)				

Dr **Share Forfeiture Account** Cr

Particulars	Amt (₹)	Particulars	Amt (₹)
To Share Capital A/c	22,500	By Share Capital	27,000
To Capital Reserve A/c	4,500		
	27,000		27,000

Solved Question 27 **Pass the necessary journal entries for forfeiture and reissue of shares in the following cases**

(i) **Premier Ltd. forfeited 600 shares of ₹ 10 each issued at a premium of ₹ 3 per share (payable with allotment) for non-payment of allotment money of ₹ 7 per share including premium. The first and final call of ₹ 3 per share was not yet made. The forfeited shares were reissued at ₹ 13 per share fully paid-up.**

(ii) **Risha Ltd. forfeited 1,000 shares of ₹ 10 each, ₹ 8 per share called-up issued at a premium of ₹ 2 per share to Atul, for non-payment allotment money of ₹ 6 per share (including premium) premium). Out of these, 800 shares were reissued at ₹ 7 per share, ₹ 8 paid-up.** CBSE 2025

Sol. (i)

JOURNAL

Date	Particulars		LF	Amt (Dr)	Amt (Cr)
	Share Capital A/c (600 ×7)	Dr		4,200	
	Security Premium A/c	Dr		1,800	
	To Share Allotment A/c				4,200
	To Share Forfeiture A/c				1,800
	(Being 600 shares forfeited)				
	Bank A/c	Dr		7,800	
	To Security Premium A/c				1,800
	To Share Capital A/c				6,000
	(Being 600 shares reissued at ₹ 13 fully paid-up)				
	Share Forfeiture A/c	Dr		1,800	
	To Capital Reserve A/c				1,800
	(Being gain on forfeiture transferred to capital reserve account)				

JOURNAL

(ii)

Date	Particulars		LF	Amt (Dr)	Amt (Cr)
	Share Capital A/c	Dr		8,000	
	Security Premium A/c	Dr		2,000	
	To Share Allotment A/c				6,000
	To Share Forfeiture A/c				4,000
	(Being 1,000 shares forfeited)				
	Bank A/c	Dr		5,600	
	Share Forfeiture A/c	Dr		800	
	To Share Capital A/c				6,400
	(Being 800 shares reissued at ₹ 7 per share ₹ 8 paid-up)				
	Share Forfeiture A/c [(800 × 4) – 800]	Dr		2,400	
	To Capital Reserve A/c				2,400
	(Being gain on 800 shares transferred to capital reserve account)				

Forfeiture and Reissue of Shares when All the Shares are not Reissued

Solved Question 28 **Manika Ltd. forfeited 500 shares of ₹ 100 each for non-payment of first call of ₹ 20 per share and second and final call of ₹ 25 per share. 250 of these shares were reissued at ₹ 50 per share fully paid-up.**
Pass the journal entries for forfeiture and reissue of shares. **CBSE 2024**

Sol.

JOURNAL

Date	Particulars		LF	Amt (Dr)	Amt (Cr)
	Share Capital A/c (500 ×100)	Dr		50,000	
	To Share First Call A/c (500 × 20)				10,000
	To Share Second and Final Call A/c (500 × 25)				12,500
	To Share Forfeited A/c				27,500
	(Being the forfeiture of 500 shares for non-payment of first and second and final call money)				
	Bank A/c (250 ×50)	Dr		12,500	
	Share Forfeited A/c	Dr		12,500	
	To Share Capital A/c (250 ×100)				25,000
	(Being 250 forfeited shares reissued as fully paid-up for ₹ 50 per share)				
	Share Forfeited A/c	Dr		1,250	
	To Capital Reserve A/c				1,250
	(Being the transfer of profit on reissue to capital reserve)				

Amount transferred to Capital Reserve

Amount forfeited on 500 shares = 27,500

Amount forfeited on 250 shares $= \frac{27{,}500}{500} \times 250 = 13{,}750$

(–) Discount allowed on 250 shares = (12,500)

₹ 1,250

Solved Question 29 Pass necessary journal entries for forfeiture and reissue of shares in the following cases

(i) Star Ltd. forfeited 8,000 shares of ₹ 100 each issued at 10% premium for non-payment of allotment money of ₹ 40 per share (including premium) and first call of ₹ 30 per share. The second and final call of ₹ 20 per share was not yet called. Out of these ₹ 6,000 shares were reissued at ₹ 80 paid-up for ₹ 70 per share.

(ii) Premier Ltd. forfeited 3,000 shares of ₹ 10 each on which the first call of ₹ 3 per share was not received and the second and final call of ₹ 2 per share was not yet called. Out of these ₹ 2,000 shares were reissued to Gita at ₹ 8 paid-up for ₹ 12 per share. **CBSE 2024**

Sol. (i) **In the Books of Star Ltd.**

JOURNAL

Date	Particulars		LF	Amt (Dr)	Amt (Cr)
	Share Capital A/c	Dr		6,40,000	
	Securities Premium A/c	Dr		80,000	
	To Share Forfeiture A/c				1,60,000
	To Share Allotment A/c				3,20,000
	To Share First Call A/c				2,40,000
	(Being 8,000 shares forfeited for non-payment of allotment and first call money)				
	Bank A/c	Dr		4,20,000	
	Share Forfeiture A/c	Dr		60,000	
	To Share Capital A/c				4,80,000
	(Being 6,000 shares reissued @ ₹ 70, ₹ 80 paid-up)				
	Share Forfeiture A/c	Dr		60,000	
	To Capital Reserve A/c				60,000
	(Being gain on reissue of 6,000 shares transferred to capital reserve)				

(ii) **In the Books of Premier Ltd.**

JOURNAL

Date	Particulars		LF	Amt (Dr)	Amt (Cr)
	Share Capital A/c	Dr		24,000	
	To Share Forfeiture A/c				15,000
	To Share First Call A/c				9,000
	(Being 3,000 shares forfeited for non-payment of first call money)				
	Bank A/c	Dr		24,000	
	To Share Capital A/c				16,000
	To Securities Premium A/c				8,000
	(Being 2,000 shares reissued for ₹ 12 per share ₹ 8 paid-up)				
	Share Forfeiture A/c	Dr		10,000	
	To Capital Reserve A/c				10,000
	(Being gain on reissue of 2,000 shares transferred to capital reserve)				

Solved Question 30 A company forfeited 8,000 shares of ₹ 10 each on which ₹ 8 were called (including ₹ 1 premium) and ₹ 6 was paid (including ₹ 1 premium). Out of these, 5,000 shares were reissued at maximum possible discount. Pass necessary journal entries. **CBSE SQP 2025**

Sol. **JOURNAL**

Date	Particulars		LF	Amt (Dr)	Amt (Cr)
	Share Capital A/c	Dr		56,000	
	To Shares Forfeited A/c				40,000
	To Calls-in-arrears A/c				16,000
	(Being shares forfeited)				
	Bank A/c (5,000 × 2)	Dr		10,000	
	Shares Forfeited A/c (5,000 ×5)	Dr		25,000	
	To Share Capital A/c (5,000 ×7)				35,000
	(Being 5,000 shares reissued at discount)				

Oversubscription and Forfeiture of Shares

Solved Question 31 **Pearl Ltd. issued a prospectus inviting applications for 40,000 shares of ₹ 10 each at a premium of 20%. The amount was payable as follows**

On application	**— ₹ 5 per share**	**On allotment**	**— ₹ 5 per share (including premium)**
On first and final call	**— Balance**		

Applications for 60,000 shares were received and allotment was made on a pro-rata basis to all the applicants. Excess money received on application was adjusted towards the amount due on allotment. Sameer who had applied for 1,200 shares failed to pay the allotment money. His shares were forfeited immediately after allotment. All the forfeited shares were reissued at ₹ 7 per share as ₹ 8 paid-up. First and final call was not yet made.

Pass necessary journal entries to record the above transactions in the book of Pearl Ltd. open 'calls-in-arrears account' wherever necessary. **CBSE 2024 C**

Sol. **In the Books of Pearl Ltd.**
JOURNAL

Date	Particulars		LF	Amt (Dr)	Amt (Cr)
	Bank A/c	Dr		3,00,000	
	To Share Application A/c				3,00,000
	(Being application money received on 60,000 shares)				
	Share Application A/c	Dr		3,00,000	
	To Share Capital A/c				2,00,000
	To Share Allotment A/c (WN 1)				1,00,000
	(Being application money transferred to share capital account, excess money received adjusted towards allotment)				
	Share Allotment A/c	Dr		2,00,000	
	To Share Capital A/c				1,20,000
	To Securities Premium A/c				80,000
	(Being amount due on allotment)				
	Bank A/c (WN 5)	Dr		98,000	
	Calls-in-arrears A/c (WN 4)	Dr		2,000	
	To Share Allotment A/c				1,00,000
	(Being allotment money received)				
	Share Capital A/c	Dr		6,400	
	Securities Premium A/c	Dr		1,600	
	To Calls-in-arrears A/c (WN 4)				2,000
	To Forfeited Shares A/c (WN 2)				6,000
	(Being 800 shares forfeited for non-payment of allotment money)				
	Bank A/c	Dr		5,600	
	Forfeited Shares A/c	Dr		800	
	To Share Capital A/c				6,400
	(Being shares reissued @ ₹ 7 per share as ₹ 8 paid-up)				
	Forfeited Shares A/c	Dr		5,200	
	To Capital Reserve A/c				5,200
	(Being gain on reissue of forfeited shares transferred to capital reserve)				

Working Notes

1. Excess on application adjusted on allotment $= 20{,}000 \times 5 =$ ₹ 1,00,000

2. Allotted shares of Sameer $= \dfrac{1{,}200 \times 40{,}000}{60{,}000} = 800$ shares

3. Excess on application of Sameer

1,200 × 5 =	6,000
(−) 800 × 5 =	(4,000)
=	2,000

4. Allotment not paid by Sameer

800 × 5 =	4,000
(−) Excess on application =	(2,000)
=	2,000

5. **Total Allotment Received**

40,000 × 5	=	2,00,000
(–) WN 2	=	(1,00,000)
(–) WN 4	=	(2,000)
Total Allotment Received =		98,000

Solved Question 32 *(Forfeiture and reissue in case of oversubscription and when there are different categories of allotment)* **Vikas Ltd. invited applications for issuing 50,000 equity shares of ₹ 10 each at par. The amount was payable as follows**

On application	—	**₹ 2 per share**
On allotment	—	**₹ 4 per share**
On first and final call	—	**Balance amount**

The issue was oversubscribed three times. Applications for 30% shares were rejected and money refunded. Allotment was made to the remaining applicants as follows

Category	Number of Shares Applied	Number of Shares Allotted
I	80,000	40,000
II	25,000	10,000

Excess money paid by the applicants who were allotted shares was adjusted towards the sums due on allotment.

Deepak, a shareholder belonging to Category I, who had applied for 1,000 shares, failed to pay the allotment money. Raju, a shareholder holding 100 shares, also failed to pay the allotment money. Raju belonged to Category II. Shares of both Deepak and Raju were forfeited immediately after allotment. Afterwards, first and final call was made and was duly received. The forfeited shares of Deepak and Raju were reissued at ₹ 11 per share fully paid-up.

Pass necessary journal entries for the above transactions in the books of the company.

Sol.

JOURNAL

Date	Particulars		LF	Amt (Dr)	Amt (Cr)
	Bank A/c (1,50,000 × 2)	Dr		3,00,000	
	To Equity Share Application A/c				3,00,000
	(Being application money received)				
	Equity Share Application A/c	Dr		3,00,000	
	To Equity Share Capital A/c				1,00,000
	To Equity Share Allotment A/c				1,10,000
	To Bank A/c				90,000
	(Being application money transferred to share capital account and excess adjusted)				
	Equity Share Allotment A/c (50,000 × 4)			2,00,000	
	To Equity Share Capital A/c				2,00,000
	(Being allotment money due)				
	Bank A/c			88,900	
	Calls-in-arrears A/c			1,100	
	To Equity Share Allotment A/c				90,000
	(Being allotment money received)				
	Equity Share Capital A/c (600 × 6)			3,600	
	To Calls-in-arrears A/c (1,000 + 100)				1,100
	To Equity Share Forfeiture A/c				2,500
	(Being shares forfeited for non-payment of allotment money)				
	Equity Share First and Final Call A/c			1,97,600	
	To Equity Share Capital A/c (49,400 × 4)				1,97,600
	(Being first call money due)				
	Bank A/c			1,97,600	
	To Equity Share First and Final Call A/c				1,97,600
	(Being first and final call money received)				

Date	Particulars		LF	Amt (Dr)	Amt (Cr)
	Bank A/c (600 × 1)	Dr		6,600	
	To Equity Share Capital A/c (600 × 1)				6,,000
	To Securities Premium A/c (600 × 1)				600
	(Being 600 shares reissued @ ₹ 11 per share)				
	Share Forfeiture A/c	Dr		2,500	
	To Bank A/c				2,500
	(Being profit on reissue transferred capital reserve)				

Analysis Table

	Shares applied I	Shares allotted II	Application money received @ ₹ 2 per share III	Application money transferred to share capital IV	Excess application money V = III − IV	Share allotment money due @ ₹ 4	Excess application money adjusted on allotment	Money refunded
I	80,000	40,000	1,60,000 (80,000 × 2)	80,000 (40,000 × 2)	80,000	1,60,000 (40,000 × 4)	80,000	—
II	25,000	10,000	50,000 (25,000 × 2)	20,000 (10,000 × 2)	30,000	40,000 (10,000 × 4)	30,000	—
III	45,000	—	90,000 (45,000 × 2)	—	—	—	—	90,000
	1,50,000	50,000	3,00,000	1,00,000	1,10,000	2,00,000	1,10,000	90,000

Working Note

Calls-in-arrears of Deepak			**Amt (₹)**
Share allotted to Deepak	$= \frac{40,000}{80,000} \times 1,000$	=	500
Application money received	= 1,000 × 2	=	2,000
(−) Amount adjusted on application	= 500 × 2	=	(1,000)
Excess application money adjusted on allotment		=	1,000
Money due on allotment	= 500 × 4	=	2,000
(−) Excess application money adjusted on allotment		=	(1,000)
Calls-in-arrears		=	1,000
Calls-in-arrears by Raju			
Share applied by Raju	$= \frac{25,000}{10,000} \times 100$	=	250
Application money received	= 250 × 2	=	500
(−) Amount adjusted on application	= 100 × 2	=	(200)
Excess application money adjusted on allotment		=	300
Money due on allotment	= 100 × 4	=	400
(−) Excess application money adjusted on allotment		=	(300)
Calls-in-arrears		=	100
Money Received on Allotment			
Total amount due on allotment		=	2,00,000
(−) Excess application money adjusted		=	(1,10,000)
Allotment money to be received		=	90,000
(−) Calls-in-arrears by Deepak		=	(1,000)
(−) Calls-in-arrears by Raju		=	(100)
Allotment money received		=	88,900

Solved Question 33 **Sangam Ltd. invited applications for issuing 80,000 equity shares of ₹ 100 each at a premium. The amount was payable as follows**

On application	**— ₹ 20 per share**
On allotment	**— ₹ 60 per share (including premium)**
On first and final call	**— ₹ 40 per share**

Applications for 1,20,000 shares were received. Allotment was made on pro-rata basis to all the applicants. Excess money received on applications was adjusted on sums due to allotment. Sitaram, who had applied for 6,000 shares failed to pay the allotment money and Harnam did not pay first and final call on 800 shares allotted to him. The shares of Sitaram and Harnam were forfeited. 4,200 of these shares were reissued for ₹ 100 per share as fully paid-up. The reissued shares included all the forfeited shares of Harnam.

Pass necessary journal entries for the above transactions in the books of Sangam Ltd.

Sol.

JOURNAL

Date	Particulars		LF	Amt (Dr)	Amt (Cr)
	Bank A/c (1,20,000 × 20)	Dr		24,00,000	
	To Equity Share Application A/c				24,00,000
	(Being application money received)				
	Equity Share Application A/c (1,20,000 × 20)	Dr		24,00,000	
	To Equity Share Capital A/c (80,000 × 20)				16,00,000
	To Equity Share Allotment A/c (40,000 × 20)				8,00,000
	(Being application money transferred to share capital account)				
	Equity Share Allotment A/c (80,000 × 60)	Dr		48,00,000	
	To Equity Share Capital A/c (80,000 × 40)				32,00,000
	To Securities Premium A/c (80,000 × 20)				16,00,000
	(Being allotment money due)				
	Bank A/c	Dr		38,00,000	
	To Equity Share Allotment A/c				38,00,000
	(Being allotment money received)				
	Equity Share First and Final Call A/c	Dr		32,00,000	
	To Equity Share Capital A/c (80,000 × 40)				32,00,000
	(Being first and final call money due)				
	Bank A/c [(80,000 – 4,000 – 800) × 40]	Dr		30,08,000	
	To Equity Share First and Final Call A/c				30,08,000
	(Being first and final call money received)				
	Equity Share Capital A/c (4,800 × 100)	Dr		4,80,000	
	Securities Premium A/c (4,000 × 20)	Dr		80,000	
	To Equity Share Allotment A/c				2,00,000
	To Equity Share First and Final Call A/c (4,800 × 40)				1,92,000
	To Share Forfeited A/c (6,000 × 20 + 800 × 60)				1,68,000
	(Being shares forfeited for non-payment)				
	Bank A/c (4,200 × 100)	Dr		4,20,000	
	To Equity Share Capital A/c				4,20,000
	(Being shares reissued @ ₹ 100 per share)				
	Shares Forfeited A/c	Dr		1,50,000	
	To Capital Reserve A/c				1,50,000
	(Being gain on reissue transferred to capital reserve account)				

Working Note

Calculation of Allotment Money not paid by Sitaram

$$\text{Number of shares allotted to Sitaram} = \frac{80,000}{1,20,000} \times 6,000 = 4,000 \text{ shares}$$

Money not paid on Allotment	**Amt (₹)**
Money paid on application (6,000 × 20)	1,20,000
(–) Amount adjusted on allotment (4,000 × 20)	(80,000)
Excess application money adjusted on allotment	40,000
Money due on allotment (4,000 × 60)	2,40,000
(–) Excess application money adjusted	(40,000)
Money not paid on allotment by Sitaram	2,00,000

Money Received on Allotment

Total amount due on allotment (80,000 × 60)	48,00,000
(–) Excess application money adjusted	(8,00,000)
	40,00,000
(–) Money not received from Sitaram on allotment	(2,00,000)
	38,00,000
Amount forfeited on Sitaram 3,400 shares = $1,20,000 \times \frac{3,400}{4,000}$	1,02,000
Amount forfieted on Harnam's 800 shares	48,000
	1,50,000

Solved Question 34 Diamond Ltd. issued a prospectus inviting applications for 20,000 shares of ₹ 10 each. The amount was payable as follows

On application — ₹ 4 per share On allotment — ₹ 4 per share

On first and final call — Balance

Applications for 45,000 shares were received and allotment was made as follows

Category (i) — Applicants for 35,000 shares were allotted 15,000 shares.

Category (ii) — Applicants for 10,000 shares were allotted 5,000 shares.

It was decided that excess money received on application be adjusted towards sum due on allotment and calls.

Amar, an applicant of Category (ii), who was allotted 500 shares, failed to pay the first and final call. His shares were forfeited and subsequently reissued at ₹ 2 per share as fully paid-up.

Pass necessary journal entries to record the above transactions in the books of Diamond Ltd. **CBSE 2024 C**

Sol. In the Books of Diamond Ltd.

JOURNAL

Date	Particulars		LF	Amt (Dr)	Amt (Cr)
	Bank A/c	Dr		1,80,000	
	To Share Application A/c				1,80,000
	(Being application money received on 45,000 shares)				
	Share Application A/c	Dr		1,80,000	
	To Share Capital A/c				80,000
	To Share Allotment A/c				80,000
	To Calls-in-advance A/c				20,000
	(Being application money transferred to share capital account, excess money received adjusted towards allotment and call)				
	Share Allotment A/c	Dr		80,000	
	To Share Capital A/c				80,000
	(Being amount due on allotment)				
	Share First and Final Call A/c	Dr		40,000	
	To Share Capital A/c				40,000
	(Being amount due on 20,000 shares on first and final call)				
	Bank A/c	Dr		19,000	
	Calls-in-arrears A/c	Dr		1,000	
	Calls-in-advance A/c	Dr		20,000	
	To Share First and Final Call A/c				40,000
	(Being amount received on first and final call)				
	Share Capital A/c	Dr		5,000	
	To Calls-in-arrears A/c				1,000
	To Forfeited Shares A/c				4,000
	(Being 500 shares forfeited for non-payment of call money)				

Date	Particulars		LF	Amt (Dr)	Amt (Cr)
	Bank A/c	Dr		1,000	
	Forfeited Shares A/c	Dr		4,000	
	To Share Capital A/c				5,000
	(Being shares reissued @ ₹ 2 per share as fully paid-up)				

Solved Question 35 *(Forfeiture and reissue in case of oversubscription)* **X Ltd. invited applications for issuing 75,000 equity shares of ₹ 10 each at a premium of ₹ 5 per share.**

The amount was payable as follows

On application and allotment — ₹ 9 per share (including premium)

On first and final call — Balance amount

Applications for 3,00,000 shares were received. Applications for 2,00,000 shares were rejected and money refunded. Shares were allotted on pro-rata basis to the remaining applicants. The first and final call was made. The amount was duly received except on 1,500 shares applied by Ravi. His shares were forfeited. The forfeited shares were reissued at a discount of ₹ 4 per share.

Pass necessary journal entries for the above transactions in the books of X Ltd.

Sol.

JOURNAL

Date	Particulars		LF	Amt (Dr)	Amt (Cr)
	Bank A/c (3,00,000 × 9)	Dr		27,00,000	
	To Equity Share Application and Allotment A/c				27,00,000
	(Being share application and allotment money received on 3,00,000 shares of ₹ 9 each including premium of ₹ 5 each)				
	Equity Share Application and Allotment A/c	Dr		27,00,000	
	To Equity Share Capital A/c (75,000 × 4)				3,00,000
	To Securities Premium A/c (75,000 × 5)				3,75,000
	To Bank A/c (2,00,000 × 9)				18,00,000
	To Equity Share First and Final Call A/c				2,25,000
	(Being share application of 75,000 shares transferred to share capital, share application and allotment on 2,00,000 shares refunded and rest is adjusted on share first and final call)				
	Equity Share First and Final Call A/c	Dr		4,50,000	
	To Equity Share Capital A/c (75,000 × 6)				4,50,000
	(Being share first and final call due on 75,000 shares of ₹ 6 each)				
	Bank A/c	Dr		2,21,625	
	To Equity Share First and Final Call A/c				2,21,625
	(Being share first and final call received)				
	Equity Share Capital A/c	Dr		11,250	
	To Equity Share Forfeiture A/c				7,875
	To Equity Share First and Final Call A/c				3,375
	(Being 1,125 shares were forfeited for non-payment of share first and final call of ₹ 6 each)				
	Bank A/c (1,125 × 6)	Dr		6,750	
	Equity Shares Forfeited A/c (1,125 × 4)	Dr		4,500	
	To Equity Share Capital A/c (1,125 ×10)				11,250
	(Being 1,125 forfeited shares were reissued at a discount of ₹ 4 per share)				
	Equity Share Forfeiture A/c	Dr		3,375	
	To Capital Reserve A/c				3,375
	(Being share forfeiture transferred to capital reserve)				

Working Notes

1. **Analysis Table**

Shares applied	Shares allotted	Money received on application and allotment @ ₹ 9 each (₹)	Money transferred to share capital @ ₹ 4 each (₹)	Money transferred to securities premium reserve @ ₹ 5 each (₹)	Excess application and allotment money received (₹)	Share first and final call @ ₹ 6 each (₹)	Amount received on share first and final call after adjustment (₹)	Money refunded (₹)
2,00,000	—	18,00,000	—	—	—	—	—	18,00,000
1,00,000	75,000	9,00,000	3,00,000 (75,000 × 4)	3,75,000 (75,000 × 5)	2,25,000	4,50,000	4,46,625	—
3,00,000	75,000	27,00,000	3,00,000	3,75,000	2,25,000	4,50,000	4,46,625	18,00,000

2. Those who applied for 1,00,000 shares were allotted = 75,000 shares

Those who applied for 1,500 shares were allotted $= 75,000 \times \frac{1,500}{1,00,000} = 1,125$ shares

Share application and allotment money received on 1,500 shares of ₹ 9 each (including premium of ₹ 5 each)	=	₹	3,500
Shares allotted (1,125 × 9)	=	₹	(10,125)
Excess application and allotment money received	=	₹	3,375
Share first and final call due to 1,125 shares of ₹ 6 each	=	₹	6,750
Excess application and allotment money received	=	₹	3,375
Share first and final call not received	=	₹	3,375 (6,750 – 3,375)
Therefore, share first and final call amount received	=	₹	2,21,625 (4,50,000 – 2,25,000 – 3,375)

Comprehensive Questions

Solved Question 36 **Sai Ltd. invited applications for issuing 60,000 shares of ₹ 10 each. The amount was payable as follows**

On application	**— ₹ 5 per share**
On allotment	**— ₹ 1 per share**
On first and final call	**— Balance**

Applications were received for 58,000 shares. Rajat, the holder of 300 shares, did not pay allotment money and Usha, the holder of 500 shares, paid her entire share money along with allotment money. Rajat's shares were forfeited immediately after allotment. First and final call was made afterwards and duly received. Pass necessary journal entries for the above transactions. Open 'calls-in-arrears' and 'calls-in-advance' account, wherever required. **CBSE 2024**

Sol. **In the Books of Sai Ltd.**

JOURNAL

Date	Particulars		LF	Amt (Dr)	Amt (Cr)
	Bank A/c	Dr		2,90,000	
	To Share Application A/c				2,90,000
	(Being application amount received on 58,000 shares)				
	Share Application A/c	Dr		2,90,000	
	To Share Capital A/c				2,90,000
	(Being application amount transferred to share capital)				
	Share Allotment A/c	Dr		58,000	
	To Share Capital A/c				58,000
	(Being application amount due on 58,000 shares)				
	Bank A/c	Dr		59,700	
	Calls-in-arrears A/c (300 × 1)	Dr		300	
	To Share Allotment A/c				58,000
	To Calls-in-advance A/c (500 × 4)				2,000
	(Being allotment amount received, calls-in-arrears debited and calls-in-advance received)				

Date	Particulars		LF	Amt (Dr)	Amt (Cr)
	Share Capital A/c (300 × 6)	Dr		1,800	
	To Share Forfeiture A/c (300 × 5)				1,500
	To Calls-in-arrears A/c (300 × 1)				300
	(Being 300 shares forfeited due to non-payment of allotment money)				
	Share First and Final Call A/c (57,700 × 4)	Dr		2,30,800	
	To Share Capital A/c				2,30,800
	(Being final call amount due on 57,700 shares)				
	Bank A/c	Dr		2,28,800	
	Calls-in-advance A/c	Dr		2,000	
	To Share First and Final Call A/c				2,30,800
	(Final calls received and calls-in-advance adjusted)				

Solved Question 37 **Kavya Ltd. invited applications for issuing 30,000 shares of ₹ 10 each at a premium of ₹ 2 per share. The amount was payable as follows**

On application and allotment – ₹ 7 per share

On first and final call – ₹ 5 per share (including ₹ 2 premium)

Applications were received for 33,000 shares. Applications for 3,000 shares were rejected and money returned to the applicants. Applications for 30,000 shares were accepted in full.

The application and allotment money was duly received. The first and final call was made and money received except from a shareholder holding 500 shares. His shares were forfeited. All these shares were re-issued to Kartik as fully paid for ₹ 8 per share.

Pass necessary journal entries for the above transactions in the books of Kavya Ltd. open calls-in-arrears account wherever required. **CBSE 2024**

Sol. In the Books of Kavya Ltd.

JOURNAL

Date	Particulars		LF	Amt (Dr)	Amt (Cr)
	Bank A/c	Dr		2,31,000	
	To Share Application and Allotment A/c				2,31,000
	(Being application money received on 33,000 shares)				
	Share Application and Allotment A/c	Dr		2,31,000	
	To Share Capital A/c				2,10,000
	To Bank A/c				21,000
	(Being application money transferred to share capital account and balance refunded)				
	Share First and Final Call A/c	Dr		1,50,000	
	To Equity Share Capital A/c				90,000
	To Securities Premium A/c				60,000
	(Being application due on first and final call)				
	Bank A/c	Dr		1,47,500	
	Calls-in-arrears A/c	Dr		2,500	
	To Share First and Final Call A/c				1,50,000
	(Being first and final call received except on 500 shares)				
	Share Capital A/c (500 × 10)	Dr		5,000	
	Securities Premium A/c (500 × 2)	Dr		1,000	
	To Share Forfeiture A/c (500 × 7)				3,500
	To Calls-in-arrears A/c (500 × 5)				2,500
	(Being 500 shares forfeited due to for non-payment of first and final call)				
	Bank A/c (500 × 8)	Dr		4,000	
	Share Forfeiture A/c (500 × 2)	Dr		1,000	
	To Share Capital A/c				5,000
	(Being forfeited shares reissued as fully paid for ₹ 8 per share)				

Date	Particulars		LF	Amt (Dr)	Amt (Cr)
	Share Forfeiture A/c	Dr		2,500	
	To Capital Reserve A/c				2,500
	(Being gain on reissue of forfeited shares transferred to capital reserve account)				

Solved Question 38 KN Ltd. invited applications for issuing 6,00,000 equity shares of ₹ 10 each at a premium of ₹ 3 per share. The amount was payable as follows

On application and allotment — ₹ 3 per share
On first call — ₹ 4 per share
On second and final call — Balance (including premium)

The issue was oversubscribed by 1,50,000 shares. Applications for 50,000 shares were rejected and the application money was refunded. Shares were allotted to the remaining applicants as follows

Category I Those who had applied for 4,00,000 shares were allotted 3,00,000 shares on pro-rata basis.

Category II The remaining applicants were allotted the remaining shares.

Excess application money received with applications was adjusted towards sums due on first call. Rakesh to whom 6,000 shares were allotted (out of Category I) failed to pay the first call money. His shares were forfeited. The forfeited shares were reissued at ₹ 13 per share fully paid-up after the second call. Pass necessary journal entries for the above transactions in the books of KN Ltd.

CBSE SQP 2025

Sol.

JOURNAL

Date	Particulars		LF	Amt (Dr)	Amt (Cr)
	Bank A/c	Dr		22,50,000	
	To Share Application and Allotment A/c				22,50,000
	(Being application and allotment money received)				
	Share Application and Allotment A/c	Dr		22,50,000	
	To Equity Share Capital A/c				18,00,000
	To Share First Call A/c				3,00,000
	To Bank A/c				1,50,000
	(Being application and allotment money adjusted and excess refunded)				
	Share First Call A/c	Dr		24,00,000	
	To Equity Share Capital A/c				24,00,000
	(Being call money due)				
	Bank A/c	Dr		20,82,000	
	Calls-in-arrears A/c	Dr		18,000	
	To Share First Call A/c				21,00,000
	(Being call money received except on 6,000 shares)				
	Share Capital A/c	Dr		42,000	
	To Shares Forfeited A/c				24,000
	To Calls-in-arrears A/c				18,000
	(Being 6,000 shares forfeited)				
	Share Second Call A/c	Dr		35,64,000	
	To Share Capital A/c				17,82,000
	To Securities Premium A/c				17,82,000
	(Being second call money due)				
	Bank A/c	Dr		35,64,000	
	To Share Second Call A/c				35,64,000
	(Being second call money received)				
	Bank A/c	Dr		78,000	
	To Share Capital A/c				60,000
	To Securities Premium A/c				18,000
	(Being forfeited shares reissued)				

Date	Particulars		LF	Amt (Dr)	Amt (Cr)
	Shares Forfeited A/c	Dr		24,000	
	To Capital Reserve A/c				24,000
	(Being balance transferred to capital reserve)				

Working Notes

1. **Applied Shares of Rakesh**

   Applied : Allotted

   4,00,000 : 3,00,000

   x : 6,000

   $$x = \frac{6{,}000 \times 4{,}00{,}000}{3{,}00{,}000} = 8{,}000$$

2. **Excess on Application by Rakesh**

   $8{,}000 \times 3$ = 24,000 (Share forfeiture account)

   $(-) 6{,}000 \times 3 =$ (18,000)

   6,000

3. **First Call not paid by Rakesh**

   $6{,}000 \times 4$ = 24,000

   (–) Excess on application = (6,000)

   18,000

4. **Total First Call Received**

First call due $(6{,}00{,}000 \times 4)$	=	24,00,000
(–) First call not paid by Rakesh	=	(18,000)
Excess on application and allotment	=	(3,00,000)
		20,82,000

Solved Question 39 *(Issue of shares for cash and for consideration other than cash and forfeiture and reissue of shares issued for cash)* **'J Star Ltd'. was registered with an authorised capital of ₹ 2,00,000 divided into 20,000 shares of ₹ 10 each. 6,000 of these shares were issued to the vendor for building purchased. 8,000 shares were issued to the public and ₹ 5 per share were called-up as follows**

On application	**— ₹ 2 per share**
On allotment	**— ₹ 1 per share**
On first call	**— Balance of the called-up amount**

The amounts received on these shares were as follows

On 6,000 shares	**— Full amount called**
On 1,250 shares	**— ₹ 3 per share**
On 750 shares	**— ₹ 2 per share**

The directors forfeited 750 shares on which ₹ 2 per share were received. Pass necessary journal entries for the above transactions in the books of J Star Ltd.

Sol.

JOURNAL

Date	Particulars		LF	Amt (Dr)	Amt (Cr)
	Building A/c	Dr		60,000	
	To Vendor A/c				60,000
	(Being building purchased for ₹ 6,00,000)				
	Vendor A/c	Dr		60,000	
	To Equity Share Capital A/c				60,000
	(Being issue of 6,000 shares towards purchase consideration)				
	Bank A/c $(8{,}000 \times 2)$	Dr		16,000	
	To Equity Share Application A/c				16,000
	(Being application money received on 8,000 shares @ ₹ 2 per share)				
	Equity Share Application A/c	Dr		16,000	
	To Equity Share Capital A/c				16,000
	(Being transfer of application money)				
	Equity Share Allotment A/c	Dr		8,000	
	To Equity Share Capital A/c $(8{,}000 \times 1)$				8,000
	(Being allotment money due on 8,000 shares)				

Date	Particulars		LF	Amt (Dr)	Amt (Cr)
	Bank A/c	Dr		7,250	
	Calls-in-arrears A/c	Dr		750	
	To Equity Share Allotment A/c				8,000
	(Being allotment money received on 7,250 shares)				
	Equity Share First Call A/c	Dr		16,000	
	To Equity Share Capital A/c (8,000 × 2)				16,000
	(Being first call money due on 8,000 shares)				
	Equity Share Capital A/c (750 × 5)	Dr		3,750	
	To Share Forfeited A/c (750 × 2)				1,500
	To Calls-in-arrears A/c (750 × 3)				2,250
	(Being 750 shares forfeited due to non-payment of allotment and call)				

Missing Information

Solved Question 40 Complete the following journal entries

JOURNAL

Date	Particulars		LF	Amt (Dr)	Amt (Cr)
	Furniture and Fittings A/c	Dr		12,000	
	Land and Building A/c	Dr		10,000	
	Sundry Debtors A/c	Dr		9,000	
	Inventories A/c	Dr		17,000	
	Bank A/c	Dr		6,000	
	To Bills Payable A/c				6,000
	To …				39,000
	To …				…
	(Being assets and liabilities of M/s MB Bros. taken over)				
	…	Dr		…	
	To …				…
	To …				…
	(Being payment made by issue of 300, 10% preference shares of ₹ 100 each at a premium of 30%)				

Sol.

JOURNAL

Date	Particulars		LF	Amt (Dr)	Amt (Cr)
	Furniture and Fittings A/c	Dr		12,000	
	Land and Building A/c	Dr		10,000	
	Sundry Debtors A/c	Dr		9,000	
	Inventories A/c	Dr		17,000	
	Bank A/c	Dr		6,000	
	To Bills Payable A/c				6,000
	To **M/s MB Bros.**				39,000
	To **Capital Reserve A/c (Balancing Figure)**				**9,000**
	(Being assets and liabilities of M/s MB Bros. taken over)				
	M/s MB Bros.	Dr		**39,000**	
	To **10% Preference Share Capital A/c**				**30,000**
	To **Securities Premium A/c**				**9,000**
	(Being payment made by issue of 300, 10% preference shares of ₹ 100 each at a premium of 30%)				

Solved Question 41 BBG Ltd. had issued 1,00,000 equity shares of ₹ 10 each at a premium of ₹ 3 per share payable with application money. While passing journal entries related to the issue, some blanks are left, you are required to complete these blanks. **All India 2016**

JOURNAL

Date	Particulars		LF	Amt (Dr)	Amt (Cr)
2015					
Jan 5	....	Dr		...	
	To				...
	(Being application money received for 1,40,000 shares @ ₹ 6 per share including premium)				
Jan 17	Equity Share Application A/c	Dr		...	
	To				...
	To				...
	To				...
	To				...
	(Being application money transferred to share capital account, securities premium account, refunded for 20,000 shares for rejected applications and balance adjusted towards money due on allotment as shares were alloted on pro-rata basis)				
Jan 17	....	Dr		...	
	To				...
	(Being allotment money due @ ₹ 4 per share)				
Feb 20	....	Dr		...	
	To				...
	(Being balance allotment amount received)				
Apr 1	....	Dr		...	
	To				...
	(Being first and final call money due)				
Apr 20	....	Dr		...	
	Calls-in-arrears A/c	Dr		3,000	
	To				...
	(Being first and final call money received)				
May 20	....	Dr		...	
	To				...
	To				...
	(Being the shares forfeited on which first and final call was not received)				
Jun 15	....	Dr		...	
	....	Dr		3,000	
	To				...
	(Being forfeited shares reissued)				
......	....	Dr		...	
	To				...
	(...)				

Sol.

JOURNAL

Date	Particulars		LF	Amt (Dr)	Amt (Cr)
2015					
Jan 5	**Bank A/c** (1,40,000 × 6)	Dr		**8,40,000**	
	To **Equity Share Application A/c**				**8,40,000**
	(Being application money received for 1,40,000 shares @ ₹ 6 per share including premium)				

Date	Particulars		LF	Amt (Dr)	Amt (Cr)
Jan 17	Equity Share Application A/c	Dr		8,40,000	
	To **Equity Share Capital A/c** (1,00,000 × 3)				3,00,000
	To **Securities Premium A/c** (1,00,000 × 3)				3,00,000
	To **Equity Share Allotment A/c**				1,20,000
	To **Bank A/c** (20,000 × 6)				1,20,000
	(Being application money transferred to share capital account, securities premium account, refunded for 20,000 shares for rejected applications and balance adjusted towards money due on allotment as shares were alloted on pro-rata basis)				
Jan 17	**Equity Share Allotment A/c**	Dr		4,00,000	
	To **Equity Share Capital A/c** (1,00,000 × 4)				4,00,000
	(Being allotment money due @ ₹ 4 per share)				
Feb 20	**Bank A/c** (4,00,000 – 1,20,000)	Dr		2,80,000	
	To **Equity Share Allotment A/c**				2,80,000
	(Being balance allotment amount received)				
Apr 1	**Equity Share First and Final Call A/c**	Dr		3,00,000	
	To **Equity Share Capital A/c** (1,00,000 × 3)				3,00,000
	(Being first and final call money due)				
Apr 20	**Bank A/c**	Dr		2,97,000	
	Calls-in-arrears A/c	Dr		3,000	
	To **Equity Share First and Final Call A/c**				3,00,000
	(Being first and final call money received)				
May 20	**Equity Share Capital A/c** (1,000 × 10)	Dr		10,000	
	To **Equity Share Forfeiture A/c**				7,000
	To **Equity Share First and Final Call A/c** (1,000 × 3)				3,000
	(Being forfeited the shares on which first and final call was not received)				
Jun 15	**Bank A/c** (1,000 × 7)	Dr		7,000	
	Equity Share Forfeiture A/c	Dr		3,000	
	To **Equity Share Capital A/c** (1,000 × 10)				10,000
	(Being forfeited shares reissued)				
Oct 3	**Equity Share Forfeiture A/c**	Dr		4,000	
	To **Capital Reserve A/c**				4,000
	(Being excess amount on forfeiture transferred to capital reserve)				

Numerical Questions

Disclosure of Share Capital in Company's Balance Sheet

1. PQR Ltd. is registered with a capital of ₹ 2,00,000 equity shares of ₹ 10 each. 3,00,000 equity shares were offered for subscription to public. Applications were received for 3,00,000 shares. All calls were made and amount was duly received except final call of ₹ 2 on 40,000 shares.

Show the share capital in the balance sheet of the company.

Ans. Balance Sheet Total = ₹ 29,20,000

Issue of Shares for Cash

2. The authorised capital of ₹ 16,00,000 of JMC Ltd. is divided into 1,60,000 equity shares of ₹ 10 each. Out of these shares, 80,000 equity shares were issued to the public. The full nominal value is payable on application. All the shares were subscribed by the public and total amount was paid for.

Give necessary journal entries in the books of the company.

3. Shiksha Ltd. was registered with a capital of 1,25,000 shares of ₹ 10 each, payable as

₹ 2.5 on application

₹ 2 on allotment

₹ 2 on first call and the balance on second and final call

The whole of the above issue was applied for and amount was duly received.

Pass journal entries to record the above transactions.

4. Saumil Limited offered for subscription of 1,00,000 equity shares of ₹ 10 each at a premium of ₹ 2 per share. The amount on share was payable as under

On application ₹ 3 per share, on allotment ₹ 5 per share (including premium), on first call ₹ 4 per share. All the shares were fully subscribed, called-up and paid.

Record these transactions in the journal and cash book of the company.

5. Vasu Fabrics Ltd. issued 1,00,000 shares of ₹ 10 per share which is issued at premium. The amount payable was as follows

₹ 2 on application, ₹ 4 on allotment, ₹ 2 on first call and ₹ 3 on final call. All the shares were applied and duly allotted.

Pass necessary journal entries.

Undersubscription

6. Harleen Luxury Cars Ltd. issued 4,500 shares of ₹ 10 each issued at a premium of ₹ 2 per share, payable as ₹ 4 on application, ₹ 3 on allotment, ₹ 2 on first call and balance on final call. Applications were received for 4,200 shares and allotment is made. All the money was duly received.

You are required to journalise these transactions.

7. ABC company issued 4,00,000 shares of ₹ 10 each at a premium of 20%. The amount per share was payable as follows

Application	₹ 2
Allotment	₹ 6 (including premium)
First call	₹ 2
Final call	Balance

Public applied for 3,90,000 shares. All the money was duly received.

Pass necessary journal entries and prepare balance sheet.

Oversubscription

8. Dinesh Ltd. issued for public subscription 30,000 equity shares of ₹ 15 each at par, payable as follows

₹ 7 on application; ₹ 5 on allotment

₹ 3 on first and final call

The company received applications for 40,500 shares.

Journalise in each of the case mentioned below

Case (i) When excess applications are rejected.

Case (ii) When proportionate allotment is made.

Case (iii) When allotment is made here under

(a) Applications for 500 shares are rejected.

(b) Applicants of 2,000 shares are allotted in full.

(c) For the balance, pro-rata allotment is made.

Ans. (i) Amount to be Refunded = ₹ 73,500

(ii) Amount received at the Time of Allotment = ₹ 76,500

(iii) Amount to be Refunded = ₹ 3,500; Amount to be received at the Time of Allotment = ₹ 80,000

9. Parag Software India Ltd. invited applications for 20,000 equity shares of ₹ 100 each, payable ₹ 40 on application, ₹ 30 on allotment and ₹ 30 on call. The company received applications for 32,000 shares. Application for 2,000 shares was rejected and money returned to applicants. Applications for 10,000 shares were accepted in full and applicants for 20,000 shares allotted half of the number of shares applied and excess application money adjusted into allotment. All money due on allotment and call was received.

Pass necessary journal entries. **Competency Based Que**

10. Jeevanshi Ltd. issued 85,000, 12% preference shares of ₹ 100 each at a premium of ₹ 20 per share, payable as
(i) ₹ 30 on application
(ii) ₹ 40 on allotment (including premium)
(iii) ₹ 30 on first call
(iv) ₹ 20 on second and final call
The company received applications for 1,00,000 shares and the directors approved the following schemes of allotment.
(i) Applicants for 20,000 shares were allotted in full.
(ii) Applicants for 50,000 shares were allotted 80% of the shares applied.
(iii) Applicants for 30,000 shares were allotted $83\frac{1}{3}$% of the shares applied.
Pass the necessary journal entries. Competency Based Que

Ans. Amount to be received at the Time of Allotment = ₹ 29,50,000

11. Yash Ltd. was registered with an authorised capital of ₹ 10,00,000 divided into 7,500 equity shares of ₹ 100 each and 2,500 preference shares of ₹ 100 each. Company offered 1,100 equity shares and 550; 9% preference shares to public.
Public applied for 1,000 equity shares and 500; 9% preference shares.
These shares were offered on the following terms
Equity shares payable ₹ 10 on application, ₹ 40 on allotment and the balance in two calls of ₹ 25 each. Preference shares are payable ₹ 25 on application, ₹ 25 on allotment and ₹ 50 on first and final call. All the shares were applied for and allotted. Amount due was duly received.
Prepare cash book and pass necessary journal entries to record the above issue of shares and show how the share capital will appear in the balance sheet. Competency Based Que

Isssue of Shares for Consideration Other than Cash

12. Kumar Ltd. purchased a machinery for ₹ 10,00,000 from Gupta Ltd. 10,000 of the amount is payable by issuing a cheque immediately and balance by fully paid-up equity shares of ₹ 10 each at a premium of 10%.
Pass necessary journal entries in the books of Kumar Ltd.

Ans. Numbers of Shares = 90,000

13. Rohit Ltd. purchased assets from Rohan and Co. for ₹ 3,50,000. A sum of ₹ 75,000 was paid by means of a bank draft and for the balance due, Rohit Ltd. issued equity shares of ₹ 10 each at a premium of 10%.
Journalise the above transactions in the books of the company.

Ans. Number of Shares Issued = 25,000 shares

14. XYZ Ltd. took over assets of 15,00,000 and liabilities of PQR Ltd. for a purchase consideration of ₹ 13,68,500. ₹ 10,000 were paid is cash, ₹ 5,500 were paid by issuing a promissory note in favour of PQR Ltd. payable after two months. Issued 1,000 preference shares of ₹ 10 each at par and balance was paid by issue of equity shares of ₹ 100 each at a premium of 25%.
Journalise the above transactions in the books of the company. Competency Based Que

Ans. Number of Shares Issued = 10,744 shares

15. Daksh Ltd. purchased a running business from Vasu Bros. for a sum of 96,00,000 payable by the issue of fully paid equity shares of ₹ 20 each at a premium of 20%. The assets and liabilities consisted of the following

Plant and Machinery	₹ 50,00,000
Stock	₹ 30,00,000
Sundry Debtors	₹ 17,20,000
Sundry Creditors	₹ 6,00,000

Pass the necessary journal entries in the books of Daksh Ltd.

Ans. Goodwill = ₹ 4,80,000

16. (i) Dhruv Ltd. purchased a running business from Sunehari Ltd. for a sum of ₹ 30,00,000 by issuing 25,000 fully paid equity shares of ₹ 100 each at a premium of 20%. The assets and liabilities consisted of the machinery ₹ 9,00,000, debtors ₹ 12,50,000, stock ₹ 8,00,000, building ₹ 10,00,000 and bills payable ₹ 7,50,000.
Pass necessary journal entries in the books of Niharika Ltd. for the above transactions.
(ii) Purchased a running business from Aman Ltd. for a sum of ₹ 15,00,000. The payment of ₹ 12,00,000 was made by issue of fully paid equity shares of ₹ 10 each and balance by a bank draft.
The assets and liabilities consisted of the following Plant ₹ 3,50,000, stock ₹ 4,50,000, land and building ₹ 6,00,000, sundry creditors ₹ 1,00,000.
Pass necessary entries. Competency Based Que

Ans. (i) Capital Reserve = ₹ 2,00,000
(ii) Goodwill = ₹ 2,00,000; Number of Shares Issued = 1,20,000 shares

17. Rakesh Ltd. issued 3,500 shares of ₹ 10 each credited as fully paid to the promoters for helping on the incorporate of the company and also issued 3,000 shares of ₹ 10 each fully paid-up to the underwriters for their underwriting services.
Journalise these transactions.

Calls-in-arrears

18. Pritpal Limited issued 30,000 equity shares of ₹ 10 each, payable at ₹ 3 on application, ₹ 5 on allotment and ₹ 1 each on first and final call. Company received applications for 35,000 shares. Allotment was made on pro-rata basis. One shareholder holding 800 shares failed to pay first call money and subsequently final call.

You are required to journalise these transactions.

19. Sagar Ltd. issued 30,000 shares of ₹ 10 each at a premium of ₹ 2 per share payable as ₹ 3 on application, ₹ 5 (including premium) on allotment and the balance on first and final call. Applications were received for 52,000 shares.

The directors resolved to allot as follows

I. Applicants of 20,000 shares	10,000 shares
II. Applicants of 30,000 shares	20,000 shares
III. Applicants of 2,000 shares	Nil

Z who had applied for 4,000 shares in category I and X who was allotted 2,000 shares in category II failed to pay the allotment money.

Pass journal entries. **Competency Based Que**

Ans. Amount received on Allotment = ₹ 79,000

20. XYZ Ltd. company had an authorised capital of ₹ 6,25,000 divided into 6,250 shares of ₹ 100 each. The company issued 10,000 shares payables as ₹ 25 on application, ₹ 25 on allotment, ₹ 30 on first call and ₹ 20 on second and final call. All the shares were subscribed. Allotment was made and the money was duly received except the second and final call on 250 shares, which is transferred to calls-in-arrears account.

Pass journal entries, prepare share capital account and show how share capital will appear in the balance sheet.

Ans. Calls-in-arrears = ₹ 5,000

21. Shri Ganga Ltd. was registered with an authorised capital of ₹ 7,00,000 divided into equity shares of ₹ 10 each. It offered to the public for subscription 50,000 equity shares. The amount was payable as follows

On application	– ₹ 4 per share
On allotment	– ₹ 4 per share
On first and final call	– Balance

The issue was fully subscribed. All the amounts were duly received except the first and final call money on 4,000 equity shares.

Show the share capital in the balance sheet of the company as per Schedule III, Part I of the Companies Act, 2013. Also prepare 'notes to accounts' for the same.

Ans. Share Capital = ₹ 4,92,000

Calls-in-advance

22. ABS Ltd. invited applications for 3,000 shares of ₹ 15 per share payable as ₹ 3 on application, ₹ 6 on allotment and ₹ 4 each on first and final call. All the shares were duly applied and allotted. When asked for first call, one shareholder holding 250 shares paid the amount of final call as well.

Pass necessary journal entries.

23. Shiv Ltd. was registered with the authorised capital of ₹ 30,00,000. They issued shares of ₹ 30,000 divided into 3,000 shares of ₹ 10 each, which were offered to the public. Amount payable is ₹ 3 per share on application, ₹ 4 per share on allotment and ₹ 3 per share on first and final call. One shareholder holding 450 shares paid entire amount on allotment. Another shareholder holding 600 shares failed to pay the amount of first and final call.

Prepare journal for the above transactions.

Competency Based Que

Forfeiture of Shares

24. XYZ Ltd. issued 5,000 equity shares of ₹ 10 each at par payable on application ₹ 2 per share, on allotment ₹ 3 per share, on first call ₹ 3 per share and on second and final call ₹ 2 per share. P was allotted 40 shares.

Give necessary journal entries for forfeiture of shares in each of the following alternative cases

***Case* 1** If P did not pay allotment money and his shares were forfeited.

***Case* 2** If P did not pay allotment money and on non-payment of first call too, his shares were forfeited.

***Case* 3** If P did not pay the first call and on non-payment of second and final call too, his shares were forfeited.

25. Laxmi Ltd. issued 15,000 shares of 50 each at par, payable as follows

On application ₹ 12, on allotment ₹ 12, on first call ₹ 10, on final call balance amount. Anil, holding 100 shares failed to pay the amount of allotment and first call and his shares were forfeited after the first call. Krishna, holding 200 shares failed to pay the amount due on final call and his shares were also forfeited.

Pass necessary journal entries.

26. Lazal Ltd. invited applications for issuing 2,00,000 equity shares of ₹ 10 each, at 20% premium. Amount per share was payable as follows

₹ 5 on application, ₹ 4 (including premium) on allotment and balance on first and final call.

Public applied for 3,20,000 shares, out of which applications for 20,000 shares were rejected and shares were allotted on pro-rata basis to the remaining applications. Kavita, an applicant of 15,000 shares failed to pay allotment and call money. Her shares were forfeited.

Pass necessary journal entries for the above transactions in the books of the company. CBSE 2024

27. Ronit Ltd. was registered with an authorised capital of ₹ 75,00,000 divided into 75,000 equity shares of ₹ 100 each. The company invited applications for issuing 45,000 shares.

The amount was payable as follows

₹ 30 per share on application, ₹ 30 per share on allotment, ₹ 25 per share on first call and balance on final call.

Applications were received for 42,000 shares and allotment was made to all the applicants. Charvi, to whom 3,300 shares were allotted, failed to pay both the calls. Her shares were forfeited.

Give journal entries to record these transactions.

Competency Based Que

28. Chand Ltd. invited applications for issuing 1,00,000 equity shares of ₹ 10 each at a premium of ₹ 2 per share. The amount per share was payable as follows

₹ 4 (including premium) on application, ₹ 5 on allotment and balance on first and final call.

Applications were received for 1,80,000 shares of which applications for 30,000 shares were rejected and remaining applicants were allotted shares on pro-rata basis. Mansi holding 5,000 shares failed to pay first and final call money and her shares were forfeited.

Pass necessary journal entries for the above transactions in the books of the company. CBSE 2024

Reissue of Forfeited Shares

29. XYZ Ltd. forfeited 500 shares of ₹ 10 each for non-payment of first call of ₹ 3 per share. The final call of ₹ 2 per share is yet to be made. All the forfeited shares were reissued.

Pass the necessary journal entries in the following cases

***Case* 1** If the shares are reissued for ₹ 5 per share.

***Case* 2** If the shares are reissued for ₹ 9 per share, ₹ 8 called-up.

***Case* 3** If the shares are reissued for ₹ 8 per share; fully called-up.

***Case* 4** If the shares are reissued for ₹ 12 per share; fully called-up.

Ans. Capital Reserve in *Case* 1 = ₹ 1,000; *Case* 2 = ₹ 2,500; *Case* 3 = ₹ 1,500; *Case* 4 = ₹ 2,500

30. Xenon Ltd. forfeited a certain number of shares with a face value of ₹ 25 each due to non-payment of the final call money of ₹ 10 per share. These forfeited shares were later reissued at a discount of ₹ 12.50 per share and an amount of ₹ 11,250 was transferred to the capital reserve account.

Record the necessary journal entries to reflect the above transactions and prepare the share forfeiture account.

Ans. Number of Shares Forfeited = 4,500

31. 'XYZ Ltd.' invited applications for issuing 50,000 equity shares of ₹ 10 each at a premium of ₹ 10 per share. The amount was payable as follows

On application – ₹ 10 per share (including ₹ 5 premium)

On allotment – The balance

The issue was fully subscribed. A shareholder holding 150 shares paid the full share money with application. Another shareholder holding 100 shares failed to pay the allotment money. His shares were forfeited. Later on, these shares were reissued for ₹ 2,000 as fully paid-up.

Pass necessary journal entries for the above transactions in the books of XYZ Ltd.

Competency Based Que

Ans. Transfer to Capital Reserve = ₹ 500

32. On 1st April, 2021, Reliable Ltd. was incorporated with an authorised capital of ₹ 65,00,000 divided into 6,50,000 equity shares of ₹ 10 each. The company issued prospectus inviting applications for 3,15,000 equity shares and it received applications for 2,97,500 equity shares.

During the first year, ₹ 8 per share was called. Rohan, holding 3,500 shares and Soham, holding 7,000 shares, failed to pay the first call of ₹ 2 per share.

Soham's shares were forfeited after the first call and 5,250 of the forfeited shares were later reissued at ₹ 6 per share, fully called-up for ₹ 8.

Give journal entries to record above transactions.

Competency Based Que

Forfeiture and Reissue of Shares when all the Shares are not Reissued

33. Pass necessary journal entries for forfeiture and reissue of shares in the following cases CBSE 2024

(i) Neon Ltd. forfeited 2,000 shares of ₹ 10 each issued at a premium of ₹ 2 per share for non-payment of allotment money of ₹ 5 per share (including premium). The first and final call of ₹ 2 per share was not yet made. Out of these, 1,500 shares were reissued at ₹ 7 per share, ₹ 8 paid-up.

(ii) Mamta Ltd. forfeited 3,000 shares of ₹ 10 each on which the first call of ₹ 3 per share was not received. The second and final call of ₹ 1 per share was not yet called. Out of these, 2,000 shares were reissued at ₹ 9 per share, ₹ 9 paid-up.

Ans. (i) Capital Reserve = ₹ 6,000
(ii) Capital Reserve = ₹ 12,000

34. Atishyokti Ltd. company was registered with an authorised capital of ₹ 20,00,000 divided into 2,00,000 equity shares of ₹ 10 each, payable ₹ 3 on application, ₹ 6 on allotment (including 1 premium) and balance on call. The company offered 80,000 shares for public subscription. All the money has been duly called and received except allotment and call money on 5,000 shares held by Manish and call money on 4,000 shares held by Alok. Manish's shares were forfeited and out of these 3,000 shares were reissued ₹ 9 per share as fully paid-up.

Show share capital in the books of the company. Also prepare notes to accounts. **Competency Based Que**

Ans. Share Capital = ₹ 7,78,000

35. Shaktimaan Ltd. invited applications for issuing 1,00,000 shares of ₹ 10 each at a premium of ₹ 2 per share. The amount was payable as ₹ 4 on application (including premium), ₹ 5 on allotment and balance on call. Applications were received shares for 1,80,000 of which applications for 30,000 shares were rejected and remaining applicants were allotted on pro-rata basis. Manthan, holding 5,000 shares failed to pay call money and his shares were forfeited.

Out of these 2,000 shares were reissued at premium of ₹ 3 per share.

Prepare cash book and pass necessary entries.

Ans. Capital Reserve = ₹ 14,000

Oversubscription and Forfeiture of Shares

36. Beta Ltd. invited applications for 4,00,000 equity shares of ₹ 10 each with the following terms
₹ 5 per share payable on application
₹ 3 per share payable on allotment
₹ 2 per share payable on the first and final call
The company received applications for 5,00,000 shares. The board decided as follows
(i) No shares would be allotted to applicants for 20,000 shares.
(ii) Full allotment would be made to applicants for 80,000 shares.
(iii) The remaining available shares would be allotted on a pro-rata basis to the other applicants.
(iv) Excess application money would be adjusted towards allotment dues.

One applicant, who was allotted shares on a pro-rata basis, failed to pay the allotment and call money on 400 shares, which were subsequently forfeited. These forfeited shares were later reissued at ₹ 9 per share.

Prepare journal entries to record the above transactions.

Ans. Capital Reserve = ₹ 2,100

37. A company offered 50,000 shares of ₹ 10 each payable as ₹ 3 on application, ₹ 2.50 on allotment, ₹ 2.50 on first call and ₹ 2 on the final call.

The public applied for 76,000 shares. The shares were allotted on a pro-rata basis to the applicants of 75,000 shares. All shareholders paid the allotment money excepting one shareholder who was allotted 100 shares. These shares were forfeited. The first call was made thereafter. The forfeited shares were reissued @ ₹ 9 per share ₹ 8 paid-up. The final call was not yet made.

You are required to pass journal entries.

Ans. Transfer to Capital Reserve = ₹ 450; Amount received on Allotment = ₹ 49,900, First Call = ₹ 1,24,750

38. SMS Ltd. issued for public subscription 20,000 equity shares of ₹ 10 each at a premium of ₹ 2 per share payable as under, on application ₹ 4 per share, on allotment ₹ 5 per share (including premium) and on call ₹ 3 per share.

Applications were received for 30,000 shares. Allotment was made pro-rata to the applicants for 24,000 shares, the remaining applications being refused. Money overpaid on application was utilised towards sums due on allotment.

X, to whom 750 shares were allotted, failed to pay the allotment and call money and Z to whom 1,000 shares were allotted failed to pay the call money. These shares were subsequently forfeited. All the forfeited shares were sold to B as fully paid-up at ₹ 8 per share.

Show the journal entries to record the above transactions. **Competency Based Que**

Ans. Transfer to Capital Reserve = ₹ 7,100; Amount received on Allotment = ₹ 80,850, First and Final Call = ₹ 54,750

39. Ravi Confectioneries Ltd. invited applications for 10,00,000 equity shares of ₹ 10 each at a premium of ₹ 2 per share. The amount was payable as follows
₹ 5 on application
₹ 4 on allotment
₹ 3 on the first and final call
The company received applications for 15,00,000 shares.
Applications for 3,00,000 shares were rejected and the remaining applicants were allotted shares on a pro-rata basis.

The excess application money was adjusted towards the amount due on allotment. Vikas, who had applied for 24,000 shares, failed to pay the allotment and call money. Consequently, his shares were forfeited.

Out of these forfeited shares, 10,000 were reissued at ₹ 8 per share, fully paid-up.

(i) **Record the necessary journal entries in the books of the company.**

(ii) **Prepare the share forfeiture account.**

Competency Based Que

Ans. Capital Reserve = ₹ 40,000

Comprehensive Questions

40. Shringar Ltd. was registered with an authorised capital of ₹ 5,00,000 divided into equity shares of ₹ 10 each. The company issued a prospectus inviting applications for 20,000 equity shares.

The amount was payable as follows

On application — ₹ 3 per share
On allotment — ₹ 5 per share
On first and final call — Balance

Applications were received for 19,000 equity shares and allotment was made to all the applicants. All the amounts were duly received except the first and final call on 5,000 shares.

Present the share capital in the company's balance sheet as per Schedule III, Part I of Companies Act, 2013. Also prepare 'notes to accounts' for the same.

CBSE 2024; Competency Based Que

Ans. Share Capital = ₹ 1,80,000

41. On 1st April, 2023, Khyati Ltd. was formed with an authorised capital of ₹ 20,00,000 divided into 2,00,000 equity shares of ₹ 10 each. The company invited applications for issuing 1,80,000 equity shares. The company received applications for 1,70,000 equity shares. During the first year, ₹ 8 per share were called and final call of ₹ 2 per share has not been made yet.

Siya holding 2,000 shares and Piya holding 4,000 shares did not pay the first call of ₹ 2 per share. All the shares of Siya and Piya were forfeited after the first call.

Present the share capital in the balance sheet of Khyati Ltd. as per Schedule III, Part I of Companies Act, 2013 and also prepare 'notes to accounts' for the same.

CBSE 2024; Competency Based Que

Ans. Share Capital = ₹ 13,48,000

42. Diamond Ltd. issued a prospectus inviting applications for 20,000 shares of ₹ 10 each. The amount was payable as follows

On application — ₹ 4 per share
On allotment — ₹ 4 per share
On first and final call — Balance

Applications for 45,000 shares were received and allotment was made as follows

Category I Applicants for 35,000 shares were allotted 15,000 shares.

Category II Applicants for 10,000 shares were allotted 5,000 shares.

It was decided that excess money received on application be adjusted towards sum due on allotment and calls.

Amar, an applicant of Category II, who was allotted 500 shares, failed to pay the first and final call.

His shares were forfeited and subsequently reissued at ₹ 2 per share as fully paid-up.

Pass necessary journal entries to record the above transactions in the books of Diamond Ltd.

CBSE 2024; Competency Based Que

Ans. Capital Reserve = Nil

43. Lilly Ltd. forfeited 100 shares of ₹ 10 each issued at 10% premium (₹ 8 called-up) on which a shareholder did not pay ₹ 3 of allotment (including premium) and first call of ₹ 2.

Out of these 60 shares were reissued to Ram as fully paid for ₹ 8 per share and 20 shares to Suraj as fully paid-up @ ₹ 12 per share at different intervals of time.

Prepare share forfeiture account.

Ans. Closing Balance of Share Forfeiture Account = ₹ 80

44. CID Limited invited applications for issuing 5,00,000 equity shares of ₹ 10 each at a premium of ₹ 10 each payable with final call.

Amount per share was payable as follows

On application — ₹ 2
On allotment — ₹ 3
On first call — ₹ 2
On second and final call — Balance

Applications for 8,00,000 shares were received. Applications for 50,000 shares were rejected and the application money was refunded.

Allotment was made to the remaining applicants as follows

Category	Number of Shares Applied	Number of Shares Allotted
I	2,00,000	1,50,000
II	5,50,000	3,50,000

Excess application money received with applications was adjusted towards sums due on allotment. Balance, if any was adjusted towards future calls. Govind, a shareholder belonging to Category I, to whom 1,500 shares were allotted paid his entire share money with allotment.

Manohar belonging to Category II who had applied for 11,000 shares failed to pay 'second and final call money'. Manohar's shares were forfeited after the final call. The forfeited shares were reissued at ₹ 10 per share as fully paid-up.

Assuming that the company maintains 'calls-in-advance account' and 'calls-in-arrears account', pass necessary journal entries for the above transactions in the books of CID Limited. **Competency Based Que**

Ans. Transfer to Capital Reserve = ₹ 24,500

45. Rathi Ltd. invited applications for issuing 1,00,000 shares of ₹ 10 each at a premium of ₹ 2 per share. Amount per share was payable as follows

On application	– ₹ 4 (including premium ₹ 1)
On allotment	– ₹ 4 (including premium ₹ 1)
On first and final call	– Balance

Applications were received for 1,50,000 shares and allotment was made to the applicants as follows

(i) Applicants of 80,000 shares were allotted 60,000 shares.

(ii) Applicants of 50,000 shares were allotted 40,000 shares.

(iii) No shares were allotted to the remaining applicants and their application money was returned.

Yatin, who belonged to Category II and who had applied for 5,000 shares failed to pay the allotment and call money. His shares were forfeited. Later, half of Yatin's forfeited shares were reissued @ ₹ 18 per share as fully paid-up.

Pass the necessary journal entries to record the above transactions in the books of Rathi Ltd.

CBSE 2020; Competency Based Que

Ans. Capital Reserve = ₹ 8,000

Missing Information

46. Complete the following journal entries **Competency Based Que**

JOURNAL

Date	Particulars		LF	Amt (Dr)	Amt (Cr)
	Equity Share Capital A/c (235 × 10)	Dr		2,350	
	....	Dr		...	
	To Forfeited Shares A/c				470
	To Calls-in-arrears A/c				3,055
	(Being 235 shares forfeited for non-payment of allotment and call money)				
	Bank A/c	Dr		420	
	To				...
	To				...
	(Being 30 shares reissued at ₹ 14 per share)				
	....	Dr		...	
	To				...
	(Being ....)				

Ans. Capital Reserve = ₹ 60

47. CJF Ltd. invited applications for 40,000 equity shares of ₹ 10 each, payable as ₹ 3 on application, ₹ 4 on allotment and the balance on first and final call. The excess application money was to be adjusted against allotment only. A, a shareholder, who had applied for 300 shares, failed to pay the call money and his shares were accordingly forfeited and reissued in such a way that ₹ 625 should be transferred to capital reserve.

You are required to fill in the missing information in the journal entries given below **Competency Based Que**

JOURNAL

Date	Particulars		LF	Amt (Dr)	Amt (Cr)
	Bank A/c	Dr		2,88,000	
	To Equity Share Application A/c				2,88,000
	(Being application money received on .... shares @ ₹ 3 per share)				
	Equity Share Application A/c	Dr		...	
	To Equity Share Capital A/c				...
	To Equity Share Allotment A/c				...
	To Bank A/c				...
	(Being pro-rata allotment made to all applicants and amount in excess of allotment money refunded)				

Date	Particulars		LF	Amt (Dr)	Amt (Cr)
	Equity Share Allotment A/c	Dr		...	
	To Equity Share Capital A/c				...
	(Being allotment due on 40,000 shares)				
	Equity Share First and Final Call A/c	Dr		...	
	To Equity Share Capital A/c				...
	(Being first and final call due on 40,000 shares)				
	Bank A/c	Dr		...	
	To Equity Share First and Final Call A/c				...
	(Being call money received)				
	Equity Share Capital A/c	Dr		...	
	To Equity Share First and Final Call A/c				...
	To Share Forfeiture A/c				...
	(Being forfeiture of .... shares)				
	Bank A/c	Dr		...	
	Share Forfeiture A/c	Dr		...	
	To Equity Share Capital A/c				...
	(Being reissue of .... shares)				
	Share Forfeiture A/c	Dr		...	
	To Capital Reserve A/c				...
	(Being transferred to reserve)				

Theoretical Questions

Short Answer Type Questions

1. What is meant by private placement of shares? CBSE 2019

Ans. It means issue and allotment of shares to a selected group of persons privately and not to public in general. It is generally made by private or unlisted companies. When a company issues shares through private placement route, a special resolution to this effect should be passed.

All SEBI guidelines concerning preferential issue are applicable to private placement of shares as well.

2. State any two purposes for which securities premium can be utilised.

Or **State any three purposes other than 'issue of bonus shares' for which securities premium can be utilised.**

Or **SSS Ltd. as a paid-up share capital of ₹ 60,00,000 and a balance of ₹ 15,00,000 in the securities premium reserve account. The company management does not want to carry over this balance. State the purpose for which this balance can be utilised.** Competency Based Que

Ans. (i) In purchasing its own shares (buy-back).

(ii) Issuing fully paid bonus shares to the members.

(iii) Writing-off the expenses of, or the commission paid or discount allowed on any issue of securities or debentures of the company.

(iv) Providing for the premium payable on the redemption of any redeemable preference shares or of any debentures of the company.

(v) Writing-off preliminary expenses of the company.

3. Guru Ltd. invited applications for issuing 5,00,000 equity shares of ₹ 10 each at a premium of ₹ 5 per share. Because of favourable market conditions, the issue was oversubscribed and applications for 15,00,000 shares were received. Suggest the alternatives available to the board of directors for the allotment of shares. Competency Based Que

Ans. In case of oversubscription of shares, the board of directors has the following alternatives

(i) Excess applications fully rejected and money refunded.

(ii) Proportionate allotment made for the whole issue.

(iii) Some of the applications are rejected in full and for the balance, proportionate allotment is made.

4. Distinguish between oversubscription and undersubscription of shares issued by a company.

Ans. Difference between oversubscription of shares and undersubscription of shares are as follows

Basis	Oversubscription of Shares	Undersubscription of Shares
Shares Applied	Number of shares applied is more than the shares offered for subscription.	Number of shares applied is less than the shares offered for subscription.
Acceptance	All application are not accepted. Some are rejected. Alternatively, shares are allotted on pro-rata basis.	All the applications for shares are accepted, i.e. full allotment is made.
Refund	Excess application money is refunded or adjusted towards allotment and calls.	As all the applications are accepted, there is no excess money to be refunded.
Minimum Subscription	A company, not faces such a problem.	A company may face the problem of 'minimum subscription'.

5. Securities premium can be utilised for three purposes besides

(i) issuing fully paid bonus shares and

(ii) buy-back of shares.

State those purposes.

Ans. The three purposes are

(i) Writing-off the expenses of or the commission paid or discount allowed on any issue of securities or debentures of the company.

(ii) Providing for the premium payable on the redemption of any redeemable preference shares or of any debentures of the company.

(iii) Writing-off preliminary expenses of the company.

6. (i) If a share ₹ 10 on which ₹ 8 is called-up and ₹ 6 is paid is forfeited. State with what amount the share capital account with be debited?

(ii) If a share of ₹ 10 on which ₹ 6 has been paid is forfeited, at what minimum price it can be reissued? **Competency Based Que**

Ans. (i) On forfeiture, share capital is debited with called-up amount i.e. ₹ 8.

(ii) The total price of money collected from first issue and reissue should be equal to face value atleast. It can exceed also.

The shares can be reissued for minimum ₹ 4 per share.

7. Distinguish between calls-in-arrears and calls-in-advance.

Ans. Difference between calls-in-arrears and calls-in-advance are as follows

Basis	Calls-in-arrears	Calls-in-advance
Meaning	It is the amount called-up by the company but not paid by shareholders.	It is the amount not called-up by the company but paid by shareholders.
Interest	Interest @ 10% is charged from members.	Interest @ 12% is given to members.
Disclosure	Amount is shown by way of deduction from called-up capital.	Amount is shown as a separate item.

8. What is the difference between a partnership and a company?

Ans. The following difference are observed between partnership and joint stock company

(i) Partnership is set-up by an agreement among partners, whereas a company is set-up by registering under the Companies Act, 2013 or any other previous Companies Act.

(ii) Partnership is regulated by Indian Partnership Act, 1932 and companies are governed by Companies Act, 2013 and the provisions of SEBI.

(iii) In partnership, the liability of partnership is unlimited but in companies, the liability of shareholders is limited.

(iv) In partnership, business may be managed by all partners or some of them acting for all but in companies, the business is managed by directors, who are paid personnels.

(v) In partnership, the profits are distributed accounting to the terms of partnership deed or equally, if there is no agreement. In companies, profits to be distributed depending on the Articles of Association or the directors.

Objective Questions

Multiple Choice Questions (MCQs)

1. Subscribed capital is **CBSE 2020**

(a) that part of authorised capital which is issued to the public for subscription
(b) that part of issued capital which has been actually subscribed by the public
(c) that part of subscribed capital which has been called-up on the shares
(d) that part of subscribed capital which has not yet been called-up on the shares

2. First call amount received in advance from the shareholders before it is actually called-up by the directors is **CBSE Term I 2021, 2020**

(a) debited to calls-in-advance account
(b) credited to share allotment account
(c) debited to first call account
(d) credited to calls-in-advance account

3. Money received in advance from shareholders before it is actually called-up by the directors is

(a) debited to calls-in-advance account
(b) credited to calls-in-advance account
(c) debited to calls account
(d) None of the above

4. Balance of share forfeiture account is shown in the balance sheet under the item

(a) current liabilities and provisions
(b) reserves and surplus
(c) share capital (d) unsecured loans

5. The company has to get minimum subscription within .... from the date of issue of the prospectus. When minimum subscription has been received, the directors of the company proceed to make .... which implies a valid contract between the company and the applicants who now become the allottees and assume the status of shareholders or members.

CBSE Term I 2021; Competency Based Que

(a) 120 days, allotment of shares
(b) 130 days, application of shares
(c) 14 days, allotment of shares
(d) 15 days, allotment of shares

6. Jupiter Ltd. invited applications for issuing 25,000 equity shares of ₹ 10 each and received applications for 30,000 shares along with the application money of ₹ 2 per share. Which of the following alternative can be followed for the allotment of shares?

CBSE Term I 2021; Competency Based Que

I. Refund the excess application money and allot full shares to rest of the applicants.

II. Not to allot any share to some applications, allot full to some applicants and allot remaining on pro-rate basis.

III. Not to allot any share and refund the total application money to the applications.

Codes

(a) Only I (b) Only II
(c) Only III (d) Any one of I and II

7. That part of the authorised capital which is actually issued to the public for subscription is called **CBSE 2023**

(a) subscribed capital (b) issued capital
(c) authorised capital (d) reserve capital

8. Beeta Ltd. offered for subscription 1,00,000 equity shares of ₹ 10 each at a premium of 100% payable entirely on application. Applications were received for 5,00,000 equity shares. The company decided to allot the shares on pro-rata basis to all the applicants. The amount received by the company on application was

CBSE 2024 C

(a) ₹ 1,00,00,000 (b) ₹ 20,00,000
(c) ₹ 1,20,00,000 (d) ₹ 80,00,000

9. A company issued 10,000 shares of ₹ 10 each. Amount is payable as ₹ 2 on application, ₹ 5 on allotment and ₹ 3 on first and final call.

A shareholder who had 1,000 shares failed to pay allotment and first call amount on due date. After a month, he paid the due amount. What will be the amount received by company against issue of shares?

Competency Based Que

(a) ₹ 92,000 (b) ₹ 90,000
(c) ₹ 1,00,000 (d) ₹ 8,000

10. Xyle Ltd. forfeited 700 shares of ₹ 10 each issued at a premium of 10% for non-payment of allotment money of ₹ 5 per share (including premium) and first and final call of ₹ 3 per share. On forfeiture of these shares, 'share forfeiture account' will be credited with

CBSE 2023; Competency Based Que

(a) ₹ 7,000 (b) ₹ 1,400 (c) ₹ 4,900 (d) ₹ 2,100

11. Alfa Ltd. invited applications for 50,000 equity shares of ₹ 10 each at a premium of 30%. The whole amount was payable on application. Applications were received for 2,50,000 shares. The company decided to allot the shares on a pro-rata basis to all the applicants. The amount refunded by the company was

Competency Based Que

(a) ₹ 32,50,000 (b) ₹ 15,60,000
(c) ₹ 39,00,000 (d) ₹ 26,00,000

12. Reserve capital is that part of .... capital which cannot be called except at the time of winding-up of the company.

(a) issued (b) called-up (c) uncalled (d) nominal

13. Xeno Ltd. issued 25,000 equity shares of ₹ 10 each. The amount was payable as follows

On application	— ₹ 4 per share
On allotment	— ₹ 5 per share
On first and final call	— Balance

All the shares offered were applied for and allotted. All the money due on allotment was received except on 1,500 shares. These shares were forfeited immediately after allotment. First and final call was not yet made. At the time of forfeiture, share capital account will be debited by **Competency Based Que**

(a) ₹ 15,000 (b) ₹ 24,000
(c) ₹ 13,500 (d) ₹ 18,000

14. Zinki Ltd. forfeited a share of ₹ 100 issued at a premium of 20% for non-payment of first call of ₹ 30 per share and final call of ₹ 10 per share. The minimum price at which this share can be reissued is **CBSE 2023; Competency Based Que**

(a) ₹ 40 (b) ₹ 60
(c) ₹ 20 (d) ₹ 100

15. Singh who was allotted 200 equity share of ₹ 20 each by a company, failed to pay ₹ 8 each on final call. Shares were reissued to Kumar at ₹ 20 each. What will be the journal entry on reissue?

(a)	Bank A/c	Dr	4,000	
	To Equity Share Capital A/c			4,000
(b)	Equity Share Capital A/c	Dr	4,000	
	To Bank A/c			4,000
(c)	Bank A/c	Dr	4,000	
	To Share Forfeiture A/c			4,000
(d)	Share Forfeiture A/c	Dr	4,000	
	To Bank A/c			4,000

16. Money received in advance from shareholders before it is actually called up by the directors is

(a) debited to calls-in-advance account
(b) credited to calls-in-advance account
(c) debited to share capital account
(d) credited to share capital account

17. Offer of securities or invitation to subscribe securities to a select group of persons by a company (other than by way of public offer) is known as **CBSE 2025**

(a) sweat equity
(b) incorporation cost
(c) private placement of shares
(d) employee stock option plan

18. If a share of ₹ 10 on which ₹ 8 has been paid-up is forfeited, it can be reissued at the minimum price of

(a) ₹ 10 per share (b) ₹ 8 per share
(c) ₹ 5 per share (d) ₹ 2 per share

19. A share of ₹ 100 on which ₹ 80 is received is forfeited for non-payment of final call of ₹ 20. The minimum price at which this share can be reissued is **CBSE 2024**

(a) ₹ 120 (b) ₹ 100 (c) ₹ 80 (d) ₹ 20

20. Shiv Ltd. forfeited 500 shares of ₹ 10 each on which ₹ 7 per share was paid. These shares were reissued for ₹ 9 per share fully paid. Amount transferred to capital reserve account will be **Competency Based Que**

(a) ₹ 3,000 (b) ₹ 5,000
(c) ₹ 4,500 (d) ₹ 3,500

21. Ajay Ltd. forfeited 100 shares of ₹ 10 each for non-payment of first call of ₹ 1 per share and second and final call of ₹ 3 per share. The minimum price per share at which these shares can be reissued will be **CBSE 2025**

(a) ₹ 6 (b) ₹ 4
(c) ₹ 10 (d) ₹ 16

22. If a share of ₹ 10 issued at a premium of ₹ 2 per share, on which ₹ 8 (including premium) has been called and ₹ 6 (including premium) has been paid by the shareholder, is forfeited, then share capital account will be debited with **Competency Based Que**

(a) ₹ 10 (b) ₹ 4
(c) ₹ 8 (d) ₹ 6

23. Vandana Ltd. issued 6,000 equity shares ₹ 10 each at 10% premium. The issue was fully subscribed. Amount per share was payable as follows

On application ₹ 3, on allotment ₹ 3 (including premium), on first call ₹ 3 and on final call ₹ 2.
A, a holder of 200 shares paid the entire money along with allotment. The amount received on allotment will be .... **CBSE Term I 2021; Competency Based Que**

(a) ₹ 18,000 (b) ₹ 19,000
(c) ₹ 25,000 (d) ₹ 21,000

24. The amount of share capital which a company is authorised to issue by its Memorandum of Association is known as **CBSE 2025**

(a) nominal capital (b) issued capital
(c) reserve capital (d) subscribed capital

25. Lexa Ltd. issued 50,000 equity shares of ₹ 10 each at a premium of ₹ 2 per share. The amount was payable as follows

On application and allotment	— ₹ 7 per share (including premium)
On first and final call	— Balance

The issue was fully subscribed. All the money was duly received except the first and final call on 1,000 equity shares. These shares were forfeited. On forfeiture of these shares calls-in-arrears account will be **Competency Based Que**

(a) credited by ₹ 7,000 (b) debited by ₹ 5,000
(c) credited by ₹ 5,000 (d) debited by ₹ 7,000

26. XYZ Ltd. reissue 2,000 shares which were forfeited by crediting share forfeited account by 3,000. These shares were reissued at ₹ 9 per share. The amount transferred to capital reserve will be **Competency Based Que**

(a) ₹ 3,000 (b) ₹ 2,000
(c) ₹ 1,000 (d) Nil

27. According to Securities and Exchange Board of India (SEBI), guidelines, minimum subscription of capital cannot be less than 90% of .... **CBSE 2025**

(a) authorised capital (b) issued capital
(c) reserve capital (d) subscribed capital

28. KLB Ltd. forfeited 3,000 shares of ₹ 10 each, ₹ 8 per share called-up for non-payment of first call of ₹ 2 per share. All these shares were reissued at ₹ 7 per share, ₹ 8 paid-up. The amount transferred to capital reserve account will be **CBSE 2024; Competency Based Que**

(a) ₹ 18,000 (b) ₹ 24,000
(c) ₹ 15,000 (d) ₹ 3,000

29. A company forfeited 4,000 shares of ₹ 10 each, ₹ 8 per share called-up for non-payment of first call of ₹ 2 per share. On forfeiture of these shares, 'share capital' account will be debited with **CBSE 2023; Competency Based Que**

(a) ₹ 4,000 (b) ₹ 800
(c) ₹ 3,200 (d) ₹ 2,000

30. NUK Ltd. forfeited 1,000 shares of ₹ 10 each, fully called-up for non-payment of final call of ₹ 2 per share. 800 of these shares were reissued at ₹ 11 per share fully paid. The amount credited to capital reserve account will be **CBSE 2024; Competency Based Que**

(a) ₹ 6,400 (b) ₹ 8,000
(c) ₹ 7,200 (d) ₹ 10,000

31. Vishant Ltd. invited applications for issuing 6,000 equity shares of ₹ 10 each at 10% premium. The issue was fully subscribed. The amount per share was payable as follows

On application ₹ 3, on allotment ₹ 3 (including premium), on first call ₹ 3 and on final call ₹ 2. Ashish the holder of 200 shares paid the entire money along with allotment. The total amount received on allotment was **CBSE 2024; Competency Based Que**

(a) ₹ 18,000 (b) ₹ 19,000
(c) ₹ 25,000 (d) ₹ 21,000

32. M Ltd. forfeited 5,000 equity shares of ₹ 10 each issued at a premium of 10% for non-payment of final call of ₹ 2 per share.

The minimum amount at which these shares can be reissued as fully paid-up will be **CBSE 2024; Competency Based Que**

(a) ₹ 5,000 (b) ₹ 10,000
(c) ₹ 12,000 (d) ₹ 50,000

33. As per the provisions of Companies Act, 2013 securities premium cannot be utilised for **CBSE 2024**

(a) buy-back of shares
(b) issue of partly paid bonus shares
(c) writing-off discount on issue of debentures
(d) writing-off preliminary expenses

34. If vendors are issued fully paid shares of ₹ 1,25,000 in purchase consideration of net assets of ₹ 1,50,000, the balance of ₹ 25,000 will be credited to **CBSE 2024**

(a) statement of profit and loss
(b) goodwill account
(c) capital reserve account
(d) profit and loss adjustment account

35. If all the forfeited shares are reissued, the balance, if any, left in the 3 forfeited shares account is transferred to **CBSE 2024**

(a) general reserve account
(b) securities premium account
(c) capital reserve account
(d) statement of profit and loss

36. Sinoy Ltd. issued 20,000 shares of ₹ 10 each at a premium of ₹ 6. The amount was payable as follows

On application — ₹ 7 per share (including premium ₹ 1 per share)
On allotment — ₹ 5 per share (including premium ₹ 2 per share)
On first and final call — Balance

The issue was fully subscribed. All the money was duly received except the allotment and first and final call on 1,000 shares. These shares were forfeited. On forfeiture of these shares, the 'securities premium account' will be debited by **CBSE 2024 C**

(a) ₹ 2,000 (b) ₹ 3,000
(c) ₹ 5,000 (d) ₹ 20,000

37. Kewal Ltd. purchased sundry assets from Ganpati Ltd. for ₹ 28,60,000. The amount was paid by issuing fully paid shares of ₹ 100 each issued at a premium of 10%. The number of shares issued to Ganpati Ltd. were **Competency Based Que**

(a) 28,000 (b) 31,778
(c) 28,600 (d) 26,000

38. Sarita Ltd. forfeited 100 shares of ₹ 10 each, ₹ 8 called-up issued at a premium of ₹ 2 per share to Ramesh for non-payment of allotment money of ₹ 5 per share (including premium). The first and final call of ₹ 2 per share was not made. Out of these ₹ 70 shares were reissued to Ashok as ₹ 8 called-up for ₹ 10 per share. The gain on reissue will be **Competency Based Que**

(a) ₹ 500 (b) ₹ 400
(c) ₹ 350 (d) ₹ 300

39. The amount of share capital which a company is authorised to issue by its Memorandum of Association is called **CBSE 2024 C**

(a) issued capital (b) subscribed capital
(c) reserve capital (d) nominal capital

40. Money not received from shareholders on allotment or calls is **CBSE 2024 C**

(a) debited to calls-in-advance account
(b) credited to calls-in-advance account
(c) debited to calls-in-arrears account
(d) credited to calls-in-arrears account

41. Forfeiture of shares leads to reduction of .... capital. **CBSE SQP 2025**

(a) authorised (b) issued
(c) subscribed (d) called-up

42. Mohit had applied for 900 share and was allotted in the ratio 3 : 2. He had paid application money of ₹ 3 per share and couldn't pay allotment money of ₹ 5 per share. First and final call of ₹ 2 per share was not yet made by the company. His shares were forfeited. The following entry will be passed

Share Capital A/c	Dr	X	
To Share Forfeited A/c			Y
To Share Allotment A/c			Z

Here X, Y and Z are **CBSE SQP 2025; Competency Based Que**

(a) ₹ 6,000, ₹ 2,700, ₹ 3,300
(b) ₹ 4,800, ₹ 2,700, ₹ 2,100
(c) ₹ 4,800, ₹ 1,800, ₹ 3,000
(d) ₹ 6,000, ₹ 1,800, ₹ 4,200

43. A company forfeited 6,000 shares of ₹ 10 each, on which only application money of ₹ 3 has been paid. 4,000 of these shares were reissued at ₹ 12 per share as fully paid-up. Amount of capital reserve will be ...... **CBSE SQP 2025**

(a) ₹ 18,000 (b) ₹ 12,000
(c) ₹ 30,000 (d) ₹ 24,000

44. 2,000 shares allotted to Ms. Regal, on which ₹ 80 each called-up and ₹ 50 paid were forfeited and reissued for ₹ 70 each as ₹ 90 paid-up. Amount transferred to capital reserve account is **CBSE SQP 2025**

(a) ₹ 1,00,000 (b) ₹ 60,000
(c) ₹ 40,000 (d) ₹ 20,000

45. Shares issued as sweat equity can be
(i) issued at par. (ii) issued at discount.
(iii) issued at a premium.
Which of the following is correct? **CBSE SQP 2025; Competency Based Que**

(a) Only (i) is correct (b) Both (i) and (iii) are correct
(c) All are correct (d) Only (ii) is correct

46. If 10,000 shares of ₹ 10 each were forfeited for non-payment of final call money of ₹ 3 per share and only 7,000 of these shares were reissued @ ₹ 11 per share as fully paid-up, then what is the minimum amount that company must collect at the time of reissue of the remaining 3,000 shares? **Competency Based Que**

(a) ₹ 21,000
(b) ₹ 9,000
(c) ₹ 16,000
(d) ₹ 30,000

47. Rancho Ltd. took over assets worth ₹ 20,00,000 from PK Ltd. by paying 30% through bank draft and balance by issue of shares of ₹ 100 each at a premium of 10%. The entry to be passed by Rancho Ltd. for settlement will be **Competency Based Que**

(a)

PK Ltd.	Dr	20,00,000	
To Share Capital A/c			12,72,700
To Securities Premium A/c			1,27,270
To Bank A/c			6,00,000
To Statement of Profit and Loss			30
(Being settlement of amount due to vendors)			

(b)

PK Ltd.	Dr	20,00,000	
To Share Capital A/c			12,72,700
To Securities Premium A/c			1,27,270
To Bank A/c			6,00,030
(Being settlement of amount due to vendors)			

(c)

PK Ltd.	Dr	20,00,000	
To Share Capital A/c			12,72,700
To Securities Premium A/c			1,27,300
To Bank A/c			6,00,000
(Being settlement of amount due to vendors)			

(d)

PK Ltd.	Dr	20,00,000	
To Share Capital A/c			12,73,000
To Securities Premium A/c			1,27,300
To Bank A/c			5,99,700
(Being settlement of amount due to vendors)			

48. A company forfeited 3,000 shares of ₹ 10 each, on which only ₹ 5 per share (including ₹ 1 premium) has been paid. Out of these few shares were reissued at a discount of ₹ 1 per share were and ₹ 6,000 were transferred to capital reserve. How many shares were reissued?

(a) 3,000 shares (b) 1,000 shares
(c) 2,000 shares (d) 1,500 shares

Assertion-Reason

Direction (Q.No. 49 to 56) *Read the following Assertion (A) and Reason (R) and choose the correct alternative from the following*

Alternatives

(a) Both Assertion (A) and Reason (R) are true and Reason (R) is the correct explanation of Assertion (A)

(b) Both Assertion (A) and Reason (R) are true, but Reason (R) is not the correct explanation of Assertion (A)

(c) Assertion (A) is true, but Reason (R) is false

(d) Assertion (A) is false, but Reason (R) is true

49. **Assertion** (A) Equity shares are those shares which are not preference shares.

Reason (R) Equity shares are the least issued class of shares and carries the minimum risks and rewards of the business.

50. **Assertion** (A) Minimum subscription is the minimum amount which must be subscribed by the public.

Reason (R) Minimum subscription has been fixed at 80% of the issued amount.

51. **Assertion** (A) Calls-in-arrears is the amount which has not been called by the company but has been paid by the shareholders.

Reason (R) Calls-in-arrears will be shown as a deduction from the subscribed but not fully paid-up capital.

52. **Assertion** (A) When the shares are forfeited, share capital account is debited with the amount called-up and credited to (i) respective unpaid calls account i.e. calls-in-arrears and (ii) share forfeiture account with the amount already received on shares.

Reason (R) When the shares are forfeited, all entries relating to the shares forfeited, except those relating to securities premium, already recorded in accounting records must be reversed.

53. **Assertion** (A) Securities premium cannot be utilised for writing-off loss on sale of a fixed asset.

Reason (R) Securities premium can be applied only for the purposes mentioned in the Companies Act, 2013.

54. **Assertion** (A) Preliminary expenses are not shown in balance sheet.

Reason (R) Preliminary expenses are written-off in the same year.

55. **Assertion** (A) A company is registered with an authorised capital of ₹ 5,00,000 equity shares of ₹ 10 each of which 2,00,000 equity shares were issued and subscribed. All the money had been called-up except ₹ 2 per share which was declared as 'reserve capital'. The share capital reflected in balance sheet as 'subscribed and fully paid-up' will be zero.

Reason (R) Reserve capital can be called-up only at the time of winding-up of the company.

56. **Assertion** (A) Maximum amount of discount allowed at the time of reissue of forfeited shares should not exceed the forfeited amount.

Reason (R) The excess amount of forfeited shares account is transferred to capital reserve account.

CBSE Term I 2021

Two Statements Based MCQs

Direction (Q.No. 57 to 62) *Read the following statements carefully and choose the correct alternative*

Alternatives

(a) Statement I is correct and Statement II is incorrect

(b) Statement II is correct and Statement I is incorrect

(c) Both the statements are correct

(d) Both the statements are incorrect

57. **Statement I** A company can exist perpetually and its existence is not affected by the death, insolvency or insanity of its members.

Statement II The liability of a company's members is unlimited.

58. **Statement I** A company's shares can only be transferred with the permission of its members.

Statement II A company can enter into contracts and hold property in its own name.

59. **Statement I** A company limited by guarantee involves liability for members only during the company's operation.

Statement II An unlimited company allows creditors to claim dues from the private property of its members.

60. **Statement I** A public company is one that limits its members to 200.

Statement II Only a natural person who is an Indian citizen and resident in India can form a One Person Company (OPC).

61. **Statement I** Pro-rata allotment is made in the event shares are undersubscribed.

Statement II Issued share capital is that part of authorised share capital that is issued for subscription whether subscribed or not.

62. **Statement I** Subscribed share capital can be less than or equal to the issued share capital but cannot be more.

Statement II Securities premium reserve can be used for issuing partly paid bonus shares.

Matching

63. Match the following features with their definitions

Column I	Column II
A. Separate legal entity	(i) Shares can be freely transferred in a public company
B. Limited liability	(ii) Distinct legal identity from its members
C. Transferability of shares	(iii) Liability limited to unpaid value of shares
D. Perpetual succession	(iv) Continues to exist despite changes in membership

Codes

	A	B	C	D
(a)	(ii)	(iii)	(i)	(iv)
(b)	(iii)	(iv)	(ii)	(i)
(c)	(i)	(ii)	(iv)	(iii)
(d)	(iv)	(i)	(iii)	(ii)

64. Match the following features with the appropriate descriptions

Column I	Column II
A. Common seal	(i) Can sue or be sued in its own name
B. May sue or be sued	(ii) Acts as official signature of the company
C. Body corporate	(iii) Formed according to legal provisions
D. Transferability of shares	(iv) Freely transferable in public companies

Codes

	A	B	C	D
(a)	(ii)	(i)	(iii)	(iv)
(b)	(iii)	(ii)	(i)	(iv)
(c)	(iv)	(i)	(iii)	(ii)
(d)	(i)	(iii)	(ii)	(iv)

65. Match the types of companies with their features

Column I	Column II
A. Companies limited by shares	(i) Liability arises only in the event of winding-up
B. Companies limited by guarantee	(ii) No limit on liability; creditors can claim private property
C. Unlimited companies	(iii) Liability limited to the unpaid value of shares
D. Public company	(iv) Not a private company and not a subsidiary of one

Codes

	A	B	C	D
(a)	(iii)	(i)	(ii)	(iv)
(b)	(i)	(ii)	(iii)	(iv)
(c)	(ii)	(iii)	(i)	(iv)
(d)	(iii)	(ii)	(i)	(iv)

66. Match the following

Column I	Column II
A. Actual number of shares offered to the public.	(i) Authorised capital
B. Maximum number of shares above which company cannot issue shares to the public.	(ii) Issued capital
C. Number of shares applied by the public.	(iii) Uncalled capital
D. The amount which is called at the time of liquidation of company.	(iv) Subscribed capital

Codes

	A	B	C	D
(a)	(ii)	(i)	(iv)	(iii)
(b)	(ii)	(iii)	(i)	(iv)
(c)	(iv)	(iii)	(ii)	(i)
(d)	(iii)	(iv)	(i)	(ii)

67. Match the following

Column I	Column II
A. When shares are issued more than face value.	(i) At par
B. Application received from public is less than issued share.	(ii) At premium
C. When share are issued at face value.	(iii) Undersubscription
D. Application received from public is more than issued share.	(iv) Oversubscription

Codes

	A	B	C	D
(a)	(ii)	(i)	(iv)	(iii)
(b)	(ii)	(iii)	(i)	(iv)
(c)	(iv)	(iii)	(ii)	(i)
(d)	(iii)	(iv)	(i)	(ii)

Case Based MCQs

Direction *Read the following case study and answer the questions 68 and 69 on the basis of the same*

Vinod Ltd. having authorised capital ₹ 1,00,00,000 divided into equity shares of ₹ 100 each, invited applications for issuing 25,000 equity shares at par.

The amount per share was payable as follows

On application ₹ 20 per share, on allotment ₹ 30 per share, on first call ₹ 25 per share and on second and final call ₹ 25 per share. Applications were received for 24,000 shares and the shares were allotted to all the applicants. All calls were made and were received as follows

On 18,000 shares — Full amount
On 2,000 shares — ₹ 75 per share
On 2,500 shares — ₹ 50 per share
On 1,500 shares — ₹ 20 per share

The company forfeited those shares on which less than ₹ 75 per share were received. The forfeited shares were reissued at ₹ 95 per share fully paid-up. **CBSE Term I 2021**

68. **How much amount was received on allotment?**

(a) ₹ 6,75,000 (b) ₹ 7,20,000 (c) ₹ 6,00,000 (d) ₹ 4,80,000

69. **How much total amount was credited to share forfeiture account on forfeiture of shares?**

(a) ₹ 3,80,000 (b) ₹ 1,35,000 (c) ₹ 1,55,000 (d) ₹ 2,45,000

Direction *Read the following case study and answer the questions 70 to 75 on the basis of the same*

In the Books of XYZEE Ltd.
Balance Sheet (An Extract)
as at 31st March, 2024

Particulars	Note No.	31st March, 2023 (₹)	31st March, 2024 (₹)
I. EQUITY AND LIABILITIES			
1. **Shareholders' Funds**			
(i) Share Capital	1	44,90,000	54,90,000
(ii) Reserves and Surplus	2	2,00,000	3,60,000

Note No. 1 (For year ending 31st March, 2023)

Particulars		Amt (₹)
Share Capital		
1. **Authorised Share Capital**		
8,00,000 Equity Shares of ₹ 10 each		80,00,000
2. **Issued Share Capital**		
4,50,000 Equity Shares of ₹ 10 each		45,00,000
3. **Called-up Share Capital**		
(i) **Called-up and Fully Paid**		
₹ 10 per Share on 4,45,000 Equity Shares	44,50,000	
(ii) **Called-up and not Fully Paid**		
₹ 10 per Share on 5,000 Equity Shares	50,000	
(–) Not Paid (₹ 2 per Share on 5,000 Equity Shares)	(10,000)	44,90,000

Note No. 1 (For year ending 31st March, 2024)

Particulars		Amt (₹)
Share Capital		
1. **Authorised Share Capital**		
8,00,000 Equity Shares of ₹ 10 each		80,00,000
2. **Issued Share Capital**		
5,50,000 Equity Shares of ₹ 10 each		55,00,000
(Out of these 40,000 shares were issued to the vendors as consideration for capital asset purchased)		
3. **Called-up Share Capital**		
(i) **Called-up and Fully Paid**		
₹ 10 per Share on 5,45,000 Equity Shares	54,50,000	
(ii) **Called-up and not Fully Paid**		
₹ 10 per Share on 5,000 Equity Shares	50,000	
(–) Not Paid (₹ 2 per Share on 5,000 Equity Shares)	(10,000)	54,90,000

Note No. 2 Reserves and Surplus

Particulars	31st March, 2023 (₹)	31st March, 2024 (₹)
Capital Reserve	Nil	40,000
Securities Premium	2,00,000	3,20,000

During the year the company took over the business of Quipa Ltd. with assets of ₹ 12,00,000 and liabilities of ₹ 7,30,000. Purchase consideration was paid in cash and by issue of equity shares at par. The entire transaction resulted in capital reserve of ₹ 40,000. **CBSE SQP 2025**

70. **What is the total face value of shares issued for cash by the company during the year 2023-24?**
(a) ₹ 10,00,000 (b) ₹ 6,00,000
(c) ₹ 9,50,000 (d) ₹ 11,20,000

71. **Shares issued for cash during the year were issued at .... (assuming they were issued together)**
(a) ₹ 10 (b) ₹ 8
(b) ₹ 12 (d) ₹ 11.20

72. **On 1st April, 2024, the company forfeited all the defaulting shares. What amount will appear in the share forfeiture account at the time of forfeiture?**
(a) ₹ 40,000 (b) ₹ 50,000 (c) ₹ 10,000 (d) ₹ 60,000

73. **What will be the number of issued shares, as on 1st April, 2024, after the forfeiture of these shares?**
(a) 5,45,000 shares (b) 5,50,000 shares
(c) 4,45,000 shares (d) 5,05,000 shares

74. **If 2,000 of the forfeited shares were issued at ₹ 14 per share, what will be the amount of securities premium and capital reserve respectively as on 1st April, 2024?**
(a) ₹ 3,20,000, ₹ 40,000 (b) ₹ 3,28,000, ₹ 56,000
(c) ₹ 3,28,000, ₹ 80,000 (d) ₹ 3,20,000, ₹ 80,000

75. **What will be the amount in the 'called-up and fully paid' sub-head after the reissue of these 2,000 shares?**
(a) ₹ 54,50,000 (b) ₹ 55,00,000
(c) ₹ 54,70,000 (d) ₹ 54,80,000

Direction *Read the following case study and answer the questions 76 to 81 on the basis of the same*

Following is the extract of the balance sheet of Vikalp Ltd. as per Schedule III, Part I of Companies Act as at 31st March, 2024 along with notes to accounts **CBSE 2025**

In the Books of Vikalp Ltd.
Balance Sheet
as at 31st March, 2024

Particulars	Note No.	31st March, 2024 (₹)	31st March, 2023 (₹)
I. EQUITY AND LIABILITIES			
1. **Shareholders' Funds**			
(i) Share Capital	1	59,60,000	50,00,000

'Notes to accounts' as at 31st March, 2023

	Particulars	31st March, 2023 (₹)
1.	**Share Capital**	
	Authorised Capital	
	9,00,000 Equity Shares of ₹ 10 each	90,00,000
	Issued Capital	
	5,00,000 Equity Shares of ₹ 10 each	50,00,000
	Subscribed Capital	
	Subscribed and Fully paid-up	
	5,00,000 Equity Shares of ₹ 10 each	50,00,000
	Subscribed but not Fully paid-up	—
		50,00,000

Notes to accounts' as at 31st March, 2024

	Particulars		31st March, 2024 (₹)
1.	**Share Capital**		
	Authorised Capital		
	9,00,000 Equity Shares of ₹ 10 each		90,00,000
	Issued Capital		
	6,00,000 equity shares of ₹ 10 each		60,00,000
	Subscribed Capital		
	Subscribed and Fully Paid-up		
	5,80,000 Equity Shares of ₹ 10 each		58,00,000
	Subscribed but not Fully paid-up		
	20,000 Equity Shares of ₹ 10 each, Fully Called-up	2,00,000	
	(–) Calls-in-arrears 20,000 Equity Shares @ ₹ 2 per Share	(40,000)	1,60,000
			59,60,000

76. **The total face value of equity shares issued during the year 2023-2024 was**
(a) ₹ 10,00,000 (b) ₹ 9,80,000
(c) ₹ 4,20,000 (d) ₹11,00,000

77. **The number of shares on which the called-up amount was not received were**
(a) ₹ 1,00,000 (b) ₹ 80,000
(c) ₹ 3,00,000 (d) ₹ 20,000

78. **On 1st April, 2024 Vikalp Limited forfeited all the shares on which the called-up amount was not received. On forfeiture, 'share capital account' will be debited by**
(a) ₹ 1,60,000 (b) ₹ 40,000
(c) ₹ 2,00,000 (d) ₹ 2,40,000

79. **On forfeiture, 'share forfeiture account' will be credited with**
(a) ₹ 1,60,000
(b) ₹ 40,000
(c) ₹ 2,00,000
(d) ₹ 2,40,000

80. If all the forfeited shares are reissued at 8 per share fully paid-up, the amount credited to 'capital reserve account' will be

(a) ₹ 40,000 (b) ₹ 1,60,000
(c) ₹ 2,00,000 (d) ₹ 1,20,000

81. If the forfeited shares are reissued at the minimum permissible price, the amount credited to 'capital reserve account' will be

(a) ₹ 2,00,000 (b) ₹ 1,60,000
(c) ₹ 40,000 (d) NIL

Answers

1. (b) that part of issued capital which has been actually subscribed by the public
2. (d) credited to calls-in-advance account
3. (b) credited to calls-in-advance account
4. (c) share capital
5. (a) 120 days, allotment of shares
6. (d) Any one of I and II
7. (b) issued capital
8. (a) Amount received on application $= 5,00,000 \times 20$ $= ₹\ 1,00,00,000$
9. (c) Amount due on total shares $(10,000 \times 10)$ is ₹ 1,00,000. Complete amount was received, one shareholder paid late, but at the end amount was received. Hence, complete amount received by the company will be ₹ 1,00,000.
10. (d)

Share Capital A/c (700 × 9)	Dr	6,300
Securities Premium A/c (700 × 1)	Dr	700
To Share Allotment A/c (700 × 5)		3,500
To Share First and Final Call A/c (700 × 3)		2,100
To Share Forfeiture A/c (700 × 2)		1,400

11. (d) Amount refunded $= 2,00,000 \times 13 = ₹\ 26,00,000$
12. (c) uncalled
13. (c) Share Capital $= 1,500 \times 9 = ₹\ 13,500$
14. (a) Minimum price at which shares can be reissued is ₹ 40
15. (a) When share are reissued then money is received, so cash/bank will be debited as per accounting rule and equity share capital is increased, hence it will be credited.
16. (b) credited to calls-in-advance account
17. (c) private placement of shares
18. (d) ₹ 2 per share
19. (d) ₹ 20
20. (a) Capital Reserve = Profit on Forfeiture − Loss on Reissue $= (500 \times 7) - (500 \times 1) = ₹\ 3,000$
21. (b) Minimum Price = Nominal Value of Share − Maximum Discount which can be Allowed* $= 10 - 6 = ₹\ 4$

*Maximum discount which can be allowed $= 10 - 3 - 1 = ₹\ 6$ (forfeited) per share

22. (d) ₹ 6
23. (b) ₹ 19,000
24. (a) nominal capital
25. (c) Calls-in-arrears will be credited by $= 1,000 \times 5 = ₹\ 5,000$
26. (c) ₹ 1,000
27. (b) issued capital
28. (c) Capital Reserve = Profit on Forfeiture − Loss on Reissue $= (3,000 \times 6) - (3,000 \times 1) = ₹\ 15,000$
29. (c)

Share Capital A/c (400 × 8)	Dr	3,200
To Share First Call A/c (400 × 2)		800
To Share Forfeiture A/c (400 × 6)		2,400

30. (a) Capital Reserve

$$= \frac{\text{Profit on Forfeiture} \times \text{Reissued Shares}}{\text{Forfeited Shares}} - \text{Loss on Reissue}$$

$$= \frac{8,000 \times 800}{1,000} - 0 = ₹\ 6,400$$

31. (b) Amount received on Allotment $= (6,000 \times 3) + (200 \times 5) = ₹\ 19,000$
32. (b) Minimum Amount $= 5,000 \times 2 = ₹\ 10,000$
33. (b) issue of partly paid bonus shares
34. (c) capital reserve account
35. (c) capital reserve account
36. (c) Securities premium $= 1,000 \times 5 = ₹\ 5,000$
37. (d) Number of Shares $= \frac{28,60,000}{110} = 26,000$
38. (c) Profit on Reissue $= \frac{500 \times 70}{100} = ₹\ 350$
39. (d) nominal capital
40. (c) debited to calls-in-arrears account
41. (c) subscribed
42. (b) Shares allotted to Mohit $= \frac{900 \times 2}{3} = 600$

Share Capital $= 600 \times 8 = ₹\ 4,800$

Share Forfeiture $= 900 \times 3 = ₹\ 2,700$

Share Capital $= (600 \times 5) - 900 = ₹\ 2,100$

43. (b) Capital Reserve

$$= \left[\frac{\text{Profit on Forfeiture} \times \text{Reissued Shares}}{\text{Forfeited Shares}} - \text{Loss on Reissue}\right]$$

$$= \frac{18,000}{6,000} \times 4,000 - 0 = ₹\ 12,000$$

44. (b) Capital Reserve = Profit on Forfeiture − Loss on Reissue
$= (2{,}000 \times 50) - (2{,}000 \times 20) =$ ₹ 60,000

45. (b) Both (i) and (iii) are correct

46. (b) Minimum Amount = 3,000 × 3 = ₹ 9,000

47. (b) Number of Shares $= \dfrac{\text{Purchase Consideration}}{\text{Issue Price}}$
$= \dfrac{14{,}00{,}000}{110} = 12{,}727$ Shares

48. (c) Let us assume the company reissued 2,000 shares.
Profit on Forfeiture = 3,000 × 4 = 12,000
Loss on Reissue = 2,000 × 1 = 2,000
Capital Reserve = (12,000/3,000 × 2,000) − 2,000
= 8,000 − 2,000
= ₹ 6,000
The company reissued 2,000 shares.

49. (c) Equity shares are the most commonly issued class of shares and carries the maximum risks and rewards of the business.

50. (c) As per Companies Act, minimum subscription has been fixed at 90% of the issued amount.

51. (d) Calls-in-arrears is the amount which has not been paid by the shareholder till due date.

52. (a) Both Assertion (A) and Reason (R) are true and Reason (R) is the correct explanation of Assertion (A)

53. (a) Both Assertion (A) and Reason (R) are true and Reason (R) is the correct explanation of Assertion (A)

54. (a) As per As-26, preliminary expenses are written-off in the same year in which they are incurred.

55. (b) Both Assertion (A) and Reason (R) are true, but Reason (R) is not the correct explanation of Assertion (A)

56. (b) Both Assertion (A) and Reason (R) are true, but Reason (R) is not the correct explanation of Assertion (A)

57. (a) Statement I is correct and Statement II is incorrect

58. (b) Statement II is correct and Statement I is incorrect

59. (b) Statement II is correct and Statement I is incorrect

60. (b) Statement II is correct and Statement I is incorrect

61. (a) Pro-rata allotment is made when shares are oversubscribed.

62. (a) Statement I is correct and Statement II is incorrect

63. (a) (ii) (iii) (i) (iv)

64. (a) (ii) (i) (iii) (iv)

65. (a) (iii) (i) (ii) (iv)

66. (a) (ii) (i) (iv) (iii)

67. (a) (ii) (i) (iv) (iii)

68. (a) Amount received on Allotment
$= (18{,}000 + 2{,}000 + 2{,}500) \times 30$
$= 22{,}500 \times 30 =$ ₹ 6,75,000

69. (c) Amount credited to Share Forfeiture Account
$= (2{,}500 \times 50) + (1{,}500 \times 20)$
$= 1{,}25{,}000 + 30{,}000$
= ₹ 1,55,000

70. (a) Total face value of shares issued
= 55,00,000 − 45,00,000 = ₹ 10,00,000

71. (c) Face Value/Share = ₹ 10
Securities Premium/Share $\left(\dfrac{1{,}20{,}000}{60{,}000}\right)$ = ₹ 2
= ₹ 12

72. (a) Share forfeiture account = 5,000 × 8 = ₹ 40,000

73. (b) 5,50,000 shares

74. (b) Securities Premium = 3,20,000 + (2,000 × 4)
= ₹ 3,28,000
Capital Reserve = 40,000 + (2,000 × 8) = ₹ 56,000

75. (c) **Called-up and Fully Paid-up**
5,45,000 × 10 = 54,50,000
2,000 × 10 = 20,000
₹ 54,70,000

76. (a) Total shares issued during 2023-24
= 6,00,000 − 5,00,000 = 1,00,000
Face value = 1,00,000 × 10 = ₹ 10,00,000

77. (d) On 20,000 shares, called-up amount, was not received.

78. (c) As the amount was fully called-up, share capital will be debited by ₹ 2,00,000.

79. (a) Share forfeiture account will be credited with ₹ 1,60,000, Calculated as follows
Share Capital − Calls-in-arrears = 2,00,000 − 40,000
= ₹ 1,60,000

80. (d) Amount will be calculated as follows
Total Gain on Forfeiture = ₹ 1,60,000
(−) Discount Allowed on Reissue (20,000 × 2)
= ₹ (40,000)
Transfer to Capital Reserve = ₹ 1,20,000

81. (d) Total Gain on Forfeiture = ₹ 1,60,000
(−) Maximum Discount Allowed = ₹ (1,60,000)
Nil

08

CHAPTER

"Debenture includes debenture stock, bonds and any other instrument of a company evidencing a debt, whether constituting a charge on the assets of the company or not."

- Section 2(30) of Companies Act, 2013

YOUR STUDY GOALS

8.1 Meaning of Debentures

8.2 Issue of Debentures for Cash

8.3 Issue of Debentures for Consideration Other than Cash

8.4 Issue of Debentures as Collateral Security

8.5 Various Cases from the Point of View of Redemption

YOUR PRACTICE GOAL

- Topicwise Solved Questions (27 Solved Questions)
- Numerical Questions [34 Questions (Unsolved)]
- Theoretical Questions [5 Questions (with answers)]
- Objective Questions (61 Qs ; MCQs, A-R, Statements, Matching, Case)

Accounting for Debentures

8.1 Meaning of Debentures

A debenture (called Debenture Certificate) is an instrument acknowledging a debt, issued under the common seal of the company.

It is a contract for the repayment of the principal sum at a specified date and for the payment of interest (usually half-yearly) at a fixed rate of per cent until the principal sum is repaid.

It specifies nominal/par value of debenture, the rate of interest to be paid, periodicity of payment, the tenure of debentures and terms of redemption.

As per Companies Act, 2013, debentures shall be shown in the equity and liabilities part of the balance sheet under the major head 'non-current liabilities' and sub-head 'long-term borrowings'.

Features of Debentures

- It is a certificate or document acknowledging debt of a company.
- Mode and period of repayment of principal and interest is fixed.
- It is issued under the common seal of the company.
- It may or may not be secured.
- It is considered as external equity or long-term borrowings of the company.
- Rate of interest on debentures is fixed. It is usual to prefix 'debentures' with the rate of interest.

Important Terms Related to Debentures

- **Bond** is also an instrument of acknowledgement of debt. Bond is similar to debentures in terms of contents and texture. However, bonds can be issued without predetermined rate of interest. Traditionally, the government issued bonds but these days, bonds are issued by semi-government and non-governmental organisations also.
- **Any Other Instrument** It includes any kind of security evidencing a debt that a company may issue. e.g. A company enter into an agreement with another company for borrowing, it will also be termed as debenture.
- **Charge** According to Section 2(16) of Companies Act, 2013, "Charge means an interest or lien created on the property or assets of a company or any of its undertakings or both, as security and includes a mortgage."

  Following are included in the category of charge
  - **Fixed Charge** When the charge is created against specific assets of the enterprise, then such a charge is called a fixed charge.
  - **Floating Charge** It is a charge created on the group of assets whose value is subjected to a change in quantity and value.
- **Debenture Trust Deed** It is a document created by the company whereby trustees are appointed to protect the interest of debentureholders before they are offered for public subscription.

Types of Debentures

A company may issue different kinds of debentures, as discussed below

Smart Study Chart No. 1

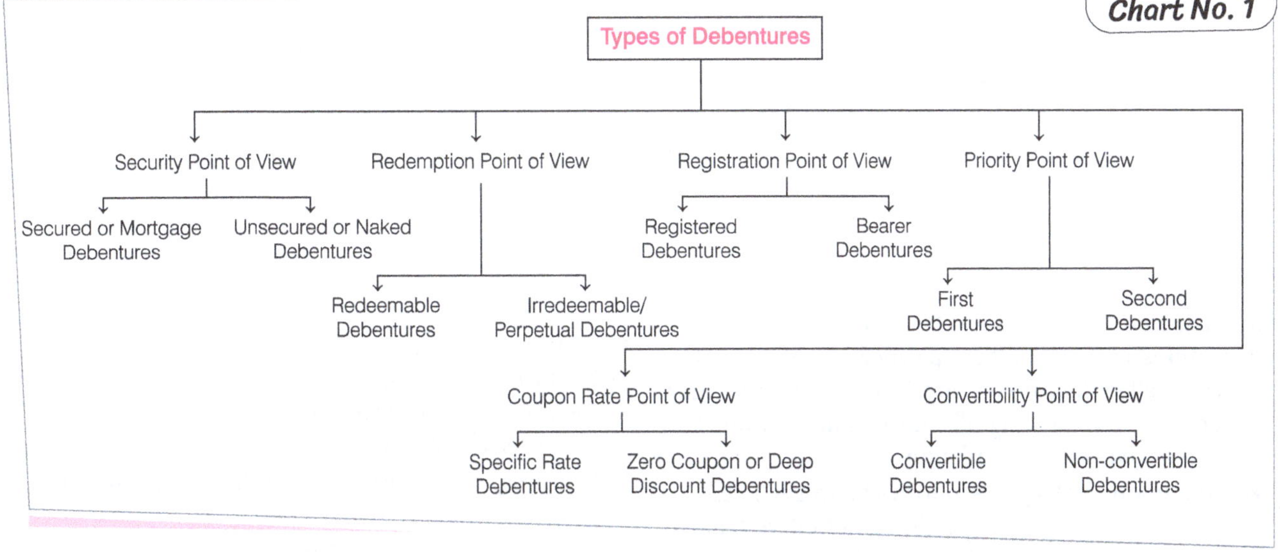

1. From the Point of View of Security

- **Secured or Mortgage Debentures** These are those debentures which are secured by either a fixed charge or a floating charge on the assets of the company.
- **Unsecured or Naked Debentures** These debentures are not secured by any charge on asset of the company. They do not have a security.

2. From the Point of View of Redemption/Tenure

- **Redeemable Debentures** These debentures are repaid at the end of specified time or by instalments during the lifetime of the company.
- **Irredeemable/Perpetual Debentures** These debentures are not repayable during the existence of the company and hence are repaid at the time of liquidation of the company.

3. From the Point of View of Registration/Records

- **Registered Debentures** These debentures are registered in the companies record in the name of the holder. These debentures are not freely transferable. The transfer of debentures in this case, requires the execution of transfer deed.
- **Bearer Debentures** These debentures are not registered in the companies record in the name of the holder.

  They are transferable by mere delivery. The company keeps no record of such debenture-holders. Payment of interest is made on the production of coupons attached to the debentures.

4. From the Point of View of Priority

- **First Debentures** These are the debentures which have to be repaid before the other debentures.
- **Second Debentures** These debentures will be repaid after the first debentures are redeemed.

5. From the Point of View of Convertibility

- **Convertible Debentures** These are the debentures which can be converted into equity shares or other securities after a specified period, at the option of the debentureholders.

  These can be further categorised as Partly Convertible Debentures (PCD) and Fully Convertible Debentures (FCD).
- **Non-convertible Debentures** The holders of these debentures have no right to convert them into equity shares.

6. From the Point of View of Coupon Rate

- **Specific Rate** (Coupon Rate) **Debentures** These debentures are issued with a specified rate of interest, which is called the **coupon rate.** The specified rate may either be fixed or floating. The floating interest rate is usually tagged with the bank rate.
- **Zero Coupon or Deep Discount Debentures** These debentures do not carry a specific rate of interest. Such debentures are issued at substantial discount and the difference between the nominal value and the issue price is treated as the amount of interest related to the duration of the debentures.

Disclosure of Debentures in Balance Sheet

Debentures being borrowings (liability) of a company are shown in the **equity and liabilities** part of the balance sheet. Debentures may be either non-current liability or a current liability.

When Non-current Liability Debentures are shown in the balance sheet under the head **non-current liabilities** and sub-head **long-term borrowings**.

When Current Liability

- Debentures are shown in the balance sheet under the head **current liabilities** and sub-head **short-term borrowings.**
- In case, debentures outstanding in the books of accounts of a company, they are shown as **long-term borrowings** under **non-current liabilities** in the balance sheet and part of it which have become due for redemption within 12 months of the date of balance sheet, will be shown under **current liabilities** as current maturities of long-term debts under **other current liabilities.**

Issue of Debentures

A company can issue debentures to raise long-term funds, provided the memorandum of association authorises it. The procedure for issuing debentures is similar to that of shares. A prospectus is issued and interested investors apply for debentures. Payment can be made in full at the time of application or in instalments (on application, allotment and calls).

As per Section 39 of the Companies Act, 2013, the condition of minimum subscription applies to all securities, including debentures.

Debentures can also be issued

- For cash
- For consideration other than cash
- As collateral security

Debentures, whether issued for cash or otherwise, may be issued

- At par
- At premium
- At discount

Key Point

Debentures can be issued at a discount, but shares cannot be issued at discount, except for sweat equity shares.

8.2 Issue of Debentures for Cash

Issue of debentures for cash may take place at par, premium and discount. Accounting entries in case of issue of debentures are same as in case of issue of shares, the difference lies only in the title or name of accounts. The amount of debentures can be collected in lumpsum or in instalments, i.e. on application, on allotment and on calls.

Journal entries required to be passed in these two instances are discussed below

I. When Debenture Amount is Received in Lumpsum (If the full amount is payable along with application)

1. **On receipt of application money**

Bank A/c Dr
  To Debenture Application and Allotment A/c
(Being application and allotment money received)

2. **On acceptance of applications money/allotment of debentures**

- **When debentures are issued at par**

Debenture Application and Allotment A/c Dr
  To X% Debentures A/c
(Being application and allotment money transferred to debenture account)

- **When debentures are issued at premium**

Debenture Application and Allotment A/c Dr
  To X% Debentures A/c
  To Securities Premium A/c
(Being application and allotment money transferred to and securities premium reserve account)

- **When debentures are issued at discount**

Debenture Application and Allotment A/c Dr
Discount on Issue of Debentures A/c Dr
  To X% Debentures A/c
(Being application and allotment money transferred debentures account and discount on issue recorded)

3. **On refund of excess application money**

Debenture Application and Allotment A/c Dr
  To Bank A/c
(Being the excess application money refunded)

II. When Debenture Amount is Received in Instalments

1. **On receipt of application money**

Bank A/c Dr
  To Debenture Application A/c
(Being application money received)

2. **On acceptance of applications**

Debenture Application A/c Dr
  To Debentures A/c
(Being application money transferred to debenture account)

3. **On adjustment of excess debenture application money**

Debenture Application A/c Dr
  To Debenture Allotment A/c
(Being adjustment of excess debenture application money)

4. **On refund of excess debenture application money**

Debenture Application A/c Dr
  To Bank A/c
(Being refund of excess debenture application money)

5. **When allotment money is due**

- **At par**

Debenture Allotment A/c Dr
  To Debentures A/c
(Being allotment money due)

- **At premium**

Debenture Allotment A/c Dr
  To Debentures A/c
  To Securities Premium A/c
(Being allotment due on debentures with premium)

- **At discount**

Debenture Allotment A/c Dr
Discount on Issue of Debentures A/c Dr
  To Debentures A/c
(Being allotment due on X% debentures)

6. **On receipt of allotment money**

Bank A/c Dr
  To Debenture Allotment A/c
(Being allotment money received)

7. **On making calls**

Debenture First and Final Call A/c	Dr
To Debentures A/c	
(Being first and final call money due)	

8. **On receipt of call money**

Bank A/c	Dr
To Debenture First and Final Call A/c	
(Being first and final call money received)	

Oversubscription of Debentures

When the number of debentures applied for is more than those offered for subscription, it is known as **oversubscription**. A company cannot allot more debentures than it has offered for subscription.
In such a situation, the company may make allotment as is made in the case of shares, i.e.

First alternative — Rejecting excess application
Second alternative — Partial or pro-rata allotment
Third alternative — A combination of the above two alternatives

8.3 Issue of Debentures for Consideration Other than Cash

When debentures are issued to vendors against purchase of assets or against purchase of business, it is termed as issue of debentures for consideration other than cash. In this case, consideration for issue of debentures is not cash but the assets or business.

Disclosure in the Balance Sheet

Debentures issued for consideration other than cash appear under the head 'non-current liabilities' and sub-head 'long-term borrowings' in the balance sheet.

Following journal entries will be passed in this case

1. On Purchase of Assets or Business

- **When assets are purchased**

Sundry Assets A/c	Dr
To Vendor's A/c	
(Being assets purchased from the vendor)	

- **When business is purchased**

Sundry Assets A/c	Dr
*Goodwill A/c	Dr
To Sundry Liabilities A/c	
To Vendor's A/c	
*To Capital Reserve A/c	
(Being business of vendor purchased)	

** Either goodwill or capital reserve will appear in the above journal entry.*

- **Goodwill account** will be debited in case the value of net assets (assets–liabilities) is less than purchase consideration to vendor.
- **Capital reserve account** will be credited in case the value of net assets is more than the purchase consideration.

2. On Issue of Debentures

Debentures issued to the vendor for consideration other than cash may be issued

- **At par**

Vendor's A/c	Dr
To X% Debentures A/c	
(Being ... debentures at ₹ ... per debenture issued to vendors)	

Number of Debentures Issued

$$= \frac{\text{Purchase Consideration}}{\text{Issue Price (Par value per debenture)}}$$

- **At premium**

Vendor's A/c	Dr
To X% Debentures A/c	
To Securities Premium A/c	
(Being ... debentures at ₹ ... each issued at a premium of ₹ ... per debenture to vendors)	

Number of Debentures Issued

$$= \frac{\text{Purchase Consideration}}{\text{Issue Price (Face value + Premium per debenture)}}$$

- **At discount**

Vendor's A/c	Dr
Discount on Issue of Debentures A/c	Dr
To X% Debentures A/c	
(Being ... debentures at ₹ ... each issued to vendors at a discount of ₹ ... per debenture)	

Number of Debentures Issued

$$= \frac{\text{Purchase Consideration}}{\text{Issue Price (Face value − Discount per debenture)}}$$

Note Par value and face value are one and the same thing.

8.4 Issue of Debentures as Collateral Security

Collateral security means additional security given to the lender in addition to the primary security. When a company takes a loan, it may provide primary security on its assets.

However, the lending institution may insist on some more assets as secondary or collateral security. In such a situation, the company may issue debentures to the lender as secondary or collateral security. Such an issue of debentures is known as 'debentures issued as collateral security'.

If the company fails to repay the loan along with the interest and the primary security is insufficient to repay the loan, only in that case the lender is free to use the debentures issued as collateral security. The lender may either present such debentures for redemption or sell them in the open market. Interest is not payable on debentures issued as collateral security.

Debentures issued as collateral security can be dealt in two ways

1. First Method (Without Passing Journal Entry)

In this method, no journal entry is passed in the books for issue of debentures as collateral security.

However, the fact that debentures have been issued as collateral security is disclosed in balance sheet, by way of information below debentures.

It is shown as long-term borrowings under non-current liabilities or as short-term borrowings under current liabilities, as the case may be.

(i) Debentures Issued as Collateral Security for Long-term Loan from Bank

Balance Sheet (Relevant extract)
as at ...

Particulars	Note No.	Amt (₹)
I. **EQUITY AND LIABILITIES**		
1. **Non-current Liabilities**		
Long-term Borrowings	1	

Notes to Accounts

Particulars	Amt (₹)
1. **Long-term Borrowings**	
Loan from Bank	
(Secured by issue of X% debentures of ₹ ... each as collateral security)	

(ii) Debentures Issued as Collateral Security for Short-term Loan from Bank

Balance Sheet (Relevant extract)
as at...

Particulars	Note No.	Amt (₹)
I. **EQUITY AND LIABILITIES**		
1. **Current Liabilities**		
Short-term Borrowings	1	

Notes to Accounts

Particulars	Amt (₹)
1. **Short-term Borrowings**	
Loan from Bank	
(Secured by issue of X% debentures of ₹... each as collateral security)	

2. Second Method (With Journal Entry)

Debentures issued as collateral security may be recorded in the books of accounts by passing a journal entry.

Following journal entry will be passed for issue of debentures as collateral security

Debenture Suspense A/c (Appears on assets side)	Dr
To X% Debentures A/c (Appears on liabilities side)	

Disclosure of Debentures Issued as Collateral Security in the Balance Sheet

In balance sheet, debentures issued as collateral security is shown separately from other debentures. As debenture issued as collateral security is related to the loan of the company, therefore, it is shown in the 'notes to accounts' in which the loan secured by debenture is shown.

Balance Sheet
as at ...

Particulars	Note No.	Amt (₹)
I. **EQUITY AND LIABILITIES**		
1. **Non-current Liabilities**		
Long-term Borrowings	1	

Notes to Accounts

Particulars		Amt (₹)
1. **Long-term Borrowings**		
Loan from Bank		...
X% Debentures of ₹ ... each Issued as Collateral Security	...	
(–) Debenture Suspense	(...)	...

When the loan is paid back, the above mentioned entry will be reversed as follows

X% Debentures A/c	Dr
To Debenture Suspense A/c	
(Being debentures issued as collateral security, now cancelled on payment of loan)	

8.5 Various Cases from the Point of View of Redemption

When a company issues debentures, it usually mentions the terms on which they will be redeemed at their maturity. Redemption of debentures means discharge of liability on account of debentures by repayment made to the debentureholders. The issue of debentures can be made at par, at premium or at a discount. However, the redemption of debentures can be made at par or at a premium only.

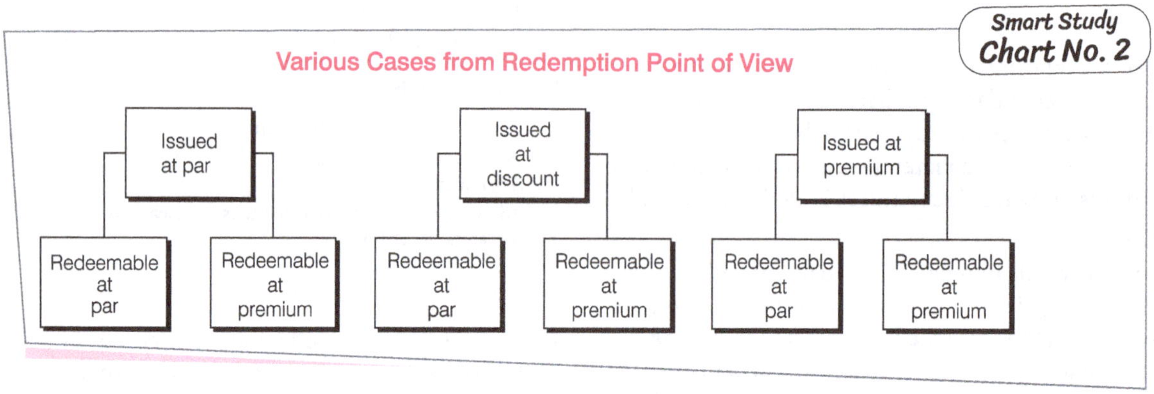

Journal entries required for each condition (assuming full payment receivable at application) are given below

1. When Debentures are Issued at Par and Redeemable at Par
(Redeemable Value is Equal to the Face Value)

(i) Bank A/c	Dr
To Debenture Application A/c	
(ii) Debenture Application A/c	Dr
To X% Debentures A/c	

2. When Debentures are Issued at Par and Redeemable at Premium
(In excess of Nominal Value)

(i) Bank A/c	Dr
To Debenture Application A/c	
(ii) Debenture Application A/c	Dr
Loss on Issue of Debentures A/c (For premium on redemption)	Dr
To X% Debentures A/c	
To Premium on Redemption of Debentures A/c	

3. When Debentures are Issued at a Discount and are Redeemable at Par

(i) Bank A/c	Dr
To Debenture Application A/c	
(ii) Debenture Application A/c	Dr
Discount on Issue of Debentures A/c	Dr
To X% Debentures A/c	

4. When Debentures are Issued at a Discount and are Redeemable at Premium

(i) Bank A/c	Dr
To Debenture Application A/c	
(ii) Debenture Application A/c	Dr
Discount on Issue of Debentures A/c	Dr
Loss on Issue of Debentures A/c (For premium)	Dr
To X% Debentures A/c (Nominal value)	
To Premium on Redemption of Debentures A/c	

In the above entry, the 'discount on issue of debentures' is also a loss on issue of debentures.
This can be further combined into one account under 'loss on issue of debentures account' as follows

Debenture Application A/c	Dr
Loss on Issue of Debentures A/c (Discount + Premium on Redemption)	Dr
To X% Debentures A/c (Nominal value)	
To Premium on Redemption of Debentures A/c	

5. When Debentures are Issued at a Premium and Redeemable at Par

(i) Bank A/c	Dr
To Debenture Application A/c	
(ii) Debenture Application A/c	Dr
To X% Debentures A/c	
To Securities Premium A/c	

6. When Debentures are Issued at a Premium and are Redeemable at Premium

(i) Bank A/c	Dr
To Debenture Application A/c	
(ii) Debenture Application A/c	Dr
Loss on Issue of Debentures A/c (For premium on redemption)	Dr
To X% Debentures A/c (Nominal value)	
To Securities Premium A/c (For premium on issue)	
To Premium on Redemption of Debentures A/c (For premium on redemption)	

Writting-off Loss/Discount on Issue of Debentures

Discount on issue of debentures is a capital loss and the amount of discount is debited to a separate account titled 'discount on issue of debentures account'.

Discount on Issue of Debentures and Loss on Issue of Debentures Former is a loss for the company, incurred at the time of issue of debentures while latter is a wider term and includes both the discount on issue of debentures and premium payable on debentures.

Writing-off Discount/Loss on Issue of Debentures It is a capital loss and written-off in the year in which debentures are issued. It can be written-off from securities premium account or statement of profit and loss. In case capital profit do not exist or is inadequate, the amount should be written-off against revenue profits of the year. Following entry is passed for writing-off discount/loss on issue of debentures

Securities Premium A/c	Dr
Statement of Profit and Loss	Dr
To Discount/Loss on Issue of Debentures A/c	

Interest on Debentures

Interest on debentures is calculated at a fixed rate on its face value and is usually payable half-yearly. Debenture interest is a charge on profit and not an appropriation of profit. Hence, interest on debentures is payable even if the company suffers a loss.

*According to Income Tax Act, 1961, a company paying interest on debentures is required to deduct income tax at the prescribed rate from the gross amount of debenture interest before any payment is made to debentureholders and it is called Tax Deducted at Source (TDS).

Entries for interest on debentures are as follows

(i) **When interest is due and tax is deducted at source**	Debenture Interest A/c	Dr	[With gross interest]
	To Debentureholders' A/c		[With net interest]
	To TDS/Income Tax Payable A/c		[With income tax deducted]
(ii) **When interest is paid**	Debentureholders' A/c	Dr	[With interest]
	To Bank or Cash A/c		[With the value of liabilities]
(iii) **When TDS is deposited in government account**	TDS Payable A/c	Dr	[With the amount of income tax deducted at source]
	To Bank A/c		
(iv) **On transfer of interest on debentures to statement of profit and loss**	Statement of Profit and Loss	Dr	[With the amount of interest]
	To Debenture Interest A/c		

Note Concept of TDS is not in syllabus. It is given here for knowledge purpose only.

**TDS concept is not in latest syllabus. However, it is given for knowledge purpose only.*

Important Points to be Remembered

- The balance of interest on debentures account is transferred to statement of profit and loss at the end of the year.
- If the amount of interest accrued and due is not paid, it is known as **interest accrued and due** or interest outstanding.
- If the date of payment of interest and accounting date are different, **interest accrued and not due** or accrued interest is to be recorded at accounting date to maintain accounting records on accrual basis.
- Interest accrued (whether due or not) on debentures is shown under the head 'current liabilities' and sub-head 'other-current liabilities'.

Smart Study **Chart No. 3**

Redemption of Debentures

Meaning

Redemption of debentures means repaying or returning the amount of debentures to the debentureholders after the period for which they were issued. It refers to extinguishing or discharging the liability on account of debentures in accordance with the terms of issue.

Sources of Redemption of Debentures

The debentures may be redeemed

- Out of capital
- Out of profits
- By covering them into shares or new debentures
- Redemption from the proceeds of fresh issue of shares and debentures

Methods of Redemption of Debentures

- Redemption of debentures in lumpsum on maturity.
- Redemption of debentures in instalments by draw of lots.
- Redemption of debentures by purchase in open market.
- Redemption of debentures by conversion.

Mind Map

Accounting for Debentures

1 Meaning of Debentures

According to **Section 2(30)** of the Companies Act, 2013, debentures include debenture stock, bonds and any other instrument of a company evidencing a debt, whether constituting a charge on the assets of the company or not.

2 Features of Debentures

- It is a certificate acknowledging debt of a company.
- Mode and period of repayment of principal and interest is fixed.
- It is issued under the common seal of the company.
- It is considered as external equity or long-term borrowings of the company.
- Rate of interest on debentures is fixed.

3 Disclosure of Debentures in Balance Sheet

1. **When Non-current Liability** Debentures are shown under the head 'non-current liabilites' and sub-head 'long-term borrowings', when they are due for redemption after 12 months from the date of issue or after the period of operating cycle.
2. **When Current Liability**
   Debentures are shown under the head 'current liabilities' and sub-head 'short-term borrowings', when they are due for redemption within 12 months from the date of balance sheet or within the period of operating cycle.

4 Issue of Debentures

- Debentures may be issued for cash, for consideration other than cash or as a collateral security.
- Debentures whether issued for cash or otherwise, maybe issued at par, at premium or at discount.

5 Accounting Treatment of Debentures

- Debentures may be issued for an amount payable in lumpsum.
- Debentures may be issued for an amount payable in installments.
- When issue is oversubscribed, following alternatives are available
  - Excess application may be rejected
  - Company may allot partially, i.e. pro-rata basis
  - Company may allot partially and reject remaining applications

6 Issue of Debentures for Other than Cash

- When debentures are issued to vendors against purchase of asset or against purchase of business, it is known as issue of debentures for consideration other than cash.
- Goodwill account will be debited, in case the value of net assets is less than purchase consideration.
- Capital reserve account will be credited, in case the value of net assets is more than the purchase consideration.

7 Issue of Debentures as Collateral Security

- The company may issue debentures to the lender as collateral security or an additional security, if lender insist on some more security. Such an issue of debentures is known as debentures issued as collateral security.
- It can be dealt in two ways
  - Without passing journal entry
  - With journal entry

8 Cases from the Point of View of Redemption

- When debentures are issued at par and redeemable at par.
- When debentures are issued at par and redeemable at premium.
- When debentures are issued at a discount and redeemable at par.
- When debentures are issued at a discount and redeemable at premium.
- When debentures are issued at premium and redeemable at par.
- When debentures are issued at a premium and redeemable at premium.

9 Accounting Treatment of Discount on Debentures

- Discount on issue of debentures is a capital loss and is debited to a separate account named as "discount on issue of debentures account".
- It is written-off in the year in which debentures are issued. It can be written-off from security premium account or statement of profit and loss.

10 Interest on Debentures

- It is calculated at a fixed rate on its face value and is usually payable half-yearly.
- It is a charge on profit and payable even if the company suffers a loss.

Topicwise Solved Questions

Disclosure of Debentures in Balance Sheet

Solved Question 1 **Shining India Ltd. issued 5,000, 8% debentures of ₹ 100 each outstanding in the books of accounts as on 31st March, 2024 to be redeemable after 5 years. Show how you will disclose debentures in the balance sheet of the company?**

Sol.

Balance Sheet

as at 31st March, 2024 (Relevant part only)

Particulars	Note No.	Amt (₹)
I. **EQUITY AND LIABILITIES**		
1. **Non-current Liabilities**		
Long-term Borrowings	1	5,00,000
		5,00,000

Notes to Accounts

Particulars	Amt (₹)
1. **Long-term Borrowings**	
5,000, 8% Debentures of ₹ 100 each	5,00,000

Issue of Debentures for Cash

Solved Question 2 ***(Issue of debentures at par)*** **A company issued 8,000, 10% debentures of ₹ 100 each, payable ₹ 20 on application and the remaining amount on allotment. The debentures are redeemable after 5 years. All the debentures were applied for and allotted. All money was received. Give the journal entries.**

Sol.

JOURNAL

Date	Particulars	LF	Amt (Dr)	Amt (Cr)
	Bank A/c (8,000 × 20) Dr		1,60,000	
	To Debenture Application A/c			1,60,000
	(Being 8,000 applications received for debentures of ₹ 100 each accompanied by the application money of ₹ 20 per debenture)			
	Debenture Application A/c Dr		1,60,000	
	To 10% Debentures A/c			1,60,000
	(Being the allotment of 8,000 debentures, application money transferred to debentures account)			
	Debenture Allotment A/c (8,000 × 80) Dr		6,40,000	
	To 10% Debentures A/c			6,40,000
	(Being the amount due on 8,000 debentures on allotment @ ₹ 80 per debenture)			
	Bank A/c Dr		6,40,000	
	To Debenture Allotment A/c			6,40,000
	(Being the amount received against allotment)			

The above entries are passed when the amount received on debentures is on the basis of instalments. If debentures are issued at par for cash which is receivable in a single instalment i.e. in lumpsum, following entries are passed

JOURNAL

Date	Particulars	LF	Amt (Dr)	Amt (Cr)
	Bank A/c Dr		8,00,000	
	To Debenture Application and Allotment A/c			8,00,000
	(Being the application money received)			
	Debenture Application and Allotment A/c Dr		8,00,000	
	To 10% Debentures A/c			8,00,000
	(Being the debenture application money transferred to debentures account)			

Solved Question 3 Ridyum Limited issued 5,000, 9% debentures of ₹ 500 each at a premium of 10%. The amount was payable as follows

On application — ₹ 200 per debenture
On allotment — Balance (including premium)

The debentures were fully subscribed and all amounts were duly received.

Pass the necessary journal entries for issue of debentures in the books of Ridyum Limited. **CBSE 2025**

Sol.

JOURNAL

Date	Particulars		LF	Amt (Dr)	Amt (Cr)
	Bank A/c	Dr		10,00,000	
	To Debenture Application A/c				10,00,000
	(Being application money received)				
	Debenture Application A/c	Dr		10,00,000	
	To 9% Debentures				10,00,000
	(Being application money transferred to 9% debentures)				
	Debenture Allotment A/c	Dr		17,50,000	
	To 9% Debentures A/c				15,00,000
	To Securities Premium A/c				2,50,000
	(Being amount due on allotment)				
	Bank A/c	Dr		17,50,000	
	To Debenture Allotment A/c				17,50,000
	(Being amount received on allotment)				

Solved Question 4 Surya Ltd. issued 2,500, 15% debentures of ₹ 100 each at a discount of 10% payable as follows ₹ 25 on application, ₹ 25 on allotment and the balance on first call. All the shares were applied and the allotment was made. All the money were duly received. Pass necessary journal entries.

Sol.

JOURNAL

Date	Particulars		LF	Amt (Dr)	Amt (Cr)
	Bank A/c	Dr		62,500	
	To Debenture Application A/c				62,500
	(Being application money received)				
	Debenture Application A/c	Dr		62,500	
	To 15% Debentures A/c				62,500
	(Being application money due)				
	Debenture Allotment A/c	Dr		62,500	
	Discount on Issue of Debentures A/c	Dr		25,000	
	To 15% Debentures A/c				87,500
	(Being allotment money due)				
	Bank A/c	Dr		62,500	
	To Debenture Allotment A/c				62,500
	(Being allotment money received)				
	Debenture First Call	Dr		1,00,000	
	To 15% Debentures A/c				1,00,000
	(Being first call money due)				
	Bank A/c	Dr		1,00,000	
	To Debenture First Call A/c				1,00,000
	(Being first call money received)				

Oversubscription and Undersubscription of Debentures

Solved Question 5 **Garvit Ltd. invited applications for issuing 3,000, 11% debentures of ₹ 100 each at a discount of 6%. The full amount was payable on application. Applications were received for 3,600 debentures. Applications for 600 debentures were rejected and the application money was refunded. Debentures were allotted to the remaining applicants. Pass the necessary journal entries for the above transactions in the books of Garvit Ltd.** CBSE 2019

Sol. JOURNAL

Date	Particulars		LF	Amt (Dr)	Amt (Cr)
	Bank A/c (3,600 × 94)	Dr		3,38,400	
	To Debenture Application and Allotment A/c				3,38,400
	(Being application money received on 3,600 debentures of ₹ 100 each at 6% discount)				
	Debenture Application and Allotment A/c	Dr		3,38,400	
	Discount on Issue of Debenture A/c (3,000 × 6)	Dr		18,000	
	To 11% Debenture A/c (3,000 × 100)				3,00,000
	To Bank A/c (600 × 94)				56,400
	(Being application money transferred to debenture account and access money refunded)				

Solved Question 6 **ABC Ltd. issued 5,000, 10% debentures of ₹ 100 each payable as ₹ 40 on application and ₹ 10 on allotment and balance on 2 equal instalments. Applications were received for 6,000 debentures. Applicants for 500 debentures were sent letter of regret and money was returned. Allotment was made proportionately to the remaining applicants. Oversubscription was applied to the amount due on allotment. Remaining amount was duly received. Make journal entries for the above transactions in the books of the company.**

Sol. JOURNAL

Date	Particulars		LF	Amt (Dr)	Amt (Cr)
	Bank A/c	Dr		2,40,000	
	To Debenture Application A/c				2,40,000
	(Being application money received)				
	Debenture Application A/c	Dr		2,40,000	
	To Bank A/c				20,000
	To Debenture Allotment A/c				20,000
	To 15% Debentures A/c				2,00,000
	(Being application money due, excess amount adjusted and refunded)				
	Debenture Allotment A/c	Dr		50,000	
	To 15% Debentures A/c				50,000
	(Being allotment money due)				
	Bank A/c	Dr		30,000	
	To Debenture Allotment A/c				30,000
	(Being allotment money received)				
	Debenture First Call A/c	Dr		1,25,000	
	To 15% Debentures A/c				1,25,000
	(Being first call money due)				
	Bank A/c	Dr		1,25,000	
	To Debenture First Call A/c				1,25,000
	(Being first call money received)				
	Debenture First Call A/c	Dr		1,25,000	
	To 15% Debentures A/c				1,25,000
	(Being first call money due)				
	Bank A/c	Dr		1,25,000	
	To Debenture First Call A/c				1,25,000
	(Being first call money received)				

Solved Question 7 *(Issue of debentures at premium, issue price payable in instalments, oversubscribed, pro-rata allotment)* **XYZ Ltd. issued 5,000, 9% debentures of ₹ 100 each at a premium of 10% payable ₹ 25 on application, ₹ 35 on allotment (including premium) and the balance on first and final call.**

Applications were received for 7,500, debentures. Allotment was made on pro-rata basis excess application money being applied towards amount due on allotment. All sums due were received by the company on due dates.

Journalise the above transactions in the books of XYZ Ltd. and prepare extract of the balance sheet showing securities premium reserve and debentures.

Sol.

In the Books of XYZ Ltd.
JOURNAL

Date	Particulars		LF	Amt (Dr)	Amt (Cr)
	Bank A/c	Dr		1,87,500	
	To 10% Debentures Application A/c				1,87,500
	(Being application money received for 7,500 debentures @ ₹ 25 each)				
	Debentures Application A/c	Dr		1,87,500	
	To 9% Debentures A/c				1,25,000
	To Debentures Allotment A/c				62,500
	(Being application money adjusted)				
	Debentures Allotment A/c	Dr		1,75,000	
	To 9% Debentures A/c				1,25,000
	To Securities Premium A/c				50,000
	(Being allotment money due on 5,000, 9% debentures)				
	Bank A/c	Dr		1,75,000	
	To Debentures Allotment A/c				1,75,000
	(Being balance of allotment money received on 5,000 debentures)				
	Debentures First and Final Call A/c	Dr		2,50,000	
	To 9% Debentures A/c				2,50,000
	(Being first and final call money due on 5,000, 9% debentures)				
	Bank A/c	Dr		2,50,000	
	To Debentures First and Final Call A/c				2,50,000
	(Being first and final call money received)				

In the Books of XYZ Ltd.
Balance Sheet
as at...

Particulars	Note No.	Amt (₹)
I. **EQUITY AND LIABILITIES**		
1. **Shareholders' Funds**		
Reserves and Surplus	1	50,000
2. **Non-current Liabilities**		
Long-term Borrowings	2	5,00,000

Notes to Accounts

Particulars	Amt (₹)
1. **Reserves and Surplus**	
Securities Premium Reserve	50,000
2. **Long-term Borrowings***	
10,000; 9% Debentures of ₹ 100 each	5,00,000

Solved Question 8 *(Undersubscription of debentures issued at par, issue price payable in instalments)* **Jerry Ltd. issued 5,000, 9% debentures of ₹ 100 each for subscription, payable ₹ 60 on application and balance on allotment. Subscription was received for 4,500 debentures. Allotment was made and due amount was received.**

Pass the journal entries for issue and allotment of debentures.

Sol. **In the Books of Jerry Ltd.**

JOURNAL

Date	Particulars		LF	Amt (Dr)	Amt (Cr)
	Bank A/c	Dr		2,70,000	
	To Debentures Application A/c				2,70,000
	(Being the application money received for 4,500, 9% debentures)				
	Debentures Application A/c	Dr		2,70,000	
	To 9% Debentures A/c				2,70,000
	(Being 4,500, 9% debentures allotted)				
	Debentures Allotment A/c	Dr		1,80,000	
	To 9% Debentures A/c				1,80,000
	(Being the allotment money due)				
	Bank A/c	Dr		1,80,000	
	To Debentures Allotment A/c				1,80,000
	(Being the allotment money received)				

The above entries are passed when the amount received on debentures is on the basis of instalments. If debentures are issued at par for cash which is receivable in a single instalment i.e. in lumpsum, following entries are passed

JOURNAL

Date	Particulars		LF	Amt (Dr)	Amt (Cr)
	Bank A/c	Dr		4,50,000	
	To Debentures Application and Allotment A/c				4,50,000
	(Being the application money received for 4500, 8% debentures @ ₹ 100 per debenture)				
	Debentures Application and Allotment A/c	Dr		4,50,000	
	To 8% Debentures A/c				4,50,000
	(Being 4,500, 8% debentures of ₹ 100 each allotted)				

Issue of Debentures for Consideration Other than Cash

Solved Question 9 **A company purchased assets of the book value of ₹ 1,98,000 from another firm. It was agreed that the purchase consideration be paid by issuing 11% debentures of ₹ 100 each. Assume debentures have been issued (i) at par (ii) at a discount of 10% (iii) at a premium of 10%.**

Pass the necessary journal entries.

Sol. **JOURNAL**

Date	Particulars		LF	Amt (Dr)	Amt (Cr)
	Assets A/c	Dr		1,98,000	
	To Vendor's A/c				1,98,000
	(Being the assets purchased from vendor for ₹ 1,98,000)				
(i)	**Issue of Debentures at Par**				
	Vendor's A/c	Dr		1,98,000	
	To 11% Debentures A/c (1,980 × 100)				1,98,000
	(Being the allotment of 1,980 (1,98,000 ÷ 100), 11% debentures of ₹ 100 each at par to the vendor)				
(ii)	**Issue of Debentures at a Discount**				
	Vendor's A/c (2,200 × 90)	Dr		1,98,000	
	Discount on Issue of Debentures A/c (2,200 × 10)	Dr		22,000	
	To 11% Debentures A/c (2,200 × 100)				2,20,000
	(Being 2,200 (1,98,000 ÷ 90) debentures of ₹ 100 each issued at a discount of 10% to the vendor)				

Date	Particulars		LF	Amt (Dr)	Amt (Cr)
(iii)	**Issue of Debentures at a Premium**				
	Vendor's A/c (1,800 × 110)	Dr		1,98,000	
	To 11% Debentures A/c (1,800 × 100)				1,80,000
	To Securities Premium A/c (1,800 × 10)				18,000
	(Being 1,800 (1,98,000 ÷ 110) debentures of ₹ 100 each issued at a premium of 10% to the vendor)				

Solved Question 10 Apoorv Ltd. acquired building worth ₹ 15,50,000, Machinery worth ₹ 11,40,000 and furniture worth ₹ 1,10,000 from Dhruv Ltd. and took over its liabilities of ₹ 2,00,000 for a purchase consideration of ₹ 25,00,000. Apoorv Ltd. paid the purchase consideration by issuing 12% debentures of ₹ 100 each at a premium of 25%.

Pass the necessary journal entries in the books of Apoorv Ltd. for the above transactions. **CBSE 2025**

Sol.

JOURNAL

Date	Particulars		LF	Amt (Dr)	Amt (Cr)
	Building A/c	Dr		15,50,000	
	Machinery A/c	Dr		11,40,000	
	Furniture A/c	Dr		1,10,000	
	To Sundry Liabilities				2,00,000
	To Dhruv Ltd.				25,00,000
	To Capital Reserve A/c (Balancing Figure)				1,00,000
	(Being acquisition of assets and liabilities recorded, difference credited capital reserve account)				
	Dhruv Ltd.	Dr		25,00,000	
	To 12% Debentures				20,00,000
	To Securities Premium A/c				5,00,000
	(Being 20,000, 12% debentures issued to Dhruv against purchase consideration)				

Working Note

Number of Debentures $= \frac{25,00,000}{125} = 20,000$

Solved Question 11 Sunrise Ltd. acquired assets of ₹ 3,60,000 and took over creditors of ₹ 1,00,000 from Moonlight Ltd. for an agreed purchase consideration of ₹ 4,80,000. Sunrise Ltd. issued 9% debentures of ₹ 100 each at a discount of 4% in satisfaction of the purchase consideration.

Pass necessary journal entries in the books of Sunrise Ltd. Show your workings clearly. **CBSE 2024**

Sol.

In the Books of Sunrise Ltd.

JOURNAL

Date	Particulars		LF	Amt (Dr)	Amt (Cr)
	Sundry Assets A/c	Dr		3,60,000	
	Goodwill A/c	Dr		2,20,000	
	To Creditors A/c				1,00,000
	To Moonlight Ltd.				4,80,000
	(Being assets acquired and liabilities taken over from Moonlight Ltd.)				
	Moonlight Ltd.	Dr		4,80,000	
	Discount on Issue of Debentures A/c	Dr		20,000	
	To 9% Debentures A/c				5,00,000
	(Being purchase consideration settled by issuing 5,000, 9% debentures at 4% discount)				

Working Note

Number of Debentures = Purchase Consideration/Issue Price = 4,80,000/96 = 5,000

Solved Question 12 Ajanta Ltd. purchased machinery worth ₹ 36,00,000 from Sujata Ltd. Ajanta Ltd. paid half the amount to Sujata Ltd. through a bank draft and the balance by issuing 8% debentures of 100 each at a discount of 10%. Pass the necessary journal entries in the books of Ajanta Ltd. for the above transactions. **CBSE 2025**

Sol.

JOURNAL

Date	Particulars		LF	Amt (Dr)	Amt (Cr)
	Machinery A/c	Dr		36,00,000	
	To Sujata Ltd.				36,00,000
	(Being machinery bought from Sujata Ltd.)				
	Sujata Ltd.	Dr		36,00,000	
	Discount on Issue of Debentures A/c	Dr		2,00,000	
	To Bank A/c				18,00,000
	To 8% Debentures A/c				20,00,000
	(Being 20,000, 8% debentures issued at 10% discount to Sujata Ltd. against purchase consideration of ₹ 18,00,000.				

Working Note

Number of debentures $= \frac{18,00,000}{90} = 20,000$

Solved Question 13 **Buddha Limited took over assets of ₹ 40,00,000 and liabilities of ₹ 6,50,000 of Ginny Limited. Buddha Limited issued 30,000, 8% debentures of ₹ 100 each at 10% discount, to be redeemed at 5% premium along with cheque of ₹ 5,00,000. Pass necessary journal entries in the books of Buddha Ltd.** CBSE SQP 2025

Sol.

JOURNAL

Date	Particulars		LF	Amt (Dr)	Amt (Cr)
	Assets A/c	Dr		40,00,000	
	To Liabilities A/c				6,50,000
	To Ginny Ltd. A/c				32,00,000
	To Capital Reserve A/c				1,50,000
	(Being business taken over and capital reserve recorded)				
	Ginny Ltd. A/c	Dr		32,00,000	
	Loss on Issue of Debentures A/c	Dr		4,50,000	
	To 8% Debentures A/c				30,00,000
	To Premium on Redemption of Debentures				1,50,000
	To Bank A/c				5,00,000
	(Being purchased consideration discharged)				

Solved Question 14 **Sheetal Ltd. purchased building worth ₹ 2,50,000, plant and machinery worth ₹ 2,00,000, furniture worth ₹ 40,000 and took over liabilities of ₹ 30,000 from Poonam Ltd. for a purchase consideration of ₹ 4,40,000. The purchase consideration was paid by issuing 12% debetures of ₹ 100 each at a premium of 10%.**
Pass the necessary journal entries in books of Sheetal Ltd. to record the above transactions. CBSE 2024 C

Sol.

In the Books of Sheetal Ltd.

JOURNAL

Date	Particulars		LF	Amt (Dr)	Amt (Cr)
	Building A/c	Dr		2,50,000	
	Plant and Machinery A/c	Dr		2,00,000	
	Furniture A/c	Dr		40,000	
	To Sundry Liabilities A/c				30,000
	To Poonam Ltd.				4,40,000
	To Capital Reserve A/c				20,000
	(Being assets and liabilities taken over)				
	Poonam Ltd.	Dr		4,40,000	
	To 12% Debentures A/c				4,00,000
	To Securities Premium A/c				40,000
	(Being 4,000 12% debentures issued at premium for consideration other than cash)				

Working Note

Number of Debentures $= \frac{\text{Purchase Consideration}}{\text{Issue Price}} = \frac{4,40,000}{110} = 4,000$ debentures

Issue of Debentures as Collateral Security

Solved Question 15 **Arihant Ltd. secured a loan of ₹ 1,60,000 from Punjab National Bank issuing 2,000, 9% debentures of ₹ 100 each as collateral security. How will you show issue of debentures in the balance sheet**

(i) Without passing journal entry? **(ii) When journal entry is passed?**

Sol. (i) **First Method** (When journal entry is not passed)

Balance Sheet (An Extract)
as at...

Particulars	Note No.	Amt (₹)
I. **EQUITY AND LIABILITIES**		
1. **Non-current Liabilities**		
Long-term Borrowings	1	1,60,000
		1,60,000

Notes to Accounts

Particulars	Amt (₹)
1. **Long-term Borrowings**	
Punjab National Bank (Secured by issue of 2,000, 9% debentures of ₹ 100 each as collateral security)	1,60,000

(ii) **Second Method** (When journal entry is passed)

JOURNAL

Date	Particulars		LF	Amt (Dr)	Amt (Cr)
	Debenture Suspense A/c	Dr		2,00,000	
	To 9% Debentures A/c				2,00,000
	(Being the issue of 2,000, 9% debentures of ₹ 100 each as collateral security for a loan from a bank as per board's resolution)				

Balance Sheet (An Extract)
as at...

Particulars	Note No.	Amt (₹)
I. **EQUITY AND LIABILITIES**		
1. **Non-current Liabilities**		
Long-term Borrowings	1	1,60,000
		1,60,000

Notes to Accounts

Particulars		Amt (₹)
1. **Long-term Borrowings**		
Loan from Punjab National Bank		1,60,000
2,000, 9% Debentures of Par Value of ₹ 100 each Issued as Collateral Security	2,00,000	
(−) Debenture Suspense	(2,00,000)	—
		1,60,000

Solved Question 16 **Zenith Ltd. issued 3,000, 8% debentures at a face value of ₹ 100 each, payable in cash. Additionally the company secured a loan of ₹ 1,30,000 from Global Bank, offering ₹ 1,50,000 worth of 9% debentures as collateral security. As per the agreement, the bank must release the debentures immediately upon repayment of the loan. How will the debentures be shown in the company's balance sheet, assuming the debentures issued as collateral have been recorded in the books?**

Sol.

Balance Sheet
as at...

Particulars	Note No.	Amt (₹)
I. EQUITY AND LIABILITIES		
1. Non-current Liabilities		
Long-term Borrowings	1	4,30,000
		4,30,000

Notes to Accounts

Particulars		Amt (₹)
1. Long-term Borrowings		
Loan from Bank		1,30,000
Debentures		
3,000, 8% Debentures of ₹ 100 each		3,00,000
1,500, 9% Debentures of ₹ 100 each Issued as Collateral Security	1,50,000	
(–) Debenture Suspense	(1,50,000)	—
		4,30,000

Solved Question 17 **CDS Ltd. issued 5,000, 8% debentures of ₹ 100 each at a premium of 10% on 1st April, 2023. It purchased fixed assets of the value of ₹ 1,25,000 and took over current liabilities of ₹ 20,000 and issued 8% debentures at a premium of 5% to the vendor. On the same date it took loan from the bank for ₹ 50,000 and issued 8% debentures as collateral security. Record the relevant journal entries in the books of CDS Ltd. Ignore interest.**

Sol.

JOURNAL

Date	Particulars	LF	Amt (Dr)	Amt (Cr)
2023				
Apr 1	Bank A/c Dr		5,50,000	
	To 8% Debenture Application and Allotment A/c			5,50,000
	(Being the application money received on 5,000 debentures @ ₹ 110 each)			
Apr 1	8% Debenture Application and Allotment A/c Dr		5,50,000	
	To 8% Debenture A/c			5,00,000
	To Securities Premium A/c			50,000
	(Being the transfer of application money to debentures account and securities premium reserve account)			
Apr 1	Fixed Assets A/c Dr		1,25,000	
	To Current Liabilities A/c			20,000
	To Vendor's A/c			1,05,000
	(Being the purchase of assets and liabilities)			
Apr 1	Vendor's A/c Dr		1,05,000	
	To 8% Debentures A/c			1,00,000
	To Securities Premium A/c			5,000
	(Being the issue of 1,000 debentures of ₹ 100 each at 5% premium calculated as follows $\frac{1,05,000}{105}$ = 1,000 debentures)			
Apr 1	Bank A/c Dr		50,000	
	To Bank Loan A/c			50,000
	(Being the loan taken, secured by the issue of ₹ 50,000 debentures)			
Apr 1	8% Debentures Suspense A/c Dr		50,000	
	To 8% Debentures A/c			50,000
	(Being the issue of debentures as collateral security)			

Various Cases from the Redemption Point of View

Solved Question 18 **Pass necessary journal entries for issue of debentures for the following transactions** **CBSE 2024**

(i) Kajal Ltd. issued 30,000, 11% debentures of ₹ 100 each at a discount of 10%, redeemable at a premium of 5%.

(ii) Ninja Ltd. issued 32,000, 8% debentures of ₹ 100 each at a premium ₹ 20 per debenture, redeemable at a premium of ₹ 10 per debenture.

(iii) Him Ltd. issued 40,000, 13% debentures of ₹ 100 each at par, redeemable at a premium of 10%.

Sol. (i)

In the Books of Kajal Ltd.
JOURNAL

Date	Particulars	LF	Amt (Dr)	Amt (Cr)
	Bank A/c Dr		27,00,000	
	To Debenture Application and Allotment A/c			27,00,000
	(Being receipt of application money on 30,000, 11% debentures of ₹ 100 each at a discount of 10%)			
	Debenture Application and Allotment A/c Dr		27,00,000	
	Loss on Issue of Debentures A/c Dr		4,50,000	
	To 11% Debentures A/c			30,00,000
	To Premium on Redemption of Debentures A/c			1,50,000
	(Being transfer of debenture application money and provision for premium on redemption of debentures made)			

(ii)

In the Books of Ninja Ltd.
JOURNAL

Date	Particulars	LF	Amt (Dr)	Amt (Dr)
	Bank A/c Dr		38,40,000	
	To Debenture Application and Allotment A/c			
	(Being receipt of application money on 32,000, 8% debentures of ₹ 100 each at a premium of ₹ 20 per debenture)			38,40,000
	Debenture Application and Allotment A/c Dr		38,40,000	
	Loss on Issue of Debentures A/c Dr		3,20,000	
	To 8% Debentures A/c			32,00,000
	To Securities Premium A/c			6,40,000
	To Premium on Redemption of Debentures A/c			3,20,000
	(Being transfer of debenture application money and provision for premium on redemption of debentures made)			

(iii)

In the Books of Him Ltd.
JOURNAL

Date	Particulars	LF	Amt (Dr)	Amt (Cr)
	Bank A/c Dr		40,00,000	
	To Debenture Application and Allotment A/c			40,00,000
	(Being receipt of application money on 40,000, 13% debentures of ₹ 100 each)			
	Debenture Application and Allotment A/c Dr		40,00,000	
	Loss on Issue of Debentures A/c Dr		4,00,000	
	To 13% Debentures A/c			40,00,000
	To Premium on Redemption of Debentures A/c			4,00,000
	(Being transfer of debenture application money and provision for premium on redemption of debentures made)			

Solved Question 19 Pass necessary journal entries for the issue of debentures in the following cases

(i) Issued 50,000, 9% debentures of ₹ 100 each at par redeemable at par.
(ii) Issued 10,000, 8% debentures of ₹ 100 each at 7% premium redeemable at par.
(iii) Issued 750, 8% debentures of ₹ 100 each at 10% discount redeemable at par.
(iv) Issued 1,000, 9% debentures of ₹ 100 each at 5% premium redeemable at 8% premium.
(v) Issued 500, 9% debentures of ₹ 100 each at 10% discount redeemable at 10% premium. CBSE Term II 2022

Sol.

JOURNAL

Date	Particulars		LF	Amt (Dr)	Amt (Cr)
(i) (a)	Bank A/c	Dr		50,00,000	
	To Debenture Application and Allotment A/c				50,00,000
	(Being the application money received on 50,000, 9% debenture of ₹ 100 each)				
	Debenture Application and Allotment A/c	Dr		50,00,000	
	To 9% Debentures A/c				50,00,000
	(Being the application money transferred to debentures account)				
(ii)	Bank A/c	Dr		10,70,000	
	To Debenture Application and Allotment A/c				10,70,000
	(Being the application money received)				
	Debenture Application and Allotment A/c	Dr		10,70,000	
	To 8% Debentures A/c				10,00,000
	To Securities Premium A/c				70,000
	(Being the application money transferred to debentures account)				
(iii)	Bank A/c	Dr		67,500	
	To Debenture Application and Allotment A/c				67,500
	(Being the application money received)				
	Debenture Application and Allotment A/c	Dr		67,500	
	Discount on Issue of Debentures A/c	Dr		7,500	
	To 8% Debentures A/c				75,000
	(Being the application money transferred to debentures account)				
(iv)	Bank A/c	Dr		1,05,000	
	To Debenture Application and Allotment A/c				1,05,000
	(Being the application money received)				
	Debenture Application and Allotment A/c	Dr		1,05,000	
	Loss on Issue of Debentures A/c	Dr		8,000	
	To 8% Debentures A/c				1,00,000
	To Securities Premium A/c				5,000
	To Premium on Redemption of Debentures A/c				8,000
	(Being the application money transferred to debentures account)				
(v)	Bank A/c	Dr		45,000	
	To Debenture Application and Allotment A/c				45,000
	(Being the application money received)				
	Debenture Application and Allotment A/c	Dr		45,000	
	Loss on Issue of Debentures A/c	Dr		10,000	
	To 8% Debentures A/c				50,000
	To Premium on Redemption of Debentures A/c				5,000
	(Being the application money transferred to debentures account)				

Solved Question 20 Pass journal entries relating to issue of debentures in the books of Novex Ltd. in each of following cases

(i) Issued 30,000, 10% debentures of ₹ 100 each at a premium of 10%, redeemable at par.
(ii) Issued 4,000, 10% debentures of ₹ 100 each at a premium of 15%, redeemable at a premium of 10%.
(iii) Issued 5,000, 10% debentures of ₹ 100 each at a discount of 5%, redeemable at a premium of 10%.

Sol.

In the Books of Novex Ltd.

JOURNAL

Date	Particulars	LF	Amt (Dr)	Amt (Cr)
(i)	Bank A/c Dr		33,00,000	
	To Debenture Application and Allotment A/c			33,00,000
	(Being debenture application money received)			
	Debenture Application and Allotment A/c Dr		33,00,000	
	To 10% Debentures A/c			30,00,000
	To Securities Premium A/c			3,00,000
	(Being debenture application money transferred to debentures and securities premium account)			
(ii)	Bank A/c Dr		4,60,000	
	To Debenture Application and Allotment A/c			4,60,000
	(Being debenture application money received)			
	Debenture Application and Allotment A/c Dr		4,60,000	
	Loss on Issue of Debentures A/c Dr		40,000	
	To 10% Debentures A/c			4,00,000
	To Securities Premium A/c			60,000
	To Premium on Redemption of Debentures A/c			40,000
	(Being debenture application money transferred to debentures and securities premium account and provision for premium on redemption of debentures made)			
(iii)	Bank A/c Dr		4,75,000	
	To Debenture Application and Allotment A/c			4,75,000
	(Being debenture a application money received)			
	Debenture Application and Allotment A/c Dr		4,75,000	
	Loss on Issue of Debentures A/c Dr		75,000	
	To 10% Debentures A/c			5,00,000
	To Premium on Redemption of Debentures A/c			50,000
	(Being debenture application money transferred to debentures and provision for premium on redemption of debentures made)			

Solved Question 21 **Pass the necessary journal entries for 'issue of debentures' for the following**

(i) Arman Ltd., issued 750, 12% debentures of ₹ 100 each at a discount of 10% redeemable at a premium of 5%.

(ii) Sohan Ltd. issued 800, 9% debentures of ₹ 100 each at a premium of ₹ 20 per debenture redeemable at a premium of ₹ 10 per debenture.

X Ltd. obtained a loan of ₹ 4,00,000 from IDBI Bank. The company issued 5,000, 9% debentures of ₹ 100 each as a collateral security for the same. Show how these items will be presented in the balance sheet of the company? **CBSE SQP 2025**

Sol.

JOURNAL

Date	Particulars	LF	Amt (Dr)	Amt (Cr)
(i) (a)	Bank A/c Dr		67,500	
	To Debenture Application and Allotment A/c			67,500
	(Being application received)			
(b)	Debenture Application and Allotment A/c Dr		67,500	
	Loss on Issue of Debentures A/c Dr		11,250	
	To 12% Debentures A/c			75,000
	To Premium Redemption of Debentures A/c			3,750
	(Being debentures issued at discount redeemable at premium)			
(ii)	Bank A/c Dr		96,000	
	To Debenture Application and Allotment A/c			96,000
	(Being application received)			

Date	Particulars		LF	Amt (Dr)	Amt (Cr)
	Debenture Application and Allotment A/c	Dr		96,000	
	Loss on Issue of Debentures A/c	Dr		8,000	
	To 12% Debentures A/c				8,000
	To Securities Premium A/c				16,000
	To Premium on Redemption A/c				80,000
	(Being debentures issued at discount redeemable at premium)				

Balance Sheet Sunrise of Ltd. (An Extract)

Particulars	Note No.	Amt (₹)
I. **EQUITY AND LIABILITIES**		
1. **Non-current Liabilities**		
Long-term Borrowings	1	4,00,000

Notes to Accounts

Particulars	Amt (₹)
1. **Long-term Borrowings**	
Loan from IDBI (Secured by issue of 5,000, 9% debentures of ₹ 100 each as collateral security)	4,00,000

Writing-off Loss on Issue of Debentures

Solved Question 22 **Rohit Ltd. has issued 25,000, 8% debentures of ₹ 100 each at a discount of 9% on 1st April, 2023. The company has balance of ₹ 2,50,000 in securities premium reserve. Pass necessary journal entries for issue of debentures and to write-off discount/loss on issue of debentures. The debentures are redeemable after 5 years at a premium of 7%.**

Sol. **JOURNAL**

Date	Particulars		LF	Amt (Dr)	Amt (Cr)
	Bank A/c	Dr		22,75,000	
	To Debenture Application and Allotment A/c				22,75,000
	(Being application money received)				
	Debenture Application and Allotment A/c	Dr		22,75,000	
	Loss on Issue of Debentures A/c	Dr		4,00,000	
	To 8% Debentures A/c				25,00,000
	To Premium on Redemption				1,75,000
	(Being debenture issued at discount)				
	Statement of Profit and Loss A/c	Dr		1,50,000	
	Securities Premium A/c	Dr		2,50,000	
	To Loss on Issue of Debenture A/c				4,00,000
	(Being loss on issue of debentures transferred to statement of profit and loss)				

Solved Question 23 **On 1st April, 2024, Light Ltd. issued, 4,00,000, 6% debentures of ₹ 100 each at a discount of 5%,**
The amount per debenture was payable as follows
On application ₹ 80 per debenture, on allotment Balance
The debentures were fully subscribed and all money was duly received.
Pass necessary journal entries for issues of debentures. Show how the amounts will appear in balance sheet. **CBSE 2020 (M)**

Sol. **JOURNAL**

Date	Particulars		LF	Amt (Dr)	Amt (Cr)
2019 Apr 1	Bank A/c (4,00,000 × 80)	Dr		3,20,00,000	
	To Debenture Application A/c				3,20,00,000
	(Being the application money on 4,00,000 debentures @ ₹ 80 received)				

Date	Particulars		LF	Amt (Dr)	Amt (Cr)
	Debenture Application A/c	Dr		3,20,00,000	
	To 9% Debentures A/c				3,20,00,000
	(Being the debenture application money transferred to debentures account)				
	Debenture Allotment A/c (4,00,000 × 15)	Dr		60,00,000	
	Discount on Issue of Debentures A/c (4,00,000 × 5)	Dr		20,00,000	
	To 9% Debentures A/c (4,00,000 × 20)				80,00,000
	(Being the allotment money due on 4,000 debentures)				
	Bank A/c	Dr		60,00,000	
	To Debenture Allotment A/c				60,00,000
	(Being the amount received on allotment)				

Note The amount demanded on allotment is presumed as net of discount.

Balance Sheet
as at ...

Particulars	Note No.	Amt (₹)
I. EQUITY AND LIABILITIES		
1. Non-current Liabilities		
Long-term Borrowings	1	4,00,00,000
Total		4,00,00,000
II. ASSETS		
1. Current Assets		
Cash and Cash Equivalents	2	4,00,00,000
Total		4,00,00,000

Notes to Accounts

Particulars	Amt (₹)
1. Long-term Borrowings	
4,00,000, 9% Debentures of ₹ 100 each	4,00,00,000
2. Cash and Cash Equivalents	
Cash at Bank	4,00,00,000

Interest on Debentures

Solved Question 24 **Tata Ltd. issued 5,000, 10% debentures of ₹ 100 each on 1st April, 2020. The issue was fully subscribed. According to the terms of issue, interest on debentures is payable half-yearly on 30th September and 31st March. Pass the necessary entries related to the debenture interest for the half-yearly ending on 31st March, 2021 and transfer of interest on debentures to statement of profit and loss.**

Sol. **JOURNAL**

Date	Particulars		LF	Amt (Dr)	Amt (Cr)
2020					
Sep 30	Debenture Interest A/c $\left(5,00,000 \times \frac{10}{100} \times \frac{6}{12}\right)$	Dr		25,000	
	To Debentureholders' A/c				25,000
	(Being amount of interest due for 6 months)				
	Debentureholders' A/c	Dr		25,000	
	To Bank A/c				25,000
	(Being interest paid to debentureholders)				
2021					
Mar 31	Debenture Interest A/c $\left(5,00,000 \times \frac{10}{100} \times \frac{6}{12}\right)$	Dr		25,000	
	To Debentureholders' A/c				25,000
	(Being amount of interest due for 6 months)				

Date	Particulars		LF	Amt (Dr)	Amt (Cr)
	Debentureholders' A/c	Dr		25,000	
	To Bank A/c				25,000
	(Being interest paid to debentureholders)				
	Statement of Profit and Loss	Dr		50,000	
	To Debenture Interest A/c				50,000
	(Being interest on debentures account transferred to statement of profit and loss)				

Solved Question 25 **On 1st April, 2023, MS Ltd. issued 8,000, 9% debentures of ₹ 1,000 each at a discount of 6%, payable as ₹ 400 an application and balance on allotment. These debentures were to be redeemed at a premium of 5% after 3 years. The company closes its book on 31st March every year. Interest on 9% debentures is payable on 30th September and 31st March every year.**

Pass necessary journal entries for the issue of 9% debentures and debenture interest for the year ended 31st March, 2024.

Sol.

JOURNAL

Date	Particulars		LF	Amt (Dr)	Amt (Cr)
2020					
Apr 1	Bank A/c (8,000 × 400)	Dr		32,00,000	
	To Debenture Application A/c				32,00,000
	(Being debenture application money received)				
	Debenture Application A/c	Dr		32,00,000	
	To 90% Debentures A/c				32,00,000
	(Being 8,000, 9% debentures allotted)				
	Debenture Allotment A/c	Dr		43,20,000	
	Loss on Issue of Debentures A/c [(8,000 × 60) + 4,00,000]	Dr		8,80,000	
	To 9% Debentures A/c (8,000 × 600)				48,00,000
	To Premium on Redemption of Debentures A/c (8,000 × 50)				4,00,000
	(Being debenture application money transferred to debentures account)				
	Bank A/c	Dr		43,20,000	
	To Debenture Allotment A/c				43,20,000
	(Being allotment money received)				
Sep 30	Debenture Interest A/c	Dr		3,60,000	
	To Debentureholders' A/c				3,60,000
	(Being amount of interest due)				
	Debentureholders' A/c	Dr		3,60,000	
	To Bank A/c				3,60,000
	(Being interest paid to debentureholders deposited with government)				
2021 Mar 31	Debenture Interest A/c	Dr		3,60,000	
	To Debentureholders' A/c				3,60,000
	(Being amount of interest due)				
	Debentureholders' A/c	Dr		3,60,000	
	To Bank A/c				3,60,000
	(Being interest paid to debentureholders' deposited with government)				
	Statement of Profit and Loss	Dr		7,20,000	
	To Debenture Interest A/c (3,60,000 + 3,60,000)				7,20,000
	(Being annual debenture interest transferred to statement of profit and loss)				

Working Note

Loss on Issue of Debentures

Discount on Issue = 8,000 × 60 = 4,80,000

(+) Premium on Redemption = 8,000 × 50 = 4,00,000

= ₹ 8,80,000

Debenture Interest for Six Months = $80,00,000 \times \frac{9}{100} \times \frac{6}{12}$ = ₹ 3,60,000

Missing Information

Solved Question 26 Vashya Ltd. issued 30,000, 10% debentures of ₹ 100 each as collateral security for a loan of ₹ 25,00,000 taken from Bank of India. Fill in the blanks for the journal entry for issue of debentures as a collateral security.

CBSE 2020

In the Books of Vashya Ltd.
JOURNAL

Date	Particulars		LF	Amt (Dr)	Amt (Cr)
	...... A/c	Dr		...	
	To ...... A/c				...
	(Being ₹ 30,00,000, 10% debentures issued as collateral security for a loan of ₹ 25,00,000)				

Sol.

In the Books of Vashya Ltd.
JOURNAL

Date	Particulars		LF	Amt (Dr)	Amt (Cr)
	Debenture Suspense A/c	Dr		**30,00,000**	
	To **10% Debentures** A/c				**30,00,000**
	(Being ₹ 30,00,000, 10% debentures issued as a collateral security for a loan of ₹ 25,00,000)				

Solved Question 27 Fill in the blanks in the following case

JOURNAL

Date	Particulars		LF	Amt (Dr)	Amt (Cr)
	....	Dr		...	
	To				...
	(Being application money received on 2,000, 12% debentures of ₹ 100 each issued at a premium of 10% and redeemable at a premium of 10%)				
	....	Dr		...	
	....	Dr		...	
	To				...
	To				...
	To				...
	(...................................)				

Sol.

JOURNAL

Date	Particulars		LF	Amt (Dr)	Amt (Cr)
	Bank A/c (2,000 × 110)	Dr		**2,20,000**	
	To **Debenture Application and Allotment A/c**				**2,20,000**
	(Being application money received on 2,000, 12% debentures of ₹ 100 each issued at a premium of 10% and redeemable at a premium of 10%)				
	Debenture Application and Allotment A/c	Dr		**2,20,000**	
	Loss on Issue of Debentures A/c (2,000 × 10)	Dr		**20,000**	
	To **12% Debentures A/c** (2,000 × 100)				**2,00,000**
	To **Securities Premium A/c** (2,000 × 10)				**20,000**
	To **Premium on Redemption of Debentures A/c** (2,000 × 10)				**20,000**
	(Being amount received on issue of 12% debentures adjusted)				

Numerical Questions

Disclosure of Debentures in Balance Sheet

1. Brilliant Horizons Ltd. issued 6,000, 9% debentures of ₹ 120 each, recorded in the company's books as of 31st March, 2024, with a redemption period of 5 years.

Present how these debentures would be disclosed in the company's balance sheet?

Issue of Debentures for Cash

2. Galaxy Ltd. issued 3,000, 12% debentures of ₹ 100 each, with payment terms as follows
₹ 30 on application, ₹ 40 on allotment and the remaining balance on the first call. The issue was fully subscribed, allotments were made and all payments were received on time.

Record the necessary journal entries.

3. (i) PQR Ltd. issued 2,000, 9% debentures of ₹ 100 each payable as follows
₹ 25 on application, ₹ 25 on allotment and ₹ 50 on first and final call.

Applications were received for all the debentures along with the application money and allotment was made. The call money was also received on the due date.

Pass necessary journal entries in the books of the company.

(ii) MET Ltd. issued 10,000, 9% debentures of ₹ 100 each as per payable on application by 1st April, 2024. Debentures were allotment on 5th April, 2024.
Pass necessary journal entries in the books of company.

4. (i) XYZ Ltd. issued 5,000, 10% debentures of ₹ 100 each, at a premium of ₹ 10 per debenture payable as follows

On application	₹ 25
On allotment	₹ 45 (including premium)
On first and final call	₹ 45

The debentures were fully subscribed and all money was duly received. Record the necessary entries in the books of the company.
Show how the amounts will appear in the balance sheet?

(ii) ABC Ltd. issued 5,000, 10% debentures of ₹ 100 each at a premium of 10%, payable along with application. Application were received for all the debentures issued allotment was made.
Pass the journal entries. Competency Based Que

5. Stellar Ltd. issued 15,000, 6% debentures of ₹ 60 each at a discount of ₹ 10, payable as ₹ 25 on application, ₹ 20 on allotment and the remaining balance on the final call. The entire issue was fully subscribed and all payments were received promptly.

Prepare the necessary journal entries.

Oversubscription and Undersubscription of Debentures

6. Rashmi Ltd. issued 2,000, 6% debentures of ₹ 100 each. The whole amount was payable at the time of application. Applications were received for 2,500 debentures. Company issued debentures to all the applicants on pro-rata basis.

Give journal entries.

7. XYZ Ltd. issued 4,000, 12% debentures of ₹ 100 each, payable as ₹ 50 on application, ₹ 20 on allotment and the remaining balance in two equal instalments. Applications were received for 5,000 debentures. Applications for 400 debentures were rejected and the money was refunded. Allotment was made on a pro-rata basis to the remaining applicants. The excess application money was adjusted towards the allotment. All subsequent payments were received on time.

Record the journal entries for these transactions in the company's books. Competency Based Que

8. Brightstar Ltd. issued 8,000, 10% debentures of ₹ 100 each, with payment terms as ₹ 30 on application, ₹ 50 on allotment and the balance in two equal calls. Applications were received for 9,000 debentures. The company rejected applications for 800 debentures and returned the money.

The remaining applicants were allotted debentures proportionately, with the excess application money applied to the allotment. All due amounts were received in full.

Prepare journal entries for the above transactions.

9. MJC Ltd. issued 2,000, 9% debentures of ₹ 100 each on the following terms.

₹ 20 on application, ₹ 20 on allotment, ₹ 30 on first call, ₹ 30 on final call.

The public applied for 2,400 debentures. Applications for 1,800 debentures were accepted in full. Applications for 400 debentures were allotted 200 debentures and applications for 200 debentures were rejected.

Pass necessary journal entries. **Competency Based Que**

10. Dhatu Ltd. invited applications for issuing 4,000, 11% debentures of ₹ 100 each at a premium of ₹ 50 per debenture. Full amount was payable on application. Applications were received for 5,000 debentures. Applications for 1,000 debentures were rejected and application money was refunded. Debentures were allotted to the remaining applicants.

Pass necessary journal entries for the above transactions in the books of Dhatu Ltd.

Issue of Debentures for Consideration other than Cash

11. ABC Ltd. purchased assets of the book value of ₹ 8,00,000 and took over the liabilities of ₹ 1,00,000 from XYZ Ltd. It was agreed that the purchase consideration, settled at ₹ 7,60,000, be paid by issuing debentures of ₹ 100 each.

What journal entries will be made in the following three cases if debentures are issued (i) at par (ii) at a discount of 10% and (iii) at a premium of 10%? It was agreed that any fraction of debentures be paid in cash.

Competency Based Que

Ans. Goodwill = ₹ 60,000 (i) 7,600 debentures of ₹ 100 each (ii) 8,444 debentures of ₹ 100 each and paid cash ₹ 40 (iii) 6,909 debentures of ₹ 100 each and paid cash ₹ 10

12. XYZ Ltd. purchased furniture from ABC Ltd. as follows

(i) By issuing 250, equity shares of ₹ 10 each at a premium of 10%.

(ii) By issuing 50, 10% debentures of ₹ 100 each at a discount of 10%.

(iii) Balance in cash ₹ 12,500.

Pass necessary journal entries.

13. Radiant Ltd., issued 40,000, 12% debentures of ₹ 100 each at a premium of 20%. Additionally, the company acquired machinery worth ₹ 16,00,000 from ABC Machinery Traders. Half of the amount was settled by accepting a bill of exchange and the remaining was paid by issuing 12% debentures of ₹ 100 each at a premium of 25% in favour of ABC Machinery Traders.

Record the necessary journal entries in the books of Radiant Ltd. for the above transactions and provide detailed working notes. **Competency Based Que**

Ans. Number of Debentures = 6,400

14. Priti Ltd. purchased assets worth ₹ 5,40,000 and took over liabilities of ₹ 1,20,000 of Payal Ltd. for a purchase consideration of ₹ 5,28,000.

Priti Ltd. paid half the amount by cheque and the balance was settled by issuing 10% debentures of ₹ 100 each at a premium of 10%?

Pass necessary journal entries for the above transactions in the books of Priti Ltd. **CBSE 2024**

Ans. Goodwill = 1,08,000; Number of Debentures = 2,400

15. Sumi Ltd. acquired assets of ₹ 8,00,000 and took over sundry creditors of ₹ 2,00,000 from Pandora Ltd. for a purchase consideration of ₹ 9,00,000, The payment was made by issuing a cheque of ₹ 4,60,000 and remaining by issue of 9% debentures of ₹ 100 each at a premium of 10%.

Pass necessary journal entries for the above transactions in the books of Sumi Ltd.

Competency Based Que

Ans. Goodwill = 3,00,000

Number of Debentures = 40,000

16. Gundola Ltd. took over assets of ₹ 9,00,000 and liabilities of ₹ 3,00,000 from AK Ltd. for an agreed purchase consideration of ₹ 14,00,000.

The payment was made through a bank draft of ₹ 5,00,000 and the remaining by issue of 8% debentures at a discount of 10%.

Record necessary journal entries in the books of Gundola Ltd. for the above transactions.

CBSE 2024; Competency Based Que

Ans. Goodwill ₹ 8,00,000; Number of Debentures = 10,000

17. On 1st April, 2023, Simple Ltd. took over assets of ₹ 5,00,000 and liabilities of ₹ 1,00,000 from Temur Ltd. at an agreed value of ₹ 16,00,000.

Simple Ltd. paid the amount to Temur Ltd. as follows

(i) Issued a bank draft of ₹ 1,00,000.

(ii) Issued 8% debentures of ₹ 100 each at a premium of 50% in satisfaction of the balance amount of purchase consideration.

Pass the necessary journal entries in the books of Simple Ltd. to record the above transaction.

CBSE 2024 C; Competency Based Que

Ans. Goodwill = ₹ 12,00,000

Number of Debentures = 10,000

18. ABC Ltd. issued 500, 10% debentures of ₹ 1,000 each credited as fully paid-up to the promoters for their services to incorporate the company. It also issued 100, 10% debentures of ₹ 1,000 each credited as fully paid-up to the underwriters towards their commission.

Pass the journal entries.

Issue of Debentures as Collateral Securities

19. Black Spot Ltd. took a loan of ₹ 10,00,000 from a bank giving ₹ 12,000, 9% debentures of ₹ 100 each as collateral security.

How will you show issue of debentures in the balance sheet of the company

(i) Without passing journal entry?

(ii) When journal entry is passed?

20. A company had ₹ 10,00,000, 12% debentures outstanding as on 1st April, 2023. During the year, company took a loan of ₹ 2,00,000 from XYZ Bank for which the company placed with the bank, debentures for ₹ 2,50,000 as collateral security.

Pass journal entries, if any. Also show how the debentures and bank loan will appear in the companies balance sheet as at 31st March, 2024? **Competency Based Que**

21. Omega Ltd. issued 3,500 debentures bearing 8% interest at a nominal value of ₹ 100 each, fully payable in cash. Additionally, the company obtained a loan of ₹ 1,20,000 from Horizon Bank, pledging debentures worth ₹ 1,40,000 as collateral security.

According to the terms of the agreement, the pledged debentures will be released by the bank immediately after the repayment of the loan.

How will these debentures appear in the company's balance sheet, assuming the collateral arrangement has been recorded in the books?

22. Alpha Ltd., issued 6,000, 9% debentures of ₹ 100 each at a premium of 15% on 1st April, 2023. The company acquired fixed assets worth ₹ 1,50,000 and assumed current liabilities of ₹ 30,000, settling the balance by issuing 9% debentures at a premium of 10% to the vendor.

On the same date, the company secured a loan of ₹ 60,000 from a bank, providing 9% debentures as collateral security.

Pass the necessary journal entries in the books of Alpha Ltd. and prepare the relevant extract of the balance sheet as at 31st March, 2024, ignore interest calculations. **Competency Based Que**

Various Cases from the Redemption Point of View

23. Give journal entries for the issue of debentures in the following conditions.

(i) Issued 2,000, 9% debentures of 100 each at par, redeemable also at par.

(ii) Issued 2,000, 9% debentures of 100 each at a discount of 2%, redeemable at par.

(iii) Issued 2,000, 9% debentures of 100 each at a premium of 5%, redeemable at par.

(iv) Issued 2,000, 9% debentures of 100 each at par but redeemable at 5% premium.

(v) Issued 2,000, 9% debentures of 100 each at a discount of 2%, redeemable at a premium of 5%.

(vi) Issued 2,000, 9% debentures of 100 each at a premium of 5%, redeemable at a premium of 10%.

24. On 1st April, 2024, ABC Ltd. issued 10,000, 9% debentures of ₹ 100 each at a discount of 10%, redeemable at par after 5 years.

The issue price is payable along with application. The debentures were subscribed. It has a balance of ₹ 1,75,000 in securities premium reserve.

Pass journal entries for issue of debentures and writing-off the discount and prepare discount on issue of debentures account.

25. On 1st January, 2024, CDM Ltd. issued 6,000, 8% debentures of ₹ 100 each at par, redeemable at 5% premium. The debentures were to be redeemed after the end of fourth year.

Prepare loss on issue of debentures account.

26. Record the journal entries for the following debenture transactions (ignore entries for the write-off of capital losses) **Competency Based Que**

(i) Titan Ltd. issued 6,000, 12% debentures of ₹ 100 each at a discount of 8%, redeemable at par after 6 years.

(ii) Nova Ltd. issued 4,000, 10% debentures of ₹ 100 each at a discount of 5%, redeemable at a premium of 12% after 5 years.

27. Pass journal entry for issue of debentures if ₹ 80,000, 15% debentures of ₹ 100 each issued at a premium of 10% redeemable at a premium of 10%.

Writing-off Loss on Issue of Debentures

28. Fiza Ltd. has issued 15,00,000, 9% debentures of ₹ 20 each at a discount of ₹ 6 per debenture on 1st October, 2019. The company has a balance of ₹ 1,00,000 in securities premium reserve account on the same date.

Pass necessary journal entries for issue of debentures and to write-off discount on issue of debentures.

Competency Based Que

29. On 1st November, 2024, Maharaj Ltd. issued 20,000, 10% debenturs of ₹ 100 each at a discount of 5%. The debentures were fully subscribed. It has a balance of ₹ 75,000 in securities premium reserve which the company decided to use for writing-off the discount on issue of debentures.

Pass the journal entries for issue of debentures and writing-off the discount. Also prepare discount on issue of debentures account. **Competency Based Que**

Interest on Debentures

30. DLF Ltd. issued 20,000, 10% debentures of ₹ 100 each on 1st April, 2024. The issue was fully subscribed. According to the terms of issue, interest on the debentures is payable half-yearly on 30th September and 31st March.

Pass necessary journal entries related to the debenture interest for the half-yearly ending 31st March, 2025 and transfer of interest on debentures of the year to the statement of profit and loss.

Ans. Debenture Interest for half-year = ₹ 1,00,000

31. ABC Ltd. issued ₹ 1,00,000, 6% debentures of ₹ 10 each at a premium of ₹ 2 per debenture on 1st April, 2024. The issue was fully subscribed and interest will be paid at the end of each financial year.

Pass necessary journal entries for the year 2024-25.

Ans. Debenture Interest for Full Year = ₹ 6,000

32. A Ltd., issued 1,000, 10% debentures of ₹ 200 each on 1st April, 2024 at a discount of 10% redeemable at a premium of 10%.

Give journal entries relating to the issue of debentures and debenture interest for the period ending 31st March, 2025 assuming that interest was paid half-yearly on 30th September and 31st March.

Ans. Debenture Interest for half-year = ₹ 10,000

Missing Information

33. **Fill in the missing information in the following**

Competency Based Que

JOURNAL

Date	Particulars	LF	Amt (Dr)	Amt (Cr)
	Bank A/c Dr		...	
	To 12% Debenture Application and Allotment A/c			...
	(Being application money received on .... debentures of ₹ 100 each issued at a discount of 10%)			
	12% Debenture Application and Allotment A/c Dr		18,00,000	
	Loss on Issue of Debentures A/c Dr		...	
	To 12% Debentures A/c			...
	To Premium on Redemption A/c			...
	(Being transfer of application money to debentures account, issued at a discount of 10% and redeemable at a premium of 5%)			

34. **Fill in the blanks in the following case**

Competency Based Que

JOURNAL

Date	Particulars	LF	Amt (Dr)	Amt (Cr)
	Sundry Assets A/c Dr		18,00,000	
	.... Dr		...	
	To Sundry Creditors A/c			2,00,000
	To			...
	(Being business of Rohit and Co. purchased for a consideration of ₹ 20,00,000)			
	.... Dr		20,00,000	
	.... Dr		...	
	To 8% Debentures A/c			...
	(Being paid to Rohit and Co. by issue of ....., 8% debentures of ₹ 150 each at a discount of ₹ 50 per debenture)			

Theoretical Questions

Short Answer Type Questions

1. How is 'discount on issue of debentures' treated in the books of accounts? NCERT

Ans. Discount on issue of debentures is a capital loss and the amount of discount of debited to a separate account named discount on issue of debentures account.

It is written-off in the year in which debentures are issued. It can be written-off from securities premium reserve account or statement of profit and loss.

Following entry is passed for writing-off discount on debentures

Securities Premium/Statement of Profit and Loss	Dr
To Discount on Issue of Debentures A/c	

2. Distinguish between shares and debentures.

Ans. Difference between shares and debentures

Basis	Shares (Equity)	Debentures
Meaning	Shares are the denomination (parts) of share capital.	Debentures are the denomination of loan.
Return	Dividend is received on shares.	Interest is received on debentures.
Assured Return	Rate of dividend on equity shares is not assured.	Rate of interest on debentures is assured.
Security	Shares are not secured.	Debentures are ordinarily secured.
Repayment	Money received on equity shares is not required to be returned except on dissolution.	Money received through debentures has to be repaid as per the terms of their issue.
Status	The holders of equity shares are the owners of the company.	The holders of debentures are the creditors of the company.
Convertibility	Shares cannot be converted into debentures.	Debentures can be converted into shares.
Issue at Discount	Shares cannot be issued at discount except sweat equity shares.	There are no restrictions on issue of debentures at discount.

3. Differentiate between shareholders and debentures-holders.

Ans. Difference between shareholders and debentureholders

Basis	Shareholders	Debentureholders
Meaning	Holders of shares are called the shareholders.	Holders of debentures are called the debentureholders.
Owners/ Creditors	Shareholders are the owners of the company.	Debentureholders are just the creditors of the company.
Dividend/ Interest	Shareholders are entitled to receive dividend from the company.	Debentureholders get interest from the company.

4. What is meant by oversubscription of debentures? What alternatives are available to a company in case of oversubscription?

Ans. When the number of debentures applied for is more than those offered for subscription, it is known as oversubscription. A company cannot allot more debentures than it has offered for subscription. In such a situation, the company may make allotment as is made in the case of shared that is

First alternative – Rejective excess application
Second alternative – Partial or pro-rata allotment
Third alternative – A combination of the above two alternatives

5. What is meant by issue of debentures for consideration other than cash? How are these debentures disclosed in the balance sheet? NCERT

Ans. When debentures are issued to vendors against purchase of assets or against purchase of business, it is termed as issue of debentures of consideration other than cash. In this case, consideration for issue of debenture is not cash but the assets or business.

Disclosure in the Balance Sheet Debentures issued for consideration other than cash appear under the head 'non-current liabilities' and sub-head 'long-term borrowings' in the balance sheet.

Objective Questions

Multiple Choice Questions (MCQs)

1. **Debentures which are transferable by mere delivery are**
(a) registered debentures (b) first debentures
(c) bearer debentures (d) secured debentures

2. **When debentures are issued at a discount and are redeemable at a premium, which of the following accounts is debited at the time of issue?** **CBSE 2020**
(a) Debentures account
(b) Premium on redemption of debentures account
(c) Loss on issue of debentures account
(d) None of the above

3. **Convertible debentures cannot be issued at a discount if**
(a) they are to be immediately converted
(b) they are not to be immediately converted
(c) Both (a) and (b)
(d) None of the above

4. **Discount on issue of debentures is shown under the following head in the balance sheet.**
(a) Statement of profit and loss
(b) Other non-current assets
(c) Debentures account
(d) None of the above

5. **When debentures are issued at par and are redeemable at a premium, the loss on such an issues debited to**
(a) statement of profit and loss
(b) debentures applications and allotment account
(c) loss on issue of debentures account
(d) All of the above

6. **Debentures on which a company does not give any undertaking for the repayment of money borrowed are called** **CBSE 2025**
(a) bearer debentures
(b) secured debentures
(c) perpetual debentures (d) registered debentures

7. **The debentures which do not carry a specific rate of interest are called**
(a) zero coupon rate debentures
(b) specific coupon rate debentures
(c) unsecured debentures
(d) secured debentures

8. **Which of the following statements is incorrect about debentures?** **Competency Based Que**
(a) Interest on debentures is an appropriation of profits
(b) Debentureholders are the creditors of a company
(c) Debentures can be issued to vendors at discount
(d) Interest is not paid on debentures issued as collateral security

9. **Excess value of net assets over purchase consideration at the time of purchase of business is credited to**
(a) general reserve (b) capital reserve
(c) vendors' account (d) Both (a) and (b)

10. **Which of the following statements is incorrect?** **CBSE 2023; Competency Based Que**
(a) Interest on debentures is a charge and not an appropriation
(b) Debentures can be issued at discount
(c) Debentureholders do not have voting rights
(d) Debentures cannot be converted into shares

11. **Name the sub-head under which the 'premium on redemption of debentures' appears in balance sheet.**
(a) Shareholders' fund (b) Non-current liabilities
(c) Long-term borrowings (d) None of these

12. **When debentures are issued at a discount but are redeemable at a premium, which of the following account will be credited at the time of issue?**
(a) Discount on issue of debentures account
(b) Loss on issue of debentures account
(c) Premium on redemption of debentures account
(d) Security premium account

13. **If the amount of debentures issued is more than the amount of the net assets taken over by a company, the difference will be treated as** **CBSE 2025**
(a) capital reserve (b) goodwill
(c) purchase consideration (d) general reserve

14. **...... is not paid on debentures issued as collateral security.**
(a) Interest (b) Mortgage
(c) Neither (a) or (b) (d) Both (a) and (b)

15. **Premium on redemption of debentures is a .... account.**
(a) personal (b) liability
(c) Both (a) and (b) (d) None of these

16. **Which of the following statements is/are incorrect?** **Competency Based Que**
I. **Premium received on debentures is credited to securities premium account.**
II. **Loss on issue of debentures is written-off in the year the debentures are issued from statement of profit and loss.**
III. **Debentures are normally shown as long-term borrowings under non-current liabilities.**

Codes
(a) I and III (b) Only I
(c) Only II (d) Only III

17. Rohit Ltd. issued 2,000, 9% debentures of ₹ 100 each at ₹ 95 per debenture. 9% debentures account will be credited by **CBSE 2023**

(a) ₹ 1,90,000 (b) ₹ 1,10,000
(c) ₹ 2,00,000 (d) ₹ 10,000

18. On 1st April, 2019 a company took a loan of ₹ 80,00,000 on security of land and building. This loan was further secured by issue of 40,000, 12% debentures of ₹ 100 each as collateral security. On 31st March, 2024, the company defaulted on repayment of the principal amount of this loan. Consequently on 1st April, 2024, the land and building were taken over and sold by the bank for ₹ 70,00,000. For the balance amount, debentures were sold in the market on 1st May, 2024. From which date would the interest on debentures become payable by the company? **CBSE SQP 2025; Competency Based Que**

(a) 1st April, 2019 (b) 31st March, 2024
(c) 1st April, 2024 (d) 1st May, 2024

19. Misha Ltd. issued 6,000, 8% debentures of ₹ 100 each at ₹ 96 per debenture. 8% debentures account will be credited by **CBSE 2024; Competency Based Que**

(a) ₹ 5,76,000 (b) ₹ 24,000
(c) ₹ 6,00,000 (d) ₹ 60,000

20. Maharaja Ltd. took over assets of ₹ 15,00,000 and liabilities of ₹ 2,00,000 of Dolphin Ltd. for an agreed purchase consideration of ₹ 12,60,000. It was agreed that the purchase consideration will be paid by issuing 11% debentures of ₹ 100 each at 10% discount. The number of debentures issued will be **CBSE 2024; Competency Based Que**

(a) 13,000 (b) 12,600
(c) 10,000 (d) 14,000

21. Maira Ltd. took over assets of ₹ 12,00,000 and liabilities of ₹ 4,00,000 of Subav Ltd., for an agreed purchase consideration of ₹ 9,00,000.

The amount was payable by issue of 11% debentures of ₹ 100 each at 10% discount. The number of debentures issued will be **CBSE 2023; Competency Based Que**

(a) 9,000 (b) 10,000
(c) 8,000 (d) 11,000

22. Arnav Ltd. purchased assets worth ₹ 24,00,000. It issued 9% debentures of ₹ 100 each at a discount of 4% for payment of the purchase consideration. The number of debentures issued to vendor were **CBSE 2024; Competency Based Que**

(a) 24,000 (b) 25,000
(c) 30,000 (d) 28,000

23. On 1st May, 2023, Amrit Ltd. issued 10,000, 10% debentures of ₹ 100 each at a premium of 10% redeemable at a premium of 10%. Loss on issue of debentures will be **CBSE 2024; Competency Based Que**

(a) ₹ 2,00,000 (b) ₹ 1,30,000 (c) ₹ 1,00,000 (d) ₹ 80,000

24. Anrav Ltd. issued 10,000, 9% debentures of ₹ 100 each at a premium of 5%, redeemable at a premium of 10%. Loss on issue of debentures account will be debited by **Competency Based Que**

(a) ₹ 10,00,000 (b) ₹ 1,00,000
(c) ₹ 1,50,000 (d) ₹ 1,05,000

25. The following journal entry appears in the books of Latvion Ltd.

JOURNAL

Date	Particulars		LF	Amt (Dr)	Amt (Cr)
	Bank A/c	Dr		4,75,000	
	Loss on Issue of Debentures A/c	Dr		75,000	
	To 12% Debentures A/c				5,00,000
	To Premium on Redemption of Debentures A/c				50,000

The discount on issue of debentures is **CBSE 2025; Competency Based Que**

(a) 15% (b) 5% (c) 10% (d) 95%

26. Nagar Ltd. issued 6,000, 11% debentures of ₹ 100 each at a discount of 10% redeemable at a premium. 'discount on issue of debentures' and 'premium on redemption of debentures' were accounted for through 'loss on issue of debentures account'. If the amount of 'loss on issue of debentures' was ₹ 90,000, then the amount of premium on redemption of debentures was **CBSE 2024 C; Competency Based Que**

(a) ₹ 60,000 (b) ₹ 90,000
(c) ₹ 1,20,000 (d) ₹ 30,000

27. On 1st April, 2022, Surya Ltd. issued 10,000, 12% debentures of ₹ 100 each at a premium of 5%. The total amount of interest on debentures for the year ended 31st March, 2023 will be **CBSE 2024 C**

(a) ₹ 1,20,000 (b) ₹ 50,000
(c) ₹ 1,00,000 (d) ₹ 1,26,000

28. Moon Ltd. issued 40,000, 10% debentures of ₹ 100 each at certain rate of discount and were to be redeemed at 20% premium. Exiting balance of securities premium before issuing of these debentures was ₹ 12,00,000 and after writing-off loss on issue of debentures, the balance in securities premium was ₹ 2,00,000. At what rate of discount these debentures were issued? **CBSE SQP 2025; Competency Based Que**

(a) 10% (b) 5%
(c) 25% (d) 15%

29. **Zeba Limited issued 15,000, 9% debentures of ₹ 100 each at 10% discount on 1st April, 2023. It has a balance of ₹ 1,00,000 in securities premium account. The 'discount on issue of debentures' of ₹ 1,50,000 will be written-off** CBSE 2025

(a) ₹ 1,00,000 out of securities premium account and ₹ 50,000 out of statement of profit and loss
(b) ₹ 50,000 out of securities premium account and 1,00,000 out of statement of profit and loss
(c) ₹ 1,50,000 out of securities premium account
(d) ₹ 1,50,000 out of statement of profit and loss

30. **Alexa Ltd. purchased building from Siri Ltd. for ₹ 18,00,000. The consideration was paid by issue of 6% debentures of ₹ 100 each at a discount of 20%. The 6% debentures account is credited with** Competency Based Que

(a) ₹ 10,40,000 (b) ₹ 10,00,000
(c) ₹ 9,60,000 (d) ₹ 6,40,000

Assertion-Reason

Direction (Q. No. 31 to 40) *Read the following Assertion (A) and Reason (R) and choose the correct alternative from the following*

Alternatives

(a) Both Assertion (A) and Reason (R) are true and Reason (R) is the correct explanation of Assertion (A)
(b) Both Assertion (A) and Reason (R) are true, but Reason (R) is not the correct explanation of Assertion (A)
(c) Assertion (A) is true, but Reason (R) is false
(d) Assertion (A) is false, but Reason (R) is true

31. **Assertion** (A) Irredeemable debentures are also known as perpetual debentures.

Reason (R) The company does not give any undertaking for the repayment of money borrowed by issuing such debentures. They are repayable on the winding-up of the company or on the expiry of a long period.

32. **Assertion** (A) Debentures being borrowings of the company are shown on asset side of the balance sheet.

Reason (R) Debentures may be either non-current liability or current liability.

33. **Assertion** (A) Shares represent ownership in the company, whereas debentures are acknowledgement of debt.

Reason (R) Debentureholders do not have voting rights, while shareholders enjoy voting rights in the company.

34. **Assertion** (A) A company can issue debentures for raising long-term borrowings.

Reason (R) The power to issue debentures must be mentioned in articles of association.

35. **Assertion** (A) The payment of interest on debentures is a charge on profits and must be paid even in the absence of profits.

Reason (R) Interest on debentures is a prefixed amount, unlike dividends on shares, which vary based on profits.

36. **Assertion** (A) Debentures are unsecured instruments that do not carry any charge on the assets of the company.

Reason (R) Debentures are generally issued for a specified period and are repayable upon expiry.

37. **Assertion** (A) A fixed charge on secured debentures is created against specific assets held by the company for operational purposes.

Reason (R) Fixed charges cover all the assets of a company except those assigned to secured creditors.

38. **Assertion** (A) Redeemable debentures are repaid on the expiry of a specified period, either in lumpsum or instalments.

Reason (R) Redeemable debentures can only be issued at par and not at a premium.

39. **Assertion** (A) Interest on bearer debentures is paid to a person who produces the interest coupon attached to such debentures.

Reason (R) Bearer debentures are transferred by way of delivery and the company does not keep any record of those debentureholders. CBSE 2024

40. **Assertion** (A) Discount on the issue of debentures to be written-off after 12 months from the balance sheet date is shown under 'other non-current assets.'

Reason (R) Discounts on the issue of debentures are considered a deferred revenue expenditure, which is allocated over the lifetime of the debentures.

Two Statements Based MCQs

Direction (Q. No. 41 to 48) *Read the following statements carefully and choose the correct alternative*

Alternatives

(a) Statement I is correct and Statement II is incorrect
(b) Statement II is correct and Statement I is incorrect
(c) Both the statements are correct
(d) Both the statements are incorrect

41. **Statement I** Interest on debentures is calculated at the fixed percentage on the issue price.

Statement II Debenture is evidence of company's borrowings.

42. **Statement I** The balance of interest on debentures account is transferred to statement of profit and loss at the end of the year.

Statement II Dividend is received on debentures.

43. **Statement I** A debenture is a written acknowledgement of a debt under the common seal of a company.

Statement II Shares are a part of the owned capital of a company, while debentures are part of the borrowed capital.

44. **Statement I** The return on shares is called a dividend, while the return on debentures is called interest.

Statement II Debentureholders generally have voting rights in the company.

45. **Statement I** Secured debentures are backed by a charge on the company's assets, which may be fixed or floating.

Statement II Unsecured debentures usually have a fixed charge on the company's specific assets.

46. **Statement I** Redeemable debentures are repayable either at par or at a premium upon the expiry of a specified period.

Statement II Irredeemable debentures are also called perpetual debentures as they are repayable only during the company's winding-up.

47. **Statement I** The Companies Act, 2013 does not prohibit the issue of debentures at a discount.

Statement II Discount on the issue of debentures is classified under 'other current assets' if it is to be written-off within 12 months of the balance sheet date.

48. **Statement I** Debentures issued as collateral security create an immediate liability for the company, requiring them to record the transaction through a journal entry in all cases.

Statement II When no journal entry is passed for debentures issued as collateral security, a note is appended below the loan in the balance sheet indicating the security.

Matching

49. **Match the following pairs based on their characteristics**

Column I	Column II
A. Debentures	(i) Secured and carry a charge on assets.
B. Shares	(ii) Represent ownership of the company.
C. Convertible debentures	(iii) Can be converted into shares.

Codes

	A	B	C		A	B	C
(a)	(ii)	(i)	(iii)	(b)	(i)	(ii)	(iii)
(c)	(iii)	(ii)	(i)	(d)	(i)	(iii)	(ii)

50. **Match the following**

Column I	Column II
A. Debentures secured by either a fixed charge or a floating charge	(i) Bearer debentures
B. Debentures not repayable during the existence of the company	(ii) Naked debentures
C. Debentures transferable by mere delivery	(iii) Mortgage debentures
D. Debentures not secured by any charge on asset	(iv) Perpetual debentures

Codes

	A	B	C	D		A	B	C	D
(a)	(iii)	(iv)	(i)	(ii)	(b)	(ii)	(iii)	(i)	(iv)
(c)	(iv)	(ii)	(i)	(iii)	(d)	(iii)	(i)	(iv)	(ii)

51. **Match the following types of debentures with their features**

Column I	Column I
A. Zero coupon debentures	(i) Issued without a specific interest rate.
B. Redeemable debentures	(ii) Repayable during the company's lifetime.
C. Secured debentures	(iii) Backed by a charge on the company's assets.

Codes

	A	B	C		A	B	C
(a)	(i)	(iii)	(ii)	(b)	(ii)	(i)	(iii)
(c)	(i)	(ii)	(iii)	(d)	(iii)	(ii)	(i)

52. **Match the following**

Column I	Column II
A. Received oversubscription	(i) Debenture suspense account
B. Debentures issued to promoters	(ii) Rejection of excess application
C. Issue debentures as collateral security	(iii) Goodwill

Codes

	A	B	C		A	B	C
(a)	(i)	(ii)	(iii)	(b)	(ii)	(iii)	(i)
(c)	(ii)	(i)	(iii)	(d)	(iii)	(ii)	(i)

Case Based MCQs

Direction *Read the case study and answer the question 53 to 55 on the basis of the same*

Maverick Ltd. is a company engaged in manufacturing industrial equipment. To expand its operations, the company secured a loan of ₹ 50,00,000 from Apex Bank. As a primary security, Maverick Ltd. mortgaged its land valued at ₹ 60,00,000. However, Apex Bank insisted on additional collateral security. Consequently, Maverick Ltd. issued 5,000, 10% debentures of ₹ 1,000 each as collateral security.

The debentures were issued at a discount of 5% and are to be redeemed at par after 7 years. The company decided not to record the journal entry of issue of debentures as collateral security in its books.

Additionally, the company issued 3,000, 9% convertible debentures at ₹ 900 each (face value ₹ 1,000), redeemable at a premium of 10% after 5 years.

53. **What is the redeemable value of the 9% convertible debentures issued by Maverick Ltd.?**

(a) ₹ 1,000 (b) ₹ 900
(c) ₹ 1,100 (d) ₹ 950

54. **Where would Maverick Ltd. disclose the debentures issued as collateral security in its balance sheet?**

(a) Under 'share capital'
(b) Under 'non-current Liabilities' as a note below the loan
(c) Under 'reserves and surplus'
(d) Under 'current liabilities'

55. **What will be the amount of long-term borrowings in the balance sheet of the company?**

(a) ₹ 1,10,00,000 (b) ₹ 50,00,000
(c) ₹ 60,00,000 (d) ₹ 80,00,000

Direction *Read the following case study and answer the questions 56 to 58 on the basis of the same*

'Golden Blankets Ltd'. are the manufacturers of woollen blankets. Blankets of the company are exported to many countries. The company decided to distribute blankets free of cost to five villages of Kashmir valley destroyed by the recent floods. It also decided to employ 100 young persons from these villages in their newly established factory at Solan in Himachal Pradesh. To meet the requirements of funds for starting its new factory, the company issued 50,000, 10% debentures of ₹ 10 each and 2000, 8% debentures of ₹ 100 each to the vendor of the machinery purchased for ₹ 7,00,000.

56. **How many debentures are issued in total?**

(a) 50,000 (b) 20,000 (c) 70,000 (d) 52,000

57. **How many debentures should be issued, if 8% debentures of ₹ 100 each are issued at 20% discount amounting to ₹ 2,00,000?**

(a) 2,500 (b) 1,000
(c) 1,500 (d) 2,000

58 **Total interest payable by the company will amount to**

(a) ₹ 52,000 (b) ₹ 5,200
(c) ₹ 66,000 (d) ₹ 16,000

Direction *Read the following case study and answer the questions 59 to 61 on the basis of the same*

Moonlight India Ltd. is to produce and distribute green energy in the backward areas of India. It has also taken up a project of giving vocational training to the girls belonging to the backward areas of Rajasthan. To meet the requirements of funds to serve the purpose, company issued 40,000 debentures of ₹ 100 each at a premium of ₹ 25, payable as follows

₹ 20 per debenture on application

₹ 45 per debenture on allotment (including premium of ₹ 15)

₹ 60 per debenture on first and final call (including premium of ₹ 10)

The issue was oversubscribed by 20,000 debentures. Applicants of 16,000 were allotted only 2,000 debentures and applicants of 2,000 debentures were sent letter of regret.

Excess amount received at the time of application was to be adjusted only against allotment and payments exceeding the amount due in the allotment were to be refunded. All the money due on allotment and calls was duly received.

59. **Amount refunded to debentureholders will be**

(a) ₹ 2,60,000 (b) ₹ 2,50,000
(c) ₹ 2,30,000 (d) ₹ 2,00,000

60. **What amount will be received on allotment?**

(a) ₹ 16,30,000 (b) ₹ 16,00,000
(c) ₹ 18,00,000 (d) ₹ 18,30,000

61. **What pro-rata allotment is made in this case other than the one already mentioned?**

(a) 44,000 : 40,000 (b) 42,000 : 38,000
(c) 60,000 : 40,000 (d) 42,000 : 36,000

Answers

1. (c) bearer debentures
2. (c) Loss on issue of debentures account
3. (a) they are to be immediately converted
4. (b) Other non-current assets
5. (c) loss on issue of debentures account
6. (c) perpetual debentures
7. (a) zero coupon rate debentures
8. (a) Interest on debentures is an appropriation of profits
9. (b) capital reserve
10. (d) Debentures cannot be converted into shares
11. (c) The 'premium on redemption of debentures' appears under the head 'non-current liabilities' and sub-head 'long-term borrowings'.
12. (c) Premium on redemption of debentures account will be credited with the same amount that will be paid at the time of redemption.

13. (b) goodwill
14. (a) Interest
15. (c) Both (a) and (b)
16. (c) Loss on issue of debentures can be written-off from securities premium account or statement of profit or loss.
17. (c) Debentures account will be credited with $(2,000 \times 100) = ₹\ 2,00,000$
18. (d) 1st May, 2024
19. (c) 8% debenture account $= 6,000 \times 100 = ₹\ 6,00,000$
20. (d) Number of debenture $= \frac{12,60,000}{90} = 14,000$
21. (b) Number of debentures issued $= \frac{9,00,000}{(100-10)}$ $= 10,000$ debentures
22. (b) Number of debenture $= \frac{24,00,000}{96} = 25,000$
23. (c) Loss on issue of debenture $= 10,00,000 \times \frac{10}{100}$ $= ₹\ 1,00,000$
24. (b) Loss on issue of debentures $= 10,00,000 \times \frac{10}{100}$ $= ₹\ 1,00,000$
25. (b) Discount on Issue = Loss on issue − Premium on Redemption
$= 75,000 - 50,000 = ₹\ 25,000$
Rate of Discount $= \frac{25,000}{5,00,000} \times 100 = 5\%$
26. (d) Premium on redemption of debentures
$= 90,000 - \left(6,00,000 \times \frac{10}{100}\right) = ₹\ 30,000$
27. (a) Interest on debentures $= 10,00,000 \times \frac{12}{100} = ₹\ 1,20,000$
28. (b) Total loss $= 12,00,000 - 2,00,000 = ₹\ 10,00,000$
Loss on redemption $= 40,00,000 \times \frac{20}{100} = ₹\ 8,00,000$
Loss on issue $= 10,00,000 - 8,00,000 = ₹\ 2,00,000$
% of loss $= \frac{2,00,000}{40,00,000} \times 100 = 5\%$
29. (a) Discount on issue $= (15,000 \times 100) \times 10\% =$ ₹ 1,50,000
(−) Written-off from securities premium = ₹ (1,00,000)
Written-off from statement of profit and loss ₹ 50,000
30. (b) 6% debentures $= \frac{8,00,000}{80} \times 10,000 \times 100 = ₹\ 10,00,000$
31. (a) Both Assertion (A) and Reason (R) are true and Reason (R) is the correct explanation of Assertion (A)
32. (d) Debentures being borrowings of the company are shown on equity and liability side of the balance sheet.
33. (a) Both Assertion (A) and Reason (R) are true and Reason (R) is the correct explanation of Assertion (A)
34. (c) The power to issue debentures must be mentioned in memorandum of association.
35. (a) Both Assertion (A) and Reason (R) are true and Reason (R) is the correct explanation of Assertion (A)
36. (d) Assertion (A) is false, but Reason (R) is true
37. (c) Assertion (A) is true, but Reason (R) is false
38. (c) Assertion (A) is true, but Reason (R) is false
39. (a) Both Assertion (A) and Reason (R) are true and Reason (R) is the correct explanation of Assertion (A)
40. (a) Both Assertion (A) and Reason (R) are true and Reason (R) is the correct explanation of Assertion (A)
41. (b) Interest on debentures is calculated at the fixed percentage on the face value, not on the issue price.
42. (a) Statement I is correct and Statement II is incorrect
43. (c) Both the statements are correct
44. (a) Statement I is correct and Statement II is incorrect
45. (a) Statement I is correct and Statement II is incorrect
46. (c) Both the statements are correct
47. (a) Statement I is correct and Statement II is incorrect
48. (b) Statement II is correct and Statement I is incorrect
49. (b) (i) (ii) (iii)
50. (a) (iii) (iv) (i) (ii)
51. (c) (i) (ii) (iii)
52. (a) (i) (ii) (iii)
53. (c) Redeemable Value $= 1,000 + \left(1,000 \times \frac{10}{100}\right) = ₹\ 1,100$
54. (b) Under 'non-current liabilities' as a note below the loan
55. (d) Long-term borrowings $= 50,00,000 + 30,00,000$ $= ₹\ 80,00,000$
56. (d) 10% debentures = 50,000
8% debentures = 2,000
Total number of debentures issued = 52,000
57. (a) Number of debentures issued = 2,00,000/80
= 2,500
58. (c) 50,000, 10% debenture @ ₹ 10 = 5,00,000 × 10/100
= ₹ 50,000
2,000, 8% debenture @ ₹ 100 each = 2,00,000 × 8/100
= ₹ 16,000
Total interest = 50,000 + 16,000 = ₹ 66,000
59. (c) Excess money received on application not adjusted in any call will be refunded
Excess money received $(20,000 \times 20) = ₹\ 4,00,000$
Adjusted on allotment $(2,000 \times 45 + 4,000 \times 20)$
$= ₹\ 1,70,000$
Therefore, total amount refunded is (4,00,000 −1,70,000)
= ₹ 2,30,000
60. (a) Allotment money due $(40,000 \times 45)$ = 18,00,000
(−) Excess money adjusted = (1,70,000)
Amount received = 16,30,000
61. (b) Out of 60,000 applications, applicants of 16,000 debentures were allotted 2,000 debentures and applications of 2,000 debentures were rejected. So, pro-rata will be made to the remaining shareholders, i.e. 42,000 de benture applications were allotted 38,000 debentures.

PART B
FINANCIAL STATEMENT ANALYSIS

01 CHAPTER

"Financial statements provide a summary of accounts of a business enterprise, the balance sheet reflecting the assets, liabilities and capital as on a certain date and income statement showing the results and operations during a certain period."

– John N Myer

YOUR STUDY GOALS

1.1 Meaning of Financial Statements
1.2 Balance Sheet
1.3 Statement of Profit and Loss

YOUR PRACTICE GOAL

- Topicwise Solved Questions (10 Solved Questions)
- Numerical Questions [12 Questions (Unsolved)]
- Theoretical Questions [35 Questions (with answers)]
- Objective Questions (60 Qs ; MCQs, A-R, Statements, Matching, Case)

Financial Statements of a Company

1.1 Meaning of Financial Statements

Financial statements are the end product of an accounting process. Financial statements are historical in nature and are prepared following the accounting concepts and principles.

These statements provide information about the financial performance of an entity for an accounting period and also discloses its financial position at the end of the period.

Section 129 of the Companies Act, 2013 requires every company to prepare its financial statements every year in the form prescribed, i.e. Schedule III of the Companies Act, 2013.

A set of financial statements as per **Section 2(40)** of the **Companies Act, 2013** includes

1. **Balance Sheet** It is a statement of assets and liabilities, showing the financial position of an enterprise at a given date. It is also known as position statement.
2. **Statement of Profit and Loss** It shows the net result of business operations during an accounting period. It is also known as income statement.
3. **Cash Flow Statement** It is a statement prepared in accordance with AS-3, to show inflow and outflow of cash and cash equivalents.
4. **Statement of Changes in Equity** It shows changes in equity during a year.
5. **Notes to Accounts** It is any explanatory note annexed to any document referred above.

Characteristics of Financial Statements

- Financial statements relate to a specific past period and thus are historical in nature.
- Financial statements are expressed in monetary terms.
- Financial statements show profitability through statement of profit and loss and financial position through balance sheet.

Nature of Financial Statements

1. **Recorded Facts** Financial statements are prepared on the basis of facts recorded in accounting books. The figures of various accounts such as cash in hand, cash at bank, bills receivable, sundry debtors, fixed assets, etc., are taken as per the figures recorded in the accounting books.
2. **Accounting Conventions** Certain accounting conventions such as the conventions of consistency, conservatism and full disclosure are required to be followed while preparing financial statements. The use of accounting conventions makes financial statements comparable, simple and realistic.
3. **Postulates/Concepts** Financial statements are prepared on certain basic assumptions known as postulates or concepts such as going concern concept, money measurement concept, realisation concept, etc.
4. **Personal Judgements** Personal opinion, judgements and estimates also effect the financial statements. e.g. Which method is to be followed for depreciating assets or for valuing inventory, depends on the personal judgement of the management.

Financial Year

As per **Section 2(41)** of the **Companies Act, 2013**, all companies are required to have a uniform financial year which shall be a period from 1st April to 31st March every year.

Objectives of Financial Statements

- To provide information on economic resources (assets) and obligations (liabilities) of an enterprise.
- To provide information about the earning capacity.
- To provide sufficient and reliable information to various parties interested in financial statements.
- To serve as the basis for future planning and implementation of various operations.
- To provide information about the cash flows.
- To help to judge the effectiveness of management.
- To disclose various accounting policies.
- To give a true and fair view of the financial performance (i.e. profit earned or loss suffered) of the business.
- To give a true and fair view of the financial position (i.e. assets/equity and liabilities) of the business.

Smart Study Chart No. 1

Essentials of Financial Statements

- **Accurate Information** It should disclose the factual information about the financial position and the working of the business.
- **Understandability** It should be prepared in accordance with the accepted accounting principles for better understanding.
- **Comparable** It should disclose information in a manner that the user can compare the information of the same entity over the years (intra-firm comparison) and also compare the reporting company's financial information with that of other companies (inter-firm comparison).
- **Verifiable** Information disclosed by the financial statements should be verifiable from the records of the company.
- **Relevant** Information disclosed by the financial statements should be in accordance with the legal requirements.
- **Timeliness** It should be prepared and presented within a reasonable period after the end of accounting period.

Uses and Importance of Financial Statements

Financial statements provide essential information about an organisation's performance, aiding stakeholders in making informed economic decisions. Their uses and importance include

1. **Reporting Management Performance** Highlight gaps between management performance and share-holders' expectations by showcasing results to owners.
2. **Basis for Fiscal Policies** Financial statements serve as inputs for government policies on taxation and industry regulation, linked to companies' financial performance.
3. **Basis for Granting Credit** Financial statements help credit institutions in evaluating a company's financial health before granting loans.
4. **Investors Guidance** Financial statements help prospective investors to assess solvency and profitability for decision-making.
5. **Investment Evaluation** Financial statements provide shareholders with details about the safety, returns and status of their investments.
6. **Support to Trade Associations** Financial statements assist trade associations in offering member services, setting standard ratios and designing uniform accounting systems.

Limitations of Financial Statements

1. **Historical Data** Financial statements reflect past performance and do not provide insights into future growth, which is a key concern for shareholders and investors.
2. **Subject to Personal Judgements** Decisions like stock valuation or provision for depreciation depend on personal judgement, making financial statements prone to bias.
3. **Varied Accounting Practices** Different methods, such as straight line or written down value method for depreciation, lead to variations in reported profits or losses.
4. **Exclusion of Qualitative Factors** Non-monetary elements like management quality, labour efficiency and public relations are not expressed in monetary terms.
5. **Ignores Price Level Changes** Assets are recorded at historical cost, disregarding current market values and inflation impacts.

Smart Study
Chart No. 2

Users of Financial Statements

Internal Users

- **Owners** Analyse financial strength, cash position and profitability to assess risk and returns on their investments.
- **Management** Uses financial data for decisions on pricing, cost control, new investments and efficient business operations to maximise profits.
- **Employees** Interested in profits for bonuses, timely remuneration and job security.

External Users

- **Banks and Financial Institutions** Evaluate business performance to ensure loan repayment and financial stability.
- **Present and Future Investors** Assess profitability and safety of their investments.
- **Creditors or Suppliers** Analyse creditworthiness to determine reliability for extending credit.
- **Government and Authorities** Use financial data for tax assessment, national income calculations and policy-making.
- **SEBI and Regulatory Bodies** Monitor financial practices to protect investors and ensure compliance.
- **Consumers** Assess a company's ability to provide goods at reasonable prices.

Annual Report and its Contents

As per law, the annual reports of a company, should disclose the prescribed information to enable the users to make informed judgements and decisions. The information is disclosed in the financial statements, directors' report and by separate statements being part of the annual report.

A complete set of annual report of a company has

- A report by the board of directors, containing
  - Report in terms of Section 134 of the Companies Act, 2013.
  - Director's responsibility statement.
  - Report on corporate governance.
  - Management discussion and analysis.
- Auditors' report to the shareholders.
- Financial statements
  - Balance sheet as at the end of financial year.
  - Statement of profit and loss for the year ended.
  - Cash flow statement.
- Notes to accounts
  - Accounting policies adopted by the company.
  - Notes giving information of items in the balance sheet and statement of profit and loss.
  - Additional information required to be disclosed in terms of Part III of Schedule III of the Companies Act, 2013.

1.2 Balance Sheet

Balance sheet may be defined as a statement of assets and liabilities of the company at a particular date. It is prepared and presented in the form prescribed in Schedule III, Part I of the Companies Act, 2013. It must exhibit a true and fair view of financial position of company at the close of the year.

Characteristics of Balance Sheet

- It shows the financial position of the business at a specific point of time.
- It shows the relationship between assets and equity and liabilities. Assets = Liabilities + Owner's Equity.
- It is prepared on a particular date and not for a period.
- It is influenced by the personal judgements and accounting assumptions and not based on absolute facts.

Format of Balance Sheet

Name of the Company ...
Balance Sheet
as at ...

Particulars	Note No.	Figures as at the End of the Current Reporting Period (₹)	Figures as at the End of the Previous Reporting Period (₹)
I. EQUITY AND LIABILITIES			
1. Shareholders' Funds			
(i) Share Capital		...	...
(ii) Reserves and Surplus		...	...
*(iii) Money Received against Share Warrants		...	...
***2. Share Application Money Pending Allotment**		...	...
3. Non-current Liabilities			
(i) Long-term Borrowings		...	...
*(ii) Deferred Tax Liabilities (Net)		...	...
*(iii) Other Long-term Liabilities		...	...
(iv) Long-term Provisions		...	...
4. Current Liabilities			
(i) Short-term Borrowings		...	...
(ii) Trade Payables		...	...
(iii) Other Current Liabilities		...	...
(iv) Short-term Provisions		...	...
Total		...	...
II. ASSETS			
1. Non-current Assets			
(i) Property, Plant and Equipment and Intangible Assets			
(a) Property, Plant and Equipment		...	...
(b) Intangible Assets		...	...
*(c) Capital Work-in-progress		...	...
*(d) Intangible Assets under Development		...	...
(ii) Non-current Investments		...	...
*(iii) Deferred Tax Assets (Net)		...	...
(iv) Long-term Loans and Advances		...	...
*(v) Other Non-current Assets		...	...
2. Current Assets			
(i) Current Investments		...	...
(ii) Inventories		...	...
(iii) Trade Receivables		...	...
(iv) Cash and Cash Equivalents		...	...
(v) Short-term Loans and Advances		...	...
(vi) Other Current Assets		...	...
Total		...	...

Note *As per CBSE circular, the accounting treatment of star marked items will not be evaluated.

Details of Contents under the Head 'Equity and Liabilities'

1. Shareholders' Funds

Shareholders' funds mean funds belonging to the shareholders. They are categorised in three categories, which are discussed below

(i) **Share Capital** It is the amount invested by the shareholders as capital in the company. It includes both equity and preference share capital. The disclosure of share capital in the balance sheet is limited to following

Balance Sheet
as at ...

Particulars	Note No.	Figures as at the End of the Current Reporting Period (₹)	Figures as at the End of the Previous Reporting Period (₹)
I. **EQUITY AND LIABILITIES**			
1. **Shareholders' Funds**			
Share Capital	1	...	...

Notes to Accounts

Particulars		Year Ended ... (₹)
1. **Share Capital**		
Authorised Capital		
... Shares of ₹ ... each		...
Issued Capital		
... Shares of ₹ ... each		...
Subscribed Capital		
Subscribed and Fully Paid-up		
... Shares of ₹ ... each		...
Subscribed but not Fully Paid-up		
... Shares of ₹ ... each	...	
(–) Calls-in-arrears	(...)	...
Forfeited Shares		...
		...

Important Points Related to Share Capital

- Equity share capital and preference share capital are to be shown separately.
- Forfeited shares amount, (i.e. amount originally paid-up) is shown by adding it to subscribed capital. But in case of profit on reissue of forfeited shares, it is transferred to capital reserve.
- Amount of calls-in-arrears is shown as deduction from 'called-up capital' or 'subscribed capital' to ascertain the paid-up capital of the company and shown as liability in the balance sheet.
- Calls-in-arrears from directors and officers of the company have to be disclosed.

(ii) **Reserves and Surplus** It is a part of shareholders' funds and may be free reserve or committed reserve. It may be received as securities premium or may have been appropriated out of surplus of statement of profit and loss or may be the balance of statement of profit and loss.

Schedule III of the Companies Act, 2013 has prescribed the heads of reserves and surplus to be

- Capital reserve
- Securities premium
- Capital redemption reserve
- Debenture redemption reserve
- Revaluation reserve (accounting treatment not to be evaluated)
- Share options outstanding account (accounting treatment not to be evaluated)
- Other reserves – general reserve, tax reserve, subsidy reserve, amalgamation reserve (restricted to general reserve only)
- Surplus i.e. balance in statement of profit and loss

Important Points Related to Reserves and Surplus

- A reserve specifically represented by earmarked investments shall be termed as 'fund.'
- 'Debit' balance of statement of profit and loss shall be shown as a negative figure under the head 'surplus.'
- The balance of 'reserves and surplus' after adjusting negative balance of surplus, if any, shall be shown under the head 'reserves and surplus' even if the resulting figure is 'negative'.

*(iii) **Money Received against Share Warrants** (Not to be evaluated) Share warrants are the financial instruments which give holder the right to acquire equity shares at a specified date and at a specified time.

Hence, effectively, share warrants are nothing, but the amount which would ultimately form part of the 'shareholders' funds'. As shares are yet to be issued against the same, these cannot be part of share capital, but the same should be reflected as a separate line item under 'shareholders' funds'.

*2. Share Application Money Pending Allotment

It is the amount received as application money for allotment of shares against which shares are yet to be allotted.

3. Non-current Liabilities

A non-current liability is a liability which is not classified as current liability. The term 'current liabilities' is defined in Schedule III of the Companies Act, as follows

- It is expected to be settled in the company's normal **operating cycle**.
- It is held primarily for the purpose of being traded.
- It is due to be settled within 12 months after the reporting date.
- The company does not have an unconditional right to defer settlement of the liabilities for atleast 12 months after the reporting date.

Hence, the liabilities which are not classified as current shall be classified as non-current.

Operating Cycle

It means the time between the acquisition of assets for processing and their realisation in cash or cash equivalents. It may vary from few days to few years. Where the operating cycle cannot be identified, it is assumed to have a duration of 12 months.

Operating Cycle in a Trading Firm Operating cycle in a trading firm is shown below

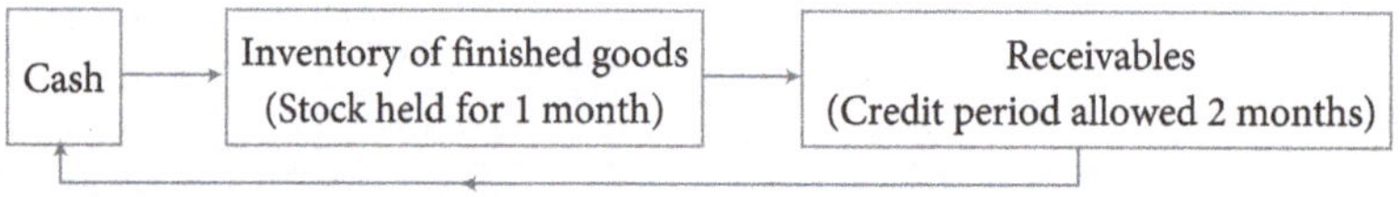

Hence, operating cycle =1 month + 2 months = 3 months

Operating Cycle in a Manufacturing Firm Operating cycle in a manufacturing firm is shown below

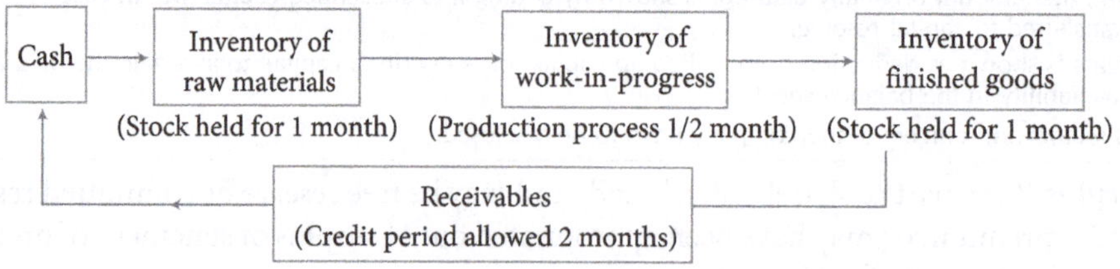

Hence, operating cycle = 1 month + $\frac{1}{2}$ month + 1 month + 2 months = $4\frac{1}{2}$ months

Non-current liabilities are classified as

(i) **Long-term Borrowings** These are loans repayable after 12 months from the balance sheet date or the operating cycle period. For instance, if the balance sheet is dated 31st March, 2024, long-term borrowings will include amounts due after 31st March, 2025 (e.g. Debentures, long-term loans).

Key Points

- Long-term borrowings are categorised as secured or unsecured, with the nature of security specified separately.
- Bonds/Debentures should be listed in descending order of maturity or conversion, starting with the farthest redemption or conversion date. For bonds/debentures redeemable in instalments, the first instalment's due date is considered the maturity date.
- Current maturities of long-term borrowings must be shown under other current liabilities, not under long-term borrowings or short-term borrowings.

*(ii) **Deferred Tax Liabilities** (Net) It arises when accounting income (i.e. income arrived according to accounting principles) is more than the taxable income (i.e. income arrived according to the Provisions of Income Tax Act). Deferred tax is calculated every year and adjusted to the existing balance.

*(iii) **Other Long-term Liabilities** Long-term liabilities (other than long-term borrowings) are classified as other long-term liabilities.

They are classified into

→ **Trade Payables** If they are agreed to be settled after 12 months of the date of balance sheet or after the period of operating cycle.

→ **Others** If they are payable after more than 12 months of the date of balance sheet or after the period of operating cycle.

(iv) **Long-term Provisions** All provisions for which the related claims are expected to be settled beyond 12 months after the balance sheet date are classified as long-term provisions.

4. Current Liabilities

As per Schedule III of the Companies Act, 2013, current liabilities are

- Expected to be settled within the operating cycle (or 12 months if the cycle is undefined).
- Due within 12 months of the reporting date.
- Held for trading purposes.
- Without an unconditional right to defer settlement for at least 12 months.

All other liabilities are classified as non-current liabilities.

Current liabilities are classified as

(i) **Short-term Borrowings** It includes loans repayable within 12 months, including loans on demand, deposits, advances from related parties, and bank overdrafts or cash credit limits.

(ii) **Trade Payables** It refers to amounts payable for goods or services in the normal course of business, including sundry creditors and bills payable. It is classified as current only if due within 12 months of the balance sheet or the operating cycle.

(iii) **Other Current Liabilities** Liabilities not covered under short-term borrowings, trade payables or short-term provisions, are shown under this head e.g. Unpaid dividends, interest accrued, income received in advance, calls-in-advance and current maturities of long-term borrowings.

(iv) **Short-term Provisions** Provisions expected to be settled within 12 months or the operating cycle are classified as short-term provisions and shown under current liabilities, e.g. Provision for doubtful debts, tax, proposed dividend, etc.

Details of Contents Under the Head 'Assets'

1. Non-current Assets

A non-current asset is an asset which is not classified as current asset.

Current assets as defined in Schedule III of the Companies Act, 2013 is as follows

- It is expected to be realised in or is intended for sale or consumption in the company's normal operating cycle. Where the normal operating cycle cannot be identified, it is assumed to have a duration of 12 months.
- It is held primarily for the purpose of being traded.
- It is expected to be realised within 12 months after the reporting date.
- It is cash or cash equivalents unless it is restricted from being exchanged or used to settle a liability for atleast 12 months after the reporting date.

All other assets shall be classified as non-current assets. Non-current assets are classified as follows

(i) **Property, Plant and Equipment and Intangible Assets** (Fixed Assets) They are classified as follows

- **Property, Plant and Equipment** (Tangible Assets) Those assets which have physical existence i.e. they can be physically seen and touched are tangible assets. e.g. Land, building, plant and equipment, furniture and fixtures, vehicles, office equipments, etc.
- **Intangible Assets** Those assets which do not have physical existence i.e. which cannot be seen and touched are intangible assets.

- *__Capital Work-in-progress__ It means amount incurred on construction or development of tangible assets.
- *__Intangible Assets under Development__ It means amount incurred on development of intangible assets such as patent, intellectual property rights, etc., which are being developed by the company.

(ii) **Non-current Investments** Investments intended to be held for more than 12 months and not meant for resale are classified as non-current investments.

They are classified as

→ **Trade Investments** These are investments in shares or debentures of another company to promote trade or business.

→ **Others Investments** These are investments which not related to trade, e.g. Investment in property, equity instruments, preference shares, government securities, debentures and mutual funds.

*(iii) **Deferred Tax Assets** (Net) It arises when accounting income (i.e. income arrived according to accounting principles) is less than the taxable income (i.e. income arrived according to the provisions of Income Tax Act).

(iv) **Long-term Loans and Advances** These are those loans and advances which are receivable by the company in cash or kind after a period of 12 months from the date of balance sheet.

They are classified into

- Capital advances
- Security deposits
- Other loans and advances (nature to be specified) If a debenture is to be redeemed partly within 12 months and balance after 12 months, the amount to be redeemed within 12 months should be disclosed as current and balance should be shown as non-current.

*(v) **Other Non-current Assets** (not to be evaluated) All long-term assets which do not fall in the above categories or classification are shown under this head.

e.g. Advance given to an employee, repayment of which is to be after 12 months from the date of the balance sheet.

2. Current Assets

As per Schedule III of the Companies Act, 2013, current assets are

- Realised, sold or consumed within the operating cycle (or 12 months if the cycle is undefined).
- Held for trading purposes.
- Realised within 12 months from the reporting date.
- Cash or cash equivalents.

Current assets are classified as

(i) **Current Investments** Short-term investments held for less than 12 months from the balance sheet date, are termed as current investments.

These can include trade or other investments such as equity instruments, preference shares, government securities, debentures and mutual funds, etc.

(ii) **Inventories**

It is the term used for stock. It is the tangible asset held by an enterprise for

- the purpose of sale in the ordinary course of business.
- the purpose of using it in the production of goods meant for sale or services to be rendered.

Inventory is valued on the principle of 'cost or net realisable value' (i.e. market price) whichever is lower.

Inventories include the following

- Raw materials
- Work-in-progress
- Finished goods
- Stores and spares
- Goods acquired for trading
- Loose tools

(iii) **Trade Receivables** These are amount due for goods sold or services rendered in the normal course of business, including debtors and bills receivable.

Receivables expected to be realised within 12 months or the operating cycle, are classified as current. Receivables due beyond 12 months or the operating cycle are shown as 'other non-current assets' under 'non-current assets'.

Provision for doubtful debts is treated as

- Shown as a deduction under trade receivables.
- Classified as long-term provisions or short-term provisions based on the receivables' classification.

(iv) **Cash and Cash Equivalents** It is the new term used for cash in hand and cash at bank.

Schedule III requires that cash and cash equivalents be classified or shown as follows

- Balance with banks
- Cheques, drafts on hand
- Cash in hand
- Others
- Earmarked balances with banks (e.g. Unpaid dividend)
- Balance with banks held as margin money
- Book deposits with more than 12 months maturity

(v) **Short-term Loans and Advances** These loans and advances are receivable in cash or kind, within 12 months of the balance sheet date or the operating cycle.

(vi) **Other Current Assets** They include all current assets which are not classified under other categories, such as prepaid expenses, accrued incomes and advance taxes, which must be disclosed separately.

*3. Contingent Liabilities and Capital Commitments

(i) **Contingent Liabilities** Those liabilities which may or may not arise because they are dependent on a happening in future. It is not recorded in the books of accounts but is disclosed in the notes to accounts for the information of the users. It is classified into claims against the company not acknowledged as debts, guarantees, other money for which the company is contingently liable.

(ii) **Capital Commitments** Financial commitments due to activities agreed by the company to be undertaken by it in future.

It is classified into

- Estimated amounts of contracts remaining to be executed on capital accounts and not provided for.
- Uncalled liability on shares and other investments partly paid.
- Other commitments (nature to be specified).

*As per CBSE circular, the accounting treatment of star marked items are not to be evaluated, however they have been given for the purpose of knowledge of students.

1.3 Statement of Profit and Loss

Statement of profit and loss shows the net result of business operations i.e. financial performance (profit earned or loss suffered) during an accounting period. The vertical form for preparing statement of profit and loss is prescribed under Schedule III, Part II of the Companies Act, 2013.

Characteristics of Statement of Profit and Loss

- It is prepared for a specific accounting period and not on a particular date.
- It is a historical document as it is prepared for a past period.
- It shows the financial performance of the business (i.e. profit earned or loss suffered during the period).

Format of Statement of Profit and Loss

Particulars	Note No.	Figures for the Current Reporting Period (₹)	Figures for the Previous Reporting Period (₹)
I. **Revenue from Operations**		...	...
II. **Other Income**		...	...
III. **Total Revenue** (I + II)		...	...
IV. **Expenses**			
Cost of Materials Consumed		...	...
Purchases of Stock-in-trade		...	...
Changes in Inventories of Finished Goods		...	...
Work-in-progress and Stock-in-trade		...	...
Employees Benefits Expenses		...	...
Finance Costs		...	...
Depreciation and Amortisation Expenses		...	...

	Particulars	Note No.	Figures for the Current Reporting Period (₹)	Figures for the Previous Reporting Period (₹)
	Other Expenses		...	...
	Total Expenses		...	...
V.	**Profit before Tax** (III – IV)		...	...
VI.	(–) Tax		...	...
VII.	**Profit after Tax** (V – VI)		...	...

Details of Contents of Statement of Profit and Loss

In statement of profit and loss only, so much information is to be disclosed as required. The remaining information is to be disclosed in the notes to accounts. e.g. Revenue from operations is to be shown as one consolidated amount and its components, i.e. sale of products, sale of services, etc., are to be shown in the notes to accounts.

1. Revenue from Operations

Revenue from operations means revenue earned by the company from its business operations (i.e. its operating activities) e.g. Sale of products is an operating activity for a manufacturing company or a trading company. Similarly, interest earned on loans and advances or dividend earned by a financing company is revenue from operations for a financing company.

Revenue from operations is to be classified into

- Sale of products (Net)
- Sale of services (Net)
- Other operating revenues such as sale of scrap

In the case of a finance company, revenue from operations shall include revenue from

- Interest income
- Dividend income
- Income from financial services
- Net gain/loss on sale of investments

2. Other Income

Other income means revenue that is not revenue from operations.

Other income is to be classified into

- Interest income (In case of a company other than a finance company).
- Dividend income (In case of a company other than a finance company).
- Net gain on sale of fixed assets.
- Other non-operating income (Net of expenses directly attributable to such income).
- Excess provision written back.
- Bad debts recovered.
- Rent received.
- Income from sale of investment.
- Sale of miscellaneous items.
- Refund of income tax.
- Discounts received, commission received.

3. Expenses

Expenses are to be classified into

(i) **Cost of Materials Consumed** It relates to a manufacturing company. It will consist of raw materials and other materials consumed in the process of manufacturing. In simple words,

Cost of Materials Consumed
= Opening Inventory of Materials + Purchases of Materials – Closing Inventory of Materials

(ii) **Purchases of Stock-in-trade** It relates to companies engaged in trading, i.e. purchase and sale of goods. Thus, it means and includes goods purchased with the purpose to resell. If the company carries out further processing on the goods purchased, then they do not remain as stock-in-trade but become part of materials consumed.

(iii) **Changes in Inventories of Finished Goods, Work-in-progress and Stock-in-trade** It is the difference between the opening inventories and closing inventories. It is to be disclosed separately for raw materials, work-in-progress and stock-in-trade. Net difference can be positive or negative between opening inventory and closing inventory.

(iv) **Employees Benefit Expenses** These are those expenses which are incurred on employees of the company. It will include expenses on

- Salaries and wages
- Bonus, leave encashment, etc.
- Staff welfare expenses such as canteen expenses, medical expenses, expenses on Employees Stock Option Scheme (ESOS), Employees Stock Purchase Plan (ESPP), etc.
- Contribution to provident fund and other funds

- Employee State Insurance (ESI)
- Gratuity payments
- Contribution to gratuity fund employees benefit expenses may be further categorised into direct and indirect expenses

(v) **Finance Cost** It means expenses incurred on borrowings (loans taken) by the company. It is classified into

- **Interest Expenses** It includes interest paid on term loans from bank, overdraft, cash credit limit from bank, debentures, public deposits and bonds.
- **Other Borrowing Costs** It includes discount or loss on issue of debentures written-off, premium payable on redemption of debentures written-off, loan processing charges, guarantee charges, commitment charges, commission paid for deposit mobilisation.

  Bank charges will not be shown under this head because it is not interest on borrowings but is a cost for services availed from the bank. It will be shown under 'other expenses'.

(vi) **Depreciation and Amortisation Expenses** Depreciation means writing-off the amount related to fixed tangible assets over their useful life. Depreciation is the diminution in the value of fixed assets whereas, amortisation means writing-off intangible assets.

(vii) **Other Expenses** All other expenses, which do not fall in the above categories, are shown or classified under 'other expenses'.

Other expenses may further be categorised into direct expenses, indirect expenses and non-operating expenses.

e.g. Consumption of loose tools (spare parts), stores, power and fuel, carriage, carriage inwards and carriage outwards, freight, manufacturing expenses, rent, rates and taxes (excluding tax on income), insurance less prepaid (if any), discount allowed, commission allowed, bad debts written-off, provision for bad debts, repairs to machinery, building and other fixed assets, trade expenses, administration, office and telephone expenses, excise duty paid, prior period expenses, bank charges, loss on sale of fixed assets, lease rent and computer hiring charges, director's fees, audit fee, conveyance expenses, travelling expenses, courier expenses, telephone and internet expenses, entertainment expenses, business promotion expenses, share issue expenses written-off, underwriting commission on issue of shares written-off.

*4. Exceptional Items

They are not defined in Schedule III. It has been defined in AS-5 on net profit or loss for the period, prior period items and changes in accounting policies.

Exceptional item is an income or expense that arises from transactions that are clearly distinct from ordinary activities of the business.

Exceptional items, as examples will include

- Reducing the value of inventories to net realisable value.
- Disposal of fixed assets.
- Disposal of long-term investments.
- Legislative changes having retrospective application.
- Reversals of provisions.

*5. Extraordinary Items

They are also not defined in Schedule III. However, it has been defined in AS-5 on net profit or loss for the period, prior period items and changes in accounting policies.

Extraordinary items are incomes or expenses that arise from events or transactions that are clearly distinct from ordinary activities of the enterprise and are not expected to recur frequently or regularly.

e.g. Compensation paid under voluntary retirement scheme.

*Exceptional items, extraordinary items and profit (loss) from discontinued operations are excluded from the syllabus. However, they have been given for the knowledge of students.

Quick View

Classification of various items of balance sheet under main head, sub-head and sub-sub-head (if any)

Items	Main Head	Sub-head	Sub-sub-head
• Debentures	Non-current Liabilities	Long-term Borrowings	
• Public Deposits	Non-current Liabilities	Long-term Borrowings	
• Securities Premium	Shareholders' Funds	Reserves and Surplus	
• Capital Reserve	Shareholders' Funds	Reserves and Surplus	
• Forfeited Shares Account	Shown in notes to accounts of share capital		
• Interest Accrued and Due on Debentures	Current Liabilities	Other Current Liabilities	
• Bills Payable	Current Liabilities	Trade Payables	
• Advance Received from Customers	Current Liabilities	Other Current Liabilities	
• Sundry Creditors	Current Liabilities	Trade Payables	
• Unclaimed Dividend	Current Liabilities	Other Current Liabilities	
• Calls-in-arrears	Shareholders' Funds	Subscribed Capital (Shown by way of deduction)	
• Interest Accrued but not Due on Debentures	Current Liabilities	Other Current Liabilities	
• Loose Tools	Current Assets	Inventories	
• Calls-in-advance	Current Liabilities	Other Current Liabilities	
• Premium on Redemption of Debentures	Non-current Liabilities	Other Long-term Liabilities	
• Balance with Banks	Current Assets	Cash and Cash Equivalents	
• Tax Reserve	Shareholders' Funds	Reserves and Surplus	
• Interest on Calls-in-advance	Current Liabilities	Other Current Liabilities	
• Stores and Spares	Current Assets	Inventories	
• Mining Rights	Non-current Assets	Property, Plant and Equipment and Intangible Assets	Intangible Assets
• Encashment of Employees Earned Leave Payable on Retirement	Non-current Liabilities	Long-term Provisions	
• Vehicles	Non-current Assets	Property, Plant and Equipment and Intangible Assets	Property, Plant and Equipment
• Subsidy Reserve	Shareholders' Funds	Reserves and Surplus	
• Provision for Doubtful Debts	Current Assets	Deduction from Trade Receivables	
• Sundry Debtors	Current Assets	Trade Receivables	
• Long-term Investments	Non-current Assets	Non-current Investments	
• Shares of XYZ Ltd.	Non-current Assets	Non-current Investments	
• Prepaid Insurance	Current Assets	Other Current Assets	
• Arrears of Fixed Cumulative Preference Dividend	As a footnote as contingent liability		
• Interest Accrued and Due on Secured Loans	Current Liabilities	Other Current Liabilities	

Items	Main Head	Sub-head	Sub-sub-head
• Interest Accrued but not Due on Unsecured Loans	Current Liabilities	Other Current Liabilities	
• Debenture Redemption Reserve	Shareholders' Funds	Reserves and Surplus	
• Capital Redemption Reserve	Shareholders' Funds	Reserves and Surplus	
• Advances from Customers (Long-term)	Non-current Liabilities	Other Long-term Liabilities	
• Trade Payables	Current Liabilities		
• Provision for Tax	Current Liabilities	Short-term Provisions	
• Surplus (i.e. balance in statement of profit and loss) (Cr)	Reserves and Surplus		
• Surplus (i.e. balance in statement of profit and loss) (Dr)	Reserves and Surplus	As negative amount	
• Mortgage Loan	Non-current Liabilities	Long-term Borrowings	
• Patents and Brand/Trademarks	Non-current Assets	Property, Plant and Equipment and Intangible Assets	Intangible Assets
• Investments	Non-current Assets	Non-current Investments	
• General Reserve	Shareholders' Funds	Reserves and Surplus	
• Bills Receivable	Current Assets	Trade Receivables	
• Deposit with Custom Authorities	Non-current Assets	Long-term Loans and Advances	
• Land and Buildings	Non-current Assets	Property, Plant and Equipment and Intangible Assets	Property, Plant and Equipment
• Interest Accrued on Investment	Current Assets	Other Current Assets	
• Unamortised Loss on Issue of Debentures (To be written-off after 12 months from the date of balance sheet)	Non-current Assets	Other Non-current Assets	
• Stock-in-trade	Current Assets	Inventories	
• Goodwill	Non-current Assets	Intangible Assets	
• Cash at Bank	Current Assets	Cash and Cash Equivalents	
• Authorised Capital	Share Capital		
• Outstanding Salary	Current Liabilities	Other Current Liabilities	
• Shares Options Outstanding Account	Shareholders' Funds	Reserves and Surplus	
• Government Securities	Non-current Assets	Non-current Investments	
• Commission Received in Advance	Current Liabilities	Other Current Liabilities	
• Uncalled Liability on Partly Paid Shares	Commitments in notes to accounts		
• Prepaid Rent	Current Assets	Other Current Assets	
• Computer Software under Development	Non-current Assets	Property, Plant and Equipment and Intangible Assets	Intangible Assets
• Bill Discounted but not Matured	Contingent liabilities in notes to accounts		
• Office Furniture	Non-current Assets	Property, Plant and Equipment and Intangible Assets	Property, Plant and Equipment
• Livestock	Non-current Assets	Property, Plant and Equipment and Intangible Assets	Property, Plant and Equipment
• Bills of Exchange	Current Assets	Trade Receivables	

Items	Main Head	Sub-head	Sub-sub-head
• Work-in-progress	Current Assets	Inventories	
• Advances Recoverable in Cash	Current Assets	Other Current Assets	
• Deferred Tax Assets (Net)	Non-current Assets	Deferred Tax Assets (Net)	
• Bonds	Non-current Liabilities	Long-term Borrowings	
• Unpaid Dividend	Current Liabilities	Other Current Assets	
• Dividend not Paid on Cumulative Preference Shares	Contingent liabilities in the notes to accounts		
• Share Application Money Pending Allotment	Share application money pending allotment is shown as a separate line item between equity and non-current liabilities		
• Loans Repayable on Demand	Current Liabilities	Short-term Borrowings	
• Preliminary Expenses	Reserves and Surplus	Deducted from Securities Premium Reserve	
• Contingent Liabilities and Commitments	To be shown as notes to accounts below the balance sheet		
• Trade Receivables	Current Assets		
• Inventories	Current Assets		
• Proposed Dividend	Current Liabilities	Short-term Provisions	

Important Note

According to CBSE Circular No. Acad-43/2013 dated 2nd July, 2013 on Schedule VI of the Companies Act, 1956 (Now Schedule III of the Companies Act, 2013) accounting treatment of certain items is not to be evaluated in the examination, but their presentation in the balance sheet can be examined.

According to the circular, accounting treatment of following will not be evaluated

- Reserves and surplus: (Revaluation reserve, share options outstanding and other reserves are not to be evaluated. However, general reserve can be evaluated);
- Money received against share warrants;
- Share application money pending allotment;
- Deferred tax liabilities (Net);
- Other long-term liabilities;
- Intangible assets: (Masthead and publishing titles, copyrights and patents and other intellectual property rights, services and operating rights and licenses and franchise are not to be evaluated);
- Capital work-in-progress;
- Intangible assets under development;
- Deferred tax assets (Net);
- Other non-current assets;
- Cash and cash equivalents: (Earmarked balance with banks, balances with banks held as margin money or security against borrowings, guarantees, other commitments and bank deposits with more than 12 months maturity are not to be evaluated); and
- Treatment of unamortised expenses.

Also, accounting treatment of other current assets is restricted to prepaid expenses, accrued incomes and advance tax only.

The expression' not to be evaluated' used in the circular, means that a student will not be examined for the above items in the examination in the topics of comparative statements, common size statements, accounting ratios and cash flow statement.

Mind Map

Financial Statements of a Company

1 Meaning of Financial Statements

- Financial statements are the end product of an accounting process.
- As per **Section 2 (40)** of the Companies Act, 2013, financial statements of a company include
  - Balance Sheet
  - Statement of Profit and Loss
  - Cash Flow Statement
  - Statement of Changes in Equity
  - Notes to Accounts

2 Nature of Financial Statements

- These are prepared on the basis of facts recorded.
- Certain accounting conventions are required to be followed while preparing statements.
- These are prepared on the basis of accounting concepts.
- They include personal judgements.

3 Objectives of Financial Statements

- To provide information of assets and liabilities.
- To provide information about earning capacity.
- To provide information to various parties.
- To provide information about cash flows.
- To give a true and fair view of financial performance of business.
- To give a true and fair view of financial position of business.

4 Importance of Financial Statements

- It provides basis for formulation of fiscal policy of the government.
- It provides basis for granting of loans by institutions.
- It helps investors to assess solvency of the company.
- It provides help to investors to know status, safety and return of their investments.

5 Limitations of Financial Statements

- These are historical in nature as they do not reflect the future prospects.
- These are affected by personal judgements.
- They ignore qualitative elements.
- They ignore price level changes.

6 Users of Financial Statements

- Internal users (include owners, management and employees).
- External users (include financial institutions, investors, creditors, government, SEBI, consumers etc).

Format of Balance Sheet
as per Schedule III, of Companies Act, 2013

Particulars	Note No.	Current Year (₹)	Previous Year (₹)
I. EQUITY AND LIABILITIES			
1. **Shareholder's Funds**			
(i) Share Capital		...	...
(ii) Reserves and Surplus		...	...
2. Share Application Money Pending Allotment		...	...
3. **Non-current Liabilities**			
(i) Long-term Borrowings		...	...
(ii) Long-term Provisions		...	...
4. **Current Liabilities** (Short-term borrowings, trade payables, other current liabilities, short-term provisions)		...	...
Total		...	...
II. ASSETS			
1. **Non-current Assets**			
(i) Property, Plant and Equipment and Intangible Assets		...	...
(ii) Non-current Investments		...	...
(iii) Long-term Loans and Advances		...	...
2. **Current Assets** (Current investments, inventories, trade receivablas, cash and cash equivalents, short-term loans and advances, other current assets)		...	...
Total		...	...

Format of Statement of Profit and Loss

Particulars	Note No.	Current Year (₹)	Previous Year (₹)
I. **Revenue from Operations**		...	...
II. **Other Income**		...	...
III. **Total Revenue** (I + II)		...	...
IV. **Expenses**			
Cost of Materials Consumed		...	...
Purchases of Stock-in-trade		...	...
Changes in Inventories of Finished Goods		...	...
Work-in-progress and Stock-in-trade		...	...
Employees Benefits Expenses		...	...
Finance Costs		...	...
Depreciation and Amortisation Expenses		...	...
Other Expenses		...	...
Total Expenses		...	...
V. **Profit before Tax** (III–IV)		...	...
VI. (–) **Tax**		(...)	(...)
VII. **Profit after Tax** (V – VI)		...	...

Topicwise Solved Questions

Balance Sheet

Solved Question 1 **FYI Ltd. has the following balances on 1st April, 2023**

General Reserve	₹ 1,00,000
Securities Premium	₹ 50,000
Statement of Profit and Loss	₹ (3,50,000)

During the year ended 31st March, 2024, it incurred a loss of ₹ 2,25,000. Show how these items will appear in the balance sheet and notes to accounts.

Sol. **An Extract of Balance Sheet**
as at 31st March, 2024

Particulars	Note No.	31st March, 2024 (₹)	31st March, 2023 (₹)
I. EQUITY AND LIABILITIES			
1. **Shareholders' Funds**			
Reserves and Surplus	1	(4,25,000)	(2,00,000)

Notes to Accounts

Particulars		Amt (₹)
1. **Reserves and Surplus**		
Securities Premium		50,000
General Reserve		1,00,000
Surplus		
Balance in Statement of P & L (Opening)	(3,50,000)	
Surplus (Loss) for the Period	(2,25,000)	(5,75,000)
		(4,25,000)

Solved Question 2 **Show the following items in a company's balance sheet as at 31st March, 2024**

Particulars	Amt (₹)
Trade Receivables	3,00,000
Inventories	5,00,000
Cash	10,000
Cheques, Drafts on Hand	50,000
Bank Overdraft	75,000
Land and Building	20,00,000
Goodwill	2,00,000
Patents	1,00,000

Sol. **An Extract of Balance Sheet**
as at 31st March, 2024

Particulars	Note No.	31st March, 2024 (₹)	31st March, 2023 (₹)
I. EQUITY AND LIABILITIES			
1. **Current Liabilities**			
Short-term Borrowings	1	75,000	—
II. ASSETS			
1. **Non-current Assets**			
(i) Property, Plant and Equipment and Intangible Assets			
(a) Property, Plant and Equipment	2	20,00,000	—
(b) Intangible Assets	3	3,00,000	—
2. **Current Assets**			
(i) Inventories		5,00,000	—
(ii) Trade Receivables		3,00,000	—
(iii) Cash and Cash Equivalents	4	60,000	—

Notes to Accounts

Particulars	Amt (₹)
1. **Short-term Borrowings**	
Bank Overdraft	75,000
2. **Property, Plant and Equipment**	
Land and Building	20,00,000
3. **Intangible Assets**	
Goodwill	2,00,000
Patents	1,00,000
	3,00,000
4. **Cash and Cash Equivalents**	
Cash	10,000
Cheques, Drafts on Hand	50,000
	60,000

Solved Question 3 **Following balances have been extracted from the books of Vardhman Ltd. on 31st March, 2018.**

Equity share capital (2,00,000 equity shares of ₹ 10 each) ₹ 20,00,000, securities premium ₹ 4,00,000, 12% debentures ₹ 10,00,000, creditors ₹ 4,00,000, dividend payable ₹ 1,00,000, surplus i.e. balance in statement of profit and loss (debit) ₹ 1,00,000, land and building ₹ 18,00,000, government bonds ₹ 10,00,000, intangible asset (patent) ₹ 7,00,000, discount on issue of 12% debentures ₹ 2,00,000, cash at bank ₹ 1,00,000. Debentures were issued on 1st April, 2014 redeemable after 5 years, i.e. on 31st March, 2019. Surplus, i.e. balance in statement of profit and loss is before writing-off discount on issue of debentures.

Prepare the balance sheet of the company as per Schedule III, Part I of the Companies Act, 2013.

Sol. **Balance Sheet**
as at 31st March, 2018

Particulars	Note No.	31st March, 2018 (₹)
I. EQUITY AND LIABILITIES		
1. **Shareholders' Funds**		
(i) Share Capital	1	20,00,000
(ii) Reserves and Surplus	2	2,60,000
2. **Non-current Liabilities**		
Long-term Borrowings	3	10,00,000
3. **Current Liabilities**		
(i) Trade Payables	4	4,00,000
(ii) Other Current Liabilities	5	1,00,000
Total		37,60,000
II. ASSETS		
1. **Non-current Assets**		
(i) Property, Plant and Equipment and Intangible Assets		
(a) Property, Plant and Equipment	6	18,00,000
(b) Intangible Assets	7	7,00,000
(ii) Non-current Investments	8	10,00,000
(iii) Other Non-current Assets	9	1,20,000
2. **Current Assets**		
(i) Cash and Cash Equivalents	10	1,00,000
(ii) Other Current Assets	11	40,000
Total		37,60,000

Notes to Accounts

Particulars	Amt (₹)
1. **Share Capital**	
Authorised Capital	
... Equity Shares of ₹ 10 each	...
Issued Capital	
... Equity Shares of ₹ 10 each	...
Subscribed Capital	
Subscribed and Fully Paid-up	
2,00,000 Equity Shares of ₹ 10 each	20,00,000
2. **Reserves and Surplus**	
Securities Premium	4,00,000
(–) Surplus, i.e. Balance in Statement of Profit and Loss*	(1,40,000)
	2,60,000
*Surplus i.e. Balance in Statement of Profit and Loss is after Writing-off ₹ 40,000 being 1/5th of Discount on Issue of 12% Debentures	
3. **Long-term Borrowings**	
12% Debentures	10,00,000
4. **Trade Payables**	
Creditors	4,00,000
5. **Other Current Liabilities**	
Dividend Payable	1,00,000
6. **Property, Plant and Equipment**	
Land and Building	18,00,000
7. **Intangible Assets**	
Patent	7,00,000
8. **Non-current Investments**	
Government Bonds	10,00,000
9. **Other Non-current Assets**	
Unamortised Discount on Issue of Debentures	1,20,000
10. **Cash and Cash Equivalents**	
Cash at Bank	1,00,000
11. **Other Current Assets**	
Unamortised Discount on Issue of Debentures	40,000

Statement of Profit and Loss

Solved Question 4 **Compute revenue from operations, other income and total income for a non-financial company from the following particulars**

Sales ₹ 60,00,000, sales return ₹ 3,00,000, sale of scrap ₹ 1,20,000, sale of miscellaneous items ₹ 15,000, refund of income tax ₹ 30,000, interest on time deposits ₹ 60,000.

Sol.

Particulars		Amt (₹)
I. **Revenue from Operations**		
Sales	60,00,000	
(–) Sales Return	(3,00,000)	57,00,000
Sales of Scrap		1,20,000
II. **Other Income**		
Sale of Miscellaneous Items	15,000	
Refund of Income Tax	30,000	
Interest on Time Deposits	60,000	1,05,000
Total Income (I + II)		59,25,000

Solved Question 5 **Calculate revenue from operations, other income and total revenue of a financial company from the following information. Miscellaneous income ₹ 10,000, interest on loans ₹ 55,00,000, dividend ₹ 2,00,000, profit on sale of building ₹ 30,00,000.**

Fees received for arranging loans ₹ 4,00,000, profit on sale of investments ₹ 1,00,000.

Sol. **Revenue from Operations**

Particulars		Amt (₹)
I. **Revenue from Operations**		
Interest on Loans		55,00,000
Dividend		2,00,000
Fees Received for Arranging Loans		4,00,000
Profit on Sale of Investment		1,00,000
		62,00,000
II. **Other Income**		
Profit on Sale of Building	30,00,000	
Miscellaneous Income	10,000	30,10,000
III. **Total Revenue** (I + II)		92,10,000

Solved Question 6 Calculate cost of materials consumed from the following

Particulars	Amt (₹)
Inventory of materials as at 1st April, 2023	80,000
Inventory of materials as at 31st March, 2024	1,00,000
Purchase of materials during the accounting year 2023-24	3,08,000
Return of materials purchased	3,000

Sol.

		Amt (₹)
Opening Inventory of Materials		80,000
(+) Purchase of Materials	3,08,000	
(–) Return of Materials	(3,000)	3,05,000
		3,85,000
(–) Closing Inventory of Materials		(1,00,000)
Cost of Material Consumed		2,85,000

Solved Question 7 From the following information for the year ended 31st March, 2024, prepare notes to accounts to determine the amount to be shown in statement of profit and loss against 'change in inventory'.

Particulars	Opening Inventory (₹)	Closing Inventory (₹)
Finished Goods	35,00,000	32,90,000
Work-in-progress (Semi-finished Goods)	17,50,000	21,00,000
Stock-in-trade	28,00,000	25,55,000
Materials	3,50,000	5,25,000

Sol. Notes to Accounts

Particulars		Year ended 31st March, 2024 (₹)
Changes in Inventories of Finished Goods, Work-in-progress and Stock-in-trade		
Opening Inventory of Finished Goods	35,00,000	
(–) Closing Inventory of Finished Goods	(32,90,000)	2,10,000
Opening Inventory of work-in-progress (WIP)	17,50,000	
(–) Closing Inventory of Work-in-progress	21,00,000	(3,50,000)
Opening Inventory of Stock-in-trade	28,00,000	
(–) Closing Inventory of Stock-in-trade	(25,55,000)	2,45,000
Total		1,05,000

Solved Question 8 From the following information for the year ended 31st March, 2018, prepare notes to accounts on employees benefit expenses.

(i) Wages ₹ 4,80,000
(ii) Salaries ₹ 7,20,000
(iii) Entertainment expenses ₹ 30,000
(iv) Bonus ₹ 1,00,000
(v) Gratuity paid ₹ 2,40,000
(vi) Conveyance expenses ₹ 50,000
(vii) Medical expenses ₹ 80,000

Sol. Notes to Accounts

Particulars	Amt (₹)
Employees Benefit Expenses	
Wages	4,80,000
Salaries	7,20,000
Bonus	1,00,000
Gratuity Paid	2,40,000
Medical Expenses	80,000
	16,20,000

Note Entertainment and conveyance expenses are not part of employees benefit.

Solved Question 9 From the following information of Evergreen Ltd. for the year ended 31st March, 2024, prepare the notes to accounts on finance costs.

(i) Interest paid on term loan ₹ 5,00,000
(ii) Interest paid on bank overdraft ₹ 70,000
(iii) Discount on issue of debentures written-off ₹ 20,000
(iv) Interest received on fixed deposits ₹ 50,000
(v) Bank charges ₹ 19,000
(vi) Interest paid on deposits ₹ 1,50,000

Sol. Notes to Accounts

Particulars	Amt (₹)
Finance Costs	
Interest on Term Loan	5,00,000
Interest Paid on Bank Overdraft	70,000
Interest Paid on Deposits	1,50,000
Discount on Issue of Debentures Written-off	20,000
	7,40,000

Solved Question 10 Prepare statement of profit and loss from the following information extracted from the books of NGO Ltd. as at 31st March, 2024

Particulars	Amt (₹)
Sales	25,00,000
Purchase of Stock-in-trade	15,00,000
Wages	5,00,000
Interest Received	30,000
Bonus	60,000
Gratuity Paid	40,000
Opening Stock-in-trade	1,50,000
Closing Stock-in-trade	2,50,000
Cost of Material Consumed	2,00,000
Salaries	30,000
Sale of Scrap	5,000
Depreciation of Machinery	10,000
10% Debentures (Issued on 1st April, 2023)	2,00,000

Sol. **Statement of Profit and Loss**
for the year ended 31st March, 2024

Particulars	Note No.	Amt (₹)
I. Revenue from Operations	1	25,05,000
II. Other Income	2	30,000
III. Total Revenue (I + II)		25,35,000

Particulars	Note No.	Amt (₹)
IV. Expenses		
Purchase of Stock-in-trade		15,00,000
Changes in Inventories of Stock-in-trade	3	(1,00,000)
Employee Benefit Expenses	4	6,30,000
Cost of Material Consumed		2,00,000
Depreciation and Amortisation		10,000
Finance Cost	5	20,000
Total Expenses		22,60,000
Profit before Tax (III – IV)		2,75,000

Notes to Accounts

Particulars		Amt (₹)
1. **Revenue from Operations**		
Sales		25,00,000
Sales of Scrap		5,000
		25,05,000
2. **Other Income**		
Interest Received		30,000
3. **Changes in Inventories of Stock-in-trade**		
Opening Inventory	1,50,000	
(–) Closing Inventory	(2,50,000)	(1,00,000)
4. **Employee Benefit Expenses**		
Wages		5,00,000
Bonus		60,000
Gratuity Paid		40,000
Salaries		30,000
		6,30,000
5. **Finance Cost**		
Interest on Debentures (10% of ₹ 2,00,000)		20,000

Numerical Questions

Balance Sheet

1. ZTE Ltd. has an authorised capital of ₹ 20,00,000 divided into equity shares of ₹ 10 each. The company invited applications for 1,50,000 equity shares.

The amount was payable as follows

On application ₹ 3, on allotment ₹ 5 and on final call ₹ 2.

The public applied for 1,40,000 shares and all the money was duly received.

Show how share capital will appear in the balance sheet of the company? Also prepare notes to accounts.

Ans. Subscribed and Fully Paid Capital = ₹ 14,00,000

2. ABC Ltd. has the following balances on 1st April, 2023

General Reserve ₹ 2,25,000
Statement of Profit and Loss ₹ 1,00,000

During the year ended 31st March, 2024, it incurred a loss of ₹ 1,00,000.

How would you show these items in the balance sheet and notes to accounts?

3. Show the following items in a company's balance sheet as at 31st March, 2024 **Competency Based Que**

Particulars	Amt (₹)
Provision for Taxation	75,000
Provision for Employee Benefits (Maturing within 12 months)	10,000
Public Deposit	2,00,000
Calls-in-advance	12,500
Outstanding Expenses	5,000
Computer Software	3,00,000
Vehicles	25,00,000
Office Equipment	5,00,000
Trademark	1,00,000

Ans. Notes to Accounts : Other Current Liabilities = ₹ 17,500; Short-term Provisions = ₹ 85,000; Tangible Assets = ₹ 30,00,000; Intangible Assets = ₹ 4,00,000

4. Prepare balance sheet of the company as per Schedule III of the Companies Act, 2013. **Competency Based Que**

Particulars	Amt (₹)
10% Debentures of ₹ 100 each	3,80,000
Stock-in-trade (Inventories)	80,000
Goodwill	40,000
Provision for Tax	12,000

Totalling of balance sheet is not required.

Ans. Long-term Borrowings (10% debentures) = ₹ 3,80,000; Short-term Provisions (Provisions for tax) = ₹ 12,000; Property, Plant and Equipment and Intangible Assets (Goodwill) = ₹ 40,000; Current Assets (Inventories) = ₹ 80,000

Statement of Profit and Loss

5. Compute revenue from operations, other income and total income for a non-financial company from the following particulars

Total sales ₹ 3,00,000, sales return ₹ 15,000, sale of scrap ₹ 6,000, dividend received ₹ 750, refund of income tax ₹ 1,500, interest on debentures ₹ 3,000.

Ans. Revenue from Operations = ₹ 2,91,000; Other Income = ₹ 5,250; Total Income = ₹ 2,96,250

6. **Determine revenue from operations, other income and total revenue for a financial company using the following details**

Interest received on debentures ₹ 27,50,000, dividend received ₹ 1,00,000, profit on sale of building ₹ 15,00,000, bad debts recovered ₹ 5,000, fees received for arranging loans ₹ 2,00,000, profit on sale of investments ₹ 50,000.

Ans. Revenue from Operations = ₹ 31,00,000; Other Income ₹ 15,05,000; Total Income = ₹ 46,05,000

7. **From the following information, calculate revenue from operations and other income for a manufacturing company.** **Competency Based Que**

For the year ended 31st March, 2024.

Particulars	Amt (₹)
Sale of Products	17,50,000
Sale of Services	2,25,000
Commission Received in the Normal Course of Business	15,000
Excise Duty Paid	75,000
Dividends Received from Shares	25,000
Interest Received on Deposits	80,000
Loss on Sale of Investments	10,000
Income from Sub-letting	48,000
Expenses for Collecting Rent	4,000

Ans. Revenue from Operations = ₹ 19,15,000; Other Income = ₹ 1,39,000

8. **Calculate cost of material consumed from the information given below** **Competency Based Que**

Opening Inventory	
Raw Material	₹ 1,25,000
Work-in-progress	₹ 4,75,000
Finished Goods	₹ 2,25,000
Raw Material Purchased during the Year	₹ 9,75,000
Closing Inventory	
Raw Material	₹ 3,15,000
Work-in-progress	₹ 1,25,000
Finished Goods	₹ 4,75,000

Ans. Cost of Raw Material Consumed = ₹ 7,85,000

9. **From the following information of JCB Ltd. for the year ended 31st March, 2024, calculate amount that will be shown in note to accounts on changes in inventories of finished goods, work-in-progress and stock-in-trade.**

Particulars	Opening Inventory (₹)	Closing Inventory (₹)
Finished Goods	2,50,000	2,75,000
Work-in-progress (WIP)	2,25,000	2,12,500
Stock-in-trade	3,25,000	3,00,000

Ans. Change in Inventories of Finished Goods = ₹ (25,000); Work-in-progress = ₹ 12,500; Stock-in-trade = ₹ 25,000; Net Change = ₹ 12,500

10. **From the following information for the year ended 31st March, 2024, prepare notes to accounts on employees benefit expenses.**

(i) Wages and Salaries	₹ 7,50,000
(ii) Bonus Paid	₹ 2,50,000
(iii) Entertainment Expenses	₹ 50,000
(iv) Contribution towards Provident Fund	₹ 75,000

Ans. ₹ 10,75,000

11. **From the following information, prepare notes to accounts on finance costs**

Interest paid to bank ₹ 37,500, interest on debentures ₹ 29,000, loss on issue of debentures written-off ₹ 13,750 and commitment charges ₹ 7,500.

Ans. ₹ 87,750

12. **Prepare statement of profit and loss from the following balances extracted from the books of Aisha Ltd. as 31st March, 2024.** **Competency Based Que**

Particulars	Amt (₹)
Sale	7,50,000
Cost of Materials Consumed	8,00,000
10% Debentures (Issued on 1st April, 2023)	1,00,000
Depreciation on Machinery	15,000
Wages	9,00,000
Salaries	30,000
Sale of Scrap	5,000

Ans. Revenue from Operations = ₹ 7,55,000; Employee benefit Expenses = ₹ 1,20,000; Finance Cost = ₹ 10,000

Theoretical Questions

Short Answer Type Questions

1. Under which head the following items of a non-financial company will be shown?

(i) Sale of scrap
(ii) Dividend received
(iii) Sales
(iv) Profit on sale of investment
(v) Interest earned
(vi) Profit on sale of fixed asset

Ans. **Revenue from Operations** Sales, sale of scrap.

Other Income Interest earned, profit on sale of fixed asset, dividend received, profit on sale of investment.

2. Under which head the following items of a financial company will be shown?

(i) Dividend received
(ii) Refund of income tax
(iii) Interest earned
(iv) Profit on sale of property, plant and equipment
(v) Profit on sale of investment

Ans. **Revenue from Operations** Interest earned, dividend received, profit on sale of investment.

Other Income Profit on sale of property, plant and equipment, refund of income tax.

3. Identify which of the following items will be shown in the notes to accounts on employee benefit expenses?

(i) Wages (ii) Staff welfare expenses
(iii) Bonus
(iv) Office expenses
(v) Expenses on employees stock option scheme
(vi) Salaries
(vii) Leave encashment expenses
(viii) Entertainment expenses
(ix) Gratuity paid

Ans. Items to be shown in the notes to accounts on employee benefits expenses are

Salaries, staff welfare expenses, wages, bonus, gratuity paid, leave encashment expenses, expenses on employees stock option scheme.

4. Identify the items to be shown in the notes to accounts on finance cost

(i) Interest paid on bank overdraft
(ii) Bank charges
(iii) Interest paid on public deposit
(iv) Interest paid on term loan
(v) Guarantee charges
(vi) Commission paid for deposit mobilisation
(vii) Loss on issue of debentures written-off

Ans. All items except bank charges will be shown in the notes to accounts on finance cost. Bank charges are not included in finance cost because they are not incurred in connection with loan but for availing the services provided by the bank.

5. Out of the following, identify the items to be shown in the notes to accounts on other expenses.

(i) Carriage inwards
(ii) Salaries
(iii) Rent for factory
(iv) Computer software amortised
(v) Depreciation on computer
(vi) Commission allowed
(vii) Leave encashment expenses
(viii) Bad debts written-off
(ix) Internet expenses
(x) Audit fee

Ans. Items to be shown in notes to accounts on other expenses are
Carriage inwards, rent for factory, commission allowed, audit fee, bad debts written-off, internet expenses.

6. State under which major heading will the following items be presented in the statement of profit and loss of a company? **Competency Based Que**

(i) Sale of products (ii) Wages
(iii) Sale of scrap (iv) Interest earned
(v) Bonus (vi) Material purchased
(vii) Goodwill amortised

Ans.

S. No.	Items	Major Heads
(i)	Sale of Products	Revenue from Operations
(ii)	Wages	Employee Benefit Expenses
(iii)	Sale of Scrap	Revenue from Operations
(iv)	Interest Earned	Other Income
(v)	Bonus	Employee Benefit Expenses
(vi)	Material Purchased	Cost of Material Consumed
(vii)	Goodwill Amortised	Depreciation and Amortisation Expenses

7. State under which major heading will the following items be presented in the statement of profit and loss of a company? **Competency Based Que**

(i) Interest on public deposit
(ii) Entertainment expenses
(iii) Interest expenses

(iv) Purchase of stock-in-trade
(v) Discount on issue of debentures written-off
(vi) Interest on term loan

Ans.

S. No.	Items	Major Heads
(i)	Interest on Public Deposit	Finance Cost
(ii)	Entertainment Expenses	Other Expenses
(iii)	Interest Expenses	Other Expenses
(iv)	Purchase of Stock-in-trade	Purchase of Stock-in-trade
(v)	Discount on Issue of Debentures Written-off	Finance Cost
(vi)	Revenue from Services Rendered	Revenue from Operations
(vii)	Interest on Term Loan	Finance Cost

8. Classify the following items under major heads and sub-heads (if any) in the balance sheet of a company as per Schedule III, Part I of the Companies Act, 2013.
CBSE 2025; Competency Based Que

(i) Work-in-progress (ii) Securities premium
(iii) Creditors

Ans.

S. No.	Items	Heads	Sub-heads
(i)	Working-in-progress	Current Assets	Inventories
(ii)	Securities Premium	Shareholders' Funds	Reserve and Surplus
(iii)	Creditors	Current Liabilities	Trade Payables

9. Name any five items that can be disclosed under 'current investments'.

Ans. The items that can be disclosed under 'current investments' are as follows
(i) Investment in equity instruments.
(ii) Investment in preference shares.
(iii) Investment in government or trust securities.
(iv) Investment in debentures or bonds.
(v) Investment in mutual funds.

10. Name any five items that can be disclosed under 'long-term borrowings'.

Ans. The items that are presented under 'long-term borrowings' are
(i) Bonds/Debentures (ii) Term loans
(iii) Deferred payment liabilities
(iv) Deposits
(v) Loans and advances from related parties

11. List the items which are shown under the heading 'current liabilities' as per Schedule III, Part I of the Companies Act, 2013.

Ans. Items shown under the heading 'current liabilities' are
(i) Short-term borrowings (ii) Trade payables
(iii) Other current liabilities
(iv) Short-term provisions

12. List the items which are shown under the heading 'current assets' as per Schedule III, Part I of the Companies Act, 2013.

Ans. The items which are shown under the heading 'current assets' are
(i) Current investments
(ii) Inventories
(iii) Trade receivables
(iv) Cash and cash equivalents
(v) Short-term loans and advances
(vi) Other current assets

13. Show the major headings into which the equity and liabilities side of a company's balance sheet is organised and presented as per Schedule III, Part I of the Companies Act, 2013.

Ans. The major heading into which the equity and liabilities side is organised are
(i) Shareholders' funds
(ii) Share application money pending allotment
(iii) Non-current liabilities
(iv) Current liabilities

14. List the items, which are shown under the heading 'shareholders' funds' as per Schedule III, Part I of the Companies Act, 2013.

Ans. The items that are presented under 'shareholders' funds are
(i) Share capital
(ii) Reserves and surplus
(iii) Money received against share warrants

15. List the items which are shown under the heading 'non-current assets' as per Schedule III, Part I of the Companies Act, 2013.

Ans. The items which are shown under the heading 'non-current assets' are
(i) Property, plant and equipment and intangible assets
(ii) Non-current investments
(iii) Deferred tax assets (Net)
(iv) Long-term loans and advances
(v) Other non-current assets

16. List the items which are shown under 'property, plant and equipment and intangible assets' as per Schedule III, Part I of the Companies Act, 2013.

Ans. The items which are shown under 'property, plant and equipment and intangible assets' are
(i) Property, plant and equipment
(ii) Intangible assets (iii) Capital work-in-progress
(iv) Intangible assets under development

17. Name the items that can be disclosed under 'short-term borrowings.'

Ans. The items that can be disclosed under 'short-term borrowings' are

(i) Loans repayable on demand
(ii) Bank overdraft or cash credit from banks
(iii) Loans from other parties repayable with 12 months from the date of loan
(iv) Deposits
(v) Other loans and advances (nature to be specified)

18. Name the items that can be disclosed under 'short-term provisions'.

Ans. The items that can be disclosed under 'short-term provisions' are

(i) Provision for employee benefits
(ii) Provision for expenses
(iii) Provision for tax
(iv) Proposed dividend
(v) Other provisions

19. Name the items that can be disclosed under 'long-term loans and advances.'

Ans. The items that can be disclosed under 'long-term loans and advances' are

(i) Capital advances (ii) Security deposits
(iii) Other loans and advances

20. List the items that are included under the head 'non-current investments.'

Ans. The items that are included under the head 'non-current investments' are

(i) Investment in property
(ii) Investment in equity instruments
(iii) Investment in preference shares
(iv) Investment in debentures or bonds
(v) Investment in mutual funds

21. Name any five items of property, plant and equipment.

Ans. The five items of property, plant and equipment are

(i) Land (ii) Building
(iii) Plant and equipment
(iv) Furniture and fixtures
(v) Vehicles

22. Name any five items of intangible assets.

Ans. The five items of intangible assets are

(i) Goodwill (ii) Brand/Trademark
(iii) Computer software
(iv) Mining rights
(v) Licenses and franchise

23. Name any two items that are shown under the head 'other current liabilities' and any two items that are shown under the head 'other current assets' in the balance sheet of a company as per Schedule III of the Companies Act, 2013.

Ans. The two items shown under the head 'other current liabilities' are

(i) Unpaid dividends
(ii) Income received in advance

The two items shown under the head 'other current assets' are

(i) Prepaid expenses
(ii) Advance taxes

24. List any four items of 'reserves' that are shown under the heading 'reserves and surplus' in the balance sheet of a company as per Schedule III of the Companies Act, 2013.

Ans. The four items shown under the heading 'reserves and surplus' are

(i) Capital reserve
(ii) Securities premium
(iii) Capital redemption reserve
(iv) Debenture redemption reserve

25. Classify the following items under major heads and sub-heads (if any) in the balance sheet of the company as per Schedule III, Part I of the Companies Act, 2013. **CBSE 2024 C; Competency Based Que**

(i) Copyrights
(ii) Interest accrued on investments
(iii) Long-term investment in shares

Ans.

S. No.	Items	Major Heads	Sub-heads
(i)	Copyrights	Non-current Assets	Fixed Assets (Property, Plant and Equipment and Intangible Assets) – Intangible Assets
(ii)	Interest accrued on Investments	Current Assets	Other Current Assets
(iii)	Long-term Investment in Shares	Non-current Assets	Non-current Investments

26. Identify the major heads under which of the following items will be shown in the balance sheet of a company as per Schedule III of Companies Act, 2013? **Competency Based Que**

(i) Provision for tax
(ii) Loans payable on demand
(iii) Computer and related equipment
(iv) Goods acquired for trading

Ans.

S. No.	Items	Major Heads
(i)	Provision for Tax	Current Liabilities
(ii)	Loans Payable on Demand	Current Liabilities
(iii)	Computer and Related Equipment	Non-current Assets
(iv)	Goods Acquired for Trading	Current Assets

27. (i) Give the meaning of 'long-term provisions'.

(ii) List any four items other than 'stock-in-trade' that are presented under the sub-head 'inventories' as per Schedule III of the Companies Act, 2013.

Ans. (i) Long-term provisions are the provisions against which liability will arise after 12 months of the date of balance sheet or after the period of operating cycle. e.g. Provision made for retirement benefits payable to employees who will retire after 12 months from the date of balance sheet, provision for warranty claims that relates to the period after 12 months of the date of balance sheet.

(ii) The items other than 'stock-in-trade' that are presented under the sub-head 'inventories' are

(a) Raw material (b) Work-in-progress

(c) Finished goods (d) Stores and spares

28. Classify the following items under major heads and sub-heads (if any) in the balance sheet of a company as per Schedule III, Part I of the Companies Act, 2013.
CBSE 2023; Competency Based Que

(i) Licenses and franchise
(ii) Loans repayable on demand
(iii) Accrued income

Ans.

S. No.	Items	Major Heads	Sub-heads
(i)	Licenses and Franchise	Non-current Assets	Intangible Assets
(ii)	Loans Repayable on Demand	Current Liabilities	Short-term Borrowings
(iii)	Accrued Income	Current Assets	Other Current Assets

29. Classify the following items under major heads and sub-heads (if any) in the balance sheet of the company as per Schedule III Part I of the Companies Act, 2013.
CBSE 2024; Competency Based Que

(i) Long-term loans from bank
(ii) Loose tools
(iii) Outstanding expenses

Ans.

S. No.	Items	Major Heads	Sub-heads
(i)	Long-term Loans from Bank	Non-current Liabilities	Long-term Borrowings
(ii)	Loose Tools	Current Assets	Inventories
(iii)	Outstanding Expenses	Current Liabilities	Other Current Liabilities

30. Classify the following items under major heads and sub-heads (if any) in the balance sheet of a company as per Schedule III, Part I of the Companies Act, 2013.
CBSE 2024; Competency Based Que

(i) Calls-in-advance (ii) Mining rights
(iii) Loose tools

Ans.

S. No.	Items	Heads	Sub-heads
(i)	Calls-in-advance	Current Liabilities	Other Current Liabilities
(ii)	Mining Rights	Non-current Assets	Fixed Assets (Property, Plant and Equipment and Intangible Assets) – Intangible Assets
(iii)	Loose Tools	Current Assets	Inventories

31. State under which major headings and sub-headings will the following items be presented in the balance sheet of a company as per Schedule III, Part I of the Companies Act, 2013? **CBSE 2019; Competency Based Que**

(i) Prepaid insurance
(ii) Investment in debentures
(iii) Calls-in-arrears (iv) Unpaid dividend
(v) Capital reserve (vi) Loose tools
(vii) Capital work-in-progress
(viii) Patents being developed by the company.

Ans.

S. No.	Major Heads	Sub-heads
(i)	Current Assets	Other Current Assets
(ii)	Non-current Assets	Non-current Investments
(iii)	Shareholders' Funds	Share Capital (Notes to accounts)
(iv)	Current Liabilities	Other Current Liabilities
(v)	Shareholders' Funds	Reserves and Surplus
(vi)	Current Assets	Inventories
(vii)	Non-current Assets	Property, Plant and Equipment and Intangible Assets
(viii)	Non-current Assets	Intangible Assets under Development

32. Under which major headings and sub-headings will the following items be presented in the balance sheet of a company as per Schedule III, Part I of the Companies Act, 2013? **CBSE 2019; Competency Based Que**

(i) Interest accrued and due on debentures
(ii) Loose tools
(iii) Accrued interest on calls-in-advance
(iv) Interest due on calls-in-arrears
(v) Trademarks
(vi) Premium on redemption of debentures
(vii) Plant and machinery
(viii) Patents

Ans.

S. No.	Major Heads	Sub-heads
(i)	Current Liabilities	Other Current Liabilities
(ii)	Current Assets	Inventories
(iii)	Current Liabilities	Other Current Liabilities
(iv)	Current Assets	Other Current Assets
(v)	Non-current Assets	Property, Plant and Equipment and Intangible Assets
(vi)	Non-current Liabilities	Other Non-current Liabilities
(vii)	Non-current Assets	Property, Plant and Equipment (Tangible)
(viii)	Non-current Assets	Property, Plant and Equipment and Intangible Assets

33. Under which major heads and sub-heads will the following items be placed in the balance sheet of the company as per Schedule III, Part I of the Companies Act, 2013?

(i) Cheques and bank drafts in hand
(ii) Loose tools
(iii) Securities premium
(iv) Long-term investments with maturity period less than six months
(v) Work-in-progress (vi) Mining rights
(vii) Publishing titles
(viii) Debtors **All India 2019; Competency Based Que**

Ans.

S. No.	Major Heads	Sub-heads
(i)	Current Assets	Cash and Cash Equivalents
(ii)	Current Assets	Inventories
(iii)	Shareholders' Fund	Reserves and Surplus
(iv)	Current Assets	Current Investments
(v)	Current Assets	Inventories
(vi)	Non-current Assets	Intangible Assets
(vii)	Non-current Assets	Intangible Assets
(viii)	Current Assets	Trade Receivables

34. Classify the following items under major heads and Sub-heads (if any) in the balance sheet of a company as per Schedule III, Part I of the Companies Act, 2013. **CBSE 2024; Competency Based Que**

(i) Accrued income
(ii) Capital advances
(iii) Capital work-in-progress

Ans.

S. No.	Items	Major Heads	Sub-heads
(i)	Accrued Income	Current Assets	Other Current Assets
(ii)	Capital Advances	Non-current Assets	Long-term Loans and Advances
(iii)	Capital Work-in-progress	Non-current Assets	Property, Plant and Equipment

35. Find the heads and sub-heads under which of the following items will appear in the balance sheet of a company as per Schedule III, Part I of Companies Act, 2013?

(i) Furniture and fixture
(ii) Advance paid to contractor for building under construction
(iii) Accrued income
(iv) Loans repayable on demand to bank
(v) Employees earned leaves payable on retirement
(vi) Employees earned leaves encashable

CBSE SQP 2025; Competency Based Que

Ans.

S. No.	Items	Heads	Sub-heads
(i)	Furniture and Fixture	Non-current Assets	Property, Plant and Equipment
(ii)	Advance paid to Contractor for Building under Construction	Non-current Assets	Long-term Loans and Advances
(iii)	Accrued Income	Current Assets	Other Current Assets
(iv)	Loans Repayable on Demand to Bank	Current Liabilities	Short-term Borrowings
(v)	Employees earned Leaves payable on Retirement	Non-current Liabilities	Long-term Provisions
(vi)	Employees earned Leaves Encashable	Current Liabilities	Short-term Provisions

Objective Questions

Multiple Choice Questions (MCQs)

1. 'Loose tools' appear in the company's balance sheet under the head/sub-head. CBSE 2020

(a) Inventory (b) Non-current assets
(c) Other current assets (d) Stores and spare parts

2. 'Calls-in-advance' appears in the company's balances sheet under the head. CBSE 2020

(a) Non-current assets (b) Current liabilities
(c) Shareholders' funds (d) Non-current liabilities

3. 'Public deposits' appear in the company's balance sheet under the head/sub-head. CBSE 2020

(a) Intangible assets (b) Current liabilities
(c) Shareholders' funds (d) Non-current liabilities

4. 'Income received in advance' appears in the balance sheet of a company under the sub-head .... CBSE 2020 (M)

(a) other current liabilities
(b) other current assets
(c) other non-current liabilities
(d) None of the above

5. 'Prepaid insurance' appears in the balance sheet of a company under the sub-head .... CBSE 2020 (M)

(a) other current liabilities
(b) other current assets
(c) other non-current liabilities
(d) None of the above

6. ABC Ltd. provides the following information for the year ending 31st March, 2024

(i) Equity share capital = ₹ 10,00,000
(ii) Long-term borrowings = ₹ 5,00,000
(iii) Fixed assets = ₹ 12,00,000
(iv) Trade receivables = ₹ 3,00,000
(v) Reserves and surplus = ₹ 1,50,000
(vi) Cash and cash equivalents = ₹ 1,50,000

Calculate the total equity and liabilities to be reported in the balance sheet. Competency Based Que

(a) ₹ 17,50,000 (b) ₹ 18,50,000
(c) ₹ 16,50,000 (d) ₹ 15,00,000

7. 'Security deposits' appear in the balance sheet of a company under the sub-head .... CBSE 2020 (M)

(a) other current liabilities (b) other current assets
(c) other non-current liabilities
(d) None of the above

8. 10% debentures are included in

(a) current liability
(b) property, plant and equipment and intangible assets
(c) current assets
(d) None of the above

9. Prepaid rent is a

(a) current asset
(b) property, plant and equipment and intangible assets
(c) current liability
(d) None of the above

10. Staff welfare expenses are included in

(a) cost of material consumed
(b) revenue from operation
(c) employees benefit expense
(d) None of the above

11. External users of financial statements are

(a) banks (b) suppliers
(c) Both (a) and (b) (d) director of company

12. In a trading firm, if stock of finished goods held for a month and credit period is 2 months, then operating cycle will be for .... month(s).

(a) one (b) two
(c) three (d) four

13. Per share value of equity share capital and preference share capital is shown as

(a) par value (b) issued price
(c) face value (d) Either (a) or (c)

14. The reserve set aside for a defined purpose and treated as a charge against revenue is known as

(a) capital reserve (b) general reserve
(c) hidden reserve (d) specific reserve

15. Under which heading and sub-heading sundry debtors are shown?

(a) Property, plant and equipment and intangible assets, trade receivables
(b) Current assets, trade receivables
(c) Property, plant and equipment and intangible assets, trade payables
(d) Current assets, trade payables

16. If expected period of payment of trade payables is 10 months and operating cycle is of 15 months it is a .... liability.

(a) non-current (b) current
(c) Either (a) or (b) (d) None of these

17. **Statement of profit and loss is also known as ....**
(a) income statement (b) assets statement
(c) liabilities statement (d) None of these

18. **Minimum subscription prescribed for allotment of shares is ...... of share issued.**
(a) 100% (b) 90% (c) 50% (d) 30%

19. **From the following information, compute cost of materials consumed.** **Competency Based Que**

Opening inventory of materials ₹ 2,50,000, purchased ₹ 20,00,000, closing inventory of materials ₹ 3,00,000.
(a) ₹ 20,50,000 (b) ₹ 19,50,000
(c) ₹ 14,50,000 (d) ₹ 25,50,000

20. **From the following information, compute revenue from operations for a financial company.** **Competency Based Que**

Miscellaneous income ₹ 2,500, interest on loan ₹ 4,00,000, dividend ₹ 50,000, profit on sale of building ₹ 7,50,000.
(a) ₹ 7,52,500 (b) ₹ 12,02,500
(c) ₹ 4,50,000 (d) ₹ 7,52,500

21. **From the following information, calculate other incomes.** **Competency Based Que**

Sales of product ₹ 54,000, sale of services ₹ 60,000, commission received ₹ 1,20,000, excise duty paid ₹ 3,00,000, dividend from investment ₹ 20,000.
(a) ₹ 1,40,000 (b) ₹ 2,54,000
(c) ₹ (46,000) loss (d) None of these

22. **From the following information, you are required to compute profit after tax.** **Competency Based Que**
(i) Revenue from operation = ₹ 80,00,000
(ii) Cost of material consumed = ₹ 10,00,000
(iii) Purchase of stock-in-trade = ₹ 30,00,000
(iv) Employees salary = ₹ 4,00,000
(v) Tax rate = 50%
(a) ₹ 20,00,000 (b) ₹ 24,00,000
(c) ₹ 15,00,000 (d) ₹ 18,00,000

23. **From the following information, compute total revenue for a non-financial company.** **Competency Based Que**

Sales ₹ 6,00,000, sales return ₹ 1,00,000, sale of scrap ₹ 12,500, interest on fixed deposit ₹ 15,000, dividend earned ₹ 5,000.
(a) ₹ 5,32,500 (b) ₹ 5,00,000
(c) ₹ 5,12,500 (d) ₹ 20,000

24. **A company has an operating cycle of eight months. It has accounts receivables amounting to ₹ 1,00,000 out of which ₹ 60,000 have a maturity period of 11 months. How would this information be presented in the balance sheet?** **CBSE SQP Term I 2021; Competency Based Que**
(a) ₹ 40,000 as current assets and ₹ 60,000 as non-current assets
(b) ₹ 60,000 as current assets and ₹ 40,000 as non-current assets
(c) ₹ 1,00,000 as non-current assets
(d) ₹ 1,00,000 as current assets

25. **Ajanta Ltd. issued 10% debentures of ₹ 8,00,000 on 1st April, 2019 which are redeemable in five equal yearly instalments starting from 1st April, 2022. How would this information be presented in the balance sheet as at 31st March, 2021?**
CBSE Term I 2021; Competency Based Que
(a) ₹ 8,00,000 as long-term borrowings
(b) ₹ 8,00,000 as other non-current liability
(c) ₹ 8,00,000 as current liability
(d) ₹ 1,60,000 as other current liability and ₹ 6,40,000 as long-term borrowing

26. **Which of the following will be included under shareholder's funds?**
(a) General reserve of ₹ 50,000
(b) Public deposits amounting to ₹ 1,20,000
(c) Trade receivables of ₹ 83,000
(d) Provision for taxation of ₹ 1,20,000

27. **What will be the amount shown under the head current liabilities when the following data is given? Short-term borrowings ₹ 3,00,000, trade payables ₹ 2,00,000, other current liabilities ₹ 1,00,000, short-term provisions ₹ 1,00,000.** **Competency Based Que**
(a) ₹ 5,00,000 (b) ₹ 6,00,000
(c) ₹ 4,00,000 (d) ₹ 7,00,000

28. **Which of the following item can be presented on the asset side of the balance sheet of a company?**
Competency Based Que
(a) Sundry debtors of ₹ 93,000
(b) Public deposits of ₹ 2,20,000
(c) Livestock of ₹ 1,20,000
(d) Both (a) and (c)

Assertion-Reason

Direction (Q.No. 29 to 38) *Read the following Assertion (A) and Reason (R) and choose the correct alternative from the following*

Alternatives
(a) Both Assertion (A) and Reason (R) are true and Reason (R) is the correct explanation of Assertion (A)
(b) Both Assertion (A) and Reason (R) are true, but Reason (R) is not the correct explanation of Assertion (A)
(c) Assertion (A) is true, but Reason (R) is false
(d) Assertion (A) is false, but Reason (R) is true

29. **Assertion** (A) Financial statements are based on historical costs.
Reason (R) Historical cost ensures that assets are presented at their market value.

30. **Assertion** (A) Financial statements are prepared using accounting conventions.
Reason (R) Accounting conventions like conservatism and materiality ensure reliability and comparability of financial statements.

31. **Assertion** (A) Financial statements reflect a mix of recorded facts and personal judgements.
Reason (R) Personal judgements are excluded from all aspects of financial reporting.

32. **Assertion** (A) Financial statements are prepared based on the going concern postulate.
Reason (R) This postulate assumes that the business will not continue in the foreseeable future.

33. **Assertion** (A) Financial statements of a company must be prepared in accordance with Schedule III of the Companies Act, 2013.
Reason (R) Schedule III provides a standard format for the preparation and presentation of financial statements to ensure uniformity and comparability.

34. **Assertion** (A) Financial statements include reports about the activities of a business affecting society.
Reason (R) Businesses are responsible for disclosing their impact on the social environment.

35. **Assertion** (A) Certain accounting conventions like conventions of consistency, conservatism, full disclosure, etc. are followed while preparing financial statements.
Reason (R) Use of accounting conventions makes the financial statements comparable, simple and realistic.

36. **Assertion** (A) The management uses accounting information to arrive at various decisions like determination of selling price, cost controls, investment into new ventures, etc.
Reason (R) The management has the responsibility to safeguard the customer's investment and increase its value by managing the business efficiently.

37. **Assertion** (A) The bank charges charged by the bank are included in finance cost.
Reason (R) Bank charges are an expense not incurred in connection with raising finance but for availing the services of the bank.

38. **Assertion** (A) Bills receivable are shown as trade receivables in the balance sheet of the company.
Reason (R) Debtors and bills receivable forms the part of trade receivables.

Two Statements Based MCQs

Direction (Q. No. 39 to 46) *Read the following statements carefully and choose the correct alternative*

Alternatives

(a) Statement I is correct and Statement II is incorrect
(b) Statement II is correct and Statement I is incorrect
(c) Both the statements are correct
(d) Both the statements are incorrect

39. **Statement I** Financial statements communicate financial information to both internal and external users.
Statement II Financial statements include the balance sheet, profit and loss statement, and budget statement.

40. **Statement I** Financial statements are always prepared based on current market prices.
Statement II They reflect a combination of recorded facts, accounting principles and personal judgements.

41. **Statement I** Postulates like the going concern and money measurement are fundamental assumptions in preparing financial statements.
Statement II The depreciation method used in financial statements is strictly regulated and leaves no room for personal judgement.

42. **Statement I** A company's balance sheet reflects the financial position of the business on a particular date.
Statement II The statement of profit and loss shows the financial position of a business for a particulars period.

43. **Statement I** The primary purpose of financial statements is to help external parties like investors and tax authorities in decision-making.
Statement II Financial statements also disclose the significant accounting policies followed during the reporting period.

44. **Statement I** Contingent liabilities are shown as liabilities in the balance sheet of a company.
Statement II Notes to accounts provide additional information regarding financial statements that cannot be presented in the main financial statements.

45. **Statement I** Share application money pending allotment is shown as a line item.
Statement II Contingent liabilities are shown in the balance sheet under the heading current liabilities.

46. **Statement I** Loose tools are shown as inventories in balance sheet.
Statement II Reserve capital is that part of share capital that a company resolves not to sell at any time it desires.

Matching

47. Match the terms in Column I with their correct descriptions in Column II

Column I	Column II
A. Share capital	(i) Represents accumulated profits of a company.
B. Reserves and surplus	(ii) Amount contributed by shareholders.
C. Current liabilities	(iii) Includes trade payables and short-term borrowings.
D. Non-current liabilities	(iv) Includes long-term borrowings and deferred tax liabilities.

Codes

	A	B	C	D		A	B	C	D
(a)	(ii)	(i)	(iii)	(iv)	(b)	(iii)	(ii)	(iv)	(i)
(c)	(iv)	(i)	(ii)	(iii)	(d)	(i)	(iv)	(ii)	(iii)

48. Match the following elements of financial statements with their explanations

Column I	Column II
A. Balance sheet	(i) Historical cost data from books
B. Statement of profit and loss	(ii) Position of assets, liabilities and equity
C. Cash flow statement	(iii) Income and expenditure during a period
D. Recorded facts	(iv) Cash inflows and outflows

Codes

	A	B	C	D		A	B	C	D
(a)	(iii)	(i)	(ii)	(iv)	(b)	(iv)	(ii)	(i)	(iii)
(c)	(ii)	(iii)	(iv)	(i)	(d)	(i)	(ii)	(iii)	(iv)

49. Match the following objectives of financial statements with their descriptions

Column I	Column II
A. Economic resources	(i) Information about assets and liabilities of a business
B. Earning capacity	(ii) Useful for predicting, comparing and evaluating firm's earning
C. Cash flows	(iii) Predicting, comparing and evaluating, potential cash flows
D. Effectiveness of management	(iv) Judging the management's resource utilisation

Codes

	A	B	C	D		A	B	C	D
(a)	(i)	(ii)	(iii)	(iv)	(b)	(ii)	(iii)	(i)	(iv)
(c)	(iv)	(i)	(iii)	(ii)	(d)	(iii)	(ii)	(iv)	(i)

50. Match the items given in Column I with the headings/ sub-headings (balance sheet) given in Column II as defined in Schedule III of Companies Act, 2013

CBSE SQP Term I 2021

Column I	Column II
A. Loose tools	(i) Intangible assets
B. Patents	(ii) Other current assets
C. Prepaid insurance	(iii) Long-term borrowings
D. Debentures	(iv) Inventories
E. Machinery	(v) Property, plant and equipment

Codes

	A	B	C	D	E
(a)	(i)	(ii)	(iv)	(iii)	(v)
(b)	(iv)	(i)	(ii)	(iii)	(v)
(c)	(iv)	(i)	(ii)	(v)	(iii)
(d)	(v)	(iv)	(i)	(ii)	(iii)

51. Match the items given in Column I with the correct heading/sub-heading given in Column II

CBSE Term I 2021

Column I	Column II
A. 9% debenture redeemable during the current year	(i) Intangible assets
B. Loose tools	(ii) Current liabilities
C. Copyright	(iii) Cash and cash equivalents
D. Cash at bank	(iv) Inventories

Codes

	A	B	C	D		A	B	C	D
(a)	(i)	(ii)	(iii)	(iv)	(b)	(iii)	(ii)	(iv)	(i)
(c)	(iv)	(iii)	(ii)	(i)	(d)	(ii)	(iv)	(i)	(iii)

Case Based MCQs

Direction *Read the following case study and answer the question 52 to 54 on the basis of the same*

Mohinder Ltd. a reputed manufacturing company, has been in operation for the past decade. Recently, the company expanded its operations, requiring additional financing to support its growth initiatives.

The company's financial position as of 31st March, 2024, reflects a combination of equity, reserves and various borrowings to fund its operations and expansion plans. Below is a summary of their liabilities

Particulars	Amt (₹)
Equity Share Capital	40,00,000
11% Debentures	20,00,000
General Reserves	20,00,000
Loan from SBI	16,00,000
Debenture Redemption Reserve	10,00,000
Creditors	8,00,000
Securities Premium	10,00,000
Loan Repayable on Demand	4,00,000

52. How will 11% debentures be recorded in the balance sheet?
(a) Current liabilities (b) Shareholders' funds
(c) Long-term borrowings (d) Reserves and surplus

53. What is the total amount of reserves and surplus?
(a) ₹ 50,00,000 (b) ₹ 40,00,000
(c) ₹ 30,00,000 (d) ₹ 20,00,000

54. How will loans repayable on demand be recorded in the balance sheet?
(a) Long-term borrowings
(b) Short-term borrowings
(c) Non-current liabilities
(d) Other current liabilities

Direction *From the following information extracted from the books of ABC Ltd. answer the questions 55 to 57 (keeping in mind the provisions of Companies Act, 2013).*

Particulars	Amt (₹)
10% Debentures of ₹ 100 each	2,00,000
11% Bank Loan from SBI Repayable after 5 Years	1,00,000
Stock-in-trade (Inventories)	40,000
Goodwill	50,000
Computer Software under Development	50,000
Provision for Tax	70,000

55. Computer software under development will be shown under the .... category of the sub-head property, plant and equipment and intangible assets on the assets side of the balance sheet.
(a) intangible assets
(b) property, plant and equipment
(c) capital work-in-progress
(d) None of the above

56. The total value of intangible assets that will be shown under sub-head property, plant and equipment and intangible assets on the assets side of the balance sheet is
(a) ₹ 50,000 (b) ₹ 1,00,000
(c) ₹ 1,50,000 (d) ₹ 2,20,000

57. The total value of long-term borrowings that will be shown under the head non-current liabilities on the equity and liability side of the balance sheet is
(a) ₹ 50,000 (b) ₹ 1,00,000
(c) ₹ 3,00,000 (d) ₹ 2,00,000

Direction *Read the following case study and answer the questions 58 to 60 on the basis of the same*

XYZ Ltd. is a financial company. For the year 2020-21 interest on loans given amounted to ₹ 4,00,000 and fees received for arranging loans amounted to ₹ 1,00,000. Its miscellaneous income amounted to ₹ 50,000. Further, a building was sold during the year on which XYZ Ltd. earned a profit of ₹ 70,000. Moreover, it earned a profit of ₹ 75,000 on the sale of investments during the year.

58. Profit on sale of investments will be shown as .... in the statement of profit and loss.
(a) other income (b) revenue from operations
(c) finance cost (d) None of these

59. The total value of revenue from operations that will be shown in the statement of profit and loss is ....
(a) ₹ 50,000 (b) ₹ 4,00,000
(c) ₹ 1,50,000 (d) ₹ 5,75,000

60. The total value of other income that will be shown in the statement of profit and loss is
(a) ₹ 50,000 (b) ₹ 70,000
(c) ₹ 1,20,000 (d) ₹ 1,95,000

Answers

1. (a) Inventory 2. (b) Current liabilities
3. (d) Non-current liabilities
4. (a) other current liabilities
5. (b) other current assets
6. (c) Equity and Liabilities = Equity Share Capital + Reserves and Surplus + Long-term Borrowings
$= 10,00,000 + 1,50,000 + 5,00,000 = ₹\ 16,50,000$
7. (c) other non-current liabilities
8. (d) Debentures are always treated as long-term until unless these debentures are redeemable within 12 months. Therefore, they are included in long-term liabilities.
9. (a) Prepaid rent means advance payment of rent. Since rent is paid in advance, so it will not be repaid when it will be due. So, it is a current asset.
10. (c) Staff welfare expenses means employees expenses which are paid for their benefit. These are shown in statement of profit and loss.
11. (c) Both (a) and (b)
12. (c) three
13. (d) Share capital can be issued at premium or discount but share capital amount is shown only on par value which is also known as face value.
14. (d) specific reserve

15. (b) Debtors are to be received within 12 months. So, these can be classified as current assets and these are included in trade receivables with bills receivables.

16. (b) current

17. (a) income statement

18. (b) 90%

19. (b) Cost of Materials Consumed = 2,50,000 + 20,00,000 − 3,00,000 = ₹ 19,50,000

20. (c) Revenue from Operations = Interest on Loan + Dividend
= 4,00,000 + 50,000 = ₹ 4,50,000

21. (a)

Other Incomes	**Amt (₹)**
Commission Received	= 1,20,000
Dividend from Investment Received	= 20,000
	= 1,40,000

Sale of products and services are revenue from operation and excise duty is revenue from operation in negative nature.

22. (d) **Statement of Profit and Loss**

Particulars		Amt (₹)
Revenue from Operations		80,00,000
(−) Expenses		
Cost of Material Consumed	10,00,000	
Purchase of Stock-in-trade	30,00,000	
Employees Benefit Expense	4,00,000	(44,00,000)
Profit before Tax		36,00,000
(−) Tax @ 50%		(18,00,000)
Profit after Tax		18,00,000

23. (a) Total Revenue = Revenue from Operations + Other Income
= (6,00,000 − 1,00,000) + 12,500 + (15,000 + 5,000)
= ₹ 5,32,500

24. (d) Accounts receivable or trade receivable of ₹ 1,00,000 would be shown in the balance sheet under current assets.

25. (d) ₹ 1,60,000 as other current liability and ₹ 6,40,000 as long-term borrowing

26. (a) General reserve will be included under reserves and surplus and will be a part of shareholders' funds.

27. (d) Current Liabilities = Short-term Borrowings + Trade Payables + Other Current Liabilities + Short-term Provisions Current Liabilities
= 3,00,000 + 2,00,000 + 1,00,000 + 1,00,000 = ₹ 7,00,000

28. (b) Public deposits are long-term borrowings and are non-current liabilities, hence not shown on the assets side of the balance sheet.

29. (c) Assertion (A) is true, but Reason (R) is false

30. (a) Both Assertion (A) and Reason (R) are true and Reason (R) is the correct explanation of Assertion (A)

31. (c) Assertion (A) is true, but Reason (R) is false

32. (c) Assertion (A) is true, but Reason (R) is false

33. (a) Both Assertion (A) and Reason (R) are true and Reason (R) is the correct explanation of Assertion (A)

34. (a) Both Assertion (A) and Reason (R) are true and Reason (R) is the correct explanation of Assertion (A)

35. (a) Both Assertion (A) and Reason (R) are true and Reason (R) is the correct explanation of Assertion (A)

36. (d) The management has the responsibility to safeguard the owner's investment and increase its value by managing the business efficiently.

37. (c) The bank charges charged by the bank are not included in finance cost.

38. (a) Both Assertion (A) and Reason (R) are true and Reason (R) is the correct explanation of Assertion (A)

39. (a) Statement I is correct and Statement II is incorrect

40. (b) Statement II is correct and Statement I is incorrect

41. (a) Statement I is correct and Statement II is incorrect

42. (a) Statement I is correct and Statement II is incorrect

43. (b) Statement II is correct and Statement I is incorrect

44. (b) Statement II is correct and Statement I is incorrect

45. (b) Contingent liabilities are disclosed in the notes to accounts.

46. (a) Statement I is correct and Statement II is incorrect

47. (a) (ii) (i) (iii) (iv)

48. (c) (ii) (iii) (iv) (i)

49. (a) (i) (ii) (iii) (iv)

50. (b) (iv) (i) (ii) (iii) (v)

51. (d) (ii) (iv) (i) (iii)

52. (c) Long-term borrowings

53. (b) Reserves and Surplus = General Reserve + Debentures Redemption Reserve + Securities Premium
= 20,00,000 + 10,00,000 + 10,00,000

54. (b) Short-term borrowings

55. (a) intangible assets

56. (b) Intangible Assets = Goodwill + Computer Software under Developmnet
= 50,000 + 50,000 = ₹ 1,00,000

57. (c) Long-term Borrowings = 10% Debentures + 11% Bank Loan from SBI
= 2,00,000 + 1,00,000 = ₹ 3,00,000

58. (b) Revenue from operations as it is a financial company.

59. (d) Revenue from Operations = Interest on Loans Given + Fees Received for Arranging Loans + Profit on Sale of Investments
= 4,00,000 + 1,00,000 + 75,000 = ₹ 5,75,000

60. (c) Other Income = Miscellaneous Income + Profit on Sale of Building
= 50,000 + 70,000 = ₹ 1,20,000

02 CHAPTER

Financial Statement Analysis

"Financial statement analysis is largely a study of relationships among various financial factors in a business, as disclosed by a single set of statements and a study of trends of these factors, as shown in a series of statements." *–Myer*

YOUR STUDY GOALS

2.1 Meaning of Financial Statement Analysis
2.2 Comparative Statements
2.3 Common Size Statements

YOUR PRACTICE GOAL

- Topicwise Solved Questions (15 Solved Questions)
  Numerical Questions [20 Questions (Unsolved)]
- Theoretical Questions [12 Questions (with answers)]
- Objective Questions (57 Qs ; MCQs, A-R, Statements, Matching, Case)

2.1 Meaning of Financial Statement Analysis

Financial statement analysis is the process of critically evaluating financial information contained in financial statements to understand and make decisions about a firm's operations. It involves studying relationships among various financial figures to identify the firm's strengths and weaknesses by establising relationship between items in the balance sheet and income statement.

This analysis helps creditors, investors and other stakeholders to assess the creditworthiness and earning potential of a business.

It includes both analysis and interpretation. Analysis involves methodical classification to simplify financial data and Interpretation involves explaining the meaning and significance of data. It complements analysis, as analysis is meaningless without interpretation and interpretation is impossible without analysis.

Objectives (Purposes) of Financial Statement Analysis

- To present the complex financial data in simplified and understandable form.
- To judge the financial stability of an enterprise.
- To measure the short-term and long-term solvency of enterprise.

- To measure the operating efficiency and profitability of enterprise.
- To compare intra-firm position, inter-firm position and pattern position within the industry.
- To assess the future prospects of the enterprise.
- To classify the items contained in financial statements in groups.
- To draw conclusions by making comparison between various groups.

Types of Financial Statements Analysis

Viewpoint	Description
From the viewpoint of Users	• **External Analysis** Conducted by outsiders like creditors, bankers, investors and government agencies, relying on published accounts and reports due to limited access to records. • **Internal Analysis** Performed by management using detailed internal information to assess the financial position and operational efficiency of the organisation.
From the viewpoint of its Objectivity	• **Short-term Analysis** Examines liquidity, profitability and short-term solvency of an enterprise. • **Long-term Analysis** Assesses long-term financial stability, solvency and future profit earning capacity of an enterprise.
From the viewpoint of Timespan	• **Horizontal Analysis** Also called dynamic analysis, it reviews financial data over multiple years, comparing trends against a chosen base year. It is useful for long-term planning. • **Vertical Analysis** Also called static analysis, if focuses on a single year's data, comparing divisions within a company or similar firms. Tools include ratio analysis and common size statements.
From the viewpoint of Firm	• **Intra-firm Analysis** Compares financial statements of the same enterprise across different accounting periods to identify trends. It is also known as time series analysis or trend analysis. • **Inter-firm Analysis** Compares financial statements of multiple enterprises in the same industry during the same accounting period to evaluate relative position of an enterprise compared to competitive firms. It is also known as cross sectional analysis.

Process of Financial Statement Analysis

1. **Rearrangement of Data** For analysis, data contained in financial statements is reclassified into purposive classes, so that maximum information from data under analysis, can be obtained.
2. **Comparison** After the classification of data, the data is compared. The comparison can be between data of an enterprise only or between two enterprises. Comparison helps to ascertain the growth in the enterprise and also its relative position in the industry.
3. **Analysis** Here, analysis of comparative financial data is carried out with reference to financial characteristics like profitability, solvency and liquidity.
4. **Interpretation** In this step, conclusions are drawn on the basis of comparison and analysis which is presented in the form of reports and suggestions.

Uses of Financial Statement Analysis

1. **Security Analysis** It helps the investors to know whether the firm is fulfilling their expectations with regard to payment of dividend, capital appreciation and security of money.
2. **Credit Analysis** When a firm offers credit to a new customer or a dealer, such analysis helps in determining whether to extend credit or not.
3. **Debt Analysis** It helps in determining the borrowing capacity of a prospective borrower.
4. **Dividend Decision** It helps the firm in determining the rate of dividend, i.e. how much portion of earnings to be distributed and how much to be retained.
5. **General Business Analysis** This analysis helps to assess the future growth/profit potential of the firm. This analysis reveal the trend of cost, sales, profit, etc.

Limitations of Financial Statement Analysis

- It does not consider price level changes.
- It may be misleading without the knowledge of the changes in accounting procedure followed by a firm.
- It is just a study of interim reports.
- Monetary information alone is considered in financial analysis while non-monetary aspects are ignored.
- The financial statements are prepared on the basis of ongoing concept, as such, it does not reflect the current position.

Significance (Importance) of Financial Statement Analysis

Financial statement analysis is vital for various stakeholders, as discussed below

1. **Finance Manager** Assesses the financial potential of the business, predicts future financial needs and takes appropriate actions.
2. **Management** Evaluates financial condition, profitability and solvency of enterprise to control operations and improve efficiency.
3. **Trade Creditors** Judge the company's ability to meet short-term obligations and its ongoing credit-worthiness.
4. **Bankers and Lenders** Assess profit earning capacity, solvency and repayment ability of business to ensure timely interest and principal payments.
5. **Investors** Analyse profitability, dividends, market value and growth potential of business to evaluate management efficiency and future returns.
6. **Labour Unions** Determine if the business earns fair returns to justify wage increases and settle wage agreements.
7. **Government** Uses the analysis to assess tax liabilities, monitor industries' performance and shape tax, industrial and trade policies.
8. **Regulatory Authorities** Ensure compliance related to financial statements with legal guidelines to safeguard stakeholders' interests.
9. **Customers** Interested in an enterprise's continuity, especially for long-term commitments.
10. **Tax Authorities** Evaluate accurate tax assessments based on financial performance.
11. **Researchers** Study profitability, growth and future prospects for academic or industry insights.
12. **Other Parties** Groups like economists, trade associations and media analyse financial data for their specific purposes.

Quick View : Parties Interested in Financial Statement Analysis and their Areas of Interest

Parties	Areas of Interest
Shareholders or investors or owners	(i) Profitability (ii) Financial position (iii) Future prospects of business
Management	(i) Short-term and long-term solvency (ii) Liability of the concern (iii) Profitability in relation to turnover and investments
Suppliers or creditors	(i) Profitability (ii) Short-term solvency
Bankers and lenders	(i) Financial position (ii) Profitability (iii) Long-term and short-term solvency
Employees and trade unions	(i) Profitability (ii) Financial position of the concern
Government and agencies	(i) Profitability (ii) Financial position (iii) Growth (iv) Estimating national income
Researchers	(i) Profitability (ii) Financial position (iii) Growth (iv) Future prospects

Smart Study Chart No. 1

Tools or Techniques of Financial Statement Analysis

- **Comparative Statements** Present financial statements (income statement and balance sheet) for two or more years to Identify strengths and weaknesses.
- **Common Size Statements** Express individual items of financial statements as percentages of a common base (e.g. Revenue for profit and loss or total assets for the balance sheet) for easier comparison across years.
- **Ratio Analysis** Involves calculating key financial ratios to evaluate performance and financial health.
- **Cash Flow Statement** Highlights cash inflows and outflows over a period, showing changes in the financial position.

2.2 Comparative Statements

A comparative statement presents financial statements, such as income statement and balance sheet, for two or more periods or firms, enabling the analysis of strengths and weaknesses.

It can involve intra-firm (different periods) or inter-firm (same period) comparisons and is also called **horizontal analysis.**

They are internal documents prepared by business and are not included in formal financial statements.

A comparative statement exhibits the following information

- Absolute figures for two or more years of the items appearing in financial statements.
- Changes in absolute figures of the current year as compared to the previous year taken as the base year.
- Percentage changes in absolute figures of the current year on the basis of the base year.

Objectives or Purposes of Comparative Statements

- To know the nature of changes affecting financial position and financial performance of an enterprise.
- To know the weakness and strength of the enterprise with regard to liquidity, profitability and solvency.
- To plan and forecast the financial soundness and profitability of the business.
- To compare firm's performance with the average performance of the industry.
- To present the data in a simple, understandable and comparable form so that conclusions can be drawn easily.

Types of Comparative Statements

There are two types of comparative statements
- Comparative statement of profit and loss
- Comparative balance sheet

1. Comparative Statement of Profit and Loss or Income Statement

Comparative statement of profit and loss is the horizontal analysis of income statement. It shows the operating results (i.e. net profit or loss) for two or more accounting periods, so that changes in absolute amounts and percentages may be known.

Objectives of Comparative Income Statement

- To analyse the income and expenditure for two or more years.
- To analyse the increase or decrease in the income and expenditure in terms of rupees and also in percentage.
- To review the business operations of the last year and its likely effect on the current year's operations.

Preparation of Comparative Statement of Profit and Loss or Income Statement

A comparative income statement has five columns

1. **First Column** (Particulars) The items of statement of profit and loss are entered in this column.
2. **Second Column** (Previous year's data) Figures of previous year are entered in this column.
3. **Third Column** (Current year's data) Figures of current year are entered in this column.
4. **Fourth Column** (Absolute change) Differences (increase or decrease) in figures between the previous accounting period and current accounting period are recorded in this column.

Absolute Change (₹) = Current Year's Figure − Previous Year's Figure

5. **Fifth Column** (Percentage change) The differences (increase or decrease) expressed in percentage are shown in this column.

$$\text{Percentage Change (\%)} = \frac{\text{Absolute Change}}{\text{Amount of Previous Year}} \times 100$$

Format of Comparative Statement of Profit and Loss or Income Statement

Comparative Statement of Profit and Loss
for the years ended...

Particulars (1)	**Previous Year (₹)** (2)	**Current Year (₹)** (3)	**Absolute Change** (Increase or Decrease) (₹) (4)	**Percentage Change** (Increase or Decrease) (%) (5)
I. Revenue from Operations (Net sales)	...	...	...	...
II. Other Income	...	...	...	...
III. **Total Revenue** (I + II)	...	...	...	...
IV. **Expenses**				
(a) Cost of Materials Consumed	...	...	...	...
(b) Purchases of Stock-in-trade	...	...	...	...
(c) Changes in Inventories of Finished Goods, Work-in-progress and Stock-in-trade	...	...	...	...
(d) Employees Benefit Expenses	...	...	...	...
(e) Finance Cost	...	...	...	...
(f) Depreciation and Amortisation	...	...	...	...
(g) Other Expenses	...	...	...	...
Total Expenses	...	...	...	...

Particulars (1)	Previous Year (₹) (2)	Current Year (₹) (3)	Absolute Change (Increase or Decrease) (₹) (4)	Percentage Change (Increase or Decrease) (%) (5)
V. **Profit before Tax** (III – IV)	...	...	...	...
(–) Income Tax	...	...	...	...
VI. **Profit after Tax**	...	...	...	...

2. Comparative Balance Sheet

Comparative balance sheet is the horizontal analysis of balance sheet. It analyses each item of assets, equity and liabilities for two or more accounting periods, so that changes in absolute amounts and percentages may be known.

Objectives of Comparative Balance Sheet

- To measure the financial position of an enterprise.
- To analyse different items of assets and liabilities in absolute rupees, i.e. balances on two or more comparative dates.
- To analyse increase or decrease in rupee amounts as well as in percentage by taking the data of previous years as base.
- To review the past financing and investing activities and their effect on the financial position of the enterprise.

Preparation of Comparative Balance Sheet

A comparative balance sheet has five columns

1. **First Column** (Particulars) The components or elements or items of balance sheet are entered in this column.
2. **Second Column** (Previous year's data) Data (amounts) of previous year's balance sheet are entered in this column.
3. **Third Column** (Current year's data) Data (amounts) of current year's balance sheet are entered in this column.
4. **Fourth Column** (Absolute change) Differences (increase or decrease) in amounts between the previous year and current year are shown in this column.

$$\text{Absolute Change (₹)} = \text{Current Year's Figure} - \text{Previous Year's Figure}$$

5. **Fifth Column** (Percentage change) The differences (increase or decrease) expressed as percentage, taking previous year's amount as the base are shown in this column.

$$\text{Percentage Change (\%)} = \frac{\text{Absolute Change}}{\text{Amount of Previous Year}} \times 100$$

Format of Comparative Balance Sheet

Comparative Balance Sheet
as at ...

Particulars (1)	Previous Year (₹) (2)	Current Year (₹) (3)	Absolute Change (Increase or Decrease) (₹) (4)	Percentage Change (Increase or Decrease) (%) (5)
I. **EQUITY AND LIABILITIES**				
1. **Shareholders' Funds**				
(i) Share Capital				
(a) Equity Share Capital	...	...	...	...
(b) Preference Share Capital	...	...	...	...
(ii) Reserves and Surplus	...	...	...	...
2. **Non-current Liabilities**				
(i) Long-term Borrowings	...	...	...	...
(ii) Long-term Provisions	...	...	...	...
3. **Current Liabilities**				
(i) Short-term Borrowings	...	...	...	...
(ii) Trade Payables	...	...	...	...
(iii) Other Current Liabilities	...	...	...	...
(iv) Short-term Provisions	...	...	...	...
Total	...	...	...	...

Particulars (1)	Previous Year (₹) (2)	Current Year (₹) (3)	Absolute Change (Increase or Decrease) (₹) (4)	Percentage Change (Increase or Decrease) (%) (5)
II. **ASSETS**				
1. **Non-current Assets**				
(i) Property, Plant and Equipment and Intangible Assets				
(a) Property, Plant and Equipment	...	...	...	...
(b) Intangible Assets	...	...	...	...
(ii) Non-current Investments	...	...	...	...
(iii) Long-term Loans and Advances	...	...	...	...
2. **Current Assets**				
(i) Current Investments	...	...	...	...
(ii) Inventories	...	...	...	...
(iii) Trade Receivables	...	...	...	...
(iv) Cash and Cash Equivalents	...	...	...	...
(v) Short-term Loans and Advances	...	...	...	...
(vi) Other Current Assets	...	...	...	...
Total	...	...	...	...

2.3 Common Size Statements

Common size statements present items of the balance sheet or profit and loss statement as percentages of a common base. For the profit and loss statement, the base is revenue from operations while for the balance sheet, it is the total assets or liabilities. This is also known as *vertical analysis* and simplifies comparisons across periods, helping draw meaningful conclusions.

A common size statement exhibits the following information

- Absolute figures of the items appearing in financial statements of two or more years or two or more firms.
- Percentage figure of every item appearing in financial statements as a percentage of the pre-selected base item.

Purposes or Objectives of Common Size Statements

- To present the changes in various items of assets and liabilities in relation to total of balance sheet.
- To present the changes in various items of statement of profit and loss in relation to revenue from operations.
- To establish relationship of different items of balance sheet with total assets/liabilities so that important conclusion can be drawn.
- To provide a common base for comparison.

Types of Common Size Statements

There are two types of common size statement

- Common size statement of profit and loss
- Common size balance sheet

1. Common Size Statement of Profit and Loss or Income Statement

It is the statement in which amount of revenue from operations (net sales) is assumed to be equal to 100 and other amounts are expressed as percentage of revenue from operations (net sales).

Such statement may be prepared for different periods or for two firms. It shows the relative efficiency in operating the business.

Objectives of Common Size Income Statement

- To analyse change in individual items of statement of profit and loss.
- To study the trend in different items of income/expenditure.
- To assess the efficiency.

Preparation of Common Size Statement of Profit and Loss

A common size income statement has five columns

1. **First Column** (Particulars) Items of statement of profit and loss are entered in first column.
2. **Second Column** (Previous year's data) Absolute amounts of different items (i.e. income/expenses) of statement of profit and loss for the previous year are entered in second column.
3. **Third Column** (Current year's data) Absolute amounts of different items (i.e. income/expenses) of statement of profit and loss for the current year are entered in this column.

4. **Fourth Column** (Percentage change for previous year) Percentage relation of different items of statement of profit and loss for the previous year to net sales (which is taken as 100) are entered in fourth column.
5. **Fifth Column** (Percentage change for current year) Percentage relation of different items of statement of profit and loss for the current year to net sales (which is taken as 100) are entered in fifth column.

Format of Common Size Statement of Profit and Loss or Income Statement

Common Size Statement of Profit and Loss
for the years ended...

Particulars (1)	Absolute Amounts		Percentage of Revenue from Operations (Net Sales)	
	Previous Year (₹) (2)	Current Year (₹) (3)	Previous Year (%) (4)	Current Year (%) (5)
I. Revenue from Operations (Net Sales)	...	...	...	...
II. Other Income	...	...	...	...
III. **Total Revenue** (I + II)	...	...	...	...
IV. **Expenses**				
(a) Cost of Materials Consumed	...	...	...	...
(b) Purchases of Stock-in-trade	...	...	...	...
(c) Changes in Inventories of Finished Goods, Work-in-progress and Stock-in-trade	...	...	...	...
(d) Employees Benefit Expenses	...	...	...	...
(e) Finance Cost	...	...	...	...
(f) Depreciation and Amortisation	...	...	...	...
(g) Other Expenses	...	...	...	...
Total Expenses	...	...	...	...
V. **Profit before Tax** (III – IV)	...	...	...	...
VI. (–) Income Tax	...	...	...	...
VII. **Profit after Tax**	...	...	...	...

2. Common Size Balance Sheet

It shows the percentage relation of each asset/liability to total assets/total liabilities including capital. In this, total assets or total equity and liabilities are taken as 100 and all the figures are expressed as percentage of the total.

Objectives of Common Size Balance Sheet

- To analyse the changes in individual items of balance sheet.
- To see the trend of different items of assets, equity and liabilities.
- To understand the financial strategy and also to assess the financial soundness of the company.

Preparation of Common Size Balance Sheet

A common size balance sheet has five columns

1. **First Column** (Particulars) Enter the items of balance sheet in first column.
2. **Second Column** (Previous year's data) Enter the absolute amounts of different items (assets/ liabilities) of previous year's balance sheet in second column.
3. **Third Column** (Current year's data) Enter the absolute amounts of different items (i.e. assets/ liabilities) of balance sheet for current year.
4. **Fourth Column** (Percentage change for previous year) Calculate and enter the percentage relation of different items of previous year's balance sheet to total equity and liabilities/total assets (which are taken as 100) in this column.
5. **Fifth Column** (Percentage change for current year) Calculate and enter the percentage relation of different items of current year's balance sheet to total equity and liabilities/total assets (which are taken as 100) in this column.

Format of Common Size Balance Sheet

Common Size Balance Sheet
as at ...

Particulars	Absolute Amount		Percentage of Balance Sheet Total	
	Previous Year (₹)	Current Year (₹)	Previous Year (%)	Current Year (%)
I. **EQUITY AND LIABILITIES**				
1. **Shareholders' Funds**				
(i) Share Capital				
(a) Equity Share Capital	...	...	...	...
(b) Preference Share Capital	...	...	...	...
(ii) Reserves and Surplus	...	...	...	...
2. **Non-current Liabilities**				
(i) Long-term Borrowings	...	...	...	...
(ii) Long-term Provisions	...	...	...	...
3. **Current Liabilities**				
(i) Short-term Borrowings	...	...	...	...
(ii) Trade Payables	...	...	...	...
(iii) Other Current Liabilities	...	...	...	...
(iv) Short-term Provisions	...	...	...	...
Total	...	...	100	100
II. **ASSETS**				
1. **Non-current Assets**				
(i) Property, Plant and Equipment and Intangible Assets				
(a) Property, Plant and Equipment	...	...	...	...
(b) Intangible Assets	...	...	...	...
(ii) Non-current Investments	...	...	...	...
(iii) Long-term Loans and Advances	...	...	...	...
2. **Current Assets**				
(i) Current Investments	...	...	...	...
(ii) Inventories	...	...	...	...
(iii) Trade Receivables	...	...	...	...
(iv) Cash and Cash Equivalents	...	...	...	...
(v) Short-term Loans and Advances	...	...	...	...
(vi) Other Current Assets	...	...	...	...
Total	...	...	100	100

Mind Map

Financial Statement Analysis

1 Meaning of Financial Statement Analysis

The process of critical evaluation of the financial information contained in the financial statements in order to understand and make decisions regarding the operations of the firm is called financial statement analysis.

2 Objectives of Financial Statement Analysis

- To present the complex financial data in a simple form.
- To judge the financial stability of an enterprise.
- To measure the short-term and long-term solvency of enterprise.
- To compare intra-firm position, inter-firm position and pattern position within the industry.
- To draw conclusions by making comparison between various groups.
- To assess the future prospects of the enterprise.

3 Types of Financial Statement Analysis

- External analysis (Analysis by outsiders).
- Internal analysis (By the management).
- Short-term analysis (To access the short-term solvency).
- Long-term analysis (To access long-term solvency).
- Horizontal analysis (Shows comparison for several years against a chosen base year. It is also called **dynamic analysis**).
- Vertical analysis (Also called **static analysis**. It is made to analyse financial statements of one particular year only. It compares the performance of several companies of the same type).
- Intra-firm analysis (Comparison of financial statements of a company for two or more accounting periods. It is also known as **time series analysis**).
- Inter-firm analysis (Comparison of financial statements of two or more companies for the same year. It is also known as **cross sectional analysis**).

4 Limitations of Financial Statement Analysis

- It does not consider price level changes.
- It is just a study of interim reports.
- It does not reflect the correct position.
- Non-monetary aspects are ignored.

5 Tools of Financial Statement Analysis

- Comparative statements
- Common size statements
- Ratio analysis
- Cash flow statement

6 Comparative Statements

Comparative statement is an art of presenting financial statements, i.e. income statement and balance sheet of two or more periods or firms in such a manner that it helps to assess the strength and weakness of the business entity.

Format

Format of Comparative Statement*

Particulars A	Previous Year (₹) B	Current Year (₹) C	Absolute Change (increase or Decrease) (₹) D = C – B	Percentage Change (D × 100)/ Previous Year E
All items of income statement or balance sheet, as the case may be.	...	...	...	...

* Above format is applied for both balance sheet and statement of profit and loss

7 Common Size Statements

- These are the statements in which amounts of individual items of balance sheet and statement of profit and loss as percentage of a common base.
- Revenve from operations is base for income statement while total assets or liabilities are base for balance sheet.

Format

Format of Common Size Statement**

Particulars A	Absolute Amounts		Previous Year (%) D	Current Year (%) E
	Prvious Year (₹) B	Current Year (₹) C		
All items of income statement or balance sheet as the case may be.	...	...	...	...

**Above format is applied for both balance sheet and statement of profit and loss

Topicwise Solved Questions

Comparative Statement of Profit and Loss

Solved Question 1 From the following particulars of Accent Ltd. prepare a comparative statement of profit and loss for the year ended 31st March, 2023 **CBSE 2024 C**

Particulars	Note No.	2022-23 (₹)	2021-22 (₹)
Revenue from Operations		25,00,000	20,00,000
Employee Benefit Expenses		5,00,000	4,00,000
Other Expenses		2,50,000	2,00,000
Tax Rate		50%	50%

Sol.

Comparative Statement of Profit and Loss
for the year ended 31st March, 2023

Particulars	2021-22 (₹)	2022-23 (₹)	Absolute Change (Increase or Decrease) (₹)	Percentage Change (Increase or Decrease) (%)
I. Revenue from Operations	20,00,000	25,00,000	5,00,000	25
II. **Expenses**				
(a) Employee Benefit Expenses	4,00,000	5,00,000	1,00,000	25
(b) Other Expenses	2,00,000	2,50,000	50,000	25
Total Expenses	6,00,000	7,50,000	1,50,000	25
III. **Profit before Tax** (I – II)	14,00,000	17,50,000	3,50,000	25
IV. (–) Tax @ 50%	(7,00,000)	(8,75,000)	(1,75,000)	25
V. **Profit after Tax**	7,00,000	8,75,000	1,75,000	25

Solved Question 2 Following is the statement of profit and loss of Sun India Ltd. for the year ended 31st March, 2024

Particulars	Note No.	31st March, 2024 (₹)	31st March, 2023 (₹)
Revenue from Operations		25,00,000	20,00,000
Other Incomes		1,00,000	5,00,000
Employee Benefits Expenses		60% of Total revenue	50% of Total revenue
Other Expenses		10% of Employee benefits expenses	20% of Employee benefits expenses
Tax Rate		50%	40%

You are required to prepare a comparative statement of profit and loss of Sun India Ltd. from the given statement of profit and loss.

Sol.

Comparative Statement of Profit and Loss of Sun India Ltd.
for the years ended 31st March, 2023 and 2024

Particulars	Note No.	2022-23 (₹)	2023-24 (₹)	Absolute Change (₹)	Percentage Change (%)
I. Revenue from Operations		2,00,000	25,00,000	5,00,000	25
II. Other Incomes		5,00,000	1,00,000	(4,00,000)	(80)
III. **Total Revenue** (I + II)		25,00,000	26,00,000	1,00,000	4
IV. **Expenses**					
(a) Employee Benefits Expenses		12,50,000	15,60,000	3,10,000	24.8
(b) Other Expenses		2,50,000	1,56,000	(94,000)	(37.6)
Total Expenses		15,00,000	17,16,000	2,16,000	14.4
V. **Profit before Tax** (III – IV)		10,00,000	8,84,000	(1,16,000)	(11.6)
VI. (–) Tax		(4,00,000)	(4,42,000)	(42,000)	10.5
VII. **Profit after Tax**		6,00,000	4,42,000	(1,58,000)	(26.33)

Solved Question 3 From the following information, prepare a comparative statement of profit and loss of Smart Ltd. **CBSE 2025**

Particulars	2023-24 (₹)	2022-23 (₹)
Revenue from Operations	24,00,000	20,00,000
Cost of Materials Consumed	6,00,000	4,00,000
Employee Benefit Expenses	4,00,000	2,00,000
Tax Rate	50%	50%

Sol.

Comparative Statement of Profit and Loss
for the years ended 2023 and 2024

Particulars	2022-23 (₹)	2023-24 (₹)	Absolute Change (Increase or Decrease) (₹)	Percentage Change (Increase or Decrease) (%)
I. Revenue from Operations	20,00,000	24,00,000	4,00,000	20.00
II. **Expenses**				
(a) Cost of Material Consumed	4,00,000	6,00,000	2,00,000	50.00
(b) Employee Benefit Expenses	2,00,000	4,00,000	2,00,000	100.00
III. **Total Expenses**	6,00,000	10,00,000	4,00,000	66.67
IV. **Profit before Tax** (I – III)	14,00,000	14,00,000	—	—
V. (–) Tax @ 50%	(7,00,000)	(7,00,000)	—	—
VI. **Profit after Tax**	7,00,000	7,00,000	—	—

Solved Question 4 From the following information prepare a comparative statement of profit and loss of Y Ltd. **CBSE 2024**

Particulars	31st March, 2023 (₹)	31st March, 2022 (₹)
Revenue from Operations	40,00,000	20,00,000
Purchase of Stock-in-trade	24,00,000	12,00,000
Change in Inventories (% of Purchase of Stock-in-trade)	25%	20%
Other Expenses	2,00,000	1,60,000
Tax Rate	40%	40%

Sol.

Comparative Statement of Profit and Loss of Y Ltd.
for the year ended 31st March, 2023

Particulars	Note No.	31st March, 2022 (₹)	31st March, 2023 (₹)	Absolute Change (Increase/ Decrease) (₹)	Percentage Change (Increase/Decrease) (%)
I. Revenue from Operations		20,00,000	40,00,000	20,00,000	100
II. **Expenses**					
Purchase of Stock-in-trade		12,00,000	24,00,000	12,00,000	100
Change in Inventories		2,40,000	6,00,000	3,60,000	150
Other Expenses		1,60,000	2,00,000	40,000	25
Total		16,00,000	32,00,000	16,00,000	100
III. **Profit before Tax**		4,00,000	8,00,000	4,00,000	100
(–) Tax @ 40%		(1,60,000)	(3,20,000)	1,60,000	100
IV. **Profit after Tax**		2,40,000	4,80,000	2,40,000	100

Solved Question 5 Prepare comparative statement of profit and loss from the following information

Particulars	31st March, 2024	31st March, 2023
Revenue from Operations	₹ 40,00,000	₹ 30,00,000
Cost of Material Consumed	55% of Revenue from operations	60% of Revenue from operations
Paid Wages	₹ 30,000	₹ 25,000
Other Expenses	25% of Gross profit	20% of Gross profit
Income Tax	40%	40%

Sol.

Comparative Statement of Profit and Loss
for the years ended 31st March, 2023 and 2024

Particulars	31st March, 2023 (₹)	31st March, 2024 (₹)	Absolute Change (Increase or Decrease) (₹)	Percentage Change (Increase or Decrease) (%)
I. Revenue from Operations (Sales)	30,00,000	40,00,000	10,00,000	33.33
II. **Expenses**				
(a) Cost of Material Consumed	18,00,000	22,00,000	4,00,000	22.22
(b) Operating Expenses	2,40,000	4,50,000	2,10,000	87.50
Total Expenses	20,40,000	26,50,000	6,10,000	29.90
III. **Profit before Tax** (I – II)	9,60,000	13,50,000	3,90,000	40.63
(–) Income Tax @ 40%	(3,84,000)	(5,40,000)	1,56,000	40.63
IV. **Profit after Tax**	5,76,000	8,10,000	2,34,000	40.63

Working Note

	2024 (₹)	2023 (₹)
Revenue from operations	40,00,000	30,00,000
(–) Cost of material consumed	(22,00,000)	(18,00,000)
Gross profit	18,00,000	12,00,000
Other expenses	4,50,000	2,40,000
	(25% of gross profit)	(20% of gross profit)

Note Wages is a direct expense. Hence, it is ignored because it is already included in the cost of goods sold or cost of revenue from operations.

Comparative Balance Sheet

Solved Question 6 From the following information, prepare comparative balance sheet of X Ltd.

Particulars	31st March, 2024 (₹)	31st March, 2023 (₹)
Reserve and Surplus	6,00,000	3,00,000
Share Capital	5,00,000	5,00,000
Trade Payables	6,35,000	4,50,000
Land and Buildings	8,00,000	7,50,000
Plant and Machinery	3,15,000	2,50,000
Goodwill	—	50,000
Investments	60,000	50,000
Current Assets	7,60,000	4,00,000
Long-term Borrowings	2,00,000	2,50,000

Sol.

Comparative Balance Sheet of X Ltd.
as at 31st March, 2023 and 2024

Particulars	Note No.	31st March, 2023 (₹) A	31st March, 2024 (₹) B	Absolute Change (Increase or Decrease) (₹) (B – A = C)	Percentage Change (Increase or Decrease) (%) C/A × 100 = D
I. EQUITY AND LIABILITIES					
1. **Shareholders' Funds**					
(i) Share Capital		5,00,000	5,00,000	—	—
(ii) Reserves and Surplus		3,00,000	6,00,000	3,00,000	100.00
2. **Non-current Liabilities**					
Long-term Borrowings		2,50,000	2,00,000	(50,000)	(20.00)*

Particulars	Note No.	31st March, 2023 (₹)	31st March, 2024 (₹)	Absolute Change (Increase or Decrease) (₹)	Percentage Change (Increase or Decrease) (%)
3. Current Liabilities					
Trade Payables		4,50,000	6,35,000	1,85,000	41.11
Total		15,00,000	19,35,000	4,35,000	29.0
II. ASSETS					
1. Non-current Assets					
(i) Property, Plant and Equipment and Intangible Assets					
(a) Property, Plant and Equipment	1	10,00,000	11,15,000	1,15,000	11.50
(b) Intangible Assets	2	50,000	—	(50,000)	(100.00)
(ii) Investments		50,000	60,000	10,000	20.00
2. Current Assets		4,00,000	7,60,000	3,60,000	90.00
Total		15,00,000	19,35,000	4,35,000	29.00

Notes to Accounts

Particulars	31st March, 2023 (₹)	31st March, 2024 (₹)
1. Property, Plant and Equipment		
Land and Buildings	7,50,000	8,00,000
Plants and Machinery	2,50,000	3,15,000
	10,00,000	11,15,000
2. Intangible Assets		
Goodwill	50,000	—

**Bracket denotes negative balance*

Solved Question 7 **From the following balance sheet of Hari Ltd. as at 31st March, 2023, prepare comparative balance sheet**

Balance Sheet of Hari Ltd.
as at 31st March, 2023

Particulars	Note No.	31st March, 2023 (₹)	31st March, 2022 (₹)
I. EQUITY AND LIABILITIES			
1. Shareholders' Funds			
(i) Share Capital		15,00,000	12,00,000
2. Non-current Liabilities			
Long-term Borrowings		10,00,000	5,00,000
3. Current Liabilities			
(i) Trade Payables		1,00,000	3,00,000
Total		26,00,000	20,00,000
II. ASSETS			
1. Non-current Assets			
(i) Property, Plant and Equipment and Intangible Assets		20,00,000	15,00,000
2. Current Assets			
(i) Inventories		1,50,000	1,00,000
(ii) Trade Receivables		4,50,000	4,00,000
Total		26,00,000	20,00,000

Sol.

Comparative Balance Sheet
as at 31st March, 2023

Particulars	Note No.	31st March, 2022 (₹)	31st March, 2023 (₹)	Absolute Change (Increase or Decrease) (₹)	Percentage Change (Increase or Decrease) (%)
I. **EQUITY AND LIABILITIES**					
1. **Shareholders' Funds**					
(i) Share Capital		12,00,000	15,00,000	3,00,000	25
2. **Non-current Liabilities**					
(i) Long-term Borrowings		5,00,000	10,00,000	5,00,000	100
3. **Current Liabilities**					
(i) Trade Payables		3,00,000	1,00,000	(2,00,000)	(66.7)
Total		20,00,000	26,00,000	6,00,000	30
II. **ASSETS**					
1. **Non-current Assets**					
(i) Property, Plant and Equipment and Intangible Assets		15,00,000	20,00,000	5,00,000	33.3
2. **Current Assets**					
(i) Inventories		1,00,000	1,50,000	50,000	50
(ii) Trade Receivables		4,00,000	4,50,000	50,000	12.5
Total		20,00,000	26,00,000	6,00,000	30

Common Size Statement of Profit and Loss

Solved Question 8 Prepare a 'common size statement of profit and loss' of Neurosci Ltd. for the year ended 31st March, 2023 from the following information.

Particulars	2022-23 (₹)	2021-22 (₹)
Revenue from Operations	40,00,000	20,00,000
Purchase of Stock-in-trade	4,00,000	2,00,000
Other Expenses	40,000	20,000
Tax Rate	50%	50%

Sol.

Common Size Statement of Profit and Loss of Neurosci Ltd.
for the years ended 31st March, 2022 and 2023

Particulars	Note No.	Absolute Amounts		Percentage of Revenue from Operations	
		2021-22 (₹)	2022-23 (₹)	2021-22 (%)	2022-23 (%)
I. Revenue from Operations		20,00,000	40,00,000	100	100
II. **Expenses**					
(a) Purchase of Stock-in-trade		2,00,000	4,00,000	10	10
(b) Other Expenses		20,000	40,000	1	1
Total Expenses		2,20,000	4,40,000	11	11
III. **Profit before Tax** (I – II)		17,80,000	35,60,000	89	89
IV. (–) Tax @ 50%		(8,90,000)	(17,80,000)	44.5	44.5
V. **Profit after Tax** (III – IV)		8,90,000	17,80,000	44.5	44.5

Solved Question 9 Prepare common size income statement of Tavleen Ltd. from the following statement of profit and loss.

Particulars	31st March, 2024 (₹)	31st March, 2023 (₹)
I. **Income**		
Revenue from Operations (Net sales)	5,00,000	5,00,000
Other Income	5,500	5,000
Total	5,05,500	5,05,000
II. **Expenses**		
Purchases of Stock-in-trade	3,50,000	3,25,000
Changes in Inventories of Stock-in-trade	24,000	25,000
Employees Benefit Expenses	49,000	40,000
Other Expenses	45,000	58,750
Total	4,68,000	4,48,750
III. **Profit** (I – II)	37,500	56,250

Additional Information	**2024 (₹)**	**2023 (₹)**
Other expenses include		
Provision for Tax	37,500	56,250

Sol.

Common Size Income Statement
for the years ended 31st March, 2023 and 2024

Particulars	Absolute Amounts		Percentage of Revenue from Operations (Net sales)	
	2023 (₹)	2024 (₹)	2023 (%)	2024 (%)
I. Revenue from Operations (Net sales)	5,00,000	5,00,000	100.00	100.00
II. Other Income	5,000	5,500	1.00	1.10
III. **Total Revenue** (I + II)	5,05,000	5,05,500	101.00	101.10
IV. **Expenses**				
(a) Purchases of Stock-in-trade	3,25,000	3,50,000	65.00	70.00
(b) Changes in Inventories of Stock-in-trade	25,000	24,000	5.00	4.80
(c) Employees Benefit Expenses	40,000	49,000	8.00	9.80
(d) Other Expenses	2,500	7,500	0.50	1.50
Total Expenses	3,92,500	4,30,500	78.50	86.10
V. **Profit before Tax** (III – IV)	1,12,500	75,000	22.50	15.00
(–) Provision for Tax	56,250	37,500	11.25	7.50
VI. **Profit after Tax**	56,250	37,500	11.25	7.50

Solved Question 10 From the following information prepare a common size statement of profit and loss of A Ltd. and B Ltd. for the year ended 31st March, 2023

Particulars	A Ltd. (₹)	B Ltd. (₹)
Revenue from Operations	20,00,00	10,00,000
Other Income	3,00,000	80,000
Expenses	10,40,000	4,80,000
Tax Rate	40%	40%

Sol.

In the Books of A Ltd. and B Ltd.
Common Size Statement of Profit and Loss
for the year ended 31st March, 2023

Particulars	Absolute Amounts		Percentage of Revenue from Operations	
	A Ltd. (₹)	B Ltd. (₹)	A Ltd. (%)	B Ltd. (%)
Revenue from Operations	20,00,000	10,00,000	100	100
Other Income	3,00,000	80,000	15	8
Total Revenue	23,00,000	10,80,000	115	108

Particulars	Absolute Amounts		Percentage of Revenue from Operations	
(–) Expenses	10,40,000	4,80,000	52	48
Profit before Tax	12,60,000	6,00,000	63	60
(–) Tax @ 40%	5,04,000	2,40,000	25.2	24
Profit after Tax	7,56,000	3,60,000	37.8	36

Solved Question 11 **Prepare common size statement of profit and loss from the following information**

Particulars	31st March 2024 (₹)	31st March, 2023 (₹)
Revenue from Operations	5,00,000	3,75,000
Other Income	50,000	37,500
Purchases of Stock-in-trade	3,75,000	3,00,000
Change in Inventories of Stock-in-trade	(25,000)	5,000
Other Expenses	5,000	3,750
Rate of Income Tax	50%	50%

Sol.

Common Size Statement of Profit and Loss

for the years ended 31st March, 2023 and 2024

Particulars	Note No.	Absolute Amounts		Percentage of Revenue from Operations (Net Sales)	
		31st March, 2023 (₹)	31st March, 2024 (₹)	31st March, 2023 (%)	31st March, 2024 (%)
I. Revenue from Operations		3,75,000	5,00,000	100.00	100.00
II. Other Income		37,500	50,000	10.00	10.00
III. **Total Revenue** (I + II)		4,12,500	5,50,000	110.00	110.00
IV. **Expenses**					
(a) Purchases of Stock-in-trade		3,00,000	3,75,000	80.00	75.00
(b) Change in Inventories of Stock-in-trade		5,000	(25,000)	1.33	(5.00)
(c) Other Expenses		3,750	5,000	1.00	1.00
Total Expenses		3,08,750	3,55,000	82.33	71.00
V. **Profit before Tax** (III – IV)		1,03,750	1,95,000	27.67	39.00
VI. (–) Income Tax		(51,875)	(97,500)	13.83	19.50
VII. **Profit after Tax** (V – VI)		51,875	97,500	13.84	19.50

Common Size Balance Sheet

Solved Question 12 **Following data is derived from the books of Kajal Ltd.**

Particulars	31st March, 2024 (₹)	31st March, 2023 (₹)
Share Capital	1,50,000	1,20,000
Reserve and Surplus	40,000	35,000
Trade Payables	50,000	55,000
Trade Receivables	95,000	90,000
Short-term Provisions	20,000	7,500
Property, Plant and Equipment and Intangible Assets	1,45,000	1,15,000
Long-term Provisions	40,000	32,500
Current Investments	5,000	4,000
Inventory	50,500	36,000
Cash and Cash Equivalents	4,500	5,000

You are required to prepare a common size balance sheet.

Sol.

Common Size Balance Sheet
as at 31st March, 2023 and 2024

Particulars	Note No.	Absolute Amounts		Percentage of Balance Sheet Total	
		2023 (₹)	2024 (₹)	2023 (%)	2024 (%)
I. EQUITY AND LIABILITIES					
1. **Shareholders' Funds**					
(i) Share Capital		1,20,000	1,50,000	48.00	50.00
(ii) Reserves and Surplus		35,000	40,000	14.00	13.33
2. **Non-current Liabilities**					
Long-term Provisions		32,500	40,000	13.00	13.33
3. **Current Liabilities**					
(i) Trade Payables		55,000	50,000	22.00	16.67
(ii) Short-term Provisions		7,500	20,000	3.00	6.67
Total		2,50,000	3,00,000	100.00	100.00
II. ASSETS					
1. **Non-current Assets**					
Property, Plant and Equipment and Intangible Assets		1,15,000	1,45,000	46.00	48.33
2. **Current Assets**					
(i) Current Investments		4,000	5,000	1.60	1.67
(ii) Inventory		36,000	50,500	14.40	16.83
(iii) Trade Receivables		90,000	95,000	36.00	31.67
(iv) Cash and Cash Equivalents		5,000	4,500	2.00	1.50
Total		2,50,000	3,00,000	100.00	100.00

Solved Question 13 From the given balance sheet of Moonlight Ltd., prepare a common size balance sheet **CBSE 2024 C**

Balance Sheet of Moonlight Ltd.
as at 31st March, 2023

Particulars	31st March, 2023 (₹)	31st March, 2022 (₹)
I. EQUITY AND LIABILITIES		
1. **Shareholders' Funds**		
(i) Share Capital	12,00,000	5,00,000
2. **Non-current Liabilities**		
(i) Long-term Borrowings	2,00,000	3,00,000
3. **Current Liabilities**		
(i) Trade Payables	6,00,000	2,00,000
Total	20,00,000	10,00,000
II. ASSETS		
1. **Non-current Assets**		
(i) Property, Plant and Equipment and Intangible Assets	14,00,000	7,00,000
2. **Current Assets**		
(i) Trade Receivables	4,00,000	2,50,000
(ii) Inventories	2,00,000	50,000
Total	20,00,000	10,00,000

Sol.

Common Size Balance Sheet of Moonlight Ltd.
as at 31st March, 2022 and 2023

Particulars	Absolute Amount		Percentage of Balance Sheet Total 31st March, 2022 (%)	Percentage of Balance Sheet Total 31st March, 2023 (%)
	2022 (₹)	2023 (₹)		
I. EQUITY AND LIABILITIES				
1. **Shareholders' Funds**				
(i) Share Capital	5,00,000	12,00,000	60	60
2. **Non-current Liabilities**				
(i) Long-term Borrowings	3,00,000	2,00,000	30	10

Particulars	Absolute Amount		Percentage of Balance Sheet Total	Percentage of Balance Sheet Total
	2022 (₹)	2023 (₹)	31st March, 2022 (%)	31st March, 2023 (%)
3. **Current Liabilities**				
(i) Trade Payables	2,00,000	6,00,000	20	30
Total	10,00,000	20,00,000	100	100
II. **ASSETS**				
1. **Non-Current Assets**				
(i) Property, Plant and Equipment and Intangible Assets	7,00,000	14,00,000	70	70
2. **Current Assets**				
(i) Trade Receivables	2,50,000	4,00,000	25	20
(ii) Inventories	50,000	2,00,000	5	10
Total	10,00,000	20,00,000	100	100

Missing Information

Solved Question 14 **Complete the comparative statement of profit and loss** **CBSE SQP 2025**

Particulars	2022-23 (₹)	2023-24 (₹)	Absolute change Increase or Decrease (₹)	Percentage change Increase or Decrease (%)
Revenue from Operations	16,00,000	20,00,000	...	...
(–) Employees Benefit Expenses	8,00,000	...	...	25%
(–) Other Expenses	2,00,000	...	(1,00,000)	...
Profit before Tax	6,00,000	...	...	50%
Tax @ 30%	...	...	90,000	...
Profit after Tax	4,20,000	...	2,10,000	...

Sol.

Comparative Income Statement

Particulars	2022-23 (₹)	2023-24 (₹)	Absolute change Increase or Decrease (₹)	Percentage change Increase or Decrease (%)
Revenue from Operations	16,00,000	20,00,000	**4,00,000**	**25%**
(–) Employees Benefit Expenses	8,00,000	**10,00,000**	**2,00,000**	25%
(–) Other Expenses	2,00,000	**1,00,000**	(1,00,000)	**50%**
Profit before Tax	6,00,000	**9,00,000**	**3,00,000**	50%
Tax @30%	**1,80,000**	**2,70,000**	90,000	**50%**
Profit after Tax	4,20,000	**6,30,000**	2,10,000	**50%**

Solved Question 15 **Following is the common size statement of profit and loss of Bittoo Ltd. You are required to fill in the missing figures in the comparative statement of profit and loss.**

Common Size Statement of Profit and Loss
for the years ended 31st March, 2023 and 2024

Particulars	Note No.	Absolute Amounts		Percentage of Revenue from Operations	
		2023 (₹)	2024 (₹)	2023 (%)	2024 (%)
I. Revenue from Operations		...	...	...	...
II. **Expenses**					
Cost of Materials Consumed		3,60,000	4,80,000	45	48
Employee Benefit Expenses		...	...	10	8
Depreciation		...	...	7.5	6
Other Expenses		40,000	50,000	...	...
Total Expenses		...	...	...	...
III. **Profit before Tax** (I – II)		...	...	...	...
(–) Tax		(1,04,000)	(1,48,500)	...	...
IV. **Profit after Tax** (III – IV)		...	...	...	...

Sol.

Common Size Statement of Profit and Loss
for the years ended 31st March, 2023 and 2024

Particulars	Note No.	Absolute Amounts		Percentage of Revenue from Operations	
		2023 (₹)	2024 (₹)	2023 (%)	2024 (%)
I. Revenue from Operations		**8,00,000**	**10,00,000**	**100**	**100**
II. **Expenses**					
Cost of Materials Consumed		3,60,000	4,80,000	45	48
Employee Benefit Expenses		**80,000**	**1,60,000**	10	8
Depreciation		**60,000**	**60,000**	7.5	6
Other Expenses		40,000	50,000	5	5
Total Expenses		**5,40,000**	**6,70,000**	**67.5**	**67**
III. **Profit before Tax** (I – II)		**2,60,000**	**3,30,000**	**32.5**	**33**
(–) Tax		(1,04,000)	(1,48,500)	**13**	**14.85**
IV. **Profit after Tax** (III – IV)		**1,56,000**	**1,81,500**	**19.5**	**18.15**

Working Note

First of all, figure of revenue from operations will be found out. It will be calculated on the basis of 'cost of materials consumed'

$2023 = 3,60,000 \times \frac{100}{45} = ₹\ 8,00,000 \qquad 2024 = 4,80,000 \times \frac{100}{48} = ₹\ 10,00,000$

Numerical Questions

Comparative Profit and Loss

1. **From the following statement of profit and loss of Shikha Ltd., prepare comparative statement of profit and loss for the year ended 31st March, 2023.**

In the Books of Shikha Ltd.
Statement Profit and Loss
for the year ended 31st March, 2023

Particulars	2022-23 (₹)	2021-22 (₹)
Revenue from Operations	32,00,000	20,00,000
Expenses		
Employee benefit Expenses	9,60,000	6,00,000
Other Expenses	6,40,000	4,00,000
Tax	50%	50%

2. **From the following statement of profit and loss of Saraswati Ltd. for the years ended 31st March, 2023 and 2024, prepare a comparative statement of profit and loss.** **Competency Based Que**

Particulars	Note No.	31st March, 2024	31st March, 2023
Revenue from Operations (Sales)		₹ 25,00,000	₹ 20,00,000
Employees Benefit Expenses (% of Revenue from operations)		50%	50%
Other Expenses (% of Revenue from operations)		10%	10%
Tax		40%	40%

3. **From the following information, prepare a comparative statement of profit and loss** **Competency Based Que**

Particulars	Note No.	2024	2023
Revenue from Operations		₹ 24,00,000	₹ 18,00,000
Other Incomes (% of Revenue from operations)		15%	25%
Expenses (% of Revenue from operations)		60%	50%
Tax Rate		40%	40%

4. **From the statement of profit and loss, prepare comparative income statement of Sai Ram Ltd.**

Particulars	31st March, 2024 (₹)	31st March, 2023 (₹)
I. **Income**		
Revenue from Operations	66,00,000	60,00,000
Other Income	1,20,000	1,20,000
Total	67,20,000	61,20,000
II. **Expenses**		
Purchases of Stock-in-trade	48,00,000	46,00,000
Changes in Inventories of Stock-in-trade	2,40,000	2,00,000
Employees Benefit Expenses	1,80,000	1,40,000
Finance Cost	1,20,000	1,20,000
Other Expenses	1,80,000	1,60,000
Total	55,20,000	52,20,000
III. **Profit** (I – II)	12,00,000	9,00,000
Tax is Payable @ 50%		

5. From the following information, prepare comparative statement of profit and loss for the year ended 31st March, 2023 **CBSE 2024**

Particulars	2022-23 (₹)	2021-22 (₹)
Revenue from Operations	4,00,000	2,00,000
Other Income	80,000	40,000
Employee benefit Expenses	50% of Revenue from operations	50% of Revenue from operations
Tax Rate	50%	50%

6. From the following information prepare comparative statement of profit and loss. **Competency Based Que**

Particulars	31st March, 2024	31st March, 2023
Revenue from Operations	₹ 12,50,000	₹ 10,00,000
Cost of Materials Consumed	₹ 10,50,000	₹ 8,00,000
Other Expenses	25% of Gross profit	20% of Gross profit
Income Tax	50%	50%

Comparative Balance Sheet

7. From the following information, prepare comparative balance sheet of X Ltd. **CBSE 2019 (M)**

Particulars	31st March 2024 (₹)	31st March, 2023 (₹)
Share Capital	25,00,000	25,00,000
Reserves and Surplus	6,00,000	10,00,000
Long-term Borrowings	16,00,000	15,00,000
Current Liabilities	5,00,000	4,50,000
Property, Plant and Equipment and Intangible Assets	35,00,000	25,00,000
Investments (Non-current)	10,50,000	15,00,0000
Current Assets	6,50,000	14,50,000

8. From the following information of Mathura Ltd., prepare comparative balance sheets **Competency Based Que**

Particulars	31st March, 2024 (₹)	31st March, 2023 (₹)
Reserve and Surplus	6000	30,000
Share Capital	50,000	50,000
Trade Payables	63,500	45,000
Land and Buildings	80,000	75,000
Plant and Machinery	31,500	25,000
Goodwill	—	5,000
Investments	6,000	5,000
Current Assets	76,000	40,000
Long-term Borrowings	20,000	25,000

9. From the following summarised balance sheets of Raghav Ltd. as at 31st March, 2024 and 2023, prepare a comparative balance sheet. **Competency Based Que**

Particulars	31st March, 2024 (₹)	31st March, 2023 (₹)
I. **EQUITY AND LIABILITIES**		
1. **Shareholders' Funds**		
(i) Share Capital		
(a) Equity Share Capital	30,00,000	30,00,000
(b) Preference Share Capital	7,50,000	7,50,000
(ii) Reserves and Surplus	9,00,000	7,50,000
2. **Non-current Liabilities**		
(i) Long-term Borrowings		
(a) Secured Loans	13,50,000	15,00,000
(b) Unsecured Loans	9,00,000	7,50,000
(ii) Long-term Provisions	1,15,000	1,00,000
3. **Current Liabilities**		
(i) Trade Payables (Creditors)	6,60,000	6,00,000
(ii) Short-term Provisions	50,000	50,000
Total	77,25,000	75,00,000
II. **ASSETS**		
1. **Non-current Assets**		
(i) Property, Plant and Equipment and Intangible Assets	54,00,000	45,00,000
(ii) Non-current Investments	7,50,000	7,50,000
2. **Current Assets**		
(i) Trade Receivables (Debtors)	14,75,000	20,00,000
(ii) Cash and Cash Equivalents	1,00,000	2,50,000
Total	77,25,000	75,00,000

Common Size Profit and Loss

10. Prepare common size statement of profit and loss from the following information

Particulars	31st March, 2024 (₹)	31st March, 2023 (₹)
Revenue from Operations (Sales)	1,30,000	1,00,000
Cost of Material Consumed	84,000	80,000
Other Expenses	9,000	12,000
Income Tax	50%	50%

11. From the following statement of profit and loss, prepare common size income statement

Particulars	31st March, 2024 (₹)	31st March, 2023 (₹)
I. **Income**		
Revenue from Operations (Net sales)	25,00,000	20,00,000
II. **Expenses**		
Purchases of Stock-in-trade	17,40,000	14,40,000
Changes in Inventories of Stock-in-trade	(40,000)	60,000
Depreciation and Amortisation	60,000	40,000
Other Expenses	1,00,000	60,000
Total	18,60,000	16,00,000
III. **Net Profit** (I – II)	6,40,000	4,00,000

12. From the following information of NK Ltd., prepare a common size statement of profit and loss for the years ended 31st March, 2022 and 31st March, 2023

Particulars	31st March, 2023 (₹)	31st March, 2022 (₹)
Revenue from Operations	25,00,000	20,00,000
Cost of Materials Consumed	8,00,000	6,00,000
Employee Benefit Expenses	4,00,000	4,00,000
Income Tax	20%	30%

13. **Following particulars are obtained from the books of Prerna Ltd. You are required to prepare common size statement of profit and loss**

Particulars	Note No.	2024 (₹)	2023 (₹)
Revenue from Operations		60,00,000	40,00,000
Purchases of Stock-in-trade		43,20,000	30,40,000
Changes in Inventories		1,20,000	(80,000)
Other Income		1,50,000	60,000
Other Expenses		3,60,000	2,00,000

14. **From the information extracted from the statement of profit and loss of Zee Ltd. for the year ended 31st March, 2022 and 31st March, 2023, prepare a common size statement of profit and loss** **Competency Based Que**

Particulars	Note No.	2022-23 (₹)	2021-22 (₹)
Revenue from Operations		8,00,000	10,00,000
Gross Profit		60%	70%
Other Expenses		2,20,000	2,60,000
Tax Rate		50%	50%

15. **From the following data, prepare a common size statement of profit and loss of Jatin Ltd.** **Competency Based Que**

Particulars	31st March, 2024 (₹)	31st March, 2023 (₹)
Revenue from Operations (% of Other Income)	200%	200%
Other Income	60,000	45,000
Cost of Materials consumed (% of Operating Revenue)	60%	50%
Other Expenses (% of Material Cost)	10%	20%
Tax Rate	30%	30%

Common Size Balance Sheet

16. **Prepare common size balance sheet from the following information** **Competency Based Que**

Particulars	31st March, 2024 (₹)	31st March, 2023 (₹)
Shareholder' Funds	9,00,000	6,00,000
Non-current Liabilities	3,00,000	3,00,000
Current Liabilities	3,00,000	1,00,000
Non-current Assets	10,50,000	7,00,000
Current Assets	4,50,000	3,00,000

17. **From the given balance sheet of Geox Ltd., prepare common size balance sheet.**

Balance Sheet of Geox Ltd.
as at 31st March, 2023

Particulars	Note No.	31st March, 2023 (₹)	31st March, 2022 (₹)
I. EQUITY AND LIABILITIES			
1. Shareholders' Funds			
(i) Share Capital		4,00,000	2,50,000
2. Non-current Liabilities			
(i) Long-term Borrowings		2,00,000	1,50,000
3. Current Liabilities			
(i) Trade Payables		2,00,000	1,00,000
Total		8,00,000	5,00,000
II. ASSETS			
1. Non-current Assets			
(i) Property, Plant and Equipment and Intangible Assets		4,00,000	3,50,000
2. Current Assets			
(i) Inventories		2,00,000	70,000
(ii) Trade Receivables		2,00,000	80,000
Total		8,00,000	5,00,000

18. **Prepare a common size balance sheet of X Ltd. from the following information** **CBSE 2024**

Balance Sheet of X Ltd.
as at 31st March, 2023

Particulars	Note No.	31st March, 2023 (₹)	31st March, 2022 (₹)
I. EQUITY AND LIABILITIES			
1. Shareholders' Funds			
(i) Equity Share Capital		30,00,000	15,00,000
(ii) Reserves and Surplus		10,00,000	5,00,000
2. Non-current Liabilities		20,00,000	20,00,000
3. Current Liabilities		20,00,000	10,00,000
Total		80,00,000	50,00,000
II. ASSETS			
1. Non-current Assets		40,00,000	30,00,000
2. Current Assets			
(i) Inventories		40,00,000	20,00,000
Total		80,00,000	50,00,000

Missing Information

19. **Fill in the missing figures in the following common size statement of profit and loss of Manju Ltd.** **Competency Based Que**

Common Size Statement of Profit and Loss
for the year ended 31st March, 2024

Particulars	Note No.	Absolute Amount (₹)	Percentage of Revenue from Operations (%)
I. **Revenue from Operations**		...	...
II. Other Income		2,70,000	...
III. Total Income (I + II)		...	...
IV. (–) **Expenses**			
Cost of Materials Consumed		...	50
Other Expenses		9,45,000	14
Total Expenses		...	...
Profit before Tax (III – IV)		...	...
(–) Tax		(...)	16
Profit after Tax		...	...

20. **Fill in the amounts left blank in the following common size statement of profit and loss of Somya Ltd. for the year ended 31st March, 2024.** **Competency Based Que**

Common Size Statement of Profit and Loss
for the year ended 31st March, 2024

Particulars	Absolute Change		% of Revenue From	
	2022-23 (₹)	2023-24 (₹)	2022-23 (₹)	2023-24 (₹)
I. **Revenue from Operations**	10,00,000	12,50,000	...	100
II. Other Income	50,000	12,50,000	...	10
III. **Total Revenue**	10,50,000	13,75,000	105	110
IV. **Expenses**				
(a) Cost of Materials Consumed	...	4,00,000	30	32
(b) Change in Inventory	50,000	1,00,000	...	8
(c) Employee Benefit Expenses	...	2,25,000	15	18
(d) Other Expenses	...	1,12,500	10	9
Total Expenses	6,00,000	8,37,500	...	67
V. **Profit before Tax** (III – IV)	4,50,000	5,37,500	45	43
(–) Tax	(1,00,000)	(1,25,000)	10	...
VI. **Profit after Tax**	3,50,000	4,12,500	35	33

Theoretical Questions

Short Answer Type Questions

1. Explain briefly any four objectives of analysis of financial statements. **CBSE 2019**

Or **State the objectives of 'analysis of financial statements'.**

Or **One of the objectives of 'financial statement analysis' is to judge the ability of the firm to repay its debt and assessing the short-term as well as the long-term liquidity position of the firm. State two more objectives of this analysis.**

Or **One of the objectives of 'financial statement analysis' is to ascertain the relative importance of the different components of the financial position of the firm. State two more objectives of this analysis.** **Competency Based Que**

Ans. The objectives of analysis of financial statements are as follows

(i) To measure the operating efficiency and profitability of an enterprise.

(ii) To compare the intra-firm position, inter-firm position and pattern position within the industry.

(iii) To judge the financial stability of an enterprise.

(iv) To measure the short-term and long-term solvency of enterprise.

2. Explain briefly any four limitations of analysis of financial statements. **CBSE 2019**

Or **State any four limitations of analysis of financial statements.**

Or **State any one limitation of financial statement analysis.**

Ans. The limitations of analysis of financial statements are as follows

(i) It ignores price level changes.

(ii) It is not free from bias.

(iii) It suffers from limitations of financial statements.

(iv) It ignores qualitative aspects.

3. Distinguish between vertical and horizontal analysis of financial statements. **NCERT**

Ans.

Basis	Horizontal Analysis	Vertical Analysis
Items	It deals with same items of same period.	It deals with different items of same period.
Information	It provides information in absolute and percentage terms.	It provides information in percentage terms.
Period	It requires financial statement of two or more accounting periods.	It requires financial statements of one period.
Useful	It is generally used for time series analysis.	It is generally used for cross sectional analysis.
Comparison	It is a part of comparison.	It is a step towards comparison.

4. Explain the importance of financial analysis of (i) labour unions and (ii) creditors **CBSE 2019**

Ans. (i) **Labour Unions** They analyse the financial statement to assess whether the business concern is earning a fair rate of return on capital employed and whether they should demand for increased wages or not.

So, financial statement analysis helps the labour unions in settling wage agreements.

(ii) **Creditors** A creditor, through an analysis of financial statements, judges not only the present ability of the company to meet its obligations, but also the probability of its continued ability to meet all its financial obligations.

Trade creditors are particularly interested in the firm's ability to meet their claims over a short period of time.

5. List the techniques of financial statement analysis. **NCERT**

Ans. The tools or techniques of financial statement analysis are

(i) Comparative financial statements

(ii) Common size statements

(iii) Ratio analysis

(iv) Cash flow statement

6. What do you mean by comparative statement of profit and loss? What are the objectives of preparing comparative statement of profit and loss?

Ans. Comparative statement of profit and loss is the horizontal analysis of income statement. It shows the operating results (i.e. net profit or loss) for two or more accounting periods, so that changes in absolute amounts and percentages may be known.

The **objectives** of comparative income statement are

(i) To analyse the income and expenditure for two or more years.

(ii) To analyse the increase or decrease in the income and expenditure in terms of rupees and also in percentage.

(iii) To review the business operations of the last year and its likely effect on the current year's operations.

7. What do you mean by comparative balance sheet? What are the objectives of preparing comparative balance sheet?

Ans. Comparative balance sheet is the horizontal analysis of balance sheet.

It analyses each item of assets, equity and liabilities for two or more accounting periods, so that changes in absolute amounts and percentages may be known.

The **objectives** of comparative balance sheet are

(i) To measure the financial position of an enterprise.

(ii) To analyse different items of assets and liabilities in absolute rupees, i.e. balances on two or more comparative dates.

(iii) To analyse increase or decrease in rupee amounts as well as in percentage by taking the data of previous years as base.

(iv) To review the past financing and investing activities and their effect on the financial position of the enterprise.

8. What do you mean common size statement of profit and loss? What are the objectives of preparing common size statement of profit and loss?

Ans. It is the statement in which amount of revenue from operations (net sales) is assumed to be equal to 100 and other amounts are expressed as percentage of revenue from operations (net sales).

Such statement may be prepared for different periods or for two firms. It shows the relative efficiency in operating the business.

The **objectives** associated with common size income statement are

(i) To analyse change in individual items of statement of profit and loss.

(ii) To study the trend in different items of income expenditure.

(iii) To assess the efficiency.

9. What do you mean by common size balance sheet? What are the objectives of preparing common size balance sheet?

Ans. It shows the percentage relation of each asset/liability to total assets/total liabilities including capital. In this, total assets or total equity and liabilities are taken as 100 and all the figures are expressed as percentage of the total.

The **objectives** of common size balance sheet are

(i) To analyse the changes in individual items of balance sheet.

(ii) To see the trend of different items of assets, equity and liabilities.

(iii) To understand the financial strategy and also to assess the financial soundness of the company.

Long Answer Type Questions

10. What do you mean by comparative financial statements and common size statements?

Ans. Comparative statement is an art of presenting financial statements, (i.e. income statement and balance sheet) of two or more years of a firm, in such a manner which helps to assess the weak and strong points of the business entity.

It may relate to different periods (intra-firm comparison) or different firms but for the same period (inter-firm comparison). Comparative statements analysis is also known as horizontal analysis. Comparative statements are part of management information system. They are the internal documents prepared by a business and do not form the part of the financial statements.

These are the statements in which amounts of individual items of balance sheet, statement of profit and loss for two or more years are written. These items are further converted into percentages to a common base.

For statement of profit and loss, common base is revenue from operations and for balance sheet, common base is total of balance sheet.

Comparison can be easily made with the percentage so calculated with the corresponding percentages in other periods and meaningful conclusions can be drawn. Common size analysis is also known as vertical analysis.

11. State the advantages and disadvantages of using comparative statements.

Ans. Advantages of Comparative Statements

(i) Changes in the components of assets and liabilities can easily be known at a glance through comparative balance sheet.

(ii) Comparative statement of profit and loss helps to identify the trend of changes in revenue from operations, expenses, profits, etc.

(iii) Inter-firm comparison helps the management to evaluate performance of the firm in relation to other firms in the same industry. Thus, management can identify strengths and weaknesses of the firm and can adopt appropriate corrective measures.

Disadvantages of Comparative Statements

(i) When a particular item of financial statements does not appear in the base year but appears in current year, meaningful computation of percentage change in absolute figure of that item cannot be done.

(ii) Comparative analysis cannot exhibit meaningful disclosure when uniformity in accounting concepts and conventions is not maintained over the years.

(iii) Such comparison becomes meaningless when size of firms differ.

12. **State the advantages and disadvantages of common size statements.**

Ans. **Advantages of Common Size Statements**

(i) It shows relative significance of every item in financial statements in percentage terms of its base figure.

(ii) In common size balance sheet, every item is presented in terms of total of assets or liabilities, which helps the analyst to know how much percentage of total assets has been apportioned between current and fixed assets, etc and how much percentage of total liabilities is payable to the owners and the outsiders.

(iii) It makes inter-company comparison easier. It facilitates comparison of firms with different sizes.

Disadvantages of Common Size Statements

(i) In these statements, relative importance of each component of financial statements in whole is exhibited, but no comparative study is done between the years.

(ii) In such statement, time value of money is not considered.

(iii) This analysis does not prove to be very useful for important decision-making.

Objective Questions

Multiple Choice Questions (MCQs)

1. **The process of simplifying financial data by classification is referred to as**

(a) interpretation (b) analysis
(c) forecasting (d) consolidation

2. **What does time series analysis involve?** Competency Based Que

(a) Comparing financial statements of a firm with other firms
(b) Predicting a firm's future earnings based on past trends
(c) Analysing a firm's performance over different periods
(d) Consolidating a firm's balance sheet and profit and loss accounts

3. **Which of the following is not a component of financial statement analysis?**

(a) Predicting future cash flows
(b) Judging management efficiency
(c) Preparing financial statements
(d) Assessing profitability

4. **Financial statement analysis primarily helps in** Competency Based Que

(a) preparing tax returns
(b) understanding a firm's financial health and future prospects
(c) recording day-to-day business transactions
(d) estimating inventory levels

5. **............ is not a tool of 'analysis of financial statements'.** CBSE 2025

(a) Income statement (b) Ratio analysis
(c) Comparative statements (d) Cash flow statement

6. **Horizontal analysis provides information in**

(a) absolute terms (b) percentage terms
(c) Both (a) and (b) (d) different terms

7. **The financial statements of a business enterprise include**

(a) balance sheet
(b) statement of profit and loss account
(c) cash flow statement
(d) All of the above

8. **When an analyst analyse the financial statements of an enterprise over a number of years, the analysis is called .... analysis.** CBSE SQP 2025

(a) static (b) external
(c) horizontal (d) vertical

9. **Which of the following tools helps in inter-firm and intra-firm comparisons?**

(a) Comparative statements (b) Ratio analysis
(c) Trend analysis (d) Cash flow analysis

10. **What does financial analysis help investors to determine?**

(a) Liquidity position of the firm
(b) Efficiency of management
(c) Firm's earning potential and risk
(d) Probability of future cash flows

11. **An annual report is issued by a company to its**

(a) directors (b) auditors
(c) shareholders (d) management

12. **Balance sheet provides information about financial position of enterprise**

(a) at a point in time (b) over a period of time
(c) for a period of time (d) None of these

13. **Which of the following is a tool of analysis of financial statements?** CBSE 2023; Competency Based Que

(i) Cast flow statement
(ii) Statement of profit and loss
(iii) Notes to accounts
(iv) Balance sheet

Codes
(a) Only (i) (b) (i) and (ii)
(c) Only (ii) (d) (i), (ii) and (iv)

14. **Which tool is also known as 'horizontal analysis'?**
(a) Ratio analysis
(b) Trend analysis
(c) Comparative statements
(d) Common size statements

15. **Which of the following is not a limitation of 'analysis of financial statements?** CBSE 2024 C; Competency Based Que
(a) It is just a study of the reports of the company
(b) It does not consider price level changes
(c) It ascertains the relative importance of different components of the financial position of the firm
(d) It may be misleading without the knowledge of the changes in accounting procedures followed by a firm

16. **The tool of 'analysis of financial statements' which helps to assess the profitability, solvency and efficiency of an enterprise is known as** CBSE 2024
(a) cash flow statement (b) comparative statement
(c) common size statement (d) ratio analysis

17. **Financial statement analysis includes .... and .... of financial statements.** CBSE Term I 2021
(a) analysis, preparation (b) preparation, interpretation
(c) preparation, analysis (d) analysis, interpretation

18. **Which of the following is not a limitation of 'financial statements analysis'?** CBSE 2020; Competency Based Que
(a) It is affected by personal bias
(b) Inter-firm comparative study possible
(c) Lack of qualitative analysis
(d) Ignores price level changes

19. **Which of the following are the tools of vertical analysis?** CBSE SQP Term I 2021; Competency Based Que

(i) Ratio analysis (ii) Comparative statements
(iii) Common size statements

Codes
(a) Only (iii) (b) Both (i) and (iii)
(c) Both (i) and (ii) (d) Only (i)

20. **In 'common size income statement' each item is expressed as a percentage of ....** CBSE 2025
(a) total income (b) total expenses
(c) profit after tax (d) revenue from operations

21. **Financial statement analysis is not free from .... bias.**
(a) sectional (b) personal
(c) non-personal (d) None of these

22. **.......... analysis helps in determining the borrowing capacity of a prospective buyer.**
(a) External (b) Internal
(c) Debt (d) None of these

23. **.......... may like to analyse profitability, growth, financial position and future prospects of a business.**
(a) Researchers (b) Government
(c) Customers (d) None of these

24. **Long-term borrowings of a firm on 31st March, 2016 was ₹ 5,00,000 and ₹ 8,00,000 on 31st March, 2017. What will be the absolute change and percentage change in comparative balance sheet?** Competency Based Que
(a) ₹ 4,00,000, 80% respectively
(b) ₹ 3,00,000, 60% respectively
(c) ₹ 5,00,000, 35% respectively
(d) ₹ 8,00,000, 25% respectively

25. **Revenue from operations on 31st March, 2016 was ₹ 15,00,000 and on 31st March, 2015 was ₹ 12,00,000, then what will be the percentage change in revenue from operations?** Competency Based Que
(a) 50% (b) 62% (c) 45% (d) 25%

26. **Cost of material consumed was ₹ 6,00,000 in 2016-17 and total revenue from operations was ₹ 10,00,000, then percentage of cost of material consumed to total revenue from operations is** Competency Based Que
(a) 60% (b) 30% (c) 25% (d) 18%

27. **Tangible assets are ₹ 4,00,000 on 31st March, 2016 and intangible assets are ₹ 2,00,000. Total assets of the firm are ₹ 10,00,000, then what will be the percentage of tangible assets to total assets?** Competency Based Que
(a) 48% (b) 50% (c) 40% (d) 32%

28. **Non-current investment of a firm on 31st March, 2019 was ₹ 15,00,000 and ₹ 10,50,000 on 31st March, 2020. What will be the absolute change in comparative balance sheet?** Competency Based Que
(a) ₹ 4,50,000 increase (b) ₹ 4,50,000 decrease
(c) ₹ 15,00,000 increase (d) ₹ 15,00,000 decrease

Assertion-Reason

Direction (Q.No. 29 to 38) *Read the following Assertion (A) and Reason (R) and choose the correct alternative from the following*

Alternatives
(a) Both Assertion (A) and Reason (R) are true and Reason (R) is the correct explanation of Assertion (A)
(b) Both Assertion (A) and Reason (R) are true, but Reason (R) is not the correct explanation of Assertion (A)
(c) Assertion (A) is true, but Reason (R) is false
(d) Assertion (A) is false, but Reason (R) is true

29. **Assertion** (A) Financial statement analysis helps in identifying the strengths and weaknesses of a business.

Reason (R) It involves regrouping and analysing the data provided in financial statements.

30. **Assertion** (A) Cross sectional analysis helps compare a firm's performance with its own past performance.

Reason (R) Cross sectional analysis is useful for comparing the performance of a firm with other firms in the same industry.

31. **Assertion** (A) Interpretation of financial data is not necessary for decision-making.

Reason (R) Interpretation helps explain the meaning and significance of financial data for informed decisions.

32. **Assertion** (A) Financial statement analysis is useful for assessing the solvency of a company.

Reason (R) Financial statement analysis is primarily conducted to comply with legal requirements rather than for decision-making.

33. **Assertion** (A) Internal analysis carried out by management is more detailed, extensive and correct.

Reason (R) Management has access to all the information relating to the organisation.

34. **Assertion** (A) Comparative statements are useful for making inter-firm comparisons.

Reason (R) Comparative statements involve expressing financial data in a common size format.

35. **Assertion** (A) Inter-firm analysis is a comparison of financial statements of an enterprise for two or more accounting periods.

Reason (R) Time series analysis is conducted to determine the trend of different financial variables over a period of time.

36. **Assertion** (A) A common size statement helps in comparing the financial performance of different companies.

Reason (R) In a common size statement, each item is expressed as a percentage of a common base, making comparison easier.

37. **Assertion** (A) Analysis of financial statements is done to assess the managerial efficiency.

Reason (R) Financial statement analysis helps to identify the areas where the managers have been efficient and the areas where they have been inefficient.

38. **Assertion** (A) Financial analysis helps in assessing the current profitability and operational efficiency of a firm.

Reason (R) Financial analysis enables analysts to make decisions regarding the operation and future investments in a firm by understanding its strengths and weaknesses.

Two Statements Based MCQs

Direction (Q.No. 39 to 46) *Read the following statements carefully and choose the correct alternative*

Alternatives

(a) Statement I is correct and Statement II is incorrect
(b) Statement II is correct and Statement I is incorrect
(c) Both the statements are correct
(d) Both the statements are incorrect

39. **Statement I** Financial statement analysis involves analysing the relationship among various financial facts and figures to understand a firm's profitability.

Statement II Financial analysis is complete even without interpretation.

40. **Statement I** Time series analysis compares a firm's performance over different periods.

Statement II Cross sectional analysis compares the performance of a firm with other firms.

41. **Statement I** Analysis without interpretation is useful for decision-making.

Statement II Financial statement analysis helps in estimating current financial positions and predicting future conditions.

42. **Statement I** Comparative statements provide data in a common size format to enable comparison.

Statement II Trend analysis helps observe changes in financial data over a series of years.

43. **Statement I** Financial statement analysis can reveal a firm's strengths and weaknesses.

Statement II Financial analysis is only useful for external users such as investors and creditors.

44. **Statement I** Comparative financial statements help in analysing the trend of financial performance over multiple accounting periods.

Statement II A common size statement expresses each item of a financial statement as a percentage of the total assets or total liabilities.

45. **Statement I** Financial analysis is used for credit analysis.

Statement II An objective of financial analysis to determine operating efficiency and profitability.

46. **Statement I** Financial statement analysis is free from bias.

Statement II Qualitative aspects are not ignored in the financial statement analysis.

Matching

47. **Match the terms in Column I with their respective descriptions in Column II**

Column I		Column II
A. Time series analysis	(i)	Compares performance with other firms
B. Cross sectional analysis	(ii)	Study of relationship among financial figures
C. Interpretation	(iii)	Analysing a firm's performance over time
D. Financial statement analysis	(iv)	Explains the meaning of financial data

Codes

	A	B	C	D
(a)	(iii)	(i)	(iv)	(ii)
(b)	(ii)	(iv)	(i)	(iii)
(c)	(i)	(iii)	(ii)	(iv)
(d)	(iv)	(ii)	(iii)	(i)

48. **Match the tools of analysis in Column I with their features in Column II**

Column I		Column II
A. Ratio analysis	(i)	Studies the operational results over several years
B. Cash flow analysis	(ii)	Measures profitability, solvency and efficiency
C. Comparative statements	(iii)	Compares financial data over two or more periods
D. Trend analysis	(iv)	Summarises cash inflows and outflows between two dates

Codes

	A	B	C	D		A	B	C	D
(a)	(ii)	(iv)	(iii)	(i)	(b)	(iii)	(i)	(iv)	(ii)
(c)	(iv)	(iii)	(i)	(ii)	(d)	(i)	(ii)	(iii)	(iv)

49. **Match the users of financial analysis in Column I with their objectives in Column II**

Column I		Column II
A. Finance manager	(i)	To assess the company's ability to repay its claims in the short term
B. Trade payables	(ii)	To evaluate profitability and capital structure
C. Investors	(iii)	To analyse managerial performance and financial efficiency
D. Lenders	(iv)	To determine long-term solvency and cash generation ability

Codes

	A	B	C	D
(a)	(iii)	(i)	(ii)	(iv)
(b)	(ii)	(iv)	(iii)	(i)
(c)	(iv)	(ii)	(iii)	(i)
(d)	(i)	(iii)	(ii)	(iv)

50. Match the following

Column I (Purpose)		Column II (Type of Financial Statement Analysis)
A. Users	(i)	Intra-firm analysis and inter-firm analysis
B. Objectivity	(ii)	External analysis and internal analysis
C. Time	(iii)	Short-term analysis and long-term analysis
D. Firm	(iv)	Horizontal analysis and vertical analysis

Codes

	A	B	C	D		A	B	C	D
(a)	(ii)	(iii)	(iv)	(i)	(b)	(i)	(ii)	(iii)	(iv)
(c)	(iii)	(iv)	(i)	(ii)	(d)	(iv)	(ii)	(iii)	(i)

51. Match the following

Column I		Column II
A. Significance	(i)	Comparative statements and common size statements
B. Type of analysis	(ii)	Does not consider price level changes
C. Tools of analysis	(iii)	To present the complex financial data in simplified and understandable form
D. Limitation	(iv)	Horizontal analysis and vertical analysis

Codes

	A	B	C	D		A	B	C	D
(a)	(iii)	(iv)	(i)	(ii)	(b)	(i)	(ii)	(iii)	(iv)
(c)	(iv)	(ii)	(iii)	(i)	(d)	(ii)	(iii)	(iv)	(i)

Case Based MCQs

Direction *Read the following case study and answer the questions 52 to 54 on the basis of the same*

INA Ltd. is a company that deals in manufacturing of pharmaceutical products. Raman has recently been hired as an assistant to the accountant of INA Ltd. The accountant of the firm Mr. Rajat asks Raman to go for financial statement analysis of the firm to assess the financial position of the firm.

To judge the knowledge and capabilities of Raman, Mr. Rajat asked him to analyse the financial statements from the viewpoint of various parties interested in the firm e.g. The management, the lenders, the investors, labour unions, government, etc.

52. **Which of the following statements will primarily be utilised by Raman for the purpose of financial statement analysis?**

(a) Balance sheet and cash flow statement
(b) Statement of profit and loss and cash flow statement
(c) Balance sheet and statement of profit and loss
(d) Cash flow statement and fund flow statement

53. If Raman is to analyse the financial statements for the top management, what should he consider?
(a) Short-term liquidity of the firm
(b) Ability to pay its long-term lenders
(c) To see that the resources of the firm are used most efficiently and that the firm's financial condition is sound
(d) None of the above

54. If Raman is to analyse the financial statements for the short-term lenders, what should he consider?
(a) Short-term liquidity of the firm
(b) Long-term solvency of the firm
(c) To see that the resources of the firm are used most efficiently and that the firm's financial condition is sound
(d) None of the above

Direction *Read the following case study and answer the questions 55 to 57 on the basis of the same*

The motto of 'Pharma Ltd.' a company engaged in the manufacturing of low cost generic medicines, is 'Healthy India'.

Its management and employees are hardworking, honest and motivated. The net profit of the company doubled during the year ended 31st March, 2019. Encouraged by its performance, the company decided to pay bonus to all employees at double the rate than last year. Following is the comparative statement of profit and loss of the company for the years ended 31st March, 2018 and 2019

In the Books of Pharma Ltd.
Comparative Statement of Profit and Loss
for the year ended 31st March, 2018 and 2019

Particulars	Note No.	2018-19 (₹)	2017-18 (₹)
Revenue from Operations		30,00,000	20,00,000
(−) Employees Benefit Expenses		(14,00,000)	(12,00,000)
Profit before Tax		16,00,000	8,00,000
(−) Tax Rate at 25%		(4,00,000)	(2,00,000)
Profit after Tax		12,00,000	6,00,000

55. All except .... has same percentage of change.
(a) revenue from operations (b) profit after tax
(c) tax (d) profit before tax

56. Tax liability .... by ....
(a) decreased, ₹ 4,00,000 (b) decreased, ₹ 2,00,000
(c) increased, ₹ 4,00,000 (d) increased, ₹ 2,00,000

57. If the tax rate is increased by 15% in 2018-19, then what will be the absolute change in profit after tax?
(a) ₹ 6,40,000 (b) ₹ 9,60,000
(c) ₹ 3,60,000 (d) ₹ 5,00,000

Answers

1. (b) analysis
2. (c) Analysing a firm's performance over different periods
3. (c) Preparing financial statements
4. (b) understanding a firm's financial health and future prospects
5. (a) Income statement
6. (c) Horizontal analysis provides information in absolute and percentage terms. It is undertaken to review and analyse the financial statements of a number of years and is very useful for long-term trend analysis and planning.
7. (d) All of the above
8. (c) horizontal
9. (a) Comparative statements
10. (c) Firm's earning potential and risk
11. (c) shareholders
12. (a) at a point in time
13. (a) Only I
14. (c) Comparative statements
15. (c) It ascertains the relative importance of different components of the financial position of the firm
16. (d) ratio analysis
17. (d) analysis, interpretation
18. (b) Inter-firm comparative study possible
19. (b) Comparative statement is the tool of horizontal analysis.
20. (d) revenue from operations
21. (b) personal
22. (c) Debt
23. (a) Researchers
24. (b) Absolute change = 8,00,000 − 5,00,000 = ₹ 3,00,000

$$\text{Percentage Change} = \frac{\text{Change} \times 100}{\text{Previous Years Balance}} = \frac{3,00,000 \times 100}{5,00,000} = 60\%$$

25. (d) Absolute change = 15,00,000 − 12,00,000 = ₹ 3,00,000

$$\text{Percentage Change} = \frac{\text{Absolute Change} \times 100}{\text{Previous Year Figures}} = \frac{3,00,000 \times 100}{12,00,000} = 25\%$$

26. (a) Percentage of Cost of Material Consumed to Total Revenue from Operations

$$= \frac{\text{Cost of Material Consumed} \times 100}{\text{Total Revenue from Operations}}$$

$$= \frac{6,00,000 \times 100}{10,00,000} = 60\%$$

27. (c) Percentage of Tangible Assets

$$= \frac{\text{Tangible Assets}}{\text{Total Assets}} \times 100 = \frac{4,00,000 \times 100}{10,00,000} = 40\%$$

28. (b) ₹ 4,50,000 decrease

29. (a) Both Assertion (A) and Reason (R) are true and Reason (R) is the correct explanation of Assertion (A)

30. (d) Assertion (A) is false, but Reason (R) is true

31. (d) Assertion (A) is false, but Reason (R) is true

32. (c) Assertion (A) is true, but Reason (R) is false

33. (a) Both Assertion (A) and Reason (R) are true and Reason (R) is the correct explanation of Assertion (A)

34. (c) Assertion (A) is true, but Reason (R) is false

35. (c) Intra-firm analysis is a comparison of financial statements of an enterprise for two or more accounting periods.

36. (a) Both Assertion (A) and Reason (R) are true and Reason (R) is the correct explanation of Assertion (A)

37. (a) Both Assertion (A) and Reason (R) are true and Reason (R) is the correct explanation of Assertion (A)

38. (a) Both Assertion (A) and Reason (R) are true and Reason (R) is the correct explanation of Assertion (A)

39. (a) Statement I is correct and Statement II is incorrect

40. (c) Both the statements are correct

41. (b) Statement II is correct and Statement I is incorrect

42. (b) Statement II is correct and Statement I is incorrect

43. (a) Statement I is correct and Statement II is incorrect

44. (c) Both the statements are correct

45. (c) Both the statements are correct

46. (b) Financial statement analysis is not free from bias. It is based on personal judgement and abilities.

Financial statement analysis takes into consideration only monetary transactions, not qualitative.

47. (a) (iii) (i) (iv) (ii) **48.** (a) (ii) (iv) (iii) (i)

49. (a) (iii) (i) (ii) (iv)

50. (a) (ii) (iii) (iv) (i)

51. (a) (iii) (iv) (i) (ii)

52. (c) Balance sheet and statement of profit and loss

53. (c) To see that the resources of the firm are used most efficiently and that the firm's financial condition is sound

54. (a) Short-term liquidity of the firm

55. (a) All have been changed by 100% but revenue from operations has changed by 50%.

56. (d) Tax liability increased from ₹ 2,00,000 to ₹ 4,00,000.

57. (c) Profit after Tax in 2017-18 = ₹ 6,00,000 (Given)
Now, Profit after Tax in 2018-19 = 16,00,000 – 6,40,000 (16,00,000 × 40%) = ₹ 9,60,000 then, Absolute Change = 9,60,000 – 6,00,000 = ₹ 3,60,000

03
CHAPTER

"The term accounting ratio is used to describe significant relationships which exist between figures shown in balance sheet, in a statement of profit and loss, in a budgetary control system or in any part of the accounting organisation." *–J Betty*

▼ **YOUR STUDY GOALS**

3.1 Ratio
3.2 Liquidity Ratios (Short-term Solvency)
3.3 Solvency Ratios (Long-term Solvency)
3.4 Activity/Performance/Turnover Ratios
3.5 Profitability Ratios

▼ **YOUR PRACTICE GOAL**

- Topicwise Solved Questions (65 Solved Questions)
- Numerical Questions [80 Questions (Unsolved)]
- Theoretical Questions [14 Questions (with answers)]
- Objective Questions (69 Qs; MCQs, A-R, Statements, Matching, Case)

Accounting Ratios

3.1 Ratio

Ratio is an arithmetical expression of relationship between two related or interdependent items. It is the numerical or quantitative relationship between two items/variables. It is calculated by dividing one item of the relationship with other.

Accounting Ratios

When ratios are calculated on the basis of accounting information, then these are called 'accounting ratios'. An accounting ratio is a mathematical expression of the relationship between two items or group of items shown in the financial statements.

Expression of Accounting Ratio

Expression	Explanation
Pure or Simple	It is expressed as a quotient, e.g. 2, that implies 2 : 1.
Percentage	It is expressed in percentage, e.g. 25%.
Times, Rate or Number	It is expressed in a number of times a particular figure is, when compared to another figure, e.g. 4 times.
Fraction	It is expressed in fraction, e.g. 3/4.

Ratio Analysis

It is a technique which involves analysing the financial statements by calculating various ratios. It is the most important and powerful tool for measuring performance of a business enterprise. It requires a fine understanding of the ways and the rules used for preparing final statements.

Objectives of Ratio Analysis

- To know the areas of the business which need more attention.
- To know about the potential areas which can be improved with the effort in desired direction.
- To provide a deeper analysis of the profitability, liquidity, solvency and efficiency levels in the business.
- To provide information for making cross sectional analysis by comparing the performance with best industry standards.
- To provide information derived from financial statements useful for making projections and estimates for the future.

Advantages of Ratio Analysis

- It helps in understanding that whether the business firm has taken the right kind of decision and how far they have helped in improving the performance.
- It helps the business in identifying the problem areas, which in turn helps the management to take remedial actions.
- It helps in explaining the changes occuring in the business which helps the management to understand the current threats and opportunities and allows the business to do its own SWOT analysis.
- It helps in simplifying the complex accounting figures and bring out their relationship.
- Accounting ratios facilitate inter and intra-firm comparisons.

Limitations of Ratio Analysis

- It is a technique of quantitative analysis and thus, ignores qualitative factors, which may be important in decision-making.
- No single standard ratio is available, against which the ratio may be measured and compared.
- If different accounting policies and procedures are followed by different firms in respect of certain items, ratios may not be comparable.
- Changes in price level affect the comparability of ratios. But no consideration is given to price level changes in the accounting variables from which ratios are computed.

Smart Study Chart No. 1

Classification or Types of Ratios

Accounting Ratios (On the basis of purpose)

Liquidity Ratios
- Current ratio/Working capital ratio
- Liquid ratio/Quick ratio/Acid test ratio

Solvency Ratios
- Debt equity ratio
- Debt to capital employed ratio
- Total assets to debt ratio
- Proprietary ratio
- Interest coverage ratio

Activity/Performance/Turnover Ratios
- Inventory (Stock) turnover ratio
- Trade receivables turnover ratio
- Trade payables turnover ratio
- Fixed assets turnover ratio
- Net assets turnover ratio
- Working capital turnover ratio

Profitability Ratios
- Gross profit ratio
- Operating ratio
- Operating profit ratio
- Net profit ratio
- Return on investment

3.2 Liquidity Ratios (Short-term Solvency)

These ratios help to assess the enterprise's ability to meet its short-term financial obligations.

The two ratios of this category are

- Current ratio or working capital ratio
- Liquid ratio or quick ratio or acid test ratio

I. Current Ratio or Working Capital Ratio

Current ratio explains the relationship between current assets and current liabilities of a business. It is computed by dividing current assets with current liabilities.

Formula $$\text{Current Ratio} = \frac{\text{Current Assets}}{\text{Current Liabilities}}$$

Current Assets	Current Liabilities
These are the assets that are either in the form of cash or cash equivalents or can be converted into cash or cash equivalents in a short time, i.e. within a year from the date of balance sheet or within the period of an operating cycle. **Items Included in Current Assets** • Current investments. • Inventories (Excluding loose tools, stores and spares). • Trade receivables (Bills receivable and sundry debtors less provision for doubtful debts). • Cash and cash equivalents (Cash in hand, cash at bank, cheques/drafts in hand). • Short-term loans and advances. • **Other current assets (Prepaid expenses, interest receivable, etc). **Current assets can also be calculated as** Current Assets = Current Liabilities + Working Capital *or* Current Assets = Total Assets – Non-current Assets	These are those liabilities which are repayable in a short time, i.e. within a year from the date of balance sheet or within the period of an operating cycle. **Items Included in Current Liabilities** • Short-term borrowings. • Trade payables (Bills payable and sundry creditors). • Other current liabilities (Current maturities of long-term debts, interest accrued but not due on borrowings, interest accrued and due on borrowings, outstanding expenses, unclaimed dividend, calls-in-advance, etc). • Short-term provisions. **Current assets can also be calculated as** Current Liabilities = Current Assets – Working Capital *or* Current Liabilities = Total Debts – Long-term Debt

Note **As per CBSE circular, 'other current assets' except prepaid expenses, accrued incomes and advance tax, are not to be evaluated.

Objective and Significance of Current Ratio

- Current ratio is computed to assess the short-term financial position of the enterprise. It is an indicator of the enterprises ability to meet its short-term obligations (i.e. its current liablities).
- Normally, **2 : 1** is considered as ideal current ratio. However, it is subject to change from business to business and industry to industry.
- Higher the ratio, the better it is, as the firm will be able to pay its current liabilities. If the current ratio is less than **2 : 1**, it indicates the lack of liquidity and shortage of working capital.

II. Liquid Ratio or Quick Ratio or Acid Test Ratio

Quick ratio shows the relationship between quick (liquid) assets and current liabilities. It is computed by dividing quick assets with current liabilities.

Formula $$\text{Liquid Ratio} = \frac{\text{Liquid Assets } or \text{ Quick Assets}}{\text{Current Liabilities}}$$

Liquid/Quick Assets	Current Liabilities
These are the assets which are either in the form of cash or cash equivalents or can be converted into cash within a very short period. **Items Included in Liquid/Quick Assets** • Current investments. • Trade receivables (Bills receivable, debtors, provisions for doubtful debts). • Cash and cash equivalents. • Short-term loans and advances. • Other current assets except prepaid expenses. Items excluded in liquid assets are inventories, prepaid expenses. Liquid/Quick Assets = Current Assets – Inventories – Prepaid Expenses Inventory is not considered as liquid assets because it takes some time before it is converted into cash. Similarly, prepaid expenses are not considered as liquid assets because they are expenses paid in advance and thus, cannot be converted into cash and are thus excluded from liquid assets.	These are those liabilities which are repayable in a short time, i.e. within a year from the date of balance sheet or within the period of an operating cycle. **Items Included in Current Liabilities** • Short-term borrowings. • Trade payables (Bills payable and sundry creditors). • Other short-term liabilities. • Short-term provisions. **Current liabilities can also be calculated as** Current Liabilities = Current Assets – Working Capital *or* Current Liabilities = Total Debts – Debt

Objective and Significance of Liquid Ratio

- Liquid ratio is computed to assess the short-term liquidity of the enterprise. It indicates whether the firm is in a position to pay its current liabilities within a month or immediately.
- Normally, a quick ratio of **1 : 1** is considered satisfactory. Higher the quick ratio, better the short-term financial position.

3.3 Solvency Ratios (Long-term Solvency)

Solvency means firm's ability to meet its long-term liabilities. So, solvency ratios are calculated to judge the long-term financial position of the business. They help to determine the ability of the business to service and repay its debt in the long-run.

The following ratios are normally computed for evaluating solvency of the business

- Debt equity ratio (Debt to equity ratio)
- Total assets to debt ratio
- Interest coverage ratio
- Debt to capital employed ratio
- Proprietary ratio

I. Debt Equity Ratio (Debt to Equity Ratio)

Debt equity ratio expresses the relationship between **long-term debt** (external equities) and the **equity** (internal equities), **i.e. shareholders' funds.** It is computed by dividing long-term debts with shareholders funds.

Formula $\text{Debt to Equity Ratio} = \dfrac{\text{Debt (Long-term External Equities)}}{\text{Equity (Shareholders' Funds)}}$

Debts or External Equities	Equity or Shareholders' Funds
These are the liabilities of the enterprise towards the outsiders. It thus, includes long-term borrowings and long-term provisions. These are shown as non-current liabilities in the equity and liabilities part of the balance sheet. **Debt can also be calculated as** Debt = Total Debts – Current Liabilities *or* Debt = Capital Employed – Equity where, Capital Employed = Equity + Debt **Note** As per CBSE circular, 'other long-term liabilities' is not to be evaluated, hence it is not included in external equities or long-term debts.	Equity *or* Shareholders' Funds = Equity Share Capital + Preference Share Capital + Reserves and Surplus *or* *Non-current Assets (Property, Plant and Equipment + Intangible Assets + Non-current Trade Investments + Long-term Loans and Advances) + Working Capital – Non-current Liabilities (Long-term Borrowings + Long-term Provisions) Working Capital = Current Assets – Current Liabilities **Equity can also be calculated as** Equity = Capital Employed – Non-current Liabilities *or* Equity = Total Assets – Total Debts **Note** *As per CBSE circular, accounting treatment of 'other non-current assets' is not to be evaluated.

Objective and Significance of Debt Equity Ratio

- Debt equity ratio is computed to ascertain the long-term financial position of the firm, i.e. to assess the ability of the firm to meet its long-term liabilities.
- A debt equity ratio of **2 : 1** may be considered satisfactory. It is also called 'leverage ratio'.
- Lower the debt equity ratio, higher degree of protection is enjoyed by the long-term lenders.
- A high ratio, on the other hand, is considered risky as it may put the firm into difficulty in meeting its obligation to outsiders.

II. Debt to Capital Employed Ratio

Debt to capital employed ratio expresses the relation between **long-term debt** and **capital employed/net assets** (total of external and internal funds).

Formula $\text{Debt to Capital Employed Ratio} = \dfrac{\text{Long-term Debt}}{\text{Capital Employed (}\textit{or}\text{ Net Assets)}}$

Here,

Long-term Debt = Same as in case of 'debt equity ratio'.

Capital Employed = Long-term Debt + Shareholders' Funds *or* Net Assets = Total Assets – Current Liabilities

Debt to capital employed ratio can also be computed in relation to total assets. In that case, it can be defined as the ratio of **total debt** and **total assets**.

Formula $$\text{Debt to Capital Employed Ratio} = \frac{\text{Total Debts}}{\text{Total Assets}}$$

Here, Total Debts = Long-term Debts + Current Liabilities

Total Assets = Non-current Assets + Current Assets

or Total Assets = Shareholders' Funds + Long-term Debts + Current Liabilities

Objectives and Significance of Debt to Capital Employed Ratio

- Like debt equity ratio, it shows proportion of long-term debts in capital employed.
- Low ratio provides security to lenders and high ratio helps management in trading on equity.

III. Total Assets to Debt Ratio

Total assets to debt ratio establishes relationship between **total assets** and **total long-term debts.** It is computed by dividing total assets with debts.

Formula $$\text{Total Assets to Debt Ratio} = \frac{\text{Total Assets}}{\text{Debts}}$$

Total Assets	Debts
It includes • *Non-current Assets [Property, Plant and Equipment and Intangible Assets + Non-current Investments + Long-term Loans andAdvances] • Current Assets [Current Investments + Inventories +Trade Receivables + Cash and Cash Equivalents + Short-term Loans and Advances + Other Current Assets] **Total Assets can also be calculated as** Total Assets = Shareholders' Funds + Non-current Liabilities + Current Liabilities *or* Total Assets = Shareholders' Funds + Total Debts *or* Total Assets = Capital Employed + Current Liabilities	It refers to debts that will mature after one year. It includes • Long-term borrowings • Long-term provisions **Debt can also be calculated as** Debt = Total Debts – Current Liabilities *or* Debt = Capital Employed – Equity

Note *As per CBSE circular, accounting treatment of other non-current assets, other long-term liabilities and deferred tax assets (net) is not to be evaluated.

Objectives and Significance of Total Assets to Debt Ratio

- This ratio measures the safety margin available to the providers of long-term debts.
- A higher ratio indicates a larger safety margin for lenders, as the use of debts is lower in financing the assets.
- A lower ratio indicates risky financial position as it implies the use of debts is higher in financing the assets.

IV. Proprietary Ratio

Proprietary ratio depicts the relationship between **proprietors' funds** and **total assets.** This ratio shows the portion of shareholders' funds in the total assets of the business. It is computed by dividing shareholders funds with total assets. It is expressed as pure ratio.

Formula $$\text{Proprietary Ratio} = \frac{\text{Proprietors' Funds or Shareholders' Funds}}{\text{Total Assets}}$$

Here, **Proprietors' Funds or Shareholders' Funds** = Same as in case of 'debt equity ratio'.

Total Assets = Same as in case of 'total assets to debt ratio'.

Objective and Significance of Proprietary Ratio

- Proprietary ratio shows the extent to which the total assets have been financed by the proprietor.
- Higher the ratio, greater the satisfaction for lenders and creditors, as the firm is less dependent on external sources of finance.
- A low proprietary ratio indicates that long-term lenders are less secured and they may face the risk of repayment of their debt.

V. Interest Coverage Ratio

Interest coverage ratio depicts the relationship between the **net profit before interest and tax** and **interest payable on long-term debts**. It is also known as debt service ratio.

Since, interest is a charge on profit, net profit taken to calculate the ratio is before interest and tax.

Formula $$\text{Interest Coverage Ratio} = \frac{\text{Net Profit before Interest and Tax}}{\text{Interest on Long-term Debt}}$$

Objective and Significance of Interest Coverage Ratio

- Interest coverage ratio shows how many times the interest charges are covered by the profit available to pay interest.
- This ratio measures the safety margin for long-term lenders.
- The higher the ratio, more secured the lender is, (in respect of payment of interest regularly). The ideal interest coverage ratio is 6 to 7 times.

3.4 Activity/Performance/Turnover Ratios

Activity/Turnover ratios show how efficiently a company is using its assets to generate sales. These ratios express the number of times assets employed (or for that matter, any constituent of assets) is turned into sales during an accounting period. These are also known as efficiency/performance ratios.

These ratios are usually calculated on the basis of revenue from operations (sales) or cost of revenue from operations (cost of sales). The important activity/turnover ratios are

- Inventory (Stock) Turnover Ratio
- Trade Receivables or Debtors Turnover Ratio
- Trade Payables or Creditors Turnover Ratio
- Working Capital Turnover Ratio
- Net Asset/Capital Employed Turnover Ratio
- Fixed Assets Turnover Ratio

I. Inventory (Stock) Turnover Ratio

It determines the number of times stock is turned into sales during the accounting period under consideration. Inventory turnover ratios shows the relationship between the **cost of goods sold, i.e. cost of revenue from operations** during a given period and the **average amount of inventory** carried during that period.

Formula $$\text{Inventory Turnover Ratio} = \frac{\text{Cost of Revenue from Operations, i.e. Cost of Goods Sold}}{\text{Average Inventory}}$$

Cost of Revenue from Operations i.e. Cost of Goods Sold = Cost of Materials Consumed + Purchases of Stock-in-trade + Changes in Inventories of Finished Goods, Work-in-progress and Stock-in-trade + Direct Expenses

or = Opening Inventory + Net Purchases + Direct Expenses − Closing Inventory

or = Revenue from Operations (Sales) − Gross Profit

$$\textbf{Average Inventory} = \frac{\text{Opening Inventory} + \text{Closing Inventory}}{2}$$

Objective and Significance of Inventory Turnover Ratio

- Inventory turnover indicates the rate at which inventory is converted into revenue from operations (i.e. sales). It indicates whether the inventory has been efficiently used or not.
- Higher the ratio, the better it is, since it indicates inventory is being sold quickly. However, high turnover needs to be interpreted carefully as it may be due to buying in small lots and selling quickly at low margin to realise cash.
- Low turnover of inventory may be due to bad buying, obsolete stock, etc. and is a danger signal.

II. Trade Receivables or Debtors Turnover Ratio

Debtors turnover ratio depicts the relationship between credit revenue from operations, i.e. net credit sales and average trade receivables (debtors + bills receivables) of the year.

Formula

$$\text{Debtors Turnover Ratio} = \frac{\text{Net Credit Revenue from Operations (Net Credit Sales)}}{\text{Average Trade Receivables}}$$

Net Credit Revenue from Operations

= Credit Revenue from Operations – Sales Return

or = Revenue from Operations – Cash Revenue from Operations

$$\text{Average Trade Receivables} = \frac{\text{Opening Receivables (Debtors + Bills Receivable)} + \text{Closing Receivables (Debtors + Bills Receivable)}}{2}$$

Key Points

- In case, credit sales are not given in the question, then credit sales equal to total sales.
- If opening receivables are not given, closing receivables are taken as average receivables.
- Debtors will be taken at gross value, i.e. before provision.

Objective and Significance of Debtors Turnover Ratio

- Trade receivables turnover ratio indicates the speed with which the amount is collected from debtors.
- Higher the ratio, better it is, since it indicates that debts are being collected more quickly.
- A lower trade receivable turnover ratio indicates the inefficient credit sales policy of the management.

Debt Collection Period or Average Collection Period

It provides an approximation of the average time that it takes to collect debtors.

It is determined as follows

$$\text{Debt Collection Period} = \frac{\text{365 Days / 52 Weeks / 12 Months}}{\text{Trade Receivables } or \text{ Debtors' Turnover Ratio}} = \ldots\ldots \text{ Number of Days/Weeks/Months (as the case may be)}$$

III. Trade Payables or Creditors Turnover Ratio

Creditors turnover ratio shows the relationship between **net credit purchases** and **total payables** or **average payables**, whereas average payment period signifies the credit period enjoyed by the enterprise in paying creditors.

Formula $$\text{Trade Payables } or \text{ Creditors Turnover Ratio} = \frac{\text{Net Credit Purchases}}{\text{Average Trade Payables}}$$

Net Credit Purchases = Net Purchases – Cash Purchases

$$\textbf{Average Trade Payables} = \frac{\text{Opening Payables (Creditors + Bills Payable)} + \text{Closing Payables (Creditors + Bills Payable)}}{2}$$

Point to Remember

In the absence of opening creditors and bills payable, closing creditors and bills payable can be used average trade payables.

Objective and Significance of Creditors or Trade Payables Turnover Ratio

- Trade payables turnover ratio indicates the speed with which amount is being paid to the creditors.
- A higher creditors turnover ratio indicates that the firm pays its suppliers quickly which increases its credit worthiness and *vice-versa*.

Average Payment Period or Average Age of Payables

It provides an approximation of the average time taken to make payment to the creditors. It is determined as follows

$$\text{Average Payment Period} = \frac{\text{365 Days / 52 Weeks / 12 Months}}{\text{Trade Payables } or \text{ Creditors Turnover Ratio}} = \text{........ Number of Days/Weeks/Months (as the case may be)}$$

IV. Working Capital Turnover Ratio

Working capital turnover ratio depicts the relationship between **revenue from operations i.e. sales and working capital**.

Formula

$$\text{Working Capital Turnover Ratio} = \frac{\text{Revenue from Operations (Net Sales)}}{\text{Working Capital}^*}$$

or

$$= \frac{\text{Cost of Revenue from Operations i.e. Cost of Goods Sold}}{\text{Working Capital}^*}$$

***Working Capital** = Current Assets (Excluding Fictitious Assets) – Current Liabilities

Objective and Significance of Working Capital Turnover Ratio

- The ratio indicates how efficiently working capital has been utilised in making revenue from operations.
- A high working capital ratio indicates efficient utilisation of working capital.
- A low working capital turnover ratio indicates, working capital has not been utilised efficiently.

V. Net Asset/Capital Employed Turnover Ratio

Net asset turnover ratio expresses the relationship between **revenue from operations** and **net assets** (capital employed) in the business.

Formula

$$\text{Net Assets/Capital Employed Turnover Ratio} = \frac{\text{Revenue from Operations}}{\text{Capital Employed}}$$

Where, **Capital Employed** = Long-term Debt + Shareholders' Funds *or* Net Assets = Total Assets – Current Liabilities

VI. Fixed Asset Turnover Ratio

Fixed asset turnover ratio expresses relationship between **net revenue from operations** and **net fixed assets**.

Formula

$$\text{Fixed Asset Turnover Ratio} = \frac{\text{Net Revenue from Operations}}{\text{Net Fixed Assets}}$$

Objective and Significance of Fixed Asset Turnover Ratio

- The fixed asset turnover ratio reveals how efficient a company is at generating sales from its existing fixed assets.
- A higher ratio implies that management is using its fixed assets more effectively.

3.5 Profitability Ratios

Profitability ratios measure the profitability of a business. Profitability ratios help in assessing the overall efficiency with which a business is being managed. These ratios are calculated to analyse the earning capacity of the business which is the outcome of utilisation of resources employed in the business.

Various profitability ratios commonly used to analyse the profitability of the business are

- Gross profit ratio
- Operating ratio (Operating cost ratio)
- Operating profit ratio
- Net profit ratio
- Return on investments (Return on capital employed, rate of return)

I. Gross Profit Ratio

It depicts the relationship between **gross profit** and **revenue from operations** of an enterprise.

Formula

$$\text{Gross Profit Ratio} = \frac{\text{Gross Profit}}{\text{Revenue from Operations (Net Sales)}} \times 100$$

Revenue from Operations, i.e. Sales (Both Cash and Credit) – Sales Return

Gross Profit = Revenue from Operations i.e. Sales – Cost of Goods Sold *or* Cost of Revenue from Operations

or = Opening Inventory (Excluding Spare Parts and Loose Tools) + Purchases + Direct Expenses – Closing Inventory (Excluding Spare Parts and Loose Tools)

or

In case, statement of profit and loss is given, cost of revenue from operations, i.e. cost of goods sold is computed by adding Cost of Materials Consumed + Purchases of Stock-in-trade + Changes in Inventories of Finished Goods, Work-in-progress and Stock-in-trade + Direct Expenses

or Revenue from Operations – Gross Profit

Objective and Significance of Gross Profit Ratio

- Gross profit ratio shows the margin of profit available on revenue from operations.
- Higher the gross profit ratio, the better it is, as no ideal ratio is fixed for gross profit ratio.
- Gross profit ratio should be adequate enough not only to cover the operating expenses but also to provide for depreciation, interest on loans, dividends and creation of reserves.

Key Point

Direct expenses may be given as notes on employees benefits expenses and other expenses. If direct expenses are not given, it may be assumed that there is no such expense.

II. Operating Ratio (Operating Cost Ratio)

Operating ratio establishes the relationship between **operating cost** and **revenue from operations i.e. net sales**. It shows the proportion of cost of revenue from operations and operating expenses to revenue from operations.

Formula

$$\text{Operating Ratio} = \frac{\text{Operating Cost}}{\text{Revenue from Operations (Net Sales)}} \times 100$$

or

$$= \frac{\text{Cost of Revenue from Operations} + \text{Operating Expenses}}{\text{Revenue from Operations (Net Sales)}} \times 100$$

Operating Cost It is the cost which is associated with the operating activities of the business, e.g. Employees benefits expenses and other expenses. Non-operating incomes and expenses are excluded.

Non-operating income is shown in the statement of profit and loss as other income. Non-operating expenses are given in the notes to accounts on 'other expenses' in the statement of profit and loss. It may be given as additional information. If no information is given for non-operating expenses, it is taken as nil.

Alternatively, operating cost may be calculated as follows

Operating Cost

= Cost of Materials Consumed + Purchases of Stock-in-trade + Changes in Inventories of Finished Goods, Work-in-progress and Stock-in-trade + Employees Benefits Expenses + Depreciation and Amortisation Expenses + Other Expenses (Other than Non-operating Expenses)

Cost of Revenue from Operations

= Cost of Materials Consumed + Purchases of Stock-in-trade + Change in Inventories of Finished Goods, Work-in-progress and Stock-in-trade + Direct Expenses

Objective and Significance of Operating Ratio

- This ratio is a test of the operational efficiency of the business. It shows the extent of revenue from operations that is absorbed by cost of revenue from operations and operating expenses.
- A rise in this ratio will indicate a decline in efficiency.
- It is a cost ratio and hence, lower the ratio, the better it is.

or = Revenue from Operations – Gross Profit

or = Opening Inventory (Excluding Spare Parts and Loose Tools) + Net Purchase + Direct Expenses – Closing Inventory (Excluding Spare Parts and Loose Tools)

Operating Expenses = Employees Benefit Expenses + Other Expenses (Other than Non-operating Expenses) + Depreciation and Amortisation Expenses

or = Office Expenses + Administrative Expenses + Selling and Distribution Expenses + Employees Benefit Expenses + Depreciation and Amortisation Expenses

III. Operating Profit Ratio

Operating profit ratio establishes the relationship between **operating profit** and **revenue from operations i.e. net sales.**

Formula $$\text{Operating Profit Ratio} = \frac{\text{Operating Profit}}{\text{Revenue from Operations (Net Sales)}} \times 100$$

Operating Profit = Gross Profit + Other Operating Income – Other Operating Expenses

or = Net Profit (Before Tax) + Non-operating Expenses/Losses* – Non-operating Income**

or = Revenue from Operations – Operating Cost

***Non-operating Expenses** These are those expenses which are not incurred to earn profit. e.g. Interest on long-term borrowings, loss on sale of fixed or non-current assets.

****Non-operating Incomes** These are those incomes which are not earned from the operating activities of the business. e.g. Interest earned on investments, profit on sale of fixed or non-current assets.

It is to be noted that operating profit ratio and operating ratio are complementary to each other and thus, if one of the two ratios are deducted from 100, another ratio is obtained. e.g. If the operating profit ratio is 30%, it means that the operating ratio is 70%.

$$\text{Operating Ratio} + \text{Operating Profit Ratio} = 100$$

Objective and Significance of Operating Profit Ratio

- This ratio indicates the part of revenue from operations available after absorbing cost of revenue from operations and operating expenses.
- It helps to analyse the performance of business and throws light on the operational efficiency of the business. It is very useful for inter-firm as well as intra-firm comparisons.
- It is a profit ratio, hence, higher the ratio, the better it is.

IV. Net Profit Ratio

Net profit ratio establishes the relationship between **net profit** and **revenue from operations i.e. net sales.**

Formula $$\text{Net Profit Ratio} = \frac{\text{Net Profit after Tax}}{\text{Revenue from Operations (Net Sales)}} \times 100$$

Net Profit = Revenue from Operations – Cost of Revenue from Operations – Operating Expenses – Non-operating Expenses + Non-operating Income – Tax

Objective and Significance of Net Profit Ratio

- Net profit ratio measures the rate of net profit earned on revenue from operations.
- This ratio is an indicator of the overall efficiency of the business.
- It is a profit ratio, hence, higher the ratio, the better it is. It has great importance for investors.

V. Return on Investments (RoI) or Return on Capital Employed

This ratio establishes the relationship between **net profit before interest, tax and preference dividend** and **capital employed** (equity + debts). This ratio shows how efficiently the internal (equity) sources and external (debts) sources are being used or employed in business. It is also known as yield on capital.

Formula

$$\text{Return on Investments (RoI)} = \frac{\text{Net Profit before Interest, Tax and Preference Dividend}}{\text{Capital Employed}} \times 100$$

Capital employed can be calculated from liabilities side approach and assets side approach as follows

When Liabilities Approach is Followed

It is computed by adding

- Shareholders' funds (i.e. share capital, reserves and surplus).
- Non-current liabilities (i.e. long-term borrowings, long-term provisions).

Point to Remember

As per CBSE circular, accounting treatment of money received against share warrants, share application, money pending allotment, deferred tax liabilities (net), other long-term liabilities, deferred tax assets (net), other non-current assets and other current assets (unamortised expenses) are not to be evaluated.

When Assets Approach is Followed

It is computed by adding

- Non-current assets, i.e.
  - (a) Property, plant and equipment and intangible assets
  - (b) Non-current trade investments (it is assumed that all non-current investments are trade investments).
  - (c) Long-term loans and advances.
- Working capital (Current Assets – Current Liabilities).

Point to Remember

Since, non-operating assets are excluded while determining capital employed, income from non-operating assets should also be excluded from profit.

Objective and Significance of Return on Investments

- This ratio measures how efficiently the capital employed in the business is being used.
- Return on investment is a fair indicator of the profitability of any concern and helps in inter-firm and inter-industry comparison.
- It is a profit ratio. Hence, higher the ratio, the better it is.

Quick View

	Ratio	Formula	Explanation
		Liquidity Ratios	
1.	**Current Ratio**	$\frac{\text{Current Assets}}{\text{Current Liabilities}} = \ldots : \ldots$	**Current Assets** = Current Investments + Inventories (Excluding Stores and Spares and Loose Tools) + Trade Receivables (Net of Provision for Doubtful Debts) + Cash and Cash Equivalents + Short-term Loans and Advances + Other Current Assets
2.	**Liquid Ratio/ Acid Test Ratio/ Quick Ratio**	$\frac{\text{Quick Assets } or \text{ Liquid Assets}}{\text{Current Liabilities}} = \ldots : \ldots$	**Current Liabilities** = Short-term Borrowings + Trade Payables + Other Current Liabilities + Short-term Provisions **Quick Assets** = Current Assets – Inventories – Prepaid Expenses
		Solvency Ratios	
1.	**Debt Equity Ratio**	$\frac{\text{Debt}}{\text{Equity (Shareholders' Funds)}} = \ldots : \ldots$	**Debt** = Long-term Borrowings (i.e. Debentures, Mortgage, Public Deposits) + Long-term Provisions **Shareholders' Funds** = Share Capital + Reserves and Surplus *or* = Non-current Assets (Property, Plant and Equipment + Intangible Assets + Non-current Investments + Long-term Loans and Advances) + Working Capital* – Non-current Liabilities (Long-term borrowings + Long-term Provisions) *Working Capital = Current Assets – Current Liabilities
2.	**Debt to Capital Employed Ratio**	$\frac{\text{Long-term Debt}}{\text{Capital Employed}} = \ldots$	**Long-term Debt** = Long-term Borrowings + Long-term Provisions **Capital Employed** = Long-term Debt + Shareholders' Funds
3.	**Total Assets to Debt Ratio**	$\frac{\text{Total Assets}}{\text{Long-term Debts}} = \ldots : \ldots$	**Total Assets** = Non-current Assets (Property, Plant and Equipment + Intangible Assets + Non-current Investments + Long-term Loans and Advances) + Current Assets [Current Investments + Inventories (Including Stores and Spares and Loose Tools) + Trade Receivables + Cash and Cash Equivalents + Short-term Loans and Advances] + Other Current Assets
4.	**Proprietary Ratio**	$\frac{\text{Shareholders' Funds or Proprietors' Funds}}{\text{Total Assets}} = \ldots\%$	
5.	**Interest Coverage Ratio**	$\frac{\text{Net Profit before Interest and Tax}}{\text{Interest on Long-term Debt}} = \ldots\text{times}$	**Profit before Interest and Tax** = Profit after Tax + Tax + Interest
		Activity Ratios/Turnover Ratios	
1.	**Inventory** (Stock) **Turnover Ratio**	$\frac{\text{Cost of Revenue from Operations}}{\text{Average Inventory}} = \ldots \text{ times}$	**Average Inventory or Stock** $= \frac{\text{Opening Inventory} + \text{Closing Inventory}}{2}$
2.	**Trade Receivables or Debtors Turnover Ratio**	$\frac{\text{Credit Revenue from Operations}}{\text{Average Trade Receivables}} = \ldots \text{ times}$	**Average Trade Receivables** $= \frac{(\text{Opening Debtors} + \text{Opening Bills Receivables}) + (\text{Closing Debtors} + \text{Closing Bills Receivables})}{2}$
3.	**Trade Payables or Creditors' Turnover Ratio**	$\frac{\text{Net Credit Purchases}}{\text{Average Trade Payables}} = \ldots \text{ times}$	**Average Trade Payables** $= \frac{(\text{Opening Creditors} + \text{Opening Bills Payable}) + (\text{Closing Creditors} + \text{Closing Bills Payable})}{2}$
4.	**Working Capital Turnover Ratio**	$\frac{\text{Revenue from Operations}}{\text{Working Capital}} = \ldots \text{ times}$	**Working Capital** = Current Assets – Current Liabilities Current Assets = As per current ratio Current Liabilities = As per current ratio
5.	**Net Assets Turnover Ratio**	$\frac{\text{Revenue from Operations}}{\text{Capital Employed}} = \ldots \text{ times}$	**Capital Employed** = Long-term Debt + Shareholders' Funds
6.	**Fixed Assets Turnover Ratio**	$\frac{\text{Net Revenue from Operations}}{\text{Net Fixed Assets}} = \ldots \text{ times}$	

		Profitability Ratios	
1.	**Gross Profit Ratio**	$\frac{\text{Gross Profit}}{\text{Revenue from Operations}} \times 100 = \ldots\%$	**Gross Profit** = Revenue from Operations – Cost of Revenue from Operations **Cost of Revenue from Operations** = Opening Inventory (Excluding Stores and Spares and Loose Tools) + Net Purchases Direct Expenses – Closing Inventory (Excluding Stores and Spares and Loose Tools) *or* = Revenue from Operations – Gross Profit *or* = Cost of Materials Consumed + Purchases of Stock-in-trade + Change in Inventories of Finished Goods, Work-in-progress and Stock-in-trade + Direct Expenses If direct expenses are not given, assume it to be nil.
2.	**Operating Ratio**	$\frac{\text{Cost of Revenue from Operations} + \text{Operating Expenses}}{\text{Revenue from Operations}} \times 100 = \ldots\%$	**Cost of Revenue from Operations** = Opening Inventory (Excluding Stores and Spares and Loose Tools) + Net Purchases + Direct Expenses – Closing Inventory (Excluding Stores and Spares and Loose Tools) *or* = Revenue from Operations – Gross Profit *or* = Cost of Materials Consumed + Purchases of Stock-in-trade + Change in Inventories of Finished Goods, Work-in-progress and Stock-in-trade + Direct Expenses If direct expenses are not given, assume it to be nil. **Revenue from Operations** = Sales – Sales Return **Operating Expenses** = Employees Benefit Expenses + Other Expenses (Other than Non-operating Expenses)
3.	**Operating Profit Ratio**	$\frac{\text{Operating Profit}}{\text{Revenue from Operations}} \times 100 = \ldots\%$	**Operating Profit** = Net Profit (Before Tax) + Non-operating Expenses – Non-operating Income *or* = Gross Profit + Operating Income – Operating Expenses **Non-operating Expenses** = Interest on Long-term Borrowings + Loss on Sale of Fixed Assets *or* Non-current Assets **Non-operating Income** = Interest Received on Investments + Profit on Sale of Fixed Assets *or* Non-current Assets
4.	**Net Profit Ratio**	$= \frac{\text{Net Profit after Interest and Tax}}{\text{Revenue from Operations}} \times 100 = \ldots\%$	**Net Profit before Interest and Tax** = Gross Profit + Other Income – Indirect Expenses
5.	**Return on Investment or Return on Capital Employed**	$= \frac{\text{Net Profit before Interest Tax and Preference Dividend}}{\text{Capital Employed}} \times 100$ $= \ldots\%$	**Capital Employed** *Liabilities approach* Share Capital + Reserves and Surplus + Long-term Borrowings + Long-term Provisions *Assets approach* Non-current Assets (Tangible Assets + Intangible Assets) + Non-current Investments + Long-term Loans and Advances + Working Capital Working Capital = Current Assets – Current Liabilities (Assume that all non-current investments are trade investments). (Interest on non-trade investments should be deducted from profit before interest, tax and dividend).

Mind Map

Accounting Ratios

1 Meaning of Accounting Ratios

When ratios are calculated on the basis of accounting information, then these are called accounting ratios. An accounting ratio is a mathematical expression of the relationship between two items shown in the financial statements.

2 Expression of Accounting Ratios

- **Pure or Simple** It is expressed as a quotient, e.g. 2, that implies 2 : 1.
- **Percentage** It is expressed in percentage, e.g. 25%.
- **Times, Rate or Number** It is expressed in a number of times, e.g. 4 times.
- **Fraction** It is expressed in fraction, e.g. 3/4.

3 Ratio Analysis

It is a technique which involves analysing the financial statements by calculating various ratios. It is the most important and powerful tool for measuring performance of a business enterprise.

4 Objectives and Advantages of Ratio Analysis

Objectives

- To know the areas of the business which need more attention.
- To provide a deeper analysis of the profitability, liquidity, solvency and efficiency in business.
- To help in estimations for the future.
- To provide information for making cross sectional analysis.

Advantages

- It helps in taking right decision for improving the performance.
- It helps in identifying the problem areas.
- It helps business to do it's SWOT analysis.
- Accounting ratios facilitate inter and intra-firm comparisons.

5 Limitations of Ratio Analysis

- It ignores qualitative factors.
- No single standard ratio is available.
- It ignores price level changes.
- Forecasting of future trends is based only on historical facts.

6 Liquidity Ratios

These ratios help to assess short-term solvency. They are of two types

- Current Ratio = $\frac{\text{Current Assets}}{\text{Current Liabilities}}$
- Liquid Ratio = $\frac{\text{Liquid Assets}}{\text{Current Liabilities}}$
- Ideal ratio of current ratio and liquid ratio is 2 : 1 and 1 : 1 respectively.

7 Solvency Ratios

Solvency ratios are calculated to judge the long-term financial position of the business. Following are the solvency ratios

- Debt Equity Ratio = Debt/Equity
- Debt to Capital Employed Ratio = Debt/Capital Employed
- Total Assets to Debt Ratio = Total Assets/Debts
- Proprietary Ratio = Shareholder's Funds/Total Assets
- Interest Coverage Ratio = Net Profit before Tax/Interest on Long-term Debt

8 Activity/Turnover Ratios

Activity ratio shows how efficiently a company is using its assets to generate sales.

The important activity ratios are

- Inventory Turnover Ratio = Cost of Revenue from Operations/Average Inventory
- Trade Recievables Turnover Ratio = Net Credit Revenue from Operations/ Average Trade Recievables
- Trade Payables Turnover Ratio = Net Credit Purchases/Average Trade Payables
- Working Capital Turnover Ratio = Net Revenue from Operations/Working Capital
- Net Asset Turnover Ratio = Revenue from Operations/Capital Employed
- Fixed Asset Turnover Ratio = Net Revenue from Operations/Net Fixed Assets

9 Profitability Ratios

Profitability ratios measure the profitability of a business. These ratios are calculated to analyse the earning capacity of the business. Various profitability ratios are

- Gross Profit Ratio = $\frac{\text{Gross Profit}}{\text{Net Revenue from Operations}} \times 100$
- Operating Ratio = $\frac{\text{Operating Cost}}{\text{Net Revenue from Operations}} \times 100$
- Operating Profit Ratio = $\frac{\text{Operating Profit}}{\text{Net Revenue from Operations}} \times 100$
- Net Profit Ratio = $\frac{\text{Net Profit after Tax}}{\text{Net Revenue from Operations}} \times 100$
- Return on Investments = $\frac{\text{Net Profit before Interest, Tax and Preference Dividend}}{\text{Capital Employed}} \times 100$

Topicwise Solved Questions

Liquidity Ratios

Solved Question 1 **Calculate current ratio from the following information given below**

Debtors ₹ 5,00,000, inventories ₹ 1,60,000, loose tools ₹ 5,000, short-term investments ₹ 60,000, marketable securities ₹ 20,000, trade payables ₹ 30,000, bills payable ₹ 5,000, 10% debentures ₹ 60,000, machinery ₹ 40,000.

Sol. $\text{Current Ratio} = \dfrac{\text{Current Assets*}}{\text{Current Liabilities**}} = \dfrac{7,35,000}{3,00,000} = 2.45:1$

*Current Assets = Debtors + Inventories − Loose Tools + Short-term Investments + Marketable Securities

= 5,00,000 + 1,60,000 − 5,000 + 60,000 + 20,000

= ₹ 7,35,000

**Current Liabilities = Trade Payables = ₹ 3,00,000

Solved Question 2 **Siyaraman Fabrics Ltd. non-current assets, current assets, equity and non-current liabilities is ₹ 6,00,000, ₹ 2,00,000, ₹ 3,00,000 and ₹ 4,50,000 respectively. Calculate current ratio.**

Sol. $\text{Current Ratio} = \dfrac{\text{Current Assets*}}{\text{Current Liabilities**}} = \dfrac{2,00,000}{50,000} = 4:1$

*Current Assets = ₹ 2,00,000 (Given)

**Current Liabilities = Non-current Assets + Current Assets − Equity − Non-current Liabilities

= 6,00,000 + 2,00,000 − 3,00,000 − 4,50,000 = ₹ 50,000

Solved Question 3 **Calculate current ratio if working capital of Khushi Ltd. is ₹ 4,50,000 and its current assets are ₹ 6,00,000 excluding inventories of ₹ 40,000.**

Sol. $\text{Current Ratio} = \dfrac{\text{Current Assets*}}{\text{Current Liabilities**}} = \dfrac{6,40,000}{1,90,000} = 3.37:1$

*Current Assets = 6,00,000 + 40,000 (Inventories)

= ₹ 6,40,000

**Current Liabilities = Current Assets − Working Capital

= 6,40,000 − 4,50,000 = ₹ 1,90,000

Solved Question 4 **A company had current assets ₹ 3,00,000 and current liabilities ₹ 1,40,000. Afterwards, it purchased goods worth ₹ 20,000 on credit. Calculate the current ratio after the purchase of goods.** **CBSE 2019**

Sol. New Current Assets = 3,00,000 + 20,000 = ₹ 3,20,000

New Current Liabilities = 1,40,000 + 20,000 = ₹ 1,60,000

$\text{Current Ratio} = \dfrac{\text{Current Assets}}{\text{Current Liabilities}} = \dfrac{3,20,000}{1,60,000} = 2:1$

Solved Question 5 **Working capital is ₹ 4,50,000, total assets are ₹ 22,30,000 (excluding inventory of ₹ 20,000), non-current assets are ₹ 16,50,000. Calculate current ratio.**

Sol. $\text{Current Ratio} = \dfrac{\text{Current Assets*}}{\text{Current Liabilities**}} = \dfrac{6,00,000}{1,50,000} = 4:1$

*Current Assets = Total Assets + Inventory − Non-current Assets

= 22,30,000 + 20,000 − 16,50,000 = ₹ 6,00,000

**Current Liabilities = Current Assets − Working Capital

= 6,00,000 − 4,50,000 = ₹ 1,50,000

Solved Question 6 **From the following extracts of Ramanyan Edtech Ltd. calculate current ratio.**

Balance Sheet (Extract)
In the Books of Ramanyan Ltd.

Particulars	Amt (₹)
Equity Share Capital	6,00,000
Reserve and Surplus	2,00,000
Balance in Statement of Profit and Loss	(50,000)
Non-current Liabilities	4,00,000
Non-current Assets	11,00,000
Trade Receivables	80,000
Inventories (including loose tools ₹ 2,000)	1,40,000

Sol. $\text{Current Ratio} = \dfrac{\text{Current Assets*}}{\text{Current Liabilities**}} = \dfrac{2,18,000}{1,68,000} = 1.30:1$

*Current Assets = Trade Receivables + Inventories − Loose Tools

= 80,000 + 1,40,000 − 2,000 = ₹ 2,18,000

**Current Liabilities = Non-current Assets + Current Assets − Shareholders' Funds − Non-current Liabilities

= 11,00,000 + 2,18,000 − (6,00,000 + 2,00,000 − 50,000) − 4,00,000

= ₹ 1,68,000

Solved Question 7 **Easy Private Ltd. had current assets of ₹ 2,00,000. The company paid a current liability of ₹ 50,000. After this payment the current ratio was 3 : 1. Calculate**

(i) Current liabilities and working capital after the payment.

(ii) Current liabilities and working capital before the payment.

Sol. $\text{Current Ratio} = \dfrac{\text{Current Assets}}{\text{Current Liabilities}}$

Current Assets = ₹ 2,00,000 (Given)

Current Assets after Payment = 2,00,000 – 50,000
= ₹ 1,50,000

Hence, Current Liabilities after Payment
$= \frac{1,50,000}{3} =$ ₹ 50,000

(i) **Current Liabilities and Working Capital After Payment**

Current Liabilities = ₹ 50,000

Working Capital = Current Assets – Current Liabilities
= 1,50,000 – 50,000 = ₹ 1,00,000

(ii) **Current Liabilities and Working Capital before Payment**

Current Liabilities before Payment
= 50,000 + 50,000 = ₹ 1,00,000

Working Capital = Current Assets – Current Liabilities
= 2,00,000 – 50,000 = ₹ 1,50,000

Solved Question 8 **A business has a current ratio of 3 : 1 and quick ratio of 1.2 : 1. If working capital is ₹ 1,80,000, calculate total current assets and inventory.** **CBSE 2024**

Sol. Let current liabilities be = x

$$\text{Current Ratio} = \frac{\text{Current Assets (CA)}}{\text{Current Liabilities (CL)}} = \frac{3}{1} = \frac{\text{CA}}{x}$$

∴ Current Assets (CA) = $3x$

Now, Working Capital = Current Assets – Current Liabilities

$1,80,000 = 3x - x$

∴ x (Current Liabilities) = ₹ 90,000

So, Current Assets = $3x = 3 \times 90,000 =$ ₹ 2,70,000

$$\text{Now, Quick Ratio} = \frac{\text{Liquid Assets (LA)}}{\text{Current Liabilities (CL)}}$$

$$\frac{1.2}{1} = \frac{\text{Liquid Assets}}{90,000}$$

∴ Liquid Assets = ₹ 1,08,000

Also, Liquid Assets = Current Assets – Inventory

1,08,000 = 2,70,000 – Inventory

So, Inventory = 2,70,000 – 1,08,000 = ₹ 1,62,000

Solved Question 9 **What will be the liquid ratio if in the books of Vijay Cosmetics Ltd. current assets are ₹ 2,00,000 and current liabilities, inventories, prepaid expenses and trade receivables are ₹ 1,00,000, ₹ 50,000, ₹ 15,000 and ₹ 75,000 respectively?**

Sol. $$\text{Liquid Ratio} = \frac{\text{Liquid Assets*}}{\text{Current Liabilities}} = \frac{1,35,000}{1,00,000} = 1.35 : 1$$

*Liquid Assets = Current Assets – Inventories – Prepaid Expenses
= 2,00,000 – 50,000 – 15,000 = ₹ 1,35,000

Solved Question 10 **Calculate the quick ratio of Zing Ltd. when its inventory is of ₹ 80,000, working capital amounts to ₹ 3,75,000 and current assets to ₹ 6,00,000.**

Sol. $$\text{Liquid Ratio} = \frac{\text{Liquid Assets*}}{\text{Current Liabilities**}} = \frac{5,20,000}{2,25,000} = 2.32 : 1$$

*Liquid Assets = Current Assets – Inventory
= 6,00,000 – 80,000 = ₹ 5,20,000

**Current Liabilities = Current Assets – Working Capital
= 6,00,000 – 3,75,000 = ₹ 2,25,000

Solved Question 11 **Find quick ratio from the following information**

Working capital ₹ 3,50,000, total debts ₹ 8,25,000, long- term debts ₹ 4,00,000, inventories ₹ 1,25,000.

Sol. $$\text{Quick Ratio} = \frac{\text{Liquid Assets*}}{\text{Current Liabilities**}} = \frac{6,50,000}{4,25,000} = 1.52 : 1$$

**Current Liabilities = Total Outside Liabilities – Long-term Debts
= 8,25,000 – 4,00,000 = ₹ 4,25,000

Current Assets = Working Capital + Current Liabilities
= 3,50,000 + 4,25,000 = ₹ 7,75,000

*Liquid Assets = Current Assets – Inventory
= 7,75,000 – 1,25,000 = ₹ 6,50,000

Solved Question 12 **The working capital of Elite Dresses Ltd. is ₹ 10,00,000. Its current ratio is 1.8 : 1 and the value of inventory is ₹ 2,50,000. Compute its quick ratio. Also find the value of its current assets and current liabilities.**

Sol. Let current liabilities be x.

$$\text{Current Ratio} = \frac{\text{Current Assets}}{\text{Current Liabilities}} \Rightarrow 1.8 = \frac{\text{CA}}{x}$$

∴ Current Assets = $1.8x$

Working Capital = Current Assets – Current Liabilities

∴ $10,00,000 = 1.8x - x$

⇒ $x = 12,50,000$

So, Current Assets = 12,50,000 × 1.8 = ₹ 22,50,000 and
Current Liabilities = ₹ 12,50,000

Liquid Assets = Current Assets – Inventory
= 22,50,000 – 2,50,000 = ₹ 20,00,000

$$\text{Quick Ratio} = \frac{\text{Liquid Assets}}{\text{Current Liabilities}} = \frac{20,00,000}{12,50,000} = 1.6 : 1$$

Solved Question 13 **X Ltd. has a current ratio of 3.5 : 1 and quick ratio of 2 : 1. If excess of current assets over quick assets is represented by inventories of ₹ 16,000 and prepaid expenses of ₹ 8,000, calculate** **CBSE 2024 C**

(i) Current liabilities

(ii) Current assets

(iii) Quick assets

Sol. (i) $\text{Current Ratio} = \dfrac{\text{Current Assets}}{\text{Current Liabilities}}$

$$\frac{3.5}{1} = \frac{\text{Current Assets}}{\text{Current Liabilities}}$$

$\Rightarrow$ Current Assets = 3.5 Current Liabilities

$$\text{Quick Ratio} = \frac{\text{Quick Assets}}{\text{Current Liabilities}}$$

$$\Rightarrow \frac{2}{1} = \frac{\text{Quick Assets}}{\text{Current Liabilities}}$$

$$\frac{2}{1} = \frac{\text{Current Assets} - \text{Inventories} - \text{Prepaid Expenses}}{\text{Current Liabilities}}$$

$$\frac{2}{1} = \frac{3.5\text{ Current Liabilities } - 16{,}000 - 8{,}000}{\text{Current Liabilities}}$$

2 Current Liablilities = 3.5 Current Liabilities − 16,000 − 8,000

1.5 Current Liabilities = 24,000

$$\therefore \text{ Current Liabilities} = \frac{24{,}000}{1.5} = ₹\ 16{,}000$$

(ii) Current Assets = 3.5 Current Liabilities
= 3.5 × 16,000 = ₹ 56,000

(iii) Quick Assets = 56,000 − 16,000 − 8,000 = ₹ 32,000

Solved Question 14 **Bihari Footwears Ltd. current assets are ₹ 5,00,000, current ratio is 2.5 : 1 and quick ratio is 1 : 1. Calculate.**

(i) Current liabilities **(ii) Liquid assets**
(iii) Inventories

Sol. Current Assets = ₹ 5,00,000; Current Ratio = 2.5 : 1
Quick Ratio = 1 : 1

(i) $\text{Current Ratio} = \dfrac{\text{Current Assets}}{\text{Current Liabilities}}$

$$\Rightarrow \frac{2.5}{1} = \frac{5{,}00{,}000}{\text{Current Liabilities}}$$

2.5 × Current Liabilities = 5,00,000

$$\text{Current Liabilities} = \frac{5{,}00{,}000}{2.5} = ₹\ 2{,}00{,}000$$

(ii) $\text{Quick Ratio} = \dfrac{\text{Quick Assets}}{\text{Current Liabilities}}$

$$\Rightarrow \frac{1}{1} = \frac{\text{Quick Assets}}{2{,}00{,}000}$$

2,00,000 = Quick Assets

(iii) Inventories = Current Assets − Quick Assets
= 5,00,000 − 2,00,000 = ₹ 3,00,000

Solved Question 15 **The quick ratio of Vinny Ltd. is 2 : 1. Its prepaid salary account shows ₹ 10,000 balance. Find its current ratio if its current liabilities are ₹ 1,20,000.**

Sol. $\text{Current Ratio} = \dfrac{\text{Current Assets}}{\text{Current Liabilities}} = \dfrac{2{,}50{,}000}{1{,}20{,}000} = 2.09 : 1$

$$\text{Quick Ratio} = \frac{\text{Quick Assets}}{\text{Current Liabilites}}$$

$$2 = \frac{\text{Quick Assets}}{1{,}20{,}000}$$

$\Rightarrow$ Quick Assets = 2 × 1,20,000 = ₹ 2,40,000

Current Assets = Quick Assets + Prepaid Salary
= 2,40,000 + 10,000
= ₹ 2,50,000

Solved Question 16 **The quick ratio of Sigma Ltd. is 1.2 : 1. Its current assets are of ₹ 75,000 and current liabilities amount to ₹ 40,000. Find the value of inventory.**

Sol. $\text{Quick Ratio} = \dfrac{\text{Liquid Assets}}{\text{Current Liabilities}}$

$$\Rightarrow 1.2 = \frac{\text{Liquid Assets}}{40{,}000}$$

$\Rightarrow$ Liquid Assets = ₹ 48,000

Inventory = Current Assets − Liquid Assets
= 75,000 − 48,000
= ₹ 27,000

Solved Question 17 **State, giving reasons which of the following transactions would improve, reduce or not change the current ratio, if the current ratio of a company is 2 : 1.**

(i) Goods purchased on credit.
(ii) Payments made to creditors.
(iii) Sale of a machine for ₹ 40,000 (Book value ₹ 30,000).
(iv) Sold goods for ₹ 20,000 (Cost ₹ 15,000).
(v) 8% debentures, face value ₹ 50,000 were redeemed.
(vi) Goods purchased for cash.
(vii) Cash received from debtors.

Sol. (i) **Reduced** Both current assets and current liabilities will be increased by same amount.

(ii) **Improved** Both current assets and current liabilities will be decreased by same amount.

(iii) **Improved** Only current assets will be increased in the ratio.

(iv) **Improved** Current assets will be increased by net amount of ₹ 5,000 as cash will be increased by ₹ 20,000 and inventory will be decreased by ₹ 15,000. There is no effect on liability.

(v) **Improved** Matured debentures are the part of current liabilities. Hence, both current assets and current liabilities will be decreased by same amount.

(vi) **No Change** As inventory will be increased and cash will be decreased also. Hence, there is not effect on current assets and current liabilities.

(vii) **No Change** There will be increase in cash and decrease in debtors. Hence, effect on current assets will be zero. These is also no effect on current liabilities.

Solvency Ratios

Solved Question 18 **From the information given below, calculate the debt equity ratio of Fragrance Ltd.**

Particulars	Amt (₹)
Share Capital	
25,000 Equity Shares of ₹ 10 each	2,50,000
Reserve Fund	60,000
Surplus, i.e. Balance in the Statement of Profit and Loss	40,000
Debentures	6,00,000
Long-term Provisions	1,00,000
Outstanding Expenses	15,000

Sol. $\text{Debt to Equity Ratio} = \frac{\text{Debt}^*}{\text{Equity}^{**}} = \frac{7,00,000}{3,50,000} = 2:1$

*Debt = Debentures + Long-term Provisions
= 6,00,000 + 1,00,000 = ₹ 7,00,000

**Shareholders' Funds/Equity = Equity Share Capital + Reserves + Surplus
= 2,50,000 + 6,00,000 + 40,000 = ₹ 3,50,000

Solved Question 19 **Calculate debt to equity ratio from the following information**

Total assets ₹ 3,50,000, total debts ₹ 2,50,000 and current liabilities ₹ 80,000.

Sol. $\text{Debt to Equity Ratio} = \frac{\text{Debt}^*}{\text{Equity}^{**}} = \frac{1,70,000}{1,00,000} = 1.7:1$

*Debt = Total Debts − Current Liabilities
= 2,50,000 − 80,000 = ₹ 1,70,000

**Equity *or* Shareholders' Funds = Total Assets − Total Debts
= 3,50,000 − 2,50,000 = ₹ 1,00,000

Solved Question 20 **Calculate debt equity ratio from the following information**

Share capital ₹ 1,80,000, general reserve ₹ 60,000, profit before interest and tax ₹ 70,000, 10% loan ₹ 80,000, tax paid ₹ 8,000, sales during the year ₹ 3,00,000.

Sol. $\text{Debt Equity Ratio} = \frac{\text{Debt}}{\text{Equity}} = \frac{80,000}{2,94,000} = 0.27:1$

Debt = ₹ 80,000 (Loan Given)

Equity = Share Capital + General Reserve + Balance in Statement of Profit and Loss
= 1,80,000 + 60,000 + 54,000 = ₹ 2,94,000

Balance in Statement of Profit and Loss = Net Profit before Interest and Tax − Interest − Tax
= 70,000 − 8,000 − 8,000 = ₹ 54,000

Solved Question 21 **From the following information which relates to Suriya Ltd. compute debt to equity ratio**

	Amt (₹)
Long-term borrowings	**2,00,000**
Long-term provisions	**1,00,000**
Current liabilities	**50,000**
Non-current assets	**3,60,000**
Current assets	**90,000**
Share capital	**65,000**
Reserves and surplus	**35,000**

Sol. $\text{Debt Equity Ratio} = \frac{\text{Debt}^*}{\text{Equity (Shareholders' Funds)}^{**}}$

$= \frac{3,00,000}{1,00,000} = 3:1$

*Debt = Long-term Borrowings + Long-term Provisions
= 2,00,000 + 1,00,000 = ₹ 3,00,000

**Shareholders' Funds = Non-current Assets + Current Assets − Non-current Liabilities − Current Liabilities

or Non-current Assets + Current Assets − (Long-term Borrowings + Long-term Provisions) − Current Liabilities
= 3,60,000 + 90,000 − (2,00,000 + 1,00,000 + 50,000)
= 4,50,000 − 3,50,000 = ₹ 1,00,000

or Shareholders' Funds = Share Capital + Reserves and Surplus
= 65,000 + 35,000 = ₹ 1,00,000

Point to Remember

Long-term provisions are a component of debt, as provision is an amount set aside out of profit to meet a known liability, amount of which is not yet determined.

Solved Question 22 **Assuming that the debt equity ratio is 2 : 1. State, giving reasons, whether this ratio will increase or decrease or will have no change in each one of the following cases**

(i) Purchase of a property, plant and equipment on long-term deferred payment basis.
(ii) Purchase of a property, plant and equipment on a credit of 2 months.
(iii) Sale of property, plant and equipment (Book value ₹ 40,000 at a loss of ₹ 5,000).
(iv) Sale of property, plant and equipment (Book value ₹ 40,000 for ₹ 50,000).
(v) Issue of new shares for cash.
(vi) Issue of bonus shares.
(vii) Redemption of debentures for cash.
(viii) Conversion of debenture into equity shares.
(ix) Declaration of final dividend.

Sol. (i) **Increase** Total long-term debts are increased, but total shareholders' funds remain unchanged.

(ii) **No Effect** Neither the total long-term debts nor the total shareholders' funds are affected.

(iii) **Increase** Total shareholders' funds are decreased by the amount of loss, but total long-term debts remain unchanged.

(iv) **Decrease** Total shareholders' funds are increased by the amount of profit, but total long-term debts remain unchanged.

(v) **Decrease** Total shareholders' funds are increased by the amount of cash received, but total long-term debts remain unchanged.

(vi) **No Effect** Neither the total long-term debts nor the total shareholders' funds are affected since there is only a conversion of accumulated profits into share capital.

(vii) **No Effect** Long-term debts and total shareholders' funds remain unchanged.

(viii) **Decrease** Total long-term debts are decreased and total shareholders' funds are increased by the same amount.

(ix) **Increase** Total shareholders' funds are decreased by the amount of profits appropriated for dividend but long-term debts remain unchanged. Upon the declaration of dividend by the company, the profits to the extent of dividend declared become a current debt and hence shareholders' funds are decreased and current liabilities are increased by the amount of dividend declared.

Solved Question 23 **Calculate total assets to debt ratio of Modern Breads Ltd. from the given information**

Shareholders' funds ₹ 7,50,000, total debts ₹ 10,00,000, current liabilities ₹ 2,50,000.

Sol. Total Assets to Debt Ratio $= \frac{\text{Total Assets}^*}{\text{Debt}^{**}}$

$= \frac{17,50,000}{7,50,000} = 2.33 : 1$

*Total Assets = Shareholders' Funds + Total Debts

= 7,50,000 + 10,00,000 = ₹ 17,50,000

**Debt = Total Debt – Current Liabilities

= 10,00,000 – 2,50,000 = ₹ 7,50,000

Solved Question 24 **Calculate total assets to debt ratio of APX Future Ltd. from the following information**

Total assets ₹ 8,00,000, total debts ₹ 6,00,000, creditors ₹ 80,000, bills payable ₹ 40,000, bank overdraft ₹ 60,000, outstanding expenses ₹ 40,000.

Sol. Total Assets to Debt Ratio $= \frac{\text{Total Assets}}{\text{Debt}^*}$

$= \frac{8,00,000}{5,80,000} = 1.38 : 1$

*Debt = Total Debts – All Current Liabilities

= 8,00,000 – 80,000 – 40,000 – 60,000 – 40,000

= ₹ 5,80,000

Solved Question 25 **From the following information, calculate total assets to debt ratio of Commerce Ltd. Capital employed ₹ 15,00,000, investments ₹ 1,75,000, land ₹ 5,00,000, trade receivables ₹ 1,50,000, cash and cash equivalents ₹ 80,000, marketable securities ₹ 10,000, short-term deposits ₹ 5,000, equity share capital ₹ 6,00,000, 8% debentures ₹ 1,75,000, capital reserve ₹ 25,000, surplus, i.e. balance in the statement of profit and loss ₹ (15,000).**

Sol. Total Assets to Debt Ratio $= \frac{\text{Total Assets}^*}{\text{Debt}^{**}}$

$= \frac{9,05,000}{8,90,000} = 1.02 : 1$

*Total Assets = Investments + Land + Trade Receivables + Cash and Cash Equivalents

= 1,75,000 + 5,00,000 + 1,50,000 + 80,000 = ₹ 9,05,000

Shareholders' Funds = Equity Share Capital + Capital Reserve + Surplus

= 6,00,000 + 25,000 – 15,000 = ₹ 6,10,000

**Debt = Capital Employed – Shareholders' Funds

= 15,00,000 – 6,10,000 = ₹ 8,90,000

Note Marketable securities and short-term deposits are equivalent to cash which is already added.

Solved Question 26 **From the information given below, calculate the proprietary ratio of Samiksha Ltd.**

Equity share capital ₹ 5,00,000, 12% preference share capital ₹ 2,50,000, general reserve ₹ 1,50,000, surplus, i.e. balance in the statement of profit and loss ₹ 50,000, 10% debentures ₹ 12,00,000, current liabilities ₹ 5,50,000, property, plant and equipment ₹ 16,00,000, trade investments (long-term) ₹ 1,50,000, current assets ₹ 5,00,000.

Sol. Proprietary Ratio $= \frac{\text{Shareholders' Funds}^*}{\text{Total Assets}^{**}}$

$= \frac{9,50,000}{22,50,000} = 0.42 : 1$

*Shareholders' Funds = Equity Share Capital + Preference Share Capital + General Reserve + Surplus

= 5,00,000 + 2,50,000 + 1,50,000 + 50,000

= ₹ 9,50,000

**Total Assets = Property, Plant and Equipment + Trade Investments + Current Assets

= 16,00,000 + 1,50,000 + 5,00,000

= ₹ 22,50,000

Solved Question 27 **The proprietary ratio of M Ltd. is 0.80 : 1. State with reasons whether the following transactions will increase, decrease or not change the proprietary ratio**

(i) **Obtained a loan from bank ₹ 2,00,000 payable after five years.**
(ii) **Purchased machinery for cash ₹ 75,000.**
(iii) **Redeemed 5% redeemable preference shares ₹ 1,00,000.**
(iv) **Issued equity shares to the vendors of machinery purchased for ₹ 4,00,000.**

Sol. (i) **Decrease** Loan obtained from bank will increase the total assets but the shareholders' funds will remain the same, so proprietary ratio will decrease.

(ii) **No Change** Machinery purchased for cash will increase and simultaneously decrease the total assets therefore proprietary ratio will remain unchanged.

(iii) **Decrease** Redemption of preference shares will decrease total assets and shareholders' funds, simultaneously so proprietary ratio will decrease.

(iv) **Increase** Machinery purchased by issue of equity shares will increase total assets and shareholders' funds, simultaneously so proprietary ratio will increase.

Solved Question 28 **Profit after tax amounted to ₹ 6,00,000 and tax rate was 20%. If earnings before interest and tax was ₹ 10,00,000 and nominal value of debentures amounted to ₹ 25,00,000 (assuming the only debt of the company), determine the rate of interest on debentures.**

CBSE SQP 2025

Sol. Net Profit before Interest and Tax = Profit after Tax + Tax + Interest

10,00,000 = 6,00,000 + 1,50,000 (6,00,000 × 20/80) + Interest

∴ Interest = ₹ 2,50,000

Interest on Debentures = Nominal Value of Debentures × Rate of Interest/100

2,50,000 = 25,00,000 × Rate of Interest/100

∴ Rate of Interest = 10%

Solved Question 29 **From the following details obtained from the financial statements of YZ Ltd. for the year ended 31st March, 2024. Calculate interest coverage ratio.**

Net profit after tax ₹ 8,00,000

₹ 20,00,000, 10% debentures of ₹ 100 each

Tax rate 20%

State its significance also. Will the ratio change if during the year 2023-24, the company decides to redeem debentures of ₹ 4,00,000 and expects to maintain the same rate of net profit and assume that the tax rate will not change.

Sol. Interest Coverage Ratio

$$= \frac{\text{Net Profit before Interest and Tax}}{\text{Fixed Interest Charges}}$$

Net Profit before Interest and Tax = Net Profit after Tax + Tax + Interest on Long-term Debt

= 8,00,000 + 2,00,000 + 2,00,000

= ₹ 12,00,000

$$\text{Interest Coverage Ratio} = \frac{12,00,000}{2,00,000} = 6 \text{ times}$$

Significance It shows number of times interest on long-term debt is covered by profits available.

The interest coverage ratio will improve if the company redeems debentures assuming same rate of net profit and the tax rate will be same.

Activity Ratios

Solved Question 30 **From the following information, calculate inventory turnover ratio**

Cost of revenue from operations ₹ 5,60,000, inventory (opening) ₹ 60,000, inventory (closing) ₹ 80,000.

Sol. Inventory Turnover Ratio

$$= \frac{\text{Cost of Revenue from Operations}}{\text{Average Inventory}} = \frac{5,60,000}{70,000} = 8 \text{ times}$$

Average Inventory

$$= \frac{\text{Opening Inventory} + \text{Closing Inventory}}{2}$$

$$= \frac{60,000 + 80,000}{2} = ₹\ 70,000$$

Solved Question 31 **From the given information calculate inventory turnover ratio**

Revenue from operations ₹ 8,00,000, gross profit ₹ 50,000, purchases made during the year ₹ 10,00,000, opening inventory = ₹ 2,50,000.

Sol. Inventory Turnover Ratio

$$= \frac{\text{Cost of Revenue from Operations}^{*}}{\text{Average Inventory}^{**}} = \frac{7,50,000}{3,75,000} = 2 \text{ times}$$

Cost of Revenue from Operations = Revenue from Operations − Gross Profit

= 8,00,000 − 50,000 = ₹ 7,50,000

*Cost of Revenue from Operations = Opening Inventory + Purchases + Direct Expenses − Closing Inventory

Closing Inventory = Opening Inventory + Purchases − Cost of Revenue from Operations

= 2,50,000 + 10,00,000 − 7,50,000

= ₹ 5,00,000

**Average Inventory

$$= \frac{\text{Opening Inventory} + \text{Closing Inventory}}{2}$$

$$= \frac{2,50,000 + 5,00,000}{2} = ₹\ 3,75,000$$

Solved Question 32 **From the following information obtained from the books of Kundan Ltd. calculate the inventory turnover ratio for the years 2015-16 and 2016-17**

	2015-16 (₹)	2016-17 (₹)
Inventory on 31st March	7,00,000	17,00,000
Revenue from Operations	50,00,000	75,00,000

Gross profit is 25% on cost of revenue from operations. In the year 2015-16, inventory increased by ₹ 2,00,000.

CBSE 2018

Sol. **For 2015-16**

Inventory Turnover Ratio

$$= \frac{\text{Cost of Revenue from Operations}^*}{\text{Average Inventory}^{**}}$$

$$= \frac{40,00,000}{6,00,000} = 6.67 \text{ times}$$

*Cost of Revenue from Operations = Revenue from Operations − Gross Profit

$$= 50,00,000 - 10,00,000 \left(50,00,000 \times \frac{25}{125}\right) = ₹\ 40,00,000$$

**Average Inventory

$$= \frac{\text{Operating Inventory + Closing Inventory}}{2}$$

$$= \frac{5,00,000\ (7,00,000 - 2,00,000) + 7,00,000}{2}$$

= ₹ 6,00,000

For 2016-17

Inventory Turnover Ratio

$$= \frac{\text{Cost of Revenue from Operations}^*}{\text{Average Inventory}^{**}}$$

$$= \frac{60,00,000}{12,00,000} = 5 \text{ times}$$

*Cost of Revenue from Operations = Revenue from Operations − Gross Profit

$$= 75,00,000 - 15,00,000 \left(75,00,000 \times \frac{25}{125}\right)$$

= ₹ 60,00,000

$$^{**}\text{Average Inventory} = \frac{7,00,000 + 17,00,000}{2} = ₹\ 12,00,000$$

Solved Question 33 **From the given information, calculate inventory turnover ratio**

Revenue from operations (sales) ₹ 4,00,000, gross profit 25% on cost, closing inventory was 1/4th of opening inventory, opening inventory was 25% of cost of revenue from operations.

Sol. Gross profit is 25% on cost, so sale = 100 + 25 = ₹ 125

$$\text{Gross Profit on Sale} = \frac{25}{125} \times 100 = 20\%$$

Hence, Gross Profit = 4,00,000 × 20% = ₹ 80,000

Cost of Revenue from Operations = 4,00,000 − 80,000 = ₹ 3,20,000

Opening Inventory = 3,20,000 × 25% = ₹ 80,000

$$\text{Closing Inventory} = \frac{80,000}{4} = ₹\ 20,000$$

$$\text{Average Inventory} = \frac{\text{Opening} + \text{Closing}}{2} = \frac{80,000 + 20,000}{2}$$

= ₹ 50,000

Inventory Turnover Ratio

$$= \frac{\text{Cost of Revenue from Operations}}{\text{Average Inventory}}$$

$$= \frac{3,20,000}{50,000} = 6.4 \text{ times}$$

Solved Question 34 **Cash revenue from operations ₹ 50,000, credit revenue from operations ₹ 1,50,000, gross profit 30% on revenue from operations, inventory turnover ratio 2 times.**

Calculate opening inventory and closing inventory in each of the following cases

***Case* 1 If opening inventory is 1/3rd of the inventory at the end.**

***Case* 2 If closing inventory is 25% less than the inventory in the beginning.**

***Case* 3 If opening inventory is 75% of closing inventory and closing inventory is 30% of revenue from operations.**

Sol. Revenue from Operations = Cash Revenue from Operations + Credit Revenue from Operations

= 50,000 + 1,50,000 = ₹ 2,00,000

Cost of Revenue from Operations

= Revenue from Operations − Gross Profit

$$= 2,00,000 - \left(2,00,000 \times \frac{30}{100}\right)$$

= 2,00,000 − 60,000 = ₹ 1,40,000

Inventory Turnover Ratio

$$= \frac{\text{Cost of Revenue from Operations}}{\text{Average Inventory}}$$

$$2 = \frac{1,40,000}{\text{Average Inventory}}$$

$$\text{Average Inventory} = \frac{1,40,000}{2} = ₹\ 70,000$$

***Case* 1** If opening inventory is 1/3rd of the inventory at the end.

Let Closing Inventory be x

$$\therefore \text{Opening Inventory} = \frac{1}{3} \text{ of } x \text{ or } \frac{x}{3}$$

Average Inventory

$$= \frac{\text{Opening Inventory} + \text{Closing Inventory}}{2}$$

$$70{,}000 = \frac{\frac{x}{3}+x}{2};\ 70{,}000 \times 2 = \frac{x}{3}+x;\ \left[1{,}40{,}000 = \frac{4x}{3}\right]$$

$$4x = 1{,}40{,}000 \times 3$$

$$x = \frac{4{,}20{,}000}{4} = ₹\ 1{,}05{,}000 \quad \text{(Closing Inventory)}$$

$$\therefore \text{Opening Inventory} = \frac{1{,}05{,}000}{3} = ₹\ 35{,}000$$

Case 2 If closing inventory is 25% less than the inventory in the beginning.

Let Opening Inventory be x

$\therefore$ Closing Inventory $= x - 0.25x = 0.75x$

Average Inventory

$$= \frac{\text{Opening Inventory} + \text{Closing Inventory}}{2}$$

$$70{,}000 = \frac{x+0.75x}{2};\ 1{,}40{,}000 = 1.75x$$

$$x = \frac{1{,}40{,}000}{1.75} = ₹\ 80{,}000 \quad \text{(Opening Inventory)}$$

$\therefore$ Closing Inventory $= 0.75 \times 80{,}000 = ₹\ 60{,}000$

Case 3 If opening inventory is 75% of closing inventory and closing inventory is 30% of revenue from operations.

Closing Inventory = 30% of Revenue from Operations

= 30% of 2,00,000 = ₹ 60,000

Opening Inventory = 75% of 60,000 = ₹ 45,000

Solved Question 35 **A businessman carries an average inventory of ₹ 9,000. His inventory turnover ratio is 8 times. If he sells goods at a profit of 25% on sales, find out his profit.**

Sol. Inventory Turnover Ratio

$$= \frac{\text{Cost of Revenue from Operations, i.e. Cost of Goods Sold*}}{\text{Average Inventory (at cost)}}$$

$$8 = \frac{\text{Cost of Revenue from Operations}}{9{,}000}$$

$\Rightarrow$ *Cost of Revenue from Operations = ₹ 72,000

Revenue from Operations = Cost of Revenue from Operations + Gross Profit

Let Revenue from Operations be x.

Then, gross profit be $\frac{1}{4}x$.

$$x = 72{,}000 + \frac{1}{4}x \quad or \quad x - \frac{1}{4}x = 72{,}000$$

$$x = 72{,}000 \times \frac{4}{3} = ₹\ 96{,}000$$

Revenue from Operations = ₹ 96,000

$$\text{Gross Profit} = 96{,}000 \times \frac{25}{100} = ₹\ 24{,}000$$

Solved Question 36 **State, giving reason, which of the following transactions would increase, decrease or not change the inventory turnover ratio.**

(i) Sale of goods for ₹ 25,000 (costing ₹ 20,000).

(ii) Increase in the value of closing stock by ₹ 12,000.

(iii) Goods purchased for ₹ 50,000.

(iv) Purchase return amounting to ₹ 5,000.

(v) Goods costing ₹ 15,000 distributed as free samples.

(vi) Goods costing ₹ 5,000 withdrawn for personal use.

Sol. (i) The given transaction will increase the stock turnover ratio, as cost of goods sold increases and average stock decreases.

(ii) The given transaction will decrease the ratio, as cost of goods sold will decrease and average stock will increase.

(iii) The given transaction will decrease the ratio because cost of goods sold will remain unchanged but average stock will increase.

(iv) The given transaction will improve the ratio, as cost of goods sold remains unchanged, but average stock decreases.

(v) and (vi) In both the instances, the stock turnover ratio will improve as cost of goods sold remains unchanged but average stock decreases.

Solved Question 37 **From the following information, calculate opening trade receivables and closing trade receivables** **CBSE 2025**

Trade receivables turnover ratio 4 times

Closing trade receivables were ₹ 20,000 more than that in the beginning

Cost of revenue from operations ₹ 6,40,000

Cash revenue from operations $\frac{1}{3}$rd of credit revenue from operations

Gross profit ratio 20%

Sol. Trade Receivables Turnover Ratio

$$= \frac{\text{Net Credit Revenue from Operations**}}{\text{Average Trade Receivables}}$$

$$4 = \frac{6{,}00{,}000}{\text{Average Trade Receivables}}$$

$$\text{Average Trade Receivables} = \frac{6{,}00{,}000}{4} = ₹\ 1{,}50{,}000$$

Let credit sale be x

Total Revenue from Operations* = Cash Revenue from Operations + Credit Revenue from Operations**

$$8{,}00{,}000 = \frac{x}{3} + x$$

$$x = \frac{8{,}00{,}000 \times 3}{4} = ₹\ 6{,}00{,}000$$

*Revenue from Operations = Cost of Revenue from Operations + Gross Profit

$$= 6{,}40{,}000 + \left(6{,}40{,}000 \times \frac{25}{100}\right)$$
$$= 6{,}40{,}000 + 1{,}60{,}000$$
$$= ₹\ 8{,}00{,}000$$

Now, Average Trade Receivables

$$= \frac{\text{Opening Trade Receivables} + \text{Closing Trade Receivables}}{2}$$

$$1{,}50{,}000 = \frac{x + x + 20{,}000}{2}$$

(Assuming opening trade receivables as x)

$$2x + 20{,}000 = 3{,}00{,}000$$
$$2x = ₹\ 2{,}80{,}000$$
$$\therefore\ x = \frac{2{,}80{,}000}{2} = ₹\ 1{,}40{,}000 \text{ (Opening trade receivables)}$$

So, Closing Trade Receivables = 1,40,000 + 20,000
= ₹ 1,60,000

Solved Question 38 **From the following details, calculate trade receivables turnover ratio and average collection period**

	Amt (₹)
Total Revenue from Operations for the Year (Total Sales)	**1,12,500**
Cash Revenue from Operations (Cash Sales)	
20% of Total Revenue from Operations	
Revenue from Operations Returns (Out of Credit Revenue from Operations)	**10,000**
Trade Receivables	
Opening Balance	**4,000**
Closing Balance	**6,000**

Sol. Trade Receivables Turnover Ratio

$$= \frac{\text{Credit Revenue from Operations*}}{\text{Average Trade Receivables**}} = \frac{80{,}000}{5{,}000} = 16 \text{ times}$$

Cash Revenue from Operations = 20% of 1,12,500
= ₹ 22,500

$$\therefore\ \text{*Credit Revenue from Operations} = 1{,}12{,}500 - 22{,}500 - 10{,}000 = ₹\ 80{,}000$$

**Average Trade Receivables

$$= \frac{\text{Opening Trade Receivables} + \text{Closing Trade Receivables}}{2}$$

$$= \frac{4{,}000 + 6{,}000}{2} = ₹\ 5{,}000$$

Average Collection Period

$$= \frac{\text{Days in a Year}}{\text{Trade Receivables Turnover Ratio}}$$

$$= \frac{365}{16} = 23 \text{ days}$$

Solved Question 39 **Calculate trade recievable turnover ratio from the following information**

Credit sales ₹ 8,00,000, cash received from debtors ₹ 6,50,000, discount allowed ₹ 60,000, goods returned by debtors ₹ 15,000, opening debtors ₹ 80,000.

Sol. Trade Recievable Turnover Ratio $= \frac{\text{Net Credit Sales}}{\text{Average Debtors}}$

$$= \frac{7{,}85{,}000}{1{,}17{,}500} = 6.68 \text{ times}$$

Net Credit Sales = Credit Sales − Sales Return
= 8,00,000 − 15,000 = ₹ 7,85,000

$$\text{Average Debtors} = \frac{\text{Opening Debtors} + \text{Closing Debtors}}{2}$$

$$= \frac{80{,}000 + 1{,}55{,}000}{2} = ₹\ 1{,}17{,}500$$

Closing Debtors = Opening Debtors + Credit Sales − Cash Received − Discount Allowed − Sales Returns

$$= 80{,}000 + 8{,}00{,}000 - 6{,}50{,}000 - 60{,}000 - 15{,}000$$
$$= ₹\ 1{,}55{,}000$$

Solved Question 40 **Net credit sales (credit revenue from operations) of M/s Moon Agro Ltd. amounted to ₹ 12,50,000. Its debtors and bills receivables at the end of the year amounted to ₹ 1,20,000 and ₹ 80,000 respectively. Calculate trade receivables turnover ratio and collection period in terms of days, weeks and months.**

Sol. Debtors' Turnover Ratio $= \frac{\text{Net Credit Sales}}{\text{Average Trade Receivables}}$

$$= \frac{12{,}50{,}000}{1{,}20{,}000 + 80{,}000} = \frac{12{,}50{,}000}{2{,}00{,}000} = 6.25 \text{ times}$$

Average Collection Period

In days $= \frac{365}{6.25} = 58.4$ days; In months $= \frac{12}{6.25} = 1.9$ months

In weeks $= \frac{52}{6.25} = 8.32$ weeks

Solved Question 41 **Revenue from operations (net credit sales) for 2017-18 are ₹ 35,000 and debtors' turnover ratio is 8 times. Calculate the debtors at the end, if debtors in the beginning are ₹ 1,400 less than those at the end.**

Sol. Debtors Turnover Ratio

$$= \frac{\text{Revenue from Operations (Net Credit Sales)}}{\text{Average Debtors}}$$

$$8 = \frac{35{,}000}{\text{Average Debtors}}$$

$$\text{Average Debtors} = \frac{35{,}000}{8} = ₹\ 4{,}375$$

Let Closing Debtors = x; Opening Debtors = $x - 1{,}400$

$$\text{Average Debtors} = \frac{\text{Opening Debtors} + \text{Closing Debtors}}{2}$$

$$4{,}375 = \frac{x - 1{,}400 + x}{2}$$

$$2x = (4{,}375 \times 2) + 1{,}400 \Rightarrow x = 10{,}150/2 = ₹\ 5{,}075$$

Closing Debtors = ₹ 5,075

Opening Debtors = 5,075 − 1,400 = ₹ 3,675

Solved Question 42 **Calculate trade payable turnover ratio and average payable period.**

Total purchase ₹ 90,000, cash purchase is $\frac{1}{2}$ of credit purchase, opening creditors ₹ 20,000, closing creditors ₹ 30,000.

Sol. Trade Payable Turnover Ratio

$$= \frac{\text{Net Credit Purchase}}{\text{Average Trade Payables}} = \frac{60{,}000}{25{,}000} = 2.4 \text{ times}$$

Total Purchase = Cash Purchase + Credit Purchase

Let the credit purchase is x

$$90{,}000 = \frac{x}{2} + x \Rightarrow 90{,}000 = \frac{3x}{2}$$

$$x = \frac{1{,}80{,}000}{3} = ₹\ 60{,}000 \text{ (Credit Purchase)}$$

$$\text{Average Trade Payables} = \frac{20{,}000 + 30{,}000}{2} = ₹\ 25{,}000$$

$$\text{Payable Period} = \frac{365}{2.4} = 152 \text{ days}$$

Solved Question 43 **From the following information, calculate opening and closing inventory** **CBSE 2025**

Gross Profit Ratio 25%

Revenue from operations ₹ 8,00,000

Inventory turnover ratio 4 times

Opening inventory was 2 times of the closing inventory.

Sol. Inventory Turnover Ratio

$$= \frac{\text{Cost of Revenue from Operations}}{\text{Average Inventory}}$$

$$4 = \frac{\text{Sales} - \text{Gross Profit}}{\text{Average Inventory}}; \quad 4 = \frac{8{,}00{,}000 - (8{,}00{,}000 \times 25\%)}{\text{Average Inventory}}$$

$$4 = \frac{8{,}00{,}000 - 2{,}00{,}000}{\text{Average Inventory}}$$

$$\therefore \text{Average Inventory} = \frac{6{,}00{,}000}{4} = ₹\ 1{,}50{,}000$$

Now, let the closing inventory be x

Now, Average Inventory

$$= \frac{\text{Opening Inventory} + \text{Closing Inventory}}{2}$$

$$1{,}50{,}000 = \frac{2x + x}{2}$$

$$x = \frac{3{,}00{,}000}{3} = ₹\ 1{,}00{,}000 \text{ (Closing Inventory)}$$

Opening Inventory = 2 × Closing inventory

= 2 × 1,00,000 = ₹ 2,00,000

Solved Question 44 **Calculate the working capital turnover ratio of M/s Pankaj Dresses on the basis of information given below**

Cost of revenue from operations ₹ 5,00,000, current assets ₹ 2,50,000, current liabilities ₹ 1,50,000.

Sol. Working Capital Turnover Ratio

$$= \frac{\text{Cost of Revenue from Operations}}{\text{Working Capital}} = \frac{5{,}00{,}000}{1{,}00{,}000} = 5 \text{ times}$$

Working Capital = Current Assets − Current Liabilities

= 2,50,000 − 1,50,000 = ₹ 1,00,000

Solved Question 45 **Calculate working capital turnover ratio from the following information**

Revenue from operations ₹ 6,00,000, current assets ₹ 2,50,000, total assets ₹ 4,00,000, non-current liabilities ₹ 2,00,000 and shareholders' funds ₹ 1,00,000.

Sol. Working Capital Turnover Ratio

$$= \frac{\text{Revenue from Operations}}{\text{Working Capital}} = \frac{6{,}00{,}000}{1{,}50{,}000 \text{ (Note)}} = 4 \text{ times}$$

Working Note

Working Capital = Current Assets − Current Liabilities

= 2,50,000 − 1,00,000* = ₹ 1,50,000

*Current Liabilities = Total Assets − Non-current Liabilities − Shareholders' Funds

= 4,00,000 − 2,00,000 − 1,00,000 = ₹ 1,00,000

Solved Question 46 **Calculate working capital turnover ratio from the following information**

Current assets ₹ 1,75,000, current liabilities ₹ 60,000, cost of revenue from operations ₹ 8,00,000, gross profit 20% of revenue from operations, shareholders funds ₹ 5,00,000.

Sol. Working Capital Turnover Ratio

$$= \frac{\text{Revenue from Operations}^{*}}{\text{Working Capital}^{**}} = \frac{10{,}00{,}000}{1{,}15{,}000} = 8.7 \text{ times}$$

*Revenue from Operations = Cost of Revenue from Operations + Gross Profit

$$= 8{,}00{,}000 + 2{,}00{,}000 \left(8{,}00{,}000 \times \frac{25}{100}\right)$$

= ₹ 10,00,000

**Working Capital = Current Assets − Current Liabilities

= 1,75,000 − 60,000 = ₹ 1,15,000

Solved Question 47 **From the following information, calculate net asset turnover ratio**

Preference share capital ₹ 40,000, plant and machinery ₹ 80,000, equity share capital ₹ 60,000, land and building ₹ 50,000, general reserve ₹ 10,000, motor car ₹ 20,000, balance in statement of profit and loss ₹ 30,000, furniture ₹ 10,000, 15% debentures ₹ 20,000, inventory ₹ 18,000, 14% loan ₹ 20,000, debtors ₹ 11,000, creditors ₹ 14,000, bank ₹ 8,000, bills payable ₹ 5,000, cash ₹ 3,000, outstanding expenses ₹ 1,000.

Revenue from operations for the year were ₹ 3,00,000.

Sol. Net Asset Turnover Ratio $= \dfrac{\text{Revenue from Operations}}{\text{Capital Employed}^*}$

$= \dfrac{3,00,000}{1,80,000} = 1.67$ times

*Capital Employed = Share Capital + Reserves and Surplus + Long-term Debt
= (40,000 + 60,000) + (10,000 + 30,000) + 20,000 + 20,000
= ₹ 1,80,000

Solved Question 48 **From the following information, calculate fixed asset turnover ratio**

Plant and machinery ₹ 16,00,000, land and building ₹ 10,00,000, motor car ₹ 4,00,000, furniture ₹ 2,00,000, inventory ₹ 3,60,000, debtors ₹ 2,20,000, creditors ₹ 2,80,000, bank ₹ 1,60,000, bills payable ₹ 1,00,000, cash ₹ 40,000, outstanding expenses ₹ 20,000. Revenue from operations for the year were ₹ 60,00,000.

Sol. Fixed Asset Turnover Ratio

$= \dfrac{\text{Net Revenue from Operations}^*}{\text{Property, Plant and Equipment}^{**}} = \dfrac{60,00,000}{32,00,000}$

= 1.88 times

*Revenue from Operations = ₹ 60,00,000

**Property, Plant and Equipment = Plant and Machinery + Building + Motor Car + Furniture
= 16,00,000 + 10,00,000 + 4,00,000 + 2,00,000
= ₹ 32,00,000

Profitability Ratios

Solved Question 49 **Calculate gross profit ratio from the following information**

Inventory turnover ratio 6 times, average inventory ₹ 4,00,000, goods are sold at a profit of 25% on cost. **CBSE 2023**

Sol. Gross Profit Ratio $= \dfrac{\text{Gross Profit}}{\text{Revenue from Operations}^*} \times 100$

$= \dfrac{6,00,000}{30,00,000} \times 100 = 20\%$

Inventory Turnover Ratio

$= \dfrac{\text{Cost of Revenue from Operations}}{\text{Average Inventory}}$

$6 = \dfrac{\text{Cost of Revenue from Operations}}{4,00,000}$

∴ Cost of Revenue from Operations = ₹ 24,00,000

So, Gross Profit = 25% on Cost of Revenue from Operations

$= \dfrac{25}{100} \times 24,00,000 =$ ₹ 6,00,000

*Revenue from Operations = Gross Profit + Cost of Revenue from Operations
= 6,00,000 + 24,00,000 = ₹ 30,00,000

Solved Question 50 **Calculate gross profit ratio from the following information**

Cash sales are 25% of total sales, purchase ₹ 3,45,000, credit sales ₹ 3,00,000, excess of closing inventory over opening inventory ₹ 25,000.

Sol. Gross Profit Ratio $= \dfrac{\text{Gross Profit}}{\text{Revenue from Operations}} \times 100$

$= \dfrac{80,000}{4,00,000} \times 100 = 20\%$

Working Note

Calculation of Revenue from Operations, i.e. Net Sales = Credit Sales + Cash Sales

Let Revenue from Operations, i.e. Net Sales be x

Credit Sales (Given) = ₹ 3,00,000

∴ Cash Sales = 25% of x or $\dfrac{x}{4}$

$x = \dfrac{x}{4} + 3,00,000$ (Credit Sales)

$4x = x + 12,00,000;\ 3x = 12,00,000$

$x =$ ₹ 4,00,000 (Revenue from Operations, i.e. Net Sales)

Cash Sales $= 4,00,000 \times \dfrac{25}{100} =$ ₹ 1,00,000

Cost of Revenue from Operations (Cost of Goods Sold)
= Purchases + Change in Inventories*
= Purchases − Excess of Closing Inventory over Opening Inventory
= 3,45,000 − 25,000 = ₹ 3,20,000

Gross Profit = Revenue from Operations, i.e. Net Sales
= Cost of Revenue from Operations (Cost of Goods Sold)
= 4,00,000 − 3,20,000 = ₹ 80,000

*Change in Inventories = Opening Inventories − Closing Inventories
Excess of closing inventory over opening inventory means negative change. Hence, it is deducted.

Solved Question 51 **Calculate operating ratio from the following information**

Purchases ₹ 30,000, cash sales ₹ 45,000, excess of closing inventory over opening inventory ₹ 3,000, selling and distribution expenses ₹ 1,500, cash revenue from operations are 33.33% of revenue from operations.

Sol. Operating Ratio

$= \dfrac{\text{Cost of Revenue from Operations i.e. Cost of Goods Sold + Operating Expenses, i.e. Selling and Distribution Expenses}}{\text{Revenue from Operations, i.e. Net Sales}} \times 100$

$= \dfrac{27,000 + 1,500}{1,35,000} \times 100$

$= 21.11\%$

Cash revenue from operations are 1/3 of revenue from operations

∴ Revenue from Operations (Net Sales)

$$= \frac{3}{1} \times \text{Cash Revenue from Operations}$$

$$= \frac{3}{1} \times 45{,}000 = ₹\ 1{,}35{,}000$$

Cost of Revenue from Operations, i.e.

Cost of Goods Sold = Purchases − Excess of Closing Inventory Over Opening Inventory

= 30,000 − 3,000 = ₹ 27,000

Solved Question 52 **From the following information calculate operating ratio**

Revenue from operations ₹ 6,80,000, rate of gross profit on cost 25%, selling expenses ₹ 1,44,000, administrative expenses ₹ 73,000.

Sol. Operating Ratio $= \frac{\text{Operating Cost*}}{\text{Net Sales}} \times 100$

$$= \frac{7{,}61{,}000}{6{,}80{,}000} \times 100 = 111.91\%$$

*Operating Cost = Cost of Goods Sold** + Operating Expenses

= 5,44,000 + 1,44,000 + 73,000

= ₹ 7,61,000

**Gross Profit $= \frac{1}{4}$ on Cost *or* $\frac{1}{5}$ on Sales

$$= \frac{1}{5} \times 6{,}80{,}000 = ₹\ 1{,}36{,}000$$

Let Cost of Goods Sold be $= x$

$$\Rightarrow \quad 1{,}36{,}000 = \frac{1}{4} \times x$$

$$\Rightarrow \quad x = ₹\ 5{,}44{,}000$$

Note Operating expenses include selling and administrative expenses.

Solved Question 53 **Calculate operating profit ratio under the following cases**

***Case* 1 Revenue from operations (Net sales) ₹ 10,00,000, operating profit ₹ 1,50,000.**

***Case* 2 Revenue from operations (Net sales) ₹ 12,00,000, operating cost ₹ 10,40,000.**

***Case* 3 Revenue from operations (Net sales) ₹ 14,40,000, gross profit 20% on sales, operating expenses ₹ 72,000.**

***Case* 4 Revenue from operations ₹ 5,00,000, cost of revenue from operations ₹ 4,00,000, operating expenses ₹ 20,000.**

Sol. ***Case* 1** Operating Profit Ratio

$$= \frac{\text{Operating Profit}}{\text{Revenue from Operations (Net Sales)}} \times 100$$

$$= \frac{1{,}50{,}000}{10{,}00{,}000} \times 100 = 15\%$$

***Case* 2** Operating Profit Ratio

$$= \frac{\text{Operating Profit}}{\text{Revenue from Operations (Net Sales)}} \times 100$$

$$= \frac{1{,}60{,}000}{12{,}00{,}000} \times 100 = 13.33\%$$

Working Note

Operating Profit = Revenue from Operations − Operating Cost

= 12,00,000 − 10,40,000 = ₹ 1,60,000

***Case* 3** Operating Profit Ratio

$$= \frac{\text{Operating Profit}}{\text{Revenue from Operations (Net Sales)}} \times 100$$

$$= \frac{2{,}16{,}000}{14{,}40{,}000} \times 100 = 15\%$$

Working Note

Operating Profit = Gross Profit − Operating Expenses

= 20% of 14,40,000 − 72,000

= 2,88,000 − 72,000 = ₹ 2,16,000

***Case* 4** Operating Profit Ratio

$$= \frac{\text{Operating Profit}}{\text{Revenue from Operations}} \times 100 = \frac{80{,}000}{5{,}00{,}000} \times 100 = 16\%$$

Operating Profit = Gross Profit − Operating Expenses

= 5,00,000 − 4,00,000 − 20,000 = ₹ 80,000

Solved Question 54 **Calculate the operating profit ratio from the following data**

Opening inventory ₹ 5,000, purchases ₹ 50,000, revenue from operations (gross) ₹ 75,000, closing inventory ₹ 7,500, administrative expenses ₹ 2,500, selling expenses ₹ 6,000, dividend on shares ₹ 1,500, loss by theft ₹ 1,000, sales return ₹ 1,500.

Sol. Operating Profit Ratio

$$= \frac{\text{Operating Profit*}}{\text{Revenue from Operations (Net Sales)**}} \times 100$$

$$= \frac{17{,}500}{73{,}500} \times 100 = 23.80\%$$

*Operating Profit = Revenue from Operations (Net Sales) − (Purchases + Changes-in-inventories of Stock-in-trade + Other Expenses, i.e. Administrative Expenses and Selling Expenses)

= 73,500 −[50,000 −2,500 (7,500 −5,000) + 2,500 + 6,000]

= ₹ 17,500

**Revenue from Operations (Net Sales)

= Sales (Gross) − Sales Return

= 75,000 − 1,500

= ₹ 73,500

Solved Question 55 **Calculate gross profit ratio from the following information**

Revenue from operations ₹ 10,00,000, purchases ₹ 3,60,000, carriage inwards ₹ 50,000, employee benefit expenses ₹ 1,00,000 (including wages of ₹ 60,000), opening inventory ₹ 60,000 and average inventory ₹ 80,000. **CBSE SQP 2025**

Sol. $$\text{Gross Profit Ratio} = \frac{\text{Gross Profit}^{***}}{\text{Revenue from Operations}^{\#}} \times 100$$

$$= \frac{5,70,000}{10,00,000} \times 100 = 57\%$$

#Revenue from Operations = ₹ 10,00,000

***Gross Profit = Revenue from Operations − Cost of Revenue from Operations*

= 10,00,000 − 4,30,000 = ₹ 5,70,000

*Cost of Revenue from Operations = Purchases + Opening Inventory + Direct Expenses − Closing Inventory**

= 3,60,000 + 60,000 + 50,000 + 60,000 − 1,00,000

= ₹ 4,30,000

Average Inventory

$$= \frac{\text{Opening Inventory} + \text{Closing Inventory}}{2}$$

$$\Rightarrow \quad 80,000 = \frac{60,000 + \text{Closing Inventory}}{2}$$

**Closing Inventory = ₹ 1,00,000

Solved Question 56 **Revenue from operations ₹ 4,00,000, gross profit ratio 25%, operating ratio 90%, non-operating expenses ₹ 2,000, non-operating income ₹ 22,000. Calculate net profit ratio.**

Sol. $$\text{Net Profit Ratio} = \frac{\text{Net Profit}}{\text{Revenue from Operations}} \times 100$$

$$= \frac{60,000}{4,00,000} \times 100 = 15\%$$

Working Notes

1. Opening Profit Ratio = 100 − Operating Ratio
   = 100 − 90 = 10%
2. Operating Profit = 4,00,000 × 10/100 = ₹ 40,000
3. Net Profit = Operating Profit + Non-operating Incomes − Non-operating Expenses
   = 40,000 + 22,000 − 2,000 = ₹ 60,000

Solved Question 57 **Gross profit ratio of a company was 25%. Its cash sales were ₹ 1,00,000 and credit sales were 90% of the total sales. If the indirect expenses of the company were ₹ 10,000, calculate net profit ratio.**

Sol. Net Profit Ratio

$$= \frac{\text{Net Profit}}{\text{Revenue from Operations (Net Sales)}} \times 100$$

$$= \frac{2,40,000}{10,00,000} \times 100 = 24\%$$

Total Revenue from Operations = Cash Sales + Credit Sales

= 1,00,000 + 9,00,000 = ₹ 10,00,000

Cash Sales = ₹ 1,00,000

Credit Sales = 90% of Revenue from Operations, i.e. Net Sales

It means cash sales were 10% of the revenue from operations, i.e. net sales

∴ Revenue from Operations, i.e.

$$\text{Net Sales} = \frac{\text{Cash Sales}}{10} \times 100$$

$$\text{Sales (Cash + Credit)} = \frac{1,00,000 \times 100}{10} = ₹\ 10,00,000$$

$$\text{Gross Profit} = 10,00,000 \times \frac{25}{100} = ₹\ 2,50,000$$

Net Profit = Gross Profit − Indirect Expenses

= 2,50,000 − 10,000 = ₹ 2,40,000

Solved Question 58 **Calculate net profit ratio from the following statement of profit and loss of Anand Ltd. for the year ended 31st March, 2024.**

Particulars	Note No.	Amt (₹)
I. **Revenue from Operations** (Net Sales)		25,00,000
II. **Expenses**		
Purchases of Stock-in-trade		17,40,000
Changes in Inventories of Stock-in-trade		(54,000)
Employees Benefit Expenses		2,40,000
Finance Costs		10,000
Depreciation and Amortisation Expenses		16,000
Other Expenses	1	88,000
Total Expenses		20,40,000
III. **Net Profit** (I – II)		4,60,000

Notes to Accounts

Particulars	Amt (₹)
1. **Other Expenses**	
Carriage	10,000
Administrative and General Expenses	20,000
Provision for Tax	58,000
	88,000

Sol. Net Profit Ratio

$$= \frac{\text{Net Profit after Tax}}{\text{Revenue from Operations (Net Sales)}} \times 100$$

$$= \frac{4,60,000}{25,00,000} \times 100 = 18.40\%$$

Solved Question 59 **Calculate return on investment/ capital employed from the following information**

Opening inventory ₹ 40,000, closing inventory ₹ 50,000, carriage inwards ₹ 8,000, purchases ₹ 1,20,000, current assets ₹ 60,000, current liabilities ₹ 30,000, non-current assets ₹ 90,000, indirect expenses ₹ 15,000, revenue from operations ₹ 2,00,000, other current assets ₹ 5,000.

Sol. Return on Investment

$$= \frac{\text{Net Profit before Interest and Tax}^*}{\text{Capital Employed}^{**}} \times 100$$

$$= \frac{67{,}000}{1{,}20{,}000} \times 100 = 55.83\%$$

*Net Profit before Interest and Tax = Gross Profit – Indirect Expenses

$$= 82{,}000 - 15{,}000 = ₹\ 67{,}000$$

Gross Profit = Sales – Cost of Goods Sold

$$= 2{,}00{,}000 - 1{,}18{,}000 = ₹\ 82{,}000$$

Cost of Goods Sold = Opening Stock + Purchases + Carriage Inwards – Closing Stock

$$= 40{,}000 + 1{,}20{,}000 + 8{,}000 - 50{,}000$$

$$= ₹\ 1{,}18{,}000$$

**Capital Employed = Non-current Assets + Current Assets – Current Liabilities

$$= 90{,}000 + 60{,}000 - 30{,}000 = ₹\ 1{,}20{,}000$$

Comprehensive Illustrations

Solved Question 60 **From the following information related to Naveen Ltd., calculate**

(i) Return on investment (ii) Total assets to debt ratio

Fixed assets ₹ 75,00,000, current assets ₹ 40,00,000, current liabilities ₹ 27,00,000, 12% debentures ₹ 80,00,000 and net profit before interest, tax and dividend ₹ 14,50,000.

Sol. (i) Return on Investment

$$= \frac{\text{Net Profit before Interst, Tax and Dividend}}{\text{Capital Employed}^*} \times 100$$

$$= \frac{14{,}50{,}000}{88{,}00{,}000} \times 100 = 16.48\%$$

*Capital Employed

= Fixed Assets + Current Assets – Current Liabilities

$$= 75{,}00{,}000 + 40{,}00{,}000 - 27{,}00{,}000 = ₹\ 88{,}00{,}000$$

(ii) Total Assets to Debt Ratio

$$= \frac{\text{Total Assets}^*}{\text{Debt}} = \frac{1{,}15{,}00{,}000}{80{,}00{,}000} = 1.44 : 1$$

*Total Assets = Fixed Assets + Current Assets

$$= 75{,}00{,}000 + 40{,}00{,}000$$

$$= ₹\ 1{,}15{,}00{,}000$$

Solved Question 61 **From the given information calculate the following**

(i) Cost of revenue from operations
(ii) Opening and closing inventory
(iii) Quick assets (iv) Current assets

Additional Information

Inventory turnover ratio 6 times, inventory at the end is ₹ 6,000 more than the inventory in the beginning, revenue from operations (all credits) ₹ 2,40,000, gross profit 25% on cost, current liabilities ₹ 80,000, quick ratio 0.80 : 1.

Sol. (i) Let cost be = ₹ 100

Gross profit be = ₹ 25

Revenue from Operations = 100 + 25 = ₹ 125

Revenue from Operations (All Credits) = ₹ 2,40,000

$$\therefore \text{Cost of Revenue from Operations} = 2{,}40{,}000 \times \frac{100}{125}$$

Cost of Revenue from Operations = ₹ 1,92,000

(ii) Let Opening Inventory be = x

Closing inventory be = $x + 6{,}000$

Average Inventory

$$= \frac{x + x + 6{,}000}{2} = \frac{2x + 6{,}000}{2} = x + 3{,}000$$

Inventory Turnover Ratio

$$= \frac{\text{Cost of Revenue from Operations}}{\text{Average Inventory}}$$

$$6 = \frac{1{,}92{,}000}{x + 3{,}000}$$

$$6x + 18{,}000 = 1{,}92{,}000$$

$$6x = 1{,}92{,}000 - 18{,}000$$

$$x = \frac{1{,}74{,}000}{6} = 29{,}000$$

Opening Inventory $\Rightarrow x$

$\Rightarrow$ $29{,}000 = x + 6{,}000$

Closing Inventory = 29,000 + 6,000 = ₹ 35,000

(iii) $$\text{Quick Ratio} = \frac{\text{Quick Assets}}{\text{Current Liabilities}}$$

$$0.80 = \frac{\text{Quick Assets}}{80{,}000}$$

Quick Assets = ₹ 64,000

(iv) Current Assets = Quick Assets + Inventory

= 64,000 + 35,000 = ₹ 99,000

Solved Question 62 **Calculate the current ratio and debt equity ratio from the following information** **CBSE 2020**

	Amt (₹)
Non-current assets	**16,00,000**
Current assets	**4,00,000**
Working capital	**2,00,000**
Non-current liabilities	**12,00,000**

Sol. (i) Current Liabilities = Current Assets – Working Capital

$= 4,00,000 - 2,00,000 = ₹\ 2,00,000$

$$\text{Current Ratio} = \frac{\text{Current Assets}}{\text{Current Liabilities}} = \frac{4,00,000}{2,00,000} = 2:1$$

(ii) Equity = Total Assets – Liabilities

$= 20,00,000 - 14,00,000 = ₹\ 6,00,000$

$$\text{Debt Equity Ratio} = \frac{\text{Debt}}{\text{Equity}} = \frac{12,00,000}{6,00,000} = 2:1$$

Solved Question 63 **Calculate (i) cost of revenue from operations (ii) Opening inventory and closing inventory (iii) Quick assets and current assets from the following information**

Current liabilities	**₹ 80,000**
Quick ratio	**0.8**
Gross profit ratio	**1/4 of cost**
Revenue from operation (credit)	**₹ 2,50,000**

Inventory at the end is ₹ 10,000 more than the inventory is the beginning. Inventory turnover ratio 5 times.

Sol. Gross Profit Ratio $= \frac{1}{4}$ i.e. 25% on cost (Given)

Hence, Gross Profit on Sales $= \frac{25}{125} \times 100 = 20\%$

Cost of Revenue from Operations = Revenue from Operations – Gross Profit

$= 2,50,000 - (2,50,000 \times 20\%) = 2,50,000 - 50,000$

$= ₹\ 2,00,000$

$$\text{Average Inventory} = \frac{\text{Cost of Revenue from Operations}}{\text{Inventory Turnover Ratio}} = \frac{2,00,000}{5} = ₹\ 40,000$$

$$\text{Average Inventory} = \frac{\text{Opening Inventory} + \text{Closing Inventory}}{2}$$

$$40,000 = \frac{x + x + 10,000}{2} \quad \text{(Let the opening inventory is } x\text{)}$$

$2x + 10,000 = 80,000$

$$x = \frac{80,000 - 10,000}{2} = \frac{70,000}{2} = ₹\ 35,000$$

(Opening Inventory)

Closing Inventory $= 35,000 + 10,000 = ₹\ 45,000$

$$\text{Quick Ratio} = \frac{\text{Quick Assets}}{\text{Current Liabilities}} \Rightarrow 0.8 = \frac{\text{Quick Assets}}{80,000}$$

Quick Assets $= 80,000 \times 0.8 = ₹\ 64,000$

Current Assets = Quick Assets + Inventory (Closing)

$= 64,000 + 45,000 = ₹\ 1,09,000$

Missing Information

Solved Question 64 **Following is the comparative balance sheet of Venayak Ltd.**

Comparative Balance Sheet
as at 31st March, 2023 and 2024

Particulars	Note No.	31st March, 2023 (₹)	31st March, 2024 (₹)	Absolute Change (₹)	Percentage Change (%)
I. EQUITY AND LIABILITIES					
1. **Shareholders' Funds**					
(i) Share Capital		...	6,00,000	2,00,000	...
(ii) Reserve and Surplus		80,000	...	...	25.00
2. **Non-current Liabilities**					
Long-term Borrowings		2,00,000	...	50,000	...
3. **Current Liabilities**					
Trade Payables		...	80,000	10,000	...
Total		...	...	...	...
II. ASSETS					
1. **Non-current Assets**					
Property, Plant and Equipment and Intangible Assets		6,00,000	...	1,80,000	...
2. **Current Assets**					
(i) Trade Receivables		...	1,50,000	50,000	...
(ii) Cash and Cash Equivalents		...	1,00,000	50,000	...
Total		...	...	...	...

You are required to

(i) Fill the missing figures

(ii) Calculate total assets to debt ratio for both years.

Sol. (i)

Comparative Balance Sheet
as at 31st March, 2023 and 2024

Particulars	Note No.	31st March, 2023 (₹)	31st March, 2024 (₹)	Absolute Change (₹)	Percentage Change (%)
I. EQUITY AND LIABILITIES					
1. **Shareholders' Funds**					
(i) Share Capital		**4,00,000**	6,00,000	2,00,000	**50.00**
(ii) Reserve and Surplus		80,000	**1,00,000**	**20,000**	25.00
2. **Non-current Liabilities**					
Long-term Borrowings		2,00,000	**2,50,000**	50,000	**25.00**
3. **Current Liabilities**					
Trade Payables		**70,000**	80,000	10,000	**14.28**
Total		**7,50,000**	**10,30,000**	**2,80,000**	**37.33**
II. ASSETS					
1. **Non-current Assets**					
Property, Plant and Equipment and Intangible Assets		6,00,000	**7,80,000**	1,80,000	**30.00**
2. **Current Assets**					
(i) Trade Receivables		**1,00,000**	1,50,000	50,000	**50.00**
(ii) Cash and Cash Equivalents		**50,000**	1,00,000	50,000	**50.00**
Total		**7,50,000**	**10,30,000**	**2,80,000**	**37.33**

(ii) Total Assets to Debt Ratio $= \dfrac{\text{Total Assets}}{\text{Debt}}$

(a) On 31st March, 2023 $= \dfrac{7{,}50{,}000}{2{,}00{,}000} = 3.75 : 1$

(b) On 31st March, 2024 $= \dfrac{10{,}30{,}000}{2{,}50{,}000} = 4.12 : 1$

Solved Question 65 Following is the comparative balance sheet of PQ Ltd.

Comparative Balance Sheet of PQ Ltd.
as at 31st March, 2023 and 2024

Particulars	Note No.	31st March, 2023 (₹)	31st March, 2024 (₹)	Absolute Change (₹)	Percentage Change (%)
I. EQUITY AND LIABILITIES					
1. **Shareholders' Funds**					
(i) Share Capital		6,00,000	...	3,00,000	50.00
(ii) Reserve and Surplus		...	8,80,000	80,000	...
2. **Non-current Liabilities**					
Long-term Borrowings		3,20,000	...	(1,00,000)	...
3. **Current Liabilities**					
(i) Short-term Borrowings		...	5,50,000	50,000	10,000
(ii) Trade Payables		85,000	...	15,000	...
(iii) Other Current Liabilities		35,000	40,000	5,000	14.28
Total		...	...	...	...

Particulars	Note No.	31st March, 2023 (₹)	31st March, 2024 (₹)	Absolute Change (₹)	Percentage Change (%)
II. ASSETS					
1. **Non-current Assets**					
(i) Property, Plant and Equipment and Intangible Assets					
(a) Property, Plant and Equipment		16,00,000	...	1,40,000	...
(b) Intangible Assets		3,40,000	...	...	...
2. **Current Assets**					
(i) Inventory		...	3,80,000	80,000	...
(ii) Cash and Cash Equivalents		...	1,30,000	30,000	...
Total		...	...	...	...

You are required to

(i) Fill in the missing figures. **(ii) Compute debt equity ratio for both the years.**

Sol. (i)

Comparative Balance Sheet of PQ Ltd.

as at 31st March, 2023 and 2024

Particulars	Note No.	31st March, 2023 (₹)	31st March, 2024 (₹)	Absolute Change (₹)	Percentage Change (%)
I. EQUITY AND LIABILITIES					
1. **Shareholders' Funds**					
(i) Share Capital		6,00,000	**9,00,000**	3,00,000	50.00
(ii) Reserve and Surplus		**8,00,000**	8,80,000	80,000	**10.00**
2. **Non-current Liabilities**					
Long-term Borrowings		3,20,000	**2,20,000**	(1,00,000)	**(3.2)**
3. **Current Liabilities**					
(i) Short-term Borrowings		**5,00,000**	5,50,000	50,000	10.00
(ii) Trade Payables		85,000	**1,00,000**	15,000	**17.65**
(iii) Other Current Liabilities		35,000	40,000	5,000	14.28
Total		**23,40,000**	**26,90,000**	**3,50,000**	**14.95**
II. ASSETS					
1. **Non-current Assets**					
(i) Property, Plant and Equipment and Intangible Assets					
(a) Property, Plant and Equipment		16,00,000	**17,40,000**	1,40,000	**6.25**
(ii) Intangible Assets		3,40,000	**4,40,000**	**1,00,000**	**29.42**
2. **Current Assets**					
(i) Inventory		**3,00,000**	3,80,000	80,000	**29.67**
(ii) Cash and Cash Equivalents		**1,00,000**	1,30,000	30,000	**30**
Total		**23,40,000**	**26,90,000**	**3,50,000**	**14.95**

(ii) Debt Equity Ratio $= \frac{\text{Long-term Debt}}{\text{Shareholders' Funds}}$

(a) On 31st March, 2023 $= \frac{3,20,000}{14,00,000} = 0.23:1$

(b) On 31st March, 2024 $= \frac{2,20,000}{17,80,000} = 0.13:1$

Numerical Questions

Liquidity Ratios

1. Compute the current ratio from the following information.

Non-current investments ₹ 1,00,000, current investments ₹ 60,000, inventory (including spares parts) ₹ 3,35,000, debtors ₹ 1,50,000, bills receivable ₹ 30,000, creditors ₹ 1,20,000, long-term borrowing ₹ 1,80,000, short-term borrowing ₹ 40,000, provision for tax ₹ 15,000, cash and bank balance ₹ 30,000, loose tools and spare parts ₹ 15,000.

Ans. Current Ratio = 3.37 : 1

2. Ramaya Ltd. working capital is ₹ 6,00,000, total debts are ₹ 18,50,000, 10% debentures are ₹ 16,00,000.

Calculate current ratio.

Ans. Current Ratio = 3.4 : 1

3. Calculate current ratio from the following.

Working capital ₹ 3,15,000, current assets ₹ 4,20,000 and inventory ₹ 2,00,000 excluding loose tools ₹ 20,000.

Ans. Current Ratio = 4 : 1

4. Krishna Ltd. current ratio was 2 : 1. It paid ₹ 25,000 to a creditor.

Calculate current ratio after payment if current liabilities before payment were ₹ 50,000.

Ans. Current Ratio = 3 : 1

5. A company had current assets of ₹ 1,50,000 and current liabilities of ₹ 70,000. Afterwards it purchased goods for ₹ 10,000 on credit.

Calculate current ratio after the purchase.

Ans. Current Ratio = 2 : 1

6. Visakha Ltd. paid ₹ 40,000 to its creditors. On that date following information is given

Total assets ₹ 12,00,000, non-current assets ₹ 10,00,000. After the payment, current ratio was 2 : 1. Determine

(i) The size of current liabilities and working capital after the payment.

(ii) Also determine the size of these two items before the payment was made. **Competency Based Que**

Ans. (i) Current Liabilities = ₹ 80,000; Working Capital = ₹ 80,000

(ii) Current Liabilities = ₹ 1,20,000; Working Capital = ₹ 80,000

7. If current ratio is 2 : 1. State giving reasons which of the following transactions would improve ratio, which would reduce it and which would not change it? **Competency Based Que**

(i) Goods purchased on credit.
(ii) Sale of machine for ₹ 50,000.
(iii) Issue of equity shares for cash.
(iv) Payment made to a creditor ₹ 50,000 in full settlement of ₹ 52,000.
(v) Redemption of debentures.

Ans. (i) Reduce (ii) Increase (iii) Increase (iv) Increase (v) Increase

8. The ratio of current assets ₹ (3,00,000) to current liabilities ₹ (2,00,000) is 1.5 : 1. The accountant of the firm is interested in maintaining a current ratio of 2 : 1, by paying-off a part of the current liabilities.

Compute the amount of current liabilities that should be paid, so that the current ratio at the level of 2 : 1 may be maintained. **Competency Based Que**

Ans. Current liabilities amounting to ₹ 1,00,000 should be paid-off

9. The ratio of current assets ₹ (3,00,000) to current liabilities is 2.4 : 1. The accountant of this firm is interested in maintaining a current ratio of 2 : 1 by acquiring some current assets on credit.

You are required to suggest him the amount of current assets which must be acquired for this purpose. **Competency Based Que**

Ans. Current assets amounting to ₹ 50,000 should be purchased

10. Calculate liquid ratio.

If current assets are ₹ 25,000 excluding inventory ₹ 6,500 and prepaid expenses ₹ 500 and working capital ₹ 15,000.

Ans. Liquid Ratio = 1.47 : 1

11. From the following data, calculate current ratio and liquid ratio. **Competency Based Que**

	Amt (₹)
Liquid assets	75,000
Inventories (includes loose tools of ₹ 20,000)	35,000
Prepaid salary	5,000
Prepaid insurance	3,000
Working capital	60,000
Advance tax	10,000

Ans. Current Ratio = 3 : 1; Liquid Ratio = 2.5 : 1

12. **Calculate quick ratio from the following information.** Working capital ₹ 3,50,000, total equity and liabilities ₹ 12,00,000, non-current liabilities ₹ 10,00,000, inventory ₹ 40,000, advance tax ₹ 20,000. **Competency Based Que**

Ans. Quick Ratio = 2.45 : 1

13. Working capital of a company is ₹ 4,00,000. Its current ratio is 2.5 : 1.

Calculate value of **Competency Based Que**

(i) **current liabilities**

(ii) **current assets**

(iii) **liquid ratio/quick ratio/acid test ratio, assuming inventories of ₹ 2,00,000.**

Ans. (i) Current Liabilities = ₹ 2,66,667

(ii) Current Assets = ₹ 6,66,667 (iii) Liquid Ratio = 1.74 : 1

14. **A firm has a current ratio of 4 : 1 and quick ratio of 2.5 : 1. If inventories are ₹ 10,000 find out total current assets and total current liabilities.** **Competency Based Que**

Ans. Current Liabilities = ₹ 6,667; Current Assets = ₹ 26,668

15. A company's current ratio and quick ratio are 3 : 1 and 1.75 : 1 respectively. Current liabilities are ₹ 3,50,000.

Calculate current assets, liquid assets and inventory. **Competency Based Que**

Ans. Current Assets = ₹ 10,50,000; Liquid Assets = ₹ 1,95,000; Inventory = ₹ 1,65,000

16. Current assets of a company are ₹ 3,60,000. Its current ratio is 2.4 : 1 and acid test ratio is 1.3 : 1.

Calculate the value of current liabilities, liquid assets and inventories. **Competency Based Que**

Ans. Current Liabilities = ₹ 1,50,000; Liquid Assets = ₹ 1,95,000; Inventory = ₹ 1,65,000

17. Quick ratio 1 : 8, current assets ₹ 40,000, current liabilities ₹ 15,000.

Calculate the value of inventory.

Ans. Inventory = ₹ 13,000

18. **The quick ratio of a company is 2 : 1. State giving reasons, which of the following would improve, reduce or not change the ratio.** **Competency Based Que**

(i) Purchase of machinery for cash.

(ii) Purchase of goods on credit.

(iii) Sale of furniture at cost.

(iv) Sale of goods at a profit.

(v) Cash received from debtors.

Ans. (i) Reduce (ii) Reduce (iii) Improve (iv) Improve (v) No change

19. **Which of the following transactions would increase, decrease or not change the debt equity ratio is debt equity ratio is 2 : 1?** **Competency Based Que**

(i) Purchase of machine for ₹ 10,00,000 of which 80% payment is to be made immediately and remaining 20% after 20 months.

(ii) Refund of tax ₹ 20,000 during the year.

(iii) Dividend declared by shareholders.

(iv) Dividend proposed by directors of the company.

(v) Redemption of 8% debentures.

(vi) Buy-back of shares of a company.

(vii) Repayment of bank loan.

(viii) Sale of plant and machinery at loss.

Ans. (i) Increase (ii) Decrease (iii) Increase (iv) No change (v) No change (vi) No change (vii) Decrease (viii) Increase

Solvency Ratios

20. **Calculate debt equity ratio from the following information.**

Particulars	Amt (₹)
Equity Share Capital	2,00,000
Preference Share Capital	80,000
General Reserve	55,000
Securities Premium	15,000
Profit and Loss Balance	(15,000)
10% Debentures	3,50,000
Loan from Bank	1,25,000
Current Liabilities	20,000

Ans. Debt Equity Ratio = 1.41 : 1.

21. **Calculate debt equity ratio from the following.**

(i) Total assets ₹ 2,75,000

(ii) Total debt ₹ 1,50,000

(iii) Current liabilities ₹ 20,000

Ans. Debt Equity Ratio = 1.04 : 1

22. **From the following information, calculate debt equity ratio.** **Competency Based Que**

Equity share capital ₹ 25,000, general reserve ₹ 2,500, statement of profit and loss (profit after interest and tax) ₹ 7,500, 9% debentures ₹ 10,000, creditors ₹ 7,500, land and building ₹ 32,500, equipments ₹ 7,500, debtors ₹ 7,250 and cash ₹ 2,750. Sales for the year ended 31st March, 2021 were ₹ 75,000. Tax rate 50%.

Ans. Debt Equity Ratio = 0.29 : 1

23. **Calculate debt to capital employed ratio.**

	Amt (₹)
Property, plant and equipment	10,00,000
Computer software	80,000
Patent	2,00,000
Current assets	6,00,000
Inventory	3,00,000
Total debt	4,50,000
8% debentures	3,00,000

Ans. Debt to Capital Employed Ratio = 0.17 : 1

24. **Assuming that the debt equity ratio is 2 : 1, state, giving reasons, whether this ratio would increase, decrease or remain unchanged in the following cases** **Competency Based Que**

(i) Purchase of fixed asset on a credit of 2 months.
(ii) Purchase of fixed asset on a long-term deferred payment basis.
(iii) Issue of new shares for cash.
(iv) Issue of bonus shares.
(v) Sale of fixed asset at a loss of ₹ 3,000.

Ans. (i) No change (ii) Increase (iii) Decrease (iv) No change (v) Increase

25. **Calculate debt to capital employed ratio from the following details.**

Particulars	Amt (₹)
Property, Plant and Equipment	12,00,000
Goodwill	60,000
10% Long-term Borrowings	8,00,000
Trade Investments	1,20,000
Non-trade Investments	1,40,000
Inventory (Including loose tools ₹ 10,000)	4,60,000
Cash and Cash Equivalents	90,000
Take Payables	40,000

Ans. Debt to Capital Employed Ratio = 0.43 : 1

26. **Compute total assets to debt ratio from the following information.** **Competency Based Que**

Property, plant and equipment ₹ 12,80,000, non-current investments ₹ 1,60,000, current assets ₹ 6,08,000, total debts ₹ 14,80,000, trade payables ₹ 1,12,000, outstanding expenses ₹ 20,000, bank overdraft ₹ 68,000.

Ans. Total Assets to Debt Ratio = 1.6 : 1

27. **From the following information, calculate total assets to debt ratio.** **Competency Based Que**

Particulars	Amt (₹)	Particulars	Amt (₹)
Capital Employed	11,10,000	Equity Share Capital	5,00,000
Current Liabilities	85,000	8% Debentures	1,50,000

Particulars	Amt (₹)	Particulars	Amt (₹)
Property, Plant and Equipment (Gross)	7,50,000	Capital Reserve	1,20,000
Accumulated Depreciation	90,000	Surplus, i.e. Balance in Statement of Profit and Loss (Dr)	25,000
Non-current Investments	3,50,000	Cash and Cash Equivalents	75,000
Trade Receivables	1,10,000		

Ans. Total Assets to Debt Ratio = 0.25 : 1

28. **From the following information, calculate proprietary ratio.** **Competency Based Que**

Particulars	Amt (₹)	Particulars	Amt (₹)
Equity Share Capital	2,50,000	Reserves and Surplus	3,00,000
Preference Share Capital	2,50,000	Current Assets	10,00,000
Property, Plant and Equipment	17,00,000		
Long-term Trade Investment	5,00,000		

Ans. Proprietary Ratio = 25% *or* 0.25 : 1

29. **Assuming that proprietary ratio 0.6 : 1, state giving reasons, whether the ratio will increase, decrease or will not change in each one of the following cases** **Competency Based Que**

(i) Issue of new equity for cash.
(ii) Issue of equity shares against purchase of machinery.
(iii) Issue of debentures against purchase of machinery.
(iv) Redemption of debentures for cash.
(v) Conversion of debentures into preference shares.
(vi) Buy-back of its own shares by a company.
(vii) Purchase of a fixed asset for cash.
(viii) Purchase of a fixed asset on long-term deferred payment basis.

Ans. (i) Increase (ii) Increase (iii) Decrease (iv) Increase (v) Increase (vi) Decrease (vii) No change (viii) Decrease

30. **From the following details obtained from the statements of Krishna Ltd. for the year ended 31st March, 2024, calculate interest coverage ratio.** **Competency Based Que**

Net profit after tax ₹ 10,00,000
₹ 15,00,000, 10% debentures of ₹ 100 each
Tax ratio 20%

State its significance also. Will the ratio change if during the year 2023-24, the company decides to redeem debentures of ₹ 5,00,000 and expects to maintain the same rate of net profit and assume that the tax rate will not change.

Ans. Interest Coverage Ratio = 9.33 times

31. **From the following information calculate 'interest coverage ratio'.**

Profit after interest and tax	₹ 4,97,000
Rate of income tax	30%
12% debentures	₹ 6,00,000
Interest on bank loan	₹ 28,000

Ans. Interest Coverage Ratio = 8.1 times

Activity Ratios

32. **Compute inventory turnover ratio.**

Inventory (beginning of the year) ₹ 80,000, inventory (at the end of the year) ₹ 1,20,000, purchase ₹ 2,20,000, wages ₹ 60,000, carriage inward ₹ 20,000, revenue from operations ₹ 4,50,000.

Ans. Inventory Turnover Ratio = 2.6 times

33. **Calculate inventory turnover ratio for 2023 and 2024.** **Competency Based Que**

	2023 (₹)	2024 (₹)
Revenue from operations (at gross profit of 20% on cost of revenue from operations)	75,00,000	93,60,000
Inventory on 31st March	11,00,000	15,00,000

Ans. Inventory Turnover Ratio 2023 = 5 times ; 2024 = 6 times

34. **From the following information, calculate inventory turnover ratio.**

Purchase ₹ 6,00,000, carriage inwards ₹ 12,000, wages ₹ 10,000, revenue from operatives ₹ 8,00,000, opening inventory ₹ 80,000, gross loss 15% on revenue from operations.

Ans. Inventory Turnover Ratio = 1.53 times

35. Revenue from operations of Car Trade.com is ₹ 15,75,000. Rate of gross profit on cost is 20%. Inventory in the beginning was 20% of sales and that at the end exceeded opening inventory by ₹ 10,000.

Calculate the stock turnover ratio of the company.

Ans. Stock Turnover Ratio = 4.10 times

Hint Gross Profit = ₹ 2,62,500

36. Net sales of Kamayani Sarees was ₹ 3,75,000. It's gross profit amounted to ₹ 75,000. The opening inventory was ₹ 25,000, which was ₹ 5,000 more than the closing inventory.

Calculate it's stock turnover ratio. **Competency Based Que**

Ans. Stock Turnover Ratio = 13.33 times

37. Cost of revenue from operations ₹ 2,00,000, inventory turnover ratio 6 times.

Find out the value of opening inventory and closing inventory if opening inventory is ₹ 10,000 less than the closing inventory.

Ans. Opening Inventory = ₹ 28,333; Closing Inventory = ₹ 38,333

38.

Cash revenue from operations	₹ 1,00,000
Credit revenue from operations	₹ 5,00,000
Gross profit	₹ 1,20,000
Inventory turnover ratio	4 times

Calculate the value of opening and closing inventory in each of the following cases. **Competency Based Que**

***Case* I** If closing inventory was ₹ 1,00,000 in excess of opening inventory.

***Case* II** If closing inventory was 2 times that in the beginning.

***Case* III** If closing inventory was 2 times more than that in the beginning.

***Case* IV** If closing inventory was 3 times that in the beginning.

Ans.

Particulars	Case I (₹)	Case II (₹)	Case III (₹)	Case IV (₹)
Opening	70,000	80,000	60,000	60,000
Closing	1,70,000	1,60,000	1,80,000	1,80,000

39. **From the following information, determine the amount of gross profit and revenue from operations.**

Average inventory ₹ 90,000, inventory turnover ratio 4 times, gross profit 25% of revenue from operations.

Ans. Revenue from Operations = ₹ 4,80,000; Gross Profit = ₹ 1,20,000

40. **State giving reason, which of the following transactions would increase, decrease or not change the inventory ratio.** **Competency Based Que**

(i) Goods purchased for ₹ 40,000.

(ii) Sale of goods for ₹ 25,000 (cost ₹ 30,000).

(iii) Decrease in the value of closing inventory by ₹ 20,000.

(iv) Increase in the value of closing inventory by ₹ 10,000.

(v) Goods costing ₹ 5,000 as distributed samples

Ans. (i) Decrease (ii) Increase (iii) Increase (iv) Decrease (v) Increase

41. **Calculate opening and closing trade receivables from the following information.** **Competency Based Que**

Cash revenue from operations = 1/3rd of Credit Revenue from Operations

Cost of revenue from operations = ₹ 1,80,000

Gross profit = 25% of revenue from operations trade receivables at the end were 3 times that of in the beginning.

Trade receivables turnover ratio = 3 times

Ans. Opening Trade Receivables = ₹ 30, 000

Closing Trade Receivables = ₹ 90, 000

42. Calculate trade receivables turnover ratio if total sales of the year (net) is ₹ 87,500, sales return out of credit sales is ₹ 5,000, cash sales (net) is 20% of total net sales, opening sundry debtors are ₹ 4,000 and closing sundry debtors are ₹ 6,000.

Ans. Trade Receivables Turnover Ratio = 14 times

43. Calculate trade receivables turnover ratio from the following. Competency Based Que

Credit revenue from operations ₹ 2,50,000, opening trade receivables ₹ 25,000 and closing trade receivables were ₹ 25,000 also.

State, giving reason, the impact of following transactions on trade receivables turnover ratio.

(i) Cash received from debtors ₹ 15,000.
(ii) Goods sold on credit ₹ 25,000.
(iii) Revenue from operations return ₹ 5,000.
(iv) Purchased goods on credit ₹ 20,000.

Ans. Trade Receivables Turnover Ratio = 10 times;
(i) Increase (ii) Decrease (iii) Increase (iv) No change

44. Calculate trade receivables turnover ratio and average collection period if credit revenue from operations for the year is ₹ 3,00,000 and debtors and bills receivables at the year end were ₹ 30,000 and ₹ 20,000 respectively.

Ans. Trade Receivables Turnover Ratio = 6 times; Collection Period = 2 months, 61 days

45. Calculate trade receivable turnover ratio.

Collection from trade receivables ₹ 4,20,000, discount allowed ₹ 28,000, sales returns ₹ 30,000, closing trade receivables ₹ 60,000, closing trade receivables were ₹ 10,000 more than opening trade receivables.

Ans. Trade Receivable Turnover Ratio = 8.87 times

46. Calculate trade receivables turnover ratio from the following information. Competency Based Que

Trade receivables Opening	₹ 10,000
Closing	₹ 12,500
Provision for doubtful debt Opening	₹ 1,000
Closing	₹ 1,250
Total revenue from operations	₹ 1,00,000
Cash revenue from operations	₹ 43,750

Ans. Trade Receivable Turnover Ratio = 5 times

47. ₹ 1,75,000 is the credit revenue from operations. If trade receivables turnover ratio is 8 times, calculate trade receivables in the beginning and at the end of the year. Trade receivables at the end is ₹ 7,000 more than that in the beginning.

Ans. Trade Receivables in the Beginning = ₹ 18,375
Trade Receivables in the End = ₹ 25,375

48. Calculate trade payables turnover ratio.

Credit purchases during the year ₹ 3,10,000, purchase return (out of credit purchases) ₹ 10,000.

Creditors opening ₹ 50,000, closing ₹ 70,000		
Bills payable Opening		**₹ 12,500**
	Closing	**₹ 17,500**

Ans. Trade Payables Turnover Ratio = 4 times

49. Calculate creditors turnover ratio and average payable period. Competency Based Que

If total purchases is ₹ 12,40,000, purchase return is ₹ 40,000, cash purchases are twice of credit purchases. Creditors in the beginning of the year are ₹ 1,00,000 and creditors at the end of the year are ₹ 1,50,000.

Ans. Credit Turnover Ratio = 3.2 times; Average Payable Period = 112.5 days

50. Calculate working capital turnover ratio from the following information.

Current assets ₹ 1,60,000, current liabilities ₹ 20,000, cost of revenue from operations ₹ 10,00,000, gross profit 25% on cost.

Ans. Working Capital Turnover Ratio = 8.92 times

51. Calculate working capital turnover ratio.

If revenue from operations is ₹ 24,00,000, working capital is ₹ 6,00,000, total assets are ₹ 16,00,000, non-current liabilities are ₹ 8,00,000 and shareholders' funds are ₹ 4,00,000.

Ans. Working Capital Turnover Ratio = 4 times

52. Calculate working capital turnover ratio.

If working capital is ₹ 1,25,000, cost of revenue from operations ₹ 5,00,000, gross profit on sales 20%.

Ans. Working Capital Turnover Ratio = 5 times

53. Calculate net asset turnover ratio. Competency Based Que

Equity share capital ₹ 6,00,000, general reserve ₹ 1,20,000, balance in statement of profit and loss (Dr) ₹ 20,000, security premium ₹ 20,000, long-term borrowing ₹ 2,80,000, long-term provisions ₹ 50,000, current liabilities ₹ 80,000, current assets ₹ 1,00,000, cost of sales ₹ 36,00,000, gross profit 25% of sales.

Ans. Net Asset Turnover Ratio = 4.57 : 1

54. Calculate fixed asset turnover ratio from the following information. Competency Based Que

Inventory ₹ 50,000, revenue from operations ₹ 15,00,000, machinery ₹ 4,00,000, bank ₹ 1,00,000, furniture ₹ 50,000, debtors ₹ 60,000, building ₹ 2,50,000, bills payable ₹ 60,000, car ₹ 1,00,000.

Ans. Fixed Asset Turnover Ratio = 1.88 times

Profitability Ratios

55. Calculate gross profit ratio from the following. Competency Based Que

Opening inventory ₹ 60,000, purchases ₹ 2,00,000, closing inventory ₹ 40,000, returns outward ₹ 30,000, freight inward ₹ 15,000, revenue from operations ₹ 3,00,000, auditor fees ₹ 5,000.

Ans. Gross Profit Ratio = 41.67%

56. Calculate the amount of gross profit.

If average stock ₹ 80,000, inventory turnover ratio 6 times, selling price 25% above cost.

Ans. Gross Profit = ₹ 1,20,000

57. Calculate gross profit ratio from the following information. Competency Based Que

Cash revenue from operations was 1/3 rd of total revenue from operations, cash revenue from operations was ₹ 70,000, cash purchase was 25% of credit purchase. cash purchase was ₹ 25,000. Opening inventory ₹ 15,000, closing inventory was ₹ 5,000 more than opening inventory. Carriage ₹ 6,000.

Ans. Gross Profit Ratio = 40%

Hint Cost of Revenue from Operations = Opening Inventory + Purchase + Carriage − Closing Inventory

58. From the following details of a business concern, ascertain the gross profit ratio.

Particulars	2017 (₹)	2018 (₹)
Revenue from Operations (Sales)	12,000	16,000
Gross Profit	4,000	6,000

Ans. 2017 Gross Profit Ratio = $33\frac{1}{3}\%$

2018 Gross Profit Ratio = $37\frac{1}{2}\%$

59. Calculate the gross profit ratio from the following information. Competency Based Que

	Amt (₹)
Credit revenue from operations	1,50,000
Cash revenue from operations (being 25% of total revenue from operations)	
Purchases	1,60,000
Excess of closing inventory over opening inventory	20,000

Ans. Gross Profit Ratio = 30%

60. Calculate operating ratio. Competency Based Que

if purchases are cash sales are ₹ 22,500, excess of closing inventory over opening inventory is ₹ 1,500, selling and distribution expenses ₹ 750, cash revenue from operations are 33.33% of revenue from operations.

Ans. Operating Ratio = 21.11%

61. Revenue from operations ₹ 4,50,000, gross profit 25% on cost, operating expenses ₹ 45,000.

Calculate operating ratio.

Ans. Operating Ratio = 90%

62. Calculate operating profit ratio in the following cases.

(i) Revenue from operations ₹ 6,00,000, operating profit ₹ 1,20,000.

(ii) Revenue from operations ₹ 5,00,000, cost of revenue from operations ₹ 4,00,000, operating expenses ₹ 20,000.

(iii) Revenue from operations ₹ 10,00,000, net profit ₹ 2,00,000, non-operating income ₹ 20,000, non-operating expenses ₹ 15,000.

Ans. (i) 20% (ii) 16% (iii) 19.5%

63. Revenue from operations ₹ 4,50,000, gross profit 25% on cost, operating expenses ₹ 22,500.

Calculate operating profit ratio.

Ans. Operating Profit Ratio = 15%

64. Calculate operating profit ratio from the following information. Competency Based Que

	Amt (₹)
Revenue from operations, i.e. net sales	95,99,200
Cost of revenue from operations i.e. cost of goods sold	48,80,400
Wages	6,08,000
Office and administrative expenses	5,02,400
Selling and distribution expenses	9,00,800
Interest on loan	1,00,000
Income from investment	1,20,000
Loss by theft	60,000

Ans. Operating Profit Ratio = 34.54%

65. Calculate net profit ratio from the following information.

Revenue from operations (sales) ₹ 10,00,000, gross profit ratio 30%, operating ratio 80%, non-operating expenses ₹ 15,000, non-operating income ₹ 25,000.

Ans. Net Profit Ratio = 21%

66. Gross profit ratio of a company was 20%. Its credit revenue from operations were ₹ 9,00,000 and its cash revenue from operations were 10% of the total revenue from operations. If the indirect expenses of the company were ₹ 25,000.

Calculate its net profit ratio. Competency Based Que

Ans. Net Profit Ratio = 17.5%

67. Calculate net profit ratio from the following Statement of profit and loss of New Delhi Sales Ltd. for the year ended 31st March, 2024.

Particulars	Note No.	Amt (₹)
I. Revenue from Operations (Sales)		3,50,000
II. Expenses		
Purchases of Stock-in-trade		1,74,000
Employees Benefit Expenses		40,000
Finance Costs		1,000
Depreciation and Amortisation		1,000
Total Expenses		2,16,000
III. Net Profit (I–II)		1,34,000

Ans. Net Profit Ratio = 38.28%

68. Net profit before interest and tax ₹ 4,00,000, 15% long- term debt ₹ 8,00,000 and shareholders' funds ₹ 4,00,000.

Calculate return on investment. **Competency Based Que**

Ans. Return on Investment = ₹ 33.33%

69. Calculate return on capital employed from the following information

Opening inventory ₹ 60,000, closing inventory ₹ 80,000, carriage inwards ₹ 6,000, wages ₹ 8,000, purchases ₹ 1,60,000, shareholders' funds ₹ 2,00,000, total debts ₹ 3,00,000, non-current assets ₹ 4,00,000, short-term loan from PNB ₹ 1,20,000, auditor fees expenses ₹ 12,000, revenue from operations ₹ 4,20,000.

Ans. Return on Capital Employed = 74.2%

70. Calculate gross profit ratio from the following.

Credit revenue from operations ₹ 3,00,000, cash revenue from operations 20% of total revenue from operations, purchase ₹ 3,00,000, decrease in inventory ₹ 10,000

Ans. Gross Profit Ratio = 17.33%

71. Gross profit of Sanaya Ltd. is 20% on cost of revenue from operations. Its cash revenue from operations is 1/2 of credit revenues from operations. If cash revenue from operations are ₹ 4,00,000.

Calculate gross profit ratio.

Ans. Gross Profit Ratio = 16.67%

72. Calculate operating ratio from the following.

Competency Based Que

Credit revenue from operations	₹ 6,00,000
Employee benefit expenses	₹ 40,000
Selling and distribution expenses	₹ 25,000
Depreciation and amortisation	12,000
Gross profit on cost	40%
Cash revenue from operation	$\frac{1}{4}$th of total revenue from operations

Ans. Operating Ratio = 81.05%

73. Calculate operating profit ratio from the following.

Competency Based Que

Revenue from operations	₹ 6,00,000
Gross profit	25% on cost
Administration expenses	₹ 20,000
Depreciation	₹ 15,000
Interest on bank loan	₹ 8,000

Ans. Operating Profit Ratio = 14.16%

Comprehensive Questions

74. From the following information, determine the opening inventory and the closing inventory.

Inventory turnover ratio 5 times, revenue from operations ₹ 8,00,000, gross profit ratio 25%, closing inventory was ₹ 20,000 more than the opening inventory. **CBSE 2020**

Ans. Opening Inventory = ₹ 1,10,000, Closing Inventory = ₹ 1,30,000

75. From the following information, calculate any two of the following ratios **Competency Based Que**

(i) Current ratio **(ii) Debt to equity ratio**

(iii) Inventory turnover ratio

Revenue from operations (net sales) ₹ 5,00,000, opening inventory ₹ 7,000, closing inventory ₹ 4,000 more than the opening inventory, net purchase ₹ 1,00,000 less than net sales, operating expenses ₹ 30,000, liquid assets ₹ 75,000, prepaid expenses 2,000, current liabilities ₹ 60,000, 9% debentures 3,00,000, long-term loan from bank ₹ 1,00,000, equity share capital ₹ 10,00,000, 8% preference share capital ₹ 2,00,000.

Ans. (i) Current Ratio = 1.47 : 1
(ii) Debt to Equity Ratio = 0.33 : 1
(iii) Inventory Turnover Ratio = 44 times

76. On the basis of following information calculate (i) Liquid ratio (ii) Gross profit ratio (iii) Operating ratio.

Competency Based Que

Networking capital	₹ 1,90,000
Current assets	₹ 2,90,000
Inventory	₹ 1,00,000
Revenue from operations	₹ 16,00,000
Gross profit	20% on sales
Operating expenses	₹ 1,60,000

Ans. Liquid Ratio = 1.9 : 1; Gross Profit Ratio = 20%; Operating Ratio = 90%

77. Calculate trade receivable turnover ratio from the following.

Revenue from operations (credit)		₹ 4,20,000
Returns inward		₹ 40,000
Trade receivables on 1st April, 2024		₹ 60,000
Trade Receivables on 31st March, 2025	90,000	
(−) Provision for Doubtful Debts	(10,000)	₹ 80,000

Ans. Trade Receivable Turnover Ratio = 506.67 times

78. Calculate

(i) **Gross profit ratio**

(ii) **Operating ratio**

(iii) **Operating profit ratio**

(iv) **Inventory turnover ratio and**

(v) **Working capital turnover ratio from the following figures.** **Competency Based Que**

Purchase	₹ 15,20,000
Direct expenses	₹ 3,20,000
Opening inventory	₹ 2,80,000
Closing inventory	₹ 3,60,000
Selling and distribution expenses	10% of sales
Revenue from operations	₹ 40,00,000
Current assets including inventory	₹ 8,00,000
Current liabilities	₹ 1,40,000

Ans. (i) Gross Profit Ratio = 56% (ii) Operating Ratio = 54% (iii) Operating Profit Ratio = 46% (iv) Inventory Turnover Ratio = 5.5 times (v) Working Capital Turnover Ratio = 6.06 times

Missing Information

79. Following is the comparative balance sheet of New Ltd. for consecutive years. **Competency Based Que**

Comparative Balance Sheet of New Ltd.
as at 31st March, 2023 and 2024

Particulars	Note No.	31st March, 2023 (₹)	31st March, 2024 (₹)	Absolute Change (₹)	Percentage Change (%)
I. EQUITY AND LIABILITIES					
1. **Shareholders' Funds**					
(i) Share Capital		6,00,000	8,00,000	...	...
(ii) Reserve and Surplus		4,00,000	...	1,80,000	...
2. **Non-current Liabilities**					
(i) Long-term Borrowing		...	9,00,000	2,00,000	...
(ii) Long-term Provisions		80,000	...	(10,000)	...
3. **Current Liabilities**					
Trade Payables		...	2,20,000	40,000	...
Total		...	...	...	...
II. ASSETS					
1. **Non-current Assets**					
(i) Property, Plant and Equipment and Intangible Assets Property, Plant and Equipment		14,00,000	...	5,50,000	...
(ii) Intangible Assets		2,00,000	2,20,000	1,20,000	...
2. **Current Assets**					
(i) Trade Receivables		2,20,000	...	60,000	...
(ii) Cash and Cash Equivalents		...	1,20,000	(20,000)	...
Total		...	...	...	...

You are required to

(i) Fill the missing figures in the comparative balance sheet. **(ii) Compute debt to equity ratio for both years.**

80. Following is the balance sheet of APJ Fabrics Ltd. Competency Based Que

Comparative Balance Sheet of APJ Fabrics Ltd.
as at 31st March 2023 and 2024

Particulars	Note No.	31st March, 2023 (₹)	31st March, 2024 (₹)	Absolute Change (₹)	Percentage Change (%)
I. EQUITY AND LIABILITIES					
1. **Shareholders' Funds**					
(i) Share Capital		10,00,000	1,00,000	...	...
(ii) Reserve and Surplus		3,40,000	...	(20,000)	...
2. **Non-current Liabilities**					
(i) Long-term Borrowing		...	8,00,000	(1,00,000)	...
3. **Current Liabilities**					
(i) Short-term Borrowings		2,00,000	5,00,000	3,00,000	150
(ii) Trade Payables		...	...	(...)	...
Total		26,20,000	27,05,500	...	...
II. ASSETS					
1. **Non-current Assets**					
Property, Plant and Equipment and Intangible Assets		18,00,000	18,00,000	...	...
2. **Current Assets**					
(i) Inventory		4,20,000	...	...	14.28
(ii) Trade Receivables		...	3,90,000	20,000	...
(iii) Cash and Cash Equivalents		...	...	...	...
Total		26,20,000	27,05,500	85,500	3.26

Additional Information

(i) Trade receivables as at 31st March, 2022 were ₹ 1,80,000.

(ii) Revenue from operations (net) for the year 31st March, 2023 is ₹ 60,00,000 and for the year 31st March, 2024 is ₹ 80,00,000. Net credit revenue from operations being 40% of revenue from operations in both the years.

You are required to

(a) Fill the missing figures in comparative balance sheet.

(b) Calculate trade receivable turnover ratio for both years.

Theoretical Questions

Short Answer Type Questions

1. **The quick ratio of a company is 1.5 : 1. State with reason which of the following transactions would**

(a) increase (b) decrease or

(c) not change the ratio. Competency Based Que

(i) Paid rent ₹ 3,000 in advance.

(ii) Trade receivable included a debtor Shri Ashok who paid his entire amount due ₹ 9,700.

Ans. (i) Decrease the ratio.

Reason Payment of advance rent of ₹ 3,000, will reduce the value of quick assets. Hence, the quick ratio is decreased.

(ii) Not change the ratio.

Reason As there is a simultaneous increase and decrease in quick asset, i.e. cash and debtor, therefore, it will not affect the value of current asset.

2. **X Ltd. has a current ratio at 3 : 1. Its management is interested in maintaining this ratio at 4 : 1. What are the choices to do so?**

Ans. Choices to do so are

(i) To pay a current liability.

(ii) To sell stock-in-trade at profit.

(iii) To issue equity/debt for cash.

(iv) To sell fixed assets.

3. The liquidity of a business firm is measured by its ability to satisfy its long-term obligations as they become due. Comment. NCERT; Competency Based Que

Ans. Yes, it is true that the liquidity of a business firm is measured by its ability to pay its long-term obligations as they become due.

Here, the long-term obligation means payment of principal amount on the due date and payment of interest on the regular basis.

For measuring the long-term solvency of any business, we calculate the following ratios

(i) Debt equity ratio (ii) Proprietary ratio

4. "It is a technique which involves regrouping of data by application of arithmetical relationships." Identify the technique and state its two advantages. CBSE 2023; Competency Based Que

Ans. The technique of regrouping of data by application of arithmetical relationship is ratio analysis.

Its two advantages are

(i) Ratio analysis is an useful device for analysing financial statements.

(ii) With the help of ratio analysis, comparison of profitability and financial soundness can be made between one firm and another firm in same industry.

5. The average age of inventory is viewed as the average length of time inventory is held by the firm or as the average number of day's sales in inventory. Explain. NCERT; Competency Based Que

Ans. Inventory turnover ratio is a relationship between the cost of goods sold during a particular period of time and the cost of average inventory during a particular period. It is expressed in number of times.

Inventory turnover ratio indicates the number of times, the stock has been turned over during the period and evaluates the efficiency with which a firm is able to manage its inventory.

6. X Ltd. has a inventory turnover ratio at 3 times. Its management is interested in maintaining this ratio at 4 times. What are the two choices to do so? Competency Based Que

Ans. Choices to do so are (any two)

(i) To increase revenue from operations quantity.

(ii) To reduce closing inventory.

(iii) To increase revenue from operations quantity and to reduce closing inventory.

7. X Ltd. has a creditors turnover ratio at 3 times. Its management is interested in maintaining this ratio at 4 times. What are the two choices to do so? Competency Based Que

Ans. Choices to do so are (any two)

(i) To increase credit purchases.

(ii) To reduce closing trade payables.

(iii) To increase credit purchases and to reduce closing trade payables.

8. X Ltd. has a gross profit ratio at 25%. Its management is interested in maintaining this ratio at 30%. What are the two choices to do so? Competency Based Que

Ans. Choice to do so are (any two)

(i) To increase selling prices of stock-in-trade.

(ii) To reduce cost of revenue from operations.

(iii) To increase selling prices of stock-in-trade and to reduce cost of revenue from operations.

9. The operating ratio of a company is 80%. State, giving reasons, which of the following transactions will (a) increase (b) decrease or (c) not alter the operating ratio. Competency Based Que

(i) Credit purchases of goods ₹ 5,000.

(ii) Sales return ₹ 200.

(iii) Payment to creditors ₹ 1,000.

(iv) Selling expenses ₹ 800.

(v) Cash sales ₹ 10,000 (vi) Purchase return ₹ 100.

Ans. (i) Credit purchases of goods will increase operating ratio because purchase of goods increases the operating cost without any increase in net sales.

(ii) Sales return will increase operating ratio because it reduces net sales.

(iii) Payment to creditors will not change operating ratio because it does not affect either net sales or operating cost.

(iv) Selling expenses will increase operating ratio because payment of selling expenses increases the operating expenses.

(v) Cash sales will decrease operating ratio because cash sales increases the net sales.

(vi) Purchase return will decrease operating ratio because purchases return decreases the operating cost without any increase in net sales.

10. X Ltd. has a operating profit ratio at 15%. Its management is interested in maintaining this ratio at 20%. What are the two choices to do so? Competency Based Que

Ans. Choices to do so are (any two)

(i) To increase selling prices of stock-in-trade.

(ii) To reduce cost of revenue from operations.

(iii) To reduce operating expenses.

11. The current ratio of a company is 2 : 1. State giving reasons, which of the following transactions would improve, reduce or not change the ratio. CBSE 2023; Competency Based Que

(i) Purchased goods on credit ₹ 40,000.
(ii) Sale of furniture of ₹ 8,000 at a loss of ₹ 2,000.
(iii) Cash received from trade receivables ₹ 15,000.
(iv) Issued equity shares ₹ 6,00,000.

Ans. (i) **Reduce** Both the current asset and current liabilities are increased by the same amount.
(ii) **Improve** Current assets are increased but current liabilities remain unchange.
(iii) **Not Change** Neither the current assets nor the current liabilities are affected, since there is a conversion of one current asset into another current asset.
(iv) **Improve** Current liabilities remain unchanged but current assets are increased by the amount of cash received on issue of shares.

12. **X Ltd. has a net profit ratio at 15%. Its management is interested in maintaining this ratio at 20%. What are the two choices to do so if gross profit ratio cannot be changed?**

Ans. Choices to do so are (any two)
(i) To reduce operating expenses.
(ii) To reduce non-operating expenses.
(iii) To increase non-operating incomes.
(iv) To reduce operating expenses and non-operating expenses and to increase non-operating incomes.

13. **Quick ratio of a company is 1 : 1. State, with reason, whether the following transactions will increase, decrease or not change the ratio**
(i) Paid insurance premium in advance ₹ 10,000.
(ii) Purchased goods on credit ₹ 8,000.
(iii) Issued fully paid equity shares of ₹ 1,00,000.
(iv) Issued 9% debentures of ₹ 5,00,000 to the vendor for machinery purchased.

CBSE 2019; Competency Based Que

Ans. (i) **Decrease** As payment of insurance premium will decrease the quick assets.
(ii) **Decrease** As purchase of goods on credit will increase the current liabilities.
(iii) **Increase** As issue of equity shares will increase quick assets.
(iv) **No Change** As issue of debentures to vendor of machinery would have no impact on quick assets and current liabilities.

14. **The operating ratio of a company is 80%. State whether the following transactions will increase, decrease or not change the ratio**
(i) Purchased goods on credit ₹ 20,000.
(ii) Paid wages ₹ 5,000.
(iii) Redeemed ₹ 8,000, 9% debentures.
(iv) Sold goods ₹ 50,000 for cash.

CBSE 2019; Competency Based Que

Ans. (i) **No Change** As both purchase and closing stock will increase, so there will be no effect on cost of goods sold.
(ii) **Increase** As wages paid will increase the operating cost.
(iii) **No Change** As redemption of debentures is a non-operating activity.
(iv) **Decrease** As goods sold will increase the net sales.

Objective Questions

Multiple Choice Questions (MCQs)

1. **Ratios that are calculated for measuring the efficiency of operations of business based on effective utilisation of resources are known as** **CBSE 2024 C**
(a) liquidity ratios (b) turnover ratios
(c) solvency ratios (d) profitability ratios

2. **If quick assets are ₹ 80,000 and inventories are ₹ 10,000 the current assets will be ....**
(a) ₹ 80,000 (b) ₹ 90,000
(c) ₹ 70,000 (d) None of these

3. **The quick ratio of a company is 1 : 1. Which of the following transactions will result in increase of this ratio?** **CBSE 2024 C**
(a) Purchase of inventory ₹ 1,50,000 through cheque
(b) Sold inventory on credit ₹ 50,000
(c) Outstanding expenses of ₹ 40,000 paid
(d) Machinery purchased for cash ₹ 50,000

4. **......... will result in increase in liquid ratio without affecting the current ratio.** **CBSE SQP 2025**
(a) Sale of stock at cost price (b) Sale of stock at loss
(c) Sale of stock at profit (d) Sale of investments at cost

5. **The quick ratio of a company is 1 : 1. Which of the following transactions will result in increase in quick ratio?** **CBSE 2025**
(a) Cash received from debtors (b) Sold goods on credit
(c) Purchased goods on credit (d) Purchased goods on cash

6. **Current assets ₹ 80,000, current liabilities ₹ 50,000, inventory ₹ 5,000 and advance tax is ₹ 5,000. Liquid ratio will be** **Competency Based Que**
(a) 1.6 : 1 (b) 1.4 : 1 (c) 1.8 : 1 (d) None of these

7. **Suriya Ltd. has current assets of ₹ 90,000 and current liabilities of ₹ 45,000. The company paid ₹ 15,000 to its creditors. The current ratio after payment will be**

(a) 2 : 1 (b) 2.5 : 1
(c) 3 : 1 (d) None of these

8. **"8% debentures of ₹ 50,000 were redeemed." What will be the affect of this transaction on current ratio?**

(a) Improved (b) Reduced
(c) Will not be affected (d) None of these

9. **Assume liquid ratio is 1.4 : 1. Cash paid to creditors would ....** Competency Based Que

(a) improve liquid ratio
(b) reduce liquid ratio
(c) not affect liquid ratio
(d) increase inventory turnover ratio

10. **...... is also known as the acid test ratio.** CBSE 2024

(a) Current ratio (b) Quick ratio
(c) Gross profit ratio (d) Return on investment ratio

11. **Quick ratio of Megamart Ltd. is 1.5 : 1. Which of the following transactions will result in decrease in this ratio?** CBSE 2024; Competency Based Que

(a) Sale of goods costing ₹ 10,000 for ₹ 12,000
(b) Cash collected from trade receivables ₹ 41,000
(c) Purchase of goods for cash ₹ 38,000
(d) Creditors were paid ₹ 11,000

12. **Total assets ₹ 20,00,000, shareholders funds ₹ 10,00,000, current liabilities ₹ 5,00,000. Debt equity ratio will be ....**

(a) 1 : 1 (b) 2 : 1
(c) 0.5 : 1 (d) 1.5 : 1

13. **Calculate capital employed from the following. Total debt ₹ 4,00,000, 10% long-term debt ₹ 3,80,000, non-current assets ₹ 8,80,000, current assets ₹ 2,40,000, cash and cash equivalents ₹ 1,40,000.** Competency Based Que

(a) ₹ 8,00,000 (b) ₹ 9,50,000
(c) ₹ 12,80,000 (d) ₹ 11,00,000

14. **Repayment of bank loan (long-term debt) will .... debt to capital employed ratio when it is 0.5 : 1.** Competency Based Que

(a) reduce (b) improve
(c) not affect (d) None of these

15. **Interest coverage ratio is also known as**

(a) debt service ratio (b) proprietary ratio
(c) debt to equity ratio (d) None of these

16. **If net profit after tax is ₹ 3,60,000, tax rate 40% and 12% debentures of ₹ 40,00,000 is outstanding then calculate net profit before interest and tax and interest coverage ratio.** Competency Based Que

(a) ₹ 10,80,000, 2.5 times (b) ₹ 10,80,000, 2.25 times
(c) ₹ 6,00,000, 2.25 times (d) ₹ 6,00,000, 2.5 times

17. **Unless specified, trade investments are known as ....**

(a) short-term investments
(b) current investments
(c) non-current investments
(d) None of the above

18. **Shareholders funds ₹ 15,00,000, non-current liabilities ₹ 5,00,000, current liabilities ₹ 3,00,000. Calculate total assets to debt ratio.** Competency Based Que

(a) 5.6 : 1 (b) 5 : 1
(c) 4.6 : 1 (d) 3.6 : 1

19. **Proprietary ratio will be .... if preference share capital is ₹ 5,00,000, equity share capital is ₹ 8,00,000, debentures ₹ 4,00,000, statement of profit and loss balance is ₹ 50,000.** Competency Based Que

(a) 0.77 : 1 (b) 0.79 : 1
(c) 0.99 : 1 (d) 0.69 : 1

20. **Issue of equity shares for cash will .... debt equity ratio i.e. 2 : 1.**

(a) improve (b) reduce
(c) not affect (d) None of these

21. **What will be the impact of issuing ₹ 5,00,000 equity share to vendor for building purchased on the debt and equity of X Ltd.?** CBSE Term I 2021; Competency Based Que

(a) Debt will increase and equity will decrease
(b) Debt will remain same and equity will increase
(c) Debt will decrease and equity will increase
(d) Debt will remain same and equity will decrease

22. **Aggregate of shareholders' funds and total debts**

(a) total debts (b) capital employed
(c) total assets (d) non-current assets

23. **Difference between capital employed and non-current liabilities is**

(a) shareholders' funds (b) capital employed
(c) total debts (d) total assets

24. **Non-current assets of a firm are ₹ 13,00,000, current assets are ₹ 4,50,000 and shareholders' funds are ₹ 10,75,000, total debt will be** Competency Based Que

(a) ₹ 21,75,000 (b) ₹ 6,75,000
(c) ₹ 10,75,000 (d) ₹ 19,25,000

25. **From the following information, calculate interest coverage ratio.** CBSE Term I 2021; Competency Based Que

Net profit after tax	**₹ 6,00,000**
10% debentures	**₹ 50,00,000**
Tax rate	**40%**

(a) 1.2 times (b) 3 times
(c) 2 times (d) 5 times

26. Cost of revenue from operations can be obtained by following formulas.
(a) Opening Inventory + Purchase + Direct Expenses – Closing Inventory
(b) Revenue from Operations – Gross Profit
(c) Revenue from Operations + Gross Loss
(d) All of the above

27. If cost of goods sold is ₹ 3,60,000, average inventory is ₹ 40,000, opening stock is ₹ 20,000 less than closing stock. What will be the value of opening stock? **Competency Based Que**
(a) ₹ 10,000 (b) ₹ 30,000
(c) ₹ 40,000 (d) None of these

28. Revenue from operations ₹ 6,00,000, gross profit ratio 25% closing inventory is ₹ 60,000 which is ₹ 20,000 more than opening inventory. Calculate inventory turnover ratio. **Competency Based Que**
(a) 8 times (b) 9 times (c) 5 times (d) 4 times

29. Total sale is ₹ 4,00,000. Cash sale is 1/3rd of credit sale. Calculate credit sale. **Competency Based Que**
(a) ₹ 4,00,000 (b) ₹ 2,00,000
(c) ₹ 1,00,000 (d) ₹ 3,00,000

30. Total revenue from operations is ₹ 6,00,000. Cash sale is 20% of credit sale. Closing debtors and bills receivable are ₹ 1,00,000 and ₹ 60,000 respectively. Trade receivable turnover ratio will be **Competency Based Que**
(a) 3.12 times (b) 5.25 times
(c) 5.50 times (d) 6.50 times

31. If average collection period is 3 months and net credit revenue from operations is ₹ 4,00,000, then what will be value of average inventory? **Competency Based Que**
(a) ₹ 1,00,000 (b) ₹ 80,000
(c) ₹ 2,00,000 (d) ₹ 1,20,000

32. The credit sale of M/s Dinesh & Sons is ₹ 21,00,000. It's debtors and bills receivables at the end of the accounting period amounted to ₹ 2,00,000 and ₹ 1,50,000 respectively. What will be the debtor's turnover ratio? **Competency Based Que**
(a) 4 times (b) 5 times (c) 6 times (d) 7 times

33. From the following information, the 'proprietor's funds' are **CBSE 2023; Competency Based Que**

Current assets	₹ 20,00,000
Non-current assets	₹ 40,00,000
Long-term borrowings	₹ 25,00,000
Proprietary ratio	25%

(a) ₹ 10,00,000 (b) ₹ 14,00,000
(c) ₹ 24,00,000 (d) ₹ 15,00,000

34. ABC Co. extends credit terms of 45 days to its customers. Its credit collection would be considered poor if its average collection period was **NCERT; Competency Based Que**
(a) 30 days (b) 36 days (c) 47 days (d) 37 days

35. .... ratios indicate the speed at which activities of the business are being performed. **CBSE Term I 2021**
(a) Profitability (b) Turnover
(c) Solvency (d) Liquidity

36. The ...... measures the activity of a firm's inventory.
(a) net profit ratio (b) operating ratio
(c) inventory turnover ratio (d) profitability ratio

37. The ...... may indicate that the firm is experiencing stock outs and lost sales.
(a) average collection period
(b) average payment period
(c) Neither (a) nor (b)
(d) None of the above

38. If operating ratio is 30% then operating profit ratio will be ..... .
(a) 40% (b) 70%
(c) 60% (d) 80%

39. Formula for return on investment ratio is ....
(a) $\frac{\text{Net Profit after Interest}}{\text{Capital Employed}} \times 100$
(b) $\frac{\text{Net Profit before Interest and Tax}}{\text{Capital Employed}} \times 100$
(c) $\frac{\text{Net Profit before, Interest, Tax and Preference Dividend}}{\text{Capital Employed}} \times 100$
(d) None of the above

40. Calculate operating ratio, if cost of revenue from operations ₹ 50,000, revenue from operations ₹ 1,50,000 and operating expenses ₹ 20,000. **Competency Based Que**
(a) 45% (b) 46.7% (c) 48.1% (d) 42.2%

41. Calculate operating profit ratio of revenue from operations is ₹ 2,50,000, operating profit ₹ 37,500. **Competency Based Que**
(a) 25% (b) 12% (c) 13.33% (d) 15%

42. As on 31st March, 2024 the following information of Bartan Manfacturing Ltd. is available
Net profit ratio = 40%
Operating profit ratio = 50%
On 1st April, 2024 it was came to notice that the accountant had omitted recording the interest received on investment of ₹ 2,00,000 for the financial year 2023-24. The required rectification was done.

What will be the effect of the same on net profit and operating profit ratio?

CBSE SQP 2025 (M); Competency Based Que

(a) Net profit ratio will increase and operating profit ratio will decrease
(b) Both net profit ratio and operating profit ratio will increase
(c) Net profit ratio will increase and operating profit ratio will have no change
(d) Net profit ratio will remain same and operating profit ratio will increase

43. If opening inventory is ₹ 60,000. Cost of revenue from operations is ₹ 5,00,000 and inventory turnover ratio is 5 times then closing inventory will be

Competency Based Que

(a) ₹ 1,60,000 (b) ₹ 1,40,000
(c) ₹ 80,000 (d) ₹ 2,00,000

44. If operating ratio is 65%, operating profit ratio will be ....

CBSE Term I 2021

(a) 20% (b) 25%
(c) 35% (d) 30%

45. From the following information, calculate inventory turnover ratio.

Revenue from operations ₹ 2,00,000, average inventory ₹ 20,000, gross profit ratio 10%.

CBSE Term I 2021; Competency Based Que

(a) 9 times (b) 10 times
(c) 12 times (d) 20 times

46. Which of the following equation is correct? CBSE 2023

(a) Cost of Revenue from Operations = Revenue from Operations + Gross Profit
(b) Cost of Revenue from Operations = Opening Inventory – Net Purchases + Direct Expenses – Closing Inventory
(c) Cost of Revenue from Operations = Opening Inventory + Closing Inventory
(d) Cost of Revenue from Operations = Revenue from Operations – Gross Profit

Assertion-Reason

Direction (Q.No. 47 to 54) *Read the following Assertion (A) and Reason (R) and choose the correct alternative from the following*

Alternatives

(a) Both Assertion (A) and Reason (R) are true and Reason (R) is the correct explanation of Assertion (A)
(b) Both Assertion (A) and Reason (R) are true, but Reason (R) is not the correct explanation of Assertion (A)
(c) Assertion (A) is true, but Reason (R) is false
(d) Assertion (A) is false, but Reason (R) is true

47. **Assertion** (A) Liquid assets do not include inventory and prepaid expenses.

Reason (R) Inventory and prepaid expenses are not include in current assets because these takes time for converting into cash.

48. **Assertion** (A) If current ratio is 2 : 1, goods purchased on credit will improve the ratio.

Reason (R) If both current assets and current liabilities increases with same amount then ratio is reduced.

49. **Assertion** (A) A higher debt equity ratio from its ideal ratio is considered risky.

Reason (R) If ratio is higher than its ideal ratio i.e. 2 : 1, it means long-term borrowings are more than twice to equity funds.

50. **Assertion** (A) Inventories and prepaid expenses are not considered as quick assets.

Reason (R) Inventories take some time before it is converted into cash while prepaid expenses can be converted into cash.

51. **Assertion** (A) The debt to equity ratio will increase at the time of issue of equity shares for cash.

Reason (R) Issue of equity shares will increase the shareholders' funds but the long-term debts will remain the same.

52. **Assertion** (A) A high debt equity ratio is risky.

Reason (R) It may put the firm into difficulty to pay long-term debts. CBSE Term I 2021

53. **Assertion** (A) Current ratio establishes relationship between current assets and current liabilities.

Reason (R) The objective of this ratio is to measure the ability of the firm to meet its short-term obligations as and when due without relying upon the realisation of inventories. CBSE Term I 2021

54. **Assertion** (A) Return on investment explains the overall utilisation funds by a business enterprise.

Reason (R) It measures return (net profit before interest and tax) on total funds (capital employed).

CBSE Term I 2021

Two Statements Based MCQs

Direction (Q.No. 55 to 60) *Read the following statements carefully and choose the correct alternative*

Alternatives

(a) Statement I is correct and Statement II is incorrect
(b) Statement II is correct and Statement I is incorrect
(c) Both the statements are correct
(d) Both the statements are incorrect

55. **Statement I** Liquidity ratio measures long-term solvency of the company.

Statement II Gross profit helps in fixing selling prices and assessing efficiency of trading activities.

56. **Statement I** Declaration of final dividend will increase debt equity ratio.

Statement II Loose tools and spare parts will not be included in inventory while calculating total assets for the purpose of total asset to debt ratio.

57. **Statement I** Capital Employed = Non-current Assets + Working Capital.

Statement II Capital Employed = Debt + Equity.

58. **Statement I** Operating profit is arrived at by deducting all operating expenses from gross profit.

Statement II Non-operating expenses are added to net profit for arriving at net profit.

59. **Statement I** Mortgage loan and bank loan will be taken as long-term borrowings.

Statement II Provision for employee benefits and provision for gratuity are long-term provision.

60. **Statement I** Payment of dividend payable will improve current ratio.

Statement II Sale of goods for cash ₹ 20,000 (Cost ₹ 25,000) will improve current ratio.

Matching

61. Match the following

Column I	Column II
A. Current ratio	(i) Solvency ratio
B. Debt equity ratio	(ii) Liquidity ratio
C. Trade receivable turnover ratio	(iii) Profitability ratio
D. Gross profit ratio	(iv) Activity ratio

Codes

	A	B	C	D		A	B	C	D
(a)	(ii)	(i)	(iv)	(iii)	(b)	(ii)	(i)	(iii)	(iv)
(c)	(i)	(ii)	(iv)	(iii)	(d)	(i)	(ii)	(iii)	(iv)

62. Match the following

Column I	Column II
A. Debt + Equity	(i) Cost of revenue from operations
B. Net Purchases + Wages	(ii) Capital employed
C. Total Sale – Cash Sale	(iii) Credit sale
D. Total Debt – Current Liabilities	(iv) Non-current liabilities

Codes

	A	B	C	D		A	B	C	D
(a)	(ii)	(i)	(iii)	(iv)	(b)	(i)	(ii)	(iii)	(iv)
(c)	(i)	(iv)	(iii)	(ii)	(d)	(ii)	(iii)	(i)	(iv)

63. Match the following

Column I	Column II
A. If average inventory is 80,000 and opening inventory is 1/4th of closing inventory, then opening inventory will be	(i) ₹ 40,000
B. If average inventory is ₹ 80,000 and opening inventory is ₹ 20,000 less than closing inventory, then closing inventory will be	(ii) ₹ 32,000
C. If average inventory is ₹ 90,000 and closing inventory is 2 times the opening inventory, then opening inventory will be	(iii) ₹ 90,000
D. If average inventory is ₹ 60,000 and opening inventory is half of closing inventory, then opening inventory will be	(iv) ₹ 60,000

Codes

	A	B	C	D
(a)	(ii)	(iii)	(iv)	(i)
(b)	(ii)	(iii)	(i)	(iv)
(c)	(iii)	(ii)	(i)	(iv)
(d)	(iv)	(i)	(ii)	(iii)

64. Match the following

Column I	Column II
A. Total assets to debt ratio	(i) Profitability ratio
B. Inventory turnover ratio	(ii) Solvency ratio
C. Liquid ratio	(iii) Activity ratio
D. Return on investment	(iv) Liquidity ratio

Codes

	A	B	C	D		A	B	C	D
(a)	(iii)	(iv)	(i)	(ii)	(b)	(i)	(iii)	(ii)	(iv)
(c)	(iv)	(ii)	(i)	(iii)	(d)	(ii)	(iii)	(iv)	(i)

65. Match the following

Column I	Column II
A. Return on capital employed	(i) Pure ratio
B. Receivables turnover ratio	(ii) %
C. Proprietary ratio	(iii) Times
D. Quick ratio	(iv) Pure ratio or %

Codes

	A	B	C	D		A	B	C	D
(a)	(iv)	(iii)	(i)	(ii)	(b)	(iii)	(ii)	(iv)	(i)
(c)	(ii)	(iii)	(iv)	(i)	(d)	(i)	(iii)	(iv)	(ii)

Case Based MCQs

Direction *Read the following hypothetical extract of Amol Ltd. and answer the questions 66 and 67 on the basis of the same*

Year Amount	2024 (in ₹)	2023 (in ₹)	2022 (in ₹)
Outstanding Expenses	1,00,000	80,000	50,000
Prepaid Expenses	6,00,000	5,00,000	7,00,000
Trade Payables	36,00,000	32,00,000	28,00,000
Inventory	24,00,000	20,00,000	22,00,000
Trade Receivables	22,00,000	16,00,000	20,00,000
Cash in Hand	34,00,000	24,00,000	30,00,000
Revenue from Operations	48,00,000	36,00,000	40,00,000
Gross Profit Ratio	12%	15%	18%

66. Current ratio for the year 2024 will be ……… .
(a) 2 : 1 (b) 1.6 : 1 (c) 2.32 : 1 (d) 2.4 : 1

67. Quick ratio for the year 2023 will be ……… .
(a) 1.22 : 1 (b) 1.8 : 1 (c) 0.94 : 1 (d) 1.25 : 1

Direction *Read the following case study and answer the questions 68 and 69 on the basis of the same*
The external examiner appointed by CBSE presented following information before the students

Particulars	Amt (₹)
Equity Share Capital	20,00,000
Reserve and Surplus	6,00,000
General Reserve	2,00,000
Profit and Loss Balance	(1,00,000)
Total Assets	90,00,000
Current Liabilities	1,20,000
Working Capital	4,80,000

68. What will be the debt to equity ratio?
(a) 2.25 : 1 (b) 2.29 : 1
(c) 3 : 1 (d) 2.5 : 1

69. What will be the current ratio?
(a) 4 : 1 (b) 5 : 1
(c) 3 : 1 (d) 6 : 1

Answers

1. (b) Turnover ratios

2. (b) Quick Assets = Current Assets − Inventory
80,000 = Current Assets − 10,000
Current Assets = 80,000 + 10,000 = ₹ 90,000

3. (b) Sold inventory on credit ₹ 50,000

4. (a) Sale of stock at cost price

5. (b) Sold goods on credit

6. (b) Liquid Ratio = Liquid Assets/Current Liabilities
$$= \frac{80,000 - 5,000 - 5,000}{50,000} = \frac{70,000}{50,000} = 1.4 : 1$$

7. (b) Current Ratio after Payment $= \frac{90,000 - 15,000}{45,000 - 15,000}$
$$= \frac{75,000}{30,000} = 2.5 : 1$$

8. (a) After payment of debentures, both current assets and current liabilities will be reduced by same amount.

9. (a) improve liquid ratio

10. (b) Quick ratio

11. (c) Current liabilities will remain unchanged but liquid assets are decreased by outflow of cash.

12. (c) Debt Equity Ratio $= \frac{\text{Debt}}{\text{Equity}} = \frac{5,00,000}{10,00,000} = 0.5 : 1$

Debts = Total Assets − Shareholders' Funds − Current Liabilities
= 20,00,000 − 10,00,000 − 5,00,000 = ₹ 5,00,000

13. (d) Capital Employed = Non-current Assets + Current Assets − Current Liabilities
= 8,80,000 + 2,40,000 − 20,000 = ₹ 11,00,000
Current Liabilities = Total Debt − Long-term Debt
= 4,00,000 − 3,80,000 = ₹ 20,000

14. (a) Assume bank loan is ₹ 1,00,000 which is paid and debt to capital employed ratio is $\frac{5,00,000}{10,00,000} = 0.5 : 1$

After payment $= \frac{5,00,000 - 1,00,000}{10,00,000 - 1,00,000} = \frac{4,00,000}{9,00,000} = 0.44 : 1$

15. (a) debt service ratio

16. (b) Net Profit before Tax but after Interest
$$= 3,60,000 \times \frac{100}{60} = ₹\ 6,00,000$$
Net Profit before Interest and Tax = 6,00,000 + 4,80,000
= ₹ 10,80,000

Interest Coverage Ratio $= \frac{10,80,000}{4,80,000} = 2.25$ times

17. (c) non-current investments

18. (c) Total Assets to Debt Ratio $= \frac{23,00,000}{5,00,000} = 4.6 : 1$

Total Assets = Shareholders' Funds + Non-current Liabilities + Current Liabilities
= 15,00,000 + 5,00,000 + 3,00,000 = ₹ 23,00,000
Debt = ₹ 5,00,000

19. (a) Proprietary Ratio $= \frac{13,50,000}{17,50,000} = 0.77 : 1$

Shareholders' Funds $= 5,00,000 + 8,00,000 + 50,000$
$= ₹\ 13,50,000$

Total Assets = Shareholders' Funds + Debentures
$= 13,50,000 + 4,00,000 = ₹\ 17,50,000$

20. (b) Issue of equity shares for cash will increase equity and decrease cash and cash equivalent. There will be no effect on debt.

21. (b) Debt will remain same and equity will increase

22. (c) total assets **23.** (a) shareholders' funds

24. (b) Total Debt = Non-current Assets + Current Assets – Shareholders' Funds
$= 13,00,000 + 4,50,000 - 10,75,000 = ₹\ 6,75,000$

25. (b) Interest Coverage Ratio

$$= \frac{\text{Net Profit before Interest and Tax}}{\text{Interest on Long-term Debt}} = \frac{15,00,000}{5,00,000} = 3 \text{ times}$$

Net Profit before Interest and Tax

$$= 6,00,000 \times \frac{100}{60} + 5,00,000 = ₹\ 15,00,000$$

26. (d) All of the above

27. (b) Let closing inventory $= x$

Then, opening inventory $= x - 20,000$

Average Inventory

$$= \frac{\text{Opening Inventory} + \text{Closing Inventory}}{2}$$

$$= \frac{x - 20,000 + x}{2} = 40,000$$

$$2x = 80,000 + 20,000$$

$$x = \frac{1,00,000}{2} = ₹\ 50,000$$

Opening $= 50,000 - 20,000 = ₹\ 30,000$

28. (b) Average Inventory

$$= \frac{\text{Opening Inventory} + \text{Closing Inventory}}{2}$$

$$= \frac{(60,000 - 20,000) + 60,000}{2} = ₹\ 50,000$$

Gross Profit $= 6,00,000 \times 25\% = ₹\ 1,50,000$

Cost of Revenue from Operations = Sale – Gross Profit
$= 6,00,000 - 1,50,000 = ₹\ 4,50,000$

Inventory Turnover Ratio

$$= \frac{\text{Cost of Revenue from Operations}}{\text{Average Inventory}} = \frac{4,50,000}{50,000} = 9 \text{ times}$$

29. (d) Let credit sale $= x$, then cash sale $= \frac{x}{3}$

Hence, $x + \frac{x}{3} = 4,00,000$

$$\frac{4x}{3} = 4,00,000 \Rightarrow x = \frac{12,00,000}{4} = ₹\ 3,00,000$$

30. (a) Let the credit sale $= x$, then cash sale $= \frac{x}{5}$

Now, $x + \frac{x}{5} = 6,00,000$

$$x = \frac{6,00,000 \times 5}{6} = ₹\ 5,00,000$$

Average Trade Receivables $= 1,00,000 + 60,000$
$= ₹\ 1,60,000$

Trade Receivable Turnover Ratio

$$= \frac{\text{Net Credit Sales}}{\text{Average Trade Receivables}} = \frac{5,00,000}{1,60,000} = 3.12 \text{ times}$$

31. (a) Average Collection Period

$$(3) = \frac{12}{\text{Trade Receivable Turnover Ratio}}$$

∴ Trade Receivable Turnover Ratio = 4 times

Also, Trade Receivable Turnover Ratio

$$= \frac{\text{Credit Revenue from Operations}}{\text{Average Inventory}}$$

32. (c) Debtors Turnover Ratio $= \frac{\text{Net Credit Sales}}{\text{Average Inventory}}$

$$= \frac{21,00,000}{3,50,000} = 6 \text{ times}$$

33. (d) Proprietary Ratio = Proprietors Funds/Total Assets

$$\frac{1}{4} = \frac{\text{Proprietors Funds}}{20,00,000 + 40,00,000}$$

Proprietors Funds $= \frac{60,00,000}{4} = ₹\ 15,00,000$

34. (c) 47 days **35.** (b) Turnover

36. (c) inventory turnover ratio

37. (b) average payment period

38. (b) Operating Ratio + Operating Profit Ratio = 100%
30 + Operating Profit Ratio = 100%
Operating Profit Ratio = 70%

39. (c) $\frac{\text{Net Profit before, Interest, Tax and Preference Dividend}}{\text{Capital Employed}} \times 100$

40. (b) Operating Ratio

$$= \frac{\text{Cost of Revenue from Operations} + \text{Operating Expenses}}{\text{Revenue from Operations}} \times 100$$

$$= \frac{50,000 + 20,000}{1,50,000} \times 100 = \frac{70,000}{1,50,000} \times 100 = 46.7\%$$

41. (d) Operating Profit Ratio

$$= \frac{\text{Operating Profit}}{\text{Revenue from Operations}} \times 100 = \frac{37,500}{2,50,000} \times 100 = 15\%$$

42. (c) Net profit ratio will increase and operating profit ratio will have no change

43. (b) Inventory Turnover Ratio $= \frac{\text{Cost of Goods Sold}}{\text{Average Inventory}}$

$$5 = \frac{5,00,000}{\text{Average Inventory}}$$

$\Rightarrow$ Average Inventory = ₹ 1,00,000

Average Inventory

$$= \frac{\text{Opening Inventory} + \text{Closing Inventory}}{2}$$

$$1,00,000 = \frac{60,000 + \text{Closing Stock}}{2}$$

Closing Inventory = 2,00,000 − 60,000 = ₹ 1,40,000

44. (c) Operating Profit Ratio = 100% − 65% = 35%

45. (a) Cost of Revenue from Operations

= Revenue from Operations − Gross Profit

= 2,00,000 − (2,00,000 × 10%)

= ₹ 1,80,000

Inventory Turnover Ratio

$$= \frac{\text{Cost of Revenue from Operations}}{\text{Average Inventory}}$$

$$= \frac{1,80,000}{20,000} = 9 \text{ times}$$

46. (d) Cost of Revenue from Operations = Revenue from Operations – Gross Profit

47. (a) Both Assertion (A) and Reason (R) are true and Reason (R) is the correct explanation of Assertion (A)

48. (d) Goods purchased on credit will increase the current assets and current liabilities by same amount hence ratio will be reduced.

49. (a) Both Assertion (A) and Reason (R) are true and Reason (R) is the correct explanation of Assertion (A)

50. (d) Inventories take some time before it is converted into cash and prepaid expenses are the expenses paid in advance and cannot be converted into cash.

51. (d) The debt to equity ratio will decrease at the time of issue of equity shares for cash.

52. (a) Both Assertion (A) and Reason (R) are true and Reason (R) is the correct explanation of Assertion (A)

53. (c) Assertion (A) is true, but Reason (R) is false

54. (a) Both Assertion (A) and Reason (R) are true and Reason (R) is the correct explanation of Assertion (A)

55. (b) Liquidity ratios measures short-term solvency not the long-term solvency of a company.

56. (a) For calculating total asset to debt ratio, loose tools and spares is included in inventory.

57. (c) Both the statements are correct

58. (c) Both the statements are correct

59. (c) Both the statements are correct

60. (a) Sale of goods for cash ₹ 20,000, (cost ₹ 25,000) will reduce current assets by ₹ 5,000 hence ratio will be reduced.

61. (a) (ii) (i) (iv) (iii)

62. (a) (ii) (i) (iii) (iv)

63. (a) (A) $80,000 = \frac{\frac{x}{4} + x}{2} \Rightarrow x = ₹\ 1,28,000$

So, Opening Inventory $= \frac{1,28,000}{4} = 32,000$ (ii)

(B) $80,000 = \frac{x - 20,000 + x}{2}$

$2x = 1,60,000 + 20,000$

(Closing) $x = \frac{1,80,000}{2} = ₹\ 90,000$ (iii)

(C) $90,000 = \frac{x + 2x}{2}$

$3x = 1,80,000 \Rightarrow x = ₹\ 60,000$ (iv)

(D) $60,000 = \frac{\frac{x}{2} + x}{2} \Rightarrow \frac{3x}{2} = 1,20,000$

$x = 80,000$ (Closing)

$\therefore$ Opening Inventory $= \frac{80,000}{2} = ₹\ 40,000$ (i)

64. (d) (ii) (iii) (iv) (i)

65. (c) (ii) (iii) (iv) (i)

66. (c) Current Ratio for 2024

$$= \frac{\text{Current Assets}}{\text{Current Liabilities}} = \frac{86,00,000}{37,00,000} = 2.32 : 1$$

Current Assets = Inventory + Trade Receivables + Cash in Hand + Prepaid Expenses

= 24,00,000 + 22,00,000 + 34,00,000 + 6,00,000

= ₹ 86,00,000

Current Liabilities = Outstanding Expenses + Trade Payables

= 1,00,000 + 36,00,000 = ₹ 37,00,000

67. (a) Quick Ratio $= \frac{\text{Quick Assets}}{\text{Current Liabilities}} = \frac{40,00,000}{32,80,000} = 1.22$

Quick Assets = Trade Receivables + Cash in Hand

= 16,00,000 + 24,00,000 = ₹ 40,00,000

Current Liabilities = Outstanding Expenses + Trade Payables

= 80,000 + 32,00,000 = ₹ 32,80,000

68. (b) Debt to Equity Ratio $= \frac{\text{Debt}}{\text{Equity}} = \frac{61,80,000}{27,00,000} = 2.29 : 1$

69. (b) Current Ratio $= \frac{\text{Current Assets}}{\text{Current Liabilities}} = \frac{6,00,000}{1,20,000} = 5 : 1$

04

CHAPTER

Cash Flow Statement

Cash flow statement is a financial statement that shows the movement of cash and cash equivalents in a business from operating, investing and financing activities, during an accounting period.

YOUR STUDY GOALS

4.1 Meaning of Cash Flow Statement
4.2 Cash Flow from Operating Activities
4.3 Cash Flow from Investing Activities
4.4 Cash Flow from Financing Activities
4.5 Preparation of Cash Flow Statement

YOUR PRACTICE GOAL

- Topicwise Solved Questions (26 Solved Questions)
- Numerical Questions [32 Questions (Unsolved)]
- Theoretical Questions [4 Questions (with answers)]
- Objective Questions (65 Qs ; MCQs, A-R, Statements, Matching, Case)

4.1 Meaning of Cash Flow Statement

A cash flow statement is a statement showing inflows (receipts) and outflows (payments) of cash and cash equivalents of the business during a particular period. It is a statement showing the changes in the financial position of a business concern during different intervals of time.

Important terms related to cash flow statement

1. Cash Flows

Cash flows are inflows and outflows of cash and cash equivalents which imply movement of cash in and out from non-cash items. Receipt of cash from a non-cash item is termed as **cash inflow**, while cash payment in respect of such items is termed as **cash outflow**.

Accounting Standard-3 (Revised)

It states that cash flows exclude movement between items that constitute cash or cash equivalents because these components are part of the cash management of an enterprise rather than part of its operating, investing and financing activities.

2. Cash and Cash Equivalents

As per AS-3, cash comprises cash in hand and demand deposits with banks and cash equivalents means short-term highly liquid investments that are readily convertible into known amounts of cash and which are subject to an insignificant risk of changes in value. Cash and cash equivalent include the following

- Cash in hand
- Cash at bank
- Current investment
- Short-term investment or marketable securities
- Cheques and drafts in hand

3. Non-cash Transactions

Those transactions in which flow (inflow or outflow) of cash and cash equivalents does not take place are called non-cash transactions. Non-cash transactions are ignored while preparing cash flow statement because these do not involve cash. e.g.

- Issue of equity shares or debentures against purchase of an asset.
- Issue of equity shares on conversion of convertible debentures.
- Charging of depreciation on a fixed tangible asset.
- Amortisation of a fixed intangible asset.
- Writing-off of a old fixed tangible asset.
- Declaration of final dividend on shares.

Objectives of Cash Flow Statement

- To ascertain the sources (receipts) of cash and cash equivalents of the enterprise from its operating, investing and financing activities of the enterprise.
- To ascertain the applications (payments) of cash and cash equivalents under operating, investing and financing activities of the enterprise.
- To ascertain the net change in cash and cash equivalents i.e. the difference between sources and applications under operating, investing and financing activities of the enterprise.

Benefits/Importance of Cash Flow Statement

- It facilitates the management for implementing short-term financial plan.
- Cash flow helps in assessing the liquidity and solvency of the enterprise i.e. its ability to meet its liabilities on time.
- It highlights the factors which are responsible for lower cash balance inspite of increase in income or *vice-versa*.
- A comparison of the actual cash flows with the budgeted cash flows of the years shows the extent to which cash and cash equivalents were generated and applied.
- Cash flow statement helps the investors and other outsiders to analyse the financial position of the enterprise and they take proper decisions on the basis of such analysis.
- It helps in determining cash flow from operating, investing and financing activities separately as well as net change in cash and cash equivalents.
- To helps in determining how much dividend should be paid.

Classification of Business Activities

Accounting Standard-3 (Revised) requires that the changes resulting in inflows and outflows of cash and cash equivalents should be classified into following three activities for the purpose of preparing cash flow statement

- Cash flow from operating activities
- Cash flow from investing activities
- Cash flow from financing activities

4.2 Cash Flow from Operating Activities

Operating activities are the **principal revenue producing activities** of the enterprise and other activities that are not investing or financing activities. Cash flow from operating activities being the principal revenue producing activities of the enterprise, generally result from the transactions and other events that determine the net profit or loss.

Principal Revenue Producing Activities

It means the business activities being carried out by the enterprise from which it earns profit.

e.g.

Enterprise	Principal Revenue Producing Activity
(i) For a trading company	Purchase/Sale of goods.
(ii) For a finance company	Dealing in securities, giving/taking loans.
(iii) For an insurance company	Receipt of premiums, payment of claims, annuities.
(iv) For a computer manufacturing company	Manufacturing and selling of computers.

Smart Study Chart No. 1

Operating Activities

Cash Inflow

For a Trading Company
- Cash sales of goods
- Cash received from trade receivables (i.e. debtors and bills receivables)
- Cash receipts from commission, fees, royalty

For a Finance Company
- Cash received for interest and dividends
- Proceeds from sale of securities
- Loans and advances repaid by third parties

For an Insurance Company
- Premium and claims received

For a Real Estate (Infrastructure) **Company**
- Rent received

Cash Outflow

For a Trading Company
- Cash purchases of goods
- Payment to trade payables (i.e. creditors and bills payable)
- Operating expenses paid (e.g. Salaries and wages, administration expenses, selling expenses)
- Income tax paid (related to operating activities only)

For a Finance Company
- Cash paid for interest
- Payment for purchase of securities
- Loans and advances to third parties

For an Insurance Company
- Cash receipts of premium and claims paid

For a Real Estate (Infrastructure) **Company**
- Rent paid

Calculation of Cash Flow from Operating Activities

To calculate cash flow from operating activity, the amount of net profit (as per statement of profit and loss) is required to be adjusted for non-cash and non-operating expenses, appropriation of profit, provisions and changes in working capital, etc.

According to Revised Accounting Standard (AS-3) There are two methods for calculating cash flow from operating activities – direct method or indirect method. As per the syllabus, only indirect method has been discussed.

Indirect Method for Calculating Cash Flow from Operating Activities

Under indirect method, cash flow from operating activities is calculated from the statement of profit and loss and balance sheet.

Steps to be followed for calculation of cash flow from operating activities are

Step 1 Determine net profit before tax and extraordinary items

It is calculated as follows

Particulars		Amt (₹)
Difference between Closing Balance and Opening Balance of Surplus i.e. Balance in Statement of Profit and Loss		...
(+) Proposed Dividend of Previous Year		...
Interim Dividend paid During the Year		...
Transfer to Reserves		...
Provision for Tax (Current year)		...
*Extraordinary Items Debited to Statement of Profit and Loss		...
(–) Refund of Tax Credited to Statement of Profit and Loss	...	
Extraordinary Items Credited to Statement of Profit and Loss	...	(...)
Net Profit before Tax and Extraordinary Items		...

**Star marked items will not be evaluated.*

The treatment of above mentioned items has been discussed in the table given below

Items	Treatment
1. **Proposed Dividend** When proposed dividend for current year and previous year are given in the additional information.	**Add** the previous year proposed dividend to profit (operating activities). **Deduct** the previous year proposed dividend in financing activities.

Items	Treatment
2. **Interim Dividend** When interim dividend paid is given in adjustment.	**Add** to the current year's profit. **Deduct** in financing activity.
3. ***Deferred Tax Liabilities** (Net)	The difference between the opening balance and closing balance is **added** to the net profit.
4. **Transfer to Reserves**	Transfer out of surplus to other reserves is **added** to net profit as it is an appropriation of net profit for the year. Decrease in general reserve will be **deducted** from surplus to determine net profit before tax because it is utilisation of past reserves.
5. **Provision for Tax** (i) When only opening and closing balance of provision for tax are given in the balance sheet.	**Add** closing balance to the profit. **Deduct** opening balance at the end to assess cash flow from operating activities.
(ii) When opening and closing balance of provision for tax are given in the balance sheet and provision for tax made during the year is given in additional information.	In such a case, prepare provision for tax account **Add** provision made during the year (Given) to profit. **Deduct** tax paid at the end (Balancing figure in provision for tax account) to assess cash flow from operating activities.
(iii) When opening and closing balance of provision for tax are given in the balance sheet and tax paid during the year is given in adjustment.	In such a case, prepare provision for tax account **Add** provision made during the year (Balancing figure in provision for tax account) to profit. **Deduct** tax paid (Given) at the end to assess cash flow from operating activities.
(iv) When only tax paid during the year or provision for tax made during the year is given in the additional information.	**Add** the amount to the profit (Operating activities) as provision for tax made during the year. **Deduct** the amount at the end (Operating activities) as income tax paid during the year.

[Deduct at the end (operating activities)]

(Add in profit)

Dr **Provision for Tax Account** Cr

Particulars	Amt (₹)	Particulars	Amt (₹)
To Bank A/c (Tax paid)	...	By Balance b/d	...
To Balance c/d	...	By Statement of Profit and Loss (Provision made)	...

Items	Treatment
6. ***Extraordinary Items**	Extraordinary items shown as an expense in the statement of profit and loss are **added** to the net profit while items shown as income in the statement of profit and loss are **deducted**. Towards the end, previously added items are **deducted** while previously deducted items are **added** to compute cash flow from operating activities. Profit before tax means profit before tax and appropriation of profit say transfer to general reserve and dividend, etc. Therefore, transfer if any from profit to other reserves or dividend, etc. is **added** to net profit to arrive at net profit before tax.
7. ***Deferred Tax Assets** (Net)	The difference between the opening balance and closing balance is **deducted** from the net profit.
8. **Taxes on Income and Refund of Tax**	Generally, income tax paid (net of tax refund) is classified as an operating activity and shown separately. However, if the taxes are identified with the financing or investing activity, then cash flow on account of taxes is classified as financing or investing activity.

Step 2 Adjustments for non-cash and non-operating items

In this step, net profit before tax and extraordinary items is adjusted for non-cash and non-operating items. Non-cash and non-operating items, expenses and losses are **added** back. Non-operating incomes and gains are **deducted.**

1. **Non-cash and Non-operating Items, Expenses and Losses** (Items that are added)	
(i) **Provision for Expenses**	It is **added** to net profit. The provisions may be for doubtful debts, discount on debtors or expenses. Provision for doubtful debts and provision for discount on debtors are shown in current assets by way of deduction from trade receivables. The provision does not involve cash.

(ii) **Depreciation and Amortisation**	It is **added** to net profit before tax and extraordinary items. Fall in the value of property, plant and equipment is depreciation. Fall in value of intangible assets is shown as amortisation.
(iii) **Bad Debts**	It is **added** to net profit before tax and extraordinary items, as it is an expense, which does not result in outflow of cash.
(iv) **Loss on Sale of Property, Plant and Equipment and Investments**	It is **added** to net profit before tax and extraordinary items. The gross receipts from sale of fixed assets and investments are shown as inflow of cash under investing activity. If the amount of depreciation or profit or loss on sale of fixed assets is not given, then fixed assets account is prepared to know depreciation or profit/loss on sale of fixed assets.
(v) **Interest on Borrowings**	Interest on long-term borrowings (debentures, etc) and short-term borrowings (bank overdraft and cash credit) is **added** back to net profit before tax and extraordinary items, being an expense relating to financing activity. It is shown as an outflow of cash under financing activity.
2. **Non-operating Incomes and Gains** (Items that are deducted)	
(i) **Interest and Dividend Received**	They are **deducted** from net profit before tax and extraordinary items and are shown as inflow of cash under investing activity.
(ii) **Rent Received**	It being related to investments, is **deducted** from net profit before tax and extraordinary items, and is shown as cash inflow under investing activity.
(iii) **Gain** (Profit) **on Sale of Property, Plant and Equip- ment and Investments**	It is **deducted** from net profit before tax and extraordinary items. The gross receipts are shown as inflow of cash under investing activity.
(iv) **Re-transfer of Excess Provision**	They should be deducted from profit because they do not affect the flow of cash in the current year in any way.

The amount after the above adjustments is operating profit before working capital changes.

Important Points Related to Interest and Dividend and Rent

1. Interest and Dividend

Type of Company	Dividend Paid	Dividend Received	Interest Paid	Interest Received
Finance company	Financing activity (Outflow)	Operating activity (Inflow)	Operating activity (Outflow)	Operating activity (Inflow)
Non-finance company	Financing activity (Outflow)	Investing activity (Inflow)	Financing activity (Outflow)	Investing activity (Inflow)

2. Rent

Type of Company	Rent Paid	Rent Received
Real estate (Infrastructure company)	Operating activity (Outflow)	Operating activity (Inflow)
Non-infrastructure company	Operating activity (Outflow)	Investing activity (Inflow)

Note An investing company is a finance company.

Step 3 Adjustment in respect of changes in current assets and current liabilities

In this step, operating profit before working capital changes, is adjusted for changes in working capital (i.e. current assets and current liabilities).

The amount after above adjustment is cash generated from operations.

Note • As per CBSE syllabus, bank overdraft and cash credit are to be taken as short-term borrowings and are shown as financing activity.
• Increase or decrease of individual items of current assets and current liabilities are shown separately.

Step 4 Adjustment in respect of income tax paid

In this step, income tax paid (net of refund of income tax) is deducted from cash generated from operations. The amount after above adjustment is cash flow from operating activities before extraordinary items.

****Step 5*** Adjustment in respect of extraordinary items

Here, extraordinary items are deducted or added from cash flow from operating activities before extraordinary items. The amount after adjustment is net cash flow (inflow or outflow) from operating activities.

Format of Cash Flow from Operating Activities
(As per Accounting Standard-3 Revised)

Particulars		Amt (₹)
Cash Flow from Operating Activities		
Net Profit before Taxation and Extraordinary Items		...
Adjustments for Non-cash and Non-operating Items		
(+) Items to be Added		
Depreciation	...	
Interest on Short-term Borrowings and Long-term Borrowings	...	
Preliminary Expenses/Discount on Issue of Debentures Written-off	...	
Loss on Sale of Property, Plant and Equipment	...	
Increase in Provision for Doubtful Debts	...	
Interest Paid on Bank Overdraft/Cash Credit	...	
Goodwill, Patents and Trademarks Amortised	...	...
(–) Items to be Deducted		
Interest Income	...	
Dividend Income	...	
Rental Income	...	
Gain (Profit) on Sale of Property, Plant and Equipment	...	(...)
Operating Profit before Working Capital Changes		...
(+) Decrease in Current Assets and Increase in Current Liabilities	...	
(–) Increase in Current Assets and Decrease in Current Liabilities	(...)	
Cash Generated from Operations		...
(–) Income Tax Paid (Net of tax refund received)		(...)
Cash Flow before Extraordinary Items		...
*(+/–) Extraordinary Items		...
Net Cash from (or used in) Operating Activities		...

Note Bracket denotes minus items.

4.3 Cash Flow from Investing Activities

As per AS-3, investing activities are the activities related to acquisition and disposal of long-term assets and other investments, not included in cash equivalents. These activities include transactions involving purchase and sale of the long-term productive assets like machinery, land and building, etc, which are not held for resale.

Smart Study Chart No. 2

Investing Activities

Cash Inflow
- Proceeds from sale of property, plant and equipment
- Proceeds from sale of investments (Non-current and current, other than marketable securities)
- Interest received on debentures
- Dividend received on shares
- Rent received from property held as investment (Whether short-term or long-term)

Cash Outflow
- Purchase of property, plant and equipment
- Purchase of non-current investments
- Income tax paid (Related to investing activities only)
- Loans and advances granted (Whether short-term or long-term)
- Brokerage paid on purchase of investment

Format of Cash Flow from Investing Activities

Particulars	Amt (₹)
Cash Flow from/used in Investing Activities	
Proceeds from Sale of Investments (Other than marketable securities)	...
Sale of Property, Plant and Equipment and Intangible Assets	...
Interest Received	...
Dividend Received (For non-financial companies)	...
Rent Received	...
Purchase of Property, Plant and Equipment and Intangible Assets	(...)
Purchase of Investments (Other than marketable securities)	(...)
Net Cash from/used in Investing Activities	...

Note Bracket denotes minus items.

Preparation of Fixed Assets Account and Accumulated Depreciation Account

Sometimes, to ascertain the amount of property, plant and equipment (fixed asset) purchased or sold, profit/loss on sale of fixed asset and to ascertain the amount of depreciation charged, we may be required to prepare fixed asset account and depreciation account. These accounts can be prepared in two ways as discussed below

- Fixed asset account on written down value basis.
- Fixed asset account on original cost basis.

Ways of Preparation

Case 1 **Fixed Asset Account on Written Down Value Basis**

In this case, depreciation is charged to the asset account and the balance of the asset account shows the written down value of the asset, which is also called the book value.

Dr **Fixed Assets Account** (At written down value) Cr

Particulars	Amt (₹)	Particulars	Amt (₹)
To Balance b/d	...	By Bank A/c (Sale Proceeds)	...
To Bank A/c (Purchases)	...	By Statement of Profit and Loss (Loss on sale of fixed asset)*	...
To Statement of Profit and Loss (Gain on sale of fixed asset)*	...	By Depreciation A/c	...
		By Balance c/d	...
	...		...

Either of the two will come.

Case 2 **Fixed Asset Account on Original Cost Basis**

When property, plant and equipment is shown at original cost and accumulated depreciation account is separately maintained, in that case, depreciation is not directly charged to the asset account. The depreciation for the period is debited to the depreciation account and credited to accumulated depreciation account. In the balance sheet, asset appears at its original cost and the accumulated depreciation is shown either by deducting from fixed asset account (shown at cost) or on the liabilities side of balance sheet.

Dr **Fixed Assets Account** (At cost) Cr

Particulars	Amt (₹)	Particulars	Amt (₹)
To Balance b/d	...	By Bank A/c (Sale Proceeds)	...
To Statement of Profit and Loss (Profit on sale of fixed asset)*	...	By Accumulated Depreciation A/c (Accumulated depreciation on fixed asset sold)	...
To Bank A/c (Purchase of fixed asset)	...	By Statement of Profit and Loss (Loss on sale of fixed asset)*	...
		By Balance c/d	...
	...		...

Either of the two will appear.

Dr **Accumulated Depreciation Account** Cr

Particulars	Amt (₹)	Particulars	Amt (₹)
To Fixed Asset A/c (Accumulated depreciation on fixed asset sold)	...	By Balance b/d	...
To Balance c/d	...	By Statement of Profit and Loss (Depreciation charged for current year)	...
	...		...

4.4 Cash Flow from Financing Activities

Financing activities are the activities which result in change in the size and composition of the owner's capital (including preference share capital) and borrowings (including debentures) of the enterprise from other sources. It includes proceeds from issue of shares or other similar instruments, issue of debentures, loans, bonds, other short-term or long-term borrowings and repayment of amount borrowed.

Smart Study Chart No. 3

Financing Activities

Cash Inflow

- Proceeds from issue of shares for cash
- Proceeds from issue of debentures for cash
- Proceeds from long-term borrowings
- Securities premium reserve received
- Interest received on calls-in-arrears
- Increase in balance of bank overdraft or cash credit account

Cash Outflow

- Payment of loans (Short-term and long-term)
- Payment for redemption of preference shares, debentures for cash
- Payment for buy-back of equity shares
- Payment of dividend (Equity and preference shares)
- Payment of interest on loans and debentures (Short-term and long-term)
- Premium paid on redemption of preference shares, debenturesIncome tax paid (related to financing activities only)
- Payment of interim dividend and previous year's proposed dividend
- Brokerage and underwriting commission paid on issue of shares and debentures
- Decrease in balance of bank overdraft or cash credit account
- Payment of interest on bank overdraft/cash credit.
- Payment of preliminary expenses (including share issue expenses)

Important Points to be Remembered

- An increase in share capital due to bonus issue will not be shown in the cash flow statement, since it is the capitalisation of reserves.
- When shares or debentures are issued at a premium, the cash flow statement shows the total cash received from the issue (i.e. face value of shares + premium).
- Conversion of debentures into shares is not shown in the cash flow statement.
- Increase in underwriting commission means payment of underwriting commission in raising share capital/debentures. It is cash outflow in financing activities.
- Bank overdraft and cash credit are short-term borrowings. Thus, these two items are shown under financing activities.

Format of Cash Flow from Financing Activities

Particulars	Amt (₹)
Cash Flow from/used in Financing Activities	
Proceeds from Issue of Shares (Including premium)	...
Proceeds from Issue of Debentures (Including premium but excluding discount)	...
Loans Raised (Whether short-term or long-term)	...
Payment for Redemption of Preference Shares	(...)
Payment for Redemption of Debentures	(...)
Payment for Buy-back of Equity Shares (Including premium)	(...)
Repayment of Loans (Short-term or long-term)	(...)
Interim Dividend	(...)
Final Dividend	(...)
Interest Paid on Debentures/Loans	(...)
Net Cash Flow from/used in Financing Activities	...

Note Bracket denotes minus items.

4.5 Preparation of Cash Flow Statement

On the basis of calculation of business activities, given below are the steps to be followed for preparation of cash flow statement

***Step* 1** Compute the cash flow from operating activities.

***Step* 2** Compute the cash flow from investing activities.

***Step* 3** Compute the cash flow from financing activities.

***Step* 4** Calculate the net increase or decrease in cash and cash equivalents (i.e. *Step 4 = Step 1+ Step 2 + Step 3*).

***Step* 5** Add cash and cash equivalents balance in the beginning to the net increase or decrease in cash equivalents in order to obtain the cash and cash equivalents at the end.

Format of Cash Flow Statement

Indirect Method [As per Accounting Standard–3 (Revised)]
for the year ended...

Particulars		Amt (₹)
A. **Cash Flow from Operating Activities**		
Net Profit before Taxation and Extraordinary Items**		...
Adjustments for		
(+) **Items to be Added**		
Depreciation	...	
Goodwill, Patents and Trademarks Amortised	...	
Interest on Borrowings and Debentures	...	
Loss on Sale of Property, Plant and Equipment and Intangible Assets	...	
Increase in Provision for Doubtful Debts	...	...
(–) **Items to be Deducted**		
Interest Income	(...)	
Dividend Income	(...)	
Rental Income	(...)	
Gain (Profit) on Sale of Property, Plant and Equipment and Intangible Assets	(...)	(...)
Decrease in Provision for Doubtful Debts		
Operating Profit before Working Capital Changes		...
(+) Decrease in Current Assets and Increase in Current Liabilities		...
(–) Increase in Current Assets and Decrease in Current Liabilities		(...)
Cash Generated from Operations		...
(–) Income Tax Paid (Net of tax refund received)		(...)
Cash Flow before Extraordinary Items		...
*(+/–) Extraordinary Items		...
Net Cash from (or used in) Operating Activities		...
B. **Cash Flow from Investing Activities**		
Proceeds from Sale of Property, Plant and Equipment	...	
Proceeds from Sale of Investments (Other than marketable securities)	...	
Proceeds from Sale of Intangible Assets	...	
Interest and Dividend Received (For non-financial companies only)	...	
Rent Received	...	
Purchase of Property, Plant and Equipment	(...)	
Purchase of Investments (Other than marketable securities)	(...)	
Purchase of Intangible Assets like Goodwill	(...)	
*(+/–) Extraordinary Items	...	
Net Cash from (or used in) Investing Activities		...
C. **Cash Flow from Financing Activities**		
Proceeds from Issue of Shares and Debentures	...	
Proceeds from Other Long-term Borrowings	...	
Increase/Decrease in Bank Overdraft and Cash Credit	...	
Final Dividend Paid	(...)	
Interim Dividend Paid	(...)	

Particulars		Amt (₹)
Interest on Debentures and Loans	(...)	
Repayment of Loans	(...)	
Redemption of Debentures/Preference Shares	(...)	
*(+/−) Extraordinary Items	...	
Net Cash from (or used in) Financing Activities		...
D. **Net Increase/Decrease in Cash and Cash Equivalents** (A + B + C)		...
E. (+) **Cash and Cash Equivalents in the Beginning of the Year**		
Cash in Hand	...	
Cash at Bank	...	
Short-term Deposits	...	
Marketable Securities	...	...
F. **Cash and Cash Equivalents at the End of the Year**		
Cash in Hand	...	
Cash at Bank	...	
Short-term Deposits	...	
Marketable Securities	...	
		...

**For calculation of net profit before tax and extraordinary items refer to page 491.

Key Points

- Increase/Decrease in unpaid interest on debentures/loans affects the cash flow from financing activities and not from the operating activities.
- Increase/Decrease in unclaimed dividend affects the cash flow from financing activities and not from the operating activities.
- Increase/Decrease in accrued interest on investments affects the cash flow from investing activities and not from the operating activities.

Some Items that Need Consideration while Preparing Cash Flow Statement

Items	In case of increase ↑	In case of decrease ↓
Land	Cash used in investing activities	Cash from investing activities
Comment Since land is a non-depreciable asset, decrease in its value will always be considered as sale.		
Property, Plant and Equipment (except land) [Tangible fixed assets]	Cash used in investing activities	Decrease in value will either be depreciation or sale. If question mentions the amount of depreciation, then decrease will be taken as sales (being the missing figure). If question mentions sales, then decrease will be taken as depreciation (being the missing figure). Depreciation will be added to profits to arrive at net profit before working capital changes. Sales will be shown as cash from investing activities.
Intangible assets (copyright, trademark, patent, goodwill)	Cash used in investing activities	Treated as amortisation and added back to current year's profit to calculate cash flow from operating activities.
Long-term investments	Cash used in investing activities	Cash from investing activities
Underwriting commission	Cash used in financing activities	Decrease in underwriting commission will be added back to current year's profit to calculate cash flow from operating activities.
Short-term investments	It is a part of cash and cash equivalents.	
Discount on issue of debentures	The increase in discount should be deducted from the face value of debentures and only net proceeds shall be treated as cash flows from financing activities.	Decrease in discount on issue of debentures will be added back to current year's profit to calculate cash from operating activities.
Comment No treatment, if securities premium has been used for writing-off discount on issue of debentures.		
Equity share capital	Cash from financing activities	It means buy back of shares and treated as cash used in financing activities.
Preference share capital	Cash from financing activities	It means redemption of shares and treated as cash used in financing activities.

Items	In case of increase ↑	In case of decrease ↓
Debentures	Cash from financing activities	It means redemption of debentures and treated as cash used in financing activities.
Securities premium	The increase in securities premium will be added to the face value of debentures/shares issued and the total amount will be treated as cash flow from financing activities.	No treatment is required, it should be ensured that amount of decrease in securities premium has been utilised for the purposes for which it can be utilised by Section 52 (2) of the Companies Act, 2013 and the amount of decrease in securities premium has not been included in current year's profits.
General reserve	It will be added to current year's profit for calculating cash flow from operating activities.	It will be deducted from current year's profit for calculating cash flow from operating activities.
Provision for doubtful debts	(i) **When All Debtors are Good** (Treat as appropriation)	
	The increase in doubtful debts will be added back to current year's profit to arrive at operating profit before working capital changes.	The decrease in doubtful debts will be deducted from current year's profit to arrive at operating profit before working capital changes.
	(ii) **When Debtors are Not Good** (Treat as current liability)	
	The increase in doubtful debts will be added in operating profit before working capital changes to arrive at cash generated from operating activities.	The decrease in doubtful debts will be deducted from operating profit before working capital changes to arrive at cash generated from operating activities.
Current assets other than items of cash and cash equivalents	Increase in current assets other than cash and cash equivalents will be deducted from operating profit before working capital changes to arrive at cash generated from operations.	Decrease in current assets other than cash and cash equivalents will be added in operating profit before working capital changes to arrive at cash generated from operations.
Current liabilities other than items of cash and cash equivalents	Increase in current liabilities will be added back to operating profit before working capital changes to arrive at cash generated from operations.	Decrease in current liabilities will be deducted from operating profit before working capital changes to arrive at cash generated from operations.
Bank overdraft/Cash credit	Cash from financing activities.	Cash used in financing activities.
Cash and cash equivalents	As per Para 7 of AS-3 (Revised), cash flows exclude movement between items that constitute cash or cash equivalents because these components are part of the cash management of an enterprise rather than part of its operating, investing and financing activities.	
Proposed dividend	**Previous Year's Dividend** (i) Add back to current year's profit to arrive at net profit before tax and extraordinary items. (ii) It is cash used in financing activities.	
Provision for tax	**Previous Year's Provision** (i) Add back to current year's profit to arrive at net profit before tax and extraordinary items. (ii) It is cash used in financing activities.	

Comment If question mentions either provision made (debited to statement of profit and loss account) during the year or actual tax paid, then prepare provision for tax account and find the other. Provision made during the year will be added to current year's profit to arrive at net profit before working capital changes. Tax paid is deducted from cash from operations to arrive at net cash from operating activities.

Mind Map

Cash Flow Statement

1 Meaning of Cash Flow Statement

Cash flow statement is a statement showing inflows (receipts) and outflows (payments) of cash and cash equivalents of the business during a particular period.

2 Important Terms related to Cash Flow Statement

- **Cash Flows** They are inflows and outflows of cash and cash equivalents.
- **Cash and Cash Equivalents** As per AS-3, cash comprises cash in hand and demand deposits with banks. Cash equivalents means short-term highly liquid investments that are readily convertible into cash and which are subject to an insignificant risk of change in value.
- **Non-cash Transactions** Those transactions in which flow of cash and cash equivalents does not take place are called non-cash transactions. These transactions are ignored while preparing cash flow statement.

3 Objectives of Cash Flow Statement

- To ascertain the sources of cash and cash equivalents from its operating, investing and financing activities of enterprise.
- To ascertain the applications of cash and cash equivalents under operating, investing and financing activities.
- To ascertain the net change in cash and cash equivalents under operating, investing and financing activities.

4 Importance of Cash Flow Statement

- It helps management to prepare short-term financial plan.
- It helps in determining how much dividend should be paid.
- It helps investors and other outsiders to analyse financial position of the business.
- Cash flow helps in assessing the liquidity and solvency of the enterprise.
- It highlights the factors responsible for lower cash balance inspite of increase in income or *vice-versa*.
- It helps in determining cash flow from operating, investing and financing activites separately as well as net change in cash and cash equivalents.

5 Classification of Business Activities

Business activities, for the purpose of preparing cash flow statement, are classified into following three activities

- ***Cash Flow from Operating Activities*** These are principal revenue producing activities.
- ***Cash Flow from Investing Activities*** These are related to acquisition and disposal of long-term assets and other investments, not included in cash equivalents.
- ***Cash Flow from Financing Activities*** These are the activities which result in change in the size and composition of owner's capital and borrowings.

6 Format of Cash Flow Statement

Particulars		Amt (₹)
A. **Cash Flow from Operating Activities**		
Net Profit before Tax and Extraordinary Items		...
Adjustmens for Non-cash and Non-operating Items		
(+) Items to be Added	...	
(−) Items to be Deducted	(...)	...
Operating Profit before Working Capital Changes		...
(+) Decrease in Current Assets and Increase in Current Liabilities		...
(−) Increase in Current Assets and Decrease in Current Liabilities		(...)
Cash Generated from Operations		...
(−) Income Tax Paid (Net of Tax Refund)		(...)
Net Cash Flow from (or used in) Operating Activities		...
B. **Cash Flow from Investing Activities**		
Sales Proceeds of Property, Plant and Equipment and Intangible Assets, Investment	...	
Rent, Interest and Dividend Received	...	
Purchase of Property, Plant and Equipment and Intangible Assets, Investments	...	
Net Cash Flow from (or used in) Investing Activities		...
C. **Cash Flow from Financing Activities**		
Proceeds from Issue of Shares and Debentures, Other Long-term Borrowings	...	
Increase/Decrease in Bank Overdraft and Cash Credit	...	
Dividend, Interest Paid	(...)	
Loan Repayment, Redemption of Shares/Debentures	(...)	
Net Cash Flow from (or used in) Financing Activities		...
Net Increase/Decrease in Cash and Cash Equivalents (A + B + C)		...
(+) Cash and Cash Equivalents in the Beginning		...
Cash and Cash Equivalents at the End of the Year		...

Topicwise Solved Questions

Operating Activities

Solved Question 1 Suryansh Ltd. earned net profit after tax ₹ 22,000 for the year ended 31st March, 2024. Below is extract from balance sheet as 31st March, 2024.

Particulars	31st March, 2024 (₹)	31st March, 2023 (₹)
Inventories	6,900	7,200
Trade Receivables	8,500	5,500
Prepaid Expenses	1,800	600
Trade Payables	7,200	6,500
Provision for Tax	1,200	1,800

Depreciation charged on plant and machine ₹ 5,100, insurance claim received ₹ 2,000 and gain on sale of investments of ₹ 400 appeared in the statement of profit and loss for the year ended 31st March, 2024.

Calculate cash flow from operating activities.

Sol. **Cash Flow from Operating Activities**

Particulars		Amt (₹)
Net Profit after Tax as per Statement of Profit and Loss		22,000
(+) Provision for Tax (Current Year)		1,200
		23,200
(–) Extraordinary Item		
Insurance Claim Received		(2,000)
Net Profit before Tax and Extraordinary Items		21,200
(+/–) Non-cash and Non-operating Items		
(+) Depreciation on Plant and Machinery		5,100
		26,300
(–) Gain (Profit) on Sale of Investments		(400)
Operating Profit before Working Capital Changes		25,900
(+) Decrease in Current Assets and Increase in Current Liabilities		
Inventories	300	
Trade Payables	700	1,000
		26,900
(–) Increase in Current Assets		
Trade Receivables	3,000	
Prepaid Expenses	1,200	(4,200)
Cash Generated from Operations		22,700
(–) Income Tax Paid (Note)		(1,800)
Cash Flow from Operating Activities before Extraordinary Items		20,900
Extraordinary Items		
(+) Insurance Claim Received		2,000
Cash Flow from Operating Activities		22,900

Key Point
Previous year's provision for tax is the amount of tax paid and current year's provision for tax is treated as provision for tax made during the year.

Solved Question 2 From the following information, calculate cash flow from operating activities. **CBSE SQP 2025**

Particulars	31st March, 2024 (₹)	31 March, 2023 (₹)
Surplus i.e. Balance in Statement of Profit and Loss	5,00,000	6,00,000
Provision for Tax	1,20,000	1,00,000
Trade Receivables	2,40,000	2,00,000
Trade Payables	2,00,000	1,50,000
Goodwill	1,50,000	2,00,000

Additional Information

Proposed dividend for the year ended 31st March, 2023 and 31st March, 2024 was ₹ 1,50,000 and ₹ 1,80,000 respectively.

Sol. **Cash Flow from Operating Activities**

Particulars		Amt (₹)
Profit Earned during the Year		(1,00,000)
(+) Proposed Dividend of Previous Year	1,50,000	
Provision for Tax for Current Year	1,20,000	2,70,000
Profit before Tax and Extraordinary Items		1,70,000
Non-operating and Non-cash Items		
(+) Goodwill Amortised	50,000	50,000
Operating Profit before Tax and Change in Working Capital		2,20,000
(+) Increase in Trade Payable	50,000	
(–) Increase in Trade Receivables	(40,000)	10,000
Cash Generated from Operations		2,30,000
(–) Income Tax Paid		(1,00,000)
Cash Flow from Operating Activities		1,30,000

Solved Question 3 In 2021, two young Indian entrepreneurs, Vaishali Bhatia and Vivek Bhatia decided to start an online auto portal. At that time, there were no major players in the market and they saw an opportunity to fill the gap.

They used a user-friendly website and mobile app which made it easy for users to research and buy cars. It was converted into a company 'Car Easy Ltd.' in 2018. From the following balance sheet of the company as on 31st March, 2022. Calculate 'cash flow from operating activities'. **CBSE 2023**

Balance Sheet of 'Car Easy Ltd.'
as at 31st March, 2022

Particulars	Note No.	31st March, 2022 (₹)	31st March, 2021(₹)
I. EQUITY AND LIABILITIES			
1. Shareholders' Funds			
(i) Share Capital		9,00,000	3,00,000
(ii) Reserves and Surplus	1	75,000	3,60,000

Particulars	Note No.	31st March, 2022 (₹)	31st March, 2021(₹)
2. **Non-current Liabilities**			
Long-term Borrowings	2	2,40,000	1,80,000
3. **Current Liabilities**			
(i) Trade Payables		18,000	60,000
(ii) Short-term Provisions	3	2,04,000	2,10,000
Total		14,37,000	11,10,000
II. ASSETS			
1. **Non-current Assets**			
Property, Plant and Equipment	4	10,08,000	5,76,000
2. **Current Assets**			
(i) Inventories		3,54,000	3,87,000
(ii) Cash and Cash Equivalents		75,000	1,47,000
Total		14,37,000	11,10,000

Notes to Accounts

Particulars	31st March, 2022 (₹)	31st March, 2021 (₹)
1. **Reserve and Surplus**		
Surplus i.e. Balance in Statement of Profit and Loss	75,000	3,60,000
2. **Long-term Borrowings**		
10% Debentures	2,40,000	1,80,000
3. **Short-term Provisions**		
Provision for Tax	2,04,000	2,10,000
4. **Property, Plant and Equipment**		
Machinery	11,52,000	6,45,000
Accumulated Depreciation	(1,44,000)	(69,000)
	10,08,000	5,76,000

Additional Information

(i) 10% debentures were issued on 31st March, 2021.

(ii) Tax of ₹ 80,000 was paid during the year.

Sol. **Cash Flow from Operating Activities**
for the year ended 31st March, 2022

Particulars	Amt (₹)
Net Profit before Tax	(2,11,000)
Adjustment for Non-cash and Non-operating Items	
(+) Interest on Debentures	24,000
Depreciation	75,000
Operating Profit before Working Capital Changes	(1,12,000)
(+) Decrease in Current Assets and Increase in Current Liabilities	
Inventories	33,000
(−) Increase in Current Assets and Decrease in Current Liabilities	
Trade Payables	(42,000)
(−) Payment of Tax	(80,000)
Net Cash Flow from (used in) Operating Activities	(2,01,000)

Working Notes

1. **Calculation of Net Profit before Tax**

Particulars	Amt (₹)
Balance of Reserves and Surplus on 31st March, 2022	75,000
(−) Balance of Reserves and Surplus on 31st March, 2021	(3,60,000)
	(2,85,000)
(+) Provision for Tax	74,000
	(2,11,000)

2. Interest on debentures $= 2{,}40{,}000 \times \frac{10}{100} =$ ₹ 24,000

3.

Provision for Tax Account

Dr | | | Cr

Particulars	Amt (₹)	Particulars	Amt (₹)
To Bank A/c (Payment Made)	80,000	By Balance b/d	2,10,000
To Balance c/d	2,04,000	By Statement of Profit and Loss (Provision Made)	74,000
	2,84,000		2,84,000

Solved Question 4 Following is the balance sheet of Bharat Gas Ltd. as at 31st March, 2023

Balance Sheet of Bharat Gas Ltd.
as at 31st March, 2023

Particulars	Note No.	31st March, 2023 (₹)	31st March, 2022 (₹)
I. EQUITY AND LIABILITIES			
1. **Shareholders' Funds**			
(i) Share Capital		14,00,000	10,00,000
(ii) Reserves and Surplus	1	5,00,000	4,00,000
2. **Non-current Liabilities**			
Long-term Borrowings		5,00,000	1,40,000
3. **Current Liabilities**			
(i) Trade Payables		1,00,000	60,000
(ii) Short-term Provisions	2	80,000	60,000
Total		25,80,000	16,60,000
II. ASSETS			
1. **Non-current Assets**			
(i) Property, Plant and Equipment and Intangible Assets			
(a) Property, Plant and Equipment	3	16,00,000	9,00,000
(b) Intangible Assets	4	1,40,000	2,00,000
2. **Current Assets**			
(i) Inventories		2,50,000	2,00,000
(ii) Trade Receivables		5,00,000	3,00,000
(iii) Cash and Cash Equivalents		90,000	60,000
Totals		25,80,000	16,60,000

Notes to Accounts

Particulars	31st March, 2023 (₹)	31st March, 2022 (₹)
1. **Reserves and Surplus**		
Balance in Statement of Profit and Loss	5,00,000	4,00,000
	5,00,000	4,00,000

Particulars	31st March, 2023 (₹)	31st March, 2022 (₹)
2. **Short-term Provisions**		
Provision for Taxation	80,000	60,000
	80,000	60,000
3. **Property, Plant and Equipment**		
Machinery	18,50,000	10,00,000
(–) Accumulated Depreciation	(2,50,000)	(1,00,000)
	16,00,000	9,00,000
4. **Intangible Assets**		
Goodwill	1,40,000	2,00,000
	1,40,000	2,00,000

Additional Information

During the year a machine costing ₹ 3,00,000 on which accumulated depreciation was ₹ 45,000 was sold for ₹ 1,35,000. Calculate 'cash flow from operating activities'. **CBSE 2024**

Sol. **Cash Flow from Operating Activities**
for the year ended 31st March, 2023

Particulars		Amt (₹)
Cash Flow from Operating Activities		
Net Profit before Tax (1,00,000 + 80,000)		1,80,000
Adjustment for		
(+) Accumulated Depreciation (WN 2)	1,95,000	
Loss on Sale of Machinery (WN 1)	1,20,000	
Goodwill Written-off	60,000	3,75,000
Operating Profit before Working Capital Changes		5,55,000
(–) Increase in Current Assets and Decrease in Current Liabilities		
Inventories	(50,000)	
Trade Receivables	(2,00,000)	(2,50,000)
(+) Decrease in Current Assets and Increase in Current Liabilities		
Trade Payables	40,000	40,000
Cash Generated from Operations		3,45,000
(–) Payment of Tax		(60,000)
Net Cash Flow from Operating Activities		2,85,000

Working Notes

1. Dr **Machinery Account** Cr

Particulars	Amt (₹)	Particulars	Amt (₹)
To Balance b/d	10,00,000	By Accumulated Depreciation A/c	45,000
To Cash A/c (Purchase) (Balancing Figure)	11,50,000	By Cash A/c (Sale)	1,35,000
		By Loss on Sale	1,20,000
		By Balance c/d	18,50,000
	21,50,000		21,50,000

2. Dr **Accumulated Depreciation Account** Cr

Particulars	Amt (₹)	Particulars	Amt (₹)
To Machinery A/c	45,000	By Balance b/d	1,00,000
To Balance c/d	2,50,000	By Statement of Profit and Loss (Balancing Figure)	1,95,000
	2,95,000		2,95,000

Solved Question 5 **From the following information, calculate cash flow from operating activities**

Statement of Profit and Loss
for the year ended 31st March, 2024

Particulars	Amt (₹)
I. **Revenue from Operations** (Sales)	8,00,000
II. **Expenses**	
Purchases of Stock-in-trade	7,50,000
Changes in Inventories of Stock-in-trade (Opening Stock – Closing Stock) (50,000 – 2,50,000)	(2,00,000)
Employees Benefit Expenses	75,000
Depreciation and Amortisation	50,000
Other Expenses	20,000
	6,95,000
III. **Net Profit** (I – II)	1,05,000
IV. (–) Tax Expense (Provision for Tax)	(25,000)
V. **Profit after Tax** (III – IV)	80,000

Additional Information

Particulars	2023 (₹)	2024 (₹)
Debtors	62,500	75,000
Bills Receivable	20,000	15,000
Creditors	42,500	37,500
Inventories	55,000	67,500
Salaries Outstanding	5,000	7,500
Prepaid Insurance	12,500	13,750
Provision for Tax	7,500	5,000

Sol. **Cash Flow from Operating Activities**

Particulars		Amt (₹)
Net Profit before Tax and Extraordinary Items (WN 1)		1,05,000
Adjustments for		
(+) Depreciation and Amortisation		50,000
Operating Profit before Working Capital Changes		1,55,000
(+) Decrease in Current Assets and Increase in Current Liabilities		
Bills Receivable	5,000	
Outstanding Salaries	2,500	7,500
		1,62,500
(–) Increase in Current Assets and Decrease in Current Liabilities		
Sundry Debtors	(12,500)	
Inventories	(12,500)	
Prepaid Insurance	(1,250)	
Sundry Creditors	(5,000)	(31,250)
Cash Generated from Operations		1,31,250
(–) Income Tax Paid (WN 2)		(27,500)
Net Cash Flow from Operating Activities		1,03,750

Working Notes

1. **Calculation of Net Profit before Tax and Extraordinary Items**

Particulars	Amt (₹)
Net Profit as per Statement of Profit and Loss	80,000
(+) Provision for Tax	25,000
	1,05,000

2. Dr **Provision for Tax Account** Cr

Particulars	Amt (₹)	Particulars	Amt (₹)
To Bank A/c (Balancing Figure)	27,500	By Balance b/d	7,500
To Balance c/d	5,000	By Statement of Profit and Loss (Provision Made)	25,000
	32,500		32,500

Solved Question 6 **Calculate net cash flow from operating activities from the following balance sheet of Annie Ltd.**

Particulars	Note No.	31st March, 2024 (₹)	31st March, 2023 (₹)
I. EQUITY AND LIABILITIES			
1. **Shareholders' Funds**			
(i) Share Capital	1	4,75,000	4,75,000
(ii) Reserves and Surplus	2	1,55,000	(10,000)
2. **Non-current Liabilities** (8% Debentures)		90,000	35,000
3. **Current Liabilities**			
(i) Short-term Borrowings (8% Bank Loan)		15,000	20,000
(ii) Trade Payables		60,000	55,000
(iii) Short-term Provisions (Provision for Tax)		25,000	20,000
Total		8,20,000	5,95,000
II. ASSETS			
1. **Non-current Assets**			
(i) Property, Plant and Equipment and Intangible Assets			
(a) Property, Plant and Equipment		4,85,000	3,65,000
(b) Intangible Assets (Goodwill)		7,500	20,000
(c) Non-current Investments		62,500	40,000
2. **Current Assets**			
(i) Current Investments		2,500	7,500
(ii) Inventories		97,500	50,000
(iii) Trade Receivables		1,00,000	1,00,000
(iv) Cash and Cash Equivalents		65,000	12,500
Total		8,20,000	5,95,000

Notes to Accounts

Particulars	2024 (₹)	2023 (₹)
1. **Share Capital**		
Equity Share Capital	3,75,000	3,25,000
5% Preference Share Capital	1,00,000	1,50,000
	4,75,000	4,75,000
2. **Reserves and Surplus**		
General Reserve	75,000	60,000
Statement of Profit and Loss	75,000	(70,000)
Securities Premium	5,000	—
	1,55,000	(10,000)

Additional Information

During the year, a piece of machinery costing ₹ 25,000 on which depreciation charged was ₹ 10,000 was sold for ₹ 10,000. Depreciation provided on machinery ₹ 30,000. Dividend on equity shares @ 8% was paid on opening balance. Income tax ₹ 22,500 was provided. Additional debentures were issued at par on 1st October, 2023 and bank loan was repaid on the same date. At the end of the year, preference shares were redeemed at a premium of 5%.

Sol.

Calculation of Net Cash Flow from Operating Activities

Particulars		Amt (₹)
Cash Flow from Operating Activities		
Net Profit before Tax (WN 1)		2,16,000
Adjustments For		
(+) Depreciation on Property, Plant and Equipment	30,000	
Loss on Sale of Machinery (WN 2)	5,000	
Interest on Debentures [(35,000 × 8/100) + (55,000 × 8/100 × 6/12)]	3,020	
Interest on Bank Loan [(20,000 × 8/100 × 6/12) + (20,000 × 8/100 × 6/12)]	1,400	
Goodwill Amortised	12,500	
Premium on Redemption of Preference Shares	2,500	54,420
Operating Profit before Working Capital Changes		2,70,420
(+) Decrease in Current Assets and Increase in Current Liabilities		
Trade Payables	5,000	
(−) Increase in Current Assets and Decrease in Current Liabilities		
Inventories	(47,500)	(42,500)
Net Cash Flow from Operating Activities before Tax		2,27,920
(−) Tax Paid (WN 3)		(17,500)
Net Cash Inflow from Operating Activities after Tax		2,10,420

Working Notes

1. **Calculation of Net Profit before Tax**

Particulars	Amt (₹)
Net Profit as per Statement of Profit and Loss (75,000 + 70,000)	1,45,000
(+) Transfer to Reserve	15,000
(+) Dividend on Equity Shares	26,000
(+) Dividend on Preference Shares	7,500
(+) Provision for Tax	22,500
Net Profit before Tax	2,16,000

2. Dr **Machinery Account** Cr

Particulars	Amt (₹)	Particulars	Amt (₹)
To Balance b/d	3,65,000	By Depreciation A/c	30,000
To Bank A/c (Purchases) (Balancing Figure)	1,65,000	By Bank A/c (Sale)	10,000
		By Loss on Sale A/c (Statement of Profit and Loss)	5,000
		By Balance c/d	4,85,000
	5,30,000		5,30,000

3. Dr **Provision for Tax Account** Cr

Particulars	Amt (₹)	Particulars	Amt (₹)
To Bank A/c (Balancing Figure)	17,500	By Balance b/d	20,000
To Balance c/d	25,000	By Provision for Tax A/c (Statement of Profit and Loss)	22,500
	42,500		42,500

Solved Question 7 From the following balance sheet of Jay Ltd. as at 31st March, 2022, calculate cash flows from operating activities

CBSE Term II 2022

Balance Sheet
as at 31st March, 2022

Particulars	Note No.	31st March, 2022 (₹)	31st March, 2021 (₹)
I. **EQUITY AND LIABILITIES**			
1. **Shareholders' Funds**			
(i) Share Capital	1	50,00,000	30,00,000
(ii) Reserves and Surplus	2	10,00,000	6,00,000
2. **Non-current Liabilities**			
Long-term Borrowings	3	8,00,000	4,00,000
3. **Current Liabilities**			
(i) Trade Payables		2,00,000	3,00,000
(ii) Other Current Liabilities	4	3,00,000	1,00,000
(iii) Short-term Provisions	5	1,50,000	1,00,000
Total		74,50,000	45,00,000
II. **ASSETS**			
1. **Non-current Assets**			
(i) Property, Plant and Equipment and Intangible Assets			
(a) Property, Plant and Equipment	6	60,00,000	40,00,000
(b) Intangible Assets	7	4,00,000	4,00,000
2. **Current Assets**			
(i) Inventories		7,00,000	40,000
(ii) Cash and Cash Equivalents		3,50,000	60,000
Total		74,50,000	45,00,000

Notes to Accounts

Particulars	2022 (₹)	2021 (₹)
1. **Share Capital**		
Equity Share Capital	50,00,000	30,00,000
2. **Reserves and Surplus**		
Surplus Balance in the Statement of Profit and Loss	10,00,000	6,00,000
3. **Long-term Borrowings**		
10% Debentures	8,00,000	4,00,000
4. **Other Current Liabilities**		
Outstanding Rent	3,00,000	1,00,000
5. **Short-term Provisions**		
Provision for Tax	1,50,000	1,00,000
6. **Property, Plant and Equipment**		
Land	60,00,000	40,00,000
7. **Intangible Assets**		
Patents	4,00,000	4,00,000

Additional Information

₹ 4,00,000, 10% debentures were issued on 31st March, 2022.

Sol.

Cash Flow from Operating Activities
for the year ended 31st March, 2022

Particulars		Amt (₹)
Cash Flow from Operating Activities		
Net Profit before Tax and Extraordinary Items (WN 1)		5,50,000
Adjustments for		
(+) Interest on Debentures		40,000
Operating Profit before Working Capital Change		5,90,000
(+) Decrease in Current Assets and Increase in Current Liabilities : Outstanding Rent	2,00,000	
(−) Increase in Current Assets and Decrease in Current Liabilities : Trade Payables	(1,00,000)	
Inventories	(6,60,000)	(5,60,000)

Particulars	Amt (₹)
Cash Generated from Operations	30,000
(–) Income Tax Paid	(1,00,000)
Net Cash Used in Operating Activities	(70,000)

Working Note

1. **Net Profit before Tax and Extraordinary Items**

Net Profit for the year (10,00,000 – 6,00,000)	=	4,00,000
(+) Provision for tax	=	1,50,000
		₹ 5,50,000

Investing Activities

Solved Question 8 **Calculate cash flow from investing activities from the following information**

Particulars	31st March, 2023 (₹)	31st March 2024 (₹)
Plant and Machinery	3,00,000	3,80,000
Goodwill	60,000	90,000
15% Long-term Investments	4,50,000	2,50,0000
Investment in Shares of JMC Ltd.	10,00,000	16,00,000

Additional Information

(i) **8% dividend was received from JMC Ltd.**

(ii) **A machine costing ₹ 40,000 (depreciation provided there on ₹ 8,000) was sold for ₹ 27,000. Depreciation charged during the year was ₹ 38,000.**

Sol. **Cash Flow from Investing Activities**

Particulars	Amt (₹)
Sale of Plant and Machinery	27,000
Purchase of Plant and Machinery	(1,50,000)
Purchase of Goodwill	(30,000)
Purchase of Shares of JMC Ltd.	(6,00,000)
Sale of Long-term Investments	1,50,000
Dividend Received from JMC Ltd.	1,28,000
Interest received (4,50,000 × 15%)	67,500
Net Cash Used in Investing Activities	(4,07,500)

Working Note

Dr **Plant and Machinery Account** Cr

Particulars	Amt (₹)	Particulars	Amt (₹)
To Balance b/d	3,00,000	By Bank A/c	27,000
To Bank A/c (Balancing Figure) (Purchase)	1,50,000	By Statement of Profit and Loss	5,000
		By Depreciation A/c	38,000
		By Balance c/d	3,80,000
	4,50,000		4,50,000

Note It is assumed that long-term investment are sold and investment are made in JMC Ltd. on 31st March, 2024. It can also be assumed as on 1st April, 2023 but in this case answer will differ.

Solved Question 9 **From the following information, calculate cash flow from investing activities**

Particulars	31st March, 2024 (₹)	31st March, 2023 (₹)
Machinery (Cost)	28,00,000	20,00,000
Accumulated Depreciation	6,50,000	4,00,000

Additional Information

(i) **Machinery costing ₹ 50,000 (book value ₹ 40,000) was lost by fire and insurance claim of ₹ 32,000 was received.**

(ii) **Depreciation charged during the year was ₹ 3,50,000.**

(iii) **A part of machinery costing ₹ 2,50,000 was sold at a loss of ₹ 20,000.** **CBSE SQP 2025**

Sol. **Cash Flow from Investing Activities**

Particulars	Amt (₹)
Sale of Machinery	1,40,000
Claim Received from Insurance Company	32,000
Machinery Purchased	(11,00,000)
Cash Outflow from Investing Activities	(9,28,000)

Working Notes

1. Dr **Accumulated Depreciation Account** Cr

Particulars	Amt (₹)	Particulars	Amt (₹)
To Machinery A/c (Previous Depreciation on Machine Damaged)	10,000	By Balance b/d	4,00,000
To Machinery A/c (Previous Depreciation on Machine Sold)	90,000	By Depreciation A/c (Charged During the Year)	3,50,000
To Balance c/d	6,50,000		
	7,50,000		7,50,000

2. Dr **Machinery Account** Cr

Particulars	Amt (₹)	Particulars	Amt (₹)
To Balance b/d	20,00,000	By Accumulated Depreciation A/c	1,00,000
To Bank A/c (Balancing Figure)	11,00,000	By Insurance Company A/c	32,000
		By Loss by Fire A/c	8,000
		By Bank A/c (2,50,000 – 90,000 – 20,000)	1,40,000
		By Loss on Sale A/c	20,000
		By Balance c/d	28,00,000
	31,00,000		31,00,000

Solved Question 10 From the following information, calculate cash flow from investing activities of NTPC Ltd.

Particulars	31st March, 2024 (₹)	31st March, 2023 (₹)
Investments @ 10%	7,00,000	3,50,000
Property, Plant and Equipment	17,00,000	12,00,000

Additional Information

(i) Half of the investments held in the beginning of the year were sold at 20% profit.

(ii) Depreciation on property, plant and equipment was ₹ 80,000 for the year.

(iii) Interest received on investments ₹ 70,000.

(iv) Dividend received on investments ₹ 50,000.

Sol. **Cash Flow from Investing Activities**

Particulars	Amt (₹)
Proceeds from Sale of Investments	2,10,000
Purchase of Investments (WN 1)	(5,25,000)
Purchase of Property, Plant and Equipment (WN 2)	(5,80,000)
Interest Received	70,000
Dividend Received	50,000
Cash Used in Investing Activities	(7,75,000)

Working Notes

1. Dr **Investment Account** Cr

Particulars	Amt (₹)	Particulars	Amt (₹)
To Balance b/d (Opening)	3,50,000	By Bank A/c (Sale)	2,10,000
To Profit on Sale of Investments (Statement of Profit and Loss)	35,000	By Balance c/d	7,00,000
To Bank A/c (Purchase of Investments) (Balancing Figure)	5,25,000		
	9,10,000		9,10,000

Sale of Investments = 50% of 3,50,000 + 20% of 1,75,000
= 1,75,000 + 35,000 = ₹ 2,10,000

2. Dr **Property, Plant and Equipment Account** Cr

Particulars	Amt (₹)	Particulars	Amt (₹)
To Balance b/d (Opening)	12,00,000	By Depreciation A/c	80,000
To Bank A/c (Purchases) (Balancing Figure)	5,80,000	By Balance c/d	17,00,000
	17,80,000		17,80,000

Solved Question 11 From the following particulars of Ruparel Ltd., calculate 'cash flow from investing activities'. Show your working clearly. **CBSE 2024 C**

Particulars	31st March, 2023 (₹)	31st March, 2022 (₹)
Goodwill	3,00,000	1,00,000
Patents	1,60,000	2,80,000
Machinery	12,40,000	10,20,000
10% Investments	1,60,000	60,000

Additional Information

(i) Patents of ₹ 1,20,000 were sold at book value.

(ii) Depreciation charged during the year on machinery was ₹ 1,40,000. A machine having a book value of ₹ 80,000 was sold for ₹ 50,000.

(iii) On 31st March, 2023, 10% investments were purchased for ₹ 1,80,000 and some investments were sold at a profit of ₹ 20,000.

Interest received on investments was ₹ 6,000.

Sol. **Cash Flow from Investing Activities**

Particulars	Amt (₹)
Purchase of Machinery (WN 1)	(4,40,000)
Sale of Machinery	50,000
Purchase of Investment	(1,80,000)
Sale of Investments (WN 2)	1,00,000
Sale of Patents	1,20,000
Purchase of Goodwill	(2,00,000)
Interest Received	6,000
Net Cash used in Investing Activities	(5,44,000)

Working Notes

1. Dr **Machinery Account** Cr

Particulars	Amt (₹)	Particulars	Amt (₹)
To Balance b/d	10,20,000	By Depreciation A/c	1,40,000
To Bank A/c (Bal. Fig.)	4,40,000	By Bank A/c (Sale)	50,000
		By Statement of Profit and Loss	30,000
		By Balance c/d	12,40,000
	14,60,000		14,60,000

2. Dr **10% Investment Account** Cr

Particulars	Amt (₹)	Particulars	Amt (₹)
To Balance b/d	60,000	By Bank A/c (Sale) (Balancing Figure)	1,00,000
To Statement of Profit and Loss (Gain)	20,000	By Balance c/d	1,60,000
To Bank A/c	1,80,000		
	2,60,000		2,60,000

Solved Question 12 **From the following balances and additional information given below. Calculate cash flow from investing activities.**

Particulars	31st March, 2024 (₹)	31st March, 2023 (₹)
Goodwill	1,40,000	1,00,000
Patents	70,000	1,10,000
Machinery	6,20,000	5,10,000
10% Long-term Investment	80,000	30,000
Investment in Land	50,000	50,000
Shares of PQR Ltd.	50,000	50,000

Additional Information

(i) Patents were written-off to the extent of ₹ 10,000 and some patents were sold at a profit of ₹ 6,000.

(ii) A machine costing ₹ 70,000 (depreciation provided thereon ₹ 30,000) was sold for ₹ 25,000. Depreciation charged during the year was ₹ 70,000.

(iii) On 31st March, 2024, 10% investments were purchased for ₹ 90,000 and some investments were sold at a profit of ₹ 10,000. Interest on investment was received on 31 March, 2024.

(iv) PQR Ltd. paid dividend @ 8% on its shares.

(v) A plot of land was purchased out of surplus funds for investment purposes and let out for commercial use and rent received ₹ 20,000.

Sol. **Cash Flow from Investing Activities**

Particulars	Amt (₹)
Purchase of Goodwill	(40,000)
Proceeds from Sale of Patents (WN 1)	36,000
Proceeds from Sale of Machinery	25,000
Purchase of Machinery (WN 2)	(2,20,000)
Purchase of 10% Investments	(90,000)
Proceeds from Sale of Investments (WN 3)	50,000
Interest Received (10% on ₹ 30,000)	3,000
Dividend Received (8% on ₹ 50,000)	4,000
Rent Received	20,000
Net Cash Used in Investing Activities	(2,12,000)

Working Notes

1. Dr **Patents Account** Cr

Particulars	Amt (₹)	Particulars	Amt (₹)
To Balance b/d	1,10,000	By Statement of Profit and Loss (Written-off)	10,000
To Statement of Profit and Loss (Profit on Sale)	6,000	By Bank A/c (Balancing Figure) (Sale of Patents)	36,000
		By Balance c/d	70,000
	1,16,000		1,16,000

2. Dr **Machinery Account** Cr

Particulars	Amt (₹)	Particulars	Amt (₹)
To Balance b/d	5,10,000	By Statement of Profit and Loss (Depreciation)	70,000
To Bank A/c (Balancing Figure) (Purchase)	2,20,000	By Bank A/c (Sale)	25,000
		By Statement of Profit and Loss (Loss on Sale) (70,000 – 30,000 – 25,000)	15,000
		By Balance c/d	6,20,000
	7,30,000		7,30,000

3. Dr **10% Investment Account** Cr

Particulars	Amt (₹)	Particulars	Amt (₹)
To Balance b/d	30,000	By Bank A/c (Balancing Figure) (Sale)	50,000
To Bank A/c (Purchase)	90,000	By Balance c/d	80,000
To Statement of Profit and Loss (Profit on Sale)	10,000		
	1,30,000		1,30,000

Financing Activities

Solved Question 13 **From the following particulars of Vijeta Ltd. calculate net cash flow from financing activities.**

Particulars	31st March, 2024 (₹)	31st March, 2023 (₹)
Equity Share Capital	20,00,000	16,00,000
10% Preference Share Capital	2,00,000	6,00,000
Securities Premium	2,60,000	2,20,000
10% Debentures	6,00,000	3,00,000

Additional Information

Dividend on preference shares and an interim dividend on equity shares @ 15% were paid on 30th September, 2023. Preference shares were redeemed on 31st March, 2024 at a premium of 5%. Such premium has been provided out of profits. New shares and debentures were issued on 1st October, 2023.

Sol. **Calculation of Net Cash Flow from Financing Activities**

Particulars	Amt (₹)
Issue of Equity Share Capital (including Securities Premium)	4,40,000
Issue of Debentures (6,00,000 – 3,00,000)	3,00,000
Redemption of Preference Shares (4,00,000 + 20,000)	(4,20,000)
Interest Paid on Debentures	(45,000)
Interim Dividend Paid on Equity Shares (16,00,000 × 15/100)	(2,40,000)
Dividend Paid on Preference Shares	(60,000)
Net Cash Used in Financing Activities	(25,000)

$$\text{Interest on Debentures} = \left(3,00,000 \times \frac{10}{100} \times \frac{6}{12}\right) + \left(6,00,000 \times \frac{10}{100} \times \frac{6}{12}\right) = 15,000 + 30,000 = ₹\ 45,000$$

Solved Question 14 **From the following information of Lata Opticals Ltd. Calculate cash flow from financing activities.**

Particulars	31st March, 2024 (₹)	31st March 2023 (₹)
Equity Share Capital	10,00,000	6,00,000
12% Debentures	—	1,20,000
Bank Overdraft	70,000	90,000
10% Debentures	3,20,000	—

Additional Information

(i) 12% Debentures were redeemed on 30th June 2023 and 10% debentures were issued at 10% discount on the same date.
(ii) Interest paid on bank overdraft @ 10% p.a. overdraft was repaid on 1st October, 2023.
(iii) During the year 2023-24, Lata opticals Ltd. issued bonus shares amounting ₹ 2,00,000.

Sol. **Cash Flow from Financing Activities**

Particulars	Amt (₹)
Issue of Equity Shows	2,00,000
Redemption of Debentures	(1,20,000)
Repayment of Bank Overdraft	(20,000)
Issue of 10% Debenture (3,20,000 – 32,000)	2,88,000
Interest Paid on Debentures	(27,600)
Interest Paid on Bank Overdraft	(8,000)
Net Cash Flow from Financing Activities	3,12,400

Working Notes

1. Interest on Debentures $= 1{,}20{,}000 \times \frac{12}{100} \times \frac{3}{12} =$ ₹ 3,600

$= 3{,}20{,}000 \times \frac{10}{100} \times \frac{9}{12} =$ ₹ 24,000

2. Interest on Bank Overdraft $= \left(90{,}000 \times \frac{10}{100} \times \frac{6}{12}\right) + \left(70{,}000 \times \frac{10}{100} \times \frac{6}{12}\right) = 4500 + 3500 =$ ₹ 8,000

3. Bonus shares are issued to existing shareholders without charging any amount. Hence, there is no flow of cash.

Solved Question 15 **Calculate cash flow from financing activities from the information given below.**

Particulars	31st March, 2024 (₹)	31st March, 2023 (₹)
Equity Share Capital	15,00,000	10,00,000
12% Debentures	—	1,50,000
10% Debentures	2,50,000	—
Bank Overdraft	40,000	50,000

Additional Information

(i) During the year 2023-24, X Ltd. issued bonus shares in the ratio of 2 : 1 by capitalising reserve.

(ii) 12% Debentures were redeemed on 1st July, 2023 and new 10% debentures were issued on the same date at a discount of 5%.

(iii) Proposed dividend on equity share capital for previous year ended 31st March, 2023 was paid @ 8%.

(iv) Interest paid on bank overdraft ₹ 5,000.

Sol. **Cash Flow from Financing Activities**

Particulars	Amt (₹)
Redemption of 12% Debentures	(1,50,000)
Proceeds from Issue of 10% Debentures (2,50,000 – 12,500 Discount)	2,37,500
Interest Paid on Debentures (WN 2)	(23,250)
Decrease in Bank Overdraft	(10,000)
Proposed Dividend Paid on Equity Share Capital (8% on ₹ 10,00,000)	(80,000)
Interest Paid on Bank Overdraft	(5,000)
Net Cash Used in Financing Activities	(30,750)

Working Notes

1. Bonus shares are issued to existing equity shareholders without charging any amount from them. Hence, bonus shares are not shown in cash flow statement because there is no flow of cash. Bonus shares are issued in the ratio of 2 : 1. It means a shareholder holding 2 shares is issued 1 bonus share. As such, ₹ 5,00,000 bonus shares are issued.
2. Interest on Debentures

12% on 1,50,000 for 3 months = ₹ 4,500

10% on 2,50,000 for 9 months = ₹ 18,750

23,250

Solved Question 16 **From the following information, calculate cash flow from financing activities.**

Particulars	31st March, 2024 (₹)	31st March, 2023 (₹)
Equity Share Capital	4,00,000	3,00,000
12% Preference Share Capital	—	1,00,000
14% Debentures	50,000	—

Additional Information

(i) Equity shares were issued at a premium of 15%.

(ii) 12% preference shares were redeemed at a premium of 5%.

(iii) 14% debentures were issued at a discount of 1%.

(iv) Dividend paid on old preference shares ₹ 12,000.

(v) Interest paid on debentures ₹ 7,000.

(vi) Underwriting commission of equity shares ₹ 5,000.

(vii) Proposed dividend on equity shares for the year ended 31st March, 2024 ₹ 60,000.

(viii) Proposed dividend on equity shares for the year ended 31st March, 2023 ₹ 45,000.

Sol. **Cash Flow from Financing Activities**

Particulars	Amt (₹)
Proceeds from Issue of Equity Share Capital (1,00,000 + Securities Premium 15,000 – Underwriting Commission 5,000)	1,10,000
Redemption of Preference Shares (1,00,000 + Premium on Redemption 5,000)	(1,05,000)
Proceeds from Issue of Debentures (50,000 – 500)	49,500
Proposed Dividend on Equity Shares for the year ended 31st March, 2023	(45,000)
Dividend Paid on Preference Shares	(12,000)
Interest Paid on Debentures	(7,000)
Net Cash Used in Financing Activities	(9,500)

Important Problems Solving Points

- Proposed dividend for previous year i.e. for the year ended 31st March, 2023 is declared (approved) in the year ended 31st March, 2024. Hence it will be added back to net profit to determine net profit before tax. It will also be shown under financing activities as outflow of cash.
- Proposed dividend for current year i.e. for the year ended 31st March, 2024 will be declared (approved) in the next financial year. Hence, it will have no effect on cash flow statement.

Solved Question 17 **On 31st March, 2024 following is the Balance Sheet of Bhavik Limited**

In the Books of Bhavik Ltd.

Balance Sheet

as at 31st March, 2024

Particulars	Note No.	31st March, 2024 (₹)	31st March, 2023 (₹)
I. **EQUITY AND LIABILITIES**			
1. **Shareholders' Funds**			
(i) Share Capital		12,00,000	10,00,000
(ii) Reserves and Surplus	1	4,00,000	3,00,000
2. **Non-current Liabilities**			
Long-term Borrowings	2	6,00,000	10,00,000
3. **Current Liabilities**			
(i) Trade Payables		5,00,000	1,00,000
(ii) Short-term Provisions	3	3,00,000	4,00,000
Total		30,00,000	28,00,000
II. **ASSETS**			
1. **Non-current Assets**			
(i) Property, Plant and Equipment and Intangible Assets			
(a) Property Plant and Equipment	4	19,00,000	15,00,000
(ii) Non-current Investments		3,00,000	4,00,000
2. **Current Assets**			
(i) Inventories		4,50,000	3,50,000
(ii) Trade Receivables		2,50,000	4,50,000
(iii) Cash and Cash Equivalents		1,00,000	1,00,000
Total		30,00,000	28,00,000

Notes to Accounts

Particulars	31st March, 2024 (₹)	31st March, 2023 (₹)
1. **Reserves and Surplus**		
Balance in Statement of Profit and Loss	4,00,000	3,00,000
2. **Long-term Borrowings**		
10% Debentures	6,00,000	10,00,000
3. **Short-term Provisions**		
Provision for Tax	3,00,000	4,00,000
4. **Property Plant and Equipment**		
Plant and Machinery	21,50,000	16,00,000
(–) Accumulated Depreciation	(2,50,000)	(1,00,000)
	19,00,000	15,00,000

Additional Information

(i) During the year a piece of machinery costing ₹ 8,00,000 accumulated depreciation thereon ₹ 50,000 was sold for ₹ 6,50,000.

(ii) Debentures were redeemed on 31st March, 2024.

Calculate

(a) Cash flow from investing activities.

(b) Cash flow from financing activities. **CBSE 2025**

Sol. (a) **Cash Flow from Investing Activities**

Particulars	Amt (₹)
Sale Proceeds of Plant and Machinery	6,50,000
Purchase of Plant and Machinery (WN)	(13,50,000)
Sale Proceeds from investment (Non-current)	1,00,000
Net Cash used in Investing Activities	(6,00,000)

Working Note

Dr **Plant and Machinery Account** Cr

Particulars	Amt (₹)	Particulars	Amt (₹)
To Balance b/d	16,00,000	By Bank A/c (Sale)	6,50,000
To Bank A/c (Balancing figure) (Purchase)	13,50,000	By Accumulated Deprecation A/c	50,000
		By Statement of Profit and Loss (Loss)	1,00,000
		By Balance c/d	21,50,000
	29,50,000		29,50,000

(b) **Cash Flow from Financing Activities**

Particulars	Amt (₹)
Interest Paid on Debentures	(1,00,000)
Debentures Redeemed	(4,00,000)
Issues of Share Capital	2,00,000
Net Cash used in Financing Activities	(3,00,000)

Note Debentures are redeemed on 31st March, 2024, hence interest will be paid on opening balance, i.e. 10,00,000 × 10% = ₹ 1,00,000

Solved Question 18 K Ltd. a manufacturing company obtained a loan of ₹ 6,00,000, advanced a loan of ₹ 1,00,000 and purchased machinery for ₹ 5,00,000. Calculate the amount of cash flow from financing and investing activities. **CBSE 2019**

Sol. **Cash Flow from Investing Activities**

Particulars	Amt (₹)
Loan Given	(1,00,000)
Purchase of Machinery	(5,00,000)
Cash Used in Investing Activities	(6,00,000)

Cash Flow from Financing Activities

Particulars	Amt (₹)
Loan Taken	6,00,000
Cash Flow from Financing Activities	6,00,000

Cash Flow Statement

Solved Question 19 **From the following balance sheet of Shri Ganpati Industries Ltd., prepare cash flow statement as per AS-3 (Revised).**

Particulars	Note No.	31st March, 2024 (₹)	31st March, 2023 (₹)
I. EQUITY AND LIABILITIES			
1. Shareholders' Funds			
(i) Share Capital	1	5,00,000	4,00,000
(ii) Reserves and Surplus (General Reserve)		2,44,000	1,02,000
2. Non-current Liabilities			
10% Debentures		2,00,000	1,25,000
3. Current Liabilities			
(i) Short-term Borrowings (Bank Overdraft)		12,000	10,000
(ii) Trade Payables		15,000	83,000
(iii) Short-term Provisions (Provision for Taxation)		18,000	11,000
Total		9,89,000	7,31,000
II. ASSETS			
1. Non-current Assets			
(i) Property, Plant and Equipment and Intangible Assets			
(a) Property, Plant and Equipment	2	8,60,000	6,10,000
(ii) Long-term Investments		50,000	30,000
2. Current Assets			
(i) Trade Receivables		61,000	80,000
(ii) Cash and Cash Equivalents		18,000	11,000
Total		9,89,000	7,31,000

Notes to Accounts

Particulars	2024 (₹)	2023 (₹)
1. Share Capital		
Equity Share Capital	3,50,000	2,00,000
15% Preference Share Capital	1,50,000	2,00,000
	5,00,000	4,00,000
2. Property, Plant and Equipment		
Machinery	10,10,000	7,10,000
(–) Accumulated Depreciation	(1,50,000)	(1,00,000)
	8,60,000	6,10,000

Additional Information

(i) **Preference shares were redeemed on 31st March, 2024 at a premium of 10%.**

(ii) **Dividend at 12% was paid to equity shares for the year 2022-23.**

(iii) **Fresh debentures were issued on 1st April, 2023.**

Sol.

Cash Flow Statement
for the year ended 31st March, 2024

Particulars		Amt (₹)
A. Cash Flow from Operating Activities		
Net Profit before Taxation and Extraordinary Items (WN 1)		2,14,000
Adjustments for		
(+) Interest on Debentures	20,000	
Depreciation (WN 3)	50,000	
Premium on Redemption of 15% Preference Shares	5,000	75,000
Operating Profit before Working Capital Changes		2,89,000
(+) Decrease in Current Assets and Increase in Current Liabilities		
Trade Receivables		19,000

Particulars		Amt (₹)
(–) Decrease in Current Liabilities and Increase in Current Assets		
Trade Payables		(68,000)
Cash Generated from Operations		2,40,000
(–) Payment of Tax		(11,000)
Net Cash Flow from Operating Activities		2,29,000
B. **Cash Flow from Investing Activities**		
Purchase of Machinery (WN 2)	(3,00,000)	
Investments Purchased	(20,000)	
Net Cash Used in Investing Activities		(3,20,000)
C. **Cash Flow from Financing Activities**		
Increase in Bank Overdraft	2,000	
Issue of Equity Shares	1,50,000	
Redemption of 15% Preference Share Capital at Premium (50,000 + 5,000)	(55,000)	
Issue of Debentures	75,000	
Interest Paid on Debentures	(20,000)	
Dividend Paid on Preference Shares	(30,000)	
Dividend Paid on Equity Shares	(24,000)	
Net Cash Flow from Financing Activities		98,000
Net Increase in Cash and Cash Equivalents (A + B + C)		7,000
(+) Cash and Cash Equivalents at the Beginning of the Period		11,000
Cash and Cash Equivalents at the End of the Period		18,000

Working Notes

1. **Calculation of Net Profit before Taxation and Extraordinary Items**

Particulars	Amt (₹)
Increase in Reserves and Surplus	1,42,000
(+) Provision for Taxation	18,000
	1,60,000
(+) Dividend on Preference Shares (2,00,000 × 15%)	30,000
	1,90,000
(+) Dividend on Equity Shares (2,00,000 × 12%)	24,000
	2,14,000

2. Dr **Machinery Account** Cr

Particulars	Amt (₹)	Particulars	Amt (₹)
To Balance b/d	7,10,000	By Balance c/d	10,10,000
To Cash A/c (Purchase)(Balancing Figure)	3,00,000		
	10,10,000		10,10,000

3. Dr **Accumulated Depreciation Account** Cr

Particulars	Amt (₹)	Particulars	Amt (₹)
To Balance c/d	1,50,000	By Balance b/d	1,00,000
		By Statement of Profit and Loss (Balancing Figure)	50,000
	1,50,000		1,50,000

Solved Question 20 From the following information, prepare a cash flow statement.

Particulars	Note No.	31st March, 2024 (₹)	31st March, 2023 (₹)
I. **EQUITY AND LIABILITIES**			
1. **Shareholders' Funds**			
(i) Share Capital		15,75,000	13,50,000
(ii) Reserves and Surplus	1	9,67,500	5,73,750
2. **Non-current Liabilities**			
Long-term Borrowings	2	4,95,000	7,20,000

Particulars	Note No.	31st March, 2024 (₹)	31st March, 2023 (₹)
3. **Current Liabilities**			
(i) Trade Payables		5,62,500	3,60,000
(ii) Other Current Liabilities	3	27,000	45,000
(iii) Short-term Provisions	4	1,71,000	1,57,500
Total		37,98,000	32,06,250
II. **ASSETS**			
1. **Non-current Assets**			
(i) Property, plant and Equipment and Intangible Assets			
(a) Property, Plant and Equipment	5	21,37,500	18,00,000
(ii) Non-current Investments		3,85,000	3,85,000
2. **Current Assets**			
(i) Inventories		5,31,000	3,82,500
(ii) Trade Receivables		6,97,500	5,96,250
(iii) Other Current Assets (Prepaid Expenses)		27,000	22,500
(iv) Cash and Cash Equivalents		20,000	20,000
Total		37,98,000	32,06,250

Notes to Accounts

Particulars	2024 (₹)	2023 (₹)
1. **Reserves and Surplus**		
General Reserve	5,62,500	4,50,000
Surplus, i.e. Balance in Statement of Profit and Loss	3,82,500	1,23,750
Capital Reserve	22,500	—
	9,67,500	5,73,750
2. **Long-term Borrowings**		
10% Debentures	4,95,000	7,20,000
3. **Other Current Liabilities**		
Outstanding Expenses	27,000	45,000
4. **Short-term Provisions**		
Provision for Tax	1,71,000	1,57,500
5. **Property, Plant and Equipment**		
Plant and Machinery (Cost)	27,00,000	22,50,000
(−) Accumulated Depreciation	(5,62,500)	(4,50,000)
	21,37,500	18,00,000

Additional Information

(i) During the year, plant and machinery with a net book value of ₹ 22,500 (accumulated depreciation ₹ 67,500) was sold for ₹ 18,000.

(ii) During the year, investment costing ₹ 1,80,000 was sold at a profit of 12.5% on cost, which is transferred to capital reserve and also investment costing ₹ 1,80,000 was purchased.

(iii) Tax of ₹ 1,23,750 was paid during the year.

(iv) At the beginning of the year, debentures of ₹ 2,25,000 were redeemed at par.

(v) Interest on debentures paid during the year ₹ 49,500.

(vi) Contingent liability

	2024 (₹)	2023 (₹)
Proposed dividend	**76,500**	**67,500**

Sol.

Cash Flow Statement
for the year ended 31st March, 2024

Particulars		Amt (₹)
A. **Cash Flow from Operating Activities**		
Net Profit before Tax and Extraordinary Items (WN 1)		5,76,000
Adjustments for		
(+) Depreciation (WN 3)	1,80,000	
Interest on Debentures	49,500	
Loss on Sale of Fixed Assets	4,500	2,34,000

Particulars		Amt (₹)
Operating Profit before Working Capital Changes		8,10,000
(+) Decrease in Current Assets or Increase in Current Liabilities		
Trade Payables		2,02,500
(–) Increase in Current Assets or Decrease in Current Liabilities		
Inventories	(1,48,500)	
Trade Receivables	(1,01,250)	
Prepaid Expenses	(4,500)	
Outstanding Expenses	(18,000)	(2,72,250)
Cash Generated from Operations		7,40,250
(–) Income Tax Paid		(1,23,750)
Cash Flow from Operating Activities		6,16,500
B. **Cash Flow from Investing Activities**		
Proceeds from Sale of Assets (Machinery)	18,000	
Proceeds from Sale of Investments (1,80,000 + 22,500)	2,02,500	
Purchase of Machinery (WN 2)	(5,40,000)	
Purchase of Investments	(1,80,000)	(4,99,500)
Cash Used in Investing Activities		
C. **Cash Flow from Financing Activities**		
Proceeds from Issue of Shares	2,25,000	
Repayment of Debentures	(2,25,000)	
Interest Paid on Debentures	(49,500)	
Proposed Dividend Paid	(67,500)	
Cash Used in Financing Activities		(1,17,000)
Net Increase in Cash and Cash Equivalents (A + B + C)		—
(+) Cash and Cash Equivalents in the Beginning of the Year		20,000
Cash and Cash Equivalents at the End of the Year		20,000

Working Notes

1. **Calculation of Net Profit before Tax and Extraordinary Items**

Particulars		Amt (₹)
Surplus i.e. Balance in Statement of Profit and Loss (Closing)	3,82,500	
(–) Surplus i.e. Balance in Statement of Profit and Loss (Opening)	(1,23,750)	2,58,750
(+) Proposed Dividend for the Previous Year	67,500	
Transfer to Reserve	1,12,500	
Provision for Tax (WN 4)	1,37,250	3,17,250
Net Profit before Tax and Extraordinary Items		5,76,000

2. Dr **Plant and Machinery Account** Cr

Particulars	Amt (₹)	Particulars	Amt (₹)
To Balance b/d	22,50,000	By Bank A/c	18,000
To Bank A/c (Purchase) (Balancing Figure)	5,40,000	By Accumulated Depreciation A/c	67,500
		By Loss on Sale (Statement of Profit and Loss)	4,500
		By Balance c/d	27,00,000
	27,90,000		27,90,000

3. Dr **Accumulated Depreciation Account** Cr

Particulars	Amt (₹)	Particulars	Amt (₹)
To Plant and Machinery A/c (Transfer)	67,500	By Bank A/c	4,50,000
To Balance c/d	5,62,500	By Depreciation A/c (Statement of Profit and Loss) (Balancing Figure)	1,80,000
	6,30,000		6,30,000

4. Dr **Provision for Tax Account** Cr

Particulars	Amt (₹)	Particulars	Amt (₹)
To Bank A/c (Tax Paid)	1,23,750	By Balance b/d	1,57,500
To Balance c/d	1,71,000	By Statement of Profit and Loss (Provision for Tax) (Balancing Figure)	1,37,250
	2,94,750		2,94,750

Solved Question 21 **Prepare cash flow statement for Shiv Ltd. from the following balance sheet.**

Particulars	Note No.	2024 (₹)	2023 (₹)
I. EQUITY AND LIABILITIES			
1. **Shareholders' Funds**			
(i) Share Capital		2,37,500	2,00,000
(ii) Reserve and Surplus	1	58,000	(15,000)
2. **Non-current Liabilities**			
Long-term Borrowings	2	1,25,000	1,00,000
3. **Current Liabilities**			
(i) Trade Payables		55,000	25,000
(ii) Short-term Provisions	3	8,000	5,000
Total		4,83,500	3,15,000
II. ASSETS			
1. **Non-current Assets**			
(i) Property, plant and Equipment and Intangible Assets			
(a) Property, Plant and Equipment	4	2,26,000	85,000
(b) Non-current Investments		22,500	20,000
2. **Current Assets**			
(i) Current Investments		15,000	25,000
(ii) Inventory		1,00,000	75,000
(iii) Trade Receivables		28,000	88,000
(iv) Cash and Bank		92,000	22,000
Total		4,83,500	3,15,000

Notes to Accounts

Particulars	2024 (₹)	2023 (₹)
1. **Reserve and Surplus**		
Securities Premium	30,000	—
Profit and Loss Balance	28,000	(15,000)
	58,000	(15,000)
2. **Long-term Borrowings**		
15% Debentures	1,25,000	1,00,000
3. **Short-term Provision**		
Provision for Doubtful Debts	7,000	5,000
Provision for Repairs	1,000	—
	8,000	5,000
4. **Property, Plant and Equipment**	2,50,000	1,00,000
(–) Accumulated Depreciation	(24,000)	(15,000)
	2,26,000	85,000

Additional Information

(i) Interim dividend paid during the year ₹ 18,000.

(ii) Non-current investment costing ₹ 5,000 were sold at a profit of 40%.

(iii) A machine costing ₹ 10,000 (accumulated depreciation ₹ 4,000) were sold for ₹ 8,500.

(iv) Additional debentures amounting to ₹ 25,000 were issued at par on 1st August, 2023. Interest on debentures has been paid regularly.

Sol.

Cash Flow Statement
for the year ended 31st March, 2024

Particulars		Amt (₹)
A. **Cash Flow from Operating Activities**		
Net Profit before Tax (WN 1)		61,000
Adjustments for Non-cash and Non-operating Items		
(+) Depreciation on Property, Plant and Equipment (WN 3)	13,000	
Provision for Doubtful Debts	2,000	
Provision for Repairs	1,000	
Interest Paid on Long-term Borrowings (Debentures)	17,500	33,500
		94,500
(–) Profit on Sale of Non-current Investments	(2,000)	
Profit on Sale of Property, Plant and Equipment	(2,500)	(4,500)
Operating Profit before Working Capital Changes		90,000
(+) Decrease in Current Assets		
Trade Receivables	60,000	
(+) Increase in Current Liabilities		
Trade Payables	30,000	90,000
		1,80,000
(–) Increase in Current Assets		
Inventory		(25,000)
Net Cash Flow from Operating Activities		1,55,000
B. **Cash Flow from Investing Activities**		
Purchase of Property, Plant and Equipment (WN 2)	(1,60,000)	
Sale of Property, Plant and Equipment	8,500	
Purchase of Non-current Investments (WN 4)	(7,500)	
Sale of Non-current Investments	7,000	
Net Cash used in Investing Activities		(1,52,000)
C. **Cash Flow from Financing Activities**		
Proceeds from Issue of Share Capital	37,500	
Security Premium Received on Issue of Share Capital	30,000	
Proceeds from Long-term Borrowings (Debentures)	25,000	
Payment of Interim Dividend	(18,000)	
Interest Paid on Long-term Borrowings	(17,500)	
Net Cash Flow from Financing Activities		57,000
Net Increase in Cash and Cash Equivalents (A + B + C)		60,000
(+) Cash and Cash Equivalents in the Beginning of the Period		47,000
Cash and Cash Equivalents at the End of the Period		1,07,000

Working Notes

1. **Calculation of Net Profit before Tax**

Particulars	Amt (₹)
Balance of Statement of Profit and Loss as on 31st March, 2024	28,000
(–) Balance of Statement of Profit and Loss as on 31st March, 2023	15,000
[28,000 – (– 15,000)]	43,000
(+) Interim Dividend Paid	18,000
	61,000

2. Dr **Machine Account** (On Original Cost) Cr

Particulars	Amt (₹)	Particulars	Amt (₹)
To Balance b/d	1,00,000	By Bank (sale)	8,500
To Profit on the Sales of Fixed Tangible Assets	2,500	By Accumulated Dep. A/c (Being Depreciation on Fixed Tangible Assets Sold)	4,000
To Bank A/c (Balancing Figure) (Purchase)	1,60,000	By Balance b/d	2,50,000
	2,62,500		2,62,500

3. Dr **Accumulated Depreciation Account** Cr

Particulars	Amt (₹)	Particulars	Amt (₹)
To Fixed Tangible Assets A/c (Being the Transfer of Depreciation on Fixed Tangible Assets)	4,000	By Balance c/d	15,000
To Balance c/d	24,000	By Depreciation A/c (Balancing Figure) (Current Year's Depreciation)	13,000
	28,000		28,000

4. Dr **Non-current Investments Account** Cr

Particulars	Amt (₹)	Particulars	Amt (₹)
To Balance c/d	20,000	By Bank A/c (Sale Proceeds)	7,000
To Profit on Sale of Non-current Investments	2,000	By Balance c/d	22,500
To Bank A/c (Balancing Figure) (Purchases)	7,500		
	29,500		29,500

5. **Cash and Cash Equivalents**

Particulars	2020 (₹)	2019 (₹)
Cash and Bank	92,000	22,000
Current Investments	15,000	25,000
	1,07,000	47,000

Solved Question 22 From the following balance sheet of XYZ Ltd. as at 31st March, 2024, prepare cash flow statement

Particulars	Note No.	31st March, 2024 (₹)	31st March, 2023 (₹)
I. EQUITY AND LIABILITIES			
1. Shareholders' Funds			
(i) Share Capital		1,75,000	1,50,000
(ii) Reserves and Surplus	1	35,000	25,000
2. Non-current Liabilities			
Long-term Borrowings (12% Debentures)		40,000	50,000
3. Current Liabilities			
(i) Short-term Borrowings (Bank Loan)		7,500	12,500
(ii) Trade Payables		82,500	30,000
Total		3,40,000	2,67,500
II. ASSETS			
1. Non-current Assets			
(i) Property, Plant and Equipment and Intangible Assets			
(a) Property, Plant and Equipment	2	2,05,000	1,50,000
(ii) Non-current Investments		20,000	25,000
2. Current Assets			
(i) Inventories		26,000	15,000
(ii) Trade Receivables		30,000	20,000
(iii) Cash and Cash Equivalents		59,000	57,500
Total		3,40,000	2,67,500

Notes to Accounts

Particulars	31st March, 2024 (₹)	31st March, 2023 (₹)
1. **Reserves and Surplus**		
Capital Reserve	1,000	—
General Reserve	16,500	10,000
Surplus i.e. Balance in Statement of Profit and Loss	17,500	15,000
	35,000	25,000
2. **Property, Plant and Equipment**		
Machinery (Cost)	2,35,000	1,75,000
(–) Accumulated Depreciation	(30,000)	(25,000)
	2,05,000	1,50,000

Additional Information

(i) During the year, machinery costing ₹ 10,000 (accumulated depreciation of ₹ 7,500 was sold at for ₹ 6,000).
(ii) During the year, non-current investments were sold at a profit of 20%, which is transferred to capital reserve.
(iii) Debentures were redeemed at par on 1st April, 2023.
(iv) Tax of ₹ 7,500 was paid during the year.
(v) Interim dividend paid during the year amount to ₹ 12,500.
(vi) Board had proposed final dividend for the previous year (year ended 31st March, 2023) @ 10%. The shareholders did not declare (approve) the proposed dividend.

Sol.

Star Ltd. Cash Flow Statement
for the year ended 31st March, 2024

Particulars		Amt (₹)
A. **Cash Flow from Operating Activities**		
Net Profit before Tax and Extraordinary Items (WN 1)		29,000
(+) Non-cash and Non-operating Expenses		
Depreciation on Machinery (WN 3)	12,500	
Interest on Debentures (12% of ₹ 40,000)	4,800	17,300
		46,300
(–) Gain (Profit) on Sale of Machinery (WN 2)		(3,500)
Operating Profit before Working Capital Changes		42,800
(+) Increase in Current Liabilities		
Trade Payables		52,500
		95,300
(–) Increase in Current Assets		
Inventories	(11,000)	
Trade Receivables	(10,000)	(21,000)
Cash Generated from Operating Activities before Tax		74,300
(–) Tax Paid		(7,500)
Cash Flow from Operating Activities		66,800
B. **Cash Flow from Investing Activities**		
Purchase of Machinery (WN 2)	(70,000)	
Proceeds from Sale of Machinery	6,000	
Proceeds from Sale of Non-current Investments (WN 4)	6,000	
Cash Used in Investing Activities		(58,000)
C. **Cash Flow from Financing Activities**		
Proceeds from Issue of Shares	25,000	
Interim Dividend Paid	(12,500)	
Redemption of Debentures	(10,000)	
Interest on Debentures Paid	(4,800)	
Bank Loan Repaid	(5,000)	
Cash Used in Financing Activities		(7,300)
Increase in Cash and Cash Equivalents (A + B + C)		1,500
(+) **Cash and Cash Equivalents in the Beginning of the Period**		57,500
Cash and Cash Equivalents at the End of the Period		59,000

Working Notes

1.

Particulars	Amt (₹)
Calculation of Net Profit before Tax and Extraordinary Items	
Surplus i.e. Balance in Statement of Profit and Loss (Closing)	17,500
(–) Surplus i.e. Balance in Statement of Profit and Loss (Opening) Profit for the Year	(15,000)
Profit for the Year	2,500
(+) Transfer to General Reserve (16,500 – 10,000)	6,500
Provision for Tax	7,500
Interim Dividend Paid	12,500
Net Profit before Tax and Extraordinary Items	29,000

2. Dr **Machinery Account** Cr

Particulars	Amt (₹)	Particulars	Amt(₹)
To Balance b/d	1,75,000	By Accumulated Depreciation A/c	7,500
To Gain (Profit) on Sale of Machinery A/c* (Statement of Profit and Loss)	3,500	By Bank A/c (Sales)	6,000
		By Balance c/d	2,35,000
To Bank A/c (Balancing Figure) (Purchase)	70,000		
	2,48,500		2,48,500

Particulars	Amt (₹)
*Sale Value	6,000
(–) Book Value on the Date of Sale (i.e. 10,000 – 7,500)	2,500
Gain (Profit) on Sale of Machinery	3,500

3. Dr **Accumulated Depreciation Account** Cr

Particulars	Amt (₹)	Particulars	Amt (₹)
To Machinery A/c (Transfer)	7,500	By Balance b/d	25,000
To Balance c/d	30,000	By Depreciation A/c (Statement of Profit and Loss) (Balancing Figure)	12,500
	37,500		37,500

4. Dr **Non-current Investment Account** Cr

Particulars	Amt (₹)	Particulars	Amt (₹)
To Balance b/d	25,000	By Bank A/c (Sales)*	6,000
To Capital Reserve A/c (Gain)*	1,000	By Balance c/d	20,000
	26,000		26,000

*Calculation of Sale Value and Gain (Profit) on sale of Non-current Investments (NCI)
Book Value of Investments Sold = Opening Book Value = Closing Book Value = 25,000 – 20,000 = ₹ 5,000
Gain (Profit) on Sale = 20% × 5,000 = ₹ 1,000
Sale Value of Non-current Investments = Book Value + Gain (Profit) = 5,000 + 1,000 = ₹ 6,000

5. As the Gain (Profit) on sale of non-current investment has not been transferred to statement of profit and loss but to capital reserve, it will not be adjusted while calculating operating profit before working capital changes.
6. The shareholders did not declare (approve) the proposed dividend. Since it was not declared, it was neither accounted in the books of account nor paid during the year. Hence, in cash flow statement, it is not considered.

Solved Question 23 **From the following information, prepare cash flow statement**

Balance Sheet
as at 31st March 2023-24

Particulars	Note No.	31st March, 2024 (₹)	31st March, 2023 (₹)
I. **EQUITY AND LIABILITIES**			
1. **Shareholders' Funds**			
(i) Share Capital		50,000	40,000
(ii) Reserve and Surplus	1	3,200	3,000
2. **Non-current Liabilities**			
Long-term Borrowings	2	7,000	6,000

Particulars	Note No.	31st March, 2024 (₹)	31st March, 2023 (₹)
3. **Current Liabilities**			
(i) Short-term Borrowings	3	6,800	12,500
(ii) Trade Payables		15,800	17,000
(iii) Short-term Provisions (Provision for Tax)		4,200	3,000
(iv) Other Current Liabilities	4	1,000	—
Total		88,000	81,500
II. **ASSETS**			
1. **Non-current Assets**			
Property, Plant and Equipment (Machine)	5	25,000	30,000
2. **Current Assets**			
(i) Inventories		35,000	30,000
(ii) Trade Receivables		24,000	20,000
(iii) Cash and Cash Equivalents		3,500	1,200
(iv) Prepaid Expenses		500	300
Total		88,000	81,500

Notes to Accounts

Particulars	31st March, 2024 (₹)	31st March, 2023 (₹)
1. **Reserve and Surplus**		
General Reserve	2,000	2,000
Profit and Loss Balance	1,200	1,000
	3,200	3,000
2. **Long-term Borrowings**		
15% Debentures	7,000	6,000
3. **Short-term Borrowings**		
Cash Credit	6,800	12,500
4. **Other Current Liabilities**		
Dividend Payable	1,000	—
5. **Machine**	40,000	41,000
(–) Accumulated Depreciation	(15,000)	(11,000)
	25,000	30,000

Additional Information

(i)

Contingent Liability	31st March, 2024 (₹)	31st March, 2023 (₹)
Proposed Dividend	5,800	5,000

(ii) Provision for tax made ₹ 4,700.

(iii) A machine was sold for ₹ 5,000, cost being ₹ 10,000 and depreciation till date of sale is ₹ 3,000.

(iv) An interim dividend paid during the year ₹ 4,500.

Sol.

Cash Flow Statement
for the year ended 31st March, 2024

Particulars		Amt (₹)
A. **Cash Flow from Operating Activities**		
Net Profit before Tax (WN 1)		14,400
Adjustments for Non-cash and Non-operating Items		
(+) Depreciation (WN 4)	7,000	
Loss on Sale of Machine	2,000	
Interest on Debentures	900	9,900
Operating Profit before Working Capital Changes		24,300
(–) Increase in Current Assets		
Inventories	(5,000)	
Trade Receivables	(4,000)	
Prepaid Expenses	(200)	

Particulars		Amt (₹)
(–) Decrease in Current Liabilities		
Trade Payables	(1,200)	(10,400)
Cash Generated from Operating Activities		13,900
(–) Income Tax Paid (WN 5)		(3,500)
Net Cash from Operating Activities		10,400
B. **Cash Flow from Investing Activities**		
Sale of Machine	5,000	
Purchase of Machine (WN 3)	(9,000)	
Net Cash Used in Investing Activities		(4,000)
C. **Cash Flow from Financing Activities**		
Issue of Share Capital	10,000	
Issue of Debentures	1,000	
Interest on Debentures (WN2)	(900)	
Decrease in Cash Credit (WN 6)	(5,700)	
Payment of Proposed Dividend (for 2023) (5,000 – Dividend Payable 1,000) (WN 7)	(4,000)	
Interim Dividend Paid	(4,500)	
Net Cash Used in Financing Activities		(4,100)
Net Increase in Cash and Cash Equivalents		2,300
(+) Cash and Cash Equivalents in the Beginning of the Period		1,200
Cash and Cash Equivalents at the End of the Period		3,500

Working Notes

1. **Calculation of Net Profit before Tax**

Particulars	Amt (₹)
Profit and Loss Balance on 31st March, 2024	1,200
(–) Profit and Loss Balance on 31st March, 2023	(1,000)
	200
(+) Proposed Dividend for Previous Year	5,000
Interim Dividend Paid	4,500
Provision for Tax made during the Current Year	4,700
	14,400

2. It is assumed that new debentures have been issued at the end of current accounting period. Hence interest on debentures is 15% on ₹ 6,000.

3. Dr **Property, Plant and Equipment Account** (On Original Cost) Cr

Particulars	Amt (₹)	Particulars	Amt (₹)
To Balance b/d	41,000	By Bank (Sale)	5,000
To Bank (Balancing Figure) (Purchase)	9,000	By Accumulated Depreciation A/c (Being Depreciation on Fixed Assets Sold)	3,000
		By Statement of P and L (Loss on Sale of Fixed Assets)	2,000
		By Balance c/d	40,000
	50,000		50,000

4. Dr **Accumulated Depreciation Account** Cr

Particulars	Amt (₹)	Particulars	Amt (₹)
To Property, Plant and Equipment A/c (Transfer of Depreciation on Fixed Assets Sold)	3,000	By Balance b/d	11,000
To Balance c/d	15,000	By Statement of Profit and Loss (Balancing Figure) (Current Year's Depreciation)	7,000
	18,000		18,000

5. Dr **Provision for Tax Account** Cr

Particulars	Amt (₹)	Particulars	Amt (₹)
To Bank (Balancing Figure) (Payment Made)	3,500	By Balance b/d	3,000
To Balance c/d (Given)	4,200	By Statement of Profit and Loss (Provision made in 2020) (Given)	4,700
	7,700		7,700

6. Decrease in cash credit will be treated as financing activity.
7. Dividend payable will be deducted from last year's 'Proposed Dividend' to ascertain the actual payment for dividend.

Solved Question 24 From the following balance sheet of XYZ Ltd., prepare its cash flow statement for the year 2023-2024 (as per AS-3)

Particulars	Note No.	31st March, 2024 (₹)	31st March, 2023 (₹)
I. EQUITY AND LIABILITIES			
1. **Shareholders' Funds**			
(i) Share Capital		3,30,000	3,20,000
(ii) Reserve and Surplus	1	50,000	40,000
2. **Non-current Liabilities**			
Long-term Borrowings	2	1,60,000	1,50,000
3. **Current Liabilities**			
(i) Trade Payables		32,000	51,300
(ii) Short-term Provisions (Provision for Tax)		3,000	2,700
Total		5,75,000	5,64,000
II. ASSETS			
1. **Non-current Assets**			
(i) Property, Plant and Equipment and Intangible Assets			
(a) Property, Plant and Equipment	3	3,95,000	3,46,000
(b) Intangible Assets	4	5,000	4,000
(ii) Non-current Investments		60,000	60,000
2. **Current Assets**			
(i) Current Investments	5	1,000	3,000
(ii) Trade Receivables		5,000	4,000
(iii) Inventories		60,000	80,000
(iv) Cash and Bank		49,000	67,000
Total		5,75,000	5,64,000

Notes to Accounts

Particulars	31st March, 2024 (₹)	31st March, 2023 (₹)
1. **Reserve and Surplus**		
General Reserve	35,000	28,000
Statement of Profit and Loss	15,000	12,000
	50,000	40,000
2. **Long-term Borrowings**		
10% Debentures	1,60,000	1,50,000
3. **Property, Plant and Equipment**		
Plant and Machinery	3,95,000	3,46,000
4. **Intangible Assets**		
Goodwill	5,000	4,000
5. **Current Investments**		
Marketable Securities	1,000	3,000

Additional Information

(i) The debentures were issued on 1st April, 2023.

(ii) Machinery costing ₹ 7,000 (accumulated depreciation thereon ₹ 1,000) was sold for ₹ 4,500.

(iii) Machinery costing ₹ 80,000 was purchased during the year.

(iv) Interim dividend of ₹ 1,100 was paid during the year.

(v) Proposed dividend for the year ended 31st March, 2024 was ₹ 2,000 and for the year ended 31st March, 2023 was ₹ 1,300.

Sol.

Cash Flow Statement
for the year ended 31st March, 2024

Particulars		Amt (₹)
A. **Cash Flow from Operating Activities**		
Net Profit before Tax (WN 1)		15,400
Adjustments for Non-cash and Non-operating Items		
(+) Loss on Sale of Machinery	1,500	
Current Year's Depreciation on Plant and Machinery (WN 2)	25,000	
Interest on Debentures	16,000	42,500
Operating Profit before Working Capital Changes		57,900
(+) Decrease in Current Assets		
Inventory		20,000
		77,900
(−) Increase in Current Assets		
Trade Receivables	(1,000)	
Decrease in Current Liabilities		
Trade Payables	(19,300)	(20,300)
		57,600
(−) Payment of Tax		(2,700)
Net Cash Flow from Operating Activities		54,900
B. **Cash Flow from Investing Activities**		
Purchase of Machinery	(80,000)	
Purchase of Goodwill	(1,000)	
Sale of Machinery	4,500	
Net Cash Used in Investing Activities		(76,500)
C. **Cash Flow from Financing Activities**		
Proceeds from Issue of Share Capital	10,000	
Proceeds from Issue of Debentures	10,000	
Payment of Interim Dividend	(1,100)	
Payment of Proposed Dividend of Last Year	(1,300)	
Payment of Interest on Debentures	(16,000)	
Net Cash Flow from Financing Activities		1,600
Net Decrease in Cash and Cash Equivalents		(20,000)
(+) Cash and Cash Equivalents in the Beginning of the Period (WN 3)		70,000
Cash and Cash Equivalents at the End of the Period		50,000

Working Notes

1. **Calculation of Net Profit before Tax**

Particulars	Amt (₹)
Profit and Loss Balance on 31st March, 2024	15,000
(−) Profit and Loss Balance on 31st March, 2023	(12,000)
	3,000
(+) Interim Dividend Paid	1,100
Proposed Dividend for Previous Year	1,300
Provision for Taxation for Current Year	3,000
Transfer to General Reserve	7,000
	15,400

2. Dr **Machine Account** Cr

Particulars	Amt (₹)	Particulars	Amt (₹)
To Balance b/d	3,46,000	By Bank (Sale)	4,500
To Bank (Purchase)	80,000	By Loss on Sale	1,500
		By Depreciation (Balancing Figure)	25,000
		By Balance c/d	3,95,000
	4,26,000		4,26,000

3.

Particulars	31st March, 2024 (₹)	31st March, 2023 (₹)
Cash and Cash Equivalent		
Cash and Bank	49,000	67,000
Marketable Securities	1,000	3,000
	50,000	70,000

Missing Information

Solved Question 25 **From the given notes to accounts and cash flow statement of Vijay Prakash cosmetic Ltd. Complete the missing figures.**

Notes to Accounts

Particulars	31st March, 2024 (₹)	31st March 2023 (₹)
1. **Share Capital**		
Equity Share Capital	12,00,000	10,50,000
2. **Reserve and Surplus**		
Balance in Statement of Profit and Loss	1,20,000	85,000
General Reserve	90,000	70,000
Securities Premium	60,000	35,000
	2,70,000	1,90,000
3. **Cash and Cash Equivalents**		
Cash at Bank	9,65,000	2,00,000

Additional Information

(i) Depreciation for 2023-24, charged ₹ 55,000. (ii) Plant (Book Value ₹ 35,000) at a loss of ₹ 10,000.

Cash Flow Statement

for the year ended 31st March, 2024

Particulars		Amt (₹)
A. **Cash Flow from Operating Activities**		
Net Profit before Tax (WN)		...
Adjustment for		
Depreciation		...
Loss on Sale of Machine		...
Operating Profit before Working Capital Changes		...
(+) Decrease in Current Assets		
Trade Receivables	1,80,000	
(+) Increases in Current Liabilities		
Trade Payables	...	3,00,000
(–) Increase in Current Assets		
Inventories	70,000	
(–) Decrease in Current Liabilities		
Other Current Liabilities	(20,000)	...
Net Cash Flow from Operating Activities		...
B. **Cash Flows from Investing Activities**		
Sale of Plant	...	
Sale of Building	3,50,000	
Purchase of Plant and Machinery	(90,000)	
Purchase of Patents	...	
Net Cash Flow from Investing Activities		...
C. **Cash Flow Flow from Financing Activities**		
Proceeds from Issue of Shares at Premium	...	
Net Cash Flow from Financing Activities		...
Net Increase in Cash and Cash Equivalents		7,65,000
Cash and Cash Equivalent of the Beginning of the Period		2,00,000
Cash and Cash Equivalent at the End of the Period		9,65,000

Sol.

Cash Flow Statement
for the year ended 31st March, 2024

Particulars		Amt (₹)
A. **Cash Flow from Operating Activities**		
Net Profit before Tax (WN)		**55,000**
Adjustment for		
Depreciation		**55,000**
Loss on Sale of Machine		**10,000**
Operating Profit before Working Capital Changes		**1,20,000**
(+) Decrease in Current Assets		
Trade Receivables	1,80,000	
(+) Increases in Current Liabilities		
Trade Payables	**1,20,000**	3,00,000
(–) Increase in Current Assets		
Inventories	70,000	
(–) Decrease in Current Liabilities		
Other Current Liabilities	(20,000)	**90,000**
Net Cash Flow from Operating Activities		**3,30,000**
B. **Cash Flow from Investing Activities**		
Sale of Plant	**25,000**	
Sale of Building	3,50,000	
Purchase of Plant and Machinery	(90,000)	
Purchase of Patents	**(25,000)**	
Net Cash Flow from Investing Activities		**2,60,000**
C. **Cash Flow from Financing Activities**		
Proceeds from Issue of Shares at Premium	**1,75,000**	
Net Cash Flow for Financing Activities		**1,75,000**
Net Increase in Cash and Cash Equivalents		7,65,000
(+) Cash and Cash Equivalent of the Beginning of the Period		2,00,000
Cash and Cash Equivalent at the End of the Period		9,65,000

Working Note

Calculation of Profit before Tax	**Amt (₹)**
Surplus (Closing – Opening) (1,20,000 – 85,000)	35,000
(+) Transfer to General Reserve	20,000
	55,000

Solved Question 26 **From the given notes to account and cash flow statement of Steve Ltd. complete the missing figures.**

Particulars	31st March, 2024 (₹)	31st March 2023 (₹)
1. **Reserve and Surplus**		
General Reserve	6,00,000	3,50,000
Profit and Loss Balance	1,90,000	1,40,000
	7,90,000	4,90,000
2. **Long-term Borrowings**		
Debentures	...	1,90,000
3. **Provision for Tax**	1,20,000	90,000
4. **Intangible Assets** (Goodwill)	1,40,000	2,00,000

Cash Flow Statement
for the year ended 31st March 2024

Particulars		Amt (₹)
A. **Cash Flows From Operating Activities**		
(+) Net Profit before Tax (WN)	...	
Adjustment for Non-Cash and Non-operating Items		
(+) Intangible Assets Written-off	...	
Operating Profit before Working Capital Changes		...
(+) Decrease in Current Assets		

Particulars		Amt (₹)
Inventory	95,000	
(–) Increase in Current Assets		
Trade Receivables	(...)	
(–) Decrease in Current Liabilities		
Trade Payables	(1,90,000)	(...)
Cash Generated from Operations		...
(–) Payment of Tax		...
Net Cash Flow from Operating Activities		...
B. **Cash Flow from Investing Activities**		
Sale of Land and Building	8,40,000	
Purchase of Plant and Machinery	(...)	
Sale of Non-current Investments	1,20,000	
Net Cash Flow from Investing Activities		...
C. **Cash Flow from Financing Activities**		
Issue of Shares	1,00,000	
Redemption of Debentures	(...)	
Net Cash Used in Financing Activities		(...)
Net Increase in Cash and Cash Equivalents		2,15,000
(+) Opening Cash and Cash Equivalents		1,45,000
Closing Cash and Cash Equivalents		3,60,000

Sol.

Cash Flow Statement
for the year ended 31st March, 2024

Particulars		Amt (₹)
A. **Cash Flow from Operating Activities**		
(+) Net Profit before Tax (WN)	**4,20,000**	
Adjustment for Non-cash and Non-operating Items		
(+) Intangible Assets Written-off	**60,000**	
Operating Profit before Working Capital Changes		4,80,000
(+) Decrease in Current Assets		
Inventory	95000	
(–) Increase in Current Assets		
Trade Receivables	**(50,000)**	
(–) Decrease in Current Liabilities		
Trade Payables	(1,90,000)	**(1,45,000)**
Cash Generated from Operations		**3,35,000**
(–) Payment of Tax		**(90,000)**
Net Cash Flow from Operating Activities		**2,45,000**
B. **Cash Flow from Investing Activities**		
Sale of Land and Building	8,40,000	
Purchase of Plant and Machinery	**(9,00,000)**	
Sale of Non-current Investments	1,20,000	
Net Cash Flow from Investing Activities		**60,000**
C. **Cash Flow from Financing Activities**		
Issue of Shares	1,00,000	
Redemption of Debentures	**(1,90,000)**	
Net Cash Used in Financing Activities		**(90,000)**
Net Increase in Cash and Cash Equivalents		2,15,000
(+) Opening Cash and Cash Equivalents		1,45,000
Closing Cash and Cash Equivalents		3,60,000

Working Note

Calculation of Net Profit before Tax	**Amt (₹)**
Closing-Opening (Surplus) (1,90,000 – 1,40,000)	50,000
(+) Transferred to Reserve	2,50,000
Provision of Tax	1,20,000
	4,20,000

Numerical Questions

Operating Activities

1. The net income of Visakha Ltd. for the year ended 31st March, 2024 was ₹ 2,44,500. Depreciation charged for the year was ₹ 43,500. Income for the year was arrived at after adjusting for gain on sale of land ₹ 52,500, loss on sale of equipment ₹ 24,000 and writing-off cost of equity issue ₹ 12,500.

Particulars	31st March, 2024 (₹)	31st March, 2023 (₹)
Inventory	83,500	92,500
Trade Recievables	72,500	71,000
Prepaid Expenses	4,000	6,000
Marketable Securities	16,000	8,500
Trade Payables	53,500	47,500
Expenses Outstanding	4,500	6,500
Cash Credit	40,000	30,000

Calculate cash flow from operating activities.

Ans. Cash Flow from Operating Activities = ₹ 2,85,500

2. Compute cash flow from operating activities from the following.

Particulars	31st March, 2024 (₹)	31st March, 2023 (₹)
Debtors	4,00,000	3,50,000
Creditors	70,000	80,000
Bills Receivable	55,000	45,000
Bills Payable	35,000	40,000
Outstanding Expenses	8,000	6,000
Prepaid Expenses	3,000	8,000
Accrued Income	14,000	12,000
Income Received in Advance	5,000	7,000
Marketable Securities	10,500	12,500

Operating profit before working capital changes was ₹ 4,50,000.

Ans. Cash Flow from Operating Activities = ₹ 3,78,000

3. From the following balances, calculate cash flow from operating activities. **Competency Based Que**

Particulars	31st March, 2024 (₹)	31st March, 2023 (₹)
Balance of Profit and Loss	1,40,000	1,60,000
Provision for Depreciation	40,000	30,000
Prepaid Insurance	4,500	4,000
Goodwill	16,000	20,000
Provision for Doubtful Debts	6,000	5,000
Balance of Trade Receivables	49,000	70,000
Short-term Deposits into Bank	12,500	15,000

Ans. Cash Flow from Operating Activities = ₹ 15,500

4. From the following information, calculate net profit before tax and extraordinary items. **Competency Based Que**

Particulars	Amt (₹)
Surplus i.e. Balance in Statement of Profit and Loss (Opening)	30,000
Surplus i.e. Balance in Statement of Profit and Loss (Closing)	72,000
Dividend Paid (Proposed dividend for the previous year)	22,000
Interim Dividend Paid during the Year	18,000
Transfer to Reserve	15,000
Provision for Tax made during the Current Year	25,000
Refund of Tax	1,200
Loss at Inventory due to Earthquake	45,000
Insurance Claim Received for above Loss	36,000

Ans. Net Profit = ₹ 1,29,800

5. Parul Ltd. reported a profit of ₹ 8,00,000 for the year ended 31st March, 2024 after considering the following

	Amt (₹)
(i) Tax provided during the year	25,000
(ii) Amortisation of goodwill	80,000
(iii) Profit on sale of land	40,000
(iv) Writing-off preliminary expenses	1,000
(v) Machinery costing ₹ 4,00,000 (book value being ₹ 1,80,000) was sold during the year at a loss of ₹ 1,70,000	

Extract of its balance sheet in the beginning and at the end of the year is given below

Particulars	31st March, 2024 (₹)	31st March, 2023 (₹)
Accounts Receivable	2,00,000	1,60,000
Stock	1,20,000	1,50,000
Cash at Bank	80,000	1,00,000
Trade Payables	85,000	1,05,000
Expenses Payable	60,000	50,000
Provision for Taxation	30,000	50,000
Investments (Short-term)	50,000	20,000
Plant and Machinery (Net value)	9,40,000	13,00,000
Proposed Dividend	1,20,000	1,00,000

You are required to calculate cash flow from operating activities as per Accounting Standard-3. **Competency Based Que**

Ans. Cash Flow from Operating Activities = ₹ 12,11,000

6. Calculate cash flow from operating activities from the following.

Particulars	2023 (₹)	2024 (₹)
Surplus i.e. Balance in Statement of Profit and Loss	(30,000)	(45,000)
Plant and Machinery	2,60,000	2,20,000
10% Debentures	3,50,000	4,50,000
Trade Receivables	2,90,000	2,30,000
Creditors	1,60,000	1,40,000
Provision for Doubtful Debts	22,000	24,000
8% Non-current Investment	1,80,000	2,40,000
Goodwill	25,000	30,000
Inventories	5,40,000	4,80,000
Short-term Loans	35,000	40,000

Additional Information

(i) New debentures have been issued on 31st December, 2023.

(ii) New investment were made on 31st March, 2024.

Ans. Cash Flow from Operating Activities = ₹ 1,50,100

7. Compute cash flow from operating activities from the following statement of profit and loss of Kamini Ltd.

Statement of Profit and Loss of Kamini Ltd.
for the year ended 31st March, 2024

Particulars	Note No.	Amt (₹)
I. Revenue from Operations (Sales)		2,00,000
II. **Expenses**		
Cost of Materials Consumed		5,000
Purchases of Stock-in-trade		50,000
Other Expenses		30,000
Total Expenses		85,000
III. Profit before Tax (I – II)		1,15,000

Additional Information

(i) Trade receivables decrease by ₹ 5,000 during the year.

(ii) Prepaid expenses increase by ₹ 500 during the year.

(iii) Trade payables increase by ₹ 1,500 during the year.

(iv) Outstanding expenses increased by ₹ 300 during the year.

(v) Other expenses included depreciation of ₹ 3,500.

Ans. Cash Flow from Operating Activities = ₹ 1,24,800

8. From the following balance sheet of Annapoorna Ltd. compute cash flow from operating activities. Competency Based Que

Particulars	Note No.	31st March, 2024 (₹)	31st March, 2023 (₹)
I. **EQUITY AND LIABILITIES**			
1. **Shareholders' Funds**			
(i) Share Capital		40,000	25,000
(ii) Reserve and Surplus	1	25,000	15,000
2. **Non-current Liabilities**			
Long-term Borrowings	2	35,000	25,500
3. **Current Liabilities**			
(i) Trade Payables		17,500	12,500
Total		1,17,500	78,000
II. **ASSETS**			
1. **Non-current Assets**			
(i) Property, Plant and Equipment and Intangible Assets			
(a) Property, Plant and Equipment	3	36,000	28,000
(b) Intangible Assets	4	28,000	30,000
(ii) Non-current Investments		18,000	8,000
2. **Current Assets**			
(i) Inventory		10,500	6,000
(ii) Cash and Cash Equivalents		25,000	6,000
Total		1,17,500	78,000

Notes to Accounts

Particulars	31st March, 2024 (₹)	31st March, 2023 (₹)
1. **Reserve and Surplus**		
General Reserve	18,000	12,000
Profit and Loss Balance	7,000	3,000
	25,000	15,000

Particulars	31st March, 2024 (₹)	31st March, 2023 (₹)
2. **Long-term Borrowings**		
12% Debentures	35,000	25,500
3. **Property, Plant and Equipment**		
Machinery	47,000	33,000
(–) Provision for Depreciation	(11,000)	(5,000)
	36,000	28,000
4. **Intangible Assets**		
Goodwill	28,000	30,000

Additional Information

(i) Debentures were issued on 31st March, 2024.
(ii) Investments were made on 1st October, 2023.
(iii) Rate of interest on investments is 8%.

Ans. Cash Flow from Operating Activities = ₹ 20,920

Investing Activities

9. From the following information, calculate cash flow from investing activities. Competency Based Que

Particulars	31st March, 2024 (₹)	31st March, 2023 (₹)
Plant and Machinery	12,00,000	9,00,000
Investment (Long-term)	2,00,000	80,000
Land (At cost)	1,50,000	3,00,000

Additional Information

(i) Depreciation charged on plant and machinery ₹ 60,000 during the year 2023-24.
(ii) Plant and machinery with a book value of ₹ 1,20,000 was sold for ₹ 80,000.
(iii) Land was sold at a profit of ₹ 1,20,000.
(iv) No investment was sold during the year.

Ans. Net Cash used in Investing Activities = ₹ 2,50,000

10. From the following particulars of Anandnayi Ltd., calculate cash flow from investing activities. Competency Based Que

Particulars	31st March, 2024 (₹)	31st March, 2023 (₹)
Shares in Groundnut Ltd.	90,000	90,000
Investments (in land)	80,000	80,000
8% Long-term Investments	1,80,000	1,50,000
Machinery	11,40,000	9,80,000
Patents	1,20,000	1,60,000
Goodwill	1,60,000	80,000

Additional Information

(i) Patents were written-off to the extent of ₹ 40,000 and some patents were sold at a profit of ₹ 20,000.
(ii) On 31st March, 2024, company purchased investments for ₹ 60,000 and some investment were sold at a profit of ₹ 25,000. Interest on investment was received on 31st March, 2024.
(iii) Dividend received from Groundnut Ltd. @ 10%.
(iv) A plot of land was purchased out of surplus funds for investment purpose and let out for commercial use and rent received ₹ 15,000.
(v) A machine costing ₹ 1,20,000 (depreciation provided thereon ₹ 40,000) was sold for ₹ 60,000. Depreciation charged during the year ₹ 70,000.

Ans. Net Cash used in Investing Activities = ₹ 1,11,000

11. From the following information, calculate net cash flow from operating activities and investing activities.

Particulars	31st March, 2024 (₹)	31st March, 2023 (₹)
Profit and Loss A/c	2,40,000	60,000
Provision for Tax	30,000	30,000
Trade Payables	90,000	24,000
Non-current Investments	48,000	60,000
Current Assets (Inventories and trade receivables)	3,12,000	2,76,000

Additional Information

Tax paid during the year was ₹ 18,000. At the end of the year, some investments costing ₹ 42,000 were sold at a loss of 30%.

Ans. Net Cash Inflow from Operating Activities = ₹ 2,22,600;
Net Cash used in Investing Activities = ₹ 600

12. The balances in machinery account and provision for depreciation account as on 31st March, 2023 and 2024 are given below

Particulars	31st March, 2023 (₹)	31st March, 2024 (₹)
Machinery	3,80,000	4,50,000
Provision of Depreciation	1,32,000	1,50,000

During the year, a machine costing ₹ 80,000 accumulated depreciation thereon ₹ 24,000 was sold ₹ 46,000.

Your are required to compute the following Competency Based Que

(i) Amount of machinery purchased.
(ii) Depreciation charged for the year.
(iii) Loss/Gain on sale of machinery.

Ans. (i) ₹ 1,50,000 (ii) ₹ 6,000 (iii) ₹ 10,000 (Loss)

13. **From the following information, calculate amount of cash flow from investing activities.**

Particulars	31st March, 2023 (₹)	31st March, 2024 (₹)
Furniture and Fitting	7,50,000	8,00,000
Non-current Investments	25,000	60,000
Land (at cost)	4,00,000	3,20,000

Additional Information

(i) Land was sold at a gain of ₹ 35,000.

(ii) Depreciation charged on furniture and fitting was ₹ 37,500.

(iii) Furniture having book value ₹ 80,000 was sold for ₹ 65,000.

Ans. Net Cash used in Investing Activities = ₹ 22,500

14. **From the following balance sheets of Rajshree Ltd for the years ended 31st March, 2024 and 2023 and additional information, calculate cash flow from investing activities.**

Particulars	Note No.	31st March, 2024 (₹)	31st March, 2023 (₹)
I. EQUITY AND LIABILITIES			
1. Shareholders' Funds			
(i) Share Capital		15,00,000	10,00,000
(ii) Reserves and Surplus		20,00,000	17,00,000
2. Current Liabilities		9,00,000	7,00,000
Total		44,00,000	34,00,000
II. ASSETS			
1. Non-current Assets			
(i) Property, Plant and Equipment and Intangible Assets			
(a) Property, Plant and Equipment	1	24,00,000	24,00,000
(ii) Non-current Investments		10,00,000	6,00,000
2. Current Assets			
(i) Trade Receivables		6,00,000	2,20,000
(ii) Cash and Cash Equivalents		4,00,000	1,80,000
Total		44,00,000	34,00,000

Notes to Accounts

Particulars	2024 (₹)	2023 (₹)
1. Property, Plant and Equipment		
Land	6,00,000	6,00,000
Building	8,00,000	8,00,000
Plant and Machinery	10,00,000	10,00,000
	24,00,000	24,00,000

Additional Information

During the year, the company sold machinery (at book value of ₹ 3,00,000) for ₹ 2,40,000. Depreciation charged for the year ₹ 60,000.

Ans. Cash used in Investing Activities = ₹ 5,20,000

Financing Activities

15. **From the following particulars, calculate cash flow from financing activities.**

Particulars	31st March, 2024 (₹)	31st March, 2023 (₹)
10% Preference Share Capital	—	3,00,000
Equity Share Capital	8,50,000	6,50,000
10% Debentures	1,50,000	—

Additional Information

(i) Preference shares were redemed at 10% premium. (ii) Debentures were issued on 1st October, 2023 at discount of 10%.
(iii) Dividend paid on preference shares ₹ 30,000. (iv) Underwriting commission was paid ₹ 8,000.

Ans. Net Cash used in Financing Activities = ₹ 90,500

16. **Calculate cash flow from financing activities from the following extracts of balance sheet of Pureman Ltd.**

Particulars	2024 (₹)	2023 (₹)
Equity Share Capital	16,00,000	12,00,000
12% Preference Share Capital	6,00,000	7,50,000
12% Debentures	8,00,000	6,00,000

Additional Information

(i) Interim dividend on equity shares at the end of current year was paid @15%.

(ii) Dividend on preference shares was paid.

(iii) Preference shares were redeemed at a premium of 5% at the last date of current year. Premium was charged from profit.

(iv) Fresh shares and debentures were issued on the last date of current year.

Ans. Cash Flow from Financing Activities = ₹ 1,30,500

17. **Daynight Ltd. provides you the following information. Calculate cash flow from financing activities.**

Competency Based Que

Particulars	31st March, 2024 (₹)	31st March, 2023 (₹)
Equity Share Capital	1,25,000	1,00,000
8% Preference Share Capital	20,000	—
10% Debentures	—	30,000
Investment in Shares	15,000	10,000

Additional Information

(i) During the year 2023-24, XYZ Ltd. issued bonus shares in the raio of 4 : 1 by capitalising reserve.

(ii) 10% debentures were redeemed on 1st January, 2024 at a premium of 5%.

(iii) Preference dividend paid ₹ 800.

(iv) Dividend received on investments ₹ 1,000.

Ans. Cash used in Financing Activities = ₹ 14,550

18. XYZ Mutuals, a mutual fund company provides you the following information

Proposed dividend 2023 – ₹ 20,000; 2024 – ₹ 15,000

Additional Information

Equity share capital raised during the year ₹ 3,00,000

10% Bank loan repaid was ₹ 1,00,000

Dividend received during the year was ₹ 20,000

Find out cash flow from financing activity.

Ans. Cash Flow from Financing Activities = ₹ 1,80,000

19. From the following extracts taken from the balance sheets of M/s XYZ Ltd., on 31st March and the additional information provided, you are required to calculate

(i) **Cash flow from operating activities.**

(ii) **Cash flows from financing activities.**

Competency Based Que

Equity and Liabilities	31st March, 2024 (₹)	31st March, 2023 (₹)
Equity Share Capital	15,00,000	10,00,000
10% Preference Share Capital	50,000	1,00,000
Securities Premium Reserve A/c	47,500	—
Profit and Loss Balance	4,00,000	2,00,000
10% Debentures	5,00,000	5,00,000

Additional Information

(i) Fresh equity shares were issued on 31st March, 2024 at a premium of 10%.

(ii) Interim dividend was paid on equity shares @ 8%.

(iii) Preference shares were redeemed on 31st March, 2024 premium of 5%. Premium on redemption was charged against premium received on issue of fresh equity shares.

Ans. Cash Flow from Operating Activities = ₹ 3,40,000

Cash Flow from Financing Activities = ₹ 3,57,500

20. **Following is the balance sheet of Mahadev Ltd. as at 31st March, 2024. Calculate cash flow from investing and financing activities.**

Competency Based Que

In the Books of Mahadev Ltd.
Balance Sheet
as at 31st March, 2024

Particulars	Note No.	31st March, 2024 (₹)	31st March, 2023 (₹)
I. EQUITY AND LIABILITIES			
1. Shareholders' Funds			
(i) Share Capital		15,00,000	13,00,000
(ii) Reserve and Surplus	1	5,00,000	2,50,000
2. Non-current Liabilities			
10% Long-term Borrowings		4,00,000	2,50,000
3. Current Liabilities			
(i) Short-term Borrowings (Bank Overdraft)		1,80,000	1,90,000
(ii) Short-term Provisions (Provision for Tax)		1,40,000	80,000
Total		27,20,000	20,70,000

Particulars	Note No.	31st March, 2024 (₹)	31st March, 2023 (₹)
II. ASSETS			
1. **Non-current Assets**			
(i) Property, Plant and Equipment and Intangible Assets			
(a) Property, Plant and Equipment (Machine)		22,00,000	16,00,000
(b) Intangible Assets (Goodwill)		2,00,000	1,60,000
2. **Current Assets**			
(i) Current Investments		1,20,000	1,40,000
(ii) Inventories		90,000	80,000
(iii) Cash at Bank		1,10,000	90,000
Total		27,20,000	20,70,000

Notes to Accounts

Particulars	31st March, 2024	31st March, 2023
1. **Reserves and Surplus**		
Balance in Statement of Profit and Loss	5,00,000	2,50,000

Additional Information

(i) A machinery book value of which was ₹ 50,000 was sold for ₹ 65,000 and depreciation charged for the year was ₹ 1,60,000.

(ii) Long-term borrowing was raised on 1st October, 2023.

Ans. Cash used in Investing Activities = ₹ 7,85,000; Cash Inflow from Financing Activities = ₹ 3,07,500

Cash Flow Statement

21. **Following are the balance sheet of Winter Ltd. Prepare a cash flow statement.**

Particulars	Note No.	31st March, 2024 (₹)	31st March, 2023 (₹)
I. EQUITY AND LIABILITIES			
1. **Shareholders' Funds**			
(i) Share Capital		20,000	20,000
(ii) Reserves and Surplus	1	7,200	(3,700)
2. **Non-current Liabilities**			
Long-term Borrowings	2	7,500	5,000
3. **Current Liabilities**			
(i) Trade Payables		4,400	4,600
(ii) Short-term Provisions	3	2,400	3,000
Total		41,500	28,900
II. ASSETS			
1. **Non-current Assets**			
(i) Property, Plant and Equipment and Intangible Assets			
(a) Property, Plant and Equipment	4	6,200	14,000
(b) Non-current Investments		200	1,000
2. **Current Assets**			
(i) Inventory		20,000	6,000
(ii) Trade Receivables		12,100	5,600
(iii) Cash and Cash Equivalents		3,000	2,300
Total		41,500	28,900

Notes to Accounts

Particulars	31 March, 2024 (₹)	31st March, 2023 (₹)
1. **Reserves and Surplus**		
General Reserve	2,200	—
Profit and Loss	5,000	(3,700)
	7,200	(3,700)
2. **Long-term Borrowings**		
Public Deposits	7,500	5,000
3. **Short-term Provisions**		
Provision for Taxation	2,000	2,500
Provision for Doubtful Debts	400	500
	2,400	3,000
4. **Property, Plant and Equipment**		
Land	—	10,000
Plant and Machinery	10,000	8,000
Accumulated Depreciation	(3,800)	(4,000)
	6,200	14,000

Additional Information

(i) A piece of machinery was sold for ₹ 800 during the year 2023-24. Its original cost was ₹ 2,000 and depreciation of ₹ 1,500 has been provided on it.

(ii) Non-current investments were sold at a loss of 40%.

(iii) Land was sold for ₹ 15,000.

(iv) Interest paid on public deposits amounted to ₹ 600.

Ans. Cash Used in Operating Activities = ₹ 13,480; Cash Flow from Investing Activities = ₹ 12,280;

Cash Flow from Financing Activities = ₹ 1,900

Hint Non-current investments costing ₹ 800 are sold for ₹ 480.

22. **Prepare cash flow statement of Tarun Footwears Ltd. as at 31st March, 2024 from the following balance sheets.**

Competency Based Que

Balance Sheet of Tarun Footwears Ltd.
as at 31st March, 2023 and 31st March, 2024

Particulars	Note No.	31st March, 2024 (₹)	31st March, 2023 (₹)
I. **EQUITY AND LIABILITIES**			
1. **Shareholders' Funds**			
(i) Share Capital (Equity Share Capital)		10,00,000	8,00,000
(ii) Reserve and Surplus (Statement of Profit and Loss)	1	6,00,000	5,50,000
2. **Non-current Liabilities**			
Long-term Borrowings (10% Debentures)		3,00,000	1,20,000
3. **Current Liabilities**			
(i) Short-term Borrowings (Bank Overdraft)		40,000	45,000
(ii) Trade Payables (Creditors)		80,000	65,000
(iii) Short-term Provisions	1	50,000	35,000
Total		20,70,000	16,15,000
II. **ASSETS**			
1. **Non-current Assets**			
(i) Property, Plant and Equipment and Intangible Assets			
(a) Property, Plant and Equipment	2	16,95,000	12,00,000
(b) Intangible Assets		85,000	95,000

Particulars	Note No.	31st March, 2024 (₹)	31st March, 2023 (₹)
2. **Current Assets**			
(i) Inventory		1,80,000	2,20,000
(ii) Trade Receivables		50,000	55,000
(iii) Cash and Bank Balances		60,000	45,000
Total		20,70,000	16,15,000

Notes to Accounts

Particulars	31st March, 2024 (₹)	31st March, 2023 (₹)
1. **Short-term Provisions**		
Provision for Taxation	50,000	35,000
2. **Property, Plant and Equipment**		
Plant and Machinery	17,85,000	12,70,000
(–) Accumulated Depreciation	(90,000)	(70,000)
	16,95,000	12,00,000

Additional Information

(i) A part of machine, costing ₹ 60,000, accumulated depreciation thereon being ₹ 15,000 was sold for ₹ 25,000.

(ii) Tax paid ₹ 22,000.

(iii) Interest paid on debentures ₹ 30,000.

Ans. Cash Flow from Operating Activities = ₹ 2,20,000; Cash used in Investing Activities = ₹ 5,50,000; Cash Flow from Financing Activities = ₹ 3,45,000

23. From the following balance sheet of SK Coal Ltd. as at 31st March, 2024, prepare its cash flow statement.

Competency Based Que

Particulars	Note No.	31st March, 2024 (₹)	31st March, 2023 (₹)
I. **EQUITY AND LIABILITIES**			
1. **Shareholders' Funds**			
(i) Share Capital	1	3,50,000	2,50,000
(ii) Reserve and Surplus	2	1,25,000	1,62,500
2. **Non-current Liabilities**			
Long-term Borrowings	3	1,00,000	1,25,000
3. **Current Liabilities**			
Short-term Provisions	4	25,000	12,500
Total		6,00,000	5,50,000
II. **ASSETS**			
1. **Non-current Assets**			
(i) Property, Plant and Equipment and Intangible Assets			
(a) Property, Plant and Equipment (Machinery)		2,50,000	1,50,000
(b) Non-current Investments		1,00,000	70,000
2. **Current Assets**			
(i) Inventories		75,000	1,00,000
(ii) Trade Receivables		90,000	75,000
(iii) Cash and Cash Equivalents		85,000	1,55,000
Total		6,00,000	5,50,000

Notes to Accounts

Particulars	31st March, 2024 (₹)	31st March, 2023 (₹)
1. **Share Capital**		
Equity Share Capital	3,00,000	1,50,000
12% Preference Share Capital	50,000	1,00,000
	3,50,000	2,50,000
2. **Reserves and Surplus**		
General Reserve	67,500	1,87,500
Surplus i.e. Balance in Statement of Profit and Loss	57,500	(25,000)
	1,25,000	1,62,500
3. **Long-term Borrowings**		
9% Debentures	1,00,000	1,25,000
4. **Short-term Provisions**		
Provision for Tax	25,000	12,500

Additional Information

(i) Machinery costing ₹ 50,000 on which depreciation charged was ₹ 35,000, was sold at a profit of 20% on book value. Depreciation charged during the year amounted to ₹ 35,000.

(ii) Preference shares were redeemed at par on 31st March, 2024.

(iii) Equity shares were issued on 1st April, 2023 and debentures were redeemed on 1st January, 2024.

(iv) The company declared and paid interim dividend on equity shares @ ₹ 40 per share out of general reserve. It did not propose final dividend on equity shares.

(v) Non-current investments costing ₹ 30,000 were sold at a profit of 20%.

(vi) Income tax ₹ 22,500 was provided.

Ans. Cash Flow from Operating Activities = ₹ 1,53,687; Cash Flow from Investing Activities = ₹ (1,56,000);
Cash Flow from Financing Activities = ₹ (67,687)

24. **Prepare cash flow statement from the following balance sheet.**

Balance Sheet of Junaid Ltd.
as at 31st March, 2024 and 2023

Particulars	Note No.	31st March, 2024 (₹)	31st March, 2023 (₹)
I. EQUITY AND LIABILITIES			
1. **Shareholders' Funds**			
(i) Share Capital		2,25,000	2,25,000
(ii) Reserve and Surplus	1	2,39,000	1,78,000
2. **Non-current Liabilities**			
Long-term Borrowings	2	85,000	—
3. **Current Liabilities**			
(i) Trade Payables		54,500	1,01,500
(ii) Short-term Provisions	3	17,500	20,000
Total		6,21,000	5,24,500
II. ASSETS			
1. **Non-current Assets**			
(i) Property, Plant and Equipment and Intangible Assets			
(a) Property, Plant and Equipment	4	1,60,000	2,00,000
(b) Intangible Asset (Goodwill)		30,000	25,000

Particulars	Note No.	31st March, 2024 (₹)	31st March, 2023 (₹)
2. **Current Assets**			
(i) Current Investments		35,000	39,000
(ii) Inventory		85,000	1,07,500
(iii) Trade Receivables		2,27,500	1,05,000
(iv) Cash and Bank Balances		83,500	48,000
Total		6,21,000	5,24,500

Notes to Accounts

Particulars	31st March, 2024 (₹)	31st March, 2024 (₹)
1. **Reserve and Surplus**		
Retained Earnings	2,39,000	1,78,000
2. **Long-term Borrwings**		
Mortgage Loan	85,000	—
3. **Short-term Provisions**		
Provision for Taxation	17,500	20,000
4. **Property, Plant and Equipment**		
Land	50,000	1,20,000
Plant and Machinery	1,10,000	80,000
	1,60,000	2,00,000

Additional Information

(i) Gain on sale of land ₹ 30,000.

(ii) Depreciation was provided @ 10% on last year balance.

(iii) Interest paid on mortgage loan was ₹ 15,000.

(iv) Provision for income tax made during the year 2023-24 was ₹ 18,000.

Ans. Cash used in Operating Activities = ₹ 95,500; Cash Flow from Investing Activities = ₹ 57,000; Cash Flow from Financing Activities = ₹ 70,000

25. You are required to prepare a cash flow statement (as per AS-3) for the year 2023-24 from the following balance sheets.

Balance Sheets of Janaki India Ltd.
as at 31st March, 2024 and 31st March, 2023

Particulars	Note No.	31st March, 2024 (₹)	31st March, 2023 (₹)
I. **EQUITY AND LIABILITIES**			
1. **Shareholders' Funds**			
(i) Share Capital (Equity Share Capital)		1,50,000	1,00,000
(ii) Reserves and Surplus (Statement of Profit and Loss)		60,000	35,000
2. **Non-current Liabilities**			
(i) Long-term Borrowings (8% Debentures)		75,000	60,000
3. **Current Liabilities**			
(i) Short-term Borrowings (Bank Overdraft)		9,500	2,500
(ii) Trade Payables (Creditors)		40,500	40,000
(iii) Short-term Provisions	1	41,000	30,800
Total		3,76,000	2,68,300
II. **ASSETS**			
1. **Non-current Assets**			
(i) Property, Plant and Equipment and Intangible Assets			
(a) Property, Plant and Equipment	2	1,02,100	91,500
(ii) Non-current Investment		65,000	60,000

Particulars	Note No.	31st March, 2024 (₹)	31st March, 2023 (₹)
2. **Current Assets**			
(i) Inventories		70,750	62,500
(ii) Trade Receivables		32,300	32,250
(iii) Cash and Bank Balances		1,05,850	22,050
Total		3,76,000	2,68,300

Notes to Accounts

Particulars	31st March, 2024 (₹)	31st March, 2023 (₹)
1. **Short-term Provisions**		
Provision for Taxation	40,000	30,000
Provision for Doubtful Debts	1,000	800
	41,000	30,800
2. **Property, Plant and Equipment** (Tangible)		
Plant and Machinery	1,21,500	1,11,500
(–) Accumulated Depreciation	(19,400)	(20,000)
	1,02,100	91,500

Additional Information

During the year 2023-24

(i) A part of the machine was sold for ₹ 10,500 at a profit of ₹ 2,000.

(ii) The company charged ₹ 1,500 as depreciation on its plant and machinery.

(iii) New debentures were issued on 31st March, 2024, at a discount of 10%.

(iv) Interest of ₹ 4,800 paid on debentures.

(v) Contingent Liability

	31st March, 2024 (₹)	31st March, 2023 (₹)
Proposed Dividend	25,000	20,000

Ans. Cash Flow from Operating Activities = ₹ 53,200; Cash used in Investing Activities = ₹ 15,100; Cash Flow from Financing Activities = ₹ 45,700

26. **Prepare cash flow statement from the following balance sheet of Anupriya Designer Ltd.**

Balance Sheet of Anupriya Designer Ltd.
as at 2024 and 2023

Particulars	Note No.	31st March, 2024 (₹)	31st March, 2023 (₹)
I. EQUITY AND LIABILITIES			
1. **Shareholders' Funds**			
(i) Share Capital		3,00,000	2,25,000
(ii) Reserve and Surplus	1	50,000	25,000
2. **Non-current Liabilities**			
Long-term Borrowings	2	85,000	55,000
3. **Current Liabilities**			
(i) Trade Payables		25,000	13,000
(ii) Short-term Provisions	3	22,000	12,000
Total		4,82,000	3,30,000
II. ASSETS			
1. **Non-current Assets**			
(i) Property, Plant and Equipment and Intangible Assets			
(a) Property, Plant and Equipment	4	1,65,000	90,000
(b) Intangible Assets (Goodwill)		22,000	25,000

Particulars	Note No.	31st March, 2024 (₹)	31st March, 2023 (₹)
2. **Current Assets**			
(i) Inventory		85,000	40,000
(ii) Trade Receivables		1,40,000	1,30,000
(iii) Cash and Bank Balances		70,000	48,000
Total		4,82,000	3,30,000

Notes to Accounts

Particulars	31st March, 2024 (₹)	31st March, 2023 (₹)
1. **Reserve and Surplus**		
Balance in Profit and Loss	50,000	25,000
2. **Long-term Borrowing**		
8% debentures	85,000	55,000
3. **Short-term Provisions**		
Provision for Taxation	22,000	12,000
4. **Property, Plant and Equipment**		
Plant and Machinery	2,20,000	1,25,000
(–) Provision for Depreciation	(55,000)	(35,000)
	1,65,000	90,000

Additional Information

(i) A piece of machine costing ₹ 40,000 (accumulated depreciation thereon ₹ 8,000) was sold for ₹ 30,000.

(ii) Provisions of ₹ 15,000 was made during current year.

(iii) Debentures were issued at the beginning of the year.

(iv) Proposed dividend for year 2022-23 was ₹ 24,000 and for the year 2023-24 was ₹ 35,000.

Ans. Cash Flow from Operating Activities = ₹ 52,800; Cash used in Investing Activities = ₹ 1,05,000; Cash Flow from Financing Activities = ₹ 74,200

27. Following is the balance sheets of Vande Ltd.

Balance Sheet of Vande Ltd.
as at 31st March, 2024

Particulars	Note No.	31st March, 2024 (₹)	31st March, 2023 (₹)
I. **EQUITY AND LIABILITIES**			
1. **Shareholders' Funds**			
(i) Share Capital	1	60,000	55,000
(ii) Reserves and Surplus	2	12,800	7,000
2. **Current Liabilities**			
(i) Trade Payables		12,200	8,000
(ii) Short-term Provisions	3	4,500	4,000
Total		85,500	74,000
II. **ASSETS**			
1. **Non-current Assets**			
(i) Property, Plant and Equipment and Intangible Assets			
(a) Property, Plant and Equipment		37,000	28,000
(b) Intangible Assets (Goodwill)		12,000	11,500

Particulars	Note No.	31st March, 2024 (₹)	31st March, 2023 (₹)
2. **Current Assets**			
(i) Current Investments		1,000	700
(ii) Inventory		15,200	10,000
(iii) Trade Receivables		15,700	15,700
(iv) Cash and Cash Equivalents		8,600	8,100
Total		85,500	74,000

Notes to Accounts

Particulars	31st March, 2024 (₹)	31st March, 2023 (₹)
1. **Share Capital**		
Equity Share Capital	50,000	40,000
10% Preference Share Capital	10,000	15,000
	60,000	55,000
2. **Reserves and Surplus**		
Securities Premium	1,000	—
General Reserve	7,000	4,000
Surplus i.e. Balance in Statement of Profit and Loss	4,800	3,000
	12,800	7,000
3. **Short-term Provision**		
Provision for Tax	5,000	4,000

Additional Information

(i) Proposed dividend for the years ended 31st March, 2024 and 2023 were ₹ 6,000 and ₹ 5,000 respectively.
(ii) A machine costing ₹ 5,000 (depreciation provided thereon ₹ 3,000) was sold for ₹ 1,000.
(iii) Depreciation charged during the year was ₹ 2,000.
(iv) Interim dividend paid ₹ 2,000. (v) Income tax paid ₹ 3,500.

Prepare a cash flow statement for the year ended 31st March, 2024, complying with AS-3 (Revised).

Ans. Cash Flow from Operating Activities = ₹ 15,800; Cash used in Investing Activities = ₹ 12,500; Cash used in Financing Activities = ₹ 2,500

28. From the following balance sheet of XYZ Ltd. prepare a cash flow statement

Particulars	Note No.	31st March, 2024 (₹)	31st March, 2023 (₹)
I. **EQUITY AND LIABILITIES**			
1. **Shareholders' Funds**			
(i) Share Capital		15,000	12,000
(ii) Reserves and Surplus		17,800	7,500
2. **Non-current Liabilities**			
Long-term Borrowings	1	—	5,000
3. **Current Liabilities**			
(i) Trade Payables		3,150	6,700
(ii) Short-term Provisions (Provision for Tax)		4,200	3,000
Total		40,150	34,200
II. **ASSETS**			
1. **Non-current Assets**			
(a) Property, Plant and Equipment and Intangible Assets			
(i) Property, Plant and Equipment	2	20,800	14,000
(ii) Intangible Assets	3	3,500	2,000

Particulars	Note No.	31st March, 2024 (₹)	31st March, 2023 (₹)
2. **Current Assets**			
(i) Inventory		10,500	12,000
(ii) Trade Receivables		3,350	3,700
(iii) Cash and Cash Equivalents		2,000	2,500
Total		40,150	34,200

Notes to Accounts

Particulars	31st March, 2024 (₹)	31st March, 2023 (₹)
1. **Long-term Borrowings**		
15% Debentures	—	5,000
2. **Tangible Assets**		
Building	8,000	10,000
Plant and Machinery	12,800	4,000
	20,800	14,000
3. **Intangible Assets**		
Goodwill	3,500	2,000

Additional Information

	31st March, 2024 (₹)	31st March, 2023 (₹)
(i) Contingent Liability Proposed Dividend	1,500	1,200

(ii) Depreciation of ₹ 1,000 was provided on plant and machinery.

(iii) Gain on sale of a part of building ₹ 2,500.

(iv) Debentures were redeemed on 1st April, 2023.

(v) Provision for tax made during the year ₹ 5,000.

Ans. Cash Flow from Operating Activities = ₹ 9,500 ; Cash used in Investing Activities = ₹ 6,800; Cash used in Financing Activities = ₹ 3,200

29. Prepare cash flow statement from the following balance sheets

Balance Sheet of Solemon Ltd.
as at 31st March, 2024 and 31st March, 2023

Particulars	Note No.	31st March, 2024 (₹)	31st March, 2023 (₹)
I. **EQUITY AND LIABILITIES**			
1. **Shareholders' Funds**			
(i) Share Capital		6,00,000	4,80,000
(ii) Reserve and Surplus	1	(1,40,000)	(80,000)
2. **Non-current Liabilities**			
Long-term Borrowings	2	2,20,000	1,70,000
3. **Current Liabilities**			
(i) Short-term Borrowings (Cash Credit)		34,000	28,000
(ii) Trade Payables		55,000	67,000
(iii) Other Current Liabilities (Outstanding Expenses)		18,000	15,000
Total		7,87,000	6,80,000
II. **ASSETS**			
1. **Non-Current Assets**			
(i) Property, Plant and Equipment and Intangible Assets			
(a) Property, Plant and Equipment		5,20,000	4,10,000
(ii) Non-current Investment		56,000	46,000

Particulars	Note No.	31st March, 2024 (₹)	31st March, 2023 (₹)
2. **Current Assets**			
(i) Current Investment		32,000	35,000
(ii) Inventory		60,000	1,04,000
(iii) Trade Receivables		37,000	40,000
(iv) Cash and Cash Equivalents		82,000	45,000
Total		7,87,000	6,80,000

Notes to Accounts

Particulars	31st March, 2024 (₹)	31st March, 2023 (₹)
1. **Reserve and Surplus**		
Profit and Loss Balance	(1,40,000)	(80,000)
2. **Long-term Borrowings**		
9% Debentures	2,20,000	1,70,000

Additional Information

A piece of machinery costing ₹ 65,000 on which depreciation charged was ₹ 34,000 was sold for ₹ 26,000. During the year, machinery was purchased for ₹ 2,50,000. Share issue expenses of 10,000 were incurred and written-off from the statement of profit and loss in 2023-24.

Ans. Cash Flow from Operating Activities = ₹ 1,17,300; Cash used in Investing Activities = ₹ 2,34,000; Cash Flow from Financing Activities = ₹ 1,50,700

30. **From the given balance sheet of Raman House Ltd., prepare cash flow statement.** **Competency Based Que**

Balance Sheet of Raman House Ltd.
as at 31st March, 2024 and 31st March, 2023

Particulars	Note No.	31st March, 2024 (₹)	31st March, 2023 (₹)
I. EQUITY AND LIABILITIES			
1. **Shareholders' Funds**			
(i) Share Capital		3,75,000	3,00,000
(ii) Reserve and Surplus	1	96,000	(20,000)
2. **Non-current Liabilities**			
Long-term Borrowing	2	1,50,000	1,00,000
3. **Current Liabilities**			
(i) Trade Payables		60,000	35,000
(ii) Short-term Provisions	3	15,000	10,000
Total		6,96,000	4,25,000
II. ASSETS			
1. **Non-current Assets**			
(i) Property, Plant and Equipment and Intangible Assets			
(a) Property, Plant and Equipment	4	3,52,000	1,50,000
(b) Non-current Investment		55,000	45,000
2. **Current Assets**			
(i) Current Investment		40,000	35,000
(ii) Inventory		1,20,000	1,10,000
(iii) Trade Receivables		37,000	40,000
(iv) Cash and Bank Balances		92,000	45,000
Total		6,96,000	4,25,000

Notes to Accounts

Particulars	31st March, 2024 (₹)	31st March, 2023 (₹)
1. **Reserve and Surplus**		
Securities Premium	50,000	—
Profit and Loss Balance	46,000	(20,000)
	96,000	(20,000)
2. **Long-term Borrowings**		
12% debentures	1,50,000	1,00,000
3. **Short-term Provisions**		
Provision for Depreciation	5,000	2,000
Provision for Taxation	10,000	8,000
	15,000	10,000
4. **Property, Plant and Equipment**		
Plant and Machinery	3,92,000	1,78,000
(–) Provision for Depreciation	(40,000)	(28,000)
	3,52,000	1,50,000

Additional Information

(i) A piece of machine costing ₹ 40,000 (accumulated depreciation thereon ₹ 12,000) was sold for ₹ 22,000.
(ii) Non-current Investment costing ₹ 12,000 were sold at a profit of 20%.
(iii) Interim dividend paid during the year ₹ 22,000.
(iv) Additional debentures were issued on 1st October, 2023.

Ans. Cash Flow from Operating Activities = ₹ 1,53,600; Cash used in Investing Activities = ₹ 2,39,600; Cash Flow from Financing Activities = ₹ 1,38,000

Missing Information

31. **Complete the missing figures from the given notes to accounts and cash flow statement of Surbhi Garments Ltd.** **Competency Based Que**

Particulars	31st March, 2024 (₹)	31st March, 2023 (₹)
1. **Reserve and Surplus**		
General Reserve	11,00,000	7,00,000
Profit and Loss Balance	4,00,000	(1,50,000)
2. **Long-term Borrowings**		
Public Deposits	3,50,000	—
3. **Short-term Provision**		
Income Tax Provision	1,10,000	1,30,000

Additional Information

(i) Depreciation written-off on plant and machinery ₹ 1,20,000.
(ii) Company paid interim dividend during the year ₹ 1,40,000.
(iii) Public deposits was taken on 1st October, 2023 @ 10% p.a. Interest has been paid upto date.

Cash Flow Statement
as at 31st March, 2024

Particulars		Amt (₹)
A. **Cash Flow from Operating Activities**		
Net Profit before Tax (WN 1)		...
Adjustments for Non-cash and Non-operating Items		
(+) Depreciation	...	
Interest Paid	...	...
Operating Profit before Working Capital Changes		...
(+) Decrease in Current Assets		
Trade Receivables	...	
Increase in Current Liabilities	...	
Trade Payables	1,40,000	2,30,000
(–) Increase in Current Assets		
Inventory		(3,60,000)
Cash Generated from Operations		...
(–) Tax Paid		(...)
Net Cash Flow from Operating Activities		...
B. **Cash Flow from Investing Activities**		
Purchase of Plant and Machinery	...	
Net Cash Used in Inventing Activities		...

Particulars		Amt (₹)
C. **Cash Flow from Financing Activities**		
Raising of Public Deposits	...	
Interim Dividend Paid	...	
Interest Paid	...	
Net Cash used in Financing Activities		...
Net Increase in Cash and Cash Equivalents (A + B + C)		4,40,000
(+) Cash and Cash Equivalents in the Beginning		...
Cash and Cash Equivalents at the End		7,40,000

32. **Complete the missing figures from the given notes to accounts and cash flow statement of Narmada Ltd.**

Competency Based Que

Particulars	31st March, 2024 (₹)	31st March, 2023 (₹)
1. **Share Capital**		
Equity Share Capital	4,00,000	3,50,000
Preference Share Capital	2,00,000	1,40,000
	6,00,000	4,90,000
2. **Reserve and Surplus**		
General Reserve	70,000	90,000
Profit and Loss Balance	1,80,000	1,10,000
	2,50,000	2,00,000

Additional Information

(i) A machine book values ₹ 80,000 was sold for ₹ 60,000 and dividend was paid ₹ 20,000.

(ii) Debentures of ₹ 40,000 were redeemed during the year. Interest paid on debentures amounted to ₹ 15,000.

Cash Flow Statement
as at 31st March, 2024

Particulars		Amt (₹)
A. **Cash Flow from Operating Activities**		
Net Profit before Tax (WN 1)		...
Adjustments for Non-cash and Non-operating Items		
(+) Interest on Debentures	...	
Loss on Sale of Machinery	...	...
Operating Profit before Working Capital Changes		...
(−) Increase in Current Assets		
Inventory	(30,000)	
Trade Receivables	...	(65,000)
Net Cash Flow from Operating Activities		...
B. **Cash Flow from Investing Activities**		
Sale of Machine	...	
Purchase of Machine	...	
Net Cash Used in Inventing Activities		...
C. **Cash Flow from Financing Activities**		
Issue of Equity Share Capital	...	
Issue of Preference Share Capital	...	
Redemption of Debentures	(...)	
Interest Dividend Paid	(...)	
Interest Paid on Debentures	(...)	
Net Cash Flow from Financing Activities		...
Net Increase/Decrease in Cash and Cash Equivalent		...
(+) Opening Cash Equivalents		70,000
Closing Cash Equivalents		90,000

Theoretical Questions

Short Answer Type Questions

1. **How the various activities are classified (as per AS-3 revised) while preparing cash flow statement?**

Ans. (i) **Cash Flow from Operating Activities** Operating activities are the **principal revenue producing activities** of the enterprise and other activities that are not investing or financing activities. Cash flows from operating activities being the principal revenue producing activities of the enterprise, generally result from the transactions and other events that determine the net profit or loss.

(ii) **Cash Flow from Investing Activities** As per AS-3, investing activities are the activities related to acquisition and disposal of long-term assets and other investments, not included in cash equivalents. These activities include transactions involving purchase and sale of the long-term productive assets like machinery, land and building, etc which are not held for resale.

(iii) **Cash Flow from Financing Activities** Financing activities are the activities which result in change in the size and composition of the owner's capital (including preference share capital) and borrowings (including debentures) of the enterprise from other sources. It includes proceeds from issue of shares or other similar instruments, issue of debentures, loans, bonds, other short-term or long-term borrowings and repayment of amount borrowed.

2. **Explain the terms 'cash flows.'** **CBSE 2019; NCERT**

Ans. Cash flows are inflows and outflows of cash and cash equivalents which imply movement of cash in and out from non-cash items.

Receipt of cash from a non-cash item is termed as **cash inflow** while cash payment in respect of such items is termed as **cash outflow**.

3. Explain the major cash inflow and outflows from investing activities. NCERT

Ans. Cash Inflows

(i) Proceeds from sale of fixed assets.
(ii) Proceeds from sale of investments (Non-current and current other than marketable securities).
(iii) Interest received.
(iv) Dividend received.
(v) Rent received (Whether short-term or long-term).

Cash Outflows

(i) Purchase of fixed assets.
(ii) Purchase of investments (Non-current and current other than marketable securities).
(iii) Income tax paid (Related to investing activities only).
(iv) Loans and advanced granted (Whether short-term or long-term).
(v) Brokerage paid on purchase of investment.

4. Explain the major cash inflows and outflows from financing activities. NCERT

Ans. Cash Inflows

(i) Proceeds from issue of shares for cash.
(ii) Proceeds from issue of debentures for cash.
(iii) Proceeds from long-term borrowings.
(iv) Securities premium reserve received.
(v) Interest received on calls-in-arrears.
(vi) Increase in balance of bank overdraft or cash credit account.

Cash Outflows

(i) Payment of loans.
(ii) Redemption of preference shares, debentures for cash.
(iii) Buy-back of equity shares.
(iv) Payment of dividends
(v) Payment of interest on loans and debentures
(vi) Premium paid on redemption of preference shares and debentures
(vii) Income tax paid (related to financing activities only)
(viii) Loans repaid
(ix) Brokerage and underwriting commission paid on issue of shares and debentures
(x) Decrease in balance of bank overdraft or cash credit account.

Objective Questions

Multiple Choice Questions (MCQs)

1. What is highly liquid investment?

(a) Cash convertible investment
(b) Short-term investment
(c) Cash equivalents
(d) None of the above

2. Short-term highly liquid investments qualify as cash equivalents if they are realisable into know amounts of cash from the date of acquisition within a period of CBSE 2025

(a) 6 months or less
(b) 9 months or less
(c) 12 months or less (d) 3 months or less

3. Which of the following item is not included in cash and cash equivalents? CBSE 2025

(a) Trade receivables
(b) Demand deposits with bank
(c) Short-term marketable securities
(d) Cheques in hand

4. Provision for tax is .... to net profit in operating activities.

(a) added (b) deducted
(c) No treatment (d) None of these

5. Cash flow from operating activity means cash flow from business operation because

(a) cash flow from operating activity is outside the business
(b) cash flow from operating activity is taken from investment
(c) cash flow from cash inflow and outflow from operating activity are the core activity
(d) Both (a) and (c)

6. Following is the extract from the balance sheet of ABC Ltd. Competency Based Que

Particulars	31st March, 2024 (₹)	31st March, 2023 (₹)
Surplus i.e. Balance in Statement of Profit and Loss	4,50,000	3,00,000
Proposed Dividend	1,75,000	1,50,000

Calculate net profit before tax and extraordinary items.

(a) ₹ 3,00,000 (b) ₹ 1,25,000
(c) ₹ 3,25,000 (d) ₹ 1,75,000

7. Provision for depreciation on plant

Opening balance ₹ 60,000, closing balance ₹ 65,000.

An item of plant costing ₹ 20,000 having book value of ₹ 14,000 was sold for ₹ 18,000 during the year.

Calculate the amount of depreciation to be added back to net profit before tax and extraordinary items.

Competency Based Que

(a) ₹ 6,000 (b) ₹ 9,000
(c) ₹ 5,000 (d) ₹ 11,000

8. **Which of the following statements is/are correct?**

Competency Based Que

(i) Cash flow statement is not a replacement of fund flow statement.
(ii) Cash flow statement is a substitute of income statement.
(iii) Cash flow statement records only cash items.
(iv) Cash flow statement records only cash equivalents items.

Codes

(a) Only (i) (b) Both (ii) and (iii)
(c) Only (iv) (d) All of these

9. **Which of the following will be added while calculating cashflow from operating activities?**

(a) Interest paid on debentures
(b) Depreciation
(c) Amortisation (d) All of the above

10. **ABC Ltd. made a profit of ₹ 60,000 after considering the following items** **Competency Based Que**

(i) Depreciation written-off	₹ 8,000
(ii) Interest paid	₹ 4,000
(iii) Gain on sale of machine	₹ 6,000

Operating profit before working capital changes will be

(a) ₹ 78,000 (b) ₹ 66,000
(c) ₹ 72,000 (d) ₹ 80,000

11. **Which of the following transactions will result in no inflow of cash?**

(a) Cash withdrawn from bank ₹ 6,000
(b) Deposit ₹ 10,000 as short-term deposits
(c) Purchase of marketable securities ₹ 6,000
(d) All of the above

12. **Which of the following is a limitation of cash flow statement?**

(a) There is possibility of window dressing
(b) It igneous non-cash transactions
(c) It is historical in nature (d) All of the above

13. **Which accounting standard is prescribed by Institute of Chartered Accountants of India?**

(a) AS-4 (b) AS-26 (c) AS-3 (d) AS-25

14.

Particulars	Purchased (₹)	Sold (₹)
Investments	2,00,000	1,80,000
Goodwill	3,00,000	—

From the above information, 'cash flows from investing activities' will be **CBSE 2024; Competency Based Que**

(a) inflow ₹ 3,20,000
(b) outflow ₹ 3,20,000
(c) outflow ₹ 20,000 (d) inflow ₹ 20,000

15. **Which of the following will be deducted while calculating cash flow from operating activities?**

(a) Gain on sale of furniture
(b) Increase in general reserve
(c) Loss on sale of machine
(d) Amortisation

16. **If balance in securities premium is increased, how it is treated while preparing cash flow statement?**

(a) Added while calculating net profit before tax
(b) Shown as cash inflow under financing activities
(c) Shown under investing activities
(d) Both (a) and (b)

17. **Insurance claim received by Iye Ltd. of ₹ 2,00,000 for loss of machinery due to earthquake will be recorded in cash flow statement in which of the following manner?**

Competency Based Que

(a) Added under operating activity as extraordinary items and subtracted from operating activity also
(b) Subtracting under operating activity as extraordinary items and added to operating activities also
(c) Added under operating activity as extraordinary items and outflow under investing activity
(d) Subtracted under operating activity and inflow under investing activity

18. **If a machine original cost of which is ₹ 50,000 and accumulated depreciation on which is ₹ 18,000, sold for ₹ 35,000 then while preparing cash flow statements, its effect on cash will be ....** **Competency Based Que**

(a) cash flow from financing activities ₹ 35,000
(b) cash flow from financing activities ₹ 15,000
(c) cash flow from investing activities ₹ 35,000
(d) cash flow from investing activities ₹ 15,000

19. **For a company manufacturing garments, procurement of raw material, incurrence of manufacturing expenses, sale of garments are classified .... activities.**

CBSE 2020 (M)

(a) operating (b) investing
(c) financing (d) None of these

20. **Which of the following transactions will result in cash outflow from operating activities?** **CBSE 2024 C**

(a) Payment to creditors
(b) Proceeds from sale of investments
(c) Dividend received by a non-finance company
(d) Depreciation charged on furniture

21. Which of the following statements is/are incorrect? Competency Based Que

(i) Debentures issued for consideration other than cash are shown as inflow under financing activity.

(ii) Depreciation is added to net profit before tax and extraordinary items, they being non-cash expense.

Codes

(a) Only (i) (b) Only (ii)
(c) Both (i) and (ii) (d) None of these

22. X Ltd. has balance in provision for tax account of ₹ 25,000 and ₹ 37,500 as on 31st March, 2019 and 2020. It made a provision of tax during the year ₹ 32,500. The amount of tax paid during the year was Competency Based Que

(a) ₹ 25,000 (b) ₹ 30,000 (c) ₹ 20,000 (d) ₹ 37,500

23. Pink Ltd. has the machinery opening balance of ₹ 35,00,000 and closing balance of ₹ 47,60,000. Depreciation for the year was ₹ 4,00,000. Calculate purchase value of machinery. Competency Based Que

(a) ₹ (35,00,000) (b) ₹ (16,60,000)
(c) ₹ 47,60,000 (d) ₹ (8,30,000)

24. City Pulse Ltd. took a loan from financing company in the year 2016 for ₹ 25,00,000 and balance at the starting of 2017 financial year, i.e. on 1st April, 2017 was ₹ 15,00,000. What kind of activity and amount has been transacted? Competency Based Que

(a) ₹ (10,00,000) has been inflow, i.e. amount is paid to financing company
(b) ₹ 10,00,000 has been outflow, i.e. amount is paid to financing company
(c) ₹ 10,00,000 has been outflow, i.e. amount is received from financing company
(d) None of the above

25. Surya Ltd. had investment of ₹ 4,08,000 as on 31st March, 2016 and investment of ₹ 3,36,000 as on 31st March, 2017. During the year, Surya Ltd. sold 80% of it's investment being held in the beginning of period at a profit of ₹ 1,34,400. Determine cash flow from investing activity. Competency Based Que

(a) ₹ 5,42,400 (b) ₹ 2,06,400
(c) ₹ 6,10,000 (d) None of these

26. While computing cash from operating activities, which of the following item(s) will be added to the net profit? CBSE SQP 2025

(i) Decrease in value of inventory
(ii) Increase in share capital
(iii) Increase in the value of trade receivables
(iv) Increase in the amount of outstanding expenses

Codes

(a) Only (i) (b) (i) and (ii)
(c) (i) and (iii) (d) (i) and (iv)

27. Which of the following statements is incorrect? CBSE SQP 2025; Competency Based Que

(a) Investments in shares are excluded from cash equivalents unless they are in substantial cash equivalents
(b) Short-term marketable securities which can be readily converted into cash are treated as cash equivalents
(c) In case of a financial enterprise, interest received and dividend received are classified as operating activities while dividend paid and interest paid are financing activities
(d) Dividend tax, i.e. tax paid on dividend should be classified as financing activity along with dividend paid

28. What will be the effect of transaction 'payment of employee benefit expenses' on the cash flow statement?

(a) Outflow from operating activities CBSE 2024
(b) Outflow from investing activities
(c) Outflow from financing activities
(d) No effect on cash flow

29. Opening balance and closing balance of investment was ₹ 10,00,000 and ₹ 20,00,000 respectively for Vimal Ltd. Half of the investment held in the beginning of the year were sold at 20% profit. Calculate purchase value of investment? Competency Based Que

(a) ₹ (10,00,000) (b) ₹ (15,00,000)
(c) ₹ (20,00,000) (d) ₹ (6,00,000)

30. Sale of patents of ₹ 50,00,000 will result in CBSE 2024 C

(a) cash inflow of ₹ 50,00,000 from financing activities
(b) cash outflow of ₹ 50,00,000 from financing activities
(c) cash outflow of ₹ 50,00,000 from investing activities
(d) cash inflow of ₹ 50,00,000 from investing activities

31. While preparing cash flow statement, if net cash flow from operating, investing and financing activities is negative the same is .... to opening cash balance to obtain .... cash balance. CBSE 2020 (M)

(a) deducted, opening (b) deducted, closing
(c) Neither (a) nor (b) (d) None of these

32. Which of the following transactions are shown under financing activities while preparing cash flow statement? CBSE 2023

(i) Issue of equity shares
(ii) Cash received from debtors
(iii) Redemption of debentures
(iv) Cash paid against trade payables

Codes

(a) Only (i) (b) (i) and (ii)
(c) (ii) and (iii) (d) (i), (ii) and (iv)

33. Income tax paid is classified under CBSE 2024 C

(a) operating activities (b) investing activities
(c) financing activities (d) cash and cash equivalents

34. **'Interest received on investments' will come under which type of activity from the following, while preparing cash flow statement of a non-financial enterprise.** CBSE 2023

(a) Investing activity (b) Financing activity
(c) Operating activity (d) Both (b) and (c)

35. **'Dividend paid' by a financial enterprise will come under which kind of activity from the following while preparing cash flow statement.** CBSE 2023

(a) Operating activity (b) Investing activity
(c) Financing activity (d) Both (b) and (c)

36. **X Ltd. purchased machinery of ₹ 5,00,000 issuing a cheque of ₹ 1,25,000 and 10% debentures of ₹ 3,75,000. In the cash flow statement the transaction will be shown as** Competency Based Que

(a) investing activity outflow ₹ 5,00,000, financing activity inflow ₹ 3,75,000 as receipt of debentures
(b) investing activity outflow ₹ 1,25,000
(c) financing activity inflow ₹ 3,75,000
(d) None of the above

37. **Paid ₹ 7,00,000 to acquire shares in KL Ltd. and received a dividend of ₹ 20,000 after acquisition. These transactions will results in** CBSE 2020; Competency Based Que

(a) cash used in investing activities ₹ 7,00,000
(b) cash generated from financing activities ₹ 7,20,000
(c) cash generated from financing activities ₹ 6,80,000
(d) cash used in investing activities ₹ 6,80,000

38. **Shri Niwas Ltd. has the opening balance of furniture ₹ 4,00,000 and closing balance ₹ 4,20,000 and depreciation opening and closing balance ₹ 1,00,000 and ₹ 1,10,000. During the year, a furniture costing ₹ 40,000 with its accumulated depreciation of ₹ 24,000 was sold for ₹ 20,000. Calculate purchase value of furniture.** Competency Based Que

(a) ₹ 40,000 (b) ₹ 50,000
(c) ₹ (60,000) (d) ₹ 76,000

Assertion-Reason

Direction (Q.No. 39 to 47) *Read the following Assertion (A) and Reason (R) and choose the correct alternative from the following*

Alternatives

(a) Both Assertion (A) and Reason (R) are true and Reason (R) is the correct explanation of Assertion (A)
(b) Both Assertion (A) and Reason (R) are true, but Reason (R) is not the correct explanation of Assertion (A)
(c) Assertion (A) is true, but Reason (R) is false
(d) Assertion (A) is false, but Reason (R) is true

39. **Assertion** (A) Cash deposited into bank will not result in flow of cash and cash equivalents.

Reason (R) Cash deposited into bank is movement between cash and cash equivalents.

40. **Assertion** (A) XYZ Limited purchased a machine on hire purchase installment. Payment of installment will be classified as investing activity.

Reason (R) Principal amount of hire purchase installment will be shown as investing activity and interest will be classified as financing activity.

41. **Assertion** (A) Payment of income tax is an operating activity.

Reason (R) Tax paid on gain of sale of building is an investing activity.

42. **Assertion** (A) Increase in provision for doubtful debt will not result in flow of cash.

Reason (R) It is a non-cash item.

43. **Assertion** (A) Issue of bonus shares are shown as inflow under financing activity.

Reason (R) Bonus shows are issued out of reserves, hence there is no inflow of cash.

44. **Assertion** (A) An investment normally qualifies as a cash equivalent only when its maturity is of three months or less from the date of acquisition.

Reason (R) There is significant risk of change in value.

45. **Assertion** (A) Purchase and sale of shares on behalf of customers is an operating activity.

Reason (R) They are being purchased for their customers.

46. **Assertion** (A) An inflow or outflow between components of cash and cash equivalent is not considered.

Reason (R) It is called management of cash.

47. **Assertion** (A) Cash flow ignores two basic accounting principles *viz* 'full disclosure' and 'accrual concept'.

Reason (R) It facilitates the management for short-term plans.

Two Statements Based MCQs

Direction (Q.No. 48 to 56) *Read the following statements carefully and choose the correct alternative*

Alternatives

(a) Statement I is correct and Statement II is incorrect
(b) Statement II is correct and Statement I is incorrect
(c) Both the statements are correct
(d) Both the statements are incorrect

48. **Statement I** Increase in inventory should be deducted while calculating cash flow from operating activity.

Statement II Decrease creditors should be added while calculating cash flow from operating activity.

49. **Statement I** Proposed dividend for previous year is added for calculating net profit before tax.

Statement II Proposed dividend in current year is shown as outflow of cash under financing activity.

50. **Statement I** 'Shree Ltd.' was carrying on a business of packaging in Delhi and earned good profits in the past years. The company wanted to expand its business and required additional funds. To meet its requirements, the company issued equity shares of ₹ 30,00,000. It purchased a computerised machine of ₹ 20,00,000. During the current year the net profit of the company was ₹ 15,00,000.

Cash flows from operating, investing and financing activities from the above transactions will be ₹ 15,00,000, (₹ 20,00,000), ₹ 30,00,000 respectively.

Statement II The patents of X Ltd. increased from ₹ 3,00,000 in 2021-22 to ₹ 3,50,000 in 2022-23. It will be taken as purchase of patents of 50,000 and will be shown under cash outflow from investing activities. **CBSE SQP 2025**

51. **Statement I** Snow Limited earned a profit of ₹ 2,00,000 after charging depreciation of ₹ 50,000 on machinery. So, operating profit before working capital changes would be ₹ 2,50,000.

Statement II Depreciation is added back to net profit as it does not result in any cash flow. **CBSE 2025**

52. **Statement I** Debentures issued as collateral security will result in inflow of cash.

Statement II Purchase of marketable securities will result in no flow of cash.

53. **Statement I** Decrease in bank overdraft is shown under financing activities.

Statement II Interest paid on bank overdraft is shown under financing activities.

54. **Statement I** Cash paid for acquistion of intangible activities is shown under investing activities.

Statement II Cash received from sale of debentures of other company is shown under investing activities for a non-financial company.

55. **Statement I** Payment of preliminary expenses is shown under financing activities of company.

Statement II Cash advances and loans made to third parties are shown under investing activities.

56. **Statement I** Financing activities relate to long-term funds or capital of an enterprise.

Statement II Separate disclosure of cash flows arising from financing activities is important because they represent the extent to which expenditures have been made for resources intended to generate future income and cash flows. **CBSE 2024**

Matching

57. Match the following

Column I	Column I
A. Increase in cash credit	(i) Investing activity
B. Sale of machine by a dealer of machines	(ii) Operating activity
C. Short-term deposits	(iii) Cash and cash equivalents
D. Received rent on property held as an investment	(iv) Financing activity

Codes

	A	B	C	D		A	B	C	D
(a)	(iv)	(ii)	(iii)	(i)	(b)	(iv)	(ii)	(i)	(iii)
(c)	(i)	(iii)	(ii)	(iv)	(d)	(i)	(ii)	(iii)	(iv)

58. Match the following

Column I	Column I
A. Goods sold on credit	(i) Financing activity
B. Cash paid for purchase of marketable securities	(ii) Cash and cash equivalents
C. Sale of machine	(iii) Operating activity
D. Issue of shares	(iv) Investing activity

Codes

	A	B	C	D		A	B	C	D
(a)	(iii)	(ii)	(iv)	(i)	(b)	(iii)	(iv)	(ii)	(i)
(c)	(i)	(ii)	(iii)	(iv)	(d)	(i)	(ii)	(iv)	(iii)

59. Match the following

Column I	Column I
A. Increase in general reserve	(i) Added for calculation of net profit before tax
B. Increase in provision for doubtful debts	(ii) Added to net profit before tax for obtaining operating profit before working capital changes
C. Decease in creditors	(iii) Deducted from operating profit before working capital changes
D. Income tax paid	(iv) Deducted from cash generated from operating for obtains net cash from operating activities

Codes

	A	B	C	D		A	B	C	D
(a)	(i)	(ii)	(iii)	(iv)	(b)	(i)	(ii)	(iv)	(iii)
(c)	(i)	(iv)	(iii)	(ii)	(d)	(i)	(iii)	(iv)	(ii)

60. Match the following

Column I	Column II
A. Buy-back of own shares	(i) Operating activity
B. Purchase and sale of securities by a finance company	(ii) Financing activity
C. Receipt of dividend	(iii) Investing activity

Codes

	A	B	C
(a)	(iii)	(i)	(ii)
(b)	(ii)	(i)	(iii)
(c)	(iii)	(ii)	(i)
(d)	(ii)	(iii)	(i)

61. Match the following

Column I	Column II
A. Purchase of goodwill	(i) Operating activity
B. Royalty recieved	(ii) Cash equivalents
C. Interest paid on debentures by non-finance company	(iii) Investing activity
D. Marketable securities	(iv) Financing activity

Codes

	A	B	C	D
(a)	(iii)	(i)	(iv)	(ii)
(b)	(i)	(ii)	(iii)	(iv)
(c)	(iv)	(iii)	(ii)	(i)
(d)	(ii)	(iv)	(i)	(iii)

Direction *Read the following case study and answer the questions 62 and 63 on the basis of the same*

Cash flow from operating activities of Universe Ltd. for the year ended 31st March, 2024 was ₹ 18,000. The balance sheet along with notes to accounts of Starline Ltd. as at 31st March, 2024 is given below

Balance Sheet
as at 31st March, 2024

Particulars	Note No.	31st March, 2024 (₹)	31st March, 2023 (₹)
I. EQUITY AND LIABILITIES			
1. **Shareholders' Funds**			
(i) Share Capital		18,00,000	10,00,000
(ii) Reserves and Surplus	1	50,000	40,000
2. **Non-current Liabilities**			
Long-term Borrowings	2	1,00,000	4,00,000
3. **Current Liabilities**			
Short-term Provisions	3	2,50,000	3,60,000
Total		22,00,000	18,00,000
II. ASSETS			
1. **Non-current Assets**			
(i) Property, Plant and Equipment and Intangible Assets			
(a) Property, Plant and Equipment	4	14,00,000	10,00,000
(b) Intangible Assets	5	1,80,000	70,000
2. **Current Assets**			
(i) Current Investments		30,000	1,90,000
(ii) Trade Receivables		2,90,000	3,10,000
(iii) Cash and Cash Equivalents		3,00,000	2,30,000
Total		22,00,000	18,00,000

Notes to Accounts

Particulars	31st March, 2024 (₹)	31st March, 2023 (₹)
1. **Reserves and Surplus**		
Surplus (Balance in Statement of Profit and Loss)	50,000	40,000
2. **Long-term Borrowings**		
8% Debentures	1,00,000	4,00,000
3. **Short-term Provisions**		
Provision for Tax	2,50,000	3,60,000

Particulars	31st March, 2024 (₹)	31st March, 2023 (₹)
4. **Property, Plant and Equipment**		
Plant and Machinery	15,20,000	10,90,000
(–) Accumulated Depreciation	(1,20,000)	(90,000)
	14,00,000	10,00,000
5. **Intangible Assets**		
Goodwill	1,80,000	70,000

You are given the following additional information

(i) A machinery of the book value of ₹ 40,000 (depreciation provided thereon ₹ 12,000) was sold at a loss of ₹ 6,000.

(ii) 8% debentures were redeemed on 1st July, 2023.

62. How much amount is received on the sale of plant and machinery?

(a) ₹ 22,000 (b) ₹ 34,000 (c) ₹ 16,000 (d) ₹ 20,000

63. How much amount is invested in plant and machinery in the current year?

(a) ₹ 4,76,000 (b) ₹ 4,70,000 (c) ₹ 4,76,500 (d) ₹ 4,75,000

Direction *Read the following case study and answer the questions 64 and 65 on the basis of the same*

Following is the balance sheet of G Ltd. as at 31st March, 2024 and additional information

Balance Sheet

as at 31st March, 2024

Particulars	Note No.	31st March, 2024 (₹)	31st March, 2023 (₹)
I. **EQUITY AND LIABILITIES**			
1. **Shareholders' Funds**			
(i) Share Capital		8,00,000	6,00,000
(ii) Reserves and Surplus	1	3,30,000	2,20,000
2. **Non-current Liabilities**			
Long-term Borrowings	2	1,60,000	1,00,000
3. **Current Liabilities**			
Trade Payables		1,65,000	1,95,000
Total		14,55,000	11,15,000
II. **ASSETS**			
1. **Non-current Assets**			
(i) Property, Plant and Equipment	3	9,50,000	6,05,000
(ii) Non-current Investments		1,35,000	1,00,000
2. **Current Assets**			
(i) Current Investments		80,000	40,000
(ii) Trade Receivables		90,000	2,00,000
(iii) Cash and Cash Equivalents		2,00,000	1,70,000
Total		14,55,000	11,15,000

Notes to Accounts

Particulars	31st March, 2024 (₹)	31st March, 2023 (₹)
1. **Reserves and Surplus**		
Surplus i.e Balance in Statement of Profit and Loss	3,30,000	2,20,000
2. **Long-term Borrowings**		
10% Debentures	1,60,000	1,00,000
3. **Property, Plant and Equipment**		
Machinery (Cost)	10,70,000	70,00,000
(–) Accumulated Depreciation	(1,20,000)	(95,000)
	9,50,000	6,05,000

Additional Information

10% debentures ₹ 60,000 were issued on 1st April, 2023.

64. For how many months, the interest on debentures would be provided on the debentures issued on 1st April, 2023?

(a) 12 months (b) 7 months (c) 5 months (d) No interest

65. How much depreciation is charged on machinery for the current year?

(a) ₹ 15,000 (b) ₹ 75,000 (c) ₹ 50,000 (d) ₹ 25,000

Answers

1. (c) Cash equivalents mean short-term highly liquid investments that are readily convertible into known amounts of cash and which are subjected to an insignificant risk of changes in value.
2. (d) 3 months or less
3. (a) Trade receivables
4. (a) Provision for tax is identified and classified as operating activity and it is added to net profit.
5. (c) Cash flow from operating activity means cash flow from business operation. As inflow and outflow of cash from operating activity are the core activities for business, by which business generate profit.
6. (a) Net Profit before Tax and Extraordinary Items
   = Difference between Closing and Opening Surplus + Proposed Dividend (2023)
   = 1,50,000 + 1,50,000 = ₹ 3,00,000
7. (d) Depreciation Charged during the Year = Closing Balance + Accumulated Depreciation on Machine Sold – Opening Balance
   = 65,000 + 6,000 – 60,000 = ₹ 11,000
8. (a) Only (i)
9. (d) All of the above
10. (b) Operating Profit before Working Capital Changes
    = Net Profit + Depreciation + Interest Paid – Gain on Sale of Machine
    = 60,000 + 8,000 + 4,000 – 6,000 = ₹ 66,000
11. (d) All of the above
12. (d) All of the above
13. (c) AS-3
14. (b) Calculation of Cash Flow from Investing Activities

Purchase of Investment	(2,00,000)
Sale of Investment	1,80,000
Purchase of Goodwill	(3,00,000)
Outflow	(3,20,000)

15. (a) Gain on sale of furniture
16. (b) Shown as cash inflow under financing activities
17. (b) Subtracting under operating activity as extraordinary items and added to operating activities also
18. (c) cash flow from investing activities ₹ 35,000
19. (a) operating
20. (a) Payment to creditors
21. (a) Only (i)
22. (c) Amount of Tax Paid = Opening Balance + Provision Made – Closing Balance
    = 25,000 + 32,500 – 37,500 = ₹ 20,000
23. (b) Purchased Value of Machine = Depreciation for the Year + Closing Balance – Opening Balance
    = 4,00,000 + 47,60,000 – 35,00,000 = ₹ 16,60,000
24. (b) ₹ 10,00,000 has been outflow, i.e. amount is paid to financing company
25. (b) Balancing Figure of Purchase of Investment = Sale + Closing Balance – Opening balance – Gain on sale
    = ₹ 2,54,400
    Cash Flow from Investing Activities = Sale of Investments – Purchase of Investments
    = 4,60,800 – 25,440 = ₹ 2,06,400
26. (d) (i) and (iv)
27. (a) Investments in shares are excluded from cash equivalents unless they are in substantial cash equivalents
28. (a) Outflow from operating activities
29. (b) Purchase Value of Investment = Opening Balance + Profit on Sale – Sale of Investment – Closing balance
    = 10,00,000 + 1,00,000 – 6,00,000 – 20,00,000
    = ₹ (15,00,000)
30. (d) cash inflow of ₹ 50,00,000 from invsting activities
31. (b) deducted, closing
32. (c) Issue of equity shares increases the share capital and redemption of debentures decreases long-term borrowing hence are shown under financing activity.
33. (a) operating activities
34. (a) Investing activity

35. (c) Financing activity

36. (b) investing activity outflow ₹ 1,25,000

37. (d) Cash used in Investing Activities = Purchase of Shares + Dividend Recieved

= (7,00,000) + 20,000 = ₹ (6,80,000)

38. (c) Purchase Value of Furniture = Sale of Furniture + Accumulated Depreciation on Furniture Sold + Closing Balance of Furniture – Gain on Sale of Furniture – Opening Balance

= 20,000 + 24,000 + 4,20,000 – 4,000 – 4,00,000

= ₹ (60,000)

39. (a) Both Assertion (A) and Reason (R) are true and Reason (R) is the correct explanation of Assertion (A)

40. (d) Assertion (A) is false, but Reason (R) is true

41. (b) Both Assertion (A) and Reason (R) are true, but Reason (R) is not the correct explanation of Assertion (A)

42. (a) Both Assertion (A) and Reason (R) are true and Reason (R) is the correct explanation of Assertion (A)

43. (d) Issue of bonus shown are not shown under financing activity because bonus shares are not issued for cash.

44. (c) Cash and cash equivalents have no significant risk of change in their value.

45. (d) Its not an operating activity but brokerage received is an operating activity.

46. (a) Both Assertion (A) and Reason (R) are true and Reason (R) is the correct explanation of Assertion (A)

47. (b) Both Assertion (A) and Reason (R) are true, but Reason (R) is not the correct explanation of Assertion (A)

48. (a) Decrease in creditors results in outflow hence deducted while calculation of cash flow from operating activities.

49. (a) Previous year's proposed dividend is shown as outflow under financing activity rather than current year's proposed dividend.

50. (c) Both the statements are correct

51. (c) Both the statements are correct

52. (b) Debentures issued as collateral security does not result in inflow of cash.

53. (c) Both the statements are correct

54. (c) Both the statements are correct

55. (c) Both the statements are correct

56. (c) Both the statements are correct

57. (a) (iv) (ii) (iii) (i)

58. (a) (iii) (ii) (iv) (i)

59. (a) (i) (ii) (iii) (iv)

60. (b) (ii) (i) (iii)

61. (a) (iii) (i) (iv) (ii)

62. (a) Sale = Book Value – Loss

= 40,000 – 12,000 – 6,000 = ₹ 22,000

63. (b) Sale + Closing Balance + Loss on Sale – Opening Balance

= 34,000 + 15,20,000 + 6,000 – 10,90,000

= ₹ 4,70,000

64. (a) 12 months

65. (d) Current year Depreciation = 1,20,000 – 95,000

= ₹ 25,000

HOW TO MAKE A PROJECT ?

A project report is a written statement of what the analyser analyses in his/her evaluation. The project report needs to be prepared with great care and consideration.

A project report should

- be handwritten
- be concise
- be clear
- have diagrammatic presentation
- have a length of 25 to 30 pages
- have topics with suitable headings
- end up with conclusion

Elements

Try to ensure that your report contains the following elements

Title Page

This should include the project title, name of the company on which you are conducting your research and name of the student. You can also list the name of your school, class and subject teacher.

Acknowledgement

It is usual to thank those individuals, who have provided particularly useful assistance, technical or otherwise, during your project. In this, you pleased your supervisor as he/she will have invested quite a lot of time in overseeing your progress. You can also give a note of thank to the department of the company, which provides you a relevant data.

Content Page

This should list the main sections and sub-sections of your report. Choose self-explanatory titles with their respective pages and use double spacing for clarity. Content should be impressive and explanatory so that the reader would clearly understand the motto of the project.

Introduction

This is one of the most important component of the project report. It should begin with a clear statement of what the project is about, so that the nature and scope of the project can be understood by a reader. It should summarise everything which you set out to achieve and provide a clear summary of the project's background, relevance and main contributions. The introduction should set the context for the project and should provide the reader with a summary of the key things to look out for in, the remainder of the report. It is useful in stating the main objectives of the project as part of the introduction.

Background

The background section of the report should set the project into action, it specifies the problem of the company, what remedial actions were taken by the company, what are its effects. It proposed the layout of whole project.

Body of Report

The central part of the report usually consists of three or four sections detailing the technical work undertaken during the project. The structure of these sections is highly project dependent. They can reflect the chronological development of the project. It includes the detailed description regarding the matter of the project.

Evaluation

This might involve quantitative and qualitative evaluation such as expressibility, functionality, ease-of-use, etc of a product. At some point, you should also evaluate the strengths and weaknesses of what you have done. It includes certain questionnaires, sampling test which help in evaluating the result on the basis of truths and facts.

Conclusions

The conclusion should list the things, which have been learnt as a result of the work you have done. It shows the ultimate response of the project undertaken by a student. It should be expressive and impressive so that a reader would clearly evaluate the result and rated you on the basis of your presentation.

Project Work

Title of the Project	....
Company Chosen for the Project	....
Name	....
School	....
Year	....
Class	XII A
Submitted to	....

Acknowledgement

I would like to extend my sincere and heartfelt gratitude to my accounts teacher Mr/Ms. .... who has helped me in this endeavour and has always been very cooperative and without his/her help, cooperation, guidance and encouragement, the project couldn't have been what it evolved to be.

I extend my heartfelt thanks to my faculty for their guidance and constant supervision as well as, for providing me the necessary information regarding the project.

I am also thankful to my parents for their cooperation and encouragement.

At last but not least, gratitute to all my friends who helped me (directly or indirectly) to complete this project within a limited time frame.

Name of the Student..............................

Roll No..

Certificate

This is to certify that Mr/Ms .... of Class XII A of .... School, Meerut, has completed his/her project file under my supervision.

He/She has taken proper care and shown utmost sincerity in completion of this project. I certify that this project is up to my expectation and as per guidelines issued by CBSE.

Mr/Ms...............

(PGT Accounts/Head of Commerce Department)

INDEX

S.No.	Title of Project Work	Page No.	Remarks	Teacher's Signature
1.	Comprehensive			
2.	Specific Project 1— Cash Flow Statement			
3.	Specific Project 2— Ratio Analysis			

Project 1 Comprehensive

Case Study of an Individual, Willing to Set-up a Small-scale Business in Retail Sector

Mr Sultan Raza, a business school graduate from US came back to India with a thought to open a retail outlet on a small-scale with an initial capital investment of ₹ 5,00,000 for selling packaged and frozen foods in Mumbai, as people in Mumbai are quite busy and don't have time for cooking. He then finalised the business plan, capital requirement, etc. He opened a bank account with Punjab National Bank, in which he deposited ₹ 3,50,000.

He selected a suitable place for the store, renovated it, purchased furniture of ₹ 1,00,000 and paid the amount by cheque. He employed a helper for his shop.

The other transactions during the year were

Particulars	Amt (₹)
Purchases	
On Credit (from Ajay)	2,00,000
On Cash (from Ashok)	80,000
Sales	
On Credit (from Vijay)	1,40,000
On Cash (from Vinod)	1,00,000
Paid Travelling Expenses in Cash	30,000
Paid Salary to Helper in Cash	20,000
Received from Debtor Vijay in Full Settlement by Cheque	1,30,000
Deposited Cash into Bank	50,000
Paid to Creditor Ajay by Cheque in Full Settlement	1,95,000

He withdrew for his personal use an amount of ₹ 30,000 by cheque. *You are required to*

1. Journalise these transactions after considering the following information
   (a) Value of goods unsold on 31st March, 2025, valued at cost ₹ 1,70,000
   (b) Depreciate furniture @ 2%
   (c) Telephone bill for the month of March 2025 not yet paid ₹ 15,000
2. Open ledger and prepare trial balance.
3. Prepare financial statements for the year ended 31st March, 2025 and also calculate the profitability ratios i.e. gross profit ratio, net profit ratio and also comment on the profitability of the company, comparing its performance with the industry standards. Industry standard being 50% and 20% respectively for gross profit and net profit.

Detailed Study of the Project

Introduction

The project is to prepare accounting record of Mr Sultan Raza for the accounting year 2024-25 and also to prepare trial balance, trading and profit and loss account and balance sheet. Necessary data has been provided for the project work.

Execution of Project Work

1. Preparation of journal, ledger and trial balance.
2. Preparation of financial statements for the year ending 31st March, 2025.
3. Computation of gross profit ratio and net profit ratio to assess profitability and to compare with the industry standards.

JOURNAL

Date	Particulars		LF	Amt (Dr)	Amt (Cr)
	Cash A/c	Dr		5,00,000	
	To Capital A/c				5,00,000
	(Being capital introduced in the business)				
	Bank A/c	Dr		3,50,000	
	To Cash A/c				3,50,000
	(Being bank account opened)				
	Furniture A/c	Dr		1,00,000	
	To Bank A/c				1,00,000
	(Being furniture purchased and payment made by cheque)				
	Purchases A/c	Dr		2,00,000	
	To Ajay				2,00,000
	(Being goods purchased on credit)				
	Purchases A/c	Dr		80,000	
	To Cash A/c				80,000
	(Being goods purchased for cash)				
	Vijay	Dr		1,40,000	
	To Sales A/c				1,40,000
	(Being goods sold on credit)				
	Cash A/c	Dr		1,00,000	
	To Sales A/c				1,00,000
	(Being goods sold for cash)				
	Travelling Expenses A/c	Dr		30,000	
	To Cash A/c				30,000
	(Being travelling expenses paid)				
	Salary A/c	Dr		20,000	
	To Cash A/c				20,000
	(Being salary paid)				
	Bank A/c	Dr		1,30,000	
	Discount A/c	Dr		10,000	
	To Vijay				1,40,000
	(Being amount received from Vijay in full settlement)				
	Bank A/c	Dr		50,000	
	To Cash A/c				50,000
	(Being cash deposited in bank)				
	Ajay	Dr		2,00,000	
	To Bank A/c				1,95,000
	To Discount A/c				5,000
	(Being payment made to Ajay in full settlement)				
	Drawings A/c	Dr		30,000	
	To Bank A/c				30,000
	(Being amount withdrawn for personal purpose from bank)				

General Ledger of Mr Sultan Raza

Capital Account

Particulars	Amt (₹)	Particulars	Amt (₹)
		By Cash A/c	5,00,000
To Balance c/d	5,00,000		
	5,00,000		5,00,000

Cash Account

Particulars	Amt (₹)	Particulars	Amt (₹)
To Capital A/c	5,00,000	By Bank A/c	3,50,000
To Sales A/c	1,00,000	By Travelling Expenses A/c	30,000
		By Purchases A/c	80,000
		By Bank A/c	50,000
		By Salary A/c	20,000
		By Balance c/d	70,000
	6,00,000		6,00,000

Bank Account

Particulars	Amt (₹)	Particulars	Amt (₹)
To Cash A/c	3,50,000	By Ajay	1,95,000
To Vijay	1,30,000	By Furniture A/c	1,00,000
To Cash A/c	50,000	By Drawings A/c	30,000
		By Balance c/d	2,05,000
	5,30,000		5,30,000

Furniture Account

Particulars	Amt (₹)	Particulars	Amt (₹)
To Bank A/c	1,00,000	By Depreciation A/c	2,000
		By Balance c/d	98,000
	1,00,000		6,00,000

Depreciation Account

Particulars	Amt (₹)	Particulars	Amt (₹)
To Furniture A/c	2,000	By Profit and Loss A/c	2,000
	2,000		2,000

Purchases Account

Particulars	Amt (₹)	Particulars	Amt (₹)
To Ajay	2,00,000	By Trading A/c	2,80,000
To Cash A/c	80,000		
	2,80,000		2,80,000

Sales Account

Particulars	Amt (₹)	Particulars	Amt (₹)
To Trading A/c	2,40,000	By Vijay	1,40,000
		By Cash A/c	1,00,000
	2,40,000		2,40,000

Ajay's Account

Particulars	Amt (₹)	Particulars	Amt (₹)
To Bank A/c	1,95,000	By Purchases A/c	2,00,000
To Discount A/c	5,000		
	2,00,000		2,00,000

Vijay's Account

Particulars	Amt (₹)	Particulars	Amt (₹)
To Sales A/c	1,40,000	By Bank A/c	1,30,000
		By Discount A/c	10,000
	1,40,000		1,40,000

Travelling Expenses Account

Particulars	Amt (₹)	Particulars	Amt (₹)
To Cash A/c	30,000	By Profit and Loss A/c	30,000
	30,000		30,000

Salary Account

Particulars	Amt (₹)	Particulars	Amt (₹)
To Cash A/c	20,000	By Profit and Loss A/c	20,000
	20,000		20,000

Discount Account

Particulars	Amt (₹)	Particulars	Amt (₹)
To Vijay	10,000	By Ajay	5,000
		By Profit and Loss A/c	5,000
	10,000		10,000

Telephone Expenses Account

Particulars	Amt (₹)	Particulars	Amt (₹)
To Outstanding Expenses A/c	15,000	By Profit and Loss A/c	15,000
	15,000		15,000

Outstanding Expenses Account

Particulars	Amt (₹)	Particulars	Amt (₹)
To Balance c/d	15,000	By Telephone Expenses A/c	15,000
	15,000		15,000

Drawings Account

Particulars	Amt (₹)	Particulars	Amt (₹)
To Bank A/c	30,000	By Balance c/d	30,000
	30,000		30,000

Trial Balance
as at 31st March, 2025

Name of the Account	Debit (₹)	Credit (₹)
Cash	70,000	—
Bank	2,05,000	—
Purchases	2,80,000	—
Sales	—	2,40,000
Travelling Expenses	30,000	—
Salary	20,000	—
Telephone Expenses	15,000	—
Depreciation	2,000	—
Discount	5,000	—
Capital	—	5,00,000
Furniture	98,000	—
Outstanding Expenses	—	15,000
Drawings	30,000	—
Total	7,55,000	7,55,000

Financial Statements

Trading and Profit and Loss Account
for the year ended 31st March, 2025

Particulars	Amt (₹)	Particulars	Amt (₹)
To Opening Stock A/c	—	By Sales A/c	2,40,000
To Purchases A/c	2,80,000	By Closing Stock A/c	1,70,000
To Gross Profit c/d	1,30,000		
	4,10,000		4,10,000
To Travelling Expenses A/c	30,000	By Gross Profit b/d	1,30,000
To Salary A/c	20,000		
To Telephone Expenses A/c	15,000		
To Discount A/c	5,000		
To Depreciation A/c	2,000		
To Net Profit Transferred to Capital A/c	58,000		
	1,30,000		1,30,000

Balance Sheet
as at 31st March, 2025

Particulars		Amt (₹)	Particulars		Amt (₹)
Capital			**Fixed Assets**		
Balance	5,00,000		Furniture	1,00,000	
(+) Profit for Year	58,000		(–) Depreciation	(2,000)	98,000
(–) Drawings	(30,000)	5,28,000			
Current Liabilities			**Current Assets**		
Outstanding Expenses		15,000	Stock		1,70,000
			Cash		70,000
			Bank		2,05,000
		5,43,000			5,43,000

Profitability Ratios

$$\text{Gross profit ratio} = \frac{\text{Gross profit}}{\text{Revenue from operations (Net sales)}} = \frac{1{,}30{,}000}{2{,}40{,}000} \times 100 = 54.17\%$$

$$\text{Net profit ratio} = \frac{\text{Net profit}}{\text{Revenue from operations (Net sales)}} \times 100 = \frac{58{,}000}{2{,}40{,}000} \times 100 = 24.17\%$$

Conclusions

1. The gross profit ratio of Mr Sultan is 54.17% against industry standard of 50%, which is quite good.
2. The net profit ratio of firm is 24.17% against the industry standard of 20%, which is also good and a healthy sign for the firm.

Viva Questions

1. **What do you mean by closing stock?**
2. **Why is it necessary to prepare the trial balance?**
3. **What does a trading account show?**
4. **What is gross profit?**
5. **What does profit and loss account show?**
6. **Give two characteristics of a balance sheet.**
7. **How is closing stock (inventory) valued?**
8. **What is meant by financial statements?**
9. **Why is the journal called 'book of prime entry' or 'book of original entry'?**
10. **Why is the ledger called as the 'book of final entry'?**

Answers

1. Goods lying unsold at the closing date of accounting year is called closing stock. It includes stock of raw material, semi-finished goods and finished goods.
2. Trial balance is a statement of debit and credit balances of accounts in the ledger. Trial balance helps in
   (*i*) Testing the arithmetical accuracy of the transactions recorded in the books of accounts.
   (*ii*) Preparing the financial statements.
3. Trading account shows the gross profit, i.e. excess of net sales over cost of goods sold, earned during the year.
4. Gross profit is the excess of sales over cost of goods sold.
5. It shows the net profit earned, i.e., gross profit less indirect expenses incurred during the year.
6. (*i*) A balance sheet is prepared at a particular point of time. It shows the financial position of the firm at a particular date.
   (*ii*) It is a summary of balances of ledger accounts that have not been closed by transfer to trading and profit and loss account.
7. It is valued at cost or net realisable value, whichever is lower.
8. Financial statements are the end product of an accounting process which begins with the identification of accounting information and recording thereof in the books of primary entry.
9. A journal is called a 'book of original entry' (or prime entry) as all the business transactions are first of all recorded in this book.
10. Ledger is called the 'book of final entry' as it is the ultimate destination of all the transactions.

Project 2 Specific Project Based on Cash Flow Statement

Preparation of Cash Flow Statement from the Balance Sheet of a Company

From the following balance sheet of Vardhman Ltd as at 31st March, 2024 and 2025 and additional information, prepare cash flow statement and interpret the results thereof.

Vardhman Ltd
Balance Sheet
as at 31st March, 2024 and 2025

Particulars	Note No.	31st March, 2025 (₹)	31st March, 2024 (₹)
I. EQUITY AND LIABILITIES			
1. **Shareholders' Funds**			
(a) Share Capital		1,00,000	1,00,000
(b) Reserves and Surplus (Balance in statement of profit and loss)		49,000	48,000
2. **Non-current Liabilities**			
Long-term Borrowings	1	45,000	30,000
3. **Current Liabilities**			
Trade Payables		41,000	36,000
Total		2,35,000	2,14,000
II. ASSETS			
1. **Non-current Assets**			
Property, Plant and Equipment	2	1,71,000	1,50,000
2. **Current Assets**			
(a) Trade Receivables		38,400	35,000
(b) Inventories		22,000	25,000
(c) Cash and Cash Equivalents		3,600	4,000
Total		2,35,000	2,14,000

Notes to Accounts

Particulars			31st March, 2025 (₹)	31st March, 2024 (₹)
1. **Long-term Borrowings**				
Loan from Z Ltd			20,000	—
Loan from Bank			25,000	30,000
			45,000	30,000
3. **Property, Plant and Equipment**				
Land			30,000	20,000
Building			55,000	50,000
Plant and Machinery	1,22,000	1,07,000		
(–) Depreciation	(36,000)	(27,000)	86,000	80,000
			1,71,000	1,50,000

Additional Information

During the year, ₹ 26,000 were paid as interim dividend.

Detailed Study of the Project

Introduction

The project is to prepare cash flow statement of Vardhman Ltd for the year ended 31st March, 2025 in accordance with the Accounting Standard-3 (Revised) issued by the Institute of Chartered Accountants of India. Also, the company's results are to be interpreted.

The necessary data i.e. the balance sheet of Vardhman Ltd as at 31st March, 2024 and 31st March, 2025 alongwith the relevant information and notes to accounts for the year ended 31st March, 2025 is provided.

Execution of Project Work

(*i*) Cash flow statement of Vardhman Ltd as per AS-3 (Revised) for the year ended 31st March, 2025 is prepared following the indirect method.

(*ii*) Cash flow statement prepared is analysed and observations are made.

(*iii*) Graphical presentation of results of different business activities to show cash generated (or used) under operating, investing and financing activities is given below

Cash Flow Statement
for the year ended 31st March, 2025

Particulars		Amt (₹)
A. **Cash Flow from Operating Activities**		
Net Profit before Tax and Extraordinary Items (WN)		27,000
Adjustment for Non-cash and Non-operating Expenses		
(+) Depreciation		9,000
Operating Profit before Working Capital Changes		36,000
(+) *Decrease in Current Assets and Increase in Current Liabilities*		
Inventories	3,000	
Trade Payables	5,000	
(–) *Increase in Current Assets and Decrease in Current Liabilities*		
Trade Receivables	(3,400)	4,600
Net Cash Flow from Operating Activities		40,600
B. **Cash Flow from Investing Activities**		
Purchase of Buildings	(5,000)	
Purchase of Land	(10,000)	
Purchase of Plant and Machinery	(15,000)	
Net Cash used in Investing Activities		(30,000)
C. **Cash Flow from Financing Activities**		
Proceeds of Loan from Z Ltd	20,000	
Repayment of Bank Loan	(5,000)	
Payment of Interim Dividend	(26,000)	
Net Cash used in Financing Activities		(11,000)
Net Decrease in Cash and Cash Equivalents		(400)
Cash and Cash Equivalents in the Beginning of the Year		4,000
Cash and Cash Equivalents at the End of the Year		3,600

Working Note

Calculation of Net Profit before Tax and Extraordinary Items

Particulars	Amt (₹)
Closing Balance as per Statement of Profit and Loss on 31st March, 2025	49,000
(–) Opening Balance as per Statement of Profit and Loss as on 1st April, 2024	(48,000)
Profit for the Year	1,000
(+) Interim Dividend Paid	26,000
Net Profit before Tax and Extraordinary Items	27,000

Interpretation of Results

Cash flow statement analysis of Vardhman Ltd shows the inflow and outflow of cash separately from the three different activities namely, operating activities, investing activities and financing activities. Cash generated from operating activities amounted to ₹ 40,600 which has been invested in purchasing building ₹ 5,000, land ₹ 10,000, machinery ₹ 15,000 as is shown under cash used in investing activities. The remaining cash of ₹ 10,600 from operating activities is used for meeting the deficit of cash from financing activities amounting to ₹ 11,000. Thus, resulting in net cash outflow of ₹ 400 from all the three activities together. Increase in trade receivables is not good. Increase in turnover may have lead to increase in trade receivables. However, it should be analysed with bad debts and debt collection period to reach any logical conclusion.

Company has generated cash from its operating activities which is a good sign. The inflow from operating activities will help the company to finance its growth plans. Besides it also meets the expectation of shareholders regarding return on their investment.

Result to Different Activities

Business Activities	Amt (₹)
Cash from Operating Activites	40,600
Cash used in Investing Activites	(30,000)
Cash used in Financing Activities	(11,000)

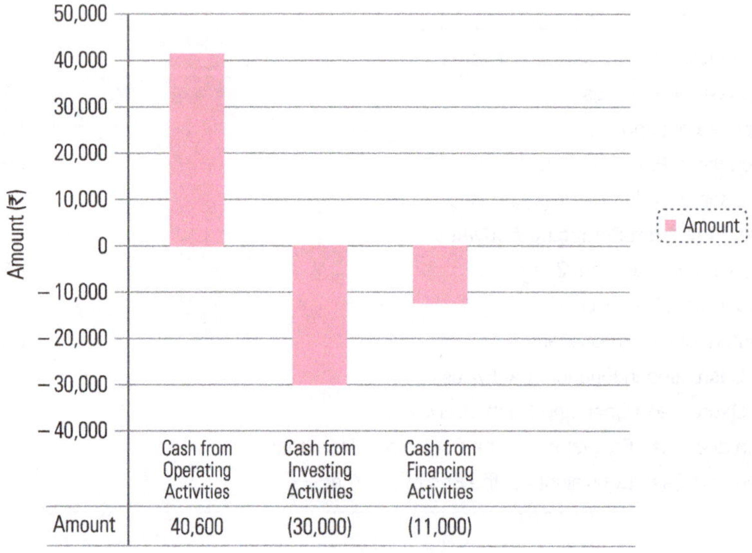

Project Work

Viva Questions

1. **What do you mean by cash flow statement?**
2. **What is meant by operating activities?**
3. **What is meant by financing activities?**
4. **What is meant by investing activities?**
5. **What is meant by cash equivalents?**
6. **While calculating cash flow from operating activities, what is the treatment of depreciation?**
7. **The cash generated from operating activities of the company amounts to ₹ 40,600. Do you consider it healthy for the company?**
8. **Why depreciation written back is not considered while preparing the cash flow statement?**
9. **Give an example of investing activity.**
10. **Give an example of financing activity.**

Answers

1. It is a statement prepared to show inflow and outflow of cash and cash equivalents.
2. Operating activities are the principal revenue producing activities of the enterprise and other activities that are not investing or financing activities.
3. Financing activities are activities that result in changes in the size and composition of the owner's capital and borrowings of the enterprise.
4. Investing activities are the acquisition and disposal of long-term assets and other investments not included in cash equivalents.
5. Cash equivalents are short-term, highly liquid investments that are readily convertible into known amount of cash and which are subject to an insignificant risk of changes in value.
6. While calculating cash flow from operating activities, depreciation is added back to the net profit, as it is a non-cash expenditure.
7. Yes, it is healthy for the company as the cash generated from operating activities is utilised in investing and financing activities that means business is generating adequate cash to finance the purchase of assets as well as payment of loan and interest.
8. As it is not a cash transaction.
9. Purchase of building.
10. Repayment of bank loan.

Project 3

Specific Project Based on Ratio Analysis of Reliance Industries Ltd

About the Company

The Reliance Group, founded by Dhirubhai H Ambani (1932-2002), is India's largest private sector enterprise, with businesses in the energy and materials value chain. Group's annual revenues are in excess of US$ 66 billion. The flagship company, Reliance Industries Limited, is a Fortune Global 500 company and is the largest private sector company in India.

The Group's activities span exploration and production of oil and gas, petroleum refining and marketing, petrochemicals (polyester, fibre intermediates, plastics and chemicals), textiles, retail, infotel and special economic zones.

Reliance enjoys global leadership in its businesses, being the largest polyester yarn and fibre producer in the world and among the top five to ten producers in the world in major petrochemical products.

Major Group companies are Reliance Industries Limited, including its subsidiaries and Reliance Industrial Infrastructure Limited.

Reliance
Industries Limited
Growth is Life

Performance Evaluation of Reliance Industries Limited through Ratio Analysis

Following is the balance sheet and statement of profit and loss of Reliance Industries Ltd for the year ended 31st March, 2024 and 2025. (Imaginary Figures)

Reliance Industries Limited
Balance Sheet
as at 31st March, 2025 (₹ in crore)

Particulars	Note No.	as at 31st March, 2025 (₹)		as at 31st March, 2024 (₹)	
I. EQUITY AND LIABILITIES					
1. Shareholders' Funds					
(a) Share Capital	1	3,229		3,271	
(b) Reserves and Surplus	2	1,76,766		1,62,825	
			1,79,995		1,66,096
2. Share Application Money Pending Allotment	1		25		
3. Non-current Liabilities					
(a) Long-term Borrowings	3	43,012		48,034	
(b) Deferred Tax Liability (Net)	4	12,193		12,122	
4. Cuurent Liabilities			55,205		60,156
(a) Short-term Borrowings	5	11,511		10,593	
(b) Trade Payables	6	45,787		40,324	
(c) Other Current Liabilities	7	21,640		13,713	
(d) Short-term Provisions	8	4,348		4,258	
			83,286		68,888
Total			3,18,511		2,95,140
II. ASSETS					
1. Non-current Assets					
(a) Property, Plant and Equipment and Intangible Assets	9	82,962		88,001	
(i) Property, Plant and Equipment	9	26,786		25,722	
(ii) Intangibel Assets	9	13,525		3,695	
(b) Capital Work-in-progress	9	5,591		4,059	
(c) Intangible Assets under Development	10	24,143		26,979	
(d) Non-current Investments	11	21,528		14,340	
(e) Long-term Loans and Advances					
			1,74,535		1,62,796
2. Current Assets					
(a) Current Investments	12	28,366		27,029	
(b) Inventories	13	42,729		35,955	
(c) Trade Receivables	14	11,880		18,424	
(d) Cash and Bank Balances	15	49,547		39,598	
(e) Short-term Loans and Advances	16	10,974		11,089	
(f) Other Current Assets	17	480		249	
			1,43,976		1,32,344
Total			3,18,511		2,95,140

Reliance Industries Limited
Statement of Profit and Loss
for the year ended 31st March, 2025

Particulars	Note No.	2024-25 (₹ in crore)	2023-24 (₹ in crore)
Income			
Revenue from Operations	18	3,60,297	3,29,904
Other Income	19	7,998	6,192
Total Revenue		3,68,295	3,36,096
Expenses			
Cost of Materials Consumed	20	3,06,127	2,74,814
Purchases of Stock-in-trade		502	1,441
Changes in Inventories of Finished Goods		(3,317)	(872)
Stock-in-process and Stock-in-trade	21		
Employee Benefits Expense	22	3,354	2,862
Finance Costs	23	3,036	2,667
Depreciation and Amortisation Expense	24	9,465	11,394
Other Expenses	25	22,844	18,040
Total Expenses		3,42,011	3,10,346
Profit before Tax		26,284	25,750
Tax Expenses			
Current Tax		(5,244)	(5,150)
Deferred Tax		(37)	(560)
Profit for the Year		21,003	20,040
Earnings per Equity Share of Face Value of ₹ 10 each			
Basic and Diluted (in ₹)	26	64,82	61,21

Additional Information

The company's closing inventory on 31st March, 2025 was ₹ 29,825. You are required to calculate accounting ratios for each of two years i.e. 2024 and 2025 and comment briefly on the results of the business using these ratios.

(*i*) Current ratio
(*ii*) Quick ratio
(*iii*) Inventory turnover ratio
(*iv*) Fixed assets turnover ratio
(*v*) Current assets turnover ratio
(*vi*) Total assets turnover ratio
(*vii*) Debt collection period
(*viii*) Net profit ratio
(*ix*) Earning per share
(*x*) Return on total assets

Detailed Study of the Project

Introduction

The project is to compute accounting ratios i.e. current ratio, quick ratio, fixed assets turnover ratio, current assets turnover ratio, total assets turnover ratio, inventory turnover ratio, debt collection period, net profit ratio, earning per share and return on total assets and also to comments on these ratios. The necessary data to compute the accounting ratios has been provided i.e., balance sheet and statement of profit and loss.

Execution of Project Work

1. Two liquidity ratios i.e. current ratio and quick ratio have been computed and analysed to make observations on the short-term financial position of the company.
2. Debt collection period has been computed to assess whether the company is able to collect its debts efficiently.
3. Earning per share has been computed to assess the return on share.
4. Activity ratio i.e. inventory turnover ratio is computed to assess whether the company is able to use its inventories efficiently.
5. Activity ratio i.e. fixed assets turnover ratio, current assets turnover ratio, total assets turnover ratio are computed and analysed.
6. Profitability ratios i.e. net profit ratio and have been computed to assess the profitability of the company.
7. Return on total assets has been computed and analysed to assess whether the company has used its fixed assets efficiently.

Computation of Various Ratios

		2024	2025
1.	Current ratio $= \frac{\text{Current assets}}{\text{Current liabilities}}$	$\frac{1,32,344}{68,888} = 1.92 : 1$	$\frac{1,43,976}{83286} = 1.72 : 1$
2.	Quick ratio $= \frac{\text{Quick assets}}{\text{Current liabilities}}$ [Quick assets = Currrent assets-Inventories]	$\frac{96,389}{68,888} = 1.39 : 1$	$\frac{1,01247}{83286} = 121 : 1$
3.	Inventory turnover ratio $= \frac{\left[\text{Cost of revenue from operations , i.e. Cost of goods sold}\right]}{\text{Average inventory}}$ [Cost of revenue form operations = Cost of material consumed + Purchases of stock-in-trade + Changes in inventories of finished goods] Average inventories $= \frac{\text{Opening inventory} + \text{Closing inventory}}{2}$	$\frac{2,75,383}{32,890} = 837$ times	$\frac{303,312}{39,342} = 7.71$ times
4.	Fixed assets turnover ratio $= \frac{\text{Revenue operation i.e. sales}}{\text{Fixed assets}}$ [Fixed assets include tangible as well as intangible fixed assets]	$\frac{3,29,904}{1,13,723} = 2.90$ times	$\frac{360,279}{1,09,748} = 3.28$ times
5.	Current assets turnover ratio $= \frac{\text{Revenue from operations i.e. sales}}{\text{Current assets}}$	$\frac{3,29,904}{1,32,344} = 2.49$ times	$\frac{3,60,297}{1,43,976} = 2.50$ times
6.	Total assets turnover ratio $= \frac{\text{Revenue from operations i.e. sales}}{\text{Total assets}}$ [Total assets include both non-current assets and current assets other than deferred tax assets (net) and ficticious assets]	$\frac{3,29,904}{2,95,140} = 1.12$ times	$\frac{3,60,297}{3,18,511} = 1.13$ times

		2024	2025
7.	Debt collection period = $\frac{\text{Accounts receivable}}{\text{Average daily credit sales}}$	$\frac{18,424}{3,29,904} \times 365 = 20$ days	$\frac{11,880}{3,60,297} \times 365 = 12$ days
8.	Net profit ratio = $\frac{\text{Net profit after tax}}{\text{Revenue from operations}} \times 100$	$\frac{20,040}{3,29,904} \times 100 = 6\%$	$\frac{21,003}{3,60,297} \times 100 = 5.8\%$
9.	Earning per share = $\frac{\text{Net profit available for equity shareholders}}{\text{Number of equity shares}}$	$\frac{20,040}{237} = 61.2$ per share	$\frac{21,003}{324} = 64.82$ per share
10.	Return on total assets = $\frac{\text{Profit after tax}}{\text{Total assets}}$	$\frac{20,400}{2,95,140} \times 100 = 6.78\%$	$\frac{21,003}{3,18,511} \times 100 = 6.59\%$

Conclusions

1. Against the accepted norm for current ratio i.e., 2 : 1, the current ratio of Reliance Ltd is 1.9 2 : 1 in 2024 and 1.72 : 1 in 2025. The current ratios of both the years are quite close to the accepted norm i.e., it indicates that the company has a comfortable current assets position and it is in a good position to meet its current liabilities on time. However, the ratio has declined in 2025 as compared to 2024.
2. Against the accepted norm for quick ratio i.e., 1 : 1, the quick ratio of Reliance Ltd is 1.30 : 1 in 2024 and 1.21 : 1 in 2025. It indicates that the company has a good liquidity position and is better placed to meet its current liabilities at a short notice.
3. After analysing all the activity ratios of two years i.e., fixed assets turnover ratio, current assets turnover ratio, total assets turnover ratio and inventory turnover ratio, it has been observed that the company is making better utilisation of available resources to achieve sales. Although, inventory turnover ratio has declined in 2025 to 7.71 from 8.37 in 2024, but still the ratio is satisfactory.
4. Earning per share has increased from ₹ 61.2 per share in 2024 to ₹ 64.48 per share in 2025. It is a good sign for the company. This situation is very much favourable. A high EPS would mean higher market price of a company's share.
5. Debt collection period provides an approximation of the average time that it takes to collect debtors. The debt collection period has reduced to 12 days in 2025 from 20 days in 2024 which is a good sign for the company.
6. Return on total assets is favourable. The ratio is almost same in both the years. It indicates that the fixed assets are utilised efficiently.
7. Net profit ratio of both the years are almost same. Net profit ratio is a result of better gross profit ratio, it means company is either making more economical purchases or products are better priced or both.

Viva Questions

1. **What is quick ratio?**
2. **What is meant by debt collection period?**
3. **What is the significance of return on total assets ratio?**
4. **Why is ratio analysis important for a business?**
5. **What is Earning Per Share (EPS)?**
6. **What do you understand by inventory turnover ratio?**
7. **What are other names for quick ratio?**
8. **What are quick assets?**
9. **Is the quick ratio of Reliance Ltd satisfactory?**
10. **How is average inventories calculated?**

Answers

1. Quick ratio is a relationship of quick assets with current liabilities.
2. Debt collection period indicates the number of days within which payment is collected from debtors.
3. This ratio measures the profitability of investments which reflects managerial efficiency. The higher the ratio, the better is the profit earning capacity of the company or vice-versa.
4. Ratio analysis helps in
   (*i*) Understanding the short-term and long-term financial position of the business.
   (*ii*) Assessing the operating efficiency of the business.
5. The ratio of dividend on shares depends upon the amount of profit earned by a company. Whatever profits remain after meeting all expenses and paying preference shares dividend, belong to equity shareholders. These are the profits earned on equity share capital. The Earning Per Share (EPS) is calculated by dividing the profit available to equity shareholders by the number of shares issued.
6. Inventory turnover ratio means the number of times inventories are turned to generate sales.
7. Liquid ratio and acid test ratio.
8. Quick assets are current assets less inventories and prepaid expenses.
9. The quick ratio of Reliance Ltd is satisfactory in both the years. It indicates that the company has a good liquidity position.
10. Opening and closing inventories are added and divided by 2 to calculate average inventories

SAMPLE QUESTION PAPER 1

A Highly Simulated Sample Question Paper for CBSE Class XII Examination

ACCOUNTANCY

Time : 3 Hours **Max. Marks : 80**

General Instructions

1. This question paper contains **34** questions. **All** questions are compulsory.
2. This question paper is divided into **two** Parts: **Part A** and **B**.
3. **Part-A** and **B** are compulsory for all the candidates.
4. Question Nos. **1 to 16** (Part-A) and **27 to 30** (Part-B) are multiple choice questions carrying **1** mark each.
5. Question Nos. **17 to 20** (Part-A) and **31 & 32** (Part-B) are short answer type questions, carrying **3** marks each.
6. Question Nos. from **21, 22** (Part-A) and **33** (Part-B) are long answer type-I questions, carrying **4** marks each.
7. Question Nos. from **23 to 26** (Part-A) and **34** (Part-B) are long answer type-II questions, carrying **6** marks each.
8. There is no overall choice. However, an internal choice has been provided in few questions in each of the parts.

PART-A
(Accounting for Partnership Firms and Companies)

1. If a partner withdraws equal amount at end of each quarter, then .... are to be considered for interest on total drawings. (1)

(a) 5.5 months (b) 6 months
(c) 4.5 months (d) 7.5 months

2. A company issued 25,000 shares and received applications for 35,000 shares. Company wants to allot shares to everyone who has applied. What will be the ratio for allotment? (1)

(a) 6:7 (b) 7:5 (c) 5:7 (d) 7:6

3. V, S and T are partners in a firm with profit sharing ratio 3 : 2 : 1 respectively. The extract of their balance sheet is as follows

Liabilities	Amt (₹)	Assets	Amt (₹)
Workmen Compensation Reserve	48,000		

At the time of retirement of T, if liability for workmen compensation to the extent of ₹ 24,000 is to be created, then at what amount will workmen compensation reserve be shown in new balance sheet? (1)

(a) ₹ 48,000 (b) ₹ 72,000
(c) ₹ 24,000 (d) Not to be shown in new balance sheet

Or Sonu and Monu are partners sharing profits and losses in the ratio of 3 : 2. Tonu is admitted for 1/5th share in profits of the firm which he gets entirely from Sonu. Find out the new profit sharing ratio.

(a) 12 : 8 : 5 (b) 8 : 12 : 5
(c) 2 : 2 : 1 (d) 2 : 2 : 2

4. Assertion (A) At the time of change in profit sharing ratio, it is important to determine the sacrificing ratio and gaining ratio.

Reason (R) At the time of change in profit sharing ratio, gaining partner compensates the sacrificing partner by paying him proportionate amount of goodwill. (1)

Alternatives

(a) Both Assertion (A) and Reason (R) are true and Reason (R) is the correct explanation of Assertion (A)
(b) Both Assertion (A) and Reason (R) are true, but Reason (R) is not the correct explanation of Assertion (A)
(c) Assertion (A) is true, but Reason (R) is false
(d) Assertion (A) is false, but Reason (R) is true

Or With context to debit side of partners' current account, pick the odd one out.

(a) Drawings (b) Interest on drawings
(c) Salary (d) None of these

5. The 'share of premium for goodwill' brought in by the new partner is divided in which ratio? (1)

(a) In new ratio (b) In old ratio
(c) In sacrificing ratio (d) None of these

6. Calculate the interest for the year 2022, when 6% debentures are issued for ₹ 20,00,000 of ₹ 100 each. (1)

(a) ₹ 1,60,000 (b) ₹ 1,20,000
(c) ₹ 12,000 (d) ₹ 12,00,000

Or Which of the following statements is incorrect about shares?

(a) Pro-rata allotment is made in the event shares are oversubscribed.
(b) Issued share capital is that part of authorised share capital that is issued for subscription whether subscribed or not.
(c) Subscribed share capital can be less than or equal to the issued share capital but cannot be more.
(d) Securities premium reserve can be used for issuing partly paid bonus shares.

7. P, Q and R are partners sharing profits in 5 : 4 : 3 ratio. P has given to R a guarantee of minimum ₹ 10,000 profit. For the year ending 31st March, 2024, firm's profit is ₹ 28,800. P's share in profit will be (1)

(a) ₹ 9,200 (b) ₹ 9,600 (c) ₹ 7,200 (d) ₹ 12,000

8. Jhunjhun, a partner paid loan of the firm of ₹ 1,00,000 at the time of dissolution. Pass the journal entry for this transaction. (1)

(a) Jhunjhun's Capital A/c	Dr	1,00,000	
To Realisation A/c			1,00,000
(b) Realisation A/c	Dr	1,00,000	
To Loan A/c			1,00,000
(c) Realisation A/c	Dr	1,00,000	
To Jhunjhun's Capital A/c			1,00,000

(d) None of the above

Or A firm having the assets of ₹ 2,00,000 and liabilities of ₹ 84,000 earns the annual profit of ₹ 18,000. The rate of normal profit being 12%, the amount of goodwill by capitalisation of super profit method, will be ....

(a) ₹ 13,290 (b) ₹ 36,000
(c) ₹ 34,000 (d) ₹ 4,080

9. A and B are partners sharing profits in 2 : 1 ratio. They have fixed capitals of ₹ 45,000 and ₹ 30,000 respectively. After closing the accounts for the year ending 31st March, 2024 it was discovered that interest on capital was provided @ 6% p.a. instead of 8% p.a. In the adjusting entry. (1)

(a) A will be credited by ₹ 900 and B will be credited by ₹ 600
(b) A will be debited by ₹ 100 and B will be credited by ₹ 100
(c) A will be credited by ₹ 100 and B will be debited by ₹ 100
(d) A will be debited by ₹ 900 and B will be debited by ₹ 600

10. X and Y are partners sharing profits in 1 : 1 ratio. Their were having fixed capitals of ₹ 2,00,000 and ₹ 1,00,000 respectively. After closing the accounts for the year ending 31st March, 2024 it was discovered that interest on capital @ 8% was omitted to be provided.

They following adjusting entry will be passed

X's Capital A/c Dr A

To Y's Capital A/c B

Here A and B will be (1)

(a) A = ₹ 4,000, B = ₹ 4,000
(b) A = ₹ 16,000, B = ₹ 16,000
(c) A = ₹ 8,000, B = ₹ 8,000
(d) A = ₹ 6,000, B = ₹ 6,000

11. 'X', 'Y' and 'Z' were partners sharing profits in the ratio of $\frac{1}{2}, \frac{3}{10}$ and $\frac{1}{5}$. 'X' retires. The new ratio will be (1)

(a) 5 : 2 (b) 1 : 1 (c) 3 : 2 (d) 5 : 1

12. Ashish and Avnish are partners sharing profits in the ratio of 10 : 2. Ankit is admitted and the new profit sharing ratio is now 10 : 6 : 4. At the date of admission, general reserve appears in the books at ₹ 48,000. Avnish's share in the reserve will be (1)

(a) ₹ 8,000 (b) ₹ 40,000 (c) ₹ 14,400 (d) None of these

13. 'X' Limited purchased the assets from 'Y' Limited for ₹ 16,20,000. 'X' Limited issued 10% debentures of ₹ 10 each at 10% discount against the payment. The number of debentures issued by 'X' Limited will be (1)

(a) 16,200 (b) 18,000 (c) 1,80,000 (d) 1,62,000

14. Which of the following is/are method(s) of valuation of goodwill?

(i) Average profit method (ii) Super profit method (iii) Capitalisation method (1)

Codes

(a) Only (i) (b) (i) and (ii) (c) (ii) and (iii) (d) (i), (ii) and (iii)

15. A company 'Vansh Ltd.' has purchased an asset costing ₹ 22,00,000. Vendor issued 10% debentures of ₹ 100 each at 10% premium as consideration against asset purchased. Calculate number of debentures to be issued. (1)

(a) 26,000 debentures
(b) 24,000 debentures
(c) 20,000 debentures
(d) 22,000 debentures

Or XYZ Ltd. called first call money of ₹ 3 per share on its 50,000 shares. A shareholder holding 2,750 shares failed to pay the amount. How much amount will be due on first call?

(a) ₹ 1,41,750 (b) ₹ 1,57,000 (c) ₹ 1,50,000 (d) ₹ 1,47,750

16. A, B and C are partners sharing profits in the ratio of 5 : 3 : 2. They have admitted Z into the partnership for 1/6th share. Investment fluctuation fund appears in the balance at ₹ 13,500 and investment (cost) at ₹ 1,50,000. If the market value of investments is ₹ 1,45,000. Investment fluctuation fund will be shown at .... (1)

(a) ₹ 13,500 (b) ₹ 10,000 (c) ₹ 5,000 (d) ₹ 6,500

17. Complete the following journal entries. (3)

JOURNAL

Date	Particulars		LF	Amt (Dr)	Amt (Cr)
	Land and Building A/c	Dr		18,00,000	
	Plant A/c	Dr		9,20,000	
	Stock A/c	Dr		3,20,000	
	Debtors A/c	Dr		2,80,000	
	.... A/c	Dr		...	
	To Sundry Creditors A/c				2,60,000
	To Blue Bath Ltd.				32,00,000
	(..)				

Date	Particulars	LF	Amt (Dr)	Amt (Cr)
	.... Dr		...	
	To			...
	To			...
	To			...
	(Being purchase consideration settled by issue of 2,50,000 equity shares of ₹ 10 each at 20% premium and balance amount by cheque)			

18. Josh and Krish are partners sharing profits and losses in the ratio of 3 : 1. Their capitals at the end of the financial year 2021-2022 were ₹ 1,50,000 and ₹ 75,000. During the year 2021-22, Josh's drawings were ₹ 20,000 and the drawings of Krish were ₹ 5,000. Profit before charging interest on capital for the year was ₹ 16,000 which was duly credited to their accounts. Krish had brought additional capital of ₹ 16,000 on 1st October, 2021. Calculate interest on capital @ 12% per annum for the year 2021-2022. (3)

Or

Preeti, Mona and Nisha shared profits in the ratio of 3 : 2 : 1. The profits of the last three years were ₹ 1,40,000, ₹ 84,000 and ₹ 1,06,000 respectively. These profits were by mistake, shared equally for all the three years. It is now decided to correct the error. Pass necessary journal entry for the same.

19. Niharika Ltd. purchased a running business from Sunehari Ltd. for a sum of ₹ 30,00,000 by issuing 25,000 fully paid equity shares of ₹ 100 each at a premium of 20%. The assets and liabilities consisted of the following

Machinery ₹ 9,00,000, debtors ₹ 12,50,000, stock ₹ 8,00,000, building ₹ 10,00,000 and bills payable ₹ 7,50,000.

Pass necessary journal entries in the books of Niharika Ltd. for the above transactions. (3)

Or

Priyanka Ltd. has a registered capital of ₹ 25,00,000 divided into 1,00,000 equity shares of ₹ 10 each and 15,000, 8% preference shares of ₹ 100 each. The company issued 5,000 preference shares on which the amount was payable as follows

₹ 30 on application; ₹ 25 on allotment; ₹ 25 on first call and the balance of ₹ 20 on final call

The issue was fully subscribed. Pass necessary journal entries, when it was the policy of the company to maintain only one account for application and allotment.

20. Makkar Ltd. invited applications for 4,000 equity shares of ₹ 10 each at the issue price of ₹ 10. The amount payable alongwith application is ₹ 10. This issue was fully subscribed. Give the journal entries for the above transactions. (3)

21. Vikas and Vivek were partners in a firm sharing profits in the ratio of 3 : 2. On 1st April, 2022, they admitted Vandana as a new partner for 1/8th share in the profits with a guaranteed profit of ₹ 1,50,000. The new profit sharing ratio between Vivek and Vikas will remain the same but they decided to bear any deficiency on account of guarantee to Vandana in the ratio 2 : 3. The profit of the firm for the year ended 31st March, 2023 was ₹ 9,00,000.

Prepare profit and loss appropriation account of Vikas, Vivek and Vandana for the year ended 31st March, 2023. (4)

22. Pass the necessary journal entries for the following transactions on the dissolution of firm of Anju, Manju and Sanju (who were sharing profits in the ratio of 2 : 2 : 1) after the transfer of all assets (other than cash) and external liabilities to realisation account.

(i) Debtors were of ₹ 62,100. Anju takes over debtors amounted to ₹ 60,000 at ₹ 58,600 and the remaining debtors were sold to a debt collecting agency at 50% of the value.

(ii) Sundry assets were of ₹ 58,500. Manju is to take over some sundry assets at ₹ 36,000 (being 10% less than the book value). Sanju is to take over remaining sundry assets at 80% of the book value.

(iii) Sanju assumes the responsibility of discharge of Mrs. Sanju's loan of ₹ 5,750 together with accrued interest of ₹ 1,150. (4)

23. The capital accounts of A and B stood at ₹ 4,00,000 and ₹ 3,00,000 respectively after necessary adjustments in respect of the drawings and the net profits for the year ended 31st March, 2022. It was subsequently ascertained that 5% per annum interest on capital and drawings was not taken into account in arriving at the net profit.

The drawings of the partners had been: A ₹ 12,000 drawn at the end of each quarter and B ₹ 18,000 drawn at the end of each half year. The profits for the year as adjusted amounted to ₹ 2,00,000. The partners share profits in the ratio of 3 : 2. You are required to pass journal entries and show adjusted capital accounts of the partners. (6)

24. (i) Wadhwa Ltd. issued 60,000, 15% debentures of ₹ 10 each credited as fully paid to the promoters for their services and issued 15,000, 15% debentures of ₹ 10 each credited as fully paid to the underwriters for the underwriting services. Journalise these transactions.

(ii) Prabhu Darbaar Pvt. Ltd. issued 20,000, 9% debentures of ₹ 100 each to the public at 10% discount on 1st April, 2021. These debentures are redeemable after 6 years at a premium of 10%.

Pass the necessary journal entries for issue of debentures and writing-off 'loss on issue of debentures' in same year of issue, if company has a balance of ₹ 1,60,000 in its securities premium reserve account. (6)

25. Raja Ltd. invited applications for 1,00,000 equity shares of ₹ 10 each. The shares were issued at a premium of ₹ 5 per share. The amount was payable as follows

On application and allotment ₹ 8 per share (including premium ₹ 3).

The balance including premium on the first and final call.

Applications for 1,50,000 shares were received. Applications for 10,000 shares were rejected and pro-rata allotment was made to the remaining applicants on the following basis

(i) Applicants for 80,000 shares were allotted 60,000 shares.

(ii) Applicants for 60,000 shares were allotted 40,000 shares.

P, who belonged to the first category and was allotted 300 shares, failed to pay the first call money.

Q, who belonged to the second category and was allotted 200 shares, also failed to pay the first call money. Their shares were forfeited. The forfeited shares were reissued @ ₹ 12 per share fully paid-up. Pass necessary journal entries and prepare cash book. (6)

Or

Maharaja Ltd. was incorporated on 1st April, 2020 with registered office in Mumbai. As funds were required the company invited applications for 2,00,000 equity shares of ₹ 10 each at a premium of ₹ 4 per share.

The amount was payable as follows

On application ₹ 6 (including premium ₹ 2) On allotment ₹ 7 (including premium ₹ 2)

Balance on first and final call

Applications for 3,00,000 shares were received. Allotment was made to all the applicants as pro-rata basis Z, to whom 400 shares were allotted failed to pay allotment and call money. A, who had applied for 300 shares failed to pay the call money. Their shares were forfeited after final call. 400 of the forfeited shares (including all shares of A) were reissued @ ₹ 8 per share as fully paid-up.

(i) What amount is received at the time of application?

(a) ₹ 12,00,000 (b) ₹ 18,00,000 (c) ₹ 30,00,000 (d) ₹ 42,00,000

(ii) What is the excess amount received alongwith application money adjusted with allotment?

(a) ₹ 14,00,000 (b) ₹ 4,00,000 (c) ₹ 6,00,000 (d) ₹ 10,00,000

(iii) What is the amount received on allotment?

(a) ₹ 8,01,600 (b) ₹ 14,00,000 (c) ₹ 8,00,000 (d) ₹ 7,98,400

(iv) What is the amount received on first and final call?

(a) ₹ 1,99,400 (b) ₹ 2,00,000 (c) ₹ 1,99,700 (d) ₹ 1,99,800

(v) Amount debited to share capital account at the time of forfeiture will be

(a) ₹ 6,000 (b) ₹ 6,800 (c) ₹ 4,600 (d) ₹ 2,200

(vi) What is the amount of forfeiture transferred to capital reserve?

(a) ₹ 3,200 (b) ₹ 2,400 (c) ₹ 2,800 (d) ₹ 4,000

26. The following is the balance sheet as at 31st December, 2022 of A and B, who share profits and losses in the ratio of 3 : 2.

Balance Sheet
as at 31st December, 2022

Liabilities		Amt (₹)	Assets		Amt (₹)
Capital A/cs			Plant and Machinery		10,000
A	10,000		Land and Building		8,000
B	10,000	20,000	Debtors	12,000	
General Reserve		15,000	(–) Provision for Doubtful Debts	(1,000)	11,000
Workmen's Compensation Fund		5,000	Stock		12,000
Creditors		10,000	Cash		9,000
		50,000			50,000

On 1st January, 2023, they agreed to admit C into partnership on the following terms
(i) Provision of doubtful debts would be increased by ₹ 2,000.
(ii) The value of land and building would be increased to ₹ 18,000.
(iii) The value of stock would be increased by ₹ 4,000.
(iv) A worker being injured in the factory and a claim of ₹ 2,000 was declared for him.
(v) C brought in as his share of goodwill ₹ 10,000 in cash.
(vi) Capital account of A and B will be adjusted by opening cash account.
(vii) C would bring further cash as would make his capital equal to 20% of the total capital of the new firm after the above revaluation and adjustments are carried out.

Prepare revaluation account, partners' capital account and balance sheet of the firm after C's admission. **(6)**

Or P, Q and R were equal partners. Their balance sheet as at 31st March, 2022 is

Balance Sheet
as at 31st March, 2022

Liabilities		Amt (₹)	Assets		Amt (₹)
Bills Payable		20,000	Bank		20,000
Creditors		40,000	Stock		20,000
General Reserve		30,000	Furniture		28,000
Profit and Loss A/c		6,000	Debtors	45,000	
Capital A/cs			(–) Provision for Doubtful Debts	(5,000)	40,000
P	60,000		Land and Building		1,20,000
Q	40,000				
R	32,000	1,32,000			
		2,28,000			2,28,000

Q retired on 1st April, 2022. P and R decided to continue the business as equal partners on the following terms
(i) Goodwill of the firm was valued at ₹ 57,600.
(ii) The provision for doubtful debts to be maintained @ 10% on debtors.
(iii) Land and building to be increased to ₹ 1,32,000.
(iv) Furniture to be reduced by ₹ 8,000.
(v) Rent outstanding (not provided for as yet) was ₹ 1,500.

The remaining partners decided to bring in sufficient cash in the business to pay-off Q and to maintain a bank balance of ₹ 24,800. They also decided to readjust their capitals as per their new profit sharing ratio. Prepare the necessary ledger accounts and the balance sheet.

PART-B
(Financial Statement Analysis)

27. Which of the following items can be presented on the assets side of the balance sheet of company?

(i) Sundry debtors (ii) Public deposits (iii) Livestock (iv) Cash credit **(1)**

Codes

(a) Only (i) (b) (i) and (iii) (c) (ii) and (iii) (d) (i) and (iv)

Or From the following information, you are required to calculate cost of material consumed.

Opening inventory of materials ₹ 30,00,000, opening stock-in-trade ₹ 8,00,000, material purchased ₹ 1,00,00,000, purchase of stock-in trade ₹ 60,00,000, closing inventory of material ₹ 10,00,000, closing inventory of stock ₹ 6,00,000.

(a) ₹ 60,00,000 (b) ₹ 1,20,00,000 (c) ₹ 80,00,000 (d) None of these

28. Which of the following statement is incorrect? **(1)**

(a) Issue of debentures for ₹ 75,000 is a financing cash flow
(b) Dividend paid on equity shares amounting to ₹ 24,000 is a financing cash flow
(c) Purchase of investment for ₹ 40,000 cash is a financing cash flow
(d) Cash proceeds from issue of equity shares is a financing cash flow

29. Statement I Cash flow statement is not a replacement of fund flow statement.

Statement II Cash flow statement is a substitute of income statement. **(1)**

Alternatives

(a) Statement I is correct and Statement II is incorrect (b) Statement I is incorrect and Statement II is correct
(c) Both statements are correct (d) Both statements are incorrect

30. **Balance Sheet** (Extract)

Liabilities	Amt (₹)	Assets	Amt (₹)
Borrowings: 10% Debentures	6,00,000	Inventories	4,80,000
Trade Payables	9,36,000	Trade Receivables	3,60,000
Short-term Provisions	24,000	Cash and Cash Equivalents	91,200

Additional Information

50% of the debentures are repaid by issuing shares amounting to ₹ 3,00,000.

Based on the above information, you are required to calculate the liquid ratio for the company. **(1)**

(a) 1 : 1 (b) 0.47 : 1 (c) 2 : 1 (d) 1 : 2

Or Gross profit of a firm is ₹ 9,00,000 and revenue from operations ₹ 27,00,000. What will be the gross profit ratio?

(a) 34% (b) 38% (c) 33.3% (d) 33%

31. From the following balance sheet, calculate the ratios. **(3)**

(i) Debt equity ratio (ii) Proprietary ratio

Balance Sheet
as at ...

Particulars	Amt (₹)
I. **EQUITY AND LIABILITIES**	
1. **Shareholders' Funds**	
(i) Equity Share Capital	30,00,000
(ii) Reserves and Surplus	12,00,000
2. **Non-current Liabilities**	
Long-term Borrowings (12% Debentures)	10,00,000
3. **Current Liabilities**	
(i) Short-term Borrowings	4,00,000
(ii) Trade Payables	24,00,000
Total	80,00,000

Particulars	Amt (₹)
II. ASSETS	
1. **Non-current Assets**	
(i) Property, Plant and Equipment and Intangible Assets	33,00,000
(ii) Long-term Investments	3,20,000
2. **Current Assets**	
(i) Inventories	18,20,000
(ii) Trade Receivables	24,80,000
(iii) Cash and Cash Equivalents	80,000
Total	80,00,000

32. What is meant by analysis of financial statements? State any two objectives of such an analysis. (3)

33. (i) Current ratio of a company is 2 : 1 and quick ratio is 1 : 1. If value of inventory is ₹ 10,000 and prepaid insurance is ₹ 5,000, then calculate the value of current assets, current liabilities and liquid assets.

(ii) Calculate value of opening stock and closing stock from the following information
Sales ₹ 5,00,000, gross profit is 20% of net sales, return inward is ₹ 20,000, return outward is ₹ 50,000, purchases ₹ 2,50,000, opening stock is 2 times of the closing stock. (4)

Or From the following information, prepare comparative statement of profit and loss.

Particulars	31st March, 2017 (₹)	31st March, 2018 (₹)
Revenue from Operations (% of other income)	250%	250%
Other Income	1,20,000	1,44,000
Cost of Materials Consumed (% of operating revenue)	60%	55%
Expenses (% of material cost)	10%	20%
Tax Rate	30%	30%

34. From the following, calculate the net cash flow from operating activities

Particulars	Note No.	31st March, 2022 (₹)	31st March, 2021 (₹)
I. EQUITY AND LIABILITIES			
1. **Shareholders' Funds**			
(i) Share Capital	1	1,87,500	1,87,500
(ii) Reserves and Surplus	2	77,500	(5,000)
2. **Non-current Liabilities** (8% Debentures)		65,000	37,500
3. **Current Liabilities**			
(i) Short-term Borrowings		10,000	12,500
(ii) Trade Payables		30,000	27,500
(iii) Short-term Provisions		12,500	10,000
Total		3,82,500	2,70,000
II. ASSETS			
1. **Non-current Assets**			
(i) Property, Plant and Equipment (Net)		2,15,000	1,55,000
(ii) Intangible Assets		3,750	10,000
(iii) Non-current Investments		31,250	20,000
2. **Current Assets**			
(i) Current Investments		1,250	3,750
(ii) Inventories		48,750	25,000
(iii) Trade Receivables		50,000	50,000
(iv) Cash and Cash Equivalents		32,500	6,250
Total		3,82,500	2,70,000

Notes to Accounts

Particulars	2022 (₹)	2021 (₹)
1. **Share Capital**		
Equity Share Capital	1,37,500	1,12,500
5% Preference Share Capital	50,000	75,000
	1,87,500	1,87,500
2. **Reserves and Surplus**		
General Reserve	37,500	30,000
Statement of Profit and Loss	37,500	(35,000)
Securities Premium Reserve	2,500	—
	77,500	(5,000)
3. **Short-term Borrowings**		
8% Bank Loan	10,000	12,500
4. **Short-term Provisions**		
Provision for Tax	12,500	10,000
5. **Intangible Assets**		
Goodwill	3,750	10,000

Additional Information

During the year, a piece of machinery costing ₹ 15,000 on which depreciation charged was ₹ 5,000 was sold for ₹ 5,000. Depreciation provided on fixed assets ₹ 15,000. Dividend on equity shares @ 8% was paid on opening balance.

Income tax ₹ 11,250 was provided. Additional debentures were issued at par on 1st October, 2021 and bank loan was repaid on the same date. At the end of the year, preference shares were redeemed at a premium of 5%. (6)

Answers

1. (c) **2.** (c) **3.** (c) *Or* (c) **4.** (a) *Or* (c) **5.** (c) **6.** (b) *Or* (d) **7.** (a)
8. (c) *Or* (c) **9.** (b) **10.** (a) **11.** (c) **12.** (a) **13.** (c) **14.** (d)
15. (c) *Or* (c) **16.** (c)

18. Interest on Josh's Capital = ₹ 18,960; Interest on Krish's Capital = ₹ 8,160

Or Debit Nisha's Capital A/c and Credit Preeti's Capital A/c with ₹ 55,000

19. Capital reserve = ₹ 2,00,000

21. Profit share Vikas = ₹ 4,50,000, Vivek = ₹ 3,00,000, Vandana = ₹ 1,50,000

23. Partners' capital accounts A = ₹ 3,98,790, B = ₹ 3,01,210; Capitals on 1st April, 2018 A = ₹ 3,28,000, B = ₹ 2,56,000; Interest on capital A = ₹ 16,400, B = ₹ 12,800; Interest on drawings A = ₹ 900, B = ₹ 450

25. Capital reserve = ₹ 4,100 *Or* (i) (b) (ii) (c) (iii) (d) (iv) (a) (v) (a) (vi) (b)

26. Profit on revaluation = ₹ 12,000; Capital A/cs A = ₹ 36,000, B = ₹ 24,000, C = ₹ 15,000; Balance sheet total = ₹ 87,000

Or Profit on revaluation = ₹ 3,000; Capital A/cs P and R = ₹ 87,900 each; Balance sheet total = ₹ 2,37,300

27. (b) *Or* (b) **28.** (c) **29.** (a) **30.** (b) *Or* (c)

31. (i) Debt equity ratio = 0.2381 : 1 (ii) Proprietary ratio = 0.525 : 1

33. (i) Current assets = ₹ 30,000; Current liabilities = ₹ 15,000; Liquid assets = ₹ 15,000

(ii) Opening stock = ₹ 3,68,000; Closing stock = ₹ 1,84,000

34. Cash flow from operating activities = ₹ 1,06,500

SAMPLE QUESTION PAPER 2

A Highly Simulated Sample Question Paper for CBSE Class XII Examination

ACCOUNTANCY

Time : 3 Hours **Max. Marks : 80**

General Instructions

1. This question paper contains **34** questions. **All** questions are compulsory.
2. This question paper is divided into **two** Parts: **Part A** and **B**.
3. **Part-A** and **B** are compulsory for all the candidates.
4. Question Nos. **1 to 16** (Part-A) and **27 to 30** (Part-B) are multiple choice questions carrying **1** mark each.
5. Question Nos. **17 to 20** (Part-A) and **31 & 32** (Part-B) are short answer type questions, carrying **3** marks each.
6. Question Nos. from **21, 22** (Part-A) and **33** (Part-B) are long answer type-I questions, carrying **4** marks each.
7. Question Nos. from **23 to 26** (Part-A) and **34** (Part-B) are long answer type-II questions, carrying **6** marks each.
8. There is no overall choice. However, an internal choice has been provided in few questions in each of the parts.

Part-A
(Accounting for Partnership Firms and Companies)

1. Under what circumstances, a partner can get exemption from sharing losses in a firm? (1)
(a) If he is a senior citizen (b) If he is a minor (c) If he is retiring partner (d) All of these

Or If the debit side of realisation account exceeds the credit side, then it signifies
(a) profit on realisation (b) loss on realisation (c) Neither profit nor loss (d) None of these

2. X and Y are sharing profits and losses in the ratio of 3 : 2. Z is admitted with 1/5th share in profits of the firm which he gets entirely from X. Find out the new profit sharing ratio. (1)
(a) 12 : 8 : 5 (b) 8 : 12 : 5 (c) 2 : 2 : 1 (d) 2 : 2 : 2

3. A firm earns ₹ 1,10,000. The normal rate of return is 10%. The assets of the firm amounted to ₹ 11,00,000 and liabilities to ₹ 1,00,000. Value of goodwill by capitalisation of average actual profits will be (1)
(a) ₹ 2,00,000 (b) ₹ 10,000 (c) ₹ 5,000 (d) ₹ 1,00,000

4. Amox Ltd. is registered with a capital of 10,00,000 equity shares of ₹ 10 each. 6,00,000 equity shares were offered for subscription to public. Applications were received for 6,00,000 shares. All calls were made and amount was duly received except final call of ₹ 2 on 80,000 shares. What will be the amount of share capital shown in the balance sheet? (1)
(a) ₹ 60,00,000 (b) ₹ 58,40,000 (c) ₹ 5,84,000 (d) ₹ 6,00,000

Or If a share of ₹ 10 on which ₹ 8 has been called and ₹ 6 is paid is forfeited, the share capital account should be debited with
(a) ₹ 8 (b) ₹ 10 (c) ₹ 6 (d) ₹ 2

5. What will be the journal entry for shares reissued at discount? (1)
(a) Bank A/c Dr
To Share Capital A/c
To Securities Premium Reserve A/c

(b) Bank A/c Dr
Share Forfeiture A/c Dr
To Share Capital A/c

(c) Share Capital A/c Dr
To Bank A/c
To Share Forfeiture A/c

(d) Share Capital A/c Dr
Securities Premium Reserve A/c Dr
To Bank A/c

6. KK, KN and KH are partners sharing profits and losses in the ratio of 2 : 2 : 1. KH retires on 31st December, 2022. Extract of the balance sheet of the firm as at 31st December, 2022 is as follows

Liabilities	Amt (₹)	Assets	Amt (₹)
		Land and Building	40,00,000

If the land and building is revalued at ₹ 48,00,000 how will you show the effect of change in value of land and building in revaluation account? (1)

(a) Land and building account ₹ 8,00,000 (Cr)
(b) Land and building account ₹ 8,00,000 (Dr)
(c) Land and building account ₹ 48,00,000 (Cr)
(d) Land and building account ₹ 48,00,000 (Dr)

Or

X and Y were partners in a firm sharing profits and losses in the ratio of 2 : 1. With effect from 1st January, 2020, they decided to share profits and losses equally. Individual partner's gain or sacrifice due to change in the ratio will be

(a) Gain by X $\frac{1}{6}$, Sacrifice by Y $\frac{1}{6}$
(b) Sacrifice by X $\frac{1}{6}$, Gain by Y $\frac{1}{6}$
(c) Gain by X $\frac{1}{2}$, Sacrifice by Y $\frac{1}{2}$
(d) Sacrifice by X $\frac{1}{2}$, Gain by Y $\frac{1}{2}$

7. State the order of share capitals of the following types according to the Schedule III, Part I of the companies balance sheet.

(i) Subscribed share capital (ii) Authorised/Registered share capital (iii) Issued share capital (1)

Codes

(a) (i), (ii), (iii) (b) (ii), (iii), (i) (c) (iii), (ii), (i) (d) No specified order

8. Ram and Shyam are partners sharing profits in the ratio of 3 : 2. They admit Tarun as a new partner. After his admission, the profit sharing ratio becomes 5 : 5 : 3. On the date of Tarun's admission, goodwill of the firm is valued at ₹ 13,00,000. The amount of goodwill brought in by Tarun will be (1)

(a) ₹ 5,00,000 (b) ₹ 10,00,000 (c) ₹ 3,00,000 (d) ₹ 13,00,000

Or Ram, Raghav and Raghu are partners in a firm sharing profits in the ratio of 5 : 3 : 2. As per partnership deed, Raghu is to get a minimum amount of ₹ 10,000 as profit. Net profit for the year is ₹ 40,000. Calculate deficiency (if any) to Raghu.

(a) ₹ 750 (b) ₹ 2,000 (c) ₹ 1,500 (d) None of these

9. X and Y are partners with capitals of ₹ 6,50,000 and ₹ 5,50,000 respectively. The admit Z as a partner with 1/4th share in profit. Z brought ₹ 6,50,000 as capital.

Entry for premium of goodwill credited to sacrificing partner is

Z's Capital A/c Dr A
To X's Capital A/c B
To Y's Capital A/c C

Here A, B and C will be (1)

(a) A = ₹ 1,87,500, B = ₹ 93,750, C = ₹ 93,750
(b) A = ₹ 6,50,000, B = ₹ 3,25,000, C = ₹ 3,25,000
(c) A = ₹ 6,00,000, B = ₹ 3,25,000, C = ₹ 2,75,000
(d) None of these

10. An old customer whose account was written-off as bad debts has promised to pay ₹ 15,000 in full settlement of his account of ₹ 25,000.

How will it affect revaluation account? (1)

(a) Revaluation account will be credited with ₹ 25,000
(b) Revaluation account will be debited with ₹ 10,000
(c) Revaluation account will be credited with ₹ 15,000
(d) Revaluation account will be credited with ₹ 10,000

11. When debentures are issued at a discount and are redeemable at a premium, which of the following accounts is debited at the time of issue? (1)

(a) Debentures account
(b) Premium on redemption of debentures account
(c) Loss on issue of debentures account
(d) None of these

12. The capital balance of a partner at the end of the year (after adjusting for his drawings ₹ 3,500 and his share in the profit ₹ 2,300) is ₹ 12,000. Interest on capital is payable to him at 5% per annum. What will be the amount of interest on capital? (1)

(a) ₹ 660
(b) ₹ 600
(c) ₹ 540
(d) None of these

13. On dissolution of a firm, partner's loan account is transferred to (1)

(a) realisation account
(b) partners' capital account
(c) partners' current account
(d) None of these

14. Which of the following statements is incorrect about debentures? (1)

(a) Premium received on debentures is credited to securities premium reserve
(b) Loss on issue of debentures is written-off in the year the debentures are issued from statement of profit and loss
(c) Debentures are normally shown as long-term borrowings under non-current liabilities
(d) None of the above

15. **Assertion** (A) Change in profit sharing ratio among existing partners results in reconstitution of partnership firm.
Reason (R) The relationship among partner changes at the time of change in profit sharing ratio. (1)

Alternatives

(a) Both Assertion (A) and Reason (R) are true and Reason (R) is the correct explanation of Assertion (A)
(b) Both Assertion (A) and Reason (R) are true, but Reason (R) is not the correct explanation of Assertion (A)
(c) Assertion (A) is true, but Reason (R) is false
(d) Assertion (A) is false, but Reason (R) is true

16. X, Y and Z are partners in the ratio of 5 : 3 : 2. Before Y's salary of ₹ 3,400 firm's profit is ₹ 19,400. How much in total, Y will receive from the firm? (1)

(a) ₹ 3,400 (b) ₹ 8,000 (c) ₹ 4,800 (d) ₹ 8,200

Or Ram is a partner in a firm. He withdraws regularly ₹ 6,000 at the end of every month for the six months ending 31st March, 2021. If interest on drawings is charged @ 10% p.a., the interest charged will be

(a) ₹ 750 (b) ₹ 900 (c) ₹ 1,050 (d) ₹ 1,800

17. Cameroon Ltd. invited applications for issuing 10,000, 12% debentures of ₹ 100 each at a premium of ₹ 70 per debenture. The full amount was payable on application.

Applications were received for 13,500 debentures. Applications for 3,500 debentures were rejected and application money was refunded. Debentures were allotted to the remaining applications.

Pass necessary journal entries in the books of Cameroon Ltd for the above transactions. (3)

Or Warren Hasting Ltd. took a loan of ₹ 10,00,000 from a bank giving ₹ 12,00,000, 9% debentures as collateral security. Pass journal entry regarding the issue of debentures if any and show this loan in the balance sheet of the company.

18. Y and Z who were sharing profits and losses in the ratio of 3 : 1 respectively, decided to dissolve the firm on 31st March, 2021. Complete the following realisation account, partners' capital account and bank account. (3)

Dr **Realisation Account** Cr

Particulars	Amt (₹)	Particulars		Amt (₹)
To Sundry Assets A/c	60,000	By Sundry Liabilities A/c		
To Bank A/c (Trade creditors)	14,250	Trade Creditors	15,000	
To Bank A/c (Loan from Mrs. Y)	4,750	Loan from Mrs. Y	5,000	20,000
To Bank A/c (Expenses)	500	By Bank A/c (Sundry assets realised)		55,000
		By		...
	79,500			79,500

Dr **Partners' Capital Account** Cr

Particulars	Y (₹)	Z (₹)	Particulars	Y (₹)	Z (₹)
To Balance b/d	—	5,000	By Balance b/d	50,000	—
To Profit and Loss A/c (Loss)	3,000	1,000	By Bank A/c (Cash brought in)	—	7,125
To Realisation A/c	...	...			
To Bank A/c	...	—			
	50,000	7,125		50,000	7,125

Dr **Bank Account** Cr

Particulars	Amt (₹)	Particulars	Amt (₹)
To Balance b/d	1,000	By	...
To Realisation A/c (Assets realised)	55,000	By	...
To Z's Capital A/c (Cash brought in)	7,125	By	...
		By Y's Capital A/c (Final payment)	43,625
	63,125		63,125

19. The partnership agreement between Maneesh and Girish provides that

(i) Profits will be shared equally.
(ii) Maneesh will be allowed a salary of ₹ 400 per month.
(iii) Girish who manages the sales department will be allowed a commission equal to 10% of the net profits, after allowing Maneesh's salary.
(iv) 7% interest will be allowed on partners' fixed capital.
(v) 5% interest will be charged on partners' annual drawings.
(vi) The fixed capitals of Maneesh and Girish are ₹ 1,00,000 and ₹ 80,000 respectively. Their annual drawings were ₹ 16,000 and ₹ 14,000 respectively. The net profit for the year ending 31st March, 2006 amounted to ₹ 40,000.

Prepare firm's profit and loss appropriation account. (3)

Or X and Y are partners in a firm. They admitted Z as a partner without capital for 1/3rd share in the profits of the firm. The new partnership agreement provides for the following

(i) 10% of the trading profit will be donated to Prime Minister's Relief Fund.
(ii) 5% of the trading profit will be donated to the National Blind Relief Fund.
(iii) Products will be sold at a discount of 15% on maximum retail price to the people living below poverty line.
(iv) New retail shops will be opened in the naxal affected areas of the country.
(v) New jobs of sales persons will be reserved for the girls belonging to scheduled castes and scheduled tribes.

Trading profit of the firm for the year ended 31st March, 2022 was ₹ 5,00,000. Prepare 'profit and loss appropriation account' of X, Y and Z for the year ended 31st March, 2022.

20. X, Y and Z are partners sharing profits and losses in the ratio of 2 : 2 : 1. Y retires from the firm on 31st March, 2020. On the date of Y's retirement, the following balances appeared in the books of the firm

Advertisement suspense account	₹ 25,000
Contingency reserve	₹ 15,000
Workmen's compensation reserve	₹ 20,000
Loss in business account	₹ 15,000

Pass the necessary journal entries for the adjustment of these items on Y's retirement. (3)

21. Parth Ltd. was registered with a capital of ₹ 10,00,000 in shares of ₹ 20 each. It invited applications for 50,000 shares. The amount is payable as ₹ 5 on application, ₹ 10 on allotment and ₹ 5 on first and final call. Give journal entries for the above transactions and also show the cash book of the firm, when the public has subscribed for 46,500 shares. (4)

22. A, B and C are partners. Their capitals as on 1st April, 2021 were A ₹ 1,00,000, B ₹ 2,00,000 and C ₹ 3,00,000. Profits for the year 2020-21 amounting to ₹ 1,20,000 were distributed in the ratio of capitals without providing for the following

(i) Interest on capitals A ₹ 10,000, B ₹ 20,000, C ₹ 30,000.
(ii) Interest on drawings A ₹ 6,000, B ₹ 10,000, C ₹ 16,000.
(iii) A's salary of ₹ 2,000 per month and B's commission of ₹ 8,000.

The partnership deed was silent as to the sharing of profits and losses. Pass the necessary single adjusting entry. (4)

23. A, B and C were partners sharing profits and losses in the ratio of 5 : 3 : 2 respectively. On 31st December, 2022, their balance sheet stood as under

Balance Sheet
as at 31st December, 2022

Liabilities		Amt (₹)	Assets	Amt (₹)
Sundry Creditors		50,000	Goodwill	25,000
Employees Provident Fund		5,000	Leasehold	1,00,000
Contingency Reserve		20,000	Patents	30,000
Employees Compensation Reserve		10,000	Machinery	1,50,000
Capital A/cs			Stock	50,000
A	1,50,000		Debtors	40,000
B	1,25,000		Cash at Bank	40,000
C	75,000	3,50,000		
		4,35,000		4,35,000

C died on 1st May, 2023 and it was agreed that

(a) Goodwill to be valued at 2½ years' purchase of last four years' average profits which were I = ₹ 65,000, II = ₹ 60,000, III = ₹ 80,000 and IV = ₹ 75,000.
(b) Machinery be valued at ₹ 1,40,000, patents be valued at ₹ 40,000, leasehold be valued at ₹ 1,25,000 on 1st May, 2023.
(c) For the purpose of calculating C's share in the profits to 2023, the profits in 2023 should be taken to have accrued on the same scale as in 2022.
(d) A sum of ₹ 21,000 to be paid immediately to the executors of C and the balance to be paid in four equal half-yearly instalments together with interest @ 10% per annum. (6)

(i) Amount of deceased partner's share of goodwill be
(a) ₹ 11,667 (b) ₹ 35,000 (c) ₹ 14,000 (d) ₹ 30,000

(ii) What will be the share of deceased partner in profit till his death?
(a) ₹ 5,000 (b) ₹ 15,000 (c) ₹ 10,000 (d) ₹ 6,000

(iii) What will be C's share in the reserve on the date of his death?
(a) ₹ 4,000 (b) ₹ 2,000 (c) ₹ 7,000 (d) ₹ 6,000

(iv) What will be C's share in profits on revaluation?
(a) ₹ 5,000 (b) ₹ 25,000 (c) ₹ 10,000 (d) ₹ 6,000

(v) Amount due to C to be transferred to his executors, account will be
(a) ₹ 75,000 (b) ₹ 1,26,000 (c) ₹ 1,21,000 (d) None of these

(vi) What amount is paid to C's executors?
(a) ₹ 1,21,000 (b) ₹ 1,00,000 (c) ₹ 21,000 (d) None of these

24. (i) Vikram Ltd. issued 4,000, 10% debentures of ₹ 100 each, payable as follows ₹ 25 on application, ₹ 35 on allotment and ₹ 40 on first and final call. All the debentures were applied. Aniket, the holder of 200 debentures paid the entire amount on his holding on allotment. Pass entries.

(ii) PQR Ltd. issued 24,000, 8% debentures of ₹ 100 each at a discount of 5% payable 25% on application, 20% on allotment and balance after three months. Pass necessary journal entries in the books of the company, assuming that the amounts were received as they became due. (6)

25. Batra Ltd. issued 20,000 shares of ₹ 100 each at a premium of ₹ 25 per share, payable as follows
₹ 20 per share on application
₹ 45 per share on allotment (including premium of ₹ 15)
₹ 60 per share on first and final call (including premium of ₹ 10)

The issue was oversubscribed by 10,000 shares. Applicants of 8,000 shares were allotted only 1,000 shares and applicants of 1,000 shares were sent letters of regret. Excess amount received at the time of application was to be adjusted only against allotment and overpayments exceeding the amount due on allotment were to be refunded. All the money due at the time of allotment and call was duly received. Pass necessary entries in the books of the firm. (6)

Or On 1st April, 2021, Vardhman Ltd. made an issue of 2,00,000 equity shares of ₹ 10 each at a premium of ₹ 8 per share, payable as follows
₹ 7 on application (including ₹ 2 premium); ₹ 4 on allotment (including ₹ 2 premium); ₹ 3 on first call (including ₹ 2 premium); ₹ 4 on second and final call (including ₹ 2 premium)

Applications were received for 3,00,000 shares, of which applications for 60,000 shares were rejected and their money were refunded. Rest of the applicants were issued shares on pro-rata basis and their excess money was adjusted towards allotments. X, to whom 400 shares were allotted, failed to pay the allotment money and his shares were forfeited after allotment. Y, who applied for 960 shares failed to pay the two calls and on his such failure, his shares were forfeited.

Z, who was allotted 500 shares did not pay final call. 1,000 forfeited shares reissued as fully paid on receipt of ₹ 8 per share, the whole of Y's shares being included. Prepare the cash book and pass the necessary journal entries.

26. A and B were partners sharing profits and losses in the ratio of 3 : 2. On 31st December, 2022, their balance sheet was as follows

Balance Sheet
as at 31st December, 2022

Liabilities		Amt (₹)	Assets	Amt (₹)
Capital A/cs			Land and Building	80,000
A	60,000		Plant and Machinery	40,000
B	50,000	1,10,000	Stock	22,000
Reserves		20,000	Sundry Debtors	16,000
Sundry Creditors		32,000	Cash	4,000
		1,62,000		1,62,000

On the above date, C was admitted into partnership on the following terms
(i) C was to pay ₹ 40,000 as capital and ₹ 20,000 as goodwill for 1/4th share in profits.
(ii) Land and buildings were to be revalued at ₹ 90,000 and plant and machinery at ₹ 50,000. Stock was to be written down by ₹ 4,000. Creditors included ₹ 1,000 no longer payable.
(iii) Capital of all partners of the new firm were to be in the profit sharing ratio and for this purpose current accounts were to be opened.

Prepare revaluation account, partners' capital account and balance sheet. (6)

Or Xavier, Yusuf and Zaman were partners in a firm sharing profits in the ratio of 4 : 3 : 2. On 1st April, 2021, their balance sheet was as follows

Balance Sheet
as at 1st April, 2021

Liabilities		Amt (₹)	Assets		Amt (₹)
Sundry Creditors		41,400	Cash at Bank		33,000
Capital A/cs			Sundry Debtors	30,450	
Xavier	1,20,000		(–) Provision for Doubtful Debts	(1,050)	29,400
Yusuf	90,000		Stock		48,000
Zaman	60,000	2,70,000	Plant and Machinery		51,000
			Land and Building		1,50,000
		3,11,400			3,11,400

Yusuf had been suffering from ill health and thus gave a notice of retirement from the firm. An agreement was, therefore, entered into as on 1st April, 2021, the terms of which were as follows

(i) That land and building be appreciated by 10%.

(ii) The provision for bad debts is no longer necessary.

(iii) That stock be appreciated by 20%.

(iv) That goodwill of the firm be fixed at ₹ 54,000. Yusuf's share of the same be adjusted into Xavier's and Zaman's capital accounts, who are going to share future profits in the ratio of 2 : 1.

(v) The entire capital of the newly constituted firm be readjusted by bringing in or paying necessary cash so that the future capitals of Xavier and Zaman will be in their profit sharing ratio.

Prepare revaluation account and partners' capital account.

PART-B
(Financial Statement Analysis)

27. From the following information, calculate the amount of cash flow from financing activities.

Particulars	31st March, 2023 (₹)	31st March, 2022 (₹)
Equity Share Capital	20,00,000	18,00,000
Securities Premium Reserve	5,20,000	5,00,000
12% Debentures	2,00,000	3,00,000

Additional Information

Interest paid on debentures ₹ 36,000. (1)

(a) ₹ 36,000 (b) ₹ 2,20,000 (c) ₹ 84,000 (d) ₹ 1,36,000

Or The net amount of source or use of cash when a fixed asset (having book value ₹ 1,20,000) is sold at a loss of ₹ 40,000 in term of cash flow will be ....

(a) ₹ 1,20,000 (b) ₹ 40,000 (c) ₹ 80,000 (d) ₹ 1,60,000

28. Which of the following statement is incorrect? (1)

(a) Term loan from bank is shown under the sub-head long-term borrowings

(b) Internet expenses, carriage inwards, commission allowed are shown in notes to accounts on other expenses

(c) Share issue expenses to be written-off after 12 months is classified as other current assets

(d) Commission paid for deposit mobilisation is included in other borrowing cost

Or The most commonly used tools for financial analysis are

(a) horizontal analysis (b) vertical analysis

(c) ratio analysis (d) All of these

29. Which of the following does not indicate long-term financial solvency?

(i) Debt equity ratio (ii) Debt ratio (iii) Liquidity ratio (iv) Equity ratio (1)

Codes

(a) (i) and (iv) (b) Only (iii) (c) (ii) and (iv) (d) Only (iv)

30. **Statement I** Purchase and sale of shares on behalf of customers is an operating activity.

Statement II They are being purchased for their customers. (1)

Alternatives

(a) Statement I is correct and Statement II is incorrect
(b) Statement I is incorrect and Statement II is correct
(c) Both statements are correct
(d) Both statements are incorrect

31. From the following balance sheet of Varsha Ltd. as at 31st March, 2021, calculate the return on investment for the year 2020-2021.

Balance Sheet
as at 31st March, 2021

Particulars	Note No.	31st March, 2021 (₹)
I. EQUITY AND LIABILITIES		
1. **Shareholders' Funds**		
(i) Share Capital	1	16,50,000
(ii) Reserves and Surplus (Balance of statement of profit and loss)		3,75,000
2. **Non-current Liabilities**		
12% Debentures		12,00,000
3. **Current Liabilities**		
Trade Payables		5,10,000
Total		37,35,000
II. ASSETS		
1. **Non-current Assets**		
(i) Property, Plant and Equipment and Intangible Assets	2	28,50,000
(ii) Non-current Investment	3	2,25,000
2. **Current Assets**		6,60,000
Total		37,35,000

Notes to Accounts

Particulars	Amt (₹)
1. **Share Capital**	
Equity Share Capital	15,00,000
Preference Share Capital	1,50,000
	16,50,000
2. **Property, Plant and Equipment and Intangible Assets**	
Property, Plant and Equipment	34,50,000
(–) Depreciation	(6,00,000)
	28,50,000
3. **Non-current Investment**	
10% Trade Investment	1,50,000
10% Other Investment (Face value ₹ 1,05,000)	75,000
	2,25,000

Additional Information

Net profit before tax but after interest for the year 2020-21 is ₹ 6,07,500 and tax rate is 40% (3)

32. From the following, calculate
(i) Current ratio (ii) Working capital turnover ratio (3)

Particulars	Amt (₹)	Particulars	Amt (₹)
Non-current Assets	50,000	Total Assets	1,00,000
Shareholders' Fund	60,000	Non-current Liabilities	20,000
Revenue from Operations	1,50,000		

33. Mention about any four parties which are interested in financial statement analysis. (4)

Or From the following information for the year ended 31st March, 2022, prepare notes to accounts on finance costs

Particulars	Amt (₹)
Interest paid on Cash Credit	1,10,000
Interest paid on Debentures	1,75,000
Commitment Charges	10,000
Bank Charges	2,250
Interest paid on Public Deposits	40,000
Commission paid for Deposit Mobilisation	8,000

34. Prepare a cash flow statement from the following information of Mr. Rajesh (a proprietor).

Balance Sheet

Liabilities	31st March, 2022 (₹)	31st March, 2021 (₹)	Assets	31st March, 2022 (₹)	31st March, 2021 (₹)
Capital	1,60,000	1,50,000	Cash	5,000	4,000
Bank Loan	10,000	20,000	Debtors	40,000	35,000
Mr. Rajesh's Loan	20,000	5,000	Stock	25,000	20,000
Creditors	42,000	30,000	Land	36,000	25,000
Depreciation Provision	15,000	10,000	Building	55,000	50,000
			Machinery	86,000	81,000
	2,47,000	2,15,000		2,47,000	2,15,000

(i) During the year 2021-22, Mr. Rajesh had withdrawn ₹ 21,000 for personal use.

(ii) A part of the machinery costing ₹ 10,000 (accumulated depreciation ₹ 8,000) was sold for ₹ 5,000. (6)

Answers

1. (b) *Or* (b) **2.** (c) **3.** (d) **4.** (b) *Or* (a) **5.** (b) **6.** (a) *Or* (b) **7.** (b)
8. (c) *Or* (b) **9.** (a) **10.** (c) **11.** (c) **12.** (a) **13.** (d) **14.** (b)
15. (a) **16.** (d) *Or* (a)
19. Share of profit Manish = ₹ 10,290; Girish = ₹ 10,290
Or Share of profit X, Y, Z = ₹ 1,41,667 each
21. Cash book balance = ₹ 9,30,000
22. Debit B's Capital A/c with ₹ 2,000, C's Capital A/c with ₹ 26,000 and credit A's Capital A/c with ₹ 28,000
23. (i) (b) (ii) (a) (iii) (d) (iv) (a) (v) (c) (vi) (c)
26. Profit on revaluation = ₹ 17,000; Balance in capital A/cs A = ₹ 93,150, B = ₹ 62,100, C = ₹ 51,750;
Balance sheet total = ₹ 2,49,750
Or Profit on revaluation = ₹ 25,650; Capital A/cs Xavier = ₹ 1,97,100, Zaman = ₹ 98,550; Yusuf's loan A/c = ₹ 1,16,550
27. (c) *Or* (c) **28.** (c) *Or* (d) **29.** (b) **30.** (b) **31.** 23.52% **32.** (i) 2.5 : 1 (ii) 5 times
33. *Or* Finance costs = ₹ 3,43,000
34. Cash flow from operating activities = ₹ 43,000 ; Cash flow from investing activities = ₹ 26,000
Cash flow from financing activities = ₹ 16,000

SAMPLE QUESTION PAPER 3

A Highly Simulated Sample Question Paper for CBSE Class XII Examination

ACCOUNTANCY

Time : 3 Hours **Max. Marks : 80**

General Instructions

1. This question paper contains **34** questions. **All** questions are compulsory.
2. This question paper is divided into **two** Parts: **Part A** and **B**.
3. **Part-A** and **B** are compulsory for all the candidates.
4. Question Nos. **1 to 16** (Part-A) and **27 to 30** (Part-B) are multiple choice questions carrying **1** mark each.
5. Question Nos. **17 to 20** (Part-A) and **31 & 32** (Part-B) are short answer type questions, carrying **3** marks each.
6. Question Nos. from **21, 22** (Part-A) and **33** (Part-B) are long answer type-I questions, carrying **4** marks each.
7. Question Nos. from **23 to 26** (Part-A) and **34** (Part-B) are long answer type-II questions, carrying **6** marks each.
8. There is no overall choice. However, an internal choice has been provided in few questions in each of the parts.

PART-A

(Accounting for Partnership Firms and Companies)

1. 'A' and 'B' were partners in a firm. They share profits in 2 : 3 ratio. They close their accounts on 31st December every year. 'A' withdrew a fixed sum of ₹ 2,000 at the beginning of every month starting from 1st July, 2022. You have to calculate interest on drawings while rate of interest is 12%. (1)

(a) ₹ 420 (b) ₹ 720 (c) ₹ 440 (d) ₹ 580

2. XYZ Ltd. issued 20,000 equity shares of ₹ 10 each at a premium of ₹ 2 payable alongwith application. All the shares were applied and duly allotted. What will be the total amount at the time of application? (1)

(a) ₹ 2,00,000 (b) ₹ 2,20,000 (c) ₹ 2,40,000 (d) ₹ 2,60,000

3. Rights of a partner consists which of the following? (1)

(a) Right to inspect books of accounts
(b) Right to not allow the admission of new partner
(c) Right to conduct affairs of business
(d) All of these

Or Goodwill of firm is ₹ 53,750. Find the number of years' purchased if the average profits are ₹ 21,500.

(a) 1 (b) 1.5 (c) 2 (d) 2.5

4. A firm has an unrecorded investment of ₹ 5,000. Entry in the firm's journal on admission of a partners will be (1)

(a) Unrecorded Investment A/c	Dr	5,000	
To Revaluation A/c			5,000
(b) Partners' Capital A/c	Dr	5,000	
To Unrecorded Investment A/c			5,000
(c) Revaluation A/c	Dr	5,000	
To Unrecorded Investment A/c			5,000

(d) None of the above

Or P and Q are partners with the profit sharing ratio of 1 : 2. They decided to change this ratio to 2 : 1 with effect from 1st April, 2021. In adjustment entry, Q's account will be ...... by .... assuming goodwill of firm is valued at ₹ 15,000.

(a) debited, ₹ 10,000 (b) credited, ₹ 10,000
(c) credited, ₹ 5,000 (d) debited, ₹ 5,000

5. Which of the following is correct with regard to usage of balance of share forfeiture account?

(i) Provide for discount given at the time of reissue
(ii) Write-off preliminary expenses (iii) Write-off bad debts (1)

Codes

(a) (i) and (ii) (b) Only (i) (c) Only (iii) (d) (i) and (ii)

6. A, B and C are partners sharing profits and losses in the ratio of 2 : 2 : 1. The extract of their balance sheet is as follows

Liabilities	Amt (₹)	Assets	Amt (₹)
		Stock	2,40,000

If the value of stock is to be reduced by ₹ 40,000, then what will be the amount of stock at which it will be shown in reconstituted balance sheet? (1)

(a) ₹ 2,80,000 (b) ₹ 40,000 (c) ₹ 2,00,000 (d) ₹ 2,40,000

Or P and Q are partners in a firm. They decided to dissolve the firm. Assets other than cash ₹ 1,60,000, cash ₹ 25,000, total liabilities ₹ 1,75,000. On dissolution, assets realised ₹ 1,25,000 and liabilities paid ₹ 1,40,000. Net profit or loss on realisation is

(a) profit ₹ 25,000 (b) loss ₹ 25,000 (c) loss ₹ 15,000 (d) No profit no loss

7. Which account is debited, when some amount of any installment of share capital is not received from any shareholder by the company? (1)

(a) Calls-in-advance (b) Calls-in-arrears (c) Cash (d) Share allotment

Or Capital which is called only at the time of winding-up of the company is called

(a) capital reserve (b) reserve capital (c) secure capital (d) authorised capital

8. 'A' and 'B' are partners sharing profits and losses in the ratio of 5 : 3. On admission, 'C' brings ₹ 70,000 cash and ₹ 48,000 against goodwill. New profit sharing ratio between 'A', 'B' and 'C' is 7 : 5 : 4. The sacrificing ratio among 'A' and 'B' is (1)

(a) 4 : 1 (b) 4 : 7 (c) 5 : 4 (d) 3 : 1

9. A computer purchased on 1st October, 2022 for ₹ 40,000 debited to office expenses account is to be brought into account on 31st March, 2024 charging depreciation @ 10% p.a. on written down value basis. What will be the effect on revaluation account? (1)

(a) Revaluation account will be credited with ₹ 38,000 (b) Revaluation account will be debited with ₹ 34,200
(c) Revaluation account will be credited with ₹ 34,200 (d) Revaluation account will be credited with ₹ 40,000

10. At the time of admission of a new partner, a liability for claim, included is creditors for ₹ 20,000 is settled at ₹ 16,000. The following entry will be passed

Creditors A/c	Dr	A	
To Bank A/c			B
To Revaluation A/c			C

Here, A, B and C will be (1)

(a) A = ₹ 20,000, B = ₹ 4,000 and C = ₹ 16,000 respectively (b) A = ₹ 20,000, B = ₹ 16,000 and C = ₹ 4,000 respectively
(c) A = ₹ 16,000, B = ₹ 80,000 and C = ₹ 80,000 respectively (d) A = ₹ 20,000, B = ₹ 10,000 and C = ₹ 10,000 respectively

11. In the profit and loss appropriation account, net profit is always taken after (1)

(a) interest on partner's loan (b) manager's commission
(c) Both (a) and (b) (d) None of these

12. 'P', 'Q' and 'R' are partners sharing profits in the ratio of 2 : 1 : 1. 'R' retires and assets and liabilities are revalued, resulting in a profit of ₹ 12,000. 'R's' share will be (1)

(a) ₹ 6,000 (b) ₹ 3,000 (c) ₹ 2,000 (d) None of these

13. A company forfeited 700 shares of ₹ 10 each on which only ₹ 5 per share was paid. Out of these 200 shares were reissued at ₹ 9 per share. What amount will be transferred from share forfeiture account to capital reserve account? (1)

(a) ₹ 800 (b) ₹ 200 (c) ₹ 3,500 (d) ₹ 2,500

14. Which of the following statements is incorrect about shares? (1)

(a) Shares cannot be issued at discount
(b) The liability of every shareholder of the company is unlimited
(c) A private limited company with only one person as its member is called one person company
(d) Shareholders receive dividend from the company as a benefit against their investment

15. Net profit of a firm is ₹ 9,900. Manager is entitled to a commission of 10% on profits before charging his commission. Manager's commission will be (1)

(a) ₹ 990 (b) ₹ 900 (c) ₹ 1,100 (d) ₹ 970

Or Raj is a partner in a firm. He withdraw regularly ₹ 4,000 every month for the six months ending 31st March, 2020. If interest on drawings is charged @ 8% p.a., the interest charged will be

(a) ₹ 960 (b) ₹ 560 (c) ₹ 400 (d) ₹ 480

16. **Assertion** (A) Minimum subscription is the minimum amount which must be subscribed by the public.
Reason (R) Minimum subscription has been fixed at 80% of the issued amount. (1)

Alternatives

(a) Both Assertion (A) and Reason (R) are true and Reason (R) is the correct explanation of Assertion (A)
(b) Both Assertion (A) and Reason (R) are true, but Reason (R) is not the correct explanation of Assertion (A)
(c) Assertion (A) is true, but Reason (R) is false
(d) Assertion (A) is false, but Reason (R) is true

17. A Ltd. forfeited 300 shares of ₹ 10 each fully called-up, held by Zee for non-payment of allotment money of ₹ 3 per share and final call of ₹ 4 per share. He had paid the application money of ₹ 3 per share. These shares were reissued to Cee for ₹ 8 per share. Pass necessary journal entries. (3)

Or X Ltd. purchased machinery for ₹ 5,00,000 from Y Ltd. Half of the amount was paid by accepting a bill of exchange drawn by Y Ltd. payable after three months. The balance was paid by issue of equity shares of ₹ 10 each at a premium of 25%. Pass necessary journal entries in the books of X Ltd. for these transactions.

18. P, Q and R were partners in a firm sharing profits and losses in 2 : 2 : 1 ratio. The firm closes its books on 31st March every year. P died three months after the last accounts were prepared. On that date, the goodwill of the firm was valued at ₹ 90,000.

On the death of a partner, his share of profit in the year of death was to be calculated on the basis of the average profit of the last four years. The profits of last four years were

I. ₹ 2,00,000 II. ₹ 1,80,000 III. ₹ 2,10,000 IV. ₹ 1,70,000 (Loss)

Pass the necessary journal entries to adjust P's share of goodwill and profit. (3)

Or Pass necessary journal entries for recording the following transactions at the time of dissolution of the firm.

(i) Z, a partner agreed to pay-off his wife's loan ₹ 20,000.
(ii) X, a partner takes over an unrecorded asset (typewriter) at ₹ 300.
(iii) Undistributed balance (debit) of profit and loss account ₹ 30,000. The firm has three partners X, Y and Z.
(iv) Y, who undertakes to carry out the dissolution proceedings is allowed ₹ 2,000 for the same.
(v) Partner Y's loan paid-off ₹ 10,000.
(vi) ₹ 10,000 bills payable settled at ₹ 8,000.

19. Complete the following journal entries (3)

JOURNAL

Date	Particulars		LF	Amt (Dr)	Amt (Cr)
	Sundry Assets A/c	Dr		20,00,000	
	....	Dr		...	
	To Sundry Liabilities A/c				3,00,000
	To Vendor's A/c				17,60,000
	(Being the purchase consideration for acquiring the business)				

Date	Particulars	LF	Amt (Dr)	Amt (Cr)
	.... Dr		...	
	To 10% Debentures A/c (10,000 × 100)			10,00,000
	To			...
	To			...
	To			...
	(Being the purchase consideration settled by issue of 10,000, 10% debentures of ₹ 100 each at a premium of 10%, 6,000 equity shares of ₹ 100 each and 60,000 in cash)			

20. P and Q were partners in a firm sharing profits and losses equally. Their fixed capitals were ₹ 2,00,000 and ₹ 3,00,000 respectively. The partnership deed provided for interest on capital @12% per annum. For the year ended 31st March, 2016, the profits of the firm were distributed without providing interest on capital. Pass necessary adjustment entry to rectify the error. (3)

21. Ayaan and Husna are partners. Ayaan's capital is ₹ 2,50,000 and Husna's capital is ₹ 1,60,000. Interest is payable @ 8% p.a. Husna is entitled to a salary of ₹ 3,000 per month for extra time, she devotes to the business. Profit for the current year before interest and salary to Husna is ₹ 1,00,000. Divide the profit between Ayaan and Husna. Also, calculate total closing capital of each partner at the end of the year. (4)

22. Bina, Rahul and Priya were partners in a firm having capitals of ₹ 6,000, ₹ 6,000 and ₹ 8,000 respectively. Their current account balances were: Bina ₹ 1,000; Rahul ₹ 500 and Priya ₹ 200 (Dr).

According to the partnership deed, the partners were entitled to interest on capital @ 5% p.a. Priya being the working partner was also entitled to a salary of ₹ 600 p.a. The profits were to be divided as

(i) The first ₹ 2,000 in proportion to their capitals.

(ii) Next ₹ 3,000 in the ratio of 5 : 3 : 2. (iii) Remaining profits to be shared equally.

The firm made a profit of ₹ 15,600 before charging any of the above items.

Prepare profit and loss appropriation account. (4)

23. (i) X Ltd. purchased machinery from Y Ltd. and paid to Y Ltd. as follows

(a) By issuing 5,000, equity shares of ₹ 10 each at a premium of 10%.

(b) By issuing 100, 9% debentures of ₹ 100 each at a discount of 10%.

(c) Balance by accepting a bill of exchange of ₹ 25,000 payable after one month.

Pass necessary journal entries in the books of X Ltd. for the purchase of machinery and making payment to Y Ltd.

(ii) Rashmi Ltd. issued 2,000, 6% debentures of ₹ 100 each. The whole amount was payable at the time of application. Applications were received for 2,500 debentures. Company issued debentures to all the applicants on pro-rata basis. Give journal entries. (6)

24. L, M and N were equal partners. On 31st March, 2022, their balance sheet stood as under

Balance Sheet
as at 31st March, 2022

Liabilities		Amt (₹)	Assets	Amt (₹)
Creditors		1,00,800	Cash	7,400
Reserve		24,000	Stock	40,200
Capital A/cs			Debtors	1,25,200
L	60,000		Investments	32,000
M	50,000		Furniture	13,000
N	30,000	1,40,000	Building	47,000
		2,64,800		2,64,800

The firm was dissolved on that date. For the purpose of dissolution, investments were valued at ₹ 36,000 and L took over the investments at this value. Fixed assets realised ₹ 59,400 whereas stock and debtors realised ₹ 1,60,000. Expenses of realisation amounted to ₹ 2,600. Creditors allowed a discount of ₹ 1,600. In addition, one bill receivable for ₹ 3,000 under discount was dishonoured as the acceptor had become insolvent and was unable to pay anything and hence, the bill had to be met by the firm.

Prepare realisation account, partners' capital account and cash account showing how the accounts would finally be settled among the partners. (6)

25. Makkar Ltd. was registered with an authorised capital of ₹ 20,00,000 divided in ₹ 10 per equity share. It invited applications for issuing 1,00,000 equity shares at a premium of ₹ 2 per share. The amount was payable as follows

On application	₹ 4 per share (including premium)
On allotment	₹ 3 per share
On first and final call	Balance amount

Applications were received for 1,30,000 shares. Applications for 10,000 shares were rejected and the application money received on them was refunded. Pro-rata allotment was made to the remaining applications.

Amount overpaid on these applications was adjusted towards the amount due on allotment. Raj, who had applied for 1,200 shares, failed to pay the allotment and call money.

The company forfeited his shares, out of which 800 shares were reissued to Mohan at ₹ 9 per share fully paid-up.

You are required to

(i) Pass the journal entries in the books of the company through calls-in-arrears account.
(ii) Prepare the share allotment account. **(6)**

Or XYZ Ltd. invited applications for issuing 10,00,000 equity shares of ₹ 10 each payable as follows

On application and allotment	₹ 4 per share (including premium ₹ 1)
On first call	₹ 4 per share
On second and final call	₹ 3 per share

Applications for 15,00,000 shares were received and pro-rata allotment was made to all the applicants. Excess application money was adjusted on the sums due on calls. A shareholders who had applied for 6,000 shares did not pay the first and the second and final call. His shares were forfeited. 90% of the forfeited shares were reissued of ₹ 8 per share fully paid-up.

(i) Excess money received on application adjusted towards calls is
(a) ₹ 30,00,000 (b) ₹ 10,00,000 (c) ₹ 20,00,000 (d) ₹ 40,00,000

(ii) What amount is received on, first and final call?
(a) ₹ 19,92,000 (b) ₹ 39,92,000 (c) ₹ 20,00,000 (d) ₹ 19,84,000

(iii) What amount is received on second and final call?
(a) ₹ 29,76,000 (b) ₹ 30,00,000 (c) ₹ 29,88,000 (d) ₹ 10,00,000

(iv) Amount debited to equity share capital account at the time of forfeiture will be
(a) ₹ 40,000 (b) ₹ 20,000 (c) ₹ 12,000 (d) ₹ 8,000

(v) Amount credited to share forfeiture account at the time of forfeiture will be
(a) ₹ 40,000 (b) ₹ 12,000 (c) ₹ 20,000 (d) ₹ 8,000

(vi) What is the amount of forfeiture transferred to capital reserve?
(a) ₹ 18,000 (b) ₹ 10,800 (c) ₹ 7,200 (d) ₹ 12,800

26. The balance sheet of R and L, who are partners in a firm sharing profits in the ratio of 3 : 2 was as follows

Balance Sheet

as at ...

Liabilities		Amt (₹)	Assets		Amt (₹)
Capital A/cs			Machinery		6,000
R	6,000		Buildings		4,800
L	4,800	10,800	Debtors	7,200	
General Reserves		9,000	(−) Provision	(600)	6,600
Workmen's Compensation Fund		3,000	Stock		7,200
Creditors		7,200	Cash		5,400
		30,000			30,000

They agreed to admit D into partnership for 1/5th share of profits on the following terms

(i) Provision for doubtful debts would be increased by ₹ 1,200.
(ii) The value of land and building would be increased to ₹ 10,800.
(iii) The value of stock would be increased by ₹ 2,400.
(iv) The liability against workmen's compensation fund is determined at ₹ 1,200.

(v) D brought in as his share of goodwill ₹ 6,000 in cash. D would bring further cash as would make his capital equal to 20% of the total capital of the new firm, after the above revaluation and adjustments are carried out.

Prepare revaluation account, partners' capital account and the balance sheet of the firm after D's admission. (6)

Or The balance sheet of Zee, Pee and Cee who were sharing profits in proportion to their capitals is given below

Balance Sheet
as at ...

Liabilities		Amt (₹)	Assets		Amt (₹)
Sundry Creditors		36,000	Goodwill		54,000
Workmen Compensation Reserve		59,400	Cash at Bank		33,000
Employees Provident Fund		5,400	Sundry Debtors	30,000	
Capital A/cs			(–) Provision for Doubtful Debts	(600)	29,400
Zee	1,20,000		Stock		48,000
Pee	90,000		Plant and Machinery		51,000
Cee	60,000	2,70,000	Factory Land and Building		1,50,000
			Advertisement Expenditure A/c		5,400
		3,70,800			3,70,800

Pee retires and the following re-adjustments of the assets and liabilities have been agreed upon before the ascertainment of the amount payable by the firm to Pee.

(i) That the stock be depreciated by 6%.
(ii) That the provision for doubtful debts be brought up to 5% on debtors.
(iii) That the factory land and building be appreciated by 20%.
(iv) That a provision of ₹ 4,620 be made in respect of outstanding legal charges.
(v) That the goodwill of the entire firm be fixed at ₹ 64,800 and Pee's share of the same be adjusted into the accounts of Zee and Cee who are going to share in future in the proportion of five-eighths and three-eighths respectively. (No goodwill account is to be raised).
(vi) That the entire capital of the firm as newly constituted be fixed at ₹ 1,68,000 between Zee and Cee in the proportion of five-eighths and three-eighths after passing entries in their accounts for adjustments (i.e. actual cash to be paid-off or to be brought in by the continuing partners as the case may be).

Pass the necessary journal entries to give effect to the above arrangement and prepare the balance sheet of new firm transferring the amount due to retiring partner to a separate loan account in his name.

PART-B

(Financial Statement Analysis)

27. Which of the following statements is correct? (1)

(a) Payment of outstanding liabilities will not change the current ratio
(b) Sale of furniture costing ₹ 10,000 of loss of ₹ 2,000 will reduce the current ratio
(c) Goods costing ₹ 10,000 withdrawn for personal use will reduce the gross profit ratio
(d) Purchase of machinery for cash will reduce the quick ratio

Or $\frac{\text{Total Assets}}{\text{Debt}}$ is used for calculating

(a) Debtors Turnover Ratio (b) Debt Equity Ratio (c) Debt Turnover Ratio (d) Total Assets of Debt Ratio

28. Current liabilities of a company are ₹ 3,50,000. Its current ratio is 3 : 1 and acid test ratio is 1.75 : 1. What will be the value of liquid assets? (1)

(a) ₹ 6,10,700 (b) ₹ 10,50,000 (c) ₹ 8,10,000 (d) ₹ 6,12,500

29. What are the principal revenue during activities for as insurance company?

(i) Receipt of premium (ii) Payment of claims (iii) Purchase and sale of land (iv) Giving and taking loans (1)

Codes

(a) Only (i) (b) (i) and (ii) (c) (ii) and (iii) (d) (iii) and (iv)

Or

Balance Sheet (Extract)

Particulars	31st March, 2020 (₹)	31st March, 2019 (₹)
Investments @ 10%	10,00,000	5,00,000

Additional Information

Half of the investments held in the beginning of the year were sold @ 10% profit. Interest and dividend received on investments ₹ 70,000 and ₹ 50,000 respectively.

How much amount as per above information, will be shown in investing activity for cash flow statement prepared on 31st March, 2020?

(a) Outflow ₹ 3,55,000
(b) Outflow ₹ 3,25,000
(c) Inflow ₹ 3,55,000
(d) Inflow ₹ 1,20,000

30. **Statement I** Dividend paid is always shown as operating activity.

Statement II Depreciation and amortisation, being non-cash expenses, are deducted from net profit before tax and extraordinary items. (1)

Alternatives

(a) Statement I is correct and Statement II is incorrect
(b) Statement I is incorrect and Statement II is correct
(c) Both statements are correct
(d) Both statements are incorrect

31. From the following details, calculate debtors turnover ratio and average receivable period in terms of months. (3)

Total sales for the year	₹ 1,75,000
Cash sales	20% of total sales
Sales return out of credit sales sales	₹ 10,000
Sundry debtors	
Opening balance	₹ 8,000
Closing balance	₹ 12,000

32. Calculate current assets of a company from the following information

Stock turnover ratio = 4 times

Stock at the end is ₹ 20,000 more than the stock in the beginning

Sales ₹ 3,00,000 and gross profit ratio is 20% of sales.

Current liabilities = ₹ 40,000, Quick ratio = 0.75 (3)

33. Prepare balance sheet of XYZ Ltd. as at 31st March, 2023 from the following information (4)

Particulars	Amt (₹)	Particulars	Amt (₹)
Equity Share Capital	40,00,000	Surplus i.e. Balance in Statement of Profit and Loss (Cr)	6,00,000
12% Preference Share Capital	20,00,000		
Property, Plant and Equipment and Intangible Assets (At cost)	93,20,000	Stock	12,00,000
		Sundry Debtors	16,00,000
Depreciation Written-off till Date	33,20,000	Cash	3,00,000
Investments	8,00,000	Loans and Advances	1,00,000
Current Liabilities	16,00,000	Provision for Taxation	4,00,000
12% Debentures	12,00,000	Workmen Compensation Reserve	2,00,000

Or

List the items which are shown under the heading 'current liabilities' as per Schedule III, Part I of the Companies Act, 2013.

34. Batra Ltd. made a profit of ₹ 1,20,000 after considering the following during the year 31st March, 2022.

(i) Depreciation of property, plant and equipment ₹ 30,000

(ii) Amortisation of goodwill ₹ 20,000

(iii) Loss on sale of machine ₹ 10,000

(iv) Profit on sale of building ₹ 20,000

(v) Transfer to general reserve ₹ 30,000

(vi) Interim dividend paid ₹ 20,000

(vii) Dividend received on investment ₹ 10,000

(viii) Provision for taxation made ₹ 16,000

The following additional information is also available to you

Particulars	31st March, 2021 (₹)	31st March, 2022 (₹)
Accounts Receivable	60,000	50,000
Accounts Payable	30,000	70,000
Prepaid Expenses	5,000	3,000

Calculate cash flow from operating activities. (6)

Answers

1. (a) **2.** (c) **3.** (d) *Or* (d) **4.** (a) *Or* (c) **5.** (b) **6.** (c) *Or* (d)

7. (b) *Or* (b) **8.** (d) **9.** (c) **10.** (b) **11.** (c) **12.** (b)

13. (a) **14.** (b) **15.** (a) *Or* (d) **16.** (c)

17. Capital reserve = ₹ 300 *Or* Number of shares issued = 20,000 shares

21. Profit transferred to partner's capital A/c = ₹ 31,200; Closing capital Ayaan = ₹ 2,85,600, Husna = ₹ 2,24,400

22. To partner's current account Bina = ₹ 5,100, Rahul = ₹ 4,500, Priya = ₹ 4,400

24. Loss on realisation = ₹ 6,000; Cash paid to L, M and N = ₹ 30,000, ₹ 56,000, ₹ 36,000 respectively.

25. Amount received on allotment after calls-in-arrears = ₹ 2,17,800; Transferred to capital reserve = ₹ 1,440

Or (i) (c) (ii) (a) (iii) (c) (iv) (a) (v) (c) (vi) (b)

27. (d) *Or* (d) **28.** (a) **29.** (b) *Or* (a) **30.** (a) **32.** Value of current assets = ₹ 1,00,000

33. Balance sheet total = ₹ 1,00,00,000 **34.** ₹ 2,52,000

CBSE
Examination Paper 2025

Accountancy

Time : 3 Hours **Max. Marks : 80**

General Instructions

1. This question paper contains **34** questions. **All** questions are compulsory.
2. This question paper is divided into **two** Parts: **Part A** and **B**.
3. **Part-A** and **B** are compulsory for all the candidates.
4. Question Nos. **1 to 16** (Part-A) and **27 to 30** (Part-B) are multiple choice questions carrying **1** mark each.
5. Question Nos. **17 to 20** (Part-A) and **31 & 32** (Part-B) are short answer type questions, carrying **3** marks each.
6. Question Nos. from **21, 22** (Part-A) and **33** (Part-B) are long answer type-I questions, carrying **4** marks each.
7. Question Nos. from **23 to 26** (Part-A) and **34** (Part-B) are long answer type-II questions, carrying **6** marks each.
8. There is no overall choice. However, an internal choice has been provided in few questions in each of the parts.

PART A
(Accounting for Partnership Firms and Companies)

1. Arun, Bashir and Joseph were partners in a firm sharing profits and losses in the ratio of 5 : 3 : 2. They admitted Daksh as a new partner who acquired his share entirely from Arun. If Arun sacrificed 1/5th from his share to Daksh, Daksh's share in the profits of the firm will be **(1)**

(a) $\frac{1}{10}$ (b) $\frac{1}{5}$ (c) $\frac{3}{10}$ (d) $\frac{2}{5}$

2. Eliza, Fenn and Garry were partners in a firm sharing profits and losses in the ratio of 4 : 3 : 1. Fenn was guaranteed ₹ 25,000 as his share in the profits. Any deficiency arising on that account was to be met by Eliza. The firm earned a profit of ₹ 80,000 for the year ended 31st March, 2024. The amount of profit credited to Fenn's capital account will be **(1)**

(a) ₹ 30,000 (b) ₹ 40,000 (c) ₹ 25,000 (d) ₹ 10,000

3. Wayne, Shann and Bryan were partners in a firm. Shann had advanced a loan of ₹ 1,00,000 to the firm. On 31st March, 2024 the firm was dissolved. After transferring various assets (other than cash and bank) and outside liabilities to realisation account, Shaan took over furniture of book value of ₹ 90,000 in part settlement of his loan amount.

For the payment of balance amount of Shaan's loan, bank account will be credited with **(1)**

(a) ₹ 1,00,000 (b) ₹ 90,000
(c) ₹ 1,90,000 (d) ₹ 10,000

4. Pulkit and Ravinder were partners in a firm sharing profits and losses in the ratio of 3 : 2. Sikander was admitted as a new partner for 1/5th share in the profits of the firm. Pulkit, Ravinder and Sikander decided to share future profits in the ratio of 2 : 2 : 1. Sikander brought ₹ 5,00,000 as his capital and ₹ 10,00,000 as his share of premium for goodwill. The amount of premium for goodwill that will be credited to the old partners' capital accounts will be **(1)**

(a) Pulkit's capital account ₹ 10,00,000
(b) Pulkit's capital account ₹ 6,00,000 and Ravinder's capital account ₹ 4,00,000
(c) Pulkit's capital account ₹ 5,00,000 and Ravinder's capital account ₹ 5,00,000
(d) Pulkit's capital account ₹ 2,00,000

5. Kajal and Laura were partners in a firm sharing profits and losses in the ratio of 5 : 3. They admitted Maddy for for 1/4th share in future profits.

Maddy brought ₹ 8,00,000 as his capital and ₹ 4,00,000 as his share of premium for goodwill. Kajal, Laura and Maddy decided to share profits in future in the ratio of 2 : 1 : 1. After all adjustments in respect of goodwill, revaluation of assets and liabilities etc. Kajal's capital was 15,00,000 and Laura's capital was ₹ 8,00,000. It was agreed that partners' capitals should be in proportion to their new profit sharing ratio taking Maddy's capital as base. The adjustment was made by bringing in or withdrawing the necessary cash as the case may be. The cash brought in by Kajal was (1)

(a) ₹ 1,00,000 (b) ₹ 8,00,000
(c) ₹ 16,00,000 (d) ₹ 12,00,000

6. **Assertion** (A) The maximum number of partners in a partnership firm is 50.

Reason (R) By virtue of the Companies Act 2013, the central government is empowered to prescribe maximum number of partners in a firm. The central government has prescribed the maximum number of partners in a firm to be 50. (1)

Alternatives

(a) Both Assertion (A) and Reason (R) are true and Reason (R) is the correct explanation of Assertion (A)
(b) Both Assertion (A) and Reason (R) are true, but Reason (R) is not the correct explanation of Assertion (A)
(c) Assertion (A) is true, but Reason (R) is false
(d) Assertion (A) is false, but Reason (R) is true

7. Nandita and Prabha were partners in a firm. Nandita withdrew ₹ 3,00,000 during the year for personal use. The partnership deed provides for charging interest on drawings @ 10% p.a. Interest on Nandita's drawings for the year ended 31st March, 2024 will be (1)

(a) ₹ 9,000 (b) ₹ 30,000 (c) ₹ 18,000 (d) ₹ 15,000

8. Radhika, Mehar and Shubha were partners in a firm sharing profits and losses in the ratio of 9 : 8 : 7. If Radhika's share of profit at the end of the year amounted to ₹ 5,40,000, Shubha's share of profit will be (1)

(a) ₹ 5,40,000 (b) ₹ 4,80,000
(c) ₹ 60,000 (d) ₹ 4,20,000

9. Suhas and Vilas were partners in a firm with capitals of ₹ 4,00,000 and ₹ 3,00,000 respectively. They admitted Prabhas as a new partner for 1/5th share in future profits. Prabhas brought ₹ 2,00,000 as his capital. Prabhas' share of goodwill will be (1)

(a) ₹ 1,00,000 (c) ₹ 10,00,000
(b) ₹ 9,00,000 (d) ₹ 20,000

10. Offer of securities or invitation to subscribe securities to a select group of persons by a company (other than by way of public offer) is known as (1)

(a) sweat equity (b) incorporation cost
(c) private placement of shares
(d) employee stock option plan

11. Ajay Ltd. forfeited 100 shares of ₹ 10 each for non-payment of first call of ₹ 1 per share and second and final call of ₹ 3 per share. The minimum price per share at which these shares can be reissued will be (1)

(a) ₹ 6 (b) ₹ 4
(c) ₹ 10 (d) ₹ 16

12. The amount of share capital which a company is authorised to issue by its Memorandum of Association is known as .... (1)

(a) nominal capital (b) issued capital
(c) reserve capital (d) subscribed capital

Or According to Securities and Exchange Board of India (SEBI), guidelines, minimum subscription of capital cannot be less than 90% of ....

(a) authorised capital (b) issued capital
(c) reserve capital (d) subscribed capital

13. Debentures on which a company does not give any undertaking for the repayment of money borrowed are called (1)

(a) bearer debentures
(b) secured debentures
(c) perpetual debentures
(d) registered debentures

Or If the amount of debentures issued is more than the amount of the net assets taken over by a company, the difference will be treated as

(a) capital reserve (b) goodwill
(c) purchase consideration (d) general reserve

14. The following journal entry appears in the books of Latvion Ltd.

JOURNAL

Date	Particulars		LF	Am (Dr)	Am (Cr)
	Bank A/c	Dr		4,75,000	
	Loss on Issue of Debentures A/c	Dr		75,000	
	To 12% Debentures A/c				5,00,000
	To Premium on Redemption of Debentures A/c				50,000

The discount on issue of debentures is (1)

(a) 15% (b) 5% (c) 10% (d) 95%

Or Zeba Limited issued 15,000, 9% debentures of ₹ 100 each at 10% discount on 1st April, 2023. It has a balance of ₹ 1,00,000 in securities premium account. The 'discount on issue of debentures' of ₹ 1,50,000 will be written-off

(a) ₹ 1,00,000 out of securities premium account and ₹ 50,000 out of statement of profit and loss
(b) ₹ 50,000 out of securities premium account and ₹ 1,00,000 out of statement of profit and loss
(c) ₹ 1,50,000 out of securities premium account
(d) ₹ 1,50,000 out of statement of profit and loss

15. Anisha, Deepa and Charu were partners sharing profits and losses in the ratio of 5 : 3 : 2. On 31st March, 2024, they decided to change their profit sharing ratio to 2 : 3 : 5. Each partner's gain or sacrifice due to change in profit sharing ratio will be (1)

(a) Anisha's sacrifice $\frac{3}{10}$; Charu's gain $\frac{3}{10}$
(b) Anisha's gain $\frac{3}{10}$; Charu's sacrifice $\frac{3}{10}$
(c) Anisha's sacrifice $\frac{3}{10}$; Deepa's gain $\frac{3}{10}$
(d) Deepa's gain $\frac{3}{10}$; Charu's sacrifice $\frac{3}{10}$

Or Preet and Saral were partners sharing profits and losses in the ratio of 3 : 2. On 31st March, 2024 they decided to change their profit sharing ratio to 1 : 1. On the date of reconstitution goodwill of the firm was valued at ₹ 1,00,000. The journal entry for treatment of goodwill on account of change in profit sharing ratio will be

(a) Preet's Capital A/c	Dr	1,00,000	
To Saral's Capital A/c			1,00,000
(b) Saral's Capital A/c	Dr	1,00,000	
To Preet's Capital A/c			1,00,000
(c) Preet's Capital A/c	Dr	10,000	
To Saral's Capital A/c			10,000
(d) Saral's Capital A/c	Dr	10,000	
To Preet's Capital A/c			10,000

16. Ishan, Jatin and Kapil were partners in a firm sharing profits and losses in the ratio of 5 : 4 : 1. Jatin retired and his share was taken up by Ishan and Kapil in the ratio 1 : 1. The new profit sharing ratio between Ishan and Kapil after Jatin's retirement will be (1)

(a) 5 : 1 (b) 1 : 1
(c) 5 : 4 (d) 7 : 3

Or Sakshi, Kiara and Gunjan were partners in a firm sharing profits and losses in the ratio of 3 : 2 : 1. Kiara retired on 1st April, 2023. After all adjustments the amount due to Kiara was ₹ 5,00,000. The payment was to be made in two yearly instalments of ₹ 2,50,000 each plus interest @ 10% per annum on the unpaid balance. The amount of first instalment paid on 31st March, 2024 will be

(a) ₹ 3,00,000 (b) ₹ 2,75,000
(c) ₹ 5,50,000 (d) ₹ 2,50,000

17. Anubha and Yuvika were partners in a firm sharing profits and losses in the ratio of 3 : 2. From 1st April, 2024, they decided to share future profits and losses in the ratio of 2 : 3. On this date, their balance sheet showed a balance of ₹ 50,000 in general reserve and a debit balance of ₹ 2,50,000 in profit and loss account. Partners decided to write-off profit and loss account but decided not to distribute the general reserve. Pass the necessary journal entries for the above transactions on the reconstitution of the firm. Show your workings clearly. (3)

18. Sunny and Ujjwal were partners in a firm sharing profits and losses in the ratio of 3 : 2. On 1st April, 2024 Timmy was admitted as a new partner for 1/5th share in profits which he acquired equally from Sunny and Ujjwal. On the date of Timmy's admission the balance sheet of Sunny and Ujjwal showed investments at ₹ 5,00,000 and a balance of ₹ 2,00,000 in investment fluctuation reserve.

Pass necessary journal entries for treatment of investment fluctuation reserve on the date of Timmy's admission in each of the following cases

(i) Market value of investments was ₹ 5,00,000.
(ii) Market value of investments was ₹ 3,00,000.
(iii) Market value of investments was ₹ 2,00,000. (3)

19. Apoorv Ltd. acquired building worth ₹ 15,50,000, Machinery worth ₹ 11,40,000 and furniture worth ₹ 1,10,000 from Dhruv Ltd. and took over its liabilities of ₹ 2,00,000 for a purchase consideration of ₹ 25,00,000. Apoorv Ltd. paid the purchase consideration by issuing 12% debentures of ₹ 100 each at a premium of 25%.

Pass the necessary journal entries in the books of Apoorv Ltd. for the above transactions. (3)

Or Ajanta Ltd. purchased machinery worth ₹ 36,00,000 from Sujata Ltd. Ajanta Ltd. paid half the amount to Sujata Ltd. through a bank draft and the balance by issuing 8% debentures of 100 each at a discount of 10%. Pass the necessary journal entries in the books of Ajanta Ltd. for the above transactions.

20. Aakash and Baadal entered into partnership on 1st October, 2023 with the capitals of ₹ 80,00,000 and ₹ 60,00,000 respectively. They decided to share profits and losses equally. Partners were entitled to interest on capital capital @ 10% per annum as per the provisions of the partnership deed.

Baadal is given a guarantee that his share of profit, after charging interest on capital will not be less than ₹ 7,00,000 per annum. Any deficiency arising on that account shall be met by Aakash. The profit of the firm for the year ended 31st March, 2024 amounted to ₹ 13,00,000.

Prepare profit and loss appropriation account for the year ended 31st March, 2024. (3)

Or Parul and Rajul were partners in a firm, sharing profits and losses in the ratio of 5 : 3. The balance in their fixed capital accounts on 1st April, 2023 were Parul ₹ 6,00,000 and Rajul ₹ 8,00,000.

The partnership deed provided for allowing interest on capital at 12% per annum. The net profit of the firm for the year ended 31th March, 2024 was ₹ 1,26,000.

Prepare profit and loss appropriation account for the year ended 31st March, 2024. Show your working clearly.

21. Ridyum Limited issued 5,000, 9% debentures of ₹ 500 each at a premium of 10%. The amount was payable as follows

On application — ₹ 200 per debenture
On allotment — Balance (including premium)

The debentures were fully subscribed and all amounts were duly received.

Pass the necessary journal entries for issue of debentures in the books of Ridyum Limited. (4)

22. Simar, Tanvi and Umara were partners in a firm sharing profits and losses in the ratio of 5 : 6 : 9.

On 31st March, 2024 their balance sheet was as follows

Balance Sheet of Simar, Tanvi and Umara
as at 31st March, 2024

Liabilities		Amt (₹)	Assets	Amt (₹)
Capital A/cs			Fixed Assets	25,00,000
Simar	13,00,000		Stock	10,00,000
Tanvi	12,00,000		Debtors	8,00,000
Umara	14,00,000	39,00,000	Cash	7,00,000
General Reserve		7,00,000	Profit and Loss Account (2023-24)	2,00,000
Trade Payables		6,00,000		
		52,00,000		52,00,000

Umara died on 30th June, 2024. The partnership deed provided for the following on the death of a partner

(i) Goodwill of the firm be valued at 3 years purchase of average profits for the last 5 years. The profit/loss for the previous four years were
2022-23 ₹ 3,10,000 (loss)
2021-22 ₹ 3,00,000 (profit)
2020-21 ₹ 4,00,000 (profit)
2019-20 ₹ 2,50,000 (profit)

(ii) Umara's share of profit or loss till the date of her death was to be calculated on the basis of profit or loss for the year ended 31st March, 2024.

(a) Calculate goodwill of the firm.

(b) Pass the necessary journal entry for the treatment of goodwill on Umara's death.

(c) Calculate Umara's share in the profit or loss of the firm till the date of her death.

(d) Pass the necessary journal entry to record Umara's share of profit or loss till the date of her death. (4)

23. Pass necessary journal entries for the following transactions on dissolution of the firm of Rajesh, Somesh and Yogesh after various assets (other than cash) and third party liabilities have been transferred to realisation account.

(i) Rajesh took over stock of ₹ 4,00,000 at a discount of 20%.

(ii) Somesh agreed to take over the firm's furniture, not recorded in the books of the firm at ₹ 80,000.

(iii) Land and building of the book value of ₹ 60,00,000 was sold for ₹ 90,00,000 through a broker who charged 10% commission.

(iv) Ashish, an old customer, whose account for ₹ 70,000 was written-off as bad in the previous year, paid 60% of the amount.

(v) Sundry creditors of ₹ 3,00,000 were settled at a discount of 10%.

(vi) Realisation expenses amounting to ₹ 21,000 were paid by Yogesh. (6)

24. Following is the extract of the balance sheet of Vikalp Ltd. as per Schedule III, Part I of Companies Act as at 31st March, 2024 along with notes to accounts (6)

In the Books of Vikalp Ltd.
Balance Sheet
as at 31st March, 2024

Particulars	Note No.	31st March, 2024 (₹)	31st March, 2023 (₹)
I. EQUITY AND LIABILITIES			
1. Shareholders' Funds			
(i) Share Capital	1	59,60,000	50,00,000

Notes to Accounts

	Particulars	31st March, 2023 (₹)
1.	**Share Capital**	
	Authorised Capital	
	9,00,000 Equity Shares of ₹ 10 each	90,00,000
	Issued Capital	
	5,00,000 Equity Shares of ₹ 10 each	50,00,000
	Subscribed Capital	
	Subscribed and Fully paid-up	
	5,00,000 Equity Shares of ₹ 10 each	50,00,000
	Subscribed but not Fully paid-up	—
		50,00,000

Notes to Accounts

	Particulars		31st March, 2024 (₹)
1.	**Share Capital**		
	Authorised Capital		
	9,00,000 Equity Shares of ₹ 10 each		90,00,000
	Issued Capital		
	6,00,000 Equity Shares of ₹ 10 each		60,00,000
	Subscribed Capital		
	Subscribed and Fully Paid-up		
	5,80,000 Equity Shares of ₹ 10 each		58,00,000
	Subscribed but not Fully paid-up		
	20,000 Equity Shares of ₹ 10 each, Fully Called-up	2,00,000	
	(–) Calls-in-arrears 20,000 Equity Shares @ ₹ 2 per Share	(40,000)	1,60,000
			59,60,000

(i) The total face value of equity shares issued during the year 2023-2024 was
(a) ₹ 10,00,000 (b) ₹ 9,80,000
(c) ₹ 4,20,000 (d) ₹11,00,000

(ii) The number of shares on which the called-up amount was not received were
(a) ₹ 1,00,000 (b) ₹ 80,000
(c) ₹ 3,00,000 (d) ₹ 20,000

(iii) On 1st April, 2024 Vikalp Limited forfeited all the shares on which the called-up amount was not received. On forfeiture, 'share capital account' will be debited by
(a) ₹ 1,60,000 (b) ₹ 40,000
(c) ₹ 2,00,000 (d) ₹ 2,40,000

(iv) On forfeiture, 'share forfeiture account' will be credited with
(a) ₹ 1,60,000 (b) ₹ 40,000 (c) ₹ 2,00,000 (d) ₹ 2,40,000

(v) If all the forfeited shares are reissued at ₹ 8 per share fully paid-up, the amount credited to 'capital reserve account' will be
(a) ₹ 40,000 (b) ₹ 1,60,000 (c) ₹ 2,00,000 (d) ₹ 1,20,000

(vi) If the forfeited shares are reissued at the minimum permissible price, the amount credited to 'capital reserve account' will be
(a) ₹ 2,00,000 (b) ₹ 1,60,000
(c) ₹ 40,000 (d) Nil

25. Alexia Limited invited applications for issuing 1,00,000 equity shares of ₹ 10 each at premium of ₹ 10 per share. The amount was payable as follows

On application ₹ 9 per share (including premium ₹ 6 per share)

On allotment ₹ 8 per share (including premium ₹ 4 per share)

On first and final call ₹ 3 per share.

Applications were received for 1,50,000 equity shares and allotment was made as follows

Category A Applicants for 90,000 shares were allotted 70,000 shares.

Category B Applicants for 60,000 shares were allotted 30,000 shares.

Excess money received on application was adjusted towards allotment and first and final call.

Shekhar, who had applied for 1,200 shares failed to pay the first and final call. Shekhar belonged to category B.

Pass necessary journal entries for the above transactions in the books of Alexia Limited. Open calls-in-arrears and calls-in- advance account, wherever necessary. (6)

Or Pass the necessary journal entries for forfeiture and reissue of shares in the following cases

(i) Premier Ltd. forfeited 600 shares of ₹ 10 each issued at a premium of ₹ 3 per share (payable with allotment) for non-payment of allotment money of ₹ 7 per share including premium. The first and final call of ₹ 3 per share was not yet made. The forfeited shares were reissued at ₹ 13 per share fully paid-up.

(ii) Risha Ltd. forfeited 1,000 shares of ₹ 10 each, ₹ 8 per share called-up issued at a premium of ₹ 2 per share to Atul, for non-payment allotment money of ₹ 6 per share (including premium) premium). Out of these, 800 shares were reissued at ₹ 7 per share, ₹ 8 paid-up.

26. Bittu and Chintu were partners in a firm sharing profit and losses in the ratio of 4 : 3. Their balance sheet as at 31st March, 2024 was as follows

Balance Sheet of Bittu and Chintu
as at 31st March, 2024

Liabilities		Amt (₹)	Assets	Amt (₹)
Capital A/cs			Fixed Assets	15,40,000
Bittu	8,00,000		Stock	3,50,000
Chintu	6,00,000	14,00,000	Debtors	1,40,000
General Reserve		2,10,000	Bank	70,000
Creditors		4,90,000		
		21,00,000		21,00,000

On 1st April, 2024, Diya was admitted in the firm for 1/7th share in the profits on the following terms

(i) New profit sharing ratio between Bittu, Chintu and Diya will be 3 : 3 : 1.

(ii) Fixed assets were found to be overvalued by ₹ 1,40,000.

(iii) Creditors were paid ₹ 4,20,000 in full settlement.

(iv) Diya brought proportionate capital and ₹ 5,60,000 as her share of goodwill premium by cheque.

Prepare revaluation account and partners' capital account. (6)

Or Rupal, Shanu and Trisha were partners in a firm sharing profits and losses in the ratio of 4 : 3 : 1. Their balance sheet as at 31st March, 2024 was as follows

Balance Sheet of Rupal, Shanu and Trisha
as at 31st March, 2024

Liabilities		Amt (₹)	Assets	Amt (₹)
Capital A/cs			Fixed Assets	8,20,000
Rupal	8,00,000		Stock	2,80,000
Shanu	6,00,000		Debtors	5,00,000
Trisha	2,00,000	16,00,000	Cash	7,20,000
General Reserve		3,20,000		
Creditors		4,00,000		
		23,20,000		23,20,000

Trisha retired from the firm on 1st April, 2024 on the following terms

(i) Trisha's share of profit was entirely taken by Shanu.
(ii) Fixed assets were found to be undervalued by ₹ 2,40,000.
(iii) Stock was revalued at ₹ 2,00,000.
(iv) Goodwill of the firm was valued at ₹ 8,00,000 on Trisha's retirement.
(v) The total capital of the new firm was fixed at ₹ 16,00,000 which was adjusted according to the new profit sharing ratio of the partners. For this necessary cash was paid-off or brought in by the partners as the case may be.

Prepare revaluation account and partners' capital account.

PART-B
(Financial Statement Analysis)

27. The quick ratio of a company is 1 : 1. Which of the following transactions will result in increase in quick ratio? (1)
(a) Cash received from debtors
(b) Sold goods on credit
(c) Purchased goods on credit
(d) Purchased goods on cash

28. **Statement I** Snow Limited earned a profit of ₹ 2,00,000 after charging depreciation of ₹ 50,000 on machinery. So, operating profit before working capital changes would be ₹ 2,50,000.

Statement II Depreciation is added back to net profit as it does not result in any cash flow. (1)

Alternatives
(a) Statement I is correct and Statement II is incorrect
(b) Statement II is correct and Statement I is incorrect
(c) Both the statements are correct
(d) Both the statements are incorrect

29. ...... is not a tool of 'analysis of financial statements'. (1)
(a) Income statement
(b) Ratio analysis
(c) Comparative statements
(d) Cash flow statement

Or In 'common size income statement' each item is expressed as a percentage of ....
(a) total income
(b) total expenses
(c) profit after tax
(d) revenue from operations

30. Short-term highly liquid investments qualify as cash equivalents if they are realisable into know amounts of cash from the date of acquisition within a period of (1)
(a) 6 months or less
(b) 9 months or less
(c) 12 months or less
(d) 3 months or less

Or

Which of the following item is not included in cash and cash equivalents?
(a) Trade receivables
(b) Demand deposits with bank
(c) Short-term marketable securities
(d) Cheques in hand

31. Classify the following items under major heads and sub-heads (if any) in the balance sheet of a company as per Schedule III, Part I of the Companies Act, 2013. (3)
(i) Work-in-progress
(ii) Securities premium
(iii) Creditors

32. From the following information, prepare a comparative statement of profit and loss of Smart Ltd. (4)

Particulars	2023-24 (₹)	2022-23 (₹)
Revenue from Operations	24,00,000	20,00,000
Cost of Materials Consumed	6,00,000	4,00,000
Employee Benefit Expenses	4,00,000	2,00,000
Tax Rate	50%	50%

33. From the following information, calculate opening trade receivables and closing trade receivables. (4)

Trade receivables turnover ratio 4 times

Closing trade receivables were ₹ 20,000 more than that in the beginning

Cost of revenue from operations ₹ 6,40,000

Cash revenue from operations 1/3rd of credit revenue from operations

Gross profit ratio 20%

Or From the following information, calculate opening and closing inventory

Gross profit ratio 25%

Revenue from operations ₹ 8,00,000

Inventory turnover ratio 4 times

Opening inventory was 2 times of the closing inventory.

34. On 31st March, 2024 following is the balance sheet of Bhavik Limited.

In the Books of Bhavik Ltd.
Balance Sheet
as at 31st March, 2024

Particulars	Note No.	31st March, 2024 (₹)	31st March, 2023 (₹)
I. **EQUITY AND LIABILITIES**			
1. **Shareholders' Funds**			
(i) Share capital		12,00,000	10,00,000
(ii) Reserves and Surplus	1	4,00,000	3,00,000
2. **Non-current Liabilities**			
Long-term borrowings	2	6,00,000	10,00,000
3. **Current Liabilities**			
(i) Trade Payables		5,00,000	1,00,000
(ii) Short-term Provisions	3	3,00,000	4,00,000
Total		30,00,000	28,00,000
II. **ASSETS**			
1. **Non-current Assets**			
(i) Property, Plant and Equipment and Intangible Assets			
(a) Property, Plant and Equipment	4	19,00,000	15,00,000
(ii) Non-current Investments		3,00,000	4,00,000
2. **Current Assets**			
(i) Inventories		4,50,000	3,50,000
(ii) Trade Receivables		2,50,000	4,50,000
(iii) Cash and Cash Equivalents		1,00,000	1,00,000
Total		30,00,000	28,00,000

Notes to Accounts

Particulars	31st March, 2024 (₹)	31st March, 2023 (₹)
1. **Reserves and Surplus**		
Balance in Statement of Profit and Loss	4,00,000	3,00,000
2. **Long-term Borrowings**		
10% Debentures	6,00,000	10,00,000
3. **Short-term Provisions**		
Provision for Tax	3,00,000	4,00,000
4. **Property, Plant and Equipment**		
Plant and Machinery	21,50,000	16,00,000
(–) Accumulated Depreciation	(2,50,000)	(1,00,000)
	19,00,000	15,00,000

Additional Information

(i) During the year a piece of machinery costing ₹ 8,00,000 accumulated depreciation thereon ₹ 50,000 was sold for ₹ 6,50,000.

(ii) Debentures were redeemed on 31st March, 2024.

Calculate

(a) Cash flow from investing activities.

(b) Cash flow from financing activities. (6)

Answers

1. (b) $\frac{1}{5}$

2. (a) Fenn's share in profit $= 80{,}000 \times \frac{3}{8} =$ ₹ 30,000 which is more than the guaranteed amount. Hence Fenn's capital account will be credited with ₹ 30,000.

3. (d) Balance amount to be paid for Shaan's loan

$= 1{,}00{,}000 - 90{,}000 =$ ₹ 10,000

4. (d) Only Pulkit is sacrificing as $= \frac{3}{5} - \frac{2}{5} = \frac{1}{5}$ Sacrifice

Pulkit's capital will be credited with ₹ 2,00,000 as premium for goodwill.

Pulkit's share in premium for goodwill

$=$ ₹ $10{,}00{,}000 \times \frac{1}{5} =$ ₹ 2,00,000

5. (a) Capital of new firm taking Maddy's capital as base $= 8{,}00{,}000 \times 4 =$ ₹ 32,00,000

New capital of Kajal $= 32{,}00{,}000 \times \frac{2}{4} =$ ₹ 16,00,000

Cash brought in by Kajal = New Capital – Adjusted Capital

$= 16{,}00{,}000 - 15{,}00{,}000 =$ ₹ 1,00,000

6. (a) Both Assertion (A) and Reason (R) are true and Reason (R) is the correct explanation of Assertion (A)

7. (d) Interest on Drawings $= 3{,}00{,}000 \times \frac{10}{100} \times \frac{6}{12} = ₹\ 15{,}000$

8. (d) Total Profit = Share of Profit of Radhika × Reciprocal of her Share $= 5{,}40{,}000 \times \frac{24}{9}$

$= ₹\ 14{,}40{,}000$

Shubha's Share in Profit $= 14{,}40{,}000 \times 7/24 = ₹\ 4{,}20{,}000$

9. (d) Hidden Goodwill = Capital of Firm taking Prabhas Base − Net Worth

$= (2{,}00{,}000 \times 5) - (2{,}00{,}000 + 4{,}00{,}000 + 3{,}00{,}000)$

$= 10{,}00{,}000 - 9{,}00{,}000 = ₹\ 1{,}00{,}000$

Prabhas' share in goodwill $= 1{,}00{,}000 \times \frac{1}{5} = ₹\ 20{,}000$

10. (c) private placement of shares

11. (b) Minimum Price = Nominal Value of Share − Maximum Discount which can be allowed*

$= 10 - 6 = ₹\ 4$

*Maximum discount which can be allowed

$= 10 - 3 - 1 = ₹\ 6$ (forfeited) per share

12. (a) nominal capital *Or* (b) issued capital

13. (c) perpetual debentures

Or (b) goodwill

14. (b) Discount on Issue = Loss on Issue − Premium on Redemption

$= 75{,}000 - 50{,}000$

$= ₹\ 25{,}000$

Rate of Discount $= \frac{25{,}000}{5{,}00{,}000} \times 100 = 5\%$

Or (a) Discount on Issue $= (15{,}000 \times 100) \times 10\% = ₹\ 1{,}50{,}000$

(−) Written-off from Securities Premium $= ₹\ (1{,}00{,}000)$

Written-off from Statement of Profit and Loss ₹ 50,000

15. (a) Anisha $= \frac{5}{10} - \frac{2}{10} = \frac{3}{10}$ Sacrifice

Deepu $= \frac{3}{10} - \frac{3}{10} =$ Nil; Charu $= \frac{2}{10} - \frac{5}{10} = -\frac{3}{10}$ Gain

Or (d) Preet's $= \frac{3}{5} - \frac{1}{2} = \frac{6-5}{10} = \frac{1}{10}$ Sacrifice

Saral's $= \frac{2}{5} - \frac{1}{2} = \frac{4-5}{10} = -\frac{1}{10}$ Gain

Saral will compensate ₹ 10,000 $\left(1{,}00{,}000 \times \frac{1}{10}\right)$ to Preet

16. (d) Ishan's New Ratio = Old share + Share taken

$= \frac{5}{10} + \left(\frac{4}{10} \times \frac{1}{2}\right)$

$= \frac{5}{10} + \frac{4}{20} = \frac{7}{10}$

Kapil's New Ratio = Old Share + Share Taken

$= \frac{1}{10} + \left(\frac{4}{10} \times \frac{1}{2}\right) = \frac{1}{10} + \frac{2}{10} = \frac{3}{10}$

Or (a) Interest due on 31st March, 2024 $= 5{,}00{,}000 \times \frac{10}{100}$

$= ₹\ 50{,}000$

Amount of First Installment $= 2{,}50{,}000 + 50{,}000$

$= ₹\ 3{,}00{,}000$

17. Refer to Solved Question 10 of Chapter-3 (Part-A).

18. Refer to Solved Question 26 of Chapter-4 (Part-A).

19. Refer to Solved Question 10 of Chapter-8 (Part-A).

Or Refer to Solved Question 12 of Chapter-8 (Part-A).

20. Refer to Solved Question 28 of Chapter-1 (Part-A).

Or Refer to Solved Question 17 of Chapter-1 (Part-A).

21. Refer to Solved Question 3 of Chapter-8 (Part-A).

22. Refer to Solved Question 29 of Chapter-5 (Part-A).

23. Refer to Solved Question 4 of Chapter-6 (Part-A).

24. (i) (a) Total shares issued during 2023-24

$= 6{,}00{,}000 - 5{,}00{,}000 = 1{,}00{,}000$

Face value $= 1{,}00{,}000 \times 10 = ₹\ 10{,}00{,}000$

(ii) (d) On 20,000 shares, called-up amount was not received.

(iii) (c) As the amount was fully called-up, share capital will be debited by ₹ 2,00,000.

(iv) (a) Share forfeiture account will be credited with ₹ 1,60,000, calculated as follows

Share Capital − Calls-in-arrears $= 2{,}00{,}000 - 40{,}000$

$= ₹\ 1{,}60{,}000$

(v) (d) Amount will be calculated as follows

Total Gain on Forfeiture	= ₹ 1,60,000
(−) Discount Allowed on reissue (20,000 × 2)	= ₹ (40,000)
Transfer to Capital Reserve	= ₹ 1,20,000

(vi) (d)

Total Gain on Forfeiture	= ₹ 1,60,000
(−) Maximum Discount Allowed	= ₹ (1,60,000)
	Nil

25. Refer to Solved Question 21 of Chapter-7 (Part-A).

Or Refer to Solved Question 27 of Chapter-7 (Part-A).

26. Refer to Solved Question 37 of Chapter-4 (Part-A).

Or Refer to Solved Question 26 of Chapter-5 (Part-A).

27. (b) Sold goods on credit

28. (c) Both the statements are correct

29. (a) Income statement

Or (d) revenue from operations

30. (d) 3 months or less *Or* (a) Trade receivables

31. Refer to Theoretical Question 8 of Chapter-1 (Part-B).

32. Refer to Solved Question 3 of Chapter-2 (Part-B).

33. Refer to Solved Question 37 of Chapter-3 (Part-B).

Or Refer to Solved Question 43 of Chapter-3 (Part-B).

34. Refer to Solved Question 17 of Chapter-4 (Part-B).